TRAVELS IN
ARABIA DESERTA

TRAVELS IN
ARABIA DESERTA

BY

CHARLES M. DOUGHTY

With an Introduction by
T. E. LAWRENCE

IN TWO VOLUMES

VOLUME II

DOVER PUBLICATIONS, INC.
NEW YORK

Published in Canada by General Publishing Company, Ltd., 30 Lesmill Road, Don Mills, Toronto, Ontario.

Published in the United Kingdom by Constable and Company, Ltd., 10 Orange Street, London WC2H 7EG.

This Dover edition, first published in 1979, is an unabridged and unaltered republication of the definitive version of the third edition published in London in 1936 by Jonathan Cape Ltd. The work was originally published in 1888 by Cambridge University Press. The second edition was published in London by P. Lee Warner in January, 1921, and the third edition was first issued by the same publisher in October, 1921.

International Standard Book Number: 0-486-23826-1
Library of Congress Catalog Card Number: 79-52396

Manufactured in the United States of America
Dover Publications, Inc.
180 Varick Street
New York, N.Y. 10014

CONTENTS TO VOL. II

CHAPTER I
IBN RASHÎD'S TOWN
PAGE

Curious questioning of the townspeople. A Moor hakîm had visited Hâyil. He cast out demons. The jins. Superstitious fears of the Arabs. Exorcists. A counterfeit Christian vaccinator cut off in the desert. Advantage of the profession of medicine. Hamûd sends his sick infant son to the Nasrâny hakîm, who cures also Hamûd's wife. Diseases at Hâyil. The great Kasr. The guest-chambers. Hâyil house-building. Wards of the town. Artificers. Visit to S'weyfly. The mákbara has swallowed up the inhabitants. Deaf and dumb man-at-arms of the Emir. Mâjid shooting with ball. English gunpowder. Gulf words heard at Hâyil. Palms and a gum-mastic tree in Ajja. 'The coming of Mohammed foretold in the Enjil.' Hamûd's tolerant urbanity. Another audience. The princely family of Ibn Rashîd. Telâl a slayer of himself. Metaab succeeded him. His nephews, Telâl's sons, conspire to kill him. Metaab dies by their shot. Bunder prince. Mohammed who fled to er-Riâth returns upon assurance of peace. He is again conductor of the Bagdad pilgrims; and returns to Hâyil with the yearly convoy of temmn for the public kitchen. Bunder rides forth with his brother Bedr and Hamûd to meet him. Mohammed slays (his nephew) Bunder. Hamûd's speech to the people. Tragedies in the Castle. Mohammed's speech in the Méshab. He sits down as Muhafûth. Bedr taken and slain. Mohammed slays the slayer. Hamûd's nature. Mohammed the Emir is childless. His moderation and severity. The princely bounty. The Shammar state. Villages and hamlets. The public dues and taxes and expense of government. The Prince's horses sold in India. His forces. Ibn Rashîd's forays. He " weakens " the Aarab. The Shammar principality   15–37

CHAPTER II
LIFE IN HÂYIL

The great tribes beyond Ibn Rashîd. *Akhu Noora*. The princely families. The Prince Mohammed childless. His " Christian wife." Abd el-Azîz the orphan child of Telâl, and his half-brother Bunder's orphan. Secret miseries of Princes. The family of Abeyd. A song of Abeyd. Abeyd could be generous. Fáhd. The poor distracted soul sells his daughter to his father Abeyd. Feyd. Sleymàn. Abdullah. Wealth of Abeyd's family. Hamûd's daughter. The government of Ibn Rashîd. Beginning of the Shammar state. By some the Emir is named *Zálim*, a tyrant. A tale of Metaab's government. A Christian Damascene tradesman visits Hâyil. Discord among tribes of the Emir's domination. The Rajajîl es-Sheukh. Imbârak. The Moors' garrison in the tower Mârid at Jauf. Their defection and the recovery of Jauf. Tale of the Ottoman expedition against Jauf. Words of Sherarát tribesmen, to the sheykhs in Jauf. Ibn Rashîd rides to save Jauf. Ibn Rashîd and the Ottoman pasha. Beduins among the rajajîl. Men of East Nejd and of er-Riâth come to serve the Western Emir. Ibn Saûd is " ruined." A messenger from er-Riâth. Kahtân tribesmen at Hâyil. Their speech. The Wady Dauâsir country. Hayzàn their sheykh. He threatens to stab the Nasrâny. People's tales of the Kahtân. 'Their graves are crows' and eagles' maws.' Ibn Rashîd's lineage. Kindreds of Shammar. Rashîd, a lettered Beduwy. A fanatic kâdy. Dispute with the pedant kâdy. " The Muscovs of old possessed the land of Nejd." Inscriptions at Gubba. Study of letters in Nejd. Their nomad-like ignorance of the civil world. A village schoolmaster. A prophecy of Ezekiel. Plain words among the Arabs. Travelled men in Hâyil. Wintry weather. An outrage in the coffee-hall. The coffee-server called before the Emir. [*Note :* itinerary from Hâyil to Kuweyt.]   38–61

5

CONTENTS

CHAPTER III
DEPART FROM HÂYIL: JOURNEY TO KHEYBAR

PAGE

The 'Persian pilgrimage.' Imbârak's words. Town thieves. Jauf pilgrims in Hâyil. Beduins on pilgrimage. The Caravan to Mecca arrives from the North. An Italian hajjy in Hâyil. The Persians passed formerly by el-Kasîm. Murderous dangers in Mecca. Concourse at Hâyil.—The Kheybar journey. Violent dealing of Imbârak. Ibn Rashîd's passport. Departure from Hâyil. Gofar. Seyadîn, Beduin pedlars. El-Kasr village. Biddîa hamlet. Adventure in the desert. Eyâda ibn Ajjuèyn. Kâsim ibn Barák. Sâlih the rafîk. "It is the angels." The Wady er-Rummah. Kâsim's sister. Set forward again with Sâlih. The Nasrâny abandoned at strange tents. The hospitable goodness of those nomads. Thaifullah. Set forth with Ghroceyb from the menzil of Eyâda. The Harra in sight. Heteym menzil in the Harra. Lineage of the Heteym. The lava-field. The division of waters of Northern Arabia. The dangerous passage. The great Harrat (Kheybar). El Hâyat, village. Cattle paths in the Harra. An alarm near Kheybar. Locusts. Ghroceyb in trouble of mind. Wady Jellâs. Kheybar village. The Húsn. An antique Mesjid   62–93

CHAPTER IV
KHEYBAR. "THE APOSTLE'S COUNTRY."

The night at Kheybar. Abd el-Hâdy. Ahmed. The gunner's belt. Kheybar by daylight. Medina soldiery. Muharram. Sirûr. The Nasrâny brought before the village governor. Amm Mohammed en-Nejûmy. Amân. The Gallas. Evening in the soldiers' kahwa. Ibrahîm the kâdy. Abdullah's tale of the Engleys. Hejâz Arabic. A worthy negro woman. Amm Mohammed's house. Umm Kîda. Brackish soil. Wadies of Kheybar. The Albanians. Kheybar genealogy. The Nasrâny accused. The villagers in fear of his enchantments. Friendship with Amm Mohammed. Our well labour. His hunting. Kasr en-Néby. El-Asmîeh. Blood-sprinkling. Hospitality of the sheykh of the hamlet. Gatûnies. Barrows upon the Harra. Magicians come to Kheybar to raise treasures. The Húsn rock   94–123

CHAPTER V
THE KHEYABÂRA

Kheybar witches. Dakhîlullah, the Menhel. Ibrahîm. Our garden labour. Their custom to labour for each other without wages. Housebuilding. The negro villagers are churlish and improvident. Famine in the land. Kheybar "THE LAND'S WEALTH." Antique Kheybar conquered by the Annezy. The ancient partnership of Beduins and villagers. Sirûr. The villagers' rights in the soil. Their husbandry is light. Afternoons and evenings at Kheybar. The Asiatic priests' mystery of stabbing and cutting themselves. Villagers going out for wood are surprised by a ghrazzu. 'The work of the Dowla is mere rapine.' Kheybar occupied by the Dowla. The Beduins taxed. A day of battle with the Aarab. Vility of a Turkish colonel. Perfidy of the Fukara. The Kheyâbara sup of their hostile (nomad) partners' camels. The ears of the slain are cut off. The Medina soldiery at Kheybar. The cholera. Wandering hills. Fabulous opinion, in the East, of Kheybar. Abdullah's letter to the Governor of Medina. Abdullah's tales. His tyranny at Kheybar. Sedition in the village. The village kindreds. Abdullah's stewardship. Dakhîl the post. Aly, the religious sheykh, an enemy to death. The Nejûmy's warning to Abdullah, spoken in generous defence of the Nasrâny. The ostrich both bird and camel. Amm Mohammed had saved other strangers   124–156

CHAPTER VI
THE MEDINA LIFE AT KHEYBAR

Amm Mohammed's Kurdish family. His life from his youth. His son Haseyn. His easy true religion. He is a chider at home. Ahmed. A black fox. The kinds of gazelles.

CONTENTS

The Nejûmy a perfect marksman. His marvellous eye-sight. The ignorances of his youth. A transmuter of metals. A brother slain. His burning heart to avenge him. A Beduin marksman slain, by his shot, in an expedition. A running battle. He is wounded. Fiend-like men of the Bashy Bazûk. The Muatterîn at Damascus. Religious hospitality of the Arabs. Syrian tale of a bear. Mohammedan and Christian cities. Mohammed (in his youth) went in a company, from Medina, to rob a caravan of pilgrims. He saves a pilgrim's life. The *Lahabba* of Harb, a kindred of robbers. Tales of the Lahabba. Imperfect Moslems in the Haj. A Christian found at Medina. His martyr's death. A friar in Medina. Another Christian seen by Mohammed in Medina. Yahûd and Nasâra. 'Whose Son is Jesus?' Mohammed answers the salutation of just men, from his tomb. The martyrs' cave at Bedr Honeyn. Dakhîl returns not at his time. The Nasrâny's life in doubt. Amm Mohammed's good and Abdullah's black heart. Dakhîl arrives in the night. Atrocious words of Abdullah. "The Engleys are friends and not rebels to the Sooltân." Andalusîa of the Arabs. An English letter to the Pasha of Medina. Abdullah's letter. Spitting of some account in their medicine   157–184

CHAPTER VII
GALLA-LAND. MEDINA LORE

The Abyssinian Empire. *Galla-land*. Perpetual warfare of (heathen) Gallas and (Christian) Abyssinians. A renegade Frank or Traveller at Mecca and Medina. *Subia* drink. A hospitable widow at (Tâyif). "The Nasâra are the Sea's offspring." Wady Bîshy. Muharram's death. The Nasrâny accused. Sale of Muharram's goods. Aly, the (deadly) enemy of the Nasrâny. The Ferrâ. El-Auâzim. Thegîf. The Nejûmy in Hâyil. A Roman invasion of ancient Arabia. Aelius Gallus sent by Augustus, with an army, to occupy the riches of *A. Felix*. Season of the Haj. Alarms. Tidings from the War. Palm plait. Quern stones wrought by the Arabs. New Alarms. Antique building on the Harra. Yanbâ. The Kheybar valleys. Harrats of Medina. The Hálhal. The Húrda. Clay summer-houses of W. Aly Beduins. The Kheyábara abstain from certain meats. Another Ageyly's death. — His grave 'violated by the witches'. Tales of the jân. A man wedded with a jin wife at Medina   185–215

CHAPTER VIII
DELIVERANCE FROM KHEYBAR

Amm Mohammed's wild brother-in-law. The messenger arrives from Medina. The Nasrâny procures that the water is increased at Kheybar. Ayn er-Reyih. Abu Middeyn, a derwish traveller. A letter from the Pasha of Medina. Violence of Abdullah. Might one forsake the name of his religion, for a time? Amm Mohammed would persuade the Nasrâny to dwell with him at Kheybar. Abu Bakkar. '*All is shame in Islam.*' The Engleys in India, and at Aden. The Nasrâny's Arabic books are stolen by a Colonel at Medina. Return of the camel-thief. Heteym cheeses. Wedduk. The villagers of el-Hâyat. Humanity loves not to be requited. 'God sends the cold to each one after his cloth.' Mutinous villagers beaten by Abdullah. *Deyik es-súdr*. Departure from Kheybar. Hamed. Love and death. Amm Mohammed's farewell. Journey over the Harra. Come to Heteym tents. Habâra fowl. Stormy March wind. The Hejjûr mountains. Eagles. Meet with Heteym. 'The Nasâra inhabit in a city closed with iron.' Solubbies from near Mecca. The rafîks seeking for water. Certain deep and steyned wells "were made by the jân." Blustering weather. The Harra craters. "God give that young man (Ibn Rashîd) long life!"   216–248

CHAPTER IX
DESERT JOURNEY TO HÂYIL. THE NASRÂNY IS DRIVEN FROM THENCE

Eyâda ibn Ajjuèyn, seen again. Uncivil Heteym hosts. Ghroceyb. Sâlih, again. Nomad names of horses. Strife with the rafîks. A desolate night in the khála. *Zôl*. Come to tents and

CONTENTS

good entertainment. A rautha in the desert. Hunters' roast. The Tîh, or phantom thelûl in the Sherarát country. Eyâd, his person. Múthir, a poor Bishry. Braitshàn, a Shammar sheykh. An Heteymy's blasphemy. Poor Beduins' religious simplicity. A Beduin boy seeking a herdsman's place. The first hamlet in J. Shammar. Another grange in the desert. 'Between the dog and the wolf.' The village el-Kasr. Tidings that the Emir is absent from Hâyil. Beny Temîn. Hâyil in sight. Gofar. Come to Hâyil, the second time. Aneybar left deputy for Ibn Rashîd in the town. The Nasrâny is received with ill-will and fanaticism. Aneybar is now an adversary. A Medina Sherîf in Hâyil. A Yémeny stranger who had seen the Nasrâny in Egypt. Tidings of the war, which is ended. The great Sheykh of el-Ajmân. The Sherîf. The townspeople's fanaticism in the morning; a heavy hour. Depart, the second time, with trouble from Hâyil. Come again to Gofar. B. Temîn and Shammar   249–286

CHAPTER X
THE SHAMMAR AND HARB DESERTS IN NEJD

Herding supper of milk. A flight of cranes. An evil desert journey, and night, with treacherous rafîks. Aly of Gussa again. Braitshàn's booths again. "Arabs love the smooth speaking." Another evil journey. A menzil of Heteym; and parting from the treacherous rafîks. Nomad thirst for tobacco. A beautiful Heteym woman. Solubba. Maatuk and Noweyr. "Nasâra" passengers. Life of these Heteym. Burial of the Nasrâny's books. Journey to the Harb, eastward. Gazelles. Camel-milk bitter of wormwood. Heteym menzils. Come to Harb Aarab. False rumour of a foray of the Waháby. El-Aûf. An Harb sheykh. An Harb bride. Khálaf ibn Náhal's great booth. Khálaf's words. Seleymy villagers. Mount again, and alight by night at tents. Motlog and Tollog. Come anew to Ibn Náhal's tent. Ibn Náhal, a merchant Beduin. His wealth. A rich man rides in a ghrazzu, to steal one camel; and is slain. Tollog's inhospitable ferîj. Wander to another menzil. "Poor Aly." An Ageyly descried. A new face. A tent of poor acquaintance   287–319

CHAPTER XI
JOURNEY TO EL-KASÎM: BOREYDA

Beduin carriers. Set out with Hàmed, a Shammary. False report of the foray of Ibn S'aud and the Ateyba. The digging of water-pits in the khála. Ibn Rashîd's forays. Solubba. Beny Aly. Semîra, anciently Dîrat Ruwàlla. Terky, a Medina Beduin. A ráhla of Beny Sâlem. The Atáfa. A tempest of rain. Triple rainbow. Lightning by night in the desert. Religious Beduw. A gentle host. A Harb menzil pitched ring-wise. *el-Fúrn*, a kindred of Harb. Sâra mountain. The first village of el-Kasîm. Ayûn. Gassa. Watchtowers. Bare hospitality in el-Kasîm. The deep sand-land and its inhabitants. Aspect of Boreyda. The town. The Emir's hostel. The Nasrâny is robbed in the court yard. Jeyber, the Emir's officer. The Kasr Hajellân. Abdullah, the Emir's brother. Boreyda citizens; the best are camel masters in the caravans. Old tragedies of the Emirs. The town. A troubled afternoon. Set out on the morrow for Aneyza. Well sinking. Ethel trees   320–356

Appendix to Chap. XI

The Triple Rainbow. — Note by Prof. P. G. Tait, Sec. R.S.E.   356

CHAPTER XII
ANEYZA

The Nefûd (of el-Kasîm). Passage of the Wady er-Rummah. The Nasrâny, forsaken by the rafîk, finds hospitality; and enters Aneyza. Aspect of the town. The Emir *Zâmil*. His uncle Aly. The townspeople. *Abdullah el-Khenneyny*. His house and studies. Breakfast

CONTENTS 9

with Zâmil. The Nasrâny is put out of his doctor's shop by the Emir Aly. A Zelot. Breakfast PAGE
with el-Khenneyny. Eye diseases. Small-pox in the town. The streets of Aneyza. The
homely and religious life of these citizens. Women are unseen. *Abdullah el-Bessàm*. A dinner
in his house. The Bessàm kindred. Nâsir es-Smîry. The day in Aneyza. Jannah. el-
Khenneyny's plantation. *Hàmed es-Sâfy, Abdullah Bessàm,* the younger, and Sheykh *Ibn
Ayith*. An old Ateyba sheykh : Zelotism. The infirm and destitute. The Nasrâny's friends.
A tale of Ômar, the first Calif. Archæology. The Khenneyny. The vagabond Medina
Sherîf arrives at Aneyza. The good Bessàm   357–391

CHAPTER XIII
LIFE IN ANEYZA

Rumours of warfare. A savage tiding from the North. The Meteyr Aarab. The 'Ateyba.
A Kahtâny arrested in the street. A capital crime. Friday afternoon lecture. The *Muttowwa*.
Bessàm and Khenneyny discourse of the Western Nations. An Arabic gazette. " *The touchstone of truth.*" The *Shazlîeh*. An erudite Persian's opinion of The three (Semitic) religions.
European evangelists in Syria. An Arabian's opinions of Frankish manners (which he had
seen in India). An inoculator and leech at Aneyza. The Nasrâny without shelter. A learned
personage. Mohammed. The Semitic faiths. " Sheykh " Mohammed. Laudanum
powder medicine. A message from Boreyda. Discourse of religion. A Jew's word. The
small-pox. *Yahya's* household. Maladies. A short cure for distracted persons ; story of a
Maronite convent in Lebanon. Stone-workers at Aneyza. An outlying homestead. Money
borrowed at usury. Oasis husbandry. An Aneyza horsebroker. Ants' nests sifted for bread.
Arabian sale horses ; and the Northern or Gulf horses. El-'Eyarîeh. The Wady er-Rummah
northward. *Khâlid bin Walîd*. Owshazîeh. Deadly strife of well-diggers. Ancient man in
Arabia. The Nasrâny is an outlaw among them. Thoughts of riding to Sîddûs and er-Riâth.
The Arabic speech in el-Kasîm   392–426

CHAPTER XIV
THE CHRISTIAN STRANGER DRIVEN FROM ANEYZA; AND RECALLED

Yahya's homestead. Beduins from the North. Rainless years and murrain. Picking
and stealing in Aneyza. Handicrafts. Hurly-burly of fanatic women and children against
the Nasrâny. Violence of the Emir Aly, who sends away the stranger by night. Night
journey in the Nefûd. The W. er-Rummah. Strife with the camel driver. Come to
Khóbra in the Nefûd. The emir's kahwa. The emir's blind father. Armed riders of Boreyda.
Medicine seekers. The town. An 'Aufy. The cameleer returns from Zâmil ; to convey the
stranger again to Aneyza ! Ride to el-Helâlîeh. El-Búkerîeh. Helálîeh oasis. Night journey in
the Nefûd. Alight at an outlying plantation of Aneyza (appointed for the residence of the
Nasrâny). Visit of Abdullah el-Khenneyny.— Rasheyd's jenèyny. Sâlih. Joseph Khâlidy. A
son of Rasheyd had visited Europe ! Rasheyd's family. Ibrahîm. The Suez Canal. The
field labourers. El-Wéshm. A labouring lad's tales. Ruin of the Wahâby. Northern limits
of Murra and other Southern Aarab. A foray of Ibn Rashîd   427–456

Appendix to Chap. XIV
The 'Ateyba Aarab   457

CHAPTER XV
WARS OF ANEYZA. KAHTÂN EXPELLED FROM EL-KASÎM

The Wahâby governor driven out by the patriot Yahya. Aneyza beleaguered by Ibn
S'aud. The second war. A sortie. Aneyza women in the field. The words of Zâmil. A
strange reverse. Words of Yahya. A former usurping Emir was cut off by Zâmil. Zâmil's

homely life. The Emir's dues. Well-waters of Aneyza. Well-driving and irrigation. PAGE
Evenings in the orchard. The kinds of palms. Locusts. The Bosra caravan arrives. Violence
of Ibrahîm. Rasheyd visits his jenèyny. The hareem. The small-pox. Bereaved households.
The jehâd. Arabian opinion of English alms-deeds. The Meteyr Aarab gather to Aneyza.
Warfare of the town, with the Meteyr, against the (intruded) Kahtân. Morning onset of
Meteyr. Zâmil approaches. Final overthrow and flight of the Kahatîn. Hayzàn is slain.
The Kahtân camp in the power of Meteyr. A Moghrebby enthralled among those Kahtân
is set free. The Meteyr and the town return from the field. Beduin wives wailing for their
dead. ' When the Messiah comes will he bid us believe in Mohammed ? ' The great sheykh
of the Meteyr. The departure of the Mecca caravan is at hand. Hàmed el-Yahŷa. The
Nasrâny removes to the Khenneyny's palm-ground 458–485

CHAPTER XVI
SET OUT FROM EL-KASÎM, WITH THE BUTTER CARAVAN FOR MECCA

Abdullah el-Khenneyny; — a last farewell. Sleymàn, a merchant-carrier in the kâfily.
The camp at 'Auhellàn. The *emir el-kâfily*. The setting-out. Noon halt. Afternoon march.
The evening station. Er-Russ. The Abàn mountains. Ibrahîm, the emir. Simûm wind.
The last desert villages. A watering. Beduin rafîks. — *Are not these deserts watered by the
monsoon rains?* An alarm. Caravaners and Beduins. The landscape seyls to the W.
er-Rummah. Camels and cameleers. 'Afîf, a well-station. Signs of hunters. Caravan paths
to Mecca. *Wady Jerrîr*. Mountain landmarks, *Thúlm* and *Khâl*. Water tasting of alum.
The *Harrat el-Kisshub*. Thirst in the caravan. Sleymàn's opinion of English shippers.
A pleasant watering-place. *El-Moy*: cries in the evening menzil. *Er-Rukkaba*. Beduins.
Sh'aara watering. *Harrat 'Ashîry*. *Er-Rî'a*. *Es-Seyl* [KURN EL-MENÂZIL. Head of the
W. el-Humth. New aspect of Arabia. The caravaners about to enter Mecca take the ihràm.
The Hathèyl. The *ashràf* descend from Mohammed. Arrive at the 'Ayn (ez-Zeyma).
Mecca is a city of the Tehâma. The Nasrâny leaves the Nejd caravan at the station before
Mecca; and is assailed by a nomad sherîf 486–521

CHAPTER XVII
TÂYIF. THE SHERÎF, EMIR OF MECCA

Maabûb and Sálem. The Nasrâny captive. Troubled day at the 'Ayn. Night journey
with Mecca caravaners. Return to es-Seyl. The Seyl station. The Nasrâny assailed again.
A Mecca personage. An unworthy Bessàm. A former acquaintance. '*Okatz*. The path
beyond to et-Tâyif. Night journey. Alight at a sherîf's cottage near Tâyif. Poor women of
the blood of Mohammed. Aspect of et-Tâyif. The town. The Nasrâny is guest of a Turkish
officer. Evening audience of the Sherîf. Sherîf Hasseyn, Emir of Mecca. The Sherîf's
brother Abdillah. Turkish officers' coffee-club. A bethel stone. Zeyd, a Bîshy. Harb
villages and kindreds. Sâlem brings again their booty. A Turkish dinner. " What meat is for
the health." Three bethels. Mid-day shelter in an orchard 522–551

CHAPTER XVIII
WADY FÂTIMA

Ghraneym. His unequal battle with the Kahtân. A second audience of the Sherîf.
The tribes of ashràf. The dominion of the Sherîf. Gog and Magog. The *Rôb'a el-Khâly*.
Tâyif is in fear of the Muscôv. The Koreysh. Set out to ride to Jidda. " The English are
from the Tâyif dîra." A love-sick sherîf. A renowned effigy. The maiden's mountain.
New dates. The Wady Fâtima. Tropical plants. The shovel-plough. Another Harra.
Bee-hive-like cottages. The Tehâma heat. A rich man in both worlds. Mecca-country civil

CONTENTS

life and hospitality. A word of S'aud Ibn S'aud when he besieged Jidda. A thaif-Ullah. A poor negro's hospitality. End of the Fâtima valley. The Mecca highway to Jidda. Sacred doves. Witness-stones. Apes of the Teháma. A wayside Kahwa. — Jidda in sight! Melons grown in the sand without watering. Works and cisterns of Jidda water-merchants. 'Eve's grave.' Enter the town. — A hospitable consulate   552–574

Appendix to Vol. II

Geology of the Peninsular of the Arabs   575–6

INDEX AND GLOSSARY OF ARABIC WORDS   577

VOLUME TWO

CHAPTER I

IBN RASHÎD'S TOWN

Curious questioning of the townspeople. A Moor hakîm had visited Hâyil. He cast out demons. The jins. Superstitious fears of the Arabs. Exorcists. A counterfeit Christian vaccinator cut off in the desert. Advantage of the profession of medicine. Hamûd sends his sick infant son to the Nasrâny hakîm, who cures also Hamûd's wife. Diseases at Hâyil. The great Kasr. The guest-chambers. Hâyil house-building. Wards of the town. Artificers. Visit to S'weyfly. The mákbara has swallowed up the inhabitants. Deaf and dumb man-at-arms of the Emir. Májid shooting with ball. English gunpowder. Gulf words heard at Hâyil. Palms and a gum-mastic tree in Ajja. 'The coming of Mohammed foretold in the Enjîl.' Hamûd's tolerant urbanity. Another audience. The princely family of Ibn Rashîd. Telâl a slayer of himself. Metaab succeeded him. His nephews, Telâl's sons, conspire to kill him. Metaab dies by their shot. Bunder prince. Mohammed who fled to er-Riâth returns upon assurance of peace. He is again conductor of the Bagdad pilgrims. He comes again to Hâyil with the yearly convoy of temmn for the public kitchen. Bunder rides forth with his brother Bedr and Hamûd to meet him. Mohammed slays (his nephew) Bunder. Hamûd's speech to the people. Tragedies in the Castle. Mohammed's speech in the Méshab. He sits down as Muhafûth. Bedr taken and slain. Mohammed slays the slayer. Hamûd's nature. Mohammed the Emir is childless. His moderation and severity. The princely bounty. The Shammar state. Villages and hamlets. The public dues and taxes and expense of government. The Prince's horses sold in India. His forces. Ibn Rashîd's forays. He " weakens " the Aarab. The Shammar principality.

WHEN I returned in the afternoon from the ascent of the Sumrâ I found it was already a matter of talk in the town. The first persons met with approached to ask me, " What have you found there — anything ? tell us ! certainly you went to see something yonder, — and else wherefore had the Nasrâny climbed upon those high rocks, and paid pence for an ass ? " As I passed by the sûk tradesmen beckoned to me from the shops, they too would speak with me of the adventure.

My former friends durst no more be seen openly in the Nasrâny's company ; it might be laid to their charge, that they also favoured the kafir. As I walked on the morrow in the town, one of the young patricians of those daily about the Emir came to question me : — the most of these complacent young gallants, as I might perceive them, through their silken shining petticoats, are some of the vilest spirits in Hâyil. With many shallow impatient gestures, and plucking my mantle, " Khalîl, said he, what dost thou here, so far from the sûk? Why wander round about? what brings thee into this place? what seekest, what seest thou? Is Hâyil a good town? the air, is it well? — and when wilt thou depart?" As I came again a Beduwy who sat in the upper end of the Méshab saluted me friendly, he was of the Wélad Aly sheykhs, and had seen the Nasrâny at el-Héjr. We sat down together, and another came to me of those effeminate young silken Arabs, masking in the insolent confidence of the Emir. The cockerel disdainfully breaking our talk, I cut him off with — " Pass on, young man, my ears ache of thy ignorance and malevolent speech." The young man left us in anger, and as he was gone, " Khalîl, said the friendly Beduwy, I speak it of fellowship, deal not so plainly with this townspeople; believe me they will take up thy words, he also that you now sent away will not cease to hate thee extremely; and billah the young man is of their principal houses, and one nigh to the Emir. — Ay! here is another manner of life, than that to which thou hast been wont in the desert, and we are not here in the desert, neither be these the Beduw:" — and himself, a messenger from the rebellious tribe, he seemed somewhat to be daunted in the tyrannical shadow of the place.

Some friendly persons coming to visit me, after I had flitted from my old beyt to the next makhzan, said, " Khalîl is the second hakîm we have seen in this lodging." — " Who was the hakîm in this chamber before me?" — " A Moghreby, a doctor indeed, [better than Khalîl,] there was none like him to write hijâbs, and upon every one he received three reals: — why, Khalîl, write you no hijâbs? Write, man, and the whole town will be at thy door, and every one with two dollars, or three, in his hand. Thou mightest be enriched soon, that now never canst thrive in this selling of medicines, the Arabs desire no medicines. — But the Moghreby, wellah, holding his hijâbs a moment in the smoke, delivered them to those who paid him reals, and the people found them very availing. If such were the Moghreby's hijâbs, is not Khalîl a Nasrâny, and therefore one who might write even better than he? — Ah! how that man was powerful in his 'reading' (spells)! He cast out the demons of possessed persons, and he bound the jân, wellah, in yonder corner." — "What bound he in that corner?" — "*Ahl el-aard*, (the demon-folk, which inhabit under the earth,) they make men sick, and the possessed beat themselves, or they fall down, raging and foaming."

Aly el-Aŷid, my neighbour in the next houses, who was beholden to me for some faithful (medical) service, brought me a lamp of tallow, saying, ' He would not have a friend sleep here in the darkness, the demons might affray me ; ' and, looking round, " This Makhzan, he said, is full of jân (since the Moghreby's casting out so many), I myself durst not sleep in this place." — " But tell me, who has seen these jân, and what is their likeness ? " — " I have seen them, Khalîl, some tall, and some be of little stature, their looks are very horrible ; certain of them have but one eye in the midst of their faces ; other jins' visages be drawn awry in fearful manner, or their face is short and round, and the lips of many jins hang down to their middles." Aly el-Aŷid came early on the morrow to my beyt to know how I fared, and seeing not an hour of his tallow burned, he called me foolhardy to sleep without light. But pointing upward, he showed me a worse case, the great beam was half broken in the midst ! the load of the earthen heaped ceiling threatened ruin and destruction, and therefore they had lodged none here of late : — but even that abandoned makhzan Hamûd had conceded to the Nasrâny unwillingly. The wavering branches of a palm which grew in Hamûd's orchard-grounds, sliding ghostly in the open casement by night, might, I thought, be the jân of their unquiet consciences. By day little chirping sparrows of the Méshab were my guests, and more than other, amiable company.

I found professors of exorcism (as before said) at Hâyil : they were two vile and counterfeit persons. One of them was a man growing into years ; I had seen him at Abeyd's kahwa, and by certain of his answers he surprised me, and by his knowledge of letters : this person was a foreigner from East Nejd, but now he dwelt at Gofar. He seemed afraid in that presence to answer me ; perhaps he durst not speak frankly, or much above his breath. That other was a young man of Hâyil, and he came secretly to my makhzan, to learn some mastery in the art, from the Nasrâny. He asked me, ' what were my manner to lay strong constraint upon the demons, and the words of my powerful spells, *kerreya*.' ' He had a book too written full of very strong *readings* at home, and he sped very well by it, for he could cast out the jins more than any person besides. This was a smooth fellow, Nature had favoured him in all, and for his sweet voice the shrew was sometimes called in (he boasted) to sing before the Emir.

That Moghreby, with his blind arts, lived at Hâyil in the popular favour, and he had won much silver; also to the lone man they lent a pretty widow to wife, — "wherefore should he live without house-wifery?" Abdullah, a slave of the Emir, came to the Nasrâny upon a day with a like proffer, and Mâjid showed me a pleasant Galla maiden of his father's household, saying, that did I consent, she should be mine. The poor girl was gentle and modest, and without unwillingness; but because I would not lead my life thus, they ascribed it to the integrity of the Christian faith, and had the more tolerance of me in the rest. Word that 'the Princes suffered at Hâyil, and even favoured the Nasrâny' was spread by Beduins returning from the capital, into all the next parts of Arabia; and afterward I came nowhither in Nejd, until I arrived at the Kasîm villages, where they had not heard of the wandering Nasrâny, and by the signs they all knew me. They told me also of a Nasrâny (some Syrian by likelihood or Mesopotamian), who years before, coming to Hâyil, had taken the people's money for pretended vaccination. "But Ullah, they said, cut him off, for he was met with and slain in the desert by the Aarab."

Little was my practice of medicine, yet this name procured me entrance amongst them, and the surest friends. A man of medicine is not found in Nejd; but commonly they see some Ajamy hakîm, once a year, at Hâyil amongst the Persian pilgrims. I was called to visit suffering persons; yet because they would not leave with me the smallest pledge of their good faith, I remained with hardly any daily patients. Hamûd now sent to me an infant son, *Feysal*, that seemed to be of a very good disposition, and was sick of fever and dysentery. The child whom they brought to me, languishing and likely to die, I left, when I departed from Hâyil, nearly restored to health. I was called also to Hamûd's wife in his family house. I found her clad as other Arabian women in a simple calico smock dyed in indigo, her face was blotted out with the heathenish veil-clout; I gave her a medicine and she in a few days recovered. Of all their ailings most common (we have seen already) are eye-diseases, — it is the poorer, that is the misdieted people, who are the sooner affected — then diseases of the intestines, agues, old rheumatism; and men, the ignominy of the Meccawy's religion, too often complain of inability. The morbus gallicus is common at Hâyil, and in the neighbourhood; I saw many hypochondriacs [they are a third of all the Arabians]. There were brought to me cases of a sudden kind of leprosy;

the skin was discoloured in whitish spots, rising in the space of two or three days in the breast and neck. Cancer was not uncommon, and partial paralysis with atrophy of the lower limbs.

I enquired when was the Kasr founded? — which though claybuilt is of a certain noble aspect. The wall is near eight feet in thickness at the ground, and more than forty in height, and seems to be carried about a great space. Upon the public place, I measured this castle building, one hundred and ten paces, with two towers. The doorway of the Kasr, under the tower in the midst, is shut at evening by a rude door of heavy timber, in which is a little wicket, only to be entered stooping — and that before dark, is put-to. The wall and foundation of the huge clay building is from old times and was laid by some of the former sheykhs (surely men of ambitious mind) at Hâyil, before Abdullah. The Méshab in front is twenty-five paces over, and the makhzans built in face of the castle are nine in number. [*v.* the fig., Vol. I. p. 639.] To every makhzan is a door with a wooden lock opening into a little court, and beyond is the guest-chamber without door, square and dark, some fifteen feet by twelve feet. If any rubba would have fuel in the cold winter days, they must ask it of the Emir sitting in the public mejlis. Telâl built the makhzans, and the great mesjid; his father Abdullah had ended the building of the Kasr, only one year before his decease. The clay of the house-building at Hâyil is disposed in thick layers, in which are bedded, as we saw at Môgug, flat brick-blocks, long dried in the sunny air, set leaning wise, and very heavy, of great strength and endurance. The copes of the house-walling at Hâyil, and the sills of their casements, are often finished above with a singular stepped pinnacle (fig., Vol. I. p. 147), which resembles the strange sculptured cornice of the Petra and Héjr frontispices.

Their streets — I came in then from living long in the wilderness — I thought well set out; the rows are here of one-storied houses. There is no seeming of decay, but rather of newness, and thriving and spending: their capital village is seen, as her inhabitants, well arrayed. Hâyil is divided into eleven wards, a twelfth is S'weyfly. All the settlements in nomad Arabia, even the smallest hamlets, with the incorrupt desert about them, have a certain freshness and decent aspect above that which the traveller arriving from the West may have seen in Syria. The village Arabians — come of the nomad blood — are happy (where God's peace is not marred by striving factions) under the mild and just government of their homeborn sheykhs ; and in their green palm islands, they have much of the free-born and civil mind of the desert. At Hâyil, and Teyma, the stranger's eye may mark certain little close frames set high upon the front walling of many dàrs, and having the form of right-angled triangles ; he will see them to be timbered above the doorways. These are shooting-down sconces (like the machicolations of our mediæval fortresses), for defence of the door of the household.

As for the administration of the town, there are no dues at Hâyil for maintenance of ways or public lighting,—which is unknown even at Damascus — nor so much as for watchmen : yet the streets are clean, and draffe is cast out into certain pits and side places. Irrigation water drawn by camel labour from their deep wells, though not of the best, is at hand in sebîls and conduits ; to these common pools the town housewives resort to fill their pans and their girbies, and for the household washing. Dogs are not seen by day in any Nejd villages, but some lost hounds which remain without the most oases, will prowl by their streets in the night-time. Of household animals, there are in nearly all the settlements small kine for their sweet milk and as light plough-beasts, asses for riding and carriage, cats to quit them of vermin, besides poultry.

The artificers in Hâyil are few and of the smith's caste, workers in metal and wood, in which there are some who turn small and brittle ethelware bowls. Their thelûl saddle here is other than that of Teyma and westwards, in which the pillars are set upright. There is a petty industry among women of sewing and embroidering, with silk and metal thread, the mantles which are brought down (in the piece) from Jauf and Bagdad, — none are made here. I saw in the sûk fine skein-silks, folded in printed papers, and such the shopkeepers ofttimes put in my hands to read for them ; — but the language was English ! and when I found the title it was THE BOMBAY GAZETTE. Their hareem plait the common house-matting of the tender springing palm-leaf, as in all the oases. There are besides a few men of builders' and carpenters' craft, rude workers, nearly without tools, and pargeters in jiss or *jips*, a gypsum-stone which is brought from the mountain, and found clotted together, like mortar, in the desert sand. The jips, broken and ground to a flour-like powder, they mix with water, and spread it for the border and lining-walls of hearth-pits : this dries quickly to a hard white crust, shining like marble, that will bear the fire. The wood and hay gatherers who go far out into the wilderness, are *Kusmân*, laborious foreigners from el-Kasîm ; the nomad-spirited townspeople of Jebel Shammar are not good for such drudging labour.

I went out of Hâyil another day towards S'weyfly. Beyond Wâsit I walked by fields where men were labouring, and one threw clods at the Nasrâny, but the rest withheld him ; I went on between the two Samras, and beside the wide seyl bed, being there half a stone-cast over. The soil is now good loam, no more that sharp granite grit of Hâyil ; the dates are good, they are the best of the country. — The first houses I found to be but waste walls and roofless, and the plantations about them forsaken ; the languishing palm-stems showed but a dying crown of rusty leaves. I had not perceived a living person in these fields, that were once husbanded upon both sides of the large-bedded torrent. The pest, which destroyed the Jebel villages, came upon them, after a year of dearth, when the date harvest had failed, and the price of corn (three sahs to the real) was risen more than twofold. Strange it seems to us, used to public remedies, that in none of the merchants, more than in cattle, nor in the Prince himself, was there any readiness of mind to bring in grain from a distance : — the Moslem religion ever makes numbness and death in some part of the human understanding. The wába being come upon them there died in two months in this small village two hundred persons. The few which remained at S'weyfly were feeble even now, and had lost their health, so that it was said of them, " They might hardly bear the weight of their mantles." The cruel disease seized upon men sooner than women and children.

At length I came where a few persons were loitering abroad ; I saluted them in passing, and asked " Who has here a coffee-house, and where are the inhabitants ? " They saw he was a stranger who enquired this of them and responded with a desolate irony, " They lie in yonder mákbara ! " I went forward where I heard the shrilling of a suány. A woman (since the men were dead) was driving that camel-team at the well. It is eight fathoms here to water ; all their wells are brackish, and sweet water to drink must be fetched from Hâyil ' for money.' Brackish water in a sweet soil is best for the palm irrigation ; but if the palms be rooted in any saltish or bitter earth, as at Kheybar, they have need of a fresh irrigation water : and always for some little saltiness in the soil or water, palm-plants thrive the better. Such water to drink is very unwholesome in these climates, and was a cause they think of so many dying here in the pestilence. In old time, they say, when S'weyfly was ancient Hâyil, the wells in this part were sweet, that is until the new planting above them had spent the vein of good water. One led the stranger in hospitable manner to the best house which remained, to drink coffee. We entered a poor clay room, long unswept, and in the sun a swarming place of flies; this was their kahwa. The three or four ghastly looking and weakly speaking men who followed us in to drink were those that survived in the neighbourhood; and it seemed as if the nightmare lay yet upon them. Kindly they received the guest, and a tray was presently set before me of their excellent dates. The S'weyfly villagers, for this hospitable and gentle humour, are said to resemble rather the Beduw then Hâyil townspeople. Enough it seemed to them that the stranger was the hakîm, they would not cavil with a guest or question of his religion.

Whilst I sat with them at the coffee, there entered, with his sword, a deaf and dumb young man, whom I knew in Hâyil, one of the Prince's armed rajajîl: and with vehement signs and maffling cries he showed us he was come out from Hâyil to seek me. The poor fellow had always a regard of me in the town, and would suffer none to trouble me. I have seen him threaten even Mâjid in my chamber with angry looks, and shake his stick at the princeling boy, who too much, he thought, molested me. He now made them signs — drawing the first finger across his throat — that he feared for me so far abroad. All the way homeward the poor man blamed me, as if he would say "Why adventure so far alone, and thou art in danger to be waylaid?" I made him signs I went to visit sick people, that were in need of medicines. Lower where we passed he showed me smiling a few palm trees and a field which were his own. I heard he was a stranger (as are so many of the Emir's men) from el-Aruth. At my first arriving at Hâyil, when they beckoned to him that I was not of their religion, he quickly signified his friendly counsel ' that I should pray as the rest.' The poor Speechless uttered his soul in a single syllable, *Ppahppah*; that is nearly the first voice in children and dumb creatures, beginning in M-, B-, W-, which is all one. This P is not found in all the large Arabic alphabet, but any foreign taken-up words having in them that initial letter they must pronounce with F- or else with B-. All his meaning was now very well understood by the people of Hâyil; they made him kindly answers with movement of the lips, as in speaking, and of his wistful life-long comparison, he could guess again their minds: but if any mocked, with great bursting forth of *Ppahs* and chattering, and furious eyes, and laying hand upon his sword, he threatened their lives, or suddenly he drew it forth rattling, to the half, in the scabbard. Of his long sufferance of the malice of the world might be this singular resolution in him, to safeguard another manner of deaf and dumb person. He rode in the band upon his thelûl, and served very well, they said, in the Prince's ghrazzus.

As I returned to town I met with Mâjid and his company carrying guns in the fields, his uncle Fáhd was with them. Thus they went out daily, shooting with ball at a white paper set up in an orchard wall at a hundred and twenty paces. I sat down with Fáhd to see the practice; their shots from the long Arabic matchlocks struck at few fingers' distance all round the sheet, but rarely fell within it. The best was Ghrânim, when he was one amongst them, for looking through spectacles, he would send his ball justly at the first shot into the midst of the white;—this firing with the match does not unsettle the aim. They shot with 'powder Engleysy,' of a tin flask, whereupon I read in a kind of stupor, HALL, DARTFORD! There are many sea-borne wares of the Gulf-trade seen at Hâyil, and the people take as little thought from whence they come to them, as our country people of China tea-chests; European are many things of their most necessary use, as the husbandman's spades and crowbars, pigs of lead with the English stamp, iron and tinning metal; their clothing is calico of Manchester and Bombay. All their dealings are in foreign money; reals of Spain, Maria Theresa dollars, and Turkish mejîdy crowns; gold money is known more than seen among them. They call *doubloon* the piece of 5 Turkish pounds, English sovereigns *ginniyát* or *bintu*, and the 20 fr. piece *lira fransâwy*. For small silver in the Hâyil sûk they have Austrian sixpences, and certain little gross Persian coins, struck awry, and that for the goodly simplicity of the workmanship resemble the stamps of the old Greek world. With the love of novelty which is natural even to Semitic souls, they are also importers with their foreign merchandise of some Gulf words, especially from the Persian, as they will say for a dromedary *shittr*, rather than of their own wealth in the current Arabic, (*hajîn*,) *thelûl*, *rikàb*, (*hadùj*), *mátîyah*, *rohòl*, *hâshy*, *hurra*.

Mâjid invited me, if I stayed till winter, to take part in their hunting expeditions in Ajja. Then the young franklins and men of Hâyil, and even the Princes, go out to the mountain to shoot at the bedûn, driving asses with them to carry their water: they commonly stay out a week thus and trust to shooting the game for their supper. In many small wadies of Ajja are wild palms watered by springs, or growing with their roots in the seyl ground. The owners are Beduin families which come thither only in the time of the date gathering: the date is smaller than the fruit of trees which are husbanded. There grows a tree in Ajja, named *el-aràr*, from which flows a sort of gum-mastica, " it resembles the tamarisk." Ajja is greater, and a score of miles longer, than the sister mountain Selma.

Hamûd I saw daily; I went to dine with him again, and as we sat in the evening, he said to me, " Is there not something written in the Enjîl, of Mohammed?"—" Nay, nothing, and I know of it every word."—" But is there not mentioned that a prophet, by name *Hamed*, should come after;—and that is Mohammed?" I answered shortly again: " No, there *is not*." Hamûd startled, he believed me, his humanity persuaded him that I could not intend any offence—and that were without remission—towards the religion. I said further: " If such were found in the Enjîl, I would be a Mosleman; do you read this word in the koran!" Hamûd did not answer, he sat on gravely musing. It was an enigma to me what they might mean by a prediction of Hamed or Mohammed (which is one) in the Christian scriptures.—We read in the sixth verset of the koran chapter 61, " *And said Îsa-bin-Miriam, O Beny Israel, I am the apostle of Ullah, to confirm the Towrât* (Mosaic Scriptures) *and to show unto you the coming of an apostle,—his name shall be Ahmed*" (The Glorious). To such Ahmed or Glorious One responds in the tongue of the New or Hellenic Scriptures the word Περικλυτός, ' very illustrious.' Therefore their barbaric doctors bray that the malicious Nasâra have miswritten Παράκλητος, ' Comforter' [which word is but four times found, and namely, in the last testament of Christ, from the xiv. to the xvi. chapters of St. John].

Hamûd took pleasure to question, and commune with me of our religion; he smiled with pious admiration to hear the Nasrâny stranger repeat after him some part of their canonical prayers, and say ' he held them thus far for godly,' as the fâtiha, commonly said in the beginning of their devotion, which sounds in their full and ripe Nejd utterance of a certain surprising beauty and solemnity : the sense of the text is this : " In the name of the God of the Bowels of Mercies. The praise be unto God, the Lord of all worlds [creatures], the God of the Bowels and Mercies, Sovereign of the day of doom ; we adore Thee, we for help do cry unto Thee. Lead us in the right way ; the way of those unto whom Thou hast been gracious, with whom Thou art not wroth, and which be not gone astray." Hamûd, even in his formal religion, was of a tolerant urbanity : religion was in him the (politic) religion of rulers. In the palm ground without his kahwa, he has (in their town manner) a raised place for prayers ; this was a square platform in clay, with a low cornice, bestrewn with clean gravel, and so large that a coffee company might kneel in it and bow themselves to the ground. Hamûd prayed in this oratory in the day-time, as imâm, before the men of his household. Some day whilst they prayed, Aly, that ribald foot-follower of Mâjid, laid hands suddenly on my mantle to have drawn me among them. But Hamûd stayed in his prayers to smile towards one and the other, and with a sign forbade that the stranger should suffer any displeasure. In all the house-courts at Hâyil, and in their orchard grounds, there is made some such praying-stand ; it may be a manner of the reformed religion in Nejd, and like to this we have seen prayer-steads in the open deserts defended from the common by a border of stones. Every such raised clay *masálly*, littered with pure gravel, is turned towards the sanctuary of Arabia.

A week passed and then the Emir Mohammed came again from the wilderness : the next afternoon he called for me after the mejlis. His usher found me slumbering in my makhzan ; worn and broken in this long year of famine and fatigues, I was fallen into a great languor. The Prince's man roused me with haste and violence in their vernile manner : " Stand up thou and come off ; the Emir calls thee ; " and because I stayed to take the kerchief and mantle, even this, when we entered the audience, was laid against me, the slave saying to the Emir that ' Khalîl had not been willing to follow him ! '

Mohammed had gone over from the mejlis with the rajajîl to Abeyd's kahwa. The Emir sat now in Hamûd's place, and Hamûd where Sleymàn daily sat. The light scimitar, with golden hilt, that Mohammed carries loose in his hand, was leaned up to the wall beside him ; the blade is said to be of some extremely fine temper. He sat as an Arabian, in his loose cotton tunic, mantle and kerchief, with naked shanks and feet, his sandals, which he had put off at the carpet, were set out before him. I saluted the Emir, *Salaam aleyk*. — No answer : then I greeted Hamûd and Sleymàn, now of friendly acquaintance, in the same words, and with *aleykom es-salaam* they hailed me smiling comfortably again. One showed me to a place where I should sit down before the Emir, who said shortly " From whence ? " — " From my makhzan." — ' And what found I there to do all the day, ha ! and what had I seen in the time of my being at Hâyil, was it well ? ' When the Prince said, " Khalîl ! " I should have responded in their manner *Aunak* or *Labbeyk* or *Tawîl el-Ummr*, " O Long-of-age ! and what is thy sweet will ? " but feeling as an European among these light-tongued Asiatics, and full of mortal weariness, I kept silence. So the Emir, who had not responded to my salutation, turned abruptly to ask Hamûd and Sleymàn : *Mâ yarúdd?* ' how ! he returns not one's word who speaks with him ? ' Hamûd responded kindly for me, ' He could not tell, it might be Khalîl is tired.' I answered after the pause, " I am lately arrived in this place, but *aghrûty*, I suppose it is very well." The Emir opened his great feminine Arab eyes upon me as if he wondered at the not flattering plainness of my speech ; and he said suddenly, with an emphasis, before the company, " Ay, I think so indeed, it is very well ! — and what think you Khalîl, it is a good air ? " — " I think so, but the flies are very thick." — " Hmm, the flies are very thick ! and went you in the pilgrimage to the Holy City (Jerusalem) ? " — " Twice or thrice, and to *J. Tôr*, where is the mountain of our Lord Mûsa." — Some among them said to the Emir, " We have heard that monks of the Nasâra dwell there, their habitation is built like a castle in the midst of the khála, and the entry is by a window upon the wall ; and who would come in there must be drawn up by a wheelwork and ropes." The Emir asked, " And have they riches ? " — " They have a revenue of alms." The Emir rose, and taking his sandals, all the people stood up with him, — he beckoned them to be seated still, and went out to the plantation. In the time of his absence there was silence in all the company ; when he returned he sat down again without ceremony. The Prince, who would discern my mind in my answers, asked me, " Were dates good or else bad ? " and I answered " *battâl, battâl*, very bad." — " Bread is better ? and what in your tongue is bread ? " he repeated to himself the name which he had heard in Turkish, and he knew it in the Persian ;

Mohammed, formerly conductor of the pilgrimage, can also speak in that language.

The Emir spoke to me with the light impatient gestures of Arabs not too well pleased, and who play the first parts, — a sudden shooting of the brows, and that shallow extending of the head from the neck, which are of the bird-like inhabitants of nomadic Nejd, and whilst at their every inept word's end they expect thy answer. The Emir was favourably minded toward me, but the company of malignant young fanatics always about him, continually traduced the Nasrâny. Mohammed now Prince was as much better than they, as he was of an higher understanding. When to some new question of the Emir I confirmed my answer in the Beduin wise, By his life, *hayâtak*, he said to Hamûd, "Seest thou? Khalîl has learned to speak (Arabic) among the Annezy, he says *aghrûty*." — "And what might I say, O el-Muhafûth? I speak as I heard it of the Beduw." The Prince would not that I should question him of grammar, but hearing me name him so justly by his title, Warden (which is nearly that in our history of Protector), he said mildly, "Well, swear By the life of Ullah!" (The other, since they are become so clear-sighted with the Wahâby, is an oath savouring of idolatry.) I answered somewhat out of the Prince's season, "— and thus even the nomads use, in a greater occasion, but they say, *By the life of thee*, in a little matter." As the Prince could not draw from me any smooth words of courtiers, Hamûd and Sleymàn hastened, with their fair speech, to help forth the matter and excuse me. "Certainly, they said, Khalîl is not very well to-day, eigh, the poor man! he looks sick indeed!" — And I passed the most daylight hours, stretched weakly upon the unswept floor of my makhzan, when the malignants told the Emir I was writing up his béled; so there ofttimes came in spies from the Castle, who opened upon me suddenly to see in what manner the Nasrâny were busied. — *Emir*: "And thy medicines are what? hast thou *tiryâk*?" [thus our fathers said treacle, θηριαχ-, the antidote of therine poisons]. In an extreme faintness, I was now almost falling into a slumber, and my attention beginning to waver I could but say, — "What is tiryâk? — I remember, but I have it not, by God there is no such thing." *Sleymàn*: "Khalîl has plenty of salts Engleys (magnesia) — hast thou not, Khalîl?" At this dull sally, and the Arabian Emir being so much in thought of poison, I could not forbear to smile, — an offence before rulers. Sleymàn then beginning to call me to give account in that presence of the New Continent, he would I should say, if we had not dates there, but the " Long-of-Days " rose abruptly and haughtily, — so rose all the rest with him, and they departed.

A word now of the princely family and of the state of J. Shammar: and first of the tragedies in the house of Ibn Rashîd. Telâl returning from er-Riâth (whither he was accustomed, as holding of the Waháby, to go every year with a present of horses) fell sick, *musky*, poisoned, it was said, in his cup, in East Nejd. His health decayed, and the Prince fell into a sort of melancholy frenzy. Telâl sent to Bagdad for a certain Persian hakîm. The hakîm journeyed down to Hâyil, and when he had visited the Prince, he gave his judgment unadvisedly: " This sickness is not unto death, it is rather a long disease which must waste thy understanding."—Telâl answered, " Aha, shall I be a fool?— wellah *mejnûn! wa ana el*-Hâkim, and I being the Ruler?" And because his high heart might not longer endure to live in the common pity, one day when he had shut himself in his chamber, he set his pistols against his manly breast, and fired them and ended. So Metaab, his brother, became Emir at Hâyil, as the elder of the princely house inheriting Abdullah their father's dignity: Telâl's children were (legally) passed by, of whom the eldest, Bunder, afterwards by his murderous deed Emir, was then a young man of seventeen years. Metaab I have often heard praised as a man of mild demeanour, and not common understanding; he was princely and popular at once, as the most of his house, politic, such as the great sheukh el-Aarab, and a fortunate governor. Metaab sat not fully two years, — always in the ambitious misliking of his nephew Bunder, a raw and strong-headed young man. Bunder, conspiring with his next brother, Bedr, against their uncle, the ungracious young men determined to kill him.

They knew that their uncle wore upon his arm " an amulet which assured his life from lead," therefore the young parricides found means to cast a silver bullet. — Metaab sat in his fatal hour with his friends and the men-at-arms before him in the afternoon mejlis, which is held, as said, upon the further side of the Méshab, twenty-five paces over in face of the Kasr. — Bunder and Bedr were secretly gone up from the apartments within to the head of the castle wall, where is a terrace and parapet. Bunder pointing down his matchlock through a small trap in the wall, fired first; and very likely his hand wavered when all hanged upon that shot, for his ball went a little awry and razed the thick head-band of a great Beduin sheykh *Ibn Shalàn*, chief of the strong and not unfriendly Annezy tribe er-Ruwàlla in the north, who that day arrived from his dîra, to visit Prince Ibn Rashîd. Ibn Shalàn, hearing the shot sing about his ears, started up, and (cried he) putting a hand to his head, " Akhs, Mohafûth, wouldst thou murder me! " The Prince, who sat on, and would not save himself by an unseemly flight, answered the sheykh with a constant mild face, " Fear not ; thou wilt see that the shot was levelled at myself." A second shot struck the Emir in the breast, which was Bedr's.

Bunder being now Prince, sat not a full year out, and could not prosper: in his time, was that plague which so greatly wasted the country. Mohammed who is now Emir, when his brother Metaab was fallen, fled to er-Riâth, where he lived awhile. The Waháby prince, Abdullah Ibn Saûd, was a mean to reconcile them, and Bunder, by letters, promising peace, invited his uncle to return home. So Mohammed came, and receiving his old office, was governor again of the Bagdad haj caravan. Mohammed went by with the convoy returning from Mecca to Mesopotamia, and there he was to take up the year's provision of temmn for the Mothîf (if you would believe them, a thousand camel-loads, — 150 tons!) Mohammed finding only Thuffîr Aarab at el-Méshed, hired camels of them with promise of safe-conduct going and returning, in the estates of Ibn Rashîd; for they were Beduw from without, and not friendly with the Jebel. The journey is two weeks' marches of the nomads for loaded camels. — Mohammed approaching Hâyil, sent before him to salute the Emir saying, " Mohammed greets thee, and has brought down thy purveyance of temmn for the Mothîf." — " Ha! is Mohammed come? answered Bunder, — he shall not enter Hâyil." Then Bunder, Bedr, and Hamûd rode forth, these three together, to meet Mohammed; and at Bunder's commandment the town gates behind them were shut.

Mohammed sat upon his thelûl, when they met with him, as he had ridden down from the north, and said Bunder, " Mohammed, what Beduw hast thou brought to Hâyil? — the Thuffîr! and yet thou knowest them to be gôm with us!" *Mohammed :* " Wellah, yâ el-Mohafûth, I have brought them *bî wéjhy*, under my countenance! (and in the Arabian guise he stroked down his visage to the beard) —

because I found none other for the carriage of your temmn." Whilst Bunder lowered upon him, Hamûd, who was in covenant with his cousin Mohammed, made him a sign that his life was in doubt, — by drawing (it is told) the forefinger upon his gullet. Mohammed spoke to one of the town who came by on horseback, " Ho there ! lend me thy mare awhile," making as though he would go and see to the entry and unloading of his caravan. Mohammed, when he was settled on horseback, drew over to the young Prince and caught Bunder's " horns," and with his other hand he took the crooked broad dagger, which upon a journey they wear at the belt. — " *La ameymy, la ameymy*, do it not, do it not, little 'nuncle mine ! " exclaimed Bunder in the horror and anguish of death. Mohammed answered with a deadly stern voice, " Wherefore didst thou kill thine uncle ? *wa hu fî batn-ak*, and he is in thy belly (thou hast devoured him, dignity, life, and all)," and with a murderous hand-cast he struck the blade into his nephew's bowels ! — There remained no choice to Mohammed, when he had received the sign, he must slay his elder brother's son, or himself be lost ; for if he should fly, how might he have outgone the godless young parricides ? his thelûl was weary, he was weary himself ; and he must forsake the Thuffîr, to whom his princely word had been plighted. — Devouring is the impotent ambition to rule, of all Arabians who are born near the sheykhly state. Mohammed had been a loyal private man under Metaab ; his brother fallen, what remained but to avenge him ? and the garland should be his own.

Bunder slain, he must cut off kindred, which else would endanger him. The iniquity of fortune executed these crimes by Mohammed's hand, rather than his own execrable ambition. — These are the tragedies of the house of Ibn Rashîd ! their beginning was from Telâl, the murderer of himself : the fault of one extends far round, such is the cursed nature of evil, as the rundles of a stone dashed into water, trouble all the pool. There are some who say that Hamûd made Bunder's dying sure with a pistol-shot, — he might do this, because his lot was bound up in Mohammed's life : but trustworthy persons in Hâyil have assured me that Hamûd had no violent hand in it. — Hamûd turning his horse's head, galloped to town and commanded to ' keep the gates close, and let no man pass out or enter for any cause ' ; and riding in to the Méshab he cried : " Hearken, all of you ! a Rashîdy has slain a Rashîdy, — there is no word for any of you to say !

let no man raise his voice or make stir, upon pain of my hewing off his head wellah with this sword."

In Hâyil there was a long silence, the subject people shrunk in from the streets to their houses ! Beduins in the town were aghast, inhabitants of the khála, to which no man " may set doors and bars," seeing the gates of Hâyil to be shut round about them.

An horrible slaughter was begun in the Kasr, for Mohammed commanded that all the children of Telâl should be put to death, and the four children of his own sister, widow of one *el-Jabbâr* of the house *Ibn Aly*, (that, till Abdullah won all, were formerly at strife with the Rashîdy family for the sheykhship of Hâyil, — and of them was Mohammed's own mother). Their uncle's bloody command was fulfilled, and the bleeding warm corses, deceived of their young lives, were carried out the same hour to the burial ; there died with them also the slaves, their equals in age, brought up in their fathers' households, — their servile brethren, that else would be, at any time, willing instruments to avenge them.

All Hâyil trembled that day till evening and the long night till morning, when Mohammed, standing in the Méshab with a drawn sword, called to those who sat timidly on the clay banks, — the most were Beduins — " Yâ Moslemîn ! I had not so dealt with them, but because I was afraid for this ! (he clapped the left palm to the side of his neck), and as they went about to kill me, *ana sabáktahum*, I have prevented them." Afterward he said : — " And they which killed my brother Metaab, think ye they had spared me ? " " And hearing his voice, we sat (an eyewitness, of the Meteyr, told me) astonished, every one seeing the black death before him." — Then Mohammed sat down in the Emir's place as Muhafûth. Bye and bye some of the principal persons at Hâyil came into the Méshab bending to this new lord of their lives, and giving him joy of his seized authority. Thus ' out dock in nettle,' Bunder away, Mohammed began to rule ; and never was the government, they say, in more sufficient handling.

— Bedr had started away upon his mare for bitter-sweet life to the waste wilderness : he fled at assr. On the morrow, fainting with hunger and thirst, and the suffered desolation of mind and weariness, he shot away his spent horse, and climbed upon a mountain. — From thence he might look far out over the horror of the world, become to him a vast dying place ! Mohammed had sent horsemen to scour the khála, and take him; and when they found Bedr in the rocks they would not listen to his lamentable petitions: they killed him there without remedy, and hastily loading his body they came again the same day to Hâyil. The chief of them as he entered, all heated, to Mohammed, exclaimed joyfully, " Wellah, O Muhafûth, I bring thee glad tidings ! it may please thee come with me whereas I will show thee Bedr lies dead ; this hand did it, and so perish all the enemies of the Emir ! " But Mohammed looked grimly upon the man, and cried, " Who commanded thee to kill him ? I commanded thee, son of an hound ? when, thou cursed one ? Ullah curse thy father, akhs ! hast thou slain Bedr ? " and, drawing his sword, he fetched him a clean back-stroke upon the neck-bone, and swapt off at once (they pretend) the miserable man's head. Mohammed used an old bitter policy of tyrants, by which they hope to make their perplexed causes seem the more honest in the thick eye-sight of the common people. " How happened it, I asked, that Bedr, who must know the wilderness far about, since the princely children accompany the ghrazzus, had not ridden hardily in some way of escape ? Could not his mare have borne him an hundred miles ? — a man of sober courage, in an extremity, might have endured, until he had passed the dominion of Ibn Rashîd, and entered into the first free town of el-Kasîm." It was answered, " The young man was confused in so great a calamity, and jâhil, of an inept humour, and there was none to deliver him."

Hamûd and Mohammed allied together, there was danger between them and Telâl's sons ; and if they had not forestalled Bunder and Bedr, they had paid it with their lives. The massacres were surely contrary to the clement nature of the strong man Hamûd. Hamûd, who for his pleasant equal countenance, in the people's eyes, has deserved to be named by his fellow citizens *Azîz*, " a beloved," is for all that, when contraried out of friendship, a lordly man of outrageous incontinent tongue and jabbâr, as his father was ; and doubtless he would be a high-handed Nimrod in any instant peril. Besides, it is thus that Arabs deal with Arabs ; there are none more pestilent, and ungenerous enemies. Hamûd out of hospitality, is as all the Arabs of a somewhat miserable humour, and I have heard it uttered at Hâyil, " Hamûd *khára !* " that is draffe or worse. These are vile terms of the Hejâz, spread from the dens of savage life, under criminal governors, in the Holy Cities ; and not of those schools of speaking well and of comely manners, which are the kahwa in the Arabian oases and the mejlis in the open khála. — A fearful necessity was laid upon Mohammed: for save by these murders of his own nigh blood, he could not have sat in any daily assurance. Mohammed is childless, and ajjr, a man barren in himself; the loyal Hamûd el-Abeyd has many children.

His instant dangers being thus dispersed, Mohammed set himself to the work of government, to win the opinion of his proper merit; and affecting popular manners, he is easier of his dispense than was formerly Telâl. Never Prince used his authority, where not resisted, with more stern moderation at home, but he is pitiless in the excision of any unsound parts of the commonwealth. When Jauf fell to him again by the mutiny of the few Moghrâreba left in garrison, it is said, he commanded to cut off the right hands of many that were gone over to the faith of the Dowla. Yet Jauf had not been a full generation under the Jebel; for Mohammed himself, then a young man, was with his uncle Abeyd at the taking of it, and he was wounded then by a ball in the foot which lodged in the bone; — the shot had lately been taken from him in Hâyil by a Persian hakîm, come down, for the purpose, from Mesopotamia.

As for any bounty in such Arabian Princes, it is rather good laid out by them to usury. They are easy to loose a pound to-day, which within a while may return with ten in his mouth. The Arabs say, "Ibn Rashîd uses to deal with every man *aly aklu*, according to his understanding." Fortune was to Mohammed's youth contrary, a bloody chance has made him Ruler. In his government he bears with that which may not be soon amended; he cannot by force only bridle the slippery wills of the nomads; and though his heart swell secretly, he receives all with his fair-weather countenance, and to friendly discourse; and of few words, in wisely questioning them, he discerns their minds. Motlog, sheykh of the Fejîr, whom he misliked, he sends home smiling; and the Prince will levy his next year's *mîry* from the Fukara, without those tribesmen's unwillingness. The principal men of Teyma, his good outlying town, whose well was fallen, depart from him with rewards. Mohammed smooths the minds of the common people; if any rude Beduin lad call to him in the street, or from the mejlis (they are all arrant beggers), "Aha! el-Muhafûth, God give thee long life! as truly as I came hither, in such a rubba, and wellah am naked," he will graciously dismiss him with "*bismillah*, in God's name! go with such an one, and he will give thee garments," — that is a tunic worth two shillings at Hâyil, a coarse worsted cloak of nine shillings, a kerchief of sixpence; and since they are purchased in the gross at Bagdad, and brought down upon the Emir's own camels, they may cost him not ten shillings.

What is the state and authority for which these bitter Arabians contended? Ibn Rashîd is master, as I can understand, of some thirty oases, of which there are five good desert towns: Sh'kâky, Jauf, Hâyil, Gofar, Teyma, with a population together of 12,000 to 13,000 souls: others are good villages, as *el-Kasr, Mógug, Aly, Mustajidda, Feyd, er-Rautha, Semîra, el-Hâyat*, and more, with hardly 5000 persons. There are, besides the oases, many outlying hamlets in the desert of Jebel Shammar inhabited by a family or two or three households, that are colonists from the next villages; in the best may be a score of houses, in the least are not ten inhabitants; such are *Jefeyfa, el-Agella, el-Gussa, Biddîa, Haleyfa, Thùrghrod, Makhaûl, Otheym*. Some among them are but granges, which lie forsaken, after the April harvest is carried, until the autumn sowing and the new months of irrigation: but the palm hamlets have stable inhabitants, as Biddîa, Thûrghrod. So the settled population of Jemel Shammar may be hardly 20,000 souls: add to these the tributary nomads, Beny Wáhab, — the Fejîr, 800, and half tribe of Wélad Aly in the south, 1600 — say together 2500; then Bishr in the south, say 3000, or they are less; northern Harb in the obedience of Ibn Rashîd, say 2000; southern Shammar, hardly 2000; midland Heteym, say 1500; Sherarát, say 2500; and besides them no more. In all, say 14,000 persons or less: and the sum of stable and nomad dwellers may be not much better than 30,000 souls.

The burden of the Emir's public contribution is levied in the settlements, upon the fruits of corn and dates, — we have seen that it was in Teyma nearly £1 sterling for every head; and among nomads, (who have little regard of any government set up for the public advantage,) it was in the Fukara, a poor tribe, about £1 sterling for eight or ten persons. Other than these exactions there are certain dues, of which I am not well informed, such as that payment to be made of sixty reals upon every camel-load of Hameydy tobacco, which is brought in, at the sûk gates of Hâyil. In this not improbable course of conjecture I can compute the state revenues of Ibn Rashîd, partly in kind, and partly paid in silver, to be nearly £40,000, of which hardly the twentieth part is gathered among his nomads. The private rents of the Prince are also very large. The price and fruits of all confiscated possessions are brought yearly into the beyt el-mâl, or public treasure-house.

The ordinary government expenses, for the castle service, for the maintenance of the armed band, the slave grooms of his stud and the herdsmen of his live wealth in the wilderness, stewards, mutasállims, his residents in outlying towns as Teyma and Jauf, the public hospitality at Hâyil, and for the changes of clothing, may be nearly £12,000. His extraordinary expenses are nearly £1000 yearly in gunpowder and provision for the general ghrazzus, and yearly gifts. His bribes are according to the shifting weather of the world, to great Ottoman government men ; and now on account of Kheybar, he was gilding some of their crooked fingers in Medina. These disbursements are covered by his selling, most years, Nejd horses (all stallions) in India ; which, according to the request, are shipped at Kuweyt, commonly about two score together : — his stud servants, who convey them, are absent from Hâyil, upon the India expedition, about two months.

In a necessity of warfare Ibn Rashîd might summon to the field, I suppose, without much difficulty, 2000 fighting men from his villages, riders upon camels (the most thelûls), but not all provided with fire-arms ; and to ride in an expedition not easily to a fourth of the number. Among the subject Beduw he might raise at a need, of the tribes more bound to him, or most fearing him as nigh neighbours, Shammar, Bishr, Harb, Heteym, as I can estimate of my knowledge of the land, eight hundred or nine hundred : of the B. Wáhab, as borderers, always of doubtful trust, and not seldom rebels, two hundred and fifty ; of the oppressed Sherarát, who would gladly turn from him to the Dowla, if the Syrian government would stand by them, nearly another two hundred ; that is altogether to the number of 1300 nomad Arabians, namely dromedary riders (only a few principal sheykhs are horsemen) — and two-third parts of them armed with matchlocks, the remnant riding as they may, with swords, clubs, spears and lances. The Prince is said to have " four hundred horses," lent out to men of his trust and interest among the submitted tribes ; they are riders in his yearly expeditions. In the Prince's general ghrazzus there ride, his rajajîl and Hâyil towns-men and men of the next villages, about four hundred men, and nearly as many of the tributary Beduw that are ready at the word of the Emir to mount with him in the hope of winning : and to all a day is given and the assembling place. The Arabians, dwelling in a dead country, think that a marvellous muster of human lives which they see assemble to Ibn Rashîd's forays. They will tell you " All the way was full of riders betwixt Hâyil and Gofar ! " — since it is hardly twelve miles, that were but a rider, in their loose array, for every twenty paces ; and eight hundred or nine hundred armed Arabs mounted upon dromedaries, even in the eyes of Europeans, were a noble spectacle.

The Prince Mohammed is pitiless in battle, he shoots with an European rifle ; Hamûd, of ponderous strength, is seen raging in arms by the Emir's side, and, if need were, since they are sworn together to the death, he would cover him with his body. The princes, descended from their thelûls, and sitting upon horseback in their " David shirts of mail," are among the forefighters, and the wings of the men-at-arms, shooting against the enemy, close them upon either hand. The Emir's battle bears down the poor Beduw, by weight and numbers ; for the rajajîl, and his riders of the villages, used to the civil life, hear the words of command, and can maintain themselves in a body together. But the bird-witted Beduins who, in their herding life, have no thought of martial exercises, may hardly gather, in the day of battle, under their sheukh, but like screaming hawks they fight dispersedly, tilting hither and thither, every man with less regard of the common than of his private interest, and that is to catch a beggarly booty : the poor nomads acknowledge themselves to be betrayed by tóma, the greediness of gain. Thus their resistance is weak, and woe to the broken and turned to flight ! None of the Emir's enemies are taken to quarter until they be destroyed : and cruel are the mercies of the rajajîl and the dire-hearted slaves of Ibn Rashîd. I have known when some miserable tribesmen made prisoners were cast by the Emir's band into their own well-pits : — the Arabians take no captives. The battles with nomads are commonly fought in the summer, about their principal water-stations, where they are long lodged in great standing camps.

Thus the Beduins say " It is Ibn Rashîd that weakens the Beduw ! " Their resistance broken, he receives them among his confederate tributaries, and delivers them from all their enemies from his side. A part of the public spoil is divided to the rajajîl, and every man's is that commonly upon which he first laid his hand. Ibrahîm the Algerian, one of them who often came to speak with me of his West Country, said that to every man of the Emir's rajajîl are delivered three or four reals at the setting out, that he may buy himself wheat, dates and ammunition; and there is carried with them sometimes as much as four camel loads of powder and lead from Hâyil, which is partly for the Beduw that will join him by the way.

But to circumscribe the principality or dominion in the deserts of Ibn Rashîd: — his borders in the North are the Ruwàlla, northern Shammar and Thuffîr marches, nomad tribes friendly to the Jebel, but not his tributaries. Upon the East his limits are at the dominion of Boreyda, which we shall see is a principality of many good villages in the Nefûd of Kasîm, as el-Ayun, Khubbera, er-Russ, but with no subject Beduw. The princely house of Hâyil is by marriage allied to that usurping peasant *Weled Mahanna* tyrant of Boreyda, and they are accorded together against the East, that is Aneyza, and the now decayed power of the Waháby beyond the mountain. In the South, having lost Kheybar, his limits are at about an hundred miles from el-Medina; the deserts of his dominion are bounded westwards by the great haj-way from Syria, — if we leave out the B. Atîeh — and all the next territory of the Sherarát is subject to him, which ascends to J. Sherra and so turns about by the *W. Sirhân* to his good northern towns of Jauf and Sh'kâky and their suburbs. In a word, all that is Ibn Rashîd's desert-country lying between Jauf, el-Kasîm and the Derb el-Haj; north and south some ninety leagues over, and between east and west it may be one hundred and seventy leagues over. And the whole he keeps continually subdued to him with a force (by their own saying) of about five hundred thelûl riders, his rajajîl and villagers; for who may assemble in equal numbers out of the dead wilderness, or what were twice so many wild Beduins, the half being almost without arms, to resist him?

CHAPTER II

LIFE IN HÂYIL

The great tribes beyond Ibn Rashîd. *Akhu Noora.* The princely families. The Prince Mohammed childless. His "Christian wife." Abd el-Azîz the orphan child of Telâl, and his brother orphan child of Bunder. Secret miseries of Princes. The family of Abeyd. A song of Abeyd. Abeyd could be generous. Fáhd. The poor distracted soul sells his daughter to his father Abeyd. Feyd. Sleymàn. Abdullah. Wealth of Abeyd's family. Hamûd's daughter. The government of Ibn Rashîd. Beginning of the Shammar state. By some the Emir is named *Zâlim,* a tyrant. A tale of Metaab's government. A Christian Damascene tradesman visits Hâyil. Discord among tribes of the Emir's domination. The Rajajîl es-Sheukh. Imbârak. The Moors' garrison in the tower Mârid at Jauf. Their defection and the recovery of Jauf. Tale of the Ottoman expedition against Jauf. Words of Sherarát tribesmen, to the sheykhs in Jauf. Ibn Rashîd rides to save Jauf. Ibn Rashîd and the Ottoman pasha. Beduins among the rajajîl. Men of East Nejd and of er-Riâth come to serve the Western Emir. Ibn Saûd ruined. A messenger from er-Riâth. Kahtân tribesmen at Hâyil. Their speech. The Wady Daûasir country. Hayzàn their sheykh. He threatens to stab the Nasrâny. People's tales of the Kahtân. 'Their graves are crows' and eagles' maws.' Ibn Rashîd's lineage. Kindreds of Shammar. Rashîd, a lettered Beduwy. A fanatic kâdy. Dispute with the pedant kâdy. "The Muscovs of old possessed the land of Nejd." Inscriptions at Gubba. Study of letters in Nejd. Their nomad-like ignorance of the civil world. A village schoolmaster. A prophecy of Ezekiel. Plain words among the Arabs. Travelled men in Hâyil. Winter weather. An outrage in the coffee-hall. The coffee-server called before the Emir.

THE great tribes partly or wholly west of the Derb el-Haj are too far from him; they fear not Ibn Rashîd in their dangerous encumbered dîras. Beginning from the north, they are the B. Sókhr in the Belka, now submitted to the government of Syria, then B. Atîeh, and backward of them the stout nomad nation of the Howeytát, so far extended betwixt the two seas, Bíllî behind the Harra, and their neighbours the noble and ancient stock of Jeheyna: besides the southern Harb, nomads and villagers, in Hejâz, and all whose soil seyls into the Wady el-Humth. Between Mecca country and el-Kasîm is the great nomad territory, more than one hundred leagues over, (the best I have seen in the wilderness of Arabia), of the Ateyba nation; they are stout in arms, and civil-spirited Beduins, and Ibn Rashîd's capital enemies. There hardly passed a year in which Ibn Rashîd did not invade them, and they again were the bane of the next Aarab of his federation, especially of the midland Heteym, upon the W. er-Rummah, and their Harb neighbours. — Such are his estates, and this is the government of Ibn Rashîd, a name now so great in the (after the masterstrokes of the Waháby) timid Upper or Nomadic Arabia.

Between affection and fear, the desert people call him, and he will name himself (it is the pleasant oath of his house) *Akhu Noora*. Thus Abdullah, the first Muhafûth, in Hâyil, swore after the Nejd urbanity and magnanimity by his little sister, " As I am akhu (the brother of) Noora." Telâl after him, and Metaab, swore likewise thus, and so does Mohammed ; for a second Noora, Abdulla's daughter, was their sister, now deceased. — That is a formidable utterance of the Ruler, above the jest, were it spoken against a man's life ! I have heard a man, who had no sister, swear pleasantly by his infant daughter, " I am Abu (the father of) *Atheba !* " So it is in friendship a pretty adulation, and may be a knavish irony, to say to one, " O thou akhu of Such (naming her) ; " — as much as " O magnanimous, that even in thy weak things art worthy to be named among the valiant." I have heard nomad lads (Bishr) exclaim, *Ána akhu Chokty (ákhty)* ! I am the brother of Sissy, my little sister ; and akin to this, in the Beduin urbanity, is that (old man's) word of sober astonishment, *Ána weled abûy !* I (am) the son of my father.

To speak shortly of the princely families : Mohammed (as said) is ajjr, made sterile by some pernicious medicine, given him in a sickness, " when by this only he might be saved from death." In such he is unhappy, it is impossible he should strengthen himself by his own offspring. Mohammed has the four wives of their religious licence, two are *hathariyát*, ' women of the settlements,' and other two are *beduwiyát*. By strange adventure, one of those townswomen, we have seen, is named " a Christian." This I often heard ; but what truth there might be in their words, I cannot tell. What countrywoman she was, I could not learn of them. ' She came to Hâyil few years before with her brother, a young man who showing them masteries, and fencing with the lance upon horseback,' had delighted these loose riding and unfeaty Arabians. " The Christian became a Mosleman in Hâyil," and departing, he left his sister wife of the lord of the land. Might this, I mused, have been some horse-player from Egypt or the northern border countries ? — but where my words would be quickly misreported by tale-bearers in the Castle, to ask at large of the Prince's matter were not prudent. The other town wife is a sister of *Hásan*, Weled Mahanna, tyrant of Boreyda ; and Hamûd has a daughter of this Emir Hásan, among his wives.

Mohammed puts away and takes new wives, at his list, " month by month : " howbeit the princely wretch cannot purchase the common blessing ! his children are as dead within him, and the dreaded inhabitant of yonder castle remains a desolate man, or less than a man, in the midst of his marriages. But the childless Emir cherishes as his own son the little orphan child, *Abd el-Azîz*, the flesh which is left in the world of his brother Metaab, and has a father's tenderness of his daily thriving and learning, that he himself oversees. The child brought him every day his task, versets of the koran, written, as the Arabian oasis children use, in their ink made of the soot of pomegranate rinds, upon a wooden tablet, which is whitened with jiss or pipe-clay : for another school-day the ink is washed out, and the plate new whitened. Abd el-Azîz came often to my makhzan, and he asked me to give him some better ink and sheets of paper, and percussion caps for a little pistol which had been given him by his uncle Mohammed. If Mâjid came in then, Abd el-Azîz would rise and go out, — and I saw there was no word or sign of fellowship between them. Abd el-Azîz came alone, or with another princely child, (whom Mohammed had spared,) — it was the orphan of Bunder ! A Galla slave-boy of a very good nature accompanied them.

Those princely children by an horrible confusion of wedlock were half-brothers, born of one mother, of an uncle and nephew, of whom one had murdered the other ! and the young parricide, whom no man mourned, was now gone by the murderous avenging hand of Mohammed his next uncle (to-day Emir) to his bloody grave. — Bunder having murdered the Prince his uncle, took to wife the widow of the slain and mother of Abd el-Azîz, — his aunt ; and the parricide begat upon her a son. The murderous young man spared his uncle's infant, for the present, and might look, by such an healing of the breach of blood, to lay up some assurance for himself against a day when this little orphan of murdered Metaab should be grown. — Would Abd el-Azîz seek in that day the life of the father of his half-brother, with whom he had been bred, the same being his step-father, his " uncle " and his cousingerman, and yet the same by whom his own father was done to death long ago ? Now Mohammed succeeding, the danger from the side of the children is changed : will Bunder's son, if he may come to years, for

Abd el-Azîz's sake, and because he himself was preserved, pardon in Mohammed his father's cutting off? — but that horrid deed was not in men's sight unjust.

The little Abd el-Azîz shows the gait and countenance of his uncle the Emir, and carries a little sword which his mother has given him; yet there is somewhat in the child of sad orphan looks, of the branch planted alone by waters not of his natural parentage. Already his mind seemed to muse much of these things; I have heard him say to himself, when he came to visit me, " Ha! it was he, *ellathi thábah* — who killed such an one or other," and the horrible word seemed to be of presage, it was so light upon the child's lips. — O God! who can forecast their tragedies to come! what shall be the next vengeance and succession and forestalling of deaths between them? The eyes painted, their long hair shed in the midst and plaited in love-locks all round their orphan heads, and with the white tunics to their feet, these two princely children had the tender fresh looks of little maidens. Upon that other part may stand Mâjid, for who is after the Prince to-day but his cousin Hamûd? Of this perhaps the children's early shunning each other; — it was Abd el-Azîz who shunned Mâjid. But is it for aught that was practised against his parentage by Hamûd? perhaps they already had determined in their young hearts the destruction of each other. Mâjid also is a pleasant grandson of his father's brother, and like a nephew to the Emir. Mâjid, grandson of Abeyd, is as his father, of a cheerful popular spirit, but less loyal; and there is some perilous presentiment in him, an ambitious confidence that he shall himself one day be the Ruler. Abd el-Azîz, grandson of Abdullah, is an eagle's young; and in his day, if he may so long live, he will pierce through an hand that holds him with a stroke of his talons; but he seems to be of a gentle heart, and if God please that this child be afterwards Emir in Hâyil, he is like to be a good princely man, like his father Metaab. — Such for all their high looks, which is but sordid prince-craft, are the secret miseries of the Emirs' lives at Hâyil; and an horror must hang over Mohammed, or he is not a man, in his bloody solitude. In Kasîm I heard men say of Mohammed ibn Rashîd, " He has committed crimes which before were not known in the world!"

To speak then of the family of Abeyd, of which Hamûd is now head. Abeyd was conductor of the military power of J. Shammar, in Abdullah his brother and in his nephew Telâl's days. He was a martial man, and a Waháby more than is now Hamûd, born in easier times. He was a master of the Arabian warfare, a champion in the eyes of the discomfited Aarab. Abeyd, as said, was an excellent kassâd, he indited of all his desert warfare ; his boastful rimes, known wide in the wilderness, were ofttimes sung for me, in the nomad booths. The language of the kasasîd is as a language apart from the popular speech ; but here I may remember some plain and notable verse of Abeyd, as that which says, " By this hand are fallen of the enemies ninety men. Smitten to death the Kusmân perished before me, until the evening, when my fingers could not be loosed from the handle of the sword ; the sleeve of my garment was stiffened with the blood of war." This he made of the repulse of an ill-commanded and worse starred expedition, sent out by the great Kasîm town Aneyza, against Ibn Rashîd. — " And how happened it, I asked, that Abeyd, one man, could make so monstrous a slaughter of the men contending against him in battle ? " *Answer :* " When the Kusmân were broken and turned to flight, Abeyd pursuing, whilst the day lasted, struck down so many of the fugitives (from the backward) that they were numbered as ninety men ; " and a worthy and principal person who told me the tale put it to Abeyd's glory that he had killed many thus !

Abeyd could be generous, where the Arabs are so least, with an adversary : and clad in his hauberk of mail which they call Davidian, — for David, say they, first found the ringed armour, and Ullah made the crude iron easy to be drawn in his prophetic fingers — the jeopardy of the strong leader was not very great in the field of battle. One day in his bitter warfare with the Annezy *Ibn Mujállad*, Beduins of el-Kasîm and nomad inheritors of the palm valleys *el-Háyat* (in the Harrat Kheybar), the sheykh of the tribe espying this prince their destroyer in the battle, with a great cry defied him, and tilted desperately against him ; but Abeyd (though nettled with his injuries, yet pitying a man whom he had sorely afflicted) let the Beduwy pass under his romhh, calling to him ' that he would not kill a man [having upon him only a cotton tunic] who ran thus wilfully to his own destruction.'

Abeyd was in his latter days the old man of the saffron beard at home, a mild father of the Arabian household ; he was dead, according to their saying, seven years before my coming to Hâyil, and two years after the decease of Telâl. Of Abeyd's children we have seen Fáhd, the elder, had been set aside for the weakness of his understanding, a man now at the middle age, of a very good countenance, well-grown, and of such stature nearly as his next brother Hamûd, who had supplanted him. He was of a gentle virtuous disposition, and with a sort of cheerful humility consenting to the will of others, only some obscure drawing of the brows, a perplexed secret sadness of face and troubled unsteadfastness of the eyes, were tokens in him of the distracted mind. He was an onlooker with the placid day-long musing of the Moslemîn, and little he said; he was thus in some sort at Hâyil the happiest of mankind, — the only man's life that feared nothing. Fáhd passed his daily hours in Abeyd's kahwa, and Hamûd now sat in their father's hall in Abeyd's room, and next by him in a seat of honour sat Sleymàn: and Fáhd had no stately place, but he sat upon the common sitting-carpet with the younkers of the princely households, and with the officers of the Emir and any visiting sheykhs of the tribes and villages. Fáhd was become as it were a follower of Hamûd and the companion and play-fellow of Hamûd's son Mâjid. Mâjid his nephew said to me, " I love him, he is so quiet and peaceable a man;" but yet he did not name him *ammy*, mine uncle. At the supper-time Fáhd departed, who was the father of a family. From his home Fáhd returned again to the paternal coffee-house to sit out the evening, and modestly he would attend awhile in the closet where kahwa was made, if he came in then, until " the Emir " (Hamûd) had ended all the saying of his superstitious devotion.

When the princes forayed, Fáhd was left in Hâyil. Upon a time he would needs ride out to them and came to his father in the field; so said Abeyd, " How now, my son! why comest thou hither? " — " Father, I would ride in the ghrazzu and take part in the spoil;" and Abeyd, " Well, go home to thy house in Hâyil and abide our coming again, which shall be soon, it may please Ullah; this is my will, and thou shalt lose nothing." The Semitic greediness of the prey wrought in his infirm heart: and another time the poor man brought forth his fair growing daughter to Abeyd, saying, ' It was time now to sell her away ' (to be a bond-woman); and Abeyd falling fatherly in with his son's distracted humour gave him *fulûs*, silver, for the price of his granddaughter, and bade Fáhd keep her still for him. The third brother, to read anything in his pale vicious looks, was an umbratile young man, and very fanatical; he lived apart near the Méshed gate, and came never to sit amongst his brethren in their father's hall. I met with him one or two times in a month, passing in the public street, and he cast upon me only sour glances; he passed his time perhaps with the hareem, and seemed not to be held in any estimation at Hâyil. The fourth younger brother was Feyd, a good plain-hearted almost plebeian young man of seventeen years. Yet in him was some misshaping of nature, for I found in his jaws a double row of teeth. Sometimes in the absence of the Princes in the spring holidays or upon warfare, Feyd was left deputy-Emir, to hold the daily mejlis — at such times nearly forsaken — in Hâyil. After him was one Sleymàn, as I remember, a boy of little worth, and another, Abdullah, of his nephew Mâjid's age, sordid spirits and fitter to be bound prentices to some ratcatcher than to come into any prince's hall and audience. The last had fallen in his childhood from a height and put an arm out of joint; and as a bone-setter is not found in these countries, and "it were not worth" to send to Mesopotamia, they had let 'Ullah provide for him,' and his arm now hanged down withered. He came very often to my makhzan, to beg some trifle of the stranger: sore eyes added to his unlovely looks, he asked for medicine, but "I will not pay thee, said he, and I have not half a dollar." Fanatical he was, and the dastardly lad would even threaten me. The Hâyil princes (*bred up in the company of bond-servants*) are perhaps mostly like vile-spirited in their youth. When, rarely, Abdullah entered their father's kahwa, Hamûd called the boy cheerfully and made him sit down beside him; and casting his brother's arm about the child's neck, as the Arabians will (caressing equally their own young sons and their youngest brethren) he asked gently of his mirth and what he did that day; but the ungracious boy hardly responded and soon shrunk sourly away. — Such were the old eagle Abeyd's children, *affûn*, crow's eggs, all of them born with some deficiency of nature, except Hamûd only. So it seems the stock was faulty, it were strange if there lingered no alloy in the noble substance of Hamûd; and the temper of his mind, though good, is not very fine; but this may be found in the Emir Mohammed.

Abeyd's family are wealthy, were it only of their landed possessions in Hâyil; they have palms also at Jauf, — and an Arabian man's spending for his household, except it come by the Mohammedan liberty of wiving, is small in our comparison. Besides they are rich with the half fruits of el-Hâyat, which of old appertained to the inheriting Annezy; but when those were driven out by Abeyd, their rents were given by Telâl to his uncle and his heirs. Abeyd's family are also happy in this,

IBN RASHÎD'S GOVERNMENT

that no vengeance clouds the years before them for kinsmen's blood. The wild nomads look on and speak with an awe of the last damnable deeds in the house of Abdullah : in their own little commonwealths of uncles' sons in the desert, are not such impious ambitions. Feyd and Abdullah lived yet minors in their brother Hamûd's house in Hâyil, where almost daily I came to treat Feysal, and when I knocked at the ring it was opened to me sometimes by a slave woman, the child's nurse, sometimes by Feyd himself. I have found him stand quarrelling with a carpenter, and they scolded together with the Arabian franchise as equals. Or it was Abdullah that opened, and sometimes Hamûd's daughter came to the door, a pleasant girl, with her father's smiling ingenuous looks, clad only in her poor calico smock, dipped in indigo, without any ornament, and not to discern from the other village maidens of like age ; and such perhaps was Tamar David's daughter, who kneaded and baked bread. Simple was their place, a clay court and dwelling-chambers beyond, a house of hareem and eyyâl, where no strangers were admitted. I saw a line and a cross together, rudely chalked upon the wall of the doorway, IX — it is the wasm of Ibn Rashîd. The children of the sheukh mingled with the people in the town ; they went only more freshly clad than other men's sons. Girls are like cage birds bred up in their houses ; young maidens are not seen abroad in the public streets. At fifteen years the sheykhly boys ride already in the ghrazzus ; having then almost two years been free of their schoolmaster, of whom there is little to learn but their letters.

To consider the government of Ibn Rashîd, which is for the public security in a great circuit of the nomad country : — the factious strifes had been appeased in the settlements, even the disorders of the desert were repressed by the sword of the Waháby religion, and the land of Ishmael became *béled amân*, a peaceable country. In the second generation a sheykhly man, Abdullah Ibn Rashîd, of one of the chief Hâyil houses, who had become a principal servitor of the Waháby Prince at er-Riâth, was sent home by Ibn Saûd to his own town in Jebel Shammar: — to be his constable of the west marches of Nejd, " TO GOVERN ANNEZY," and namely the southern tribes of that Beduin nation, landlords in the palm valleys of the Harrat Kheybar. Abdullah soon seated himself by the sword at Hâyil, and prevailing all round, he became muhafûth of a new state, tithing villages and tribes ; yet of the zikâ, brought into his government treasury, yielding no tribute to er-Riâth, other than a present of horses which he led with him in his yearly visit to Ibn Saûd. This homage is now disused, — in the decay of the Waháby state ; and Ibn Rashîd is to-day the greatest prince in Nejd. His is a ruling of factious Arabs by right of the sword ; none of them not persuaded by fear would be his tributaries. The Beduw and oasis dwellers are not liegemen (as they see it) to any but their natural sheykhs. Townsmen have said to me ofttimes of Ibn Rashîd, even in Hâyil, *Henna mamlukîn,* ' we dwell here as bondsmen under him.' A northern nomad patient, pointing backward, whilst he sat within my makhzan door, as if he feared to be descried through wood and walls, murmured to me between his teeth, " The Inhabitant of yonder Kasr is ZÂLIM, a strong-handed tyrant." At Hâyil, where are no stocks, tortures, nor prison, punishment is sudden, at the word of the Ruler ; and the guilty, after his suffering, is dismissed.

The Emirs in Hâyil have austerely maintained the police of the desert. — This was told me of Metaab's time : One of the few salesmen to the tribes from the Syrian countries, who from time to time have arrived at Hâyil, was stripped and wounded, as he journeyed in the Sherarát dîra. The stranger came to Hâyil and complained of this outrage to the Emir. Metaab sent riders to summon the sheykhs of the Sherarát to find, and immediately deliver the guilty persons, which was done accordingly, they not daring to disobey Ibn Rashîd, and the riders returned with a prisoner. Metaab commanded the nomad to stand forth in the mejlis, and enquired of the stranger if this were he ? When he answered, " It is he," said the Emir, " Sherâry hound ! how durst thou do this violence ? " Metaab bade the stranger take the Sherâry's lance which had been brought with him, and as he had done unto him so to do to the fellow again. " What must I do, O el-Muhafûth ! " — " Pierce him, and kill him too, if it please thee ! " But the tradesman's heart was now cold, and he could not strike the man, but entreated the Emir, since he had his things again, to let him go. I have known certain Damascene salesmen to the Beduw, that had visited Hâyil, and one of them was a Christian, who traded every year to the W. Sirhân and Jauf. The man understanding that mantles were dear in the Jebel, had crossed the Nefûd with a camel-load to Hâyil. Telâl, the prince, spoke to him kindly, and was content that he should remain there awhile and sell his wares ; only exhorting him " not to shave the chin," — the guise of

Damascus Christians and the young coxcombs among the town Moslems.

Tribes agreeing ill together in Ibn Rashîd's confederacy (we have seen) are not in general suffered to molest each other: yet there are some nomads (whether because Hâyil would weaken them, or they are too outlying from him, and not so much bound to keeping of good neighbourhood) who complaining to the Emir of inroads made by Aarab of his subjection, have received his hard answer: " This lies between you and I will be no party in your Beduin dissensions." All the great sheykhs of Arabs are very subtle politic heads: and I think *it would be hard to find a fault in Ibn Rashîd's government,* — yet my later Kasîm friends (his enemies at Aneyza) dispraised it.

— A word of the armed band, *rajajîl es-sheukh*. Ibn Rashîd is much served (as said) by foreigners (adventurers, and fugitives) from East Nejd: and such will be faithful servants of the Emir, with whom they stand or fall. Besides these, there are nearly two hundred men in his salary, of the town. Captain of the guard, the Prince's chamberlain at home, and his standard-bearer in battle, was *Imbârak*, a pleasant but fanatic strong man. He was a stranger from el-Aruth, and had been promoted from the low degree by succeeding Emirs, for his manly sufficiency, until he was become now, in his best years, the executive arm of Ibn Rashîd.

Among the strangers, in my time, in Hâyil, that lived of Ibn Rashîd's wages, were certain Moghrebies. These Moors were at the taking of Jauf, in the expedition from Syria. Unto them, at the departure of the Pasha, was committed one of the two towers, *Mârid*; and the other to a few Syrian soldiery. — These were left in garrison with a kaimakàm, or Resident for the Dowla. But when a time passed, and they had not received their stipends, the bitter and hot-headed men of the West said in their disdain, 'They would call in Ibn Rashîd'! They went also to assail the soldiery of Syria, who though in the same case, yet as men that would return to their homes, held " for the Sooltàn," against them. The Moors had the upper hand, and when this tiding was brought in haste to Hâyil, the Emir returned with his armed men, and reoccupied the place which he had lately lost with so much displeasure. The Moors, — fifteen persons — were transported to Hâyil; where they became of the Prince's armed service. One of them (grown unwieldy to ride) had been made the porter of his castle gate, and no man may pass in thereat but by that Moor's allowance. Sometimes when the sheukh are absent, the Moorish men-at-arms are left in Hâyil, and lodged in the Kasr by night, *for fear of any irruption of the wild Beduw*, who have heard marvels reported of Ibn Rashîd's treasury : for *there is no peace among the Ishmaelites, nor assurance even in the Prince's capital !*

Jauf was thus recovered, by the defection of the Moors, four years before my coming to Hâyil. The men were now wedded and established in the town ; only two had departed. Another of them, Haj Ibrahîm an Algerian, who had been a soldier in his youth (he remembered the words of command) in the French service, was little glad of the Arabian Emir's small salary, and the lean diet of the Mothîf ; and he said, as ever his little son, born in Hâyil, should be of age for the journey, he would take his leave. He and the Moors despised the Arabians as ' a benighted wild kind of people.'

The tale of Jauf may help our estimation of the value in the field of Arabian numbers, against troops under Turkish command, armed with rifles. In or about the year 1872, an expedition was sent by the government of Syria (the Turk, at that time, would extend his dominion in Arabia) to reduce the desert town of Jauf, fifty leagues eastward from the haj road, to the obedience of the Sultan. The small force was assembled at Maan camp. Mahmûd, who went with them, has told me they were seventy irregular soldiery, and the rest a motley crew of serving men in arms ; among them those Moghrebies had been hired in Damascus to go upon the expedition. Mohammed Aly, who rode also with the Pasha, gave me their numbers more than the truth, — troopers two hundred, police soldiery (*zabtîyah*) one hundred, besides fifty ageyl of the haj service. The Kurdy Pasha, Mohammed Saîd, commanded them.

Ten marches to Jauf in the desert are counted from Maan, with laden camels. Great care was had to provide girbies, for there is little water to find by the way. " But, said Mahmûd, by the mercy of Ullah, it rained plentifully, as we were setting out, so that we might drink of the standing pools where we would, in our daily marches." The ninth evening the Pasha halted his soldiery at three or four leagues from Jauf, and bade them kindle many watch-fires in the plain : — and they of the town looking from their towers, saw this light in the sky, as if all the wilderness had burned. In the first watch some Sherarát came by them, — nomads well disposed towards the Dowla, in as much as they think themselves grieved by (the tyranny of) Ibn Rashîd; they related marvels that night in Jauf of the great army of the askars of the Sooltàn! "We passed, said they, where they lie encamped; and they cannot be less than forty thousand men. We saw them, wellah a score or two about every fire; at some they were beating the tambour, at some they danced; and their companies are without number: you might walk four hours among their camp-fires! — and what help is there in Ibn Rashîd, O ye inhabitants of Jauf!" — The sheukh went out and delivered the keys the same night, and surrendered themselves to the Pasha, who in the morning peaceably occupied the place.

When word came to the Prince in Hâyil, that his good town in the North had been taken by the Dowla, Ibn Rashîd sent a letter thus written to the Ottoman Pasha: "As thou hast entered Jauf without fight, now in like manner depart from it again; and if not, I come to put you out."

Ibn Rashîd rode over the Nefûd from Hâyil, with his rajajîl and villagers upon thelûls; and a great cloud of his Beduw followed him (Mohammed Aly said ten thousand in all, that is perhaps one thousand at most). There were some old cannon in the towers: but the Pasha levelled against the Arabians an "English" piece of steel mountain artillery, which had been borne upon a mule's back in the expedition. The first ball struck a Beduin rider in the middle, from a wonderful distance; and naught remained of him but his bloody legs, hanging in the shidàd. The hearts of the Arabians waxed cold at that sight, — the black death, when they thought themselves secure, was there in the midst of them! also the bullets of the Dowla fell to them from very far off; nevertheless they passed on to the assault. Mahmûd and the seventy stood without the gates with their small arms to resist them, and the rest repulsed them with musketry from the towers. Ibn Rashîd perceiving that his rajajîl and the multitude of Beduw could not avail him, that his enemies were within walls, and this beginning against him had been made by the Dowla, invited the Pasha to a parley; and trusted to find him a Turk reasonable, greedy to be persuaded by his fee. They met and, as the Arabs speak, "understood each other." Mohammed Ibn Rashîd said: "I give you then Jauf." — *Mohammed Saîd*: "We are in Jauf; and if the Lord will we may go on to take Hâyil." In the end it was accorded between them that Jauf should be still the Prince's town but tributary to the Dowla; Ibn Rashîd covenanted to pay every year for the place, at Damascus, 1500 mejîdy crowns : and a kaimakàm with his Syrian garrison was to be resident in the place. Each of these principal men looked upon the other with a pleasant admiration ; and in that they became friends for their lives.

In the mixed body of the rajajîl, I found some Beduins. Poverty had persuaded them to abandon the wandering life in the desert. Small was the Prince's fee, but that was never in arrear, and a clay house in Hâyil and rations. Certain among the strangers at Hâyil had been formerly servants of the Waháby ! — I knew a company of Riâth men, a sort of perpetual guests of the Emir. They rode in all Ibn Rashîd's ghrazzus, and the Prince who lent them their thelûls, bestowed upon them, from time to time, a change of clothing and four or five reals ; and with that won in the forays, there came in, they reckoned, to each of them twenty reals by the year ; and they had their daily rations in the Mothîf. This life they now led six years, they were unwedded, and one among them was a blind man, who when his fellows forayed must abide at home. — Their house was one of the many free lodgings of the Emir, — a walled court, for their beasts, and two clay chambers, beyond the sûk, in the upper street leading to Gofar. There I went to visit them often, for another was a scholar who knew many ancient lays of the nomad tribes and the muallakát, which he read to me from a roll of parchment. They have often told me that if I went to er-Riâth I should be well treated. I asked, " What has brought you to leave your homes and come to encamp without your families at Hâyil ? " — " Ibn Saûd (answered the scholar, with an Arabian gesture, balancing his outstretched hand down to the ground) is every day sinking lower and lower, but Ibn Rashîd is *ha-ha-ha-ha-ha* coming up thus up-up-up ! and is always growing." It was said now at Hâyil " *Ibn Saûd khurbân* " (is ruined).

Abdullah the Waháby prince, son of old blind Feysal, was come himself two years before into these parts, a fugitive, driven from his government by the rebellion of his younger brother Saûd. Abdullah wandered then awhile, bare of all things, pitching his tent among the western Beduw within the jurisdiction of Ibn Rashîd. The Emir Mohammed sent to Abdullah el-Waháby offering him sheep and camels and horses and all things necessary, only forbidding him to enter Hâyil : but Saûd soon dying, Abdullah returned in peace, to that little which remained to him of his former dominion. Abdullah took at that time a sister of Mohammed Ibn Rashîd for one of his wives ; — but she dying he had afterward a sister of Hamûd : yet, since the past year, some enmity was said to be sprung up between them ; and that is in part because Mohammed ever bitterly harries the great tribe of Ateyba, which are the old faithful allies (though no more tributaries) of Abdullah the Wahâby. — There came a messenger from er-Riâth whilst I was at Hâyil. As I sat one day with him at coffee, the man seeing me use a lead pencil, enquired of the company, "Tell me, ye who know him, is the Nasrâny a magician!" other than this he showed no dislike towards me, but looked with the civil gentleness of an Arabian upon the guest and the stranger. And someone saying to him, "Eigh now! if this (man) go to er-Riâth what thinkest thou, will they kill him?" he answered mildly, "Nay, I think they would treat him with gentleness, and send him forward on his journey; have not other Nasrânies visited er-Riâth (peaceably)!"

Hâyil is now a centre of nomadic Arabia on this side *J. Tueyk*, and within the Syrian haj road. Embassies often arrive from tribes, not his tributaries, but having somewhat to treat with the Emir Ibn Rashîd. Most remarkable of these strange Aarab were some Kahtân Beduins, of that ancient blood of el-Yémen and called the southern stock of the Arabs, — as is the Abrahamid family of Ishmael of the north Arabians. The men wondered to hear that any named them *Beny Kahtân*. "This (they said) is in the loghrat of Annezy." Jid or grandsire of their nation they told me to be the 'prophet *Hûd*,' and their beginning to be from the mountain country *et-Tôr* in *Asîr. Ismayîn* (Ishmael) they said, was brother of Hûd their patriarch. These men had not heard of Hûd's sepulchre in the southern country, nor have they any tradition (it sounded like old wives' tales to them) of the dam-breach at *Mâreb*, [from which is fabled the dispersion of the ancient Arabs in the little world of Arabia]. One of them sang me some rimes of a ditty known to all the Kahtân, in which is the stave, "The lance of Neby Hûd, raught to the spreading firmament." Some of them asked me, "Wellah! do the Nasâra worship *asnâm*," graven images? — I think this book-word is not in the traditions of the northern Arabs. The Kahtân now in Hâyil were two rubbas : they had ridden with the young man their great sheykh *Hayzàn*, from el-Kasîm ; in which country their division of the tribe were intruders these two years, and that was partly into the forsaken Annezy dîra of the Ibn Mujállad expelled by Abeyd. They were two hundred tents, and had been driven from their Yémen dîra, — where the rest remain of their nomad kindred.

These southern tribesmen wandering in Ibn Rashîd's borders, sent, now the second time, to treat with the Prince of Shammar, offering themselves to become his Aarab, and pay tithings to Hâyil; but Ibn Rashîd, not willing that this dire and treacherous tribe should be established in Nejd, dismissed them with such words; — 'They might pasture in his neighbourhood as guests, giving no occasion against themselves, but that he looked upon them as aliens, and should neither tax them, nor give any charge to the tribes concerning them.' The messengers of Kahtân responded, "Wellah! O Muhafûth, be we not thy brethren? is not Ibn Rashîd *Jaafary*, of the fendy *Abda Shammar*, which is from the *Abîda* of Kahtân?" But the prince Mohammed responded hardly, "We know you not, your speech is strange in our hearing, and your manners are none of ours: go now, we are not of you, we will neither help you nor hurt you." Abhorred at er-Riâth, — since by their treachery the old power of the Wahâby was broken, — the Nejd Aarab pressing upon them, and the Ateyba from the southward, these intruded Kahtân were now compassed in by strong enemies.

The men seemed to me to speak very well in the Nomad Arabic, with little difference from the utterance of Nejd Beduins, save perhaps that they spoke with a more eloquent fulness. When they yet dwelt in the south country, they drew their provision of dates from the W. Dauâsir; one of them told me the palms there lasted — with no long intermissions — for three thelûl journeys: it is a sandy bottom and all their waters are wells. Those of the valley, he said, be not bad people, but "good to the guest." It is their factions which so much trouble the country, the next villages being often in feud one with another. *El-Aflâj* (plur. of *Fálaj*— Peleg, as some learned think — which may signify 'the splitting of the mountain') is in Jebel Tuey(k)ch, and the villagers are Dauâsiries. From er-Riâth he counted to el-Aflâj three, and to *W. Bîsha* twelve thelûl journeys, and he named to me these places by the way, *el-Ferra, el-Sulèyl, Lèyla, el-Bedîya, Sélla, El-Hadda, Hámmr, es-Sîhh*: some of them asked me if I had heard tell of the *Kasr Ibn Shaddâd*. The 'wild oxen' are in their country, which they also name wothyhî. Certainly these men of Kahtân differed not in the least gestures from any other Beduw whom I have known; they were light-coloured and not so swarthy, as are many of the northern Aarab.

The Kahtân who talked with me in the Méshab were pleased when I confirmed the noble antiquity of their blood, in the ears of the tribesmen of Nejd, who until that hour had never heard anything in the matter. The men invited me to visit them at evening in their makhzan, when they would be drinking kahwa with the sheykh. These Kahtân came not into the great public coffee-hall of the Kasr, whether because of the (profane) bibbing there of tobacco smoke, or that they were at enmity with most of the tribesmen : they drank the morning and mid-afternoon and evening cup apart, in their own makhzan ; but they received the coffee-berries from the Emir's kitchen. After supper I sought them out : their young sheykh Hayzàn immediately bid me sit down on the saddle-skin beside him, and with a good grace he handed to me the first cup of kahwa. This was a beautiful young man, of manly face and stature ; there was nothing in him that you would have changed, he was a flower of all whom I have seen among the Arabians : his life had never suffered want in the khála. In his countenance, with a little ferocity of young years, appeared a pleasant fortitude : the milk-beard was not yet sprung upon Hayzàn's hardy fresh face. His comeliness was endowed with the longest and greatest braided side-locks, which are seen among them ; and big he was, of valiant limbs : — but all this had no lasting !

They were in some discourse of religion ; and their fanatic young sheykh pronounced the duty of a Moslem to lie in three things chiefly, — " the five times daily prayers, the fast in Ramathán, and the tithe or yielding of zîka." — How the Semites are Davids ! they are too religious and too very scelerat at once ! Their talk is continually (without hypocrisy) of religion, which is of genial devout remembrance to them, as it is to us a sad, uncomfortable, untimely and foreign matter. Soon after, their discourse began to turn upon my being a Nasrâny. Then Hayzàn said to one of his rubba, " Give me there my kiddamîyyah," which is their crooked girdle-knife. Then holding the large blade aloft, and turning himself upon me, he said, *Sully aly en-Néby,* ' Give glory to the apostle,' so I answered, " We all worship the Godhead. I cannot forsake my name of Nasrâny, neither wouldst thou thine if thou be'st a worthy man." — But as he yet held the knife above my breast, I said to him, " What dagger is that ? and tell these who are present whether thy meaning be to do me a mischief ? " Then he put it down as if he were ashamed to be seen by the company savagely threatening his coffee guest ; and so returning to his former behaviour, he answered all my questions. " Come, he said, in the morning, and we will make thee coffee ; then ask me of all that you please, and I will tell thee as it is." When I said, " You have many Yahûd in your Yémen country," the fanatic young man was much troubled to hear it. " And that knife, is from whence ? " — " From Nejrân." — " And in Nejrân be not your sânies Yahûdies ? was not the smith who made this dagger-blade a Yahûdy ? " The ignorant young Beduin, who thought I must know the truth, hissed between his teeth : *Ullah yusullat aleyhim*, " The Lord have the mastery of them (to bring evil upon them)." — When I returned on the morrow, I found Hayzàn alone ; the young sheykh, with an uncommon courtesy, had awaited me, for they think it nothing not to keep their promises. So he said, " Let us go to the rubba in the next makhzan, they have invited us, and we will drink our coffee there."

When I came another evening to the Kahtân, to hear their lays, Hayzàn did not return my greeting of peace. Soon after I had taken the cup, the young sheykh as before bade one bring him his kiddamîyyah ; and handling the weapon with cruel looks, he turned himself anew upon me, and insisted, saying, " *Sully aly en-Néby*." I answered, " Oh ! ignorant Beduwy, how is it that even with your own religion I am better acquainted than thyself ! " — " Thou art better acquainted with my religion than myself ! *sully aly en-Néby*." — (Some of the Kahtân company now said, " Hayzàn, nay ! he is a guest.") — " If thou mayest come even to the years of this beard, thou wilt have learned, young man, not to offer any violence to the guest." I thought if I said ' the guest of the lord of yonder castle,' he might have responded, that the Prince permitted him ! In the same moment a singular presentiment, almost a persuasion, possessed my soul, that the goodly young man's death was near at hand ; and notwithstanding my life daily threatened in a hazardous voyage and this infirm health, that I should survive him. " Your coffee, I added, was in my throat when you lifted the knife against me ; but tell me, O ye of the Kahtân, do ye not observe the rites of the other Aarab ? " Some of them answered me, " Ay, Ullah ! that do we ; " but Hayzàn was silent, for the rest of the company were not with him, and the Arabs are never of one assent, save in blind dogma of religion : this is for one's safety who adventures among them. — Hayzàn, a few months afterward, by the retaliation of fortune, was slain (in battle) by my friends. This case made the next day some idle talk in the town, and doubtless was related in the palace, for Imbârak asked me of it in the great kahwa : — " Khalîl, what of the Kahtân ? and what of Hayzàn, when he took the knife to stab thee, fearedst thou not to die ? " — " If I feared for every word, judge thyself, had I entered your Arabian country ? but tell me, did the young ignorant well, thinkest thou ? " — Imbârak, who was in such times a spokesman for the Emir, kept silence.

Very ugly tales are current of the Kahtân in the mouths of Nejd Arabians. It is commonly reported that they are eaters of the flesh of their enemies ; and there is a vile proverb said to be of these human butchers, ' *eth-thail*, the rump, is the best roast.' They are esteemed faithless, " wood at a word, and for every small cause ready to pluck out their weapons." A strange tale was told me in Kasîm, by certain who pretended they had it of eye-witnesses : ' Some Kahtân riders returning weary and empty from a ghrazzu passed by er-Russ ; and finding an *abd* or bondsman of the village without in the khála, they laid hands on him and bound him, and carried the negro away with them. Before evening the Kahtânies, alighted in the Nefûd, the men were faint with the many days suffered hunger ; — and they said among themselves, ' We will kill the captive and eat him : ' they plucked also bushes and gathered fuel for a great fire. — The black man would be cast in, when they had cut his throat, and roasted whole ; as the manner is of passengers and hunters in the wilderness to dress their game. But in that appeared another band riding over the sand-dunes ! The Kahtân hastily remounted on their thelûls ; and seeing them that approached to be more than their number, they stayed not, but, as Beduw, they turned their beasts to flight. Those that now arrived were some friendly Kasîm villagers, who loosing the poor bondsman heard from him his (unlikely) tale.' — But most fanatic are these scelerats, and very religious even in their crimes. So it is said of them proverbially in Nejd, " El-Kahtân murder a man only for his drinking smoke, and they themselves drink human blood." But sheykhly persons at Aneyza have told me that " el-Kahtân in el-Yémen do confirm their solemn swearing together by drinking human gore ; also a man of them may not wive, nor loose his leathern band, until he have slain an enemy." Another sheykh of Kahtân visited Hâyil two years before, — and after discourse of their affairs the Prince Ibn Rashîd said to him : " In all my riding southwards through the Beduin country we never saw a Kahtân burying place ! " The sheykh, it is reported, answered him (in a boast), " Ay wellah Muhafûth, thou hast seen the graves of Kahtân, *in the air !* — the crows and the rákham and the ágab : " he would say their carcases are cast out unburied, — that which happens in the wild battle-fields of Arabia ; the fallen of the losers' side remain without burial. It was so with Kahtân when this Hayzàn was slain in the summer : a week after I passed by, and the caravaners avoided that sinister neighbourhood !

Somewhat has been said of Ibn Rashîd's lineage. Shammar is not, as the most great nomad tribes, reputed to spring from one Jid, but according to the opinion in Nejd, is of mixed ancestry. Others say the name of their patriarch is *Shimmer*. The divisions by fendies or lineages of Shammar were given me by a lettered nomad of Annezy Sbáa living at Hâyil. The fendy *Abda* is from the fendy *Abîda* of Kahtân whereof the *Jaafar* kindred, of which is Ibn Rashîd's house ; the other fendies are many and not of one descent, — *Sinjâra, Tumân, Èslam, Deghreyrat, Ghreyth, Amûd, Faddâghra, Thâbit, Afarît, ez-Zumeyl, Hammazân, Saiyeh, Khûrussy, Zûba, Shammar-Toga* (in Irâk).

No man of the inhabitants of the wilderness knows letters ; and it was a new pleasure to me to meet here with a lettered Beduwy, as it were an eye among their dull multitude, for he was well taught and diligent, and his mind naturally given to good studies. This was one *Rashîd* who had been bred a scholar at er-Riâth ; but had since forsaken the decaying Wahâby state and betaken himself to Hâyil, where he was become a man of Hamûd's private trust and service. He made every year some scholarly journey, into distant provinces. He was last year, he told me, in the land of Israel, where he had visited Bethlehem, " the place (he said devoutly) where the Messiah was born," and the Holy (City). There is in these Arabians such a facility of mind, that it seems they only lack the occasion, to speed in any way of learning ; — that were by an easy imitation. Rashîd was a good man of liberal understanding [I could have wished for such a rafîk in my Arabian travels], but too timid as a Beduwy under masters : almost he dared not be seen in the town to discourse with the Nasrâny, lest it should displease any great personage. There is reported to be a far outlying settlement in al-Aruth, of Shammar lineage, the name of the village is *Aleyî* and the kindred *Kurunîyah*.

One day I found Rashîd carrying my book of Geography in the Méshab. As he said that Mâjid sent him with it to some learned man in Hâyil, a kâdy, I accompanied him ; but come to his dàr we found not the learned person at home. I heard the kâdy had compiled *shájr*, a tree, of genealogies, in which he exhibited the branching from the stock of all their Arabian lines. I went another day to visit him, and could not soon find his distant house, because a swordsman of the Emir, whom I met stalking in his gay clothes, sent me upon a false way about ; and when I arrived I found the shallow fellow sitting there before me ! so knavish they are in a trifle, and full of Asiatic suspicions. When I reproached him the fellow could not answer a word, only feeling down the edge of his sword, he let me divine that he had the best will in the world to have tried his force and the temper of the metal upon my neck. The same man was afterwards not less ready to defend me from the insolence of others.

I greeted the kâdy, who hardly saluted me again : *Mâtha turîd*, quoth the pedant ; — and this is all their learning, to seem well taught in the Arabic tongue. He was sitting under his house wall in the dust of the street. All their gravity is akin to levity, and first showing me his watch, he asked, " What is this written upon the face of it ? " Then he sent for a book, and showed me in the fly-leaf his copies of some short antique inscriptions which he had found scored upon the rocks in this neighbourhood (they were written in a kind of Himyaric character), and he asked of me, " Are these *Yunâny* (of Javan), in the Greek tongue, or Muscovy ? — *the Muscovs of old inhabited this country*." I answered, " Art thou so ignorant then even of your own language ! This is the Himyaric, or ancient Yemenish writing of Arabia. I heard thou wast a learned man, and upon that common ground we might be friends. Though thy name be Moslem and mine is Messîhy we all say ' There is an only Godhead.' " — " The impiety is not unknown to me of the Messihiyûn ; they say ' Ullah childed, and that the only God is become more Gods ' ! Nay ! but if thou wilt turn from the way of idolatry to be a Moslem, we may be accorded together." — " I become a Moslem ! I think thou wouldst not become a Nasrâny ; neither will I take on me the name of your religion, *ebeden* ! (ever) : yet may we be friendly in this world, and seekers after the true knowledge." —

"Knowledge of the Messihiyûn! that is a little thing, and next to unlearning." — " How art thou called learned! being without knowledge even of your own letters. The shape is unknown to you of the dry land, the names of the hundred countries and the great nations; but we by navigation are neighbours to all nations, we encompass the earth with our speech in a moment. Says not Sleymàn bin Daûd, ' It is the glory of man's solicitous spirit to search out the sovereign works of the Lord '? ye know not those scriptures, but our young children read these things with understanding." — The pedant could not find his tongue; he might feel then, like a friar out of his cell, that he was a narrow soul, and in fault to have tempted the stranger in argument. He was mollified, and those that sat with him.

Afterwards, meeting with Rashîd, he said, " How found you him, he knows very much?" — " The koran, the muallakát, the kamûs and his jots, and his titles (the vowel points in their skeleton writing), and he knows nothing else." — " It is the truth, and I can think thou didst not like him;" for it seems, the learned and religious kâdy was looked upon as a crabbed fellow in his own town. As we were talking of the ancient scored inscriptions, in Abeyd's kahwa, Mâjid's tutor said to Hamûd, " Have we not seen the rocks full of them at *Gubba?*" Gubba is the outlying small Nefûd village next to J. Shammar, upon the way to Jauf.

In Nejd I have found the study of letters in most honour amongst the prosperous merchants at Aneyza. At Hâyil it was yet in the beginning: though Hamûd and the Prince are said to be possessors (but who may ever believe them!) of two or three thousand volumes. I found in Abeyd's kahwa not above a dozen in their cotton cases, and bound in red leather:—but the fewer they were, the more happy I esteemed them, as princes, not to be all their lives going still to school. Hamûd sometime asked me of the art of printing, ' Could I not show him the manner?' but when I answered he might buy himself a printer's press from Bagdad, for not much money, he was discouraged, for they will spend nothing. It is wonderful in what nomad-like ignorance of the natural world they all pass their lives! Some evening Hamûd asked me, " Do the Nasâra, Khalîl, see the moon?" — his meaning might be — ' The new moon is the ensign of the Sultan of Islam, the moon then is of the Moslemîn;—therefore the moon is not of the other religions!'

There were in Hâyil four common schools. The master of one of them, a depraved looking fanatical young man, daily uttered the presumptuous saws of his self-liking heart of gall to the ignorant assembly in the kahwa : sordid was his voice, and the baseness of his snake-looking eyes a moral pestilence. Upon a day he called upon me loudly, and smiling in his manner, before them all, " Khalîl, why so steadfast in a false way ? Wouldst thou come to my house, to-morrow, I will lay before thee the proofs, and they shall be out of your own scriptures. Thou shalt read the prophecy of *Hazkiyal* and the other testimonies ; and then, if the Lord will, thou mayest say, ' I that was long time blind, do now see and bear witness that God is One, and Mohammed is the apostle of God.' " — " Will you make my head ache in the Prince's coffee-hall about your questions of religion ! where I come but to drink a cup with my friends." The Beduins answered for me, " He has well said ; peace, thou young man, and let this stranger be." — " But it is of the great hope I have, hissed the holy ribald, of this man's conversion ; for was it not so with the Yahûdy before him ? "

Desiring to see a book at Hâyil and in Arabic " of Ezekiel the prophet " ! I went the next afternoon to his dàr, which I found by the Méshab, near the common draught-yard, as unsavoury as himself. " Ah ! he said, welcome, also I hope thou art come disposed to receive the truth." He set dates before the stranger, and fetched me his wise book ; which I found to be a solemn tome of some doctor of Islam, who at a certain place quoted a voice of the prophet, but in other than barbarous ears of little meaning. The Arabs have a curious wit for the use of this world, but they are all half-rational children in religion. " Well ! (I asked) is there no more than this ? and I was almost in hope to have reformed myself ! " But now the young man, who looked perhaps that I should have taken his vanity upon trust, was displeased with himself, and so I left him. This schoolmaster was maintained by the State ; he dined miserably in the Mothîf, and received, besides, a few reals in the year, and a change of clothing.

The Arabs are to be won by gentleness and good faith, they yield to just arguments, and before I left Hâyil the most of my old foes wished me well in their hearts. To use an unflattering plainness of speech was also agreeable to the part of sûwahh, or wandering anchorite in the fable of human life. The best that I met with here, were some who had been in Egypt and Syria, or conductors of the Emir's sale-horses to Bombay, where they told me, with a pleasant wonder, they had seen the horse-race; men who viewed a stranger, such as themselves had been in another soil, with eyes of good-will and understanding. "This people (they would say) have learned no good manners, they have not corrected themselves by seeing foreign countries: else why do they molest thee, Khalîl, about your religion; in which no man ought to be enforced.— But we have instructed ourselves in travel; also we have seen the Nasâra, their wealth, their ingenuity, and justice and liberality."

The weather, sultry awhile after my coming to Hâyil, was now grown cold. Snow, which may be seen the most winters upon a few heads of Arabian mountains, is almost not known to fall in the Nejd wilderness, although the mean altitude be nearly 4000 feet. They say such happens about "once in forty years." It had been seen two winters before, when snow lay on the soil three days: the camels were couched in the menzils, and many of them perished in that unwonted cold and hunger.

A fire was kindled morning and evening in the great kahwa, and I went there to warm myself with the Beduins. One evening before almost anyone came in, I approached to warm myself at the fire-pit. — " Away! (cried the coffee-server, who was of a very splenetic fanatical humour) and leave the fire to the guests that will presently arrive." Some Beduins entered and sat down by me. " I say, go back!" cries the coffee-keeper. " A moment, man, and I am warm; be we not all the Prince's guests?" Some of the Beduw said in my ear: " It were better to remove, not to give them an occasion." That káhwajy daily showed his rancour, breaking into my talk with the Beduw, as when someone asked me " Whither wilt thou next, Khalîl?"—" May it please Ullah (cries the coffee-server) to jehennem!" I have heard he was one of servile condition from Aneyza in Kasîm; but being daily worshipfully saluted by guesting Beduin sheykhs, he was come to some solemn opinion of himself. To cede to the tyranny of a servant might, I thought, hearten other fanatics' audacity in Hâyil. The coffee-server, with a frenetic voice, cried to a Beduwy sitting by, " Reach me that camel-stick " (which the nomads have always in their hands,) and having snatched it from him, the slave struck me with all his decrepit force. The Beduins had risen round me with troubled looks, — they might feel that they were not themselves safe; none of these were sheykhs, that durst say any word, only they beckoned me to withdraw with them, and sit down with them at a little distance. It had been perilous to defend myself among dastards ; for if it were told in the town that the Nasrâny laid heavy hands on a Moslem, then the wild fire had kindled in many hearts to avenge him. The Emir must therefore hear of the matter and do justice, or so long as I remained in Hâyil every shrew would think he had as good leave to insult me. I passed by the gallery to the Emir's apartment, and knocking on the iron door, I heard the slave-boy who kept it within say to the guard that it was Khalîl the Nasrâny. The Emir sent out Nasr to enquire my business, and I went to sit in the Méshab. Later someone coming from the Kasr who had been with the Emir, said that the Emir sent for the coffee-server immediately, and said to him, " Why ! Ullah curse thy father, hast thou struck the Nasrâny ? "— " Wellah, O el-Muhafûth (the trembling wretch answered) I touched him not ! " — so he feared the Emir, who said then to some of the guard " Beat him ! " — but Hamûd rose and going over to Mohammed, he kissed his cousin's hand, asking him, for his sake, to spare the coffee-server, ' who was a *mesquin* (meskîn).' " Go káhwajy, said the Emir, and if I hear any more there shall nothing save thee, but thou shalt lose thy office." Because I forsook the coffee-hall, the second coffee-server came many times to my makhzan, and wooed me to return among them ; but I responded, " Where the guests of the Emir are not safe from outrage — ? "

Note.—Ibn Rashîd's horses, for the Indian market, are shipped at Kuweyt. The itinerary is, from Hâyil to el-Khâsira, 9 stounds ;— Bak'a, 8 ;—Khathrâ, 18 ;—el-Feṣaṣ, Umm Arthama (the well there 32 fathoms), 28 ;—el-Wakbâ, 24 ;—el-Ḥafr (in the Wady er-Rummah, the well 35 fathoms), 24 ;—Arrak'i (where there is little water), 16 ;—el-Jahrâ (on the sea coast), 30 ; el-Kuweyt, 9. [*Abu Daûd, sheykh el-Ageyl, Damascus.*]

CHAPTER III

DEPART FROM HÂYIL: JOURNEY TO KHEYBAR

The 'Persian pilgrimage.' Imbârak's words. Town thieves. Jauf pilgrims in Hâyil. Beduins on pilgrimage. The Caravan to Mecca arrives from the North. An Italian hajjy in Hâyil. The Persians passed formerly by el-Kâsim. Murderous dangers in Mecca. Concourse at Hâyil. — The Kheybar journey. Violent dealing of Imbârak. Ibn Rashîd's passport. Departure from Hâyil. Gofar. Seyadîn, Beduin pedlars. El-Kasr village. Biddîa hamlet. Adventure in the desert. Eyâda ibn Ajjuèyn. Kâsim ibn Barák. Sâlih the rafîk. "It is the angels." The Wady er-Rummah. Kâsim's sister. Set forward again with Sâlih. The Nasrâny abandoned at strange tents. The hospitable goodness of those nomads. Thaifullah. Set forth with a rafîk from the menzil of Eyâda. Ghroceyb. The Harra in sight. Heteym menzil in the Harra. Lineage of the Heteym. The lava-field. The division of waters of Northern Arabia. The dangerous passage. The great Harrat (Kheybar). El-Hâyat, village. Cattle paths in the Harra. An alarm near Kheybar. Locusts. Ghroceyb in trouble of mind. Wady Jellâs. Kheybar village. The Húsn. An antique Mesjid.

THE Haj were approaching;—this is Ibn Rashîd's convoy from Mesopotamia of the so-called 'Persian pilgrimage' to Mecca:— and seeing the child Feysal had nearly recovered, I thought after that to depart, for I found little rest at all or refreshment at Hâyil. Because the Emir had spoken to me of mines and minerals, I conjectured that he would have sent some with me on horseback, seeking up and down for metals:— but when he added "There is a glancing sand in some parts of the khála like scaly gold," I had answered with a plainness which must discourage an Arab. Also Hamûd had spoken to me of seeking for metals.

Imbârak invited me one morning to go home with him "to kahwa," he had a good house beside the mesjid, backward from the Méshab. We found his little son playing in the court: the martial father took him in his arms with the tenderness of the Arabians for their children. An European would bestow the first home love upon the child's mother; but the Arabian housewives come not forth with meeting smiles and the eyes of love, to welcome-in their husbands, for they are his espoused servants, he purchased them of their parents, and at best, his liking is divided. The child cried out, "Ho! Nasrâny, thou canst not look to the heaven!"—"See, my son, I may look upon it as well, I said, as another and better;—*taal húbbiny!* come thou and kiss me;" for the Arab strangers kiss their hosts' young children.—When some of the young courtiers had asked me, *Fen rubbuk*, 'Where is thy Lord God?' I answered them very gravely, *Fî kull makán*, 'The Lord is in every place;' which word of the Nasrâny pleased them strangely, and was soon upon all their tongues in the Kasr.

"Khalîl, said Imbârak, as we sat at the hearth, we would have thee to dwell with us in Hâyil; only become a Moslem, it is a little word and soon said. Also wouldst thou know more of this country, thou shalt have then many occasions in being sent for the Emir's business here and there. The Emir will promote thee to an high place and give thee a house where thou mayest pass thy life in much repose, free from all cares, wellah in only stretching the limbs at thy own hearth-side. Although that which we can offer be not more than a man as thou art might find at home in his country, yet consider it is very far to come again thither, and that thou must return through as many new dangers."—Imbârak was doubtless a spokesman of the Emir, he promised fair, and this office I thought might be the collecting of taxes; for in handling of money they would all sooner trust a Nasrâny.

Those six or seven reals which came in by the sale of my nâga,—I had cast them with a few small pieces of silver into a paper box with my medicines, I found one day had been stolen, saving two reals and the small money; that either the Arab piety of the thief had left me, or his superstition, lest he should draw upon himself the Christian's curse and a chastisement of heaven. My friends' suspicion fell upon two persons. The dumb man, who very often entered my lodging, for little cause, and a certain Beduwy, of the rajajîl at Hâyil, of a melancholy malignant humour; he had bought my camel, and afterward he came many times to my makhzan, to be treated for ophthalmia. I now heard him named a cut-purse of the Persian Haj, and the neighbours even affirmed that he had cut some of their wezands. When I spoke of this mischief to Hamûd, he affected with the barbaric sleight of the Arabs not to believe me. I looked then in my purse, and there were not thirty reals! I gave my tent to the running broker and gained four or five more. The dellâl sold it to some young patrician, who would ride in this winter pilgrimage of 160 leagues and more in the khála, to Mecca. Imbârak set his sword to the dumb man's throat, but the dumb protested with all the vehement signs in the world that this guilt was not in him. As for the Beduwy he was not found in Hâyil.

Already the fore-riders of the Haj arrived: we heard that the pilgrims this year were few in number. I saw now the yearly gathering in Hâyil of men from the villages and the tribes that would follow with the caravan on pilgrimage, and of petty tradesmen that come to traffic with the passing haj:—some of them brought dates from Kasîm above a hundred miles distant. A company from the Jauf villages lodged in the next makhzans; they were more than fifty persons, that had journeyed ten days tardily over the Nefûd in winter rain and rough weather: but that is hardly a third of their long march (of seven hundred miles) to Mecca. I asked some weary man of them, who came to me trembling in the chill morning, how he looked to accomplish his religious voyage and return upwards in the cold months without shelter. "Those, he answered, that die, they die; and who live, God has preserved them." These men told me they reckon from Jauf eight, to el-Méshed and to Damascus nine camel journeys; to Maan are five thelûl days, or nine nights out with loaded camels. Many poor Jaufies come every year into the Haurân seeking labour, and are hired by the Druses to cleanse and repair their pools of rain-water:—it is the jealous manner of the Druses, who would live by themselves, *to inhabit where there is scarcity of water*. Much salt also of the Jauf deserts is continually carried thither. The Jauf villagers say that they are descended from Mesopotamians, Syrians and from the Nejd Arabians. The sûk in Hâyil was in these days thronged with Beduins that had business in the yearly concourse, especially to sell camels. The Méshab was now full of their couching thelûls. The multitude of visiting people were bidden, at the hours, in courses, by Mufarrij and those of the public kitchen, and led in to break their fasts and to sup in the Mothîf.

Three days later the Haj arrived, they were mostly *Ajam*, strangers 'of outlandish speech'; but this word is commonly understood of Persia. They came early in an afternoon, by my reckoning, the 14th of November. Before them rode a great company of Beduins on pilgrimage; there might be in all a thousand persons. Many of the Aarab that arrived in Hâyil were of the Syrian Annezy, Sbáa, whose dîra is far in the north-west near Aleppo. With this great yearly convoy came down trains of laden camels with wares for the tradesmen of Hâyil; and I saw a dozen camels driven in through the castle gate, which carried bales of clothing, for the Emir's daily gifts of changes of garments to his visiting Beduins. The Haj passed westwards about the town, and went to encamp before the Gofar gate, and the summer residency, and the Mâ es-Sáma. The caravan was twelve nights out from Bagdad. I numbered about fifty great tents: they were not more, I heard, than half the hajjies of the former season; but this was a year of that great jehâd which troubled el-Islam, and the most Persians were gone (for fear) the long sea way about to the port of Mecca. I saw none of them wear the Persian bonnets or clad as Persians: the returning pilgrimage is increased by those who visit el-Medina, and would go home by el-Méshed.

I wondered to mark the perfect resemblance of the weary, travel-stained, and ruffianly clad Bagdad akkâms to those of Damascus; the same moon-like white faces are of both the great mixed cities. In their menzil was already a butcher's market, and I saw saleswomen of the town sitting there with baskets of excellent girdle-bread and dates; some of those wives — so wimpled that none might know them — sold also buttermilk! a traffic which passes for less than honest, even in the towns of nomad Arabia. Two days the pilgrims take rest in Hâyil, and the third morrow they depart. The last evening, one stayed me in the street, to enquire, whether I would go with the Haj to Mecca! When I knew his voice in the dusk I answered only, "*Ambar*, no!" and he was satisfied. Ambar, a home-born Galla of Ibn Rashîd's house, was now *Emir el-Haj*, conductor of the pilgrim convoy — this was, we have seen, the Emir Mohammed's former office; Aneybar was his elder brother, and they were freemen, but their father was a slave of Abdullah Ibn Rashîd. Aneybar and Ambar, being thus libertine brethren of the succeeding Emirs, were holders of trusts under them; they were also welfaring men in Hâyil.

On the morrow of the setting out of the Haj, I stood in the menzil to watch their departure. One who walked by in the company of some Bagdad merchants, clad like them and girded in a kumbâz, stayed to speak with me. I asked, 'What did he seek?' — 'I thought the hajjy would say *medicines*: but he answered, "If I speak in the French language, will you understand me?"—" I shall understand it! but what countryman art thou?" I beheld a pale alien's face with a chestnut beard : — who has not met with the like in the mixed cities of the Levant? He responded, " I am an Italian, a Piedmontese of Turin." — " And what brings you hither upon this hazardous voyage? good Lord! you might have your throat cut among them; are you a Moslem?" — " Ay." — " You confess then their ' none îlah but Ullah, and Mahound, apostle of Ullah' — which they shall never hear me utter, may Ullah confound them!" — " Ay, I say it, and I am a Moslem; as such I make this pilgrimage."

— He told me he was come to the Mohammedan countries, eight years before; he was then but sixteen years of age, and from Damascus he had passed to Mesopotamia : the last three years he had studied in a Mohammedan college, near Bagdad, and received the circumcision. He was erudite in the not short task of the Arabic tongue, to read, and to write scholarly, and could speak it with the best, as he said, " without difference." For a moment, he treated in school Arabic, of the variance of the later Arabian from the antique tongue, as it is found in the koran, which he named with a Mohammedan aspiration *es-sherîf*, ' the venerable or exalted scripture.' With his pedant teachers, he dispraised the easy babble-talk of the Aarab. When I said I could never find better than a headache in the farrago of the koran; and it amazed me that one born in the Roman country, and under the name of Christ, should waive these prerogatives, to become the brother of Asiatic barbarians in a fond religion! he answered with the Italic *mollitia* and half urbanity, — " Aha! well, a man may not always choose, but he must sometime go with the world." He hoped to fulfil this voyage, and ascend with the returning Syrian Haj : he had a mind to visit the lands beyond Jordan, and those tribes [B. Hameydy, B. Sókhr], possessors of the best blood horses, in Moab; but when he understood that I had wandered there, he seemed to pass over so much of his purpose. It was in his mind to publish his Travels when he returned to Europe. Poor (he added) he was in the world, and made his pilgrimage at the charges, and in the company, of some bountiful Persian personage of much devotion and learning : — but once returned to Italy, he would wipe off all this rust of the Mohammedan life. He said he heard of me, " the Nasrâny," at his coming to Hâyil, and of the Jew-born Abdullah : he had visited the Moslemanny, but " found him to be a man altogether without instruction."

There was a hubbub in the camp of the taking up tents and loading of baggage and litters; some were already mounted: — and as we took hands, I asked, "What is your name? and remember mine, for these are hazardous times and places." The Italian responded with a little hesitation — it might be true, or it might be he would put me off — *Francesco Ferrari*. Now the caravan was moving, and he hastened to climb upon his camel.

From Hâyil to Mecca are five hundred miles at least, over vast deserts, which they pass in fifteen long marches, not all years journeying by the same landmarks, but according to that which is reported of the waterings (which are wells of the Aarab), and of the peace or dangers of the wilderness before them. Ibn Rashîd's Haj have been known to go near by Kheybar, but they commonly hold a course from Mustajidda or the great watering of *Semîra*, to pass east of the *Harrat el-Kesshub*, and from thence in other two days descend to the underlying Mecca country by *W. Laymûn*. It is a wonder that the Ateyba, (the Prince's strong and capital enemies) do not waylay them: but a squadron of his rajajîl ride to defend the Haj.

Formerly this convoy from Mesopotamia to Mecca passed by the way of el-Kasîm, with the kâfilas of Aneyza, or of Boreyda; in which long passages of the deserts, those of the Persian belief were wont to suffer harshness and even violence, especially by the tyranny of Mahanna, the usurping *jemmâl* or " cameleer " sheykh of Boreyda, of whom there is many a tale told. And I have heard this of a poor Ajamy: When the caravan arrived in the town, he was bound at the command of Mahanna and beaten before him; the Emir still threatening the needy stranger, — " Son of an hound, lay me down thy four *giniyát*, and else thou diest in this place." The town Arabs when crossed are very uncivil spirits, and their hostility turning to a beastly wildness, they set no bounds to their insane cruelty; it is a great prudence therefore not to move them. — It was now twelve years since all the " Persian " overland pilgrims use to come down from el-Méshed under the strong conduct of the Prince of Shammar: — to him they pay toll, (if you can believe the talk) ' an hundred reals ' for each person. — I saw a mare led through the town, of perfect beauty: the Emir Mohammed sent her (his yearly present) with the Haj to the sherîf of Mecca. It was eight o'clock when the Haj departed; but the thelûl riders of Hâyil were still leaving the town to overtake the slow camel-train till mid-day.

When in the favourable revolution of the stars I was come again to peaceable countries, I left notice of the Italian wanderer " Ferrari " at his consulate in Syria, and have vainly enquired for him in Italy : — I thought it my duty, for how dire is the incertitude which hangs over the heads of any aliens that will adventure themselves in Mecca, — where, I have heard it from credible Moslems, that *nearly no Haj passes in which some unhappy persons are not put to death as intruded Christians.* A trooper and his comrade, who rode with the yearly Haj caravans, speaking (unaffectedly) with certain Christian Damascenes (my familiar acquaintance), the year before my setting out, said ' They saw two strangers taken at Mona in the last pilgrimage, that had been detected writing in pocket-books. The strangers being examined were found to be " Christians " ; they saw them executed, and the like happened most years !' Our Christian governments too long suffer this religious brigandage ! Why have they no Residents, for the police of nations in Mecca ? Why have they not occupied the direful city in the name of the health of nations, in the name of the common religion of humanity, *and because the head of the slave trade is there ?* It were good for the Christian governments, which hold any of the Mohammedan provinces, to consider that till then they may never quietly possess them. Each year at Mecca every other name is trodden down, and the " Country of the Apostle " is they pretend inviolable, where no worldly power may reach them. It is " The city of God's house," — and the only God is God only of the Moslemîn.

Few or none of the pilgrim strangers while lying at Hâyil had entered the town, — it might be their fear of the Arabians. Only certain Bagdad derwishes came in, to eat of the public hospitality ; and I saw besides but a company of merry adventurers, who would be bidden to a supper in Arabia, for the novelty. In that day's press even the galleries of the Mothîf were thronged ; there I supped in the dusk, and when I rose, my sandals, the gift of Hamûd, were taken. From four till half-past six o'clock rations had been served for " two to three thousand " persons ; the Emir's cheer was but boiled temmn and a little samn.

It is a passion to be a pointing-stock for every finger and to maintain even a just opinion against the half-reason of the world. I have felt this in the passage of Arabia more than the daily hazards and long bodily sufferance : yet some leaven is in the lump of pleasant remembrance ; it is oftentimes by the hearty ineptitude of the nomads. In the throng of Aarab in these days in the Méshab, many came to me to speak of their infirmities ; strangers where I passed called to me, not knowing my name, " Ho ! thou that goest by, el-hakîm there ! " others, when they had received of me (freely) some faithful counsel, blessed me with the Semitic grace, " God give peace to that head, the Lord suffer not thy face to see the evil." And such are phrases which, like their brand-marks, declare the tribes of nomads : these were, I believe, northern men. One, as I came, showed me to his rafîk, with this word : *Urraie urraie, hu hu !* ' Look there ! he (is) he, this is the Nasrâny.' — *Cheyf Nasrâny?* (I heard the other answer, with the hollow drought of the desert in his manly throat), *agûl! weysh yúnsurhu?* He would say, " How is this man victorious, what giveth him the victory ? " In this strange word to him the poor Beduwy thought he heard *nasr*, which is *victory*. A poor nomad of Ruwàlla cried out simply, when he received his medicines : ' Money he had none to give the hakîm, wellah ! he prayed me be content to receive his shirt.' And, had I suffered it, he would have stripped himself, and gone away naked in his sorry open cloak, as there are seen many men in the indigence of the wilderness and, like the people of India, with no more than a clout to cover the human shame ; and when I let him go, he murmured, *Jîzak Ullah kheyr*, ' God recompense thee with good,' and went on wondering, whether the things ' which the Nasrâny had given him for nothing, could be good medicines ? '

I thought no more of Bagdad, but of Kheybar ; already I stayed too long in Hâyil. At evening I went to Abeyd's kahwa to speak with Hamûd ; he was bowing then in the beginning of his private devotion, and I sat down silently, awaiting his leisure. The son of Abeyd at the end of the first bout looked up, and nodding cheerfully, enquired, " Khalîl, is there need, wouldst thou anything immediately ? " — " There is nothing, the Lord be praised." — " Then I shall soon have ended." As Hamûd sat again in his place, I said, ' I saw the child Feysal's health returning, I desired to depart, and would he send me to Kheybar ? ' Hamûd answered, ' If I wished it.' — " But why, Khalîl, to Kheybar, what is there at Kheybar ? go not to Kheybar, thou mayest die of fever at Kheybar ; and they are not our friends, Khalîl, I am afraid of that journey for thee." I answered, " I must needs adventure thither, I would see the antiquities of the Yahûd, as I have seen el-Héjr."

— "Well, I will find some means to send thee; but the fever is deadly, go not thither, eigh Khalîl! lest thou die there." — Since I had passed the great Aueyrid I desired to discover also the Harrat Kheybar, such another vulcanic Arabian country, and wherein I heard to be the heads of the W. er-Rummah, which westward of the Tueyk mountains is the dry waterway of all northern Arabia. This great valley which descends from the heads above el-Hâyat and Howeyat, to the Euphrates valley at ez-Zbeyer, a suburb of Bosra, has a winding course of "fifty camel marches."

Hamûd, then stretching out his manly great arm, bade me try his pulse; the strokes of his heart-blood were greater than I had felt any man's among the Arabians, the man was strong as a champion. When they hold out their forearms to the hakîm, they think he may well perceive all their health: I was cried down when I said it was imposture. " Yesterday a Persian medicaster in the Haj was called to the Kasr to feel the Emir's pulse. The Persian said, ' Have you not a pain, Sir, in the left knee?' the Prince responded, ' Ay, I feel a pain there by God!' — and no man knew it!"

The Haj had left some sick ones behind them in Hâyil: there was a welfaring Bagdad tradesman, whose old infirmities had returned upon him in the way, a foot-sore camel driver, and some poor derwishes. The morrow after, all these went to present themselves before the Emir in the mejlis, and the derawîsh cried with a lamentable voice in their bastard town Arabic, *Janâbak!* ' may it please your grace.' Their clownish carriage and torpid manners, the barbarous border speech of the north, and their illiberal voices, strangely discorded with the bird-like ease and alacrity and the frank propriety in the tongue of the poorest Arabians. The Emir made them a gracious gesture, and appointed them their daily rations in the Mothîf. Also to the tradesman was assigned a makhzan; and at Hâyil he would pass those two or three months well enough, sitting in the sun and gossiping up and down the sûk, till he might ride homeward. Afterward I saw led-in a wretched young man of the Aarab, who was blind; and spreading his pitiful hands towards the Emir's seat, he cried out, *Yâ Tawîl el-Ummr! yâ Weled Abdullah!* ' Help, O Long-of-days, thou Child of Abdullah!' The Emir spoke immediately to one over the wardrobe, and the poor weled was led away to receive the change of clothing.

Afterwards, I met with Imbârak. "Wouldst thou (he said) to

Kheybar? there are some Annezy here, who will convey thee." When I heard their menzils were in the Kharram, and that they could only carry me again to Misshel, and were to depart immediately : I said that I could not so soon be ready to take a long journey, and must call in the debts for medicines. "We will gather them for thee ; but longer we cannot suffer thee to remain in our country : if thou wouldst go to Kheybar, we will send thee to Kheybar or to el-Kasîm, we will send thee to el-Kasîm." — "To Kheybar, yet warn me a day or two beforehand, that I may be ready."

The morning next but one after, I was drinking kahwa with those of er-Riâth, when a young man entered out of breath, he came, he said, to call me from Imbârak. Imbârak when I met him, said, "We have found some Heteym who will convey thee to Kheybar."—'And when would they depart?'—"To-morrow or the morning after." But he sent for me in an hour to say he had given them handsel, and I must set out immediately. "Why didst thou deceive me with *to-morrow?*" — "Put up thy things and mount." — "But will you send me with Heteym ! " — "Ay, ay, give me the key of the makhzan and make up, for thou art to mount immediately." — "And I cannot speak with the Emir ? " — "*Ukhlus!* have done, delay not, or wellah ! the Emir will send, to take off thy head." — "Is this driving me into the desert to make me away, covertly?" — "Nay, nothing will happen to thee." — "Now well let me first see Hamûd." There came then a slave of Hamûd, bringing in his hand four reals, which he said his "uncle" sent to me. So there came Zeyd, the Moghreby porter of the Kasr ; I had shown him a good turn by the gift of medicines, but now quoth the burly villain, "Thou hast no heart (understanding) if thou wouldst resist Imbârak ; for this is the captain and there ride behind him five hundred men."

I delayed to give the wooden key of my door, fearing lest if they had flung the things forth my aneroid had been broken, or if they searched them my pistol had been taken ; also I doubted whether the captain of the guard (who at every moment laid hand to the hilt of his sword) had not some secret commission to slay the Nasrâny there within. His slaves already came about me, some plucked my clothes, some thrust me forward ; they would drive me perforce to the makhzan. — "Is the makhzan thine or ours, Khalîl ? " — "But Imbârak, I no longer trust thee : bear my word to the Emir, 'I came from the Dowla, send me back to the Dowla,'" The Arab swordsman with *fugh!* spat in my face. "Heaven send thee confusion that art not ashamed to spit in a man's face." — "Khalîl, I did it because thou saidst 'I will not trust thee.'" I saw the Moghreby porter go and break open my makhzan door, bursting the clay mortice of the wooden lock. The slaves plucking me savagely again, I let go the loose Arab upper garments in their hands, and stood before the wondering wretches in my shirt. "A shame! I said to them, and thou Imbârak *dakhîl-ak*, defend me from their insolence." As Imbârak heard 'dakhîl-ak,' he snatched a camel-stick from one who stood by, and beat them back and drove them from me.

They left me in the makhzan and I quickly put my things in order, and took my arms secretly. Fáhd now came by, going to Abeyd's kahwa: I said to him, "Fáhd, I will enter with thee, for here I am in doubt, and where is Hamûd?" The poor man answered friendly, "Hamûd is not yet abroad, but it will not be long, Khalîl, before he come." — *Imbârak*: "Wellah, I say the Emir will send immediately to cut off thy head!" *Mâjid* (who passed us at the same time, going towards Abeyd's Kahwa): "Eigh! Imbârak, will the Emir do so indeed?" and the boy smiled with a child's dishonest curiosity of an atrocious spectacle. As I walked on with Fáhd, Imbârak retired from us, and passed through the Kasr gate, perhaps then he went to the Emir. — Fáhd sighed, as we were beyond the door, and "Khalîl, please Ullah, said the poor man, it may yet fall out well, and Hamûd will very soon be here." I had not sat long, when they came to tell me, 'the Emir desired to see me.' I said, "Do not deceive me, it is but Imbârak who knocks." *Fáhd*: "Nay, go Khalîl, it is the Emir."

When I went out, I found it was Imbârak, who with the old menaces, called upon me to mount immediately. "I will first, I answered, see Hamûd:" so he left me. The door had been shut behind me, I returned to the makhzan, and saw my baggage was safe; and Fáhd coming by again, "Hamûd, he said, is now in the house," and at my request he sent back a servant to let me in. After a little, Hamûd entering, greeted me, and took me by the hand. I asked, 'Was this done at the commandment of the Emir?' *Hamûd*: "By God, Khalîl, I can do nothing with the Emir; *hu yáhkam aleyna* he rules over us all." — "Some books of mine, and other things, were brought here." — "Ha! the eyyâl have taken them from thy makhzan, they shall be restored." When I spoke of a knavish theft of his man Aly — he was gone now on pilgrimage — Hamûd exclaimed : " The Lord take away his breath ! " — He were not an Arab if he had proffered to make good his man's larceny. " What intended you by that money you lately sent me ? " — " My liberality, Khalîl, why didst thou refuse it ? " — " Is it for medicine and a month's daily care of thy child, who is now restored to health ? " — " It was for this I offered it, and we have plenty of quinine ; wilt thou buy an handful of me for two reals ? " He was washing to go to the midday public prayer, and whilst the strong man stayed to speak with me it was late. " There is a thing, Hamûd." — " What is that, Khalîl ? " and he looked up cheerfully. " Help me in this trouble, for that bread and salt which is between us." — " And what can I do ? Mohammed rules us all." — " Well, speak to Imbârak to do nothing till the hour of the afternoon mejlis, when I may speak with the Emir." — " I will say this to him," and Hamûd went to the mesjid.

After the prayer I met the Prince himself in the Méshab ; he walks, as said, in an insolent cluster of young fanatics, and a half score of his swordsmen close behind them. — Whenever I had encountered the Emir and his company of late, in the streets, I thought he had answered my greeting with a strutting look. Now, as he came on with his stare, I said, without a salutation, *Arûhh*, ' I depart.' " *Rûhh*, So go," answered Mohammed. " Shall I come in to speak with thee ? " — " *Meshghrûl !* we are too busy."

When at length the afternoon mejlis was sitting, I crossed through them and approached the Emir, who sat enforcing himself to look gallantly before the people ; and he talked then with some great sheykh of the Beduw, who was seated next him. Mohammed Ibn Rashîd looked towards me, I thought with displeasure and somewhat a base countenance, which is of evil augury among the Arabs. " What (he said) is thy matter ? " — " I am about to depart, but I would it were with assurance. To-day I was mishandled in this place, in a manner which has made me afraid. Thy slaves drew me hither and thither, and have rent my clothing ; it was by the setting on of Imbârak, who stands here : he also threatened me, and even spat in my face." The Emir enquired, under his voice, of Imbârak, ' what had he done,' who answered, excusing himself. I added, " And now he would compel me to go with Heteym ; and I foresee only mischance." " Nay (said the Emir, striking his breast), fear not ; but ours be the care for thy safety, and we will give thee a passport," — and he said to Nasr, his secretary, who sat at his feet — " Write him a schedule of safe-conduct."

I said, " I brought thee from my country an excellent telescope." The cost had been three or four pounds ; and I thought, ' if Ibn Rashîd receive my gift, I might ask of him a camel ' : but when he said, " We have many, and have no need," I answered the Emir with a frank word of the desert, *weysh aad*, as one might say, ' What odds ! ' Mohammed Ibn Rashîd shrunk back in his seat, as if I had disparaged his dignity before the people ; but recovering himself, he said, with better looks and a friendly voice, " Sit down." Mohammed is not ungenerous, he might remember in the stranger his own evil times. Nasr having ended his writing, upon a small square of paper, handed it up to the Emir, who perused it, and daubing his Arabic copper seal in the ink, he sealed it with the print of his name. I asked Nasr, " Read me what is written herein," and he read, " That all unto whose hands this bill may come, who owe obedience to Ibn Rashîd, know it is the will of the Emir that no one *yaarud aley*, should do any offence to, this Nasrâny." Ibn Rashîd rising at the moment, the mejlis rose with him and dispersed. I asked, as the Emir was going, " When shall I depart ? " — " At thy pleasure." — " To-morrow ? " — " Nay, to-day." He had turned the back, and was crossing the Méshab.

" Mount ! " cries Imbârak : but, when he heard I had not broken my fast he led me through the Kasr, to the Mothîf and to a room behind, which is the public kitchen, to ask the cooks what was ready. Here they all kindly welcomed me, and Mufarrij would give me dates, flour and samn for the way, the accustomed provision from the Emir, but I would not receive them. The kitchen is a poor hall, with a clay floor, in which is a pool and conduit. The temmn and barley is boiled in four or five coppers : other three stand there for flesh days (which are not many), and they are so great that in one of them may be seethed the brittled meat of a camel. So simple is this palace kitchen of nomadic Arabia, a country in which he is feasting who is not hungry ! The kitchen servants were one poor man, perhaps of servile condition, a patient of mine, and five or six women under him ; besides there were boys, bearers of the metal trays of victual for the guests' suppers. — When I returned to the Méshab, a nomad was come with his camel to load my baggage : yet first he entreated Imbârak to take back his real of earnest-money and let him go. The Emir had ordered four reals to be given for this voyage, whether I would or no, and I accepted it in lieu of that which was robbed from my makhzan ; also I accepted the four reals from Hamûd for medicines.

"Imbârak, swear, I said, as we walked together to the sûk, where the nomads would mount, that you are not sending me to the death." — " No, by Ullah, and Khalîl nothing I trust will happen to thee." — " And after two journeys in the desert will the Aarab any more observe the word of Ibn Rashîd ? " — " We rule over them ! — and he said to the nomads, Ye are to carry him to *Kâsim ibn Barák* (a great sheykh of the midland Heteym, his byût were pitched seventy miles to the southward), and he will send him to Kheybar." — The seller of drugs from Medina, a good liberal Hejâz man, as are many of that partly Arabian city, came out, as we passed his shop, to bid me God speed, " Thou mayest be sure, he said, that there is no treachery, but understand that the people (of Hâyil and Nejd) are Beduw." — " O thou (said the nomad to me) make haste along with us out of Hâyil, stand not, nor return upon thy footsteps, for then they will kill thee."

Because I would not that his camel should kneel, but had climbed upon the overloaded beast's neck standing, the poor pleased nomad cried out, " Lend me a grip of thy five ! " that is the five fingers. A young man, Ibrahîm, one of the Emir's men — his shop was in the end of the town, and I had dealt with him — seeing us go by, came out to bid me farewell, and brought me forward. He spoke sternly to the nomads that they should have a care for me, and threatened them, that ' If anything befell me, the Emir would have their heads.' Come to the Mâ es-Sáma, I reached down my water-skin to one of the men, bidding him go fill it. " Fill the kafir's girby ! nay, said he, alight, Nasrâwy, and fill it thyself." Ibrahîm then went to fill it, and hanged the water at my saddle-bow. We passed forth and the sun was now set. My companions were three, — the poor owner of my camel, a timid smiling man, and his fanatic neighbour, who called me always the Nasrâwy (and not Nasrâny), and another and older Heteymy, a somewhat strong-headed holder of his own counsel, and speaking the truth uprightly. So short is the twilight that the night closed suddenly upon our march, with a welcome silence and solitude, after the tumult of the town. When I responded to all the questions of my nomad company with the courtesy of the desert, " Oh ! wherefore, cried they, did those of Hâyil persecute him ? Wellah the people of Hâyil are the true Nasâra ! " We held on our dark way three and a half hours till we came before Gofar ; there we alighted and lay down in the wilderness.

When the morrow was light we went to an outlying kasr, a chamber or two built of clay-brick, without the oasis, where dwelt a poor family of their acquaintance. We were in the end of November (the 21st by my reckoning) ; the nights were now cold at this altitude of 4000 feet. The poor people set dates before us and made coffee ; they were neither settlers upon the soil nor nomads, but Beduw. Weak and broken in the nomad life, and forsaking the calamities of the desert, they had become 'dwellers in clay' at one of the Jebel villages, and *Seyadîn* or traffickers to the Aarab. They buy dates and corn in harvest time, to sell later to the *hubts* or passing market parties of nomad tribesmen. When spring is come they forsake the clay-walls and, loading their merchandise upon asses, go forth to trade among the Aarab. Thus they wander months long, till their lading is sold ; and when the hot summer is in they will return with their humble gains of samn and silver to the oasis. From them my companions took up part of their winter provision of dates, for somewhat less than the market price in Hâyil. These poor folk, disherited of the world, spoke to me with human kindness ; there was not a word in their talk of the Mohammedan fanaticism. The women, of their own thought, took from my shoulders and mended my mantle which had been rent yesterday at Hâyil ; and the house-father put in my hand his own driving-stick made of an almond rod. Whilst I sat with them, my companions went about their other business. Bye and bye there came in a butcher from Hâyil. (I had bought of him three pounds of mutton one morning, for fourpence), and with a loud good humour he praised the Nasrâny in that simple company.

The men were not ready till an hour past midday ; then they loaded their dates and we departed. Beyond Gofar we journeyed upon a plain of granite grit ; the long Ajja mountain trended with our course upon the right hand. At five we alighted and I boiled them some temmn which I carried, but the sun suddenly setting upon us, they skipt up laughing to patter their prayers, and began to pray as they could, with quaking ribs ; and they panted yet with their elvish mirth. — Some wood-gatherers of Hâyil went by us. The double head of the Sumrâ Hâyil was still in sight at a distance of twenty-five miles. Re-mounting we passed in the darkness the walls and palms of el-Kasr, thirteen miles from Gofar, under the cliffs of Ajja; an hour further we alighted in the desert to sleep.

I saw in the morning the granite flanks of Ajja strangely blotted, as it were with the shadows of clouds, by the running down of erupted basalts; and there are certain black domes upon the crest in the likeness of volcanoes. [*v.* fig.] Two hours later we were in a granitic mountain ground *el-Mukhtelif*. Ajja upon the right hand now stands far off and extends not much further. We met here with a young man of el-Kasr riding upon his thelûl in quest of a strayed well-camel.

A view of J. Ajja below el-Kasr

Rock-partridges were everywhere calling and flying in this high granite country, smelling in the sun of the (resinous) sweetness of southernwood.

About four in the afternoon we went by an outlying hamlet *Biddîa*, in the midst of the plain, but encompassed by lesser mountains of granite and basalt. This small settlement, which lies thirty-five miles W. of S. from el-Kasr, was begun not many years ago by projectors from Môgug; there are only two wells and four households. When I asked my companions of the place, they fell a coughing and laughing, and made me signs that only coughs and rheums there abounded. — A party of Shammar riding on dromedaries overtook us. They had heard of Khalîl and spoke friendly, saying that there lay a menzil of their Aarab not far before us (where we might sup and sleep). And we heard from them these happy tidings of the wilderness in front, " The small cattle have yeaned, and the Aarab have plenty of léban; they pour out (to drink) till the noon day! " One of them cried to me : " But why goest thou in the company of these dogs? " — he would say ' Heteymies.'

A great white snake, *hánash*, lay sleeping in the path: and the peevish owner put it to the malice of the Nasrâny that I had not sooner seen the worm, and struck away his camel, which was nearly treading on it; and with his lance he beat in pieces the poisonous vermin. When the daylight was almost spent my companions climbed upon every height to look for the black booths of the Aarab. The sun set and we journeyed on in the night, hoping to espy the Beduin tent-fires. Three hours later we halted and lay down, weary and supperless, to sleep in the khála. The night was chill and we could not slumber; the land-height was here 4000 feet.

We loaded and departed before dawn. Soon after the day broke we met with Shammar Aarab removing. Great are their flocks in this dîra, all of sheep, and their camels are a multitude trooping over the plain. Two herdsmen crossed to us to hear tidings: "What news, they shouted, from the villages? how many sahs to the real?"—Then, perceiving what I was, one of them who had a lance lifted it and said to the other, 'Stand back, and he would slay me.' "Nay do not so! wellah! (exclaimed my rafîks), for this (man) is in the safeguard of Ibn Rashîd, and we must billah convey him, upon our necks, to Ch(K)âsim Ibn Barák." Heteymies in presence of high-handed Shammar, they would have made no manly resistance; and my going with these rafîks was nearly the same as to wander alone, save that they were eyes to me in the desert.

In the slow march of the over-loaded camels I went much on foot; the fanatic who cried Nasrâwy, Nasrâwy! complained that he could not walk, he must ride himself upon my hired camel. Though weary I would not contradict them, lest in remembering Hâyil they should become my adversaries. I saw the blown sand of the desert lie in high drifts upon the mountain sides which encompassed us; they are granite with some basalt bergs.—We were come at unawares to a menzil of Shammar. Their sheykh hastened from his booth to meet us, a wild looking carl, and he had not a kerchief, but only the woollen head-cord *maasub* wound about his tufted locks. He required of me dokhân; but I told them I had none, the tobacco-bag with flint and steel had fallen from my camel a little before.—"Give us tobacco (cried he), and come down and drink kahwa with us, and if no we will *nô'kh* (make kneel) thy camel, and take it perforce."—"How (I said), ye believe not in God! I tell you I have none by God, it is *ayib* (a shame) man to molest a stranger, and that only for a pipe of tobacco." Then he let me pass, but they made me swear solemnly again that I had none indeed.

As we journeyed in the afternoon and were come into Heteym country we met with a sheykhly man riding upon his thelûl : he would see what pasture was sprung hereabout in the wilderness. The rafîks knew him, and the man said he would carry me to Kheybar himself, for tómâ (gain). This was one whom I should see soon again, *Eyâda ibn Ajjuèyn*, an Heteymy sheykh. My rafîks counselled me to go with him : ' He is a worthy man, they said, and one with whom I might safely adventure.' — The first movements of the Arabs from their heart, are the best, and the least interested, and could the event be foreseen it were often great prudence to accept them ; but I considered the Emir's words, — that I should go to Kâsim ibn Barák sheykh of the Beny Rashîd ' who would send me to Kheybar,' and his menzil was not now far off. This Kâsim or Châsim, or *Jâsîm*, they pronounce the name diversely, according to their tribes' loghrat, my companions said was a great sheykh, " and one like to Ibn Rashîd " in his country.

The sun set as we came to the first Heteym booths, and there the rafîks unloaded. Kâsim's beyt we heard was built under a brow yonder, and I mounted again with my rafîk Sâlih, upon his empty camel, to ride thither. And in the way said Sâlih, " When we arrive see that thou get down lightly ; so the Aarab will hold of thee the more as one inured to the desert life." Kâsim's tent was but a hejra, small and rent ; I saw his mare tied there, and within were only the hareem. One of them went to call the sheykh, and Sâlih hastily put down my bags : he remounted, and without leave-taking would have ridden away ; but seizing his camel by the beard I made the beast kneel again. " My rafîk, why abandon me thus ? but Sâlih thou shalt deliver all the Emir's message to Kâsim ; " — we saw him coming to us from a neighbour beyt.

Kasîm was a slender young man, almost at the middle age. At first he said that he could not receive me. ' How ! (he asked), had the Emir sent this stranger to him, to send him on to Kheybar, when he was at feud with those of Kheybar ! ' Then he reproached Sâlih who would have ' forsaken me at strange tents.' — I considered how desperate a thing it were, to be abandoned in the midst of the wilderness of Arabia, where we dread to meet with unknown mankind more than with wild beasts! "You, Kâsim, have heard the word of Ibn Rashîd, and if it cannot be fulfilled at least I have alighted at thy beyt and am weary; here, I said, let me rest this night, *wa ana dakhîlak*, and I enter under thy roof."

He now led me into his booth and bade me repose: then turning all his vehement displeasure against Sâlih, he laid hands on him and flung him forth — these are violences of the Heteym — and snatched his mantle from him. "Away with thee! he cried, but thy camel shall remain with me, whereupon I may send this stranger to Kheybar; Ullah curse thy father, O thou that forsakedst thy rafîk to cast him upon Aarab." Sâlih took all in patience, for the nomads when they are overborne make no resistance. Kâsim set his sword to Sâlih's throat, that he should avow to him all things without any falsity, and first what tribesman he was. Sâlih now acknowledged himself to be of *Bejaida*, that is a sub-tribe of Bishr; he was therefore of Annezy, but leading his life with Noâmsy Heteymies he passed for an Heteymy. Many poor families both of Annezy and Harb join themselves to that humbler but more thriving nomad lot, which is better assured from enemies; only they mingle not in wedlock with the Heteym. So Kâsim let Sâlih go, and called to kindle the fire, and took up himself a lapful of his mare's provender and littered it down to Sâlih's camel; so he came again and seated himself in the tent with the hypochondriacal humour of a sickly person. "Who is there, said he, will go now and seek us kahwa that we may make a cup for this stranger? — thy name?" — "Khalîl." — "Well, say Khalîl, what shall I do in this case, for wellah, I cannot tell; betwixt us and those of Kheybar and the Dowla there is only debate and cutting of throats: how then says the Emir, that I must send thee to Kheybar?" — Neighbours came in to drink coffee, and one answered, "If Khalîl give four reals I will set him down, billah, at the edge of the palms of Kheybar and be gone." *Kâsim:* "But Khalîl says rightly he were then as much without Kheybar as before."

The coffee-drinkers showed me a good countenance; "Eigh! Khalîl (said Kâsim), hadst thou complained to me that the man forsook thee, he who came with thee, wellah I would have cut off his head and cast it on this fire: accursed be all the *Anûz* [nation of Annezy]." — "Well, if Kheybar be too difficult, you may send me to Hannas sheykh of the Noâmsy; I heard he is encamped not far off, and he will receive me friendly." — "We shall see in the morning." A scarce dish of boiled temmn without samn, and a little old rotten léban was set before me, — the smallest cheer I had seen under worsted booths; they had no fresh milk because their camel troops were âzab, or separated from the menzil, and pasturing towards Baitha Nethîl, westward.

The night closed in darkly over us, with thick clouds and falling weather, it lightened at once upon three sides without thunder. The nomad people said, "*It is the Angels!*" — their word made me muse of the nomads' vision in the field of Bethlehem. "The storm, they murmured, is over the Wady er-Rummah," — which they told me lay but half a thelûl journey from hence. They marvelled that I should know the name of this great Wady of middle Nejd: the head, they said, is near el-Hâyat, in their dîra, one thelûl day distant, — that may be over plain ground forty-five to seventy miles. The cold rain fell by drops upon us through the worn tent-cloth: and when it was late said Kâsim, "Sleep thou, but I must wake with my eyes upon his camel there, all night, lest that Annezy (man) come to steal it away."

When I rose with the dawn Kâsim was making up the fire; "Good morrow! he said: well, I will send thee to Hannas; and the man shall convey thee that came with thee." — "He betrayed me yesterday, will he not betray me to-day? he might even forsake me in the khála." — "But I will make him swear so that he shall be afraid." Women came to me hearing I was a mudowwy, with baggl or dry milk shards, to buy medicines; and they said it was a provision for my journey. Kâsim's sister came among the rest and sat down beside me. Kâsim, she said, was vexed with the rîhh or ague-cake, and what medicine had I? These women's veil is a blue calico clout suspended over the lower face; her eyes were wonderfully great, and though lean and pale, I judged that she was very beautiful and gracious; she leaned delicately to examine my drugs with the practised hands of a wise woman in simples. When she could find no medicine that she knew, she said, with a gentle sweet voice, "Give then what thou wilt, Khalîl, only that which may be effectual." Although so fair, and the great sheykh's sister, yet no man of the Beduins would have wedded with her; because the Heteym "are not of the stock" of the Aarab.

Now came Sâlih, and when he saw his camel restored to him, he was full of joy, and promised all that Kâsim would; and he swore mighty oaths to convey me straightway to Hannas. We mounted and rode forth; but as we were going I drew bridle and bound Sâlih by that solemn oath of the desert, *aly el-aûd wa Rubb el-mabûd*, that he would perform all these things : if he would not swear, I would ride no further with him. But Sâlih looking back and trembling cried, " I do swear it, billah, I swear it, only let us hasten and come to our rafîks, who have awaited us at the next tents."

We set out anew with them, and quoth Sâlih, " I was never in such fear in my life, as when Châsim set his sword to my neck ! " We marched an hour and a half and approached another Heteym menzil of many beyts : as we passed by Sâlih went aside to them to enquire the tidings. Not far beyond we came upon a brow, where two lone booths stood. My companions said the (overloaded) camels were broken, they would discharge them there to pasture an hour. When we were come to the place they halted.

In the first tent was an old wife : she bye and bye brought out to us, where we sat a little aloof, a bowl of milk shards and samn, and then, that which is of most comfort in the droughty heat, a great bowl of her butter-milk. " Canst thou eat this fare ? said Sâlih, — the Heteym have much of it, they are good and hospitable." The men rose after their breakfast and loaded upon the camels, — but not my bags ! — and drove forth. I spoke to the elder Heteymy, who was a worthy man, but knitting the shoulders and turning up his palms he answered gravely, " What can I do ? it is Sâlih's matter, wellah, I may not meddle in it ; but thou have no fear, for these are good people, and amongst them there will no evil befall thee." " Also Eyâda ibn Ajjuèyn, said Sâlih, is at little distance." — " But where is thy oath, man ? " The third fanatic fellow answered for him, " His oath is not binding, which was made to a Nasrâwy ! " — " But what of the Emir ? and Kâsim is not yet far off." *Sâlih :* " As for Kâsim we curse both his father and his mother ; but thou be not troubled, the Heteym are good folk and this will end well." — To contend with them were little worth ; they might then have published it that I was a Nasrâny, I was as good quit of such rafîks, — here were but two women — and they departed.

— " It is true, quoth the old wife, that Eyâda is near, yesterday I heard their dogs bark." In the second tent was but her sick daughter-in-law ; their men were out herding. The old wife looked somewhat grim when the hubt had forsaken me ; afterwards she came where I sat alone, and said, " Be not sorrowful ! *ana khâlatak*, for I am thy mother's sister." Soon after that she went out to bear word to the men in the wilderness of this chance. Near by that place I found the border of a brown vulcanic flood, a kind of trachytic basalt : when the sun was setting I walked out of sight, — lest seeing the stranger not praying at the hour I had been too soon known to them.

Not much after the husband came home, a deaf man with the name of happy augury *Thaifullah* : kindly he welcomed me, and behind him came three grown sons driving-in their camels ; and a great flock of sheep and goats followed them with many lambs and kids. I saw that (notwithstanding their Heteym appearance of poverty) they must be welfaring persons. Thaifullah, as we sat about the evening fire, brought me in a bowl of their evening milk, made hot ; — " We have nothing, he said, here to eat, no dates, no rice, no bread, but drink this which the Lord provideth, though it be a poor supper." I blessed him and said it was the best of all nourishment. " Ay, thus boiled, he answered, it enters into the bones." When he heard how my rafîks forsook me to-day he exclaimed, ' Billah if he had been there, he had cut off their heads.' That poor man was very honourable ; he would hardly fill his galliûn once with a little tittun that I had found in the depths of my bags, although it be so great a solace to them ; neither suffered he his young men to receive any from the (forlorn) guest whom the Lord had committed to them, to-day. These were simple, pious and not (formal) praying Arabs, having in their mouths no cavilling questions of religion, but they were full of the godly humanity of the wilderness. ' He would carry me in the morning (said my kind host) to Eyâda ibn Ajjuèyn, who would send me to Kheybar.'

It was dim night, and the drooping clouds broke over us with lightning and rain. I said to Thaifullah, " God sends his blessing again upon the earth." — " Ay verily," he answered devoutly, and kissed his pious hand towards the flashing tempest, and murmured the praises of Ullah. — How good ! seemed to me, how peaceable ! this little plot of the nomad earth under the dripping curtains of a worsted booth, in comparison with Hâyil town !

When the morning rose the women milked their small cattle ; and we sat on whilst the old housewife rocked her blown-up milk-skin upon her knees till the butter came ; they find it in a clot at the mouth of the semîly. I saw soon that little butter seething on the fire, to be turned into samn, and they called me to sup the pleasant milk-skim with my fingers. They throw in now a little meal, which brings down the milkiness; and the samn or clarified butter may be poured off. The sediment of the meal thus drenched with milky butter is served to the guest; and it is the most pleasant sweet-meat of the poor nomad life. Afterward the good old woman brought me the samn (all that her flocks had yielded this morning), in a little skin (it might be less than a small pint) : this was her gift, she said : and would I leave with them some fever medicine ? I gave her doses of quinine. She brought forth a large bowl of butter-milk ; and when we had drunk a good draught Thaifullah laid my bags upon a camel of his. We mounted, and rode southward over the khála.

We journeyed an hour and approached Eyâda's menzil, the worsted booths were pitched in a shelving hollow overlooking a wide waste landscape to the south : I saw a vast blackness beyond, — that was another Harra (the *Harrat Kheybar*) — and rosy mountains of granite. Sandstones, lying as a tongue between the crystalline mountains and overlaid by lavas, reach southward to Kheybar. — " When we come to the tents thus and thus shalt thou speak to them, said Thaifullah : say thou art a mudowwy arrived from Hâyil, and that thou wouldst go over to Kheybar ; and for two reals thou shalt find some man who will convey thee thither."

We alighted and Thaifullah commended me to Eyâda ; I was (he said) a skilful mudowwy, — so he took his camel again and departed. This was that Heteymy sheykh whom I had two days before seen chevying in the wilderness : — he might have understood then (from some saying of the fanatic) that I was not a right Moslem, for now when I saluted him and said I would go to Kheybar with him, he received me roughly. He was a sturdy carl, and with such ill-blooded looks as I have remarked in the Fehját, which are also of Heteym. *Eyâda :* " Well, I said it yesterday, but I cannot send thee to Kheybar." — Some men were sitting before his tent — " Ho ! which of you, he said, will convey the man to Kheybar, and receive from him what — ? three reals." One answered, " I will carry him, if he give me this money." I promised, and he went to make ready ; but returning he said, " Give me four reals, — I have a debt, and this would help me in it." *Eyâda :* " Give him four, and go with him." I consented, so the sheykh warranted me that the man would not forsake his rafîk, as did those of the other day.

"Nay, trust me, this is *Ghroceyb*, a sheykh, and a valorous man." — " Swear, O Ghroceyb, by the life of this stem of grass, that thou wilt not forsake me, thy rafîk, until thou hast brought me to Kheybar!" — " I swear to bring thee thither, but I be dead." *Eyâda*: " He has a thelûl too, that can flee like a bird." *Ghroceyb* : " See how the sun is already mounted! let us pass the day here, and to-morrow we will set forward." — " Nay, but to-day," answered the sheykh, shortly, so that I wondered at his inhospitable humour, and Ghroceyb at this strangeness. The sheykh did not bid me into his tent, but he brought out to us a great bowl of butter-milk. The hareem now came about me, bringing their little bowls of dry milk shards, and they clamoured for medicines. I have found no Beduins so willing as the Heteym to buy of the mudowwy. After my departure, when they had proved my medicines, they said that Khalîl was a faithful man; and their good report helped me months later, at my coming by this country again.

Ghroceyb told me that from hence to Baitha Nethîl was half a (thelûl) journey, to Hâyil three, to Teyma four, to el-Ally four and a half; and we should have three nights out to Kheybar. When we had trotted a mile, a yearling calf of the thelûl, that was grazing in the desert before us, ran with their sidelong slinging gait (the two legs upon a side leaping together) to meet the dam, and followed us lowing, — the mother answered with sobs in her vast throat; but Ghroceyb dismounted and chased the weanling away. We rode upon a plain of sand. Nigh before us appeared that great craggy blackness — the Harra, and thereupon certain swart hills and crests, *el-Hélly* : I perceived them to be crater-hills of volcanoes! A long-ranging inconsiderable mountain, *Bothra*, trended with our course upon the left-hand, which I could not doubt to be granitic. Ghroceyb encouraged his thelûl with a pleasant *gluck*! with the tongue under the palate, — I had not heard it before; and there is a diversity of cattle-calls in the several tribes of the Arabian khála.

We entered upon that black Harra. The lava field is now cast into great waves and troughs, and now it is a labyrinth of lava crags and short lava sand-plains. — This is another member of the vulcanic country of West Arabia, which with few considerable breaches, extends from Tebûk through seven degrees of latitude to the borders of Mecca.

We found clayey water, in a cavern (after the late showers), and

Ghroceyb alighted to fill our girby. At half-afternoon we saw a goatherd loitering among the wild lavas. The lad was an Heteymy, he knew Ghroceyb, and showed us where the beyts were pitched, in a deep place not far off. Here Ghroceyb came to his own kindred; and we alighted at the tent of his brother. The cragged Harra face is there 4300 feet above sea-level. Their hareem were veiled like those of Kâsim's encampment, and they wore a braided forelock hanging upon their foreheads. In the evening we were regaled with a caldron of temmn, and the host poured us out a whole skinful of thick butter-milk.

One of those men was a hunter; the Heteym and the Sherarát surpass the Beduw in the skill, and are next to the Solubba. In the last season he had killed two ostriches, and sold the skins (to that Damascus feather merchant who comes down yearly with the Haj) for 80 reals: 40 reals for an ostrich skin! (the worth of a good camel) — a wonderful price it seems to be paid in this country. Of the lineage of the Heteym I could never learn anything in Arabia. They are not of so cheerful a temper, and they lack the frank alacrity of mind and the magnanimous dignity of Beduins. Ghroceyb spoke of his people thus, " Jid el-Heteym is *Rashîd* and we — the midland Heteym — are the *Beny Rashîd*. Those Heteymies at the Red Sea bord, under el-Wejh, are the *Gerabîs*, our kindred indeed but not friendly with us. The B. Rashîd are as many as the B. Wáhab " (nearly 600 beyts, not much above 2000 souls). Of the Sherarát akin to the Heteym he said, " We may wed with them and they with us, — but there is cattle stealing between us; they are 800 beyt." He told me that in former days, some camels having been reaved by a Noâmsy ghrazzu from the Gerabîs, the sheykh Ibn Nômus (father of Hannas), ordained their restitution, saying, " Wellah they be our kindred."

In the early morning Ghroceyb milked our thelûl and brought me this warm bever; and after that, in the fatigue of the long way to be passed almost without her tasting herbage, her udder would be dried up, and the Beduwy fetched in a hurr to cover her; [at such times doubtless in the hope that she may bear a female]. We were called away to breakfast in another booth where they set before us dates fried in samn, and bowls of butter-milk. All was horrid lava-field far before us, and we should be " two nights out without Aarab," and the third at Kheybar.

Gloomy were these days of drooping grey clouds in the golden-aired

Arabia. We journeyed quickly by the camel paths (*jiddar*, pl. *jiddrân*) worn, since ages, in the rolling cinders and wilderness of horrid lavas. Hither come Bishr and Heteym nomads in the early year with their cattle, to seek that rabîa which may be sprung among the lava clefts and pits and little bottoms of volcanic sand. Before noon we were among the black hills (*hilliân*) which I had viewed before us since yesterday; they are cones and craters of spent volcanoes. Our path lay under the highest *hilly*, which might be of four hundred or five hundred feet. Some are two-headed, — it is where a side of the crater is broken down. Others are seen ribbed, that is they are guttered down from the head. *All is here as we have seen in the Harrat el-Aueyrid.* We passed over a smooth plain of cinders; and, at the roots of another hilly, I saw yellowish soft tufa lying under the scaly crags of lavas. From hence we had sight of the Kharram, a day distant to the westward; lying beyond the Harra in a yellow border of Nefûd; the white sand lay in long drifts upon the high flanks of the mountain.

There was now much ponded rain upon these vulcanic highlands; and in a place I heard the heavy din of falling water! We came to a cold new tarn, and it seemed a fenny mountain lake under the setting sun! from this strange desert water issued a wild brook with the rushing noise of a mill-race. Having gone all the daylight, we drew bridle in a covert place, where we might adventure to kindle our fire. My rafîk was never come so far in this sea of lava, but he knew the great landmarks. He went about to pull an armful of the scanty herbage in the crevices, for his fasting thelûl; I gathered dry stems to set under our pot, poured in water and began our boiling, which was but of temmn. When Ghroceyb came again I bid him mind the cooking; but said he, "What can I do? I, billah, understand it not." — "Yet I never saw the nomad who could not shift for himself upon a journey." — "I eat that which the hareem prepare and have never put my hand to it." — He had brought for himself only two or three handfuls of dry milk shards! in Ghroceyb was the ague-cake of old fever, and he could eat little or nothing. In this place I found the greatest height which I had passed hitherto in Arabia, nearly 6000 feet. And here I have since understood to be the division of waters between the great wady bottoms of northern Arabia; namely the W. er-Rummah descending from the Harra to the north-eastward, and the W. el-Humth.

This night was mild, and sheltered in the wild lavas, as between walls, we were warm till the morning.

We mounted in the morrow twilight; but long after daybreak the heavens seemed shut over us, as a tomb, with gloomy clouds. We were engaged in the horrid lava beds; and were very oftentimes at fault among sharp shelves, or finding before us precipitous places. The vulcanic field is a stony flood which has stiffened; long rolling heads, like horse-manes, of those slaggy waves ride and over-ride the rest: and as they are risen they stand petrified, many being sharply split lengthwise, and the hollow laps are partly fallen down in vast shells and in ruinous heaps as of massy masonry. The lava is not seldom wreathed as it were bunches of cords; the crests are seen also of sharp glassy lavas, *lâba* (in the plural *lûb*); lâba [v. vol. I, p. 468] is all that which has a likeness to molten metal. — That this soil was ever drowned with burning mineral, or of burning mountains, the Aarab have no tradition. As we rode further I saw certain golden-red crags standing above the black horror of lavas; they were sandstone spires touched by the scattered beams of the morning sun. In the sheltered lava bottoms, where grew gum-acacias, we often startled *gatta* fowl (" sand-grouse "); they are dry-fleshed birds and not very good to eat, say the nomads. There is many times seen upon the lava fields a glistering under the sun as of distant water; it is but dry clay glazed over with salt.

Ghroceyb spread forth his hands devoutly; he knew not the formal prayers, but wearied the irrational element with the lowings of his human spirit in this perilous passage. " Give, Lord, that we see not the evil! and oh that this be not the day of our deaths and the loss of the thelûl!" My rafîk knew not that I was armed. Ghroceyb, bearing his long matchlock, led on afoot betwixt running and walking, ever watching for a way before the thelûl, and gazing wide for dread of any traversing enemies. Upon a time turning suddenly he surprised me as I wrote with a pencil [a reading of the aneroid]. " Is it well, O Khalîl? quoth my rafîk, how seest thou (in your magical art of letters), is there good or else evil toward? canst thou not write something (a strong spell) for this need?" Then seeing me ride on careless and slumbering for weariness he took comfort. My pistol of six chambers gave me this confidence in Arabia, for must we contend for our lives I thought it might suffice to defend me and my company, and Ghroceyb was a brave companion. Ghroceyb's long piece must weigh heavily upon the strenuous man's sick shoulders, and I spoke to him to hang it at the saddle-bow of me his rafîk ; to this he consented, ' so I did not loop the shoulder-cord about the peak ; it must hang simply, he said, that in any appearance of danger he might take it again at the instant.'

Two hours after the sunrise we passed the Harra borders, and came without this lava field upon soil of sandstone. The vulcanic country which we had crossed in seventeen hours is named Harrat *el-Ethnân*, of the great crater-hill of that name *J. Ethnân* ; the dîra is of the Noâmsa Heteym. We came in an hour by a descending plain of red sand-rock, to a deep cleft, *es-Shotb*, where we drove down the dromedary at short steps, upon the shelves and ledges. In the bottom were gum-acacias, and a tree which I knew not, it has leaves somewhat like the mountain ash. " The name of it is *thirru*, it has not any use that we know," said Ghroceyb. Beyond the grove were some thin effluxions of lava run down upon the sandstone soil, from the vulcanic field above. By noon we had passed the sand-rock and came again upon the main Harra beyond, which is all one eastward with the former Harra ; and there we went by a few low craters. The whole — which is the *Harrat Kheybar* — lies between north-west and south-east four days in length ; and that may be, since it reaches to within a thelûl journey of Medina, an hundred great miles. The width is little in comparison, and at the midst it may be passed in a day.

Ghroceyb now said : " But wouldst thou needs go to Kheybar? — *tûahi*, hearest thou ? shall I not rather carry thee to el-Hâyat ? " — My rafîk was in dread of going to Kheybar, the Dowla being there : those criminals-in-office (I understood it later) might have named him an enemy and seized the poor nomad's thelûl, and cast him into prison ; but el-Hâyat was yet a free village in the jurisdiction of Ibn Rashîd. Ghroceyb I knew afterward to be an homicide, and there lay upon him a grievous debt for blood ; it was therefore he had ridden for four reals with me in this painful voyage. From Eyâda's menzil we might have put the Harra upon our left hand, and passed by easy sand-plains [where I journeyed in the spring] under the granite mountains ; but Ghroceyb would not, for in the open there had been more peril than in this cragged way of the Harra.

An hour from the Shotb I found the altitude to be 5000 feet. Before mid-afternoon upon our right hand, beyond the flanks of the

Harra and the low underlying sand-plain, appeared a world of wild ranging mountains *Jebâl Hejjûr*, twenty-five miles distant, in dîrat of the Wélad Aly. We went all day as fugitives in this vulcanic country. Sunset comes soon in winter, and then we halted, in a low clay bottom with tall acacias and yellow ponds of rain water. Ghroceyb hopshackled her with a cord and loosed out the two days' fasting thelûl to browse the green branches. There we cooked a little temmn; and then laid ourselves down upon the fenny soil and stones in a mizzling night-rain to slumber.

When the day began to spring we set forward, and passed over a brook running out from ponded water in the lava-field. The weather was clearer, the melting skies lifted about us. The vulcanic country is from henceforward plain, and always descending and full of jiddrân. Before and below our path, we had now in sight the sharp three-headed mountain, *Atwa*, that stands beside Kheybar : Ghroceyb greeted the landmark with joy. 'Beyond Atwa was but a night out, he said, for thelûl riders to Medina.' Upon our left hand a distant part of the Harra, *Harrat el-Abyad*, showed white under the sun and full of␣hilliân. Ghroceyb said, " The hills are whitish, the lava-field lies about them ; the white stone is burned-like, and heavy as metal." Others say " The heads only of the␣hilliân are white stone, the rest is black lava." — Those white hills might be limestone, which, we know, lies next above the Hisma sand-rock.

Already we saw the flies of the oasis : Kheybar was yet covered from sight by the great descending limb of the Harra ; we felt the air every moment warmer and, for us, faint and breathless. All this country side to Jebâl Hejjûr seyls down by the wady grounds *el-Khâfutha* and *Gumm'ra* to the Wady el-Humth. Ghroceyb showed me a wolf's footprints in the vulcanic sand. At the half-afternoon we were near Kheybar, which lay in the deep yonder, and was yet hidden from us. Then we came upon the fresh traces of a ghrazzu : they had passed down towards Kheybar. We rode in the same jiddar behind them ! — the footprints were of two mares and two camels. Ghroceyb made me presently a sign to halt ; he came and took his gun in silence, struck fire to the match and ran out to reconnoitre. He stayed behind a covert of lavas, from whence he returned to tell me he saw two horsemen and two *ráduffa* (radîfs), upon thelûls, riding at a long gunshot before us : they had not seen us. And now, blowing his match, he enquired very earnestly, ' Were I able with him to resist them ? ' — Contrary to the will of Ghroceyb I had stayed this day, at noon, ten minutes, to take some refreshment : but for this we had met with them as they came crossing from the westward, and it is too likely that blood had been shed between us. We stood awhile to give them ground, and when they were hidden by the unequal lava-field, we passed slowly forward. The sun was now going low in the west, — and we would be at Kheybar this night ere the village gate should be shut.

Locusts alighted by our path, and I saw aloft an infinite flight of them drifted over in the evening wind. Ghroceyb asked again, 'If I were afraid of the Dowla.' — " Am I not a Dowlany ? they are my friends." — " Wellah, *yâ sámy*, my namesake, couldst thou deliver me and quit the thelûl, if they should take me ? " — " Doubt not ; they of the Dowla are of my part."

Now we descended into a large bottom ground in the lava-field, *el-Húrda*, full of green corn : — that corn I saw ripen before my departure from Kheybar ! Here Ghroceyb dreaded to meet with the ghrazzu, — the robbers might be grazing their mares in the green corn of the settlement. Where we came by suânies, wild doves flew up with great rattling of wings, from the wells of water. I thought these should be the fields of Kheybar, and spoke to Ghroceyb to carry me to the *Jériat Wélad Aly*. There are three villages, named after the land-inheriting Annezy tribes, *Jériat Bishr* (that is Kheybar proper), *Jériat W. Aly*, at the distance of half a mile, and at two miles the hamlet *Jériat el-Fejîr*. — Jériat is said for ķeriat in the loghrat of these nomads.

Ghroceyb saw only my untimely delay, whilst he dreaded for his thelûl, and was looking at every new turn that we should encounter the enemies who had ridden down before us. I drew bridle, and bade my rafîk — he stepped always a little before me on foot — promise to bring me to none other than the Wélad Aly village. My visiting Kheybar, which they reckon in '*The Apostle's Country*,' was likely to be a perilous adventure ; and I might be murdered to-night in the tumult if it went ill with me : but at the W. Aly hamlet I should have become the guest of the clients of Motlog and Méhsan, great sheykhs of that tribe. Ghroceyb saw me halt, as a man beside himself ! and he came hastily, to snatch the thelûl's halter ; then he desperately turned his matchlock against me, and cried, " Akhs ! why would I compel him to do me a mischief ? " — " Thou canst not kill thy rafîk ! now promise me and go forward." He promised, but falsely. — Months after I heard he had told his friends, when he was at home again, that ' he had found the stranger a good rafîk, only in the journey's end, as we were about entering Kheybar, I would have taken his thelûl ' !

We passed the corn-fields of the Húrda without new alarms, and came upon the basalt neck of the Harra about the oasis' valleys, which is called *el-figgera* (in the pl. *el-fuggar*) Kheybar. Ghroceyb mounted with me, and he made the thelûl run swiftly, for the light was now failing. I saw ruins upon the figgera of old dry building and ring-walls : some are little yards of the loose basalt blocks, which the Beduw use to dry their dates in the sun, before stiving the fruit in their sacks. After a mile, we came to a brow, and I saw a palm forest in a green valley of Kheybar below us, but the village not yet. The sun set as we went down by a steep path. At the left hand was an empty watch-tower, one of seven lately built by the now occupying Medina government, upon this side, to check the hostile Annezy [Bishr and Fejîr]. This human landmark seemed to me more inhuman than all the Harra behind us ; for now I remembered Medáin Sâlih and the danger of the long unpaid, and sometimes to be dreaded, Turkish soldiery. How pleasant then seemed to me the sunny drought of the wilderness, how blessed the security of the worsted booths in the wandering villages ! These forts are garrisoned in the summer and autumn season.

We came through palm-groves in a valley bottom, *W. Jellâs*, named after that old division of Annezy, which having long since forsaken Kheybar, are at this day — we have seen — with the Ruwàlla in the north. The deep ground is mire and rushes and stagnant water, and there sunk upon our spirits a sickly fenny vapour. In the midst we passed a brook running in a bed of green cresses. Foul was the abandoned soil upon either hand, with only few awry and undergrown stems of palms. The squalid ground is whitish with crusts of bitter salt-warp, *summakha* [written *subbakha*], and stained with filthy rust : whence their fable, that ' this earth purges herself of the much blood of the Yahûd, that was spilt in the conquest of Kheybar.' The thelûl which found no foot-hold under her sliding soles, often halted for fear. We came up between rough walling, built of basalt stones, and rotten palm-stocks, and clots of black clay. — How strange are these dank Kheybar valleys in the waterless Arabia ! A heavy presentiment of evil lay upon my heart as we rode in this deadly drowned atmosphere.

We ascended on firm ground to the entering of Kheybar, that is Jériat Bishr, under the long basalt crag of the ancient citadel *el-Húsn*. In the falling ground upon the left hand stands an antique four-square building of stone, which is the old mesjid from the time, they say, of Mohammed; and in the precinct lie buried the *Ashab en-Néby*, — those few primitive Moslemîn, partisans and acquaintance of the living " apostle," that fell in the (poor) winning of Kheybar.

At the village gate a negro woman met us in the twilight, of whom I enquired, whether *Bou (Abu) Ras* were in the town? — I had heard of him from the Moghrebies in Hâyil as a safe man: he was a Moghreby negro trader settled in those parts; also I hoped to become his guest. But he was gone from the place, since the entrance of the (tyrannical) Dowla — being now, as they say, *shebbaan*, or having gotten his suffisance of their poor riches, — to live yet under the free Nejd government at el-Hâyat. — She answered timidly, bidding the strangers a good evening, " She could not tell, and that she knew nothing."

CHAPTER IV

KHEYBAR. "THE APOSTLE'S COUNTRY"

The night at Kheybar. Abd el-Hâdy. Ahmed. The gunner's belt. Kheybar by daylight. Medina soldiery. Muharram. Sirûr. The Nasrâny brought before the village governor. Amm Mohammed en-Nejûmy. Amân. The Gallas. Evening in the soldiers' kahwa. Ibrahîm the kâdy. Abdullah's tale of the Engleys. Hejâz Arabic. A worthy negro woman. Amm Mohammed's house. Umm Kîda. Brackish soil. Wadies of Kheybar. The Albanians. Kheybar genealogy. The Nasrâny accused. The villagers in fear of his enchantments. Friendship with Amm Mohammed. Our well labour. His hunting. Kasr en-Néby. El-Asmîeh. Blood-sprinkling. Hospitality of the sheykh of the hamlet. Gatûnies. Barrows upon the Harra. Magicians come to Kheybar to lift treasures. The Húsn rock.

WE passed the gates made of rude palm boarding into the street of the Hejâz negro village, and alighted in the dusk before the house of an acquaintance of Ghroceyb. The host, hearing us busy at the door of his lower house, looked down from the casement and asked in the rasping negro voice what men we were? Ghroceyb called to him, and then he came down with his brother to receive the guests. They took my bags upon their shoulders, and led us up by some clay stairs to their dwelling-house, which is, as at el-Ally, an upper chamber, here called *suffa*. The lower floor, in these damp oases, is a place where they leave the orchard tools, and a stable for their few goats which are driven in for the night. This householder was named *Abd el-Hâdy*, 'Servitor of Him who leadeth in the way of Truth,' a young man under the middle age, of fine negro lineaments. — These negro-like Arabians are not seldom comely.

Our host's upper room was open at the street side with long casements, *tâga*, to the floor; his roof was but a loose strawing of palm stalks, and above is the house terrace of beaten clay, to which you ascend [they say *erkâ!*] by a ladder of two or three palm beams, with steps hacked in them. Abd el-Hâdy's was one of the better cottages, for he was a substantial man. Kheybar is as it were an African village in the Hejâz. Abd el-Hâdy spread his carpet and bade us welcome, and set before us Kheybar dates, which are yellow, small and stived together; they are gathered ere fully ripe [their Beduin partners' impatience, and distrust of each other!] and have a drug-like or fenny savour, but are "cooler" than the most dates of the country and not unwholesome. After these days' efforts in the Harra we could not eat; we asked for water to quench our burning thirst. They hang their sweating girbies at the stair-head, and under them is made a hole in the flooring, that the drip may fall through. The water, drawn, they said, from the spring head under the basalt, tasted of the ditch; it might be sulphurous. We had left our thelûl kneebound in the street.

Many persons, when they heard say that strangers had arrived, came up all this evening to visit us; — the villagers were black men. Ghroceyb told them his tale of the ghrazzu; and the negroes answered "Wellah! except we sally in the morning to look for them — !" They feared for the outlying corn lands, and lest any beast of theirs should be taken. There came with the rest a tall and swarthy white man, of a soldiery countenance, bearing a lantern and his yard-long tobacco-pipe: I saw he was of the mixed inhabitants of the cities. He sat silent with hollow eyes and smoked tobacco, often glancing at us; then he passed the *chibûk* to me and enquired the news. He was not friendly with Abd el-Hâdy, and waived our host's second cup. The white man sat on smoking mildly, with his lantern burning; after an hour he went forth [and this was to denounce us, to the ruffian lieutenant at Kheybar]. My rafîk told me in a whisper, "That was *Ahmed*; he has been a soldier and is now a tradesman at Kheybar." — His brother was *Mohammed en-Nejûmy*, he who from the morrow became the generous defender of my adversity at Kheybar: they were citizens of Medina. It was near midnight when the last coffee-drinkers departed; then I whispered to Ghroceyb: "Will they serve supper, or is it not time to sleep?" "My namesake, I think they have killed for thee; I saw them bring up a sheep, to the terrace, long ago." — "Who is the sheykh of the village?" — "This Abd el-Hâdy is their sheykh, and thou wilt find him a good man." My rafîk lied like a (guileful) nomad, to excuse his not carrying me to the W. Aly village.

Our host and his brother now at length descended from the house-top, bearing a vast metal tray of the seethed flesh upon a mess of thùra (it may be a sort of millet): since the locusts had destroyed their spring corn, this was the only bread-stuff left to them at Kheybar.

The new day's light beginning to rise Ghroceyb went down to the street in haste; "Farewell, he said, and was there any difference between us forgive it, Khalîl;" and taking my right hand (and afraid perchance of the stranger's malediction) he stooped and kissed it. Hâdy, our host's brother, mounted also upon the croup of his thelûl; this strong-bodied young negro with a long matchlock upon his shoulder rode forth in his bare tunic, girded only with the *házam* or gunner's belt. Upon the baldric are little metal pipes, with their powder charges, and upon the girdle leather pouches for shot, flint and steel, and a hook whereupon a man — they go commonly barefoot — will hang his sandals. The házams are adorned with copper studs and beset with little rattling chains; there are some young men who may be seen continually *muházamîn*, girded and vain-glorious with these little tinkling ornaments of war. It is commonly said of tribes well provided with firearms "They have many muházamîn." — Hâdy rode to find the traces of the ghrazzu of yesterday.

Some of the villagers came up to me immediately to enquire for medicines: they were full of tedious words; and all was to beg of me and buy none. I left them sitting and went out to see the place, for this was Kheybar.

Our host sent his son to guide me; the boy led down by a lane and called me to enter a doorway and see a spring. I went in: — it was a mesjid! and I withdrew hastily. The father (who had instructed the child beforehand) hearing from him when we came again that I had left the place without praying, went down and shut his street door. He returned and took his pistol from the wall, saying, 'Let us go out together and he would show me round the town.' When we were in the street he led me by an orchard path out of the place.

We came by a walled path through the palms into an open space of rush-grass and black vulcanic sand, *es-Sefsáfa*: there he showed me the head of a stream which welled strongly from under the figgera. The water is tepid and sulphurous as at el-Ally, and I saw in it little green-back and silver-bellied fishes: — all fish are named *hût* by the Arabians. "Here, he said, is the (summer) menzil of the Dowla, in this ground stand the askars' tents." We sat down, and gazing into my face he asked me, 'Were I afraid of the Dowla?' "Is the Dowla better or Ibn Rashîd's government?" — "The Dowla delivered us from the Beduw, — but is more burdenous."

We passed through a burial ground of black vulcanic mould and salt-warp: the squalid grave-heaps are marked with head-stones of wild basalt. That funeral earth is chapped and ghastly, bulging over her enwombed corses, like a garden soil, in springtime, which is pushed by the new-aspiring plants. All is horror at Kheybar! — nothing there which does not fill a stranger's eye with discomfort.

— " Look, he said, this is the spring of our Lord Aly ! — I saw a lukewarm pool and running head of water. — Here our Lord Aly [Fatima's husband] killed *Márhab*, smiting off his head ; and his blade cleft that rock, which thou seest there divided to the earth : " — so we came beyond. — " And here, he said, is Aly's mesjid " [already mentioned]. The building is homely, in courses of the wild basalt blocks : it is certainly ancient. Here also the village children are daily taught their letters, by the sheykh of the religion.

When we had made the circuit, " Let us go, he said, to the *Emir*." So the villager named the aga or lieutenant of a score of Ageyl from Medina. Those thelûl riders were formerly Nejd Arabians ; but now, because the Dowla's wages are so long in coming, the quick-spirited Nejders have forsaken that sorry service. The Ageyl are a mixed crew of a few Nejders (villagers, mostly of el-Kasîm, and poor Nomads), and of Gallas, Turks, Albanians, Egyptians, Kurdies and Negroes. The Ageyl at Kheybar now rode upon their feet : some of their thelûls were dead, those that remained were at pasture (far off) with the nomads. They all drew daily rations of corn for their thelûls alive and dead ; and how else might the poor wretches live ? who had not touched a cross of their pay (save of a month or twain) these two years. A few of the government armed men at Kheybar were zabtîyah, men of the police service. — " The Aga is a Kurdy," quoth Abd el-Hâdy.

We ascended, in a side street, to a suffa, which was the soldiers' coffee-room : swords and muskets were hanging upon pegs in the clay walls. Soon after some of them entered ; they were all dark-coloured Gallas, girded (as townsmen) in their white tunics. They came in with guns from some trial of their skill, and welcomed us in their (Medina) manner, and sat down to make coffee. I wondered whilst we drank together that they asked me no questions ! We rose soon and departed. As we stepped down the clay stair, I heard a hoarse voice saying among them, " I see well, he is *adu* (an enemy) ; " — and I heard answered, " But let him alone awhile."

It was time I thought to make myself known. When I asked where was the Kurdy Aga ? my host exclaimed, " You did not see him ! he sat at the midst of the hearth." That was *Abdullah es-Siruân*, chief of the Medina crew of soldiery: his father was "a Kurdy," but he was a black man with Galla looks, of the younger middle age, — the son of a (Galla) bond-woman. I was new to discern this Hejâz world, and the town manner of the Harameyn. In the street I saw two white faces coming out of a doorway; they were infirm soldiery, and the men, who walked leaning upon long staves of palm-stalks, seemed of a ghastly pallor in the dreadful blackness of all things at Kheybar: they came to join hands with me, a white man, and passed on without speaking. One of them with a hoary beard was an Albanian, *Muharram*; the other was an Egyptian. When we were again at home Abd el-Hâdy locked his street door; and coming above stairs, "Tell me, said he, art thou a Moslem? and if no I will lay thy things upon a cow and send thee to a place of safety." — "Host, I am of the Engleys; my nation, thou mayest have heard say, is friendly with the Dowla, and I am of them whom ye name the Nasâra."

Abd el-Hâdy went out in the afternoon and left his street-door open! There came up presently *Sálem* a Beduin Ageyly, to enquire for medicines, and a Galla with his arms, *Sirûr*; — he it was who named me adu. — "Half a real for the fever doses!" (salts and quinine), quoth Sâlem. The Galla murmured, 'But soon it would be seen that I should give them for nothing'; and he added, "This man has little understanding of the world, for he discerns not persons: ho! what countryman art thou?" — "I dwell at Damascus." — "Ha! and that is my country, but thou dost not speak perfectly Araby; I am thinking we shall have here a Nasrâny: oho! What brings thee hither?" — "I would see the old Jews' country." — "The Jews' country! but this is *dîrat er-Rasûl*, the apostle's country:" so they forsook me. And Abd el-Hâdy returning, "What, said he, shall we do? for wellah all the people is persuaded that thou art no Moslem." — "Do they take me for an enemy! and the aga...?" — "Ah! he is *jabbàr*, a hateful tyrant." My host went forth, and Sirûr came up anew;—he was sent by the aga. 'What was I?' he demanded. — "An Engleysy, of those that favour the Dowla." — "Then a Nasrâny; sully aly en-Néby, — come on!" and with another of the Ageyl the brutal black Galla began to thrust me to the stairs. Some villagers who arrived saying that this was the police, I consented to go with them. "Well, bring him (said the bystanders), but not with violence." — "Tell me, before we go further, will ye kill me without the house?" I had secretly taken my pistol under my tunic, at the first alarm.

At the end of the next street one was sitting on a clay bench to judge me, — that dark-coloured Abyssinian 'Kurdy,' whom I heard to be the soldiers' aga. A rout of villagers came on behind us, but without cries. — In what land, I thought, am I now arrived! and who are these that take me (because of Christ's sweet name!) for an enemy of mankind? — Sirûr cried, in his bellowing voice, to him on the clay bench, " I have detected him, — a Nasrâny!" I said, " What is this! I am an Engleysy, and being of a friendly nation, why am I dealt with thus?" " By Ullah, he answered, I was afraid to-day, art thou indeed an Engleysy, art thou not a Muskôvy?" — " I have said it already!" — " But I believe it not, and how may I trust thee?" — " When I have answered, here at Kheybar, *I am a Nasrâny*, should I not be true in the rest?" — " He says well; go back, Abd el-Hâdy, and fetch his baggage, and see that there be nothing left behind." The street was full of mire after the late rain; so I spoke to Abdullah, and he rising led to an open place in the clay village which is called *es-Saheym*, ' the little pan.' — " By God (added Abdullah es-Siruân, — the man was illiterate), if any books should be found with thee, or the what-they-call-them, — charts of countries, thou shalt never see them more: they must all be sent to the Pasha at Medina. But hast thou not an instrument, — ah! and I might now think of the name, — I have it! the air-measure? — And from whence comest thou?" — " From Hâyil; I have here also a passport from Ibn Rashîd." Abdullah gave it to a boy who learned in the day school, — for few of the grown villagers, and none of those who stood by, knew their letters. *Abdullah*: " Call me here the sheykh *Sâlih*, to read and write for us." A palm-leaf mat was brought out from one of the houses and cast before us upon a clay bench. I sat down upon it with Abdullah. — A throng of the black villagers stood gazing before us.

So Sâlih arrived, the sheykh of this negro village — an elder man, who walked lame — with a long brass inkstand, and a leaf of great paper in his hand. *Siruân*: " Sâlih, thou art to write all these things in order. [My great camel-bags were brought and set down before him.] Now have out the things one by one; and as I call them over, write, sheykh Sâlih. Begin: a camel-bridle, a girby, bags of dates, hard milk and temmn; — what is this?" — " A medicine box." — " Open it!" As

I lifted the lid all the black people shrunk back and stopped their nostrils. Sirûr took in his hands that which came uppermost, a square compass, — it had been bound in a cloth. "Let it be untied!" quoth Abdullah. The fellow turning it in his hand, said, "Auh! this is *sabûny*," (a square of Syrian soap), so Abdullah, to my great comfort, let it pass. But Abd el-Hâdy espying somewhat, stretched forth his hand suddenly, and took up a comb; "Ha! ha!" cries my host (who till now had kindly harboured me; but his lately good mind was turned already to fanatical rancour — the village named him *Abu Summakh*, 'Father Jangles') what is this perilous instrument, — ha! Nasrâny? Abdullah, let him give account of it; and judge thou if it be not some gin devised by them against the Moslemîn!"

Next came up a great tin, which I opened before them: it was full of tea, my only refreshment. "Well, this you may shut again," said Abdullah. Next was a bundle of books. "Aha! exclaimed the great man, the former things — hast thou written them, sheykh Sâlih? — were of no account, but the books! — thou shalt never have them again." Then they lighted upon the brass reel of a tape measure. "Ha! he cries, tell me, and see thou speak the truth (*alemny b'es sahîhh*), is not this the sky-measure?" "Here, I said to him, I have a paper, which is a circular passport from the Wàly of Syria." — "Then read it, sheykh Sâlih." Sâlih poured over the written document awhile; — "I have perused it, he answered, but may perceive only the names, because it is written in *Turki*, [the tongue was Arabic, but engrossed in the florid Persian manner!], and here at the foot is the seal of the Pasha," — and he read his name. "Ho! ho! (cries Sirûr) that Pasha was long ago; and he is dead, I know it well." — A sigh of bodily weariness that would have rest broke from me. "Wherefore thus? exclaimed the pious scelerat Abdullah, only stay thee upon *el-Mowla* (the Lord thy God)."

— To my final confusion, they fetched up from the sack's bottom the empty pistol case! — in that weapon was all my hope. "Aha! a pistol case! cried many voices, and, casting their bitter eyes upon me, oh thou! where is the pistol?" I answered nothing; — in this moment of suspense, one exclaimed, "It is plain that Ibn Rashîd has taken it from him." — "Ay, answered the black villagers about me, he has given it to Ibn Rashîd; Ibn Rashîd has taken it from him, trust us, Abdullah." — A pistol among them is always preciously preserved in a gay holster; and they could not imagine that I should wear a naked pistol under my bare shirt. After this I thought 'Will they search my person?' — but that is regarded amongst them as an extreme outrage; and there were here too many witnesses. He seemed to assent to their words, but I saw he rolled it in his turbid mind, 'what was become of the Nasrâny's pistol?' The heavy weapon, worn continually suspended from the neck, not a little molested me; and I could not put off my Arab cloak (which covered it) in the sultry days. — So he said, " Hast thou money with thee? — and we may be sure thou hast some. Tell us plainly, where is it, and do not hide it; this will be better for thee, — and, that I may be friends with thee! also it must be written in the paper; and tell us hast thou anything else? — mark ye O people, I would not that a needle of this man's be lost!" — " Reach me that tin where you saw the tea: in the midst is my purse, — and in it, you see, are six liras!" The thief counted them, with much liking, in his black palm; then shutting up the purse he put it in his own bosom, saying, " Sâlih, write down these six liras Fransâwy. I have taken them for their better keeping; and his bags will be under key in my own house."

There came over to me Ahmed, whom I had seen last evening; he had been sitting with the old tranquillity amongst the lookers-on, and in the time of this inquisition, he nodded many times to me friendly. " *Mâ aleyk, mâ aleyk*, take comfort, he said, there shall no evil happen to thee." — *Abdullah :* " Abd el-Hâdy, let him return to lodge with thee; also he can cure the sick." The negro answered, " I receive again the kafir! — Only let him say the testimony and I will receive him willingly." — " Then he must lodge with the soldiery; thou *Amân* — a Galla Ageyly — take him to your chamber: Khalîl may have his provisions with him and his box of medicines."

I saw the large manly presence standing erect in the backward of the throng — for he had lately arrived — of a very swarthy Arabian; he was sheykhly clad, and carried the sword, and I guessed he might be some chief man of the irregular soldiery. Now he came to me, and dropping (in their sudden manner) upon the hams of the legs, he sat before me with the confident smiling humour of a strong man; and spoke to me pleasantly. I wondered to see his swarthiness, — yet such are commonly the Arabians in the Hejâz — and he not less to see a man so 'white and red.' This was Mohammed en-Nejûmy, Ahmed's brother, who from the morrow became to me as a father at Kheybar. " Go now, said Abdullah, with the soldier." — " Mâ aleyk, mâ aleyk," added some of the better-disposed bystanders. *Abdullah :* " You will remain here a few days, whilst I send a post to the Pasha (of Medina) with the books and papers." — " Ho ! ye people, bellows Sirûr, we will send to the Pasha ; and if the Pasha's word be to cut his head off, we will chop off thy head Nasrâny." " Trouble not thyself, said some yet standing by, for this fellow's talk, — he is a brute." Hated was the Galla bully in the town, who was valiant only with their hareem, and had been found *khòaf*, a skulking coward, in the late warfare.

So I came with Amân to the small suffa which he inhabited with a comrade, in the next house. They were both *Habûsh*, further-Abyssinians, that is of the land of the Gallas. Lithe figures they are commonly, with a feminine grace and fine lineaments ; their hue is a yellow-brown, ruddy brown, deep brown or blackish, and that according to their native districts, — so wide is the country. They have sweet voices and speak not one Galla tongue alike, so that the speech of distant tribes is hardly understood between them. Amân could not well understand his comrade's talk (therefore they spoke together in Arabic), but he spoke nearly one language with Sirûr. Amân taught me many of his Galla words ; but to-day I remember no more than *bîsàn*, water. Though brought slaves to the Hejâz in their childhood, they forget not there their country language : so many are now the Gallas in Mecca and Medina, that *Hábashy* is currently spoken from house to house. Some of the beautiful Galla bondwomen become wives in the citizen families, even of the great, others are nurses and house servants ; and the Arab town children are bred up amongst them. — The poor fellows bade me be of good comfort, and all would now end well, after a little patience : one set bread before me, and went out to borrow dates for their guest. They said, " As for this negro people, they are not men but oxen, apes, sick of the devil and niggards." — These Semite-like Africans vehemently disdain the Sudân, or negro slave-race. " Great God ! " I have heard them say at Kheybar, " can those woolly polls be of the children of Adam ? "

We heard Mohammed en-Nejûmy upon the clay stairs. He said, " It is the first time I ever came here, but for thy sake I come." At night-fall we went forth together, lighting our way with flaming palm-branches, to the soldiers' kahwa. Abdullah, whom my purse had enriched to-day, beckoned me to sit beside him. Their talk took a good turn, and Mohammed en-Nejûmy pronounced the famous formula : *kull wáhed aly dînu*, ' every man in his own religion ! ' — and he made his gloss, " this is to say the Yahûdy in his law, the Nasrâny in his law and the Moslem in his law ; aye, and the kafir may be a good faithful man in his belief." The Nejûmy was an heroic figure, he sat with his sword upon his knees, bowing and assenting, at every word, to the black villain Abdullah : this is their Turkish town courtesy. Sometimes (having heard from me that I understood no Turkish) they spoke together in that language. Mohammed answered, after every clement saw of the black lieutenant, the pious praise [though it sounded like an irony], *Ullah yubèyith wejh-ak,* ' the Lord whiten thy visage (in the day of doom) ! ' There was some feminine fall in the strong man's voice, — and where is any little savour of the mother's blood in right manly worth, it is a pleasant grace. He was not altogether like the Arabs, for he loved to speak in jesting-wise, with kindly mirth : though they be full of knavish humour, I never saw among the Arabians a merry man !

Mohammed and Ahmed were sons of a Kurdy sutler at Medina ; and their mother was an Harb woman of the Ferrâ, a palm settlement of that Beduin nation in the Hejâz, betwixt the Harameyn. We drunk round the soldiers' coffee ; yet here was not the cheerful security of the booths of hair, but town constraint and Turkish tyranny, and the Egyptian plague of vermin. They bye and bye were accorded in their sober cups that the Nasâra might pass everywhere freely, only they may not visit the Harameyn : and some said, " Be there not many of Khalîl's religion at Jidda ? the way is passed by riders in one night-time from Mecca " [many in the Hejâz pronounce *Mekky*]. Abdullah said at last, " Wellah, Khalîl is an honest man, he speaks frankly, and I love him." I was soon weary, and he sent his bondman to light me back to my lodging. Hearing some rumour, I looked back, and saw that the barefoot negro came dancing behind me in the street with his drawn sword.

Abdullah said to me at the morning coffee, that I might walk freely in the village ; and the black hypocrite enquired 'had I rested well ? ' When it was evening, he said, " Rise, we will go and drink coffee at the house of a good man." We went out, and some of his soldiers lighted us with flaming palm leaves to the cottage of one *Ibrahîm el-kâdy*. Whilst we sat in his suffa, there came up many of the principal villagers. Ibrahîm set his best dates before us, made up the fire, and began to prepare kahwa, and he brought the village governor his kerchief full of their green tobacco.

Then Abdullah opened his black lips — to speak to them of my being found at Kheybar, a stranger, and one such as they had not seen in their lives. " What, he said, are these Nasâra ? — listen all of you ! It is a strong nation : were not two or three Nasrânies murdered some years ago at Jidda ? — well, what followed ? There came great war-ships of their nation and bombarded the place : but you the Kheyâbara know not what is a ship ! — a ship is great, well nigh as the Hûsn (the old acropolis). They began to shoot at us with their artillery, and we that were in the fortress shot again ; but oh ! where was the fortress ? or was there, think ye, any man that remained in the town ? no, they all fled ; and if the Lord had not turned away that danger, we could not have resisted them. And who were those that fought against Jidda ? I tell you the Engleys, the people of this Khalîl : the Engleys are high-handed, ay wella, jabâbara !

" Shall I tell you a tale ? — There was in the city of Sham a tumult and a slaughter of the Nasâra ; the youngest of you all might have heard of it, if ye heard anything at Kheybar. Listen all of you ! I would have each one of you consider how I fear for myself, and wherefore I do well in preserving this Khalîl [The Ottoman lieutenant in Kheybar makes his apology, to the black audience, for not murdering me yesterday !] I tell you, sirs, that the Nasâra are mighty nations ; — but whether that killing of the Nasâra in es-Sham were or were not expedient, we are not now to consider. The Pasha of es-Sham — and, mark ye, he is a Pasha of pashas and governor over a great province, — and Sham is a city so great that by comparison Medina might be called a village ; he being also *mushîr*, marshal of the Sultàn's army in Syria — was attached, at the commandment ye are to understand of the Sooltàn ! I tell you, his arms were bound behind his back ; and he was led forth like a common criminal before the people ; and as the Sooltàn had commanded in his firmàn — ye wot all of you that a firmàn of the Sooltàn of Islam must needs be obeyed — his head was struck off ! His punishment was followed by the suffering, in like manner, of many more who had borne the chief parts in slaying the Nasâra ; — and you may understand that they were Moslemîn ! Ah my friends ! we must all be governed by reason, but ye know little of the world." — A black adulator answered him, " Eigh me ! Abdullah says sooth ; for what are the Kheyâbara ! or know we any other thing than the husbandry of these palms ? and our thoughts hardly pass the Harra ; and if some of us take a journey it is but to go to Medina : and they are few that in former years have visited Hâyil ! "

Siruân: "Ye know now, what a power have the Nasâra with the Sooltàn, and in what peril I stand ! I could tell you more of these Engleys : some even of the ships of the Sooltàn are commanded by Engleysies. Have none among you heard of a great ship of war, from Stambûl, with a treasure on board for the pay of the army, that was lost on the coasts yonder ? Well, her commander was an Engleysy ; a man with a terrible visage, and so great mustachios, that you might have tied them behind his ears. I have seen him, and wellah there is none of you who had not been afraid to look in his face. He was in his drink, — for ye know it is so with them ! they drink ' the fermented,' which is forbidden to the Moslemîn. The watch sent word to him where he sat drunken, after nightfall, ' Master *kobtàn*, we heard breakers, the ship is running on shoals, give the word to put the helm about.' He answered them, ' Ullah confound you all ! and hold on your course.' A little after they came to him saying, ' Sir, we are now amongst the reefs ; ' and he, ' What reefs ? I tell you sail on to jehennem ! ' — for he had lost his mind. The great ship fell presently upon the rocks, and foundered, beaten by the waves, in the wild darkness : there were drowned upon her 800 persons and this kobtàn, — and those treasure chests were afterward fished by divers.

" And now shall I tell you what is a *konsul* of theirs : konsul is a Resident of their nation in all chief cities, — but, ye understand well, not in the Harameyn, which may be entered only by the Moslemîn. Well, If I cut off a man's head, and might run under the banner of a konsul, none might lay hands upon me there, — and why ? because I am under his protection. Such power, ye can understand, they have not of themselves, but by a firmàn of the Sooltàn. — Shall I tell you of a visit which I made myself to a konsul, at Jidda : he was the konsul of the Engleys, and this Khalil's konsul ! and if Khalîl came there, and were in need, that konsul would send him home to his own country, — the distance, by land, were twelve months' journey, eigh Khalîl ? One winter we were stationed at Mecca, and I was sent to bring up five hundred sacks of rice, for the soldiery. I went down to Jidda in company of Such-an-one whom some of you here know : and as we were sitting in the government house, we heard that the *Konsul el-Engleys* was at the door, and he would speak with the Pasha. The Pasha made us a sign, as he came in, that we should not rise, — and ye wot why ? — because the konsul was a Nasrâny ! the konsul was admitted, and we remained sitting. We talked together ; and that konsul could speak Araby well, — better than Khalîl. When he learned our business, that we were come about the government service, and were strangers at Jidda, he invited us to his house ; — this they call *el-Konsulato*. We went there to see him the next day ; it was a great building ! and we were led on from one room to another. Life of Ullah ! we passed through five doors before we reached him, — five doors ! " — " Then the man it seems lived in much fear for himself ! (laughed the Nejûmy), may not one door suffice among them ? " — " But I would have you understand the magnificence of that Nasrâny, and — *ouff!* what was his coffee service ? believe me, sirs, mere silver ! his coffee tray an ell wide of splendid plate ! Begin ye now to see ? — what then must be their government ! But the wealth of them is nearly incredible ! " — (Abdullah rolled his black head.) *En-Nejûmy :* " The Nasâra must be *guwiyîn*, a strong people ; it is very well. And thou sayest, that they injure none, but they be first aggrieved ; and the Engleys are the Sooltàn's friends, and Khalîl is Engleysy : is it thus, sheykh Khalîl ? " *Abdullah :* " And that konsul's *kawasses* (javelin men) seemed more stately than the kawasses of the Pasha ! wellah the silver knops upon their sticks were greater than the knops upon the sticks of the Pasha himself, — the Pasha of Mecca ! "

Abdullah, though ignorant in school-lore, spoke with that popular persuasion of the Turkish magistrates, behind whose fair words lies the crude handling of the sword. The Arabs and Turks whose books are men's faces, their lively experience of mankind, and whose glosses are the common saws and thousand old sapient proverbs of their oriental world, touch near the truth of human things. They are old men in policy in their youth, and have little later to unlearn ; but especially they have learned to speak well. Abdullah, and the Medina soldiery, and the black Kheyâbara spoke Medina Arabic. Their illiberal town speech resembles the Syrian, but is more full and round, with some sound of ingenuous Arabian words : the tanwîn is not heard at Kheybar. I thought the Nejûmy spoke worst among them all ; it might be he had learned of his father, a stranger, or that such was the (Hejâz) speech of his Harb village : his brother spoke better. Medina, besides her motley (now half Indian) population, is in some quarters a truly Arabian town ; there is much in her of the Arabian spirit : every year some Arabians settle there, and I have met with Medina citizens who spoke nearly as the upland Arabians.

I was his captive, and mornings and evenings must present myself before Abdullah. The village governor oppressed me with cups of coffee, and his official chibûk, offered with comely smiles of his black visage ; until the skeleton three days' hospitality was ended. The soldiery were lodged in free quarters at Kheybar, where are many empty houses which the owners let out in the summer months to the salesmen who arrive then from Medina. Abdullah was lodged in one of the better houses, the house of a black widow woman, whose prudent and beneficent humour was very honourably spoken of in the country. If any marketing nomads dismounted at her door, she received them bountifully ; if any in the village were in want, and she heard of it, she would send somewhat. Freely she lent her large dwelling, for she was a loyal woman who thought it reason to give place to the officer of the Dowla. Although a comely person in her early middle age, yet she constantly refused to take another mate, saying ' She was but the guardian of the inheritance for her two sons.' She already provided to give them wives in the next years. The Kheybar custom is to mortgage certain palm-yards for the bride-money ; but thus the soil (which cannot bring forth an excessive usury) not seldom slips, in the end, quite out of the owner's hands. But this honest negro wife imagined new and better ways : she frankly sold two béleds, and rode down with the price to Medina ; and bought a young Galla maiden, well disposed and gracious, for her elder son's wife : and she would nourish the girl as a daughter until they should both be of the age of marriage. The Kheyâbara are wont to match with the (black) daughters of their village ; but the Galla women might be beloved even by white men.

Abdullah once called me to supper : he had a good Medina mess of goat's flesh and french-beans. When we rose he smiled to those about him and boasted " *Hàg Ullah !* ' it is God's truth,' seeing Khalîl has eaten this morsel with me, I could not devise any evil against him ! " Another time I came up weary in the afternoon, when the soldiery had already drunk their coffee and departed; yet finding a little in the pot I set it on the coals, and poured out and sipped it. — Abdullah, who sat there with one or two more, exclaimed, " When I see Khalîl drink only that cup, wellah I cannot find it in my heart to wish him evil : " — this was the half-humane black hypocrite!

The Nejûmy, who — since a white man is the black people's " uncle " — was called in the town *Amm Mohammed*, did not forget me; one forenoon I heard his pleasant voice at the stair head : " *Sheykh Khalîl, sheykh Khalîl, hŷ !* come, I want thee." He led me to his house, which was in the next street, at the end of a dark passage, from whence we mounted to his suffa. The light, *eth-thów*, entered the dwelling room at two small casements made high upon the clay wall, and by the ladder-trap in the roof: it was bare and rude. — " Sit down, sheykh Khalîl, this is my poor place, said he; we live here like the Beduw, but the Lord be praised, very much at our ease, and with plenty of all things : " Amm Mohammed was dwelling here as a trader. A Bishr woman was his housewife; and she had made us an excellent dish of moist girdle-cakes, *gors*, sopped in butter and wild honey. " This honey comes to me, said he, from the Beduw, in my buying and selling, and I have friends among them who bring it me from the mountains." The fat and the sweet [in the Hebrew Scriptures — where the fat of beasts is forbidden to be eaten — Fat things, milk and honey, or butter and honey, oil olive and honey] are, they think, all-cure; they comfort the health of the weak-dieted. There is a tribe of savage men upon the wide *Jebel Rodwa* (before Yanba), who " are very long lived and of marvellous vigour in their extreme age; and that is (say the Arabs) because they are nourished of venison (el-bedûn) and wild honey." When we had eaten, " I and thou are now brethren, said the good man; and, sheykh Khalîl, what time thou art hungry come hither to eat, and this house is now as thine own : undo the door and come upstairs, and if I am not within say to this woman, thou wouldst eat dates or a cake of bread, and she will make ready for thee." He told me that at first the negro villagers had looked upon me as a soldier of the Dowla; but he said to them, ' Nay, for were the stranger a soldier he had gone to alight at the Siruân's or else at my beyt.' When, the day after, they began to know me, there had been a sort of panic terror among the black people. ' I was *sáhar*, they said, a warlock, come to bewitch their village '; and the hareem said " Oh ! look ! how red he is ! "

Amm Mohammed : " This is a feast day (*Aŷd eth-thahîa*), shall we now go and visit the acquaintance ? " — We went from house to house of his village friends : but none of them, in their high and holy day, had slain any head of cattle, — they are reputed niggards ; yet in every household where we came a mess was set before us of girdle-bread sopped in samn. " I warn thee, sheykh Khalîl, said my friend, we must eat thus twenty times before it is evening."

" In these days, whilst we are sending to Medina, said Abdullah the Siruân, thou canst cure the sick soldiery ; we have two at *Umm Kîda*, another is here. Sirûr, and you Sâlem, go with him, take your arms, and let Khalîl see Muharram." — " I cannot walk far." — " It is but the distance of a gunshot from the *Sefsáfa*."

— We came thither and descended behind the figgera, into another valley *W. es-Sillima*, named thus because in the upper parts there is much wild growth of *slîm* acacia trees. The eyes of the Arab distinguish four kinds of the desert thorns : *tólh* (the gum-acacia), *sámmara*, *sillima* and *siála* ; the leaves of them all are like, but the growth is diverse. The desert smiths cut tólh timber for their wood work, it is heavy and tough ; the other kinds are too brittle to serve them. The sámmara is good for firewood ; it is sweet-smelling, and burns with a clear heat leaving little ash, and the last night's embers are found alive in the morning. They have boasted to me of this good fuel, — " We believe that the Lord has given you many things in your plentiful countries, but surely ye have not there the sámmara ! " W. Sillima descends from the Harra beyond the trachytic mount Atwa, and gives below the basalt headland *Khusshm es-Sefsáfa* into *W. Zeydîeh*, the valley of the greater Kheybar village and the antique citadel. W. Sillima is here a rusty fen, white with the salt-warp, summakha, exhaling a sickly odour and partly overgrown with sharp rushes, *el-girt*, which stab the shanks of unwary passengers. — Such is, to the white man, the deadly aspect of all the valley-grounds of Kheybar !

If you question with the villagers, seeing so much waste bottom-soil and barrenness about them, they answer, " There is more already upon our hands than we may labour." The summakha soil, which is not the worst, can be cured, if for two or three seasons the infected salt-crusts be pared with the spade : then the brackish land may be sowed, and every year it will become sweeter. A glaze of salt is seen upon the small clay bottoms in the Harra ; yet of the many springs of Kheybar, which are warm and with some smack of sulphur, there is not one brackish : they rise between certain underlying clays and the basalt, which is fifty feet thick, at the edge of the figgera. The large Kheybar valleys lie together, like a palm leaf, in the Harra border : they are gashes in the lava-field — in what manner formed it were not easy to conjecture — to the shallow clays beneath. Where an underlying (sandstone) rock comes to light it is seen scaly (burned) and discoloured.

— We came up by walled ways through palm grounds and over their brook, to the village Umm Kîda : this is Jériat W. Aly. The site, upon the high wady-bank of basalt, is ancient, and more open and cheerful, and in a better air than the home village. We ascended near the gateway to a suffa, which was the soldiers' quarters ; the men's arms hanged at the walls, and upon the floor I saw three pallets. — The Turkish comrades bade us welcome in the hard manner of strangers serving abroad at wages, and tendered their chibûks. Two of them were those pale faces, which I had first seen in Kheybar ; the third was *Mohammed*, a Kurdy, from some town near *Tiflis* (in Russian Armenia). Muharram was a tall extenuated man, and plainly European. He had worn out forty years in military service in the Hejâz, about Medina and Mecca, and never the better : I asked him where was his *fustân* ? He answered smiling, with half a sigh, " There was a time when we wore the petticoat, and many of the Arnaût were prosperous men at Medina ; but now they are dispersed and dead." He wore yet his large tasseled red bonnet, which seemed some glorious thing in the rusty misery of Kheybar ! His strength failed him here, the fever returned upon him : I gave him rhubarb in minute doses, and quinine. This poor man was pleased to speak with me of *Béled er-Rûm*, that is Greekland, Hellas, bordering on his native country ; and he had heard of the English at Corfu. The Egyptian was an unsavoury fellah, but thankful for my medicines : he told me that certain Franks, traders, came every year for grain to his Nile village, which was some days' march from *Kosèyr*, a port of the Red Sea in front of Wejh : he had only honour to report of them. When I asked him " And was *Ismaiel Pasha*, the Khedewy, a good ruler ? " he answered, " Akhs ! *that is a cursed man*." — I said to Mohammed, the Kurdy, "You are the only man of the strangers, whom I do not hear groan at Kheybar." — But the others answered for him, " He too is often ailing, and has only lately risen from his bed of fever."

The Kurdy, who was one of the police soldiers, moved always with a formidable clattering of arms. He told me that he had once served in an English family at Tiflis! their bountiful humour and the purity of their manners, he highly commended. He had learned to speak, with the full Turkish mouth, a little Medina Arabic, and would civilly greet me in the forenoons, in the city guise, with *keyf usbaht*, 'how have you passed the morning? — you have risen well?' Besides these, two or three Ageylies were stationed at Umm Kîda in another house: one of them (a Nejd man from Kasîm) remembered me! for I had spoken with him at Damascus, in the time of the Haj, when I would ride to Medáin Sâlih. — The fellow had promised then immediately, with a mighty oath, to mount me in the troop, and convey me not only to Medáin, but (if I would) to Medina also and Mecca! — His head was too light for my enterprise. Now meeting with me here in Arabia, as we descended to the street, he said, "It is I! and dost thou not know me?"

Muharram, though "rich," and the hakîm was come from the village to give him remedies, had made us no coffee; — such, in the eyes of the Arabs, are always the Albanians. 'I love not the Arnaût (I have heard Abdullah and the Nejûmy say), they are selfish and wretched, and in land where they are strangers they desire not even the welfare one of another.' When we left them I bade my companions find where I might breakfast, since I could not return fasting. They knocked at a door, and we ascended to the suffa of one of the principal cottages. — They live more cleanly here in the hamlet, and are less negro-like than the most in the village: they are land-partners of the Allayda, W. Aly. The householder spread his matting, and fetched dates; and sat down beside us with the alacrity and smiling acquiescence of Arabian hosts: and presently as their custom is, there came up many idle persons to sit with the strangers. They were landowners and such as went not out to labour themselves, having bond-servants or eyyâl that wrought for them in the plantations. Seeing these more Arab-looking, and even copper-coloured village faces, and that some young men here wore their negro locks braided as the Nomads, I enquired, had they no tradition of their ancestry. They answered me: "We are Jeheyna; — but is there nothing of Kheybar written in your books?" — "Are not the Kheyâbara from the Sudàn? — or from whence have they these lips and noses?" — "Nay, we are tribesmen of Jeheyna, we are Aarab." They said also, " We are *kôm* (the stock or people of) Márhab." *Sirûr* (with his ribald malice), " Come up, ye people of Umm Kîda ! and let this wise stranger feel each of your noses (khusshm), and declare to you what ancestry ye be of, and where is every man's natural béled." Among the Kheyâbara it rarely happens that some welfaring negro villager takes a lone Beduwîa to wife. — After an hour the good man set before us a hot mess, which was of boiled millet. Those of the Bishr village find some diversity in the speech of this hamlet, not a mile from them, and say, " how they puff off their words ! " — My third Ageyly patient was in the home village, a Nejd man from Boreyda : in his evil day he had been sent to Kheybar ; where he was now low with famine and fever. Abdullah, who embezzled the fifth part of the soldiers' pay, enquired of me affectedly before them all, ' What might he do for him?' — " Give him a little broth and meat, he is dying of hunger."

The guest in the Arabic countries sees the good disposition of his host, after three days, turned as the backside of a carpet. — Each morning, after I had presented myself to the village tyrant at the kahwa, I went to breathe the air upon the figgera above the Sefsáfa. I might sit there in the winter sun, without the deadly damps of the valley, to meditate my time away ; and read the barometer unespied, and survey the site of Kheybar (*v.* next page), and the brick-red and purple-hued distance of mountains in the immense Arabian landscape beyond. One day having transcribed my late readings of the aneroid, I cast down the old papers, and, lest the wind should betray me, laid stones on them : but my vision never was good, and there were eyes that watched me, though I saw no man. As I walked there another day a man upon a house-top, at Umm Kîda, fired his gun at me. The morning after, seeing two men approach with their matchlocks, I returned to the village : and found Abdullah sitting with malevolent looks. " What is this, he said, that I hear of thee ? — children of Umm Kîda saw you bury papers, I know not what ! They have taken them up, and carried them to the hamlet, where all the people were troubled ; and a sheykh, a trusty man, has been over here to complain to me. What were the papers ? [in their belief written full of enchantments :] — and now the sheykhs have solemnly burned them." Besides a Beduwy had been to Abdullah accusing the Nasrâny ' that he saw me sitting upon the Harra with a paper in my hand.'

Abdullah told me, that as I returned yesterday, by the path, through the plantations, two young men of Umm Kîda sate behind the clay

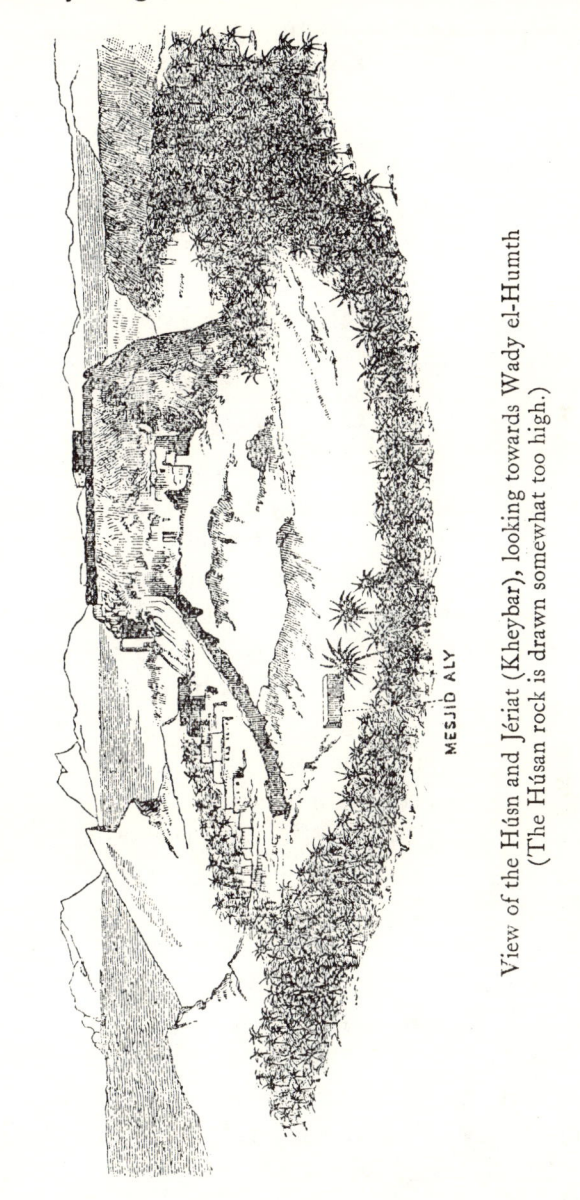

View of the Húsn and Jériat (Kheybar), looking towards Wady el-Humth (The Húsan rock is drawn somewhat too high.)

MESJID ALY

walling with their matchlocks ready, and disputed whether they should take my life; and said one to the other, " Let me alone, and I will shoot at him : " but his fellow answered, " Not now, until we see further ;

for if his blood were shed we know not whom it might hurt." *Abdullah :* "What hast thou done, Khalîl ? what is this that I hear of thee ? The chief persons come to me accusing thee ! and I do tell thee the truth, this people is no more well-minded towards thee. Observe that which I say to thee, and go no more beyond the gates of the village ; — I say go not ! I may protect thee in the village, in the daytime : by night go not out of thy chamber, lest some evil befall thee ; and the blame be laid upon me. For Ullah knoweth — and here the malevolent fanaticism kindled in his eyes — who is there might not come upon thee with his knife ! — a stroke, Khalîl, and thou art dead ! But the slayer was not seen, and the truth of it might never be known. Only in the day-time visit thine acquaintance, and sit in friendly houses. I have said go not beyond the gates ; but if thou pass them, and thou art one day slain, then am I clean of it ! Canst thou look through walling ? a shot from behind some of their (clay) walls may take thy life ; there are some here who would do it, and that as lightly as they shoot at crows, because thou art an alien, and now they have taken thee for an enemy ; and that they have not done it hitherto, wellah it was for my sake."

Abdullah, born in the rude and dark places of Medina, came not much behind the negro villagers in their mad fantasies ; and to all their fable-talk he lent his large ass's ears. The tyrannical wretch threatened me another day that, if I would go any more wandering without the village, he would put me in prison. I said to him : "If any think they have cause against me, send for the persons and call me ; and let the matter be examined before thee." — But the superstitious doubt of those written papers long clouded the village governor's mind ! Another day being at coffee in Ibrahîm's house, I said to the villagers present : "Is it true which Abdullah the Siruân says, that the Kheyâbara have an evil opinion of me ?" They answered, "We think well of thee." Ibrahîm added, "A stranger is a guest, whoso he be, without question of his religion." — Among these black villagers of the *Dîrat er-Rasûl*, the coffee server says, in handing down his tray (upon the left hand), "Sully aly en-Néby !" and they religiously respond, "Upon whom be peace." In sighing, yawning and stretching themselves, they exclaim *Yá Rasûl Ullah !* 'aha missionary of God !' As they sit at the morning coffee the negro peasants recount their yesternights' dreams, and draw from them prognostics : and oftentimes those heavy lips disputed of their pedigrees, seeking to attribute to themselves the coveted nobility.

THE FRIENDSHIP OF AMM MOHAMMED

Amm Mohammed said to me, smiling, "Knowest thou, that all the Kheyâbara tremble for fear of thee?" — "And how should they be afraid of one man, who is infirm and poor, and a stranger?" — "This is the manner of them, they are like beasts, and have no understanding: they say of thee thou art a magician! Fie! I am afraid of thee, sheykh Khalîl; and what thinkst thou the asses say to me? — 'Oho! Amm Mohammed, how canst thou eat with him! or art thou not in dread that he will bewitch thee?' — was there ever such a beast-like malice? And I tell them that though I eat with thee I am never the worse: yet they say, 'Trust well that Khalîl is of a kind of enchantment, he is not born of human nature, he is not of the children of Adam:' — but they themselves what are they? the children of apes; and when they say 'He is a Nasrâny!' I answer them, and so am I — a Nasrâny!"

Such was the amity that grew daily betwixt me and this estimable person. At first he called me often to eat with him; then seeing me bare of necessary things (Abdullah had now my purse) he took me altogether to his house to live with him, in the daytime. Some evenings we went abroad, — '*nedowwer* (said he,) *el-haky wa el-káhwa*, — seeking pleasant chat and coffee,' to friendly houses. At night, since his home was but an upper chamber, I withdrew to sleep in Amân's suffa. At each new sunrising I returned to him: after his prayers we breakfasted, and when the winter sun began to cast a little golden heat, taking up our tools, a crowbar, a spade and a basket, we went forth to an orchard of his; and all this was devised by Mohammed, that I might not be divided from him. He carried also (for my sake) his trusty sword, and issuing from the sordid village I breathed a free air, and found some respite in his happy company, in the midst of many apprehensions.

Amm Mohammed set himself to open a water-pit in a palm ground of his next the troops' summer quarters; the ground-water lies about a spade deep in the valley bottom of Kheybar, but the soil rising there and shallowing out under the figgera, he must break down an arms' length through massy basalt. We passed the days in this idle business: because he saw his guest full of weariness he was uneasy when in my turn I took up the bar. "Sit we down, sheykh Khalîl, a breathing while! *nésma*: nay, why make earnest matter of that which is but our pastime, or what haste is there so all be ended before the summer?"

A good crowbar is worth at Kheybar five reals; their (Medina) *husbandmen's-tools are fetched from the coast.* The exfoliated upper basalt was easy to be broken through : but next lies the massy (crystalline) rock, which must be riven and rent up by force of arms ; and doubtless all the old spring-heads of Kheybar have been opened thus ! — Seldom at this season there arrived a hubt, or company of marketing nomads : then his wife or son called home Amm Mohammed, and the good man returned to the village to traffic with them.

Amm Mohammed — endowed with an extraordinary eyesight — was more than any in this country, a hunter. Sometimes, when he felt himself enfeebled by this winter's (famine) diet of bare millet, he would sally, soon after the cold midnight, in his bare shirt, carrying but his matchlock and his sandals with him : and he was far off, upon some high place in the Harra, by the day dawning, from whence he might see over the wide vulcanic country. When on the morrow I missed the good man, I sat still in his suffa, full of misgiving till his coming home again ; and that was near mid-day. Only two or three days of autumn rain had fallen hereabout, and the new blade was hardly seen to spring ; the gazelles and the wild goats had forsaken this side of the Harra : Amm Mohammed therefore found nothing. — At Kheybar they name the stalker of great ground game *gennàs* : *seyàd* is the light hunter with hawk and hound, to take the desert hare.

He led me with him sometime upon the Harra, to see certain ancient inscriptions ; they were in Kufic, scored upon the basalt rock, and full of *Ullah* and *Mohammed*. Many old Arabic inscriptions may be seen upon the scaly (sandstone) rocks which rise in the valley, half an hour below the place. I found no more of heathen Arabic than two or three inscriptions, each of a few letters. (*Doc. Épigr.* pl. xxviii.) They are scored upon a terrace of basalt, under the Khusshm es-Sefsáfa, with images of animals : I found the wild ox, but not the elephant, the giraffe, and other great beasts of the African continent, which Amân told me he had seen there.

One forenoon we went over the figgera towards the third hamlet of Kheybar, *el-Asmîeh*, or Jériat el-Fejîr. After a long mile's way, in Wady Zeydîeh, under a low brow where those sand-rocks rise from the valley ground, we passed by a lone antique building — the walls are of rude stone courses — which is venerable in their religious eyes, and the name of it is *Kasr en-Néby*, ' the Prophet's cottage.' For they say, that " Mohammed, returning some time from Damascus, drew here the bridle of his thelûl, and would have made her kneel, but gnats swarming up about him, he rode on to lodge at Umm Kîda ; and, where his dromedary couched, that spring welled forth whereof they now drink. The old Arabian dwelling is but a ground chamber with a door and casement. It is maintained by the devotion of the Kheyâbara, who build-in any fallen stones, and renew the roof with fresh palm beams from time to time. The Nejûmy had an outlying plot of corn ground in this valley side: and good part of it cost him no more, he laughed, than an old cutlass and the scabbard. In the border of his field were some graves of those who had perished in the plague, few years before, — that in which his brother Ahmed sickened to death ; the heaps were now hoary with summakha. Amm Mohammed (little nice) had now a mind to take up the bones, for said he, ' It would enlarge his ground, and he might sow more corn there.' But the good man promising to do after my rede, I made answer that he should reverence the dead, and not remove them. We found a skull under a dôm palm, amongst the wild rocks, — " Ha ! he said musing, this is of some Beduwy fallen in last year's warfare ; a hound has carried away the head, and left it here."

We went beside our path in the wide valley (of the now joint wadies Sillima and Zeydîeh), to visit the ruins of a village, in the midst, seated upon a crag of basalt : he called it *el-Gereyeh*. — The walls of her strait streets are of dry courses of the Harra stones. Small were those antique dwellings, every house is no more than a narrow chamber, and the earthen floor is advanced, like a step, — as the use is in the Arabic countries, above the doorway and entry, where they leave their sandals. This site is not only well chosen for defence, but the ancient date-eaters overlooked their palm-valleys in a better air. Those old inhabitants, far beside the great trade road, were by likelihood *mesakîn* : though we searched through the ruined hamlet, I saw not an ornament, nor an inscription. We found but a great mortar, in the street, and pitted blocks of basalt, wherein — as the use now is — they brayed their corn stuffs for boiling. The housewives of Israel beat even their manna in a mortar ; and this was a sapient saying among them, ' *Though thou bray a fool in a mortar, amongst wheat* with a pestle, yet will not this foolishness depart from him.'

We came to the mouth of the W. Jellâs, where I saw wide watery grounds that might be husbanded. There is another ruinous village upon the next basalt figgera, the name of it, he said, is *Gériat Abu Robaï*. Those ruins were such as we had viewed in el-Gereyeh ; and I saw there a small four-square tower finished as a pyramid above, — it was but an earthen heap within, and might be a sepulchre. Under this old village, is a spring of the sweetest water. Amm Mohammed gazed about us; and said, "Wellah the ancients had more wit (than this people that now is), for they built upon free overlooking headlands in a better air!" I saw el-Asmîeh not far off, upon a height of the figgera: but here he would have turned back. — *El-Nejûmy* : " Nay, we will not enter, lest it should be said, we went to eat the bread of any man." — " Yet let us go and repose an hour in the sheykh's house, and drink coffee, and be gone." That hamlet is ancient: the few families are land-partners with the Fukara. They are not Kheyâbara, but colonists from el-Hâyat, where they have yet possessions. El-Hâyat is a Nejd negro village, and the people are of more liberal mind than they of lowland Kheybar. The palms growing here in sweeter soil, are more robust than the palms about the Bishr village.

We now ascended the rock to their gate, and the first met civilly saluted us, " Welcome sheykhs, and what news from the jéria?" The sheykh's kahwa hearth we found to be but a fire in the street, and a palm mat! for he was building. This sheykh — and in general they of el-Hâyat are such — was a man of the Arabian hospitality; so that it was commonly said of him, in Kheybar, "He will sacrifice a sheep, if but a (strange) child come there." The good man brought us clotted dates, and sat down with much goodwill to make his guests kahwa. I asked wherefore the corner of his new building had been sprinkled with gore? They wondered to hear me question them thus (and felt in their hearts that I was an alien)! they thought I should have known that it was the blood of a goat which had been sacrificed [to the jân] for the safety of the workmen, " lest, as they said, any one should be wounded." Labourers, since all the householders at el-Asmîeh are substantial persons, must be hired from " the jéria."

— Bye and bye we rose to depart, but that good man held our cloaks and made us sit down again. One who came then to speak with the sheykh was the husbandman partner of Zeyd es-Sbeykán, my sheykhly friend among the Fukara. Though the yearly rent of their plantations might be valued at hundreds of reals, the thriftless peasant was always behind hand with old indebtedness: Amm Mohammed said, 'he had not sometimes a ready real to buy himself a new shirt-cloth!' — Of our host he told me an incredible thing! ' that he had 2000 to 3000 reals by the year (say £400 sterling), and he could spend it all. His *béleds* (béled is at Kheybar palm-yard) were so many that he hardly knew some of them: and if any poor man came to settle there, he would give him the fruit of two or three béleds only to keep them; he bestows much upon his poorer acquaintance, both villagers and nomads; and in his bountiful hospitality.' The palms of these Kheybar valleys are innumerable: the far outlying are abandoned to the Beduw, and yield but wild fruits.

When we had sat three hours, till the afternoon, our host called us, and those who were sitting at the hearth with us, to an inner room; where he set down before us a vast trencher of his hospitality; two boiled kids were heaped in it, on a mess of thùra. He said with host's smiles, that such was poor cheer, but his sheep were at that hour out of call, and, after the locusts, they had none other grain than this bare millet (thùra). He stood a moment comforting his guests to eat, and added, ' might it do us good ' : he would not sit down with us, since, by their magnanimous fiction, the host is the servant of his guests. — The growing thùra is a cane-like stem with a flaggy head of many hard corns; the harvest is in the early autumn, the stalks are good provender for camels. The thùra corn is dry and woody; and in common years the villagers eat none, — they sell it to the nomads: and the desert housewives patiently seething this cheap grain in butter-milk make of it a wholesome porridge. Amm Mohammed's Beduwîa prepared very well our daily messes of this harsh meal. Yet many of the villagers could not eat it; they chose rather to live of their date-fruit, though already they had not half enough. The Kheyâbara (negroes) say that the valley dates are to their stomach " as fresh meat."

Amm Mohammed looked, as we came again over the figgera, to see if the new blade began now to spring: he said at last, " There will be no rabîa this year ! " — If the green herb were sprung in the land he would have called-in some of his goats from the Heteym; and gone forth, to wander like the nomads upon the Harra: and then, he said, I should have been with him. — He had gone out last year with his Beduin wife and most of the *geyatîn* (sing. gatûny, indigent Beduin squatters at Kheybar): they made themselves booths of their palm matting; and lodged in hollow places. Amm Mohammed led me round by a site, *Másr*, which overlooks the plain-like W. Jellâs : we sought for inscriptions, but found only ruins of old walling such as there are upon all the *fuggar* about Kheybar. — I wondered to see the stalwart man so often sit down complaining that he was weary ! and neither could he labour long at once in the garden : the ignorances of his youth, and pernicious drugs, had brought down his strength, and the fever of Kheybar. As we went, he looked on the ground for bullets, which had been shot in the last year's warfare.

Many times we went by certain bowl-shaped and dry-built vaults of the rude lava stones, none of them above six feet large and high ; some have a ring-border of stones laid about them (*v.* fig.). — Are they not

Section of vaulted barrows upon the Harra near Kheybar

grave chambers ? and such as the rijjûm in the Harrat el-Aueyrid, and the nawamîs of Sinai ? To bury upon the basalt floor, must needs be by building. It was the ancient manner to the ends of the world to lay the dead ancestors in barrows of earth or stone. I said to Amm Mohammed, "What thinkest thou, are they not tombs ?" — " Eigh ! it may be so ; and now I remember sometimes in my hunting to have seen bones in them."

In the evening he showed me morsels of glassy quartz, which he had found from time to time upon the Harra, — vehemently hoping that they might be diamonds. The good man said cheerfully, in his disappointment, " At least they will be beautiful to have set in rings." Such is the Orientalism, the fond dream, of the Arabs, — to be rich upon a day, before we die, by the benign influence of the stars, without our labour : then would one live — on this side the grave — voluptuously, and be a bountiful householder. Even Amm Mohammed believed with the rest, that I might find them a thing if I would : for this cause also Abdullah, after his violent iniquity, sought to win favour with the Nasrâny. Sometimes with a smiling hypocrisy he threatened me, crying ' Confess, Khalîl ! and I was ungrateful not to remember his kindness ; for had he not saved my life in the beginning, when he might (as easily) have broken my pan with a pistol shot : confess, Khalîl ! or the felon's mind was to hang me upon yonder breastwork of the Húsn,' — where certain " guide stones " appeared. " Ay, wellah !

answered him the old sheykh Sâlih, and might one interpret those signs they would lead him to a treasure." — In the dry walling of the ancient acropolis, built of rude basalt blocks, are five white stones, near the southern end above the village, and laid in such enigmatical order as the stars in their constellations. — ' And if I would not fall out of his favour, added the village tyrant, — and what then could save me ? — I must sally to-morrow with him upon the Húsn ; and he would have the tools borne up before us. — And if I were of the súwahh, that seek no part in the sliding riches of this world, yet they were not men of that perfection ; they loved well the use of this world and to live richly : and would I none of it wherefore should I envy them the silver ? '

— Alas ! how might I persuade them that there is no such lore ? when already certain strangers had attempted to raise the hid treasures of Kheybar : and they held that the silent Nasrâny, from a far country, should have some more deep sight in the cabalistical learning. Sâlih added this toothless argument, ' All (outlandish) strangers would to Kheybar ! — for what other cause could it be than to seek fortune at Kheybar ? '

They have often told me of a Moghreby that came hither to raise hidden treasures : — it is always in the people's faith a Moor who is master of the magical art. ' This Moor sacrificed [to the jân] in the night, a black cock ; he read his spells, and a great black fowl alighted beside him. He read on, and a strange black steer (it was none of the village cattle, but a phantom) ascended from the valley palms ! The earth rumbled ; and rose as it were in billows, gaping and shutting; and in that earthy womb appeared an infinite treasure. Then the wise man commanded his black slave to hew off a foot of the black bull with his sword : but the bondsman's heart failing him at this point, the enchantment was broken ; — and all that pelf of wealthy metal was turned (they said who saw it) to such vile and brittle matter as the sea shells. Then the Moghreby flung a magical writing into the well, and there ascended a smoke, which he commanded the slave to smite with his mantle ; and there rained down upon them pieces of pure gold. — Another enchantment was made by night in a field nigh Umm Kîda : the ground was seen swelling and rolling ; but in neither could the master of the spells come to the looked-for end of his labour.'

Another treasure-trover had been here in these years, namely that Yahûdy who perished miserably in the valleys of Kheybar. [*v.* Vol. I.

p. 193.] I heard some say he came to them from Yanba, — others said from el-Ally.

One day I ascended with Sâlem the Bishr Ageyly to the Húsn ; and he also told me of " a Yahûdy " who had made an incantation in the night : the earth wallowed and yawned ; but the spell had been broken by the untimely intruding of some villagers, — and all that glittering metal was turned to brittle chalk-scales before their eyes.

The Húsn or Acropolis rock of ancient Kheybar ; from the side of the Bishr village

The Yahûdy, he told me, had visited Kheybar, with the Beduw. The Húsn, or citadel rock of basalt, stands solitary in the wady Zeydîeh ; and upon its southern skirt is built the clay (Bishr) village. The length of the walled platform is two hundred paces, and the breadth ninety : the floor is deep mould [that may be partly of the old (clay) buildings which are melted away] upon the uneven rock. The Siruân digging there (to repair the ancient wall with a clay breastwork, and build a covert for the soldiery), found potsherds, broken glass, egg-shells, date-stones and dung of horses. — Strangely shouldering upon the Húsn flanks, from the valley ground above the village, are seen the twin heads of two antique clay pyramids [*v.* the fig.], whose lower parts are cased with dry building of trimmed stones. Those pyramids are of clay bricks, and they enclose an ancient covered well ! so that, in times of public danger, the townspeople in the acropolis should not lack water.

"From hence, said Sâlem, we shot at the Beduw [his own tribesfolk!] and the Beduw shot against us from yonder figgera. We killed we know not how many, for there fell some of them in the palms, and after the Beduins fled, none sought them ; but in a day or two the stench of the dead was horrible : one man was wounded of our side." — "Sâlem, I know that thou art an Auájy : tell me didst thou fire upon thine own tribesfolk ? " — " Ay ! I fired upon them, and so did another, *Eyâd*, and so did another, *Merjàn*, and another, a gatûny. We that eat the bread of the Dowla must fight for the Dowla, even against our own people : — but why came they to bring war upon us ? " — The same afternoon I saw that gatûny drinking coffee at Abdullah's ; and the Siruàn said, " See Khalîl, how they be all of them at my commandment ! this Beduwy here killed his own tribesmen in the war, aha-ha-ha ! " — " Ay billah (the fellow answered), and if Abdullah bid me rise now and cut the wezand of any one in the company, I would do it."

CHAPTER V

THE KHEYÂBARA

Kheybar witches. Dakhîlullah, the Menhel. Ibrahîm. Our garden labour. Their custom to labour for each other without wages. House-building. The negro villagers are churlish and improvident. Famine in the land. Kheybar "THE LAND'S WEALTH." Antique Kheybar conquered by the Annezy. The ancient partnership of Beduins and villagers. Sirûr. The villagers' rights in the soil. Their husbandry is light. Afternoons and evenings at Kheybar. The Asiatic priests' mystery of stabbing and cutting themselves. Villagers going out for wood are surprised by a ghrazzu. 'The work of the Dowla is mere rapine.' Kheybar occupied by the Dowla. The Beduins taxed. A day of battle with the Aarab. Vility of a Turkish colonel. Perfidy of the Fukara. The Kheyâbara sup of their hostile (nomad) partners' camels. The ears of the slain are cut off. The Medina soldiery at Kheybar. The cholera. Wandering hills. Fabulous opinion, in the East, of Kheybar. Abdullah's letter to the Governor of Medina. Abdullah's tales. His tyranny at Kheybar. Sedition in the village. The village kindreds. Abdullah's stewardship. Dakhîl the post. Aly, the religious sheykh, an enemy to the death. The Nejûmy's warning to Abdullah, spoken in generous defence of the Nasrâny. The ostrich both bird and camel. Amm Mohammed had saved other strangers.

WHENEVER in the late evenings I returned to Amân's lodging, I found that our door was barred! and I must stand in the street, with my flaming palm branch, calling and knocking to awaken Amân; and he would rise and come down to undo for me: he was now alone, since his Galla comrade, for some displeasure, had forsaken him. Though I daily asked Amân, why did he bar me out? he answered nothing; but one night the poor fellow acknowledged that, after dusk, he was in ghostly fear of the hags of Kheybar; and showing me our palm rafters, "Wellah, he said, sheykh Khalîl, one of them, sitting on such a beam, may ride in the night-time to Medina and return ere day, and no man know it; for they will be found in their houses when the people waken." — "How may a witch that has an husband gad abroad by night, and the goodman not know it?" — "If she take betwixt her fingers only a little of the ashes of the hearth, and sprinkle it on his forehead, the dead sleep will fall upon him till the morning. But though one knew his wife to be a witch, yet durst he not show it, nor put her away, — for she might cause him to perish miserably! yet the most witches are known, and one of them, he added darkly, is a neighbour of ours. When it is the time to sleep they roam through the village ways : and I warn thee, sheykh Khalîl ! — for a thing which we looked not for may happen in a moment ! have a care in thy coming home by night." — " I would willingly see them." — " Eigh ! speak not so foolhardily, — except thou know some powerful spells to say against them. I have heard that _Dakhîlullah_ [a menhel, or man of God] once meeting with the witches did cry against them words which the Lord put into his heart, out of the koran, and they fled from him shrieking that the pains of hell were come upon them. — The witches, said the melancholy Amân, are of all ages : they have a sheykh over them, who is a man, and he also is known." — " And, why are they not punished ? " — " Wellah it is for fear of their malice ! The hags assemble in dead hours of the night, and sitting in a place of ordures, they strip off their smocks, and anoint their bodies with cow milk [which in Arabia is esteemed medicinal] ; and then the witches cry, ' We be issued from the religion of Islam.' So they gad it in the dim streets, and woe worth any man returning lateward if they meet with him ! For they will compel him to lie with them ; and if he should deny them they will change him into the form of some beast — an ox, a horse, or an ass : and he shall afterward lose his mind, and in the end perish miserably. But they eat wellah the heart (and he is not aware of it) of him who consents to them, and suck the blood of his living body ; and after this he will become a fool, and be a dazing man all his days."

There were few at Kheybar that could not tell of some night's fearful jeopardy of their precious soul and body. Amm Mohammed at his first coming hither, being then a robust young man and his heart not misgiving him, had many times lurked behind his casement, in the night shadow, in wait for the witches. And he learned certain texts, against that hard adventure, out of a book which he had that time by him ; for his purpose was to leap down his stair-head as ever he heard them before the house, throw up the street door and break out upon them. Yet, for all his watching, he told me, he had never seen the witches ; and he now inclined to my (incredulous) opinion. " Wellah, sheykh Khalîl, we are _ghrashemîn_, rude (he said) and ignorant ; and such tales, out of their black blockheads, may be but _mushrak !_ (meddling superstitious vanities to the dishonouring of the only God)." — But sheykh Sâlih said one evening, " I have seen them myself ! It was in my father's days when I was a child, as I came late homeward from a neighbour's house : and what did I see in the street ! — wellah Such-a-woman (he named her) go by all naked, and I saw her gross belly, and her eyes rolling like fire. I shrunk into a doorway, and had but time and sense — I knew little else for I was yet untaught — to cry *Ullahu akhbar!* and start to my father's threshold : and there I fell down in a swoon ; and so the neighbours found me ! Ay ! I knew her right well, — I could not be mistaken, and some of you are of age to remember her."

Dakhîlullah, as his father before him, was the maul of the village witches. This poor man, at certain times when the spirit moved him, went forth by night, with a great cry in his mouth, and proclaimed the kingdom of God and Mohammed through the village ways. One night as Dakhîlullah issued from his house he saw the man whom the village whispered to be 'sheykh of the witches,' going in the street a little before him. Dakhîlullah ran and leapt upon his back, and beating him in the head, he cried at his ears, " Say, thou cursed one ! La îlah ill' Ullah ; say, La îlah ill' Ullah !" The startled man, who thought the fiend was fallen on his neck, ran the length of the street under him, and fell down in a swoon ; but Dakhîlullah wrung from him the words of the testimony before leaving him, 'There is no îlah but Ullah.' — Dakhîl though otherwise poor in spirit, feared no after-claps of the beaten and mishandled man ; for the saving religion defended and maintained him.

One of these nights I was wakened by a judgment-voice which resounded through the village streets ! — and I heard a strong footfall coming roundly on in haste through the silent *aswâk*. It was Dakhîlullah, and his words were, *Yâ abeyd Illah, la îlah ill' Ullah, wâhed Ullah!* 'Ho, ye worshippers of the Lord, there is none God but the Lord, the Lord is one !' and he strode through the Saheyn, and went-on thus till he was out of hearing. Amân sat up in the cold moonlight ; he listened devoutly and said to me, 'Dakhîlullah was calling to the Moslemîn.' After a space, when Dakhîlullah had gone through all that side of the village, we heard the portentous voice with the same words and his mighty tread coming about again. Only a wall of clods parted us from our neighbours : I could hear them rake their embers, and the voices of the rude families inhabiting about our little open place ; they took up the burden and repeated long and devoutly his La îlah ill'

Ullah ! I looked out, and saw in every casement the red firelight : they had blown their embers, it wanted not much to the day, and none might sleep more.

— The sickly Amân said to me with a pious sigh, " Oh ! what sweetness is there in believing ! Trust me, dear comrade, it is a thing above that which any heart may speak ; and would God thou wert come to this (heavenly) knowledge ; but the Lord will surely have a care of thee, that thou shouldst not perish without the religion. Ay, how good a thing it were to see thee a Moslem, and become one with us ; but I know that the time is in God's hand : the Lord's will be done. — But ah ! what a marvellous Providence, sheykh Khalîl, has brought us here together ! I born at six months' distance, and thou as far in the other parts of the world ; and when we speak one may understand the other ! " — Full was the tender and weary human heart of this poor Galla ; and I could not perceive that anything in him was barbarous, or uncivil : he had grown up in a foreign land in the divine school of affliction and poverty.

Dakhîlullah was a dull man, all the day after this night-wrestling and effusion of his spirits. At other times, the poor negro was a simple soul, and for fear of certain persons in the village, about some question of inheriting land, he had lately been a fugitive among the nomads. He was a neighbour of ours, and in his trouble he reverted to the magnanimous defence of the Nejûmy ! and he saw me always with a good eye, since I was the friend of Mohammed. When we passed forth to our labour in the morning, he sat drooping in the street upon the public clay benches. — Amm Mohammed enquired, with a little hardness and irony in his voice : " Why thus ? up ! and go to thy work, man." Dakhîl only answered sadly, *Nay !* — I questioned Mohammed, and drew from him an unwilling answer, that ' Dakhîlullah was a MENHEL.' When the religious passion was upon him, he could not forbear ; he must go forth and prophesy through the town.

Certain days later, any sick persons might enquire of him ; and Dakhîlullah would answer them [as he was taught by the spirit] and prescribe remedies. Amm Mohammed tells me it is the second day of the week after, when the infirm or their friends resort to him, 'bearing coffee and incense.' — " And woman' (he spoke to his wife) see thou forget not ! the seventh day from to-day carry our sick bint to him, with a present of dates, and we shall hear what he says." — In that day, the seer responded, 'That because Mohammed was a harsh man in his household their babe should die ; — but let the father sacrifice a sheep for the life of his child.' — Amm Mohammed as he heard this answer, exclaimed in disdain, "The slave's divination is *waswassat*, a making religious mystery by whispers ; and all this I begin to believe, with sheykh Khalîl, is not in the religion. — Dahkîl is an ass, a fool, and he tells my wife that because I am of hard speech, the little daughter must die ! and thy daughter Khalîl, for, since thy medicines saved her life, she is a child of thine."

Her sickness was dysentery and fever ; and we were in dread, from day to day, of the babe's dying. Two infant children, which his housewife had borne him, before her, were dead, and he yearned for the child's life : I counselled them to send her out of Kheybar, to the Beduw. — I daily wondered to see almost no young children in Kheybar ! The villagers answered me, "The children (*bizrán*) die in this air ! — it is the will of Ullah." The most pestilent season at Kheybar, which they call the *hamîm*, is the still and sultry month (the summer's heat then entering), when the new date berries are first formed in the trees ; — this is between March and April, and as soon as the corn is carried. — If the valley fever come upon the grown negro people, they do but languish a day or two.

Ibrahîm was a prosperous young man of the Arabian mind, and comely manners ; and save for some rasping of the negro gullet when he spoke, you had not remembered his colour. He was unlettered, and when I praised his boy's reading, he sighed and said, "I have only this child left." Ibrahîm was rich, he had four wives, though nearly every wedded man of these villagers leads his life with an only housewife. They live on together, and she is the mother of his children : upon the men's part they are far from the lightness of the Beduins, and the feminine infidelity is little heard of amongst them. Their women are not veiled ; and many are the bonny young faces (almost Ethiopian) of their sex at Kheybar. In their houses there is no separation of the hareem : the Kheybar dwelling is commonly but an upper chamber, and in presence of village guests, or of nomad friends, the negro women come to sit at the hearth, and take their part in the common talk ; and that is often with a loud tongue, and harsh plainness of understanding. If guests lodge in their suffa by night, the hareem go out to sleep with some hareem of the neighbours. — 'Aha ! said Ibrahîm, it was not so with him formerly ; his wives had been all years with child, and many were born to him : but he lost their babes again in the hamîm. Now his hareem had left off bearing, and he was much in doubt of evil eyes ; there were many witches at Kheybar !' — He would hear the hakîm's counsel. — I bade him send his son, in the hot months, to some friendly tribe in the khála.

That power or passion which came upon Dakhîlullah, Amm Mohammed told me, was ES-SULÂT, — the Prayer ; he might mean the Spirit of Prayer. The same strife of spirit had been in his father before him : the hags fled from the religious sound of his voice : " he could even perceive the odour of witches passing his house, and would hurl down upon them, carrying away the door in his hand." — One day after, Dakhîl came of his own accord to help us in the garden ; he wrought till the midday, but had not much strength : so said his noonday prayers with a devout simplicity, and ate his due of dates and departed. The poor soul desired me to cure his ophthalmia. — When afterwards I said to Mohammed, " Your Seer is bleareyed ! " he laughed maliciously.

As we opened our well-pit, we found veins of jips, and jiss (which they distinguish, the last is perhaps pipe-clay) under the mould of the valley, with banded clays, which are seen parched and flawed above with the old vulcanic heat. — " Thy lore is good, said Mohammed, [I had spoken of geology,] verily this soil is laid in stages." — Some will take that fat white clay for soap to wash their cotton garments : but at better leisure they use the bruised stalks of the alkaline plant er-rimth. With our well rubbish we built a loose terrace wall, *thofîra*, and sifted (*jérula*) mould upon it, using the labourer's palm basket, *muâra*. Mohammed would make of this ground a (Medina) garden of potherbs and fruit trees ; which hitherto were not planted at Kheybar, — not even the sweet-meat palm el-helwa, nor vines [but these may not prosper here] : because the Beduins formerly overran all in their lawless levity.

There was an honest vainglory in Amm Mohammed to show himself a citizen and a loyal man, and to be seen in company with the officers of the Dowla : the *quondam* trooper maintained a horse at Kheybar, chiefly that in the months of the military occupation he might ride, like a sheykhly person, with those great ones. Now he foresaw the brave time when he should bid the Medina officers to this ground, which would be his herb-garden; where sitting dangle-legs upon our terrace wall, they should partake of his summer fruits. Mohammed was of a metal which I have seen in all countries: strong men and large-bodied, yet infirm soon, with sweet and clear, almost feminine, voices. He was of a mild and cheerful temper, confident, tolerant, kind, inwardly God-fearing, lightly moved: his heart was full of a pleasant humour of humanity. Loving mankind he was a peacemaker, not selfish of his own, true and blithe in friendship, of a ready and provident wit, both simple and sly, eluding enmities; — an easy nature passing over all hard and perplexed matter, content with the natural course of the world, manly and hardy, but not long-breathed in any enterprise.

If I reminded Mohammed of our task, which lay whole days abandoned, he answered cheerfully, that when he might see me once safe out of Kheybar, he would bring-in a bevy of stout young villagers, and our long labour would be sped in a few hours. — When our iron would no more bite on the metallic durity of the deeper rock in the well-pit, I brought a mantle-full of palm leaf-butts to fire the stone: they use thus to find the joints of the intractable basalt, which is to be suddenly chilled with water. I struck a spark and blew the flame in a shred of palm-bast; and kindled a raging fire. "Aha! hast thou set on fire jehennem? laughed Amm Mohammed, or to speak it mouthing-like, as the Turks, jehendem." — There was lately a governor of Medina of this mad name, *Jehendem Pasha!* As all was burned low, we found nothing to take up the water. "Alas! laughed he, jehennem has burned in vain:" then, at my bidding, he hastily daubed our basket with clay, and cast on water. Ahmed called his brother *laab*, a play-fellow. Though Mohammed had passed his fiftieth year, he was young in honest glee as one who had not found a trouble in the world.

They have an old world's custom here, to labour for each other without wages, besides that which the young men must eat. When one has any need he calls to some likely young man of his acquaintance, 'Come thou and work for me to-day,' — be it to dig, to plough, to sow, to reap, to water, to build. — The workmen leave their labour at high noon (when the work-day is ended at Kheybar) and follow him home, where his housewife has made them ready their dinner; — that should not be of dates, but some of their bread or corn messes. Mohammed had a purpose to build himself a house, since this was not his own wherein he now dwelt. — " Yet, said he, it must cost me some sacks of wheat, to fill so many days their hungry bellies. It is not known, he often said, how well we live at Kheybar, saving that this air is not good. I am better here than at Medina, where we pay the water-carrier to drink water, we pay for firewood, and one must buy his horse provender."

To his house-building he told me he would call only the best workers of the eyyâl, and say to them, " I build a beyt, come and make clods with me to-day." These are half-spadefuls of the fenny black earth, rolled in their hands for bricks, and left to harden a few days in the sun ; they are then to be turned. When the sun of ten days has baked the crusts, and the white summakha is seen upon them, they may be carried for building : the builders have puddled earth for mortar. They lay the foundation of two or three courses of rude stones (*v.* Vol. I. p. 176 ; and confer Jer. li. 26], and thereupon build clods, two bricks thick, but without any craft or care, to knit them with cross-laying : they dress all rudely to the eye, and it suffices them. When the young men go out for beams, they seek windcast palms in the béleds ; and whereso they find any they take them, since fallen palm timber is only cumber at Kheybar. The balk is girded with ropes, and a score of good fellows will draw it home with a song ; and return for more until they have enough. The stair is made of stones and clay : the suffa floor is a palm deep of stamped earth, upon a matwork of palm branches ; and in the midst is made the square clay hearth, of a span height with a border. They now want nothing to garnish their houses, but a little matting.

The negroes are poor in the abundance of their palm valleys, and of an improvident, churlish, and miserable humour : yet it is said, that in the date harvest they can be open-handed. Many palm yards and seed grounds may be counted to almost every household ; but they lie partly untilled, and there is much indebtedness and poverty amongst them, even in good years. " Mine, said Amm Mohammed, are but ten béleds, — there is hardly another here who has so few, and many have fifty or sixty : yet none of them fare better than I ; and that is but of a little providence and good husbandry. I thank God, there is always in my house to eat ; but the half of them have not oftentimes enough." — I knew a wasteful young man who had been rich, but to-day he was almost undone. He had spent palm grounds and palm grounds to purchase him wives and more wives ; for, as he was a sot, he might not live many weeks in peace with any of them : I saw that the nomad marketers would not trust him now with one real's worth of samn, for payment (to be made in dates) at the coming harvest ! — The sah measure at Kheybar is the good old standard of Medina, the greatest that I have seen in Arabia. The sah may be nigh two pints at Teyma, two and a half at Hâyil, at el-Ally nearly three, and at Kheybar, five ; their *medega* (a small palm basket) is a twelve-sah measure, five medegas are one *mejellád*. A skin of dates is called here as at Medina *hashîah*.

There had been a famine in the desert seven years before. That was after four rainless winters, so that there sprang no after rabîa ; and the cattle of the Beduins died away to the half. Then many poor tribesmen came down to seek some relief in these valleys ; and Amm Mohammed told me that the Kheyâbara entertained them until their own began to give out. He said, " You might see the Beduw, an hour before sunset, creeping up from the street, by twos and threes, to the people's suffas ; and they would sit silently at an hearth till the supper hour." — Such a general charity might hardly be procured by public laws in other countries ! — An unwilling householder will but say, " Why guest it so often with me, *and hinder others' coming*, wherefore do I see thee here every day ? seek other houses ! " In all this wealth of land, few of the Kheyâbara have any little ready money. It was said of old crooked Sâlih, the sheykh, whose palm grounds were more than other men's — ' that he had in his chest perhaps 200 or 300 reals.' The greenness and plenty of the Kheybar valleys is a proverb in the desert, and the tribesmen make a pretty etymology of the name : " What, say they, is Kheybar but *Kheyr-el-barr*, THE LAND'S WEALTH."

The seats of the Annezy Aarab soon after the conquest of Mosaic Kheybar were a little, says the tradition, above Medina, between the W. el-Humth and the W. er-Rummah [where wander now the W. Aly and Heteym, and part of the Harb nation]. — '*Okilla* a slave of Márhab, the Emir of ancient Kheybar, had gathered a remnant of his villagers, and was become their sheykh. One year when the Annezy passed by with their cattle, they pitched by the (friendly) Kheybar valleys, as in a place of much water. A maiden of the Aarab entered Kheybar to see the daughters of the town : and there a young man was wounded with her love, who enticed the gazing damsel and forced her ; — he was the

VILLAGE & BEDUIN LAND-PARTNERSHIP

sheykh Okilla's son! The poor young woman went home weeping; — and she was a sheykh's daughter. This felony was presently reported in the nomads' menzil! and 'It was not to be borne that a virgin should suffer violence!' said all the Beduw.

The Annezy sheykhs sent to require satisfaction from the sheykh of Kheybar; who answered them shortly that the Annezy should no more water there. On the morrow the town sheykh, Okilla, rode to the nomads' menzil, with a few horsemen, and defied them. The Beduw set furiously upon them; and Okilla fell, and there were slain many of his people. The Beduw now overran all; they conquered the villages, and bound themselves by oath not to give their daughters to the Kheyâbara for ever — 'Thenceforward the Kheyâbara took bondwomen for wives; and at this day they are become a black people.' — The Beduw left the villagers to husband the palm valleys, for the half fruits with them; and removed in the wilderness.

Every possession is reckoned at Kheybar upon the Beduin partnership; even the villagers' houses are held betwixt them and the absent nomads. At midsummer the Annezy tribes (which remain in the south) descend to gather their part of the date harvest. Every béled is thus a double inheritance; there is a Beduin landlord and a black villager partner, and each may say 'it is mine.' The villagers are free husbandmen: they may sell their half-rights to others, they may even neglect their holdings, without contradiction of the Beduwy; and the tribesman cannot put another in his room. If the villager sow the soil, the harvest is all his own; the absent Beduwy has no part therein: yet if the Beduwy (as there be some few impoverished tribesmen) dwell at Kheybar and become a settler (gatûny), he may do the like, entering to the half with his negro partners and sowing the inheritance. In the home géria were fifteen poor (Bishr) Beduins that did so: they were bankrupts of the desert come to settle upon that little (landed) good which yet remained to them inalienable. These village Beduins are not misseen by the Kheyâbara, who willingly lend the poor gatûnies their ploughs and plough-oxen, and the husbandman's tools.

The absent tribesmen's land-right is over no more than the palms. As these decay the villager should set new plants, and the Beduwy is holden to pay him for every one a real: but if his land-partner be poor and cannot requite him, he may leave their ground unplanted, or he may sow the soil for himself. Nevertheless the Beduin lordship remains in the land, and his nomad partner may, at any time, require the village partner to set palms there, for the half fruit, only requiting his labour : or the villager may plant an old palm ground, and reckon the Beduin's indebtedness in their future harvests. Good village partners will provide against the decay of their plantations ; for where they see any old stem they cherish an offset, that when this fails they may have another palm, in its room. Yet so there is the less order in their béleds, the offset stems grow over-thwartly, and are in their season the sooner to fall.

Besides the villagers possess in their singular right certain open lands, which (from antiquity) were never planted with palms ; such are their fields towards *Kasr en-Néby*, and that upland bottom of sweet (but not deep) earth, el-Húrda, where are many old wells ; — they say " three hundred," that is, very many. We have seen what is their landed wealth ; and if I consented to remain at Kheybar, almost every considerable householder, they promised, would bestow upon me a béled : and first Amm Mohammed gave me that ground where we laboured, with its fifteen *aydàn*, or stems of palms : last year he had bought the villager's right for sixty reals. Sheykh Sâlih gave me the next béled, but like his liberality, it was not large. Every palm-yard has a high-built wall about it, because formerly (in the season of dates) the Beduins were knavish climbers and pilferers by day and night. The béled wall is built and repaired by the villager's labour ; the Beduin is to pay him for every length of a palm-leaf rod, a real.

If a Beduwy, for any instant need — as to make an atonement for bloodshed — must sell his inheritance of land, he sells it to some tribesmen, and not to the negro husbands. When landlord tribes or kindreds forsake the country and become Aarab of another dîra, as the Sbáa, Ruwàlla and Jellâs, the reversion is to the Annezy that remain in the land ; and the former rights remain in abeyance. Any stranger at Kheybar may use the idle soil of a béled in partnership with the villager. The stranger's seed corn is sown in the field, and the villager's is all the husbandry. — ploughing and watering and harvesting ; and the grain will be halved between them. Thus did Ahmed, thus did Sirûr, who was of a thriving nature ; the Galla had three good plots sown down this year, and he drank milk of his own little troop of goats : he was the only man of the miserable soldiery that prospered at Kheybar. ' Eigh ! said the ribald, lifting his eyes to heaven, if only his Lord would leave him here other two or three years ! — then would he be fully at his ease, and a welfaring person.'

— It happened (strangely) that this Sirûr had been somewhile a soldier of the kella at Medáin ; and (as Amân said) the bondsman of Haj Nejm, but he had conveyed himself away from thence : he knew also Teyma and el-Ally. Once he had been beset in the Ally boghrâz by Beduw, but said the smooth scelerat, ' Rubb-hu, his Lord delivered him ' : — he was thus an unwilling witness to the truth of all that I said, of those places. — Only with this infamous slave I had forsworn all patience ; it might seem imprudent, but to batter such spirits in breach was often my best defence. Whenever Abdullah entered the coffee-room his audience, and even the Nejûmy, rose to the black village governor, and I remained sitting. — Amm Mohammed, when I twitted him, at home, answered cheerfully ' that he did not lout to Abdullah, but to the Dowla.' — If any man were displeased, I answered them not. Abdullah, at such times, sitting silent, and a little confused, waited that some other should take up the word to censure me, as his bully Sirûr ; — and no man besides was well affected to the Siruân. Sheykh Sâlih one afternoon coming in after me, — " Room (cries the bellowing voice of Sirûr) for sheykh Sâlih, rise ! make room, Khalîl, for the sheykh." — " Sâlih, I said, may find another seat." Abdullah, who felt himself a slave, might not, in such thing, question with the white Nasrâny ; and Sâlih mildly let his lame weight down in the next place. Sirûr murmured, and barked, so I turned and said to him plainly, " I have wandered in many lands, many years, and with a swine such as thou art, I have not met in any place." The timid Hajâz audience were astonished at my words ; the most stared into the fire, and mused in their hearts that the Nasrâny had not said amiss. Abdullah rolled himself, rose a little from me in his seat, and looked down ; — the Nejûmy was present, whom he feared. Sirûr made a countenance not to hear, and " What is it ? (he enquired of the next sitters) eigh ! tell me what has Khalîl said ? " But they, as Arabs, where is matter of contention, held their peace ; and seeing that none favoured him, he found not another word. — " The slave, said Amm Mohammed, as we came home, has not the heart of a chicken ! "

All their tillage is light. The husbandmen go out after sunrise, when they have eaten, to the plantations. They plough with a pair of their small oxen, and when they have broken a *fuddân*, or hide of the mouldy earth, in the few hours before high noon, they think it is enough! Their plough is little more than a heavy sharpened stake, which may stir the soil to the depth of an handbreadth. Another day it will be sown down with the same hasty hands; there is no dressing, and this is all their care till the harvest, save in their hour in the week of the public water, when they will let in the brook upon their field, and it floods at once all the pans of irrigation. Thus one man's hands may minister to the field labour of a Kheybar household, though their acres be many. In the spring time they marry the palm blossoms, and lop the sere leaf-branches: the villager, armed with a heavy bill, hitches himself upon the scaly palm stem sitting in a sling of palm-bast. Sâlih, the sheykh of Kheybar, was a cripple; he sat continually at home, and a slave lad tilled all his possessions. Haseyn's two hands, — the lad was not yet sixteen years of age, — sufficed for nearly all his father's husbandry. In this Kheybar is unlike the Nejd oases, that [saving in the Húrda] here is no well labour; they may keep holiday all the days of the week and go nearly empty-handed. When it is hot noon they think it time that the people of God should rest from worldly toil, — the sun is already hot over their black heads even in the winter season; they come home to the street shadows, and eat dates in their suffas. They sit abroad, in the idle afternoons, on the public clay benches; and some will take part in, and some look upon the others' pastimes, as the *bîát*: some of the younger sort carry out their long guns to the palms a-birding. — They play bîát at Kheybar not with two but with seven rows of seven pits each. The negro women sit in their house-tops platting palm-straws, and often singing at their labour.

After the sun's going down the young men blow their double pipe of reeds, *mizmàr*, through the village ways: and most evenings they gathered in the Saheyn or in the other open place, *er-Rahabba*. Then the great tambour was fetched, and they kindled a fire of palm leaf-stalks to give them light to the dance. — The young men step counter, lifting their black shanks to the measure, which is beaten to them with loud stirring strokes; and smiting swords to bucklers they bless the shimmering blades about their shining black faces. They tread forth, training the shifting-feet, and beat the ground; and winding their bodies, they come on anew, with a boisterous song, — and that is some thousand-times-repeated simple verse. Their sword dance may last an hour or two ; and commonly there stands a bevy, to look on, of the black but comely village lasses, who at the first sound of the tambour have run down from the mothers' suffas : or those maidens dance apart. Many times when I came by them, returning homeward from Amm Mohammed, with my flaming palm-torch, the young men redoubled their warlike rumour ; and they that had them fired their pistols, there was a sudden brandishing of cutlasses aloft, and with vehement cries, they clattered them on their shields : they all showed me the white teeth, and shouted " aha, aha, Khalîl ! "

Many a night they kept this morris dance in the Saheyn, and the uneasy light of their bonfire shining in at our casement, the thunder-dints of the tambour, and the uncivil uproar of the negro voices, wasted our rest, which was our only refreshment at Kheybar. — Then the poor infirm Amân could not contain his illhumour : " A wildfire, he said, fall upon them ! akhs ! who but the Kheyâbara might suffer such a trouble of beastly noises ? " Upon the great feast *ayd eth-thahîa* there was all day a dinning of the tambour and a dancing through the town, to the Saheyn. Where finding my comrade who sat drooping upon the public benches, " How, I said, always musing ! hast thou not a light foot to lift with the rest in this feast ? be merry man whilst thou art alive." The poor Galla smiled a moment and forgot his melancholy ; then he responded, with a reproachful look, " I am a *Tourk* as thou art a Tourk : the Turks hold aloof from the people's levities."

Amm Mohammed said to me of the Kheyâbara, " They are *ahl hàwà* and *wàhamy*, an aery, whimsical people." Even he (a city Moslem) reproved their blowing the mizamîr, for the sound of the shrilling reeds is profane in their grave religious hearing : but the horrid swelling din of the tambour pleases them wonderfully. He said to me, " The tambour is the music-sound [the organ-tones] of the religion of Islam." — Herdsmen and nomad children blow up shawms of green grass stalks in the sweet spring season ; the toy is named by them *hawwâma*.

The Nejûmy's third younger brother, who two years ere this had been killed by a ghrazzu of Jeheyna in the way hither from Medina, was nigh the end of his life initiated in that strange mystery of Asiatic religions, which is yet practised by certain derwishes in Mohammedan countries. There is a school of them at Damascus, and I have found certain of them in the W. Bárada. They wound themselves, in their fury ; and it seems to us, without after hurt ! In festival processions, roused by the religious din of the tambour, and inflamed by the fanatical people's shouting, those unhappy men rip up their bellies, strike skewers through their two cheeks, and stab knives into the fleshy parts of their bodies. All this we may see them do; and after three days they are whole again in appearance! Amm Mohammed told me, gravely, 'It might be by a medicine; it was no trick, — and this he had ascertained from his brother, who had never deceived him.'

One day when we were at our garden labour a company of villagers went over the figgera, to gather wood. Dakhîlullah and another remained to keep watch from a rock above the Sefsáfa, where a rude summer barrack had been built of clay for the Medina soldiery. An hour passed: then suddenly they cried to the Nejûmy, 'They saw smoke as of shooting whither the wood gatherers had gone.' Amm Mohammed caught up his matchlock, and leaving his mantle and kerchief with me, bareheaded, and in his shirt as he was, and without sandals, the strong man ran out with them to the rescue. Others saw them run, and the alarm was soon in the village. Abdullah the Siruân called his Ageylies to arm and follow him; every Kheybary had taken his weapons, and they all hied over the Harra. Also Amân tottered forth, with his dying face, in the wild rocks, under the load of his musket: but Abdullah bade the sick askar return to his rest.

Mohammed's béled lay somewhat open; he had often warned me not to be found there alone, for dread of murderous shots from the béleds about: but if I returned towards the town I must meet with hotheads running to battle, with arms in their hands; besides Amm Mohammed had left his clothing with me, and I thought it were not for the valiant man to return through the streets unclad. I remained therefore to labour in the garden: and in those long hours of silence, I was a worshipper in the temple, and a devout witness of the still life of Nature. And when I paused great herb-eating rats sallied from the four ruinous clay walls: every rat cropped a nettle stalk, and carried back the tall leaf in his mouth to his cave, and returned for more pasture.

At the mid-afternoon I heard such a warlike hubbub, that I supposed the enemy must be breaking into our village: the shouting and shots seemed to be in the midst of the béleds. — Now came Amm Mohammed out of breath, and he wondered to find me yet there. Seeing his heated looks, I enquired quickly, " What of the battle ? " — " It was but a ghrazzu, and we have beaten them off ; there was some far-off shooting, — no man is hurt. And this noise of shooting (in the air) is of the eyyâl returning : must they not brave it a little and cool their black blood ere they enter the houses : — and now hie thee ! sheykh Khalîl, let us homeward and eat támr."

After supper we went to the soldiers' kahwa ; where they chatted of that day's adventure. Abdullah cursed the Beduw and all their father's kin ; and he lamented for his tender black feet, which had been bruised upon the ruggedness of the Harra. The Nejûmy answered, with his pleasant Turkish adulation, which seemed an irony in so manly and free a mouth, " Poor thou ! I do pity thee, Abdullah ; the sharp lavas made as well my (naked) soles to bleed." When we sat at home I blamed this dissimulation ; but the Nejûmy answered smiling, " It is not amiss to smooth him with a fair word, since such is the way of them : slave, and cursed one, and tyrannical fool, though he be, yet is he not here the officer of the Dowla ? "

The wood-gatherers had been met by a Bishr ghrazzu, who stripped the more forward of them. Then succour arriving, the Beduw (who saw many long guns among them) held off, and the villagers ran in to save their asses : there was after this only a distant firing of matchlocks, and the Nomads rode from them. In all the village, only the lame sheykh Sâlih had stayed at home. Hearing that I remained in the garden Abdullah said, " You might have been assailed there, O Foolhardy ; and if one day thou art killed thus, the blame will be laid upon me : now do no more so, lest I put thee in prison ! — Now sirs, let everyone speak his mind, — and we are the Dowla ! I say, for the time to come how may we bridle these insolencies of the Beduw ? " — Abdullah himself slept upon it, and, at the morrow's coffee-drinking, he cries, " I have found it ! and clapped his thigh, *âs' Ullah, temmém,* yes, and it please God, perfectly ; — *ana werrîk,* I shall show you, that I know the office of a governor at Kheybar ! There will, I say, be twenty horse-riders stationed at Kheybar : this shall be my request when next I write to the Bashat el-Medina ! "

Their wood-gathering is often with peril ; since not content, as in the most oases, to burn the sickly reeking palm fuel, the Kheyâbara go to seek the sere sammara timber (with asses for carriage and their housewives, who will bear home some upon their heads) far over the

Harra. — There was a murmuring now in the town, because Abdullah imposed upon them a contribution of this hard-won fuel for himself, and for the soldiery.

The Dowla was at Kheybar now five years : I enquired of prudent villagers what comparison they made of the present and their former state. They answered, that though the zikát of Ibn Rashîd was a little more than is levied by the Dowla, yet Ibn Rashîd's exactors, which were a dozen armed thelûl riders, came upon them in the date harvest only : they remained few days, and theirs was a short tyranny ; whereas this now resident Dowla is continually grieving them. Ibrahîm the Kády added in my ear, *Wa shúghrol-hum bes en-náhab*, ALL THEIR BUSINESS IS RAPINE. — Nevertheless the Dowla defend the villagers from the Beduw, that beforetime maltreated them, binding and beating them, naming them theirs and their fathers' slaves to do all their wild behests, as to bring in forage. They not seldom forcibly entered their clients' houses, to make booty of grain ; Beduins have outraged the negro women, and they behaved themselves in all things inordinately, as masters : and whereso they thrust into any village house, a sheep or else a goat must be slain to their supper. In the date harvest before the Turkish occupation, Misshel the Auájy had sacked Sâlih the sheykh's house ! — Sâlih was pleased to hear me condemn the churlish hospitality of that great Beduin sheykh.

At the hands of Ibn Rashîd's men they fared little better : for whereso the Nejders found any gay sword or matchlock among them, they carried it away 'for the Emir's armoury,' enforcing their wills with cruel blows ; and the Kheyâbara could have no redress at Hâyil ! — At length the villagers of Umm Kîda, who had been sorely vexed and mishandled by them, sent messengers to the Pasha of Medina, beseeching him to receive them into the protection of the Dowla : — and they were heartened to this by their W. Aly partners.

That good Pasha — his name is not now in my remembrance — was an uncorrupt and charitable personage, such as there are only few among them. He had lately distributed copies of the koran to all who could read them, in these parts: — the copy which Amm Mohammed possessed was one of them. — The Pasha lent a pious ear to the tale of these black villagers : he heard their griefs and the name (Ibn Rashîd) of that great sheykh who oppressed them, and where their valleys lay, which they affirmed to be in his lordship's province ; and the good gentleman promised them some relief.

— From that time the Turks began to think of the utility of Kheybar, a name which had been hitherto as good as unknown in Medina. The summer after the Pasha sent thither some companies of infantry with a squadron of horse, and a troop of Ageyl, — it might be the year 1874. They came in five marches to Kheybar, where they found none to oppose them.

The Beduins descended peaceably, and gathered their dates with the Kheyâbara : but in the day of their departure they found watches of the soldiery, set in all the heads of the ways, to levy a toll of half a real upon every outborne camel-load of their own fruits ! The Beduw had never heard in the khála of any duty of theirs toward the Dowla ; besides many of them had not a piece of silver ! The poor nomads spend that little money they bring with them, in the harvest-market, for their clothing and about their other needs.

The tribes descended in the second season of the Medina occupation : but seeing the guard lessened they began to contemn them and would not pay the taxes. " Let the Dowla take them, they said, if they would have them." — The Medina government saw that they must increase the summer camp at Kheybar ; and the Bishr were now in heart against them, by the setting on of Ibn Rashîd. Early therefore in the third summer a regiment, with cavalry, and a troop of Ageyl riders, were sent to Kheybar. Their tents were pitched at the Sefsáfa ; also the Húsn was occupied and repaired by the Ageyl, under this Abdullah Siruân.

The date harvest approached, and the Annezy descended from the Harra, the Fukara came first. Their yearly menzil is at *es-Suffuk*, under the Asmîeh ; and there the principal sheukh, Motlog, Rahŷel and Zeyd, have their good clay (summer) houses. They had sworn, by the way, to the Bishr to take part with them, both against the Dowla and against the W. Aly.

The Turkish officers rode that night to visit the Fejîr in their encampment. The mejlis of the sheykhs and tribesmen assembled immediately in Motlog's clay beyt, " to hear the words of the Dowla." — Motlog and the sheukh answered, " We are come hither to gather the fruits of our own palms ; and if ye be at war with Bishr, we are for neither of you." — " Do ye promise this ? " — " We promise you." — When the officers returned they appointed a station to the W. Aly for the morrow ; bidding them observe the Fejîr, and be in readiness if need were to resist them.

When the sun was rising the Aarab were seen from the Húsn " like locusts " leaping upon the Harra ; the Siruân beat a loud alarm upon the tambour. The soldiery at the Sefsáfa had slept upon their arms ! — Eighty Ageyls were sent out, as light skirmishers, against the Beduw. When a noise of their shooting began to be heard, upon the figgera, the colonel who commanded bade his soldiers (of the line) not to budge from about him. He entered himself the clay chamber, which was his lodging, and locked himself in, and (because his casements were made low to the ground, to let in the freshing air) he lay down flat upon the floor !

— The Beduins came bravely on with their shouting and singing ; they were armed with spears and swords, only few had matchlocks. The Ageyl, that had advanced dispersedly over the rugged Harra, fell back before them, until they might all run together, — then they stayed ; and so they returned in a body against the nomads. Thus running upon both sides and shooting, they were long in distant battle ; and the Ageylies had the better. At length one fell upon the side of the Beduw, who was a principal sheykh : then the Aarab ceased firing, their powder also was nearly spent, and they turned to fly. Misshel (their great sheykh) made haste to save himself upon his thelûl ; and first drew bridle, they say, at a day's distance.

As for the colonel, at the Sefsáfa, when the noise of their shooting had somewhile ceased in his ears, he rose and came forth. The coward had heard the scurrilous tongues of his own soldiery infaming him, 'the dog-son vile traitor to the Dowla, that had not sent them to the support of those few, whose lives were so long jeopardised upon the Harra.' — This man is said to have lost a regiment in el-Yémen, and to have purchased another colonelship for his money.

The armed villagers of Kheybar (Amm Mohammed was their captain), in the Húsn, had fired with powder against their land partners, till one of them fell wounded ; and only then they rammed down lead. — The Fukara held themselves coy ; but when they saw Bishr broken and flying, they ran in and made booty of their booths and utensils. Their wild deed was not afterward reproved, nor for such had the Bishr any rancour against them, — they had else lost their stuff to the Dowla ; and in like case they themselves had done the like ! — Much more strange and unnatural was the deed of the Bishr geyatîn ! for they took part with the Dowla, and with the black villagers, against their own nomad brethren. Besides, we have seen, there were certain Ageylies of the same tribe, who fought against their own tribesfolk.

One of those traitors fell the same year into his people's hands; but after vehement words they let him go; and Misshel had since sent to say, that any such guilty tribesman might return to him when he would, and nothing should be laid against him: — so easy are the Aarab to forgive every treachery! *for they put all to the account of necessity.* Those men having served some years under the government of Medina, the arrears of their pay now amounted to hundreds of reals; and in this was all the hope of their lives for the time to come. Amm Mohammed's wife's brother, a (Bishr) gatûny, was with the villagers' cattle in W. Jellâs; but as ever he heard the shots he went to join the part of his nomad kinsmen. When it was evening, Amm Mohammed went thither with an armed company of the young Kheyâbara, to bring home the beasts of the village; and he led his brother-in-law secretly in again to Kheybar. The Aarab were now out of heart, and those with him were strong-bodied young negroes, more sturdy, he said, to fight than the Beduw. If Beduins met with him he thought he had only to say, " It is I the Nejûmy, and these with me Kheyâbara, come to drive our cattle home," and they would let him pass; they were partners, and this quarrel was only with the tyrannical Dowla.

After night-fall, the watch on the Húsn heard a sound of distant chanting, in the palms: — some of the Beduw were gathering their dates in W. Zeydîeh. Then Amm Mohammed led down a band of villagers to go and take them by surprise. They found the nomads' camels couched without those plantations; and drew their swords and houghed them. Then the Nejûmy and the Kheyâbara with (the battle-cry) *Ullahu akhbar*, ' God is All Might,' leapt over the orchard walls, and fired their pieces. The nomads within the grove, hearing shots and the shout of their enemies rushing upon them, ran to save themselves, and broke out at the further end of the palms. — Mohammed and the black villagers returned well laden with the flesh of the enemies' camels: and an hundred Kheybar households supped well at the cost of their Beduin partners: — so ended this warfare of a day; but that will be long remembered among them.

On the morrow the colonel sent to bring in the heads of the fallen desert men whom he called ' rebels to the Dowla.' — Amân had counted eighty heads laid out at the Sefsáfa, — a lesson of barbarous rulers to their subject people ! A post rider carried their ears, powdered with salt, in a sack, to Medina : — five reals for every pair of ears would be distributed to the poor soldiery. Of the Ageyl two men were fallen : one of them being infirm had been overrun at little distance, — his brain-pan was found shattered by a Beduin mace ; but none saw it. That poor man was an Albanian and Amân's amm, who had paid the price of his childhood to the merchant driver at Jidda : he had early enfranchised him, and a kindly affection remained in the gentle breast of Amân towards his housefather. The poor Galla showed me the grave-heap of his dead " uncle," and afflicted himself that he could not garnish it, in this deep misery of the strangers' life at Kheybar.

Amân told me he fled in the beginning, when the Ageyl were put to the worse, till he might go no more for weakness : and where first he found an hollow place he cowered down among the rocks, hoping in God to be hidden ; but gazing backward he saw an huge Beduwy with a long lance, that was stealing upon him. Then he fired his musket from the hip and fled affrighted, without looking again. He heard the enemies leaping all about him, whilst he hasted as he could and ran feebly on the Harra, from stone to stone ; and ' the Lord turned away their eyes that they should not see him.' — He said of the colonel, " He was a Stambûly, a cursed man, who cared not though we had all perished ; and he was only colonel for his money, for aha ! in the Dowla all is now bought and sold ! " — They pretend that ' Ibn Rashîd sent three hundred men of Shammar to help the Bishr ' : they found also certain green tubes, where the shooting had been, which ' were Persian cartridges from Ibn Rashîd.'

Amm Mohammed, a loyal citizen of Medina, thought better of the public security since the occupation : from that time he began to buy palms, and to be established at Kheybar. — The soldiery also are pilferers of orchards ; and the villagers say, " We cannot lead armed men to the officers, and if we accuse any soldiers in the camp they will answer, ' Ye are mistaken,' and so we are dismissed with a scorn : " the Medina soldiery are mostly Shwâm. Amm Mohammed, deriding their Syrian speech, told me his adventure with some of them that climbed over his orchard walls. The clownish fellows, seeing so swarthy a man, clad only in a tunic and kerchief, mistook him for one of the Aarab. Certain of them would have empressed his ass ; and the churls were confused when the strong man began to drive them with his drawn sword to their menzil : and there they saw the captain rise to greet him ! — Although he entreated for them, they were led away to be beaten.

A better order has been established at Kheybar ; gates have been put to the village streets, and every housewife must daily sweep before her own doors, or be beaten by the Siruân ; — and Abdullah told me he had beaten many. The ways were formerly foul with pestilent ordures, in the giddy heat of the summer sun ; and the passing stranger or soldier who had drawn there his breath, was in danger to fall down anon, deadly sick. In the first year 'well nigh all the soldiers died' of cholera and the valley fever. Amm Mohammed thought that hardly a score of them lived to re-enter the walls of Medina ! and the negro villagers now say this proverb with horrid laughter ; " *Kheybar is the grave of the asàker.*" " Kheybar, said the melancholy Amân, in his Albanian-learned Arabic, is *kábr ed-dunnia*, the whole world's sepulchre." There came a military doctor from Medina, with new remedies, to cure the sick ; but he himself sickened in the morning, and he was laid a yard deep, in his shroud, ere midday, in the subbakha earth — dead at Kheybar ! " I have cleansed the town, quoth Abdullah, and now they see it done, even this people is grateful to me."

Kheybar is but one long thelûl journey from Medina, yet lying out of the common ways even this name, as said, had been scarce known in the Holy City ; or it sounded in their ears with a superstitious strangeness, — for who has not heard told in the Haj fables, of the Yahûd Kheybar ? At Medina is an iron-plated door (it closes now the soldiers' quarters), which passes for the ancient castle-gate of Kheybar : " Our lord Aly, they say, flung forth the leaves from his two hands when he won the place ; and one of them fell down upon a hill at Medina, but the other fell at Bagdad." It is said likewise of the mountain *Ehad* near to el-Medina, whereon is the sepulchre of *Hamzy* uncle of the Néby, that of old time this jebel was at Kheybar but it has since flitted to the Holy City : and some of their wise men contend that J. Hamzy was formerly at Bagdad. The rude Moslemîn can persuade themselves in this sort : " J. Hamzy stands at Medina ; but was formerly in another part ; therefore this mountain has removed hither ! " Upon a time I laughed a little with Amm Mohammed, " Your lord Aly threw stiffly ! it is about a score of the longest cannon shots to Medina." — " But this is not all, Khalîl, for they say that once our lord Aly stood and lifted the universal world." — " And where then was your lord Aly ? must he not stand out of the world to remove it ? " The Nejûmy answered, " Now I think upon it, sheykh Khalîl, I am well-nigh of thy opinion, that these are but the sayings of vain superstition and not in the religion." I made Amm Mohammed a globe of the clay we cast up in our digging, and portraied the seas and continents upon it. He was pleased, but could not easily follow my words, since the whole world is flat in their estimation : he let his tools fall and cried, laughing, " Said not the Kheyâbara well of thee, sheykh Khalîl, that thou art a magician ? — but hyak, let us homeward and eat támr."

It is certain that the Jews have at this day a fabulous opinion of Kheybar ; some of them (in the East) have told me that 'the Yahûd Kheybar are the *Beny Rechab*.' — And even Orientalists in Europe have asked me " Be there now no Jews at all at Kheybar ? " I have known a missionary to the Jews in the Levant who at his first coming thither, if he had not fallen sick, would have set forth, riding on an ass, to pass the great deserts toward Kheybar ; moved with a youthful zeal to convert those fabulous lost sheep to the religion of the Nasâra ! But let none any more jeopardy his life for Kheybar ! — I would that these leaves might save the deaths of some : and God give me this reward of my labour ! for who will, he may read in them all the tale of Kheybar. Merchants of Kasîm have related to me, that " there are descendants of the Yahûd Kheybar in Bagdad, who are accounted noble (*asîly*) among the Jews ; there are besides rich traders of them in India ; " — but their words were, I found, as strange tales in the ears of the respectable (Bagdad) merchant Jews in Bombay.

In the third week of my being in this captivity at Kheybar, the slave-spirited Abdullah wrote to the Pasha of Medina. Since the village governor knew no letters, the black sheykh Sâlih was his scrivener and wrote after him : " Upon such a day of the last month, when the gates of Kheybar were opened in the morning, we found a stranger without waiting to enter. He told us that a Beduwy with whom he arrived in the night had left him there and departed. When we asked him what man he was ? he answered ' an Engleysy ' ; and he acknowledged himself to be a Nasrâny. And I not knowing what there might be in this matter have put the stranger in ward, and have seized his baggage, in which we have found some books and a paper from Ibn Rashîd. So we remain in your Lordship's obedience, humbly awaiting the commandments of your good Lordship." — " Now well, said Abdullah ; and seal it, Sâlih. Hast thou heard this that I have written, Khalîl ? " — " Write only the truth. When was I found at your gates ? I rode openly into Kheybar." — " Nay, but I must write thus, or the Pasha might lay a blame upon me and say, ' Why didst thou suffer him to enter ? ' — That Heteymy lodged in the place all night, and he was a gomâny! also his thelûl lay in the street, and I did not apprehend him : — Oh God ! where was then my mind ? I might [the thief murmured] have taken his dromedary ! Listen, everyone of you here present ! for the time to come ye are to warn me when any strangers arrive, that if there be anything against them, they may be arrested immediately."

Abdullah had in these days seized the cow of an orphan, — for which all the people abhorred him — a poor minor without defence, that he might drink her milk himself : so he wrote another letter to the Pasha, " I have sequestered a cow for arrears of taxes, and will send her unto your lordship ; the beast is worth fifteen reals at Kheybar, and might be sold for fifty at el-Medina." In a third paper he gave up his account of the village tithing to the Dowla : all the government exactions at Kheybar were together 3600 reals. [For this a regiment of soldiers must march every year to (their deaths at) Kheybar !] Abdullah's men being not fully a score were reckoned in his paysheet at forty. If any man died, he drew the deceased's salary himself to the end of his term of service. Once every year he will be called to muster his asâkar ; but then with some easy deceit, as by hiring or compelling certain of the village, and clothing them for a day or two, he may satisfy the easy passing over of his higher officers ; who full of guilty bribes themselves look lightly upon other men's criminal cases. Abdullah added a postscript. " It may please your honour to have in remembrance the poor askars that are hungry and naked, and they are looking humbly unto your good Lordship for some relief." In thirty and two months they had not been paid ! — what wonder though such wretches, defrauded by the Ottoman government, become robbers ! Now they lifted up their weary hearts to God and the Pasha, that a new *khúsna*, or ' paymaster's chest of treasure,' from Stambûl might be speedily heard of at el-Medina. These were years of wasting warfare in Europe ; of which the rumour was heard confusedly at this unprofitable distance. So

Abdullah sealed his letters which had cost him and his empressed clerk three days' labour, until their black temples ached again.

These were days for me sooner of dying than of life ; and the felonious Abdullah made no speed to deliver me. The government affairs of the village were treated-of over cups of coffee ; and had Sâlih not arrived betimes, Abdullah sent for him with authority. The unhappy sheykh with a leg short came then in haste, and the knocking of his staff might be heard through the length of the street, whilst the audience sat in silence, and the angry blood seemed to boil in the black visage of Abdullah. When he came up, ' Why wast thou not here ere this, sheykh Sâlih ? ' he would say, in a voice which made the old man tremble ; Sâlih answered nothing, only rattling his inkstand he began to pluck out his reed pens. The village sheykh had no leisure now to look to his own affairs ; and for all this pain he received yearly from the government of Medina the solemn mockery of a scarlet mantle : but his lot was now cast in with the Dowla which he had welcomed ; and he might lose all, and were even in danger of his head, if Ibn Rashîd entered again.

It is the custom of these Orientals to sit all day in their coffee halls, with only a resting-while at noon. To pass the daylight hours withdrawn from the common converse of men were in their eyes unmanly ; and they look for no reasonable fellowship with the hareem. Women are for the house-service ; and only when his long day is past, will the householder think it time to re-enter to them. Abdullah drank coffee and tobacco in his soldiers' kahwa ; where it often pleased him to entertain his company with tales of his old prowess and prosperity at Medina : and in his mouth was that round kind of utterance of the Arabic coffee-drinkers, with election of words, and dropping with the sap of human life. Their understanding is like the moon, full upon this side of shining shallow light ; but all is dimness and deadness upon the side of science. He told us what a gallant horseman he had been, — he was wont to toss a javelin to the height, wellah, of the minarets in Medina ; and how he went like a gentleman in the city, and made his daily devout prayers in the *háram* ; nor might he ever be used to the rudeness of thelûl riding, because nature had shaped him a gentle cavalier. He had ridden once in an expedition almost to el-Héjr ; and as they returned he found an hamlet upon a mountain, whose inhabitants till that day, wellah, had not seen strangers. He had met with wild men when he rode to Yanba, — that was upon the mountain Rodwa; those hill-folk [Jeheyna] besides a cotton loin-cloth, go naked. One of them an ancient, nearly ninety years of age, ran on before his horse, leaping like a wild goat among the rocks; and that only of his good will, to be the stranger's guide. He boasted he had bought broken horses for little silver, and sold them soon for much; so fortunate were his stars at Medina. In the city he had a chest four cubits long, a cubit deep and wide; and in his best time it was full of reals, and lightly as they came to his hand he spent them again. He had a Galla slave-lad at Medina who went gaily clad, and had sweetmeats and money, so that he wondered; but upon a day, his infamy being known, Abdullah drew a sword and pursued his bondsman in the street and wounded him, and sold him the day after to one of his lovers for five reals. — It seems that amongst them a householder may main or even slay his bond-servant in his anger and go unpunished, and the law is silent; for as Moses said, HE IS HIS CHATTEL.

Sometimes he would speak of his adverse fortunes, that he might show us also his criminal audacity. Upon a time he was brought before the military court for disobedience; and the Pasha commanded to take away his girdle weapons. — Among them there is not a greater despite than to lay forcible hands upon a man's person. As the 'archer' approached, Abdullah drew one of his pistols, and fired, but missed him; and drawing the other, "This (he said to the Pasha) is for thine own head:" the Governor of Medina answered, "Is he a man, or a sheytân?" Then they disarmed and bound him. "I lay many weeks in the ward, quoth Abdullah, and oh! what was the horror of that prison, a pit, and the damp ground, and the creeping vermin! I bribed the gaoler every day, wellah with a real, to leave me a little while unloosed, only that I might rub myself; but when there came a new Pasha, I was shortly in favour again." He told with wonder of some offenders who cast by night into the city prison, had wound and wrung their limbs quite out of the gyves and escaped; and one of them, because his foot could not pass the fetter, had cut away the heel, and was fled with his fellows! — The like is mentioned by Herodotus, of a Greek prisoner who never afterward showed himself to be of a worthy or manly nature: — for will not a rat as desperately deliver herself, leaving even her limb in the trap?

Abdullah carried the ensign and had borne himself well in the Ageyl expeditions from Medina. Twice he boasted he had been enveloped by the enemies, *wa fúkny rubby*, but his Lord delivered him. — He could speak too, with the sententious unction of the Oriental towns, of the homely human life. 'There were, he said, two honest men of even fortune, that one was seen ever alike freshly clad, the other went ill-favouredly clad : — and wot ye wherefore, Sirs ? — I shall show you. That one had a good diligent housewife, but the other was the husband of a foolish woman. — And who is the best of women ? I shall tell you, — and mark well these be the words of the Néby, — it is she that can keep silence !' He had too some peaceable tales of the men of God, of Islam, as this [the like is read in the Greek Legends of the Eremite Fathers] : — There was an holy man who passed the days of his mortality in adoration ; so that he forgate to eat. Then the Lord commanded ; and the neighbour ants ascending upon his dreaming flesh, continually cast their grains into the saint's mouth and fostered him.

Abdullah was sick some days with the valley fever, and his wife also. He had taken her at Kheybar ; the young woman was of a copper colour and daughter of the sheykh's brother. Abdullah desired my remedies, but his conscience durst not trust the Nasrâny ; he turned therefore for relief to Sâlih who had an old book of remedies and enchantments. Sâlih read therein, ' that one should drink a coffee-cupful of butter with pepper in the morning fasting ; ' he wrote also a charm for Abdullah, to be tied in a knot of his kerchief. — " Is he sick, the *melâun?* exclaimed Amm Mohammed, now would God he might die also !" Almost none that were not Beduw asked me for medicines : in the winter-time there is not much fever at Kheybar.

In his fever days Abdullah, laying aside the cares of office, would ease his aching brows, in telling us endless Oriental tales (of Medina) : — these are the townspeople's solace, as the public plays are pleasant hours of abandonment to the citizens of Europe. The matter is most what that which was heart's joy to the good old knight in the noble English poet, " When any man hath been in poor estate and climbeth up and wexeth fortunate." But their long process grows in European ears (for tediousness) to a confused babble of sounds. He told of the climbing up of the fortunate son from the low degree to wedding with kings' daughters ; mingling in his tale many delightful standings by the way, — perils and despairs, gifts of precious jewels, the power of talismans, the finding of hid treasures, and the blissful rencounters as "𝔱𝔥𝔢 𝔧𝔬𝔶 𝔱𝔥𝔞𝔱 𝔩𝔞𝔰𝔱𝔢𝔱𝔥 𝔢𝔳𝔢𝔯𝔪𝔬," of separated affections; the sound of the trumpet and the battle, and thereafter the secure and happy days. — Yet their fables appear to us barbarous and out of joint, and (as all their dedale art) thing which cannot satisfy our conscience, inasmuch as they are irrational. Amm Mohammed tasted these tales and the lively invention of Abdullah; and such were pleasant entertainments to the Medina men and full of happy wonder to the Gallas. When they praised his telling, " But how much better had it been, said he, if I might have told it you in *Turki*," (which is an high sounding tongue and spoken with a full mouth). If any nomads were present or geyatîn, I saw them sit and weary themselves to listen; they found no savour in Abdullah's brain-sick matter, neither understood they very well those quaint terms of townsfolk.

The Kheyâbara inured to the short tyranny of the Beduins were not broken to this daily yoke of the Dowla. They had no longer sanctuary in their own houses, for Abdullah summoned them from their hearths at his list; their hareem were beaten before their faces; — and now his imposition of firewood! Abdullah sent for the chief murmurers of the village, and looking gallantly, he sought with the unctuous words of Turkish governors to persuade them. " Are not the soldiers quartered by order of the Dowla upon you in this village? and I say, sirs, they look unto you for their fuel, — what else should maintain this kahwa fire? which is for the honour of Kheybar, and where ye be all welcome. Listen! — under his smiles he looked dangerous, and spoke this proverb which startled me: — the military authority is what? *It is like a stone, whereupon if anyone fall he will be broken, but upon whom the Dowla shall fall he will be broken in pieces.* I speak to you as a friend, *the Dowla has a mouth gaping wide* [it is a criminal government which devours the subject people], and that cries evermore *hât-hât-hât*, give! give! — And what is this? O ye the Kheyâbara, I am mild heretofore; I have well deserved of you: but if ye provoke me to lay upon you other burdens, ye shall see, and I will show it you! It had been better for you that you had not complained for the wood, for now I think to tax your growing tobacco. — I have reckoned that taking one field in eight, I shall raise from Kheybar a thousand reals, and this I have left to you free hitherto. And whatsoever more I may lay upon you, trust me Sirs it will be right well received, and for such I shall be highly commended at Medina."

Kheybar is three sheykh's sûks. *Atewy*, a sturdy carl, chief of the upper sûk under the Húsn, answered for himself and his, 'that they would no longer give the wood.' Abdullah sent for him; but Atewy would not come. Abdullah imprisoned two of Atewy's men: Atewy said it should not be so; so the men of his sûk caught up bucklers and cutlasses and swore to break up the door and release them. Half of the Ageyl askars at Kheybar could not, for sickness, bear the weight of their weapons; and the strong negroes, when their blood was moved, contemned the Siruân's pitiful band of feeble wretches. Abdullah sent out his bully Sirûr, with the big brazen voice, to threaten the rioters: but the Galla coward was amazed at their settled countenance, and I saw him sneak home to Abdullah; who hearing that the town was rising, said to the father of his village housewife, "And wilt thou also forsake me?" The man answered him, "My head is with thy head!"

Abdullah who had often vaunted his forwardness to the death in any quarrel of the Dowla, now called his men to arm; he took down his pair of horseman's pistols from the wall, with the ferocity of the Turkish service, and descended to the street; determined 'to persuade the rioters, and if no wellah he would shed blood.' — He found the negroes' servile heat somewhat abated: and since they could not contend with 'the Dowla,' they behaved themselves peaceably: Abdullah also promised them to release the captives.

Abdullah re-entered the kahwa, — and again he summoned Atewy; who came now, — and beginning some homely excuses, "Well, they cared not, he said, though they gave a little wood for Abdullah's sake, only they would not be compelled." Abdullah, turning to me, said, "*Wheu!* now hast thou seen, Khalîl, what sheytâns are the Kheyâbara! and wast thou not afraid in this hurly-burly? I am at Kheybar for the Dowla, and these soldiers are under me; but where wert thou to-day, if I had not been here?" — "My host's roof had sheltered me, and after that the good will of the people." — "Now let the Kheyâbara, he cried, see to it, and make him no more turmoils; or by Ullah he would draw on his boots and ride to Medina! and the Pasha may send you another governor, not easy as I am, but one that will break your backs and devour you: and as for me, wellah, I shall go home with joy to mine own house and children."

I enquired of Mohammed of those three suks (which are three

kinships or factions) at Kheybar ; and they are here set down, as he told me, for an example of the Arabian corporate life. [v. Vol. I. p. 527.] — The kindred of the *Khutherân*, which are above half the inhabitants of Kheybar, their head is Sâlih : they are three affinities, *el-Kirrân*, which are Sâlih's alliance ; the second *el-Jerràr*, sheykh *Auwàd* ; — his is an hereditary office, to be arbiter in the village ; the man was unlettered. Black-skinned as the rest, but of almost Arabic lineaments, he was called at Kheybar a Moghreby ; the land of his fathers, he told me, was *Sûs* in Morocco. — The third affinity *Noâba*, sheykh Ibrahîm, whose is the hereditary office in the village to determine the midda, or ransom for manslaughter. The second kindred is *el-Muhállif*, under sheykh Atewy, in four affinities, *el-Hadèyd*, *Guâd*, *Asheyfát*, *Sherrân*. The third kindred Amm Mohammed has not recorded, unless it were of those dwelling at Umm Kîda, whose inhabitants are named *el-Ateyfát* ; they are two affinities, the *Sellût*, — whose kinships are three, *Hennânia*, *el-Hîara*, *Afâra* — and *Mejarîd*, whose kinships are *Shellalî*, *Zîarra*, *Tueym*. In the Bishr or chief jériat of Kheybar, may be two hundred houses and more; in Umm Kîda eighty houses ; the hamlet el-Asmîeh is ten or twelve households. We may reckon at hardly one thousand all the village inhabitants of the valleys of Kheybar.

Abdullah, who knew the simple properties of numbers, told them upon his fingers in tens ; but could not easily keep the count, through his broken reckoning rising to thousands. — And devising to deliver a Turkish bill of his stewardship, he said, with a fraudulent smile : ' We may be silent upon such and such little matters, that if the Pasha should find a fault in our numbers we may still have somewhat in hand wherewith to amend it.' The unlettered governor made up these dispatches in the public ear, and turning often to his audience he enquired, ' Did they approve him, Sirs ? ' and only in some very privy matter he went up with sheykh Sâlih to indite upon his house-terrace. Abdullah hired Dakhîl (not the Menhel), one of the best of the black villagers, to carry his government budget, for four reals, to Medina. Dakhîl, who only at Kheybar, besides the Nejûmy, was a hunter, fared on foot : and because of the danger of the way he went clad (though it was mid-winter) in an old (calico) tunic ; he left his upper garment behind him.

Many heavy days must pass over my life at Kheybar, until Dakhîl's coming again ; the black people meanwhile looked with doubt and evil meaning upon the Nasrâny, — because the Pasha might send word to put me to death. Felonous were the Turkish looks of the sot Abdullah, whose robber's mind seemed to be suspended betwixt his sanguinary fanaticism and the dread remembrance of Jidda and Damascus : the brutal Sirûr was his privy counsellor. — Gallas have often an extreme hatred of this name, Nasrâny : it may be because their border tribes are in perpetual warfare with the Abyssinian Christians.

Abdullah had another counsellor whom he called his ' uncle,' — *Aly*, the religious sheykh, crier to prayers, and the village schoolmaster. Looking upon Aly's mannikin visage, full of strange variance, I thought he might be a little lunatic : — of this deformed rankling complexion, and miserable and curious humour, are all their worst fanatics. I enquired of Amm Mohammed, and he remembered that Aly's mother had died out of her mind. Aly was continually breathing in the ass's ears of Abdullah that the Nasrâny was *adu ed-dîn*, ' enemy of the faith ; ' and ' it was due to the Lord (said he) that I should perish by the sword of the Moslemîn. Let Abdullah kill me ! cries the ape-face ; and if it were he durst not himself, he might suffer the thing to be done. And if there came any hurt of it, yet faithful men before all things must observe their duty to Ullah.' — The worst was that the village sheykh Sâlih, otherwise an elder of prudent counsel, put-to his word that Aly had reason !

The Nejûmy hearing of the counsels of Abdullah cared not to dissemble his disdain. He said of Aly, " The hound, the slave ! and all the value of him [accounting him in his contempt a bondman] is ten reals : and as for the covetous fool and very ass Abdullah, the father of him bought the dam of him for fifty reals ! " — But their example heartened the baser spirits of the village, and I heard again they had threatened to shoot at the kafir, as I walked in the (walled) paths of their plantations. Amm Mohammed therefore went no more abroad, when we were together, without his good sword. And despising the black villagers he said, " They are apes, and not children of Adam ; Oh ! which of them durst meddle in my matter ? were it only of a dog or a chicken in my house ! But sheykh Khalîl eats with me every day in one dish." The strong man added, ' He would cut him in twain who laid an hand on Khalîl ; and if any of them durst sprinkle Khalîl with water, he would sprinkle him with his blood ! '

Abdullah, when we sat with him, smiled with all his Turkish smiles upon the Nejûmy ; and Amm Mohammed smiled as good to his black face again. " But (quoth he) let no man think that I am afraid of the

Dowla, nor of sixty Dowlas; for I may say, Abdullah, as once said the ostrich to the Beduwy, 'If thou come to take camels, am I not a bird? but comest thou hither a-fowling, behold, Sir! I am a camel.' So if the Aarab trouble me I am a Dowlâny, a citizen of the illustrious Medina, — where I may bear my sword in the streets [which may only officers and any visiting Beduw], because I have served the Dowla. And, if it go hard with me upon the side of the Dowla, I am *Harby*, and may betake me to the *Ferrâ* (of the Beny Amr); that is my mother's village, in the mountains [upon the middle *derb*] between the Harameyn: there I have a patrimony and an house. The people of the Ferrâ are my cousins, and there is no Dowla can fetch me from thence, neither do we know the Dowla; for the entry is strait as a gateway in the jebel, so that three men might hold it against a multitude." — And thus the Nejûmy defended my solitary part, these days and weeks and months at Kheybar; — one man against a thousand! Yet dwelling in the midst of barking tongues, with whom he must continue to live, his honest heart must sometimes quail (which was of supple temper, as in all the nomad blood). And so far he gave in to the popular humour that certain times, in the eyes of the people, he affected to shun me: for they cried out daily upon him, that he harboured the Nasrâny! — "Ah! Khalîl, he said to me, thou canst not imagine all their malice!"

Neither was this the first time that Mohammed en-Nejûmy had favoured strangers in their trouble. — A Medina tradesman was stripped and wounded in the wilderness as he journeyed to Kheybar; and he arrived naked. The black villagers are inhospitable; and the Medina citizen sitting on the public benches waited in vain that some householder would call him. At last Ahmed went by; and the stranger, seeing a white man, — one that (in this country) must needs be a fellow citizen of Medina, said to him, "What shall I do, my townsman? of whom might I borrow a few reals in this place, and buy myself clothing?" *Ahmed*: "At the street's end yonder is sitting a tall white man! ask him:" — that was Mohammed. — "Ah! Sir, said the poor tradesman, finding him; thou art so swarthy, that I had well nigh mistaken thee for a Beduwy!" Amm Mohammed led him kindly to his house and clothed him: and the wounded man sojourned with his benefactor and Ahmed two or three months, until they could send him to Medina. "And now when I come there, and he hears that I am in the city, said Amm Mohammed, he brings me home, and makes feast and rejoicing." — This human piety of the man was his thank-offering to the good and merciful Providence, that had prospered him and forgiven him the ignorances of his youth!

Another year, — it was in the time of Ibn Rashîd's government — when the Nejûmy was buying and selling dates and cotton clothing in the harvest-market at Kheybar, some Annezy men came one day haling a naked wretch, with a cord about his neck, through the village street: it was an Heteymy; and the Beduins cried furiously against him, that he had withheld the khûwa, ten reals! and they brought him to see if any man in Kheybar, as he professed to them, would pay for him; and if no, they would draw him out of the town and kill him. The poor soul pleaded for himself, "The Nejûmy will redeem me:" so they came on to the Rahabba, where was at that time Mohammed's lodging, and the Heteymy called loudly upon him. Mohammed saw him to be some man whom he knew not: yet he said to the Annezy, "Loose him." — "We will not let him go, unless we have ten reals for him." — "But I say, loose him, for my sake." — "We will not loose him." — "Then go up Ahmed, and bring me ten reals from the box." "I gave them the money, said Mohammed, and they released the Heteymy. I clothed him, and gave him a waterskin, and dates and flour for the journey, and let him go. A week later the poor man returned with ten reals, and driving a fat sheep for me."

Mohammed had learned (of a neighbour) at Medina to be a gunsmith, and in his hands was more than the Arabian ingenuity; his humanity was ever ready. A Bedûwy in the fruit harvest was bearing a sack of dates upon Mohammed's stairs; his foot slipped, and the man had a leg broken. Mohammed, with no more than his natural wit, which they call *háwas*, set the bone, and took care of him until he recovered; and now the nomad every year brings him a thankoffering of his samn and dried milk. Mohammed, another time, found one wounded and bleeding to death: he sewed together the lips of his wound with silken threads, and gave him a hot infusion of *saffron* to drink, the quantity of a fenjeyn, two or three ounces, which he tells me *will stay all hæmorrhages.* The bleeding ceased, and the man recovered.

CHAPTER VI

THE MEDÎNA LIFE AT KHEYBAR

Amm Mohammed's Kurdish family. His life from his youth. His son Haseyn. His easy true religion. He is a chider at home. Ahmed. A black fox. The kinds of gazelles. The Nejûmy a perfect marksman. His marvellous eye-sight. The ignorances of his youth. A transmuter of metals. A brother slain. His burning heart to avenge him. A Beduin marksman slain, by his shot, in an expedition. A running battle. He is wounded. Fiend-like men of the Bashy Bazûk. The Muatterîn at Damascus. Religious hospitality of the Arabs. Syrian tale of a bear. Mohammedan and Christian cities. Mohammed (in his youth) went in a company, from Medina, to rob a caravan of pilgrims. He saves a pilgrim's life. The *Lahabba* of Harb, a kindred of robbers. Tales of the Lahabba. Imperfect Moslems in the Haj. A Christian found at Medina. His martyr's death. A friar in Medina. Another Christian seen by Mohammed in Medina. Yahûd and Nasâra. Jesus, whose Son? Mohammed answers the salutation of just men, from his tomb. The martyrs' cave at Bedr Honeyn. Dakhîl returns not at his time. The Nasrâny's life in doubt. Amm Mohammed's good and Abdullah's black heart. Dakhîl arrives in the night. Atrocious words of Abdullah. "The Engleys are friends and not rebels to the Sooltân." Andalusîa of the Arabs. An English letter to the Pasha of Medina. Abdullah's letter. Spitting of some account in their medicine.

AMM MOHAMMED'S father was a Kurdy of Upper Syria, from the village Beylân, near Antioch (where their family yet remain); their name is in that language *Yelduz*, in Arabia Nejûmy, [of *nejm*, star]. The old Nejûmy was purveyor in Medina to the Bashy Bazûk. He brought up his provision convoys himself by the dangerous passage from Yanbâ; the good man had wedded an Harb woman, and this delivered him from their nation; moreover he was known upon the road, for his manly hospitable humour, to all the Beduw. He received for his goods the soldiers' bills on their pay (ever in arrear), with some abatement; which paper he paid to his merchants at the current rate. And he became a substantial trader in the Holy City.

He was a stern soldier and severe father; and dying he left to his three sons, who were Bashy Bazûk troopers, no more than the weapons in their right hands and the horses;—he had six or eight Syrian hackneys in his stable. He left them in the service of the Dowla, and bade them be valiant: he said that this might well suffice them in the world. All his goods and the house he gave to their mother, besides a maintenance to the other women; and he appointed a near kinsman to defend her from any recourse against her of his sons. — The horses they sold, and the price was soon wasted in riot by Mohammed, the elder of the young brethren: and then to replenish his purse he fell to the last unthrift of gaming. And having thus in a short novelty misspent himself, his time and his substance, he found himself bare: and he had made his brethren poor.

When the Bashy Bazûk were disbanded, Mohammed and Ahmed took up a humble service; they became dustmen of the temple, and carried out the daily sweeping upon asses, for which they had eightpence wages. Besides they hired themselves as journeymen, at sixpence, to trim the palms, to water the soil, to dig, to build walls in the orchards. Weary at length of his illiberal tasks Mohammed turned to his father's old friends, and borrowed of them an hundred reals. He now became a salesman of cotton wares in the sûk; but the daily gain was too little to maintain him, and in the end he was behind the hand more than four hundred reals.

With the few crowns that remained in his bag he bought a broken mill-horse, and went with her to Kheybar; where the beast browsing (without cost to him) in the wet valleys, was bye and bye healed; and he sold her for the double in Medina. Then he bought a cow at Kheybar, and he sold his cow in the city for double the money. And so going and coming, and beginning to prosper at Kheybar, he was not long after master of a cow, a horse, and a slave; which he sold in like manner, and more after them: — and he became a dealer in clothing and dates in the summer market at Kheybar. When in time he saw himself increased, he paid off two hundred reals of his old indebtedness. Twelve years he had been in this prosperity, and was now chief of the autumn salesmen (from Medina), and settled at Kheybar: for he had dwelt before partly at el-Hâyat and in Medina.

The year after the entering of the Dowla Ahmed came to live with him. He could not thrive in the Holy City; where passing his time in the coffee houses, and making smoke of his little silver, he was fallen so low that Mohammed sent the real which paid for his brother's riding, in a returning hubt, to Kheybar; — where arriving in great languor he could but say, 'His consolation was that his good brother should bury him!' — Mohammed, with the advantage of his summer trading, purchased every year (the villagers' right in) a béled for forty or fifty reals.

AMM MOHAMMED'S EASY TRUE RELIGION

He had besides three houses, bought with his money, and a mare worth sixty reals. His kine were seven, and when they had calved, he would sell some, and restore one hundred reals more to his old creditors. A few goats taken up years ago in his traffic with the nomads, were become a troop; an Heteymy client kept them with his own in the khála. Also his brother had prospered: "See, said Mohammed, he lives in his own house! Ahmed is now a welfaring trader, and has bought himself a béled or two."

Haseyn, Amm Mohammed's only son, was bred up by his Harb grandmother at Medina; and his father had only lately sent for him to Kheybar. In another year he would choose for the sixteen years' old lad a Beduwîa wife. He chid his son early and late, for so he said, his own father had done by his sons: — he hoped in this untimely marriage to strengthen himself by the early birth of grandsons. The good man said he would make at that time three portions of all that he had, one for himself, one should be Ahmed's, and one for his son Haseyn. The lad's mother died young, and the Nejûmy, who had dearly loved her, remained for years unwedded: another wife of his had died earlier; — they were Medina Hareem. When he was formerly at Kheybar, he had some neighbour woman to come in and cook for him, and fetch his water and wood. At length because the people blamed his lonely life he took a Beduwîa; but she not long enduring the townsman's hard usage, and imprisoned in the valleys of Kheybar, entreated Mohammed to let her go, and he divorced her: the housewife that he now had was of the same tribe. To strengthen himself, he said, he would purchase a stout negro slave, after the wedding of his boy Haseyn. In the third year he thought to give him his freedom, and a wife, with certain palms for their living: and this freed family would be his servants, and partisans of his children for ever.

His was an heart full of human mirth, even in matter of religion. He would say, "They tell of Paradise and of Jehennem, but I ask them: 'How, Sirs, can ye know it? has any man returned to us from such places?'" With all this the Nejûmy was devout, only not a formal man, in his religion. He asked me, "What say they in your belief is chiefly a man's duty to Godward?" — "To love the Lord with all thy heart, and thy neighbour as thine own soul." — "But that is easy, Khalîl! God knoweth that I love Him! I would only that He be not weary of my so many times calling upon Him (in my daily prayers):

and truly I would as well to my neighbour as to myself!" He prayed at dawn, and at noon, when he had bathed his manly breast in the warm Sefsáfa spring, — whereby is a prayer-ground, enclosed from the common, with a border of stones: in the evening he prayed again and it sufficed him; for he said, 'I am weary of praying.' And most afternoons he spelled out somewhat in his koran, when he sat at home.

On Fridays we went to our garden labour as at other times. The fanatics whispered of his little or no (formal) religion; and because he harboured an adversary of the faith, an enchanter, in his beyt. I have heard his good Beduin wife admonish him thus, smiling, "O Mohammed, yet go sometimes to the mesjid, for the people murmur that thou dost not pray!" The Nejûmy, though he disdained both them and their malice, remained a little confused; because to forsake their outward religion, is as much as to be forsaken by all the world of superstitious persons. He exclaimed in his laughing humour, "Every man is justified in his own belief! — is Ullah I say *rajol*, (a man), that He should punish poor people, only because they heard not in what sort He were pleased to be worshipped? [the miserable Adam-son's eternal salvation subjected to his feeble intellection, and impossible invention of the truth divine, in confuse matter of this world's opinion without basis reasonable and intelligible!] then were Ullah a rajol not so good as a good rajol! but God is All-good; and therefore I can think that He will show mercy unto all mankind."

Mohammed, though so worthy a man and amiable, was a soldier in his own household. When I blamed him he said, "I snib my wife because a woman must be kept in subjection, for else they will begin to despise their husbands." He chided every hour his patient and diligent Beduwîa as *melaunat ej-jins*, 'of cursed kind.' He had a mind to take another wife more than this to his liking; for, he said, she was not fair; and in hope of more offspring, though she had thrice borne him children in four or five years, — but two were dead in the sickly air of Kheybar: "a wife, quoth he, should be come of good kin, and be liberal." Son and housewife, he chid them continually; only to his guest Amm Mohammed was a mild Arabian. Once I saw him — these are the uncivil manners of the town — rise to strike his son! The Beduwîa ran between them to shelter her step-son, though to her the lad was not kind. I caught the Nejûmy's arm, yet his force bruised the poor woman; — and "wellah, she said, smiling in her tears to see the tempest abated, thy hand Mohammed is heavy, and I think has broken some of my bones." Haseyn bore at all times his father's hard usage with an honest submission.

We passed-by one day where Haseyn ploughed a field, and when I praised the son's diligence, Mohammed smiled; but in that remembering his hard custom he said, " Nay, he is idle, he will play with the lads of the village, and go a gunning."—Each morning when Haseyn returned to his father's suffa, his father began his chiding: " What! thou good-for-nothing one, should a young man lie and daze till the sun rise over him?" Hardly then his father suffered him to sit down a moment, to swallow the few dates in his hand; but he rated him forth to his labour, to keep cows in the *Hálhal*, to dig, to plough, to bring in the ass, to seek his father's strayed mare, to go about the irrigation. Week, month and year, there was no day when Haseyn might sit at home for an hour; but he must ever avoid out of his father's sight. Sometimes Mohammed sent him out before the light, fasting, far over the Harra, with some of the village, for wood; and the lad returned to break his fast at mid-afternoon. If any day his father found his son in the village before the sun was set, he pursued him with outrageous words, in the public hearing; " Graceless! why come home so soon? (or, why camest thou not sooner?) Ha! stand not, *thôr!* steer, ox, to gape upon me,—*enhaj!* remove out of my sight—thou canst run fast to play; now, *irkud! ijrî!* run about thy business. Is it to such as thou I should give a wife to-year?" Haseyn: " What wouldst thou have me to do, father?"—" Out of my sight, *kòr!* Ullah punish that face!" and he would vomit after him such ordures of the lips (from the sink of the soldiers' quarters at Medina), *akerût, kharra, térras,* or he dismissed his son with *laanat Ullah aleyk*, ' God's curse be with thee.' Haseyn returned to the house, to sup, little before nightfall. Then his father would cry: " Ha! unthrift, thou hast done nothing to-day but play in the Hálhal!—he stares upon me like an ox, *bákr!*"—" Nay but father I have done as thou badest me."—" Durst thou answer me, chicken! now make haste to eat thy supper, sirra, and begone." Haseyn, a lad under age, ate not with his father and the guest; but after them of that which remained, with his father's *jâra*, whom he called, in their manner, his mother's sister, *khálaty*.

Doubtless Mohammed had loved Haseyn, whilst he was a child, with the feminine affection of the Arabs; and now he thought by hardness to make his son better. But his harsh dealing and cries in the street made the good man to be spoken against in the negro village; and for this there was some little coldness betwixt him and his brother Ahmed. But the citizen Ahmed was likewise a chider and striker, and for such his Kheybar wife, Mohammed's housewife's sister, had forsaken him: he had a town wife at Medina. Why, I asked, was she not here to keep his house? *Ahmed:* " I bring my wife to inhabit here! only these blacks can live at Kheybar, or else, we had taken it from them long ago!" Ahmed's children died in their youth, and he was unmindful of them: " Ahmed has no feeling heart," said his brother Mohammed. I counselled Amm Mohammed to have a better care for his son's health, and let him be taught letters. " Ay, said his father, I would that he may be able to read in the koran, against the time of his marriage, for *then he ought to begin to say his prayers* (like a man)."

' Ahmed he would say is half-witted, for he spends all that ever he may get in his buying and selling for kahwa and dokhân.' Mohammed [in such he resembled the smiths' caste] used neither. " Is that a wise man, he jested, who will drink coffee and tan his own bowels?" Yet Ahmed must remember, amongst his brother's kindness, that the same was he who had made him bare in the beginning: even now the blameworthy brother's guilts were visited upon his head, and the generous sinner went scatheless! — Mohammed, wallowing in the riot of his ignorant youth at Medina, was requited with the evil which was sown by the enemy of mankind. Years after he cured himself with a violent specific, he called it in Arabic " rats' bane," which had loosened his teeth; a piece of it that Mohammed showed me was red lead. Though his strong nature resisted so many evils and the malignity of the Kheybar fevers, the cruel malady (only made inert) remained in him with blackness of the great joints. And Ahmed living with him at Kheybar and extending the indigent hand to his brother's mess, received from Mohammed's beneficent hand the contagion which had wasted him from the state of an hale man to his present infirmity of body.

The rude negro villagers resorted to Ahmed, to drink coffee and hear his city wisdom; and he bore it very impatiently that his brother named him mejnûn in the town. " Sheykh Khalîl, he said to me, how lookest thou upon sheykh Mohammed?" " I have not found a better man in all." — " But he is fond and childish." When Ahmed sickened to death in the last pestilence Mohammed brought a bull to the door and vowed a vow to slaughter him, if the Lord would restore his brother. Ahmed recovered: and then Mohammed killed the bull, his thankoffering, and divided the flesh to their friends; — and it was much for a poor man ! In these days Mohammed killed his yearly sacrifice of a goat, which he vowed once when Haseyn was sick. He brought up his goat when the beasts came home in the evening; and first taking coals in an earthen censer he put on a crumb of incense, and censed about the victim. I asked wherefore he did this? he answered: " That the sacrifice might be well pleasing to Ullah; and do ye not so?" He murmured prayers, turning the goat's head towards Mecca; and with his sword he cut her throat. When he heard from me that this was not our custom, — every man to kill his own sacrifice, he seemed to muse in himself, that we must be a faint-hearted people.

One early morning, his son going about the irrigation had found a fox drowned in our well. — Haseyn flung it out upon the land; and when we came thither, and could not at first sight find this beast, " No marvel, quoth Mohammed, for what is more sleighty than a fox ? It may be he stiffened himself, and Haseyn threw him out for dead !" — but we found the *hosenny* cast under some nettles, stark-dead indeed. From the snout to the brush his fur was of such a swart slate colour as the basalt figgera ! only his belly was whitish. Amm Mohammed drew the unclean carcase out of his ground, holding a foot in a handful of palm lace.

I told the good man how, for a fox-brush, sheykhs in my béled use to ride furiously, in red mantles, upon horses — the best of them worth the rent of some village — with an hundred yelling curs scouring before them; and leaping over walls and dykes they put their necks and all in adventure: and who is in at the hosenny's death, he is the gallant man. For a moment the subtil Arabian regarded me with his piercing eyes as if he would say, " Makest thou mirth of me !" but soon again relenting to his frolic humour, " Is this, he laughed, the chevying of the fox?"—in which he saw no grace. And the good Medina Moslem seemed to muse in spirit, ' Wherefore had the Lord endowed the Yahûd and Nasâra with a superfluity of riches, to so idle uses ?' The wolf no less, he said, is a sly beast: upon a time, he told me, as he kept his mother's goats at the Ferrâ in his youth, and a (Harb) maiden was herding upon the hillside with him, he saw two wolves approach in the plain; then he hid himself, to watch what they would do. At the foot of the rocks the old wolf left his fellow ; and the other lay down to await him : that wolf ascended like an expert hunter, pausing, and casting his eyes to all sides. The trooping goats went feeding at unawares among the higher crags ; and Mohammed saw the wolf take his advantage of ground and the wind, in such sort that a man might not do better. 'Greylegs' chose out one of the fattest bucks in the maiden's herd, and winding about a rock he sprang and bit the innocent by the throat : — Mohammed's shot thrilled the wolf's heart at the instant ; and then he ran in to cut the bleeding goat's throat (that the flesh might be lawful meat).

Besides the predatory animals, in the Arabian deserts, before mentioned [v. Vol. I. p. 373], Mohammed spoke of the *gòrta*, " a cat of the bigness of a fox ; it is neither fáhd nor nimmr : this gòrta lurks in the long bunch-grass of the Nefûd to spring upon passing gazelles." Of another beast he spoke somewhat doubtfully, *eth-thurrambàn*, — which I take to be a fabulous animal. " It is black and somewhat more of bulk than the fox ; he digs up new graves to feed on the dead corses." The Nejûmy thought he had seen one, upon a time, lying dead in a ditch. The fruit-eating jackal is not found in the khála. He named the never-drinking small gazelle of the Nefûd, *el-affery* ; and that of the Harra which, drinking water, is also of greater bulk, *el-iddimy* ; a gazelle fawn of three days old, he said, could outstrip any man. There are bedûn of great bulk and horn, upon the Harra. Last year Mohammed killed a giant bédan, the length of whose horns was five spans and an hand-breadth [more than 40 in.], and the flat of the horn a hand-breadth. Four men and himself were weary to bear the wild goat's quarters and the fell home with them.

Mohammed was a perfect marksman. When we came one morning to our well-ground, and he had his long matchlock in his hand, there sat three crows upon a *sîdr* (apple-thorn) tree that cumbered our ears with their unlucky *krâ-krâ*. " The cursed ones! " quoth Amm Mohammed, and making ready his gun, he said he would try if his eyesight were failing : as he levelled the crows flew up, but one sat on, — through which he shot his bullet from a wonderful distance. Then he set up a white bone on the clay wall, it was large as the palm of my hand, and he shot his ball through the midst from an hundred paces. He shot again, and his lead pierced the border of the former hole ! Mohammed gave the crow to some Kheyâbara, who came to look on ;

and the negro villagers kindling a fire of palm sticks roasted their bird whole, and parted it among them. — " Like will to like ! quoth the Nejûmy, and for them it is good enough."

He had this good shooting of an uncommon eyesight, which was such that very often he could see the stars at noonday : his brother, he said, could see them, and so could many more. He told me he had seen, by moments, three or four little stars about one of the wandering stars, [Jupiter's moons !] I asked then, " Sawest thou never a wandering star horned like the moon ? " — " Well, I have seen a star not always round, but like a blade hanging in the heaven." — Had this vision been in European star-gazers, the Christian generations had not so long waited for the tube of Galileo ! [to lay the first stone — hewn without hands — of the indestructible building of our sciences]. Mohammed saw the moon always very large, and the whole body at once : he was become in his elder years long-sighted.

One day Amm Mohammed made gunpowder, and I gave him (from my medicine box) a pound or two of official nitre. He prepared his charcoal of the light castor-oil wood, which grows at Kheybar to a tree : when all was well fired he whelmed a pan upon it and smothered the burning. The cake of powder was soon nearly dry, and cross-cutting it he made gross grains with a knife : perhaps they are taught by experience that this kind is safer for their long weak guns, in which they ram down heavy charges. My ' gun-salt,' white as snow, he thought excellent, and he had never seen so pure a nitre. Amm Mohammed went to prove this new powder at the Sefsáfa. — But the sharp-ringing detonation startled him, and the eye of the touch-hole was blown out. He returned saying, the English " salt " was strong, and he would he had more of it.

In so rude a country it is a praise to shoot well. Abdullah the Siruân valued himself upon his fair shooting ; — ' But what was the difference, he told us, to shoot at a living man ! ' Sometime in an expedition against the Beduw, a Medina personage said to him, ' Canst thou put a ball through that fellow yonder ? ' " I shot (he told us), but by Ullah ! I missed him ; for what man's heart will not shrink when he levels at a man, — albe it is an enemy ? — But let us to the housetop, and all try a bout at shooting." A white sheet of paper was set up for his mark at 120 yards, with a rise of sixty feet, under the breast-work of the Húsn.

Abdullah made a trivet of reeds; and balancing thereupon his long matchlock, with great deliberation, he fired; but all his shots struck somewhat wide of the mark, and none fell within it! — Such is the unmasking of vaunters, who utter their wishes, as if they were already performances, without the alliance of nature.

In Amm Mohammed were certain old grudges of conscience; and he enquired of me (whom he took to be book-learned in theology), 'Did I conclude that the Lord had forgiven him the iniquities of his youth?' Yet in things, which were not plain to him, he had but a thick-skinned religious judgment. He asked in our talk, 'Could I transmute metals?' adding: "I have seen it done; it is but the casting in of a certain powder. How! sheykh Khalîl, a traveller from far countries and have none of it by you?" He told me further, "When I dwelt at el-Hâyat [he had wrought there as a gunsmith and swordsmith to the Aarab] an Hindy alighted one day at my door. [It might be one of the Indian pilgrimage; — there are Moslem Hindies, apothecaries, who cast their eyes curiously upon the desert land of Mohammed.] The man told us he sought certain simples which grew only in these dîras. When he had sojourned a while in my house, he said to me 'Yâ Mohammed!' and I said to him 'Eigh?' and he said 'Hitherto thou hast borne all our charges, now I would show thee a good turn; hast thou here any copper pan?' I brought him a pot, and he asked for the shears. 'Now, said he, is there no man besides us two in this house? go and make the door fast.' He shred the copper into a cresset, and I blew the fire: when the metal began to relent, he poured in his medicine, — it was like a little dust. He had his ingots by him and began to cast; and there came out that bright silver money of India, which they call *rupî*. The Hindy said, 'Let us part them between us.'" — "But tell me were they silver indeed?" — "They were well-ringing and silver-like pieces that would pass; I do not say that they were very silver." — "What have you done? you two were false moneyers!" — "Khalîl, the man did me a pleasure and I did him another: but I grant you if the Dowla had been there, that we were both in danger of punishment."

The remembrance of their younger brother, who had been slain by robbers as he came in a company from Medina to visit his brethren at Kheybar, was yet a burning anguish in Mohammed's breast; — until, with his own robust hands, he might be avenged for the blood! A ghrazzu of *Móngora*, Bíllî Aarab, and five times their number, had set upon them in the way: the younger Nejûmy, who was in the force of his years, played the lion amongst them, until he fell by a pistol shot. Móngora men come not to Kheybar; therefore Mohammed devised in his heart that in what place he might first meet with any tribesman of theirs he would slay him. A year after he finding one of them, the Nejûmy led him out, with some pretence, to a desert place; and said shortly to him there, " O thou cursed one! now will I slay thee with this sword." — " Akhs! said the Beduwy, let me speak, Sir, why wilt thou kill me? did I ever injure thee?" — " But thou diest to-day for the blood of my brother, whom some of you in a ghrazzu have slain, in the way to Kheybar." — " The Lord is my witness! that I had no hand in it, for I was not among them." — " Yet thy blood shall be for his blood, since thou art one of them." — " Nay, hear me, Mohammed en-Nejûmy! and I will tell thee the man's name, — yea by Him which created us! for the man is known to me who did it; and he is one under my hand. Spare now my life, and as the Lord liveth I will make satisfaction, in constraining him that is guilty, and in putting-to of mine own, to the estimation of the midda, 800 reals." Mohammed, whose effort is short, could no more find in his cooling mood to slaughter a man that had never displeased him. He said then, that he forgave him his life, upon this promise to send him the blood-money. So they made the covenant, and Mohammed let him go.

— " That cursed Bellûwy! I never saw him more (quoth he), but now, — ha! wheresoever I may meet with any of them, I will kill him." I dissuaded him — " But there is a wild-fire in my heart, which cannot be appeased till I be avenged for the death of my brother." — " Were it not better if you take any of their tribesmen, to bind him until the blood be redeemed?" But Amm Mohammed could not hear this; the (South) Arabian custom is not to hold men over to ransom: for either they kill their prisoner outright, or, giving him a girby with water and God's curse, they let him go from them. " *Ruhh*, they will say, depart thou enemy! and perish, may it please God, in the khála." They think that a freeman is no chattel and cannot be made a booty. Women are not taken captive in the Arabian warfare, though many times a poor valiant man might come by a fair wife thus, without his spending for bride money.

Mohammed answered, " But now I am rich — the Lord be praised therefore, what need have I of money? might I but quench this heart-burning!" — " Why not forgive it freely, that the God of Mercies may forgive thee thy offences." — " Sayest thou this! — and sheykh Khalîl I did a thing in my youth, for which my heart reproaches me; but thou who seemest to be a man of (religious) learning declare unto me, whether I be guilty of that blood. — The Bashy Bazûk rode [from Medina] against the Ateyba, and I was in the expedition. We took at first much booty: then the Beduw, gathering from all sides [they have many horsemen], began to press upon us, and our troop [the soldiers ride but slowly upon Syrian hackneys] abandoned the cattle. The Aarab coming on and shooting in our backs, there fell always some among us; but especially there was a marksman who infested us. He rode upon a mare, radîf, and his fellow carried him out galloping on our flank and in advance: then that marksman alighted, behind some bush, and awaited the time to fire his shot. When he fired, the horseman, who had halted a little aloof, galloped to take him up: they galloped further, and the marksman loaded again. At every shot of his there went down horse or rider, and he killed my mare: then the aga bade his own slave take me up on his horse's croup. ' Thou O young man, said he, canst shoot, gallop forth with my lad and hide thee; and when thou seest thy time, shoot that Ateyby, who will else be the death of us all.' — ' Wellah Captain, I would not be left on my feet, the troop might pass from me.' — ' That shall not be, only do this which I bid thee.'

" We hastened forward, said Mohammed, when those Beduins came by on the horse: we rode to some bushes, and there I dismounted and loaded carefully. The marksman rode beyond and went to shroud himself as before; he alighted, and I was ready and shot at the instant. His companion who saw him wounded, galloped to take him up, and held him in his arms on the saddle, a little while; and then cast him down, — he was dead! and the Arabs left pursuing us." I asked, ' Wherefore, if he doubted to kill an enemy in the field, had he taken service with the soldiery?' — " Ah! it was for tóma: I was yet young and ignorant."

Amm Mohammed had the blood of another such manslaughter on his mind; but he spoke of it without discomfort. In a new raid he pursued a Beduwy lad who was flying on foot, to take his matchlock from him, — which might be worth twelve reals; the weled, seeing himself overtaken by a horseman of the Dowla, fired back his gun from the hip, and the ball passed through the calf of Mohammed's leg, who 'answered the melaun, as he said, *trang*'! — with a pistol shot: the young tribesman fell grovelling, beating his feet, and wallowed snatching the sand in dying throes. Mohammed's leg grew cold, and only then he felt himself to be wounded: he could not dismount, but called a friend to take up the Beduwy's gun for him. Mohammed's father (who was in the expedition) cut off his horseman's boot, which was full of blood, and bound up the hurt: and set him upon a provision camel and brought him home to Medina; and his wound was whole in forty days.

He showed me also that a bone had been shot away of his left wrist; that was in after years. — Amm Mohammed was coming up in a convoy of tradesmen from Medina, with ten camel-loads of clothing for Kheybar. As they journeyed, a strong ghrazzu of Harb met with them: then the passengers drove their beasts at a trot, and they themselves hasting as they could on foot, with their guns, fired back against the enemies. They ran thus many miles in the burning sun, till their strength began to give out and their powder was almost spent. The Beduw had by this taken the most of the tradesmen's loaded camels. Mohammed had quitted his own and the camel of a companion, when a ball shattered the bone of his left forearm. "I saw him, he said, who shot it! I fired at the melaun again, and my bullet broke all his hand." — The Aarab called now to the Nejûmy (knowing him to be of their kindred), "What ho! Mohammed son of our sister! return without fear, and take that which is thine of these camels." He answered them, "I have delivered mine already," and they, "Go in peace." — I asked "How, being a perfect marksman, he had not, in an hour, killed all the pursuers." — "But know, Khalîl, that in this running and fighting we fire almost without taking sight."

A market company of Heteym, which lately passed by Kheybar, carrying down samn and cheeses, were "taken" when they were not far from the gates of Medina! So the Nejûmy used to say, "Wellah we hardly reckon him a man, in this country, who has not been wounded!" I wandered more than two years, in the Beduin marches, and had never mishap: and some of my rafîks have said, 'There was billah a good fortune with Khalîl for the journey.'

The Bashy Bazûk was a rake-hell service, in which good fellows might enrich themselves for the time; since vessels, money, weapons, stuff, and all was theirs, upon which they might first lay their hands in the nomad tents ; besides they had their part in the (government) booty of the Beduins' cattle. They were a crew, in those days, of reckless poor companions at Medina, that wore their white felt bonnets bounced down upon their jolly coxcombs as *shubúb*, or ' proper tall young men,' who were the sword of the Dowla : and ' every one of them, said Amm Mohammed, you might know it by their name, *Bashy Bazûk*, was his own master.' Few of them knew other father or mother than their captain; they acknowledged none other authority over them. Mohammed told me for an example of their desperate manners, that one morning as they rode, in another foray, in the heat of the year, and his comrades [with the unforbearing of townsmen] had drunk to the dregs all that remained in their girbies, they hastened to come to a weyrid. It was mid-afternoon when they arrived at the well and dismounted, and the foremost ran with his cord and leathern bucket to draw water : but as the fellow, in this passion of thirst, took up the precious humour to his own lips, " Curse thee ! cries another trooper, there is like to hell in my entrails, and drinkest thou all before me ? " — He fired his pistol in the other's breast, and snatched the leather from the dying man : but as he took it to his mouth the shot of another fiend-like trooper prevented him, who seized upon the precious inheritance ; and he the third fell in like manner. And in their devilish impatience there fell among them, one after other, seven troopers, contending, as beasts without reason, to drink first of the bloody water. Then the captain drove all his men from the well, and made them stand in a row ; and drew himself, and calling them to him one by one, he gave them to drink. When the troop returned to Medina no question was made of this hellish butchery. And why ? — " Were not these the Bashy Bazûk ? when one was dead (said Amm Mohammed), no man enquired for him ; and the most of them were strangers at Medina."

— In all the Turkish-Arabic towns, there are certain spirits not framed to the moderation of the civil life, and they fall in each other's fellowship, to loose living and riot. In the lands of Christians such would be haunters of the licensed stews and taverns ; but in the Mohammedan world they must come to their drunkenness and harlotry as law-breakers. The *muatterîn* at Damascus are not accounted public enemies, for honest citizens seldom suffer by misdoing of theirs ; only wayfarers beyond the gates by night must pass betwixt the clay walls of the orchards at their peril. The best are but city roysterers, and the worst are scourges — where the law is weak — for the backs of evildoers. Muatterîn hire themselves (it is sometimes for the good turn they would do their friends) to take up other men's desperate quarrels, and be their avengers for private wrongs.

When muatterîn meet with muatterîn, there are swelling looks and injurious words, and many times brawls between them, in the daytime. In the first heats of summer, when the *mishmish* (apricots) are ripening [of the paradise of Damascus], those lawless men go out by night in bands, to disport themselves in the orchards : they will break over the clay walls, and pluck the pleasant fruit to their supper. In such places they solace themselves, in the company of abandoned women, drinking the fiery alcohol (which is distilled from the lees of the grapes in the Christians' and Jews' houses). They are evil livers, but Arabs, with a human grace in their unworthiness ; and if a stranger approach, whilst they are eating and drinking, they would bid him sit down and fear not to partake with them — If muâtters overhear muâtters, insults will be bandied between them : and commonly they rise from the forbidden drink (with their quarter-staves), to go and set upon each other. — The battle of these ribalds is to win their adversaries' hareem.

In the hospitality of the Arabs is kinship and assurance, in their insecure countries. This is the piety of the Arab life, this is the sanctity of the Arabian religion, where we may not look for other. — Returning one day, in Syria, from a journey, I enquired the way of a countryman in the road. It was noon ; — the young man, who went by eating bread and cheese, paused and cut a piece of his girdle-cake, with a pleasant look, and presented it to the stranger : when I shook the head, he cut a rasher of cheese and put it silently to my mouth ; and only then he thought it a time to speak. — Also if a stranger enter vineyard or orchard, he is a guest of that field ; and, in the summer months, the goodman, if he be there, will bring some of his fruits to refresh him.

There is a merry tale which is often told in the mountains of Antilibanus, where are many bears, — and I have hunted them at Helbon [whose wine is mentioned in Ezekiel, in the traffic of Damascus]. — The Syrian villagers sleep out in their orchards to keep night-watch in the warmer months. A husbandman hearing a bear rout in the dark, lifted himself hastily into the boughs of the next tree, which was an almond. The sweet-toothed brute came and climbed into that tree where the trembling man sat ; and put out his paw to gather the delicate green nuts to his mouth. When the Arab saw this bear would become his guest, he cried before his thought, *kul!* 'Eat, and welcome !' The bear, that had not perceived him, hearing man's voice, gave back ; the branch snapt under his weight ! — the brute tumbled on his head, and broke his neck bone. After an hour or two the goodman, who saw this bear lie still as stone, in the starlight ! took heart to come down : and finding the brute dead, he cut his throat and plucked the fell over his ears ; which on the morrow he sold to the cobbler for sole-leather [*conf.* Ezek. xvi. 10], they eat not the flesh. — Wellah, it fell out for the poor man according to the true proverb, which saith, 'spare to speak, spare to speed !' I have known children scold a bear and beat him too as a thief, and drive him with stones from their father's orchard. But a wounded bear is perilous, and (in age) when having lost their teeth, they become flesh-eaters. Who has not noted the human manners in this breechless, handfooted, and saturnine creature ! A she-bear, with her cub, came down one winter in the deep snow, to the village of *Bludàn* in the same mountains. The people pursued them with their dogs, and caught the young one ; the mother brute, they told me, hurled back stones against them !

I have heard many a strange tale in Damascus of the muâtters of former days, and even in our fathers' lifetime, when — besides certain Franciscan monks suffered to sojourn there — no Frenjy, not disguised, ever came thither. The Nasâra might have no redress, even the Resident for the Sultan had little or no authority over them ; and the correction of intolerable wrongs was by the violent hands of the muatterîn. — Yet how sober, and peaceably full of their (not excessive) homely toil, is the life of such a Mohammedan city of 130,000 souls ! And doubtless we exceed them in passionate disorders, as much as we excel them in arts and learning, and are subject to better laws and to the Christian religion.

— Mohammed was one of the ruffling young ignorants of Medina, and partaker in their criminal excesses. A companion of his said to him upon a time, "We are nineteen good fellows going out to waylay the cursed Moghrâreba, and I am pledged to bring thee the twentieth, for thou art a strong one and canst shoot." — The wayworn pilgrims marching in Arabia are not in any assurance without the confines of

Mecca ! the Ishmaelite nomads doubt not to rob the Haj travelling from most far countries to fulfil the precept of their common religion.

Those young evil-doers of Medîna stole forth unknown to their parents, one by one, with their arms, at evening. From the meeting place they went on to lurk by the Derb el-Haj, in Wady el-Humth, at a short journey from Medina. The caravan of pilgrim Moors pass through the Hejâz armed, as in a hostile country ; for they only deny toll to the Beduw. — Of late years the valorous Moors have burned two Harb villages, betwixt the Harameyn, whose people had robbed them.

— Those pilgrims of the white burnûs rode by : in the hindward came a few stragglers. Upon these the young men ran down, with the whooping of Arabs. The Moors, who were but three men, turned and fired their guns, and wounded one of them : then the young men betook themselves to the mountain side. — They fired down, and there fell one of the three Moghrebies ; and his companions fled. The young adventurers pursued them, and took one of them ; but the other, forsaking his camel, outwent them upon his feet.

Now they had the three Moghreby men's camels ; and braving about their captive, they cried, " This is the melaun that wounded our fellow ; by the life of Ullah he shall be dead." Then the poor Moghreby gazing in Mohammed's honest face, cast his arms about his neck, saying, " O sir, I beseech thee, save my life, and defend me from these." *Mohammed* : " Ay, fellows, I say, the slain Moor is full satisfaction for this one of ours wounded ; " — but they not consenting, he said to them, " I have granted him protection : — hie ! Moghreby, — and I go, now, to see this man safe till he may come to his people." — When they were again in sight of the caravan the Moor said to him, " Come no further, lest some evil betide thee amongst them ; now bless thee Ullah and His Apostle." *Mohammed* : " How ! I have saved thee from my fellows, and canst thou not quit me from thine ? " — " Go, good sir ; I may very well deliver thee from my friends, but not from the fellowship of him that is slain."

When Mohammed returned to his companions they had divided the booty ! and they all denied him his part, crying out upon him, " But thou wast against us ! and thou hast taken away our revenge." — " Well, part it among ye, and the Lord be judge between us ! " — Mohammed had not slipped his matchlock from the leathern case.

Amm Mohammed said, there soon fell a judgment upon those loose companions : for seven of them died in the pestilence which the returning Haj brought (two months later) from Mecca. The rest perished in their young age, and they all came to evil ending ; and to-day there remained not one of them. — Such accidents, falling in with the people's superstition, we hear told in testimony of the divine authority of every religion !

The Moors who journey by land from the furthest Occident are eleven months on their religious voyage to Mecca ! and only in certain years [that was when France had disarmed the Algerians] have they paid any scot to the malignant Arabians. *El-Auf* (a great clan of Harb) are bitterly accused of outrages made upon the pilgrims marching betwixt the Harameyn, although their sheykhs receive a yearly surra from the government caravans of Syria and Egypt. The Beduin inhabitants of that flaming wilderness are more miserable than beggars. Of the Aufy sub-tribe *Lahabba* it is said, that such is their cursed calling by inheritance ! — to rob the Haj caravans. They have no camels, for in that fearful country they could not maintain them : their booths are in the mountains, where they possess only a few goats. Every year they descend at the Haj season ; and they hope, of that they may lay their hands on in those few days, to find themselves and their inhuman households till the time be come about again. Lahabbies taken in the manner excuse themselves, saying, ' they fear Ullah ! that the trade is come down to them from their fathers : and how else might they live in this dîra, wherein the Lord hath cast them ? — they and their wives and little ones ! They do but take somewhat from the pilgrims for their necessity, and, wellah it is an alms.'

These robbers have been many times denounced, by the Turkish officers, to the *Bab el-Aly* [the high ingate — after the Oriental speech — to the Sultan's government, which we call the Porte, and ridiculously the Sublime Porte] ; but the answer is always one, — ' That although the detriment be such as they have set forth, yet are those offenders neighbours of the Rasûl, and the sword ought not to be drawn between Moslemîn, *within hearing of the Néby.*'

The Haj tales of the Lahabba are as many as of the Yahûd Kheybar. This is of Abdullah the Siruân : — " There was an old Lahabby, not less praised for his prudence than for his legerdemain ; and there was a young man that would be the best among them : — ' What, said he, is this gaffer good for any more ? ' The greybeard answered, ' I choose thee, young man, for my rafîk, to rob at the next Haj ; it shall be seen then whether of us twain is the better man.' — At length the time was come : and the Haj lay encamped at evening before them. 'Partner (quoth the old man), their watch is yet awake ; abide we till midnight, when this people will be in their first sleep.'

"— They went down, and the elder bade the young man choose a tent. And there the greybeard entering boldly, brought out what he would, and laid it on the younger man's shoulders, and bade him come again quickly. — Then the greybeard whispered, 'Whether of us twain is the better man ?' — 'I durst say I am as good as thou, Partner.' The old shrew whispered, 'Well, go we to supper ; here is rice in the hajjies' pot ; put forth thy hand, bismillah !' When they had eaten their fill, the greybeard rouned to him, 'Now tell me whether of us twain is the better man.' — 'In all this I doubt not but I am as good as thou, Partner.' Then the old man caught up the pan, and let it fall on a stone ! — and with the clangour those weary sleepers — the pilgrims lie down mistrusting all things, with their weapons under their heads — awakened in dread. The young robber was nimble ; but some of their outstretched hands have caught him in the dark, and he was pulled down among them. — That old fox lay abroad on his breast (as the Beduins slumber) and breathed deep in the moonlight ! 'It was some poor old man, they said, as they saw him, — one of the wretched people of this country, who come begging in the Haj menzil to eat some poor morsel among them.' As for that younger thief, they beat him well, and bound him with their girdles to the tent-pole till morning. When the old man saw that the pilgrims slumbered again, he came and loosed his partner's bonds, and whispered, 'Tell me, young man, which is the better of us twain ?' The other answered (so soon as they were without) 'Ay, wellah, my father, thou art the better man.' " — Abdullah ended with a proverb, which might be said in English, 'The young may the old outrun but not outread.'

Amm Mohammed laughed and said: " But I could tell you that the hajjàj be not all such novices. There was a Moghreby too hard for them ; wellah in his first coming down he outwitted the Beduw. One night, when his companions were sleeping, he felt a draught of air ; and the tent skirt was lifted beside him. He opened his eyes, and saw a man put forth some of their baggage ; and the thief whispered to another without, 'Hist ! away with this, and come quickly, and I shall have more ready.' — That Moghreby felt to his knife, and lay still and drew the long breaths of a sleeper : but when he saw him stoop he rose behind the thief and fetched him a mortal stroke ! The Moor hacked the robber in pieces ; and put the limbs and his head in a sack, and stuffed an old camel-cloth upon them. When the other returned the Moghreby spoke under his breath, ' Have a care, partner, for this sack is heavy.' The Beduwy staggered forth, till he could cast his load in a safe place ; and seeing the daylight almost come he durst return no more. — He said to himself, ' but I marvel what my fellow has put in this last sack ; ' and loosing the cords, he found the bloody poll of his rafîk in the sack's mouth !"

In the yearly torrent of superstitious human life setting into the Hejâz there are some imperfect Moslems ; certain uplandish Turkomans are not circumcised ! A poor man of their nation served Amm Mohammed's father in Medina. His wife, that had borne him two children in the Holy City, as one day he changed his apparel, was aware of the reproach. She cried, ' Harrow, and wealaway !' and ran to tell his master, the old Nejûmy : who sent for his offending servant, and bade one go call a barber. And "*Taal yâ melaun*, come hither thou cursed one (cries the stern soldier), Oh ! what is this that I hear of thee ?" And he of the razors arriving the old Nejûmy bade him do his office, in God's Holy Name. When I smiled at his tale, Mohammed said, "Thou wouldst have laughed, hadst thou been there ! for my father was a right merry man.'

Dakhîl, the messenger, might ere this have returned again from Medina. Because he came not yet, the Siruân and Amm Mohammed thought it foreboded me no good ; and I remembered the fanatical words of the Turkish Emir of the Haj at el-Héjr. My life was now in the power of such men, in parts where the hap of an European traveller were for ever beyond the enquiry of his friends. Amm Mohammed told me my matter would be examined by the Pasha in council, which sits twice in the week ; and that men of years and grave citizens would be my judges.

I heard a strange tale from the Nejûmy and from Amân, that last year a Christian came to Medina ! and when the people asked him, "Who art thou, Sir ?" he responded "I am a Nasrâny." — "And what dost thou then in the (illustrious) Medina ? is not this the City of the Apostle?" — "How! say ye that the town is el-Medina? — I would go to Kheybar; and is not this Kheybar?" — "Oho! he would to Kheybar! — Kheybar where? — where, O man, is Kheybar? Ushhud, testify! and say thou, Ullah the only God, and His messenger is Mohammed, or this people will kill thee." — "I may not say as ye say, because I am a Nasrâny." — "Let the man alone now, cried some, and bring him without violence before the Pasha; for all should be done according to law, and not tumultuously, although he have deserved to die."

The disciple of Jesu was cast into prison, in Mohammed's City; but the "Sheykh of the religion" went to the Pasha, and pleaded for the life of the Messîhi stranger, and bade the governor remember Jidda and Damascus! "If aught befall this man, said he, a firmân might be sent down from Stambûl to bring us all to the answer, for our heads." The Pasha was likeminded, and commanded that an escort of soldiers should be ready, to convey the Nasrâny to the port-town, Yanba; which is six marches from Medina.

The Christian was brought through the City again, and passed the gates of Medina with his guard. But when first they were come to a desert place, one of the rake-hell askars said to him, "Ushhud! Nasrâny hound! confess the faith of Islam, thou shalt not dare to say nay; say it cursed one, or else wellahî . . . !" and the fellow levelled his musket. The Christian answered them, "Ye have heard the Pasha's injunctions, my friends, to convey me peaceably to Yanba." — "Die then kafir! — to whom should I obey? know, that in killing thee I shall obey my Lord: Ushhud! and I will not take thy life." — "Ye have a religion, so have I, ye serve God, and I serve Him; live in your religion, and let me live in mine." — "And what should that be? Yahûdy! Thou hast no religion!" "Friends (said the Christian), let us be going; and speak to this man that he leave his railing words." But he: "Not a footstep! pronounce, O hound, the testimony of the Moslemîn! or else this is thy dying place, thou misbelieving Nasrâny;" and the soldier set his musket to the Christian's breast. "Ushhud (he yells) Yahûdy! kelb! kafir! Sheytân!" — and the stranger not answering, he fired and killed him [✠ 1877]. — When the Pasha heard this tiding, he sent the soldier to prison; and there, said Amân and Amm Mohammed, the askar yet lies, awaiting the response to the letter which the Pasha had written to Stambûl; whether it were the Sultan's pleasure to release him, or else put him to death. "And this, said they, holds Abdullah's hand, and makes him dread: and they will not dare do anything against thee fearing to bring themselves in question for thy life."

— But who was the Christian Martyr? That Child of Light, in comparison with their darkness, was swarthy, "a black man, they said, but not *abd*, a negro:"— we have seen that Sicilian seamen and swarthy Neapolitan coral fishers may be mistaken on the Moorish coast for black men. [Vol. I. p. 168].

Mohammed told me that once he met with an alien at Medina, who, when he asked him 'What man art thou?' answered 'A Nasrâny.' — 'Then tell no more so and take better heed to thyself; I will not betray thee, and now the Lord be with thee.' "For what had I to do with his being a Nasrâny? is it not betwixt a man and his God what he is?" Another time Mohammed had seen [one calling himself] a Christian *ráhab* or friar feasted up and down the Apostle's city in his monk's frock. The ráhab told them, he was come down from Jerusalem, to pray at the sepulchre of Néby Mohammed! "I have heard, the Nejûmy added, that our Lord Mohammed, finding certain ráhabs dwelling in the desert, in continual fasting and prayers and in chanting the Word of God, left a commandment, that no man should molest them."

Amm Mohammed often spoke, with a joyous liberality, to the village fanatics of their prophet's dealing thus with the ráhabs: his humanity would that we were not inhumanly divided, and he found in this where our religions had kissed each other. "But tell me, sheykh Khalîl, were I in your béled and I said, 'I am a Moslem,' would they strip me and beat me, and perhaps put me to death? But what and if I changed my religion, and became a Nasrâny?" Mohammed said now, 'He must learn the English tongue whilst Khalîl stayed with him, for who can foresee the years to come, this world is so tickle, and it might one day serve him.' I told him that the Nasâra would make much of him for his strength and good shooting, his strenuous mind, his mirth and manly sincerity. "But sheykh Khalîl, tell me, when I come to your bilâd will they give me a maiden to wife?" He marvelled to hear that the Arabic tongue was unknown (to the people) in our distant countries.

Ahmed enquired, as we were sitting at coffee in his suffa, "Are there Yahûd among you? And speak they evil of your prophet?" —

" I have heard they say that the Messîh (here Ahmed answered ' Upon whom be peace ') was born of fornication ! yet so they break not the laws we suffer them to dwell among us." — " Oh ! oh ! (Ahmed gazed ghastly, his hands moved, as if they felt for his sword) tell me, they say it not openly ! our religion commands to slay him outright, who blasphemeth thus, or the Lord would be wroth with us." Ahmed was a sickly man of a good nature, crossed in many things, and some part of his heart was full of anger. When I came in he ever welcomed me and said mildly, giving me the cushion, ' *koowy*, lean on it and be easy ;' and if I sat silent, he would add, ' *éherrij*, speak to us, sheykh Khalîl.' He was both liberal and fanatic ; and though he must spell as he read, he affected some erudition in human and divine learning : it is that unwritten life-wisdom of the coffee-hearths which every day enters into the large ears of the Arabs. " Though the Nasâra, he said, do not pray as we, yet is their religion a worshipping of Ullah. There was not one prophet only in the world, but a multitude, — some say three hundred ; and as many prophets as there were in old time, so many be the ways unto Ullah. We are the Moslemîn ; but let us not be hard with men of another religion more than God, for even of the Nasâra there be some just men and perfect in their belief, which was taught to them by the holy prophet Aysa."

But another day, when he had found the places in the koran, Ahmed questioned me maliciously, " Who, he said, was Aysa's father ? " I answered, " Sayest thou, the father of the Messîh ? this is, as doctors write, a mystery which no tongue can unfold : which is to say he had none in our common understanding, except ye would say ULLAH, that is the author of all being, or this which you pronounce yourselves, *Aysa from the spirit of Ullah*." — Mohammed made me a sign with the eyes that I should say no further, dreading some sudden excandescence in his brother ; since in their gross hearing I had uttered blasphemy. When to his other saws I responded in their manner *seelimt*, ' I grant it you ; ' " Eigh ! I thought (Ahmed answered) that Khalîl had said *islimt*, I become a Moslem, and I would God it were so. Eigh ! Khalîl, why is there any difference betwixt us ? and for this thy life is in danger daily, here and everywhere ? — but then would we send thee whithersoever thou wouldest go, in peace ; we will also accompany thee to el-Medina, to visit the sepulchre of the apostle of Ullah." — Another time he said, ' that when a man of perfect righteous life, praying in the

Medina Háram, is come to the place in his devotion, where the Moslems reverently salute the sepulchre saying, *Peace be with thee, O thou Messenger of Ullah,* the Néby has been heard to respond out of his tomb, UPON YE BE PEACE!'

Amân told me of a yearly miracle in the cave at Bedr Honeyn, where lie buried the "martyrs" that fell in the Néby's first battle with the (unbelieving) citizens of Mecca. "On a certain day, when the people go thither on pilgrimage, they hear as it were a blissful murmur within of the martyrs' voices. And they only may enter in who have preserved their lives pure from grievous crimes: but the polluted, and wrong-doers, he whispered, such as this blackhearted Abdullah es-Siruân who afflicts you here!— be not able to pass; for the passage straitens before them, and in the midst they stick fast; neither may they hear the voices of those blessed ones." — Amân musing, as many poor religious men among them, with a perfect natural conscience, deplored the criminal corruption which is now in all the Sultan's service. An hundred times such humble faithful servants of the Dowla have said and sighed in my hearing, "Alas! the Sooltàn knows not that they rob him: his officers abuse their trust, and because it comes not to his hearing there is no redress."

The delay of Abdullah's messenger to Medina, was a cloud big with discomfort to me in this darkness of Kheybar. One morning I said to Amm Mohammed at our well-labour, "What shall I do if ill news arrive to-day? Though you put this sword in my hands, I could not fight against three hundred." — " Sit we down, said the good man, let us consider, Khalîl: and now thou hast said a word, so truly, it has made my heart ache, and I cannot labour more; *hŷak*, let us home to the house," — though half an hour was not yet spent. — He was very silent, when we sat again in his suffa: and "Look, he said, Khalîl, if there come an evil tiding from the Pasha, I will redeem thee from Abdullah — at a price, wellah as a man buys a slave; it shall be with my mare, she is worth sixty reals, and Abdullah covets her. He is a melaun, a very cursed one, Khalîl; — and then I will mount thee with some Beduins, men of my trust, and let thee go." — "I like not the felon looks of Abdullah." — "I will go and sound him to-day; I shall know his mind, for he will not hide anything from me. And Khalîl, if I see the danger instant I will steal thee away, and put thee in a covert place of the

Harra, where none may find thee; and leave with thee a girby and dates, that thou mayest be there some days in security, till news be come from Medina, and I can send for thee, or else I may come to thee myself."

The day passed heavily: after supper the good man rose, and taking his sword and his mantle, and leaving me in the upper chamber, he said he would go and 'feel the pulse of the melaun': he was abroad an hour. The strong man entered again with the resolute looks of his friendly worth: and sitting down as after a battle, he said, "Khalîl, there is no present danger; and Abdullah has spoken a good word for thee to-day, — ' Khalîl, it seems, does not fear Ullah; he misdoubts me, and yet I have said it already, — if the Pasha write to me to cut off Khalîl's head, that I will mount him upon a thelûl, and let him go; and we will set our seals to paper, and I will take witness of all the people of Kheybar, — to what? that Khalîl broke out of the prison and escaped. — Tell Khalîl I have not forgotten es-Sham and Jidda, and that I am not afraid of a Pasha, who as he came in yesterday may be recalled to-morrow, but of Stambûl, and wellah for my own life.'"

The post arrived in the night. Mohammed heard of it, and went over privily to Dakhîl's house to enquire the news. "There is only this, said the messenger, that the Pasha sends now for his books."

On the morrow I was summoned to Abdullah, who bade sheykh Sâlih read me the Medina governor's letter, where only was written shortly, "Send all the stranger's books, and the paper which be brought with him from Ibn Rashîd; you are to send the cow also." The Siruân bade me go with his hostess to a closet where my bags lay, and bring out the books and papers, and leave not one remaining. This I did, only asking him to spare my loose papers, since the Pasha had not expressly demanded them, — but he would not. I said, " I will also write to the Pasha; and here is my English passport which I will send with the rest." " No!" he cried, to my astonishment, with a voice of savage rage; and ' for another word he would break his chibûk over my head,' he cursed me, and cursed ' the Engleys, and the father of the Engleys." — The villain would have struck me, but he feared the Nejûmy and Dakhîl, who were present. " Ha, it is thus, I exclaimed, that thou playest with my life!" Then an hideous tempest burst from the slave's black mouth; "This Nasrâny! he yelled, who lives to-day only by my benefit, will chop words with me; Oh wherefore with my pistol, wherefore, I say, did I not blow out his brains at the first? — wellah as ever I saw thee!"

Amm Mohammed as we came home said, "Abdullah is a melaun indeed, and, but we had been there, thou hadst not escaped him to-day."— How much more brutish I thought in my heart had been the abandonment of the Levantine consulate! that, with a light heart, had betrayed my life to so many cruel deaths!

Even Amm Mohammed heard me with impatience, when I said to him that we were not subject to the Sultan. — The Sultan, who is *Khàlif* (calif), successor to the apostle of Ullah, is the only lawful lord, they think, of the whole world; and all who yield him no obedience are *âsyîn*, revolted peoples and rebels. The good man was sorry to hear words savouring, it seemed to him, of sedition, in the mouth of Khalîl. He enquired, had we learned yet in our (outlying) countries to maintain bands of trained soldiery, such as are the askars of the Sooltàn? I answered, that our arts had armed and instructed the Ottoman service, and that without us they would be naked. "It is very well, he responded, that the Engleys, since they be not âsyîn, should labour for the Sooltàn."

When I named the countries of the West, he enquired if there were not Moslemîn living in some of them. I told him, that long ago a rabble of Moghrebies had invaded and possessed themselves of the florid country of *Andalûs*. — Andalusîa was a glorious province of Islam: the Arabian plant grew in the Titanic soil of Europe to more excellent temper and stature; and there were many *bulbul* voices among them, in that land of the setting sun, gladdened with the genial wine. Yet the Arabs decayed in the fruition of that golden soil, and the robust nephews of them whom their forefathers had dispossessed, descending from the mountains, reconquered their own country. As I said this, "Wellah guwiyîn! then they must be a strong people, answered Amm Mohammed. Thou, Khalîl, hast visited many lands; and wander where thou wilt, since it is thy list, only no more in the Peninsula of the Arabs (*Jezîrat el-Arab*). Thou hast seen already that which may suffice thee; and what a lawless waste land it is! and perilous even for us who were born there; and what is this people's ignorance and their intolerance of every other religion. Where wilt thou be when God have delivered thee out of these troubles? that if ever I come into those parts I might seek thee. Tell me where to send my letter, if ever I would write to thee ; and if I inscribe it *Sheykh Khalîl, Bêled el-Engleys*, will that find thee ?"

"Here is paper, a reed, and ink : Abdullah would not have thee write to the Pasha, but write thou, and I will send the letter by Dakhîl who will not deny me, and he returns to-morrow. See in writing to the Pasha that thou lift him up with many high-sounding praises." — " I shall write but plainly, after my conscience." — " Then thou art mejnûn, and that conscience is not good, which makes thee afraid to help thyself in a danger." — " Tell me, is the Pasha a young man of sudden counsels, or a spent old magistrate of Stambûl ? " — " He is a grey-beard of equitable mind, a reformer of the officer service, and for such he is unwelcome to the ill-deserving. Yet I would have thee praise him, for thus must we do to obtain anything ; the more is the pity." I wrote with my pencil in English, — for Mohammed told me there are interpreters at Medina. I related my coming down with the Haj, from Syria, to visit Medáin Sâlih ; and, that I had since lived with the Beduw, till I went, after a year, to Hâyil ; from whence Ibn Rashîd, at my request, had sent me hither, I complained to the Pasha-governor of this wrongful detention at Kheybar, in spite of my passport from a Wàly of Syria ; also certain Beduins of the Dowla coming in, who knew me, had witnessed to the truth of all that I said. I demanded therefore, that I might proceed upon my journey and be sent forward with sure persons.

I was sitting in the soldiers' kahwa, when Abdullah wrote his new letter to the Pasha, " My humble duty to your lordship : I send now the stranger's books and papers. I did send the cow to your lordship by some Aarab going down to Medina ; but the cow broke from them, and ran back to Kheybar : she is now sick, and therefore I may not yet send her." — "Hast thou written all this, sheykh Sâlih ? — he will not be much longer, please Ullah, Bashat el-Medina ; for they say another is coming." No man hearing his fable could forbear laughing ; only the Siruân looked sadly upon it, for the cow yielded him every day a bowlful of milk, in this low time at Kheybar. Abdullah set his seal to the letters, and delivered them to Dakhîl, who departed before noon. Amm Mohammed, as he was going, put a piece of silver (from me) in Dakhîl's hand, and cast my letter, with my British passport, into the worthy man's budget, upon his back, who feigned thus that he did not see it : the manly villager was not loath to aid a stranger (and a public guest) whom he saw oppressed in his village by the criminal tyranny of Abdullah.

His inditing the letter to Medina had unsettled Abdullah's brains, so that he fell again into his fever : " Help me quickly ! he cries, where is thy book, sheykh Sâlih ; and you Beduins sitting here, have ye not some good remedies in the desert ? " Sâlih pored over his wise book, till he found him a new caudle and enchantment. — Another time I saw Sâlih busy to cure a mangy thelûl ; he sat with a bowl of water before him, and mumbling thereover he spat in it, and mumbled solemnly and spat many times ; and after a half hour of this work the water was taken to the sick beast to drink. — Spitting (a despiteful civil defilement) we have seen to be some great matter in their medicine. — Is it, that they spit thus against the malicious jân ? Parents bid their young children spit upon them : an Arabian father will often softly say to the infant son in his arms, " Spit upon bábu ! spit, my darling."

CHAPTER VII

GALLA-LAND. MEDINA LORE

The Abyssinian Empire. *Galla-land.* Perpetual warfare of (heathen) Gallas and (Christian) Abyssinians. A renegade Frank or Traveller at Mecca and Medina. *Subîa* drink. A hospitable widow (at Tâyif). " The Nasâra are an offspring of the Sea." Wady Bîshy. Muharram's death. The Nasrâny accused. Sale of Muharram's goods. Aly, the (deadly) enemy of the Nasrâny. The Ferrâ. El-Auâzim. Thegîf. The Nejûmy in Hâyil. A Roman invasion of ancient Arabia. Aelius Gallus sent by Augustus, with an army, to rob the riches of *A. Felix.* Season of the Haj. Alarms. Tidings from the War. Palm plait. Quern stones wrought by the Arabs. New alarms. Antique building on the Harra. Yanba. The Kheybar valleys. Harrats of Medina. The Hálhal. The Húrda. Clay summer-houses of W. Aly Beduins. The Kheyâbara abstain from certain meats. Another Ageyly's death. — Was his grave ' violated by the witches ' ? Tales of the jân. A man wedded with a jin wife at Medina.

MANY night hours when we could not sleep, I spent in discoursing with my sick Galla comrade, the poor friendly-minded Amân. When I enquired of the great land of the Gallas, " *El-Hábash*, quoth he, is the greatest empire of the world ; for who is there a Sooltàn to be compared with the Sooltàn of el-Hàbash ! " — " Well, we found but a little king, on this side, when the Engleys took his beggarly town, *Mágdala*." — Amân bethought him, that in his childhood when he was brought down with the slave drove they had gone by this Mágdala. ' That king, he said, could be no more than a governor or pasha, for the great Sooltàn, whose capital is at the distance of a year's journey, where he inhabits a palace of ivory. The governors and lieutenants of his many provinces gather an imperial tribute, — that is at no certain time ; but as it were once in three or four years.'

This fable is as much an article of faith with all the Gallas, as the legend which underlies our most beliefs ; and may rise in their half-rational conscience of a sort of inarticulate argument : — ' Every soil is subject to rulers, there is therefore a Ruler of Galla-land. — Galla-land the greatest country in all the world ; but the Sultan of the greatest land is the greatest Sultan : also a Sultan inhabits richly, therefore that greatest Sultan inhabits the riches of the (African) world, and his palace is all of ivory ! ' Amân said, ' The country is not settled in villages ;

but every man's house is a round dwelling of sticks and stubble, large and well framed, in the midst of his ground, which he has taken up of the hill lands about him. Such faggot-work may stand many years [; but is continually in danger to be consumed by fire, in a moment]. They break and sow as much soil as they please ; and their grain is not measured for the abundance. They have great wealth of kine, so that he is called a poor man whose stock is only two or three hundred. Their oxen are big-bodied, and have great horns : the Gallas milk only so many of their cattle as may suffice them for drinking and for butter ; they drink beer also, which they make of their plenty of corn. Though it be an high and hilly land, a loin-cloth [as anciently in the Egyptian and Ethiopian countries] is their only garment ; but such is the equal temper of the air that they need none other. The hot summer never grieves them ; in the winter they feel no more than a wholesome freshness. In their country are lions, but Ullah's mercy has slaked the raging of those terrible wild beasts ; for *the lions sicken every other day with fever, and else they would destroy the world!* The lions slaughter many of their cattle ; but to mankind they do no hurt or rarely. A man seeing a lion in the path should hold his way evenly without faintness of heart, and so pass by him ; not turning his eyes to watch the lion, for that would waken his anger. There are elephants and giraffes ; their horses are of great stature.'—I have heard from the slave drivers that a horse may be purchased in the Galla country for (the value of) a real!

'In Galla-land there is no use of money ; the people, he said, have no need to buy anything : they receive foreign trifles from the slave dealers, as beads and the little round in-folding tin mirrors. Such are chiefly the wares which the drivers bring with them,—besides salt, which only fails them in that largess of heaven which is in their country. A brick of salt, the load of a light porter, is the price of a slave among them. That salt is dug at Suâkim (by the Red Sea, nearly in face of Jidda), six months distant. The Gallas are hospitable to strangers, who may pass, where they will, through their country. When there is warfare between neighbour tribes, the stranger is safe in what district he is ; but if he would pass beyond he must cross the infested border, at his peril, to another tribe ; and he will again be in surety among them. The Galla country is very open and peaceable ; and at what cottage the stranger may alight he is received to their plenteous hospitality. They ask him whether he would drink of their ale or of their milk ? Some beast is slaughtered, and they will give him the flesh, which he can cook for himself [since the Gallas are raw-flesh eaters].

'They have wild coffee trees in their country, great as oaks; and that coffee is the best: the bean is very large. They take up the fallen berries from the ground, and roast them with samn. Coffee is but for the elders' drinking, and that seldom: they think it becomes not their young men to use the pithless caudle drink. The women make butter, rocking the milk in the shells of great gourds: they store all their drink in such vessels. Grain-gold may be seen in the sand of the torrents; but there are none who gather it. Among them [as in Arabia] is a smiths' caste; the Galla people mingle not with them in wedlock. The smiths receive payment for their labour in cattle.' I did not ascertain from Amân what is their religion: 'he could not tell; they pray, he said, and he thought that they turn themselves toward Mecca.' He could not remember that they had any books among them.

Amân had been stolen, one afternoon as he kept his father's neat, by men from a neighbour tribe. The raiders went the same night to lodge in a cottage, where lived a widow woman. When the good woman had asked the captive boy of his parentage, she said to the guests, that the child's kindred were her acquaintance, and she would redeem him with an hundred oxen; but they would not. A few days later he was sold to the slave dealer: and began to journey in the drove of boys and girls, to be sold far off in a strange land. These children with the captive young men and maidens march six months, barefoot, to the Red Sea: the distance may be 1200 miles. Every night they come to a station of the slave-drivers, where they sup of flesh meat and the country beer. Besides the aching weariness of that immense foot journey, they had not been mishandled.

'Of what nation were the slave drivers?'—this he could not answer: they were white men, and in his opinion Moslemîn; but not Arabians, since they were not at home at *Jidda*, which was then, *and is now, the staple town of African slavery, for the Turkish Empire:*—*Jidda where are Frankish consuls!* But you shall find these worthies, in the pallid solitude of their palaces, affecting (great Heaven!) the simplicity of new-born babes,—they will tell you, they are not aware of it! But I say again, in your ingenuous ears, *Jidda is the staple town of the Turkish slavery*, OR ALL THE MOSLEMÎN ARE LIARS.

— At length they came down to the flood of the Nile, which lay in a great deep of the mountains, and were ferried over upon a float of reeds and blown goat-skins. Their journey, he said, is so long because of the hollowness of the country. For they often pass valley deeps, where, from one brow, the other seems not very far off; yet in descending and ascending they march a day or two to come thither. Their aged men in Galla-land use to say, that 'the Nile comes streaming to them in deep crooked valleys, from bare and unknown country many months distant.'

"Amân, when I am free, go we to Galla-land! it will not be there as here, where for one cow we would give our left hands!" The poor Galla had raised himself upon his elbow, with a melancholy distraction, and smiling he seemed to see his country again: he told me his own name in the Galla tongue, when he was a child, in his Galla home. I asked if no anger was left in his heart, against those who had stolen and sold his life to servitude in the ends of the earth. "Yet one thing, sheykh Khalîl, has recompensed me,—that I remained not in ignorance with the heathen!—Oh the wonderful providence of Ullah! whereby I am come to this country of the Apostle, and to the knowledge of the religion! Ah, mightest thou be partaker of the same!—yet I know that all is of the Lord's will, and this also shall be, in God's good time!" He told me that few Gallas ever return to their land when they have recovered their freedom.—"And wilt thou return, Amân?" "Ah! he said, my body is grown now to another temper of the air, and to another manner of living."

There is continual warfare on the Galla border with the (hither) Abyssinians; and therefore *the Abyssinians suffer none to go over with their fire-arms to the Gallas.* The Gallas are warlike, and armed with spear and shield they run furiously upon their enemies in battle.—In the Gallas is a certain haughty gentleness of bearing, even in land of their bondage.

Amân told me the tale of his life, which slave and freed-man he had passed in the Hejâz. He was sometime at Jidda, a custom-house watchman on board ships lying in the road; the most are great barques carrying Bengal rice, with crews of that country under English captains. Amân spoke with good remembrance of the hearty hospitality of the "Nasâra" seamen. One day, he watched upon a steamship newly arrived from India, and among her passengers was a "Nasrâny," who "sat weeping, weeping, and his friends could not appease him." Amân, when he saw his time, enquired the cause; and the stranger answered him afflictedly, "Eigh me! I have asked of the Lord, that I might visit the City of His Holy House, and become a Moslem: is not Mecca yonder? Help me, thou good Moslem, that I may repair thither, and pray in the sacred places!— but ah! these detain me." When it was dark, Amân hailed a wherry; and privily he sent this stranger to land, and charged the boatman for him.

The Jidda waterman set his fare on shore; and saw him mounted upon an ass, for Mecca,— one of those which are driven at a run, in a night-time, the forty and five miles or more betwixt the port town and the Holy City.— When the new day was dawning, the "Frenjy" entered Mecca! Some citizens, the first he met, looking earnestly upon the stranger stayed to ask him, "Sir, what brings thee hither?— being it seems a Nasrâny!" He answered them, "I was a Christian, and I have required it of the Lord,— that I might enter this Holy City and become a Moslem!" Then they led him with joy, to their houses, and circumcised the man: and that renegade or traveller was years after dwelling in Mecca and in Medina.— Amân thought his godfathers had made a collection for him; and that he was become a tradesman in the sûk.— Who may interpret this and the like strange tales? which we may often hear related among them!

Amân drank the strong drink which was served out with his rations on shipboard; and in his soldiering life he made (secretly) with his comrade, a spirituous water, letting boiled rice ferment: the name of it is *subia*, and in the Hejâz heat they think it very refreshing. But the unhappy man thus continually wounding his conscience, in the end had corroded his infirm health also, past remedy.— When first he received the long arrears of his pay, he went to the slave dealers in Jidda, and bought himself a maiden, of his own people, to wife, for fifty dollars.— They had but a daughter between them: and another time when he removed from Mecca to Jidda the child fell from the camel's back; and of that hurt she died. Amân seemed not in the remembrance to feel a father's pity! His wife wasted all that ever he brought home, and after that he put her away: then she gained her living as a seamstress, but died within a while;— "the Lord, he said, have mercy upon her!" — When next he received his arrears, he remained one year idle at Mecca, drinking and smoking away his slender thrift in the coffee houses, until nothing was left; and then he entered this Ageyl service.

The best moments of his life, up and down in the Hejâz, he had passed at Tâyif. " Eigh ! how beautiful (he said) is et-Tâyif ! " He spoke with reverent affection of the Great-sherîf [he died about this time], a prince of a nature which called forth the perfect good will of all who served him. Amân told with wonder of the sherîf's garden [the only garden in Desert Arabia !] at Tâyif, and of a lion there in a cage, that was meek only to the sherîf. All the Great-sherîfs' wives, he said, were Galla women ! He spoke also of a certain beneficent widow at Tâyif, whose bountiful house stands by the wayside ; where she receives all passengers to the Arabian hospitality.

Since his old " uncle " was dead, Amân had few more hopes for this life, — he was now a broken man at the middle age ; and yet he hoped in his " brother." This was no brother by nature, but a negro once his fellow servant : and such are by the benign custom of the Arabian household accounted brethren. He heard that his negro brother, now a freed-man, was living at Jerusalem ; and he had a mind to go up to Syria and seek him, if the Lord would enable him. Amân was dying of a slow consumption and a vesical malady, of the great African continent, little known in our European art of medicine : — and who is infirm at Kheybar, he is likely to die. This year there remained only millet for sick persons' diet : " The [foster] God forgive me, said poor Amân, that I said it is as wood to eat." With the pensive looks of them who see the pit before their feet, in the midst of their days, he sat silent, wrapt in his mantle, all day in the sun, and drank tobacco. — One's life is full of harms, who is a sickly man, and his fainting heart of impotent ire ; which alienates, alas ! even the short human kindness of the few friends about him. At night the poor Galla had no covering from the cold ; then he rose every hour and blew the fire and drank tobacco.

The wives of the Kheyâbara were very charitable to the poor soldiery : it is a hospitable duty of the Arabian hareem towards all lone strangers among them. For who else should fill a man's girby at the spring, or grind his corn for him, and bring in firewood ? None offer them silver for this service, because it is of their hospitality. Only a good wife serving some welfaring stranger, as Ahmed, is requited once or twice in the year with a new gown-cloth and a real or two, which he may be willing to give her. Our neighbour's wife, a goodly young negress, served the sick Amân, only of her womanly pity, and she sat ofttimes to watch by him in our suffa. Then *Jummàr* (this was her name) gazed upon me with great startling eyes; such a strangeness and terror seemed to her to be in this name 'Nasrâny'! One day she said, at length, *Andakom hareem, fî?* " be there women in your land?" — " Ullah! (yes forsooth), mothers, daughters and wives; — am I not the son of a woman: or dost thou take me, silly woman, for *weled eth-thîb*, a son of the wolf?" — "Yes, yes, I thought so: but wellah, Khalîl, be the Nasâra born as we? ye rise not then — *out of the sea!*" — When I told this tale to Amm Mohammed, he laughed at their fondness. " So they would make thee, Khalîl, another kind of God's creature, the sea's offspring! this foolish people babble without understanding themselves when they say SEA: their 'sea' is they could not tell what kind of monster!" And Jummàr meeting us soon after in the street, must hang her bonny floc head to the loud mirth of Amm Mohammed: for whom I was hereafter *weled eth-thîb*, and if I were any time unready at his dish, he would say pleasantly, "Khalîl, thou art not then *weled eth-thîb!*" A bystander said one day, as I was rolling up a flag of rock from our mine, *Ma fî hail*, 'there is no strength.' Mohammed answered, "Nevertheless we have done somewhat, for there helped me the son of the wolf." "I am no wolfling, I exclaimed, but *weyladak*, a son of thine." "Wellah! answered the good man, surprised and smiling, thou art my son indeed."

Kurds, Albanians, Gallas, Arabs, Negroes, Nasrâny, we were many nations at Kheybar. One day a Beduwy oaf said at Abdullah's hearth, " It is wonderful to see so many diversities of mankind! but what be the Nasâra? — for since they are not of Islam, they cannot be of the children of Adam." I answered, " There was a prophet named Noah, in whose time God drowned the world; but Noah with his sons Sem, Ham, Yâfet, and their wives, floated in a vessel: they are the fathers of mankind. The Kurdies, the Turks, the Engleys, are of Yâfet; you Arabs are children of Sem; and you the Kheyâbara, are of Ham, and this Bîshy." — " Akhs! (exclaimed the fellow) and thou speak such a word again — !" *Abdullah:* " Be not sorry, for I also (thy captain) am of Ham." The Bîshy, a negro Ageyly, was called by the name of his country (in el-Yémen) the *W. Bîshy* [in the opinion of some Oriental scholars " the river Pison " of the Hebrew scriptures, *v. Die alte Geographie Arabiens*]. It is from thence that the sherîf of Mecca draws the most of his (negro) band of soldiery, — called therefore *el-Bîshy*, and they are such as the Ageyl. This Yémany spoke nearly the Hejâz vulgar, in which is not a little base metal ; so that it sounds churlish-like in the dainty ears of the inhabitants of Nejd.

We heard again that Muharram lay sick ; and said Abdullah, " Go to him, Khalîl ; he was much helped by your former medicines." — I found Muharram bedrid, with a small quick pulse : it was the second day he had eaten nothing ; he had fever and visceral pains, and would not spend for necessary things. I persuaded him to boil a chicken, and drink the broth with rice, if he could not eat ; and gave him six grains of rhubarb with one of laudanum powder, and a little quinine, to be taken in the morning.

The day after I was not called. I had been upon the Harra with Amm Mohammed, and was sitting at night in our chamber with Amân : we talked late, for, the winter chillness entering at our open casement, we could not soon sleep. About midnight we were startled by an untimely voice ; one called loudly in the corner of our place, to other askars who lodged there, ' Abdullah bade them come to him.' All was horror at Kheybar, and I thought the post might be arrived from Medina, with an order for my execution. I spoke to Amân, who sat up blowing the embers, to lean out of the casement, and enquire of them what it was. Amân looking out said, *Ey khábar, yâ*, ' Ho, there, what tidings ? ' They answered him somewhat, and said Amân, withdrawing his head, " *Ullah yurhamhu*, ' May the Lord have mercy upon him,' — they say Muharram is dead, and they are sent to provide for his burial, and for the custody of his goods." — " I have lately given him medicines ! and what if this graceless people now say, ' Khalîl killed him ' ; if any of them come now, we will make fast the door, and do thou lend me thy musket." — " Khalîl, said the infirm man sitting at the fire, trust in the Lord, and if thou have done no evil, fear not : what hast thou to do with this people ? they are hounds, apes, oxen, and their hareem are witches : but lie down again and sleep."

I went in the morning to the soldiers' kahwa and found only the Siruân, who then arrived from Muharram's funeral. " What is this ? Khalîl, cries he, Muharram is dead, and they say it was thy medicines : now, if thou know not the medicines, give no more to any man. — They say that you have killed him, and they tell me Muharram said this before he died. [I afterwards ascertained from his comrades that the unhappy man had not spoken at all of my medicines.] Mohammed el-Kurdy says that after you had given him the medicine you rinsed your hands in warm water." I exclaimed in my haste, "*Mohammed lies!*" — a perilous word. In the time of my being in Syria, a substantial Christian was violently drawn by the Mohammedan people of Tripoli, where he lived, before the kâdy, only for this word, uttered in the common hearing; and he had but spoken of it of his false Moslem servant, whose name was Mohammed. The magistrate sent him, in the packet boat, to be judged at Beyrût; but we heard that in his night passage, of a few hours, the Christian had been secretly thrust overboard!— Abdullah looked at me with eyes which said 'It is death to blaspheme the Néby!' — "Mohammed, I answered, the Kurdy, lies, for he was not present." — "I cannot tell, Khalîl, Abdullah said at last with gloomy looks, the man is dead; then give no more medicines to any creature;" and the askars now entering, he said to them, "Khalîl is an angry man, for this cause of Muharram; — speak we of other matter."

There came up Mohammed the Kurdy and the Egyptian: they had brought over the dead and buried man's goods, who yesterday at this time was living amongst them! — his pallet, his clothes, his red cap, his water-skin. Abdullah sat down to the sale of them; also, $2\frac{1}{2}$ reals were said to be owing for the corpse-washing and burying. Abdullah enquired, 'What of Muharram's money? for all that he had must be sent to his heirs; and has he not a son in Albania?' The dead man's comrades swore stoutly, that they found not above ten reals in his girdle. *Sirûr:* "He had more than fifty! Muharram was rich." The like said others of them (Amân knew that he had as much as seventy reals). *Abdullah:* "Well, I will not enter into nice reckonings; — enough, if we cannot tell what has become of his money. — Who will buy this broidered coat, that is worth ten reals at Medina?" One cried, "Half a real." *Sirûr:* "Three quarters!" *A villager:* "I will give two krûsh more." *Abdullah:* "Then none of you shall have this; I reserve it for his heirs. What comes next? a pack of cards: — (and he said with his Turkish smiles) Muharram whilst he lived won the most of his money thus, mesquin! — who will give anything? — I think these were made in Khalîl's country. The picture upon them [a river, a wood, and a German church] is what, Khalîl? Will none buy? — then Khalîl shall have them." — "I would not touch them." They were bidding for the sorry old gamester's wretched blanket and pallet, and contending for his stained linen when I left them.

If a deceased person be named in the presence of pious Mohammedans they will respond, ' May the Lord have mercy upon him !' but meeting with Ahmed in the path by the burial ground, he said, " Muharram is gone, and he owed me two reals, may Ullah confound him !" — I was worn to an extremity ; and now the malevolent barked against my life for the charity which I had shown to Muharram ! Every day Aly the ass brayed in the ass's ears of Abdullah, ' It was high time to put to death the adversary of the religion, also his delaying [to kill me] was sinful : ' and he alleged against me the death of Muharram. I saw the Siruân's irresolute black looks grow daily more dangerous : " Ullah knows, I said to the Nejûmy, what may be brooding in his black heart : a time may come when, the slave's head turning, he will fire his pistols on me." — " Thou camest here as a friend of the Dowla, and what cause had this ass-in-office to meddle at all in thy matter, and to make thee this torment ? Wellah if he did me such wrong, since there is none other remedy in our country, I would kill him and escape to the Ferrâ." Amm Mohammed declared publicly, ' His own trust in sheykh Khalîl to be such that if I bade him drink even a thing venomous, he would drink it ;' and the like said Amân, who did not cease to use my remedies. The better sort of Kheyâbara now said, that ' Muharram was not dead of my medicines, but come to the end of his days, he departed by the decree of Ullah.'

Amm Mohammed told me that the summer heat is very burdenous in the Ferrâ. The Harb villagers there are black skinned : they dwell in such clay houses as these at Kheybar : the place is built upon an height, in a palm oasis. Thither in his youth he went oftentimes on foot with his brethren, from Medina. The sun beating on that sandy soil is almost insufferable : upon a time, as they went together, he saw Ahmed totter ; and his brother fell down presently in a swoon. Mohammed drew him to the shadow of an acacia, and sprinkled a little water on his face from the girby ; and he came to himself.

El-Ferrâ was anciently, he said, of the *Auâzim*, Heteym. — Surely that is a nation of antiquity in Arabia (where they are now found dwelling so widely dispersed): and they remain, in some seats, from times before the now inhabiting Arabs! The last of the *Auâzim* of the Ferrâ was one of the richest possessors of palms; Amm Mohammed remembered him. That Heteymy ever answered to the importunity of his Harb villagers, who would buy his land, " Shall I sell mine inheritance ! " In the end — to live in more rest — the old fox said to them, " Ye see, I have an only daughter ! now who is he of your young men that would be the son-in-law of me *el-Âzimy ?* and he shall inherit my land." Of the nearly extinct Auâzim there are yet three or four nomad households which encamp with the Beny Rashîd [Heteym]. Some in scorn account the Auâzim, Solubba. To this name *Âzim*, plural Auâzim, responds Hâzim. Hâzim is a fendy of Harb, but their foes revile them as Solubbies ; and according to the tradition they are intruded strangers. In this country, westwards, is a kindred of Jeheyna, *el-Thegîf*, who are snibbed as Yahûd : — this may mean that they are of the pre-Islamite Aarab. There is a doggerel rime at Medina, *Ullah yulaan Thegîf, kiddâm tegúf,* " God curse (those Jews) the Thegîf afore thou stand still." It is said of a small jummaa among the W. Sleymàn of Bishr, that they are Solubba ; but they intermarry with the rest. In the south there remain certain welfaring Heteym in the Teháma below Mecca.

Amm Mohammed had not seen el-Ally or Teyma. The Arabs are great wanderers, *but not out of the way* (of their interest). Now that he was a rich-poor man, and at rest, he promised his heart to visit them, were it only to see their country. Mohammed had once ridden to Hâyil, when he was sojourning at el-Hâyat : he mounted with Beduins. The first day they made small account of him, a townling [and a smith], but his manly sufficiency was bye and bye better known to them. They alighted at one of the outlying hamlets of Shammar ; in which place were but two houses, and only two old men at home, who came forth to receive them. The Nejûmy said to his host, " How may ye dwell thus, in the midst of the khála ? " — " God be thanked we live here without dread, under Ibn Rashîd ; our sons herd the goats upon the mountains, and go far out for wood." Each householder killed a goat, and Mohammed commended their hospitality.

In Hâyil, he was known to many : some of his acquaintance called him daily to breakfast and to supper ; and he was bidden from kahwa to kahwa. As he sat in a friend's house, Bunder entered impetuously, with his bevy of companions and slaves — all the young princes are thus attended — to see the stranger. " What *ájneby*, foreigner, is that ? "

enquired Bunder, — and without awaiting his answer, the raw young man turned the back and flung forth again.

Mohammed had ridden westward, in the Bashy Bazûk expeditions as far as Yanba; he had ridden in Nejd with Turkish troops to the Waháby capital, er-Riâth. That was for some quarrel of the sherîf of Mecca: they lay encamped before the Nejd city fifteen days, and if Ibn Saûd had not yielded their demands, they would have besieged him. The army marched over the khála, with cannon, and provision camels; and he said they found water in the Beduin wells for all the cattle, and to fill their girbies. The Arabian deserts may be passed by armies strong enough to disperse the resistance of the frenetic but unwarlike inhabitants; but they should not be soldiers who cannot endure much and live of a little. The rulers of Egypt made war twenty years in Arabia; and they failed finally because they came with great cost to possess so poor a country. The Roman army sent by Augustus under Aelius Gallus to make a prey of the chimerical riches of Arabia Felix was 11,000 men, Italians and allies. They marched painfully over the waterless wastes six months! wilfully misled, as they supposed, by the Nabateans of Petra, their allies. In the end of their long marches, they took Nejrân by assault: six camps further southward they met with a great multitude of the barbarous people assembled against them, at a brookside. In the battle there fell *many thousands* of the Arabs! and of the Romans and allies two soldiers. The Arabians fought, as men unwont to handle weapons, with slings, swords and lances and two-edged hatchets. The Romans, at their furthest, were only two marches from the frankincense country. In returning upwards the general led the feeble remnant of his soldiery, in no more than sixty marches, to the port of el-Héjr. The rest perished of misery in the long and terrible way of the wilderness: only seven Romans had fallen in battle! — Surely the knightly Roman poet deserved better than to be afterwards disgraced, because he had not fulfilled the dreams of Caesar's avarice! Europeans, deceived by the Arabs' loquacity, have in every age a fantastic opinion of this unknown calamitous country.

Those Italians looking upon that dire waste of nature in Arabia, and grudging because they must carry water upon camels, laid all to the perfidy of their guides. The Roman general found the inhabitants of the land 'A people unwarlike, half of them helping their living by merchandise, and half of them by robbing' [such they are now]. Those ancient Arabs wore a cap, *v.* Vol. I. pp. 203, 613, and let their locks grow to the full length : the most of them cut the beard, leaving the upper lip, others went unshaven. — " The nomads living in tents of hair-cloth are troublesome borderers," says Pliny, [as they are to-day !] Strabo writing from the mouth of Gallus himself, who was his friend and Prefect of Egypt, describes so well the Arabian desert, that it cannot be bettered. " It is a sandy waste, with only few palms and pits of water : the thorn [acacia] and the tamarisk grow there ; the wandering Arabs lodge in tents and are camel graziers."

The season was come about of the Haj returning : their rumour (as all in Arabia) was full of woes and alarms ! In a sudden (tropical) rain a quarter of Mecca had been damaged by the rushing torrent ; and the pestilence was among the Hajáj : also the Great-sherîf of Mecca, journeying with the pilgrimage to Medina, was deceased in the way. — At this word *el-wâba* ! Abdullah paled in his black skin, and the Nejûmy spoke under his breath : " The death, they said, will be soon at Kheybar ! " Amm Mohammed gave his counsel at the village governor's kahwa mejlis, 'that none should dread in his heart, but let every man go about his daily tasks and leave their care unto Ullah.' *Abdullah :* " And here is Khalîl, an hakîm : your opinion, Khalîl." — " There might be a quarantine." — " *Âs' Ullah sahîhh,* — the sooth by God, and it shall be done ; ye wot where, sirs ? — under Atwa yonder." Moreover the Moors had fallen out amongst themselves at Mecca, for the inheritance of those who were dead in the plague, — which had begun among them. Finally the Moghrâreba marched out, two or three days, before the departure of the Syrian and the Egyptian caravans, for Medina. When they arrived the Pasha forbade them to enter ; he said, they might come another year to visit the Néby. But the truculent Moghrebies sent this word to the Turkish governor, " Let us visit the Néby in peace, and else will we visit him by the sword. Art thou a Nasrâny ? thou that forbiddest pilgrims to visit the Néby ! " — The Pasha yielded to their importunity, sooner than any occasion should be given. The Moors entered tumultuously, and the citizens remained shut in their houses ; dreading that in a few hours the cholera would be begun among them. It was also reported from the north that the Jurdy had been detained by the Fukara at el-Akhdar. — And thus there is no year, in Arabia, not full of a multitude of alarms !

Some returning marketers from Medina brought us word of an armistice in the great jehâd of the Religion waged with the Nasâra: The fallen of Medina in the war were fifteen men. They were soldiers of the faith serving of their free will, for there is no military conscription in the Harameyn. Amm Mohammed told me that in the beginning many had offered themselves: they issued from the gates (every man bearing his shroud) and encamped without the city; and had bound themselves with an oath never to re-enter, but it were with the victory of the Moslemîn.—The like was seen in the beginning of the Crimean war; when many young men enrolled themselves, and Mohammed, persuaded by a fellow of his, would have gone along with them; but as they were ready to sail a sickness hindered him: and the ship in which his friends had put to sea foundered in her voyage!

Now I listened with pain to the talk in Abdullah's kahwa; where they spoke of the Christians' cruelties against Mohammedan captives. 'The Nasâra had shut up many Moslems in a house, and, heaping firewood about the walls, they burned them living:— the Nasâra use also to dig a hole in a field and lay-in powder, and so they blow up a great heap of the Moslemîn.'—"Sheykh Khalîl, said Amm Mohammed, I have wondered at nothing more than to see in thee a quiet and peaceable behaviour; for we hear that the Nasâra are all violent men of nature, and great strikers."

A party of the village hareem went down in an hubt to sell their palm-leaf plait in Medina. It is in long rolls that may be stitched into matting; and of such they make their baskets. For this work they must crop the tender unfolding leaf-stalks in the heads of the palm stems. They tie the stripped leaflets in bundles, and steep them when they would use them. The plucking is not without damage to the trees: a palm thus checked will bear, they say, but the half of her natural fruits (eight months later); that were an autumn loss (for the small trees at Kheybar) of twenty piastres. And all the plait from one stem (two days' labour) is worth only three piastres or sixpence!—But it is a custom: the half loss falls upon the absent Beduwy; and the village housewives, whose hands cannot be idle, think they have gotten somewhat by this diligent unthrift. For it is their own money, and therewith they may buy themselves some light cloak, *mishlah*, and a new gown-cloth. The Kheybar palms are without number; in other Arabian oases and at Medina, but one frond (it is said) may be plucked in every palm head. The kinds of palms are many in every oasis, and they know each kind by the aspect: the tender fronds only in certain kinds are good for their palm matting. The plait from Kheybar is in some estimation at Medina : the salesmen receive much of it in payment for their wares in the autumn fair. They draw as well many camel-loads of date-stones from Kheybar, which are worth five krûsh the sah at Medina, nearly twopence a pint ! — Date-stones are steeped and ground for camels' food in all that most barren and sun-stricken lowland of the Hejâz : they are cast away in Nejd.

The bonny wife of *Hamdàn*, a neighbour of ours, came in from the returning hubt. I was sitting with her husband and some neighbours in the house, and saw that she saluted them every man with a salaam and a hearty buss : it is their honest custom, and among the Beduw of these parts the wedded women will kiss the men of their acquaintance after an absence, and receive a manly kiss of them again ; and the husbands looking on take it not amiss, for they are brethren. — Other Aarab I have seen (in Sinai) so precious, that if a woman meet an uncle's son in the desert, he and she standing off from each other at their arms' length, with a solemn countenance, they do but touch together the tips of their fingers. When she had bestowed a good smack upon Amm Mohammed, " Eigh ! saw you not, said he, my mother in the city, and how fares the old lady ? " — " She is well and sends thy wife and Haseyn this packet of sweetmeats (seeds and raisins). But O Mohammed ! she was aghast to hear of a Nasrâny living with her son in his house ; ' akhs ! said thy mother to us, what do ye tell me ye women of Kheybar ? that a Nasrâny is dwelling with my son Mohammed ? Speak to Mohammed to be quit of him as soon as ever he may ; for what should a Nasrâny bring us but the displeasure of Ullah ? ' " Amm Mohammed answered, with little reverence, " Sheykh Khalîl, hast thou heard the old woman's words ? but we are brethren, we have eaten together, and these Beduw are altogether superstitious." His aged mother came sometimes in the summer caravans from Medina to visit her sons, and pass a few weeks with Mohammed at Kheybar.

There was not a smith in the oasis : the Nejûmy since the beginning of his prosperity had given up his old tasks. Only from time to time some Solubbies come, riding upon their asses, from the Heteym menzils ; and what tinning and metal work they find at Kheybar, they have it away with them to bring it again after other days. There is nothing wrought here besides quern-stones, which every household can make for themselves. I have seen it a labour of two daylights, to beat down the chosen basalt block, and fashion it with another hard stone. The Fejîr in their sand-rock dîra beat them out of sandstone, and some poor Fukara tribesmen bring such querns with them to sell in the autumn fair at Kheybar. So I have seen Towwara Beduins carrying down pairs of granite quern-stones, which they had wrought in their own Sinai mountains, to Egypt. Granite, and lava mill-stones are made by the B. Atîeh Beduins in the Aueyrid Harra. [v. Vol. I. p. 238.] After the water-skins a pair of mill-stones is the most necessary husbandry in an Arabian household. To grind their corn is the housewives' labour; and the dull rumour of the running mill-stones is as it were a comfortable voice of food in an Arabian village, when in the long sunny hours there is often none other human sound. The drone of mill-stones may be heard before the daylight in the nomad menzils; where what for the weighty carriage, and because it is so little they have ever to grind, the quern is only found in a few sheykhly households. Many neighbours therefore borrow the use of one mill, and the first must begin at early hours. I have seen the wandering Aarab in the long summer, when they had nothing left, abandon their heavy querns in some place, where another day they might find them again. It is then they say, "The people are hungry, we have no more food; *such and such sheykhs have forsaken their mill-stones.*" — The Arab housewives can make savoury messes of any grain, seething it and putting thereto only a little salt and samn, much better than the poor of European countries!

In the Arabs of the desert is a natural ability for beating out what shapes they would in stone. We have seen the Beduins fashion their best pipe-heads (*aorfy*) thus, — and in like manner their stone coffee-pestles are wrought; they work also great beads of stone, and drill the ball with a nail for a club-stick head: some which I have seen were perfect globes of white marble, from the northern deserts " about Jauf." — I saw such ganna heads formed by them of another matter, *el-elk*; and that is they say the juice of a low-growing shrub in the Nefûd, *el-môttî*: it may be a kind of caoutchouc.

A company of young men of the village had gone out to cut wild forage, and sell dates to the ascending Haj at *Stoora*. — Now two of them arrived late in an evening (before the time) ; and of the twain one ' had lost his right mind, and the other refused to speak till the morrow.' The villagers were in suspense of mind until he should find his tongue, saying under their breaths — since there is no end of mischances in these countries — ' that some great evil was betided to the young men, their eyyâl had been slain by hostile Beduw ' ; and there wanted little that night of a public wailing. As for him who returned to them lunatic they said, " Wellah there be grounds whereupon if a man sleep, the jân will enter into him." In the morning, the village sorrow had vanished as the clouds of yesterday, and such are the most of the alarms of the Arabs! — *The heart slenderly nourished*, under that sunstricken climate, can be little robust in Arabian bodies. The absent at Stoora were in good plight, the Haj passed by ; and after few days we were delivered from the dread of the wába.

Marketers go down with the nomad hubts from Kheybar to Medina in five marches. They journey till high noon, and alight to loose out their cattle to pasture ; but in ascending empty, they make but three marches. The way to the city is reckoned twelve or fourteen thelûl hours ; Amm Mohammed had often passed it on foot, in two summer days. The villagers are guests in Medina, for the night, in houses of their acquaintance. Setting out from Kheybar they pass over more than thirty miles of the Harra lavas, whose south-west border comes down to the W. el-Humth. By the way are seen ruins of stone buildings (from the times before Mohammed) ; the people call them *Jews' houses*, and there are many like them about Medina.

Not many hours' distant from Kheybar, there are certain ruins of great dams — *Bény el-Bint*, the maiden's building, is in *W. Thammud*, an upper head of the Kheybar *wadiân* ; and *el-Hassîd* is in the wady bottom of like name, of these valleys. The dam of W. Hassîd, the ' harvest valley,' is built up of great courses receding stepwise : the lower stones are huge, but some of them have been borne out from their beds and carried down with the wild rage of winter torrents. There are sluices in the upper courses, for the issue of the falling irrigation water. The dam-head is of such width that two horsemen riding over might pass each other : — thus Amm Mohammed, somewhat magnifying his matter. Once in his younger years another strenuous man of Medina invited him to be his partner, to settle upon the good bottom under the old dam : they would bring in a colony of their friends, and buy their peace of the (Harb) Aarab [Mohammed's kindred] with an easy khûwa. But they went no further than the words, for Mohammed would not spill his best years in an uncertain adventure.

By the way, over the (wide Rodwa) mountain from Medina to Yanba, Amân and other friends told me they had seen many scored inscriptions. In the Rodwa there is good building-stone. The descent is an hour or two on this side Yanba-at-the-Palms, from whence to the port town, Yanba-at-the-Sea, is a night's journey : the villagers mount at sunset, for dread of robbers, and are at the seaside before the day breaks. The Jeheyna of the Rodwa are compared by the Medina passengers to monkeys. "They wear no more than an apron before and behind them upon a string." Yanba-at-the-Palms is such as Kheybar, several villages lying nigh together, in a natural bottom : they are inhabited by settlers of the two Beduin nations, Harb and Jeheyna. A street divides the villages *Jar* and *Hósn*, which with the next standing hamlet *el-Búthenah* are of the B. *Ibrahîm* or *Barâhimma*, Jeheyna. *Sweygy* or *Suâka*, and the next hamlet *Imbârak* are settlements of Harb. Hósn and Jar had been now four years at feud with those of Suâka, for the right of sheep pastures. In those parts is an antique site *Kseyberra*. The Sherîf of Suâka is a considerable personage : he has his residence at the sea-port, and receives a yearly surra for the Egyptian pilgrimage.

Amm Mohammed who in his hunting had gone over all the vulcanic field about, made me this topography [p. 203] of the Kheybar valleys, which are commonly said to be " seven, lying side by side in the Harra." The manly man's hand was new to the subtleties of chorography, and his map is rude. The trunk valley is *W. el-Gôras*, and lower down, where straitened to a deep channel, it is called (beginning from *Ghradîr et-Teyr*, ' the birds' pool ') *et-Tubj*, and lower *W. es-Sulsilla*, until it goes out in the great valley bottom of the Hejâz, Wady el-Humth, by Hedîeh, at the Haj-road kella. The Tubj is, in some places, so straitened betwixt mountain rocks, that a thelûl rider cannot pass ; and when the winter rains run down, there is sometimes a roaring head of waters. In most bays of the valley are ruined sites and wells of ancient hamlets. In the side wadies are great pools with thickets of cane reeds, and wild bottoms grown up with dôm palms and sidr trees.

W. Koora descends to the W. el-Humth, a little above Sûjwa kella

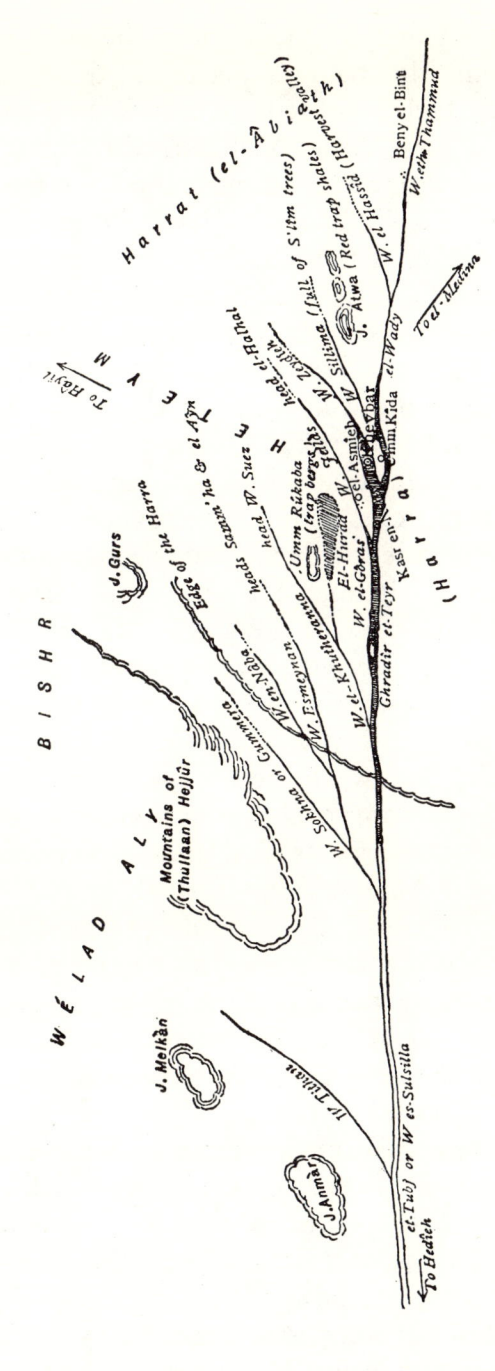

The Kheybar valleys

upon the Haj road. Further by the Derb in the same valley bottom at a day's journey from Medina is a place called *Mleylîeh*, where are " graves of the Beny Helál," obscurely set out to a wonderful length with ranges of great stones. Amm Mohammed told me, ' that in one of his passages, he stayed with certain in the caravan to measure a skeleton which the washing of the winter freshet had laid bare, of some of those antique heroes : they found the length to be twenty paces.' The site may be an alluvial bottom, with silted bones of great (perhaps living and extinct) animals, and the common waifs of water-borne blocks. — *Henakîeh* is a negro village, of forty houses, with a small guard of soldiery from Medina : to the well-water is ten to fifteen fathoms ; yet some buried springs and old broken conduits have been lately found there and repaired. It seems that the place — upon the W. el-Humth — is of several small palm groves, lying nigh together.

Amm Mohammed made me then a rude topography of the vulcanic country which lies about Medina. He said [*v.* the large Map] " Harrat *el-Anâbis* begins an hour west of the town ; Harrat *el-Auwâli* at the like distance south-west ; *Harrat Aba Rasheyd* or *Goreytha* lies southwards and eastwards ; and *Labat el-Agûl* is eastward. All these Harras (*Harâr* or *Ahrâr*) are one, — the *Harrat el-Medina.*" It lasts two or three journeys, say the Beduw, to the southward, and is a lava country with many hilliàn : and it approaches (but there is space of sand plains between them) the main Harra, which, under several names as Harrat *B. Abdillah* and Harrat *el-Kisshub* (or *Kesshub*, or *Kusshub*) is that vast vulcanic train, which comes down southward to the Mecca country, and abuts upon the Wady Fatima. — Below Kheybar, towards W. el-Humth, are certain tarns (*ghradràn*) in the wilderness [*v.* Vol. I. p. 595] and in them are many great fish, ' which drop samn, they are so fat,' say the Arabs : some of the Kheyâbara have nets, and they use to lie out a summer night to take them.

The Siruân had bound Amm Mohammed for me, since there was grown this fast friendship between us, saying, " I leave him in thy hands, and of thee I shall require him again ; " — and whenever the Nejûmy went abroad I was with him. The villagers have many small kine, which are driven every morning three miles over the figgera, to be herded in a large bottom of wet pasture, the *Hálhal*, a part of W. Jellâs. I went one day thither with Amm Mohammed, to dig up off-sets in the thickets of unhusbanded young palms. The midst of the valley is a quagmire and springs grown up with canes. The sward is not grass, though it seem such, but a minute herbage of rushes. This is the pasture of their beasts ; though the brackish rush grass, swelling in the cud, is unwholesome for any but the home-born cattle. The small Yémen kine, which may be had at Medina for the price of a good sheep, will die here : even the cattle of el-Hâyat, bred in a drier upland and valued at twelve to fifteen reals, may not thrive at Kheybar ; and therefore a good Kheybar cow is worth thirty reals. In the season of their passage plenty of water-fowl are seen in the Hálhal, and in summer-time partridges. In these thickets of dry canes the village herd-lads cut their double pipes, *mizamîr*. Almost daily some head of their stock is lost in the thicket, and must be abandoned when they drive the beasts home at evening ; yet they doubt not to find it on the morrow. The village housewives come barefoot hither in the hot sun to gather palm sticks (for firing).

Mohammed cut down some young palm stems, and we dined of the heart or pith-wood, *jummàr*, which is very wholesome ; the rude villagers bring it home for a sweetmeat, and call it, in their negro gibes, ' Kheybar cheese.' Warm was the winter sun in this place, and in the thirsty heat Amm Mohammed shewed me a pit of water ; — but it was full of swimming vermin and I would not drink. " Khalîl, said he, we are not so nice," and with *bismillah !* he laid himself down upon his manly breast and drank a heavy draught. In the beginning of the Hálhal we found scored upon a rock in ancient Arabic letters the words *Mahál el-Wái*, which was interpreted by our (unlettered) coffee-hearth scholars ' the cattle marches.' A little apart from the way is a site upon the figgera yet named *Sûk er-Ruwàlla*. There is a spring of their name in Medina ; Henakîeh pertained of old to that Annezy tribe (now far in the north) : and ' there be even now some households of their lineage.' Besides kine there are no great cattle at Kheybar ; the few goats were herded under the palms by children or geyatîn.

Another day we went upon the Harra for wood. Amm Mohammed, in his hunting, had seen some sere sammara trees ; they were five miles distant. We passed the figgera in the chill of the winter morning and descended to the W. Jellâs ; and Haseyn came driving the pack-ass. In the bottom were wide plashes of ice-cold water. " It will cut your limbs, said Mohammed, you cannot cross the water." I found it so indeed ; but they were hardened to these extremities, and the lad helped me over upon his half-drowned beast. Mohammed rode forward upon his mare, and Haseyn drove on under me with mighty strokes, for his father beckoned impatiently. To linger in such places they think perilous, and at every blow the poor lad shrieked to his *jáhash* some of the infamous injuries which his father commonly bestowed upon himself; until we came to the acacia trees. We hurled heavy Harra stones against those dry trunks, and the tree-skeletons fell before us in ruins: — then dashing stones upon them we beat the timber bones into lengths, and charged our ass and departed.

We held another way homeward, by a dry upland bottom, where I saw ancient walling of field enclosures, under red trachyte bergs, *Umm Rúkaba*, to the Húrda. The Húrda is good corn land, the many ancient wells are sunk ten feet to the basalt rock; the water comes up sweet and light to drink, but is lukewarm. Here Mohammed had bought a well and corn plot of late, and yesterday he sent hither two lads from the town, to drive his two oxen, saying to them, " Go and help Haseyn in the Húrda." They labour with diligence, and eat no more than the dates of him who bids them; at night they lie down wrapped in their cloaks upon the damp earth, by a great fire of sammara in a booth of boughs, with the cattle. They remain thus three days out, and the lads drive day and night, by turns. The land-holders send their yokes of oxen to his three-days' labour every fifteen days.

In the Kheybar valley is a spring *Ayn Selelîm*; and there says their tradition was the orchard of a Jew *Ibn Sellem*, who converting to the new religion of Medina, whilst (pagan) Kheybar yet stood, was named *Abdullah Ibn Sellàm.* — In that place, the Moghreby eyesalver had told them, might be found the buried synagogue. One day I said to the Nejûmy, " Let us go thither this fresh morning." He answered: ' That although he dreaded the neighbours' tongues, yet he would not disappoint me.' Our path lay in the width of the Kheybar valley: and where we passed under a berg of red shaly trachyte, I saw a solitary great clay house; which was a ground-room only. Mohammed told me, ' it had been the summer house of a rich Beduwy. But when the new building was ended, and the hospitable nomad first passed the threshold with his friends, the lintel fell upon his neck, and he perished by this sudden bitter death!' At the Ayn Selelîm are clay buildings — the summer houses of Allayda, sheukh of the Wélad Aly. All these tent-dwellers' houses are ground-floors only, with very many little casements to let in the freshing air, [and such as we see the Beduin summer houses in the few low palm valleys of Sinai]. I visited Motlog's beyt; there was a good house for the sheykh's family, and a long pentice for the mejlis, like a nomad tent, and turned from the sun. — The sickly heat is more tolerable by day in clay dwellings than in the worsted booths of the Aarab. These Beduin summer houses were more cleanly than the village houses.

The water of the spring is pure and light, and putting in the thermometer I found 82° F. I showed the glass tube to Amm Mohammed who, when he had examined it, said with astonishment, " Ah ! Khalîl, we are *grashimîn*, rude and ignorant ! " Then seeing some goat-herd children coming down to gaze upon us he said hastily, " Speed thee Khalîl, or they will report it in the village [that we were seen seeking for treasure], and we shall not soon have rest of this walking a mile." — " Is there a valiant man in awe of foolish tongues ! it were too mean labour, to conciliate the vile and unjust." — " Yet here is a mad world of these negroes." And truly there is nearly no Arab that durst descend alone into the tide, and set his face to contradict the multitude. — In this *Mohammed the Néby did show a marvellous spiritual courage among Arabs !* — But the Nejûmy boldly defended my life.

My Galla comrade had been put by Abdullah in the room of the deceased Muharram at Umm Kîda ; — for Amân, the freedman of an Albanian petty officer, was accounted of among them as an Albanian deputy petty officer. I returned now at night to an empty house. Abdullah was a cursed man, I might be murdered whilst I slept ; and he would write to the Pasha, ' The Nasrâny, it may please your lordship, was found slain such a morning in his lodging, and by persons unknown.' In all the Kheybar cottages is a ladder and open trap to the housetop ; and you may walk from end to end of all the house-rows by their terrace roofs, and descend by day or by night at the trap, into what house-chamber you please : thus neighbours visit neighbours. I could not pass the night at the Nejûmy's ; for they had but their suffa, so that his son Haseyn went to sleep abroad in a hired chamber with other young men in the like case. Some householders spread matting over their trap, in the winter night ; but this may be lifted without rumour, and they go always barefoot. There were evil doers not far off, for one night a neighbour's chickens which roosted upon our house terrace had been stolen; the thief, Amân thought, must be our former Galla comrade: it was a stranger, doubtless, for these black villagers eat no more of their poultry than the eggs! — This is a superstition of the Kheyâbara, for which they cannot themselves render a reason; and besides they will not eat leeks!

Another day whilst I sat in Ahmed's house there came up Mohammed the Kurdy to coffee. The Kurdy spoke to us with a mocking scorn of Muharram's death: — in his fatal afternoon, "the sick man said, 'Go Mohammed to Abdullah, for I feel that I am dying and I have somewhat to say to him.' — ' *Ana nejjàb*, am I thy post-runner? if it please thee to die, what is that to us?' — the Egyptian lay sick. In the beginning of the night Muharram was sitting up; we heard a guggle in his throat, — he sank backward and was dead! We sent word to Abdullah: who sent over two of the askars, and we made them a supper of the niggard's goods. All Muharram's stores of rice and samn went to the pot; and we sat feasting in presence of our lord [saint] Muharram, who could not forbid this honest wasting of his substance." — "The niggard's goods are for the fire" (shall be burned in hell), responded those present. I questioned the Kurdy Mohammed, and he denied before them; and the Egyptian denied it, that my medicines had been so much as mentioned, or cause at all in Muharram's death. — The Kurdy said of the jebâl in the horizon of Kheybar, that they were but as cottages in comparison with the mighty mountains of his own country.

The sickly Ageyly of Boreyda died soon after; but I had ceased from the first to give him medicines. ' He found the Nasrâny's remedies (minute doses of rhubarb) so horrible, he said, that he would no more of them.' In one day he died and was buried. But when the morrow dawned we heard in the village, that the soldier's grave had been violated in the night! — Certain who went by very early had seen the print of women's feet round about the new-made grave. 'And who had done this thing?' asked all the people. "Who, they answered themselves, but the cursed witches! They have taken up the body, to pluck out the heart of him for their hellish orgies." I passed by later with Amm Mohammed to our garden labour, and as they had said, so it seemed indeed! if the prints which we saw were not the footsteps of elvish children. — Amân carried a good fat cat to a neighbour woman of ours, and he told me with loathing, that she had eaten it greedily, though she was well-faring, and had store of all things in her beyt ; she was said to be one of the witches !

In the long evenings with the Nejûmy I learned much of their superstitious lore of the jins, which is current at Medina. " The jân are sore afraid of me," quoth Amm Mohammed. An half of the jân or jenûn, inhabiting the seven stages under the earth, are malicious (heathen) spirits, kuffâr, or kafirûn ; and an half are accounted Moslemîn." — Mohammed said, ' A chest of his father's, in which was some embroidered clothing, had been stolen when he was a young man. They sent for the conjuror, *Mundel*, to reveal to them the guilty persons.' The Mundel is in his dark science a broker, or mean, betwixt the children of Adam and the jân.

— " Who here, said the wise man, is sure of heart and strong ? " " Mohammed my son is a stout lad," answered the elder Nejûmy. — The Mundel poured water in a bowl and bade Mohammed sit-to, he must look fixedly in it, and the Mundel said over his first spells, " Now, what seest thou ? " (quoth he). — *Mohammed* : " Wellah, I see no more than this basin and water (the Mundel still spelling on his beads) : yet now it is as if I saw through a casement, and a sea is under me ; and beneath I see a wide plain, and now I see upon the plain as it were the haj arriving ! — They have pitched the pavilion of the Pasha, — I can see the Pasha sitting with his friends." — *Mundel* : " Say to him, ' O Sooltàn of the jân ! the doctor Such-an-one [the Mundel naming himself] salutes thee, and bids thee enquire, if in thy company be any jin who was by when the coffer was stolen from Yeldûzely Haseyn ; and, if he were a witness of the theft, that he name the persons.' " — The Sultan of the jân answered, " I have at the instant enquired of all my company ; none was present, and no one has heard any tiding." — The Mundel spelled on his beads, and he said again, " What seest thou now, young man ? " — *Mohammed* : " The former company has passed by, and another like company is now arriving." — " Say : ' O Sooltàn of the jân . . .,' as before." The Sooltàn of the jins responded, " I have at the instant enquired of all these ; and there is none here who has seen aught, or heard tidings." *Mundel* : " Say yet, ' Is any absent ? ' " It was answered, " There is none absent." The Mundel spelled on his beads and said, " What seest thou now ? " *Mohammed* : " The second company have passed from my sight; a third company is arriving." — " Say: ' Sooltàn of the jân ...,' as before." The Sultan answered, " I have asked of them all at the instant, and there is none here." — " Say again, ' Are all your people present?' " — " I have enquired and there is one absent, — he is in India." — *Mundel:* " Say, ' Let him be brought hither and examined.' " The Sultan of the jân spake in his company, " Which of you will bring our fellow of such a name, that is in India?" A jin answered, " I, in four days, will bring him." The Sultan said, " It is a long time." Another said, " I, in three days." A third said, " I, in two only," and a fourth, " I will bring him in a day." — " The time, quoth the Sultan, is long." — Here Amm Mohammed said a word beside the play, " Perceivest thou not, sheykh Khalîl? that it was but a malice in them to ask so many days." — So said a jin, " Give me three hours;" at the last one said, " I will bring him in a moment." — The Sultan responded: " Bring him." — " Then I saw him, said Amm Mohammed, led in like an old man; he was greyheaded, and he went lame." The Sultan of the jân questioned him, " Hast thou seen anything, or is there ought come to thy knowledge of this theft?" He answered, " Ay, for as I lay in the likeness of a dog upon the dung-hill which is before such an house, about the middle of the night, I saw a man come with the chest upon his back; he entered at the next door, and two women followed him." The jinny revealed also the persons and their names.

— The Mundel sent to call them; — and they were known in the town as ill-livers. They arrived anon; but being questioned of the theft they denied all knowledge upon their religion, and departed. Then the Mundel took three girbies, and blew them up, and he cast them from him! — In a little while the three persons came again running; that man before the women, and all of them holding their bellies, which were swollen to bursting. " Oh me! I beseech thee, cries the man. Sir, the chest is with me, only release me out of this pain and I will restore it immediately!" his women also pitifully acknowledged their guilt. — Then the Mundel spelled upon his beads backward, to reverse the enchantment, and said to Mohammed, " What seest thou?" — " I see the great plain only; — and now but this basin and the water in it." — *Mundel:* " Look up young man! rise, and walk about, whilst these wicked persons bring the stolen chest and the wares."

Amm Mohammed told this tale as if he had believed it all true ; and said further that for a while he could perceive nearly *an half part of all who bear the form of mankind to be jins* ; and many an house cat and many a street dog he saw then to be jân : the influence little by little decayed in him and he might discern them no more. Amm Mohammed startled a little when I said, " Well, tell me, what is the speech of your jân, and the fashion of their clothing ? " He answered (astutely smiling) after a moment, " It is plain that they are clad and that they speak like the Moslemîn."

— I questioned Amân of the jân ; he looked sadly upon it, and said : " I will tell thee a thing, sheykh Khalîl, which happened at Jidda within my knowledge. A bondservant, a familiar of mine, sat by a well side to wash his clothing. He cast away the first water and went with his dish to the well, to draw more ; and in that, as he leaned over the brink his money fell from him. The young man looked after his fallen silver ; — and, as he gazed, he suddenly shrieked and fell head foremost into the well ! A seller of coffee, who saw him fall in, left his tray and ran to the pit ; and whilst he looked he too fell therein. A seller of herbs ran-to ; he came to the well's mouth, and as he looked down he fell in also ; so did another, and likewise a fifth person. — When many had gathered to the cry, there spoke a seafaring man among them, ' Give me a line here ! and I will go down myself into the well and fetch them up.' They stopped his ears with cotton [lest the demons, by those ingates, should enter into the man], and giving him an incense-pot burning in his hand, they lowered him over the brink : but when he was at the half depth [wells there at the sea-bord are not fully two fathoms to the water] he cried to be taken up. The people drew up that seaman in haste ; and, he told them, when he could fetch his breath, that he saw the deep of the well gaping and shutting ! — They had sent to call a certain Moghreby ; who now arrived, bringing with him a magical writing, — which he flung into the well, and there ascended a smoke. After that the Moor said : ' *Khàlas*, it was ended, and now he would go down himself.' They bound him under the arms, and he descended without fear, and put a cord about the drowned bodies ; and one after another they were taken up. They were all dead, save only the bondman, who yet breathed weakly : he lived through that night, without sense or speech, and then died. That he was not dead already he owed it to a ring, said Amân, with a turquoise set in it. [The virtue of this stone is to disperse malign spiritual influence ; so you see blue beads hanged about the necks of cattle in the border countries.] — But the pit wherein these persons had ended their lives was filled up, the same day, by an order of the Pasha-governor."

I enquired of Amm Mohammed, " How sayest thou the jân be a-dread of thee ! canst thou lay thy strong hand upon demons ? " — " Wellah they are afraid of me, sheykh Khalîl ! last year a jin entered into this woman my wife, one evening, and we were sitting here as we sit now ; I and the woman and Haseyn. I saw it come in her eyes, that were fixed, all in a moment, and she lamented with a labouring in her throat. [I looked over to the poor wife ! who answered me again with a look of patience.] Then I took down the pistol [commonly such few fire-arms of theirs hang loaded upon the chamber-wall] and I fired it at the side of her head, — and cried to the jin, ' Aha melaun, cursed one, where be'st thou now ? ' The jin answered me (by the woman's mouth), ' In the head of her, in her eye.' — ' By which part enteredst thou into her ? ' — ' At her great toe.' — ' Then by the same, I say unto thee, depart out of her.' I spoke this word terribly and the devil left her : " but first Mohammed made the jin promise him to molest his wife no more. — " Is the devil afraid of shot ? " — " Thou art too simple, it is the smell of the sulphur ; wellah they cannot abide it."

This poor woman had great white rolling eyes and little joy in them. I have heard Haseyn say to her, " *Hu ! hu !* thou with those eyes of thine, sit further off ! thou shalt not look so upon me." — " Among the jân [he had seen them, being under the spell, in Medina] be such diversities, said Amm Mohammed, as in the children of Adam. They are long or short, gross or lean, whole or infirm, fair or foul ; there be rich and poor among them, and good and evil natures, — the evil are adversaries of mankind. They are male and female, children, grown persons and aged folk ; they come to their lives' end and die as the Adamies."

— " Certain of them, he said, are very honourable persons : there be jins of renown even in the upper world. There is a family, the *Beyt es-Shereyfa*, at el-Medina, now in the third generation, which descend from a jinnîa, or jin-woman. Their grandsire was a caravan carrier between the Harameyn. This man rode always at a little distance behind his camel train, that, if anything were fallen from the loads, he might recover it. As they journeyed upon a time he heard a voice, that saluted him : — ' Salaam aleyk, said a jin (for such he was) in the form of an old man ; I trow thou goest to Mecca.' — ' Ay.' — ' Give then this letter to my son ; thou wilt find him — a black hound, lying before the stall of the butcher, in such a street. Hold this letter to his eyes, and he will rise, and do thou follow him.'

"The carrier thrust the letter into the bosom of his tunic, and rode further. When they came to Mecca he went about his commissions. Afterward he returned to his lodging, to put on his holiday apparel ; and then he would go to pass his time in the coffee-houses. In this there fell out the letter ; and he thought as he went down the sûk he would deliver it. — He found all things as the jin foretold ; and he followed the dog. This dog led him through a ruinous quarter, and entered a forsaken house ; and there the dog stood up as a comely young man ; and said to the caravaner, ' I perceive thou hadst this letter from my father ; he writes to me of certain silver : before you set out come hither to receive my answer.' — ' We depart to-morrow from such a khân ; and thou mayest see me there.'

"The loaded camel-train was in the way, and the caravaner had mounted his thelûl, when the young jin met him, and said, ' This is the letter for my father, and (tossing him a bundle) here is that silver of which the old man spake ; tell him for me, It is verily all that I have been able to gather in this place.' The carrier thrust the bundle into his bags with the letter, and set forward.

"In the midst of the way that old elf-man stood again in his sight, and said, ' Salaam aleyk ! — Sawest thou my son, and hast thou brought me aught from him ? ' — ' Here is that thy son sends thee.' ' Thou art my guest to-day,' quoth the old jin. — ' But how then might I overtake my camels ? ' — The old jin knocked with his stick upon the ground, and it yawned before them ; and he went down leading the carrier's thelûl, and the carrier with him, under the earth, till they came to a city ; where the grey-beard jin brought him through the street to his own house. They entered ; and within doors there sat the jin's wife, and their two daughters ! — and the jin-man sat down in his hall to make the guest coffee. Before it was evening the carrier saw the jin host slaughter his thelûl ! he saw his own beast's flesh cast into the pot ; and it was afterward served for their suppers ! — ' Alas ! he said in himself, for now may I no more overtake my kâfily.'

"On the morrow, the jin said to him, ' Rise if thou wouldst depart, and let us go on together;' — and he led him his slain thelûl alive! 'I would give thee also a gift, said the old elf, as they came forth; now choose thee, what thing wouldst thou of all that thou sawest in my house?' The carrier answered boldly, 'One of thy two daughters.' — 'I pray thee ask a new request.' — 'Nay, wellah, and else I will have nothing.' — 'At your coming-by again, I will bring thee to her.' — 'What is the bride-money?' — 'I require but this of thee, that thou keep a precept, which is easy in itself, but uneasy to a hasty man: — I say if thy wife seem to do some outrage in thy sight, thou shalt abide it, for it is no more than the appearance.' So the old elf brought the caravaner above ground, and dismissed him; and the man beginning to ride was aware, as he looked up, of the walls of Medina!

"In the way returning again he received his bride, and brought her home to Medina. There they lived seven years in happy wedlock, and she had borne him two sons: — then upon a day, she caught a knife and ran with shrieks to one of their babes as it were to slay him. The poor carrier saw it, and sprang to save their child; — but in that the elf-mother and her babe vanished for ever! Of their elder son are descended the Medina family (above named): he was the father of those now living." Amm Mohammed said, "The jân may be discerned from the children of Adam only by a strangeness of the eyes; — the opening of their eyelids is sidelong-like with the nose."

The Nejûmy spoke also of a certain just kâdy of the jân whose name was very honourable (above ground) at Medina; and of his funeral in the Háram, in his own time! "One day when the Imâm had ended the noon prayer before the people, he lifted up his voice crying, *Rahamna wa rahamkom Ullah, es-sulât aly el-jenneysat el-hâthera*, 'Be merciful unto us, be merciful; to you, Ullah! our prayers for the funeral which is here present!' — A bier may be borne into the Háram (to be prayed over) at any hour of the day; and if it be at midday, the hearty response of the multitude of worshippers is heard: they affirm with a wonderful resonance, in that vast building. The people looked to all sides and marvelled, — they saw nothing! — The Imâm answered them, 'O Moslemîn, I see a corse borne in; and know that this is the bier of the just kâdy of the jân, — he deceased to-day.' Wellah when the people heard his name they all prayed over him, because that jin kâdy was reputed a just person: — wouldst thou hear a tale of his justice?

"There was a certain *muderris* or studied man in Medina, [that is one passing well seen in their old poetasters, the inept Arabic science, and solemn farrago of the koran]. One night when the great learned man was going to rest, he heard a friend's voice in the street bidding him come down quickly; so he took his mantle and went forth. His friend said then, ' Come with me I pray thee.' — When they were past the wall of the town, the learned man perceived that this was a jin in his friend's likeness ! Some more gathered to them, and he saw well that all these were jân. — They bade him stay, and said the jân, ' We be here to slay thee.' — ' Wherefore, Sirs, alas ! ' — ' Because thou hast killed our fellow to-day.' — ' If I have slain any companion of yours unwittingly, let me be judged by your laws ; I appeal to the kâdy.' The jân answered, ' We were come out to slay thee, but because thou hast appealed to the kâdy, we will lead thee to the kâdy.' They went then all together before the kâdy and accused him ; ' This *adamy* has slain to-day one of the people, and we are his kindred and fellowship : he slew him as our kinsman lay sleeping in such a palm ground, in the likeness of a serpent.' — ' Yea, truly, O honourable kâdy, I struck at a serpent there and killed him ; and is not, I pray thee, every perilous vermin slain by man, if he have a weapon or stone ? but by the Lord ! I knew him not to be a jin.' The kâdy answered, ' I find in him no cause ; but the fault lay in the little prudence of your friend that dead is : for ye be not ignorant that the snake more than all beasts is abhorred by the Beny Adam.' "

CHAPTER VIII

DELIVERANCE FROM KHEYBAR

Amm Mohammed's wild brother-in-law. The messenger arrives from Medina. The Nasrâny procures that the water is increased at Kheybar. Ayn er-Reyih. Abu Middeyn, a derwîsh traveller. A letter from the Pasha of Medina. Violence of Abdullah. Might one forsake the name of his religion, for a time? Amm Mohammed would persuade the Nasrâny to dwell with him at Kheybar. Abu Bakkar. '*All is shame in Islam.*' The Engleys in India, and at Aden. The Nasrâny's Arabic books are stolen by a Colonel at Medina. Return of the camel-thief. Heteym cheeses. Wedduk. The villagers of el-Hâyat. Humanity which loves not to be requited. 'God sends the cold to every one after his cloth.' Mutinous villagers beaten by Abdullah. *Deyik es-súdr*. Departure from Kheybar. Hamed. Love and death. Amm Mohammed's farewell. Journey over the Harra. Come to Heteym tents. Habâra fowl. Stormy March wind. The Hejjûr mountains. Eagles. Meet with Heteym. 'The Nasâra inhabit in a city closed with iron.' Solubbies from near Mecca. The rafîks seeking for water. Certain deep and steyned wells " were made by the jân." Blustering weather. The Harra craters. " God give that young man (Ibn Rashîd) long life ! "

WE looked again for Dakhîl returning from Medina. I spoke to Mohammed to send one to meet him in the way : that were there tidings out against my life (which Dakhîl would not hide from us), the messenger might bring us word with speed, and I would take to the Harra. " The Siruân shall be disappointed, answered my fatherly friend, if they would attempt anything against thy life ! Wellah if Dakhîl bring an evil word, I have one here ready, who is bound to me, a Beduwy ; and by him I will send thee away in safety." — This was his housewife's brother, a wild grinning wretch, without natural conscience, a notorious camel robber and an homicide. Their father had been a considerable Bishr sheykh ; but in the end they had lost their cattle. This wretch's was the Beduin right of the Hálhal, but that yielded him no advantage, and he was become a gatûny at Kheybar ; where his hope was to help himself by cattle-lifting in the next hostile marches. — Last year seeing some poor stranger in the summer market with a few ells of new-bought calico (for a shirt-cloth) in his hand, he vehemently coveted it for himself. Then he followed that strange tribesman upon the Harra, and came upon him in the path and murdered him ; and took his cotton, and returned to the village laughing : — he was not afraid of the blood of a stranger! The wild wretch sat by grinning when Amm Mohammed told me the tale; but the housewife said, sighing, " Alas! my brother is a kafir, so light-headed that he dreads not Ullah." The Nejûmy answered, " Yet the melaun helped our low plight last year (when there was a dearth at Kheybar); he stole sheep and camels, and we feasted many times : — should we leave all the fat to our enemies, and we ourselves perish with hunger? Sheykh Khalîl, say was this lawful for us or harâm?"

I thought if, in the next days, I should be a fugitive upon the vast lava-field, without shelter from the sun, without known landmarks, with water for less than three days, and infirm in body, what hope had I to live? — A day later Dakhîl arrived from Medina, and then (that which I had dreaded) Amm Mohammed was abroad, to hunt gazelles, upon the Harra; nor had he given me warning overnight, — thus leaving his guest (the Arabs' remiss understanding), in the moment of danger, without defence. The Nejûmy absent, I could not in a great peril have escaped their barbarous wild hands; but after some sharp reckoning with the most forward of them I must have fallen in this subbakha soil, without remedy. Ahmed was too 'religious' to maintain the part of a misbeliever against any mandate from Medina: even though I should sit in his chamber, I thought he would not refuse to undo to the messengers from Abdullah. I sat therefore in Mohammed's suffa, where at the worst I might keep the door until heaven should bring the good man home. — But in this there arrived an hubt of Heteym, clients of his, from the Harra; and they brought their cheeses and samn to the Nejûmy's house, that he might sell the wares for them. Buyers of the black village neighbours came up with them, and Mohammed's door was set open. I looked each moment for the last summons to Abdullah, until nigh midday; when Amm Mohammed returned from the Harra, whence he had seen the nomads, from far off, descending to Kheybar. — Then the Nejûmy sat down among us, and receiving a driving-stick from one of the nomads, he struck their goods and cried, " Who buys this for so much?" and he set a just price between them: and taking his reed-pen and paper he recorded their bargains, which were for measures of dates to be delivered (six months later) in the harvest. After an hour, Amm Mohammed was again at leisure; then having shut his door, he said he would go to Abdullah and learn the news.

He returned to tell me that the Pasha wrote thus, " We have now much business with the Haj ; at their departure we will examine and send again the books : in the meanwhile you are to treat the Engleysy honourably and with hospitality." I was summoned to Abdullah in the afternoon : Amm Mohammed went with me, and he carried his sword, which is a strong argument in a valiant hand to persuade men to moderation in these lawless countries. Abdullah repeated that part of the governor's order concerning the books ; of the rest he said nothing. — I afterwards found Dakhîl in the street ; he told me he had been privately called to the Pasha, who enquired of him, ' What did I wandering in this country, and whether the Nasrâny spoke Arabic ? ' (he spoke it very well himself). Dakhîl found him well disposed towards me : he heard also in Medina that at the coming of the Haj, Mohammed Said Pasha being asked by the Pasha-governor if he knew me, responded, ' He had seen me at Damascus, and that I came down among the Haj the year before to Medáin Sâlih ; and he wondered to hear that I was in captivity at Kheybar, a man known to be an Engleysy and who had no guilt towards the Dowla, other than to have been always too adventurous to wander in the (dangerous) nomadic countries.'

The few weeks of winter had passed by, and the teeming spring heat was come, in which all things renew themselves : the hamîm month would soon be upon us, when my languishing life, which the Nejûmy compared to a flickering lamp-wick, was likely (he said) to fail at Kheybar. Two months already I had endured this black captivity of Abdullah ; the third moon was now rising in her horns, which I hoped in Heaven would see me finally delivered. The autumn green corn was grown to the yellowing ear ; another score of days — so the Lord delivered them from the locust — and they would gather in their wheat-harvest.

I desired to leave them richer in water at Kheybar. Twenty paces wide of the strong Sefsáfa spring was a knot of tall rushes ; there I hoped to find a new fountain of water. The next land-holders hearkened gladly to my saw, for water is mother of corn and dates, in the oases ; and the sheykh's brother responded that to-morrow he would bring eyyâl to open the ground. — Under the first spade-stroke we found wet earth, and oozing joints of the basalt rock : then they left their labour, saying we should not speed, because it was begun on a Sunday. They remembered also my words that, in case we found a spring of water, they should give me a milch cow. On the morrow a greater working party assembled. It might be they were in doubt of the cow and would let the work lie until the Nasrâny's departure, for they struck but a stroke or two in my broken ground ; and then went, with crowbars, to try their strength about the old well-head, and see if they might not enlarge it. The iron bit in the flaws of the rock ; and stiffly straining and leaning, many together, upon their crowbars, they sprung and rent up the intractable basalt. Others who looked on, whilst the labourers took breath, would bear a hand in it: among them the Nejûmy showed his manly pith and stirred a mighty quarter of basalt. When it came to midday they forsook their day's labour. Three forenoons they wrought thus with the zeal of novices : in the second they sacrificed a goat, and sprinkled her blood upon the rock. I had not seen Arabs labour thus in fellowship. In the Arabs are indigent corroded minds full of speech-wisdom ; in the negroes' more prosperous bodies are hearts more robust. They also fired the rock, and by the third day the labourers had drawn out many huge stones : now the old well-head was become like a great bath of tepid water, and they began to call it el-hammàm. We had struck a side vein, which increased the old current of water by half as much again, — a benefit for ever to the husbandmen of the valley.

The tepid springs of Kheybar savour upon the tongue of sulphur, with a milky smoothness, save the *Ayn er-Reyih*, which is tasteless. Yellow frogs inhabit these springs, besides the little silver-green fishes. Green filmy webs of water-weed are wrapped about the channels of the lukewarm brooks, in which lie little black turreted snails, like those of W. Thirba and el-Ally [and Palmyra]. I took up the straws of caddis-worms and showed them to Amm Mohammed : he considered the building of those shell-pipes made without hands, and said ; " Oh, the marvellous works of God ; they are perfect without end ! and well thou sayest, ' that the Kheyâbara are not housed as these little vermin ! ' "

I had nearly outworn the spite of fortune at Kheybar ; and might now spend the sunny hours, without fear, sitting by the spring Ayn er-Reyih, a pleasant place little without the palms, and where only the eye has any comfort in all the blackness of Kheybar. Oh, what bliss to the thirsty soul is in that sweet light water, welling soft and warm as milk, [86° F.] from the rock ! and I heard the subtle harmony of

Nature, which the profane cannot hear, in that happy stillness and solitude. Small bright dragon-flies, azure, dun and vermilion, sported over the cistern water ruffled by a morning breath from the figgera, and hemmed in the solemn lava rock. The silver fishes glance beneath, and white shells lie at the bottom of this water world. I have watched there the young of the thób shining like scaly glass and speckled : this fairest of saurians lay sunning, at the brink, upon a stone ; and ofttimes moving upon them and shooting out the tongue he snatched his prey of flies without ever missing. — Glad were we when Jummàr had filled our girby of this sweet water.

The irrigation rights of every plot of land are inscribed in the sheykhs' register of the village ; — the week-day and the hours when the owner with foot and spade may dam off and draw to himself the public water. Amongst these rude Arabian villagers are no clocks nor watches, — nor anything almost of civil artifice in their houses. They take their wit in the daytime, by the shadowing-round of a little wand set upon the channel brink. — This is that dial of which we read in Job : ' a servant earnestly desireth the shadow . . . our days on the earth are a shadow.' In the night they make account of time more loosely. The village gates are then shut ; but the waterers may pass out to their orchards from some of the next-lying houses. Amm Mohammed tells me that the husbandmen at Medina use a metal cup, pierced with a very fine eye, — so that the cup set floating in a basin may sink justly at the hour's end.

Among the Kheyâbara was one *Abu Middeyn* (Father-two-pecks), a walker about the world. Because the negro villager's purse was light and little his understanding, he had played the derwîsh on his two feet, and beaten the soil of distant lands. And finally the forwandered man had returned from Persia ! I asked him how long was he out ? — *Answer :* " I left my new wedded wife with child, and the first I met when I came home, was mine own boy ; he was already of age to shift for himself, — and wellah I did not know him ! " This worthy was a privy hemp-smoker (as are many wandering derwishes) in the negro village ; and he comforted his slow spirits by eating-in corn like a head of cattle, wherefore the gibers of Kheybar had surnamed him, Father-of-pecks-twain. — One of those days in a great coffee company *Two-pecks* began to question the Nasrâny, that he might himself seem to allow before them all, or else solemnly to refute my pretended travels : but no man lent his idle ears to the saws of Abu Middeyn.

One afternoon when I went to present myself to the village tyrant, I saw six carrion beasts, that had been thelûls, couched before Abdullah's door ! the brutes stretched their long necks faintly upon the ground, and their mangy chines were humpless. Such could be none other than some unpaid soldiers' jades from Medina ; and I withdrew hastily to the Nejûmy. — Certain Ageylies had been sent by the Pasha ; and the men had ridden the seventy miles hither in five days ! — Such being the Ageyl, whose forays formerly — some of them have boasted to me — "made the world cold !" they are now not seldom worsted by the tribesmen of the desert. In a late expedition of theirs from Medina, we heard that 'forty were fallen, their baggage had been taken, and the rest hardly saved themselves.' — I went back to learn their tidings, and meeting with Abdullah in the street, he said, "Good news, Khalîl ! thy books are come again, and the Pasha writes, 'send him to Ibn Rashîd.'"

On the morrow, Abdullah summoned me ; he sat at coffee in our neighbour Hamdàn's house. — 'This letter is for thee, said he, (giving me a paper) from the Pasha's own hand.' And opening the sheet, which was folded in our manner, I found a letter from the Pasha of Medina ! written [imperfectly], as follows, in the French language ; with the date of the Christian year, and signed in the end with his name, — *Sábry*.

[*Ad literam.*]   Le 11 janvier 1878

                                                        [Medine]

D'aprés l'avertissement de l'autorité local, nous sommes saché votre arrivée à Khaiber, à cette occasion je suis obligé de faire venir les lettres de recommendation et les autres papiers à votre charge.

En étudiant à peine possible les livres de compte, les papiers volants et les cartes, enfin parmi ceux qui sont arrivaient-ici, jai disserné que votre idée de voyage, corriger la carte, de savoir les conditions d'état, et de trouver les monuments antiques de l'Arabie centrale dans le but de publier au monde

je suis bien satisfaisant à votre etude utile pour l'univers dans ce point, et c'est un bon parti pour vous aussi ; mais vous avez connu certainement jusqu' aujourd'hui parmi aux alantours des populations que vous trouvé, il y a tant des Bedouins témeraire, tant que vous avez le recommendion de quelque personnages, je ne regarde que ce votre voyage est dangereux parmi les Bédouins sus-indiqué ; c'est pour cela je m'oblige de vous informé à votre retour à un moment plutôt possible auprès de Cheïh d'Ibni-Réchite à l'abri de tout danger, et vous trouvrez ci-join tous vos les lettres qu'il était chez-nous, et la recommendation au dite Cheïh de ma part, et de là prenez le chemin dans ces jours à votre destination.

SABRI

"And now, I said to Abdullah, where is that money which pertains to me, — six lira!" The black village governor startled, changed his Turkish countenance, and looking felly, he said "We will see to it." The six Ageylies had ridden from Medina, by the Pasha's order, only to bring up my books, and they treated me with regard. They brought word, that the Pasha would send other twenty-five Ageylies to Hâyil for this cause. The chief of the six, a Waháby of East Nejd, was a travelled man, without fanaticism ; he offered himself to accompany me whithersoever I would, and he knew, he said, all the ways, in those parts and far southward in Arabia.

The day after when nothing had been restored to me. I found Abdullah drinking coffee in sheykh Sâlih's house. "Why, I said, hast thou not restored my things?" — "I will restore them at thy departure." — "Have you any right to detain them?" "Say no more (exclaimed the villain, who had spent my money) — a Nasrâny to speak to me thus ! — or I will give thee a buffet." — "If thou strike me, it will be at thy peril. My hosts, how may this lieutenant of a dozen soldiery rule a village, who cannot rule himself? one who neither regards the word of the Pasha of Medina, nor fears the Sultan, nor dreads Ullah himself. Sâlih the sheykh of Kheybar, hear how this coward threatens to strike a guest in thy house ; and will ye suffer it my hosts?" — Abdullah rose and struck me brutally in the face. — 'Sâlih, I said to them, and you that sit here, are you free men? I am one man, infirm and a stranger, who have suffered so long, and unjustly, — you all have seen it! at this slave's hands, that it might have whitened my beard : if I should hereafter remember to complain of him, it is likely he will lose his office." Auwad, the kâdy, who was a friend and sat by me, began some conciliating speech. 'Abdullah, he said, was to blame : Khalîl was also to blame. There is danger in such differences ; let there be no more said betwixt you both.' *Abdullah* : "Now, shall I send thee to prison?" — "I tell thee, that I am not under thy jurisdiction;" and I rose to leave them. " Sit down," he cries, and brutally snatched my cloak, " and this askar — he looked through the casement and called up one of his men that passed by — shall lead thee to prison." I went down with him, and, passing Amm Mohammed's entry, I went in there, and the fellow left me.

The door was locked, but the Beduin housewife, hearing my voice, ran down to open : when I had spoken of the matter, she left me sitting in the house, and taking the key with her, the good woman ran to call her husband who was in the palms. Mohammed returned presently, and we went out to the plantations together : but finding the chief of the riders from Medina, in the street, I told him, ' since I could not be safe here that I would ride with them to the gate of the city. It were no new thing that an Englishmen should come thither ; was there not a cistern, without the northern gate, named *Birket el-Engleysy ?*

Mohammed asked ' What had the Pasha written ? he would hear me read his letter in the Nasrâny language : ' and he stood to listen with great admiration. ' *Pitta-pitta-pitta !* is such their speech ? ' laughed he ; and this was his new mirth in the next coffee meetings. But I found the good man weak as water in the end of these evils : he had I know not what secret understanding now with the enemy Abdullah, and, contrary to his former words, he was unwilling that I should receive my things until my departure ! The Ageylies stayed other days, and Abdullah was weary of entertaining them. I gave the Waháby a letter to the Pasha ; which, as soon as they came again to town, he delivered.

Kheybar, in the gibing humour of these black villagers, is *jezîrat*, ' an island ' : it is hard to come hither, it is not easy to depart. Until the spring season there are no Aarab upon the vast enclosing Harra : Kheybar lies upon no common way, and only in the date-harvest is there any resort of Beduins to their wadiân and villages. In all the vulcanic country about there were now no more than a few booths of Heteym, and the nearest were a journey distant. — But none of those timid and oppressed nomads durst for any silver convey the Nasrâny again to Hâyil, — so aghast are they all of the displeasure of Ibn Rashîd. I thought now to go to the (Harra) village el-Hâyat, which lies in the way of them that pass between Ibn Rashîd's country and Medina : and I might there find carriage to the Jebel.

The Nejûmy blamed my plain speaking : I had no wit, he said, to be a traveller ! " If thou say among the Moslemîn that thou art a Moslem, will your people kill thee when you return home ? — art thou afraid of this, Khalîl ? " So at the next coffee meetings he said, " I have found a man that will not befriend himself ! I can in no wise persuade sheykh Khalîl : but if all the Moslemîn were like faithful in the religion, I say, the world would not be able to resist us. A young salesman of my acquaintance did not so — some of you may know him at Medina — when he was lately for his affairs at el-Meshed, where all the people are *Shîas*. The evening he arrived, as he stood in the street, some of the townspeople that went by seeing this stranger, began to question him in their [outlandish northern] speech, '*Shu bitekûn ent*' what be'st thou ? ' [in the Arabian tongue it were, *Ent min ? yâ fulàn*] be'st thou sunni or shîay ? The melaun answered them, ' Sirs I am a shîiy.' ' Then welcome, said they, dear brother ! ' — and the best of them led him home to sup with him, and to lodge. On the morrow another good man lent him a wife of his own, and bade her serve their strange brother in the time of his sojourning among them ; — and this was three months' space : and after that the pleasant young man took his leave of them, and came laughing again to Medina ; and he lives there as good a Moslem as before ! And wellah I have played the shîiy myself in my youth ! — Ye have all seen how the [schismatic] shîas are hustled by the [catholic] Haj in the Harameyn. One year a company of Persian pilgrims gave my father money that they might lodge (by themselves) in his palm ground. When I went to their tents, they said to me, ' O Haj Mohammed, be'st thou shîiy or sunni ? ' ' Eigh ! Sirs, I answered, I am a shîiy.' — ' Ah ! forgive our asking, dear brother Mohammed ; and dine with us to-day : ' and so at every meal they called for Haj Mohammed ; and when they drunk the sweet chai I drank it with them. One afternoon a Beduwy passed by and spat, as we sat supping ! — wellah, all the Persians rose from the mess, and they cried out, ' Take that dish away ! Oh ! take it away, Haj Mohammed ; it is spoiled by the beastly Beduwy man's spitting.' — But who (he added) can imagine any evil of Khalîl ? for when we go out together, he leaves in one house his cloak or his driving-stick, and in another his agâl ! he forgets his pipe, and his sandals, in other several houses. The strange negligence of the man ! ye would say he is sometimes out of memory of the things about him ! — Is this the spy, is this that magician ? but I am sorry that Khalîl is so soon to leave us, for he is a sheykh in questions of religion, and besides a peaceable man."

The Nejûmy family regarded me with affection: my medicines helped (and they believed had saved) their infant daughter; I was now like a son in the house, *wullah in-ak mithil weledna yâ Khalîl*, said they both. Mohammed exhorted me, to dwell with him at Kheybar, ' where first after long travels, I had found good friends. I should be no more molested among them for my religion; in the summer market I might be his salesman, to sit at a stall of mantles and kerchiefs and measure out cubits of calico for the silver of the poor Beduw. He would buy me then a great-eyed Galla maiden to wife.' — There are none more comely women in the Arabs' peninsula; they are gracious in the simplest garments, and commonly of a well tempered nature; and, notwithstanding that which is told of the hither Hábash countries, there is a becoming modesty in their heathen blood. — This was the good Nejûmy, a man most worthy to have been born in a happier country!

They looked for more warfare to come upon them: in the meanwhile Ibn Rashîd treated secretly at Medina, for the recovery of Kheybar. One *Abu Bakkar*, a chief personage, commanding the Ageyl at Medina, rode lately to Hâyil to confer with the Emîr; and he had returned with a saddle-bag full of reals, the Emîr's (pretended) tribute to the Sultan, and as much in the other — a gift of the subtle prince's three days' old friendship — for himself. Abu Bakkar was *Bab-el-Aarab*, ' gate for the affairs of the Nomads,' at Medina; he had been post-master, until he succeeded his father in the higher office: his mother was a Beduwîa. This Abu Bakkar was he who, from the departure of a Pasha-governor until the coming in of the new, commanded at Medina. He was leader of the Ageyl expeditions against the Aarab; and in the field he guided them himself. This valiant half-Beduin townsman had taken a wife or a by-wife from every one of the tribes about — a score or more: in this sort he made all the next Aarab his parentage and allies.

Abu Bakkar came every summer with the soldiery to Kheybar: and he gives the word at the due time, to villagers and Beduw, to begin the date-gathering, — crying, *eflah* ! He was friendly with the Nejûmy; who, good man, used this favour of the great in maintaining the cause of the oppressed. For Amm Mohammed's strong arm was a staff to the weak, and he was father of the poor in the negro village : the hungry and the improvident were welcome to his daily mess. After my departure he would go down and plead Dakhîlullah's cause at Medina, he might find thereto a little money, — " which must be given to the judges " ! When I answered " What justice can there be in such justices ? " he said sorrowfully, " *El-Islam kulluhu aŷb*, ALL IS SHAME IN ISLAM."

Mohammed asked, "What were the Engleys good for ? " I answered, " They are good rulers." — " Ha ! and what rule they ? since they be not rebels (but friends) to the Sooltàn ? " — " In these parts of the world they rule India ; an empire greater than all the Sultan's Dowlat, and the principal béled of the Moslemîn." — " Eigh ! I remember I once heard an Hindy say, in the Haj, ' God continue the *hakûmat* (government of) el-Engleys ; for a man may walk in what part he will of *el-Hind*, with a bundle of silver ; but here in these holy countries even the pilgrims are in danger of robbers ! ' " — Amm Mohammed contemned the Hindies, " They have no heart, he said, and I make no account of the Engleys, for ruling over never so many of them : I myself have put to flight a score of *Hinûd*," — and he told me the tale. " It was in my ignorant youth : one morning in the Haj season, going out under the walls (of Medina), to my father's orchard, I saw a company of Hinûd sitting before me upon a hillock, — sixteen persons : there sat a young maiden in the midst of them — very richly attired ! for they were some principal persons. Then I shouted, and lifting my lance, began to leap and run, against them ; the Hindies cried out, and all rising together they fled to save their lives ! — leaving the maiden alone ; and the last to forsake her was a young man — he perchance that was betrothed to be her husband." The gentle damsel held forth her delicate hands, beseeching him by signs to take only her ornaments : she drew off her rings, and gave them to the (Beduin-like) robber ; — Mohammed had already plucked off her rich bracelets ! But the young prodigal looking upon her girlish beauty and her distress, felt a gentleness rising in his heart and he left her [unstained]. — For such godless work the Arabs have little or no contrition ; this worthy man, whom God had established, even now in his religious years, felt none. — It may seem to them that all world's good is *kheyr Ullah*, howbeit diversely holden, in several men's hands ; and that the same (whether by subtilty, or warlike endeavour) might well enough be assumed by another.

Amm Mohammed understanding from me that the Engleys have a naval station in the peninsula of the Aarab, his bearded chin fell with a sort of national amazement! Some word of this being spoken in the soldiers' kahwa, there would no man believe me. — None of them had not heard of Âdden (Aden) : " But there be, said they, the askars of the Sultan, and not Nasrânies ; " and they derided my folly, — " Think'st thou that the Sooltàn would suffer any kafirs to dwell in the [sacred] Land of the Aarab ? — the Engleys were never at Âdden." But some answered, " Khalîl is a travelled man, who speaks truth and is seldom mistaken : if the Engleys be at Âdden, then is not Âdden on this side the sea, but upon that further (African) part." The Bîshy coming in (W. Bisha lies 120 leagues nigher our Arabian station) confirmed the Nasrâny's tale, saying, " Ay, Âdden is under the hakûmat el-Engleys." Then they all cried out, " It must be by permission of the Sooltàn ! because the Engleys are profitable to the Dowla, and not rebellious."

Twelve days after I had written to the Pasha came his rescript to Abdullah, with a returning hubt, bidding him 'beware how he behaved himself towards the Engleysy, and to send me without delay to Ibn Rashîd ; and if no Beduins could be found to accompany me, to send with me some of the Ageyl : he was to restore my property immediately, and if anything were missing he must write word again.' The black village governor was now in dread for himself; he went about the village to raise that which he had spent of my robbed liras : and I heard with pain, that (for this) he had sold the orphan's cow.

He summoned me at night to deliver me mine own. The packet of books and papers, received a fortnight before from Medina, was sealed with the pasha's signet : when opened a koran was missing and an Arabic psalter ! I had promised them to Amm Mohammed ; and where was the camel bag ? Abdullah murmured in his black throat ' Whose could be this infamous theft ? ' and sent one for Dakhîl the post. — Dakhîl told us that ' Come to Medina he went, with the things on his back, to the government palace ; but meeting with a principal officer — one whom they all knew — that personage led him away to drink coffee in his house. " Now let me see, quoth the officer, what hast thou brought? and, if that Nasrâny's head should be taken off, some thing may as well remain with me, before all goes up to the Pasha." — The great man compelled me, said Dakhîl, so I let him have the books; and when he saw the Persian camel-bag, 'This too, he said, may remain with me.' " — " Ullah curse the father of him!" exclaimed Abdullah: and, many of the askars' voices answered about him, " Ullah curse him!" I asked, " Is it a poor man, who has done this?" *Abdullah*: " Poor! he is rich, the Lord curse him! It is our colonel, Khalîl, at Medina; where he lives in a great house, and receives a great government salary, besides all the [dishonest] private gains of his office." — "The Lord curse him!" exclaimed the Nejûmy. "The Lord curse him! answered Amân (the most gentle minded of them all), he has broken the *namûs* (animus or *esprit*) of the Dowla!" *Abdullah*: " Ah! Khalîl, he is one of the great ones at Medina, and *gomâny!* (a very enemy). Now what can we do, shall we send again to Medina?" A villager lately arrived from thence said, "The colonel is not now in Medina, we heard a little before our coming away that he had set out for Mecca." — So must other days be consumed at Kheybar for this Turkish villain's wrong! in the meanwhile Sàbry Pasha might be recalled from Medina!

I sat by the Nejûmy's evening fire, and boiled tea, which he and his nomad jâra had learned to drink with me, when we heard one call below stairs; the joyous housewife ran down in haste, and brought up her brother, who had been long out cattle lifting, with another gatûny. The wretch came in jaded, and grinning the teeth: and when he had eaten a morsel, he began to tell us his adventure; — 'That come in the Jeheyna dîra they found a troop of camels, and only a child to herd them. They drove off the cattle, and drove them all that day at a run, and the night after; until a little before dawn, when, having yet a day and a half to Kheybar, they fell at unawares among tents! — it was a menzil of Harb. The hounds barked furiously at the rushing of camels, the Aarab ran from their beyts, with their arms. He and his rafîk alighting hastily, forsook the robbed cattle, and saving no more than their matchlocks, they betook themselves to the side of a mountain. From thence they shot down against their pursuers, and those shot up at them. The Harb bye and bye went home to kahwa; and the geyatîn escaped to Kheybar on foot with their weary lives!'

The next day Amm Mohammed called his robber brother-in-law to supper. The jaded wretch soon rose from the dish to kindle his pipe, and immediately went home to sleep. — Mohammed's wife returned later from milking their few goats; and as she came lighting herself upon the stairs, with a flaming palm-branch, his keen eye discerned a trouble in her looks. — " Eigh! woman, he asked, what tidings? " She answered with a sorrowful alacrity, in the Semitic wise, " Well! [a first word of good augury] it may please Ullah : my brother is very sick, and has a flux of the bowels, and is lying in great pain, as if he were to die, and we cannot tell what to do for him : — it is [the poor woman cast down her eyes] as if my brother had been poisoned; when he rose from eating he left us, and before he was come home the pains took him ! " — Mohammed responded with good-humour, " This is a folly, woman, who has poisoned the melaun? I am well, and sheykh Khalîl is well; and Haseyn and thou have eaten after us of the same mess, — but thy brother is sick of his cattle stealing ! Light us forth, and if he be ailing we will bring him hither, and sheykh Khalîl shall cure him with some medicine."

We found him easier; and led him back with us. I gave him grains of laudanum powder, which he swallowed without any mistrusting. — I saw then a remedy of theirs, for the colic pain, which might sometimes save life after drugs have failed. The patient lay groaning on his back, and his sister kneaded the belly smoothly with her housemother's hands [they may be as well anointed with warm oil]; she gave him also a broth to drink of sour milk with a head of (thûm) garlic beaten in it. At midnight we sent him away well again : then I said to Amm Mohammed, " It were easier to die once than to suffer heartache continually." — " The melaun has been twinged thus oftentimes; and who is there afraid of sheykh Khalîl? if thou bid me, little father Khalîl, I would drink poison." — The restless Beduwy was gone, the third morrow, on foot over the Harra, to seek hospitality (and eat flesh-meat) at el-Hâyat, — forty miles distant.

The Siruân asked a medicine for a chill; and I brought him camphor. " Eigh! said Abdullah, is not this *kafûr* of the dead, where-with they sprinkle the shrouds as they are borne to the burial ? — five drops of this tincture will cut off a man's offspring. What hast thou done to drink of it, Amm Mohammed ! " The good man answered, " Have I not Haseyn, and the little bint ? Wellah if sheykh Khalîl have made me from this time childless, I am content, because Khalîl has done it." The black audience were aghast; "Reach me, I said to them, that bottle and I will drink twice five drops." But they murmured, " Akhs ! and was this one of the medicines of Khalîl ?"

There came down Hetemyies with unpressed cheeses to sell in the village. — Abdullah had imagined how he might eat of the sweet-cheeses of the poor nomads, and not pay for them. He commanded the Ageylies to warn him of any hubt bringing cheeses; and when they arrived he sent out his black swaggering Sirûr to ask a cheese from them, as a present for (himself) the governor, " And else I will lay a tax, tell them, upon all cheeses which pass the gates; one in eight shall well be mine, on behalf of the Dowla." The poor nomads, hearing that tiding, loaded again upon their beasts, and drove forth, saying, ' Wellah they would return no more.'

— The black villagers sat with heavy looks on the street benches: and the Nejûmy spared not to say among them, " Is this he, the son of an ass, whom they send us to govern Kheybar? worse and worse! and Abdullah is more and more fool every day. What Aarab will come any more, I say, to Kheybar? from whence then may the people have samn and cheeses? but now they must eat their bread and their porridge *hàf* (without sauce). Is this the Dowla administered by *Abu Aly* (Abdullah)? It was better in Ibn Rashîd's time!" — It is samn put to their coarse meal and dates which makes the oasis diet wholesome: though to flesh-meat eaters it may seem that they use it inordinately, when one in a holiday will eat with his dates almost the third of a pound of precious samn. Butter thus swallowed is a singular refreshment to the wasted body; they say, " It sweats through the bones to the inward marrow, for there is nothing so subtle as samn. A girby may hold water, but no butter skin (*akka, maâun, jurn, med'hunna*) may hold clarified butter, but it be inwardly daubed with thick date syrup." Samn is the health of man in the deadly khála; the best samn has the odour of the blossoming vine. – The negroes gladly anoint their black skins with butter.

The rude unpressed Heteym cheeses, of the milk of their ewes and goats, are little more than clots of curds, and with salt they may last sweet a month. Cheeses are not made in any tribes, of my acquaintance, in Nejd. ' It is not their custom, they say, they might drink more milk than they have :' it may be in their eyes also an ignoble traffic. Yet I have found a tribe of cheese-makers in my Arabian travels, and they are *el-Koreysh*, the kinsmen of Mohammed : they carry their pleasant white cheeses to *et-Tâyif*, and to Mecca. The *Sabeans*, or ' disciples of St. John,' beside the Persian Gulf, are makers of a cheese kind in filaments : [they are praised besides as silversmiths and sword-smiths].

A market party of Heteym brought the quarters of a fat nâga that had been lost in the calving ; and Amm Mohammed bought of them the hump (to sell the lard again by measure), it might be almost an hundred weight of massy white marrow fat, without lean or sinews : cut into gobbets they filled a vast cauldron. This was set upon the fire to be boiled down to the grease, *wedduk* ; which is better they say than samn to anoint their poor diet. When it had boiled enough, the pot was set down to cool upon the clay floor, but the lard yet seethed and bubbled up. "Who, I said, is now the magician ? that can boil without fire !" "Ay, laughed his good Beduwîa, Mohammed he is the sáhar." The Nejûmy answered, " Khalîl knows not what a virtue is in wedduk ; woman, should I tell him the tale of the Solubby ? " — " Yes, tell it to Khalîl."

— " There was a Solubby and his wife, and besides him she had a lemman, a shrew that could pleasure her mother in the same kind : but the goodman kept his counsel, and showed them a simple countenance. One morrow the Solubby, taking down his matchlock, said to his faithless jâra, ' Woman, I go a hunting : from the brow of yonder hill thou mayest see a tolh tree that stands alone in the khála ; — thereat the tribesmen use to enquire of a spirit, which answers them truly. Hearest thou ! in the morning load upon the ass, and remove thither and build our beyt, and there await me. If I have any luck I shall come again the third day : ' so he left them. — The next noon, when they approached the place, the young woman ran forward, — so her heart was on fire to tell the acacia, ' Say O blissful thorn ! she cries, how may I be rid of my silly old husband ? and at the least, that my lemman might be all mine.' That old Solubby lay lurking upon his breast in the bushes ; and he answered her in another voice, ' Woman, feed him with wedduk, till forty days be out ; and after that he shall not hear nor see.' The goodman came home ; and she larded his mess with wedduk, forty days. On the morrow when she brought his breakfast, he spread his hands and felt for the bowl : when he rose, he stumbled and fell among the gear. — They saw that his eyes were set and staring ! and he fared as one that heard them not ; though they cried at his ear, he was not aware of them. In the hot midday [when the nomads slumber], her lemman came creeping to them from bush to bush ; and he made the young woman a sign. ' O stand up, thou ! said the two women, and enter boldly ; for the goodman has lost both his seeing and hearing : ' then the lemman came to them in the booth. But when the poor Solubby saw their shameful sin, he caught his spear ; and suddenly pierced them both through and killed them."

The day was at hand which should deliver me from Kheybar. Dâkhil the post was willing to convey me to Hâyil, for two of my gold pieces : but that would leave me with less than eighty shillings — too little to bring me to some friendly soil, out of the midst of Arabia. Eyâd, a Bishr Ageyly, proffered to carry me on his sick thelûl for five reals to Hâyil. I thought to go first (from this famine at Kheybar) to buy victual at el-Hâyat ; their oasis had not been wasted by locusts. Those negro Nejd villagers are hospitable, and that which the Arabians think is more than all to the welfare of their tribes and towns, the sheykh was a just and honourable person. — The Nejûmy's wife's brother had returned from thence after the three days' hospitality : and being there, with two or three more loitering Beduwies like himself, he told us that each day a householder had called them ; and " every host killed a bull to their supper ! " " It is true, said the Nejmûy ; a bull there is not worth many reals " — " The villagers of Hâyat are become a whiter people of late years ! quoth the Beduwy ; this is through their often marriages with poor women of Heteym and Jeheyna."
— Eyâd, a Beduwy, and by military adoption a townsman of Medina, was one who had drunk very nigh the dregs, of the mischiefs and vility of one and the other life. A Beduwy (mild by nature to the guest) he had not given his voice for my captivity ; but in the rest he was a lukewarm adulator of Abdullah. — All my papers were come again, *save only the safe-conduct of Ibn Rashîd*, which they had detained ! The slave-hearted Abdullah began now to call me ' Uncle Khalîl ; ' for he thought, ' What, if the Nasrâny afterward remembered his wrongs, and he had this power with the Dowla — ' ? How pitiful a behaviour might I have seen from him if our lots had been reversed at Kheybar ! He promised me provision for the way, and half the Ageyly's wages to Hâyil ; but I rejected them both.

Amm Mohammed was displeased because I would not receive from him more than two handfuls of dates : — he was low himself till the harvest, and there remained not a strike of corn in the village. I divided my medicines with the good man, and bought him a tunic and a new gun-stock : these with other reals of mine (which, since they were loose in my pockets, Abdullah had not taken from me), already spent for corn and samn in his house, might suffice that Amm Mohammed should not be barer at my departure, for all the great-hearted goodness which he had shown me in my long tribulation at Kheybar. He said, " Nay, Khalîl, but leave me happy with the remembrance, and take it not away from me by requiting me ! only this I desire of thee that thou sometimes say, ' *The Lord remember him for good*.' Am I not thy abu, art not thou my son, be we not brethren ? and thou art poor in the midst of a land which thou hast seen to be all hostile to thee. Also Ahmed would not suffer it; what will my brother say ? and there would be talk amongst the Kheyâbara." I answered, " I shall say nothing : " then he consented. So I ever used the Arabian hospitality to my possibility : yet now I sinned in so doing, against that charitable integrity, the human affection, which was in Amm Mohammed ; and which, like the waxen powder upon summer fruits, is deflowered under any rude handling. When he received my gift, it seemed to him that I had taken away his good works !

The new year had advanced to the midst of March, the days were warm soon after the sunrising ; at noon I found in the open shadow 78° F. The altitude of Kheybar is, according to my aneroid readings, 2800 feet. Medina, making comparison of the corn and date harvests, which every year are ripened there a few days later, may lie a little higher. Medina is encompassed by windy mountains, the winter is colder there, and rich citizens ruffle it in fur cloaks when a poor man is easy in his bare shirt at Kheybar. The midwinter days, at my first coming, were heavy with the latter autumn heat, and the night hours sultry with a stagnant air till morning. After Christmas the winter nights were cool, then chill, and we had a week of nights (as it seemed to us) of extreme cold (but without frost). The Arabs, whose clothing is half nakedness, lie without beds upon palm matting on the cold floor, — in which they seem to us more witless than many beasts ! only few have any piece of tent cloth to spread under them. Many poor improvident souls, and many hareem, have not so much as a mantle to wry-in their shivering bodies ; they can but roll themselves in (cold) palm mat. Amm Mohammed said : " God sendeth to every one the cold after his cloth, and the man that is nearly naked feels it not more than another who is well clad." One early morning (by my account the 11th of Feb.), when it seemed most cold, I found 51° F. ; yet some winters he had seen a film of ice upon plashes of the fenny valley. The winter air is still and warm in the sun, the heaven of a clear whitish blue, overcast with light clouds. — The time was now come to marry the palms ; the soft white blossoming shoots of the new fruit-stalks, *tólâ*, were risen in the crowns of the beautiful food stems. The Kheybar valleys are reckoned neither to the Hejâz nor to Nejd ; they are a kind of middle ground, — yet Kheybar is an Hejâz village. The higher grounds of the Harra above appertain to Nejd ; the lower desert of the W. el-Humth beyond the Hejjûr mountains is called, by the Nejd Bishr, *Teháma* [hot plain land] ; — this is not that seabord Teháma beside the Red Sea.

Abdullah had purchased other camel-bags for me, from a salesman who arrived from Medina. I agreed with Eyâd ; and on the morrow we should depart from Kheybar. — When that blissful day dawned, my rafîk found it was the 21st of the moon, *Sáfr*, and not lucky to begin our journey ; we might set out, he said, the next morning.

I saw then two men brought before Abdullah from Umm Kîda, for resisting the forced cleansing and sweeping in their sûk. Abdullah made them lie upon their breasts, in a public alley, and then, before weeping women, and the village neighbours, — and though the sheykhs entreated for them, he beat them, with green palm rods ; and they cried out mainly, till their negro blood was sprinkled on the ground. Amm Mohammed went by driving his kine to the common gathering-place of their cattle without the gates : his half-Beduin (gentle) heart swelled to see this bestial (and in his eyes inhuman) spectacle ! And with loud seditious voice as he returned, he named Abu Aly " very ass, and Yahûdy ! " to all whom he found in the village street.

The new sun rising, this was the hour of my deliverance from the long *deyik es-sudr*, the 'straitness of the breast ' in affliction, at Kheybar. Eyâd said that all his hire must be paid him ere the setting out ; because he would leave it with his wife. In a menzil of the Aarab, I had not doubted, a Beduwy is commonly a trusty rafîk ; but Eyâd was a rotten one, and therefore I had covenanted to pay him a third in departing, a third at el-Hâyat, and a third at our arriving in Hâyil. Abdullah sought to persuade me with deceitful reasons; but now I refused Eyâd, who I foresaw from this beginning would be a dangerous companion. *Abdullah:* " Let us not strive, we may find some other, and in all things, I would fain content Khalîl." Afterwards he said, " I vouch for Eyâd, and if he fail in anything, the fault be upon my head! Eyâd is an askar of mine, *the Dowla has a long arm*, and for any misdeed I might cut off his head. Eyâd's arrears of pay are now five or six hundred reals, and he durst not disobey the Dowla. Say which way you would take to Hâyil, and to that I will bind him. You may rest here a day and there a day, at your own liking, and drink whey, where you find Beduins; and to this Eyâd is willing because his thelûl is feeble. Wouldst thou as much as fifteen days for the journey? — I will give him twenty-six to go and come."

The Nejûmy, who stood as a looker-on to-day among us, was loud and raw in his words; and gave his counsel so fondly before them all, and manifestly to my hurt! that I turned from him with a heartache. The traveller should sail with every fair wind in these fanatical countries, and pass forth before good-will grew cold: I made Eyâd swear before them all to be faithful to me, and counted the five reals in his hand.

Abdullah had now a request that an Ageyly Bishr lad, *Merjàn*, should go in our company. I knew him to be of a shallow humour, a sower of trouble, and likely by recounting my vicissitudes at Kheybar to the Aarab in the way, to hinder my passage. *Abdullah:* ' He asks it of your kindness, that he might visit an only sister and his little brother at Hâyil; whom he has not seen these many years.' I granted, and had ever afterward to repent:—there is an impolitic humanity, which is visited upon us.

The Jew-like Southern Annezy are the worst natured (saving the Kahtân) of all the tribes. I marked with discomfort of heart the craven adulation of Eyâd, in his leavetaking of these wretches. Although I had suffered wrongs, I said to them (to the manifest joy of the guilty Abdullah) the last word of Peace. — My comrade Amân came along with me. The Nejûmy was gone before to find his mare; he would meet us by the way and ride on a mile with me. We went by a great stone and there I mounted: Amân took my hand feebly in his dying hand, and prayed aloud that the Lord would bring me safely to my journey's end. The poor Galla earnestly charged Eyâd to have a care of me, and we set forward.

One Hamed, a clownish young man of the village, came along with us. The Nejûmy sent him to bring in some goats of his, which he had at pasture with the next Heteym. Hamed's father (Amm Mohammed told me) had been one of the richest at Kheybar; "But it is gone from them, and now this fellow, to fill his hungry belly, must lend himself to every man's service; I choose him because he never says me nay.— His brother loved a young woman of the village, but a sheykh spoke for her; and though he was a man in years, her father gave her to him: the sheykh was Ibrahîm's father. One day when the young negro found the old wiver in the palms, and he saw no man nigh, he ran to him and broke his pan, with his mace. The sheykh not coming home, there was a stir in the village; and they sought for him in the plantations. The dead was not found till the second morrow; his corse lay under sticks and straw, which the man-slayer had cast over him. For a day or two every man asked other, 'Who has done this?' In the end a child went to the sheykh Sâlih and said, 'I will show it thee for a reward:' and the sheykh promised him. The child said, 'It was such an one, I saw him slay the sheykh; and when he hid him he saw me, and I fled without ever looking back, and ran on to the village.' — The blood-ransom was grievous; but the unhappy father chose to forsake nearly all his land, for his son's life: he made it over to Ibrahîm, the son of the slain; and there was little left for his old age." I asked, if the enriched Ibrahîm might live now out of dread of the ruffling young brethren, since he enjoyed their patrimony? "Ay, he answered, they are good friends: and the young men are beholden to him, because he accepted the blood-money, for else a brother must have died."

At little distance the Nejûmy met us, — he was on foot. He said, his mare had strayed in the palms; and if he might find her, he would ride down to the Tubj, to cut male palm blossoms of the half-wild stems there, to marry them with his female trees at home. One husband stem (to be known by the doubly robust growth) may suffice among ten female palms. — "Now God be with thee, my father Mohammed, and requite thee." — "God speed thee Khalîl," and he took my hand. Amm Mohammed went back to his own, we passed further; and the world, and death, and the inhumanity of religions parted us for ever!

We beat the pad-footed thelûl over the fenny ground, and the last brooks and plashes. And then I came up from the pestilent Kheybar wadiàn, and the intolerable captivity of the Dowla, to a blissful free air on the brow of the Harra ! In the next hour we went by many of the vaults, of wild basalt stones [v. above p. 120], which I have supposed to be barrows. After ten miles' march we saw a nomad woman standing far off upon a lava rock, and two booths of Heteym. My Beduin rafîks showed me the heads of a mountain southward, *el-Baîtha*, that they said stands a little short of Medina.

It was afternoon, we halted and loosed out the thelûl to pasture, and sat down till it should be evening. When the sun was setting we walked towards the tents : but the broken-headed Eyâd left me with Hamed and his loaded thelûl, and went with Merjàn to guest it at the other beyt. The householder of the booth where I was, came home with the flocks and camels ; he was a beardless young man. They brought us buttermilk, and we heard the voice of a negress calling in the woman's apartment, *Hamed ! yâ Hamô !* She was from the village, and was staying with these nomad friends in the desert, to refresh herself with léban. It was presently dark, but the young man went abroad again with the ass to bring in water. He returned after two hours and, without my knowledge, they sacrificed a goat : it was for this he had fetched water. The young Heteymy called me — the adulation of an abject race — *Towîl el-amr*.

After the hospitality Eyâd entered, " Khalîl, he said, hast thou reserved no morsels for me that am thy rafîk ? " — " Would a rafîk have forsaken me ? " He now counselled to hold a more westerly course, according to the tidings they had heard in the other tent, ' that we might come every day to menzils of the Aarab, and find milk and refreshment ; whereas, if I visited el-Hâyat, all the way northward to Hâyil from thence was now bare of Beduins.' — I should thus miss el-Hâyat, and had no provisions : also I assented to them in evil hour ! it had been better to have yielded nothing to such treacherous rafîks.

We departed at sunrise, having upon our right hand, in the ' White Harra ' (el-Abiath) a distant mountain, which they likewise named *el-Baitha* [other than that in the Hejâz, nigh Medina]. In that jebel, quoth my rafîks, are the highest *sháebân* (seyl-strands) of W. er-Rummah ; but all on this side seyls down to the (great Hejâz) Wady el-Humth. We passed by sharp glassy lavas ; " — *loub*," said my companions.

A pair of great lapwing-like fowl, *habâra*, fluttered before us ; I have seldom seen them in the deserts [and only at this season] : they have whitish and dun-speckled feathers. Their eggs (brown and rose, black speckled) I have found in May, laid two together upon the bare wilderness gravel [near Maan] ; they were great as turkey-eggs, and well tasting : the birds might be a kind of bustards. " Their flesh is nesh as cotton between the teeth," quoth the Bishr Sybarite Eyâd. Merjàn and Eyâd lured to them, whistling ; they drew off their long gun-leathers, and stole under the habâras ; but as Beduins will not cast away lead in the air, they returned bye and bye as they went. I never saw the Arabs' gunning help them to any game ; only the Nejûmy used to shoot at, (and he could strike down) flying partridges.

From hence the vulcanic field about us was a wilderness of sharp lava stones, where few or no cattle paths [Bishr, *jadda*] appeared ; and nomads go on foot among the rocking blocks unwillingly. A heavy toppling stone split the horny thickness of Hamed's great toe. I alighted that he might ride ; but the negro borrowed a knife and, with a savage resolution, shred away his flesh, and went on walking. In the evening halt, he seared the bloody wound, and said, it would be well enough, for the next marches. As we journeyed the March wind blustered up against us from the north ; and the dry herbage and scudding stems of sere desert bushes, were driven before the blast. Our way was uncertain, and without shelter or water ; the height of this lava-plain is 3,400 feet. Merjàn — the lad was tormented with a throbbing ague-cake (*táhal*), after the Kheybar fever, shouted in the afternoon that he saw a flock ; and then all beside his patience he shrieked back curses, because we did not follow him : the flock was but a troop of gazelles. " *Fen el-Aarab*, they said at last, the nomads where ? — *neffera !* deceitful words ; but this is the manner of the Heteymàn ! they misled us last night, Ullah send them confusion." The negro had drunk out nearly all in my small waterskin : towards evening he untied the neck and would have made a full end of it himself at a draught ; but I said to him, " Nay, for we have gone and thirsted all the day, and no man shall have more than other." The Beduins cried out upon him, " And thinkest thou that we be yet in the Saheyn ? this is the khála and no swaggering-place of the Kheyâbara." Finally, when the sun set, we found a hollow ground and sídr trees to bear off the night wind, which blew so fast and pierced our slender clothing : they rent down the sere white arms of a dead acacia, for our evening fire. Then kneading flour of the little water which remained to us, we made hasty bread under the embers. The March night was cold.

We departed when the day dawned, and held under the sandstone mountain *Gurs* : and oh, joy ! this sun being fairly risen, the abhorred land-marks of Kheybar appeared no more. We passed other vaulted cells and old dry walling upon the waste Harra, and an ancient burying-place. " See, said Eyâd, these graves of the auellîn, how they lie heaped over with stones ! " We marched in the vulcanic field — ' a land whose stones are iron,' and always fasting, till the mid-afternoon, when we found in some black sand-beds footprints of camels. At first my rafîks said the traces were of a ráhla five to ten days old ; but taking up the jella, they thought it might be of five days ago. The droppings led us over the Harra north-westward, towards the outlying plutonic coasts of J. Hejjûr. — Footprints in the desert are slowly blotted by insensible wind causing the sand corns to slide ; they might otherwise remain perfectly until the next rain. — In a monument lately opened in Egypt, fresh prints of the workmen's soles were found in the fine powder of the floor ; and they were of an hundred men's ages past ! The Beduins went to an hollow ground, to seek a little ponded rain, and there they filled the girby. That water was full of wiggling white vermin ; and we drank — giving God thanks — through a lap of our kerchiefs. [We may see the flaggy hare-lips of the camel fenced with a border of bristles, bent inwardly ; and through this brush the brute strains all that he drinks of the foul desert waters !] The Beduin rafîks climbed upon every high rock to look for the nomads : we went on till the sun set, and then alighted in a low ground with acacia trees and bushes ; there we found a dàr of the nomads lately forsaken. We were here nigh the borders of the Harra.

As the morrow's sun rose we set forward, and the camel droppings led us towards the Thullân Hejjûr. We came bye and bye to the Harra side, and the lava-border is here like the ice-brink of a glacier ; where we descended it was twenty feet in height, and a little beside us eight or ten fathoms. Beyond the Harra we passed forth upon barren steeps of plutonic gravel, furrowed by the secular rains and ascending toward the horrid wilderness of mountains, Jebâl Hejjûr. A napping gazelle-buck, started from a bush before us ; and standing an instant at gaze, he had fallen then to the shot of an European, — but the Beduins are always unready. As we journeyed I saw an hole, a yard deep, digged in the desert earth ; the rafîks answered me, ' It was for a *mejdûr* (*one sick of the small-pox*).' — They would kindle a fire in it, and after raking out the embers the sick is seated in the hot sand : such may be a salutary sweating-bath. The Arabians dread extremely the homicide disease ; and the calamity of a great sheykh of the Annezy in Kasîm was yet fresh in men's memories. — His tribesfolk removed from him in haste ; and his kindred and even his own household forsook him !

Leaving the sandstone platform mountain *el-Kh'tâm* upon the right hand, we came to the desolate mountains, whose knees and lower crags about us were traps, brown, yellow, grey, slate-colour, red and purple. Small black eagles, el-egâb, lay upon the wing above us, gliding like the shadows, which their outstretched wings cast upon the rocky coasts. Crows and rákhams hovered in the lower air, over a forsaken dàr of the nomads : their embers were yet warm, they had removed this morning. The Beduin companions crept out with their long matchlocks, hoping to shoot a crow, and have a pair of shank-bones for pipe-stems. I asked them if there had fallen a hair or feather to their shot in the time of their lives ? They protested, " Ay wellah, Khalîl ; and the gatta many times." Not long after we espied the Aarab and their camels. We came up with them a little after noon, when they first halted to encamp. The sheykh, seeing strangers approach, had remained a little in the hindward ; and he was known to my companions. These nomads were *Ferâdessa, Ibn Simry*, Heteym. We sat down together, and a weled milked two of the sheykh's nâgas, for us strangers.

This sheykh, when he knew me to be the Nasrâny, began to bluster, although I was a guest at his milk-bowl. " What ! heathen man, he cries ; what ! Nasrâny, wherefore comest thou hither ? Dost thou not fear the Aarab's knife ? Or thinkest thou, O Jew-man, that it cannot carve thy throat ? — which will be seen one day. O ye his rafîks, will they not cut the wezand of him ? Where go ye now — to Hâyil ? but Ibn Rashîd will kill him if this (man) come thither again." — The Heteym are not so civil-minded as the right Beduw ; they are often rough towards their guests, where the Beduw are gentle-natured. When I saw the man was a good blunt spirit, I derided his ignorance till he was ashamed ; and in this sort you may easily defeat the malicious simplicity of the Arabs.

We drove on our beast to their camp, and sat down before a beyt. The householder bye and bye brought us forth a bowl of lében and another of mereesy; we loosed out the thelûl to pasture, and sat by our baggage in the wind and beating sun till evening; when the host bade us enter, and we found a supper set ready for us, of boiled rice. He had been one in the Heteymy hubt which was lately taken by a foray of Jeheyna near the walls of Medina. Upon the morrow this host removed with his kindred, and we became guests of another beyt; for we would repose this day over in their menzil, where I counted thirty tents. When I gave a sick person rhubarb, his friends were much pleased for "By the smack, said they, it should be a good medicine indeed." A few persons came to us to enquire the news: but not many men were at home by day in the Heteymy menzil: for these nomads are diligent cattle-keepers, more than the Beduw.

I heard some complain of Ibn Rashîd, — ' It was he that weakened the Aarab;' Eyâd answered them, "Ay billah it is he who weakens the tribes." I asked, "How is this? without him were there any safety in the desert? — the tribes would be perpetually riding upon each other." *Eyâd*: "It is Ibn Rashîd that weakens the Aarab, for before a kabîla is subdued to him he has brought them almost to nothing: after that, he makes them to live in peace." The southern Heteym are taxed by Ibn Rashîd; and, since the Dowla is at Kheybar, they are taxed as well by the government of Medina. The Siruân had been round among them with Amm Mohammed, to collect the tithe, not long before my coming to Kheybar. The most of the Heteymán yield a khûa to all the powerful about them; and being thus released from their hostility, they are commonly more thriving than the Beduw of the same dîras. Their thelûls are the best, no Beduin tribes have so good a strain; (we shall see that best of all are the thelûls of their kindred the Sherarát). The Heteym are commonly more robust than the hunger-bitten Beduw, and their women are often beautiful.

They questioned roughly in the booth, "What are the Nasâra, what is their religion?" One among them said: "I will tell you the sooth in this as I heard it [in Medina, or in the civil north countries]: The Nasâra inhabit a city closed with iron and encompassed by the sea!" *Eyâd*: "Talk not so boisterously, lest ye offend Khalîl; and he is one that with a word might make this tent to fall about our ears." "Eigh! they answered, could he so indeed?" I found in their menzil two lives blighted by the morbus gallicus. I enquired from whence had they that malady? They answered, "From el-Medina."

At daybreak the nomad people removed. We followed with them westward, in these mountains; and ascended through a cragged passage, where there seemed to be no footing for camels. Hamed, who had left us, came limping by with one whom he had found to guide him: "Farewell, I said, *akhu Hamda*." The Kheybar villain looked up pleased and confused, because I had named him (as one of the valiant) by his sister, and he wished me God speed. We were stayed in the midst by some friends, that would milk for us ere we departed from among them. Infinite seemed to me the horrid maze of these desolate and thirsty mountains! Their name Jebâl Hejjûr may be interpreted the stony mountains:—they are of the Wélad Aly and Bishr,—and by their allowance of these Heteym. In the valley deeps they find, most years, the rabîa and good pasture bushes. These coasts seyl by W. Hejjûr to the W. el-Humth. We were now much westward of our way. The nomads removed southward; and leaving them we descended, in an hour, to a wady bottom of sand, where we found another Heteym menzil, thirty booths, of *Sueyder*, Ibn Simry. The district (of a kind of middle traps), they name *Yeterôha*: Eyâd's Aarab seldom visited this part of their dîra; and he had been here but once before. These mountains seyl, they say, by W. Khâfutha, one of the Kheybar valleys.

Merjàn found here some of his own kindred, a household or two of his Bishr clan *Bejaija* or *Bejaida*.—There are many poor families of Beduin tribesmen living (for their more welfare) in the peaceable society of the Heteym. A man, that was his cousin, laid hands on the thelûl, and drew her towards his hospitable beyt.—Our hosts of yesterday sent word of my being in the dîra to a sick sheykh of theirs, *Ibn Heyzán*, who had been hurt by a spear-thrust in a ghrazzu. Amm Mohammed lately sold some ointment of mine to the sick man's friends in Kheybar, which had been found excellent; and his acquaintance desired that I should ride to see him. I consented to wait here one day, until the return of their messenger.

When I took out my medicine book and long brass Arabic inkhorn, men and women gathered about me; it was marvels to them to see me write and read. They whispered, "He sees the invisible;—at least thou seest more than we poor folk!—it is written there!" The host had two comely daughters; they wondered to look upon the stranger's white skin. The young women's demeanour was easy, with a maidenly modesty; but their eye-glances melted the heart of the beardless lad

Merjàn, their cousin, who had already a girl-wife at Kheybar. These nomad hareem in Nejd were veiled with the face-clout, but only from the mouth downward; they wore a silver ring in the right nostril, and a braided forelock hanging upon the temples. The good-man went abroad with his hatchet, and we saw them no more till sunset, when he and his wife came dragging-in great lopped boughs of tolh trees:— where we see the trail of boughs in the khála, it is a sign of the nomad menzils. Of these they made a sheep-pen before the beyt; and the small cattle were driven in and folded for the night. They call it *hathîra*; "Shammar, they said, have another name," [*serifat*]. The host now set before us a great dish of rice.

Eyâd was treacherous, and always imagining since he had his wages, how he might forsake me: the fellow would not willingly go to Hâyil. "Khalîl, shall I leave thee here? wellah the thelûl is not in plight for a long journey." — "Restore then three reals and I will let thee go." — "Ah! how may I, Khalîl? you saw that I left the money at home." — "Then borrow it here." — "Bless me! which of these Aarab has any money, or would lend me one real?" — "All this I said at Kheybar, that thou wouldst betray me; Eyâd, thou shalt carry me to Hâyil, as thou art bounden." — "But here lies no way to Hâyil, we are come out of the path; these Aarab have their faces towards the Auájy, let us go on with them, it is but two marches, and I will leave thee there." — The ill-faith of the Arabs is a gulf to cast in the teeth of the unwary! there is nothing to hope for in man, amongst them; and their heaven is too far off, or without sense of human miseries. Now I heard from this wretch's mouth my own arguments, which he had bravely contradicted at Kheybar! On the morrow Eyâd would set out with the rising sun: I said, we will remain here to-day, as thou didst desire yesternight and obtain of me. But he loaded! and then the villanous rafîk came with his stick, and — it was that he had learned in the Turkish service — threatened to beat me, if I did not remove: but he yielded immediately.

In this menzil I found a Solubby household from *W. es-Suffera*, which is spoken of for its excessive heat, in the Hejâz, not much north of Mecca. They were here above three hundred miles from home; but that seems no great distance to the land-wandering Solubba. The man told me that when summer was in they would go to pitch, alone, at some water in the wilderness: and (having no cattle) they must live then partly of venison. "You have now asked me for an eye-medicine, can you go hunting with blear eyes?" — "It is the young men (*el-eyyâl*) that hunt; and I remain at home." — I went further by a tent where the Heteymy housewife was boiling down her léban, in a great cauldron, to mereesy. I sat down to see it: her pot sputtered, and she asked me, could I follow the spats with my eyes upward? "For I have heard say, that the Nasâra cannot look up to heaven." Harshly she chid ' my unbelief and my enmity to Ullah;' and I answered her nothing. Then she took up a ladleful of her mereesy paste, poured samn on it, in a bowl, and bade the stranger eat, saying cheerfully, "Ah! why dost thou continue without the religion? and have the Lord against thee and the people also; only pray as we and all the people will be thy kindred." — Such were the nomads' daily words to me in these deserts.

The morning after, when the messenger had not returned, we loaded betimes. The sun was rising as we rode forth; and at the camp's end another Bishr householder bade us alight, for he had made ready for us — no common morrow's hospitality; but his dish of rice should have been our supper last evening. Whilst we were eating, a poor woman came crying to me, ' to cure her daughter and stay here, — we should be her guests; and she pretended she would give the hakîm a camel when her child was well.' Eyâd was now as iniquitously bent that I should remain, as yesterday that I should remove; but I mounted and rode forth: we began our journey without water. The guest must not stretch the nomad hospitality, we could not ask them to fill our small girby with the common juice of the earth; yet when hosts send to a weyrid they will send also the guest's water-skin to be filled with their own girbies.

We journeyed an hour or two, over the pathless mountains, to a brow from whence we overlooked an empty plain, lying before us to the north. Only Merjàn had been here once in his childhood; he knew there were waterpits yonder, — and we must find them, since we had nothing to drink. We descended and saw old footprints of small cattle; and hoped they might lead to the watering. In that soil of plutonic grit were many glittering morsels of clear crystal. Merjàn, looking upon the landmarks, thought bye and bye that we had passed the water; and my rafîks said they would return upon the thelûl to seek it. They bade me sit down here and await them: but I thought the evil in their hearts might persuade them, ere they had ridden a mile, to leave me to perish wretchedly. — Now couching the thelûl, they unloaded my bags. "The way is weary, they said, to go back upon our feet, it may be long to find the themeyil ; and a man might see further from the back of the thelûl." " I will look for the water with you." — " Nay, but we will return to thee soon." — " Well go, but leave with me thy matchlock, Eyâd ; and else we shall not part so." He laid down his gun unwillingly, and they mounted and rode from me.

They were out an hour and a half : then, to my comfort, I saw them returning, and they brought water. — Eyâd now complained that I had mistrusted him ! ' And wellah no man before had taken his gun from him ; but this is Khalîl !'—" Being honest rafîks, you shall find me courteous ; — but tell me, you fired upon your own tribesmen ? "—" Ay, billah ! I an Auájy shot against the Auájy, and if I dealt so with mine own kinsmen, what would I not do unto thee ? " — " How then might I trust thee ? " *Merjàn* : " Thou sayest well, Khalîl, and this Eyâd is a light-headed coxcomb." Among the Aarab, friends will bite at friends thus, betwixt their earnest and game, and it is well taken. *Eyâd* : " Come, let us sit down now and drink tobacco ; for we will not journey all by day, but partly, where more danger is, in the night-time. Go Merjàn, gather stalks, and let us bake our bread here against the evening, when it were not well to kindle a fire." The lad rose and went cheerfully ; for such is the duty of the younger among wayfaring companions in the khála.

Merjàn put in my hand a paper, which he took from his gunner's belt, to read for him. It was a bill of his government service : To Merjàn the Bejaijy, Ageyly, is due for one year and certain months so many reals, less seventy reals to cost of thelûl." — " And your thelûl, Merjàn — ? " — " She is dead, and they [namely his fraudulent Colonel, who devours poor men thus, when they enroll themselves and have no dromedary] have written against me seventy reals, for a dying thelûl ! she was worth wellah less than ten, — so there remains for me to receive only fifteen reals ; and when, God knoweth." — " It is a sorry service." " Ay, and too iniquitous, but I think this year to make an end of it." — " You might as well serve Ibn Rashîd, who pays his rajajîl a crown less by the month, four real-Mejîdies, but that is never in arrear, besides a house and rations." — " Ay, this I think to do when I may be quit of the Dowla."

An idle hour passed, and we again set forward ; the land was a sandy plain, bordered north-eastward by distant mountains. In the midst, between hills, is a summer watering place of the Auájy, *Yemmen*.

There are ancient ten-fathom wells, and well steyned, the work, they say, of the jân. — We have passed again from the plutonic rocks to the (here dark-coloured) red sandstones. A black crater hill appeared now, far in front upon the Harra, J. Ethnàn. This sandy wilderness is of the Auájy; 'white' soil, in which springs the best pasture, and I saw about us almost a thicket of green bushes! — yet the two-third parts, of kinds which are not to the sustenance of any creature: we found there fresh foot-prints of ostriches. "Let us hasten, they said, [over this open country]," and Eyâd besought me to look in my books, and forecast the peril of our adventure; 'for *wellah yudayyik súdry*, his breast was straitened, since I had made him lay down his matchlock by me.'

We halted an hour after the stars were shining, in a low place, under a solitary great bush; and couched the thelûl before us, to shelter our bodies from the chill night wind, now rising to a hurricane, which pierced through their light Hejâz clothing. The Beduin rafîks, to comfort themselves with fire, forgot their daylight fears: they felt round in the darkness for a few sticks. And digging there with my hands, I found jella in the sand, — it was the old mûbrak, or night lair, of a camel; and doubtless some former passenger had alighted to sleep at our inn of this great desert bush: the beast's dung had been buried by the wind, two or three years. Merjàn gathered his mantle full: the precious fuel soon glowed with a red heat in our sandy hearth, and I boiled tea, which they had not tasted till now.

The windy cold lasted all night, the blast was outrageous. Hardly at dawn could they, with stiffened fingers, kindle a new fire: the rafîks sat on, — there was not warmth in their half naked bodies to march against this wild wind. — A puff whirling about our bush scattered the dying embers, "Akhs! cries Eyâd, the sot, *Ullah yulâan abu ha'l hubûb*, condemn the father of this blustering blast; and he added, *Ullah yusullat aly ha'l hattab*, God punish this firewood." We rose at last; and the Beduin rafîks bathed their bodies yet a moment in the heat, spreading their loose tunics over the dying embers. The baffling March blast raged in our teeth, carrying the sandy grit into our eyes. The companions staggered forward on foot, — we marched north-eastward: after two hours, they halted to kindle another fire. I saw the sky always overcast with thin clouds. Before noon the storm abated; and the wind chopping round blew mildly in the afternoon, from the contrary part! We approached then the black border of the Harra, under the high crater-hill Ethnàn. Ethnàn stands solitary, in a field of sharp cinder-like and rifted lavas ; the nomads say that this great *hilla* is inaccessible. Sometimes, after winter rain, they see a light reeking vapour about the volcano head : and the like is seen in winter mornings over certain deep rifts in the Harra, — ' the smell of it is like the breath of warm water.' This was confirmed to me by Amm Mohammed.

In that part there is a (land-mark) valley-ground which lies through the Harra towards el-Hâyat, *W. Mukheyat*. My small waterskin might hardly satisfy the thirst of three men in one summer's march, and this was the second journey ; we drank therefore only a little towards the afternoon, and had nothing to eat. But my mind was full to see so many seamed, guttered and naked cinder-hills of craters in the horrid black lavas before us. The sense of this word hilla, hillaya, is according to Amm Mohammed, ' that which appears evidently,' — and he told me, there is a kind of dates of that name at Medina. Eyâd said thus, " *Halla* is the Harra-hill of black powder and slaggy matter ; *hellayey* is a little Harra-hill ; *hillî* or *hellowat* (others say *hilliân*) are the Harra-hills together." — We marched towards the same hillies which I had passed with Ghroceyb. When the sun was near setting the rafîks descried, and greeted (devoutly) the new moon.

The stars were shining when we halted amidst the hillian, the eighth evening of our march from Kheybar. They thought it perilous to kindle a fire here, and we had nothing to eat ; — there should be water, they said, not far off. Eyâd rose to seek it, but in the night-time he could not find it again. — " I have been absent, he murmured, twelve years ! " He knew his landmarks in the morning ; then he went out, and brought again our girby full of puddle water. The eye of the sun was risen (as they said) ' a spear's length,' on height, when feeling ourselves refreshed with the muddy bever, we set forward in haste.

They held a course eastward over the lava country, to *Thúrghrud* : that is a hamlet of one household upon the wells of an antique settlement at the further border of the Harra. *Eyâd :* " It was found in the last generation by one who went up and down, like thyself, *yujassás*, spying out the country : " and he said I should see Thúrghrud in exchange for el-Hâyat. We went on by a long seyl and black sand-bed in the lavas, where was sprung a little rabîa : and driving the wretched thelûl to these green borders we let her graze forward, or gathering the herbs in our hands as we marched, we thrust them into her jaws. Where there grew an acacia I commonly found a little herbage, springing under the north side of the tree ; that is where the lattice of minute leaves casts a thin shadowing over the sun-stricken land, and the little autumn moisture is last dried up. I was in advance and saw camels' footprints ! Calling the rafîks I enquired if these were not of yesterday : — they said they were three days old. They could not tell me if the traces were of a ghrazzu, — that is, these Beduin Ageylies did not distinguish whether they were the smaller footprints of thelûls, passing lightly with riders, or of grazing camels ! But seeing the footing of camel-calves I could imagine that this was a drove moving between the pastures. It happened as in the former case when we found the traces of Ibn Simry's cattle, that a stranger judged nigher the truth than his Beduin company. The footprints lay always before us, and near midday, when they were in some doubt whether we should not turn and avoid them, we saw a camel troop pasturing in a green place, far in front.

The herders lay slumbering upon their faces in the green grass, and they were not aware of us, till our voice startled them with the fear of the desert. They rose hastily and with dread, seeing our shining arms ; but hearing the words of peace (salaam aleyk) they took heart. When Eyâd afterward related this adventure, " Had they been gôm, he said, we should have taken wellah all that sight of cattle, and left not one of them." So sitting down with them we asked the elder herdsman, ' How he durst lead his camels hither ? ' He answered, " *Ullah yetowil ûmr ha'l weled!* God give that young man [the Emir Ibn Rashîd] long life, under whose rule we may herd the cattle without fear. It is not nowadays as it was ten years yore, but I and my little brother may drive the 'bil to pasture all this land over." He sent the child to milk for us ; and wayworn, hungry and thirsting, we swallowed every man three or four pints at a draught : only Merjàn, because of his ague cake, could not drink much milk. The lads, that were Heteymies, had been some days out from the menzil, and their camels were jezzîn. They carried but their sticks and cloaks, and a bowl between them, and none other provision or arms. When hungry or thirsting they draw a nâga's udder, and drink their fill. They showed us where we might seek the nomads in front, and we left them.

CHAPTER IX

DESERT JOURNEY TO HÂYIL. THE NASRÂNY IS DRIVEN FROM THENCE

Eyâda ibn Ajjuèyn, seen again. Uncivil Heteym hosts. Ghroceyb. Sâlih, seen again. Nomad names of horses. Strife with the rafîks. A desolate night in the khála. Zôl. Come to tents and good entertainment. A rautha in the desert. Hunters' roast. The Tîh, or phantom thelûl in the Sherarát country. Eyâd, his person. Múthir, a poor Bishry. Braitshán, a Shammar sheykh. An Heteymy's blasphemy. Poor Beduins' religious simplicity. A Beduin boy seeking a herdsman's place. The first hamlet in J. Shammar. Another grange in the desert. 'Between the dog and the wolf.' The village el-Kasr. Tidings that the Emir is absent from Hâyil. Beny Temîm. Hâyil in sight. Gofar. Come to Hâyil, the second time. Aneybar left deputy for Ibn Rashîd in the town. The Nasrâny is received with ill-will and fanaticism. Aneybar is now an adversary. A Medina Sherîf in Hâyil. A Yémeny stranger who had seen the Nasrâny in Egypt. Tidings of the war, which is ended. The great sheykh of el-Ajmân. The Sherîf. The townspeople's fanaticism in the morning; a heavy hour. Depart, the second time, with care from Hâyil. Come again to Gofar. B. Temîm and Shammar.

WE came in the afternoon to a sandstone platform standing like an island with cliffs in the basaltic Harra; the rafîks thought we were at fault, as they looked far over the vulcanic land and could not see the Aarab. From another high ground they thought they saw a camel-herd upon a mountain far off: yet looking with my glass I could not perceive them! We marched thither, and saw a nomad sitting upon a lava brow, keeping his camels. The man rose and came to meet us; and "What ho! he cries, Khalîl, comest thou hither again?" The voice I knew, and now I saw it was Eyâda ibn Ajjuèyn, the Heteymy sheykh, from whose menzil I had departed with Ghroceyb to cross the Harra, to Kheybar!

Eyâda saluted me, but looked askance upon my rafîks, and they were strange with him and silent. This is the custom of the desert, when nomads meeting with nomads are in doubt of each other whether friends or foemen. We all sat down; and said the robust Heteymy, "Khalîl what are these with thee?" — "Ask them thyself." — "Well lads, what tribesmen be ye, — that come I suppose from Kheybar?" They answered, "We are Ageyl and the Bashat el-Medina has sent us to convey Khalîl to Ibn Rashîd." — "But I see well that ye are Beduw, and I say what Beduw?" — Eyâd answered, "*Yâ Fulàn*, O Someone — for yet I heard not thy name, we said it not hitherto, because there might be some debate betwixt our tribes." — "Oho! is that your dread? but fear nothing [at a need he had made light of them both], eigh, Khalîl! what are they? — Well then, said he, I suppose ye be all thirsty; I shall milk for thee, Khalîl, and then for these, if they would drink!" When my rafîks had drunk, Eyâd answered, "Now I may tell thee we are of Bishr." — "It is well enough, we are friends; and Khalîl thou art I hear a Nasrâny, but how didst thou see Kheybar?" — "A cursed place." — "Why wouldest thou go thither, did I not warn thee?" — "Where is Ghroceyb?" — "He is not far off, he is well; and Ghroceyb said thou wast a good rafîk, save that thou and he fell out nigh Kheybar, I wot never how, and thou wouldst have taken his thelûl." — "This is his wild talk." — "It is likely, for Khalîl (he spoke to my rafîks) is an honest man; the medicines our hareem bought of him, and those of Kâsim's Aarab, they say, have been effectual. How found ye him? is he a good rafîk?" — "Ay, this ought we to say, though the man be a Nasrâny! but billah, it is the Moslems many times that should be named Nasâra." — "And where will ye lodge to-night?" — "We were looking for the Aarab, but tell us where should we seek their beyts." — "Yonder (he said, rising up and showing us with his finger), take the low way, on this hand; and so ye linger not you may be at their menzil about the sunsetting. I may perhaps go thither myself in the evening, and to-morrow ride with you to Hâyil." — We wondered to find this welfaring sheykh keeping his own camels!

We journeyed on by cragged places, near the east border of the Harra; and the sun was going down when we found the nomads' booths pitched in a hollow ground. These also were a *ferîj* (dim. *feraij*, and pl. *ferjàn*), or partition, of Heteym. A ferîj is thus a nomad hamlet; and commonly the households in a ferîj are nigh kindred. The most nomad tribes in Nejd are dispersed thus three parts of the year, till the lowest summer season; then they come together and pitch a great standing menzil about some principal watering of their dîra.

We dismounted before the sheykh's tent; and found a gay Turkey carpet within, the uncomely behaviour of Heteym, and a miserable hospitality. They set before us a bowl of milk-shards, that can only be well broken between mill-stones. Yet later, these uncivil hosts, who were fanatical young men, brought us in from the camel-milking nearly two pailfuls of that perfect refreshment in the desert:—Eyâda came not.

These hosts had heard of the Nasrâny, and of my journey with Ghroceyb, and knew their kinsman's tale, 'that (though a good rafîk) Khalîl would have taken the thelûl, when they were nigh Kheybar.' Another said, 'It was a dangerous passage, and Ghroceyb returning had been in peril of his life ; for as he rode again over the Harra there fell a heavy rain. Then he held westward to go about the worst of the lava country ; and as he was passing by a sandy seyl, a head of water came down upon him : his thelûl foundered, and his matchlock fell from him : Ghroceyb hardly saved himself to land, and drew out the thelûl, and found his gun again.'

On the morrow we rode two hours, and came to another hamlet of Heteym. — This day we would give to repose, and went to alight at a beyt ; and by singular adventure that was Sâlih's ! he who had forsaken me in these parts when I came down (now three months ago) from Hâyil. As the man stepped out to meet us, I called him by his name, and he wondered to see me. He was girded in his gunner's belt, to go on foot with a companion to el-Hâyat, two marches distant, to have new stocks put, by a good sâny (who they heard was come thither), to their long guns. Sâlih and Eyâd were tribesmen, of one fendy, and of old acquaintance. The booth beside him was of that elder Heteymy, the third companion in our autumn journey. The man coming in soon after saluted me with a hearty countenance ; and Sâlih forewent his day's journey to the village for his guest's sake. This part of the vulcanic country is named *Hebrân*, of a red sandstone berg standing in the midst of the lavas : northward I saw again the mountains Bushra or Buthra. Having drunk of their lében, we gave the hours to repose. The elder Heteymy's wife asked me for a little meal, and I gave her an handful, which was all I had ; she sprinkled it in her cauldron of boiling samn and invited me to the skimming. The housewife poured off the now clarified samn into her butter-skin ; the sweet lees of flour and butter she served before us.

I had returned safe, therefore I said nothing ; I could not have greeted Sâlih with the Scandinavian urbanity, "Thanks for the last time :" but his wife asked me, "Is Sâlih good, Khalîl?" They had a child of six years old ; the little boy, naked as a worm, lay cowering from the cold in his mother's arms, — and he had been thus naked all the winter, at an altitude (here) of four thousand feet! It is a wonder they may outlive such evil days. A man came in who was clothed as I never saw another nomad, for he had upon him a home-spun mantle of tent-cloth; but the wind blew through his heavy carpet garment. I found a piece of calico for the poor mother, to make her child a little coat.

When the evening was come Sâlih set before us a boiled kid, and we fared well. After supper he asked me were I now appeased? — *mesquin!* he might be afraid of my evil remembrance and of my magical books. He agreed with Eyâd and Merjàn that they, in coming-by again from Hâyil, should return to him, and then all go down together to Kheybar; where he would sell his samn for dates, to be received at the harvest. Though one of the hostile Bishr, he was by adoption an Heteymy, and with Eyâd would be safe at Kheybar. — But how might they find these three booths in the wilderness after many days? Sâlih gave them the *shór* thus; "The fourth day we remove (when I come again from el-Hâyat), to such a ground: when the cattle have eaten the herb thereabout, we shall remove to such other; after ten or twelve days seek for us between such and such landmarks, and drinking of such waters." — He spoke to ears which knew the names of all bergs and rocks and seyls and hollow grounds in that vast wilderness: Eyâd had wandered there in his youth.

There came in some young men from the neighbour tents to our evening fire. And said one, "Khalîl is a travelled man from far countries; this is his life to wander through the world! and wellah I think it is the best: but he who travels has need of money. Had I silver I would do like him, I would visit foreign nations to learn their speech, and see how they lead their lives in many strange lands: for ah! what is our life? — we are like the sheep in the khála. I would set forth to-morrow with Khalîl, if he would take me with him: ay, wellah, Khalîl, I will be thy true rafîk!" Another said, "Thou hast seen the world, tell us where is the best life?" — "In the houses of hair." — "Nay, nay! this is a land of misery, and the Aarab are mesquins." Another answered, "Yet the Aarab are a valiant folk, there be none like them in the world! How seest thou the horses of the Aarab? wellah, be they not as birds?"

The Heteym have few or no horses; I asked their names. "I will tell thee some, said a good lad: — *Saera* (of sally), *el-Bûma*, *er-Raheydîn*, *es-Shûel*, *Umm es-Sghrar* (mother of the little one), *Sabigát* (that outrunneth), *Hŷha*, *Agerra*, *Saafa*, — some of them are names of mares [in their ditties] of the Beny Helál ; — *Shottifa, el-Jimerîeh, es-Shuggera* " (the bay mare, — the most Nejd horses are of this colour and chestnut reds ; grey is seldom and yet more seldom the black-haired). All these are names of mares ; the desert men make almost no account of stallions among their cattle. I asked them to tell me the names of their asses. — These were : *Deghreyma, ed-Deheysa, ej-Jámmera, el-Khéyba, el-Kowwâ, ed-Dôma, el-Wàgilla, el-Mínsilla, Sowra, el-Girthîeh, eth-Thumràn, es-Shaara* (shag-haired), *en-Nejjilla, er-Rukhsa, el-Lahá, el-Hennaba, es-Suáda, el-Gírmella, el-Khosâba, Hubbàra* [these also are mares' names]. " Oh me ! — cries Eyâd the ass, all beside his patience, what folly is this in Khalîl ? — thou our rafîk, to hearken to such ninneries ! — wellah all the people will scorn both thee and us ! " They told me also these names of the fendies of Heteym : *Ibn Barràk, Ibn Jelladàn, Ibn Dammûk* (*min el-Khluîeh* — they are snibbed as Solubbies), *Ibn Simra* or *eth-Thîabba, el-Mothâbara, el-Feradissa, Ibn Hayzàn, el-Khiarát, el-Noâmsy, el-Gabîd*.

When the morrow's light wakened us we arose and departed. We passed by the berg Hebrân, and came to a vast *niggera*, or sunken bay in the lavas : Eyâd brought me to see the place, which they name *Baedi*, as a natural wonder. This is the summer water station of those Sbáa households which wander in the south with Misshel ; when the Auájy pitch at Baitha Nethîl. In the basalt floor, littered with the old jella of the nomads' camels, are two ancient well-pits. Wild doves flew up from them, as we came and looked in ; they are the birds of the desert waters, even of such as be bitter and baneful to the Arabs. We sat to rest out a pleasant hour in the cliff's shadow (for we thought the Aarab beyond could not be far off) : and there a plot of nettles seemed to my eyes a garden in the desert ! — those green neighbours and homely inheritors, in every land, of human nature.

We rested our fill ; then I remounted, and they walked forward. Merjàn was weary and angry in the midst of our long journey. I said to him, as we went out, " Step on, lad, or let me pass, you linger under the feet of the thelûl ? " He murmured, and turning, with a malignant look, levelled his matchlock at my breast. So I said, " Reach me that gun, and I will hang it at the saddle-bow, this will be better for thee : " I spoke to Eyâd to take his matchlock from him and hang it at the peak. Eyâd promised for the lad, " He should never offend me again : forgive him now, Khalîl — because I already alighted — I also must bear with him, and this is ever his nature, full of teen." " Enough, and pass over now ; — but if I see the like again, weled, I shall teach thee thy error. Eyâd, was there ever Beduwy who threatened death to his rafîk ? " — " No, by Ullah." — " But this (man), cries the splenetic lad, is a Nasrâny, — *with a Nasrâny who need keep any law ? is not this an enemy of Ullah ?* " At that word I wrested his gun from him, and gave it to Eyâd ; and laying my driving-stick upon the lad (since this is the only discipline they know at Medina), I swinged him soundly, in a moment, and made all his back smart. Eyâd from behind caught my arms ; and the lad, set free, came and kicked me in villanous manner, and making a weapon of his heavy head-cord, he struck at me in the face : then he caught up a huge stone and was coming on to break my head, but in this I loosed myself from Eyâd. "We have all done foolishly (exclaimed Eyâd), eigh ! what will be said when this is told another day ? — here, take thy gun, Merjàn, but go out of Khalîl's sight ; and Khalîl be friends with us, and mount again. Ullah ! we were almost at mischief ; and Merjàn is the most narrow-souled of all that ever I saw, and he was always thus."

We moved on in silence ; I said only that at the next menzil we would leave Merjàn. He was cause, also, that we suffered thirst in the way ; since we must divide with him a third of my small herdsman's girby. Worse than all was that the peevish lad continually corrupted the little good nature in Eyâd, with his fanatical whisperings, and drew him from me. I repented of my misplaced humanity towards him, and of my yielding to such rafîks to take another way. Yet it had been as good to wink at the lad's offence, if in so doing I should not have seemed to be afraid of them. The Turkish argument of the rod might bring such spirits to better knowledge ; but it is well to be at peace with the Arabs upon any reasonable conditions, that being of a feminine humour, they are kind friends and implacable enemies.

The Harra is here like a rolling tide of basalt : the long bilges often rise about pit-like lava bottoms, or *niggeras*, which lie full of blown sand. Soon after this we came to the edge of the lava-field ; where upon our right hand, a path descended to Thúrghrud, half a journey distant. " Come, I said, we are to go thither." But Eyâd answered, " The way lies now over difficult lavas ! and, Khalîl, we ought to have held east- ward from the morning : yet I will go thither for thy sake, although we cannot arrive this night, and we have nothing to eat." Merjàn cried to Eyâd not to yield, that he himself would not go out of the way to Thúrghrud. *Eyâd :* " If we go forward, we may be with Aarab to-night : so Sâlih said truly, they are encamped under yonder mountain." This seemed the best rede for weary men : I gave Eyâd the word to lead forward. We descended then from the Harra side into a plain country of granite grit, without blade or bush. ' Yet here in good years, said Eyâd, they find pasture ; but now the land is máhal, because no autumn rain had fallen in these parts.' — So we marched some miles, and passed by the (granitic) Thullân Buthra.

" — But where are we come ! exclaimed the rafîks, gazing about them : there can be no Aarab in this khála ; could Sâlih have a mind to deceive us ? " The sun set over our forlorn march ; and we halted in the sandy bed of a seyl to sleep. They hobbled the thelûl's forelegs, and loosed her out in the moonlight ; but there was no pasture. We were fasting since yesterday, and had nothing to eat, and no water. They found a great waif root, and therewith we made a good fire ; the deep ground covered us, under mountains which are named *Ethmâd* (pl. of *Thammad*).

The silent night in the dark khála knit again our human imbecility and misery, at the evening fire, and accorded the day's broken fellowship. Merjàn forgot his spite ; but showing me some swelling wheals, " Dealest thou thus, he said, with thy friend, Khalîl ? the chill is come, and with it the smart." — " The fault was thine ; and I bid you remember that on the road there is neither Moslem nor Nasrâny, but we are *rufakâ, akhuân,* fellows and brethren." — " Well, Khalîl, let us speak no more of it." Merjàn went out — our last care in the night — to bring in the weary and empty thelûl ; he couched her to bear off the night wind, and we closed our eyes.

The new day rising, we stood up in our sandy beds and were ready to depart. We marched some hours through that dead plain country ; and came among pale granite hills, where only the silver-voiced siskin, *Umm Sâlema,* flitted in the rocky solitude before us. We had no water, and Eyâd went on climbing amongst the bergs at our right hand. Towards noon he made a sign and shouted, ' that Merjàn come to him with our girby.' — They brought down the skin full of water, which Eyâd had found in the hollow of a rock, overlaid with a flat stone ; the work, they supposed, of some Solubby (hunter). — Rubbing milk-shards in the water, we drank mereesy and refreshed ourselves. The height of the country is 4600 feet. We journeyed all day in this poor plight; the same gritty barrenness of plain-land encumbered with granitic and basalt bergs lay always before us. Once only we found some last year's footprints of a *ráhla*.

They watched the horizon, and went on looking earnestly for the Aarab: at half-afternoon Merjàn, who was very clear sighted, cried out " I see *zôl !* " — zôl (pl. *azzuâl*), is the looming, in the eye of aught which may not be plainly distinguished; so a blind patient has said to me, " I see the zôl of the sun." Eyâd gazed earnestly and answered, ' He thought billah he did see somewhat.' — Azzuâl in the desert are discerned moving in the farthest offing, but whether wild creatures or cattle, or Aarab, it cannot be told. When Eyâd and Merjàn had watched awhile, they said, " We see two men riding on one thelûl ! " Then they pulled off hastily their gun-leathers, struck fire, and blew the matches, and put powder to the touchholes of their long pieces. I saw in Eyâd a sort of haste and trouble ! " Why thus ? " I asked. — " But they have seen us, and now they come hither ! " — My two rafîks went out, singing and leaping to the encounter, and left me with the thelûl; my secret arms put me out of all doubt. Bye and bye they returned saying, that when those riders saw the glance of their guns they held off. — " But let us not linger (they cried) in this neighbourhood : " they mounted the thelûl together and rode from me. I followed weakly on foot, and it came into my mind, that they would forsake me.

The day's light faded, the sun at length kissed the horizon, and our hope went down with the sun : we must lodge again without food or human comfort in the khála. The Beduin rafîks climbed upon all rocks to look far out over the desert, and I rode in the plain between them. The thelûl went fasting in the mahál this second day; but now the wilderness began to amend. The sun was sinking when Merjàn shouted, ' He had seen a flock.' Then Eyâd mounted with me, and urging his thelûl we made haste to arrive in the short twilight ere it should be dark night : we trotted a mile, and Merjàn ran beside us. We soon saw a great flock trooping down in a rocky bay of the mountain in front. A maiden and a lad were herding them; and unlike all that I had seen till now there were no goats in that nomad flock. The brethren may have heard the clatter of our riding in the loose stones, or caught a sight of

A NIGHT'S HOSPITALITY IN HARB TENTS

three men coming, for they had turned their backs! Such meetings are never without dread in the khála: if we had been land-lopers they were taken tardy; we had bound them, and driven off the slow-footed flock all that night. Perchance such thoughts were in Eyâd, for he had not yet saluted them; and I first hailed the lad,—'Salaam aleyk!' He hearing it was peace, turned friendly; and Eyâd asked him "*Fen el-maâziba*, where is the place of entertainment?"—we had not seen the booths. The young Beduwy answered us, with a cheerful alacrity, "It is not far off."

We knew not what tribesmen they were. The young man left his sister with the flock, and led on before us. It was past prayer time, and none had said his devotion:—they kneeled down now on the sand in the glooming, but (as strangers) not together, and I rode by them;—a neglect of religion which is not marked in the weary wayfarer, for one must dismount to say his formal prayers. It was dusk when we came to their menzil; and there were but three booths. It had been agreed amongst us that my rafîks should not name me Nasrâny. Gently the host received us into his tent and spread down a gay Turkey carpet in the men's sitting place,—it was doubtless his own and his housewife's only bedding. Then he brought a vast bowl, full of léban, and made us slake our thirst: so he left us awhile (to prepare the guest-meal). When I asked my rafîks, what Aarab were these, Eyâd whispered, "By their speech they should be Harb."—"And what Harb?"—"We cannot tell yet." Merjàn said in my ear, "Repentest thou now to have brought me with thee, Khalîl? did not my eyes lead thee to this night's entertainment? and thou hadst else lodged again in the khála."

The host came again, and insisted gently, asking, might he take our water, for they had none. My rafîks forbade him with their desert courtesy, knowing it was therewith that he would boil the guest-meal, for us; but the goodman prevailed: his sacrifice of hospitality, a yearling lamb, had been slain already. Now upon both parts the Beduins told their tribes: these were Beny Sâlem, of Harb in Nejd; but their native dîra is upon the *sultâny* or highway betwixt the Harameyn. It was my first coming to tents of that Beduin nation; and I had not seen nomad hosts of this noble behaviour. The smiling householder filled again and again his great milk-bowl before us, as he saw it drawn low: — we drank for the thirst of two days, which could not soon be allayed. Seeing me drink deepest of three, the kind host, *maazîb*, exhorted me with *ighrtebig!* 'take thy evening drink,' and he piously lifted the bowl to my lips. "Drink! said he, for here is the good of Ullah, the Lord be praised, and no lack! and coming from the southward, ye have passed much weary country." *Eyâd:* "Wellah it is all máhal, and last night we were khlûa (lone men without human shelter in the khála); this is the second day, till this evening we found you." — "El-hamd illah! the Lord be praised therefore," answered the good householder. Eyâd told them of the ghrazzu. "And Khalîl, said our host, what is he? — a *Méshedy?* (citizen of the town of Aly's violent death or "martyrdom," *Méshed Aly*, before mentioned); methinks his speech, *rótn*, and his hue be like theirs." — "Ay, ay, (answered my rafîks), a Méshedy, an hakîm, he is now returning to Hâyil." — "An uncle's son of his was here very lately, a worthy man; he came from Hâyil, to sell clothing among the Aarab, — and, Khalîl, dost thou not know him? he was as like to thee, billah, as if ye were brethren."

We lay down to rest ourselves. An hour or two later this generous maazîb and the shepherd, his brother, bore in a mighty charger of rice, and the steaming mutton heaped upon it; their hospitality of the desert was more than one man might carry. — The nomad dish is set upon the carpet, or else on a piece of tent-cloth, that no fallen morsels might be trodden down in the earth: — and if they see but a little milk spilled (in this everlasting dearth and indigence of all things), any born Arabians will be out of countenance. I have heard some sentence of their Néby blaming spilt milk. — The kind maazîb called upon us, saying, *Gûm! kŷakom Ullah wa en-Néby, eflah!* 'rise, take your meat, and the Lord give you life, and His Prophet.' We answered, kneeling about the dish, *Ullah hŷ-îk,* 'May the Lord give thee life:' — the host left us to eat. But first Eyâd laid aside three of the best pieces, "for the maazîb, and his wives; they have kept back nothing, he said, for themselves." The nomad housemothers do always withhold somewhat for themselves and their children, but Eyâd, the fine Beduin gentleman, savoured of the town, rather than of the honest simplicity of the desert. "Ah! nay, what is this ye do? it needeth not, quoth the returning host, wellah we have enough; *eflah!* only eat! put your hands to it." "Prithee sit down with us," says Eyâd. "Sit down with us, O maazîb, said we all; without thee we cannot eat." "*Ebbeden*, nay I pray you, never." — Who among Beduins is first satisfied he holds his hand still at the dish; whereas the oasis dweller and the townling, rises and going aside by himself to wash his hands, puts the hungry and slow eaters out of countenance. A Beduwy at the dish, if he have seen the town, will rend off some of the best morsels, and lay them ready to a friend's hand : — Eyâd showed me now this token of a friendly mind.

The Beduw are nimble eaters ; their fingers are expert to rend the meat, and they swallow their few handfuls of boiled rice or corn with that bird-like celerity which is in all their deeds. In supping with them, being a weak and slow eater, when I had asked their indulgence, I made no case of this usage : since to enable nature in the worship of the Creator is more than every apefaced devising of human hypocrisy. If any man called me I held that he did it in sincerity ; and the Arabs commended that honest plainness in a stranger among them. There is no second giving of thanks to the heavenly Providence; but rising after meat we bless the man, saying (in this dîra) *Unaam Ullah aleyk*, 'the Lord be gracious unto thee,' *yâ maazîb*. The dish is borne out, the underset cloth is drawn, and the bowl is fetched to us : we drink and return to our sitting place at the hearth. Although welfaring and bountiful the goodman had no coffee ; — coffee Arabs are seldom of this hospitality.

The guest (we have seen) should depart when the morrow breaks ; and the host sends him away fasting, to journey all that day in the khála. But if they be his friends, and it is the season of milk, a good householder will detain the last night's guests, till his jâra have poured them out a draught. Our Beny Sâlem maazîb was of no half-hearted hospitality, and when we rose to depart he gently delayed us. " My wife, he said, is rocking the semîla, have patience till the butter come, that she may pour you out a little lébạn ; you twain are Beduw, but this Méshedy is not, as we, one wont to walk all day in the wilderness and taste nothing." — The second spring-time was come about of my sojourning in Arabia ; the desert land flowed again with milk, and I saw with bowings down of the soul to the divine Nature, this new sweet *rabîa*. "*Ustibbah!* (cries the good man, with the hollow-voiced franchise of the dry desert) take thy morning drink."

— I speak many times of the Arabian hospitality, since of this I have been often questioned in Europe ; and for a memorial of worthy persons. The hospitality of the worsted booths, — the gentle entertainment of passengers and strangers in a land full of misery and fear, we have seen to be religious. I have heard also this saying in the mouths of town Arabians, — " It is for the report which passing strangers may sow of them in the country : for the hosts beyond will be sure to ask of their guests, ' Where lodged ye the last night ; and were ye well entertained ? ' "

We journeyed now in a plain desert of gritty sand, which is called *Shaaba* ; beset with a world of trappy and smooth basalt bergs, so that we could not see far to any part : all this soil seyls down to the W. er-Rummah. We journeyed an hour and came by a wide *rautha*. Rautha is any bottom in the desert, which is a sinking place of ponded winter rain : the streaming showers carry down fine sediment from the upper ground, and the soil is a crusted clay and loam. Rautha may signify garden, — and such is their cheerful aspect of green shrubs in the khála : the plural is *riâth*, [which is also the name of the Waháby metropolis in East Nejd). I asked Eyâd, " Is not this soil as good and large as the Teyma oasis ? wherefore then has it not been settled ? " — " I suppose, he answered, that there is no water, or there had some wells been found in it, of the auelîn." *Gá* likewise or *khób'ra* is a naked clay bottom in the desert, where shallow water is ponded after heavy rain. *Khóbra* (or Khúbbera) is the ancient name of a principal oasis in the Nefûd of Kasîm : — I came there later.

Eyâd with a stone-cast killed a hare ; and none can better handle a stone than the Aarab : we halted and they made a fire of sticks. The southern Aarab have seldom a knife, Eyâd borrowed my penknife to cut the throat of his venison ; and then he cast in the hare as it was. When their stubble fire was burned out, Eyâd took up his hare, roasted whole in the skin, and broke and divided it ; and we found it tender and savoury meat. This is the hunters' kitchen : they stay not to pluck, to flay, to bowl, nor for any tools or vessel ; but that is well dressed which comes forth, for hungry men. In the hollow of the carcase the Beduwy found a little blood ; this he licked up greedily, with some of the *ferth* or cud, and murmured the mocking desert proverb ' I am *Shurma* (Cleft-lips) quoth the hare.' They do thus in ignorance; Amm Mohammed had done the like in his youth, and had not considered that the blood is forbidden. I said to him, " When a beast is killed, although ye let some blood at the throat, does not nearly all the gore remain in the body ? — and this you eat ! " He answered in a frank wonder, " Yes, thou sayest sooth ! the gore is left in the body, — and we eat it in the flesh ! well then I can see no difference." The desert hare is small, and the delicate body parted among three made us but a slender breakfast. Eyâd in the same place found the gallery (with two holes) of a jerboa ; it is the edible spring-rat of the droughty wilderness, a little underground creature, not weighing two ounces, with very long hinder legs and a very long tufted tail, silken pelt, and white belly [*v*. Vol. I. p. 371]; in form she resembles the pouched rats of Australia. Eyâd digged up the mine with his camel stick and, snatching the feeble prey, he slit her throat with a twig, and threw it on the embers ; a moment after he offered us morsels, but we would not taste. The jerboa and the wábar ruminate, say the hunters ; Amm Mohammed told me, that they are often shot with the cud in the mouth.

We loosed out the thelûl, and sat on in this pleasant place of pasture. Merjàn lifted the shidád to relieve her, and "Look ! laughed he, if her hump be not risen ? " — The constraint of the saddle, and our diligence in feeding her in the slow marches, made the sick beast to seem rather the better. Seeing her old brandmark was the *dubbûs* [*v*. Vol. I. p. 166], I enquired 'Have you robbed her then from the Heteym?' Eyâd was amazed that I should know a wasm ! and he boasted that she was of the best blood of the *Benát* (daughters of) *et-Tî* (or *Tîh*); he had bought her from Heteym, a foal, for forty reals : she could then outstrip the most thelûls. Now she was a carrion riding beast of the Ageyl ; and such was Eyâd's avarice that he had sent her down twice, freighted like a pack camel, with the Kheybar women's palm-plait to Medina ; for which the Beduins there laughed him to scorn. — The Tî or Tîh is a fabulous wild hurr, or dromedary male, in the Sherarát wilderness. ' He has only three ribs, they say, and runs with prodigious swiftness ; he may outstrip any horse.' The Sherarát are said to let their dromedaries stray in the desert, that haply they may be covered by the Tîh ; and they pretend to discern his offspring by the token of the three ribs. The thelûls of the Sherarát [an 'alien' Arabian kindred] are praised above other in Western Arabia : Ibn Rashîd's armed band are mounted upon the light and fleet *Sheráries*. — Very excellent also, though of little stature, are the (Howeytát) dromedaries in the Nefûd of el-Arîsh.

Eyâd seemed to be a man of very honourable presence, with his comely Jew-like visage, and well-set full black beard ; he went well clad, and with the gallant carriage of the sheykhs of the desert. Busy-eyed he was, and a distracted gazer : his speech was less honest than smooth and well sounding. I enquired 'Wherefore he wore not the horns ? — the Beduin love-locks should well become his manly [Annezy] beauty.' *Eyâd*: " I have done with such young men's vanities, since my horn upon this side was shot away, and a second ball cropt the horn on my other ; — but that warning was not lost to me ! Ay billah ! I am out of taste of the Beduin life : one day we abound with the good of Ullah, but on the morrow our halàl may be taken by an enemies' ghrazzu ! And if a man have not then good friends, to bring together somewhat for him again, wellah he must go a-begging."

Eyâd had been bred out of his own tribe, among Shammar, and in this dîra where we now came. His father was a substantial sheykh, one who rode upon his own mare ; and young Eyâd rode upon a stallion. One day a strong foray of Heteym robbed the camels of his menzil, and Eyâd among the rest galloped to meet them. The Heteymàn (nomads well nourished with milk) are strong-bodied and manly fighters ; they are besides well armed, more than the Beduw, and many are marksmen. Eyâd bore before his lance two thelûl riders ; and whilst he tilted in among the foemen, who were all thelûl riders, a bullet and a second ball cropt his braided locks ; he lost also his horse, and not his young life. " Eyâd, thou playedest the lion ! " — " Aha ! and canst thou think what said the Heteym ? — ' By Ullah let that young rider of the horse come to us when he will, and lie with our hareem, that they may bring forth valiant sons.' " — He thought, since we saw him, that Eyâda ibn Ajjuèyn had been in that raid with them.

" And when thou hast thy arrears, those hundreds of reals, wilt thou buy thee other halàl ? we shall see thee prosperous and a sheykh again ? " — " Prosperous, and a sheykh, it might well be, were I another ; but my head is broken, and I do this or that many times of a wrong judgment and fondly : — but become a Beduwy again, nay ! I love no more such hazards : I will buy and sell at Hâyil. If I sell shirt-cloth and cloaks and *mandîls* (kerchiefs) in the sûk, all the Beduw will come to me ; moreover, being a Beduwy, I shall know how to trade with them for camels and small cattle. Besides I will be Ibn Rashîd's man (one of his rajajîl) and receive a salary from him every month, always sure, and ride in the ghrazzus, and in every one take something ! " — " We shall see thee then a shopkeeper ! — but the best life, man, is to be a Beduwy." *Merjàn*: " Well said Khalîl, the best life is with the Beduw." *Eyâd*:

"But I will none of it, and ' all is not *Khúthera* and *Tunis*'; " — he could not expound to me his town-learned proverb.

— Múthir, a Bishr gatûny, was a patient of mine at Kheybar. Though now most poor he had been sometime a substantial Beduwy; like Eyâd he had wandered with Shammar. In one year, when a murrain was in Nejd, all his camels perished: then the poor man buried his tent and laid up the stuff with his date merchant (in a desert village), and left his wife, saying that he would go to that which remained to him, — his inheritance of palms at Kheybar. Afterward he heard that his jâra was dead. Now seven years were gone over him, and he had no more heart to return and require his deposit; and he said his buried tent must be rotten.

The greenness of all this empty land was a short harsh grass like wild barley with empty ears. This whilst tender is good pasture for the cattle; but later they may hardly eat it, for it pricks their throats. I saw none other springing herb of the fresh season.

We set forward; and after midday we came to six Shammar booths. The sheykh, a young man, *Braitshàn*, was known to Eyâd. My rafîks rejoiced to see his coffee-pots in the ashpit; for they had not tasted kahwa (this fortnight) since we set out from Kheybar. The beyt was large and lofty; which is the Shammar and Annezy building wise. A mare grazed in sight; a sign that this was not a poor sheykh's household. The men who came in from the neighbour tents were also known to Eyâd; and I was not unknown, for one said presently, " Is not this Khalîl, the Nasrâny ? " — he had seen me at Hâyil. We should pass this day among them, and my rafîks loosed out the thelûl to pasture. In the afternoon an old man led us to his booth to drink more coffee; he had a son an Ageyly at Medina. " I was lately there, said he, and I found my lad and his comrade eating their victuals *hâf*, without samn! — it is an ill service that cannot pay a man his bread."

They mused seeing the Nasrâny amongst them: — ' Khalîl, an adversary of Ullah, and yet like another man ! ' Eyâd answered them in mirth, " So it seems that one might live well enough although he were a kafir ! " And he told a tale, which is current for a marvel in the tribes, — for when is there heard a blasphemy in any Semitic man's mouth ? [yet *v.* Job xxi. 15]. " Ibn Nâmus (sheykh of the Noâmsy) had ridden all one night, with a strong ghrazzu; and they alighted at dawn to pray [such devout robbers they are !] The men were yet on their knees when one of them said, ' But to what effect is all this long weariness of prayers, this year after year pray-praying ? — So many prayers and every day pattering prayers, and I am never the better ; it is but casting away breath : eigh ! how long must I plough with my nose this dust of the khála ? — And now forsooth, O my Lord ! I say unto Thee, except Thou give me a thelûl to-day with a girby, I would as it were beat Thee with this camel stick ! ' — It happened ere the sun set that the Heteymy's booty, of cattle which they took the same day, was a thelûl and two girbies ; so he said at the evening fire, ' Now ye may know, fellows, ye who blamed me when I prayed at dawn, how my Lord was adread of me to-day ! ' " The man we have seen, was no right Beduwy but of the Heteymán. — Often the tongue of some poor Beduwy may slide, in matter of religion, and his simplicity will be long remembered in the idle talk of the khála. So one having solemnly pronounced the Emir's name, Ibn Rashîd, a tribesman cries out " *Sully Ullah aleyhu wa yusellim,*" — saluting him as one of the greater prophets.

— I knew a Syrian missionary in one of the villages beyond Jordan, who said upon a time to a ragged (B. Sokhr) tribesman in mockery of the elvish simplicity of the common sort of Beduw, " Hast heard thou ? — this wonderful tiding in the world ? — that the Lord is come down lately to Damascus ? " *Beduwy :* " The Lord is come down, at es-Sham ! — the Lord be praised ! but speakest thou sooth ? — is my Lord descended from heaven ! " — " Thither all the people flow unto Him ! and goest thou not up to visit thy Lord ! " — " Eigh ! I would fain go and see Him ; but look Sir, at this ! Sham is above seven journeys from hence, and how might I leave the cattle in the (open) wilderness ? "

Whilst we sat, a stranger boy came in from the khála : he trudged barefoot through the heat, from ferîj to ferîj. Poor and adventurous, he carried but a club-stick in his hand and neither food nor water. From menzil to menzil of nomads was not many hours in this spring wilderness ; and he could well find the way, for he was a Shammary. This boy of thirteen or fourteen years was seeking a herdsman's place ; and his behaviour was prudent, as haply an affectionate mother had schooled his young heart. If any one asked him of that his (weighty) enterprise, he studied a moment, and then gave answer with a manly gruffness, in few and wise words. We asked him what should be his hire ? he said, " The accustomed wages, — four she-goats at the year's end, and a cloak and a tunic," (that were about two guineas' worth). There is no expressed covenant for the hireling's meat, — the herdsmen carry a bowl with them and drink their fill of milk: this is not ill treatment. I found, making ciphers in the sand, that the lad might come to the possession in his twentieth year of fifty head of goats, or four camels.

We heard that Ibn Rashîd was not at Hâyil. " The Emir, they said, is *ghrazzai* (upon an expedition) in the north with the rajajîl; the princes [as Hamûd, Sleymàn] are with him, and they lie encamped at *Heyennîeh*," — that is a place of wells in the Nefûd, towards Jauf. The Shammar princes have fortified it with a block-house; and a man or two are left in garrison, who are to shoot out at hostile ghrazzus: so that none shall draw water there, to pass over, contrary to the will of Ibn Rashîd. We heard that Anèybar was left deputy at Hâyil. — The sky was overcast whilst we sat, and a heavy shower fell suddenly. The sun soon shone forth again, and the hareem ran joyfully from the tents to fill their girbies, under the streaming granite rocks. The sheykh bade replenish the coffee pots, and give us a bowl of that sweet water to drink. — Braitshàn's mother boiled us a supper-dish of temmn: the nomad hospitality of milk was here scant, — but this is commonly seen in a coffee sheykh's beyt.

Departing betimes on the morrow we journeyed in a country now perfectly known to Eyâd. The next hollow ground was like a bed of colocynth gourds, they are in colour and bigness as oranges. We marched two hours and came to a troop of camels: the herds were two young men of Shammar. They asked of the land backward, by which we had passed, 'Was the rabîa sprung, and which and which plants for pasture had we seen there?' Then one of them went to a milch nâga to milk for us; but the other, looking upon me, said, " Is not this Khalîl, the Nasrâny?" [he too had seen me in Hâyil]! We were here abreast of the first outlying settlements of the Jebel; and now looking on our left hand, we had a pleasant sight, between two rising grounds, of green corn plots. My rafîks said, " It is *Gussa*, a corn hamlet, and you may see some of their women yonder; they come abroad to gather green fodder for the well camels." A young man turned from beside them, with a grass-hook in his hand; and ran hither to enquire tidings of us passengers. — Nor he nor might those women be easily discerned from Beduw! After the first word he asked us for a galliûn of tobacco; — " But come, he said, with me to our kasûr; ye shall find dates and coffee, and there rest yourselves." He trussed on his neck what gathered herbs he had in his cloak, and ran before us to the settlement. We found their kasûr to be poor low cottages of a single chamber. — Gussa is a [new] desert grange of the Emir, inhabited only three months in the year, for the watering of the cornfields (here from six-fathom square well-pits sunk in the hard baked earth), till the harvest ; then the husbandmen will go home to their villages : the site is in a small wady.

Here were but six households of fifteen or twenty persons, seldom visited by tarkîes (*terâgy*). *Aly* our host set before us dates with some of his spring butter and lében : I wondered at his alacrity to welcome us, — as if we had been of old acquaintance ! Then he told them, that ' Last night he dreamed of a tarkîy, which should bring them tobacco ! ' — Even here one knew me ! and said, " Is not this Khalîl, the Nasrâny ? and he has a paper from Ibn Rashîd, that none may molest him ; I myself saw it sealed by the Emir." " How sweet, they exclaimed, is dokhàn when we taste it again ! — wellah, we are *sherarîb* (tobacco tipplers)." I said, " Ye have land, why then do ye not sow it ? " — " Well, we bib it ; but to sow tobacco, and see the plant growing in our fields, that were an unseemly thing, *makrûha* ! " When we left them near midday, they counselled us to pass by *Agella*, another like ' dîra,' or outlying corn settlement ; we might arrive there ere nightfall. — Beyond their cornfields, I saw young palms set in the seyl-strand : but wanting water, many were already sere. Commonly the sappy herb is seen to spring in any hole (that was perhaps the burrow of some wild creature) in the hard khála, though the waste soil be all bare : and the Gussa husbandmen had planted in like wise their palms that could not be watered ; the ownership was betwixt them and the Beduw.

As they had shown us we held our way, through a grey and russet granite country, with more often basalt than the former trap rocks. Eyâd showed me landmarks, eastward, of the wells *es-Sákf*, a summer water-station of Shammar. Under a granite hill I saw lower courses of two cell-heaps, like those in the Harras ; and in another place eight or more breast-high wild flagstones of granite, set up in a row. — There was in heathen times an idol's house in these forlorn mountains.

Seeing the discoloured head of a granite berg above us, the rafîks climbed there to look for water ; and finding some they filled our girby. When the sun was setting we came to a hollow path, which was likely to lead to Agella. The wilderness was again máhal, a rising wind ruffled about us, and clouds covered the stars with darkness which seemed to bereave the earth from under our footsteps. My companions would seek now some sheltered place, and slumber till morning; but I encouraged them to go forward, to find the settlement to-night. We journeyed yet two hours, and I saw some housebuilding, though my companions answered me, it was a white rock: we heard voices and barking dogs soon after, and passed before a solitary nomad booth. We were come to the "dîrat" el-Agella. Here were but two cabins of single ground-chambers and wells, and cornplots. The wind was high, we shouted under the first of the house-walls; and a man came forth who bade us good evening. He fetched us fuel, and we kindled a fire in the lee of his house, and warmed ourselves: then our host brought us dates and butter and léban, and said, 'He was sorry he could not lodge us within doors, and the hour was late to cook anything.' Afterward, taking up his empty vessels, he left us to sleep.

We had gone, they said, by a small settlement, *Hâfirat Zeylûl*; my companions had not been here before. Hâyil was now not far off, Eyâd said; "To-morrow, we will set forward in the *jéhemma*, that is *betwixt the dog and the wolf*, — which is so soon, Khalîl, as thou mayest distinguish between a hound and the wolf, (in the dawning)." — The northern blast (of this last night in March) was keen and rude, and when the day broke, we rose shivering; they would not remove now till the warm sun was somewhat risen. Yet we had rested through this night better than our hosts; for as we lay awake in the cold, we heard the shrieking of their well-wheels till the morning light. *Merjàn* : " Have the husbandmen or the Beduw the better life ? speak, Khalîl, for we know that thou wast brought up among the Beduw." — " I would sell my palms, if I had any, to buy camels, and dwell with the nomads." — " And I," said he.

As we set forward the *ajjàj* or sand-bearing wind encumbered our eyes. A boy came along with us returning to el-Kasr, which we should pass to-day: — so may any person join himself to what travelling company he will in the open Arabic countries. The wilderness eastward is a plain full of granite bergs, whose heads are often trappy basalt; more seldom they are crumbling needles of slaty trap rock. Before noon, we were in sight of el-Kasr, under Ajja, which Merjàn in his loghra pronounced *Ejja* : we had passed from the máhal, and a spring greenness was here upon the face of the desert. There are circuits of the common soil about the desert villages where no nomads may drive their cattle upon pain of being accused to the Emir : such township rights are called *h'má* [*confer* Numb. xxxv. 2–5]. We saw here a young man of el-Kasr, riding round upon an ass to gather fuel, and to cut fodder for his well camels. Now he crossed to us and cried welcome, and alighted ; that was to pull out a sour milkskin from his wallet — of which he poured us out to drink, saying, " You passengers may be thirsty ? " Then taking forth dates, he spread them on the ground before us, and bade us break our fasts : so remounting cheerfully, he said, " We shall meet again this evening in the village."

The rafîks loosed out the thelûl, and we lay down in the sand of a seyl without shadow from the sun, to repose awhile. The Ageylies chatted ; and when the village boy heard say between their talk, that there was a Dowlat at Medina, — " El-Medina ! cries he, *kus umm-ha !* " — Eyâd and Merjàn looked up like saints, with beatific visages ! and told him, with a religious awe, ' He had made himself a kafir ! for knew he not that el-Medina is one of the two sanctuaries ? ' They added that word of the sighing Mohammedan piety, " Ullah *ammr-ha*, the Lord build up Medina " — I have heard some Beduwy put thereto ' *mûbrak thelûl en-Néby*, the couching place of the prophet's dromedary,' [Christians in the Arabic border-lands will say in their sleeve, *Ullah yuharrak-ha*, ' The Lord consume her with fire ! '] It was new lore to the poor lad, who answered half aghast, that ' he meant not to speak anything amiss, and he took refuge in Ullah.' He drew out parched locusts from his scrip, and fell to eat again : locusts clouds had passed over the Jebel, he said, two months before, but the damage had been light.

The *tólâ*, or new fruit-stalks of their palms, were not yet put forth ; we saw also their corn standing green : so that the harvest in Jebel Shammar may be nearly three weeks later than at Kheybar and Medina.

At half-afternoon we made forward towards the (orchard) walls of el-Kasr, fortified with the lighthouse-like towers of a former age. Eyâd said, ' And if we set out betimes on the morrow, we might arrive in Hâyil, *há'l hazza*, about this time.' The villagers were now at rest in their houses, in the hottest of the day, and no man stirring. We went astray in the outer blind lanes of the clay village, with broken walls and cavernous ground of filthy sunny dust. Europeans look upon the Arabic squalor with loathing : to our senses it is heathenish. Some children brought us into the town. At the midst is a small open place with a well-conduit, where we watered the thelûl: that water is sweet, but lukewarm, as all ground-water in Arabia. Then we went to sit down, where the high western wall cast already a little shadow, in the public view; looking that some householder would call us.

Men stood in their cottage thresholds to look at us Beduins: then one approached, — it seems these villagers take the charge in turn, and we stood up to meet him. He enquired, "What be ye, and whence come ye, and whither will ye?" we sat down after our answer, and he left us. He came again and said '*sum!*' and we rose and followed him. The villager led us into his cottage yard; here we sat on the earth, and he brought us dates, with a little butter and thin whey: when we had eaten he returned, and we were called to the village Kahwa. Here also they knew me, for some had seen me in Hâyil. These morose peasants cumbered me with religious questions; till I was most weary of their insane fanaticism.

El-Kasr, that is *Kasr el-Asheruwát*, is a village of two hundred and fifty to three hundred souls; the large graveyard, without the place, is a wilderness of wild headstones of many generations. Their wells are sunk to a depth (the Beduins say) of thirty fathoms!

We now heard sure tidings of the Emir; his camp had been removed to *Hazzel*, that is an *aed* or jau (watering place made in hollow ground) not distant, eastwards, from Shekàky in the Ruwàlla country (where was this year a plentiful rabîa), ' and all Shammar was with him and the Emir's cattle.' They were not many days out from Hâyil, and the coming again of the Prince and his people would not be for some other weeks. These are the pastoral, and warlike spring excursions of the Shammar Princes. A month or two they lie thus in tents like the Beduw; but the end of their loitering idleness is a vehement activity: for as ever their cattle are murubba, they will mount upon some great ghrazzu, with the rajajîl and a cloud of Beduw, and ride swiftly to surprise their enemies; and after that they come again (commonly with a booty) to Hâyil. — All the desert above Kasr was, they told us, máhal. The rabîa was this year upon the western side of Ajja; and the Emir's troops of mares and horses had been sent to graze about Môgug. Eyâd enquired, ' If anything had been heard of the twenty Ageyl riders from Medina!'

The villagers of Kasr are Beny Temîm: theirs is a very ancient name in Arabia. They were of old time Beduins and villagers, and their settled tribesmen were partly of the nomad life ; now they are only villagers. They are more robust than the Beduin neighbours, but churlish, and of little hospitality. In the evening these villagers talked tediously with us strangers, and made no kahwa. Upon a side of their public coffee hall was a raised bank of clay gravel, the *manèm* or travellers' bedstead, a very harsh and stony lodging to those who come in from the austere delicacy of the desert ; where in nearly every place is some softness of the pure sand. The nights, which we had found cold in the open wilderness, were here warm in the shelter of walls. — When we departed ere day, I saw many of these Arabian peasants sleeping abroad in their mantles ; they lay stretched like hounds in the dust of the village street.

At sunrise we saw the twin heads of the Sumrâ Hâyil. Eyâd responded to all men's questions : " We go with this Khalîl to Hâyil, at the commandment of the Bashat el-Medina ; and are bearers of his sealed letter to Ibn Rashîd ; but we know not what is in the writing, — which may be to cut off all our heads ! " — also I said in my heart, ' The Turks are treacherous ! ' — But should I break the Pasha's seal ? No ! I would sooner hope for a fair event of that hazard. This sealed letter of the governor of Medina, was opened after my returning from Arabia, at a British Consulate ; and it contained no more than his commending me to ' *The Sheykh* ' Ibn Rashîd, and the request that he would send me forward on my journey.

I walked in the mornings two hours, and as much at afternoon, that my companions might ride ; and to spare their sickly thelûl I climbed to the saddle, as she stood, like a Beduwy : but the humanity which I showed them, to my possibility, hardened their ungenerous hearts. Seeing them weary, and Eyâd complaining that his soles were worn to the quick, I went on walking barefoot to Gofar, and bade them ride still. — There I beheld once more (oh ! blissful sight), the plum trees and almond trees blossoming in an Arabian oasis. We met with no one in the long main street ; the men were now in the fields, or sleeping out the heat of the day in their houses. We went by the *Manôkh*, and I knew it well ; but my companions, who had not been this way of late years, were gone on, and so we lost our breakfast. When I called they would not hear ; they went to knock at a door far beyond. They sat down at last in the street's end, but we saw no man. " Let us to Hâyil, and mount thou, Khalîl!" said the rafîks. We went on through the ruins of the northern quarter, where I showed them the road; and come near the desert side, I took the next way, but they trod in another. I called them, they called to me, and I went on riding. Upon this Eyâd's light head turning, whether it were he had not tasted tobacco this day, or because he was weary and fasting, he began to curse me; and came running like a madman, 'to take the thelûl.' When I told him I would not suffer it, he stood aloof and cursed on, and seemed to have lost his understanding. A mile beyond he returned to a better mind, and acknowledged to me, that 'until he had drunk tobacco of a morning his heart burned within him, the brain rose in his pan, and he felt like a fiend.' — It were as easy to contain such a spirit as to bind water!

I rode not a little pensively, this third time, in the beaten way to Hâyil; and noted again (with abhorrence, of race) at every few hours' end their "kneeling places"; — those little bays of stones set out in the desert soil, where wayfarers overtaken by the canonical hours may patter the formal prayer of their religion. — About midway we met the morning passengers out from Hâyil: and looking upon me with the implacable eyes of their fanaticism, every one who went by uttered the same hard words to my companions, 'Why bring ye him again?' Ambar, Aneybar's brother, came next, riding upon an ass in a company; he went to Gofar, where he had land and palms. But the worthy Galla libertine greeted us with a pleasant good humour, — I was less it might be in disgrace of the princely household than of the fanatical populace. We saw soon above the brow of the desert the white tower-head of the great donjon of the castle, and said Merjàn, "Some think that the younger children of Telâl be yet alive therein. They see the world from their tower, and they are unseen." Upon our right hand lay the palms in the desert, es-Sherafa, founded by Metaab: — so we rode on into the town.

We entered Hâyil near the time of the afternoon prayers. Because the Emir was absent, there was no business! the most shops were shut. The long market street was silent; and their town seemed a dead and empty place. I saw the renegade Abdullah sitting at a shop door; then Ibrahîm and a few more of my acquaintance, and lastly the school-master. The unsavoury pedant stood and cried with many deceitful gestures, "Now, welcome! and blessed be the Lord! — Khalîl is a

Moslem!" (for else he guessed I had not been so foolhardy as to re-enter Ibn Rashîd's town.) At the street's end I met with Aneybar, lieutenant now in (empty) Hâyil for the Emir; he came from the Kasr carrying in his hand a gold-hilted back-sword: the great man saluted me cheerfully and passed by. I went to alight before the castle, in the empty Méshab, which was wont to be full of the couching thelûls of visiting Beduins: but in these days since Ibn Rashîd was *ghrazzai*, there came no more Beduins to the town. About half the men of Hâyil were now in the field with Ibn Rashîd; for, besides his salaried rajajîl, even the salesmen of the sûk are the Prince's servants, to ride with him. This custom of military service has discouraged many traders of the East Nejd provinces, who had otherwise been willing to try their fortunes in Hâyil.

Some malignants of the castle ran together at the news, that the Nasrâny was come again. I saw them stand in the tower gate, with the old coffee-server; "Heigh! (they cried) it is he indeed! now it may please Ullah he will be put to death." — Whilst I was in this astonishment, Aneybar returned; he had but walked some steps to find his wit. "*Salaam aleyk!*" "*Aleykôm es-salaam,*" he answered me again, betwixt good will and wondering, and cast back the head; for they have all learned to strut like the Emirs. Aneybar gave me his right hand with lordly grace: there was the old peace of bread and salt betwixt us. — "From whence, Khalîl? and ye twain with him what be ye? — well go to the coffee hall! and there we will hear more." Aly el-Ayid went by us, coming from his house, and saluted me heartily.

When we were seated with Aneybar in the great kahwa, he asked again, "And you Beduw with him, what be ye?" Eyâd responded with a craven humility: "We are Heteym." — "Nay ye are not Heteym." — "Tell them, I said, both what ye be, and who sent you hither." *Eyâd:* "We are Ageyl from Medina, and the Pasha sent us to Kheybar to convey this Khalîl, with a letter to Ibn Rashîd." — "Well, Ageyl, and what tribesmen?" — "We must acknowledge we are Beduins, we are Auájy." *Aneybar:* "And, Khalîl, where are your letters?" — I gave him a letter from Abdullah es-Siruàn, and the Pasha's sealed letter. Aneybar, who had not learned to read gave them to a secretary, a sober and friendly man, who perusing the unflattering titles "*To the sheykh Ibn Rashîd,*" returned them to me unopened. — Mufarrij, the steward, now came in; he took me friendly by the hand,

and cried, " Sum ! " (i.e. short for *Bismillah*, in God's name) and led us to the mothif. There a dish was set before us of Ibn Rashîd's rusty tribute dates, and — their spring hospitality — a bowl of small camel lében. One of the kitchen servers showed me a piece of ancient copper money, which bore the image of an eagle ; it had been found at Hâyil, and was Roman.

The makhzan was assigned us in which I had formerly lodged ; and my rafîks left me to visit their friends in the town. Children soon gathered to the threshold and took courage to revile me. Also there came to me the princely child Abd el-Azîz, the orphan of Metaab : I saw him fairly grown in these three months ; he swaggered now like his uncle with a lofty but not disdainful look, and he resembles the Emir Mohammed. The princely child stood and silently regarded me, he clapt a hand to his little sword, but would not insult the stranger ; so he said : " Why returned, Khalîl Nasrâny ? " — " Because I hoped it would be pleasant to thine uncle, my darling." — " Nay, Khalîl ! nay, Khalîl ! the Emir says thou art not to remain here." I saw Zeyd the gate-keeper leading Merjàn by the hand ; and he enquired of the lad, who was of a vindictive nature, of all that had happened to me since the day I arrived at Kheybar. Such questions and answers could only be to my hurt : it was a danger I had foreseen, amongst ungenerous Arabs.

We found Aneybar in the coffee-hall at evening : " Khalîl, he said, we cannot send thee forward, and thou must depart to-morrow." — " Well, send me to the Emir in the North with the Medina letter, if I may not abide his coming in Hâyil." — " Here rest to-night, and in the morning (he shot his one palm from the other) depart ! — Thou stay here, Khalîl ! the people threatened thee to-day, thou sawest how they pressed on thee at your entering." — " None pressed upon me, many saluted me." — " Life of Ullah ! but I durst not suffer thee to remain in Hâyil, where so many are ready to kill thee, and I must answer to the Emir : sleep here this night, and please Ullah without mishap, and mount when we see the morning light." — Whilst we were speaking there came in a messenger, who arrived from the Emir in the northern wilderness : " And how does the Emir, exclaimed Aneybar with an affected heartiness of voice ; and where left you him encamped ? " The messenger, a worthy man of middle age, saluted me, without any religious misliking, he was of the strangers at Hâyil from the East provinces. *Aneybar :* " Thou hast heard, Khalîl ? and he showed me these three pauses of his malicious wit, on his fingers, *To-morrow!*— *The light!—Depart!*"—"Whither?"—"From whence thou camest;—to Kheybar: art thou of the *dîn* (their religion)?"—"No, I am not."—"And therefore the Arabs are impatient of thy life: wouldst thou be of the dîn, thou mightest live always amongst them." —"Then send me to-morrow, at my proper charge, towards el-Kasîm."

They were displeased when I mentioned the *Dowla*: Aneybar answered hardly, "What Dowla! here is the land of the Aarab, and the dominion of Ibn Rashîd. — He says Kasîm : but there are no Beduw in the town (to convey him). Khalîl! we durst not ourselves be seen in Kasîm," and he made me a shrewd sign, sawing with the forefinger upon his black throat. — "Think not to deceive me, Aneybar; is not a sister of the Emir of Boreyda, a wife of Mohammed ibn Rashîd? and are not they your allies?"—"Ullah! (exclaimed some of them), he knows everything."— *Aneybar :* "Well! well! but it cannot be, Khalîl: how sayest thou, sherîf?"

— This was an old gentleman-beggar, with grey eyes, some fortieth in descent from the Néby, clad like a Turkish citizen, and who had arrived to-day from Medina, where he dwelt. His was an adventurous and gainful trade of hypocrisy : three months or four in a year he dwelt at home; in the rest he rode, or passed the seas into every far land of the Mohammedan world. In each country he took up a new concubine; and whereso he passed he glosed so fructuously, and showed them his large letters patent from kings and princes, and was of that honourable presence, that he was bidden to the best houses, as becometh a religious sheykh of the Holy City, and a nephew of the apostle of Ullah : so he received their pious alms and returned to the illuminated Medina. Bokhâra was a *villegiatura* for this holy man in his circuit, and so were all the cities beyond as far as Càbul. In Mohammedan India, he went a begging long enough to learn the vulgar language. Last year he visited Stambûl and followed the [not] glorious Mohammedan arms in Europe; and the Sultan of Islam had bestowed upon him his imperial firmàn.—He showed me the *dedale* engrossed document, with the sign manual of the Calif upon a half fathom of court paper. And with this broad charter he was soon to go again upon an Indian voyage.

— When Aneybar had asked his counsel, "*Wellah yâ el-Mohafûth* (answered this hollow spirit), and I say the same, it cannot be; for what has this man to do in el-Kasîm? and what does he wandering up and down in all the land ; (he added under his breath), *wa yiktub el-bilâd*, and he writes up the country." *Aneybar* : " Well, to-morrow, Khalîl, depart ; and thou Eyâd carry him back to Kheybar." — *Eyâd* : " But it would be said there, ' Why hast thou brought him again ? ' wellah I durst not do it, Aneybar." Aneybar mused a little. I answered them, " You hear his words ; and if this rafîk were willing, yet so feeble is their thelûl, you have seen it yourselves, that she could not carry me." — *Eyâd* : " Wellah ! she is not able." — " Besides, I said, if you cast me back into hazards, the Dowla may require my blood, and you must every year enter some of their towns as Bagdad and Medina : and when you send to India with your horses, will you not be in the power of my fellow citizens ? " — *The Sherîf* : " He says truth, I have been there, and I know the Engleys and their Dowla : now let me speak to this man in a tongue which he will understand, — he spoke somewhat in Hindostani — what ! an Engleysy understand not the language of el-Hind ? " — *Aneybar* : " Thou Eyâd (one of our subject Beduins) ! it is not permitted thee to say nay ; I command you upon your heads to convey Khalîl to Kheybar ; and you are to depart to-morrow. — Heigh-ho ! it should be the hour of prayer ! " Some said, They had heard the *ithin* already : Aneybar rose, the Sherîf rose solemnly and all the rest ; and they went out to say their last prayers in the great mesjid.

In the next makhzan lodged a stranger, newly come from the wars : and I heard from him the first sure tidings, — ' that the Moslemîn had the worse ; but the jehâd being now at an end, they returned home. The Muskovs were big, he said, and manly bodies with great beards.' But, of all that he saw in the land of Europe, most strange seemed to him the sheep of the Nasâra, ' that they had tails like camels ' [and not the huge tallow laps of the Arabian stock]. He had come lately to Hâyil in company with the great sheykh of el-Ajmân. That sheykh of Aarab had been taken captive by the Turks, in their occupation of el-Hása, and banished to the confines of Russia. There he was seven years in durance ; and his Beduin kindred in Arabia had (in the last two years) slain the year's-mind for him, — supposing him to be deceased ! But when the valorous (unlettered) man in a strange land heard the cry to warfare for the religion, he made his humble petition to the Sultan ; and liberty was granted him to bear a lance to the jehâd in the worship of Ullah and the Apostle. — This Beduin duke was wounded, in the arm. At the armistice the Sultan bade him ask a reward; and he answered, "That I might return to my province, *Hájjar!*" — In Ramathàn he landed with this companion at Jidda: they visited Mecca and Medina, and from Medina they rode to Hâyil. Here Mohammed ibn Rashîd received him kindly, and dismissed him with his princely gift of three thelûls and a saddle-bag full of silver reals. The noble Arabian was now gone home to his country; and we heard that he had submitted himself to the Waháby.

That stranger, his rafîk, who had but one mocking eye, which seemed to look askance, said to me he had seen me three years before in Alexandria, and spoken with me! [I think it was true, — that one day meeting with him in the street, I had enquired the way of him.] To my ear the Arabian speech sounded mincing and affected-like upon his tongue. He said he was from el-Yémen, but what he was indeed (in this time of trouble) I might not further enquire. When I asked him of the sherîf from Medina, he answered with an incredulous scorn (which might have become an European), "He is no sherîf, I know him well, but a beggar come all the way hither, from Medina, with a box of candles (which they have not in these parts) for Ibn Rashîd, only to beg of him four or five reals, and receive a change of clothing. He does this every few years, though he has a good house at Medina; he runs through all the world a-begging." — "But wherefore, if he have to live?" — "It is only his avarice."

The Sherîf came, after prayers, to visit me, and his wayfaring companion, clad in their long city coats, wide girdles, superfluous slops, and red caps wound about with great calico turbans. They asked, 'Was there any water?' We were all thirsty from the journey, which is like a fever in Arabia; and I went out to ask a little water, for my guests, at the Kasr gate. It was shut: "What wouldst thou, Khalîl?" I heard a voice say in the dark, and I knew it was Aneybar; he was sitting there on Hamûd's clay settle. I asked, "Why made he this ado about my coming again to Hâyil? and seeing that I came with a letter from the Pasha of Medina?" — "Tell us not of pashas, here is Ibn Rashîd's government: to-morrow depart, there is no more to say;" and he turned to a companion, who answered him, "Ay, to-morrow early! away with the cursed Nasrâny." I asked Aneybar who was his counsellor, since I could not see him: but he answered not. — The unsavoury schoolmaster went by, and when he knew our voices, " Akhs ! quoth he, I saluted thee to-day, seeing thee arrive, as I supposed, a Moslem, but now thou wilt be slain." Aneybar was not a bad man, or fanatical, but he had a bondsman's heart, and the good was easily corrupted in him, by the despiteful reasons of others.

I went on to knock at the door of Aly el-Aŷid and ask a little water. His wife opened with " Welcome Khalîl." — " And where is Aly ? " — " My husband is gone out to sleep in the (ripening) cornfields, he must watch all night ; " she bade me enter, but I excused myself. She was young and pleasant, of modest demeanour, and had many tall children. When I was formerly at Hâyil, I often visited them, and she sat unveiled, before the hakîm, with her husband ; and he would have it so, because I was a Nasrâny. She brought me water and I returned to my makhzan.

The sherîf's companion had been in the Bagdad caravan ; afterwards he lay sick in a hospital at Medina : he met lately with the sherîf, all ready to go upon his northern journey, and they joined company. Some nomads riding to Hâyil, had carried them upon their camels for two reals each, but far ways about, so that they arrived full of weariness and impatience. When they returned to their makhzan I said I would go over presently to visit them. — Eyâd, " Is not the sherîf going to el-Méshed ? we will give him money to take thee with him, and let us see what the morning will bring forth ; look, Khalîl ! I will not forsake thee." — When we entered, the sherîf drew me out the Sultan's diploma ; he found his goggle spectacles, and when he had set them solemnly astride on his nose, the old fox took up his candle end and began to read forth. He showed us his other documents and letters mandatory, from princes and pashas, ' Only, quoth he, there lacked him one from the Engleys ! ' — He would have me write him a thing, that he might have entrance to the Consulate of our nation at Bagdad ; and he hoped there to obtain a certificate to further him in his Indian voyage. " Reach me the inkhorn, look in the bags, companion," quoth the iniquitous shrew ; who oppressed me here, and would that I should lift him up abroad ! — " Lend me that reed, and I will not fail thee, — what good deeds of thine shall I record ? wilt thou persuade Aneybar ? " — " Ugh ! " (he would as lief that I perished in this wilderness, as to thrive himself in India).

Eyâd : " Sherîf, since thou art going to Méshed, take with thee Khalîl, and we will give thee four reals ; also Khalîl shall deliver thee a writing for the Engleys." — " Ugh ! said the old shrew, four reals, four only, ugh ! we may consider of it to-morrow. He added this miserable proverb — *the Lord may work much mercy before the morning* : and — this is the only word I know of their speech, besides *bret* (*bread*), — el-Engleys *werigud*." I asked, " Did they take thee too for a spy in the Indian country ? " — " Ay, and there only can I blame their government : *I went no whither in all India, but I was watched !* and for such it is that I would obtain a certificate, another time, from a Konsulato." — " And did any threaten thee because of thy religion ? " — " Nay, that I will say for them." — " Be they not just to all without difference ? " — " They are just, out of doubt ; and (he said to Eyâd) I will tell thee a tale. One day as I journeyed in el-Hind, I hastened, I and a concubine of mine, to come to a town not far beyond to lodge : but the night falling on us short of the place, I turned aside, where I saw a military station ; because I feared for the woman, and if we should lie abroad, we were in danger of robbers.

" The [sepoy] sentinel would not suffer me to pass the gate, ' The sun, he said is set : ' then in my anger I struck him. [This is very unlike the Arabian comity ; but the holy parasite was town-bred and not wont to suffer contradiction so far from home.] The soldier reported to the guard, and their officer sent for me ; he was an Engleysy, — they are all yellow haired, and such as this Khalîl. When I told him my quality and spread my firmans before him, which ye have seen, the officer commanded to make ready for us a lodging and supper, and to give me twenty-five rupees ; and he said to me, ' You may lodge here one month, and receive daily rations.' " — " I would thou might persuade this people in Hâyil to show some humanity to strangers ! " — " Ha ! (answered the sherîf, as a citizen despising them), they are Beduw ! " and the false old man began to be merry.

" Bokhâra, he told me, is a city greater than Damascus ; the Emir, who — he added mocking — would be called *Sûltàn*, had a wide and good country ; but now (he murmured) the Muskôv are there ! " — " Well, tell us of the jehâd." — " I myself was at the wars, and am only lately come home to Medina ; " where he said, he had heard of me (detained) at Kheybar, when my matter was before the council. — " But, eigh ! the Nasâra had the upper hand ; and they have taken a province." — " Akhs ! cries Eyâd, tell us, sherîf, have the Nasâra conquered any béled of the Sooltàn ? to whom Ullah send the victory !

— Can the Nasâra prevail against the Moslemîn ? " The sherîf answered with the Mohammedan solemnity, and cast a sigh, " *Amr Ullah, amr Ullah!* it was God's ordinance." — Eyâd : " Ha ! sherîf, what thinkest thou, will the Nasâra come on hither ? " — " That is unlikely ! " Eyâd's busy broken head was full of a malicious subtlety : I said therefore, " Sherîf, thinkest thou that this land would be worth to them a cup of coffee ? " — " Well, it is all chôl, steppes, an open desolation ; aye, what profit might they have in it ! " " And the Engleys ? " — " They were of our part." — " Eyâd, you hear this from the sherîf's mouth ! " — Eyâd : " But the Nasâra take the Sultan's provinces, says the sherîf : and the Engleys are Nasâra ! "

When the morning sun rose I had as lief that my night had continued for ever. There was no going forward for me, nor going backward, and I was spent with fatigues. — We went over to the great coffee-hall. Aneybar sat there, and beside him was the old dry-hearted sherîf, who drank his morrow's cup with an holy serenity. " Eyâd affirms, I said, that he cannot, he dare not, and that he will not convey me again to Kheybar." — " To Kheybar thou goest, and that presently."

Eyâd was leading away his sick thelûl to pasture under Ajja, but the Moghréby gatekeeper withheld him by force. That Moor's heart, as at my former departure from Hâyil, was full of brutality. " Come, Zeyd, I said to him, be we not both Western men and like countrymen among these Beduw ? " — " Only become a Moslem, and we would all love thee ; but we know thee to be a most hardened Nasrâny. — Khalîl comes (he said to the bystanders) to dare us ! a Nasrâny, here in the land of the Moslemîn ! Was it not enough that we once sent thee away in safety, and comest thou hither again ! " Round was this burly man's head, with a brutish visage ; he had a thick neck, unlike the shot-up growth of the slender Nejd Arabians ; the rest of him an unwieldy carcase, and half a cart-load of tripes.

In the absence of the princely family, my soul was in the hand of this cyclops of the Méshab. I sat to talk peaceably with him, and the brute-man many times lifted his stick to smite the kafir ; but it was hard for Zeyd, to whom I had sometime shown a good turn, to chafe himself against me. The opinions of the Arabs are ever divided, and among three is commonly one mediator : — it were blameworthy to defend the cause of an adversary of Ullah : and yet some of the people of Hâyil that now gathered about us with mild words were a mean for me. The one-eyed stranger stood by, he durst not affront the storm ; but when Zeyd left me for a moment, he whispered in my ear, that I should put them off, whom he called in contempt ' beasts without understanding, Beduw ! ' — " Only seem thou to consent with them, lest they kill thee ; say ' Mohammed is the apostle of Ullah,' and afterward, when thou art come into sure countries, hold it or leave it at thine own liking. This is not to sin before God, when force oppresses us, and there is no deliverance ! "

Loitering persons and knavish boys pressed upon me with insolent tongues : but Ibrahîm of Hâyil, he who before so friendly accompanied me out of the town, was ready again to befriend me, and cried to them, " Back with you ! for shame, so to thrust upon the man ! O fools, have ye not seen him before ? " Amongst them came that Abdullah of the broken arm, the boy-brother of Hamûd. I saw him grown taller, and now he wore a little back-sword ; which he pulled out against me, and cried, " O thou cursed Nasrâny, that wilt not leave thy miscreance ! " — The one-eyed stranger whispered, " Content them ! it is but waste of breath to reason with them. Do ye — he said to the people — stand back ! I would speak with this man ; and we may yet see some happy event, it may please Ullah." He whispered in my ear, " Eigh ! there will be some mischief ; only say thou wilt be a Moslem, and quit thyself of them. Show thyself now a prudent man, and let me not see thee die for a word ; afterward, when thou hast escaped their hands, *settîn séna*, sixty years to them, and *yulaan Ullah abu-hum*, the Lord confound the father of them all ! Now, hast thou consented ? — ho ! ye people, to the mesjid ! go and prepare the *muzayyîn*: Khalîl is a Moslem ! " — The lookers-on turned and were going, then stood still ; they believed not his smooth words of that obstinate misbeliever. But when I said to them, " No need to go ! " — " Aha ! they cried, the accursed Nasrâny, Ullah curse his parentage ! " — *Zeyd* (the porter) : " But I am thinking we shall make this (man) a Moslem and circumcise him ; go in one of you and fetch me a knife from the Kasr : " but none moved, for the people dreaded the Emir and Hamûd (reputed my friend). " Come, Khalîl, for one thing, said Zeyd, we will be friends with thee ; say, there is none God but the Lord and His apostle is Mohammed : and art thou poor we will also enrich thee." — " I count your silver as the dust of this méshab : — but which of you miserable

Arabs would give a man anything ? Though ye gave me this castle, and the *beyt el-mâl*, the pits and the sacks of hoarded silver which ye say to be therein, I could not change my faith." — " *Akhs — akhs — akhs — akhs !* " was uttered from a multitude of throats : I had contemned, in one breath, the right way in religion and the heaped riches of this world ! and with horrid outcries they detested the antichrist.

— " Eigh Nasrâny ! said a voice, and what found you at Kheybar, ha ? " — " Plenty of dates O man, and fever." — " The more is the pity, cried they all, that he died not there ; but akhs ! these cursed Nasrânies, they never die, nor sicken as other men : and surely if this (man) were not a Nasrâny, he had been dead long ago." — " Ullah curse the father of him ! " murmured many a ferocious voice. Zeyd the porter lifted his huge fist ; but Aneybar appeared coming from the sûk, and Ibrahîm cries, " Hold there ! and strike not Khalîl." — *Aneybar :* " What ado is here, and (to Zeyd) why is not the Nasrâny mounted ? — did I not tell thee ? " — " His Beduw were not ready ; one of them is gone to bid his kinsfolk farewell, and I gave the other leave to go and buy somewhat in the sûk." — *Aneybar :* " And you people will ye not go your ways ? — *Sheytàn !* what has any of you to do with the Nasrâny ; Ullah send a punishment upon you all, and upon him also."

I said to Aneybar, " Let Eyâd take new wages of me and threaten him, lest he forsake me." — " And what received he before ? " — " Five reals." — " Then give him other five reals. [Two or three had sufficed for the return journey ; but this was his malice, to make me bare in a hostile land.] When the thelûl is come, mount, — and Zeyd see thou that the payment is made ; " and loftily the Galla strode from me. — Cruel was the slave's levity ; and when I had nothing left for their cupidity how might I save myself out of this dreadful country ? — *Zeyd :* " Give those five reals, ha ! make haste, or by God — ! " — and with an ugh ! of his bestial anger he thrust anew his huge fist upon my breast. I left all to the counsel of the moment, for a last need I was well armed ; but with a blow, putting to his great strength, he might have slain me. — Ibrahîm drew me from them. " Hold ! he said, I have the five reals, where is that Eyâd, and I will count them in his hand. Khalîl, rid thyself with this and come away, and I am with you." I gave him the silver. Ibrahîm led on, with the bridle of the thelûl in his hand, through the market street, and left me at a shop door whilst he went to seek Aneybar. Loitering persons gathered at the threshold where I sat ; the worst was that wretched young Abdullah el-Abeyd ; when he had lost his breath with cursing, he drew his little sword again ; but the bystanders blamed him, and I entered the makhzan.

The tradesman, who was a Meshedy, asked for my galliûn and bade me be seated ; he filled it with hameydy, that honey-like tobacco and peaceable remedy of human life. "What tidings, quoth he, in the world ? — We have news that the Queen of the Engleys is deceased ; and now her son is king in her room." Whilst I sat pensive, to hear his words ! a strong young swordsman, who remained in Hâyil, came suddenly in and sat down. I remembered his comely wooden face, the fellow was called a Moghréby, and was not very happy in his wits. He drew and felt down the edge of his blade : so said Hands-without head — as are so many among them, and sware by Ullah : "Yesterday, when Khalîl entered, I was running with this sword to kill him, but some withheld me !" The tradesman responded, "What has he done to be slain by thee ?" *Swordsman* : "And I am glad that I did it not : " — he seemed now little less rash to favour me, than before to have murdered me.

Aneybar, who this while strode unquietly up and down, in the side streets, (he would not be seen to attend upon the Nasrâny), appeared now with Ibrahîm at the door. The Galla deputy of Ibn Rashîd entered and sat down, with a mighty rattling of his sword of office in the scabbard, and laid the blade over his knees. Ibrahîm requested him to insist no more upon the iniquitous payment out of Khalîl's empty purse, or at least to make it less. "No, five reals !" (exclaimed the slave in authority,) he looked very fiercely upon it, and clattered the sword. "God will require it of thee ; and give me a schedule of safe conduct, Aneybar." He granted, the tradesman reached him an handbreadth of paper, and Ibrahîm wrote, 'No man to molest this Nasrâny.' Aneybar inked his signet of brass, and sealed it solemnly, ANEYBAR IBN RASHÎD.

"The sherîf (I said) is going to Bagdad, he will pass by the camp of the Emir : and there are some Beduw at the gate — I have now heard it, that are willing to convey me to the North, for three reals. If thou compel me to go with Eyâd, thou knowest that I cannot but be cast away : treachery O Aneybar is punished even in this world ! May not a stranger pass by your Prince's country ? be reasonable, that I may depart from you to-day peaceably, and say, the Lord remember thee for good." The Galla sat arrogantly rattling the gay back-sword in his lap, with a countenance composed to the princely awe ; and at every word of mine he clapped his black hand to the hilt. When I ceased he found no answer, but to cry with tyranny, " Have done, or else by God — " ! and he showed me a handbreadth or two of his steel out of the scabbard. " What ! he exclaimed, wilt thou not yet be afraid ? " Now Eyâd entered, and Ibrahîm counted the money in his hand : Aneybar delivered the paper to Eyâd. — " The Emir gave his passport to me." — " But I will not let thee have it, mount ! and Ibrahîm thou canst see him out of the town."

At the end of the sûk the old parasite seyyid or sherîf was sitting square-legged before a threshold, in the dust of the street. " Out, I said in passing, with thy reeds and paper ; and I will give thee a writing ? " The old fox in a turban winced, and he murmured some koran wisdom between his broken teeth. — There trotted by us a Beduwy upon a robust thelûl. " I was then coming to you, cried the man ; and I will convey the Nasrâny to el-Irâk for five reals." *Eyâd* : " Well, and if it be with Aneybar's allowance, I will give up the five reals, which I have ; and so shall we all have done well, and Khalîl may depart in peace. Khalîl sit here by the thelûl, whilst I and this Beduwy go back to Aneybar, and make the accord, if it be possible ; wellah ! I am sorry for thy sake." — A former acquaintance, a foreigner from el-Hása, came by and stayed to speak with me ; the man was one of the many in- dustrious strangers in Hâyil, where he sewed cotton quilts for the richer households. " This people, quoth he, are untaught ! all things are in the power of Ullah : and now farewell, Khalîl, and God give thee a good ending of this adventure."

Eyâd returned saying, Aneybar would not be entreated, and that he had reviled the poor Beduwy. " Up, let us hasten from them ; and as for Merjàn, I know not what is become of him. I will carry thee to Gofar, and leave thee there. — No, wellah Khalîl, I am not treacherous, but I durst not, I cannot, return with thee to Kheybar : at Gofar I will leave thee, or else with the Aarab." — " If thou betray me, betray me at the houses of hair, and not in the settlements ; but you shall render the silver." — " Nay, I have eaten it ; yet I will do the best that I may for thee."

We journeyed in the beaten path towards Gofar ; and after going a

mile, " Let us wait, quoth Eyâd, and see if this Merjàn be not coming."
At length we saw it was he who approached us with a bundle on his
head, — he brought temmn and dates, which his sister (wedded in the
town) had given him. Eyâd drew out a leathern budget, in which was
some victual for the way that he had received from the Mothîf, (without
my knowledge) : it was but a little barley meal and dates of ill kind, in
all to the value of about one shilling. We sat down, Merjàn spread his
good dates, and we breakfasted ; thus eating together I hoped they
might yet be friendly, though only misfortunes could be before me with
such unlucky rafîks. I might have journeyed with either of them but not
with both together. Eyâd had caught some fanatical suspicion in Hâyil,
from the mouth of the old Medina sherîf ! — that the Nasâra encroached
continually upon the dominion of the Sultàn, and that Khalîl's nation,
although not enemies, were not well-wishers, in their hearts, to the
religion of Islam. When I would mount ; " Nay, said Eyâd, beginning
to swagger, the returning shall not be as our coming ; I will ride
myself." I said no more ; and cast thus again into the wilderness I
must give them line. — My companions boasted, as we went, of
promises made to them both in Hâyil. — Aneybar had said, that would
they return hither sometime, from serving the Dowla, they might be of
Ibn Rashîd's (armed) service ; — Eyâd an horseman of the Emir's
riders, and Merjàn one of the rajajîl.

Two women coming out from Hâyil overtook us, as they went to
Gofar. " The Lord be praised (said the poor creatures, with a womanly
kindness) that it was not worse. Ah ! thou, — is not thy name Khalîl ? —
they in yonder town are *jabâbara*, men of tyrannous violence, that will
cut off a man's head for a light displeasure. Eigh me ! did not he so that
is now Emir, unto all his brother's children ? Thou art well come from
them, they are hard and cruel, *kasyîn*. And what is this that the people
cry, ' *Out upon the Nasrâny !* ' The Nasâra be better than the
Moslemîn." *Eyâd* : " It is they themselves that are the Nasâra, wellah,
khubithîn, full of malignity." " It is the Meshâhada that I hate, said
Merjàn, may Ullah confound them." It happened that a serving boy in
the public kitchen, one of the patients whom I treated (freely) at my
former sojourning in Hâyil, was Merjàn's brother. The Meshâhadies he
said had been of Aneybar's counsel against me. — Who has travelled in
Phoenician and Samaritan Syria may call to mind the inhumanity [the
last wretchedness and worldly wickedness of irrational religions, — that

man should not eat and drink with his brother!] of those Persian or Assyrian colonists, the *Metówali*.

Forsaking the road we went now towards the east-building of Gofar: — the east and west settlements lie upon two veins of ground-water, a mile or more asunder. The western oasis, where passes the common way is the greater; but Eyâd went to find some former acquaintance in the other with whom we might lodge. Here also we passed by forsaken palm-grounds and ruinous orchard houses, till we came to the inhabited; and they halted before the friend's dàr. Eyâd and Merjàn sat down to see if the good man (of an inhospitable race, the B. Temîm), would come forth to welcome us. Children gathered to look on, and when some of them knew me, they began to fleer at the Nasrâny. Merjàn cursed them, as only Semites can find it in their hearts, and ran upon the little mouthing knaves with his camel-stick; but now our host coming down his alley saluted Eyâd and called us to the house. His son bore in my bags to the kahwa: and they strewed down green garden stalks before the thelûl and wild herbage.

A bare dish of dates was set before us; and the good-man made us thin coffee: bye and bye his neighbours entered. All these were B. Temîm, peasant-like bodies in whom is no natural urbanity; but they are lumpish drudgers, living honestly of their own — and that is with a sparing hand. When I said to one of them, "I see you all big of bone and stature, unlike the (slender) inhabitants of Hâyil!" — He answered dispraising them, "The Shammar are *Beduw!*" Whilst we sat, there came in three swarthy strangers, who riding by to Hâyil alighted here also to drink coffee. — They carried up their zíka to the Prince's treasury; for being few and distant Aarab, his exactors were not come to them these two years: they were of Harb, and their wandering ground was nigh Medina. They mounted again immediately; and from Hâyil they would ride continually to Ibn Rashîd in the northern wilderness.

My rafîks left me alone without a word! I brought in therefore the thelûl furnitures, lest they should lead away their beast and forsake me. Eyâd and Merjàn feared no more that they must give account for me; and their wildness rising at every word, I foresaw how next to desperate, must be my further passage with them: happily for my weary life the milk-season was now in the land. — The water veins upon which their double oasis is founded flow, they say, from Ajja. The water height in their eight-fathom wells falls about a fathom in the long summer season. These B. Temîmy hosts showed a dull countenance towards 'the adversary of Ullah.' Yet the story of my former being in Hâyil was well known to them : they even told me of my old nâga, the *Khueyra*, that she had lately calved : — I would she were yet mine ! for her much milk which might sustain a man's life in full health in the desert. The nâga of any good hump has rich milk ; if her hump be low she has less and lean milk. The B. Temîm are very ancient in these districts : yet an elder nation, the *B. Taâmir*, they say, inhabited the land before them. They name their jid or patriarch *Temîm* ; he was brother of Wâil jid of the Annezy and Maazy [Vol. I. p. 270]. — My rafîks came again at evening with treacherous looks.

CHAPTER X

THE SHAMMAR AND HARB DESERTS IN NEJD

Herding supper of milk. A flight of cranes. An evil desert journey, and night with treacherous rafîks. Aly of Gussa again. Braitshán's booths again. "Arabs love the smooth speaking." Another evil journey. A menzil of Heteym; and parting from the treacherous rafîks. Nomad thirst for tobacco. A beautiful Heteym woman. Solubba. Maatuk and Noweyr. "Nasâra" passengers. Life of these Heteym. Burial of the Nasrâny's books. Journey to the Harb, eastward. Gazelles. Camel milk bitter of wormwood. Heteym menzils. Come to Harb Aarab. False rumour of a foray of the Wahâby. El-Aûf. An Harb sheykh. An Harb bride. Khálaf ibn Náhal's great booth. Khálaf's words. Seleymy villagers. Mount again and alight by night at tents. Motlog and Tollog. Come anew to Ibn Náhal's tent. Ibn Náhal, a merchant Beduin. His wealth. A rich man rides in a ghrazzu, to steal one camel, and is slain. Tollog's inhospitable ferîj. Wander to another menzil. "Poor Aly." An Ageyly descried. A new face. A tent of poor acquaintance.

AT daybreak we departed from Gofar: this by my reckoning was the first week in April. Eyâd loosed out our sick thelûl to pasture; and they drove her slowly forward in the desert plain till the sun went down behind Ajja, when we halted under bergs of grey granite. These rocks are fretted into bosses and caves more than the granite of Sinai: the heads of the granite crags are commonly trap rock. Eyâd, kindling a fire, heated his iron ramrod, and branded their mangy thelûl. —I had gone all day on foot; and the Ageylies threatened every hour to cast down my bags, though now light as Merjàn's temmn, which she also carried. We marched four miles further, and espied a camp fire; and coming to the place we found a ruckling troop of camels couched for the night, in the open khála. The herd-lad and his brother sat sheltering in the hollow bank of a seyl, and a watch-fire of sticks was burning before them. The hounds of the Aarab follow not with the herds, the lads could not see beyond their fire-light, and our *salaam* startled them: then falling on our knees we sat down by them, — and with that word we were acquainted. The lads made some of their nâgas stand up, and they milked full bowls and frothing over for us. We heard a night-fowl shriek, where we had left our bags with the thelûl: my rafîks rose and ran back with their sticks, for the bird (which they called *sirrûk*, a thief) might, they said, steal something. When we had thus supped, we lay down upon the pleasant seyl sand to sleep.

As the new day lightened we set forward. A little further we saw a flock of some great sea-fowl grazing before us, upon their tall shanks in the wilderness. — I mused that (here in Nejd) they were but a long flight on their great waggle wings from the far seabord ; a morrow's sun might see them beyond this burning dust of Arabia ! At first my light-headed rafîks mistook them for sheep-flocks, although only black fleeces be seen in these parts of Nejd : then having kindled their gun-matches, they went creeping out to approach them ; but bye and bye I saw the great fowl flag their wings over the wide desert, and the gunners returning, — I asked " from whence are these birds ? " — " Wellah from Mecca," [that is from the middle Red Sea bord.]

This soil was waste gravel, baked hard in the everlasting drought, and glowing under the soles of our bare feet ; the air was like a flame in the sun. An infirm traveller were best to ride always in the climate of Arabia : now by the cruelty of my companions, I went always on foot ; and they themselves would ride. And marching in haste, I must keep them in view, or else they had forsaken the Nasrâny : my plight was such that I thought, after a few days of such efforts, I should rest for ever. So it drew to the burning midst of the afternoon, when, what for the throes in my chest, I thought that the heart would burst. The hot blood at length spouted from my nostrils: I called to the rafîks who went riding together before me to halt, that I might lie down awhile, but they would not hear. Then I took up stones, to receive the dropping gore, lest I should come with a bloody shirt to the next Aarab : besides it might work some alteration in my rafîks' envenomed spirits ! — in this haste there fell blood on my hands. When I overtook them, they seeing my bloody hands drew bridle in astonishment ! *Merjàn:* " Now is not this a kafir ! " — " Are ye not more than kafirs, that abandon the rafîk in the way ? " They passed on now more slowly, and I went by the side of the thelûl. — " If, I added, ye abandon the rafîk, what honourable man will hereafter receive you into their tents ? " Merjàn answered, " There is keeping the faith betwixt the Moslemîn, but not with an enemy of Ullah ! "

They halted bye and bye and Eyâd dismounted : Merjàn who was still sitting upon the thelûl's back struck fire with a flint : I thought it might be for their galliûns, since they had bought a little sweet hameydy, with my money, at Hâyil : but Eyâd kindled the cord of his matchlock. I said, " This is what ? " They answered, " A hare ! " — " Where is your hare ? I say, show me this hare ! " Eyâd had yet to put priming to the eye of his piece ; they stumbled in their words, and remained confused. I said to them, " Did I seem to you like this hare ? by the life of Him who created us, in what instant you show me a gun's mouth, I will lay dead your hare's carcases upon this earth : put out the match ! " he did so. The cool of the evening approached ; we marched on slowly in silence, and doubtless they rolled it in their hollow hearts what might signify that vehement word of the Nasrâny. " Look, I said to them, *rizelleyn !* you two vile dastards, I tell you plainly, that in what moment you drive me to an extremity ye are but dead dogs ; and I will take this carrion thelûl ! "

My adventure in such too unhappy case had been nearly desperate ; nigher than the Syrian borders I saw no certain relief. Syria were a great mark to shoot at, and terribly far off ; and yet upon a good thelûl, fresh watered — for extremities make men bold, and the often escaping from dangers — I had not despaired to come forth ; and one watering in the midway, — if I might once find water, had saved both thelûl and rider. — Or should I ride towards Teyma ; two hundred miles from hence ? — But seeing the great landmarks from this side, how might I know them again ! — and if I found any Aarab westward, yet these would be Bishr, the men's tribesmen. Should I ride eastward in unknown dîras ? or hold over the fearful Nefûd sand billows to seek the Sherarát ? Whithersoever I rode I was likely to faint before I came to any human relief ; and might not strange Aarab sooner kill the stranger, seeing one arrive thus, than receive me ? My eyes were dim with the suffered ophthalmia, and not knowing where to look for them, how in the vastness of the desert landscape should I descry any Aarab ? If I came by the mercy of God to any wells, I might drink drop by drop, by some artifice, but not water the thelûl.

Taking up stones I chafed my blood-stained hands, hoping to wash them when we should come to the Aarab ; but this was the time of the spring pasture, when the great cattle are jezzîn, and oft-times the nomads have no water by them, because there is léban to drink. Eyâd thought the game turned against him ! when we came to a menzil, I might complain of them and he would have a scorn. — " Watch, said he, and when any camel stales, run thou and rinse the hands ; for wellah seeing blood on thy hands, there will none of the Aarab eat with thee." — The urine of camels has been sometimes even drunk by town caravaners in their impatience of thirst. I knew certain of the Medânite tradesmen to the Sherarát, who coming up at midsummer from the W. Sirhàn, and finding the pool dry (above Maan) where they looked to have watered, filled their bowl thus, and let in it a little blood from the camel's ear. I have told the tale to some Beduins ; who answered me, " But to drink this could not help a man, wellah he would die the sooner, it must so wring his bowels."

It was evening, and now we went again by el-Agella. When the sun was setting, we saw another camel troop not far off. The herdsmen trotting round upon some of their lighter beasts were driving-in the great cattle to a sheltered place between two hills ; for this night closed starless over our heads with falling weather. When we came to them the young men had halted their camels and were hissing to them to kneel, — *ikh-kh-kh!* The great brutes fall stiffly, with a sob, upon one or both their knees, and underdoubling the crooked hind legs, they sit ponderously down upon their haunches. Then shuffling forward one and the other fore-knee, with a grating of the harsh gravel under their vast carcase-weight, they settle themselves, and with these pains are at rest ; the fore bulk-weight is sustained upon the *zôra* ; so they lie still and chaw their cud, till the morning sun. The camel leaves a strange (reptile-like) print (of his knees, of the zôra and of the sharp hind quarters), which may be seen in the hard wilderness soil after even a year or two. The smell of the camel is muskish and a little dog-like, the hinder parts being crusted with urine ; yet is the camel more beautiful in our eyes than the gazelles, because man sees in this creature his whole welfare, in the khála. [*v.* Vol. I. pp. 260-1.]

The good herding lads milked for us largely : we drunk deep and far into the night ; and of every sup is made ere morning sweet blood, light flesh and stiff sinews. The rain beat on our backs as we sat about their watch-fire of sticks on the pure sand of the desert ; it lightened and thundered. When we were weary we went apart, where we had left our bags, and lay down in our cloaks, in the night wind and the rain. I lay so long musing of the morrow, that my companions might think me sleeping. They rested in the shelter of the next crag, where I heard them say — my quick hearing helping me in these dangers like the keen eyesight of the nomads — that later in the night they would lift their things on the thelûl and be gone. I let them turn over to sleep: then I rose and went to the place where the fire had been.

The herdsmen lay sleeping in the rain; and I thought I would tell the good lads my trouble. Their sister was herding with them, but in presence of strange menfolk she had sat all this evening obscurely in the rain, and far from the cheerful fire. Now she was warming herself at the dying embers, and cast a little cry as she saw me coming, for all is fear in the desert. 'Peace! I said to her, and I would speak with her brethren.' She took the elder by the shoulder, and rolling him, he awakened immediately, for in this weather he was not well asleep. They all sat up, and the young men, rubbing their faces asked, " Oh, what — ? and wherefore would not the stranger let them rest, and why was I not gone to sleep with my rafîks?" These were manly lads but rude; they had not discerned that I was so much a stranger. I told them, that "those with me were Annezy, Ageylies, who had money to carry me to Kheybar; but their purpose was to forsake me, and perhaps they would abandon me this night." — " Look you (said they, holding their mouths for yawning), we are poor young serving men, and have not much understanding in such things; but if we see them do thee a wrong, we will be for thee. Go now and lie down again, lest they miss thee; and fear nothing, for we are nigh thee."

About two hours before the day Eyâd and Merjàn rose, whispering, and they loaded the things on the couching thelûl; then with a little spurn they raised her silently. " Lead out (I heard Eyâd whisper), and we will come again for the guns." I lay still, and when they were passed forth a few steps I rose to disappoint them: I went with their two matchlocks in my hands to the herdsmen's place, and awaked the lads. The treacherous rafîks returning in the dark could not find their arms: then they came over where I sat now with the herdsmen. — " Ah! said they, Khalîl had of them an unjust suspicion; they did but remove a little to find shelter, for where they lay the wind and rain annoyed them." Their filed tongues prevailed with the poor herding lads, whose careless stars were unused to these nice cases; and heartless in the rain, they consented with the stronger part, — that Khalîl had misconstrued the others' simple meaning. "Well, take, they said, your matchlocks, and go sleep again, all of you; and be content Khalîl. And do ye give him no more occasion, said these upland judges : — and wellah we have not napped all this long night ! "

I went forward with the Ageylies, when we saw the morning light ; Eyâd rode. We had not gone a mile when he threatened to abandon me there in the khála ; he now threatened openly to shoot me, and raised his camel-stick to strike me ; but I laid hand on the thelûl's bridle, and for such another word, I said, I would give him a fall. Merjàn had no part in this violence ; he walked wide of us, for being of various humour, in the last hour he had fallen out with Eyâd. [In their friendly discoursing, the asseverations of these Bishr clansmen (in every clause) were in such sort ; — *Merjàn : Wellah, yâ ibn ammy*, of a truth, my cousin ! *Eyâd : Ullah hadîk*, the Lord direct thee ! — *Wa hyât rukbátak*, by the life of thy neck ! — *Weysh aleyk*, do as thou wilt, what hinders.] — " Well, Khalîl, let be now, said Eyâd, and I swear to thee a menzil of the Aarab is not far off, if the herding lads told us truly."

We marched an hour and found a troop of camels. Whilst their herdsmen milked for us, we met that Aly, who had entertained us before at Gussa ! he was here again abroad to gather forage. He told us a wife of his lay sick with fever : " and have you not a remedy, Khalîl, for the entha " (female) ? *Eyâd :* " Khalîl has kanakîna, the best of medicines for the fever, I have seen it at Medina, and if a man but drink a little he is well anon : what is the cost, Khalîl ? " — " A real." *Aly :* " I thought you would give it me, what is a little medicine, it costs thee nothing, and I will give thee fourpence ; did I not that day regale you with dates ? " Yet because the young wife was dear to him, Aly said he would go on to the Beduins' menzil, and take up a grown lamb for the payment. We came to a *ferîj* of Shammar about nine in the morning. Eyâd remembered some of those Aarab, and he was remembered by them: we heard also that Braitshàn's booths were now at half an hour's distance from hence upon our right hand. This Shammar host brought us to breakfast the best dates of the Jebel villages, clear as cornelians, with a bowl of his spring léban. Leaving there our baggage, without any mistrust (as amongst Aarab), we went over to Braitshàn's ferîj, — my rafîks hoping there to drink kahwa. A few locusts were flying and alighting in this herbage.

Sitting with Braitshàn in the afternoon, when Eyâd had walked to another booth, and Merjàn was with the thelûl, I spoke to him of my treacherous companions, and to *Ferrah*, an honest old man whom we had found here before. " What is, I asked, your counsel ? and I have entered to-day under your roof." They answered each other gravely, " Seeing that Khalîl has required of us the protection, we ought to maintain his right." But within a while they repented of their good disposition, lest it should be said, that they had taken part with the Nasrâny against a ' Míslim ' ; and they ended with these words, ' They could not go betwixt *khuiân* (companions in the journey).' They said to Eyâd, when he arrived, ' That since he had carried only my light bags, and I was come down from Hâyil upon my feet, and he had received five reals to convey me to Kheybar, and that in every place he threatened to abandon me ; let him render three reals, and leave me with the Aarab, and take the other two for his hire, and go his way.' Eyâd answered, " If I am to blame, it is because of the feebleness of my thelûl." — " Then, why, I exclaimed, didst thou take five reals to carry a passenger upon the mangy carrion ? " The Beduins laughed ; yet some said, I should not use so sharp words with my wayfellow, — " Khalîl, the Aarab love the fair speaking." I knew this was true, and that my plain right would seem less in their shallow eyes than the rafîks' smooth words.—*Eyâd :* " Well, be it thus." " Thou hast heard his promise, said they, return with *khûak*, thy way-brother, and all shall be well." — Empty words of Arabs ! the sun set ; my rafîks departed, and I soon followed them.

Our Shammar host had killed the sacrifice of hospitality : his mutton was served in a great trencher, upon temmn boiled in the broth. But the man sat aloof, and took no part in our evening talk ; whether displeased to see a kafir under his tent-cloth, or because he misliked my Annezy rafîks. I told Aly he might have the kanakîna, a gift, so he helped me to my right with Eyâd ; 'He would,' he answered.—I wondered to see him so much at his ease in the booths of the Aarab ! but his parents were Beduw, and Aly left an orphan at Gussa, had been bred up there. He bought of them on credit a good yearling ram to give me : they call it here *tully*, and the ewe lamb *rókhal*.

Aly brought me his tully on the morrow, when we were ready to depart ; and said, " See, O Khalîl, my present ! " — " I look for the fulfilment of your last night's words ; and, since you make them void, I ought not to help him in a little thing, who recks not though I perish !"

The fellow, who weighed not my grief, held himself scorned by the Nasrâny: my bags were laid upon the thelûl, and he gazed after us and murmured. The dewless aurora was rising from those waste hills, without the voice of any living creature in a weary wilderness; and I followed forth the riders, Eyâd and Merjàn.

The gravel stones were sharp; the soil in the sun soon glowed as an hearth under my bare feet; the naked pistol (hidden under my tunic) hanged heavily upon my panting chest; the air was breathless, and we had nothing to drink. It was hard for me to follow on foot, notwithstanding the weak pace of their thelûl: a little spurn of a rider's heel and she had trotted out of my sight! Hard is this human patience! showing myself armed, I might compel them to deliver the dromedary; but who would not afterward be afraid to become my rafîk? If I provoked them, they (supposing me unarmed), might come upon me with their weapons; and must I then take their poor lives! — but were that just? — in this faintness of body and spirit I could not tell; I thought that a man should forsake life rather than justice, and pollute his soul with outrage. I went training and bearing on my camel-stick, — a new fatigue — to leave a furrow in the hard gravel soil; lest if those vile-spirited rafîks rode finally out of my sight, I should be lost in the khála. I thought that I might come again, upon this trace, to Braitshàn's booths, and the Aarab. I saw the sun mount to high noon; and hoped from every new brow to descry pasturing camels, or some menzil of the Nomads.

An hour further I saw camels that went up slowly through a hollow ground to the watering. There I came up to my rafîks: they had stayed to speak with the herdsmen, who asked of the desert behind us. The Nomads living in the open wilderness are greedy of tidings; and if herdsmen see passengers go by peaceably in the desert they will run and cry after them, 'What news, ho! — Tell us of the soil, that ye have passed through? — Which Aarab be there? — Where lodge they now? — Of which waters drink they? — And, the face of them is whitherward? — Which herbs have ye seen? and what is the soil betwixt them and us? found ye any bald places (máhal)? — With whom lodged ye last night? — heard ye there any new thing, or as ye came by the way?' Commonly the desert man delivers himself after this sort with a loud suddenness of tongue, as he is heated with running; and then only (when he is nigher hand) will he say more softly, 'Peace be with thee.' — The passengers are sure to receive him mildly; and they condescend to all his asking, with *Wellah Fulàn!* 'Indeed thou Such-an-one.' And at every meeting with herdmen they say over, with a set face, the same things, in the same words, ending with the formal *wa ent sélim*, ' and thou being in peace.' — The tribesman hardly bids the strangers farewell, when he has turned the back ; or he stands off, erect and indifferent, and lets pass the tarkîeh.

I stayed now my hand upon the thelûl ; and from the next high grounds we saw a green plain before us. Our thirst was great, and Eyâd showed with his finger certain crags which lay beyond ; ' We should find pools in them,' he said (after the late showers) : but I marked in the ground [better than the inept Beduin rafîks] that no rain had fallen here in these days. We found only red pond-water, — so foul that the thirsting thelûl refused to drink. I saw there the forsaken site of a winter encampment : the signs are shallow trenching, and great stones laid about the old steads of their beyts. Now we espied camels, which had been hidden by the hollow soil, and then a worsted village ! My rafîks considered the low building of those tents, and said, " They must be of Harb ! " As we approached they exclaimed, " But see how their beyts be stretched nigh together ! they are certainly Heteym."

We met with an herdsman of theirs driving his camels to water, and hailed him — " Peace ! and ho ! what Aarab be those yonder ? " — The man answered with an unwonted frankness, " I (am an) Harby dwelling with this ferîj, and they are Heteym." — Eyâd began to doubt ! for were they of Kâsim's Heteym (enemies of the Dowla at Kheybar), he thought he were in danger. Yet now they could not go back ; if he turned from them his mangy thelûl might be quickly overtaken. The Ageylies rode on therefore with the formal countenance of guests that arrive at a nomad menzil. The loud dogs of the encampment leapt out against us with hideous affray ; and as we came marching by the beyts, the men and the hareem who sat within, only moving their eyes, silently regarded us passing strangers. We halted before the greater booth in the row, which was of ten or twelve tents.

Eyâd and Merjàn alighted, set down the packs and tied up the knee of the thelûl. Then we walked together, with the solemnity of guests, to the open half of the tent, which is the men's apartment ; here at the right hand looking forth : it is not always on the same side among the people of the desert. We entered, and this was the sheykh's beyt. Five or six men were sitting within on the sand, with an earnest demeanour (and that was because some of them knew me)! They rose to receive us, looking silently upon me, as if they would say, "Art not thou that Nasrâny?"

The nomad guest — far from his own — enters the strange beyt of hospitality, with demure looks, in which should appear some gentle token of his own manly worth. We sat down in the booth, but these uncivil hosts — Heteymies — kept their uneasy silence. They made it strange with us; and my rafîks beat their camel-sticks upon the sand and looked down: the Heteymies gazed side-long and lowering upon us. At length, despising their mumming, and inwardly burning with thirst, I said to the sly fellow who sat beside me, a comely ill-blooded Heteymy and the host's brother, "*Eskîny má*, give me a little water to drink." He rose unwillingly; and fetched a bowl of foul clay-water. When I only sipped this unwholesome bever: "*Rueyht* (he said maliciously), hast allayed thy thirst?" My companions asked for the water, and the bowl was sent round. "Drink! said the Heteymies, for there is water enough." At length there was set before us a bowl of mereesy shards and a little lében: then first they broke their unlucky silence. "I think we should know thee (quoth he of the puddle water); art not thou the Nasrâny that came to Kâsim's from Ibn Rashîd?"

They had alighted yesterday: they call the ground *Âul*, of those crags with water. The (granitic) landscape is named *Ghrólfa*; and *Sfá*, of a plutonic mountain, which appeared eastward over the plain seven miles distant; and they must send thither to fetch their water. The altitude was here 4600 feet. The flocks were driven in at the going down of the sun; and bye and bye we saw *Maatuk* — that was our host's name — struggling to master a young ram. Eyâd sent Merjàn with the words of course, "Go and withhold him." Merjàn made as though he would help the ram, saying, with the Arabs' smooth (effeminate) dissimulation, 'It should not be, nay by Ullah we would never suffer it.' "Oho! young man, let me alone, answered the Heteymy, may I not do as I please with mine own?" and he drew his slaughter-sheep to the woman's side. — Two hours later Maatuk bore in the boiled ram brittled, upon a vast trencher of temmn. He staggered under the load and caught his breath, for the hospitable man was asthmatic.

Eyâd said when we were sitting alone, "Khalîl we leave thee here, and *el-Kasîm* lies behind yonder mountains; these are good folk, and they will send thee thither." — "But how may ye, having no water-skin, pass over to the Auájy?" — "Well, we will put in to Thurghrud for a girby." — "Ullah remember your treachery, the Aarab will blame you who abandon your rafîk, also the Pasha will punish you; and as you have robbed me of those few reals he may confiscate some of your arrears." — "Oh say not so, Khalîl! in this do not afflict me; and at our departure complain not: let not the hosts hear your words, or they will not bring you forward upon your journey."

When the rest were sleeping I saw Maatuk go forth; — I thought this host must be good, although an Heteymy. I went to him and said I would speak with him. — "Shall we sit down here then, and say on," — for the Arabs think they may the better take counsel in their weak heads when sitting easily upon the béled. I told him how the rafîks had made me journey hitherto on my feet (an hundred miles) from Hâyil; how often they had threatened in the midst of the khála to forsake me, and even to kill me: should I march any longer with them? — no! I was to-day a guest in his tent; I asked him to judge between us, and after that to send me safely to el-Kasîm. — "All this will I do; though I cannot myself send thee to el-Kasîm, but to some Harb whose tents are not far from us, eastward; and we may find there someone to carry thee thither. Now, when the morning is light and you see these fellows ready to set forward, then say to me, *dakhîlak,* and we shall be for thee, and if they resist we will detain their thelûl." — "Give thy hand, and swear to me." — "Ay, I swear, said he, wullah, wullah!" but he drew back his hand; for how should they keep touch with a Nasrâny! — But in the night time whilst I slept my companions also held their council with Maatuk: and that was as between men of the same religion, and Maatuk betrayed me for his pipeful of sweet hameydy tobacco.

When it was day those rafîks laid my bags upon the thelûl, and I saw Eyâd give to Maatuk a little golden hameydy, for which the Heteymy thanked him benignly. Then, taking up their mantles and matchlocks, they raised the thelûl with a spurn: Merjàn having the bridle in his hand led forth, with *nesellim âleyk.* As they made the first steps, I said to Maatuk, "My host detain them, and *ana dakhîl-ak!* — do justly." — "Ugh! go with them, answered Maatuk (making it strange), what justice wouldst thou have, Nasrâny?" — "Where be thy last night's promises? Is there no keeping faith, Heteymy? listen! I will not go with them." But I saw that my contention would be vain ; for there was some intelligence between them.

When Eyâd and Merjàn were almost out of sight, the men in the tent cried to me, " Hasten after them and your bags, or they will be quite gone." — " I am your dakhîl, and you are forsworn ; but I will remain here." — " No ! " — and now they began to thrust me (they were Heteym). Maatuk caught up a tent-stake, and came on against me ; his brother, the sly villain, ran upon me from the backward with a cutlass. " Ha ! exclaimed Maatuk, I shall beat out his brains." — " Kill him — kill him ! " cried other frenetic voices (they were young men of Harb and Annezy dwelling in this ferîj). " Let me alone, cries his brother, and I will chop off the head of a cursed Nasrâny." " I cannot, I said to them, contend with so many, though ye be but dastards ; put down your weapons. And pray good woman ! [to Maatuk's wife who looked to me womanly over her curtain, and upbraided their violence] pour me out a little léban ; and let me go from this cursed place." — " Ah ! what wrong, she said to them, ye do to chase away the stranger ! it is harrâm, and, Maatuk, he is thy dakhîl :" she hastened to pour me out to drink. " Drink ! said she, and handed over the bowl, drink ! and may it do thee good ; " and in this she murmured a sweet proverb of their dîra, *widd el-ghrarîb ahlhu*, " the desire of the stranger is to his own people ; speed the stranger home."

" Up, I said, Maatuk, and come with me to call the Ageylies back, my strength is lost, and alone I cannot overtake them." — " I come, and wellah will do thee right with them." When we had gone hastily a mile, I said : " I can follow no further, and must sit down here ; go and call them if thou wilt." Great is their natural humanity : this Heteymy, who was himself infirm, bade me rest ; and he limped as fast as he might go and shouted after them, — he beckoned to my late rafîks ! and they tardily returned to us. " Maatuk, I said, this is the end of my journey to-day : Eyâd shall give me here Aneybar's schedule of safe conduct, and he shall restore me three reals ; also, none of you chop words with me, for I am a weary man, whom ye have driven to extremities." — *Maatuk* (to Eyâd) : " What say you to this ? it seems your rafîk is too weary to go any more, will ye carry him then on the thelûl ? " — " We will not carry him ; we can only sometimes ride upon her ourselves ; yet I will carry him — it is but half a day — to Thúrghrud, and leave him there ! " This I rejected. *Maatuk :* " Well, he shall stay with us ; and I will send Khalîl forward to the Harb with *Ibn Náhal*, for his money. Now then I say restore his money, let it be two reals, and the paper from Ibn Rashîd, — what, man ! it is his own." — *Eyâd :* " I am willing to give up the paper to Khalîl, so he write me a discharge, which may acquit me before the Pasha ; but I will not restore a real of the silver, I have spent it, — what, man ! wouldst thou have my clothes ? " — *Maatuk :* " We shall not let thee depart so ! give Khalîl one real, and lay down the schedule." — *Eyâd :* " Well, I accept : " he took out a crown, and, " This is all I have left, said he ; let Khalîl give me fourpence, for this is fourpence more than the mejîdie." — " You may think yourselves well escaped for fourpence, which is mine own : take that silver, Maatuk, *arrabûn* (earnest-money) of the three reals for conveying me as thou said'st to the Harb." He received it, but the distrustful wretch made me give him immediately the other two. I recovered thus Aneybar's safe-conduct, and that was much for my safety in the wild country. Eyâd insisted for his written discharge, and I wrote, " Eyâd, the Ageyly, of Bejaida, Bishr, bound for five reals by Abdullah Siruân, lieutenant at Kheybar, to convey me to Hâyil and engaged there by Aneybar, Ibn Rashîd's deputy, for which he received other five, to carry me again to Kheybar, here treacherously abandons me at Âul, under Sfá, in the Shammar dîra." The Ageylies took the seal from my hand, and set it to themselves twenty times, to make this instrument more sure : then Maatuk made them turn back to the menzil with my baggage. So Eyâd and Merjàn departed ; yet not without some men's crying out upon them from the tents, for their untruth to the rafîk.

These Heteymies were heavy-hearted fanatics, without the urbanity of Beduins : and Maatuk had sold me for a little tobacco. For an hour or two he embalmed his brain with the reeking drug ; after that he said, " Khalîl, *dakhîl-ak*, hast thou not, I beseech thee a little dokhân ? ah ! say not that thou hast none ; give me but a little, and I will restore to thee those three reals, and carry thee on my thelûl to Ibn Náhal." — " I have no dokhân, though you cut off my head." — " Khalîl, yet fill my galliûn once, and I will forgive thee all ! " — Had I bought a little tobacco at Hâyil, I had sped well.

One Annezy and three Harb beyts were in this Heteymy ferîj. Some of those strangers asked me in the afternoon, what tribesmen were the rafîks that had forsaken me. I answered, " Auájy and Bejaijy of Bishr." — " Hadst thou said this before to us, they had not parted so ! we had seized their thelûl, for they are *gôm*, and we have not eaten with them." Said one : " Whilst they talked I thought the speech of the younger sounded thus, ay billah it was Bejaijy." — " You might overtake them." — " Which way went they ? " — " To Baitha Nethîl, and from thence they will cross to the Auájy." Eyâd had this charge, from Kheybar to fetch the Siruân's and the Bîshy's thelûl's. [Although those Beduw were enemies of the Dowla, the Ageyl dromedaries had been privately put out to pasture among them.] In that quarter of the wilderness was sprung (this year) a plentiful *rabîa*, after the autumnal rains [Vol. I. pp. 613, 626], " so that the camels might lie down with their fills at noonday." — " How now ? (said one to another) wilt thou be my rafîk if the 'bil come home this evening ? shall we take our thelûls and ride after them : they will journey slowly with their mangy beast ; if the Lord will, we may overtake them, and cut their throats." — " Look (I said) I have told you their path, go and take the thelûl if you be able, but you shall not do them any hurt." I was in thought of their riding till the nightfall : but the camels came not.

Of Ibn Náhal's Aarab they had no late tidings. They spoke much in my hearing of Ibn Náhal ; and said the hareem — that were the best hearted in this encampment, " His tent is large, so large ! and he is rich, so rich, — ouf ! all is there liberality : and when thou comest to his tent say, ' Send me, O Ibn Náhal, to el-Kasîm,' and he will send thee."

Maatuk and his evil-eyed brother were comely ; and their sister — she dwelt in Maatuk's beyt — was one of the goodliest works of nature ; only (such are commonly the Heteymàn) not well coloured. She went freshly clad ; and her beauty could not be hid by the lurid face-clout : yet in these her flowering years of womanhood she remained unwedded ! The thin-witted young Annezy man of the North, who sat all day in the sheykh's beyt, fetched a long breath as oft as she appeared — as it were a dream of their religion — in our sight ; and plucking my mantle he would say, " Sawest thou the like ere now ! " This sheykhess, when she heard their wonted *ohs !* and *ahs !* cast upon them her flagrant great eyes, and smiled without any disdain. — She, being in stature as a goddess, yet would there no Beduwy match with her (an Heteymîa) in the way of honourable marriage ! But dissolute Beduins will mingle their blood out of wedlock with the beautiful Heteymîas; and I have heard the comely ribald Eyâd mock on thus, making his voice small like a woman's, — " Then will she come and say humbly to the man, ' Marry me, for I am with child, and shield me from the blame.' "

There was an Heteymy in this menzil who returned after an absence: I enquired, ' Where had he been in the meanwhile ? ' — " Wellah, at el-Hâyat; it is but one long day upon the thelûl, and I have wedded there a (black) wife." — " Wherefore thus ? " — " Wellah I wished for her." — " And what was the bride money ? " — " I have spent nothing." — " Or gave she thee anything ? " — " Ay billah! some palms." — " She has paid for thee!" " Well, why not ? " — " Will not thy children be black like slaves, *abîd*? " — " She is blackish-red, her children will be reddish." — " And what hast thou to do with village wives ? " — " Eigh! I shall visit her now and then; and when I come there go home to mine own house: " — and cries the half-witted nomad, " Read, Khalîl, if this thing which I have done be lawful or unlawful ? " [The negro village el-Hâyat is in the S.-E. borders of the (Kheybar) Harra; and a journey from thence toward Medina is the palm hamlet Howeyat. The (Annezy) Beduin landlords in both settlements (*v.* p. 42) were finally expulsed by Abeyd ibn Rashîd; because not conforming themselves to the will of the Emir, they had received their Ateyba neighbours — who were his enemies — as their *dakhîls*, and would have protected them against him.]

The camels were azab, Maatuk's thelûl was with them; and till their coming home we could not set out for Ibn Náhal. Some Solubba rode-in one morrow on their asses; and our people gave them pots and kettles (which are always of brass), to carry away, for tinning. I found two young Solubbies gelding an ass behind the tents ! — (the Aarab have only entire horses). The gipsies said laughing, ' This beast was an ass overmuch, and they had made him chaste!' I found an old Solubby sitting in Maatuk's tent, a sturdy greybeard; his grim little eyes were fastened upon me. I said to him, " What wouldst thou ? " — " I was thinking, that if I met with thee alone in the khála, I would kill thee." — " Wherefore, old tinker ? " — " For thy clothing and for any small things that might be with thee, Nasrâny; — if the wolf found thee in the wilderness, wert thou not afraid ? " — The Solubba offend no man, and none do them hurt [*v.* Vol. I. p. 324). I enquired of these: " Is it true that ye eat the sheep or camel which is dead of itself ? " — " We eat it, and how else might we that have no cattle eat meat in the menzils of the Aarab! Wellah, Khalîl, is this halàl or harrâm?"

A day or two after Maatuk was for no more going to Ibn Náhal; he said, " Shall I carry thee to el-Hâyat? or else I might leave thee at Semîra or at Seleyma." But I answered, " To Ibn Náhal;" and his good wife Noweyr, poor woman, looking over her tent cloth, spoke for me every day; "Oh! said she, ye are not good, and Maatuk, Maatuk! why hinder Khalîl? perform thy promise, and *widd el-ghrarîb beledhu aan el-ájnaby* (it is a refrain of the Nomad maidens ' speed the stranger on his way to his own people ;' or be it, ' the heart of the stranger is in his own country, and not in a strange land.' ") The good hareem, her neighbours, answered with that pious word of fanatical Arabia, ' We have a religion, and they have a religion ; every man is justified in his own religion.' Noweyr was one of those good women that bring the blessing to an household. Sometimes I saw her clay-pale face in their tent, without the veil ; though not in prosperous health she was daily absent in the khála, from the forenoon till the mid-afternoon ; and when I asked her wherefore she wearied herself thus? she said, and sighed, " I must fetch water from the Sfá to-day, and to-morrow visit the camels ; and else Maatuk beats me." Maatuk's hospitality was more than any Beduwy had showed me : Noweyr gave me to drink of her léban ; and he bade me reach up my hand when I was hungry to take of her new mereesy shards, which were spread to dry in the sun upon their worsted roof. If the camels came home he milked a great bowlful for the stranger, saying, it was his sádaka, or meritorious human kindness, for God's sake. In these evenings I have seen the sporting goats skip and stand, often two and three together, upon the camels' steep chines : and the great beasts that lay chawing the cud in the open moonlight, took no more heed of them than cattle in our fields, when crows or starlings light upon them.

Maatuk was afraid to further me, because of Ibn Rashîd : and they told me a strange tale. A year or two ago these Heteym carried on their camels some strangers, whom they called " Nasâra " ! — I know not whither. The Emir hearing of it, could hardly be entreated not to punish them cruelly, and take their cattle. — " Ay, this is true, O Khalîl ! " added Moweyr. — " But what Nasrânies ! and from whence ? " — " Wellah, they could not tell, the strangers were Nasâra, as they heard." The Arabs are barren-minded in the emptiness of the desert life, and retchless of all that pertains not to their living. " Nasâra," might signify in their mouths no more than " aliens not of the orthodox belief." *Maatuk:* " Ibn Rashîd is not thy friend, and the country is dangerous; abide with me, Khalîl, till the Haj come and return again, next spring." " How might I live those many months? is there food in the khála?" — " You may keep my camels." — " But how under the flaming sun, in the long summer season?" — " When it is hot thou canst sit in my booth, and drink lében; and I will give thee a wife." — Hearing his words, I rejoiced, that the Aarab no longer looked upon me as some rich stranger amongst them! When he pronounced ' wife', the worthy man caught his breath! — could he offer a bint of Heteym to so white a man? so he said further, " I will give thee an *Harbîa*."

" Years ago, quoth Maatuk, there came into our parts a Moghreby [like Khalîl], — wellah we told little by him; but the man bought and sold, and within a while we saw him thriving. He lived with Harb, and took a wife of their daughters; and the Moor had flocks and camels, all gotten at the first and increased of his traffic in samn and clothing. Now he is dead, his sons dwell with Harb, and they are well-faring." We sat in the tent, and they questioned me, ' Where is thy nation?' I shewed them the setting sun, and said we might sail thither in our shipping, *sefn*. — " Shipping (they said one to another) is *zŷmát*; but O Khalîl, it is there, in the West, we have heard to be the Kafir Nation! and that from thence the great danger shall come upon el-Islam: beyond how many floods dwell ye, we heard seven; and how many thelûl journeys be ye behind the Sooltàn?" — Coffee-drinking, though the Heteymàn be welfaring more than the neighbour Beduins, is hardly seen, even in sheykhs' tents, amongst them: there was none in Maatuk's ferîj. Aarab of Ibn Rashîd, their only enemies are the Ateyba; and pointing to the eastward, " All the peril, said Maatuk, is from thence!" — These Heteym (unlike their kindred inhabiting nearer to Medina) are never cheesemakers.

He is a free man that may carry all his worldly possession upon one of his shoulders: now I secretly cast away the superfluous weight of my books, ere a final effort to pass out of Arabia, and (saving *Die alte Geographie Arabiens*, and Zehme's *Arabien seit hundert Jahren*) gave them honourable burial in a thób's hole; heaped in sand, and laid thereon a great stone. — In this or another generation, some wallowing camel or the streaming winter rain may discover to them that dark work of the Nasrâny. Six days the Nomad tents were standing at Âul, tomorrow they would dislodge; and Maatuk now consented to carry the stranger to Ibn Náhal; for Noweyr, lifting her pale face above the woman's curtain, many times daily exhorted him, saying, "Eigh, Maatuk! detain not Khalîl against his liking; speed the stranger home."

Their camels were come; and when the morning broke, 'Art thou ready, quoth Maatuk, and I will bring the thelûl; but in faith I know not where Ibn Náhal may be found." Noweyr put a small skin of samn in her husband's wallet; to be, she said, for the stranger. We mounted, Maatuk's sly brother brought us on our journey; and hissed his last counsels in my rafîk's ear, which were not certainly to the advantage of the Nasrâny: — "Aye! aye!" quoth Maatuk. We rode on a hurr, or dromedary male (little used in these countries), and which is somewhat rougher riding. By this the sun was an hour high; and we held over the desert toward the Sfá mountain. After two hours we saw another menzil of Heteym, sheykh *Ibn Dammûk*, and their camels pasturing in the plain. Maatuk called the herdsman to us to tell and take the news; but they had heard nothing lately of Ibn Náhal.

The waste beyond was nearly máhal; we rode by some granite blocks, disposed baywise, and the head laid south-eastward, as it were towards Mecca: it might be taken in these days for a praying place. But Maatuk answered, " Such works are of the ancients in these dîras, — the B. Taâmir." We saw a very great thób's burrow, and my rafîk alighted to know ' if the edible monster were at home : ' and in that, singing cheerfully, he startled a troop of gazelles. Maatuk shrilled through his teeth and the beautiful deer bounded easily before us; then he yelled like a wild man, and they bent themselves to their utmost flight. The scudding gazelles stood still anon, in the hard desert plain of gravel, and gazed back like timid damsels, to know what had made them afraid. — In Syria, I have seen mares " that had outstripped gazelles ; " but whether this were spoken in the ordinary figure of their Oriental speech, which we call a falsehood, I have not ascertained. The nomads take the fawns with their greyhounds, which are so swift, that I have seen them overrun the small desert hare almost in a moment. I asked Maatuk, Where was his matchlock ? — He lost it, he answered, to a ghrazzu of Ateyba — that was a year ago; and now he rode but with that short cutlass, wherewith his brother had once threatened the Nasrâny. He sang in their braying-wise [which one of their ancient poets, Antara, compared to the hum of flies!] as we passed over the desert at a trot, and quavering his voice (*î-î-î-î*) to the wooden jolting of the thelûl saddle. Maatuk told me (with a sheykh's pride), that those Beduin households in his ferîj had been with him several years. In the midsummer time all the ferjân of the Ibn Barrák Heteym (under the sheykh Kâsim) assemble and pitch together near the Wady er-Rummah, " where, said he, one may find water, under the sand, at the depth of this camel-stick." — Wide we have seen to be the dispersion of the Heteym : there are some of the B. Rashîd far in the North, near Kuweyt!

Now before us appeared a steep granite mountain *Genna*; and far upon our left hand lay the watering *Benàna*, between mountains. We came after mid-day to a great troop of Heteym camels : but here was the worst grazing ground (saving the Sinai country) that I ever beheld in the wilderness ; for there was nothing sprung besides a little wormwood. The herd boys milked their nâgas for us; but that milk with the froth was like wormwood for bitterness [and such is the goats' milk in this pasture]. The weleds enquired in their headlong manner, " *El-khábar? weysh el-ellûm?* What tidings from your parts, what news is there? " — " Well, it may please Ullah." — " And such and such Aarab, beyond and beside you, where be they now? where is such a sheykh encamped, and of what waters drink they? is there word of any ghrazzus? And the country which you have passed through? — say is it bare and empty, or such that it may satisfy the cattle? Which herbs, saw ye in it, O Maatuk? What is heard of the Emir? and where left ye your households? — auh! and the ferjân and Aarab thou hast mentioned, what is reported of their pasture?" — *Maatuk :* " And what tidings have ye for us, which Aarab are behind you? what is heard of any ghrazzus? Where is Ibn Náhal? where be your booths?"

An hour or two later we found another herd of Heteym camels : and only two children kept them! Maatuk made a gesture, stroking down his beard, when we rode from them ; and said, " Thus we might have taken wellah every head of them, had they been our enemies' cattle!" Yet all this country lies very open to the inroads of Ateyba who are beyond the W. er-Rummah. Not much later we came to a menzil of Heteym, and alighted for that day. — These tent-dwellers knew me, and said to Maatuk, ' I had journeyed with a tribesman of theirs, Ghroceyb, my name was Khalîl ; and Kâsim's Aarab purchased medicines of me, which they found to be such as I had foretold them ; I was one that deceived not the Aarab.' As for Ibn Náhal, they heard he was gone over " The Wady," into the Ateyba border, (forsaken by them of late years for dread of Ibn Rashîd). The land-height was here 4200 feet, shelving to the W. er-Rummah.

At daybreak we mounted, and came after an hour's riding to other Heteym tents. All the wilderness was barren, almost máhal, and yet, full of the nomads' worsted hamlets at this season. Maatuk found a half-brother in this menzil, with their old mother ; and we alighted to sit awhile with them. The man brought fresh goat-milk and bade me drink, — making much of it, because his hospitality was *whole milk* ; 'The samn, he said, had not been taken.' Butter is the poor nomads' money, wherewith they may buy themselves clothing and town wares ; therefore they use to pour out only buttermilk to the guest. — We rode further ; the (granite) desert was now sand soil, in which after winter rain there springs the best wild pasture, and we began to find good herbage. We espied a camel troop feeding under the mountain Genna, and crossed to them to enquire the herdsman's tidings ; but Maatuk, who was timid, presently drew bridle, not certainly knowing what they were. " Yonder I said, be only black camels, they are Harb ; " [the great cattle of the south and middle tribes, Harb, Meteyr, Ateybân, are commonly swarthy or black, and none of them dun-coloured]. Maatuk answered, it was God's truth, and wondered from whence had I this lore of the desert. We rode thither and found them to be Harb indeed. The young men told us that Ibn Náhal had alighted by Seleymy to-day ; and they milked for us. We rode from them, and saw the heads of the palms of the desert village, and passed by a trap mountain, *Chebád*.

Before us, over a sandy descending plain, appeared a flat mountain *Debby* ; and far off behind Debby I saw the blue coast of some wide mountain, *el-Âlem*. " Thereby, said Maatuk, lies the way to Medina, — four days' thelûl riding." We went on in the hot noon ; and saw another camel troop go feeding under the jebel ; we rode to them and alighted to drink more milk and enquire the herdsmen's tidings. They were Harb also, and shewed us a rocky passage in the mountain to go over to Ibn Náhal. But I heard of them an adverse tiding : ' The B. *Aly* (that is all the Harb N. and E. from hence) were drawing southwards, and the country was left empty, before a ghrazzu of Ibn Saûd and the Ateyba!' — How now might I pass forward to el-Kasîm? We saw a multitude of black booths pitched under Debby; 'They were *Aûf*,' answered the herdsmen, — come up hither from the perpetual desolation of their Hejâz marches, between the Harameyn; for they heard that the rabîa was in these parts. — *El-Aûf!* that is, we have seen, a name abhorred even among their brethren; for of Aûf are the purse-cutters and pillers of the poor pilgrims. And here, then, according to a distich of the western tribes, I was come to the ends of the (known) world! for says one of their thousand rhymed saws, ' *El-Aûf warrahum ma fî shûf*, nothing is seen beyond Aûf.' I beheld indeed a desert world of new and dreadful aspect! black camels, and uncouth hostile mountains; and a vast sand wilderness shelving towards the dire imposter's city!

Genna is a landmark of the Beduin herdsmen; in the head are pools of rain-water. Descending in the steep passage we encountered a gaunt desert man riding upward on a tall thelûl and leading a mare: he bore upon his shoulder the wavering horseman's shelfa. Maatuk shrank timidly in the saddle; that witch-like armed man was a startling figure, and might be an Aûfy. Roughly he challenged us, and the rocks resounded the magnanimous utterance of his leathern gullet: he seemed a manly soul who had fasted out his life in that place of torment which is the Hejâz between the Harameyn, so that nothing remained of him but the terrific voice! — wonderfully stern and beetle-browed was his dark visage. He espied a booty in my bags; and he beheld a stranger. "Tell me, he cries, what men ye be?" — Maatak made answer meekly, "Heteymy I, and thou?" — "I Harby, and ugh! cries the perilous anatomy, who he with thee?" — "A Shâmy trading among the Aarab." — "Aye well, and I see him to be a Shâmy, by the guise of his clothing." He drew his mare to him, and in that I laid hand to the pistol in my bosom, lest this Death-on-a-horse should have lifted his long spear against us. Maatuk reined aside; but the Harby struck his dromedary, and passed forth.

We looked down from the mountain over a valley-like plain, and saw booths of the Aarab. "Khalîl, quoth Maatuk, the people is ignorant, I shall not say to any of them, ' He is a Nasrâny;' and say it not thyself. Wellah I may not go with thee to Ibn Náhal's beyt, but will bring thee to Aarab that are pitched by him." — "You shall carry me to Ibn Náhal himself. Are not these tribesmen very strait in religion? I would not light at another tent ; and thou wilt not abandon thy rafîk." — " But Khalîl there is an old controversy betwixt us for camels ; and if I went thither he might seize this thelûl." — " I know well thou speakest falsely." — " Nay, by Him who created this camel stick ! " — But the nomad was forsworn ! The Nejûmies had said to me at Kheybar, " It is well that Khalîl never met with Harb ; they would certainly have cut his throat : " — they spoke of Harb tribesmen between the sacred cities, wretches black as slaves, that have no better trade than to run behind the pilgrim-caravans clamouring, *bakshîsh* !

Here I came to upland Harb, and they are tributaries of Ibn Rashîd ; but such distinctions cannot be enquired out in a day from the ignorant. In the Nejd Harb I have found the ancient Arabian mind, more than in Annezy tribesmen. The best of the Ageyl at Kheybar was a young Harby, gentle and magnanimous, of an ascetical humour ; he was seldom seen at Abdullah's coffee drinkings, and yet he came in sometimes to Amm Mohammed, who was his half-tribesman, though in another kindred. One day he said boasting, " We the B. Sâlem are better than ye ; for we have nothing Frenjy [of outlandish usage, or wares fetched in by Turks and foreign pilgrims to the Holy Places], saving this tobacco." — Now Maatuk held over to three or four booths, which stood apart in the valley-plain ; he alighted before them, and said he would leave me there. An elder woman came out to us, where we sat on the sand beside the yet unloaded thelûl ; and then a young wife from the beyt next us. Very cleanly-gay she seemed, amongst Aarab, in her new calico kirtle of blue broidered with red worsted. — Was not this the bride, in her marriage garment, of some Beduin's fortunate youth ? She approached with the grace of the desert and, which is seldom seen, with some dewy freshness in her cheeks, — it might be of an amiable modesty ; and she was a lovely human flower in that inhuman desolation. She asked, with a young woman's diffidence, ' What would we ? ' Maatuk responded to the daughter of Harb, " Salaam, and if ye have here any sick persons, this is an hakîm from es-Sham ; one who travels about with his medicines among the Aarab, and is very well skilled : now he seeks who will convey him to el-Kasîm. I leave this Shâmy at your beyt, for I cannot myself carry him further ; and ye will send him forward." She called the elder woman to counsel ; and they answered, ' Look you ! the men are in the khála, and we are women alone. It were better that ye went over to Ibn Náhal ! — and see his great booth standing yonder!' — *Maatuk:* "I will leave him here; and when they come home (at evening) your men can see to it." But I made him mount with me to ride to Ibn Náhal.

We alighted at Ibn Náhal's great beyt; and entered with the solemnity and greeting of strangers. Ibn Náhal's son and a few young men were sitting on the sand in this wide hanging-room of worsted. We sat down and they whispered among them, that 'I was some runaway soldier, of the Dowla' [from the Holy Cities or el-Yémen]: then I heard them whisper 'Nay, I was that Nasrâny!' — They would not question with us till we had drunk kahwa.

A nomad woman of a grim stature stood upbraiding without Ibn Náhal's great booth! she prophesied bitter words in the air, and no man regarded. Her burden was of the decay of hospitality now-a-days! and Ibn Náhal [a lean soul, under a sleek skin], was gone over to another tent to be out of earshot of the wife-man's brawling. The Beduw commonly bear patiently the human anger, *zaal*, as it were trouble sent by the will of God upon them: the Aarab are light even in their ire, and there is little weight in their vehement words. If any Nomad tribesman revile his sheykh, he as a nobleman will but shrink the shoulders and go further off, or abide till others cry down the injurious mouth. But evil tongues, where the Arabs dwell in towns, cannot so walk at their large: the common railer against the sheukh in Hâyil, or in Boreyda, would be beaten by the sergeants of the Emir.

The coffee mortar rang out merrily for the guests in Ibn Náhal's booth: and now I saw the great man and his coffee companions approaching with that (half feminine) wavering gait which is of their long clothing and unmuscular bodies. They were coffee lords, men of an elegant leisure in the desert life; also the Harb go gallantly clad amongst Beduins. Khálaf ibn Náhal greeted us strangers with his easy smile, and the wary franchise of these mejlis politicians, and that ringing hollow throat of the dry desert; he proffered a distant hand: we all sat down to drink his kahwa, — and that was not very good. Khálaf whispered to his son, "What is he, a soldier?" The young man smiling awaited that some other should speak: so one of the young companions said, "We think we should know thee." *The son:* "Art not thou the Nasrâny that came last year to Hâyil?" — "I am he." — "I was at Hâyil shortly after, and heard of thee there; and when you entered, by the tokens, I knew thee." Khálaf answered among them, unmoved, "He had visited the Nasâra, that time he traded with camels to Egypt ; and they were men of a singular probity. Wellah, in his reckoning with one of them, the Christian having received too much by five-pence, rode half a day after him to make restitution !" He added, " Khalîl travels among the Aarab ! — well, I say, why not ? he carries about these medicines, and they (the Nasâra) have good remedies. Abu Fâris before him, visited the Aarab ; and wellah the princes at Hâyil favoured this Khalîl ? Only a thing mislikes me, which I saw in the manners of the Nasâra, — Khalîl, it is not honest ! Why do the men and hareem sit so nigh, as it were in the knees of each other ? "

Now there came in two young spokesmen of the Seleymy villagers, — although they seemed Beduw. They complained of the injury which Khálaf had done them to-day, sending his camels to graze in their reserve of pasture ; and threatened 'that they would mount and ride to Hâyil, to accuse him before the Emir !' Khálaf's son called them out presently to eat in the inner apartment, made (such I had not seen before) in the midst of this very long and great Beduin tent : — that hidden dish is not rightly of the Nejd Aarab, but savours of the town life and Medina. The young men answered in their displeasure, they were not hungry, they came not hither to eat, and that they were here at home. *Khálaf:* " But go in and eat, and afterward we will speak together ? " They went unwillingly, and returned anon : and when he saw them again, Khálaf, because he did them wrong, began to scold : — " Do not they of Seleymy receive many benefits from us ? buy we not dates of you and corn also ? why are ye then ungrateful ? — Ullah, curse the fathers of them, fathers of *settatásher kelb* (sixteen dogs)." Another said : " Ullah, curse them, fathers of *ethnasher kelb* (twelve dogs) ; " forms more liberal perhaps than the " sixty dogs " of the vulgar malice. These were gallants of Harb, bearing about in their Beduin garments the savour of Medina. Khálaf said, with only a little remaining bitterness, that to satisfy them, he would remove on the morrow. Seleymy (Soleyma) is a small Shammar settlement of twelve households, their wells are very deep.

When the young men were gone, Khálaf, taking again his elated countenance gave an ear to our business. He led out Maatuk, and, threatening the timid Heteymy with the displeasure of Ibn Rashîd, enquired of him of my passing in the country, and of my coming to his menzil. I went to Khálaf, and said to them, " Thou canst send me, as all the people say, to el-Kasîm ; I alighted at your beyt, and have tasted of your hospitality, and would repose this day and to-morrow ; and then let some man of your trust accompany me, for his wages, to el-Kasîm." His voice was smooth, but Khálaf's dry heart was full of a politic dissimulation : "*Mâ úkdar*, I am not able ; and how, he answered, might we send thee to el-Kasîm ? — who would adventure thither ; the people of Aneyza are our enemies." — "Khálaf, no put-offs, you can help me if you will." — "Well, hearken ! become a Moslem, and I will send thee whithersoever thou would'st ; say, 'There is no God, beside Ullah,' and I will send thee to el-Kasîm freely." — "You promise this, before witnesses ?" — "Am I a man to belie my words." — "Hear then all of you ; There is none God but Ullah ! — let the thelûl be brought round." — "Ay ! say also Mohammed is the messenger of Ullah !" — "That was not in our covenant ; the thelûl Khálaf ! and let me be going." — "I knew not that the Nasrânies could say so ; all my meaning was that you should become a Moslem. Khalîl, you may find some of the *jemmamîl* (cameleers, sing. *jemmâl*) of el-Kasîm, that come about, at this season, to sell clothing among the Aarab. Yesterday I heard of one of them in these parts [it was false] ; a jemmâl would carry thee back with him for two reals. When you have supped and drunk the evening camel milk, mount again with this Heteymy ! and he will convey thee to him ;" — but I read in his looks, that it was a fable. He went aside with Maatuk again, — was long talking with him ; and required him, with words like threatenings, to carry me from him. When we had supped, Maatuk called me to mount. I said to Ibn Náhal, "If I am forsaken in this wilderness, or there should no man receive me, and I return to thee, wilt thou then receive me ?" — Khálaf answered, 'he would receive me.'

In the first darkness of the night we rode from him ; seeking a ferîj, which Maatuk had espied as we came down from Genna. After an hour, Maatuk said, "Here is sand, shall we alight and sleep ?" — for yet we saw not their watchfires — "Let us ride on : and if all fail tell me what shall become of me, my rafîk ?" — "Khalîl, I have said it already, that I will carry thee again to live with me in my ferîj." Then a hound barked from the dark valley side : we turned up thither, and came before three tents ; where a camel troop lay chawing the cud in the night's peace : their fires were out, and the Aarab were already sleeping. We alighted and set down our bags, and kneebound the thelûl. I would now have advanced to the booths, but Maatuk withheld me, — " It were not well, he whispered ; but abide we here, and give them time, and see if there come not some to call us."

Bye and bye a man approached, and " Ugh ! said he, as he heard our salaam, why come ye not into the beyt ? " This worthy bore in his hand a spear, and a huge scimitar in the other. We found the host within, who sat up blowing the embers in the hearth ; and laid on fuel to give us light. He roused the housewife ; and she reached us over the curtain a bowl of old rotten léban, of which they make sour mereesy. We sipped their sorry night bever, and all should now be peace and confidence ; yet he of the spear and scimitar sat on, holding his weapons in his two hands, and lowered upon us. " How now, friend ! I said at last, is this that thou takest us for robbers, I and my rafîk ? " — " Ugh ! a man cannot stand too much upon his guard, there is ever peril." Maatuk said merrily, " He has a sword and we have another ! " The host answered smiling, " He never quits that huge sword of his and the spear, waking or sleeping ! " So we perceived that the poor fellow was a knight of the moonshine. I said to our host, " I am a hakîm from Damascus, and I go to el-Kasîm: my rafîk leaves me here, and will you send me thither for my money, four reals ? " He answered gently, " We will see to-morrow, and I think we may agree together, whether I myself shall convey thee, or I find another ; in the meantime, stay with us a day or two." When we would rest, the housemother, she of the rotten léban, said a thing to one of us, which made me think we were not well arrived : she was a forsaken wife of our host's brother. I asked Maatuk, " If such were the Harb manners ! " — He whispered again, " As thou seest ; and say, Khalîl, shall I leave thee here, or wilt thou return with me ? " — When the day broke, Maatuk said to them, " I leave him with you, take care of him : " so he mounted and rode from us.

Motlog (that was our host's name) : " Let us walk down to Ibn Náhal, and take counsel how we may send thee to el-Kasîm, but I have a chapped heel and may hardly go." I dressed the wound with ointment and gave him a sock ; and the Beduwy drew on a pair of old boots that he had bought in Medina. We had gone half a mile, when I saw a horseman, with his long lance, riding against us : a fierce-looking fanatical fellow. — It was he who alone, of all who sat at Khálaf's, had contraried me yesterday. This horseman was *Tollog*, my host's elder brother ! and it was his booth wherein we had passed the night! his was also that honest forsaken housewife! It were a jest worthy of the Arabs and their religion, to tell why the new wedded man chose to lie abroad at Ibn Náhal's.

"How now!" cries our horseman staring upon me like a man aghast. His brother responded simply of the Shâmy hakîm and the Heteymy. — " Akhs! which way went that Heteymy?" (and balancing his long lance, he sat up) I will gallop after him and bring him again, — Ullah curse his father! and knowest thou that this is a Nasrány?" Motlog stood a moment astonished! then the poor man said nobly, "*Wa low*, and though it be so...? he is our guest and a stranger; and that Heteymy is now too far gone to be overtaken." — Tollog rode further; he was a shrew at home and ungracious, but Motlog was a mild man. We passed by some spring pasture, and Motlog cried to a child, who was keeping their sheep not far off, to run home and tell them to remove hither. When the boy was gone a furlong he waved him back and shouted 'No!' for he had changed his mind: he was a little broken headed, — and so is every third man in the desert life. I saw, where we passed under a granite headland, some ground courses of a dry-built round chamber, such as those which, in the western dîras, I have supposed to be sepulchres.

Khálaf had removed since yesterday: we found him in his tent stretched upon the sand to slumber — it was noon. The rest made it strange to see me again, but Motlog my host worthily defended me in all. Khálaf turning himself after a while and rising, for the fox was awake, said with easy looks, " Aha! this is Khalîl back again; and how Khalîl, that cursed Heteymy forsook thee?" When he heard that Maatuk had taken wages of me he added: " Had I known this, I would have cut off his head, and seized his thelûl; — ho! there, prepare the midday kahwa." His son answered, "We have made it already and drunk round." — " Then make it again, and spare not for kahwa." Khálaf twenty days before had espoused a daughter of the village, and paid the bride money; and the Beduins whispered in mirth, that she was yet a maid. For this his heart was in bale: and the son, taking occasion to mock the Heteymy, sought in covert words his father's relief, from one called an hakîm. Ibn Náhal said at last kindly, " Since Khalîl has been left at your beyt, send him Motlog whither he desires of thee."

Ibn Náhal, rightly named *Son-of-the-Bee*, was a merchant Beduwy, he gathered sweetness and substance of all in the khála. Though not born of a sheykhly family, he had grown, by his dealing in camels, to be one of the wealthiest among the southern Aarab; and he had clients who trafficked for him, selling coffee and clothing among the Aarab. His great cattle were increased to so many that they must be herded in two droves; and yet Ibn Náhal as an iniquitous Arab found ever some sleight to keep back part of his herdsmen's slender wages. He was not a sheep-master, though the small cattle (yielding butter) be more profitable to poor nomad families; but he took up store of samn, in payment for his small merchandise. He had besides that which appeared to the Aarab a great (dead) treasure of silver, laid up in his coffer. Ibn Náhal had made his first considerable venture, years before, with a cameldrove to Egypt. The adventurous Harby passed those hundreds of desert miles, taking rafîks by the way: his tribesmen, having their eyes naturally turned towards Medina and Mecca, are unused to journey to that part. He arrived safely and his gain was seventy in the hundred. Some years later (deceived by a rumour) he made a second venture thither; but then he found that camels were cheap; and his loss was thirty in the hundred. Khálaf was without letters, — he needed them not; and when I put Aneybar's paper in his hand, he said with a grace, " We are the Beduw! we know not reading." Khálaf's life, little given to bounty, in which many might have rejoiced with him, had not much consolation of all this gathered good. The Nejd Arabians call such spirits *tájirs*, 'tradesmen.' To-day he was outwardly a sheykh of Aarab, yet being none, since the Beduw look only upon the blood; for many were the households that removed and alighted with Ibn Náhal. They were his jummaa or ferîj; he was besides Ibn Rashîd's man.

Samn was cheap this foreyear, a sah for a real in Hâyil; but Khálaf had tidings that the same was now worth two reals at Jidda. As we sat at the hearth I wondered to hear these Aarab enquire of each other, " How far is Jidda? " and some among them, blaming themselves that they were never at Mecca (on pilgrimage), even asked, " Where lies Jidda! " — Jidda, more than 400 miles from hence, were for Khálaf and his Beduin carriers no more than twelve swift camel journeys. He would go down thither in these days with many loads of clarified butter, and win silver. In all the Aarab is the spirit of barter; but in very few is a provident wit and the hardy execution of Khálaf, and civil painfulness to put their heads to a lawful enterprise. I mused, should I ride with him and see much unknown country ? — but nay, I had rather visit el-Kasîm, that middle Nefûd land of industrious Nejd citizens. All Khálaf's substance, his 300 camels, his silver and the household gear, might be valued at nearly £2000 sterling ; and that is great wealth in the poor nomad life upon the desert sand ! A Beduwy, Khálaf rode in the ghrazzus ; and he and his friends would mount to foray upon Ateyba, in one of the next days. Such Beduins will ride at least once every year of their indolent lives, to steal camels ; and that is especially when the blood is renewed in their veins in the milk season, or first eagers in the returning summer drought. If a shot attained Ibn Náhal, where, I asked them, were his thrift, and his selling of samn ?

I told this tale afterward to a friend at Aneyza ; who answered me with another. — " Also there was a very wealthy sheykh of Ateyba, one well known to us all ; his camels were five hundred, and his small cattle without number. He was now at the first grey hairs, yet could not dwell quietly at home, and leave riding in the ghrazzus, upon their Shammar foemen. In a last foray they were far entered in the enemies' country ; and having taken some inconsiderable booty, the companions turned homeward. But the Shammar horsemen outrode them, who were mounted on thelûls, and (*ghrâru aley*) set upon and surrounded the raiders ; and, being enemies to the death, they left not one alive of them " ! — Among these Harb I saw many horsemen. Tollog and Motlog, though miserable householders, had a horse and a mare between them. I saw their mare's fore-hoofs all outgrown in this sand soil : Tollog said, ' Here is no farrier, but when some Solubby comes by, he shall pare them.' — Their Harb talk sounded, in my ears, broken-like, such as the Arabic city speech, or that spoken by the Nejûmy at Kheybar. These are Aarab of Medina.

Though the rumour of Ibn Saûd's riding with Ateyba was in every man's mouth, the alarm was false ! I have not found that news is carried swiftly in Arabia, saving on the caravan roads ; yet in the season when none are passing, you may wait for long months, and hear no tidings. This alarm delayed my journey : " Have patience, said Motlog, till we hear further ; and then I will ride with thee myself, not to Aneyza — they are enemies, nor to Boreyda, but to *S'beyîeh* near *Nebhanîeh* [under the *Abanât* mountains] ; those villagers are good folk, and will send thee forward by some cameleers." But the brethren were confused, when I convinced them of their fabling to me of distances. 'How should the stranger know their country! — what then does he here?' In Arabia I entered unwillingly into villages, but it were in the fellowship of the Beduw: I heard that some of Seleyma had said, 'they would cut the Nasrâny in pieces if he ventured himself amongst them'; and yet between their words and deeds is commonly many leagues' distance.

There was here but the deadly semblance of hospitality; naught but buttermilk, and not so much as the quantity of a cup was set before me in the long day. Happy was I when each other evening their camels came home, and a short draught was brought me of the warm léban. Tollog, the gay horseman, was a glozing fanatical fellow; in Motlog was some drivelling nobility of mind: the guest's mortal torment was here the miserable hand of Tollog's cast wife. Little of God's peace or blessing was in this wandering hamlet of three brethren; the jarring contention of their voices lasted from the day rising, till the stars shone out above us. Though now their milk-skins overflowed with the spring milk, they were in the hands of the hareem, who boiled all to mereesy, to sell it later in Medina. The Beduw of high Nejd would contemn this ignoble traffic, and the decay of hospitality.

Being without nourishment I fell into a day-long languishing trance. One morrow I saw a ferîj newly pitched upon the valley side, in face of us: when none observed me, I went thither under colour of selling medicines. Few men sat at home, and they questioned with me for my name of Nasrâny; the woman clamoured to know the kinds of my simples, but none poured me out a little léban. I left them and thought I saw other tents pitched beyond: when I had gone a mile, they were but a row of bushes. Though out of sight of friends and unarmed, I went on, hoping to espy some booths of the Aarab. I descried a black spot moving far off on the rising plain, and thought it might be an herd of goats: I would go to them and drink milk. I crossed to the thin shadow of an acacia tree; for the sunbeaten soil burned my bare soles; and turning I saw a tall Beduwy issue from a broken ground and go by, upon his stalking dromedary; he had not perceived the stranger: then I made forward a mile or two, to come to the goats. I found but a young woman with a child herding them. — '*Salaam!* and could she tell me where certain of the people were pitched, of such a name?' She answered a little affrighted, 'She knew them not, they were not of her

Aarab.' — " O maiden milk for me ! " — " *Min fen halîb*, milk from whence ? we milked them early at the booths ; there is naught now in these goats' udders, and we have no vessel to draw in : " she said her tents stood yet far beyond. " And is there not hereby a ferîj for which I go seeking all this morrow ? " — " Come a little upon the hill side, and I will shew it thee : lo there ! thou mayest see their beyts." My eyes were not so good ; but I marked where she shewed with her finger and went forward. Having marched half an hour, over wild and broken ground, I first saw the menzil, when I was nigh upon them ; and turned to go to a greater booth in the circuit, wherein I espied men sitting.

Their hounds leapt out against me with open throat ; the householder ran with an hatchet, to chase them away from the stranger (a guest) arriving. — As I sat amongst them, I perceived that these were not the Beduins I sought. I asked bye and bye, " Have ye any támr (dates) ? " — also to eat with them would be for my security. The good man answered cheerfully, " We have nothing but cheese ; and that shall be fetched immediately." The host was a stranger, a fugitive of Meteyr, living with these Harb, for an homicide. He sat bruising green bark of the boughs of certain desert trees, and of the bast he would twist well-ropes : " There are, said he, some very (*ghramîk*, for *'amîk*) deep *golbân* (sing. *jellîb*, a well) in these dîras." The poor people treated me honourably, asking mildly and answering questions. I said, " I came to seek who would carry me to el-Kasîm for his wages." The man answered, " He had a good thelûl ; and could I pay five reals, he would carry me, and set me down wellah in the market-place of Aneyza ! "

When I came again to my hosts — " Whither wentest thou ? exclaimed Motlog ; to go so far from our tents is a great danger for thee : there are many who finding thee alone would kill thee, the Beduw are kafirs, Khalîl." When I told him the man's name, who would carry me to Aneyza, he added, " Have nothing to do with him ! he is a Meteyry. If he rode with thee (radîf), beware of his knife — a Meteyry cannot keep himself from treachery ; or else he might kill thee sleeping : now canst thou ride four days to el-Kasîm without sleeping ! " Such evil-speaking is common between neighbour tribes ; but I think the Meteyry would have honestly conveyed me to Aneyza. Motlog had in certain things the gentlest mind of any Arab of my acquaintance hitherto. When he saw that by moments, I fell asleep, as I sat, even in the flaming sun, and that I wandered from the (inhospitable) booths — it was but to seek some rock's shelter where, in this lethal somnolence and slowness of spirit, I might close the eyes — he said, ' He perceived that my breast was straitened (with grief) here among them : ' and since I had taken this journey to heart, and he could not carry me himself so far as Boreyda, he would seek for someone to-day to convey me thither ; — 'howbeit that for my sake, he had let pass the ghrazzu of Ibn Náhal, — for which he had obtained the loan of another horse.'

Besides him, a grim councillor for my health was Aly, he of the spear and scimitar : that untempered iron blade had been perchance the pompous side arm of some javelin man of the great officers of Medina, — a personage in the city bestowed the warlike toy upon the poor soul. " *Ana sahîbak*, I am thy very friend," quoth Aly, in the husk voice of long-suffering misery. He was of the Harb *el-Aly* : they are next from hence in the N.-E. and not of these Aarab. I asked him : " Where leftest thou thy wife and thy children and thy camels ? " He answered, " I have naught besides this mantle and my tunic and my weapons : *ana yatîm !* I am an orphan ! " This fifty years' old poor Beduin soul was yet in his nonage ; — what an hell were it of hunger and misery, to live over his age again ! He had inherited a possession of palms, with his brother, at Medina ; but the stronger father's son put out his weak-headed brother : and, said Motlog, " The poor man (reckoned a fool) could have there no redress." — " And why are these weapons always in his hands ? " — " He is afraid for a thing that happened years ago : Aly and a friend of his, rising from supper, said they would try a fall. They wrestled : Aly cast the other, and fell on him ; — and it may be there had somewhat burst in him, for the fallen man lay dead ! None accused Aly ; nevertheless the *mesquin* fled for his life, and he has gone ever since thus armed, lest the kindred of the deceased finding him should kill him."

At evening there sat with us a young kinsman of Tollog's new wife. He was from another ferîj ; and having spoken many injuries of the Nasâra, he said further, " Thou Tollog, and Motlog ! wellah, ye do not well to receive a kafir in your beyts ; " and taking for himself all the inner place at the fire, — unlike the gentle customs of the Beduins, he had quite thrust out the guest and the stranger into the evening wind ; for here was but a niche made with a lap of the tent cloth, to serve, like the rest of their inhospitality, for the men's sitting place. I exclaimed,

" This must be an Ageyly ! " — They answered, " Ay, he is an Ageyly ! a proud fellow, Khalîl." — " I have found them hounds, Turks and traitors ; by my faith, I have seen of them the vilest of mankind." — " Wellah, Khalîl, it is true." — " What Harby is he ? " — " He is *Hâzimy*." — " An *Hâzimy !* then good friends, this ignoble proud fellow is a Solubby ! " — " It is sooth, Khalîl, aha-ha-ha ! " and they laughed apace. The discomfited young man, when he found his tongue, could but answer, *subbak*, " The Lord rebuke thee." It seemed to them a marvellous thing that I should know this homely matter. — Hâzim, an ancient fendy of Harb, are snibbed as Heteym ; and Beduins in their anger will cast against any Heteymy, Sherâry or sâny the reproach of Solubby. Room was now made, and this laughter had reconciled the rest to the Nasrâny. — I had wondered to see great part of Tollog's tent shut close ; but on the morrow, when the old ribald housewife and mother of his children sat without, boiling samn, there issued from the close booth a new face, — a fair young woman, clean and comely clad ! She was Tollog's (new) bright bird in bridal bower ; and these were her love-days, without household charge. She came forth with dazing eyes in the burning sunlight.

When the next sun rose, I saw that our three tents were become four. These new comers were Seyadîn, not Solubbies, not sânies but (as we have seen) packmen of poor Beduinkin, carrying wares upon asses among the Aarab. I went to visit the strangers ; — " *Salaam !* " — " *Aleykom es-salaam* ; and come in Khalîl ! art thou here ? " — " And who be ye ! " — " Rememberest thou not when thou camest with the Heteymies and drank coffee in our kasr, at Gofar ? " The poor woman added, " And I mended thy rent mantle." " Khalîl, said the man, where is thy galliûn ? I will fill it with hameydy." Beduin-born, all the paths of the desert were known to him ; he had peddled as far as Kasîm, and he answered me truly in all that I enquired of him : — they are not unkind to whom the world is unkind ! there was no spice in them of fanaticism.

CHAPTER XI

JOURNEY TO EL-KASIM: BOREYDA

Beduin carriers. Set out with Hàmed, a Shammary. False report of the foray of Ibn Saûd and the Ateyba. The digging of water-pits in the khála. Ibn Rashîd's forays. Solubba. Beny Aly. Semîra, anciently Dîrat Ruwàlla. Terky, a Medina Beduin. A ráhla of Beny Sâlem. The Atáfa. A tempest of rain. Triple rainbow. Lighting by night in the desert. Religious Beduw. A gentle host. A Harb menzil pitched ring-wise. *el-Fúrn*, a kindred of Harb. Sára mountain. The first village of el-Kasîm. Ayûn. Gassa. Watchtowers. Bare hospitality in el-Kasîm. The deep sand-land and its inhabitants. Aspect of Boreyda. The town. The Emir's hostel. The Nasrâny is robbed in the court-yard. Jeyber, the Emir's officer. The Kasr Hajellân. Abdullah, the Emir's brother. Boreyda citizens; the best are camel masters in the caravans. Old tragedies of the Emirs. The town. A troubled afternoon. Set out on the morrow for Aneyza. Well sinking. Ethel trees.

THE same morning came two Beduins with camel-loads of temmn; which the men had brought down for Tollog and Motlog, from el-Irâk! They were of Shammar and carriers in Ibn Rashîd's Haj caravan. I wondered how after long journeying they had found our booths: they told me, that since passing Hâyil they had enquired us out, in this sort, — 'Where is Ibn Náhal?' — *Answer:* 'We heard of him in the S.E. country. — Some say he is gone over to the Ateyba marches. — When last we had word of him, he was in such part. — He went lately towards Seleyma. — you shall find his Aarab between such and such landmarks. — He is grazing about Genna.' Whilst they were unloading, a Beduin stranger, but known in this ferîj, arrived upon his camel after an absence : he had lately ridden westward 130 miles, to visit Bishr, amongst whom he had been bred up; but now he dwelt with Harb. The man was of Shammar, and had a forsaken wife living as a widow in our menzil: he came to visit their little son. Motlog counselled me to engage this honest man for the journey to Kasîm. We called him : — He answered, 'Wellah, he feared to pass so open a country, where he might lose his camel to some foraying Ateybân;' but Motlog persuaded him, saying he could buy with his wages a load of dates (so cheap in el-Kasîm) to bring home to his household. He proffered to carry me to *el-Bukkerîeh* : but we agreed for five reals that he should carry me to Boreyda. "Mount, *érkub!*" quoth the man, whose name was *Hàmed* ; he loaded my things, and climbed behind me, — and we rode forth. " Ullah bring thee to thy journey's end ! said Tollog ; Ullah, give that you see not the evil ! "

The sun was three hours high : we passed over a basalt coast, and descended to another ferîj ; in which was Hàmed's beyt. There he took his water-skin, and a few handfuls of mereesy — all his provision for riding other 450 miles — and to his housewife he said no more than this : " Woman, I go with the stranger to Boreyda." She obeyed silently ; and commonly a Beduwy in departing bids not his wife farewell : — " Hearest thou ? (said Hàmed again), follow with these Aarab until my coming home ! " Then he took their little son in his arms and kissed him. — We rode at first northward for dread of Ateybân : this wilderness is granite grit with many black basalt bergs. The marches beyond were now full of dispersed Aarab, B. Sâlem ; we saw their black booths upon every side. All these Harb were gathering towards *Semîra*, in the Shammar dîra, to be taxed there, upon a day appointed, by the collectors of Ibn Rashîd ; because there is much water for their multitude of cattle. We left the mountain landmark of Benàny at half a day's distance, west ; and held forward evenly with the course of W. el-Rummah, — the great valley now lying at a few miles' distance upon the right hand. Some black basaltic mountains, not very far off, Hàmed told me, were beyond the Wady : that great dry waterway bounds the dîrat of Harb in Nejd ; all beyond is Ateyba country. Twice as we rode we met with camel herds ; the men milked for us, and we enquired and told tidings. At sun-setting we were journeying under a steep basalt jebel ; and saw a black spot, upon a mountain sand-drift, far before us, which was a booth of the nomads ; then we saw their camels, and the thought of evening milk was pleasant to our hearts. " But seest thou ? said Hàmed, they are all males ! for they are gaunt and have low humps ; — that is because they serve for carriage : the Aarab let the cows fatten, and load not upon them."

As we approached we saw many more tents, which the brow had hidden. When we alighted, even those Beduins knew me ! — en elf of them cried out (he had seen the kafir at Hâyil), " Aha ! the Nasrâny ! " a word which made their hearts and ours cold. These tribesmen were Harb ; the women wore silver nose-rings, — among the Nomads they are not made large. Here also the (false !) report was in all their mouths, of Ibn Saûd and the foray of Ateyba, " that had arrived under the walls of Boreyda." — The open men's side, in these booths hardly the tent's third part, was made at the left hand, which is the housewife's apartment, in Annezy and Shammar beyts, in Nejd: in the Nejd Harb tents it is sometimes upon the right, but mostwhat upon the left hand; in the Heteym tents left; and in the most Billy beyts, that I have seen, left. These were dull and silent Aarab, and of no hospitality; at length the householder brought us a bowlful of their evening camel milk, and with few words he left us. At this altitude, where I found 4300 feet (the latitude being about 27°), the nights, now in the midst of April, were yet cold. Hàmed spoke to me, to visit on the morrow the village *er-Rautha*, not far before us. We heard that many were dying there of a fever, though the malady had never been known amongst them heretofore. Hàmed thought I might sell them some medicines; I answered, " We would go, if he were not afraid : " but when the sun rose he said, " It would be too far about."

We rode an hour or two, and the end of *J. Selma* appeared upon the left hand : " The mountain comes down, said Hàmed, nearly to er-Rautha." Mustijidda he told me is a village less than Teyma. Leaving our former course, we now held southward: this desert soil is an uneven plain, with many stony places, *súmt*, where our footsore camel had pain to pass. At noon we left on our right hand *Bellezzîeh*, a small corn settlement without palms. There are five houses in two *kasûr*, or yards of walling; and the hamlet, lying out in the immense wilderness, is sheltered only by the (strong) name of Ibn Rashîd: this open waste was now bare of Aarab. At half afternoon we came to water-pits, *es-Shibberîeh*: Hàmed alighted and ran on to fill our girby. The waterholes only ten feet deep (of sweet rain-water) were digged in a shaeb or freshet-strand, seyling to the wady er-Rummah. " To open a *themîla*, such as one of these, said Hàmed, is two men's labour in a day: one man digs with a stick [comp. Numb. xxi. 18], and his fellow casts out the earth in his hands " : — under this land-face of harsh gravel is soft loam. The country bordering down to the great wady is full of groundwater at little depth; for which Hàmed praised his Shammar dîra above the Bishr marches, " where is much good pasture, but only few great waters, deep to draw at and far between them; but in dîrat Shammar in every horizon there is some water-hole at least, and the Aarab may disperse themselves by families, without danger of thirsting."

When I had mixed a little mereesy Hàmed refused the offered bowl, saying he had drunk already: but I perceived that he shunned to drink with a Nasrâny; also when we came to any Aarab he ever drank of the bowl before me. The poor man of a gentle humour, and (which are so many of them) a little staggering in his brains, took it heavily that I censured his Persian-like nicety, unlike the franchise of the desert. — " But, ah! said he, let us hasten from this place for fear of Ateybân; this land lies open, and if any ghrazzu went by now, they would see us." I asked him of the Ateyba country beyond the wady: he had ridden there in Ibn Rashîd's forays. He said their dîra is sandy plains with good pasture, and there are such bergs as these (of granite and basalt), and the Aarab are rich in flocks. He had visited *Miskeh* and *Therrîeh*, which are free settlements, poor and open; and by some they are accounted to el-Kasîm: later it was my chance to journey through that vast Nomad country. Hàmed rode in all the Emir's forays: and so do many poor Beduins, to see what booty the Lord would send them; for among thelûls of dismounted enemies, cattle dispersed and abandoned tents, there will hardly not come somewhat to a ready man's hand: Hàmed had taken thus the nâga under us, and now he rode upon her in all the ghrazzus. He could not tell me if there were thelûl blood in her, ' because she had been taken from enemies, and none knew her generation.'

" What think you? I asked, is it no sin to slay men and to reave their goods?" Hàmed, yielding and assenting as a Moslem to every religious word, answered me, " Well, I think so and I thank my Lord I did never kill any man; I have but taken the booty." In such a field many thelûls of the hostile Aarab are scattered and lost. The dromedary is a dull beast, that has no feeling with her master; if he press her, it is not unlikely that the sheeplike brute will settle down, bellowing, under him, in the midst of the fray. If her rider but shake the bridle, she will stand perhaps to bray, and strive with a man when he should fly fast. Some are headstrong, and will bear their riders amongst the enemy; and the fleetest dromedary may be speedily outrun by the worst of the desert horses. Horse riders therefore though armed only with lances, and sitting loosely on their mares' backs without stirrups, have great advantage, in the desert warfare, against slow-firing matchlock men upon thelûls; and if one mounted upon an unruly dromedary have his long gun empty, when a horseman turns to assail him, he must needs cast himself down and forsake her.

J. el-Hébeshy was now in sight, a long black mountain of basalt lying beyond Semîra. — A mounted company, like a file of cavalry, came riding hitherward over the khála : they were a score of Solubbies on their asses. Hàmed would ride on to meet them for tidings, but having the bridle in my hand I held off : then one of them alighted and ran to us ; — a lad, who hailed us with a salutation I had not heard before, *Ullah y'aŷna-kom,* ' The Lord be your help ! ' They had been tinkering about Semîra ; and he told us that little beyond yonder bergs we should find the Aarab. We passed forth, and when the sun was low, said Hàmed, " The Solubby deceived us ! " for yet we saw not the Aarab. From hence he shewed me the tops of the ethel trees of Semîra : two miles further we had sight of the ferîj. These were a few booths of B. Aly, pitched in view of the settlement.

We alighted, and even here they knew the Nasrâny ! they spoke to us roughly ; but were not inhospitable. The B. Aly are dispraised by the B. Sâlem as Aarab of raw manners, and kafirs ; because not many of them have learned to say the prayer ; nor do all of them keep holy the month of ramathán : they even pretend that the B. Aly be not of the right blood of Harb. As we sat about the evening hearth, the Beduins gave back on a sudden, and rising upon their feet they left me sitting ; for they had all seen a small adder winding amongst us : then one of them with a blow of his clubbed stick beat in sunder the poisonous vermin.

At dawn we mounted to go to breakfast in Semîra. Hàmed had bartered his gun overnight in the tents to a lad, for an ewe and a lamb, worth nearly 5 reals ; the matchlock, of a very ill fashion, not worth $2\frac{1}{2}$ reals, was one he had taken in a ghrazzu : it was so short that by likelihood the rest had burst. When we lately rode with fear over the wilderness, Hàmed rammed down double lead upon the old powder ; but as he was in doubt if the gun would go off, I had made him fire it and charge anew. He went on driving his slow-footed cattle, to sell them in the settlement : but we were not come far when the weled, who had repented of his bargain, came running to overtake us. The unlucky lad cried after Hàmed, who drove so much the faster ; but a bargain amongst the iniquitous inhabitants of the desert is not binding till the third day be past. Hàmed answered him with soft words, but the sorehearted lad began to scold and delivered him his gun. Hàmed received his own again, as a Beduwy, with a good grace ; and the lad turned back his sheep, and began to hiss them home. The sun now rose before us over Jebel Hébeshy.

The small ancient town of Semîra is but an enclosure (kasr) of houses in a high wall with towers of clay; in distant sight it stands like to some lone castle upon the desert side. There are two other small wall enclosures, *kasrs*. This little borough covers I suppose not two acres; the gate is but a door in their battle wall at the south side, and there without is a dry seyl-strand of the winter rains. The tilled grounds of Semîra lie beyond, bare and uncheerful to the eye, which here looks upon no pleasant boughs of palms! their husbandry is of grain only: I saw their corn fields of well-grown wheat and barley almost ripe for the harvest. Camels cannot enter the town door; and I was unwilling to leave our bags lying abroad, in the sight of children playing; but Hàmed said that here was the manôkh, (camels' couching place,) they were safe, and no child would touch them. — We sat down to see who would call us in to breakfast. I have never arrived at the nomad menzils without a feeling of cheerfulness, but I never entered a desert village without misgiving of heart; looking for koran contentions, the dull manners of peasants and a grudging hospitality. Hàmed told me, here were thirty houses and an hundred inhabitants; the villagers are called *es-Shubâramy* of the sheykh's house *Rashîd es-Shûbramy* : and they are of that old and wide inhabiting Nejd tribe the B. Temîm.

A man came out to us; and after salaams he led us into the place to drink kahwa. We passed by small clay ways to their public coffee chamber; which was but a narrow shelter of palm branches betwixt clay walls. A few men only assembled; who lying along, upon their elbows, on the earthen floor, whilst we sipped of the first and second cups, kept a dull silence: the B. Temîm are heavy spirits and civilly incurious. Our host after coffee led us out to breakfast, in his house; and said his excuses for setting before us dates only, from the Jebel. When I asked, why had they no palm plantations? and the ground-water is so nigh, that young plants putting down roots to the moisture after the first years should have no need of irrigation? He answered, ' The palm did not prosper here.' At Semîra is perhaps too sweet an earth, and the ground-water is of the pure rain.

Hàmed who had received from me a piece of gold at the setting out, now took it forth to ask the settler, if this were so many reals. Our host answered, " It is so O Beduwy, and in Kasîm passes for somewhat more; and doubt not,—this is Khalîl." The goodman looked upon me, and I saw that he knew me; but he had been too honest to show it before the people and molest me here. He said to my rafîk, "And thou knowest who he is?" Hàmed answered, somewhat out of countenance, "Ay! — and keep this money for me, host, until my coming again." The Arabs are of an insane avidity; and Hàmed entrusted his gold to a stranger without witnesses! but for the most part the deposit will be religiously preserved by the Moslem receiver, to be rendered to the owner. The deposit may even become hereditary, — then it is laid up to be restored to the heirs [confer Ex. xxii. 7 et seq.] I asked our host of their antiquity; "All this country, he answered, was in old time dîrat Ruwàlla!" We have seen that they were once Aarab of Medina ! [p. 205], — now their marches are far in the north, more than 200 miles from hence. Our host asked me to give him medicine for his son; and I rejoiced at such times, that I had somewhat to bestow again.

Semîra, which lies in the path between J. Shammar and the Hejâz, has surely been always a principal water station. The B. Sâlem would soon arrive at these waters, to be taxed. The Beduins' stay with their troops of cattle can be only of hours; and the telling and payment is made, with the Arabic expedition, in part of two days. — How may the collectors bring all these wild Arabs to a yearly tale and muster? but the tribesmen are afraid of Ibn Rashîd, and this business is despatched easily; — the sheukh are there to declare every matter upon oath, and his neckbone is in danger who would deceive the Emir. The B. Aly are taxed at the watering *Fuâra*, one journey eastward of Semîra, nigh the W. er-Rummah. At Fuâra are wells and a spring, and corn-plots, with an only kasr of an adventuring villager from Mustijidda, who projected with that running spring, to water his tillage: but he had not greatly prospered. So few are the springs in the Arabian highlands, that it might be almost said, *There are not any*. When I returned from these Travels to Damascus, I visited the Emir *Abd el-Kâder* (he was very erudite among erudite Moslems, in the Arabic letters and school-lore of their religion); and the noble Algerian enquired of me, 'Were there many springs [in those lands, which I had visited, of Arabia] where the Aarab water their herds and flocks?' He marvelled (as another Juba) when I responded there were none indeed! that the wilderness (and oases) waters are draw-wells.

We found the camel and the bags, at their town door, as we left them : the altitude is here 3900 feet. Now we rode towards J. Hébeshy : — an hour further a voice hailed us from some bushes ! a man sat there, and his thelûl was browsing not far off. Hàmed shouted again, " Auh ! wouldst thou enquire tidings, come hither thyself ! " — Then he lighted down to see what the man meant, who sat on making signs to us ; and I rode slowly forth towards the jebel. After half an hour I saw two men hieing after me upon a thelûl : I thought they might be thieves, and had my weapon ready, — till I knew Hàmed's voice. The other was that man of the bush, who was making coffee when we passed ; and had but called us to drink with him. This worthy, *Terky* by name, was a merchant of beasts (or middle man between the nomads and the butchers) at Medina : though settled in the Holy City he was an Harby. Every spring time he rode to take up sheep in these marches. He was a weerish looking old man, full of the elvish humour of the Beduw. Upon me he gazed fast ; for he had passed by Ibn Náhal's one day after us, and there he heard of the Nasrâny : he arrived here before us, because we had fetched a circuit to the North. Terky enquired, 'Were I indeed he whom they call a Nasrâny ? ' (a name full of stupor and alarms !) and he answered himself under his breath, ' It could not be, I seemed too peaceable a man ; also Hàmed spoke well of me.' — " But come let us mend our pace, quoth he, to pass the mid-day heat with some Aarab, who they say are pitched yonder." We marched three hours and alighted at their menzil. Here my companions, when they had drunk lében, would have loitered till the next morrow ; but I was for the journey. — These Aarab were very ill-favoured and ungracious. [Though of swarthy looks, the Nejd Beduw are blackened most with smoke and dirt — especially their often nearly negro-like hands : but the skin of their bodies which is not toasted in the sun is whitish.]

When we set out again I asked my companions, " Were those Harb or Solubba ? " They answered, laughing, " Harb, of B. Aly ; — Khalîl knows everything ! they be wellah like the Solubba." As I turned in the saddle, Hàmed's nâga startled under me, and fled wildly : and before I could take hold, I was cast backward, and my cloak rending, which had caught on the hind pillar of the saddle, I was slung in the air, and fell upon my back in soft sand ; — and woe to him who is cast upon a stone ! I have seen Beduins cruelly maimed thus. It was the vice of my rafîk's camel, and he had not warned me ; there are as many mad camels in the desert as dizzy sheep among us. In falling I had a heedful thought of my aneroid barometer ; and by happy fortune the delicate instrument, which I held in my hand, was not shaken. Hàmed ran, and Terky outrode the fugitive beast upon his fleeter thelûl ; and brought her again. We marched yet three hours, and came to another Harb ferîj, where we alighted to pass the night : here Terky found some acquaintance ; and the Nasrâny was no more known among them.

When the sun is setting, the Beduins kindle their evening fire. Terky was one of those Arabs, of an infirm complexion, who are abandoned to kahwa, and think it is no day of their lives if they taste not, every third hour, the false refreshment. Had Terky been born in land of Christians, he had sat every day drunken on his bench in the village alehouse. This Beduwy rode but light ; he carried in his long-tasseled white saddle-bags no more than his coffee-roasting pan, his coffee-pot, his box of three cups, his brass pestle and mortar, and a wooden bowl for his own drinking : he had no food with him for the way, looking to sup every night with Aarab. As for clothing they have but that with them which is on their backs ; and when one comes to water he may wash his tunic, and sit in his worsted mantle, till his shirt be dry again in the sun. Already the old tippler had taken out his coffee gear ; he disposed all in order by the hearth, and said, " Who has here any kahwa ? " I whispered, that these were poor folk and had no coffee. " But abide ! said he, and we shall see it : " — and very soon a handful of the [South Arabian] berries was fetched from a yet poorer tent ! As the pot was on, there came flying to our firelight a multitude of yellow beetles, which beat upon all before them, and fell down in the ash-pit. Terky defended his pot awhile with a senile impatience ; then he drew it aside and exclaimed, " Look, Khalîl ! even so the Nasrânies will fall down into the fire ; for that is the place of them, and such is the end of them all in Jehennem, Ullah burn them up ! but I think surely thou are not one of them ; eigh ! Khalîl, say that thou art not a Nasrâny ! " — Here the host's only evening entertainment was to pour us out camel milk, and Hàmed's shallow affectation was to stay his honest hand : I said to him before them all, " Suffer him to fill our bowl ! — a plague upon ill-timed compliments." Hàmed answered under his breath, " Your customs then be not as our customs."

When the day dawned we mounted, and Terky rode with us. Beyond the long Hébeshy mountain we came upon a great plain open all round to the horizon. I had not seen such a flat since I left Syria ; for the plain landscape in Nejd is nearly everywhere encumbered with montecules and jebâl. Pyramidlike bergs, of granite, but black under the shadowing of a cloud, were landmarks before us of a watering place, *Ghraymàr*. This even land which they name *Fuèylik*, lasts from hence to the Nefûd of el-Kasîm, and my companions were here in dread of passing ghrazzus. *Terky :* " Ridest thou thus without care or fear Khalîl ! but if we see them I and Hàmed will escape upon this thelûl, and leave thee upon the nâga, and thou wilt be taken." In that there fell an April shower which shone about us like golden hairs in the sun ; and the desert earth gave up to our sense a teeming grassy sweetness. As we approached the rocks, my companions espied great cattle, and they thought it was a ghrazzu at the watering ! Then we saw them to be camel troops of the Aarab : hundreds of great cattle were standing apart or couched by their households, awaiting their turn to be watered. It was a ráhla, and these Beduins (of Harb) watered the cattle in the midst of their march. Some of their house stuff was unloaded from their bearing camels ; upon other camels sat the Harb daughters, in their saddle litters, — crated frames, trapped with wavering tongues of coloured cloths and long lappets of camel leather. In the tribes of my former acquaintance such bravery is only of a few sheykhly housewives ; but these were B. Sâlem, — tribesfolk that go well clad amongst nomads. It seemed that any one of them might have been an *Atáfa* (*v.* Vol. I. p. 101,— or *Ateyfa*), — she that from her saddle frame warbles the battle-note, with a passionate sweetness, which kindles the manly hearts of the young tribesmen, (and the Aarab are full of a wild sensibility). — They see her, each one as his spouse, without the veil, and decked as in the day of her marriage ! — The Atáfa is a sheykh's daughter ; but, said Hàmed, she may be another *mez'ûna :* it were infamous to kill an Atáfa ; yet when shots flee, her camel may fall or run furiously, and the maiden-standard is in peril. Sheep flocks were lying down in a wide seyl-strand, awaiting their waterers ; the shepherd's asses were standing with them.

This desert well, great and square mouthed, I saw to be steyned with old dry-building of basalt ; there were three fathoms to the water. The camels at the troughs, standing in old stinking sludge, were stamping for the flies. A score of Beduins in their long shirts drew upon the four sides, with a loud song, and sweated in the sun. In the throng of cattle I saw a few sheykhs with their mares ; the hounds of the nomad encampment lay panting in the shadows of the tall camels ; and suffered us strangers to pass by without a challenge ! A sheykhly man who stood nigh us, taking down his semîly, and a bowl, poured us out léban. Another enquired whither we went, and said, " He would accompany us on the morrow [el-gâbily], if we would stay over this day in his tent. — See also the rain threatens, and we shall pitch yonder not far off." *Hàmed* : " Wellah, I may not wait ; for my breast is straitened, to be at home again." — None of these Aarab knew me.

We departed and Terky remained with them. The wilderness beyond is open gravel-plain : upon our left hand was a low mountain,

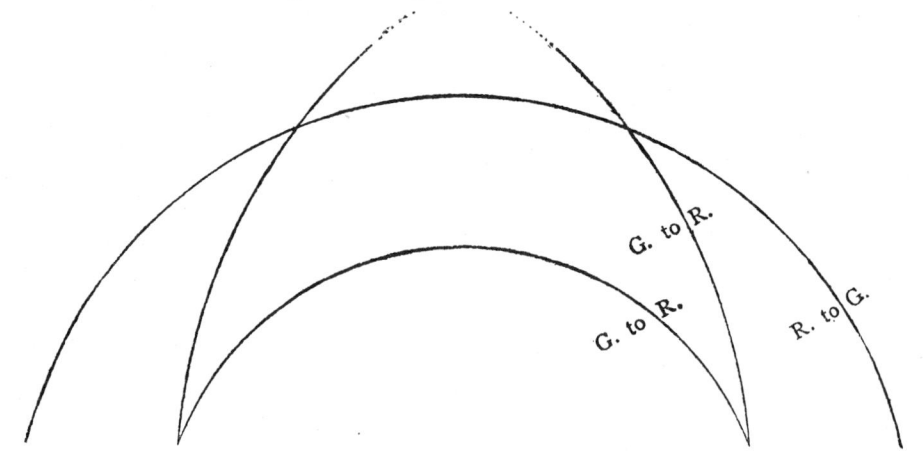

The Triple Rainbow. [G. to R. signifies *green to red* ; R. to G. *red to green*.]

whereunder are the hamlets *Makhaul* (a jau with one kasr) and *Authèym*, where are five houses. Late in the afternoon there fell great drops from the lowering skies ; then a driving rain fell suddenly, shrill and seething, upon the harsh gravel soil, and so heavily that in few moments all the plain land was a streaming plash. Our nâga settled under us stern-on to the cold tempest. Our worsted mantles were quickly wetted through ; and we cowered for shelter under the lee of the brute's body.

After half an hour the worst was past, and we mounted again. Little birds, before unseen, flitted cheerfully chittering over the wet wilderness. The low sun looked forth, and then appeared a blissful and surpassing spectacle ! a triple rainbow painted in the air before us. Over two equal bows a third was reared upon the feet of the first ; and like to it in the order of hues. — These were the celestial arches of the sun's building, a peace in heaven after the battle of the elements in the desert-land of Arabia.

The sun going down left us drowned in the drooping gloom, which was soon dark night. We held on our march in hope to meet with the Aarab, and there fell always a little rain. Serpentine lightning flickered over the ground before us, without thunder; long crested lightnings shot athwart and seemed suspended, by moments, in the wide horizon; other long cross flashes darted downward in double chains of light. The shape of all those lightnings was as an hair of wool that is fallen in water. Only sometimes we heard a little, not loud, roaring of thunder. In a lull of the weather we beheld the new moon, two days old, at her going down. The first appearing of the virgin moon is always greeted with a religious emotion in the deserts of Arabia, and we saluted her, poor night-wanderers, devoutly; the day by my reckoning should be the 23rd of April. We held on ever watching for the Beduin fires, and heard about us the night shrieks of I know not what wild birds. At length Hàmed thought he had seen a watch-fire glimmer far in front. As we rode further we saw it sometimes, and otherwhiles it was hidden by the uneven ground of the wilderness. The night darkness was very thick, the nâga stumbled, and we could not see the earth. Hàmed, whose wit ever failed a little short of the mark, began to be afraid we might fall from some cragged place: he would adventure no further. We had nothing to eat, and alighting with wet clothes, we lay down in the rain beside our camel; but the wind blew softly, and we soon slept.

The morrow broke with the cheerful voices of birds about us, as in a northern country! our clothes were dried and light again upon our backs, and we rose never the worse. We had not ridden a gunshot when we saw the booths hardly a mile in front, and trooping camels. At this happy human sight we put our nâga to the trot, and Hàmed snivelled his loud saddle-song. Some of those Aarab — they were B. Aly, came forth to meet us; for seeing my red saddle-bags of carpet stuff, they had taken me for one of those brokers [here they said *mushowwam*] from the border lands, who from time to time ride in their desert country to buy up camels. When we arrived, one spoke to his fellow, "Did I not tell thee that he was such?" and another answered, "Ay, and I knew him at the first sight." We dismounted at a booth and unloaded; and those who stood by led us toward the sheykh's beyt. "The morning coffee is ready, said they; let us go over, and there refresh yourselves, and tell us the news." Hàmed loosed out our nâga to graze; and we followed to the kahwa. — The householder, at whose tent we had alighted, came bye and bye to call us : we returned with him to breakfast, and there rested. The altitude of the plain land was here 3400 feet.

These were as all the other Beduw whom I have known, a merry crew of squalid wretches, iniquitous, fallacious, fanatical. Notwithstanding that the B. Aly are blamed as kafirs by their Harb kinsmen of the Medina dîra, the men in this menzil were perfect, more than all the tribesmen of the khála, in the formal observing of the religion. For when the sun was mounted to the mid-height, one of those desert men stood forth [Hàmed, a citizen of three great tribes, had never seen the like among Beduw] and played the *muéthin !* and being come to the last words, *es-salât wa es-salaam aleyk, yâ auwel khulk Illah wa khâtimat rusul Illah*, 'Peace be with thee, and glory, O first-born of the creation of God, and seal of the apostles of God,' those desert men gathered behind him in a row ; and they went through with their bowing, kneeling and knocking devotion, very praiseworthily ! That town religion they aped, doubtless, from the nigh-lying Kasîm, which is a Waháby country. — They called me also, " *Sull yâ, taal sull*, Come and pray thou ! " but I excused myself, and withdrew from them. I was never of any politic remembrance, that at the unlucky prayer hour I should not be found sitting in the midst of the most fanatical Arabs. — I wandered half a mile from them over the hot sand whither I saw some bushes ; but I could not be hid from their hawks' eyes : for when I returned, they said, 'The stranger had not prayed ; and oho ! — This can be no Musslim ! ' and there was some ferment amongst them.

I had eaten in a tent, and answered them shortly," What need of more questioning, my friends ? I am a Nasrâny." When they saw I took all things patiently they began to bear with me. " But how ! they said one to another, could there be any yet in the world so blind that they worshipped not Ullah ? " They gazed on me, and questioned my companion, " What is he for a rafîk ? how durst thou trust thyself with him ? — an heathen man ! " Hàmed responded mildly, ' Khalîl had been a good rafîk, and he heard good reported of him among the Aarab ; and if at any time Khalîl spoke of religion, he seemed then to have some right inkling of Ullah ; and his words sounded very nigh unto the words of the Moslemîn." The B. Aly were thus appeased, I was a passenger, and they would not molest me ; only they answered, ' Would God I might stay awhile in the well-instructed Kasîm, where the lord might make a way and enlighten me!' The good housewives said among them, *Widd el-ghrarîb béledhu.* These Beduins seeing me broken to the nomad life, enquired, 'were all my people Beduw?'

At half-afternoon Hàmed would set forward again — to pass another night in the khála! We had an evil fit yesterday, and were accorded, that if we might find the Aarab, this should be a day of repose. But now he said excusing himself, ' His breast was sore straitened, till he should be at home again!' — " This is the last quarter of the day, and see the lowering skies! where is thy understanding?" He answered : ' If I would stay, then he must forsake me ' ; and went to take his nâga : but I saw he remained to pasture her. The Beduins told me that not far before us was a ferîj of " good Aarab " ; who had lately received their summer provision of temmn from el-Irâk, and we might sup with them. I beckoned therefore to Hàmed to return with his camel. — And mounting we journeyed two hours : and came to that menzil, when the sun set : but seeing no man in the principal booth, we alighted a little apart and sat down. The householder, who was the sheykh, came soon, and some men with him, from the further tents, which were only three or four ; they stood a moment to see what we were! and then he approached, saying, " Wherefore sit ye here, rise ho ! and come into the tent." — Now I saw their sheep driven in ; and a good flock lie down before every booth : but I could see only a camel or two.

These Aarab have no goats : their small cattle are the black sheep with white heads, of high Nejd ; there was not a white fleece among them. When I asked Hàmed, " Where are their camels ? " he answered in a whisper, " They are the *Oreymát*, of Harb, that have but sheep-flocks ; they have no camels." — Here then was a new life of men inhabiting in the wilderness without camels! Hàmed added, " This is a kindred which has no heart for warfare ; their camels have been taken by ghrazzus, but they foray not again. They have no more than those few camels for carriage : yet they fare well ; for they have much samn of their ewes, which thou seest ; — and *yusûkun ez-zíka*, they pay tithing, to Ibn Rashîd." [The Harb and Shammar have all black sheep in these dîras, and few or no goats : they think their black-fleeced sheep are bigger bodied, and that the ewes yield more milk. Sheep more than other cattle languish in the sun ; we see them go drooping, in each other's shadow, and hanging their heads at noon : and surely the white-fleeces were better in a hot country.]

These Beduins, that are reckoned to the B. Sâlem, were of gentle and honest manners ; and I was never more kindly entertained in the nomad menzils. One of them — who had seen and spoken with the Nasrâny at Hâyil ! — reported very favourably of me. Here was not the half-grudging hospitality of the Medina Harb, and their tent was evenly divided : the men also were comely [which signifies in Arabia that they were well fed], and of a liberal carriage. Our sheykhly host, whose name was *Sâlem*, asked me ingenuously, ' Would I give him a remedy for his sore eyes ? ' I gave him the best medicine I had ; and he said sighing, " Who can tell if the Lord might not bless this mean unto me." Sâlem (therein the most honourable Arabian of my acquaintance) brought me immediately a present of dry milk shards, and butter : and he made us a bountiful supper of temmn with samn. When we were weary we lay down on the pure sand under his friendly tentcloth to sleep : but Sâlem, sitting-by, said he must waken all night, because the wolf — we knew it by the hounds' incessant barking — was prowling nigh us. Such were Beduins that had ceased to be cattle-reavers, in the desert !

When the day was breaking we rose to depart ; and the host brought us a great bowl of butter-milk : his was like the goodness of those B. Sâlem, in the way to Hâyil. — We journeyed two hours ; and the sun was risen with heat over the desert, when we came to a menzil of B. Aly, sixteen booths pitched ring-wise, — which hitherto I had not seen any nomads use in Arabia ; but their great cattle, lying thus within an hedge of tents and stretched cords, can hardly be robbed by night thieves. — If a camel may be raised and led forth, the rest (it is their sheep-like nature) will rise and follow ; and the steps of the pad-footed brute awaken not the slumbering Beduw. We found them coffee-Aarab, pithless day-sleepers, corroding their lives with pitiful dregs of the Môkha drug ; of malicious manners, of no hospitality. Certain of them looked upon me, and whispered and mocked together ! — all the nomads under Ibn Rashîd had heard of the forwandered Nasrâny. Dates were set before us ; and whilst we sat coffee drinking, two men went out with their matchlocks to shoot at a dog, which they called *sarûk*, a common thief. None gave him to eat, and all driving him from their beyts, they had looked to see the brute perish ; but he stole for himself more and more. Those Beduin shooters fired from thirty yards ; and they both missed him ! At the stroke of their balls in the sand, and rebutted by the (human) world, the hound fled back in the khála, with a lamentable howling ; and the shooters, that would spend no more lead, returned to the coffee-hearth. — I soon called Hàmed to mount ; lest their prayer-time should discover the Nasrâny.

We journeyed an hour or two, and fell in with a ráhla of Aarab : they were *el-Fúrn*, a kindred of Harb, called after the name of the sheykh's family, who is chief of the B. Aly ; — these were they whom Terky sought. Some young sheykhs who came riding together in advance upon their thelûls, or *rahôls* [which word is commonly heard in this dîra], approached, to enquire news of us passengers : and they knew me ! for I heard certain of them say under their breaths, " It is the kafir " ; and quoth one, " See his saddle-bags, stuffed with silver and gold ! so that they break the back of their nâga ! " Another said to us, " O you two passengers, riding upon the nâga, we go to alight yonder, under *Sâra* [a bow-shaped mountain coast of sandstone, before us] ; rest to-day in my tent."— The fellow added, in a knavish whisper to his companions, " Come over this evening and you shall see the game." I thought his mirth might be to threaten me with a knife as did the young Kahtâny sheykh at Hâyil. We excused ourselves : ' We must needs ride forward, said Hàmed, to pass certain (dangerous) way in the night time ' ; and with that word, striking our nâga, I was glad to outride them. Here we passed out of the crystalline into a sandstone soil : the height of this wilderness plain is 3300 feet. " We must go over Sâra, but not in the daylight, said Hàmed, for fear of Ateybân ; let us ride to yonder camels, and drink a little milk ; and repose there till evening." — I saw the solitary mountain *Sàk* far off in the plain of el-Kasîm, upon our right hand ; like a sharp cone, and black under a clear afternoon sky. Hàmed could even see the mountain tops el-Abanát ! — which stand at either side upon the W. er-Rummah, beyond Sàk, very far off.

We came to those herding lads ; and the younger taking my pan ran under his nâgas and milked full and frothed over for us. We sat down to drink ; and when they had heard our news, quoth the elder, " This is a man taller than any of our Aarab ! — Wherefore wander further, O stranger ? remain with us ! and a horse shall be given thee, and a mantle of scarlet, — billah with a long lance in his hand this (man) shall repulse Ateyba ! — Also they will give thee a maiden to wife." We departed from the good fellows : and I left there the speech and the franchise of the desert, for the village country of the Kasîm caravaners.

We went on riding under Sâra ; and ascended about the sunsetting in a breach of the mountain : and held on over the sandstone platform in the starlight, purposing to journey all night, which was cold and open about us.

Toward midnight, Hàmed, beginning to be afraid that we might lose ourselves, and overcome with slumber, drew bridle ; and we alighted in a place of sand and bushes ; where binding the nâga's knee we laid ourselves down to sleep. At dawn we remounted : and passing the rest of the low sandstone height as the sun came up we descended to a plain, and I saw palms of a (first) Kasîm village. "This is *er-Rauth*, said Hàmed, there are fifty houses." We found some of the village women busy abroad to cut fodder for their well-camels. Those hareem cried out, supposing we might be robbers, till we said *salaam!* — They were come forth in their old ragged smocks for dread of thieves. Hàmed, who was yet afraid of the Ateybân, enquired of them, " O hareem ! what have ye to tell us of any late ghrazzus ? " They answered, ' That a few days ago some of their women had been stripped by Beduins a little without the village walls ! '

Now before us lay the Nefûd sand of Kasîm, which begins to be driven-up in long swelling waves, that trend somewhat N. and S. Four miles further we went by the oasis *Ayûn* ; embayed in the same sandstone train, which is before called Sâra. Upon a cliff by the Nefûd side is a clay-built lighthouse-like watch-tower [the watch-tower is found in all the villages of Kasîm]. The watchman (who must be clear sighted) is paid by a common contribution : his duty is to look forth, in the spring months, from the day rising till the going down of the sun ; for this is the season, when the villagers who have called in their few milch goats from the Aarab, send them forth to pasture without the oasis. We saw the man standing unquietly in his gallery, at the tower head, in the flame of the sun ; and turning himself to every part, he watched, under the shadow of his hand, all the fiery waste of sand before him. Hàmed said, the palms at Ayûn are about half the palms of Teyma ; and here might be 400 or 500 inhabitants. Ayûn stands at the crossing of the Kasîm cameleers' paths, to J. Shammar, to the land of the north, and to the Holy Cities. My rafîk had been well content to leave me here ; where, he promised, I should meet with carriers to all parts, even to Kuweyt and Bosra, " wellah, more than in Boreyda."

Some great cattle were feeding before us in the Nefûd — they were not camels; but, oh! happy homely sight, the village kind at pasture in that uncheerful sand wilderness! I said, " I would ride to them and seek a draught of cow-milk." Hàmed answered, " Thou wilt ask it in vain, go not Khalîl! for these are not like the Beduw, but people of the *géria*, not knowing hospitality: before us lies a good village, we shall soon see the watch-tower, and we will alight there to breakfast." I saw a distant clay steeple, over the Nefûd southward. Hàmed could not tell the name of that oasis: he said, " Wellah the *geraîeh* (towns and villages) be so many in el-Kasîm!" We came in two hours to *Gassa*, a palm village, with walls, and the greatest grown palms that I had seen since Teyma, — and this said Hàmed, who knew Teyma. When I asked, what were the name Gassa, he answered, " There is a pumpkin so called:" but the Beduw are rude etymologers. Their watch-tower — *mergáb* or *garra* — is founded upon a rock above the village. The base is of rude stones laid in clay, the upper work is well built of clay bricks. We were now in Kasîm, the populous and (religious) nefûd country of the caravaners. We did not enter the place, but halted at a solitary orchard house under the garra. It was the time of their barley harvest: this day was near the last in April. The land-height I found to be now only 2800 feet.

We dismounted; the householder came out of his yard, to lead us to the kahwa, and a child bore in my bags: Hàmed brought away the head-stall and halter of our camel, for here, he said, was little assurance. The coffee-hall floor was deep Nefûd sand! When we had drunk two cups, the host called us into his store room; where he set before us a platter of dates — none of the best, and a bowl of water. The people of Kasîm are not lovers of hospitality: the poor Aarab (that are passengers without purses) say despitefully, 'There is nothing there but for thy penny!' — this is true. Kasîm resembles the border lands, and the inhabitants are become as townsmen: their deep sand country, in the midst of high Arabia, is hardly less settled than Syria. The Kusmân are prudent and adventurous: there is in them much of the thick B. Temîm blood. Almost a third of the people are caravaners, to foreign provinces, to Medina and Mecca, to Kuweyt, Bosra, Bagdad, to the Waháby country, to J. Shammar. And many of them leave home in their youth to seek fortune abroad; where some (we have seen) serve the Ottoman government in arms: they were till lately the Ageyl at Bagdad, Damascus, and Medina. — All Nejd Arabia, east of Teyma, appertains to the Persian Gulf traffic, and not to Syria: and therefore *the (foreign) colour of Nejd is Mesopotamian!* In those borderlands are most of the emigrated from el-Kasîm, — husbandmen and small salesmen ; and a few of them are there become wealthy merchants.

Arabians of other provinces viewing the many green villages of this country in their winding-sheet of sand, are wont to say half scornfully, ' Kasîm is all Nefûd.' The Nefûd of Kasîm is a sand country, through whose midst passes the great Wady [er-Rummah], and everywhere the ground water is nigh at hand. Wells have been digged and palms planted in low grounds [gá, or khóbra], with a soil of loam not too brackish or bitter : and such is every oasis-village of el-Kasîm. The chief towns are of the later middle age. The old Kasîm settlements, of which the early Mohammedan geographers make mention, are now, so far as I have enquired, ruined sites and names out of mind. The poor of Kasîm and *el-Wéshm* wander even in their own country ; young field labourers seek service from town to town, where they hear that *el-urruk*, the sweat of their brow, is likely to be well paid. Were el-Kasîm laid waste, this sand country would be, like the lands beyond Jordan, a wilderness full of poor village ruins.

Our host sat with a friend, and had sparred his yard door against any intrusion of loitering persons. These substantial men of Kasîm, wore the large silken Bagdad kerchief, cast negligently over the head and shoulders ; and under this head-gear the red Turkey cap, *tarbûsh*. Our host asked me what countryman I was. " I am a traveller, from Damascus." — " No, thou are not a Shâmy, thy speech is better than so ; for I have been in Syria : tell me, art thou not from some of those villages in the Hauràn ? I was there with the Ageyl. What art thou ? thou art not of the Moslemîn ; art thou then Yahûdy, or of the Nasâra ? " — " Yes, host, a Mesîhy ; will ye therefore drive me away, and kill me ? " — " No ! and fear nothing ; is not this el-Kasîm ? where the most part have travelled in foreign lands : they who have seen the world are not like the ignorant, they will treat thee civilly." — We heard from him that Ibn Saûd was come as far as *Mejmaâ* : but those rumours had been false of his riding in Kasîm, and in the Harb country ! Our host desired to buy quinine of the hakim ; I asked half a real ; he would pay but fourpence, and put me in mind of his inhospitable hospitality. — " Wilt thou then accompany me to Boreyda ? and I will give it thee." — " Wherefore should I pay for kanakîna ? in Kasîm thou wilt see it given away (by some charitable merchants)."

— We rode over a salt-crusted bottom beyond the village : the well-water at Gassa has a taste of this mineral. In the oasis, which is greater than er-Rauth, may be three hundred souls. The dark weather was past, the sun shone out in the afternoon ; and I felt as we journeyed here in the desert of el-Kasîm, such a stagnant sultry air, as we may commonly find in the deep Jordan plain below Jericho. At our left hand is still the low sandstone coast ; whereunder I could see palms and watch-towers of distant hamlets and villages. The soil is grit-sand with reefs of sand-rock ; beside our path are dunes of deep Nefûd sand. After five miles, we came before *Shukkûk*, which is not far from Boreyda ; it stands (as I have not seen another Arabian settlement) without walls ! in the desert side. Here we drew bridle to enquire tidings, and drink of their sweet water. We heard that *Hásan*, Emir of Boreyda, whom they commonly call *Weled* (child of) *Mahanna*, was with his armed band in the wilderness, *ghrazzai*. — Mahanna, a rich *jemmâl* or camel master at Boreyda, lent money at usury, till half the town were his debtors ; and finally with the support of the Waháby, he usurped the Emir's dignity ! — Hàmed told me yet more strangely, that the sheykh of a géria, *Káfer*, near *Kuseyby*, in these parts is a Sâny ! he said the man's wealth had procured him the village sheykhship. [It is perhaps no free oasis, but under Boreyda or Hâyil.]

Now I saw the greater dunes of the Nefûd ; such are called *tâus* and *nef'd* (pl. *anfàd*) by Beduins : and *adanát* and *kethîb* (pl. *kethbàn*) are words heard in Kasîm. " Not far beyond the dunes on our right hand (towards Aneyza) lies the W. er-Rummah," said Hàmed. We journeyed an hour and a half, and came upon a brow of the Nefûd, as the sun was going down. And from hence appeared a dream-like spectacle ! — a great clay town built in this waste sand with enclosing walls and towers and streets and houses ! and there beside a bluish dark wood of ethel trees, upon high dunes ! This is Boreyda ! and that square minaret, in the town, is of their great mesjid. I saw, as it were, Jerusalem in the desert ! [as we look down from the mount of Olives]. The last upshot sun-beams enlightened the dim clay city in glorious manner, and pierced into that dull pageant of tamarisk trees. I asked my rafîk, " Where are their palms ? " He answered, " Not in this part, they lie behind yonder great dune towards the Wady (er-Rummah)."

Hamed : " And whilst we were in the way, if at any time I have displeased thee, forgive it me ; and say hast thou found me a good rafîk? Khalîl, thou seest Boreyda! and to-day I am to leave thee in this place. And when thou art in any of their villages, say not, 'I (am) a Nasrâny,' for then they will utterly hate thee; but pray as they, so long as thou shalt sojourn in the country, and in nothing let it be seen that thou art not of the Moslemîn: do thus, that they may bear thee also goodwill, and further thee. Look not to find these townlings mild-hearted like the Beduw! but conform thyself to them; or they will not suffer thee to abide long time among them. I do counsel thee for the best — I may not compel thee! say thou art a *mudowwy*, and tell them what remedies thou hast, and for which diseases: this also must be thine art to live by. Thou hast suffered for this name of Nasrâny, and what has that profited thee? only say now, if thou canst, 'I (am a) Musslem.'"

We met with some persons of the town, without their walls, taking the evening air; and as we went by, they questioned my Beduwy rafîk: among them I noted a sinister Galla swordsman of the Emir. Hàmed answered, 'We were going to the Emir's hostel.' They said, "It is far, and the sun is now set; were it not better for you to alight at such an house? that stands a little within the gate, and lodge there this night; and you may go to the Emir in the morning." We rode from them and passed the town gate: their clay wall [vulg. *ajjidát*] is new, and not two feet thick. We found no man in the glooming streets; the people were gone home to sup, and the shops in the sûk were shut for the night: their town houses of (sandy) clay are low-built and crumbling. The camel paced under us with shuffling steps in the silent and forsaken ways: we went by the unpaved public place, *mejlis*; which I saw worn hollow by the townspeople's feet! and there is the great clay mesjid and high-built minaret. Hàmed drew bridle at the yard of the Emir's hostel, *Munôkh es-Sheukh*.

The porter bore back the rude gates; and we rode in and dismounted. The journey from er-Rauth had been nearly twenty-five miles. It was not long, before a kitchen lad bade us, "rise and say God's name." He led through dim cloistered courts; from whence we mounted by great clay stairs to supper. The degrees were worn down in the midst, to a gutter, and we stumbled dangerously in the gloom. We passed by a gallery and terraces above, which put me in mind of our convent buildings: the boy brought us on without light to the end of a colonnade, where we felt a ruinous floor under us. And there he fetched our supper, a churlish wheaten mess, boiled in water (a sort of Arabian *búrghrol,*) without samn : we were guests of the peasant Emir of Boreyda. It is the evening meal in Kasîm, but should be prepared with a little milk and butter ; in good houses this búrghrol, cooked in the broth and commonly mixed with temmn, is served with boiled mutton. — When we had eaten and washed, we must feel the way back in the dark, in danger of breaking our necks, which were more than the supper's worth. — And now Hàmed bade me his short Beduin *adieux* : he mounted his camel ; and I was easy to see my rafîk safely past the (tyrant's) gates. The moon was rising ; he would ride out of the town, and lodge in one of the villages.

I asked now to visit " the Emir," — Hásan's brother, whom he had left deputy in Boreyda ; it was answered, " The hour is late, and the Emir is in another part of the town : — *el-bâkir !* in the morning." The porter, the coffee-server, a swordsman, and other servitors of the guest-house gathered about me : the yard gates were shut, and they would not suffer me to go forth. Whilst I sat upon a clay bench, in the little moonlight, I was startled from my weariness by the abhorred voice of their barbaric religion ! the muéthin crying from the minaret to the latter prayer. — 'Ah ! I mused, my little provident memory ! what a mischance ! why had I sat on thus late, and no Emir, and none here to deliver me, till the morning ?' I asked quickly, 'Where was the sleeping place ?' Those hyenas responded, with a sort of smothered derision, ' Would I not pray along with them, ere I went to rest ? ' — they showed me to a room in the dark hostel building, which had been used for a small kahwa.

All was silent within and sounding as a chapel. I groped, and felt clay pillars, and trod on ashes of an hearth : and lay down there upon the hard earthen floor. My pistol was in the bottom of my bags, which the porter had locked up in another place : I found my pen-knife, and thought in my heart, they should not go away with whole skins, if any would do me a mischief ; yet I hoped the night might pass quietly. I had not slumbered an hour when I heard footsteps, of some one feeling through the floor ; " Up, said a voice, and follow me, thou art called before the sheykhs to the coffee hall : " — he went before, and I followed by the sound ; and found persons sitting at coffee, who seemed to be of the Emir's guard. They bade me be seated, and one reached me a cup : then they questioned me, " Art not thou the Nasrâny that was lately at Hâyil ? thou wast there with some of Annezy ; and Aneybar sent thee away upon their *jurraba* (mangy thelûl) : they were to convey thee to Kheybar ? " — " I am he." — " Why then didst thou not go to Kheybar ? " — " You have said it, — because the thelûl was jurraba ; those Beduins could not carry me thither, which Aneybar well knew, but the slave would not hear : — tell me, how knowest thou this ? " — " I was in Hâyil, and I saw thee there. Did not Aneybar forbid thy going to Kasîm ? " — " I heard his false words, that ye were enemies, his forbidding I did not hear ; how could the slave forbid me to travel, beyond the borders of Ibn Rashîd ? " — At this they laughed and tossed their shallow heads, and I saw some of their teeth, — a good sign ! The inquisitors added, with their impatient tyranny, " What are the papers with thee, ha ! go and fetch them ; for those will we have instantly, and carry them to the Emir, — and (to a lad) go thou with the Nasrâny."

The porter unlocked a store-closet where my bags lay. I drew out the box of medicines ; but my weary hands seemed slow to the bird-witted wretches that had followed me. The worst of them, a Kahtâny, struck me with his fist, and reviled and threatened the Nasrâny. " Out, they cried, with all thy papers ! " and snatched them from my hands : " We go with these, they said now, to the Emir." They passed out ; the gates were shut after them : and I was left alone in the court. The scelerat remained who had struck me : he came to me presently with his hand on his sword, and murmured, " Thou kafîr ! say *La îlah ill' Ullah* ; " and there came another and another. I sat upon the clay bench in the moonlight, and answered them, " To-morrow I will hear you ; and not now, for I am most weary."

Then they plucked at my breast (for money) ! I rose, and they all swarmed about me. — The porter had said a word in my ear, " If thou hast any silver commit it to me, for these will rob thee : " but now I saw he was one of them himself ! All the miscreants being upon me, I thought I might exclaim, " *Haramîeh*, thieves ! ho ! honest neighbours ! " and see what came of it ; but the hour was late, and this part of the town solitary. — None answered to my voice, and if any heard me, doubtless their hearts would shrink within them ; for the Arabs [inhabiting a country weakly governed and full of alarms] are commonly dastards. When I cried *thieves !* I saw my tormentors stand a little aghast : " Shout not (they said hoarsely) or by Ullah — ! " So I understood that this assailing me was of their own ribald malice, and shouted on ; and when I began to move my arms, they were such cowards that, though I was infirm, I might, I perceived, with a short effort have delivered myself from them : yet this had been worse — for then they would return with weapons ; and I was enclosed by walls, and could not escape out of the town. Six were the vile crew struggling with me : I thought it best to shout on *haramîeh!* and make ever some little resistance, to delay the time. I hoped every moment that the officer would return from the Emir. Now my light purse was in their brutish hands ; and that which most troubled me, the aneroid barometer, — it seemed to them a watch in the starlight ! The Kahtâny snatched and burst the cord by which the delicate instrument was suspended from my neck ; and ran away with it like a hound with a good bone in his mouth. They had plucked off my mantle and kerchief ; and finally the villains left me standing alone in a pair of slops : then they hied all together to the door where my bags lay. But I thought they would not immediately find my pistol in the dark ; and so it was.

— Now the Emir's man stood again at the gate, beating and calling loudly to be admitted : and the porter went like a truant to open. " What has happened ? " quoth the officer who entered. " They have stripped the Nasrâny." — " Who has done this ? " — " It was the Kahtâny, in the beginning." " And this fellow, I answered, was one of the nimblest of them ! " The rest had fled into the hostel building, when the Emir's man came in. " Oh, the shame ! (quoth the officer) that one is robbed in the Kasr of the Emir ; and he a man who bears letters from the Sooltân, what have you done ? the Lord curse you all together." " Let them, I said, bring my clothes, although they have rent them." — " Others shall be given thee by the Emir." The lurkers came forth at his call from their dark corners ; and he bade them, " Bring the stranger his clothes : — and all, he said to me, that they have robbed shall be restored, upon pain of cutting off the hand ; wellah the hand of anyone with whom is found aught shall be laid in thy bags for the thing that was stolen. I came to lead thee to a lodging prepared for thee ; but I must now return to the Emir : — and (naming them) thou, and thou, and thou, do no more thus, to bring on you the displeasure of the Emir." They answered, " We had not done it, but he refused to say, *La îlah ill' Ullah*." — " This is their falsehood ! — for to please them I said it four

or five times ; and hearken ! I will say it again, La îlah, ill' Ullah.'
— _Officer_ : " I go, and shall be back anon." — " Leave me no more
among robbers." — " Fear not, none of them will do anything further
against you " ; and he bade the porter close the gates behind him.

He returned soon : and commanded those wretches, from the Emir,
" upon pain of the hand," to restore all that they had robbed from the
Nasrâny ; he bade also the porter make a fire in the porch to give us
light. The Kahtâny swordsman, who had been the ringleader of them —
he was one of the Emir's band — adjured me to give a true account of
the money which was in my purse : ' for my words might endanger his
hand ; and if I said but the sooth the Lord would show me mercy.' —
" Dost thou think, Miserable, that a Christian man should be such as
thyself ! " — " Here is the purse, quoth the officer ; how much money
should be therein ? take it, and count thy _derâhim_ [δραχμ-]." I found
their barbarous hands had been in it ; for there remained only a few
pence ! " Such and such lacks." — _Officer :_ " Oh ! ye who have taken
the man's money, go and fetch it, and the Lord curse you." The swordsman went ; and came back with the money, — two French gold pieces
of 20 francs : all that remained to me in this bitter world. _Officer :_
" Say now, is this all thy _fulûs_ ? " — " That is all." — " Is there any
more ? " — " No ! " — The Kahtâny showed me his thanks with a
wondering brutish visage. _Officer :_ " And what more ? " — " Such
and such." — The wretches went, and came again with the small things
and what else they had time, after stripping me (it was by good fortune
but a moment), to steal from my bags. _Officer :_ " Look now, has thou
all, is there anything missing ? " — " Yes, my watch " (the aneroid
which after the pistol was my most care in Arabia) ; but they exclaimed,
" What watch ! no, we have restored all to him already." _Officer :_
" Oh, you liars, you cursed ones, you thieves, bring this man his watch !
or the (guilty) hand is forfeited to the Emir." It was fetched with
delays ; and of this they made restitution with the most unwillingness :
the metal gilt might seem to them fine gold. — To my comfort, I found
on the morrow that the instrument was uninjured : I might yet mark
in it the height of a fathom.

He said now, ' It was late, and I should pass the night here.' —
" Lend me a sword, if I must sleep in this cursed place ; and if any set
upon me again, should I spare him ? " — " There is no more danger,
and as for these they shall be locked in the coffee-hall till the morning : "

and he led away the offenders. — The officer had brought my papers : only the safe-conduct of Aneybar was not among them !

When the day broke the Emir's officer — whose name was Jeyber — returned to me : I asked anew to visit the Emir. Jeyber answered, he must first go and speak with him. When he came again, he laid my bags on his infirm shoulders saying, he would bring me to my lodging. He led me through an outlying street ; and turned into a vast ruinous yard, before a great building — now old and crumbling, that had been the Emir's palace in former days [the house walls here of loam may hardly stand above one hundred years]. We ascended by hollow clay stairs to a great hall above : where two women, his housewives, were sitting. Jeyber, tenant of all the rotten palace, was a tribesman of Kahtân. In the end was a further room, which he gave me for my lodging. " I am weary, and thou more, said he ; a cup of kahwa will do us both good : " Jeyber sat down at his hearth to prepare the morrow's coffee.

In that there came up some principal persons of the town ; clad in the (heavy) Mesopotamian wise. A great number of the well-faring sort in Boreyda are *jemmamîl*, camel masters trading in the caravans. They are wheat carriers in Mesopotamia ; they bring down clothing and temmn to Nejd ; they load dates and corn of Kasîm (when the prices serve) for el-Medina. In autumn they carry samn, which they have taken up from the country Nomads, to Mecca ; and from thence they draw coffee. These burly Arabian citizens resemble peasants ! they were travelled men ; but I found in them an implacable fanaticism.

Jeyber said when they were gone, " Now shall we visit the Emir ? " We went forth ; and he brought me through a street to a place, before the Prince's house. A sordid fellow was sitting there, like Job, in the dust of their street : two or three more sate with him, — he might be thirty-five years of age. I enquired, ' Where was Abdullah the Emir ? ' They said " He is the Emir ! " — " Jeyber (I whispered), is this the Emir ? " — " It is he." I asked the man, " Art thou Weled Mahanna ? " He answered, " Ay." " Is it (I said) a custom here, that strangers are robbed in the midst of your town ? I had eaten of your bread and salt ; and your servants set upon me in your yard." — " They were Beduw that robbed you." — " But I have lived with the Beduw ; and was never robbed in a menzil : I never lost anything in a host's tent. Thou sayest they were Beduins ; but they were the Emir's men ! " — *Abdullah* :

"I say they were Kahtân all of them." He asked to see my 'watch.' "That I have not with me; but here is a telescope!" He put this to his eyes and returned it. I said, "I give it thee; but thou wilt give me other clothing for my clothing which the Emir's servants have rent." — He would not receive my gift, the peasant would not make the Nasrâny amends; and I had not money to buy more. "To-day, said he, you depart." — "Whither?" — "To Aneyza; and there are certain cameleers — they left us yesterday, that are going to *Siddûs*: they will convey thee thither." — At Siddûs (which they suppose to have been a place of pilgrimage of the idolatrous people of the country or "Christians" before Mohammed), is an antique "needle" or column, with some scoring or epigraph. [Vol. I. p. 245.] But this was Abdullah's guile, he fabled with me of cameleers to Siddûs: and then he cries, "*Min yeshîl*, who will convey the Nasrâny on his camel to *el-Wady?*" — which I afterwards knew to signify the palms at the *Wady er-Rummah*: I said to him, 'I would rest this day, I was too weary for riding.' Abdullah granted (albeit unwillingly); for all the Arabians [inhabitants of a weary land] tender human infirmities. — "Well, as thou wilt; and that may suffice thee."

— There came a young man to bid me to coffee. "They call you said Abdullah, and go with him." I followed the messenger and Jeyber: we came to some principal house in the town; and there we entered a pleasant coffee-hall. I saw the walls pargetted with fret-work in gypsum; and about the hearth were spread Persian carpets. The sweet *ghrottha* firewood (a tamarisk kind of the Nefûd) glowed in the hearth, and more was laid up in a niche ready to the coffee maker's hand: and such is the cleanly civil order of all the better citizen households in Kasîm. Here sat a cold fanatical conventicle of well-clad persons; and a young man was writing a letter after an elder's words. But that did not hinder his casting some reproach, at every pause, upon the Christian stranger, blaspheming that which he called my impure religion. — How crabbed seemed to me his young looks, moved by the bestial spirit within! I took it to be of evil augury that none blamed him. And contemptible to an European was the solemn silence of these infantile greybeards, in whom was nothing more respectable than their apparel! I heard no comfortable word among them; and wondered why they had called me! after the second cup, I left them sitting; and returned to Jeyber's place, which is called the palace Hajellân: there a boy met me with two dry girdle-breads, from the guest-house. Such sour town bread is crude and tough; and I could not swallow it, even in the days of famine.

The *Kasr Hajellân* was built by Abdullah, son of *Abd-el-Azîz*, princes of Boreyda. Abdullah was murdered by Mahanna, when he usurped the government with the countenance of the Waháby. Mahanna was sheykh over the town for many years, and his children are Hásan (now Emir) and Abdullah.

The young sons of the Prince that was slain fled to the neighbour town of Aneyza. — And after certain years, in a spring season, when the armed band was encamped with Hásan in the Nefûd, they stole over by night to Boreyda; and lay hid in some of their friends' houses. And on the morrow, when the tyrant passed by, going to his mid-day prayers in the great mesjid, Abdullah's sons ran suddenly upon him with the knife! and they slew him there in the midst of the street. A horseman, one of the band that remained in the town, mounted and passed the gates, and rode headlong over the Nefûd; till he found the ghrazzu and Hásan. — Hásan hearing this heavy tiding gave the word to mount and the band rode hastily homeward, to be in Boreyda that night.

Abdullah in the meanwhile who, though he have a leg short, is nimble of his butchery wit, held fast in the town. In all this fear and trouble, his was yet the stronger part; and the townspeople, long daunted by the tyranny of Mahanna, were unready to favour the young homicides. And so well Abdullah wrought, that ere there was any sedition, he had enclosed the princelings in an house.

It was nightfall when Abdullah with his armed men came before their door; and to give light (to the horrid business), a bonfire was kindled in the street. Abdullah's sons and a few who were their companions within, desperately defended their lives with matchlocks, upon the house head. — Some bolder spirits that came with Abdullah advanced to the gate, under a shield they had made them of a door (of rude palm boarding), with a thick layer of dates crammed upon it. And sheltered thus from weak musketry, they quickly opened a hole, poured-in powder and laid the train. A brand was fetched! — and in the hideous blast every life within the walls perished, — besides one young man, miserably wounded; who (with a sword in his hand) would have leapt down, as they entered, and escaped; and he could not: but still flying hither and thither he cursed-on and detested them, till he fell by a shot. — Hásan arriving in the night, found the slayers of his father already slain, and the town in quiet : and he was Emir of Boreyda. — Others of the princely family of this town I saw afterward dwelling in exile at Aneyza ; and one of two old brethren, my patients, now poor and blind, was he who should have been by inheritance Emir of Boreyda !

I wandered in this waste Kasr, which, as a princely residence, might be compared with the Kasr at Hâyil ; although less, as the principality of Boreyda is less. But if we compare the towns, Hâyil is a half Beduin town-village, with a foreign sûk ; Boreyda is a great civil township of the midland Nejd life. The palace court, large as a market place, is returned to the Nefûd sand ! Within the ruinous Kasr I found a coffee-hall having all the height of the one-storied building, with galleries above — in such resembling the halls of ancient England, and of goodly proportion : the walls of sandy clay were adorned with pargetting of jis. This silent and now (it seems) time-worn Kasr, here in the midst of Desert Arabia, had been built in our fathers' days ! I admired the gypsum fretwork of their clay walls : such dedale work springs as a plant under the hands of the Semitic artificers, and is an imagery of their minds' vision of Nature ! — which they behold not as the Pythagoreans contained in few pure lines, but all-adorned and unenclosed. And is their crust-work from India ? We find a skill in raw clay-work in Syria ; clay storing-jars, pans, hearths and corn-hutches are seen in all their cottages. In Lebanon the earthen walls and pillars, in some rich peasants' houses, are curiously crusted with clay fretwork, and stained in barbaric wise.

— Admirable seemed the architecture of that clay palace ! [the sufficiency of the poorest means in the Arabs' hands to a perfect end]. The cornice ornament of these builders is that we call the shark's-tooth, as in the Mothîf at Hâyil. A rank of round-headed blind arches is turned for an appearance of lightness in the outer walling, and painted in green and red ochre. Perchance the builder of Kasr Hajellân was some Bagdad master, *muâllem* — that which we may understand of some considerable buildings, standing far from any civil soil in certain desert borders. Years before I had seen a kella among the ruins of 'Utherah in mount Seir, where is a great welling pool, a watering of the Howeytát [Vol. I. p. 74] : it was a rusty building but not ruinous ; and Mahmûd from Maan told me, 'The kella had been built in his time, *by the Beduw!*' I asked in great astonishment, "If Beduw had skill in masonry?" — *Mahmûd:* "Nay, but they fetched a muâllem from Damascus; who set them to draw the best stones from the ruins, and as he showed them so the Beduins laid the courses." In that Beduin kella were not a few loopholes and arches, and the whole frame had been built by his rude prentices without mortar! In Beduins is an easy wit in any matter not too remote from their minds; and there are tribes that in a summer's day have become ploughmen. [Vol. I. p. 54, v. also pp. 84, 85, 275, 487.] — Jeyber inhabited the crumbling walls of the old Mothîf. The new peasant lords of Boreyda keep no public hospitality; for which they are lightly esteemed by the dwellers in the desert.

I went out with Jeyber to buy somewhat in the sûk, and see the town. We passed through a market for cattle forage, mostly vetches: and beyond were victuallers' shops, — in some of them I saw hanging huge (mutton — perhaps Mesopotamian) sausages! and in many were baskets of parched locusts. Here are even cook-shops — yet unknown in the Beduin-like Hâyil — where one may have a warm mess of rice and boiled mutton, or else camel flesh for his penny. A stranger might live at Boreyda, in the midst of Nomad Arabia, nearly as in Mesopotamia; saving that here are no coffee taverns. Some of those who sat selling green stuff in the stalls were women! — Damascus is not so civil! and there are only a few poor saleswomen at Aneyza. Boreyda, a metropolis of Oasis Arabia, is joined to the northern settled countries by the trading caravans; and the B. Temîm townsmen are not unlike the half-blooded Arabs of those border provinces.

Elvish boys and loiterers in the street gaped upon the Nasrâny stranger; and they gathered as we went. Near the mejlis or market square there was sitting, on a clay bench, that Galla swordsman of the Emir, whose visage I had noted yester-evening, without the gate. The swarthy swordsman reproved Jeyber, for bringing me out thus before the people; then rising, with a stick, he laid load upon the dusty mantles of some of them, in the name of the Emir. Jeyber, liberal minded as a Beduwy, but timid more than townsfolk, hearing this talk, led me back hastily by bye-streets: I would have gone about to visit another part of the town, but he brought me again by solitary ways to his place. He promised, that he would ride with me on the morrow to

Aneyza ; " Aneyza, he said, is not far off." These towns were set down on maps with as much as a journey between them : but what was there heretofore to trust in maps of Arabia ! Jeyber, whose stature and manners showed the Beduin blood, was of Kahtân in el-Kasîm. Poor, among his tribesmen, but of a sheykhly house, he had left the desert life to be of the Emir's armed service in Boreyda. The old contrariety of fortune was written in his meagre visage ; he was little past the middle age, and his spirits half spent. The mild Beduin nature sweetened in him his Kahtâny fanaticism ; and I was to-day a thaif-ullah in his household : he maintained therefore my cause in the town, and was my advocate with the swine Abdullah. But the fanatical humour was not quenched in him ; for some one saying, " This (man) could not go to er-Riâth ; for they would kill him !" Jeyber responded, half-smiling, " Ay, they are very austere there ; they might not suffer him amongst them." He spoke also with rancour of the heterodox Mohammedanism of Nejrân [whose inhabitants are in religion *Bayâdiyyeh*, 'like the people of Mascat']. Jeyber had passed his former life in those southern countries : Wady Dauâsir, and Wady Bîsha, he said, are full of good villages.

The mid-day heat was come ; and he went to slumber in a further part of the waste building. I had reposed somewhile, in my chamber, when a creaking of the old door, painted in vermillion, startled me ! — and a sluttish young woman entered. I asked, wherefore had she broken my rest ? Her answer was like some old biblical talk ; *Tekhálliny aném fi hothnak ?* ' Suffer me to sleep in thy bosom.' — Who could have sent thus lurid quean ? the Arabs are the basest of enemies, — hoped they to find an occasion to accuse the Nasrâny ? But the kind damsel was not daunted ; for when I chided she stood to rate the stranger : saying, with the loathly voice of misery, ' Aha ! the cursed Nasrâny ! and I was about to be slain, by faithful men ; that were in the way, sent from the Emir, to do it ! and I might not now escape them.' — I rose and put this baggage forth, and fastened the door. — But I wondered at her words, and mused that only for the name of a Religion, (O Chimæra of human self-love, malice, and fear !) I was fallen daily into such mischiefs, in Arabia. — Now Jeyber came again from napping ; and his hareem related to him the adventure : Jeyber left us saying, he must go to the Emir.

Soon after this we heard people of the town flocking about our house, and clamouring under the casements, which opened backward upon a street, and throwing up stones ! and some noisy persons had broken into the great front yard ! — The stair was immediately full of them ; and they bounced at our door which the women had barred. — "Alas, said the hareem, wringing their hands, what can we do now? for the riotous people will kill thee ; and Jeyber is away." One of them was a townswoman, the other was a Beduwîa : both were good towards the guest. I sat down saying to them, "My sisters, you must defend the house with your tongues." — They were ready ; and the townswoman looking out backward chided them that made this hubbub in the street. "Ha ! uncivil people ; who be they that throw up stones into the apartment of the hareem ? akhs ! what would ye ? — ye seek what ? God send a sorrow upon you ! — Oh ! ye seek Khalîl the Nasrâny ? but here is not Khalîl ; ye fools, he is not here : away with you. Go ! I say, for shame, and Ullah curse you." — And she that kept the door cried to them that were without, "Aha ! what is your will ? — akhs ! who are these that beat like to break our door? O ye devil-sick and shameless young men ! Khalîl is not here ; he went forth, go and seek the Nasrâny, go ! We have told you Khalîl went forth, we know not whither, — akhs ! [they knocked now on the door with stones.] Oh you shameless fellows ! would ye break through folks' doors, to the hareem ? Ullah send a very pestilence upon you all ; and for this the Emir will punish you." Whilst she was speaking there was a confused thrusting and shuffling of feet without our door ; the strokes of their sticks and stones sounded hideously upon the wood. — The faithful women's tongues yet delayed them ! and I put my hope in the stars, that Jeyber would return with speed. But if the besiegers burst in to rend me in pieces, should I spare the foremost of them ? The hareem cried on, "Why beat thus, ye cursed people ? — akhs ! will ye beat down our door indeed ?"

At length came Jeyber again ; and in the name of the Emir he drove them all forth, and locked them out of his yard. — When he entered, he shrunk up his shoulders and said to me, "They are clamouring to the Emir for thy death ! 'No Nasrâny, they say, ever entered Boreyda' : there is this outcry in the town, and Abdullah is for favouring the people ! — I have now pleaded with him. If, please Ullah, we may pass this night in safety, to-morrow when my thelûl shall be come— and I have sent for her — I will convey thee by solitary lanes out of the place ; and bring thee to Aneyza." — As we were speaking, we heard those townspeople swarming anew in his court ! the foremost mounted again upon our stairs, — and the door was open. But Jeyber, threatening grievous punishments of the Emir, drove them down once more ; and out of his yard. When he returned, he asked his house-wives, with looks of mistrust, who it was had undone the gate (from within) ? which he had left barred ! He said, he must go out again, to speak with Abdullah ; but should not be long absent. I would not let him pass, till he had promised me to lock his gates, and carry the (wooden) key with him. There remained only this poor soul, and the timber of an old door, betwixt me, a lonely alien, and the fanatical wildness of this townspeople. When he came again he said the town was quiet : Abdullah, at his intercession, had forbidden to make more ado, the riotous were gone home ; and he had left the gate open.

After this there came up some other of the principal citizens, to visit me : they sat about the hearth in Bagdad gowns and loose kerchiefs and red caps ; whilst Jeyber made coffee. Amongst them appeared the great white (Medina) turban — yet spotless, though he slept in it — of that old vagabund issue of the néby ! who a month before had been a consenting witness to my mischiefs at Hâyil ! "Who art thou ? " I asked. — " Oh ! dost thou not remember the time when we were together in Hâyil ? " — " And returnest thou so soon from India ? " — " I saw the Emir, and ended my business ; also I go not to el-Hind, until after the Haj." There came in on the heels of them a young sheykh, who arrived then from Hásan's camp ; which was at half a journey, in the Nefûd. He sat down among them and began to question with me in lordly sort ; and I enquired of the absent Emir. I found in him a natural malice ; and an improbity of face which became the young man's injurious insolence. After these heavy words, he said further, " Art thou Nasrâny or Musslim ? " — " Nasrâny, which all this town knows ; now leave questioning me." — " Then the Moslemîn will kill thee, please Ullah ! Hearest thou ? the Moslemîn will kill thee ! " and the squalid young man opened a leathern mouth, that grinning on me to his misplaced lap ears, discovered vast red circles of mule's teeth. — Surely the fanatical condition in religion [though logical !] is never far from a radically ill nature ; and doubtless the javel was an offspring of generations of depraved Arab wretches. Jeyber, though I was to-day under his roof, smiled a withered half-smile of Kahtâny fanaticism, hearing words which are honey to their ears, — ' a kafir to be slain by the Moslemîn ! ' Because the young man was a sheykh and Hásan's messenger, I sat in some thought of this venomous speaking. When they departed, I said to Jeyber my conceit of that base young fanatic ; who answered, shrinking the shoulders, that I had guessed well, for he was a bad one !

— My hap was to travel in Arabia in time of a great strife of the religion [as they understood], with (God and His Apostle's enemies) the Nasâra. And now the idle fanatical people clamoured to the Emir, ' Since Ullah had delivered a Nasrâny into their hands, wherefore might they not put him to death ? ' At length the sun of this troubled day was at his going down. Then I went out to breathe the cooling air upon the terrace : and finding a broken ladder climbed to a higher part of our roof, to survey this great Arabian town. — But some townspeople in the street immediately, espying me, cried out, " Come down ! Come down ! A kafir should not overlook a beled of the Moslemîn." Jeyber brought me a ration of boiled mutton and rice (which he had purchased in the sûk) : when I had eaten he said we were brethren. He went out again to the Emir.

Jeyber returned all doubtful and pensive ! ' The people, he said, were clamouring again to Abdullah ; who answered them, that they might deal with me as they would : he had told them already, that they might have slain the Nasrâny in the desert ; but it could not be done in the town.' Jeyber asked me now, ' Would I forsake my bags, and flee secretly from Boreyda on foot ? ' I answered " No ! — and tell me sooth, Jeyber ! hast thou no mind to betray me ? " He promised as he was a faithful man that he would not. "Well, what is the present danger ? " — " I hope no more, for this night, at least in my house." — " How may I pass the streets in the morning ? " — " We will pass them ; the peril is not so much in the town as of their pursuing." — " How many horsemen be there in Boreyda, a score ? " — " Ay, and more." — " Go quickly and tell Abdullah, Khalîl says I am *rájol Dowla*, one who is safeguarded (my papers declare it) by the government of the Sooltàn : if an evil betide me (a guest) among you, it might draw some trouble upon yourselves. For were it to be suffered that a traveller, under the imperial protection, and only passing by your town, should be done to death, for the name of a religion, which is tolerated by the Sooltàn ? Neither let them think themselves secure here, in the midst of deserts ; for '_long is the arm of the Dowla!_' Remember Jidda, and Damascus ! and the guilty punished, by commandment of the Sooltàn !" Jeyber answered, ' He would go and speak these words to Abdullah.'

Jeyber returned with better looks, saying that Abdullah allowed my words: and had commanded that none should any more molest the Nasrâny ; and promised him, that no evil should befall me this night. _Jeyber :_ " We be now in peace, blessed be the Lord ! go in and rest, Khalîl ; to be ready betimes."

I was ready ere the break of day ; and thought it an hundred years till I should be out of Boreyda. At sunrise Jeyber sat down to prepare coffee ; and yet made no haste ! the promised thelûl was not come. — " And when will thy thelûl be here ? " — " At some time before noon." — " How then may we come to Aneyza to-night ? " — " I have told thee, that Aneyza is not far off." My host also asked for remedies for his old infirmities. — " At Aneyza ! " — " Nay, but now ; for I would leave them here." When he had received his medicines, Jeyber began to make it strange of his thelûl-riding to Aneyza. I thought an host would not forswear himself ; but all their life is passed in fraud and deceit. — In this came up the Kahtâny who had been ring-leader in the former night's trouble ; and sat down before his tribesman's hearth ; where he was wont to drink the morrow's cup. Jeyber would have me believe that the fellow had been swinged yesterday before Abdullah : I saw no such signs in him. The wretch who had lately injured me would now have maintained my cause ! I said to Jeyber's Beduin jâra, who sat with us, " Tell me, is not he possessed by a jîn ? " The young man answered for himself, " Ay, Khalîl, I am somewhiles a little lunatic." He had come to ask the Nasrâny for medicines, — in which surely he had not trusted one of his own religion.

— A limping footfall sounded on the palace stairs : it was the lame Emir Abdullah who entered ! leaning on his staff. Sordid was the (peasant) princeling's tunic and kerchief : he sat down at the hearth, and Jeyber prepared fresh coffee. Abdullah said, — showing me a poor man standing by the door and that came in with him ; " This is he that will carry thee on his camel to Aneyza ; rise ! and bring out thy things." — " Jeyber promises to convey me upon his thelûl." But now my host (who had but fabled) excused himself, saying, ' he would follow us, when his thelûl were come.' Abdullah gave the cameleer his wages, the quarter of a mejîdy, eleven pence. — The man took my bags upon his shoulders, and brought me by a lonely street to a camel couched before his clay cottage. We mounted and rode by lanes out of the town.

The palms and tillage of Boreyda lie all on this side, towards the W. er-Rummah, betwixt a main sand-dune and the road to Aneyza ; and last for three miles nearly (to el-Khúthar). I saw their wells, sunk in the Nefûd sand, — which is not deep, and through a bluish white underlying clay into the sand-rock : these wells, steyned with dry masonry [such in West Arabia would be reckoned works of the ancients !] are begun and ended every day in el-Kasîm. By-wells, of less cost, are digged like wide sand-pits to the clay level ; and they fence the sliding sides of sand with faggot-work. Over the well-hole, sunk square through the clay in the pit's midst, is set up a rude frame of ethel studs, for the wheel-work of their suânies ; such are commonly two-wheel pits. The steyned wells, made four-square, are for the draught of four camels ; and there are some double wells of six or eight wheels, to water greater grounds, made long-square ; the camels draw out from the two sides. To the ground-water they count seven fathoms : it is eight at the summer's end.

This clay is what ? — surely the silt of a river, which flowing of old in the W. er-Rummah, was an affluent of Euphrates. Here are wells, also of the ancients ; especially near the end of the plantations, in the site *Menzil B. Helâl*.

Boreyda was founded three to four centuries ago : the townsfolk are reckoned to the B. Temîm. They are not, I think, fully 5000 souls ; and with the nigh outlying villages and hamlets, which are suburbs to Boreyda, may be 6000 persons. When we had ridden by their palms a second mile, there met us one coming from an orchard, a young man who by his fresh clothing seemed to be of the welfaring townspeople. He asked my cameleer, whose name was *Hásan*, if he could deliver a letter for him in Aneyza ; and beginning to talk with me I found him to be a litterate. " Ah ! quoth the young franklin, thou art a Nasrâny ; in the town whither you are going, please Ullah they will make thee a Moslem ! " — He too spoke of Siddûs, and thought he had found in his crabbed books that the old name was *Kerdûs* ; and he told me, that men had worshipped *sánam*, an image, there. He looked upon me as of the sect of those ancient idolaters ! — A wonder to me was to see a new planting of ethel trees, upon the great dune of Boreyda, in this dewless and nearly rainless land, where the lowest fibres must be much above the ground-water. They set the young plants in the loose sand, and water them one year ; till they have put down long roots and begin to thrive of themselves. It is a tree seldom making clean and straight stems, but which is grown in twelve years to (brittle and heavy) timber, fit for the frames of their suânies : the green sticks and boughs will burn well. — Planted with tamarisks, the sands of Arabia might become a GREEN WOOD !

APPENDIX TO CHAP. XI

THE TRIPLE RAINBOW.—*Note by Prof. P. G. Tait, Sec. R.S.E.* — The occasional appearance of additional rainbows has been long known. They are due to sunlight reflected from a lake (or, as in the present example, a surface or surfaces of wet ground and rain water) *behind* the spectator. The elementary principles of Optics show that, in such a case, the result is the same as if there were *two suns*, the second being as far below the horizon as the true sun is above it.

CHAPTER XII

ANEYZA

The Nefûd (of el-Kasîm). Passage of the Wady er-Rummah. The Nasrâny, forsaken by his rafîk, finds hospitality; and enters Aneyza. Aspect of the town. The Emir *Zâmil*. His uncle Aly. The townspeople. *Abdullah el-Kenneyny*. His house and studies. Breakfast with Zâmil. The Nasrâny is put out of his doctor's shop by the Emir Aly. A Zelot. Breakfast with el-Kenneyny. Eye diseases. Small-pox in the town. The streets of Aneyza. The homely and religious life of these citizens. Women are unseen. *Abdullah el-Bessàm*. A dinner in his house. The Bessàm kindred. Nâsir es-Smîry. The day in Aneyza. Jannah. el-Kenneyny's plantation. *Hàmed es-Sâfy, Abdullah Bessàm*, the younger, and Sheykh *Ibn Ayith*. An old Ateyba sheykh: Zelotism. The infirm and destitute. The Nasrâny's friends. A tale of Ômar, the first Calif. Archeology. The Kenneyny. The vagabund Medina Sherîf arrives at Aneyza. The good Bessàm.

NOW we came upon the open Nefûd, where I saw the sand ranging in long banks: *adanat* and *kethîb* is said in this country speech of the light shifting Nefûd sand; *Júrda* is the sandbank's weather side, the lee side or fold is *lóghraf* [*láḥaf*]. *Júrda* or *Jorda* [in the pl. *Jérad* and *Jeràd*) is said of a dune or hillock, in which appear clay-seams, sand and stones, and whereon desert bushes may be growing. The road to Aneyza is a deep-worn drift-way in the uneven Nefûd; but in the sand (lately blotted with wind and rain) I perceived no footprint of man or cattle!— Bye and bye Hásan turned our camel from the path, to go over the dunes: we were the less likely thus to meet with Beduins not friends of Boreyda. The great tribes of these dîras, Meteyr and Ateyba, are the allies of *Zâmil*, Emir of Aneyza. — Zâmil was already a pleasant name in my ears: I had heard, even amongst his old foes of Harb, that Zâmil was a good gentleman, and that the " Child of Mahanna " (for whom, two years ago, they were in the field with Ibn Rashîd, against Aneyza) was a tyrannical churl: it was because of the Harb enmity that I had not ridden from their menzils, to Aneyza.

The Nefûd sand was here overgrown with a canker-weed which the Aarab reckon unwholesome; and therefore I struck away our camel that put down his long neck to browse; but Hásan said, " Nay; the town camels eat of this herb, for there is little else." We saw a nomad child keeping sheep: and I asked my rafîk, ' When should we come to

Aneyza?' — "By the sunsetting." I found the land-height to be not more than 2500 feet. When we had ridden slowly three hours, we fell again into the road, by some great-grown tamarisks. 'Negîl, quoth Hásan, we will alight here and rest out the hot midday hours.' I saw trenches dug under those trees by locust hunters. I asked, "Is it far now?" — "Aneyza is not far off." — "Tell me truth rafîk, art thou carrying me to Aneyza?" — "Thou believest not ; — see here !" (he drew me out a bundle of letters — and yet they seemed worn and old). "All these, he said, are merchants' letters which I am to deliver to-day in Aneyza ; and to fetch the goods from thence." — And had I not seen him accept the young franklin's letter for Aneyza ! Hásan found somewhat in my words, for he did not halt ; we might be come ten miles from Boreyda. The soil shelved before us ; and under the next tamarisks I saw a little oozing water. We were presently in a wady bottom, not a stone-cast over ; and in crossing we plashed through trickling water ! I asked, "What bed is this ?" — *Answer:* "EL-WADY" — that is, we were in (the midst of) the Wady er-Rummah. We came up by oozing (brackish) water to a palm wood unenclosed, where are grave-like pits of a fathom digged beside young palm-sets to the ground water. The plants are watered by hand a year or two, till they have put down roots to the saltish ground moisture.

It is nearly a mile to pass through this palm wood, where only few (older) stems are seen grown aloft above the rest ; because such outlying possessions are first to the destruction in every warfare. I saw through the trees an high-built court wall, wherein the husbandmen may shelter themselves in any alarms ; and Hásan showed me, in an open ground, where Ibn Rashîd's tents stood two years ago, when he came with Weled Mahanna against Aneyza. We met only two negro labourers ; and beyond the palms the road is again in the Nefûd. Little further at our right hand, were some first enclosed properties ; and we drew bridle at a stone trough, a sebîl, set by the landowner in his clay wall, with a channel from his suânies : the trough was dry, for none now passed by that way to or from Boreyda. We heard creaking of well-wheels and voices of harvesters in a field. "Here, said Hásan, as he put down my bags, is the place of repose : rest in the shadow of this wall, whilst I go to water the camel. And where is the girby? that I may bring thee to drink ; you might be thirsty before evening, when it will be time to enter the town, — thus says Abdullah ; and now open thy eyes for fear of the Beduw." I let the man go, but made him leave his spear with me.

When he came again with the waterskin, Hásan said he had loosed out the camel to pasture ; " and wellah Khalîl I must go after her, for see ! the beast has strayed. Reach me my romh, and I will run to turn her, or she will be gone far out in the Nefûd." — " Go, but the spear remains with me." " Ullah ! doubt not thy rafîk, should I go un‑armed ? give me my lance, and I will be back to thee in a moment." I thought, that if the man were faithless and I compelled him to carry me into Aneyza, he might have cried out to the fanatical townspeople : ' This is a Nasrâny ! ' — " Our camel will be gone, do not delay me." — " Wilt thou then forsake me here ? " — " No wellah, by this beard ! " I cast his lance upon the sand, which taking up, he said, " Whilst I am out, if thou have need of anything, go about the corner of the wall yonder ; so thou wilt see a palm ground, and men working. Rest now in the shadow, and make thyself a little mereesy, for thou art fasting ; and cover these bags ! let no man see them. Aneyza is but a little beyond that *ádan* there ; thou mayest see the town from thence : I will run now, and return." I let him pass, and Hásan, hieing after his camel, was hidden by the sand billows. I thought soon, I would see what were become of him, and casting away my mantle I ran barefoot in the Nefûd ; and from a sand dune I espied Hásan riding forth upon his camel — for he had forsaken me ! he fetched a circuit to go about the Wady palms homeward. I knew then that I was betrayed by the secret commission of Abdullah, and remembered his word, " Who will carry the Nasrâny *to the Wady ?* "

This was the cruellest fortune which had befallen me in Arabia ! to be abandoned here without a chief town, in the midst of fanatical Nejd. I had but eight reals left, which might hardly more than carry me in one course to the nearest coast. I returned and armed myself ; and rent my maps in small pieces, — lest for such I should be called in question, amongst lettered citizens.

A negro man and wife came then from the palms, carrying firewood towards Aneyza : they had seen us pass, and asked me simply, " Where is thy companion and the camel ? " — After this I went on under the clay walling towards the sound of suânies ; and saw a palm ground and an orchard house. The door was shut fast : I found another beyond ; and through the chinks I looked in, and espied the owner driving, — a plain-natured face. I pushed up his gate and entered at a venture with, " Peace be with thee ; " and called for a drink of water. The goodman stayed a little to see the stranger ! then he bade his young daughter fetch the bowl, and held up his camels to speak with me. " Drink if thou wilt, said he, but we have no good water." The taste was bitter and unwholesome ; but even this cup of water would be a bond between us.

I asked him to lend me a camel or an ass, to carry my things to the town, and I would pay the hire. I told further how I came hither, — with a cameleer from Boreyda ; who whilst I rested in the heat had forsaken me nigh his gate : that I was an hakîm, and if there were any sick in this place I had medicines to relieve them. — " Well, bide till my lad return with a camel : — I go (he said to his daughter) with this man ; here ! have my stick and drive, and let not the camels stand. — What be thou, O stranger, and where leftest thou thy things? come ! thou shouldst not have left them out of sight and unguarded ; how, if we should not find them — ? " — They were safe ; and taking the great bags on my shoulders, I tottered back over the Nefûd to the good man's gate ; rejoicing inwardly, that I might now bear all I possessed in the world. He bade me sit down there (without), whilst he went to fetch an ass. — " Wilt thou pay a piastre and a half (threepence) ? " There came now three or four grave elder men from the plantations, and they were going in at the next gate to drink their afternoon kahwa. The goodman stayed them and said, " This is a stranger, — he cannot remain here, and we cannot receive him in our house ; he asks for carriage to the town." They answered, he should do well to fetch the ass and send me to Aneyza. " And what art thou ? (they said to me) — we go in now to coffee ; has anyone heard the íthin ? " *Another :* " They have cried to prayers in the town, but we cannot always hear it ; — for is not the sun gone down to the âssr ? then pray we here together." They took their stand devoutly, and my host joined himself to the row ; they called me also, " Come and pray, come ! " — " I have prayed already." They marvelled at my words, and so fell to their formal reciting and prostrations. When they rose, my host came to me with troubled looks : — " Thou dost not pray, hmm ! " said he ; and I saw by those grave men's countenance, they were persuaded that I could be no right Moslem. " Well, send him forward," quoth the chief of them, and they entered the gate.

My bags were laid now upon an ass. We departed : and little

beyond the first *ádan*, as Hásan had foretold me, was the beginning of cornfields ; and palms and fruit trees appeared, and some houses of outlying orchards. — My companion said [he was afraid !] " It is far to the town, and I cannot go there to-night ; but I will leave thee with one yonder who is *ibn juâd*, a son of bounty ; and in the morning he will send thee to Aneyza." — We came on by a wide road and unwalled, till he drew up his ass at a rude gateway ; there was an orchard house, and he knocked loud and called, " *Ibrahîm !* " An old father came to the gate, who opened it to the half and stayed — seeing my clothes rent (by the thieves at Boreyda) ! and not knowing what strange person I might be : — but he guessed I was some runaway soldier from the Harameyn or el-Yémen, as there had certain passed by Aneyza of late. He of the ass spoke for me ; and then that housefather received me. They brought in my bags to his clay house ; and he locked them in a store closet ; so without speaking he beckoned with his hand, and led me out in his orchard, to the " diwân " (their clean sanded sitting-place in the field) ; and there left me.

Pleasant was the sight of their tilled ground with corn stubbles and green plots of vetches, *jet*, the well-camels' provender ; and borders of a dye-plant, whose yellow blossoms are used by the townswomen to stain the partings of their hair. When this sun was nigh setting, I remembered their unlucky prayer-hour ! and passed hastily to the further side of their palms ; but I was not hidden by the clear-set rows of trees : when I came again in the twilight, they demanded of me, ' Why I prayed not ? and wherefore had I not been with them at the prayers ? ' Then they said over the names of the four orthodox sects of Islam, and questioned with me, " To which of them pertainest thou ; or be'st thou (of some heterodox belief) a *râfuthy ?* " — a word which they pronounced with enmity. I made no answer, and they remained in some astonishment. They brought me, to sup, boiled wheat in a bowl and another of their well water ; there was no greater hospitality in that plain household. I feared the dampish (oasis) air and asked, where was the coffee chamber. *Answer :* " Here is no kahwa, and we drink none." They sat in silence, and looked heavily upon the stranger, who had not prayed.

He who brought me the bowl (not one of them) was a manly young man, of no common behaviour ; and he showed in his words an excellent understanding. I bade him sup with me. — " I have supped." —

"Yet eat a morsel, for the bread and salt between us:" he did so. After that, when the rest were away, I told him what I was, and asked him of the town. "Well, he said, thou art here to-night; and little remains to Aneyza, where they will bring thee in the morning; I think there is no danger — Zâmil is a good man: besides thou art only passing by them. Say to the Emir to-morrow, in the people's hearing, 'I am a soldier from *Béled el-Asîr*' (a good province in el-Yémen, which the Turks had lately occupied)." — Whilst we were speaking, the last íthin sounded from the town! I rose hastily; but the three or four young men, sons of Ibrahîm, were come again, and began to range themselves to pray! they called us, and they called to me the stranger with insistence, to take our places with them. I answered: "I am over-weary, I will go and sleep." — *The bread-and-salt Friend*: "Ay-ay, the stranger says well, he is come from a journey; show him the place without more, where he may lie down." — "I would sleep in the house, and not here abroad." — "But first let him pray; ho! thou, come and pray, come!" — *The Friend*: "Let him alone, and show the weary man to his rest." — "There is but the wood-house." — "Well then to the wood-house, and let him sleep immediately." One of them went with me, and brought me to a threshold: the floor was sunk a foot or two, and I fell in a dark place full of sweet tamarisk boughs. After their praying came all the brethren: they sat before the door in the feeble moonlight, and murmured, 'I had not prayed! — and could this be a Musslim?' But I played the sleeper; and after watching half an hour they left me. How new to us is this religiosity, in rude young men of the people! but the Semitic religion — so cold, and a strange plant, in the (idolatrous) soil of Europe, is like to a blood passion, in the people of Moses and Mohammed.

An hour before day I heard one of these brethren creeping in — it was to espy if the stranger would say the dawning prayers! When the morrow was light all the brethren stood before the door; and they cried to me, *Ma sulleyt*, 'Thou didst not say the prayer!'" — "Friends, I prayed." — "Where washed you then?" — This I had not considered, for I was not of the dissembler's craft. Another brother came to call me; and he led me up to the house stairs to a small, clean room: where he spread matting on the clay floor, and set before me a dish of very good dates, with a bowl of whey; and bade me breakfast, with their homely word, *fúk er-rîg*, 'Loose the fasting spittle:' (the Bed. say *rîj, for rîk*).

"Drink!" said he, and lifted to my hands his hospitable bowl. — After that he brought the ass and loaded my bags, to carry them into the town. We went on in the same walled road, and passed a ruinous open gate of Aneyza. Much of the town wall was there in sight; which is but a thin shell, with many wide breaches. Such clay walling might be repaired in few days, and Aneyza can never be taken by famine; for the wide town walls enclose their palm grounds: the people, at this time, were looking for war with Boreyda.

We went by the first houses, which are of poor folk; and the young man said he would leave me at one of the next doors, 'where lived a servant of (the Emir) *Zâmil*.' He knocked with the ring, which [as at Damascus] there is set upon all their doors, like a knocker; and a young negro housewife opened: her goodman (of the butcher's craft) was at this hour in the sûk. He was bedel or public sergeant, for Zâmil: and to such rude offices, negroes (men of a blunter metal) are commonly chosen. My baggage was set down in the little camel yard, of their poor but clean clay cottage. *Aly* the negro householder came home soon after; and finding a stranger standing in his court, he approached and kissed the guest, and led me into his small kahwa; where presently, to the pleasant note of the coffee pestle, a few persons assembled — mostly black men his neighbours. And Aly made coffee, as coffee is made even in poor houses at Aneyza. After the cup, the poor man brought-in on a tray a good breakfast: large was the hospitality of his humble fortune, and he sat down to eat with me. — Homeborn negroes, out of their warmer hearts, do often make good earnest of the shallow Arabian customs! Before the cottage row I saw a waste place, *el-Gá*; and some booth or two therein of the miserable Beduins: the plot, left open by the charity of the owner, was provided with a public pool of water running from his suânies. When later I knew them, and his son asked the Nasrâny's counsel, 'What were best to do with the ground? — because of the draffe cast there, it was noisome to the common health' — I answered, "Make it a public garden:" but that was far from their Arabian understanding.

I went abroad bye and bye with Aly to seek Zâmil; though it were *tow*, too early, said my negro host: here is the beginning of the town streets, with a few poor open stalls; the ways are cleanly. Two furlongs beyond is the sûk, where (at these hours) is a busy concourse of the townspeople: they are all men, since maidens and wives come not openly abroad. — At a cross street there met us two young gallants. "Ha! said one of them to Aly, this stranger with thee is a Nasrâny;"— and turning to me, the coxcombs bid me, "Good morrow, khawâja:" I answered them, "I am no khawâja, but an Engleysy; and how am I of your acquaintance?" — "Last night we had word of thy coming from Boreyda: Aly, whither goest thou with him?" That poor man, who began to be amazed, hearing his guest named Nasrâny, answered, "To Zâmil." — "Zâmil is not yet sitting; then bring the Nasrâny to drink coffee at my beyt. We are, said they, from Jidda and wont to see (there) all the kinds of Nasâra." They led us upstairs in a great house, by the market-square, which they call in Kasîm *el-Mejlis*: their chamber was spread with Persian carpets.

These young men were of the Aneyza merchants at Jidda. One of them showed me a Winchester (seventeen shooting) rifle! 'and there were fifty more (they pretended) in Aneyza: with such guns in their hands they were not in dread of warfare [which they thought likely to be renewed] with Ibn Rashîd: in the time of the Jehâd they had exercised themselves as soldiers at Jidda.' They added maliciously, "And if we have war with Boreyda, wilt thou be our captain?"

We soon left them. Aly led me over the open market-square: and by happy adventure the Emir was now sitting in his place; that is made under a small porch upon the Mejlis, at the street corner which leads to his own (clay) house, and in face of the clothier's sûk. In the Emir's porch are two clay banks; upon one, bespread with a Persian carpet, sat Zâmil, and his sword lay by him. Zâmil is a small-grown man with a pleasant weerish visage, and great understanding eyes: as I approached, he looked up mildly. When I stood before him Zâmil rose a little in his seat and took me by the hand, and said kindly, "Be seated, be seated!" so he made me sit beside him. I said "I come now from Boreyda, and am a hakîm, an Engleysy, a Nasrâny; I have these papers with me; and it may please thee to send me to the coast." Zâmil perused that which I put in his hand:—as he read, an uneasy cloud was on his face, for a moment! But looking up pleasant, "It is well, he responded; in the meantime go not about publishing thyself to the people, 'I am a Nasrâny;' say to them, *ana askary*, I am a (runaway Ottoman) soldier. Aly return home with Khalîl, and bring him after midday prayers to kahwa in my house : but walk not in the public places."

We passed homewards through the clothiers' street and by the butchers' market. The busy citizens hardly regarded us ; yet some man took me by the sleeve ; and turning, I saw one of those half-feminine slender figures of the Arabians, with painted eyes, and clad in the Bagdad wise. " O thou, *min eyn*, from whence ? quoth he, and art thou a Nasrâny ? " I answered, " Ay : " yet if any asked, " Who is he with thee, Aly ? " the negro responded stoutly, " A stranger, one that is going to Kuweyt." — Aneyza seemed a pleasant town, and stored with all things needful to their civil life : we went on by a well-built mesjid ; but the great mesjid is upon the public place, — all building is of clay in the Arabian city.

In these days the people's talk was of the debate and breach between the town and Boreyda : although lately Weled Mahanna wrote to Zâmil *ana weled-ak*, ' I am thy child (to serve and obey thee) ; ' and Zâmil had written, " I am thy friend." " Wellah, said Aly's gossips at the coffee hearth, there is no more passage to Boreyda : but in few days the allies of Zâmil will be come up from the east country, and from the south, as far as Wady Dauâsir." Then, they told me, I should see the passing continually through this street of a multitude of armed men.

After the noon íthin we went down to Zâmil's (homely) house, which is in a blind way out of the mejlis. His coffee room was spread with grass matting (only) ; and a few persons were sitting with him. Zâmil's elder son, *Abdullah*, sat behind the hearth, to make coffee. Tidings were brought in, that some of the townspeople's asses had been reaved in the Nefûd, by Ateybân (friendly Nomads) ! — Zâmil sent for one of his armed riders : and asked him, ' Was his dromedary in the town ? " — " All ready." — " Then take some with you, and ride on their traces, that you may overtake them to-day ! " — " But if I lose the thelûl — ? " (he might fall amongst enemies). Zâmil answered, " The half loss shall be mine ; " and the man went out. Zâmil spoke demissly, he seemed not made to command ; but this is the mildness of the natural Arab sheykhs.

— *Aly*, uncle of the Emir, entered hastily ! Zâmil some years ago appointed him executive Emir in the town ; and when Zâmil takes the field he leaves Aly his lieutenant in Aneyza. Aly is a dealer in camels ; he has only few fanatical friends. All made him room, and the great man sat down in the highest place. Zâmil, the Emir and host, sat leaning on a pillow in face of the company ; and his son Abdullah sat drinking a pipe of tobacco, by the hearth ! — but this would not be tolerated in the street. The coffee was ready, and he who took up the pot and the cups went to pour out first for Zâmil ; but the Emir beckoned mildly to serve the Emir Aly. When the coffee had been poured round, Zâmil said to his uncle, " This stranger is an hakîm, a traveller from *es-Sham* : and we will send him, as he desires, to Kuweyt." — Aly full of the Waháby fanaticism vouchsafed not so much as to cast an eye upon me. " Ugh ! quoth he, I heard say the man is a Nasrâny : wouldst thou have a Nasrâny in thy town ? " *Zâmil* : " He is a passenger ; he may stay a few days, and there can be no hurt ! " " Ugh ! " answered Aly ; and when he had swallowed his two cups he rose up crabbedly, and went forth. Even Zâmil's son was of this Waháby humour ; twenty years might be his age : bold faced was the young man, of little sheykhly promise, and disposed, said the common speech, to be a niggard. Now making his voice big and hostile, he asked me — for his wit stretched no further, " What is thy name ? " When all were gone out, Zâmil showed me his fore-arms corroded and inflamed by an itching malady which he had suffered these twenty years ! — I have seen the like in a few more persons at Aneyza. He said, like an Aarab, " And if thou canst cure this, we will give thee *fulûs !* "

Already some sick persons were come there to seek the hakîm, when I returned to Aly's ; and one of them offered me an empty *dokân*, or little open shop in a side street by the sûks. — Aly found an ass to carry my bags : and ere the mid-afternoon I was sitting in my doctor's shop : and mused, should I here find rest in Arabia ? when the muéthin cried to the assr prayers ; there was a trooping of feet, and neighbours went by to a mesjid in the end of the street. — Ay, at this day they go to prayers as hotly as if they had been companions of the Néby ! I shut my shop with the rest, and sat close ; I thought this shutter would shield me daily from their religious importunity. — " *Ullahu akhbar, Ullahu akhbar !* " chanted the muéthins of the town.

After vespers the town is at leisure ; and principal persons go home to drink the afternoon coffee with their friends. Some of the citizens returning by this street stayed to see the Nasrâny, and enquire what were his medicines ; for nearly all the Arabs are diseased, or imagine themselves to be sick or else bewitched. How quiet was the behaviour of these townsfolk, many of them idle persons and children ! but Zâmil's word was that none should molest Haj Khalîl, — so the good gentlemen, who heard I had been many times in the " Holy," (i.e. Jerusalem) called me, because it made for my credit and safety among the people. The civil countenance of these midland Arabian citizens is unlike the (Beduish) aspect of the townsmen of Hâyil, that tremble in the sight of Ibn Rashîd : here is a free township under the natural Prince, who converses as a private man, and rules, like a great sheykh of Aarab, amongst his brethren.

Zâmil's descent is from the *Sbeya*, first Beduin colonists of this loam-bottom in the Nefûd. At this day they are not many families in Aneyza ; but theirs is the Emirship, and therefore they say *henna el-úmera*, ' we are the Emirs.' More in number are the families of the *Beny Khâlid*, tribesmen of that ancient Beduin nation, whose name, before the Waháby, was greatest in Nejd ; but above an half of the town are B. Temîm. There are in Aneyza (as in every Arabian place) several wards or parishes under hereditary sheykhs ; but no malcontent factions, — they are all cheerfully subject to Zâmil. The people living in unity, are in no dread of foreign enemies.

Some principal persons went by again, returning from their friends' houses. — One of them approached me, and said, " Hast thou a knowledge of medicine ? " The tremulous figure of the speaker, with some drawing of his face, put me in mind of the Algerine Mohammed Aly, at Medáin Sâlih ! But he that stood here was a gentle son of Temîm, whose good star went before me from this day to the end of my voyage in Arabia ! Taking my hand in his hand, which is a kind manner of the Arabs, he said, " Wilt thou visit my sick mother ? "

He led me to his house gate not far distant ; and entering himself by a side door he came round to open for me : I found within a large coffee-hall, spread with well-wrought grass matting, which is fetched hither from *el-Hása*. The walls were pargetted with fretwork of jis, such as I had seen at Boreyda. A Persian tapet spread before his fire-pit, was the guests' sitting place ; and he sat down himself behind the hearth to make me coffee. This was *Abdullah el-Kenneyny*, the fortunate son of a good but poor house. He had gone forth a young man from Aneyza ; and after the first hazards of fortune, was grown to be one of the most considerable foreign merchants. His traffic was in corn, at

Bosra, and he lived willingly abroad ; for his heart was not filled in Aneyza, where he despised the Waháby straitness and fanaticism. In these days leaving his merchandise at Bosra to the care of his brother (Sâlih, who they told me little resembles him), Abdullah was come to pass a leisure year at home ; where he hoped to refresh his infirm health in the air of the Nefûd.

When I looked in this man's face he smiled kindly. — " And art thou, said he, an Engleysy ? but wherefore tell the people so, in this wild fanatical country ? I have spent many years in foreign lands, I have dwelt at Bombay, which is under government of the Engleys : thou canst say thus to me, but say it not to the ignorant and foolish people ; — what simplicity is this ! and incredible to me, in a man of *Europa*. For are we here in a government country ? no, but in land of the Aarab, where the name of the Nasâra is an execration. A Nasrâny, they think to be a son of the Evil One, and (therefore) deserving of death : an half of this townspeople are Wahábies." — " Should I not speak truth, as well here as in mine own country ? " *Abdullah* : " We have a tongue to further us and our friends, and to illude our enemies ; and indeed the more times the lie is better than the sooth. — Or dreadest thou, that Ullah would visit it upon thee, if thou assentedst to them in appearance ? Is there not in everything the good and evil ? " [even in lying and dissembling.] — " I am this second year, in a perilous country, and have no scathe. Thou hast heard the proverb, ' Truth may walk through the world unarmed.' " — " But the Engleys are not thus ! nay, I have seen them full of policy : in the late warfare between Abdullah and Saûd ibn Saûd, their Resident on the Gulf sent hundreds of sacks of rice, secretly, to Saûd [the wrongful part ; and for such Abdullah the Waháby abhors the English name]. — I see you will not be persuaded ! yet I hope that your life may be preserved : but they will not suffer you to dwell amongst them ! you will be driven from place to place." — " This seemed to me a good peaceable town, and are the people so illiberal ? " — " As many among them, as have travelled, are liberal ; but the rest no. Now shall we go to my mother ? "

Abdullah led me into an inner room, from whence we ascended to the floor above. He had bought this great new (clay) house the year before, for a thousand reals, or nearly £200 sterling. The loam brick-work at Aneyza is good, and such house-walls may stand above one hundred years. His rent, for the same, had been (before) but fifteen reals; house property being reckoned in the Arabian countries as money laid up, and not put out to usury, — a sure and lawful possession. The yearly fruit of 1000 dollars, lent out at Aneyza, were 120; the loss therefore to the merchant Abdullah, in buying this house, was each year 100 reals. But dwelling under their own roof, they think they enjoy some happy security of fortune: although the walls decay soon, it will not be in their children's time. In Abdullah's upper storey were many good chambers, but bare to our eyes, since they have few more moveables than the Beduw: all the husbandry of his great town house might have been carried on the backs of three camels! In the Arabic countries the use of bed-furniture is unknown; they lie on the floor, and the wellborn and welfaring have no more than some thin cotton quilt spread under them, and a coverlet: I saw only a few chests, in which they bestow their clothing. Their houses, in this land of sunny warmth, are lighted by open loopholes made high upon the lofty walls. But Abdullah was not so simply housed at Bosra; for there — in the great world's side, the Arab merchants' halls are garnished with chairs: and the Aneyza *tájir* sat (like the rest) upon a *takht* or carpeted settle in his counting house.

He brought me to a room where I saw his old mother, sitting on the floor; and clad — so are all the Arabian women, only in a calico smock dipped in indigo. She covered her old visage, as we entered, with a veil! Abdullah smiled to me, and looked to see " a man of Europa " smile. " My mother, said he, I bring thee el-hakîm; say what aileth thee, and let him see thine eyes: " and with a gentle hand he folded down her veil. " Oh! said she, my head; and all this side so aches that I cannot sleep, my son." Abdullah might be a man of forty; yet his mother was abashed, that a strange man must look upon her old blear eyes. — We returned to the coffee room perfect friends. " My mother, said he, is aged and suffering, and I suffer to see her: if thou canst help us, that will be a great comfort to me."

Abdullah added, " I am even now in amazement! that, in such a country, you openly avow yourself to be an Englishman; but how may you pass even one day in safety! You have lived hitherto with the Beduw; ay, but it is otherwise in the townships." — " In such hazards there is nothing, I suppose, more prudent than a wise folly." — " Then, you will not follow better counsel! but here you may trust in me: I will watch for you, and warn you of any alteration in the town." I asked, "And what of the Emir?"—"You may also trust Zâmil ; but even Zâmil cannot at all times refrain the unruly multitude."

— In the clay-built chamber of the Arabs, with casements never closed, is a sweet dry air, as of the open field ; and the perfume of a serene and hospitable human life, not knowing any churlish superfluity : yet here is not whole human life, for bye and bye we are aware of the absence of women. And their bleak walling is an uncheerfulness in our sight : pictures — those gracious images that adorn our poorest dwellings, were but of the things which are vain in the gross vision of their Mohammedan austerity. The Arabs, who sit on the floor, see the world more indolently than we : they must rise with a double lifting of the body. — In a wall-niche by the fire were Abdullah's books. We were now as brethren, and I took them down one by one : a great tome lay uppermost. I read the Arabic title *Encyclopedia Bustâny, Beyrût*,— Bustâny (born of poor Christian folk in a Lebanon village), a printer, gazetteer, schoolmaster, and man of letters, at Beyrût : every year he sends forth one great volume more, but so long an enterprise may hardly be ended. Abdullah's spectacles fell out at a place which treated of artesian wells : he pored therein daily, and looked to find some means of raising water upon his thirsty acres without camel labour.

Abdullah enriched abroad, had lately bought a palm and corn ground at home ; and not content with the old he had made in it a new well of eight camels' draught. I turned another leaf and found " Burning Mountain," and a picture of Etna. He was pleased to hear from me of the old Arab usurpers of Sicilian soil, and that this mountain is even now named after their words, *Gibello* (Jebel). I turned to " Telegraph," and Abdullah exclaimed, " Oh ! the inventions in Europa ! what a marvellous learned subtlety must have been in him who found it ! " When he asked further of my profession of medicine ; I said, " I am such as your *Solubba* smiths — better than none, where you may not find a better." — Yet Abdullah always believed my skill to be greater than so, because nearly all my reasonable patients were relieved ; but especially his own mother.

Whilst we were discoursing there came in two of the foreign-living Aneyza townsmen, a substantial citizen and his servant, clad in the Mesopotamian guise, with head-bands, great as turbans, of camel wool. The man had been *jemmâl*, a camel carrier in the Irâk traffic to Syria, —

that is in the long trade-way about by Aleppo; but after the loss of the caravan, before mentioned [Vol. I. p. 654], having no more heart for these ventures, he sold his camels for fields and ploughshares. To-day he was a substantial farmer in the great new corn settlement, *el-Amâra* (upon the river a little north of Bosra), and a client of Kenneyny's — one of the principal grain merchants in the river city. The merchant's dinner tray was presently borne in. And I rose to depart; but Abdullah made me sit down again to eat with them, though I had been bidden in another place. — I passed this one good day in Arabia; and all the rest were evil because of the people's fanaticism. At night I slept on the cottage terrace of a poor patient, Aly's neighbour; not liking the unswept dokân for a lodging, and so far from friends.

At sunrise came Aly, from Zâmil, to bid me to breakfast — the bread and salt offered to the (Christian and Frankish) stranger by the gentle philosophic Emir. We drank the morning cup, at the hearth; then his breakfast tray was served, and we sat down to it in the midst of the floor, the Emir, the Nasrâny and Aly: for there is no such ignoble observing of degrees in their homely and religious life. — The breakfast fare in Aneyza is warm girdle-bread [somewhat bitter to our taste, yet they do not perceive the bitterness, 'which might be because a little salt is ground with the corn,' said Abdullah]: therewith we had dates, and a bowl of sweet (cow) butter. A bowl of (cow) buttermilk is set by; that the breakfasters may drink of it after eating, when they rise to rinse the hands; and for this there is a metal ewer and basin. The water is poured over the fingers; and without more the breakfasters take leave: the day begins.

I went to sit in my dokân, where Zâmil sent me bye and bye, by Aly, a leg of mutton out of the butchers' sûk, "that I might dine well." Mutton is good at Aneyza: and camel's flesh is sold to poor folk. A leg of their lean desert mutton, which might weigh five or six pounds, is sold for sixpence: this meat, with scotches made in it and hung one day to the ardent sun, will last good three days. Beduins bring live gazelle fawns into the town; which are often bought by citizens to be fostered, for their children's pastime: these dearlings of the desert were valued at eight pence.

I had not long been sitting in my dokân before one came to put me out of it! he cried churlishly with averted face — so that I did not know him — to the negro Aly, who stood by, "Out! with these things!"

The negro shouted again, "The Nasrâny is here with Zâmil's knowledge ; wilt thou strive with Zâmil !" The other (who was Aly the second or executive emir) muttered between his teeth, " Zâmil quoth he, ugh ! — the dokân is mine, and I say out ! ugh ! out of my dokân, out, out !" But the negro cried as loud as he, " Zâmil he is Emir of this town, and what art thou ?" — " I am Emir." The emir Aly respected my person — to me he spoke no word, and I was ready to content him ; the shop he said was his own. But my friends had not done well to settle me there : the violence of the Waháby Aly, in contempt of the liberal Emir Zâmil, would hearten the town fanatics against the Nasrâny. — This was the comedy of the two Alyes. The white Aly spurned-to the door, and drew the bolt ; and the same day he had driven me out of the town, but Zâmil would not hear of it. I remained with my bags in the street, and idle persons came to look on ; but the negro Aly vehemently threatened, that ' Zâmil would pluck out the eyes and the tongue of any that molested me !'

The hot morning hours advanced to high noon ; and when the muéthins chanted I was still sitting in the street by my things, in the sight of the malevolent people, who again flocked by me to the mesjid. — " Ullah ! this is one who prays not," quoth every passing man. After them came a lad of the town, whose looks showed him to be of impure sinister conditions ! and bearing a long rod in his hand : therewith of his godly zeal — that is an inhuman envy and cruelty ! he had taken upon him to beat in late-lingerers to the prayers. Now he laid hands on the few lads, that loitered to gape upon the Nasrâny, and cried, " Go pray, go pray ! may Ullah confound you !" and he drove them before him. Then he threatened Aly, who remained with me ; and the poor man, hearing God named, could not choose but obey him. The shallow dastard stood finally grinning upon me, — his rod was lifted ! and doubtless he tickled in every vein with the thought of smiting a kafir, for God's sake : but he presently vailed it again, — for are not the Nasâra reputed to be great strikers ? In this time of their prayers, some Beduins [they were perhaps Kahtân] issued from a house near by, to load upon their kneeling camels. I went to talk with them and hear their *loghra* : but Beduins in a town are townsmen, and in a journey are hostile ; and with maledictions they bade me stand off, saying, " What have we to do with a kafir ?"

Aly would have me speak in the matter of the dokân to Zâmil. 1

found Zâmil in the afternoon at his house door : and he said, with mild voice, " We will not enter, because the kahwa is full of Beduw " [Meteyr sheykhs, come in to consult with the town, of their riding together against Kahtân]. We walked in his lane, and sat down under a shadowing wall in the dust of the street. " Have you lost the dokân ? said Zâmil, well, tell Aly to find you another."

— Yesterday some Aneyza tradesmen to the nomads had been robbed on the Boreyda road, and three camel loads of samn were taken from them — nearly half a ton, worth 200 reals : the thieves were Kahtân. The intruded Kahtân in el-Kasîm were of the Boreyda alliance ; and Zâmil sent a letter thither, complaining of this injury, to Abdullah. Abdullah wrote word again, " It was the wild Beduw : lay not their misdeed to our charge." Zâmil now sent out thirty young men of good houses, possessing thelûls in the town, to scour the Nefûd — [they returned six days later to Aneyza, having seen nothing]. Zâmil spoke not much himself in the town councils : but his mind was full of solicitude ; and it was said of him in these days, that he could not eat.

Aly found me so wretched a tenement, that my friends exclaimed, " It is an house of the rats ! it is not habitable." The negro answered them, He had sought up and down, but that everyone repulsed him saying, " Shall a Nasrâny harbour in my beyt ? " The ruinous house was of a miserable old man, a patient of mine, who demanded an excessive daily hire, although he had received my medicines freely. Aly on the morrow persuaded a young negro neighbour, who had a small upper chamber, empty, to house the hakîm ; promising him that the Nasrâny should cure his purblind father. — I went to lodge there : the old father was a freed-man of *Yahya's* house (afterward my friends). The negro host was a pargetter ; it was his art to adorn the citizens' coffee-halls with chequered daubing and white fretwork, of gypsum. We may see, even in the rudest villages of Arabia, the fantasy they have for whitening ; their clay casements are commonly blanched about with jis : the white is to their sense light and cheerfulness, as black is balefulness. [" A white day to thee ! " is said for " good-morrow " in the border countries : Syrian Moslems use to whiten their clay sepulchres. — Paul cries out, in this sense, " Thou whited walling ! "]

" Now ! quoth the young negro, when I entered his dwelling, let them bibble-babble that will, sixty thousand bibble-babblings," —

because for the love of his aged father, he had received the kafir. His narrow kahwa was presently full of town folk; and some of them no inconsiderable persons. It was for the poor man's honour to serve them with coffee, of the best; and that day it cost a shilling, which I was careful to restore to him. All these persons were come in to chat curiously of their maladies with the hakîm, whose counsels should cost them nothing; they hoped to defraud him of the medicines, and had determined in their iniquitous hearts to keep no good will for the Nasrâny again. And I was willing to help them, in aught that I might, without other regard.

At the next sunrise I went to breakfast with the Kenneyny: this cheerful hour is not early in that sunny climate, where the light returns with a clear serenity; and welfaring persons waken to renew the daily pleasures of prayers, coffee, and the friendly discourse of their easy lives. The meal times are commonly at hours when the Arabian people may honestly shun the burden of open hospitality. But the hours of the field labourers are those of the desert: breakfast is brought out to them at high noon, from the master's house, and they sup when the sun is going down. Every principal household possesses a milch cow in this town.

Each morning as I walked in the sûk, some that were sick persons' friends, drew me by the mantle, and led the hakîm to their houses; where they brought me forth a breakfast-tray of girdle-bread and léban. Thus I breakfasted twice or thrice daily, whilst the wonder lasted, and felt my strength revive. Their most diseases are of the eyes; I saw indeed hundreds of such patients! in the time of my being at Aneyza. The pupils are commonly clouded by night-chill cataract and small-pox cataract: many lose the sight of one or even both their eyes in childhood by this scourge; and there is a blindness, which comes upon them, after a cruel aching of years in the side of the forehead. — There is nothing feasible which the wit of some men will not stir them to attempt; also we hear of eye-prickers in Arabia: but the people have little hope in them. An eye-salver with the needle, from Shuggera, had been the year before at Aneyza. Their other common diseases are rheums and the oasis fever, and the *táhal*: I have seen the tetter among children.

— The small-pox was in the town: the malady, which had not been seen here for seven years, spread lately from some slave children brought up in the returning pilgrim caravan. Some of the town caravaners, with the profit of their sales in Mecca, use to buy slave children in Jidda, to sell them again in el-Kasîm, or (with more advantage) in Mesopotamia. They win thus a few reals : but Aneyza lost thereby, in the time of my being there, chiefly I think by their inoculation ! — " five hundred " of her free-born children ! Nevertheless the infection did not pass the Wady to Boreyda, nor to any of the Nefûd villages lying nigh about them. I was called to some of their small-pox houses, where I found the sick lying in the dark ; the custom is to give them no medicines, " lest they should lose their eyesight." And thus I entered the dwellings of some of the most fanatical citizens : my other patients' diseases were commonly old and radical. — Very cleanly and pleasant are the most homes in this Arabian town, all of clay building.

The tradesmen's shops are well furnished. The common food is cheaper at Boreyda ; at Aneyza is better cheap of " Mecca coffee " (from el-Yémen), and of Gulf clothing. Dates, which in Kasîm are valued by weight, are very good here ; and nearly 30 pounds were sold for one real.

There is an appearance of welfare in the seemly clothing of this townsfolk — men commonly of elated looks and a comely liberty of carriage. They salute one another in many words, nearly as the Beduins, with a familiar grace ; for not a few of them, who live in distant orchard houses, come seldom into the town. But the streets are thronged on Fridays ; when all the townsmen, even the field labourers, come in at midday, to pray in the great mesjid, and hear the koran reading and preaching : it is as well their market day. The poorer townspeople go clad like the Aarab ; and their kerchiefs are girded with the head-cord. These sober citizens cut the hair short — none wear the braided sidelocks of the Beduw : the richer sort (as said) have upon their heads Fez caps, over which they loosely cast a gay kerchief ; that they gird only when they ride abroad. As for the haggu or waist-band of slender leathern plait [it is called in Kasîm *hágub* or *brîm*] which is worn even by princes in Hâyil, and by the (Arabian) inhabitants of Medina and Mecca, the only wearers of it here are the hareem. The substantial townsmen go training in black mantles of light Irâk worsted : and the young patricians will spend as much as the cloth is worth, for a broidered collar in metal thread-work. The embroiderers are mostly women, in whom is a skill to set forth some careless grace of running lines, some flowery harmony in needlework — such as we see woven in the Oriental carpets. Gentle persons in the streets go balancing in their hands long rods, which are brought from Mecca.

Hareem are unseen, and the men's manners are the more gracious and untroubled : it may be their Asiatic society is manlier, but less virile than the European. They live-on in a pious daily assurance : and little know they of stings which be in our unquiet emulations, and in our foreign religion. Mohammed's sweet-blooded faith has redeemed them from the superfluous study of the World, from the sour-breathing inhospitable wine ; and has purified their bodies from nearly every excess of living : only they exceed here, and exceed all in the East, in coffee. Marriage is easy from every man's youth ; and there are no such rusty bonds in their wedlock, that any must bear an heavy countenance. The Moslem's breast is enlarged ; he finds few wild branches to prune of his life's vine, — a plant supine and rich in spirit, like the Arabic language. There is a nobility of the religious virtue among them, and nothing stern or rugged, but the hatred of the kafir : few have great hardness in their lives. — But the woman is in bondage, and her heart has little or no refreshment. Women are not seen passing by their streets, in the daytime ; but in the evening twilight (when the men sit at coffee) you shall see many veiled forms flitting to their gossips' houses : and they will hastily return, through an empty sûk, in the time of the last prayers, whilst the men are praying in the mesjids.

A day or two after my being in Aneyza, a young man of the patricians came to bid me to dinner, from his father ; who was that good man *Abdullah Abd er-Rahmàn, el-Bessàm*, a merchant at Jidda, and chief of the house of Bessàm in Aneyza. Abdullah el-Bessàm and Abdullah el-Kenneyny were entire friends, breakfasting and dining together, and going every day to coffee in each other's houses ; and they were *filasûfs* with Zâmil. Besides the Kenneyny I found there *Sheykh Nâsir, es-Smîry*, a very swarthy man of elder years, of the Waháby straitness in religion ; and who was of the Aneyza merchants at Jidda. He had lately returned — though not greatly enriched, to live in an hired house at home ; and was partner with the Kenneyny in buying every year a few young horses from the Nomads, which they shipped to Bombay for sale.

The Bessàm kindred — now principal in wealth at Aneyza, came hither sixty years before, from a village in el-Aruth. [In Pliny *Besamna* is the name of an Arabian town ; Bessàm of the Beduins is *el-Barrûd*, a village of thirty houses, south of Shuggera in the way to Mecca.] Some of them, of late years, are established in Jidda, where now the East Nejders are as commonly called [besides *es-Sherkyîn*, ' men of the East, Orientals '] *el-Bessàm !* Abdullah el-Bessàm, of B. Temîm, is a merchant Arabian honoured at home, and his name is very honourable in all Nejd ; of a joyful wise nature, full of good and gentle deeds. When Ibn Rashîd came against the town two years before, with Boreyda, Zâmil and the sheykhs sent out this man of integrity, to treat with him.

The matter was this: Ibn Saûd came with a great ghrazzu before Aneyza, and alighted to encamp between *Rasheyd's* outlying palm ground and the town. His purpose was to go against Boreyda : then Ibn Rashîd sallied from Hâyil in defence of his allies. [*v.* p. 37.] — Abdullah el-Bessàm (with his ready-writer *Ibn Ayith*) and *Abdullah el-Yahŷa*, the young sheykhly companion of Zâmil, rode forth to Ibn Rashîd, who lay encamped beyond the Wady. And he said to the Shammar Prince, " O Child of Abdullah ! we of Aneyza would to God that no difference should grow to be an occasion of warfare between Moslemîn : we desire to be a mean of peace betwixt you." *Mohammed Ibn Rashîd :* " For this also am I come out, that there might be peace." — In the end it was accorded among them, that Ibn Saûd would withdraw from these parts ; and then would Ibn Rashîd return home. Their parleying had not been without some glorious loud words of Hamûd el-Abeyd (*v. supra* p. 32] on the behalf of Ibn Rashîd ; and in such the princely man behaved himself ' like a Beduwy.' — Three days the good Bessàm was a guest in the menzil of the Shammar Emir ; and towards evening when he would depart the Prince Mohammed bade Mufarrij, ' lead round the red mare for Sheykh Abdullah ! ' But the prudent and incorrupt citizen was in no wise to be persuaded to receive a gift from Ibn Rashîd of such price. The Emir said, ' then bring the thelûl, and mount the Sheykh Abdullah thereon ! ' — This was accepted ; and Ibn Rashîd clothed the two honourable men ambassadors from Aneyza with scarlet mantles and silken kerchiefs ; and gave garments to those who followed them : and they returned to the town. — The other Bessàm houses in Aneyza, though some of them had trafficked with the Franks in the ports (saving a younger Abdullah, now of the foreign merchants in Bosra) were Wahábies. The people said of Abdullah, " he is a good man, but his sons are *afûn* (corrupted) !" That might be of the moral malaria in the port-town of Mecca ; or the unlooked-for accident of many honest fathers, that the graft of their blood in the mother's stock was faulty.

Sheykh Nâsir was of the B. Khâlid families : there is a Beduishness in them more than in the Temîmies. Though stiff in opinions, he answered me better than any man, and with a natural frankness ; especially when I asked him of the history and topography of these countries : and he first traced for me, with his pen, the situation of the southern *Harras*, — *B. Abdillah, Kesshab, Turr'a, 'Ashîry, 'Ajeyfa,* (*Rodwa, Jeheyna ;*) which, with the rest of the vulcanic train described in this work, before my voyage in Arabia, were not heard of in Europe. Not long before he had embarked some of the honest gain of his years of exile under the Red Sea climate, with two more Jidda merchants, in a lading to India. Tidings out of the caravan season may hardly pass the great desert ; but he had word in these days, by certain who came up by hap from Mecca, that their vessel had not been heard of since her sailing ! and now it was feared that the ship must be lost. These foreign merchants at the ports do never cover their sea and fire risks by an assurance, — such were in their eyes a deed of unbelief ! In the meanwhile sheykh Nâsir bore this incertitude of God's hand with the severe serenity of a right Moslem.

— This was the best company in the town ; the dinner-tray was set on a stool [the mess is served upon the floor in princes' houses in Hâyil — Vol. I. p. 646] ; and we sat half-kneeling about it. The foreign merchants' meal at Aneyza is more town-like than I had seen in Arabia : besides boiled mutton on temmn, Abdullah had his little dishes of carrots fried in butter, and bowls of custard messes or curded milk. — We sit at leisure at the European board, we chat cheerfully ; but such at the Arabs' dish would be a very inept and unreasonable behaviour ! — he were not a man but an homicide, who is not speechless in that short battle of the teeth for a day's life of the body. And in what sort (forgive it me, O thrice good friends ! in the sacrament of the bread and salt,) a dog or a cat laps up his meat, not taking breath, and is dispatched without any curiosity, and runs after to drink ; even so do the Arabs endeavour, that they may come to an end with speed : for in their eyes it were not honest to linger at the dish ; whereunto other (humbler) persons look that should eat after them. The good Bessàm, to show the

European stranger the more kindness, rent morsels of his mutton and laid them ready to my hand. — *Yerhamak Ullah*, " The Lord be merciful unto thee," say the town guests, every one, in rising from dinner, with a religious mildness and humility. Bessàm himself, and his sons, held the towel to them, without the door, whilst they washed their hands. The company returned to their sitting before the hearth ; and his elder son sat there already to make us coffee.

El-Kenneyny bid me come to breakfast with him on the morrow ; and we should go out to see his orchard (which they call here *jenèyny* ' pleasure ground '). " Abdullah, quoth sheykh Nâsir, would enquire of thee how water might be raised by some better mean than we now use at Aneyza, where a camel walking fifteen paces draws but one bucket full ! [it may be nearly three pails, 200 pails in an hour, 1500 to 2000 pails in the day's labour.] And you, a man of Europea, might be able to help us ! for we suppose you have learned geometry ; and may have read in books which treat of machines, that are so wonderful in your countries." — Nâsir's Waháby malice would sow cockle in the clean corn of our friendship, and have made me see an interested kindness in the Kenneyny ! who answered with an ingenuous asperity, that he desired but to ask Khalîl's opinion. He had imagined an artesian well flowing with water enough to irrigate some good part of Aneyza ! — I had seen to-day a hand-cart on wheels, before a smith's forge ! a sight not less strange in an Arabian town, than the camel in Europe ; it was made here for the Kenneyny. The sâny had fastened the ends of his tires unhandsomely, so that they overlapped : but his felloes, nave and spokes were very well wrought ; and in all Nejd (for the making of suâny wheels— commonly a large yard of cross measure), there are perfect wheelwrights. Abdullah's dates had been drawn home on this barrow, in the late harvest ; and the people marvelled to see how two men might wield the loads of two or three great camels !

The guests rise one after another and depart when the coffee is drunk, saying, *Yunaam Ullah aleyk*, ' The Lord be gracious unto thee ; ' and the host responds gently, *Fî amân illah*, ' (go) in the peace of the Lord.' There are yet two summer hours of daylight ; and the townsmen landowners will walk abroad to breathe the freshing air, and visit their orchards.

As for the distribution of the day-time in Aneyza : the people purchase their provision at the market stalls, soon after the sunrising; the shuttered shops are set open a little later, when the tradesmen (mostly easy-living persons and landowners) begin to arrive from breakfast. The running brokers now cry up and down in the clothiers' street, holding such things in their hands as are committed to them to sell for ready money, — long guns, spears, coffee-pots, mantles, fathoms of calico, and the like. They cry what silver is bidden; and if any person call them they stay to show their wares. Clothing-pieces brought down by the caravaners from Bagdad, are often delivered to them to the dellâls, to be sold out of hand. The tradesmen, in days when no Beduins come in, have little business: they sit an hour, till the hot forenoon, and then draw their shop shutters, and go homeward; and bye and bye all the street will be empty. — At the midday íthin the townsmen come flocking forth in all the ways, to enter the mesjids. Few salesmen return from the midday prayers to the sûk; the most go (like the patricians) to drink coffee in friends' houses: some, who have jenèynies in the town, withdraw then to sit in the shadows of their palms.

At the half-afternoon íthin, the coffee drinkers rise from the perfumed hearths, and go the third time a-praying to their mesjids. From the public prayers the tradesmen resort to the sûk; their stalls are set open, the dellâls are again a-foot, and passengers in the bazaar. The patricians go home to dine; and an hour later all the shops are shut for the day. — Citizens will wander then beyond the town walls, to return at the sun's going down, when the íthin calls men a fourth time to pray in the mesjids!

From these fourth prayers the people go home: and this is not an hour to visit friends; for the masters are now sitting to account with the field labourers, in their coffee-halls — where not seldom there is a warm mess of burghrol set ready for them. But husbandmen in far outlying palmsteads remain there all night; and needing no roof, they lie down in their mantles under the stars to sleep. Another íthin, after the sun-setting hardly two hours, calls men to the fifth or last public prayers (*súlat el-akhîr*). It is now night; and many who are weary remain to pray, or not to pray, in their own houses. When they come again from the mesjids, the people have ended the day's religion: there is yet an hour of private friendship (but no more common assemblings) in the coffee-halls of the patricians and foreign merchants.

— El-Kenneyny sent a poor kinsman of his, when we had breakfasted, to accompany me to his jenèyny, half a league distant, within the furthest circuit of town walling : he being an infirm man would follow us upon an ass. [With this kinsman of his, *Sleymàn*, I have afterward passed the great desert southward to the Mecca country.] We went by long clay lanes with earthen walling, between fields and plantations, in the cool of the morning ; but (in this bitter sun) there springs not a green blade by the (unwatered) way side ! Their cornfields were now stubbles ; and I saw the lately reaped harvest gathered in great heaps to the stamping places.

At the midst of the way is the site of an ancient settlement, *Jannah*, founded by a fendy, of that name, of B. Khâlid, some time before Aneyza [which is now called *Umm* (Mother of) *Nejd*]. — There was perpetual enmity between the two villages standing a mile asunder. Jannah had been abandoned ninety-five years ; but many living persons have seen carcases of old houses still standing there, forty years ago : pargetters dig jis on the ancient site — to-day a field. The B. Khâlid Aarab [before-time in el-Hása ; but in our days they wander in the north towards Kuweyt], are reckoned to the line of Keys ; and they are of *Yâm*, with *Murra, Ajmân, B. Hajir, el-Shamir* : the Ajmân are now also in the north near Kuweyt. Jannah, in the opinion of Sheykh Nâsir, was founded six hundred years ago [in our XIII century], three generations or four before the building of Aneyza. Jannah in the beginning of the Waháby Power, held with *Thuèyny el-Múntefik*, the great Sheykh upon the river country in the north, but Aneyza was allied with the Wahâby. The Khâlidies of Jannah were overcome in the troubles ensuing, and they forsook the place : many of them went to live in the north, the rest withdrew to Aneyza. Colonists (we have seen) of *es-Sbeya*, Keysites, were the founders of Aneyza. [Their nomad tribesmen remain in *el-Aruth* ; *Hayer* is their village, they are settlers and Beduw. More of their tribesmen are in *W. es-Sbeya*, in the borders of Nejd and the Hejâz, four journeys northwards from Mecca ; their villages are *Khórma* and *Rúnya*.] They were afterwards increased by incomers of B. Temîm, who with Korèysh are Ishmaelites in the line of *Elyâs*, brother of Keys. — So are Mozayna (Harb) from Elyâs : Elyâs is *Ibn Múthur*. Korèysh, *B. Assad* (which were before in Jebel Tŷ) Temîm, B. Khâlid, el-Múntifik, Meteyr, Ateyba, Thakîf and Sbeya are all of Múthur. — Thus Abdullah el-Bessàm, who read me this lore from his book of genealogies : and " of B. Temîm be sprung, he said, the B. Sókhr."

Kenneyny's palm and corn-ground might be three and a half acres of sand soil. The farthest bay of the town wall which fenced him was there fallen away in wide breaches : and all without the sûr is sand-sea of the Nefûd. The most had been corn land, in which he was now setting young palm plants from the Wady : for every one is paid a real. He had but forty stems of old palms, and they were of slender growth ; because of the former " weak " (empoverished) owner's insufficient watering. And such are the most small landed men in this country ; for they and their portions of the dust of this world are devoured (hardly less than in Egypt and Syria) by rich money-lenders : that is by the long rising over their heads of an insoluble usury. Abdullah's new double well-pit was six fathoms deep, sunk into the underlying crust of sand-rock ; and well steyned with dry courses of sandstone, which is hewn near Aneyza. All the cost had been 600 reals, or nearly £120 in silver : the same for four camels' draught would have cost 400 reals. Abdullah valued the ground with his well at about £600, that is above £100 an acre without the water : and this was some of their cheaper land, lying far from the town. They have thick-grown but light-eared harvests of wheat, sown year by year upon the same plots ; and corn is always dear in poor Arabia.

Here four nâgas — their camel cattle are black at Aneyza — wrought incessantly : a camel may water one acre nearly from wells of six or eight fathoms. He had opened this great well, hoping in time to purchase some piece more of his neighbour's ground. Abdullah, as all rich landed men, had two courses of well camels ; the beasts draw two months till they become lean, and they are two months at pasture in the wilderness. Every morrow Abdullah rode hither to take the air, and oversee his planting : and he had a thought to build himself here an orchard house, that he might breathe the air of the Nefûd, — when he should be come again [but ah ! that was not written in the book of life] to Aneyza. Abdullah asked, how could I, " a man of Europa," live in the khála ? and in journeying over so great deserts, had I never met with foot robbers, *henshûly!* The summer before this, he and some friends had gone out with tents, to dwell nomadwise in the Nefûd. Welfaring Aneyza citizens have canvas tents, for the yearly pilgrimage and their often caravan passages, made like the booths of the Beduw, that is cottage-wise, and open in front, — the best, I can think, under this climate.

These tilled grounds so far from the town are not fenced ; the bounds are marked by mere-stones. Abdullah looked with a provident eye upon this parcel of land, which he planted for his daughters' inheritance : he had purchased palms for his sons at Bosra. He would not that the men (which might be) born of him should remain in Arabia ! and he said, with a sad presentiment, ' Oh ! that he might live over the few years of his children's nonage.'

I found here some of his younger friends. These were *Hàmed es-Sâfy*, of Bagdad, and Abdullah Bessàm, the younger (nephew of the elder Abdullah el-Bessàm) ; and a negro companion of theirs, *Sheykh ibn Ayith*, a lettered sheykh or elder in the religion. After salaams they all held me out their forearms, — that the hakîm might take knowledge of their pulses ! Hàmed and Abdullah, unlike their worthiness of soul, were slender growths : their blood flowed in feeble streams, as their old spent fathers, and the air of great towns, had given them life. Ibn Ayith, of an (ox-like) African complexion, showed a pensive countenance, whilst I held his destiny in my hands ! — and required in a small negro voice, ' What did I deem of his remiss health ? ' The poor scholar believed himself to be always ailing ; though his was no lean and discoloured visage ! nor the long neck, narrow breast, and pithless members of those chop-fallen men that live in the twilight of human life, growing only, since their pickerel youth, in their pike's heads, to die later in the world's cold. — The negro litterate was a new man from this day, wherein he heard the hakîm's absolution ; and carried himself upright among his friends (thus they laughed to me), whereas he had drooped formerly. And Ibn Ayith was no pedant fanatic ; but daily conversing with the foreign merchants, he had grown up liberal minded. Poor, he had not travelled, saving that — as all the religious Nejdians not day-labourers — he had ridden once on pilgrimage (with his bountiful friends, who had entertained him) to Mecca ; " And if I were in thy company, quoth he, I would show thee all the historical places." His toward youth had been fostered in learning, by charitable sheykhs ; and they at this day maintained his scholar's leisure. He was now father of a family ; but besides the house wherein he dwelt he had no worldly possessions. There was ever room for him at Abdullah el-Bessàm's dish ; and he was ofttimes the good man's scrivener, for

Abdullah was less clerk than honourable merchant; and it is the beginning of their school wisdom to write handsomely. But in Ibn Ayith was no subject behaviour; I have heard him, with a manly roughness, say the kind Abdullah *nay!* to his beard. There is a pleasant civil liberty in Aneyza, and no lofty looks of their natural rulers in the town; but many a poor man (in his anger) will contradict, to the face, and rail at the long-suffering prudence of Zâmil! — saying, *Mâ b'ak kheyr.*

When I came again, it was noon, the streets were empty, and the shops shut: the íthin sounded, and the people came trooping by to the mesjids. An old Ateyba sheykh passed lateward, — he was in the town with some of his marketing tribesmen; and hearing I was the hakîm, he called to me, ' He would have a medicine for the *rîh*.' One answered, " It might cost thee a real." — "And what though this medicine cost a real, O townling (hâthery), if I have the silver!" There came also some lingering truants, who stayed to smile at the loud and sudden-tongued old Beduwy; and a merry fellow asked, amidst their laughter, were he well with his wives? " Nay, cries the old heart, and I would, billah, that the hareem had not cause. — Oho! have patience there!" (because some zealots thrust him on). — " Heardest not thou the íthin? go pray!" — " Ay, ay, I heard it, Ullah send you a sorrow! am I not talking with this mudowwy? — well, I am coming presently." — A zealot woman went by us: the squalid creature stepped to the Beduin sheykh, and drew him by the mantle. " To the prayer! cries she, old devil-sick Beduwy; thou to stand here whilst the people pray! — and is it to talk with this misbelieving person?" — " Akhs! do away thy hands! let me go, woman! — I tell thee I have said my prayers." Though he cried *akhs-akhs!* she held him by the cloth; and he durst not resist her: yet he said to me, " O thou the mudowwy! where is thy remedy for the rheums? — a wild fire on this woman! that will not let me speak." I bade him return after prayers; and the sheykh hearing some young children chide with " *Warak, warak!* why goest thou not in to pray?" he called to me as he was going, " O thou! resist them not, but do as they do; when a man is come to another country, let him observe the usage and not strive — that will be best for thee, and were it only to live in peace with them." Now the stripling with the rod was upon us! — the kestrel would have laid hands on the sheykhly father of the desert. " Oh! hold, and I go," quoth he, and they drove him before them.

My medical practice was in good credit. Each daybreak a flock of miserable persons waited for the hakîm, on my small terrace (before they went to their labour) : they importuned me for their sore eyes ; and all might freely use my eye washes. In that there commonly arrived some friendly messenger, to call the stranger to breakfast ; and I left my patients lying on their backs, with smarting eyeballs. The poorer citizens are many, in the general welfare of Aneyza. Such are the field labourers and well drivers, who receive an insufficient monthly wage. The impotent, and the forsaken in age, are destitute indeed ; they must go a-begging through the town. I sometimes met with a tottering and deadly crew in the still streets before midday ; old calamitous widows, childless aged men, indigent divorced wives, and the misshapen and diseased ones of step-dame Nature that had none to relieve them. They creep abroad as a curse in the world, and must knock from door to door, to know if the Lord will send them any good ; and cry lamentably *Yâ ahl el-karîm!* ' O ye of this bountiful household.' But I seldom saw the cheerful hand of bounty which beckoned to them or opened. One morrow when I went to visit the Emir the mesquins were crouching and shuffling at his door ; and Zâmil's son Abdullah came out with somewhat to give them : but I saw his dole was less than his outstretched hand full of dates ! " Go further ! and here is for you," quoth the young niggard : he pushed the mesquins and made them turn their backs.

I passed some pleasant evenings in the kahwas of the young friends and neighbours Hàmed and Abdullah ; and they called in Ibn Ayith, who entertained me with discourse of the Arabic letters. Hàmed regaled us with Bagdad nargîlies, and Abdullah made a sugared cooling drink of *támr el-Hind* (tamarind). To Abdullah's kahwa, in the daytime, resorted the best company in the town, — such were the honourable young Bessàm's cheerful popular manners. His mortar rang out like a bell of hospitality, when he prepared coffee. The Aneyza mortar is a little saucer-like hollow in a marble block great as a font-stone : a well-ringing mortar is much esteemed among them. Their great coffee-mortar blocks are hewn not many hours from the town eastward (near el-Mith'nib, toward J. Tueyk). An ell long is every liberal man's pestle of marble in Aneyza : it is smitten in rhythm (and that we hear at all the coffee-hearths of the Arabs). A jealous or miserable householder, who would not have many pressing in to drink with him, must muffle the musical note of his marble or knelling brasswork.

These were the best younger spirits of the (foreign) merchant houses in the town : they were readers in the Encyclopedia, and of the spirituous poets of the Arabian antiquity. Abdullah, when the last of his evening friends had departed, sitting at his petroleum lamp, and forgetting the wife of his youth, would pore on his books and feed his gentle spirit almost till the day appearing. Hàmed, bred at Bagdad, was incredulous of the world old and new ; but he leaned to the new studies. These young merchants sought counsels in medicine, and would learn of me some Frankish words, and our alphabet, — and this because their sea carriage is in the hands of European shippers. A few of these Arabians, dwelling in the trade ports, have learned to endorse their names upon Frankish bills which come to their hands, in Roman letters. Abdullah el-Bessàm's eldest son — he was now in India, and a few more, had learned to read and to speak too in English : yet that was, I can think, but lamely. Others, as the Kenneyny, who have lived in Bombay, can speak the Hindostani. Hàmed wrote from my lips (in his Arabic letters) a long table of English words, — such as he thought might serve him in his Gulf passages. His father dwelt, since thirty years, in Bagdad ; and had never revisited Aneyza : — in which time the town is so increased, that one coming again after a long absence might hardly, they say, remember himself there. El-Kenneyny told me that Aneyza was now nearly double of the town fifteen years ago ; and he thought the inhabitants must be to-day 15,000 !

My friends saw me a barefoot hakîm, in rent clothing, as I was come-in from the khála, and had escaped out of Boreyda. The younger Abdullah Bessàm sent me sandals, and they would have put a long wand in my hand ; but I answered them, " He is not poor who hath no need : my poverty is honourable." Kenneyny said to me on a morrow, when we were alone (and for the more kindness finding a Frankish word), "*Mussu* Khalîl, if you lack money — were it an hundred or two hundred reals, you may have this here of me : " but he knew not all my necessity, imagining that I went poorly for a disguise. I gave thanks for his generous words ; but which were thenceforth in my ears as if they had never been uttered. I heard also, that the good Bessàm had taken upon himself to send me forward, to what part I would. I was often bidden to his house, and seldom to Kenneyny's, who (a new man) dreaded overmuch the crabbed speech of his Waháby townspeople. The good Bessàm, as oft as he met with me, invited the stranger, benignly, to breakfast on the morrow : and at breakfast he bid me dine the same day with him, — an humanity which was much to thank God for in these extremities.

Abdullah el-Bessàm lent a friendly ear to my questions of the Arabian antiquity ; and was full of tolerance. — ' Had not Nasâra, he said, visited the Néby in Medina, and *'Amar ?* ' — Ômar, he who called to govern the new religion (of some sparkles on a waste coast, grown to a great conflagration in the World !) would bear none other style, after the deceased " apostle " than *khâlif*, his vicar. But what may be thought of the rottenness of the Roman power at that time ? when her legionaries clad in iron, could not sustain the furious running-on of weak-bodied and half-armed dissolute Arabians, in their ragged shirts ! banded [which alone can band Semites !] by the (new) passion of religion, and their robber-like greediness of the spoil ! the people through whose waste land Gallus had led a Roman army without battles five ages before, and returned with a European man's disdain of the thievish and unwarlike inhabitants ! Egypt was soon overrun, by the torrential arms of the new faith : and Bessàm told a tale, how there came a Copt to show his grief to the Commander of the believers in el-Medina. He found the magnanimous half-Beduin 'Amar busy, like any poor man in his palm-yard, to drive the well camels ; and 'Amar held up his cattle to hear the Christian's tale. The Copt alleged that the general of the Moslemîn in Egypt dealt oppressively, because in Iskanderîa (Alexandria) he would build their mesjid in a plot of his, and thereto beat down his house, — although he, the Christian, had constantly refused a price. 'Amar went in his ground till he found a bone — in the Arabs' country the scattered bones of beasts unburied are never far to seek (conf. Jud. xv. 15), and bade the Copt bear witness of that he saw him do. 'Amar with his sword cleft the head of the bone, and gave this token to the Christian, to [bind in his garment and] deliver to his lieutenant in Egypt, with his word to desist from that enterprise. 'Amar's word might remove kings, though he knew not the superfluous signs of writing, and his *tessera* was humbly obeyed by the (Arabian) his lieutenant at Alexandria. — It was 'Amar who burned the letters of the former world : it seemed to his short Semitic understanding that these had profited nothing unto the knowledge of the true God, and of His saving Religion !

Neither Bessàm nor the scholars at Aneyza could answer my simple question, "Where is *Jorda?* — named in the old (Mohammedan) itineraries 'the metropolis of Kasîm': " that name was unknown to them! They first found to answer me after other days, with much tossing of books; and the site, when they had enquired of men wont to ride in the Nefûd. — The place they suppose to be *el-Ethelly* (some outlying granges), nigh to er-Russ, at the Wady er-Rummah: where are seen 'wide ruins and foundations': and they amended my Jorda to *Járada*. Their lettered men only study to be indifferent scholars in the tedious koran learning; and they would smile at his idle curiosity, who would take in hand to write a history of their poor affairs, in the vulgar speech. The title-deeds of their grounds are perhaps the only ancient writings of the oases' dwellers. El-Bessàm's book of (pretended) genealogies was a grave volume in gilded binding of red leather: wherein I read the kinships of Amalek, Midiân, and other Arabian tribes; which were Beduins and settlers of the Mosaic and Hebrew antiquity. The good man seeing me busy to turn the leaves, gave me his book; but I would not accept it, — which a little displeased him.

They told me, 'that an agent of the Ottoman Government, with a firman from the Sultan, had been the year before in these parts; and he wrote down the names of towns and villages, and wandering tribes!' The authority [howbeit usurped by the sword] of the Turkish Sultan is acknowledged by all good Moslemîn; and the principality of Boreyda pays yearly to the Ottoman treasury in the Hejâz a (freewill) contribution, — which is not fully a thousand pounds. — But this was the answer of Aneyza; "We do not deny the tribute: send unto us and receive the same." But the Turks hitherto like not this adventuring the skin, in the sands of Arabia!

Kenneyny's thoughts were continually for the bringing up of his son; whose frail life he would launch upon the world's waves, with all that munition for the way which he had long imagined. He would have his child learn Persian and Turkish (the tongues of their Gulf neighbourhood); and French and English. In his twentieth year the young man would take his journey through the states of Europe, to view the great civil world, and those thousand new miraculous machines, which are become the nurses of human life. In Abdullah's perspicuous mind was a privy scorn of every national jealousy, and intolerance and religious arrogance; and an admiration of that natural knowledge, civility and humanity, which is now in the West parts of the world. Abdullah was of the best kind of spirits, or next to the best : he was mild, he was also austere, yet neither to a fault. He would at first send the boy Mohammed, for two years, to a school of the Moslems at Bagdad, ' since it was among the Moslemîn that his son must live.' After that he would bring him to Egypt or to Beyrût ; and he asked me of the schools at Beyrût [now once more, the Schoolmistress of the Levant]. The son, for whom Abdullah had so much busy thought, was ten years old, and had not yet learned letters. This child was born to him in Bombay of an Indian woman : I afterward heard it there, in the Nejd colony ; and that among them such alliances in the native blood are not well seen. Abdullah would have his son study much, that he might learn much ; he longed to see him continually running in the first horizons of knowledge : but seeing the slip was slender, and heir of a weak stock, I counselled his father to whelm no such damps upon him.— Abdullah who heard me speak with a sincerity not common in their deceitful world, answered finally, with a sigh, *sahih!* ' The truth indeed.'

Abdullah's youth had not been spent to pore on a squalor of school-learning ; he had not proceeded in the Universities — those shambles of good wits ; but his perspicuous understanding was well clad, and ripened in the sun of the busy human world : and running in the race he had early obtained a crown of God's good speed. His father dealt in horses, as many of the better sort in the town ; but he had remained poor and was deceased early. Then Abdullah adventuring into the world went to Bagdad, where at first (I have heard him say) he could not readily understand the outlandish northern speech. Afterward he traded ; and his trading was of a kind which [speaking with an Englishman] he said, *mâ yunfʻa* ' is good for nothing.' — Abdullah bought and sold slaves ; and in this traffic he sailed to Zanzibar, whose Sultan (of the princely family of *Âmàn*) is of the B. Temîm, and these Nejders' tribesmen. Abdullah also navigated for sugar to the Mauritius ! He was afterward a rice-shipper at Bombay, to the Arabian ports ; until he went to establish himself at Bosra : where, he told me with a merchant's pride, he had corn lying in his (open) granary to the value of £5000 ! — for shelter, he used only matting and reed shutters ; which might be drawn in any falling rain. His yearly household spending, with somewhat bestowed upon the followers of his fortunes, was now he told me £400.

Abdullah valued the greatest merchant's fortune in Aneyza at £24,000 ; upon which, if we should count twelve in the hundred, the yearly rent were ten times the ordinary trading capitals in Hâyil ! (if we might accept Hamûd's estimation). But how little can be the spending of an Arabian town household, in comparison of two or three thousand pounds !

Kenneyny's name was honourable in the liberal part of the town : ' Ullah, they said, had prospered him, and he is a good man ' ; but the Waháby envy looked upon them as a bee in their vile cobweb. None could tell me how Abdullah, " so needy in the beginning that he might hardly buy himself a pair of shoes," was now enriched in the world ; they responded only, ' the Lord had blessed him.' Market prices in the eastern wheat staples suddenly rise and fall : and for the good understanding of Abdullah all those ebbs and flows might be occasions to multiply wealth. At this day he was a corn-chandler, selling to lesser merchants upon trust, and that he said, without much carefulness of heart ; for he thought he knew (by observation) all his clients' state. — When living at Damascus, I saw the price of bread-corn excessively enhanced before the winter's end ; and imagined that with one or two hundred pounds a small granary might be opened, where poor households could buy all the year through, at little above the harvest prices. I enquired of some prudent and honest persons ; but they all answered : " It is such a curious trade, that one who has been bred a corn-chandler may scarce thrive in it." So no man had any courage to adventure with me.

When I dined again with the Bessàm, there was the Medina sherîf ! That old fox in a turban had now arrived at Aneyza, and taken up his lodging in the public hostel (*menzil es-sheukh*) ; but he breakfasted and supped solemnly at the good Bessàm's dish, who also of his charity undertook to send the holy beggar home to Medina. Abdullah was of like goodness to all, and, when the soldier-deserters lately arrived at Aneyza, it was Abdullah who piously provided for their further journey. Though the head of a wealthy kindred, and full of bountiful deeds, the good man had not much capital : when he came home to Aneyza he dwelt in an hired house ; and the most of his trading was with that which others committed to the radical integrity of Abdullah. He was a young-hearted man of the elder middle age and popular manners ; there was nothing in him too brittle for the World. His was a broad pleasant face ; he went very comely clad in the streets, and balancing the patricians' long wand in his hand : and in every place with a wise and smiling countenance he could speak or keep silence. He was a dove without gall in the raven's nest of their fanaticism : he loved first the God of Mohammed (because he was born in their religion), and then every not-unworthy person as himself. Large, we have seen, was the worshipful merchant's hospitality ; and in this also he was wise above the wisdom of the world.

CHAPTER XIII

LIFE IN ANEYZA

Rumours of warfare. A savage tiding from the North. The Meteyr Aarab. The 'Ateyba. A Kahtâny arrested in the street. A capital crime. Friday afternoon lecture. The Muttowwa. *Bessàm and Kenneyny discourse of the Western Nations. An Arabic gazette. "* The touchstone of truth." *The* Shazlîeh. *An erudite Persian's opinion of The three (Semitic) religions. European evangelists in Syria. An Arabian's opinions of Frankish manners (which he had seen in India). An inoculator and leech at Aneyza. The Nasrâny without shelter. A learned personage. Mohammed. The Semitic faiths. "Sheykh" Mohammed. Laudanum powder medicine. A message from Boreyda. Discourse of religion. A Jew's word. The small-pox. Yahŷa's household. Maladies. A short cure for distracted persons ; story of a Maronite convent in Lebanon. Stone-workers at Aneyza. An outlying homestead. Money borrowed at usury. Oasis husbandry. An Aneyza horse-broker. Ants' nests sifted for bread. Arabian sale horses ; and the Northern or Gulf horses. El-'Eyarîeh. The Wady er-Rummah northward.* Khâlid bin Walîd. *Owshazîeh. Deadly strife of well-diggers. Ancient man in Arabia. The Nasrâny is an outlaw among them. Thoughts of riding to Siddûs and er-Riâth. The Arabic speech in el-Kasîm.*

ONE of these mornings word was brought to the town, that Beduins had fallen upon harvesters in the Wady, and carried away their asses : and in the next half hour I saw more than a hundred of the young townsmen hasten-by armed to the Boreyda gate. The poorer sort ran foremost on foot, with long lances ; and the wellfaring trotted after upon thelûls with their backriders. But an hour had passed ; and the light-footed robbers were already two or three leagues distant !

There were yet rumours of warfare with Boreyda and the Kahtân. Were it war between the towns, Hásan and the Boreydians (less in arms and fewer in number) durst not adventure to meet the men of Aneyza in the Nefûd ; but would shelter themselves within their (span-thick) clay wall, leaving their fields and plantations in the power of the enemy, — as it has happened before-time. The adversaries, being neighbours, will no more than devour their fruits, whilst the orchards languish unwatered : they are not foreign enemies likely to lop the heads of the palms, whereby they should be ruined for many years.—This did Ibn Saûd's host in the warfare with Aneyza ; they destroyed the palms in the Wady : so pleasant is the sweet pith-wood to all the Arabians, and they desire to eat of it with a childish greediness.

Kahtân tribesmen were suffered to come marketing to Aneyza ; till a *hubt* of theirs returning one evening with loaded camels, and finding some town children not far from the gate, in the Nefûd, that were driving home their asses, and an *âbd* with them, took the beasts and let the children go : yet they carried away the negro, — and he was a slave of Zâmil's !

A savage tiding was brought in from the north ; and all Aneyza was moved by it, for the persons were well known to them. A great camp of Meteyr, Aarab *sadûk*, or " friends-of-trust to the town and Zâmil," (if any of the truthless nomads can be trusty !) had been set upon at four days' distance from hence by a strong ghrazzu of Kahtân, — for the pastures of Kasîm, their capital enemies. Leader of the raid was that Hayzàn, who, not regarding the rites of hospitality, had threatened me at Hâyil. The nomads (fugitive foemen in every other cause), will fight to " the dark death " for their pastures and waters. The Meteyr were surprised in their tents and outnumbered ; and the Kahtân killed some of them. The rest saved themselves by flight, and their milch camels ; leaving the slow-footed flocks, with the booths, and their household stuff in the power of their enemies ; who not regarding the religion of the desert pierced even women with their lances, and stripped them, and cut the wezands of three or four young children ! Among the fallen of Meteyr was a principal sheykh well known at Aneyza. Hayzàn had borne him through with his romh !

Those Aarab now withdrew towards Aneyza ; where their sheykhs found the townsmen of a mind to partake with them, to rid the country of the common pestilence. In their genealogies, el-Meteyr, Ishmaelites, are accounted in the descents from Keys, and from *Anmâr*, and *Rubîa* : Rubîa, Anmâr, Múthur, and Eyâd are brethren ; and Rubîa is father of Wâyil, patriarch of the Annezy. Meteyr are of old Ahl Gibly : and their home is in the great Harra which lies between the Harameyn, yet occupied by their tribesmen. Their ancient villages in that country, upon the *Derb es-Sherky* or east Haj-road to Mecca, are *El-Feréya*, *Hâthi*, *Sfeyna*, *es-Swergîeh*, in the borders of the *Harrat el-Kisshub* ; and *Hajjir* : but the most villagers of the Swergîeh valley are at this day *ashràf*, or of the " eminent " blood of the Néby. The Meteyr are now in part Ahl es-Shemâl : for every summer these nomads journey upward to pasture their cattle in the northern wilderness : their borders are reckoned nearly to Kuweyt and Bosra ; and they are next in the North to the northern Shammar. Neither are tributary but " friendly Aarab " to Ibn Rashîd. The desert marches of the Meteyr are thus almost 200 leagues over ! [They are in multitude (among the middle Arabian tribes) next after the great Beduin nation *Ateyba*, and may be almost 5,000 souls.] Their tents were more than two hundred in el-Kasîm, at this time. Each year they visit Aneyza ; and Zâmil bestows a load or two of dates upon their great sheykh, that the town caravans may pass by them, unhindered.

Other Beduin tribesmen resorting to Aneyza are the *Ateybân* (also reckoned to the line of Keys) : neither the Meteyr nor 'Ateyba were friendly with Boreyda. The 'Ateyba marches are all that high wilderness, an hundred leagues over, which lies between el-Kasîm in the north, and the Mecca country : in that vast dîra, of the best desert pastures, there is no settlement ! The 'Ateyba, one of the greatest of Arabian tribes, may be nearly 6,000 souls ; they are of more stable mind than the most Beduw ; and have been allies (as said), in every fortune, of Abdullah ibn Saûd. There is less fanaticism in their religion than moderation : they dwell between the Waháby and the Háram ; and boast themselves hereditary friends of the Sherîfs of Mecca. Zâmil was all for quietness and peace, in which is the welfare of human life, and God is worshipped ; but were it warfare, in his conduct the people of Aneyza are confident. Now he sent out an hundred thelûl riders of the citizens, in two bands, to scour the Nefûd, and set over them the son of the Emir Aly, *Yahŷa* ; a manly young man, but like his father of the strait Waháby understanding.

I saw a Kahtâny arrested in the street ; the man had come marketing to Aneyza, but being known by his speech, the by-standers laid hands on his thelûl. Some would have drawn him from the saddle ; and an Arab overpowered will [his feline and chameleon nature] make no resistance, for that should endanger him. " Come thou with us afore Zâmil," cried they. " Well, he answered, I am with you." They discharged his camel and tied up the beast's knee-bow : the salesmen in the next shops sat on civilly incurious of this adventure. — At Hâyil, in like case, or at Boreyda all had been done by men of the Emir's band, with a tyrannous clamour; but here is a free township, where the custody of the public peace is left in the hands of all the citizens. — As for the Kahtân Zâmil had not yet proclaimed them enemies of Aneyza; and nothing was alleged against this Beduwy. They bound him: but the righteous Emir gave judgment to let the man go.

Persons accused of crimes at Aneyza (where is no prison), are bound, until the next sitting of the Emir. Kenneyny told me there had been in his time but one capital punishment, — this was fifteen years ago. The offender was a woman, sister of Mufarrij! that worthy man whom we have seen steward of the prince's public hall at Hâyil: it was after this misfortune to his house that he left Aneyza to seek some foreign service. — She had enticed to her yard a little maiden, the only daughter of a wealthy family, her neighbours; and there she smothered the child for the (golden) ornaments of her pretty head, and buried the innocent body. The bereaved father sought to a soothsayer, — in the time of whose " reading " they suppose that the belly of the guilty person should swell. [See above, p. 209.] The diviner led on to the woman's house; and showing a place he bade them dig! — There they took up the little corpse! and it was borne to the burial.

— The woman was brought forth to suffer, before the session of the people and elders (musheyikh) assembled with the executive Emir. — In these Arabian towns, the manslayer is bound by the sergeants of the Emir, and delivered to the kindred of the slain, to be dealt with at their list. — Aly bade the father, " Rise up and slay that wicked woman, the murderess of his child." But he who was a religious elder (*muttowwa*), and a mild and godly person, responded, " My little daughter is gone to the mercy of Ullah; although I slay the woman yet may not this bring again the life of my child! — suffer Sir, that I spare her: she that is gone is gone." *Aly*: " But her crime cannot remain unpunished, for that were of too perilous example in the town! Strike thou! I say, and kill her." — Then the muttowwa drew a sword and slew her! Common misdoers and thieves are beaten with palm-leaf rods that are to be green and not in the dry, which (they say) would break fell and bones. There is no cutting off the hand at Aneyza; but any hardened felon is cast out of the township.

After this Zâmil sent his message to the sheykhs of Kahtân in the desert, ' that would they now restore all which had been reaved by their tribesmen they might return into friendship : and if no, he pronounced them adversaries.' Having thus discharged their consciences, these (civil) townsfolk think they may commit their cause to the arbitrage of Ullah, and their hands shall be clean from blood : and (in general) they take no booty from their enemies ! for they say " it were unlawful," — notwithstanding, I have known to my hurt, that there are many sly thieves in their town ! But if a poor man in an expedition bestow some small thing in his saddle-bag, it is indulged, so that it do not appear openly. — And thus, having nothing to gain, the people of Aneyza only take arms to defend their liberties.

One day when I went to visit Zâmil, I found a great silent assembly in his coffee-hall : forty of the townspeople were sitting round by the walls. Then there came in an old man who was sheykh of the religion ; and my neighbour told me in my ear, they were here for a Friday afternoon lecture ! Coffee was served round ; and they all drank out of the same cups. The Arabs spare not to eat or drink out of the same vessel with any man. And Mohammed could not imagine in his (Arabian) religion, to forbid this earthly communion of the human life : but indeed their incurious custom of all hands dipping in one dish, and all lips kissing in one cup, is laudable rather than very wholesome.

The Imâm's mind was somewhat wasted by the desolate koran reading. I heard in his school discourse, no word which sounded to moral edification ! He said finally—looking towards me ! " And to speak of Aysa bin Miriam, — Jesu was of a truth a Messenger of Ullah : but the Nasâra walk not in the way of Jesu, — they be gone aside, in the perversity of their minds, unto idolatry." And so rising mildly, all the people rose ; and every one went to take his sandals.

The townspeople tolerated me hitherto, — it was Zâmil's will. But the Muttowwa, or public ministers of the religion, from the first, stood contrary ; and this Imâm (a hale and venerable elder of threescore years and ten) had stirred the people, in his Friday noon preaching, in the great mesjid, against the Nasrâny. ' It was, he said, of evil example, that certain principal persons favoured a misbelieving stranger: might they not in so doing provoke the Lord to anger ? and all might see that the seasonable rain was withheld ! ' — Cold is the outlaw's life ; and I marked with a natural constraint of heart an alienation of the street faces, a daily standing off of the faint-hearted, and of certain my seeming friends. I heard it chiefly alleged against me, that I greeted with *Salaam aleyk* (Peace be with thee); which they will have to be a salutation of God's people only — the Moslemîn. El-Kenneyny, Bessàm, Zâmil were not spirits to be moved by the words of a dull man in a pulpit; in whom was but the (implacable) blind wisdom of the Wahábies of fifty years ago. I noted some alteration in es-Smîry; and, among my younger friends, in the young Abdullah Bessàm, whose nigh kindred were of the Nejd straitness and intolerance. There was a strife in his single mind, betwixt his hospitable human fellowship, and the duty he owed unto God and the religion: and when he found me alone he asked, "Wellah Khalîl, do the Nasâra hold thus and thus? contrary to the faith of Islam!" — Not so Hamed es-Sâfy, the young Bagdady; who was weary of the tedious Nejd religion: sometimes ere the íthin sounded he had shut his outer door; but if I knocked it was opened (to "*el-docteur*"), when he heard my voice. These Aneyza merchant friends commonly made tea when the Engleysy arrived: they had learned abroad to drink it in the Persian manner.

The elder Bessàm took pleasure to question with me of the Western world. — If at such time the Kenneyny were present, he assented in silence; there was not such another head in Aneyza — nor very likely in all Nejd. To Abdullah el-Kenneyny I was Arabian-like; and he was to me like an European! El-Bessàm was well-nigh middle aged when he first went down — that was fifteen years ago, to trade at Jidda. Among the nations without, his most friendly admiration was for the Engleys: he took it to be of God, that our rulers and people were of the Sultan's alliance. He could even pronounce the names of our great *wizîrs*, Palmerston, Disraeli! — and lamenting the Ottoman misrule and corruption, he said, "a grand wizîr may hardly sit three months at Stambûl! — but how long keep the Engleys their *wúzera?*" "Some of them, I responded, have continued for many years." "Aha, well done, he cries, *affârim!* well done the Engleys!" — In el-Kenneyny was an European-like contempt for the Turks: he despised even their understanding. I said, "I have found them sententious, though without science: there is a wary spirit in their discourse, which is full of human wisdom." — "No! and I have seen several Turkish Governors, at Bosra. The last one — could you believe it? had not heard of the Suez Canal! and, I say, how can men, that live in such darkness of mind, be to the furtherance of a country where they are sent to govern? A few pashas are better instructed; yet being strangers they care not for the common good. — Has not every pasha purchased his government beforehand? and what wonder then if he rake the public money into his own purse? But if there come one of those few that are good, and he undertake some public work; it is likely he will be recalled in the midst of his enterprise, — for the place has been bought over him! and another succeeding is unwilling to fulfil the projects of a former pasha."

— They spoke of the enmity of France and Prussia in Europe; and el-Kenneyny said, ' His mind misgave him, that what for Bismark, and what for Iskander (Czar Alexander) the earth ere long would be soaked with blood! He had lately seen a picture of Iskander at Bosra; it was *thŭkr*, virile!' Now I heard from their mouths all the event of the Turkish war with Russia, — begun and ended in the time of my wandering in the wilderness of Arabia: and el-Bessàm told me, with a lively pleasure, ' that the English fleet had passed the sea-strait — even contrary to the word of the Sultan! — to defend Stambûl.' [Only strong strokes can persuade the Moslemîn; since they believe devoutly that this world is theirs, and the next; and God (but for their sins) should be ever with them, and against the unbelievers. Their incurious ignorance seems not to remember the fear of their enemies, much above a score of years.] Of the late passage of the Dardanelles the sheykhly friends made an argument for the Engleysy in the intolerant town.

I marvelled at the erudition of these Arabian politicians! till I found they had it of a certain Arabic newspaper (which is set forth in face of the " Porte " at Constantinople). — The aged editor was of Christian parentage in Mount Lebanon; and when yet a young man, Ibrahîm Pasha engaged him to publish a gazette for Syria. Some years later he was Arabic reader in the Levant College at Malta: and having learned to smatter our languages, he journeyed through France, England and other States of Europe; and printed in vulgar Arabic an huge idle tome of his occidental travels. The Syrian afterward established himself at Stambûl; where he made profession of the Turks' religion: and under the favour of some great ones, founded the (excellent) Arabic gazette, in which he continues to labour [in the Mohammedan interest]. His news-sheet is current in all countries of the Arabic speech: I have found it in the Nejd merchants' houses at Bombay. In the rest I speak as I heard it related in Christian Syria, by credible persons, — theirs be the blame if they calumniate the man ! 'The Syrians, say they who sojourn amongst them, are nearly always liars, evil surmisers, of a natural vility of mind.'

— That Nasrâny-born is reputed to have blackened his scrivener's fingers in another work, whose authors are solemn *ullema* of Islam, learned in their unfounded learning ; — a loose volume full of contumely, written in answer to a little Arabic treatise of certain Christian Missionaries in India, and printed in London, *Mizàn el-hak*, 'Touchstone of the truth.' The mission book examines, with the European erudition, the religious inheritance of the Moslemîn : and when their heap is winnowed, there remains no more than this (which only Mohammed could allege in testimony of his divine mission), — the purity and beauty of the Arabs' tongue in the koran ! Had not Mohammed — from his birth a religionist ! — mused in the solitude of his spirit, in this exalted vein, more than thirty years ? till there was grown up in his soul a wood of such matter ; whereof he easily gathered the best fruits to serve his turn. [*Confer*. Mat. xiii. 52.] There was not another Arabian of his time who had walked to this length in so singular a path ; and there might no man emulate him, — reaping of that which he had not sowed in his childhood. Nevertheless in the opinion of perfect [European] scholars, the Arabic tongue in the koran is somewhat drooping from the freshness and candour which is found in their poets of the generation before Mohammed. The Arabs' speech is at best like the hollow words dropping out of the mouth of a spent old man : it was shown also in the Mizàn el-hak that in other ingenuous tongues is a nobler architecture of language. — I have heard it said in Syria, that if the Mizàn el-hak were found in a man's keeping, that the Moslems would burn his house over him ! For this and other books of damnable doctrine there was made a fanatical inquisition in my time in all their custom-houses. — Loud is the ullemas' derision (in their tedious response) of the " prattling priestlings of the Nasâra." — The Syrian Christianity attributed to the hand of that old gazetteer and *quondam* Mesîhy of *Jebel Libnàn*, the muster made therein of the atheistical opinions of certain last century philosophasters, without leaven of science.

The Moslemîn, as the rest of mankind, are nearly irrational in matter of faith; and they may hardly stumble in a religion which is so conformable to human nature; yet in their (free) cities, where men's faces are sharpened, and they see other ways about them, there are some who doubt. — It was related to me by Syrian friends, ' that the Mizàn el-hak had been, few years before, a cause of public troubles in the Turkish Capital;' where not a few persons, mostly military officers, seceded from the national religion; and became a half-christian sect assembling together secretly, to worship and hear doctrine. The rumour came to the ears of the government; and there was a persecution: some of the innovators, by commandment of the Sultan (*'Abd-el-'Azîz*), were drowned in the Bosforus; and many were deported in ships to Syria. — They are now increased at Damascus; where they are called *esh-Shazlîeh*: ' the Shazlîeh say of themselves, that they will one day be masters of the country.' They are abhorred by the Moslems; and misseen by the superstitious religion (without piety) of the Syrian Christianity. I have met with white turbans of this new school — Moslems in appearance, that in privity durst acknowledge their small or no belief in the Néby: I have seen some enter a Christian friend's shop, to drink hastily of his water crock behind the door, in the languishing days of Ramathán. — In the great Syrian city I have found another school of liberal and not credulous Musslemans. A Persian gentleman, high in office, as we were speaking one day of religions, drew on the floor before me this figure. —

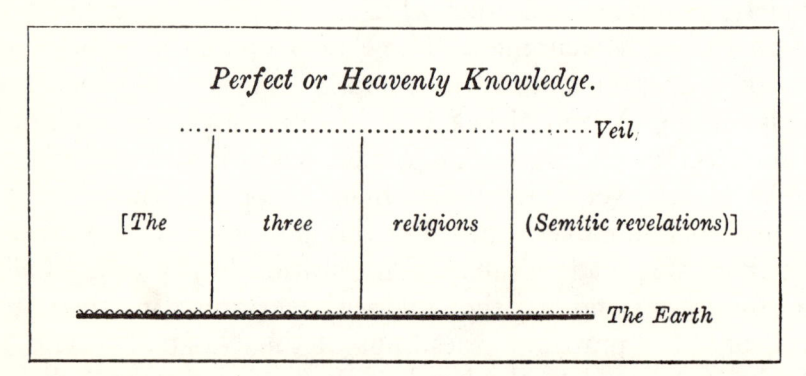

```
              Perfect or Heavenly Knowledge.
     ............................................Veil.
         |         |         |         |
   [The     three     religions   (Semitic revelations)]
     ~~~~~~~~~~~~~~~~~~~~~~~~~~~~~~ The Earth
```

" Our religions, said he — be we Jews or Christians or Moslems, arise to Godward: but they be all alike stayed at a veil (*hijâb*)! and pass not unto perfect or Divine Knowledge!"

— Syria, that bald country, which might again be made fruitful, is not of the only faith of Islam. The Nasâra are many in the land, but faint-hearted. The confederate Druses are strong weeds growing out of the Mohammedan stock, in the middle mountain and vulcanic country. In certain villages towards Antioch are other idolatrous Moslems, *en-Nuseyrîeh*. And in Phoenicia and the next borders of Palestine there are village colonies of the Persian religion. [*v.* p. 284.] — The inveterate religious divisions in this Province are not a little profitable to the weak government of their Turkish rulers.

European evangelists have been the salt of the earth in Syria these fifty years; but they speak not — for dread of death — to any Moslem! and it must be acknowledged that among Moslems they have not made five proselytes. Can Christians now return to be Jews? and how should Moslems become Christians? Those long-coated, and (in that summer country) well salaried messengers, of the European churches, preach only to the Christian folk, converting them, from bitterness to bitterness, from one to another name under the broad banner of Christ. The Arab people are in their sight as cattle; and the disciples of such teachers, upon their part, are heartless and of a nettlesome pride towards the Franks, — that Semitic pride which is a strong-sounding fibre of the Mohammedan fanaticism! They are new-whited scholars in all, save the loving meekness of Christ: and their native guile receives a Frankish colour (Italian, French, or English), whereby it may be known what countrymen were their gospellers — seldom crucified spirits. And they who received a free schooling without thankfulness, look further to receive — some are reported to embezzle! — from the same rich, and (they think too simple) beneficent Europe, a continual stipend: their own wit they hold to be 'much more subtle (*rafî'a*) than the [plain] understanding of the Franks!' — New offsets, they are of the gross Arabic stock, with little moral sense; and resemble (save in courage and in natural worth) the country Moslems. Others I have known who resenting the European harshness (and inhospitality) of their divines and teachers, prayed God, every day, that He would release them from Frenjy schoolmasters, and raise up teachers of their own: sometimes they will say shortly, "All these Frenjies (among us) are spies!" Yet would they have their apostles still to abide with them, to communicate with them the almsdeed of Europe. — Virtue is not very rare, but frustrated, in that corrupt and misgoverned country. Syrians — sterile in invention, by an easy imitation may become smatterers in the liberal arts.

—We sate about the Bessàm's (coffee) hearth — that altar of humanity of the Arab households ! Others came in ; and a young man said, " Among the customs of the Engleys, he had most marvelled to see [in India] the husbands giving place to the hareem. [The *gynolatria* of the Franks is unseemly and unmanly in the sight — beginning with the Greeks, of all Orientals.] Besides they lift the bernetta (Frankish hat) — that is the reverence used amongst them, when they meet with any dame of their acquaintance ; but to men no ! " Bessàm, with an host's comity, expected my answer. I answered, " Our hareem are well taught : it is a manly gentleness to favour the weaker part, and that gladden our lives most — which are the women and children. What says the proverb ? — *Béled el-Engleys jinnat el-hareem, wa jehennem el-khail,* ' England the paradise of women, and hell of horses ! ' " I felt the Bessàm blench, at the first clause ; but understanding the conclusion, which came roundly off in Arabic, he repeated it twenty times, with honest mirth and acceptation. — Abdullah, in my presence, was wary with a host's gentleness, to avoid (unsavoury) discourse of religion. But he was not so tender of the Yahûd ; for having lately read, in his *Gazette*, that certain merchant Jews in England were richer than the Queen's Majesty, and that the Rothschilds (whose name he knew, because they send yearly alms to Bagdad to be distributed to the poor Oriental brethren) were creditors of all Egypt, he could not forbear to cry out, " The Lord cut them off ! " " How strange, another said, that the Engleys have a Queen, and no man to rule over them ! what, Khalîl, is the name of the Queen ? " I answered, *Mansûra*, THE VICTORIOUS LADY : a name which (used in the masculine) is also of happy augury in their tongue.

Though there is not a man of medicine in Nejd, yet some modest leech may be found : and I was called to another Bessàm household to meet one who was of this town. That Bessàm, a burly body, was the most travelled of the foreign merchants : by railway he had sped through the breadth of India ; he had dwelt in the land, and in his mouth was the vulgar Hindostany. But no travel in other nations could amend his wooden head ; and like a tub which is shipped round the world he was come home never the better : there is no transmuting such metals ! His wit was thin ; and he had weakly thriven in the world. The salver sat at the Bessàm's coffee hearth ; awaiting me, with the respectable countenance of a village schoolmaster. — His little skill, he said with humility, he had gathered of reading in his few books ; and those were hard to come by. He asked me many simple questions ; and bowed the head to all my answers ; and, glad in his heart to find me friendly, the poor man seemed to wonder that the learning of foreign professors were not more dark, and unattainable !

In these last days the honest soul had inoculated all the children in the town : he acknowledged, ' that there die many thus ! — but he had read that in the cow-pox inoculation [el-'athab] of the Nasâra there die not any ! ' After hearing me he said, he would watch, mornings and evenings, at some of the town gates, when the kine are driven forth or would be returning from pasture ; if haply he might find the pocks on some of their udders. [Already Amm Mohammed had looked for it in vain, at Kheybar.] — I counselled the sheykhs to send this worthy man to the north, to learn the art for the public good ; and so he might vaccinate in these parts of Nejd. Worn as I was, I proffered myself to ride to Bagdad, if they would find me the thelûl, and return with the vaccine matter. But no desire nor hope of common advantage to come can move or unite Arabians : neither love they too well that safeguarding human forethought, which savours to them of untrust in an heavenly Providence. Their religion encourages them to seek medicines, — which God has created in the earth to the service of man ; but they may not flee from the pestilence. Certain of the foreign merchants have sometimes brought home this lymph, — so did Abdullah el-Bessàm, the last year ; yet this hardly passes beyond the walls of their houses. — I heard a new word in that stolid Bessàm's mouth (and perhaps he fetched it from India), " What dost thou, quoth he, in a land where is only *diànat el-Mohammedîa*, Mohammedan religion ? whereas they use to say *dîn el-Islam*." — India, el-Kenneyny called, " A great spectacle of religions ! "

Amm Mohammed at Kheybar and the Beduw have told me, there is a disease in camels like that which they understood from me to be the cow-pox. — The small-pox spread fast. One day at noon I found my young negro hostess sorrowing ; — she had brought-in her child very sick, from playing in the Gá : and bye and bye their other babe sickened. — I would not remain in that narrow lodging to breathe an infected air : but, leaving there my things, I passed the next days in the streets : and often when the night fell I was yet fasting, and had not where to sleep. But I thought, that to be overtaken here by the disease, would exceed all present evils. None offered to receive me into their houses ; therefore beating in the evening — commonly they knock with an idle rhythm — at the rude door of some patient, upon whom I had bestowed medicines, and hearing responded from within, *ugglot*, ' approach ' ! I entered ; and asked leave to lie down on their cottage floor [of deep Nefûd sand] to sleep. The Kenneyny would not be marked to harbour a Nasrâny : to Bessàm I had not revealed my distress. And somewhat I reserved of these Arabian friends' kindness ; that I might take up all, in any extreme need.

The deep sanded (open) terrace roof of the mesjid, by my old dokân, was a sleeping place for strangers in the town ; but what sanctity of the house of prayer would defend me slumbering ? for with the sword also worship they Ullah. — But now I found some relief, where I looked not for it : there was a man who used my medicines, of few words, sharp-set looks and painted eyes, but the son of a good mother, — a widow woman, who held a small shop of all wares, where I sometimes bought bread. He was a salesman in the clothiers' sûk, and of those few, beside the Emirs and their sons, who carried a sword in Aneyza ; for he was an officer of Zâmil's. He said to me, " I am sorry, Khalîl, to see thee without lodging ; there is an empty house nigh us, and shall we go to see it ? " — Though I found it to be an unswept clay chamber or two, I went the same day to lodge there : and they were to me good neighbours. Every morrow his mother brought me girdle-bread with a little whey and butter, and filled my water-skin : at the sunsetting (when she knew that commonly — my incurable oblivious-ness — I had provided nothing ; and now the sûk was shut), she had some wheaten mess ready for the stranger in her house, for little money ; and for part she would receive no payment ! it must have been secretly from Zâmil. This aged woman sat before me open-faced, and she treated me as her son : hers was the only town-woman's face that I have seen in middle Nejd, — where only maiden children are not veiled.

I was called to another house of the fanatical Bessàms. They would have medicines for a personage who dwelt with them ; one who, I heard, was passing " learned ; " and a fugitive (of the former Emir's house) from Boreyda. That householder hardly bade the hakîm be seated ; and poured out a tepid cup of the dregs of their last coffee, for the Nasrâny. — There sat their guest, an huge ghostly clod of B. Temîm ! He was silent ; and they beckoned that he desired a remedy of me. I cried at the ears of the dull swine, in contempt of their unkind usage, " Dost hear ? what wouldst thou of me ? " He cast down his goggle eyes — lest he should behold a kafir ! I asked, " Is this a deaf man ? " — They blench when we turn on them, knowing that the Frenjies exceed them in the radical heat and force of the spirit. The peasant divine looked up more mildly, yet would he not hold speech with one of the heathen ; but leaning over to the negro Aly, who brought me hither, he charged him, in a small dying voice, to ask, ' Had the Nasrâny a remedy for the emerods ? ' — the negro shouted these words to the company ! " It sufficeth," responded the morose pedant ; and settling his leathern chaps his dunghill spirit reverted to her wingless contemplation, at the gates of the Meccàwy's paradise. — In such religious dotage we perceive no aspect of the Truth ! which is so of kin to our better nature that we should know her, even through a rent of her veil, as the young one knows his mother.

— The most venerable image in their minds is the personage of Mohammed ; which to us is less tolerable : for the household and sheykhly virtues that were in him — mildness and comity and simplicity and good faith, in things indifferent of the daily life — cannot amend our opinion of the Arabian man's barbaric ignorance, his sleight and murderous cruelty in the institution of his religious faction ; or sweeten our contempt of an hysterical prophetism and polygamous living. — Mohammed who persuaded others, lived confident in himself ; and died persuaded by the good success of his own doctrine. What was the child Mohammed ? — a pensive orphan, a herding lad : the young man was sometime a caravan trader, — wherein he discovered his ambitious meaning, when he would not enter Damascus ! His was a soaring and wounded (because infirm) spirit, a musing solitary conscience ; and his youth was full of dim vaticination of himself, and of religious aspiration. A soul so cast will pursue the dream of those her inexpert and self-loving years : and how long soever, difficult, ay, and perilous be the circuit which lies before him, it were lighter for such an one to endure all things than fail of his presumption and (finally) to fall short of his own soul. — Mohammed, the Preacher, found no purer worshippers and witnesses of the God of Abraham than an idolatrous Christianity, and the Yahûd, ' a seed of evil-doers.' He calls them in the koran ' The

people of the [former] Scriptures, which were sent down from on high : '
but as his faction increased he came to account them — since they were
not with him — adverse factions ; and afterward his enemies.

— As moths will beat to an appearing of light in darkness ; so it is
in the preaching of a new doctrine. Arabs are naturally half-melan-
choly in the present [it is the weakness of their fibre], and they live in a
fond hope of better things : many therefore were shortly his partizans,
and valiant men became partakers of the religious fortune of Mohammed
— who had been sheltered in the beginning by the uncles and alliance
of his (considerable) sheykhly house. — Five hundred men banded in
arms — as much as the power of Ibn Rashîd — may well suffice, in
empty Arabia, for any warlike need : how much more being vehemently
knit and moved together by some contagious zeal, to the despising of
death ; and when, for one who falls, many will arise in his room ! — In
any age such might carry [as lately the Waháby] in few years, all the
wilderness land of Arabia. Sword is the key of their imagined paradise ;
and in the next decennium, those unwarlike but frenetic Arabians,
inflamed with the new greediness of both worlds, ran down like wolves
to devour the civil border-lands. — There is moreover a peaceable
conquest of the Arabian religion [that preaches a mild-hearted Godhead,
and a way of rest — in the sober and spiritual fruition of this weak
fleshly life, to the bliss of Heaven] which advances now mostly in the
African Continent ; and that may in time become a danger to Christen-
dom ! And such being Mohammed's doctrine, it has obtained a third
place among the religions of mankind.

Wide is the diversity of the Semitic faiths. The Messianic religion —
a chastisement of the soul sunning herself in the divine love — were fain
to cast her arms about the human world, sealing all men one brotherhood
with a virginal kiss of meekness and charity. The Mohammedan chain-
of-credulities is an elation of the soul, breathing of God's favour only to
the Moslemîn ; and shrewdness out of her cankered bowels to all the
world besides. — The Arabian religion of the sword must be tempered by
the sword : and were the daughter of Mecca and Medina led captive,
the Moslemîn should become as Jews ! One may be a good Moslem,
though he pass his life in the khála, without teachers. In the towns are
religious elders — not ministers of mysteries : there is no order of priesthood. Mohammed is man, an householder, the father of a family ; and
his is a virile religion : also his people walk in a large way, which is full

of the perfume of the flesh purified ; the debate betwixt carnal nature and opinion of godliness is not grievous in their hearts. — In the naturally crapulent and idolatrous Europe man himself is divine ; every age brings forth god-like heroes. And what seek we in religion ? — is it not a perfect law of humanity ? — to bind up the wounds, and heal the sores of human life ; and a pathway to heaven.

— Looking upon the religious tradition of Beny Israel, from the floor of the desert, we might imagine its rising in Jacob's family, out of the nomad Semites' vision of the *melûk*. We may read in Herodotus as in Moses of the circumcision, the superstition of meats, the priest's imposing the iniquity of the people upon the head of an animal, the vesture and ordinance of the priesthood : they were customs of the Egyptians. The bitter cry of the Hebrew prophets revived in every generation and continued the (Mosaic) tradition, which was finally established by David ; but righteousness, justice, sanctity, spring naturally in the human conscience ; they are lent to the religions : wherein divinity and human equity stand oft-times so far asunder that we might muse of a stone age in their supposed heaven !

I was bidden to another Waháby household ; and they received the hakîm not without hospitality. The house-father, a landed person, had grown sons, and named himself to me *the Sheykh Mohammed* : yet was he no sheykh, but, as friends told me (they are jealous of the sheykhly dignity), *min khulk Ullah*, ' of God's creatures,' that is one of the people. Sheykh Mohammed, who had a great town house, was purblind ; and his sons were ailing. [When I was later driven from Aneyza he sent me four pence, for medicines, for conscience' sake !] The old man gave me good words whilst I sat in their hall : — " Khalîl, I look on thee as one of my sons : couldst thou not, for the time thou art here, conform thyself to us in religion, the religion of Islam ? — I know that ye are the people of the Enjîl, and worshippers of Ullah, but not as we ; say, *Mohammed Rasûl Ullah !* and be of fellowship with the Moslemîn. Then all they that now hold aloof, will wish thee well ; and whatsoever thou wouldst ask thou shalt obtain, were it to stay here and make the pilgrimage with us, or to take thy journey to another country." — They watched me out of their false eyes ; as I responded, " Every creature is *rasûl Ullah !* "

One morning I went to breakfast there ; and he called a gossip of his, another Mohammed, a clothier in the sûk, whose mother had many years suffered incessant pain of facial neuralgia. We went afterward to see the patient, and I left with her some papers of laudanum powder. Later in the day I passed Mohammed's shop; and he told me she had swallowed the doses all at once! — I bade him hasten home; and if he found his mother slumbering to give her the potful of coffee to drink! — " Only mind the shop for me! Khalîl," — and he went. I dreaded the worst; but he returned soon, saying (to my comfort) that his mother was well. The bystanders rallied the clothier, who was a little broken-headed, insisting [the oasis Arabs are full of petulant humour] that he would have poisoned his old mother!

Sheykh Mohammed sent for me one morrow suddenly! — I found two Beduins sitting in his coffee-hall; and quoth he, " Khalîl, there is a message come for thee to go to Boreyda; and these are the men that will convey thee, and here is the letter from Abdullah (the Emir). — Come near one of you, my sons there! and read this for Khalîl." Abdullah wrote — after their formal greetings — 'They heard in Boreyda that the people of Aneyza had found the Nasrâny's remedies to be profitable; and he desired the Sheykh Mohammed, to persuade the Nasrâny to return with his messengers; to cure his sister's eyes, and to minister unto other persons.' I answered, " I was in Boreyda, and they drove me from them; also this Abdullah caused me to be forsaken in the Wady!" [I would not trust myself again in a town, where the worst of all the citizens were the ungracious usurping sheykhs.] The old man exhorted me as if he had a power to compel me; and the Beduw said (with their Asiatic fawning), " Up now Khalîl! and mount with us. Eigh! wellah they will give thee much silver: Abdullah will be kind." " Ay, trust me Khalîl! only go with them, added Sheykh Mohammed; and thou shalt have a letter from Zâmil requiring them to send thee again within a certain time." — " Let Abdullah's sister come hither; and I will cure the woman at Aneyza." — " Khalîl, I warrant thee, thou shalt win at least thirty reals by this voyage!" — " Neither for thirty mares would I return thither, farewell."

On a morrow I was in my friend's palm ground, when the sun was rising: and we sat under thick boughs of pomegranate trees. The fresh-breathing air from the Nefûd disposed our thoughts to cheerful contemplation; and in this Arabian, here in the midst of great deserts, was the brotherly discourse and the integrity of Europe! " Khalîl, quoth he, I marvel, — I have indignation at the strange fanaticism of the people! what is it?" — " They bite at me in religion! but who may certify us in these things? that are of faith, hope, authority, built not on certain ground." — "*And they who have preached religions were moved by some worldly seeking (tóm'a ed-dínya)!*" — " Every religion, and were it anciently begotten of a man's conscience, is born of human needs, and her utterance is true religion; whether we adore a Sovereign Unity, Father eternal of all Power and Life, Lord of the visible and invisible, or (with shorter spiritual ken) bow the knees to the Manifold divine Majesty in the earth and heavens. Nations hold to their religions — ' that is true [in their countries] which every man saith : ' howbeit the verity of the things alleged cannot be made manifest on this side the gate of death. And everyone will stand to his hope, and depart to the Gulf of Eternity in the common faith ; — that to clearer sight may be but a dark incongruous argument. But let us enter the indestructible temple-building of science, wherein is truth." — " Akhs! that they should persecute thee : and is there such a malignity in mankind!" — " And tell me, what can so bind to religion this people full of ungodly levity and deceitful life?" — " I think it is THE FEAR OF THE FIRE (of hell) that amazes their hearts! all the time of their lives." — "Is not death ' an end of all evils?' but by such doctrines even this last bitter comfort is taken away from the miserable!" — Fire is the divine cruelty of the Semitic religions!

As I came again to town, idle persons gathered about me in the street ; and a pleasant fellow of the people stayed to tell them a tale. — " When I was trafficking in Irâk, I had dealings with a certain Yahûdy ; who, when we spoke together, called me at every word *akhûy*, ' my brother! my brother!' but one day I cried, ' Shield me Ullah from Sheytàn! am I a Jew's brother?' The Yahûdy answered me, ' For this word, when I see thee in the flame (of hell torments) I will not fetch thee water.' And this is the confidence, friends, that have all men in their religion wherein they were born. Let us not rashly blame an alien! they have a religion and so have we. And, I say, ye do not well to pursue the Nasrâny with your uncivil words : is not Khalîl here in the countenance of the sheykhs? and those medicines that he dispenses are profitable to the Moslemîn."

The small-pox increased in the town : already they numbered thirty deaths among the sick children. The parents who called me wondered, to see the hakîm avoid to breathe the air of their infected chambers ; — since they heard from me, I had been vaccinated ! for it is a saying in these parts of Nejd, that 'if one be vaccinated, the small-pox shall never attain him.' They will tell you, ' that of all the hundreds, vaccinated by Abu Fâris, thirty years ago, none has been afterward overtaken by the disease : ' — haply the graft may be more enduring in the temper of their Arabian bodies. As I returned one evening I met a little boy in the street, — and he said dolefully, *Sully 'alâ hâ 'l ghrâdâ*, ' pray for this passed one.' The child carried a bundle, in his arms ; and I saw it was a dead babe that he bore forth, to the burial ! — At this time there died five or six children daily : and in the end ' there was not an unbereaved household.' In that disease they refuse all remedies. The only son of a patient of mine being likely to die, I would have given him a medicine, but the poor man answered, " It may yet please the Lord to save the child and his eyes." In a day or two the boy died : and finding that pensive father in the street, I said to him, " Comfort thyself ! God may send thee another ; and is the child dead ? " — " Ah ! I have even now buried him, — aha ! he is gone unto Him who made him ! "

A courtly young man led me one afternoon to an homestead out of the town, to see his sister's sick child ; the father was a kinsman of the Kenneyny's. And in the way he said to me, " Dwell here (at Aneyza), we will provide the house ; and be thou a father to us." This was *Hàmed el-Yahŷa*, third son of the patriot *Yahŷa*. So we came to a palm plantation and a rustic house ; where I was many times afterward entertained, and always kindly welcomed by the patrician family. The palm ground of not fully five acres was all their patrimony : this noble poverty had sufficed the old patriot to foster up honourably his not small family. The young man's mother welcomed the hakîm at the gate, and brought in her arms a fair-faced sick grandchild. — I had not seen such a matronly behaviour, nor seen one so like a lady, in the Arabian oases ! Yahŷa had made his wife such, taking no more than one to be the mother of his household. Hàmed brought me to his father, who was sitting in the arbour : the sire — now a poor old man bowed together and nearly blind, rose to greet the Nasrâny ; but the mother and son smiled (a little undutifully) to the stranger ; as it were to excuse the decay of his venerable person. Yahya's authority still guided the household : his sons also took to heart, and made much of their father's sayings.

— In these new friends I saw a right Arabian family : they had not ridden out of their township, save in warfaring expeditions, and to go down in the pilgrimage to Mecca ; and had never put their hands to merchandise. But old Yahya had been a busy patriot and sheykh of the bold *Khereysy*, a great (peaceable) faction of his townsmen [as there are such in all the oases] ; and theirs is one of the three standards in the battle of the men of Aneyza. The same was now the dignity of his eldest son, Abdullah, [*v.* above p. 377,] by a former wife, who was to-day the companion of Zâmil ; and 'without Abdullah el-Yahya, Zâmil did nothing at Aneyza.' The young sheykh is a dealer in camels. — In Yahya's household there was no savour of intolerance : the venerable father's voice taught his children and others, that " Khalîl is of the Messîh, and their scripture is the Enjîl, which is likewise Word of Ullah."

My medicines were well spoken of in Aneyza : the Kenneyny's mother — very dear to him, as are the Arabian mothers to their sons — had been happily relieved ; and he went about magnifying this cure to his friends and acquaintance. The good man even added ; 'And it were not too much, although he divided all that he had with Khalîl !' — The Nejders are coffee-tipplers, above all the inhabitants of the East. A coffee-server was my patient, who, in his tastings, between the cups, drunk "sixty" fenjeyns every day ; besides he thought he smoked "as many" pipes of tobacco. I bade him every week drink ten cups fewer daily ; and have done with the excess. " Verily, he exclaimed, there is a natural wisdom in the Nasâra ! more than in the Moslemîn. Khalîl can cure even without medicine : ye see in this an easy and perfect remedy, and it shall cost a man nothing !"

Even English medicaments are brought to the caravaners' town — in the Gulf trade, from India. To a phthisical patient I prescribed cod-liver oil ; and he found a bottle the same day in the sûk ! but they think it not good to drink in the hot months. The beginning of his sickness was a chill : he had been overtaken in the Nefûd by a heavy rain, and let his drenched clothing dry upon him. The malady is oftener bred of the morning chill, falling on sleepers in the open ; but this disease is not common in the desert air of Nejd. The evil, without cough, was come upon the Kenneyny ; but he hid it from me : with a narrow chest, he had passed the years since his youth in a dampish tropical climate. — I had here an epileptical patient ; I have seen but one other in Arabia ; and he was of the blacks at Kheybar. I had also a patient whose malady cannot be found in the new books of medicine ; the man was "*fascinated!*" He lamented, " It is *néfs*, a spirit, which besets me ; " and added, ' this was common in their parts — the work of the hareem, with their sly philters and maleficent drinks.' — " There, there ! (he cries), I see her wiggle-wiggling ! and she is ever thus before mine eyes. The woman was my wife, but last year I put her away ; and am in dread, she has given me a thing to drink ; whereof I shall every day fare the worse, whilst I live. The phantom is always in my head, even when I walk abroad, — wellah as we sit here I see her winding and wiggling ! " The poor fancy-stricken man, who served the Kenneyny at Bosra, was wasted and hypochondriac : his melancholy fantasy was matter of mirth (only not openly) with Hàmed of Bagdad and the younger friends.

I have seen a ready cure, in the East, for distracted persons, under the shadow of religion. Years before when wandering in the high Lebanon I descended into a deep wady — the name of it is in their tongue *Valley-of-Saints* ; wherein is a great Christian minster of the Syrian religion. One hundred and twenty are the poor religious brethren : twenty-five were ordained priests ; the rest live not in ease and leisure, of that which the toiling people have spared, but every man labours with his hands for the common living, — the most are husbandmen. Each cheerful sunrising calls them to the fields ; where every religious labourer draws apart to be alone with God in his contemplation. The handicraftsmen remain at home, namely the brothers shoemakers, and those who weave the decent black mantles without seam of all the humble friars ; others serve devoutly in the kitchen, where they bake bread for the convent, and boil their poor victual. The priests remain in the cloister to sing mass, and say their formal devotion at the canonical hours. At the knelling of the chapel bell those who are in the valley below, at their tillage, pause to bid the church prayers : the convent chapel is a great cave walled-up under the living rock. From sunset to sunset, six times in the natural day, their bells ring out to the common devotion : the brethren rise at the solemn sound in the night season, and assemble to their chapel prayers. — The winter months are austere in their airy height of the mountains : the sun, moving behind the pinnacles of that valley-side, shines but an hour upon them. The religious taste no flesh ; bread with oil and pot-herbs is their common diet ; léban and eggs they may eat twice in the week. In the deep under them is a little snow-cold river (running from above the Cedars) which turns their millstones : some brothers are millers ; and thereby is a clay building, where, in the spring time, certain of the religious husbandmen feed silkworms.

The cells of the convent are bare walls, with a little open casement, and clay floor twelve feet wide: the cloisterers are poor men, whose senses be but blunt in the use of this world ; and we might think their religious houses little cleanly. Of that society are two hermits, whose dwelling is among the rocks in the dim limestone valley : they pray continually, and a novice carries down their victual, every midday. — There are thirty convents of their order in the mountains of Lebanon ; and amongst the multitude of brethren are, they say, three holy men, unto whom it is given to work miracles. A young friar, lately ordained priest, whose office was to study, and wait upon (any visiting) strangers, seeing me suffer with rheumatism in the autumn clouds of these high places, exhorted me, with an affectionate humility, to visit one of the saints, ' to whose convent was only five little hours ; and he would ask his abbot's leave to accompany me.' One of those men of God healed all manner of infirmities ; another, he told me, had raised even the dead to life ; and of another he said, that he had given children many times to barren wives. ' He knew a sterile woman who visited the man of God : and she bare a son, according to his saying, before the year's end ; but in the journey, as she carried her babe to him for baptism, the child died. On the third day she came to the saint ; and he restored her dead child to life ! — Two men went to visit the saint, and one of them was blind : but as they were in the way the blind man saw ! then said his companion, " Wherefore should we go further ? what need have we of the man of God ? " — But whilst he was speaking, the blindness of the other fell upon him ! '

No woman may pass their cloister gate. " And is it not, I asked, a hard thing, that one who is entered into religion should be cut off from marriage ? " " Nay, he answered, it is an easy thing, it is next to nothing : and I look on a woman as I look on yonder gate-post." This young priest was epileptic, from a child ; and ' had been wont, he said, to fall every day once, till he went to the saint, with whom he abode four months; and the malady left him.' — He answered that he read only seldom in the Old Testament Scriptures; and asked me, 'if the Syrian father (and commentator of the Gospels in that tongue), the venerable Ephraim, lived before or were he after Jesus Christ? and whether the Temple, built by Solomon — with the cedars of Libnàn, were before or since Christ's time?' Besides he could not guess that wine had been in the world before the coming of the Messiah! for he thought Jesus first made it by miracle in a marriage supper. Of Noah's sons he had not heard, how many they were, nor their names. But he enquired earnestly of Sinai; and asked me 'in what part of the world lay that holy mountain, — at present?'

Finally he showed me a deep well, in their cloister yard, that he said was 'very good for the cure of any who were not in their right minds: and when the patient was drawn up it would be seen that he was come to himself.' — The poor moon-sick is let down in a dark well, and drenched in water deadly cold! and doubtless the great dread and the chill may work together to knit the fibre of all but the most distempered brains.

Poor or rich patients at Aneyza, none of them paid anything for the hakîm's service and medicines! Some welfaring persons, though I helped their lives, showed the Nasrâny no humanity again, not so much as calling me to coffee in their ungracious houses. I was happy to dispense medicines freely to poorer persons: and though I affected to chide my fraudulent debtors, I was well content with them all; since even out of their false wrangling I learned somewhat more of this Nejd country. One of the defaulters was a farmer beyond the walls; and I had these occasions of walking abroad. — Nor far beyond the Boreyda gate, the neighbours showed me a fathom-thick corner of clay walling, all that remains of a kella of the old Waháby usurpation. When Ibrahîm Pasha arrived with an Egyptian army at Aneyza, his artillery battered the clay fortress all night; and at dawn there remained nothing of the work but earthen heaps: the same day he suffered Ibn Saûd's garrison to depart from the town.

In that place is a floor of bare sand-rock, which the owner has made his well-yard; and the fifty-foot-deep well, bored therein, was the labour of Aneyza stone-workers. Their toil is so noxious (under this breathless climate), that he who in the vigorous hope of his youth is allured by the higher wage to cast in his lot with the stone-hewers may hardly come to ripe years, or even to his middle age. And the people say, in their religious wise, " It is a chastisement from Ullah ; the young men transgress heedlessly, giving themselves to an excessive labour." When the sharp flying powder has settled in the lungs, cutting and consuming them as glass, there is no power in Nature which can expel it again. — A young stone-hewer came to me ; his beard was only beginning to spring, but he was sick unto death : he could not go the length of a few houses, so his heart, he said, panted ; and he lamented to the hakîm, " My breast is broken ! " Sheykh Nâsir said " Thus they all perish early ; in two or three years they die."

I went on to the farmer's, who had a good place nigh the Kenneyny's garden. The man came from the well to meet me ; and led me into his kahwa, out of the sun ; and sat down to make coffee ! After the cup I said to him, " This is a good homestead ! I see palms and corn-land and camels ; and here are great heaps of your wheat and barley harvest ! ready to be trodden out : tell me, why keep you back the small price of my medicines ? " — " Eigh, Khalîl ! Thou dost not know how it stands with us, I would God that all these things were mine indeed, as they be mine in appearance ! Seest thou yonder camels ? — they are the Bessàm's ; and nearly all this corn will be theirs to pay for their loan ; and we must every year borrow afresh from them : wellah, it is little when I have settled with them that will remain to us. This ground was mine own, but now it is almost gone ; and I am become as it were their steward."

The wealthy Bessàm family are money-lenders at Aneyza. The rate is fifteen in the hundred for twelve months, paid in money ; but if yielded in kind, — the payment of the poor man ! for every real they are to receive a real and a half's worth, in dates or corn, at the harvest rates. This fruit they lay up till they may sell it, later in the year, at an enhanced price (to the poor Nomads). — One who came in, and was my acquaintance, thus reproached the iniquity of the farmer, " O man ! fearest thou not Ullah ? pay the hakîm his due, or know that the Lord is above thee." The farmer's son had been an Ageyly in Syria, — where he sometime served, he told me, a Nasrâny, a certain rich corn-chandler at Nazareth ; of whom he magnified the probity and hospitality.

Factions and indebtedness are the destruction of the Arab countries. " Borrowed money, they tell you, is *sweet* " [as they say of lying], — it is like a booty of other men's goods, and the day of reckoning is not yet.

The lending at usury, disallowed in the koran doctrine, is practised even in these puritan countries. The villagers are undone thereby ; and the most Beduins fall every year behindhand, thus losing a third in the use of their little money. — In Syria the Moslems lend not, for conscience sake ; but the people are greedily eaten up by other caterpillars, the Yahûd, and yet more — to the confusion of the name of Christ ! by the iniquitous Nasâra : twenty-five yearly in the hundred is a " merciful " price among them for the use of money. The soil is fallen thus into servitude : and when the mostly honest (Moslem) husbandmen-landowners, have at last mortgaged all for their debts ; and are become tenants at will to those extortioners [of that which with a religious voice, contemning the unstable condition of this world, they call " the dust " — which was theirs], they begin to forsake the villages.

— When I lived sometime among the people in Syria ; and saw that the masters of art in this kind of human malice were persons addicted to the foreign consulates, I spared not to blame the guilty ; for which cause such persons bore me slight good will. " The land, they have answered, is fruitful, above the soil in your countries : the tillage is light and of little cost." [In this twilight climate — where we live with such cost, and human needs are doubled — we sow with double labour to reap the half : the time is also doubled !]

The Arabian oasis husbandry is hardly less skilful than that we see used in the *ghrûta* of Damascus. — The oases are soil of the desert ; which is commonly fruitful under the Arabian sun, where it may be watered. Every year they sow down the same acres, with one or another kind of grain ; and yet their harvests are not light. The seed plots are dressed with loam and the dung of their well-camel yards, *ed-dímn*. The stubbles, when ploughed to be sowed down in the autumn, are laid even and balked out in pans and irrigation channels, — which in their hands is quickly performed : so that when the well-pond is let out all the little field may be flooded at once. In palm plantations every stem stands in a channel's course ; and the wet earth about their roots is refreshed by the sinking moisture as oft as the runnels are flushed, that is once or twice in the natural day. [At *el-Ally* contrariwise — it may be the Hejâz or Medina custom — the palm stems are banked up from the floor of the earth.]

My friends, when I enquired of the antiquity of the country, spoke to me of a ruined site *el-'Eyarîeh*, at little distance northward upon this side of the W. er-Rummah : and Kenneyny said " We can take horses and ride thither." I went one morning afterward with Hàmed Assâfy to borrow horses of a certain horse-broker *Abdullah*, surnamed [and thus they name every Abdullah, although he have no child] *Abu Nejm*: Abu Nejm was a horse-broker for the Indian market. There is no breeding or sale of horses at Boreyda or Aneyza, nor any town in Nejd ; but the horse-brokers take up young stallions in the Aarab tribes, which — unless it be some of not common excellence, are of no great price among them. Kenneyny would ride out to meet with us from another horse-yard, which was nigh his own plantation.

We found Abu Nejm's few sale horses, with other horses which he fed on some of his friends' account, in a field among the last palms north of the town. Two stallions feed head to head at a square clay bin ; and each horse is tethered by an hind foot to a peg driven in the ground. Their fodder is green vetches (*jet*) : and this is their diet since they were brought in lean from the desert, through the summer weeks ; until the time when the Monsoon blows in the Indian seas. Then the broker's horse-droves pass the long northern wilderness, with camels, bearing their water, in seventeen marches to Kuweyt ; where they are shipped for Bombay.

An European had smiled to see in this Arab's countenance the lively impression of his dealing in horses ! Abu Nejm, who lent me a horse, would ride in our company. Our saddles were pads without stirrups, for — like the Beduins, they use none here : yet these townsmen ride with the sharp bit of the border lands ; whereas the nomad horsemen mount without bit or rein, and sit upon their mares, as they sit on their dromedaries (that is somewhat rawly), and with a halter only. I have never heard a horseman commended among Beduins for his fair riding, though certain sheykhs are praised as spearsmen. Abu Nejm went not himself to India ; and it was unknown to him that any Nasrâny could ride: he called to me therefore, to hold fast to the pad-brim, and wrap the other hand in the horse's mane. Bye and bye I made my horse bound under me, and giving rein let him try his mettle over the sand-billows of the Nefûd, — " Ullah ! is the hakîm *khayyâl*, a horseman ? " exclaimed the worthy man.

We rode by a threshing-ground ; and I saw a team of well-camels driven in a row with ten kine and an ass inwardly (all the cattle of that homestead), about a stake, and treading knee-deep upon the bruised corn-stalks. In that yard-side I saw many ant-hills ; and drew bridle to consider the labour of certain indigent hareem that were sitting beside them.—I saw the emmets' last confusion (which they suffered as robbers), — their hill-colonies subverted, and caught up in the women's meal-sieves ! that (careful only of their desolate living) tossed sky-high the pismire nation, and mingled people and *musheyikh* in a homicide ruin of sand and grain. — And each needy wife had already some hand-fuls laid up in her spread kerchief, of this gleaning corn.

We see a long high platform of sand-rock, *Mergab er-Ràfa*, upon this side of the town. There stone is hewed and squared for well building, and even for gate-posts, in Aneyza. — Kenneyny came riding to meet us ! and now we fell into an hollow ancient way through the Nefûd leading to the 'Eyarîeh ; and my companions said, there lies such another between el-'Eyarîeh and *el-Owshazîeh* ; that is likewise an ancient town site. How may these impressions abide in unstable sand ? — So far as I have seen there is little wind in these countries.

Abdullah sat upon a beautiful young stallion of noble blood, that went sidling proudly under his fair handling : and seeing the stranger's eyes fixed upon his horse, " Ay, quoth my friend, this one is good in all." Kenneyny, who with Sheykh Nâsir shipped three or four young Arabian horses every year to Bombay, told me that by some they gain ; but another horse may be valued there so low, that they have less by the sale-money than the first cost and expenses. Abu Nejm told us his winning or losing was ' as it pleased Ullah : the more whiles he gained, but sometimes no.' They buy the young desert horses in the winter time, that ere the next shipping season they may be grown in flesh, and strong ; and inured by the oasis' diet of sappy vetches, to the green climate of India.

Between the wealthy ignorance of foreign buyers, and the Asiatic flattery of the Nejders of the Arab stables in Bombay, a distinction has been invented of Aneyza and Nejd horses ! — as well might we distinguish between London and Middlesex pheasants. We have seen that the sale-horses are collected by town dealers, *min el-Aarab*, from the nomad tribes ; and since there are few horses in the vast Arabian marches, they are ofttimes fetched from great distances. I have found " Aneyza " horses in the Bombay stables which were foaled in el-Yémen. — Perhaps we may understand by *Aneyza horses*, the horses of Kasîm dealers [of Aneyza and Boreyda] ; and by *Nejd horses*, the Jebel horses, or those sent to Bombay from Ibn Rashîd's country. I heard that a Boreyda broker's horse-troop had been sent out a few days before my coming thither.—Boreyda is a town and small Arabian state ; the Emir governs the neighbour villages, but is not obeyed in the desert. It is likely therefore that the Aneyza horse-coursers' traffic may be the more considerable. [The chief of the best Bombay stable is from Shuggera in el-Wéshm.]

As for the northern or "Gulf" horses, bred in the nomad dîras upon the river countries — although of good stature and swifter, they are not esteemed by the inner Arabians. Their flesh being only " of greenness and water " they could not endure in the sun-stricken languishing country. Their own daughters-of-the-desert, albe they are less fairly shaped, are, in the same strains, worth five of the other. — Even the sale-horses are not curried under the pure Arabian climate : they learn first to stand under the strigil in India. Hollow-necked, as the camel, are the Arabian horses : the lofty neck of our thick-blooded horses were a deformity in the eyes of all Arabs. The desert horses, nurtured in a droughty wilderness of hot plain lands beset with small mountains, are not leapers, but very sure of foot to climb in rocky ground. They are good weight carriers : I have heard nomads boast that their mares 'could carry four men.' The Arabians believe faithfully that Ullah created the horse-kind in their soil : *el-asl*, the root or spring of the horse is, they say, " in the land of the Aarab." Even Kenneyny was of this superstitious opinion ; although the horse can live only of man's hand in the droughty khála. [*Rummaky*, a mare, is a word often used in el-Kasîm : Sâlih el-Rasheyd tells me they may say *ghrôg* for a horse ; but that is seldom heard.]

We rode three miles and came upon a hill of hard loam, overlooking the Wady er-Rummah, which might be there two miles over. In the further side appear a few outlying palm plantations and granges : but that air breeds fever and the water is brackish, and they are tilled only by negro husbandmen. All the nigh valley grounds were white with *subbakha* : in the midst of the Wady is much good loam, grown up with desert bushes and tamarisks ; but it cannot be husbanded because the ground-water—there at the depth of ten feet—is saline and sterile. Below us I saw an enclosure of palms with plots of vetches and stubbles, and a clay cabin or two ; which were sheykh Nâsir's. Here the shallow Rummah bottom reaches north-eastward and almost enfolds Aneyza : at ten hours' distance, or one easy thelûl journey, lies a great rautha,

Zighreybîeh, with corn grounds, which are flooded with seyl-water in the winter rains : there is a salt bed, where salt is digged for Aneyza.

The Wady descending through the northern wilderness [which lies waste for hundreds of miles without settlement] is dammed in a place called *eth-Thueyrát*, that is a thelûl journey or perhaps fifty miles distant from Aneyza, by great dunes of sand which are grown up, they say, in this age. From thence the hollow Wady ground — wherein is the path of the northern caravans — is named *el-Bâtin* ; and passengers ride by the ruined sites of two or three villages : there are few wells by the way, and not much water in them. That vast wilderness was anciently of the B. Taâmir. The Wady banks are often cliffs of clay and gravel, and from cliff to cliff the valley may be commonly an hour (nearly three miles) over, said Kenneyny. In the Nefûd plain of Kasîm the course of the great Wady is sometimes hardly to be discerned by the eyes of strangers.

A few journeying together will not adventure to hold the valley way : they ride then, not far off, in the desert. All the winding length of the Wady er-Rummah is, according to the vulgar opinion, forty-five days or camel marches (that were almost a thousand miles): it lies through a land-breadth, measured from the heads in the Harrat Kheybar to the outgoing near Bosra, of nearly five hundred miles. — What can we think of this great valley-ground, in a rainless land? When the Wady is in flood — that is hardly twice or thrice in a century, the valley flows down as a river. The streaming tide is large, and where not straitened may be forded, they say, by a dromedary rider. No man of my time of life had seen the seyl ; but the elder generation saw it forty years before, in a season when uncommon rains had fallen in all the high country toward Kheybar. The flood that passed Aneyza, being locked by the mole of sand at eth-Thueyràt, rose backward and became a wash, which was here at the 'Eyarîeh two miles wide. And then was seen in Nejd the new spectacle of a lake indeed ! — there might be nigh an hundred miles of standing water ; which remained two years and was the repair of all wandering wings of water-fowl not known heretofore, nor had their cries been heard in the air of these desert countries. After a seyling of the great valley the water rises in the wells at Boreyda and Aneyza ; and this continues for a year or more.

We found upon this higher ground potsherds and broken glass — as in all ruined sites of ancient Arabia, and a few building-stones, and bricks ; but how far are they now from these arts of old settled countries in Nejd ! — This is the site el-'Eyarîeh or *Menzil 'Eyàr* ; where they see ' the plots of three or four ancient villages and a space of old inhabited soil greater than Aneyza ' ; they say, " It is better than the situation of the (new) town." We dismounted, and Abdullah began to say, " Wellah, the Arabs (of our time) are degenerate from the ancients, in all ! — we see them live by inheriting their labours " (deep wells in the deserts and other public works) !

— The sword, they say, of *Khâlid bin-Walîd* [that new Joshua of Islam, in the days of Ômar] devoured idolatrous 'Eyarîeh, a town of B. Temîm. The like is reported of Owshazîeh, whose site is three hours eastward : there are now some palm-grounds and orchard houses of Aneyza. *'Eyàr* and *Owshâz*, in the Semitic tradition, are " brethren." — " It is remembered in the old poets of those B. Temîm citizens (quoth my erudite companions) that they had much cattle ; and in the spring-time were wont to wander with their flocks and camels in the Nefûd, and dwell in booths like the nomads." — This is that we have seen in Edom and Moab [Vol. I. pp. 63, 78, 82] where from the entering of the spring the villagers are tent-dwellers in the wilderness about them, — for the summering of their cattle : I have seen poor families in Gilead — which had no tent-cloth — dwelling under great oaks ! the leafy pavilions are a covert from the heat by day, and from the nightly dews. Their flocks were driven-in toward the sun-setting, and lay down round about them.

Only the soil remains of the town of 'Eyàr : what were the lives of those old generations more than the flickering leaves ! the works of their hands, the thoughts and intents of their hearts, — ' their love, their hatred and envy,' are utterly perished ! Their religion is forsaken ; their place is unvisited as the cemeteries of a former age : only in the autumn landed men of Aneyza send their servants thither, with asses and panniers, to dig loam for a top-dressing. As we walked we saw white slags lying together ; where perhaps had been the workstead of some ancient artificer. When I asked ' had nothing been found here ? ' Kenneyny told of some well-sinkers, that were hired to dig a well in a new ground by the 'Eyarîeh [the water is nigh and good]. " They beginning to open their pit one of them lighted on a great earthen vessel ! — it was set in the earth mouth downward [the head of an antique grave]. Then every well-digger cried out that the treasure was his own ! none would hear his fellows' reason — and all men have reason ! From quick words they fell to hand-strokes ; and laid so sharply about them with their mattocks, that in the end but one man was left alive.

This workman struck his vessel, with an eager heart ! — but in the shattered pot was no more than a clot of the common earth !" — Abdullah said besides, 'that a wedge of fine gold had been taken up here, within their memories. The finder gave it, when he came into the town, for two hundred reals, to one who afterward sold the metal in the North, for better than a thousand.'

We returned : and Kenneyny at the end of a mile or two rode apart to his horse-yard ; where he said he had somewhat to show me another day. — I saw it later, a blackish vein, more than a palm deep and three yards wide, in the yellow sides of a loam pit : plainly the ashes of an antique fire, and in this old hearth they had found potsherds ! thereabove lay a fathom of clay ; and upon that a drift of Nefûd sand. — Here had been a seyl-bed before the land was enclosed ; but potsherds so lying under a fathom of silt may be of an high antiquity. What was man then in the midst of Arabia ? Some part of the town of Aneyza, as the mejlis and clothier's street, is built upon an old seyl-ground ; and has been twice wasted by land floods : the last was ninety years before.

I went home with Hàmed and there came-in the younger Abdullah el-Bessàm. They spoke of the ancients, and (as litterates) contemned the vulgar opinion of giants in former ages : nevertheless they thought it appeared by old writings, that men in their grandsires' time had been stronger than now ; for they found that a certain weight was then reckoned a man's burden at Aneyza, which were now above the strength of common labourers ; and that not a few of those old folk came to fourscore years and ten. There are many long-lived persons at Aneyza, and I saw more grey beards in this one town than in all parts besides where I passed in Arabia.

But our holiday on horseback to the 'Eyarîeh bred talk. 'We had not ridden there, three or four together, upon a fool's errand ; the Nasrâny in his books of secret science had some old record of this country.' Yet the liberal townsmen bade me daily, Not mind their foolish words ; and they added proverbially *el-Arab, 'akl-hum nâkis*, the Arabs are always short-witted. Yet their crabbed speech vexed the Kenneyny, a spirit so high above theirs and unwont to suffer injuries. — I found him on the morrow sitting estranged from them and offended : "Ahks, he said, this despiteful people ! but my home is in Bosra, and God be thanked ! I shall not be much longer with them. Oh ! Khalîl, thou canst not think what they call me, — they say, *el-Kenneyny bellowwy!*" — This is some outrageous villany, which is seldom heard amongst nomads ; and is only uttered of anyone when they would speak extremely. The Arabs — the most unclean and devout of lips, of mankind ! — curse all under heaven which contradicts their humour ; and the Waháby rancour was stirred against a townsman who was no partizan of their blind faction, but seemed to favour the Nasrâny. I wondered to see the good man so much moved in his philosophy ! — but he quailed before the popular religion ; which is more than law and government, even in a free town. "A pang is in my heart, says an Oriental poet, because I am disesteemed by the depraved multitude." Kenneyny was of those that have lived for the advancement of their people, and are dead before the time. May his eternal portion be rest and peace!

And seeing the daily darkening and averting of the Waháby faces, I had a careful outlaw's heart under my bare shirt ; though to none of them had I done anything but good, — and this only for the name of the young prophet of Galilee and the Christian tradition ! the simpler sort of liberals were bye and bye afraid to converse with me ; and many of my former acquaintance seemed now to shun that I should be seen to enter their friendly houses. And I knew not that this came of the Muttowwa — that (in their Friday sermons) they moved the people against me ! 'It is not reason, said these divines, in a time when the Sooltàn of Islam is busy in slaughtering the Nasâra, that any misbelieving Nasrâny should be harboured in a faithful town : and they did contrary to their duties who in any wise favoured him.' — Kenneyny though timid before the people was resolute to save me : and he and the good Bessàm were also in the counsels of Zâmil. — But why, I thought, should I longer trouble them with my religion ? I asked my friends, 'When would there be any caravan setting forth, that I might depart with them ?' They answered, "Have patience awhile ; for there is none in these days."

A fanatic sometimes threatened me as I returned by the narrow and lonely ways, near my house : "O kafir ! if it please the Lord, thou wilt be slain this afternoon or night, or else to-morrow's day. Ha ! son of mischief, how long dost thou refuse the religion of Islam ? We gave thee indeed a time to repent, with long sufferance and kindness ! — now die in thy blind way, for the Moslemîn are weary of thee. Except thou say the testimony, thou wilt be slain to-day : thou gettest no more grace, for many have determined to kill thee." Such deadly kind of arguments were become as they say familiar evils, in this long tribulation of Arabian travels ; yet I came no more home twice by the same way, in the still (prayer and coffee) hours of the day or evening ; and feeling any presentiment I went secretly armed : also when I returned (from friends' houses) by night I folded the Arab cloak about my left arm ; and confided, that as I had lived to the second year a threatened man, I should yet live and finally escape them.

In this drought of spirit there came to me a certain cameleer, Ibrahîm of Shuggera ; which is a good town, two dromedary journeys eastward in *el-Wéshm*. He proffered to carry me withersoever I would, affirming that he knew all the ways to the east and southward as far as el-Yémen. ' If I would ride, he said, to *Siddûs* : the way is ten camel marches, which he divided thus ; the first to *Míth'nib* ; the second day to *Aŷn es-Sweyna*, a small village in *Wady es-Sirr*, [this valley, in which there are springs and hamlets, seyls only into a *gá* or place of subsidence] ; we should be the third night at *el-Feytháh*, another small village ; the fourth at *Borrûd*, a small village ; the next station was his own town, Shuggera ; then *Thérmidda*, a populous and ancient place ; the seventh *er-Robba*, a small village ; the eighth *Theydich* ; the ninth *Horèymla*, a populous town ; then *Siddûs*, which is a small village in Wady Hanîfy, with *Ayeyna* and *Jebeyly* : from thence we might ride to *eth-Therr'eyyeh*, in the same valley of *el-Âruth* ; and be the twelfth night at *er-Riâth*. — Or if I thought this tedious, the way for thelûl riders is four journeys to Siddûs ; and the stations — W. es-Sirr, Shuggera, Horéymla.' When I enquired of the security of the way, — " We will ride, he said, in the night-time ; by day there is no safe passage : for since Ibn Saûd's lordship was broken, the tribes have returned to their wildness, and the country is infested by ghrazzus." — I heard from Kenneyny, that this Ibrahîm had been twice robbed, in the last months ! of his thelûl, and of the wares wherewith he went trafficking to friendly Aarab. Yet my friend thought I might adventure to ride with him, bearing a letter from Zâmil ; and return.

" If we must ride all by night, where shall we lodge in the day ? " *Ibrahîm :* " In the villages." — " And if any insult and threaten the Nasrâny — ! " — ' We will alight to rest in friendly houses ; and [he stamped upon the floor] they are all under my heel — thus ! Fear nothing if thou hast a letter from Zâmil to Abdullah ibn Saûd ; wellah for the name only of Zâmil [it is so honourable] there will none molest thee." — But I considered that the fatigues of this voyage in the darkness would be little profitable : besides I languished, so that I might expire in the saddle ere those many long journeys were ended again at Aneyza. And I valued more than all the assurance of Abdullah el-Bessàm, that I should ride in his son's company to Jidda ; for my desire was to ascertain the nature of the southern vulcanic country.

Ibrahîm had ridden sometime by the Wady Dauâsir to el-Yémen ; but that was many years ago. The Aflaj he affirmed to be in J. Tueyk, six thelûl journeys from er-Riâth ; the way is rugged and without villages. In the Aflaj he named four good palm settlements. From the Aflaj to the Wady Dauâsir " are two days through *tubj*," or mountain straits. Northward of the Aflaj is a valley which descends to *el-Hauta* (a populous town of B. Temîm, "great as Aneyza "), and reaches to *el-Khorj* (Khark). Therein are good villages, as *ed-Dillum*, *el-Yemâna*, *Najân*, *es-Sellummîeh*, *el-Atthar*, *es-Sèyeh* : then passing between er-Riâth and the Tueyk mountains it is lost in the sands. — In Bombay I afterward met with one, *Hàmed en-Nefîs*, whose father had been treasurer at er-Riâth ; and he said " Aflaj is six villages," *Siâh*, *Leyta*, *Khurrfa*, *er-Rautha*, *el-Biddea* ; — and in Wady Dauâsir he named *el-Hammam*, *es-Shotibba*, *es-Soleyil*, *Tammerra*, *el-Dam*, (three hamlets) *el-Loghrif*, *el-Ferra*, *es-Showŷg*, *el-Ayathát*.

There was a salesman who, as often as I passed by his shop, was wont to murmur some word of fanaticism. One day, as he walked in the sûk, we stayed to speak with the same person ; and when he heard my [Beduish] words, " Ha-ha ! I will never believe, he cries, but that Khalîl is Arab-born, and no Engleysy ! trust me, he was bred in some Arabic land." And in this humour the poor man led me home to coffee : he was now friendly minded. — Since those days when I had been houseless, I remained almost bedrid at home ; and there came no friends to visit me. Arabs are always thus — almost without the motions of a generous nature. I was seldom seen in the street. " It is his fear," murmured the Waháby people ; and their malevolence gathered fast.

My good friends, readers in the Gazette, though curious politicians, had no notice of geography : taking therefore a sheet of large paper I drew out a map of Europe ; and Bessàm called for his caligraph Ibn Aŷith ; who inscribed from my mouth the capital names. When our work was accomplished, he sent it round among his friends. The Semites — wide wanderers in countries which they pass upon the backs of camels, have little understanding of the circumscriptions which we easily imagine, and set down in charts. I have not found any, even among the new collegians in Syria, that have more than an infantile mind in geography. These are not Semitic arts: The Semitic arts are of human malice, and of the sensitive life. The friends enquired, if I had passed by Andalûs? — a name which ever sounds in their ears as the name of a mistress! Bessàm desired me to tell them something of all I had seen there. I spoke of Granada, Sevilla, Cordoba; and of great works celebrated in their poets, which remain to this day. But they were impatient to hear from me what were become of the Great Mesjid (the noble foundation of *Abd-er-Rahmàn*) at Cordoba [which is an acre of low roof laid upon a grove of marble columns]. I answered, "It is the metropolitan church of them to-day." When they heard that it was a Christian temple, all their jaws fell: the negro Ibn Aŷith could not forbear to utter a groan! — for doubtless they think very horribly of the Christian faith. Even the good Abdullah was cast down a moment; but in the next he caught again his pleasant countenance: and he was in that country of crabbed religion, a very cheerful man. — The bountiful is cheerful; and his honest human-heart has cause; for do not all faces answer him with cheerful looks? — Kenneyny, surveying that rude map asked me, if I were a draughtsman? he had seen the engraved pictures of the Franks; and he thought it a beautiful art.

I questioned these friends, of the Nejd speech which is heard in el-Kasîm. "It is very well, they answered, if compared with the language of Syria, Egypt, the Hejâz, Mesopotamia. Our vulgar is not the tongue of the koran: we speak as it were with another mind, and in newer wise." — To my ears all the nomads, beginning from the tribes in the Syrian and Egyptian borders, with the Nejd oases-dwellers, speak a like *rótn*; which rótn we might call Nejd Arabic, or mother-tongue of upland Arabia. In many words they deem themselves to pronounce amiss, as when they say Yahŷa for Yéhia. People's words are *âjjidat*, town-wall, *gô* for *koom*, rise, and the like. And there are some foreign words brought in among them, by those who have wandered abroad; such is *khósh* in the northern merchant's talk: they say a *khósh* man, a *khósh* house — that is one excellently good. A man of the people is *'adamy* (pl. *ou'adam*), in the discourse of some Gulf merchants.

CHAPTER XIV

THE CHRISTIAN STRANGER DRIVEN FROM ANEYZA; AND RECALLED

Yahŷa's homestead. Beduins from the North. Rainless years and murrain. Picking and stealing in Aneyza. Handicrafts. Hurly-burly of fanatic women and children against the Nasrâny. Violence of the Emir Aly, who sends away the stranger in the night-time. Night journey in the Nefûd. The W. er-Rummah. Strife with the camel driver. Come to Khóbra in the Nefûd. The emir's kahwa. The emir's blind father. Armed riders of Boreyda. Medicine seekers. The town. An 'Aufy. The cameleer returns from Zâmil; to convey the stranger again to Aneyza! Ride to el-Helâlîeh. El-Búkerîeh. Helâlîeh oasis. Night journey in the Nefûd. Alight at an outlying plantation of Aneyza (appointed for the residence of the Nasrâny). Visit of Abdullah el-Kenneyny.—Rasheyd's jenèyny. Sâlih. Joseph Khâlidy. A son of Rasheyd had visited Europe! Rasheyd's family. Ibrahîm. The Suez Canal. The field labourers. El-Wéshm. A labouring lad's tales. Ruin of the Waháby. Northern limits of Murra and other Southern Aarab. A foray of Ibn Rashîd.

A PLEASANT afternoon resort to me out of the town was Yahŷa's walled homestead. If I knocked there, and any were within, I found a ready welcome; and the sons of the old patriot sat down to make coffee. Sometimes they invited me out to sup; and then, rather than return late in the stagnant heat, I have remained to slumber under a palm in their orchard; where a carpet was spread for me and I might rest in the peace of God, as in the booths of the Aarab. One evening I walked abroad with them, as they went to say their prayers on the pure Nefûd sand. By their well Hàmed showed me a peppermint plant, and asked if it were not medicine? he brought the (wild) seed from *es-Seyl* [*Kurn el-Menâzil*], an ancient station of the Nejd caravans, in the high country before Mecca (whither I came three months later).—I saw one climb over the clay wall from the next plantation! to meet us: it was the young merchant of the rifle! whom I had not since met with, in any good company in the town. The young gallant's tongue was nimble: and he dissembled the voice of an enemy. It was dusk when they rose from prayers; then on a sudden we heard shrieks in the Nefûd! The rest ran to the cry: he lingered a moment, and bade me come to coffee on the morrow, in the town ; " Thou seest, he said, what are the incessant alarms of our home in the desert !"

— A company of northern (Annezy) Beduins entered the house at that time, with me ; the men were his guests. We sat about the hearth and there came-in a child tender and beautiful as a spring blossom ! he was slowly recovering from sickness. *Goom hubb amm-ak!* Go, and kiss thine uncle Khalîl, quoth the young man, who was his elder brother; and the sweet boy — that seemed a flower too delicate for the common blasts of the world, kissed me ; and afterward he kissed the Beduins, and all the company : this is the Arabs' home tenderness. I wondered to hear that the tribesmen were fifteen years before of this (Kasîm) *dîra* ! They had ridden from their menzil in Syria, by the water *el-Házzel* [a far way about, to turn the northern Nefûd], in a fortnight : and left their tents standing, they told me, by *Tódmor* [Palmyra] ! Their coming down was about some traffic in camels.

The small camels of Arabia increase in stature in the northern wilderness. Hàmed es-Sâfy sent his thelûl to pasture one year with these Aarab ; and when she was brought in again he hardly knew her, what for her bulk, and what for the shaggy thickness of her wool. This Annezy tribe, when yet in Kasîm, were very rich in cattle ; for some of the sheykhs had been owners of " a thousand camels " : until there came year after year, upon all the country, many rainless years. Then the desert bushes (patient of the yearly drought) were dried up and blackened, the Nomads' great cattle perished very fast ; and a thelûl of the best blood might be purchased for two reals. — These Aarab forsook the country, and journeying to the north [now full of the tribes and half tribes of Annezy], they occupied a dîrat, among their part friendly and partly hostile kinsmen.

One day when I returned to my lodging, I found that my watch had been stolen ! I left it lying with my medicines. This was a cruel loss, for my fortune was very low ; and by selling the watch I might have had a few reals : suspicion fell upon an infamous neighbour. The town is uncivil in comparison with the desert ! I was but one day in the dokân, and all my vaccination pens were purloined : they were of ivory and had cost ten reals ; — more than I gained (in twice ten months) by the practice of medicine in Arabia. I thought again upon the Kenneyny's proffer, which I had passed over at that time ; and mused that he had not renewed it ! There are many shrewd haps in Arabia ; and even the daily piastre spent for bread divided me from the coast : and what would become of my life, if by evil accident I were parted from the worthy persons who were now my friends ?

— Handicraftsmen here in a Middle Nejd town (of the sanies' caste), are armourers, tinkers, coppersmiths, goldsmiths ; and the workers in wood are turners of bowls, wooden locksmiths, makers of camel saddle-frames, well-wheel-wrights, and (very unhandsome) carpenters [for they are nearly without tools] ; the stone-workers are hewers, well-steyners and sinkers, besides marble-wrights, makers of coffee mortars and the like ; and house-builders and pargeters. We may go on to reckon those that work with the needle, seamsters and seamstresses, embroiderers, sandal makers. The sewing men and women are, so far as I have known them, of the libertine blood. The gold and silver smiths of Aneyza are excellent artificers in filigrane or thread-work : and certain of them established at Mecca are said to excel all in the sacred town. El-Kenneyny promised that I should see something of this fine Arabian industry ; but the waves of their fanatical world soon cast me from him.

The salesmen are clothiers in the sûk, sellers of small wares [in which are raw drugs and camel medicines, sugar-loaves, spices, Syrian soap from Medina, coffee of the Mecca Caravans], and sellers of victual. In the outlying quarters are small general shops — some of them held by women, where are sold onions, eggs, iron nails, salt, (German) matches, girdle-bread [and certain of these poor wives will sell thee a little milk, if they have any]. On Fridays, you shall see veiled women sitting in the mejlis to sell chickens, and milk-skins and girbies that they have tanned and prepared. Ingenuous vocations are husbandry, and camel and horse dealing. All the welfaring families are land owners. — The substantial foreign merchants were fifteen persons.

Hazardry, banquetting, and many running sores and hideous sinks of our great towns are unknown to them. The Arabs, not less frugal than Spartans, are happy in the Epicurean moderation of their religion. Aneyza is a welfaring civil town more than other in Nomadic Arabia : in her B. Temîm citizens is a spirit of industry, with a good plain understanding — howbeit somewhat soured by the rheum of the Waháby religion.

Seeing that few any more chided the children that cried after me in the street, I thought it an evil sign ; but the Kenneyny had not warned me, and Zâmil was my friend : the days were toward the end of May. One of these forenoons, when I returned to my house, I saw filth cast before the threshold ; and some knavish children had flung stones as I passed by the lonely street. Whilst I sat within, the little knaves came to batter the door ; there was a Babel of cries : the boldest climbed by the side walls to the house terrace ; and hurled down stones and clay bricks by the stair head. In this uproar I heard a skritching of fanatical women, " Yâ Nasrâny ! thou shalt be dead ! — they are in the way that will do it ! " I sat on an hour whilst the hurly-burly lasted : my door held, and for all their hooting the knaves had no courage to come down where they must meet with the kafir. At this hour the respectable citizens were reposing at home, or drinking coffee in their friends' houses ; and it was a desolate quarter where I lodged. At length the siege was raised ; for some persons went by who returned from the coffee companies, and finding this ado about Khalîl's door, they drove away the truants, — with those extreme curses which are always ready in the mouths of Arabs.

Later when I would go again into the town, the lads ran together, with hue and cry : they waylaid the Nasrâny at the corners, and cast stones from the backward ; but if the kafir turned, the troop fled back hastily. I saw one coming — a burly man of the people, who was a patient of mine ; and called to him, to drive the children away. — " Complain to Zâmil ! " muttered the ungracious churl ; who to save himself from the stones, shrank through an open door-way and forsook me. We have seen there are none better at stone-casting than the gipsy-like Arabs : their missiles sung about my head, as I walked forward, till I came where the lonely street gave upon the Boreyda road near the Gá : some citizens passed by. The next moment a heavy bat, hurled by some robust arm, flew by my face. Those townsfolk stayed, and cried " ho ! " — for the stones fell beyond them ; and one, a manly young man, shouted, " What is this, eyyâl ? akhs ! God give you confusion ; — there was a stone, that had Khalîl turned might have slain him, a guest in the town, and under the countenance of the sheykhs and Zâmil." — No one thinks of calling them cowards.

I found the negro Aly, and persuaded him to return with me ; and clear the lonely by-streets about my lodging. And this he did chasing the eyyâl ; and when his blood was warmed fetching blows with his stick, which in their nimbleness of flies lighted oftener upon the walls.

Some neighbours accused the fanatical hareem, and Aly, showing his negro teeth, ran on the hags to have beaten them; but they pitifully entreated, and promised for themselves. Yet holding his stick over one of these, 'Wellah, he cries, the tongue of her, at the word of Zâmil, should be plucked up by the roots!' After this Aly said, "All will now be peace, Khalîl!" And I took the way to the Meilis; to drink coffee at Bessàm's house.

Kenneyny was there: they sat at the hearth, though the stagnant air was sultry, — but the Arabians think they taste some refreshment when they rise from the summer fire. Because I found in these friends a cheerfulness of heart, which is the life of man — and that is so short! — I did not reveal to them my trouble, which would have made them look sad. I trusted that these hubbubs would not be renewed in the town: so bye and bye wishing them God's speed, I rose to depart. They have afterward blamed me for sparing to speak, when they might have had recourse immediately to Zâmil. — In returning I found the streets again beset nigh my house, and that the eyyâl had armed themselves with brickbats and staves. So I went down to the sûk, to speak with my neighbour, Rasheyd, Zâmil's officer. — I saw in Rasheyd's shop some old shivers of Ibrahîm Pasha's bombshells; which are used in poor households for mortars, to bray-in their salt, pepper, and the like. Rasheyd said, 'that Zâmil had heard of the children's rioting in the town. He had sent also for the hags, and threatened them; and Aly had beaten some of the lads: now there would be quietness, and I might go home'; — but I thought it was not so. I returned through the bazaar with the *deyik es-súdr* — for what heart is not straitened, being made an outlaw of the humanity about him? were it even of the lowest savages! — as I marked how many in the shops, and in the way, now openly murmured when they saw me pass. Amongst the hard faces which went by me was Aly, the executive Emir, bearing his sword; and Abdullah the grudging son of Zâmil, who likewise (as a grown child of the Emir's house) carries a sword in the streets. Then Sheykh Nâsir came sternly stalking by me, without regard or salutation! — but welcome all the experience of human life. The sun was set, and the streets were empty, when I came again to the door of my desolate house; where weary and fasting, in this trouble, I lay down and slept immediately.

I thought I had slumbered an hour, when the negro voice of Aly awakened me ! crying at the gate, " Khalîl — Khalîl ! the Emir bids thee open." I went to undo for him, and looked out. It was dark night ; but I perceived, by the shuffling feet and murmur of voices, that there were many persons. *Aly* : " The Emir calls thee ; he sits yonder (in the street) ! " I went, and sat down beside him : could Zâmil, I mused, be come at these hours ! then hearing his voice, which resembled Zâmil's, I knew it was another. " Whither, said the voice, would'st thou go, — to Zílfy ? " — " I am going shortly in the company of Abdullah el-Bessàm's son to Jidda." " No, no ! and Jidda (he said, brutally laughing) is very far off : but where wilt thou go this night ? " — " Aly, what sheykh is this ? " — " It is Aly the Emir." Then a light was brought : I saw his face which, with a Waháby brutishness, resembled Zâmil's ; and with him were some of his ruffian ministers. — " Emir Aly, Ullah lead thy parents into paradise ! Thou knowest that I am sick ; and I have certain debts for medicines here in the town ; and to-day I have tasted nothing. If I have deserved well of some of you, let me rest here until the morning ; and then send me away in peace." — " Nay, thy camel is ready at the corner of the street ; and this is thy cameleer : up ! have out thy things, and that quickly. Ho ! some of you go in with Khalîl, to hasten him." — " And whither will ye send me, so suddenly ? and I have no money ! " — " Ha-ha ! what is that to us, I say come off " : as I regarded him fixedly, the villain struck me with his fist in the face. — If the angry instinct betray me, the rest (I thought) would fall with their weapons upon the Nasrâny : — Aly had pulled his sword from the sheath to the half. " This, I said to him, you may put up again ; what need of violence ? "

Rasheyd, Zâmil's officer, whose house joined to mine from the backward — though by the doors it was a street about, had heard a rumour ; and he came round to visit me. Glad I was to see him enter, with the sword, which he wore for Zâmil. I enquired of him, if Aly's commandment were good ? for I could not think that my friends among the chief citizens were consenting to it ; and that the philosophical Zâmil would send by night to put me out of the town ! When I told Rasheyd that the Waháby Aly had struck me, he said to me apart, " Do not provoke him, only make haste, and doubtless this word is from Zâmil: for Aly would not be come of himself to compel thee." Emir Aly called from without, " Tell Khalîl to hasten ! is he not ready ? " Then he came in himself ; and Rasheyd helped me to lift the things into the bags, for

I was feeble. "Whither, he said to the Emir Aly, art thou sending Khalîl?" "To Khubbera." — " *El-Helàlîeh* were better, or *er-Russ*; for these lie in the path of caravans." — "He goes to Khubbera." "Since, I said, you drive me away, you will pay the cameleer; for I have little money." *Emir Aly*: "Pay the man his hire and make haste; give him three reals, Khalîl." — *Rasheyd*: "Half a real is the hire to Khubbera: make it less Emir Aly." — "Then be it two reals, I shall pay the other myself." — "But tell me, are there none the better for my medicines in your town?" — "We wish for no medicines." — "Have I not done well and honestly in Aneyza? answer me, upon your conscience." *Emir Aly*: "Well, thou hast." — "Then what dealing is this?" But he cried, "Art thou ready? now mount!" In the meanwhile, his ruffian ministers had stolen my sandals (left without the chamber door); and the honest negro Aly cried out for me, accusing them of the theft, "O ye, give Khalîl his sandals again!" I spoke to the brutal Emir; who answered, "There are no sandals:" and over this new mishap of the Nasrâny [it is no small suffering to go barefoot on the desert soil glowing in the sun] he laughed apace. "Now, art thou ready? he cries, mount then, mount! but first pay the man his hire." — After this, I had not five reals left; my watch was stolen: and I was in the midst of Arabia.

Rasheyd departed: the things were brought out and laid upon the couching camel; and I mounted. The Emir Aly with his crew followed me as far as the Mejlis. "Tell me (I said to him) to whom shall I go at Khubbera?" — "To the Emir, and remember his name is Abdullah el-Aly." — "Well, give me a letter for him." — "I will give thee none." I heard Aly talking in a low voice with the cameleer behind me; — words (of an adversary), which doubtless boded me no good, or he had spoken openly: when I called to him again, he was gone home. The negro Aly, my old host, was yet with me; he would see me friendly to the town's end. — But where, I mused, were now my friends? The negro said, that Zâmil gave the word for my departure at these hours, to avoid any further tumult in the town; also the night passage were safer, in the desert. Perhaps the day's hubbub had been magnified to Zâmil; — they themselves are always ready.

Aly told me that a letter from the Muttowwa of Boreyda had been lately brought to Zâmil and the sheykhs of Aneyza; *exhorting them, in the name of the common faith, to send away the Nasrâny!* — "Is this driver to trust? and are they good people at Khubbera?" Aly answered with ayes, and added, "Write back to me; and it is not far: you will be there about dawn, and in all this, believe me Khalîl, I am sorry for thy sake." He promised to go himself early to Kenneyny, with a request from me, to send 'those few reals on account of medicines': but he went not (as I afterwards learned); for the negro had been bred among Arabs, whose promises are but words in the air, and forged to serve themselves at the moment. — "Let this cameleer swear to keep faith with me." *Aly:* "Ay, come here thou Hásan! and swear thus and thus." Hásan swore all that he would; and at the town walls the negro departed. There we passed forth to the dark Nefûd; and a cool night air met us breathing from the open sand wilderness, which a little revived me to ride: we were now in the beginning of the stagnant summer heat of the lower Rummah country.

After an hour's riding we went by a forsaken orchard and ruined buildings, — there are many such outlying homesteads. The night was dim and overcast so that we could not see ground under the camel's tread. We rode in a hollow way of the Nefûd; but lost it after some miles. "It is well, said Hásan; for so we shall be in less danger of any lurking Beduins." We descended at the right hand, and rode on by a firmer plain-ground — the Wady er-Rummah; and there I saw plashes of ponded water, which remained from the last days' showers at Aneyza. The early summer in Kasîm enters with sweet April showers: the season was already sultry, with heavy skies, from which some days there fell light rain; and they looked that this weather should continue till June. Last year, I had seen, in the khála, a hundred leagues to the westward, only barren heat and drought at this season; and (some afternoons) dust-driving gusts and winds.

We felt our camel tread again upon the deep Nefûd; and riding on with a little starlight above us, to the middle night we went by a grove of their bushy fuel-tree, *ghrotha*. The excellence of this firewood, which is of tamarisk kind, has been vaunted — my friends told me, by some of their (elder) poets; "ardent, and enduring fire (they say) as the burning *ghrotha*:" and, according to sheykh Nâsir, "a covered fire of this timber may last months long, slowly burning: which has been oft proved in their time; for Aneyza caravans returning over the deserts have found embers of their former fires remaining as much as thirty days afterward." The sere wood glows with a clear red flame; and a brand will burn as a torch : they prefer it to the sammara fuel, — that we have seen in much estimation at Kheybar.

Hásan my back-rider, was of the woodman's trade. He mounted from his cottage in the night time ; at dawn he came to the trees, and broke sere boughs, and loaded ; and could be at home again in Aneyza by the half-afternoon. He was partner in the wooden beast under us — an unbroken dromedary, with Zâmil, who had advanced half the price, fifteen reals. Small were his gains in this painful and perilous industry ; and yet the fellow had been good for nothing else. I asked him wherefore he took of me for this night's journey as much as he gained, doing the like, in eight or nine days ? 'The Nefûd, he answered, was now full of unfriendly Aarab, and he feared to lose the thelûl ; he would not otherwise have adventured, although he had disobeyed Zâmil.' — He told me, this sending me away was determined to-night, in a council of the sheykhs ; he said over their names, and among them were none of my acquaintance. Hásan had heard their talk ; for Zâmil sent early to call him, and bade him be ready to carry Haj Khalîl : the Emir said at first to *el-Búkerîeh* — for the better opportunity of passing caravans ; but the rest were for Khubbera.

— Hásan dismounted about a thing I had not seen hitherto used in the Arab countries, although night passengers and Beduins are not seldom betrayed by the braying of their thelûls : he whipped his halter about the great sheep-like brute's muzzle! which cut off further complainings. I was never racked by camel riding as in this night's work, seated on a sharp pack-saddle : the snatching gait of the untaught thelûl, wont only to carry firewood, was through the long hours of darkness an agony. What could I think of Zâmil ? — was I heretofore so much mistaken in the man ?

Hásan at length drew bridle ; I opened my eyes and saw the new sun looking over the shoulder of the Nefûd : the fellow alighted to say his prayer ; also the light revealed to me the squalid ape-like visage of this companion of the way. We were gone somewhat wide in the night time ; and Hásan, who might be thirty years of age, had not passed the Nefûd to Khubbera since his childhood. From the next dune we saw the heads of the palms of el-Helàlîeh. The sand-sea lay in great windrows, banks and troughs : over these, we were now riding ; and when the sun was risen from the earth, the clay-built town of Khubbera [or

Khóbra] appeared before us, without palms or greenness. The tilled lands are not in sight ; they lie, five miles long in the bottom of the Wady er-Rummah, and thereof is the name of their _géria_. [_v._ p. 260.] Amidst the low-built Nefûd town stands a high clay watch-tower. _Hásan_ : " Say not when thou comest to the place, ' I am a Nasrâny,' because they might not receive thee." — " Have they not heard of the Nasrâny, from Aneyza ? " — " It may be ; for at this time there is much carriage of grain to the Bessàms, who are lenders there also."

We saw plashes a little beside our way. " Let us to the water," quoth Hásan. — " There is water in the girby, and we are come to the inhabited." — " But I am to set thee down there ; for thus the Emir Aly bade me." — Again I saw my life betrayed ! and this would be worse than when the Boreyda cameleer (of the same name) forsook me nigh Aneyza ; for in Aneyza was the hope of Zâmil : Khubbera, a poor town of peasant folk and ancient colony of Kahtân, is under Boreyda ; the place was yet a mile distant. — " Thou shalt set me down in the midst of the town ; for this thou hast received my reals." Hásan notwithstanding made his beast kneel under us ; I alighted, and he came to unload my bags. I put him away, and taking out a bundle in which was my pistol, the wretch saw the naked steel in my hands ! — " Rafîk, if thou art afraid to enter, I shall ride alone to the town gate, and unload ; and so come thou and take thy thelûl again : but make me no resistance, lest I shoot her ; because thou betrayest my life." " I carry this romh, answered the javel, to help me against any who would take my thelûl." — I went to unmuzzle the brute ; that with the halter in my hand I might lead her to Khubbera.

A man of the town was at some store-houses not far off ; he had marked our contention, and came running : " Oh ! what is it ? (he asked) ; peace be with you." I told him the matter, and so did Hásan who said no word of my being a Nasrâny : nor had the other seen me armed. The townsman gave it that the stranger had reason ; so we mounted and rode to the walls. But the untrained thelûl refused to pass the gates : alighting therefore we shackled her legs with a cord, and left her ; and I compelled Hásan to take my bags upon his shoulders, and carry them in before me. — So we came to the wide public place ; and he cast them down there and would have forsaken me ; but I would not suffer it. Some townspeople who came to us ruled, That I had right, and Hásan must bear the things to the kahwa of the Emir.

I heard said behind me, " It is some stranger ; " and as so many of these townspeople are cameleers and almost yearly pilgrims to the holy places, they have seen many strangers. — We entered the coffee hall ; where an old blind man was sitting alone — Aly, father of the Emir ; who rising as he heard this concourse, and feeling by the walls, went about to prepare coffee. The men that entered after me sat down each one after his age and condition, under the walls, on three sides of their small coffee-chamber. Not much after them there came in the Emir himself, who returned from the fields ; a well-disposed and manly fellah. They sent out to call my rafîk to coffee ; but Hásan having put down my things, was stolen out of their gate again. The company sat silent, till the coffee should be ready ; and when some of them would have questioned me the rest answered, " But not yet." Certain of the young men already laid their heads together, and looking up between their whispers they gazed upon me. I saw they were bye and bye persuaded that I could be none other than that stranger who had passed by Boreyda — the wandering Nasrâny.

Driven thus from Aneyza, I was in great weariness ; and being here without money in the midst of Arabia, I mused of the Kenneyny, and the Bessàm, so lately my good friends ! — Could they have forsaken me ? Would Kenneyny not send me money ? and how long would this people suffer me to continue amongst them ? Which of them would carry me any whither, but for payment ? and that I must begin to require for my remedies, from all who were not poor : it might suffice me to purchase bread, — lodging I could obtain freely. I perceived by the grave looking of the better sort, and the side glances of the rest, when I told my name, that they all knew me. One asked already, ' Had I not medicines ?' but others responded for me, " To-morrow will be time for these enquiries." I heard the emir himself say under his breath, ' they would send me to the Helàlîeh, or the *Búkerîeh.*' — Their coffee was of the worst : my Khubbera hosts seemed to be poor householders. When the coffee-server had poured out a second time the company rose to depart.

Only old Aly remained. He crept over where I was, and let himself down on his hands beside the hakîm ; and gazing with his squalid eyeballs enquired, if with some medicine I could not help his sight ? I saw that the eyes were not perished. " Ay, help my father ! said the emir, coming in again ; and though it were but a little yet that would be dear to me." I asked the emir, " Am I in safety here ? " — " I answer for it ; stay some days and cure my father, also we shall see how it will be." Old Aly promised that he would send me freely to er-Russ — few miles distant — from whence I might ride in the next (Mecca) samn kâfily, to Jidda. The men of er-Russ [pronounce *ér-Russ*] are nearly all caravaners. I enquired when the caravan would set forth ? " It may be some time yet ; but we will ascertain for thee." — " I have not fully five reals [20s.] and these bags ; may that suffice ? " — " Ay, responded the old man, I think we may find some one to mount thee for that money."

Whilst we were speaking, there came in, with bully voices and a clanking of swords and long guns, some strangers ; who were thelûl troopers of the Boreyda Prince's band, and such as we have seen the rajajîl at Hâyil. The honest swaggerers had ridden in the night time ; the desert being now full of thieves. They leaned up matchlocks to the wall, hanged their swords on the tenters, and sat down before the hearth with ruffling smiles ; and they saluted me also : but I saw these rude men with apprehension ; lest they should have a commission from Hásan to molest me : after coffee they mounted to an upper room to sleep. And on the morrow I was easy to hear that the riders had departed very early, for er-Russ : these messengers of Weled Mahanna were riding round to the oases in the principality [of Boreyda] to summon the village sheykhs to a common council.

Old Aly gave me an empty house next him, for my lodging, and had my bags carried thither. At noon the blind sire led me himself, upon his clay stairs, to an upper room ; where I found a slender repast prepared for me, dates and girdle-bread and water. He had been emir, or we might say mayor of Khubbera under Boreyda, until his blindness ; when his son succeeded him, a man now of the middle age ; of whom the old man spoke to all as ' *the emir*.' The ancient had taken to himself a young wife of late ; and when strange man-folk were not there, she sat always beside her old lord ; and seemed to love him well. They had between them a little son ; but the child was blear-eyed, with a running ophthalmia. The grey-beard bade the young mother sit down with the child, by the hakîm ; and cherishing their little son with his aged hands he drew him before me.

Old Aly began to discourse with me of religion ; enforcing himself to be tolerant the while. He joyed devoutly to hear there was an holy rule of men's lives also in the Christians' religion. — " Eigh me ! ye be good people, but not in the right way, that is pleasing unto Ullah ; and therefore it profiteth nothing. The Lord give thee to know the truth and say, there is none God but the Lord and Mohammed the apostle of the Lord." — A deaf man entering suddenly, troubled our talk ; demanding ere he sat down, would I cure his malady ? " And what, I asked, wouldst thou give the hakîm if he show thee a remedy ? " The fellow answered, " Nothing surely ! Wouldst thou be paid for only telling a man, — wilt thou not tell me ? eigh ! " and his wrath began to rise. *Aly :* " Young man, such be not words to speak to the hakîm, who will help thee if he may." — " Well tell him, I said, to make a horn of paper, wide in the mouth, and lay the little end to his ear ; and he shall hear the better." — The fellow, who deemed the Nasrâny put a scorn upon him, bore my saying hardly. " Nay, if the thing be rightly considered, quoth the ancient sheykh, it may seem reasonable ; only do thou after Khalîl's bidding." But the deaf would sit no longer. ' The cursed Nasrâny, whose life (he murmured) was in their hand, to deride him thus ! ' and with baleful looks he flung out from us. — A young man, who had come in, lamented to me the natural misery of his country ; " where there is nothing, said he, besides the incessant hugger-mugger of the suânies. I have a brother settled, and welfaring in the north ; and if I knew where I might likewise speed, wellah I would go thither, and return no more." — " And leave thy old father and mother to die ! and forget thine acquaintance ? " — " But my friends would be of them among whom I sojourned." — Such is the mind of many of the inhabitants of el-Kasîm.

On the morrow there arrived two young men riding upon a thelûl, to seek cures of the mudowwy ; the one for his eyes, and his rafîk for an old visceral malady. They were from the farthest palm and corn lands of Khubbera, — loam bottoms or rauthas in the Wady ; that last to the midway betwixt this town and er-Russ. When they heard, that they must lay down the price of the medicines, elevenpence — which is a field labourer's wages (besides his rations) for three days — they chose to suffer their diseases for other years, whilst it pleased Ullah, rather than adventure the silver. — " Nay, but cure us, and we will pay at the full : if thy remedies help us, will not the sick come riding to thee from all the villages ? " But I would not hear ; and, with many reproaches, the sorry young men mounted, to ride home again.

I found my medical credit high at Khubbera! for one of my Aneyza patients was their townswoman: the Nasrâny's eye-washes somewhat cleared her sight; and the fame had passed the Nefûd. I was soon called away to visit a sick person. At the kahwa door, the boy who led the hakîm bade me stand — contrary to the custom of Arabian hospitality — whilst he went in to tell them. I heard the child say, "The kafir is come;" and their response in like sort, — I entered then! and sat down among them; and blamed that householder's uncivil usage. Because I had reason, the peasants were speechless and out of countenance; the coffee maker hastened to pour me out a cup: and so rising I left them. — I wondered that all Khubbera should be so silent! I saw none in the streets; I heard no cheerful knelling of coffee-pestles in their clay town. In these days the most were absent, for the treading out and winnowing of their corn: the harvest was light, because their corn had been beaten by hail little before the ear ripened. The house-building of Khubbera is rude; and the place is not unlike certain village-towns of upland Syria. I passed through long uncheerful streets of half-ruinous clay cottages; but besides some butchers' stalls and a smith's forge, I saw no shop or merchandise in the town. Their mosque stands by the mejlis, and is of low clay building: thereby I saw a brackish well — only a fathom deep, where they wash before prayers. They have no water to drink in the town, for the ground is brackish; but the housewives must go out to fill their girbies from wells at some distance. The watch-tower of Khubbera, built of clay — great beneath as a small chamber, and spiring upward to the height of the gallery, is built in the midst of the acre-great Mejlis, and therein [as in all Kasîm towns] is held the Friday's market; when the nomads, coming also to pray at noon in the mesjid, bring camels and small cattle and samn.

— It was near midday: and seeing but three persons sitting on a clay bench in the vast forsaken Mejlis, I went to sit down by them. One of these had the aspect of a man of the stone age; a wild grinning seized by moments upon his half human visage. I questioned the others who sat on yawning and indifferent: and they began to ask me of my religion. The elf-like fellow exclaimed: " Now were a knife brought and put to the wezand of him! — which billah may be done lawfully, for the Muttowwa says so; and the Nasrâny not confessing, *la îlah ill' Ullah!* pronounce, *Bismillah er-rahman, er-rahîm* (in the name of God the pitiful, the God of the bowels of mercies), and cut his gullet; and *gug-gug-gug!* — this kafir's blood would gurgle like the blood of a sheep or camel when we carve her halse : I will run now and borrow a knife." — " Nay, said they, thou mayest not so do." I asked them, " Is not he a Beduwy ? — but what think ye, my friends ? says the wild wretch well or no ? " — " We cannot tell : THIS IS THE RELIGION. ! Khalîl ; but we would have no violence, — yes, he is a Beduwy." — " What is thy tribe, O thou sick of a devil ? " — " I Harby." — " Thou liest ! the Harb are honest folk : but I think, my friends, this is an *Aûfy*." — " Yes, God's life ! I am of Aûf ; how knowest thou this, Nasrâny ? — does he know everything ! " — " Then my friends, this fellow is a cut-purse, and cut-throat of the pilgrims that go down to Mecca, and accursed of God and mankind ! " The rest answered, " Wellah they are cursed, and thou sayest well : we have a religion, Khalîl, and so have ye." But the Aûfy laughed to the ears, ha-ha-hî-hî-hî ! for joy that he and his people were men to be accounted-of in the world. " Ay billah, quoth he, we be the Haj-cutters." — They laughed now upon him ; and so I left them.

When I complained of the Aûfy's words to the emir, he said — wagging the stick in his hand, " Fear nothing ! and in the meanwhile cure the old man my father : wellah, if any speak a word against thee, I will beat him until there is no breath left in him ! " — The people said of the emir, " He is poor and indebted : " much of their harvest even here is grown for the Bessàm ; who take of them ten or twelve in the hundred : if paid in kind they are to receive for every real of usury one-third of a real more. After this I saw not the emir ; and his son told me he was gone to el-Búkerîeh, to ride from thence in the night-time to Boreyda : they journey in the dark, for fear of the Beduw. Last year Abdullah the emir and fifteen men of Khubbera returning from the Haj, and having only few miles to ride home, after they left the Boreyda caravan, had been stripped and robbed of their thelûls, by hostile Beduw.

The townspeople that I saw at Khubbera were fellahîn-like bodies, ungracious, inhospitable. No man called the stranger to coffee ; I had not seen the like in Arabia, even among the black people at Kheybar : in this place may be nigh 600 houses. Many of their men were formerly Ageylies at Medina ; but the Turkish military pay being very long withheld of late, they had forsaken the service. Khubbera is a site without any natural amenity, enclosed by a clay wall : and strange it is, in this desert town, to hear no creaking and shrilling of suânies ! — The emir and his old father were the best of all that I met with in this place.

— 'The Kenneyny, I thought, will not forsake me !' but now a second day had passed. I saw the third sun rise to the hot noon ; and then, with a weary heart, I went to repose in my lodging. Bye and bye I heard some knocking at the door, and young men's voices without, — " Open, Khalîl ! Zâmil has sent for thee." I drew the bolt ; and saw the cameleer Hásan standing by the threshold ! — " Hast thou brought me a letter ? " — " I have brought none." I led him in to Aly, that the fatherly man might hear his tale. — 'Zâmil recalled me, to send me by the kâfily which was to set out for Jîdda.' — But we knew that the convoy could not be ready for certain weeks ! and I asked Aly, should I mount with no more to assure me than the words of this Hásan ? — it had been better for the old man that I continued here awhile, for his eyes' sake. " Well, said he, go Khalîl, and doubt not at all ; go in peace ! " I asked for vials, and made eye-washes to leave with him : the old sire was pleased with this grateful remembrance.

Some young men took up my bags of good will, and bore them through the streets ; and many came along with us to the gates, where Hásan had left his thelûl. — When we were riding forth I saluted the bystanders : but all those Kahtanites were not of like good mind ; for some recommended me to *Iblîs*, the most were silent ; and mocking children answered my parting word with *maa samawwy !* — instead of the goodly Semitic valediction *maa salaamy*, ' go in peace.'

We came riding four miles over the Nefûd, to the Helàlîeh : the solitary mountain Sàg, which has the shape of a pine-apple, appeared upon our left hand, many miles distant. The rock, say the Arabs, is hard and ruddy-black : — it might be a plutonic outlyer in the border of the sand country. As we approached, I saw other palms, and a high watch-tower, two miles beyond ; of another oasis, el-Búkerîeh : between these settlements is a place where they find " men's bones " mingled with cinders, and the bones of small cattle ; which the people ascribe to the B. Helàl — of whom is the name of the village, where we now arrived. El-Búkerîeh is a station of the cameleers ; and they are traffickers to the Beduw. Some of them are well enriched ; and they traded at first with money borrowed of the Bessàm.

The villagers of Helàlîeh and of Búkerîeh (ancient Sbeya colonies) would sooner be under Zâmil and Aneyza than subject to Hásan Weled Mahanna — whom they call *jabbâr* : they pay tax to Boreyda, five in the hundred. Of these five, one-fourth is for the emir or mayor of the place ; an half of the rest was formerly Ibn Saûd's, and the remnant was the revenue of the princes of Boreyda ; but now Weled Mahanna detains the former portion of the Waháby. — Their corn is valued by measure, the dates are sold by weight. At the Helàlîeh are many old wells " of the B. Helàl." Some miles to the westward is *Tholfa*, an ancient village, and near the midway is an hamlet *Shehîeh* : at half a journey from Búkerîeh upon that side are certain winter granges and plantations of Boreyda. — One cried to us, as we entered the town, " Who is he with thee, Hásan ? " — " A Nasrâny dog, answered the fellow [the only Nejd Arabian who ever put upon me such an injury], or I cannot tell what ; and I am carrying him again to Aneyza as Zâmil bids me." — Such an unlucky malignant wight as my cameleer, whose strange looking discomforts the soul, is called in this country *míshûr*, bewitched, enchanted. When I complained of the elf here in his native village — though from a child he had dwelt at Aneyza, they answered me, " Ay, he is míshûr, *mesquin* ! " — We rode through the streets and alighted where some friendly villagers showed us the kahwa.

Many persons entered with us ; and they left the highest place for the guest, which is next the coffee maker. A well-clad and smiling host came soon, with the coffee berries in his hand : but bye and bye he said a word to me as bitter as his coffee, " How farest thou ? O *adu* (thou enemy of) Ullah ! " Adu is a book word [*v*. p. 97] ; but he was a koran reader. — " I am too simple to be troubled with so wise a man : is every camel too a Moslem ? " " A camel, responded the village pedant, is a creature of Ullah, irrational ; and cannot be of any religion." — " Then account me a camel : also I pray Ullah send thee some of the aches that are in my weary bones ; and now leave finding fault in me, who am here to drink coffee." The rest laughed, and that is peace and assurance with the Arabs ; they answered him, " He says reason ; and trouble not Khalîl, who is over weary." — But the koran reader would move some great divinity matter : " Wherefore dost thou not forsake, Nasrâny, your impure religion (*dîn néjis*) ; and turn to the right religion of the Moslemîn ? and confess with us, ' There is an only God and Mohammed is his Sent One ' ? — And, with violent looks, he cries, I say to thee abjure ! Khalîl." I thought it time to appease him : the beginning of Mawmetry was an Arabian faction, and so they ever think it a sword matter. — " O What-is-thy-name, have done thou ; for I am of too little understanding to attain to your high things." It tickled the village reader's ears to hear himself extolled by a son of the ingenious Nasâra. "No more, I added: the Same who cast me upon these coasts, may esteem an upright life to be a prayer before Him. As for me, was I not born a Christian, by the providence of Ullah ? and His providence is good ; therefore it was good for me to be born a Christian ! and good for me to be born, it is good for me to live a Christian ; and when it shall please God, to die a Christian : and if I were afraid to die, I were not a Christian ! " Some exclaimed, " He has well spoken, and none ought to molest him." The pedant murmured, " But if Khalîl knew letters — so much as to read his own scriptures, he would have discerned the truth, that Mohammed is Seal of the prophets and the apostle of Ullah."

Even here my remedies purchased me some relief ; for a patient led me away to breakfast. We returned to the kahwa ; and about midafternoon the village company, which sat thick as flies in that small sultry chamber, went forth to sit in the street dust, under the shadowing wall of the Mejlis. They bade me be of good comfort, and no evil should betide me : for here, said they, the Arabs are *muhâkimîn*, ' under rulers.' [The Arabs love not to be in all things so straitly governed. I remember a young man of el-Wéshm, of honest parentage, who complained ; that in his Province a man durst not kill one outright, though he found him lying with his sister, nor the adulterer in his house : for not only must he make satisfaction, to the kindred of the slain ; but he would be punished by the laws !] — Some led me through the orchards ; and I saw that their wells were deep as those of Aneyza.

In the evening twilight I rode forth with Hásan. The moon was rising, and he halted at an outlying plantation ; where there waited two Meteyr Beduins, that would go in company with us, — driving a few sheep to their menzil near Aneyza. The mother of Hásan and some of her kindred brought him on the way. They spoke under their breath ; and I heard the hag bid her son ' deal with the Nasrâny as he found good, — so that he delivered himself ! ' — Glad I was of the Beduin fellowship ; and to hear the desert men's voices, as they climbed over the wall, saying they were our rafîks. — We journeyed in the moonlight ; and I sat crosswise, so that I might watch the shadow of Hásan's lance, whom I made to ride upon his feet. I saw by the stars that our course lay eastward over the Nefûd billows. After two hours we descended into the Wady er-Rummah. — The Beduin companions were of the mixed Aarab, which remain in this dîra since the departure of Annezy. They dwell here together under the protection of Zâmil ; and are called *Aarab Zâmil*. They are poor tribe's-folk of Meteyr and of 'Ateyba, that wanting camels have become keepers of small cattle in the Nefûd, where are wells everywhere and not deep : they live at the service of the oases, and earn a little money as herdsmen of the suâny and caravan camels. Menzils of these mixed Arabs remove together : they have no enemies ; and they bring their causes to Zâmil.

An hour after middle night we halted in a deep place among the dunes ; and being now past the danger of the way they would slumber here awhile. — Rising before dawn we rode on by the Wady er-Rummah ; which lay before us like a long plain of firm sand, with much greenness of desert bushes and growth of ghróttha : and now I saw this tree, in the daylight, to be a low weeping kind of tamarisk. The sprays are bitter, rather than — as the common desert tamarisk — saline : the Kasîm camels wreathe to it their long necks to crop mouthfuls in the march. — The fiery sun now rose on that Nefûd horizon : the Beduins departed from us towards their menzil ; and we rode forth in the Wady bottom, which seemed to be nearly an hour over. We could not be many miles from Aneyza : — I heard then a silver descant of some little bird, that flitting over the desert bushes warbled a musical note which ascended on the gamut ! and this so sweetly, that I could not have dreamed the like.

I sought to learn, from my brutish companion, what were Zâmil's will concerning me. I asked, whither he carried me ? Hásan answered, ' To the town ; ' and I should lodge in that great house upon the Gá, — the house of Rasheyd a northern merchant, now absent from Aneyza. We were already in sight of an outlying corn ground ; and Hásan held over towards a plantation of palms, which appeared beyond. When we came thither, he dismounted to speak with some whose voices we heard in the coffee-bower, — a shed of sticks and palm branches, which is also the husbandman's shelter. — Hásan told them, that Zâmil's word had been to set me down here ! Those of the garden had not heard of it : after some talk, one Ibrahîm, the chief of them, invited me to dismount and come in ; and he would ride himself with Hásan to the town, to speak with Zâmil. They told me that Aneyza might be seen from the next dunes. This outlying property of palms lies in a bay of the Wady, at little distance (southward) from el-'Eyarîeh.

They were busy here to tread out the grain: the threshing-floor was but a plot of the common ground ; and I saw a row of twelve oxen driven round about a stake, whereto the inmost beast is bound. The ears of corn can be little better than bruised from the stalks thus, and the grain is afterward beaten out by women of the household with wooden mallets. Their winnowing is but the casting up this bruised straw to the air by handfuls. A great sack of the ears and grain was loaded upon a thelûl, and sent home many times in the day, to Rasheyd's town house.

The high-walled court or kasr of this ground, was a four-square building in clay, sixty paces upon a side, with low corner towers. In the midst is the well of seven fathoms to the rock, steyned with dry masonry, a double camel-yard, and stalling for kine and asses ; chambers of a slave woman caretaker and her son, rude store-houses in the towers, and the well-driver's beyt. The cost of this castle-like clay yard had been a hundred reals, for labour ; and of the well five hundred. An only gateway into this close was barred at nightfall. Such redoubts — impregnable in the weak Arabian warfare, are made in all outlying properties. The farm beasts were driven in at the going down of the sun.

At mid-afternoon I espied two horsemen descending from the Nefûd. It was Kenneyny with es-Sâfy, who came to visit me. — Abdullah told me that neither he nor Bessàm, nor any of the friends, had notice that night of my forced departure from Aneyza. They first heard it in the morning ; when Hàmed, who had bidden the hakîm to breakfast awaited me an hour, and wondered why I did not arrive. As it became known that the Nasrâny had been driven away in the night, the townspeople talked of it in the sûk : many of them blamed the sheykhs. Kenneyny and Bessàm did not learn all the truth till evening ; when they went to Zâmil, and enquired, ' Wherefore had he sent me away thus, and without their knowledge ? ' Zâmil answered, ' That such had been the will of the mejlis,' and he could not contradict them. My friends said, ' But if Khalîl should die, would not blame be laid to Aneyza ? — since the Nasrâny had been received into the town. Khalîl was ibn juâd, and it became them to provide for his safe departure.' Bessàm, to whom nothing could be refused, asked Zâmil to recall

Khalîl ; — 'who might, added el-Kenneyny, remain in one of the outlying jeneynies, if he could not be received again into the town [because of the Waháby malice], until some kâfily were setting forth.' Zâmil consented, and sent for Hásan ; and bade him ride back to Khubbera, to fetch again Haj Khalîl. My friends made the man mount immediately ; and they named to Zâmil these palms of Rasheyd.

Abdullah said that none would molest me here ; I might take rest, until he found means for my safe departure : and whither, he asked, would I go ? — " To Jidda." He said, ' he should labour to obtain this also for me, from Zâmil ; and of what had I present need ? ' — I enquired should I see him again ? — " Perhaps no ; thou knowest what is this people's tongue ! " Then I requested the good man to advance money upon my bill ; a draft-book was in my bags, against the time of my arriving at the coast ; and I wrote a cheque for the sum of a few reals. Silver for the Kenneyny in his philosophical hours was *néjis ed-dínya* " world's dross " ; nevertheless the merchant now desired Hàmed (my disciple in English) to peruse the ciphers ! But that was surely of friendly purpose to instruct me ; for with an austere countenance he said further, " Trust not, Khalîl, to any man ! not even to me." In his remembrance might be my imprudent custom, to speak always plainly ; even in matter of religion. Here, he said, I was in no danger of the crabbed Emir Aly : when I told my friend that the Waháby mule had struck me, " God, he exclaimed, so smite Aly ! " — The bill, for which he sent me on the morrow the just exchange in silver, came to my hands after a year, in Europe : it had been paid at Beyrût. — Spanish crowns are the currency of Kasîm : I have asked, how could the foreign merchants carry their fortunes (in silver) over the wilderness ? it was answered, " in the strong pilgrimage caravans."

This tillage of Rasheyd might be nearly five acres ; a third planted with palms, the rest was unenclosed seed ground, towards the Wady. A former palm ground in this place had been destroyed in the Waháby warfare ; and the well was stopped by the besieged of Aneyza. — There remained but a desert *gá*, when Rasheyd occupied the ground, who planted palms and opened two wells. The tenement, with the young plants, was now valued at six to seven thousand reals. When Ibn Rashîd came before the town two or three years ago, with Boreyda, this jeneyny had been a camping ground of some of his cavaliers : they found here plenty of green forage. — The site was held in ancient times ; for the labourers often cast up potsherds and (burnt) bricks in their ploughing and digging.

Here one Sâlih, a salesman in the clothiers' sûk, was master (for his father) ; a tall fellah-like body, who came hither daily from the town. — If one had chalked on Sâlih's back, *Battâl ibn Battâl* (Good-for-little, son of The-Same), none reading it would not have allowed this to be rightly said. His heart was sore, his wit was short, his head was broken ; and he believed himself to be a sot in the world. — Sâlih began to say to me in the evening to my very amazement ! that he had lately travelled in Europa ; and seen those wonderful countries of the Nasâra ! the churl added, half aghast ! that it cost him " seven hundred liras (£560)." " We sailed, quoth he, from Bosra ; we touched at Stambûl ; we passed an island — the name I have not now in mind : and we landed at London. After that we visited Baris, Vienna and Italia, — great cities of the Nasâra ! " Seven months they were out : a summer month they spent in Londra, — London was wonderful ! In Baris they were a month — Baris was beautiful ! But all the people gazed on their Oriental clothing ! and after that they went clad — besides the Fez cap, as Europeans.

I asked who was his rafîk ? He answered, " *Yûsef Khâlidy*." — Now by adventure I came to Vienna in the days when Khâlidy was there ! and I had remarked two Semitic strangers in red caps in the public places ! And the name was known to me ! because they had visited the learned Orientalist *Von Kremer* : who afterwards wrote it for me (in Arabic), — YÛSEF KHÂLIDY, EL-KUDS : saying that he was a litterate Moslem, a school-teacher [a vaunter of his noble lineage, who has some-turns made profession of Christianity] in Jerusalem, who had some smattering of European languages ; and another day I might meet with him there. — I drew from my bags a bundle of letters ; and suddenly exhibited this writing to the thick eyes of Sâlih ! — who then with inept smiles as if he had been beat, began to say ; it was not himself but his brother that had been the Occidental traveller ! — one Aly, a merchant and landed man at Bosra ; where his palms " exceeded all Aneyza ! " [I have since heard that Aly el-Rasheyd was not a good name there, — and it was said, he had defaulted in his European travels !] he left this Sâlih guardian of his affairs, in his absence. It was told me at Aneyza of the same Aly, ' that upon a time he brought down (here) a stranger from the north, *a kafir*, — but they could not say whether Yahûdy, Christian or Persian; to set up some pumping gear, which should save cost of camel-labour. But ere the work was ready, the Wahábies' short patience was at an end; and the mechanic, who would not be of their religion, was driven from among them.

The words of Aly, returned from the Occident, dwelled in the ears of Sâlih. He dreamed of that dedale world of the Nasâra, full of amazing inventions! and the homely Nejd seemed to his busy broken fantasy a wilderness indeed, in comparison with all that he lately beheld with his brother's eyes in Europa. — And Sâlih, because Khalîl was an European, looked to read in my simple sayings the enigmatology of Solomon.

Ibrahîm was his brother-in-law, — a vile spirit of a pleasant humour, full of ribald jangles; and of some goodness of heart, when not crossed: he was here continually in these days to oversee the harvest work. *Fáhd*, a labouring lad of twenty and younger son of Rasheyd, was over the husbandmen, — an honest soul more than the rest; but of so stockish impenetrable nature that he had not been able to learn letters. And therefore his father banished the lubber to the fields; that at least some profit might arise to the household of his strong arms. Rude was the young man and miserable, but very diligent: he had learned at school no more than to say his prayers.

This wealthy family was new, and of the libertine blood: their lineaments were Arabian, and not swarthy. The old Rasheyd in his youth was a butcher's prentice! and carried camel-flesh and mutton on his head, from house to house. He was afterward a salesman of cotton wares and women's wimples; and very soon became a welfaring tradesman. But of this diverse voices were current in Aneyza, some saying, that " Rasheyd had found a treasure in the Hejâz, as he came again with the Haj from Mecca "; others held, that it was *the blessing*: " Ullah giveth to some, and taketh away from some in the world." — Rasheyd grew, and traded in the North: he became one of the great coast merchants; and now his traffic was chiefly at Bosra. He had merchant sons at Zbeyer and Amâra; and a third in Kuweyt. Beside them a son-in-law of his was a trader in Wady Runnya in the Bîshy country; and another son was lately a tradesman, at Aden. The old man, we heard, would come down in the next caravan. — Joining to these palms was the plantation of a poor family, also of libertine blood: but hardly to be discerned, at least by the eyes of strangers, from the full-blooded citizens.

Ibrahîm was one of the many East Nejders that, some years before, went down to dig for wages in the work of the Suez Canal: he thought there were two hundred men from el-Kasîm. And he had seen, in that enterprise, " the peoples of the Nasâra." — French, Italians, Greeks, whom he supposed to speak one language! Some parcels of the Canal had been assigned to petty undertakers: Ibrahîm wrought in the service of a Frankish woman; and the wife-man, he said, with pistols in her belt, was a stern overseer of her work-folk. There was a Babel of nations, a concourse of men of every hard and doubtful fortune: — and turbid the tide-rips of such an host of adventuring spirits on the shoals! Moslems and Christians — especially the fanatic Oriental Greeks (er-Rûm), were mingled together; and peaceable men were afraid to stray from their fellowships. He saw in these natural enmities only a war of religions: " It was the Rûm, he pretended — they had the most arms — that set upon the Moslemîn." The Greeks are execrated by el-Islam in those parts; so that even among nomads of the Sinai coast I have heard a man say to his adversary — using the Frenjy word, " Thou art worse than a *Greco!* " These disorders were repressed, Ibrahîm said, with impartiality, by the Egyptian soldiery.

Upon a time, he told us, as he and a few together went to Suez, they were waylaid by some murderous Nasâra: but there came a Nasrâny horseman; who spoke to those homicides, with authority; and persuaded them to return. — When they entered Suez, Ibrahîm saw three stripped bodies laid out in the streets, of murdered men! whose faces had been flayed that they should not be known; nevertheless they were known, by the sign of circumcision, to be of Islam.

Ibrahîm had other Suez tales of more pleasure: he could tell of his friendships with some of the Nasâra. Certain Christians, that were their neighbours, invited them upon a time to drink in the booths: but they honestly excusing themselves, the Nasrânies called them to supper; and that was prepared with a bountiful liberality. He related some half-jests and witty words, in their lame Arabic, of his Christian acquaintance. — Many a night Ibrahîm and his mates stole a balk for their cooking and coffee fire, which they buried in the day time. When I exclaimed, thief! he responded, " The timber, though it cost so much, was no man's; but bèlonged to the *Kompanîa!* " Ibrahîm returned from this moral quagmire after twelvemonths' labour; poorer in human heart, richer by a hundred or two of reals. Though not needy at home, he had journeyed seven hundred miles to be a ditcher at Suez! — but such is the natural poverty of the oasis Arabians. Ibrahîm was of the illiberal blood, and brother-in-law of Aly the Western traveller. I found their minds yet moved by the remembrance of the Suez Canal ; and some have said to me, " Might there not be made a canal through Nejd ? " — such, they thought, would be for the advantage of their country.

In this palm-yard I was to pass many a long day. The coffee-bower (*maàshush*, *mujúbbub*) was my shelter from the flaming sun ; and a camel-manger of clay in the well-yard my bed, under the stars, by night. The gnats were not many in this outlying jeneyny ; but the townspeople 'could not now sleep for them' in the stagnant air of Aneyza. From the dripping well sounded all night the shrill chirping of crickets. — Between midnight and morning is heard again the noise of the well-gear, the camels' shoveling tread ; and the voice and stripes of the well-driver. Twice in the day I took water from the well, and gathered sticks over the Nefûd, to boil an handful of rice ; and found a pleasure to watch the little there is of life in that sea of sand. Many plants and insects which I saw formerly in Sinai — that compendium of Arabia — I had not found again in the great peninsula ! The deserts of Barbary are white with the bleached shells of land-snails ; but I found none in the dewless Arabia. Only few seeds of life have passed the great deserts ! we may see here how short are the confines of some living beings. Where are the plants of the border lands ? — we hardly find a weed kind in some oases ! The same small turreted water-snail lives in the thermal (sulphurous) brooks of el-Ally, and Kheybar ; but the frog which riots in all the lukewarm springs at Kheybar, is not found thirty leagues from thence in the like waters of el-Ally, and Thirba. There are none at Aneyza or Boreyda, where are only irrigation waters, nor in any Nejd oases which I have visited : I first heard them again in the brooks of the Mecca (Teháma) country. Here — I had not seen them before in Nejd — were infinite burier beetles, creeping by day upon the desert sand : their prey is the jella of camels. The insect miners apply the robust limb-spades ; and bear up loads of sliding sand on their broad backs, and cast it from them.

The eyyâl, with other lads of the next plantation and from the 'Eyarîeh, wandered round the palms in their idle hours a-gunning.

And every bird was meat for them, beside the hoopoe with his royal crest, — which they told me was sometime king of fowls, and servant to king Solomon ; who commanded Hoopoe to seek him waters in the desert : but one day it pleased Solomon, in his sapient impatience, to curse the gay fowl ; which became unclean, and without pre-eminence. The dunghill bird, flickering by twos and threes in the orchard paths, was most common, of the (few) feathered parasites of the oasis.

Towards midday, when the sun beats sore on their kerchiefed heads, the lads come in from the field labour to the arbour of boughs, to break their fast of dates. After this they will sit on, till the meridian heat be a little abated, which is nigh the assr ; but they are not idle : for their hands are busy about the well-camel harness. Some pull palm-bast (which is steeped in water) ; some roll the fibre betwixt their palms and twist strands. Of two strands they twine a camel rope ; and of two ropes lap up a well cable. All is rudely wrought, with the Arab expedition : but these palm cables will last a good while, and the cost is little or nothing.

First among the eyyâl was a young man from Shuggera, in *el-Wéshm*, a plain country.—[Other places in Wéshm are *Shujjer*, an old village near Shuggera, *Thermidda, Marrat, Otheythia, el-Gerŷen, Kassab, el-Herreyik, el-Jereyfa, Osheyjir* (from hence came the Bessàm family), *el-Ferr'a.* The people of Shuggera are the *Beny Zeyd*, and *es-Suedda* (of Kahtân blood). North of the town is the Nefûd sand *el-Mestewwy*, and of W. *es-Sirr*, and southward a Nefûd wherein is *el-Engéll*, a pit of bubbling water. *El-Toeym* is an hamlet on the north-west, with ruins of "a town fortified with square towers, made for archers." *El-Hajîa*, or *Garat el-Hajaj*, between their town and Thermidda, is a hill with some ruins of stone building and columns : the people say 'it was a place of pilgrimage in the Time of Ignorance.'] That young man, though living by his handy-work, was a gentle endued spirit : his humanity flowed to us in the afternoon sitting, whilst he twisted bast and made strands, in the telling of tales ; and he put a life in his words, as a juggler can impress his will on some inert matter ; and thereto he had a pleasant voice. In music is an entertainment of delectable sounds flowing through our ears, with some picture of the affections ; and they ask not much more in their stories. His telling was such as I had heard at Kheybar. And sometimes he told us tales which showed forth the wisdom of proverbs — as this among them ; *A prudent man will not reveal his name in strange company.* — ' Upon a time, when the thousands of the Haj were at Mûna, a voice was heard above the rumour of the multitude, which cried, " Is there here present *Ibrahîm es-Sâlih* of *er-Russ ?* " A man of Russ, in el-Kasîm, was in the pilgrimage, of this name ; and he responded (hoping to hear of something to his advancement), " It is I." — And the stranger approached, — but suddenly he fell upon him with the sword, and killed him ! for this was the avenger of blood ! and the Kasîm villager was slain in error ; for the homicide was of er-Russ in el-Yémen ! ' — Seldom in the desert life, will one of the popular sort name before a stranger *rûh-hu*, " HIS OWN SOUL " !

But that was more worthy to be heard which the young Shuggery told me of the final ruin of the Waháby — yet unknown in Europe ! — When old blind Feysal died, Abdullah, the elder of his two sons, succeeded him at er-Riâth. But Saûd, the younger, who was of a climbing spirit, withdrew to el-Yémen ; where he gathered a multitude of partizans from the W. Bîshy and W. Dauâsir, and from the Beduin marches. With this host he returned to Nejd : and fought against his brother, and expelled him from the government ; and Abdullah became a fugitive in Ibn Rashîd's country. [*v.* above, p. 50.]

Saûd, now Ruler, would subdue the great tribe of Ateyba ; because they were confederate with Abdullah. — He set out with his armed men and the nomad allies, el-Ajmân, Aarab Dauâsir, el-Murra, Kahtân, Meteyr ; every tribe riding under a banner (*bàrak*), which had been delivered to them by Saûd. — The Ateybân wander dispersedly through immense deserts ; but word had been brought to er-Riâth that a great summer camp of them was pitched at a certain water. Saûd hasted to arrive by forced marches, before any tidings could prevent him. — It was at the hour of prayer, in an afternoon, when they came in sight of the Ateyba ; who were taken at unawares : but Beduw as they stand up in their shirts and have caught their arms, are ready to sally against their foemen. Saûd halted, and would not set-on that day ; because his men and beasts came weary, after great journeys : the Wahábies drew off before the sun set ; and alighted to encamp.

— It happened that the young Shuggery (who that year trafficked to the Aarab with a little borrowed money) was then in the Ateyba menzil, with another salesman, to sell clothing. At dawn the Aarab prayed ; and their sheykhs appointed some of the tribesmen to keep the camp behind them. — " Abide here lads, said their host to the young salesmen ; look ye to yourselves : and the event will be as it may please Ullah."

The Ateybân made haste to meet the advancing enemies, that were six times their number. At the first brunt they bore back Meteyr ; whose bàrak was taken. — And what was seen then ? The Kahtân falling on the flank of their friends ! — they are nearly the best in arms among nomads. In the next moments, they routed Ibn Saûd's horsemen, and took " two hundred " mares ! — nearly all the Waháby's stud, that had been so long in gathering. Then these hornets of men turned and fought against Meteyr ! And the Beduw remembering no more than their old enmities, went on fighting among themselves, in this infernal fray. At length the Kahtân drew off with that they had gotten ; and the valorous Ateyba remained masters of the field.

" Three hundred " were fallen of Saûd's men ; his few tents and the stuff were in the power of Ateyba : and the shorn Waháby wolf returned as he might over the deserts, to er-Riâth. By the loss of the horses the Waháby rule, which had lasted an hundred years, was weakened to death ; never — such is the opinion in Nejd — to rise again ! Founder of the Waháby reform was one Mohammed ibn Abd-el-Wáhâb, a studied religious elder, sojourning in the oasis *eth-Ther'eyyeh*, in East Nejd ; and by blood a Temîmy or, as some report, of Annezy : he won over to his puritan doctrine the Emir of the town, a warlike man, *Saûd ibn Abd-el-Azîz*. The new Waháby power grew apace and prevailed in Nejd : in the first years of this age they victoriously occupied the Hejâz ! Then Mohammed Aly, the Albanian ruler of Egypt, came with a fleet and an army as " the Sultan's deputy, to deliver the Harameyn." — We have seen Ibrahîm Pasha, his son, marching through the midst of Arabia. [*v.* p. 414]. After leaving Aneyza, he took and destroyed eth-Ther'eyyeh which was not afterward rebuilt : but the Wahábies founded their new clay metropolis at " the Rauthas " (er-Riâth). When they had rest from the Egyptian expedition, they ruled again in all Nejd and desert Arabia, as far as el-Yémen ; and the Gulf coast towns yielded tribute : but the Waháby came no more into the Hejâz. — We heard an unlikely rumour, that the Gulf Province el-Hása, occupied by the Turks, had been ceded by them to the Waháby (under tribute).

The Waháby rulers taught the Beduw to pray ; they pacified the wilderness: the villages were delivered from factions; and the people instructed in letters. I found it a reproach in Aneyza to be named *Waháby*: [this, in our plantation, was a mocking word in the mouths of the eyyâl which they bestowed on any lourdane ill-natured fellow.] — The town of er-Riâth with her suburbs, and the next village country about, is all that now remains of the Waháby dominion; which is become a small and weak principality, — such as Boreyda. Their great clay town, lately the metropolis of high Arabia, is silent; and the vast guest-hall is forsaken [the Waháby Prince's clay castle is greater than the Kasr at Hâyil]: Ibn Saûd's servants abandon his unfortunate stars and go (we have seen) to hire themselves to Mohammed ibn Rashîd. No Beduins now obey the Waháby; the great villages of East Nejd have sent back Abdullah's tax-gatherers: but they all cleave inseparably to the reformed religion. — " Abdullah has, they say, grown an over-fat man and unwieldy."

It was not in Saûd's destiny that he should live out half his age. The fatal Waháby sat Ruler two years in er-Riâth, and deceased: it is believed that he died of an old malady. The people say of Saûd, " He was not a good man: all his heart was set upon spoiling and reaving." Abdullah, being thus restored to his dignity, spared the young sons of Saûd, and suffered them to dwell still at er-Riâth. — I heard, a year later, that they had rebelled against him.

The *Morra* (or *Murra*), Kahtân, and other Aarab of el-Yémen, wander northward in the summer as far as el-Wéshm, in Middle Nejd: the young Shuggery knew many Morra, and Kahtân tribesmen, whom he saw every year in his own town: [Jeyber told me that the Kahtân marches reach northward to *el-Harich*.] Also they bring with them the rod-like horns of the Arabian antelope wothŷhi, which inhabits as well their southern sand country. The Ateybân, an honourable and hospitable Beduin nation, are reputed better fighters than the Kahtân; and not soon treacherous. They are rich in sheep and camels; and were never subject to any, save to the old Waháby Princes. They have resisted the yearly incursions of Ibn Rashîd; and the Ottoman expeditions, sent from time to time, from the holy cities, to take tribute of them perforce.

We heard that Mohammed ibn Rashîd had lately sweated his thelûls in their country. We left him *ghrazzai*, keeping his warlike spring holidays in the pastures of the north, beyond the Nefûd. From thence the Prince advanced by *ráhlas* (removes), in the nomad wise, pasturing and encamping, almost to *Sûk es-Sheukh*, at the rivers of Mesopotamia. Who could think that being there his intent was to snatch a prey in the Mecca country ? [a month distant by the pilgrimage caravans !] but none more than the Semitic Asiatics, are full of these fine fetches. You look for them another year ; and they are to-day in the midst of you ! Ibn Rashîd mounted with his armed band, and the Beduw that were with him ; and they rode swiftly over the high deserts, holding wide of the inhabited Kasîm. As he passed by, Ibn Rashîd called to him the riders of Harb, that were assembled at Semîra [p. 321] : and in a few more marches he saw the *Harrat el-Kisshub*, which borders on the Hejâz ! — They found some Ateyba upon a water, and " took them " : the booty was " thirteen thousand " camels [perhaps 130 ; for thus the Arabs use to magnify numbers ; it is a beggarly liberality — a magnanimity which costs them nothing] ; besides sheep without number. In his returning Ibn Rashîd lighted upon certain free Heteym, of the Ateyba alliance ; and he took them also. — An old Ateyba sheykh afterward told me, ' that Ibn Rashîd took but a ferrîj of his tribesfolk.' We might reckon 2000 beyts to " thirteen thousand " camels, defended by more than 2000 men, or as many as the whole Ateyba nation ! — more than enough to have sent their Shammar adversaries home weeping. Ibn Rashîd foraying, in the same dîra, in the former spring, returned empty, for tidings were gotten before him ; and the Aarab had saved themselves in Ibn Saûd's country.

APPENDIX TO CHAPTER XIV

The 'Ateyba Aarab. — *Sherîf-Nâsir,* a tribute-gatherer of the Sherîf of Mecca, and afterward my rafîk to Jidda, named to me above thirty fendies of 'Ateyba, —

Thu Ithbeyt.	*El-Jethêmma.*
El-Muzzeh'ma.	*Ed-Dajîn.*
El-Mufeyrij.	*Es-She'abîn.*
El-Murràshedda.	*El-Berrarîj.*
El-Mugótta.	*Ed-Dehussa.*
Thu Izzyàd.	*El-Meròwha.*
El-'Esomma.	*El-Menajîm.*
Er-Ruthán.	*El-Eyàlla.*
En-N'kussha.	*Erb'a.*
El-She'adda.	*El-Bat'neyn.*
Es-Suta.	*Es-Sh'hebba.*
El-Withanîn.	*Eth-Thuy Bat.*
El-Halleyfát.	*El-Monasîr.*
Ez-Zurán.	*El-Kurzân.*
Wajjidàn.	*Es-Sebbàha.*
El-Hélissa.	*El-Ateyát.*
El-Hessánna.	

He said further; that upon a time when " less than a fourth " of the tribe were gathered against Saûd ibn Saûd, he had numbered their horses — passing in a strait place — 2100. [We have seen that nomads mostly multiply a true number by 10.]

457

CHAPTER XV

WARS OF ANEYZA. KAHTÂN EXPELLED FROM EL-KASÎM

The Waháby governor driven out by the patriot Yahya. Aneyza beleaguered by Ibn Saûd. The second war. A sortie. Aneyza women in the field. The words of Zâmil. A strange reverse. Words of Yahya. A former usurping Emir was cut off by Zâmil. Zâmil's homely life. The Emir's dues. Well-waters of Aneyza. Well-driving and irrigation. Evenings in the orchard. The kinds of palms. Locusts. The Bosra caravan arrives. Violence of Ibrahîm. Rasheyd visits his jeneyny. The hareem. The small-pox. Bereaved households. The jehâd. Arabian opinion of English alms-deeds. The Meteyr Aarab gather to Aneyza. Warfare of the town, with the Meteyr, against the (intruded) Kahtân. Morning onset of Meteyr. Zâmil approaches. Final overthrow and flight of the Kahatîn. Hayzàn is slain. The Kahtân camp in the power of Meteyr. A Moghrebby enthralled among those Kahtân is set free. The Meteyr and the town return from the field. Beduin wives wailing for their dead. 'When the Messiah comes, will he bid us believe in Mohammed?' The great sheykh of the Meteyr. The departure of the Mecca caravan is at hand. Hàmed el-Yahya. The Nasrâny removes to the Kenneyny's palm-ground.

OF the late wars of Aneyza, I may relate that which I heard from my friends' mouths. *Jellowwy* [they told me he yet lived!] brother of the Prince Feysal ibn Saûd, was governor for the Waháby at Aneyza; where he daily vexed the people with his tyrannically invented exactions: for of one he would require dates, of another forage for his horses — without payment, of the rich money; and these under the name of contributions, besides yearly dues. — The chief citizens held secret council; and they determined to put out Jellowwy, and live again under an Emir of their own: the sheykhs debated who among them should lead the town in this enterprise. " He cannot be one of our house, said the Bessàms; for that might encourage Ibn Saûd to bring war on us, hoping to confiscate the riches of the Bessàm." Yahya said, " Well, my patrimony is little; and I am willing to take this danger upon me: but give me fifty swords for those of my young men [of the Kherèysy] that are poor." The Arabs are sudden in execution: and the soon gathered weapons were borne openly through the street; and cast down before Yahya, who sat in the Mejlis, with the Kherèysy. Yahya bade them take up the swords: and cried, " Who would be with us, to free Aneyza, let him now fetch his weapon ! "

The sheykh led them to the governor's gate; and beat loud! A slave answered, "Who knocks?"—"Go tell thy master, Yahya is here with his men; who say, 'Quit this town, at the instant!'"—Then they heard Jellowwy's voice within, "How, my friends! is not this a Friday? and the hour almost noon. Let us go and pray together; and then we will leave you." *Yahya*: "But I vow to God, that when we hear the íthin thou Jellowwy shalt be without the walls of Aneyza." *Jellowwy*: "You shall give me forty thelûls."—"Be it so." At Aneyza there are many thelûls of private persons always standing in their houseyards. The thelûls were fetched, and led before Jellowwy's gate. The Waháby governor with his hareem and servants loaded hastily: they mounted, and rode forth; holding their way to Boreyda. — Even for so short a passage, it seemed they had provided themselves with water: but the black girbies hanging from all the saddle bows, were filled with the Waháby prince's samn! Could an Arabian leave his butter, — as much as his *fulûs*, behind him?

Feysal ibn Saûd marched from er-Riâth to recover the rebellious town; and his vassal Ibn Rashîd came from Jebel Shammar to help him. The besieging host lay encamped on the borders of the Wâdy, till the second year [such is the indigent Arabian warfare!]; when not able to make any impression on the good borough of Aneyza, the Waháby made peace with her citizens, and withdrew from them. This warfare, which they call *harb el-awwel*, the former war, was in the years 1269 — 70 after the Héjra (twenty-five years before my coming to Aneyza). The Emir of the town was then *Abdullah ibn Yahya ibn Seleym*.

Harb eth-thâny, or their second warfare with the Waháby, was after other eight years. In 1278, the part of *Abdullah el-Azîz el-Mohammed*, Prince of Boreyda and an enemy of the Waháby tyranny, had been defeated in that town; and Abdullah fled over to Aneyza: when not yet thinking himself sure, he soon after set out, to go over to the Sherîf of Mecca. But Ibn Saûd sent men to waylay him in the deserts: and as Abdullah el-Azîz came riding, with a company of Aneyza citizens, the Wahábites met with them; and they killed the Emir there. When this tiding was brought to Aneyza, the sheykhs sent out armed riders who overtook the servants of Ibn Saûd, and fought with them in the Nefûd, crying out, "Ye have slain *eth-thaif* (the guest of) Aneyza!"—Abdullah was yet Emir; he had made Zâmil (his brother's son) executive Emir.

This honourable action of the town drew the Waháby upon them again. Mohammed ibn Saûd, brother of Feysal, a muttowwa, came to beleaguer Aneyza, "with all Arabia," namely the East Nejd villagers and Beduins, and those from el-Hása and 'Amàn. Mahanna and Boreyda was with him, and all Kasîm; and the Prince Telâl and Abeyd ibn Rashîd, with the oasis dwellers and Beduins of his jurisdiction — "from as far as the villages of Jauf." This armed multitude lay out in the Nefûd before the clay town, wherein might be not many more than a thousand able to bear arms. — But the companies of 'Amàn and el-Hása followed faintly; and as for the Kusmân, they did but make a show to fight against their countrymen!

Although now beset, the citizens were in no dread: the husbandmen still laboured within their wide town walls. "And why then, I asked, did not the enemy break your clay sûr with cannon shot?" *Answer:* "They were afraid of their own guns more than we — they could not handle them; only one shot fell in an empty space of Aneyza, and did no hurt." I have seen old cannon shot lying in the town, which they say were 'of the Waháby'; and perhaps those iron balls — so rudely round! had been wrought by the hammer of Arabian sânies.

The capital feat of arms in their second warfare was thus related to me by our well-driver: one midnight Zâmil sent out 200 matchlockmen, to lie in wait by a spring in the Wady, nigh the 'Eyarîeh. "Fear nothing, said he, for I shall be at hand to support you." When the Waháby waterers descended before day, the men of Aneyza shot at them; and the noise was heard in the enemy's menzil. This drew on them the Nejd horsemen; of whom two presently falling! the rest held off: and the day beginning to lighten, there arrived Abdullah el-Yahŷa, with his Kherèysy. A swarm of armed men came then running down from the Waháby host; and Abdullah shouted, "Upon them Khereysy!" Then the Aneyza companies advancing together, and firing, the enemy gave back, and a Waháby banner was taken: the men of Aneyza presently arrived at the tents; and the outer camp was won. — There fell many of Ibn Saûd's part; and not a few who, running whereas they thought they saw their own bàraks, lighted upon the hostile Khereysy. — The warfare of Arabians is like a warring of gipsies: they use not even to fence their menzil with an earthwork!

The Aneyza housewives were come forth to the battle driving asses and girbies. They poured out water for the thirsty fighters; and took up the wounded men. — Abdullah fell, leading the bold Kherèysy ! then the good wives laid the young sheykh upon an ass, and carried him to the town. Zâmil, galloping hither and thither (he alone of Aneyza came on horseback), shouted now to stay the slaughter, *Imbârak! Imbârak! la túktillu el-Moslemîn,* "The Lord hath blessed us, slay not our brethren in the religion!"

But suddenly there was a woeful reverse ! — When the fighting was even at their tents, there went in some principal persons to the muttowwa commander, who sat still in his pavilion : " Up, they cried, Muhâfuth ! and show thyself without the tent, that our people may take heart." " Friends, responded the holy block, kneel with me, and let us pray." And whilst they prayed, as men that wrestled for their lives, there fell a shower — it covered not so much as the breadth of the Wady ! — which quenched the matches of the lately victorious townsmen ; who with now dead firearms in their hands, and two miles from home, remained without defence. They retreated ; but were overridden by the Nejd horsemen, " more than a thousand lances " : and there perished in that flight " two hundred " of Aneyza : [this were a fifth or sixth part of all their fighting men.]

— There is a song from this time made of the patriot father Yahŷa ; who had been valiant in war, whilst yet sufficient of eye and limb, and a good marksman. — He came wandering pensively from the field to an outlying palm-ground : and went in there to repose awhile in the shadow. Certain of Aneyza who lay watching in that place hailed him, ' What did he seek ? ' — " It is a fast-day with me, and oh this thirst ! " The pious sheykh was wont twice — that is every third and fifth day in the week, to fast ; and when they fast they drink not till the going down of the sun. — " Is this a fasting day, when the enemies are broken ? drink O father of Abdullah, drink ! " — " Ay, the Lord be praised for this day ! *though I should lose Abdullah, and beside him a son.*" Abdullah's flesh wound — a shot in the thigh, was whole in a month ; and a noble life was spared to Aneyza. As for his other sons, the old patriot's blood had been a little alloyed in the children of his second marriage. — This is a country where the wounded can have no surgery for the love of God or reward.

Two lesser skirmishes are recorded of those months'-long warfaring of " *all Arabia,*" before the two-span-thick clay wall of Aneyza. Telâl became impatient of the time spent fruitlessly ; and the rest, so long absent from their households, were out of heart, and yet imperilling their lives. At last Mohammed ibn Saûd, the Muttowwa, levied the camp ; and returned with his lost labour to er-Riâth. On the town part were fallen " four hundred " men. — Only a war of religion could hearten Arabians, who are free warfarers, weakly obeying their sheykhs, to assault defended walls. Few besides Yahŷa, will jeopardy life and goods for the public welfare.

The people of Aneyza count themselves sufficient, ' if such were the mind of their sheykhs, to obtain the sovereignty of Nejd. God, say they, has given them mild and peaceable Emirs ; but were Zâmil of such stomach as Ibn Rashîd, all the country might be brought under Aneyza which lies between Wady Daûasir and Damascus.'—Yet Aneyza citizens have sometimes been aggressors ; as in that ill-counselled and worse led expedition of theirs against Ibn Rashîd, " to have his head," which was miserably defeated by Abeyd ; who in the pursuit slew so many of them : whereof the warrior-kassâd made the pæan before recorded. [*v. p. 42.*]

Zâmil has been a fortunate leader in all the warfare of his time. — When, in his early manhood, he was captain of the Aneyza troop (in a long expedition of the Waháby) in 'Amàn, he already manifested the strategist spirit and moderation which are natural to him. Zâmil's age might now be forty-five years or somewhat more. They say, ' that all their Emirs, within memory, have been men of not common worth and understanding.' Nevertheless I heard of one — perhaps he was not of the sheykhly lineage, who had usurped the Emir's dignity. He went down in a pilgrimage to Mecca : and as they returned, and were come nigh to Aneyza, he alighted to rest out the hot noon in the shadow of some outlying palms. Zâmil in the town heard of it, and mounted with his partizans ; and they found him, and slew him : there was a blood feud betwixt him and Zâmil. — When Zâmil's hands are not clean from blood, what may we look for from the other Arabs ?

There is now a good season in Aneyza, after the Waháby drought ; where Zâmil even by his own merit is first among a generation of patriots : in no place have I seen men live more happily than in this oasis. Zâmil, born in the Emir's kindred, had never travelled : wise in council, he governed the town in peace ; and upon him was all their hope in any stormy time. He has six or seven male children : a younger son, Aly (at this time a lad of thirteen years), is thought to resemble him. Zâmil, son of a former Emir, did not immediately inherit the dignity; he succeeded the next Emir, his uncle Abdullah: for their successions are not all, as in the desert life, from sire to son. Zâmil is a perfect Moslem; and he would have been a good man in any religion. He is religious for conscience's sake; and somewhat more, outwardly, because he is Emir: I have seen him stand apart in the fields at by-hours to pray. He was full of a coldly-serene circumspection, to deal prudently with the conflicts of minds in a government: all with him was fair and softly in the town. None ever appealed to him, even of the sudden-tongued and (in their causes) loud-crying Beduw, whom he did not appease with a gentle smiling wisdom, and dismiss with fair words; at the least he said, *B'il-kheyer insh' Ullah* : ' It shall be well, please God.' Zâmil can prudently dissemble displeasures; and is wont — with that lenity, which we call in Europe ' the Christian mind,' to take all in patience.

Soon after the sun is risen Zâmil breakfasts; and then he withdraws to a jeneyny of his, nigh at hand, for an hour: he will return here in the afternoon, giving himself a reasonable liberty from public cares. When the sun is rising with the first heat, Zâmil walks into the town, carrying his sword: and passes by to the Mejlis, giving the *salaam aleyk* to the salesmen seated in their shops, and to any meeting him in the street. The Emir goes on to the porch of audience, where the most days he sits but a moment; for in the homely living of a free township, there are few causes: I saw no daily mejlis in Aneyza. — The Emir *filsûf* is shortly at leisure; and may be commonly found in the forenoon hours visiting the jeneynies of patricians that are in the number of his friends. He comes home to the midday prayer; and afterward he sits in his hall or in the kahwa of some principal person. If there be any public affairs, the sheykhs assemble where Zâmil is; and their sitting may last till the assr, when the íthin calls all men again from worldly business to the public prayer.

He ' was not liberal,' this only could be alleged against Zâmil. A man radically honest, and of the old gentle blood, cannot add to his substance, but by the somewhat strait keeping of his own: el-Kenneyny said, " Zâmil lays up all he gets *míthil tájir*, like a tradesman." This humour in Zâmil was the more marked because Abdullah, before him, had been fool-large, so that he died indebted.

The Emir's dues were some two and a-half, and some five, upon corn; and of dates seven and a-half in the hundred: houses, shops and cattle are free. The rich foreign merchants [they were richer than Zâmil], whose homes are at Aneyza, pay a moderate contribution, in money, to the Emir: it is ten reals yearly. The most of so considerable revenues—which were full of envy—comes not to Zâmil's purse: there are expenses of the public service, and especially for the mothîf. — A customs' gatherer, an ill-looking fellow, visited us in Rasheyd's palms: he came spying through the jeneynies to take account of the harvest.

These were sultry days; and in the hours of most heat I commonly found (in our arbour) 97° F., with heavy skies. The wells are of five, four and three fathoms, as they lie lower towards the Wady; and a furlong beyond, the water is so nigh that young palm-sets in pits should need no watering after a year or two. The thermometer in the well-water — which in this air seemed cool, showed 87° F. A well sunk at the brim of the Nefûd yields fresh ground-water; but wells made (lower) in the gá are somewhat brackish. Corn, they say, comes up better in brackish ground; and green corn yellowing in sweet land may be restored by a timely sprinkling of salt. All the wells reek in the night air: the thermometer and the tongue may discern between well-waters that lie only a few rods asunder: the water is cooler which rises from the sandstone, and that is warmer which is yielded from crevices of the rock.

Of all wells in Aneyza, there is but one of purely sweet water! — the sheykhs sent thither to fill their girbies in the low summer season. It is in the possession of a family whose head, Abu Daûd, one of the emigrated Kusmân, lived at Damascus; where he was now sheykh of the Ageyl [Vol. I. p. 49, Vol. II. p. 61], and leader of the rear guard in the Haj caravan. [Abu Daûd told me, he had returned but once, in twenty-five years, for a month, to visit his native place!] — Water from Rasheyd's two wells was raised incessantly by the labour of five nâgas; and ran down in sandy channels (whereby they sowed water-melons, in little pits, with camel jella) to a small pool, likewise bedded in the loamy sand. These civil Arabians have not learned to burn lime, and build themselves conduits and cisterns. The irrigation pond in Kasîm lies commonly under the dim shadow of an undressed vine; which planted in the sand by water will shoot upon a trellis to a green wood. We have seen vines a covert for well-walks at Teyma. The camels labour here under an awning of palm branches.

The driving at the wells, which began in the early hours after midnight, lasts till near nine, when the day's heat is already great. — At the sun-rising you may see women (of the well-driver's family) sit with their baskets in the end of the shelving well-walk, to feed the toiling camels: they wrap a handful of vetches in as much dry forage cut in the desert; and at every turn the nâga receives from her feeder's hands the bundle thrust into her mouth. The well-cattle wrought anew from two in the afternoon, till near seven at evening, when they were fed again. The well-driver, who must break every night his natural rest, and his wife to cut trefoil and feed the camels, received three reals and a piastre — say thirteen shillings, by the month; and they must buy their own victual. A son drove the by-well, and the boy's sisters fed his pair of camels. They lived leanly with drawn brows and tasting little rest, in a land of idle rest. [Whenever I asked any of these poor souls, How might he endure perpetually? he has answered the stranger (with a sigh), That he was inured thereto from a child, and — *min Ullah!* the Lord enabled him.] — But the labouring lads in the jeneyny fared not amiss; they received 4*d.* a day besides their rations: they have less when hired by the month. I saw the young Shuggery, a good and diligent workman, agree to serve Rasheyd six months for nine reals and his rations; and he asked for a tunic (two-thirds of a real more), which was not denied him. There is no mention in these covenants of harbour; but where one will lie down on the sand, under the stars of Heaven, there is good night-lodging (the most months of the twelve), in this summer country.

The lads went out to labour from the sunrise: and when later the well-pool is let out, *yurussûn el-má*, they distributed the water running down in the channels; and thus all the pans of the field, and the furrows of the palms are flushed, twice in the day. — Of this word *russ* is the name of the Kasîm oasis er-Russ. The *jet* was flooded twice a week; and this trefoil, grown to a foot high, may be cut every fifteen days [as at Damascus]; — the soil was mere sand. The eyyâl wrought sheltered in the bower, as we have seen, in the sultry afternoons and heard tales, till vespers. Then one of them cried to prayers; the rest ran to wash, and commonly they bathed themselves in the well. It was a wonder then to see them not doubt to leap down, one upon the neck of another, from an height of thirty feet! to the water; and they plashed and swam sometime in that narrow room: they clambered up again, like lizards, holding by their fingers and toes in the joints of the stone-work. After they had prayed together, the young men laboured abroad again till the sun was setting ; when they prayed, and their supper was brought to them, from the town. Supper is the chief meal in Arabia ; and here it was a plentiful warm mess of sod wheaten stuff, good for hungry men.

The work-day ended with the sun, the rest is *keyif* : only after a long hour must they say the last prayers. The lads of the garden (without coffee or tobacco) sing the evening time away ; or run chasing each other like colts through the dim desert. On moonlight nights they played to the next palm-yards ; and ofttimes all the eyyâl came again with loud singing and beating the tambûr. The ruder merrymake of the young Arab servants and husbandmen was without villany ; and they kept this round for two or three hours : or else all sitting down in a ring together at the kasr gate, the Shuggery entertained his fellows with some new tales of marvellous adventures.

In every oasis are many date-kinds. The most at Aneyza are the *rótb* or ' moist ' (good for plain diet), of the palm-kind which is called the *es-Shúkra*, or Shuggera, of that Wéshm oasis. They have besides a dry kind, both cool and sweet, which is carried as sweetmeat in their caravan journeys. Only the date-palm is planted in Arabia: the *dôm*, or branched nut-palm, is a wilding [in the Hejâz and Teháma], — in sites of old settlements, where the ground-water is near ; and in some low desert valleys. The nut's woody rind (thrice the bigness of a goose's egg) is eaten ; and dry it has the taste of ginger-bread. — When later in the year I was in Bombay, I found a young man of Shuggera at the Arab stables : we walked through the suburbs together, and I showed him some cocoa-nut palms, — " Ye have none such, I said, in Nejd ! " " Nay, he responded austerely, not these : there is no *báraka* with them ! " — a word spoken in the (eternal) Semitic meaning, " All is vanity which is not bread."

The fruit-stalks hanged already — with full clusters of green berries — in the crowns of the female palms : the promise was of an abundant harvest, which is mostly seen after the scarcity and destruction of a locust-year. Every cluster, which had inclosed in it a spray of the male blossom, was lapped about with a wisp of dry forage ; and this defended the sets from early flights of locusts. The Nejd husbandman is every year a loser by the former and latter locusts, which are bred in the land ; besides what clouds of them are drifted over him by the winds from he knows not whither. This year there were few hitherto and weak flights ; but sometimes with the smooth wind that follows the sun-rising the flickering _jarâd_ drove in upon us : and then the lads, with palm branches of a spear's length, ran hooting in the orchard and brushed them out of the trees and clover. The fluttering insects rising before them with a _whir-r-r !_ were borne forth to the Nefûd. The good lads took up the bodies of the slain crying, " They are good and fat ; " and ran to the arbour to toast them. If I were there, they invited me to the feast : one morrow, because the hakîm said nay, none any more desired to eat ; but they cast out their scorched locusts on the sand, in the sun, where the flies devoured them. — " The jarâd, I said, devour the Beduw, and the Beduw devour the jarâd ! " — words which seemed oracles to that simple audience ; and Sâlih repeated Khalîl's proverb in the town.

The poor field labourers of Rasheyd's garden were my friends : ere the third day they had forgiven me my alien religion, saying they thought it might be as good as their own ; and they would I might live always with them. Ay, quoth the honest well-driver, " The Nasâra are of a godly religion, only they acknowledge not the Rasûl ; for they say, _Mohammed is a Beduwy_ [I thought the poor soul shot not wide from the mark, — Mohammedism is Arabism in religion] : there is no other fault in them ; and I heard the sheykhs saying this, in the town." — Some days a dulí ' bewitched ' lad laboured here, whom the rest mocked as _Kahtâny_ — another word of reproach among them [as much as man-eater], because he was from Khubbera. Other two were not honest, for they rifled my bags in the night time in Rasheyd's kasr : they stole sugar — the good Kenneyny's gift ; and so outrageously ! that they had made an end of the loaf in few days. A younger son of Rasheyd had a hand in their villany. The lads were soon after dismissed ; and we heard they had been beaten by the Emir Aly.

— It was past ten o'clock one of these nights, and dim moonlight, when Ibrahîm and Fáhd were ready with the last load of corn : — then came Ibrahîm and said to me, " We are now going home to stay in the town ; and the jeneyny will be forsaken." This was a weary tiding of ungenerous Arabs two hours before midnight when I was about to sleep ! — " What shall I do ? " — " Go with us ; and we will set thee down at the Kenneyny's palm-ground, or at his house." — " His jeneyny is open and not inhabited ; and you know that I may not return to the town : Zâmil sent me here." — " Ullah curse both thee and

Zâmil ! thou goest with us : come ! or I will shoot thee with a pistol ! [They now laid my things upon an ass.] — Drive on Fáhd ! — Come ! Khalîl, here are thieves ; and we durst not leave thee in the jeneyny alone." — " Why then in Kenneyny's outlying ground ? " — " By Ullah ! we will forsake thee in the midst of the Nefûd ! " — " If you had warned me to-day, I had sent word to Zâmil, and to Kenneyny : now I must remain here — at least till the morning." Then the slave snatched my mantle ; and in that he struck me on the face : he caught up a heavy stone, and drew back to hurl this against my head. I knew the dastardly heart of these wretches, — the most kinds of savage men are not so ignoble ! — that his wilful stonecast might cost me one of my eyes ; and it might cost my life, if I the Nasrâny lifted a hand upon one of the Moslemîn ! Here were no witnesses of age ; and doubtless they had concerted their villany beforehand. Whilst I felt secretly in the bags for my pistol, lest I should see anything worse, I spoke to the lubber Fáhd, ' that he should remember his father's honour.' A younger son of Rasheyd — the sugar-thief, braved about the Nasrâny with injuries ; and, ere I was aware in the dark, Ibrahîm struck me from behind a second time with his fist, upon the face and neck. In this by chance there came to us a young man, from the next plantation. He was a patient of mine ; and hearing how the matter stood, he said to them, " Will ye carry him away by night ? and we know not whither ! Let Khalîl remain here at least till the morning." Ibrahîm, seeing I should now be even with him, sought words to excuse his violence : the slave pretended falsely, that the Nasrâny had snibbed him (a Moslem) saying *Laanat Ullah aleyk*, " The curse of God be upon thee ! " — And he cried, " Were we here in Egypt, I had slain thee ! " — Haply he would visit upon the Nasrâny the outrages of the Suez Canal !

An Aneyza caravan was now journing from Bosra ; and in it rode the sire Rasheyd. Sâlih was called away the next forenoon by a Meteyry ; a man wont to ride post for the foreign merchants to the north. But in his last coming down he lost their budget and his own thelûl ; for he was resting a day in the Meteyr menzil, when they were surprised by the murderous ghrazzu of Kahtân. He told us, that the foreriders of the kâfily were come in ; and the caravan — which had lodged last night at *Zilfy*, would arrive at midday. This messenger of good tidings, who had sped from the town, hied by us like a roebuck :

I sat breathless under the sultry clouded heaven, and wondered at his light running. Ibrahîm said, " This Beduwy is nimble, because of the camel milk which is yet in his bones ! " — The caravan [of more than 200 camels] was fifteen days out from Bosra ; they had rested every noon-day under awnings.

— The day of the coming again of a great caravan is a day of feasting in the town. The returned-home are visited by friends and acquaintances in their houses ; where an afternoon guest-meal is served. Rasheyd now sat solemnly in that great clay beyt, which he had built for himself and the heirs of his body ; where he received also the friendly visitation of Zâmil. He had brought down seventeen loads (three tons nearly) of clothing, from his son at Kuweyt, to sell in Aneyza, for a debt of his — 3000 reals — which he must pay to the heirs of a friend deceased, *el-Kâthy*. His old servants in this plantation went hastily to Aneyza, to kiss the master's hand : and ere evening portions were sent out to them from his family supper.

I heard the story of Rasheyd from our well-driver. The Arabs covet to have many children ; and when his merchandise prospered, this new man bought him wives ; and ' had the most years his four women in child at once : and soon after they were delivered he put out the babes to suck, so that his hareem might conceive again : since forty years he wrought thus.' — " Rasheyd's children should be an hundred then, or more ! but how many has he ? " The poor well-driver was somewhat amazed at my putting him to the count ; and he answered simply, " But many of the babes die." The sire, by this butcherly husbandry in his good days, was now father of a flock ; and, beside his sons, there were numbered to him fifteen daughters. — In his great Aneyza household were more than thirty persons.

The third morrow came Rasheyd himself, riding upon a (Mesopotamian) white ass, from the town, to view his date trees in Nejd. The old multiplier alighted solemnly and ruffling in his holiday attire, a gay yellow gown, and silken kerchief of Bagdad lapped about his pilled skull. He bore in his belt — as a wayfarer come from his long journey — a kiddamîyyah and a horse-pistol ; or it might be (since none go armed at home) the old Tom-fool had armed himself because of the Nasrâny ! He was a comely person of good stature, and very swarthy : his old eyes were painted. He roamed on his toes in the garden walks, like the hoopoes, to see his palms and his vetches. Rasheyd came after an hour to the arbour, where I sat — he had not yet saluted the kafir ; and sitting down, 'Was I (he asked) that Nasrâny ? — he had heard of me.' I made the old tradesman some tea ; and it did his sorry heart good to heap in the fenjeyn my egg-great morsels of sugar. — I regaled him thus as oft as he came hither ; and I heard the old worldling said at home, 'That Khalîl is an honest person ; and wellah had made him tea with much sugar.'

He said, to soothe my weariness, 'It would not be long, please Ullah, till I might depart with a kâfily.' Then he put off his gay garments, and went abroad again in his shirt and cotton cap. — He returned to the arbour in the hot noon ; and sitting down the old man stripped himself ; and having only the tunic upon his knee, he began to purge his butcher's skin from the plague of Egypt accrued in the caravan voyage. Before the half afternoon he wandered again in the garden, and communed with the workmen like a poor man of their condition. Rasheyd looked narrowly upon every one of their tools, and he wrought somewhat himself ; and began to cleanse the stinking bed of the pool. Coming again thirsty, he went to drink of my girby, which was hanging to the air upon a palm branch ; and untying the neck he drank his draught from the mouth, like any poor camel-driver or Beduwy. — The maintenance of this outlying possession cost him yearly 200 reals ; the greater part was for camel labour. The fruits were not yet fully so much worth.

No worldly prosperity, nor his much converse abroad, could gentilize Rasheyd's ignoble understanding ; he was a Waháby after the straitest Nejd fanaticism. A son of this Come-up-from-the-shambles was, we saw, the Occidental traveller ! Another son, he who had been the merchant in Aden, came down with him in the caravan : he opened a shop in the sûk, and began selling those camel-loads of clothing stuffs. The most buyers in the town were now Meteyr tribesmen ; and one of these "locusts" was so light-handed, that he filched a mantle of Rasheyd's goods, worth 10*s.*, for which the old man made fare and chided with his sons. That son arrived one day from the town, to ask the hakîm's counsel ; he was a vile and deceitful person, full of Asiatic fawning promises. 'He would visit Aden again (for my sake) ; and sail in the same ship with me. He left a wife there, and a little son ; he had obtained that his boy was registered a British subject : if I would, he would accompany me to India.' — I sojourned in his father's plantation; and they had not made me coffee.

— 'What, said some one sitting in Rasheyd's hall (in the town), could bring a Nasrâny from the magnific cities of Europa into this poor and barren soil of Nejd?' The old merchant responded, "I know the manners of them! this is a Frenjy, and very likely a poor man who has hired out his wife, to win money against his coming home; for, trust me, they do so all of them." — The tale was whispered by his young sons in the jeneyny: and one afternoon the Shuggery asked me of it before them all, and added, "But I could not believe it." "Such imaginations, I exclaimed, could only harbour in the dunghill heart of a churl; and be uttered by a slave!" He whispered, "Khalîl speak not so openly, for here sits his son (the sugar-thief)! and the boy is a tale-bearer." — When the Shuggery had excused himself, I asked, "Are ye guiltless of such disorders?" He answered, "There are adulteries and fornication among them, secretly."

We should think their hareem less modest than precious. The Arabs are jealous and dissolute; and every Moslem woman, since she may be divorced with a word, fears to raise even a wondering cogitation in such matter. Many poor hareem could not be persuaded by their nearest friends, who had called the hakîm, to fold down so much of the face-cloth from their temples as to show me their blear eyes. A poor young creature of the people was disobedient to her mother, sooner than discover a painful swelling below the knee. Even aged negro women [here they too go veiled], that were wall-eyed with ophthalmia, would not discover their black foreheads in hope of some relief. And they have pitifully answered for themselves, 'If it be not the Lord's will here, yet should they receive their sight — where miserable mankind hope to inherit that good which they have lacked in this world! — *f' il-jinna* in the paradise.' Yahŷa's wife was prudent therein also: for when she had asked her old lord, she with a modest conveyance through the side-long large sleeves of the woman's garment, showed her painful swollen knees to the hakîm. This is their strange fashion of clothing: the woman's sleeves in Kasîm are so wonderfully wide, that if an arm be raised the gown hangs open to the knee. One must go therefore with heedfulness of her poor garment, holding the sleeves gathered under her arms; but poor townswomen that labour abroad and Beduin house-wives are often surprised by unseemly accidents. Hareem alone will sit thus in the sultry heat ; and cover themselves at the approach of strangers.

The days were long till the setting out of the samn caravan : Zâmil had delayed the town expedition, with Meteyr, against the intruded Kahtân, until the coming home of the great northern kâfily. The caravan for Mecca would not set out till that contention were determined. To this palm ground, two and a half miles from Aneyza, there came none of my acquaintance to visit the Nasrâny. Their friendship is like the voice of a bird upon the spray : if a rumour frighten her she will return no more. I had no tidings of Bessàm or of Kenneyny ! Only from time to time some sick persons resorted hither, to seek counsel of the hakîm ; who told me the Kenneyny sent them or Zâmil, saying, " In Khalîl's hand is a *báraka* ; and it may be that the Lord will relieve thee."

The small-pox was nearly at an end in the town. Sâlih had lost a fair boy, a grief which he bore with the manly short sorrow of the Moslemîn. A young daughter of Kenneyny died ; and it was unknown to him, three days ! — till he enquired for her : then they of his household and his friends said to him, " The Lord has taken the child ; and yesterday we laid her in the grave." — But Abdullah blamed them with a sorrowful severity ; " Oh ! wherefore, he said, did ye not tell me ? " — at least he would have seen her dead face. It pained me also that I was not called, — I might have been a means to save her.

I asked Sâlih to lend me some book to read : and he brought me the next day from Aneyza a great volume, in red leather, full of holy legends and dog-eared, that was, he said, " of the much reading therein of the hareem." Many of the townswomen can read in the Waháby countries ; and nearly all the children are put to learn their letters : and when a child, as they say, " is grown to a sword's length," he is taught the prayers. Sâlih lent me also a bundle of the brave Arabic gazette ; now some months old, but new in these parts of the world, and they had been brought down in the caravan. Therein I read of the jehâd : Sâlih watched me as I spelled forth, and at last he enquired, 'Were I now satisfied ? — the Sultàn [of el-Islam] is broken.' Sâlih's wooden head was full of divining malice ; and he looked that this should please me well. He found himself, in the gazette of Stambûl, so many [political, military and European] strange words, that he could not always read with understanding.

— I read to the company, how 'the Engleys sent medicines and physicians, at their proper cost, to cure the sick and wounded Moslems ; besides clothing and food, and money ; and that many wealthy persons had given out of their private purses very great sums' [which to the self-seeking misery of the Arabs appear to be beyond belief] ! and I said to them. " Well, what think ye ? those were thankworthy deeds ? were not they good to the Moslemîn ? " *Answer :* " We thank them not ; may Ullah confound them, and all kafirs ! but we give God thanks, who has moved the heathen to succour el-Islam."

When I had been more than three weeks in this desolation, I wrote on a leaf of paper, *katálny et-taab wa ej-jû'a,* ' I am slain with weariness and hunger ' ; and sent these words to Kenneyny. — I hoped ere long to remove, with Zâmil's allowance, to some of the friends' grounds ; were it Bessàm's jeneyny, on the north-east part of the town [there is the *black stone,* mentioned by some of their ancient poets, and 'whereof, they say, Aneyza itself is named'] ; or the palms of the good father Yahŷa, so kind to my guiltless cause. My message was delivered : and at sunrise on the morrow came Abdullah's serving lad, who brought girdle-bread and butter, with a skin of butter-milk ; and his master's word bidding me be of good comfort ; and they (the friends) would ere long be able to provide for my departure. — I could not obtain a little butter-milk (the wine of this languishing country) from the town. Sâlih answered, ' That though some hareem might be secretly milk-sellers in Aneyza, yet could not he, nor any of his household, have an hand in procuring it for me.' Some poor families of Meteyr came to pitch by the water-pits of abandoned stubbles nigh us ; and I went out to seek a little milk of them for dates or medicines. Their women wondered to see the (English) colour of the stranger's hair ; and said one to another, " Is this a grey-haired man, that has tinged his beard with saffron ? " — " Nay, thou mayest see it is his nature ; this is certainly a red-man, *min ha'l shottût,* from those rivers (of Mesopotamia) ; and have we not seen folk there of this hue ? — but where, O man, is thy béled ? "

The sheukh of Meteyr were now in Aneyza, to consult finally with Zâmil and the sheykhs for the common warfare. The Kahtân thought themselves secure, in the khála, that no townsfolk would ride against them in this burning season ; and as for el-Meteyr, they set little by them as adversaries. — Zâmil sent word to those who had thelûls in the town, to be ready to mount with him on the morrow. He had "written" for this expedition "six hundred" thelûls. The ghrazzu of the confederate Beduw was "three hundred thelûls, and two hundred (led) horses."

The day after el-Meteyr set forward at mid-afternoon. But Zâmil did not ride in one company with his nomad friends : the Beduins, say the townspeople, are altogether deceitful — as we have seen in the defeat of Saûd the Waháby. And I heard that some felony of the Aarab had been suffered two years before by Aneyza ! It is only Ibn Rashîd riding among the rajajîl and villagers, who may foray in assurance with his subject Beduw.

Zâmil rode out the next day, with "more than a thousand" of the town : and they say, "When Zâmil mounts, Aneyza is confident." He left Aly to govern at home : and the shops in the sûk were shut ; there would be no more buying or selling, till the expedition came home again. The morning market is not held, nor is any butcher's meat killed in these days. Although so many were in the field with Zâmil, yet 'the streets, said Sâlih, seemed full of people, so that you should not miss them !' I enquired, " And what if anyone opens his dokan — ? " *Answer :* " The emir Aly would send to shut it : but if he persisted, such an one would be called before the emir, and beaten : " only small general shops need not be closed, which are held by any old broken men or widows.

The Emir writes the names of those who are to ride in a ghrazzu ; they are mostly the younger men of households able to maintain a thelûl. Military service falls upon the substantial citizens — since there can be no warfaring a-foot in the khála : we hear not that the Waháby, poor in all military discipline, had ever foot soldiers. The popular sort that remain at home, mind their daily labour ; and they are a guard for the town. The Emir's sergeant summons all whose names have been enrolled to mount with Zâmil (on the morrow). Two men ride upon a warfaring thelûl ; the radîf is commonly a brother, a cousin, or client [often a Beduwy] or servant of the owner. — If one who was called be hindered, he may send another upon his dromedary with a backrider. If he be not found in the muster with the Emir, and have sent none in his room, it may be overlooked in a principal person ; but, in such case, any of the lesser citizens might be compelled. Zâmil was an easy man to excuse them who excused themselves ; for if one said, " Wellah, Sir, for such and such causes, I cannot ride," the Emir commonly answered him, " Stay then."

It was falsely reported that the Kenneyny was in the expedition. The infirm man sent his two thelûls with riders (which may be found among the poor townsmen and Beduins). None of Rasheyd's sons were in the field : Sâlih said, " We have two cousins that have ridden for us all." — A kinsman of Zâmil, who was with him, afterward told me their strength was 800 men, and the Meteyr were 300. Some said, that Aneyza sent 200 thelûls, that is 400 riders ; others said 500 men. — We may conjecture that Zâmil called for 300 thelûls of the town ; and there went forth 200, with 400 men, which were about a third of all the grown male citizens; and of Meteyr rode nearly 150 tribesmen. With the town were not above 20 led mares, of sheykhly persons. Kahtân were reckoned (in their double-seeing wise) 800 men; perhaps they were as many as 400, but (as southern Aarab) possessing few firearms. They had many horses, and were rich in great cattle : it was reported, ' Their mares were 150 ' ; but say they had 70 horses.

The townsmen rode in three troops, with the ensigns of the three great wards of Aneyza ; but the town banners are five or six, when there is warfare at home.

Early in the afternoon I heard this parley in the garden, between Fáhd and a poor Meteyry, — who having no thelûl could not follow with his tribesmen. *Fáhd :* " By this they are well in the way ! and please Ullah they will bring back the heads of them." — " Please Ullah ! the Lord is bountiful ! and kill the children from two years old and upward ; and the hareem shall lament ! " I said to them, " Hold your mouths, kafirs ! and worse than kafirs." *The Beduwy :* " But the Kahtân killed our children — they killed even women ! " The Meteyr were come in to encamp nigh the town walls ; and two small menzils of theirs were now our neighbours. These southern Aarab were such as other Beduw. I heard in their mouths the same nomad Arabic ; yet I could discern that they were of foreign dîras. I saw their girbies suspended in cane-stick trivets. Some of them came to me for medicines : they seemed not to be hospitable ; they saw me tolerated by Zâmil, and were not fanatical.

In these parts the town-dwellers name themselves to the Aarab, and are named of them again, *el-Moslemîn*, — a word used like *Cristiani* in the priests'-countries of Europe ; first to distinguish the human generation, and then in an illiberal straitness of the religious sense. One day I saw camels feeding towards the Wady ; and in the hope of drinking milk I adventured barefoot to them, over Rasheyd's stubbles and the glowing sand : and hailed the herdsmen ! The weleds stood still ; and when I came to them they said, after a little astonishment, " The nâgas, O man, are not in milk nor, billah, our own : these be the town camels ; and we are herding them for the *Moslemîn*." One said, " Auh ! be'st thou the hakîm ? wilt thou give me a medicine ? — and if thou come to our booths when the cattle are watered, I will milk for thee mine own nâga ; and I have but her : were our cattle here, the Beduins would milk for thee daily." — The long day passed ; then another, which seemed without end ; and a third was to me as three days : it had been told me, ' that my friends were all in the ghrazzu,' — and now Aly reigned in the town ! Sâlih bade me be easy ; but fair words in the Arabs are not to trust ; they think it pious to persuade a man to his rest.

Tidings of this foray came to Boreyda, and messengers rode out to warn the Kahtân. Zâmil made no secret of the town warfare, which was not slackness in such a politic man, but his long-suffering prudence. ' He would give the enemies time, said Sâlih, to sue for peace ' : — how unlike the hawks of er-Riâth and Jebel Shammar !

— The Kahtân were lately at *el-'Ayûn*; and the ghrazzu held thither. But in the way Zâmil heard that their menzils were upon *ed-Dellamîeh*, a water between the mountain Sàk and er-Russ. The town rode all that day and much of the night also. By the next afternoon they were nigh er-Russ ; and alighted to rest, and pitched their (canvas) tents and (carpet) awnings. Now they heard that the enemy was upon the wells *Dókhany*, a march to the southward. As they rode on the morrow they met bye and bye with the Meteyr ; and they all alighted together at noon. — The scouts of Meteyr brought them word, that they had seen the booths of the Aarab, upon *Dókhany !* and so many they could be none other than the Kahtân ; who might be taken at unawares ! — The young litterates of Aneyza boasted one to another at the coffee fires, " We shall fight then to-morrow upon the old field of *Jebel Kezâz*, by *Dókhany* ; where the Tubb'a (lord the king, signeur) of el-Yémen fought against the *Wâilyîn* (sons of Wâil, that is the Annezy), — Koleyb, sheykh Rabî'a ; and with them B. Temîm and Keys " [Kahtân against Ishmael : — that was little before the héjra]. The berg Kezâz is ' an hour ' from the bed of the Wady er-Rummah.

Zâmil and the town set forward on the morrow, when the stars were yet shining : the Meteyr had mounted a while before them, and Dókhany was at little distance. In this quarrel it was the Beduins which should fall upon their capital foemen ; and Zâmil would be at hand to support them. The town fetched a compass to envelope Kahtân from the southward.

Meteyr came upon their enemies as the day lightened : the Kahtân ran from the beyts, with their arms, sheykhs leapt upon their mares ; and the people encouraged themselves with shouting. Then seeing they were beset by Meteyr they contemned them, and cried, *jàb-hum Ullah*, " A godsend ! " — but this was a day of reckoning upon both parts to the dreary death. The Meteyr had " two hundred " mares under them ; but they were of the less esteemed northern brood. The *Kahatîn* in the beginning were sixty horse-riders. Then thirty more horsemen joined them from another great menzil of theirs pitched at little distance. The Kahtân were now more than the ghrazzu of Meteyr, who finally gave ground.

— Then first the Kahtân looked about them ; and were ware of the town bands coming on ! The Kahatîn, of whom not many were fallen, shouted one to another, in suspense of heart, " Eigh ! is it Ibn Rashîd ? — but no ! for Ibn Rashîd rides with one bàrak : but these ride like townsfolk. — Ullah ! they are *hâthr !* " — Now as the town approached some knew them, and cried, " These be the Kusmân ! — they are the *Zuâmil* (Zamils, or the people of Zâmil)." When they saw it was so, they hastened to save their milch-camels.

— Zâmil, yet distant, seeing Beduin horsemen driving off the camels, exclaimed, " Are not these the *Moslemîn* [those of our part] ? " " Nay ! answered him a sheykh of Meteyr (who came riding with the town to be a shower of the way in the khála), they are billah el-Kahtân ! " The town cavaliers were too few to gallop out against them. And now the Kahtân giving themselves to save the great cattle forsook their menzil : where they left booths, household stuff, and wives and children in the power of their foemen.

The horsemen of Meteyr pursued the flying Kahtân ; who turned once more and repulsed them: then the Aneyza cavaliers sallied to sustain their friends. The rest of the Meteyr, who alighted, ran in to spoil the enemies' tents. — And he and he, whose house-wives were lately pierced by the spears of Kahtân, or whose babes those fiend-like men slew, did now the like by their foemen, they thrust through as many hareem, and slit the throats of their little ones before the mothers' faces, crying to them, "Oh, wherefore did your men so with our little ones that other day!" Some frantic women ran on the spoilers with tent-staves; and the Meteyries, with weapons in their hands, and in the tempest of their blood, spared them not at all. — Thus there perished five or six wives, and as many children of Kahtân.

In their most tribulation a woman hid her husband's silver, 600 reals [that was very much for any Beduwy]! in a girby; and stript off her blue smock — all they wear besides the haggu on their hunger-starved bodies: and hanging the water-skin on her shoulder, she set her little son to ride upon the other. Then she ran from her tent with a lamentable cry, *weyléy, weyléy!* woe is me! and fled naked through the tumult of the enemies. The Meteyr, who saw it, supposed that one of the people had spoiled the woman, and thought shame to follow her; yet some called to her, to fling down that she bore on her shoulder: but she, playing the mad woman, cried out, 'She was undone! — was it not enough to strip a sheykh's daughter? and would they have even this water, which she carried for the life of her child!' Others shouted, to let the woman pass: and she fled fast, and went by them all; — and saved her good-man's fortune, with this cost of his wife's modesty.

There fell thirty men of Kahtân, — the most were slain in the flight; and of Meteyr ten. — These returned to bury their dead: but the human charity is here unknown to heap a little earth over the dead foemen!

A woman messenger came in from the flying Kahtân, to Zâmil. The town now alighted at the wells (where they would rear up the awnings and drink coffee): she sought safe conduct for some of their sheykhs, to come and speak with him; which Zâmil granted. — Then the men returned and kissing him as suppliants, they entreated him, 'since their flocks, and the tents and stuff, were now (as he might see) in the hands of Meteyr, to suffer them to come to the water, that they might drink and not perish.' They had sweated for their lives, and that summer's day was one of greatest heat; and having no girbies, they must suffer, in flying through the desert, an extremity of thirst.

But who might trust to words of Beduin enemies! and therefore they bound themselves with a solemn oath, — *Aleyk âhad Ullah wa amàn Ullah, in mâ akhûnak! el-khàyin yakhûnhu Ullah* — "The covenant of the Lord be with thee, and His peace! I will not surely betray thee! who betrayeth, the Lord shall him betray."

Such was the defeat of the intruded Kahtân, lately formidable even to Ibn Rashîd. [Ibn Saûd had set upon them last summer here at Dókhany! but the Kahtân repulsed the decayed Waháby!] — This good success was ascribed to the fortune of Zâmil: the townsmen had made no use of their weapons. The Meteyr sent messengers from the field to Ibn Rashîd, with a gift of two mares out of the booty of Kahtân. — Even Boreyda would be glad, that the malignant strange tribesmen were cast out of the country. — Many Kahtân perished in their flight through the khála: even lighter wounds, in that extremity of weariness and thirst, became mortal. They fled southward three days, lest their old foes, hearing of their calamity, should fall upon them: we heard, that some Ateyba had met with them, and taken "two hundred" of the saved milch camels. Certain of them who came in to el-Ethellah said, that they were destroyed and had lost 'an hundred men': — so dearly they bought the time past [now two full years] of their playing the wolf in Nejd!

When I asked what would become of the Kahtân? the Shuggery answered, "The Beduw are hounds, — that die not; and these are sheyatîn. They will find twenty shifts; and after a year or two be in good plight again." — "What can they do now?" — "They will milk the nâgas for food, and sell some camels in the villages, to buy themselves dates and cooking vessels. And they will not be long-time lodged on the ground, without shelter from the sun: for the hareem will shear the cattle that remain to them, and spin day and night; and in few weeks set up their new woven booths! besides the other Kahtân in the south will help them." — We heard after this, that the defeated Kahtân had made peace with the Ateybân; and reconciled themselves with Ibn Saûd! But how might they thus assure themselves? had the Kahtân promised to be confederate with them against Ibn Rashîd?

— Hayzàn was fallen! their young Absalom; 'a young man of a thievish false nature,' said the Beduin foes: it was he who threatened me, last year, in a guest-chamber at Hâyil: Hayzàn was slain for that

Meteyry sheykh, who lately fell by his hand in the north. A sheykhly kinsman of the dead sought him in the battle : they ran together ; and Hayzàn was borne through the body with a deadly wide wound. The young man was very robust for a Beduwy, and his strong hand had not swerved ; but his lance-thrust was fended by a shirt of mail which his foeman wore privily under his cotton tunic. That Meteyry was a manly rider upon a good horse, and after Hayzàn, he bore down other five sheykhs. — When the fortune of the day was determined by the coming of " the Zuâmil," he with his brother and his son, yet a stripling [principal sheykhs' sons soon become horsemen, and ride with their elders to the field], and a few of his Aarab, made prize of eighty milch camels ! In that day he had been struck by lances and shot in the breast, eleven times ; but the dints pierced not his " Davidian " shirt of antique chain work. They say, that the stroke of a gun-shot leaves upon the body fenced by such harness, only a grievous bruise.

A brother of Hayzàn, Terky, was fallen ; and their sheykhly sister. She was stripped, and thrust through with a spear ! — because Kahtân had stripped and slain a Meteyry sheykh's daughter. The old Kahtân sheykh — father of these evil-starred brethren, hardly escaped upon a thelûl. Hayzàn, mortally wounded, was stayed up in the saddle, in the flight, till evening ; and when they came to the next *golbân* (south of Dókhany) the young sheykh gave up the ghost : and his companions cast his warm body into one of those well-pits.

In the Kahtân camp was found a poor foreigner, — a young Móghreby derwish ! who committed himself to the charity of the townspeople. In the last pilgrimage he came to Mecca ; and had afterward joined himself to a returning kâfily of Kusmân, hoping to go up from their country to el-Irâk. But as they marched he was lost in that immense wilderness : and some wandering Kahtân found him, — what sweetness to be found, in such extreme case, by the hand of God's providence ! Yet the Kahtân who saved him, not regarding the religious bounty of the desert, made the young Moor their thrall ; and constrained him to keep sheep : and as often as they approached any village they bound him, that he should not escape them. — They had so dealt with me, and worse, if (which I once purposed) I had journeyed with some of them. — The returning " Moslemîn " brought the young Móghreby with them to Aneyza, where he remained a guest in the town, until they might send him forward. He had been with Kahtân since the winter, and said with simplicity, "I knew not that life, but they made me a Beduwy, and wellah I am become a Beduwy." — And in truth if one live any time with the Aarab, he will have all his life after a feeling of the desert.

— The fifth evening we saw a nomad horseman on the brow of the Nefûd, who descended to the booths : that was the first of them who returned from the warfare. Zâmil and the town came again on the morrow ; and we heard them, riding home under our horizon, more than two hours, with a warlike beating of tambûrs ; they arrived, in three troops, under their banners. All the Beduins came not yet : there was a wrangling among them — it is ever so, in the division of the booty. A Beduwy will challenge his own wheresoever he find it ; and as Meteyr had been lately " taken " in the north by Kahtân, many a man lighted on his cattle again, in the hand of a tribesman. The same afternoon we saw sheep driven in : they were few, and the most of them had been their own. Those who now returned from the battle brought heavy tidings, — six men were fallen of the menzils nigh us ! that were thirty households. As they heard it, the house-wives of the dead ran forth wailing, and overthrew their widowed booths. The Beduins removed when the morrow lightened, and returned to the khála. — This was the calamity of Kahtân ! and there was peace between Boreyda and Aneyza.

Now in Aneyza the jemmamîl made ready their gear ; for the samn kâfily was soon to set out for Mecca. The *zemmel*, bearing camels, were fetched in from the nomads ; and we saw them daily roaming at pasture in the Nefûd about us. A caravan departed in these days with dates and corn for Medina.

Zâmil and Kenneyny rode out one day to the Wady together, where Zâmil has a possession ; and they proposed to return by Rasheyd's plantation, to visit Khalîl. But in the hot noon they napped under the palms : Abdullah woke quaking with ague ! and they rode the next way home.

One evening there came a company of young patricians from Aneyza ; to see some sheep of theirs, which the Beduin herds had brought in, with a disease in the fleece. The gallants stripped off gay kerchiefs and mantles ; and standing in the well-troughs, they themselves washed their beasts. When it was night, they lay down on the Nefûd sand to sleep, before the shepherds' tents. Some of them were of the fanatical Bessàms; and with these came a younger son of the good Abdullah. The lad saluted me affectuously from his father; who sent me word ' that the kâfily would set out for Mecca shortly; and I should ride with Abd-er-Rahmàn (his elder son) '; I had languished now six weeks in Rasheyd's plantation.

Ere they departed on the morrow, one of the young fanatical Bessàms said to me : — " Oh, that thou wouldst believe in Mohammed ! Khalîl, is it true, that ye are daily looking for the coming again of the Messîh, from heaven? and if Aysa (Jesus) bid thee then believe on Mohammed, wilt thou obey him, and be a Moslem ? But I am sure that the Lord Aysa will so command thee ! I would that he may come quickly; and we shall see it ! " — The same day there visited us the two young men of Rasheyd's kindred that had ridden in the ghrazzu: they were very swarty, and plainly of the servile blood. One of them, who had been an Ageyly in Damascus, told me that he lately bought a horse of perfect form and strength in el-Yémen, for five hundred reals; and he hoped to sell him in es-Sham for as much again. Coffee was prepared for any who visited the jeneyny, by the young sons of Rasheyd; and in these days — the last in June — they brought cool clusters of white grapes, which were ripening in the vine.

The great sheykh of Meteyr also visited me : he was sent by Zâmil. Though under the middle age, he began to have the dropsy, and could not suffer a little fatigue : the infirm man came riding softly upon a carpet, which was bound in his thelûl-saddle. The *istiska* is better known as a horse sickness among them : he knew not what ailed him, — have not all men a good understanding of the diseases and nurture of their cattle rather than of themselves and their children ! he received my word with a heavy-heart. The horse sweats much, and is not less than man impatient of thirst : and the beginning of this evil may be, in both, a surfeit of cold water in a chilled skin. When he heard his malady would be long he said, " Yâ Khalîl ! wilt thou not go with us ? *henna rahîl*, the Aarab journey to-morrow (to their summer dîra, in the north) : thou shalt lodge in my booth; and they will serve thee well. We will milk for thee : and when thou hast cured me I will also reward thee." — " Have patience in God ! " — " I know that the blessing is from Ullah; but come Khalîl : thou wilt be in surety with us; and I will send thee again to Aneyza, or if it like thee better to Kuweyt or to Bosra." — " I am shortly to set out with the samn caravan." — " Well, that will be — we heard it now in the town — the ninth day from to-day ; come with us, and I will send thee ere that day : thereto I plight my faith." — It had been pleasant, in this stagnant heat, to breathe the air of the khála and be free again, among the Aarab ; and regaled with léban I might recover strength. I sent therefore to ask counsel of the Kenneyny : and my friend wrote again, that I could adventure with them. But the time was short, and I durst not trust in the Beduin faith.

I had passed many days of those few years whose sum is our human life, in Arabia ; and was now at the midst of the Peninsula. A month ! — and I might be come again to European shipping. From hence to the coast may be counted 450 desert miles, a voyage of at least twenty great marches in the uneasy camel-saddle, in the midsummer flame of the sun ; which is a suffering even to the homeborn Arabs. Also my bodily languor was such now, that I might not long sit upright ; besides I foresaw a final danger, since I must needs leave the Mecca kâfily at a last station before the (forbidden) city. There was come upon me besides a great disquietude : for one day twelve months before, as I entered a booth (in Wady Thirba), in the noon heat, when the Nomads slumber, I had been bitten by their greyhound, in the knee. I washed the wound ; which in a few days was healed, but a red button remained ; which now (justly at the year's end) broke, and became an ulcer ; then many like ulcers rose upon the lower limbs (and one on the wrist of the left hand). — Ah ! what horror, to die like a rabid hound in a hostile land.

The friends Kenneyny and Bessàm purchased a thelûl, in the Friday market, for my riding down to Jidda, where the beast, they thought, might fetch as much as they gave ; and if no, one of their kinsmen, who was to come up from Jidda in the returning kâfily would ride home upon her. — I received then a letter from the good Bessàm : ' All (he wrote) is ready ; but because of the uncivil mind [Waháby malice] of the people he would not now be able to send me in his son's company ! I must excuse it. But they had provided that I should ride in the company of Sleymàn el-Kenneyny [v. p. 381], to whom I might look for that which was needful [water, cooking, and the noon shelter] by the way.' — He ended in requesting me to send back a little quinine : and above his seal was written — " God's blessing be with all the faithful Moslemîn."

I sent to Zâmil asking that it might be permitted me to come one day to town, to purchase somewhat for the journey, and bid my friends farewell : but my small request could not be vouchsafed, — so much of the Waháby misery is in the good people of Aneyza.

The husbandmen of the garden — kind as the poor are kind, when they went into Aneyza on Fridays, purchased necessary things for me : the butcher's family showed me no hospitable service. — Hâmed el-Yahŷa came one of these last evenings, to visit me, riding upon his mare. This first of my returning friends — a little glozing in his words, excused himself, that he had not sooner come to see me. The hakîm being now about to depart, he would have medicines for his mother, who sent me his saddlebag-ful of a sort of ginger cakes (which they prepare for the caravan journeys), and scorched gobbets of fresh meat, that will last good a month. Hàmed was a manly young franklin with fresh looks, the son of his mother — but also the son of his father, of great strength, of an easy affectuous nature, inclined to be gentle and liberal : his beard was not yet begun to spring. The old mare was his own : to be a horseman also belongeth to nobility. He came well clad, as when these townsmen ride abroad ; his brave silken kerchief was girded with the head-band and perfumed with attar of rose, from Mecca. The young cavalier led a foal with him, which he told me he found tied in a Kahtân booth : Hàmed brought the colt home ; and said, excusing himself, ' that it had otherwise perished ! ' The colt now ran playing after the dry mare, as if she were his kindly dam. The mare had adopted the strange foal ! and wreathing back her neck she gazed for him, and snorted softly with affection.

We supped together ; and Hàmed told of their meeting with the Kahtân. He rode upon his mare, armed with a (Frankish) double gun ; but complained to me that one on horseback could not re-load. This was, I answered, their loose riding upon a pad (*maârakka*) ; I bade him use stirrups, and he held it a good counsel. — Such was the dust of the battle, that Hàmed could not number the Kahtân tents, which he supposed might be 300. The Mecca caravans pass by Dókhany ; but this year he said we should shun it, because of the fetor of the unburied carcases (of Kahtân). I enquired, if the kâfily marched through all the day's heat ! — " Nay, for then the (molten) samn might leak through the butter-skins." He thought we should journey by night, for fear of Kahtân ; and that our kâfily would be joined at er-Russ with the butter convoy descending from Boreyda. He sat on another hour with me, in the moonlight : Hàmed would not, he protested, that our friendship were so soon divided, — after my departure we might yet write one to the other. So mounting again ; he said, ' he would ride out to the gathering-place of the kâfily to bid me God-speed, on the day of our departure ' : — but I met with him no more.

It is the custom in these countries [v. Vol I. p. 42], that all who are to journey in a kâfily should assemble at a certain place, without the town : where being mustered by the vigil of the day of their departure ; when the sun is risen they will set forth.

CHAPTER XVI

SET OUT FROM EL-KASÎM, WITH THE BUTTER CARAVAN FOR MECCA

Abdullah el-Kenneyny — a last farewell. Sleymàn, a merchant-carrier in the kâfily. The camp at 'Auhellàn. An *emir el-kâfily*. The setting-out. Noon halt. Afternoon march. The evening station. Er-Russ. The Abàn mountains. Ibrahîm, the emir. Simûm wind. The last desert villages. A watering. Beduin rafîks. — *Are not these deserts watered by the monsoon rains?* An alarm. Caravaners and Beduins. The landscape seyls to the W. er-Rummah. Camels and cameleers. 'Afîf, a well-station. Signs of hunters. Caravan paths to Mecca. *Wady Jerrîr*. Mountain landmarks, *Thúlm* and *Khâl*. Water tasting of alum. The Harrat el-Kisshub. Thirst in the caravan. Sleymàn's opinion of English shippers. A pleasant watering-place. *El-Moy:* cries in the evening menzil. *Er-Rukkaba*. Beduins. *Sh'aara* watering. Harrat *'Ashîry*. *Er-Rî'a*. *Es-Seyl* [Kurn el-Menâzil]. Head of the W. el-Humth. New aspect of Arabia. The caravaners about to enter Mecca take the ihràm. The Hathèyl. The *ashràf* descend from Mohammed. Arrive at the 'Ayn (ez-Zeyma). *Mecca is a city of the Tehâma.* The Nasrâny leaves the Nejd caravan, at the station before Mecca; and is assailed by a nomad sherîf.

ON the morrow, when the sun was setting, there came a messenger for me, from Abdullah el-Kenneyny; with the thelûl upon which I should ride to Jidda. We mounted; and Rasheyd's labourers who had left their day's toil, and the poor slave woman, approached to take my hand; and they blessed me as we rode forth. We held over to the Kenneyny's plantation: where I heard I should pass the morrow. The way was not two miles; but we arrived, after the short twilight, in the dark: there my rafîk forsook me; and I lay down in that lonely palm ground to sleep, by the well side.

At the sun-rising I saw Abdullah el-Kenneyny! who arrived riding upon an ass, before the great heat. A moment later came Abdullah el-Bessàm, on foot: "Ah! Khalîl, said he, taking my hand, we are abashed, for the things thou hast suffered, and that it should have been here! but thou knowest we were overborne by this foolish people." Kenneyny asked for more of that remedy which was good for his mother's eyes; and I distributed to them my medicines. Now came Hàmed es-Sâfy; and these friends sat on with me till the sun was half an hour high, when they rose to return to breakfast, saying they would see me later. In the afternoon came es-Sâfy again; who would perfect his writing of English words. — None of my other friends and acquaintance came to visit the excommunicated Nasrâny.

The good Kenneyny arrived again riding upon the ass, in the cooling of the afternoon, with his son Mohammed. He was feeble to-day, as one who is spent in body and spirit ; and I saw him almost trembling, whilst he sat to talk with me : and the child playing and babbling about us, Abdullah bade him be still, for he could not bear it. I entreated him to forget whatsoever inquietude my coming to Aneyza had caused him : he made no answer.

It was now evening : and Sleymàn arrived, upon a thelûl, with his little son. He was riding-by to the caravan menzil, and would speak the last words with his kinsman, who lent him money for this traffic. Abdullah called to him, to set down the child ; and take up Khalîl and his bags. — I mounted with Sleymàn ; and we rode through a breach of the town wall, which bounded Kenneyny's tillage. Abdullah walked thus far with us ; and here we drew bridle to take leave of him : I gave hearty thanks, with the Semitic blessings ; and bade this gentle and beneficent son of Temîm a long farewell. He stood sad and silent : the infirm man's mortal spirit was cut off (Cruel stars !) from that Future, wherefore he had travailed — and which we should see ! [Three months later Abdullah el-Kenneyny went down in the pilgrimage to Mecca : and returned, by sea, to Bosra. But his strength failed him ; and he sought in vain a better air at *Abu Shahr*, on the Persian Coast. — In the summer of the third year after, Sleymàn a younger son of Abdullah el-Bessàm, wrote to me, from Jidda ; "Poor el-Kenneyny died some months ago, to our grief, at Bosra : he was a good man and very popular."]

We went on riding an hour or two in that hollow roadway worn in the Nefûd, by which I had once journeyed in the night-time in the way to Khubbera. It was dark when we came to the caravan menzil ; where Sleymàn hailed his drivers, that had arrived before us, with the loads. They brought us to our place in the camp ; which, for every fellowship, is where they have alighted and couched their camels. Here was a coffee fire, and I saw Sleymàn's goat-skins of samn (which were twenty-four or one ton nearly) laid by in order : four of them, each of fifteen sah (of el-Kasîm), are a camel's burden, worth thirty reals, for which they looked to receive sixty in Mecca. — Many persons from Aneyza were passing this last night in the camp with their outfaring friends and brethren. This assembling place of the Mecca kâfily is by the outlying palms, *'Auhellàn* ; where are said to be certain *ancient caves hewn in the sand-rock!* I only then heard of it, and time was not left me to search out the truth in the matter.

— But now first I learned, that no one in the caravan was going to Jidda ! they were all for Mecca. Abdullah el-Kenneyny had charged Sleymàn ; and the good Bessàm had charged his son (*Abd-er-Rahmàn*) for me, that at the station next before Mecca [whether in Wady Laymûn, or the Seyl] they should seek an *'adamy*, to convey me (without entering the *hadûd* or sacred limit) to Jidda.—The good Kenneyny, who had never ridden on pilgrimage, could not know the way ; and his perspicuous mind did not foresee my final peril, in that passage.

In our butter kâfily were 170 camels, — bearing nearly 30 tons of samn — and seventy men, of whom forty rode on thelûls, — the rest were drivers. We were sorted in small companies ; every master with his friends and hired servants. In each fellowship is carried a tent or awning, for a shelter over their heads at the noon stations, and to shadow the samn,— that is molten in the goat-skins (*jerm*, pl. *jerûm*) in the hot hours : the *jerûm* must be thickly smeared within with date syrup. Each skinful, the best part of an hundredweight, is suspended by a loop (made fast at the two ends) from the saddle-tree. Sometimes a jerm bursts in the caravan journeys, and the precious humour is poured out like water upon the dust of the waste : somewhiles the bearing-camels thrust by acacia trees, and jerms are pricked and ripped by the thorny boughs. It was well that there rode a botcher in the kâfily ; who in the evening station amended the daily accidents to butter-skins and girbies. — All this samn, worth more than £2000 in Mecca, had been taken up, since the spring, in their traffic with the Beduw : the Aneyza merchants store it for the time in marble troughs.

There is an emir, named by Zâmil, over such a great town caravan : he is one of the princely kin ; and receives for every camel a real. — El-Kenneyny had obtained a letter from Zâmil, commending me to the emir ; and charging him to provide for my safety, when I should leave the kâfily " at the Ayn." — We sat on chatting about the coffee fire, till we were weary ; and then lay down to sleep there, on the Nefûd sand.

Rising with the dawn, there was yet time to drink coffee. The emir and some young Aneyza tradesmen in Mecca, that would return with the kâfily, had remained all night in the town : they would overtake us riding upon their fleet *'omanîas*. [The thelûls of the Gulf province ' Omân or 'Amân ' are of great force and stature ; but less patient of famine and thirst than some lesser kinds. A good 'omanîa, worth 50 to 70 reals at Aneyza, may hardly be bought in the pilgrim season at Mecca — where they are much esteemed — for 150 reals.] When the sun was up the caravaners loaded, and set forward. We soon after fell into the Wady er-Rummah ; in which we journeyed till two hours before noon : and alighted on a shaeb, *es-Shibbebîeh*, to rest out the midday heat (*yugŷilûn*). In that place are some winter granges of Aneyza, of ruinous clay building, with high-walled yards. They are inhabited by well-drivers' families, from the autumn seed time till the early harvest. Here we drew brackish water, and filled our girbies. The day's sultry heat was great ; and I found under the awnings 105° F. Principal persons have canvas tents made Beduin-wise, others have awnings of Bagdad carpets. I saw but one or two round tents — bargains from the coast, and a few ragged tilts of hair-cloth [that I heard were of the Kahtân booty !] in poorer fellowships. — Sleymàn el-Kenneyny's six loads of samn were partly Abdullah's : he was a jemmâl, and the beasts were his own.

It might be three o'clock ere they removed, — and the hot sun was going down from the meridian : the signal is made with a great shout of the Emir's servant, ES-SHÎ-ÎL ! In the next instant all awnings are struck, the camels are led-in and couched, the caravaners carry out the heavy butter-skins ; and it is a running labour, with heaving above their strength, to load on their beasts, before the kâfily is moving : for the thelûl riders are presently setting forth ; and who is unready will be left in the hindward. The emir's servant stands like a shepherd before the kâfily — spreading his arms to withhold the foremost ! till the rest shall be come up ; or, running round, he cries out on the disobedient. Now they march ; and — for the fear of the desert — the companies journey nigh together. Our path southward was in the Wady Rummah, which is a wide plain of firmer sand in the Nefûd. The Abàn mountains are in sight to the westward, covered with haze. [The Abànát may be seen, lifted up in the morning twilight, from the dunes about Aneyza.] At sun-setting, we alighted by other outlying granges — that are of er-Russ, *el-Hajnowwy*, without the Wady : we were there nearly abreast of Khubbera.

Their tents are not pitched at night; but in each company the awning is now a sitting carpet under the stars; and it will be later for the master to lie on. One in every fellowship who is cook goes out to gather sticks for fuel; another leads away the beasts to browse, for the short half-hour which rests till it is dark night. With Sleymàn went three drivers: the first of them, a poor townsman of Aneyza, played the cook in our company; another was a Beduwy. — After an hour, the supper dish (of seethed wheaten stuff) is set before us. Having eaten, we sip coffee: they sit somewhile to chat and smoke tobacco; and then wrapt in our cloaks we lie down on the sand, to sleep out the short hours which remain till toward sunrising.

An hour before the dawn we heard shouted, 'THE REMOVE!' The people rise in haste; the smouldering watch-fires are blown to a flame, and more sticks are cast on to give us light: there is a harsh hubbub of men labouring; and the ruckling and braying of a multitude of camels. Yet a minute or two, and all is up: riders are mounted; and they which remain afoot look busily about them on the dim earth, that nothing be left. — They drive forth; and a new day's march begins; to last through the long heat till evening. After three hours journeying, in the desert plain, we passed before er-Russ; — whose villagers, two generations ago, spared not to fell their palm stems for a breastwork, and manfully resisted all the assaults of Ibrahîm Pasha's army. The Emir sent a thelûl rider to the place for tidings: who returned with word, that the samn caravaners of er-Russ were gone down with the Boreyda kâfily, which had passed by them two days before. Er-Russ (which they say is greater than Khubbera) appears as three oases lying north and south, not far asunder. In the first, *er-Ruêytha*, is the town; in the second, *er-Rafŷa*, a village and high watch-tower showing above the palms; the third and least is called *Shinàny*. Er-Russ is the last settlement southward and gate of el-Kasîm proper. — We are here at the border of the Nefûd; and bye and bye the plain is harsh gravel under our feet: and we re-enter that granitic and basaltic middle region of Arabia, *which lasts from the mountains of Shammar to Mecca*. The corn grounds of er-Russ are in the Wâdy er-Rummah; their palms are above.

I saw the Abànát — now half a day distant westward, to be a low jebel coast, such as Ajja, trending south. There are two mountains one behind other ; and the bed of the Wâdy (there of no great width) lies betwixt them. The northern is named *el-Eswad*, and oftener *el-Esmar*, the brown and swart coloured ; and the southerly, which is higher, *el-Ahmar*, the red mountain : this is perhaps granite ; and that basaltic.

We came at noon to *Umm Tŷeh*, other outlying granges of er-Russ, and inhabited ; where some of us, riding-in to water, found a plot of growing tobacco ! The men of Aneyza returned laughing, to tell of this adventure in the caravan menzil : for it was high noon, and the kâfily halted yonder. — From this *mogŷil* we rose early ; and journeyed forth through a plain wilderness full of basaltic and grey-red granite bergs [such as we have seen in the Harb and Shammar dîras westward]. Finally when the sun was descending, with ruddy yellow light behind the Abàn mountains, we halted to encamp.

Zâmil's letter, commending me to *Ibrahîm*, the young caravan emir, was brought to me by a client of the Bessàm to-day. Ibrahîm — he succeeded his father, who till lately had been emir of the town caravans — a sister's son of Zâmil, was a manly young sheykh of twenty years, of a gallant countenance ; and like Zâmil in his youth, though not of like parts : a smiling dissembler, confident and self-minded ; and the Waháby rust was in his soul. Such are the most young franklins in the free oases, always masking as it were in holiday apparel : but upon any turn of fortune, you find them haply to be sordid and iniquitous Arabs. Ibrahîm receiving Zâmil's letter from my hand, put it hastily into his bosom unopened ; for he would read what his uncle wrote to him concerning the Nasrâny bye and bye in a corner ! He showed me daily pleasant looks ; and sometimes as we journeyed, seeing me drooping in the saddle, he would ride to me, and put his new-kindled galliûn in my hand : and some days, he bade me come to sup with him, in the evening menzil. The young tradesmen that returned to Mecca, where they had shops, and a few of the master-caravaners mounted on thelûls, rode with Ibrahîm, in advance of the marching kâfily : now and then they alighted to kindle a fire of sticks, and make coffee. I rode, with less fatigue, among our burden camels. — Ibrahîm told me, laughing, that he first heard of me in Kuweyt (where he then arrived with a caravan), — ' That there was come a Nasrâny to Hâyil, *tûlahu thelàthy armâh*, three spears' length (they said) of stature ! for certain days the stranger had not spoken ! after that he found a mine for Ibn Rashîd, and then another!'—We lodged this night under the berg *el-Kîr*, little short of the peak *Jebel Kezâz*,—Dókhany being an hour distant, at our right hand; where are shallow water pits, and some ground-work of old building.

We journeyed on the morrow with the same high country about us, beset with bergs of basaltic traps and granite. [The steppe rises continually from el-Kasîm to et-Tâyif.] We came early to the brackish pits *er-Rukka*; and drew and replenished our girbies: this thick well-water was full of old wafted droppings of the nomads' cattle; but who will not drink in the desert, the water of the desert, must perish. Here is a four-square clay kella, with high walls and corner towers, built by those of er-Russ, for shelter when they come hither to dig gun-salt,—wherewith the soil is always infected about old water stations. We drank and rested out an hour, but with little refreshment: for the simûm—the hot land wind—was blowing, as the breath of an oven; which is so light and emptied of oxygen, that it cannot fill the chest or freshen the blood; and there comes upon man and cattle a faintness of heart.—I felt some relief in breathing through a wetted sponge.

Remounting we left *Jebel Úmmry* at the right hand, a mountain landmark of basalt which is long in sight.—I wondered seeing before us three men in the khàla! they were wood-cutters from *Therrîeh*, a desert village few hours distant to the westward; and thereby the Aneyza caravans pass some years. Not many miles north of Therrîeh is another village, Miskeh: these are poor corn settlements, without palms,—Miskeh is the greater, where are hardly fifty houses. West of Therrîeh is a hamlet, *Thorèyih*, in the mountain *Shâba*. The people of these villages are of mixed kindred from el-Kasîm, and of the nomads, and of negro blood: others say they are old colonies of Heteym. An 'Ateyby sheykh *Múthkir*, who rode rafîk in our caravan [his tribesmen are the Aarab of this vast wilderness], said, " those villagers are descended from Múthur." The nomads about them are sometimes Meteyr, sometimes Harb (intruded from the westward), sometimes 'Ateybân; but formerly those migrated Annezy were their neighbours that are now in the Syrian desert. [*v.* p. 428.]—Far to the eastward are other three desert villages, *es-Shaara*, *Doàdamy* and *Goayîeh*, which lie in the Haj way from Shuggera: the inhabitants are *Beny Zeyd*; and, it is said, 'their jid was a Solubby!'—Passing always through the same plain wilderness encumbered with plutonic bergs and mountains, we alighted at evening under the peak *Ferjeyn* ; where also I saw some old ground-courses, of great wild stones.

On the morrow we journeyed through the same high steppe, full of sharp rocks, bergs and jebâl, of trap and granite. At noon we felt no more the fiery heat of yesterday ; and I read in the aneroid that we were come to an altitude of nearly five thousand feet ! where the bright summer air was light and refreshing. Now on our left hand are the mountains *Minnîeh*, at our right a considerable mountain of granite, *Tokhfa*. Our *mogŷil* was by the watering *el-Ghról*, in hollow ground amidst trap mountains : that soil is green with growth of harsh desert bushes ; and here are two-fathom *golbân* of the ancients, well steyned. The water, which is sweet and light, is the only good and wholesome to drink in all this way, of fifteen journeys, between el-Kasîm and the Mecca country.—A day eastward from hence is a mountain, *Gabbily* ; whose rocks are said to be hewn in strange manner.

This high wilderness is the best wild pasture land that I have seen in Arabia : the bushes are few, but it is a ' white country ' overgrown with the desert grass, *nussy*. — What may be the cause that this Arabian desolation should smile more than other desolations of like soil, not far off ? I enquired of the Ateyba men who rode in the kâfily with Múthkir ; and they answered, *that this wilderness is sprinkled in the season by yearly showers*. — Is it not therefore because the land lies in the border of the monsoon or tropical rains ? which fall heavily in the early autumn, and commonly last five or six weeks at et-Tâyif. Everywhere we see some wild growth of acacias, signs doubtless of ground-water not far under : and yet in so vast a land-breadth (of three hundred miles) there is no settlement ! [This may be because the water is seldom or never sweet.] Of late years the land, lying so open to the inroads of Ibn Rashîd, has been partly abandoned by the Aarab ; and the forsaken water-pits are choked, for lack of cleansing. — After the watering, we journeyed till evening : and alighted in a place called *es-She'ab*, near the basalt mountain and water *Kabshàn*. The land-height is all one since yesterday.

The fifth morning we journeyed in the same high country, full of bergs, mostly granitic ; and often of strange forms, as the granite rock is spread sheet-wise, and even dome-wise and scale-wise : a basalt berg with a strange vein in it called ' the wolf's path' is a landmark by the way. Ere noon we crossed traces of a great ghrazzu ; which was that late foray, they said, of Ibn Rashîd against 'Ateyba. [*v.* p. 456] — Ere noon there was an alarm ! and the kâfily halted : some thought they had seen Aarab. All looked to their arms ; many fired-off their long guns to load afresh ; the weary drivers on foot, braving with their spears, began to leap and dance : the companies drew together ; and the caravan advanced in better order. Sleymàn, who among the first had plucked off his gun-case, rode now with lighted matchlock in his lap, cursing and grinding the teeth with malevolence. The like did the most of them ; for this is the caravan fanaticism, to cry to heaven for the perdition of their natural enemies ! — the human wolves of the desert. Ibrahîm sent out scouts to descry the hovering foes : who bye and bye returned with word that they found them to be but desert trees ! Then we heard it shouted, by the Emir's servant, ' To advance freely ! ' At our noon menzil we were still at the height of 4550 feet. — We rode in the afternoon through the like plain desert, full of standing hay, but most desolate : the basalt rocks now exceed the granites. And already two or three desert plants appeared, which were new to my eyes, — the modest blossoms of another climate : we saw no signs of human occupation. When the sun was setting they alighted in a place called *Umm Meshe'aib* ; the altitude is 4500 feet. We passed to-day the highest ground of the great middle desert. — In the beginning of the twilight a meteor shone brightly about us for a moment, with a beautiful blue light ; and then drooping in the sky broke into many lesser stars.

I found Múthkir in all the menzils under Ibrahîm's awning : for he alighted with the emir. The Beduin sheykh rode with us to safe-guard the caravan in all encounters with his ('Ateyba) tribesmen : and he and his two or three followers were as eyes to us in the khála. — Nevertheless the Kasîm caravaners, continually passing the main deserts from their youth, are themselves expert in land-craft. There was one among us, Sâlih (the only Arabian that I have seen cumbered with a wen in the throat), who had passed this way to and from Mecca, he thought, almost an hundred times, — that were more than four years, or fifty thousand miles of desert journeys : and he had ridden and gone not less in the north between his Kasîm town and the Gulf and river provinces. Sâlih could tell the name of every considerable rock which is seen by the long wayside. They know their paths, but not the vast wilderness beyond the landmarks.

How pleasant is the easy humour of all Beduins! in comparison with the harsher temper of townsfolk: I was bye and bye friends with Múthkir. When we spoke of the traces of Ibn Rashîd's foray, he said, "Thou hast been at Hâyil, and art a mudowwy: eigh! Khalîl, could'st thou not in some wise quit us from Ibn Rashîd — *el-Háchim!* and we would billah reward thee: it is he who afflicts 'Ateyba." He said further, "In the [north] parts from whence we come there are none our friends, but only Aneyza"; and when I enquired, Were his Aarab good folk? he answered "Eigh! — such as the people of Aneyza." Then he asked, 'If he visited me in my béled, what things would I give him? — a mare, and a maiden to wive?' — "And what wilt thou give me, Múthkir, when I alight at thy beyt?" At this word the Beduin was troubled, because his black booth of ragged hair-cloth was not very far off; so he answered, he would give me a bint, and she would be a fair one, to wive. — "But I have given thee a mare, Múthkir." — "Well, Khalîl, I will give thee a camel. We go to Mekky, and thou to Jidda; and then whither wilt thou go?" — "To India, it may please Ullah." Ibrahîm said, 'He had a mind to visit India with me; would I wait for him at Jidda? till his coming down again in the Haj — after four months!'

We removed an hour before dawn; and the light showed a landscape more open before us, with many acacia trees. Of all the wells hitherto there are none so deep as four fathoms: this land, said Múthkir, is full of *golbân* and waterpits of the Aarab. When it rains, he told me, the seyls die shortly in the soil; but if in any year it rain a flood, the whole steppe seyls down (westward) to the Wady er-Rummah. The country is full of cattle-paths, — it may be partly made by the wild goats and gazelles. Leaving on our right hand the cragged *J. She'aba*, wherein "are many bedûn," we passed by a tent-like granite landmark, *Wareysîeh*; and came to lodge at noon between black basaltic mountains, full of peaks and of seyl strands; — on this side was *Thul'aan en-Nîr*, and on that *She'ar*.

At each midday halt the town camels are loosed out to pasture. The weary brutes roam in the desert, but hardly take anything into their parched mouths: they crop only a few mouthfuls by the way in the early morning, whilst the night coolness is yet upon the ground. The great brutes, that go fainting under their loads, sweat greatly, and for thirst continue nearly without eating till seventeen days be ended ; when they are discharged at Mecca. But these beasts from Nejd suffer anew in the stagnant air of the Teháma ; where they have but few days to rest : so they endure, almost without refreshment ; till they arrive again very feeble at Aneyza. Our hardened drivers [all Arabs will — somewhat faint-heartedly — bemoan the aching life of this world !] told me with groans, that their travail in the journey was very sore ; one of them rode in the morning and two walked ; in the afternoon one walked and two rode. The march of the Kasîm caravaners is not like the slowpaced procession of the Syrian Haj ; for they drive strenuously in the summer heat, from water to water. The great desert waterings are far asunder ; and they must arrive ere the fourth day, or the beasts would faint.

The caravaners, after three days, were all beside their short Semitic patience ; they cry out upon their beasts with the passionate voices of men in despair. The drivers beat forward the lingering cattle, and go on goading them with the heel of their spears, execrating, lamenting and yelling with words of evil augury, *Yâ mâl et-teyr — hut !* eigh ! thou carrion for crows, *Yâ mâl eth-thubbah*, eigh ! butcher's meat : if any stay an instant, to crop a stalk, they cry, *Yâ mâl ej-jû'a*, O thou hunger's own ! *Yelaan Ullah abu hâ 'l ras*, or *hâ 'l kalb* or *hâ 'l hulk*, May the Lord confound the father of thy head, of thy heart, of thy long halse. — Drivers of camels must have their eyes continually upon the loaded beasts : for a camel coming to any sandy place is likely to fall on his knees to wallow there, and ease his itching skin ; — and then all must go to wreck ! They discern not their food by sight alone, but in smelling ; also a camel will halt at any white stone or bleached *jella*, as if it were some blanched bone, — which if they may find at anytime they take it up in their mouth, and champ somewhile with a melancholy air ; and that is " for the saltiness," say the Arabs. The caravaners in the march are each day of more waspish humour and fewer words; there is naught said now but with great *by-gods* ; and the drivers, whose mouths are bitter with thirst, will hardly answer each other with other than crabbed and vaunting speech ; as ' I am the son of my father ! I the brother of my little sister ! ' ' Am I the slave of thy father (that I should serve or obey thee) ? ' And an angry soul will cry out on his neighbour, *Ullah la yubârak fîk, la yujîb 'lak el-kheyr*, ' The Lord bless thee not, and send thee no good.'

The heat in our mid-day halt was 102° F. under the awnings, and rising early we made haste to come to the watering ; where we arrived two hours before the sunsetting. This is '*Afîf*, an ancient well of ten fathoms to the water, and steyned with dry building of the wild basalt blocks. — Sleymàn, and the other master caravaners, had ridden out before the approaching kâfily, with their tackle ; each one contending to arrive before other at the well's mouth, and occupy places for the watering. When we rode-in they stood there already by their gear ; which is a thick stake pight in the ground, and made fast with stones : the head is a fork, and at that they mount their draw-reel, *maḥal*, — as the nomads use at any deep golbân, where they could not else draw water. The cord is drawn by two men running out backward ; a third standing at the well-brink receives the full bucket, as it comes up ; and runs to empty it into the camel trough, — a leather or carpet-piece spread upon a hollow, which they have scraped with stick or stone and their hands in the hard gravel soil. [Vol. I. p. 428.] When so many camels must be watered at a single *jelîb*, there is a great ado of men drawing with all their might and chanting in cadence, like the Beduw. I went to drink at the camel troughs, but they bade me beware ; ' I might chance to slip in the mire, and fall over the well brink,' which, without kerb, [as in all desert golbân] is even with the soil. The well-drawers' task is not therefore without peril ; and they are weary. At their last coming down, an unhappy man missed his footing, — and fell in ! He was hastily taken up — for Arabs in the sight of such mischiefs are of a sudden and generous humanity ! and many are wont from their youth to go down in all manner of wells [*v*. Vol. I. p. 180, 554 : Vol. II. p. 465] : — His back was broken : and when the caravan departed, the sick man's friends laid him upon a camel ; but he died in the march. — To the first at the well succeeded other drawers ; and they were not all sped in three hours. This ancient well-mouth is mounded round with earth once cast up in the digging : thus the waterers, who run backward, draw easily ; and the sinking sludge returns not to infect the well.

By that well side, I saw the first token of human life in this vast wilderness, — the fresh ashes of a hunters' fire ! whereby lay the greatest pair of gazelle horns that I have seen at any time. The men doubtless were Solubba ; and some in the kâfily had seen their asses' footprints to-day. It is a marvel even to the Arabs, how these human solitaries can live by their shooting, in the khála. The Solubby may bear besides his long matchlock only a little water ; but their custom is to drink a fill of water or mereesy two hours before dawn : and then setting out, they are not athirst till noon. I now learned to do the like ; and that early draught sustained me until we halted at midday, though in the meanwhile my companions had drunk thrice.—They would hardly reach me the bowl, when they poured out for themselves to drink ; and then it was with grudges and cursing : if Sleymàn were out of hearing, they would even deny the Nasrâny altogether. Sleymàn, who was not good, said, " We all suffer by the way, I cannot amend it, and these are Arabs : Abdullah would find no better, were he here with his beard, (himself). See you this boy, Khalîl? he is one from the streets of Aneyza : that other (a Beduwy lad, of Annezy in the North) has slain, they say, his own father ; and he (the cook) yonder ! is a poor follower from the town : wellah, if I chided them, they would forsake me at the next halt ! " — It were breath lost to seek to drink water in another fellowship : one day I rode by a townsman who alighted to drink ; and ere he put up the bowl I asked him to pour out a little for me also. His wife had been a patient of mine, and haply he thought I might remember his debt for medicines ; for hastily tying up again the neck of his girby, he affected not to know me. When I called him by name ! — he could no longer refuse ; but undoing the mouth of the skin, he poured me out a little of the desert water, saying, " Such is the road and the toil, that no man remembers other ; but the word is *imshy hâl-ak !* help thyself forward." — A niggard of his girby is called *Bía'a el-má*, Water-seller, by his angry neighbours. My thelûl was of little stature, wooden and weak : in walking she could not keep pace with the rest ; and I had much ado to drive her forward. The beast, said Sleymàn, was hidebound ; he would make scotches in her side, when they were come down to Mecca.

I found here the night air, at the coolest, 72° F. ; the deep well-water being then 79° F. The land-height is 4600 feet : there were flies and gnats about the water. — The cattle were drenched again towards morning : then we were ready to set forward, but no signal was given. The sun rose ; and a little after we heard a welcome shout of the emir's servant, *El-yôm nej-î-î-îm !* We shall abide here to-day.

— There are two paths for the kâfilies going down from el-Kasîm to Mecca ; the west derb with more and better waterings, — in which the butter caravan of Boreyda and er-Russ were journeying before us—is called *es-Sultâny*, the 'highway.' The middle derb, wherein we marched, is held by convoys that would pass expediently : it is far between waterings, and there is the less likelihood of strife with Aarab summering upon any of them. — The caravaners durst not adventure to water their camels, in presence of the (fickle) Beduw : in such hap they may require the nomads to remove, who on their part will listen to the bidding of townsfolk with very evil mind. But if the Beduw be strong in number, the townspeople must make a shift to draw in haste with arms in their hands : and drive-on their half-refreshed beasts to the next cattle-pits, which in this wilderness are mostly bitter. — There is a third path, east of us, *derb Wady Sbeya*, with few and small *maweyrids* ; which is trodden by flying companies of thelûl riders. Last year the good Abdullah el-Bessàm, returning home by that way from Jidda, found the well-pit choked, when he came to one of those disused waterings, *Jelîb ibn Haddîf* ; and he with his fellowship laboured a day to clear it. The several derbs lie mostwhat so nigh together, that we might view their landmarks upon both sides.

'Afîf, where we rested, is an hollow ground like el-Ghrôl, encompassed by low basaltic mountains. I saw the rude basalt stones of this well's mouth in the desert encrusted white, and deeply scored by the Nomad's soft ropes ! Hereabout grows great plenty of that tall joint-grass (*thurrm*), which we have seen upon the Syrian Haj road. The fasting camels were driven out to pasture ; and the 'Ateyba Beduins, companions of Múthkir, went up into the *mergab* — which was the next height of basalt — to keep watch. Great was the day's heat upon the kerchiefed heads of them who herded the camels ; for the sun which may be borne in journeying, that is whilst we are passing through the air, is intolerable even to Nomads who stand still : our Beduin hind sighed to me, " Oh ! this sun ! " which broiled his shallow brains. Towards evening a sign being made from the mergab ! the caravan camels were hastily driven in. The scouts had descried *zôl*, as they supposed, of some Aarab : but not long after they could distinguish them to be four Solubbies, riding on asses.

We set forward from 'Afîf before the new day. When the sun came up we had left the low mountain train of *Átula* on our left hand ; and the wilderness in advance appeared more open : it is overgrown with hay ; and yet, Múthkir tells me, they have better pastures ! The mountains are now few : instead of bergs and peaks, we see but rocks. — I was riding in the van; and a great white gazelle-buck stood up in his lair before us: the *thobby*, which was thickgrown as a great he-goat, after a few steps stood still, to gaze on this unwonted procession of men and camels; then he ran slowly from us. The well-mounted young gallants did off their gun-leathers; and pricked after the quarry on their crop-eared thelûls, which run jetting the long necks like birds:— to return when they were weary, from a vain pursuit! Desert hares started everywhere as we passed and ran to cower under the next bushes — the pretty tips yet betraying them of their most long ears.

For two days southward this desert land is called *es-Shiffa*, which is counted three days wide; others say 'Es-Shiffa lies between er-Russ and 'Afîf; and all beyond is *el-Házzam*, for two and a half journeys:' Múthkir holds that the Házzam and the Shiffa are one. In all this vast land-breadth I had not seen the furrow of a seyl!— Our mountain marks are now *Mérdumma*, on the left; and at our right hand three conical bergs together, *Methàlitha*. *Jebel es-Sh'eyb*, which appears beyond, lies upon the *derb es-Sultâny*: there is good water [this is *Gadyta* of the old itineraries — v. *Die alte Geogr. Arabiens*; wherein we find mentioned also *Dathyna*, that is the water-pits *Dafîna*; and *Koba*, which is *Goba*, a good watering]: *J. Meshaf* stands before us. Our *mogŷil* was between the mountains '*Ajjilla* and *eth-Th'al*; the site is called *Shebrûm*, a bottom ground with acacia trees, and where grows great plenty of a low prickly herb, with purple blossoms, of the same name. In this neighbourhood are cattle-pits of the Aarab, *Sh'brâmy*.

Here at the midst of the Sheffa is an head, says Múthkir (though it be little apparent), of *Wady Jerrîr*. This is the main affluent from the east country of the Wady er-Rummah; that in some of their ancient poems is feigned to say; 'My side valleys give me to drink sip-wise; there is but Wady Jerrîr which allays my thirst,' — words that seem to witness of the (here) tropical rains! In the course of this valley, which is north-westward, are many water-holes of the Beduw. Some interpret *Rummah* ' old fretted rope ' [which might be said of its much winding]. — We journeyed again towards evening: the landscape is become an open plain about us; and the last mountain northward is vanished below our horizon. — Where we lodged at the sunset I found the land height to be 4100 feet.

We removed not before dawn: at sunrise I observed the same altitude, and again at mid-day; when the air under the awnings was

107° F. This open district is called *ed-D'aika*, which they interpret 'plain without bergs of mixed earth and good pasture.' Eastward we saw a far-off jebel ; and the head of a solitary mountain, *Khâl*, before us. Later we passed between the *Seffua* and *'Aridàn* mountains and *Thennŷib*, which is a landmark and watering-place upon the derb es-Sultâny. — Near the sunsetting we rode over a wide ground crusted with salt ; and the caravan alighted beyond.

Arriving where he would encamp, the emir draws bridle and, smiting her neck, hisses to his dromedary to kneel ; and the great infirm creature, with groans and bowing again the knees, will make some turns like a hound ere her couching down. — Strange is the centaur-like gaunt figure of the Arab dromedary rider regarded from the backward ; for under the mantled man appears — as they were his demesurate pair of straddling (camel) legs. The master caravaners ride-in after the emir to take their menzils,—having a care that the lodgings shall be disposed in circuit : then the burden camels are driven up to their places and unloaded. The unruly camel yields to kneel, being caught by the beard : if a couched camel resist, rolling and braying, lay hold on the cartilage of his nose, and he will be all tame. We may think there is peril of his teeth, Arabs know there is none ; for the great brute is of mild nature, though he show no affection to mankind. Beduins gather sappy plants and thrust them into their camels' jaws,— which I have done also a thousand times ; and never heard that anyone was bitten. [I have once — in Sinai — seen a muzzled camel.] Though they snap at each other in the march it is but a feint : a grown camel has not the upper front teeth.

Our morrow's course — the tenth from Aneyza — was toward the flat-topped and black (basaltic) conical Jebel Khâl ; and a swelling three-headed (granitic) mountain *Thúlm*. — The Nejd pilgrims cry out joyfully in their journey, when they see these jebâl, ' that, thanks be to God, they are now at the midway ! ' In the midst is the *maweyrid Shurrma*, where we alighted three hours before mid-day : here are cattle pits, but of so bitter water, that the Kusmàn could not drink. "We shall come, they said, to another watering to-morrow." There was little left in their girbies. I chose to drink here, enforcing myself to swallow the noisome bever, rather than strive with Sleymàn's drivers : the taste was like alum. But the cooks filled up some flagging skins of

'Afîf water ; and thus mingled it might serve, they thought, to boil the suppers. The three shallow pits [one is choked], with water at a fathom, are dry-steyned. In the midst of our watering, the wells were drawn dry ; and the rest of the thirsting camels were driven up an hour later to drink, when the water was risen in them again. The land-height is the same as in our yesterday's march.

Journeying from Shurrma, we began to cross salty bottoms ; and were approaching that great vulcanic country, the *Harrat el-Kisshub*. We pass wide-lying miry grounds, encrusted with subbakha ; and white as it were with hoarfrost : at other times we rode over black plutonic gravel ; and I thought I saw clear pebbles shining amongst the stones. In this desert landscape, of one height and aspect, are many *sammar* (acacia) trees : but the most were sere, and I saw none grown to timber. — A coast loomed behind Khâl : " Look ! Khalîl, said my companions, yonder is the Harrat el-Kisshub ! " a haze dimmed the Harra mountains, which I soon perceived to be crater-hills, *hilliân*. In this march I rode by certain round shallow pits, a foot deep, but wide as the beginning of water-holes ; and lying in pairs together. I hailed one of the kâfily as he trotted by ; who responded, when I showed him the place, " Here they have taken out gold ! " I asked Múthkir of it in the evening : " Ay Khalîl, he answered, we find many *rasûm*, ' traces,' in our dîra, — they are of the *auellîn*."

On the morrow we removed very early to come this day to water. When the light began to spring, I saw that our course lay even with the Harra border, some miles distant. The lower parts were shrouded in the morning haze, where above I saw the tops of crater hills. The derb es-Sultâny lies for a day and a half over this lava field. We coast it ; which is better for the camels' soles, that are worn to the quick in a long voyage. [Múthkir tells me, the lavas of the *Harrat Terr'a*, which joins to the Kisshub, are so sharp that only asses may pass them : and therein are villages and palms of 'Ateyba Aarab.] A foot-sore beast must be discharged ; and his load parted among them will break the backs of the other camels. Some Nejd caravaners are so much in dread of this accident, that in the halts they cure their camels' worn feet with urine. — Might not the camels be shod with leather? there is a stave in the moallakát [LEBEID, 23] which seems to show that such shoes were used by the (more ingenious) ancient Arabians.

Betwixt us and the lava country is the hard blackish crusted mire of yesterday; a flat without herb or stone, without footprint, and white with *subbakha*: tongues of this salty land stretch back eastward beyond our path. A little before noon we first saw footprints of nomad cattle, from the Harra-ward; — whereunder is a good watering, in face of us. In the midday halt our thirst was great: the people had nothing to drink, save of that sour and black water from Shurrma; and we could not come to the wells, till nightfall, or early on the morrow. I found the heat of the air under the awnings 107° F.; and the simûm was blowing. In the caravan fellowships they eat dates in the mogŷil, and what little burghrol or temmn may be left over from their suppers. Masters and drivers sit at meat together; but to-day none could eat for thirst. I went to the awnings of Ibrahîm and Bessàm — each of them carried as many as ten girbies — to seek a fenjeyn of coffee or of water. The young men granted these sips of water and no more: for such are Arabians on the journey: I saw they had yet many full waterskins!

That nooning was short, because of the people's thirst, — and the water yet distant. As we rode forth I turned and saw my companions drinking covertly! besides they had drunk their fills in my absence, after protesting to me that there was not any; and I had thirsted all day. I thought, might I drink this once, I could suffer till the morning. I called to the fellows to pour me out a little; 'we were rafîks, and this was the will of Abdullah el-Kenneyny': but they denied me with horrible cursing; and Sleymàn made merchant's ears. I alighted, for 'need hath no peer,' and returned to take it whether they would or no. The Beduwy, wagging his club and beginning to dance, would maintain their unworthy purpose: but Sleymàn (who feared strife) bade them then pour out for Khalîl. — It was sweet water from 'Afîf, which they had kept back and hidden this second day from the Nasrâny: they had yet to drink of it twice in the afternoon march. — Sleymàn was under the middle age, of little stature, of a sickly nature, with some sparkles of cheerful malice, and disposed to fanaticism. I had been banished from Aneyza, and among these townsmen were many of the Waháby sort;

but the most saluted me in the long marches with a friendly word, " How fares Khalîl, art thou over weary ? well ! we shall be soon at our journey's end." Once only I had heard an injurious word ; that was in the evening rest at 'Afîf, when crossing in the dark towards Ibrahîm and Múthkir I lighted on some strange fellowship, and stumbled at the butter skins. " Whither O kafir," cried their hostile voices ; but others called to them ' to hold their mouths ! — and pass by, mind them not Khalîl.'

Sleymàn told me he had sometime to do with the English shippers, on the Gulf : " they were good people, and better than the Turks. Trust thy goods, quoth he, to the Engleys ; for they will save thee harmless, if anything should be damaged or lost. But as for Turkish shipping, you must give to the labourers, and again ere they will receive your goods aboard ; besides the officer looks for his fee, and the seamen will embezzle somewhat on the ship's voyage : but with the English you shall find right dealing and good order. And yet by Ullah, if any Engleys take service with the Osmully, they become bribe-catchers, and are worse than the Turks ! " — The brazen sun, in the afternoon march, was covered with clouds : and when we had ridden in these heavenly shadows three hours, leaving the mountains *el-Kamîm* and *Hakràn* behind our backs, I saw some stir in the head of our kâfily ; and thelûl-riders parted at a gallop ! They hastened forward to seek some cattle pits, lying not far beside the way. When they came to the place, every man leapt down in a water-hole, to fill his girby ; where they stood up to their middles in the slimy water : each thirsty soul immediately swallowed his bowlful ; and only then they stayed to consider that the water was mawkish !

This is *Hazzeym es-Seyd*, a grove of acacia trees — very beautiful in the empty khála ! and here are many cattle-pits of a fathom and a half, to the water ; which rises of the rain. — Now we looked back, and saw the kâfily heading hither ! the thirsty drivers had forsaken their path. Ibrahîm, when the camels were driven in, gave the word to encamp. That water was welcome more than wholesome ; — the most were troubled with diarrhoea in the night. I felt no harm ; — nor yesterday, after drinking the Shurrma water : which made me remember with thankful mind, that in these years spent in countries, where in a manner all suffer, I had never sickened.

In the night-time Ibrahîm sent some thelûl-riders to spy out that water before us, where we had hoped to arrive yesterday ; and bring word if any Aarab were lodged upon it. — The sun rose and we yet rested in this pleasant site. And some went out with their long matchlocks amongst the thorny green trees, to shoot at doves [which haunt the *maweyrids*, but are seldom seen flying in the khála]: but by the counsel of Múthkir, Ibrahîm sent bye and bye to forbid any more firing of guns ; for the sound might draw enemies upon us. — When the sun was half an hour high, we saw our scouts returning ; who rode in with tidings, that they had seen only few Beduw at the water, which were 'Ateybàn ; and had spoken with one they found in the desert, who invited them to come and drink milk. We remained still in our places ; and the awnings were set up. — A nâga fàtir (worn out she camel) was slaughtered ; and distributed among the fellowships, that had purchased the portions of meat. Three or four such slaughter-beasts were driven down in the kâfily : and in this sort the weary caravaners taste flesh-meat, every few days.

The caravan removed at noon : the salt flats reaching back to the vulcanic coast, lay always before us ; and to the left the desert horizon. We passed on between the low *J. Hakràn* and the skirts of the Harra. At sunset the caravan entered a cragged bay in an outflow of the Harra : that lava rock is heavy and basaltic. Here is a watering place of many wells, — *el-Moy*, or *el-Moy She'ab*, or *Ameah Hakràn*, a principal *maurid* of the Aarab.

The Beduins were departed : yet we alighted in the twilight somewhat short of the place ; for ' the country in these months is full of thieves.' But every fellowship sent one to the wells with a girby, to fetch them to drink. The caravaners now encamped in a smaller circuit, for the fear of the desert : the coffee and cooking fires were kindled ; it was presently dark night, and watches were set. In each company one wakes for the rest ; and they make three watches till dawn. If any pass by the dim fire-lights, or one is seen approaching, a dozen cruel throats cry out together, *Min hâtha*, ' Who is there, who ? ' And all the fellowships within hearing shout hideously again, *Ethbah-hu!* kill-kill him ! So the beginning of the night is full of their calling and cursing ; since some will cross hither and thither, to visit their friends. When I went through the camp to seek Ibrahîm and Múthkir, and the son of Bessàm ; huge were the outcries, *Ethbah-hu !* — *Min hu hâtha?* the answer is *Ana sahib*, It is I, a friend ; or *Tâyib, mâ fî shey*, It is well, there is nothing. — Sleymàn tells me, that in their yearly pilgrimage caravan, in which is carried much merchandise and silver, they keep these night watches in all the long way of the desert.

At break of day the Kusmàn, with arms in their hands ! drove the camels to water : and their labour was soon sped, for the wells were many. The kâfily departed two hours after the sunrise, the thirteenth from Aneyza. We had not met with mankind since el-Kasîm ! but now a few Beduins appeared driving their cattle to water. The same steppe is about us : many heads of quartz, like glistening white heaps, are seen in this soil. We passed by a *dar*, or old worn camping-ground of the Aarab ; and cattle-pits of bitter water. The high coast of the Harrat el-Kisshub trends continually with our march ; I could see in it green acacias, and drift-sand banked up high from the desert : the crater-hills appeared dimly through the sunny haze. [These great lavas have overflowed plutonic rocks : — those of Kheybar and the 'Aueyrid a soil of sandstones.] The salt-flats yet lie between our caravan path and the Harra. — Such is the squalid landscape which we see in going down from Nejd to Mecca ! The height of all this wilderness is 4200 feet nearly.

We halted at high noon, sun-beaten and in haste to rear-up the awnings. A Beduwy came riding to us from the wilderness upon his thelûl. The man, who was a friendly 'Ateyby, brought word that the kâfily of Boreyda was at the water *Marràn*, under the Harra yonder. — The simûm rose, in our afternoon march, and blustered from the westward. At the sun's going down we alighted for the night : but some in the caravan, hearing that cattle-pits were not far off, rode out to fill their girbies : they returned empty, for the water was bitter and tasted, they told us, of sulphur.

On the morrow, we saw everywhere traces of the Nomads. The height of the desert soil is that which I have found daily for a hundred miles behind us. Our path lies through a belt of country, *er-Rukkaba*, which the Arabs say ' is the highest in all the way, where there always meets them a cold air,' — when they come up from the (tropical) Tehàma. Notwithstanding their opinion I found the altitude at noon and before sunset no more than 4300 feet. The heat was lighter, and we look here upon a new and greener aspect of the desert ; this high plain reaches south-eastward to et-Tâyif. Each day, when the sun as we journeyed was most hot over our heads, I nodded in the saddle and swooned for an hour or two : but looking up this noon-day methought

I saw by the sun that we were returning backward ! I thought, in those painful moments, it was a sunstroke ; or that the fatigues of Arabian travel had at length troubled my understanding : but the bitter sweat on my forehead was presently turned to a dew of comfort, in the cogitation, that we were past the summer tropic ; and the northing of the sun must reverse our bearings. I saw in the offing a great mountain bank, eastward, _J. Hatthon_, of the _B'goom_ Aarab ; and beyond is the village _Túrraba_ : under the mountain are, they say, some ancient ruins. West of our path stands the black basaltic jebel, _Néfur et-Tarîk_. The Harra has vanished from our sight : before us lies the water _Mehàditha_. — This night was fresher than other : the altitude being nearly 4600 feet. At dawn I found 73° F. and chill water in the sweating girbies.

The morrow's journey lay yet over the Rukkaba, always an open plain : the height increases in the next hours to nearly five thousand feet. I saw the acacia bushes cropped close, and trodden round in the sand — by the beautiful feet of gazelles ! At our mogŷil the heat under the awnings was 102° F. — In the evening march we saw sheep flocks of the Aarab ; and naked children keeping them. The little Beduins — nut-brown skinned under the scourge of the southern sun — were of slender growth. We espied their camels before us : the herdsmen approached to enquire tidings ; and a horseman, who sat upon his mare's bare chine, thrust boldly in among us. We saw now their black booths : these Aarab were _Sheyabîn_, of 'Ateyba. The sun was low ; and turning a little aside from the nomad menzil we alighted to encamp. — And there presently came over to us some of the nomad women, who asked to buy clothing of the caravaners : but the Kusmàn said it was but to spy out our encampment, and where they might pilfer something in the night. Their keen eyes noted my whiter skin ; and they asked quickly " Who he ? — who is that stranger with you ? "

On the morrow we journeyed in the midst of the nomad flocks — here all white fleeces. In this (now tropical) desert, I saw some solitary tall plants of a jointed and ribbed flowering cactus, _el-ghrullathî_, which is a cattle-medicine : the Aarab smear it in the nostrils of their sick camels. The soil is sand and gravel of the crystalline rocks. — Two hours before noon we rode by the head of another basaltic lava stream ; and met camels of the same Sheyabîn breasting up from the maweyrid _Sh'aara_, lying nigh before us. These 'Ateyba camels are brown coloured, with a few blackish ones among them ; and all of little stature : the herdsmen were free and well-spoken weleds. — Riding by a worsted booth standing alone, I saw only a Beduin wife and her child that sat within, and said *Salaam!* she answered again with a cheerful " Welcome — welcome," — In approaching nomads, our caravaners — ever in distrust of the desert folk — unsling their long guns, draw off the leathers, blow the matches ; and ride with the weapons ready on their knees.

Before us is a solitary black jebel, *Biss*, which is perhaps of basalt. — And now we see again the main Harra ; that we are approaching, to water at Sh'aara. Múthkir tells me, ' the great Harrat el-Kisshub is of a round figure [some say, It is one to two days to go over] ; and that the Kisshub is not solitary, but a member of the train of Harras between Mecca and Medina : the Kisshub and the Ahràr el-Medina are not widely separated.' There met us a slender Beduin lad coming up after the cattle ; and beautiful was the face of that young waterer, in his Mecca tunic of blue ! — but to Northern eyes it is the woman's colour : the black locks hanged down dishevelled upon his man-maidenly shoulders. " Hoy, weled ! (cries our rude Annezy driver, who as a Beduwy hated all Beduw not his tribesfolk). — I say fellows, is this one a male or a female ? " The poor weled's heart swelled with a vehement disdain ; his ingenuous eyes looked fiercely upon us, and almost he burst out to weep. — Sh'aara, where we now arrived, is a bay in the Harra that is here called '*Ashîry*. The end of the lava, thirty feet in height, I found to overlie granite rock, — which is whitish, slacked, and crumbling, with the suffered heat : the head of lava has stayed at the edge of the granite reef. Sh'aara is a sh'aeb or seyl-strand which they reckon to the *Wady Adzîz* and *Wady el-'Agîg*. Here are many narrow-mouthed wells of the ancients, and dry-steyned with lava stones ; but some are choked. We heard from the Aarab that the Boreyda caravan watered here last noon : since yesterday the desert paths are one. I found the altitude, 4900 feet.

The caravaners passed this night under arms. Our slumbers were full of shouted alarms, and the firing of matchlocks ; so that we lay in jeopardy of our own shot, till the morning. If any Beduin thief were taken they would hale him to the Emir's tent ; and his punishment, they told me, would be " to beat him to death." Almost daily there is somewhat missed in the kâfily ; and very likely when we mounted ere day it was left behind upon the dark earth. — In the next menzil the owner, standing up in his place, will shout, through his hollow hands,

' that he has lost such a thing ; which if anyone have found, let him now restore it, and remember Ullah.'

Some of the Beduins came to us in the morning ; who as soon as they eyed me, enquired very earnestly what man I were. Our caravaners asked them of the price of samn in Mecca. When we removed, after watering again the camels, a Beduin pressed hardily through the kâfily : he was ill clad as the best of them, but of comely carriage beside the harsh conditions of drudging townsfolk. Our bold-tongued Annezy driver cursed the father that begat him, and bade him stand off ! but the 'Ateyby drew out his cutlass to the half and, with a smile of the Beduin urbanity, went on among them : he was not afraid of townlings in his own dîra. We journeyed again : and the coast of the Harra appeared riding high upon the plain at our right hand. We found a child herding lambs, who had no clothes, but a girdle of leathern thongs. [Afterward I saw hareem wearing the like over their smocks : it may be a South Arabian guise of the *haggu*.] The child wept that he and his lambs were overtaken by so great a company of strangers : but stoutly gathering his little flock, he drove aside and turned his blubbered cheeks from us.

Here we passed beyond the large and pleasant plains of Nejd ; and entered a craggy mountain region of traps and basalts, er-Rî'a, where the altitude is nearly 5000 feet. [*Rî'a* we have seen to signify a gap and wild passage in the jebel, — I find no like word in our lowland language.] In the Rî'a grow certain gnarled bushes, *nèbba*, which I had seen last in the limestone hills of Syria : and we passed by the blackened sites of (Mecca) charcoal burners. Further in this strait we rode by cairns : some of them, which show a rude building, might be sepulchres of principal persons in old time, — the Rî'a is a passage betwixt great regions. If I asked any in the caravan, What be these heaps? they answered, " Works of the kafirs that were in the land before the Moslemîn : — how Khalîl ! were they not of thy people ? " Others said, " They are of the Beny Helál."

From this passage we ascended to the left, by a steep seyl, encumbered with rocks and acacia trees. Not much above, is a narrow brow ; where I saw a cairn, and courses of old dry building ; and read under my cloak the altitude 5500 feet, which is the greatest in all the road. There sat Ibrahîm with his companions ; and the emir's servant stood telling the camels — passing one by one, which he noted in a paper ; for upon every camel (as said) is levied a real. Few steps further the way descended again, by another torrent. — I looked in vain for ancient scored inscriptions : here are but hard traps and grey-red granite, with basalt veins.

The aspect of this country is direful. We were descending to Mecca — now not far off — and I knew not by what adventure I should live or might die on the morrow : there was not anyone of much regard in all the caravan company. Sleymàn's goodwill was mostwhat of the thought, that he must answer for the Nasrâny, to his kinsman Abdullah. Abd-er Rahmàn was my friend in the kâfily, — in that he obeyed his good father : he was amiable in himself ; and his was not a vulgar mind, but *mesquin*. I felt by his answers to-day, that he was full of care in my behalf.

It was noon when we came forth upon a high soil, straitened betwixt mountains, like a broad upland wady. This ground, from which the Nejd caravans go down in a march or two short stages, to Mecca, is called *es-Seyl* : I found the height to be 5060 feet. — The great Wady el-Humth whereunto seyls the Harb country on both sides, and the Harras between Mecca and Tebûk, is said to spring from the Wady Laymûn [*v.* Vol. I. p. 217], which lies a little below, on the right hand : the altitude considered, this is not impossible.

We have passed from Nejd ; and here is another nature of Arabia ! We rode a mile in the narrow *Seyl* plain, by thickets of rushy grass, of man's height ! with much growth of peppermint [*v.* p. 427]; and on little leas, — for this herbage is browsed by the caravan camels which pass-by daily between Mecca and Tâyif. Now the kâfily halted, and we alighted : digging here with their hands they find at a span deep the pure rain water. From hence I heard to be but a march to Tâyif : and some prudent and honest persons in the kâfily persuaded me to go thither, saying, ' It was likely we should find some Mecca cameleers ascending to et-Tâyif, and they would commit me to them, — so I might arrive at et-Tâyif this night ; and they heard the Sherîf (of Mecca) was now at et-Tâyif : and when I should be come thither, if I asked it of the Sherîf, he would send me down safely to Jidda.'

— What pleasure to visit Tâyif ! the Eden of Mecca, with sweet and cool air, and running water ; where are gardens of roses, and vineyards and orchards. But these excellencies are magnified in the common speech, for I heard some of the Kusmàn saying, 'They tell wonders of et-Tâyif! — well, we have been there ; and one will find it to be less than the report.' — The maladies of Arabia had increased in me by the way ; the lower limbs were already full of the ulcers, that are called *hub* or *bîzr* or *bethra et-támr*, 'the date button,' on the Persian Gulf Coast [because they rise commonly near the time of date harvest]. The boil, which is like the Aleppo button, is known in many parts of the Arabic world, — in Barbary, in Egypt ('Nile sores'); and in India ('Delhi boil') : it is everywhere ascribed to the drinking of unwholesome water. The flat sores may be washed with carbolic acid, and anointed with fish oil ; but the evil will run its course, there is no remedy : the time with me was nearly five months. — Sores springing of themselves are common among the Beduw. [*Comp.* also Deut. xxviii. 35.] For such it seemed better to descend immediately to Jidda ; also I rolled in my heart, that which I had read of (old) Mecca Sherîfs : besides, were it well for me to go to et-Tâyif, why had not el-Bessàm — who had praised to me the goodness of the late Sherîf — given me such counsel at Aneyza ? Now there sat a new Sherîf : he is also Emir of Mecca ; and I could not know that he would be just to a Nasrány.

The Kusmàn were busy there to bathe themselves, and put off their secular clothing : and it was time, for the tunics of the drivers and masters were already of a rusty leaden hue, by their daily lifting the loads of butterskins. — Sitting at the water-holes, each one helped other, pouring full bowls over his neighbour's head. And then, every man taking from his bundle two or three yards of new calico or towel stuff, they girded themselves. This is the *ihràm*, or pilgrims' loin-cloth, which covers them to the knee ; and a lap may be cast over the shoulder. They are henceforth bare-headed and half-naked ; and in this guise must every soul enter the sacred precincts : but if one be of the town or garrison, it is his duty only after a certain absence. In the men of our Nejd caravan, a company of butter-chandlers, that descend yearly with this merchandise, could be no fresh transports of heart. They see but fatigues before them in the Holy City ; and I heard some say, 'that the heat now in Mekky [with clouded simûm weather] would be intolerable' : they are all day in the sûks, to sell their wares ; and in the sultry nights they taste no refreshing, until they be come again hither. The fellowships would lodge in hired chambers : those few persons in the caravan who were tradesmen in the City would go home ; and so would the son of Bessàm : his good father had a house in town ; and an old slave-woman was left there, to keep it.

This is a worn camping-ground of many generations of pilgrims and caravaners ; and in summer the noon station of passengers between the Holy City and et-Tâyif. Foul rákhams were hawking up and down ; and I thought I saw mortar clods in this desert place, and some old substruction of brick building ! — My Aneyza friends tell me, that this is the old station *Kurn el-menâzil* ; which they interpret of the interlacing stays of the ancient booths, standing many together in little space. I went barefoot upon the pleasant sward in the midday sun, — which at this height is temperate ; for what sweetness it is, after years passed in droughty countries, to tread again upon the green sod ! Only the Nasrâny remained clad among them ; yet none of the Kusmàn barked upon me ; they were themselves about to arrive at Mecca ; and I might seem to them a friend, in comparison with the malignant Beduin people of this country [*el-Hathèyl*].

I found Bessàm's son, girded only in the ihràm, sitting under his awning. " Khalîl, quoth he, yonder — by good fortune ! are some cameleers from et-Tâyif : I have spoken with one of them ; and the man — who is known — is willing to convey thee to Jidda." — " And who do I see with them ? " — " They are *Jáwwa*. [Java pilgrims so much despised by the Arabians : for the Malay faces seem to them hardly human ! I have heard Amm Mohammed say at Kheybar, ' Though I were to spend my lifetime in the *Béled ej-Jáwwa*, I could not — ! wellah I could not wive with any of their hareem.' Those religious strangers had been at Tâyif, to visit the Sherîf ; and the time was at hand of their going-up, in the ' little pilgrimage,' to Medina.] Khalîl, the adventure is from Ullah : wellah I am in doubt if we may find anyone at *el-'Ayn*, to accompany thee to the coast. And I must leave the kâfily ere the next halt ; for we (the young companions with Ibrahîm) will ride this night to Mecca ; and not to-morrow in the sun, because we are bare-headed. Shall we send for Sleymàn, and call the cameleer ? — but, Khalîl, agree with him quickly ; for we are about to depart, and will leave thee here."

— That cameleer was a young man of wretched aspect ! one of the multitude of pack-beast carriers of the Arabic countries, whose sordid lives are consumed with daily misery of slender fare and broken nights on the road. In his wooden head seemed to harbour no better than the wit of a camel, so barrenly he spoke. *Abd-er-Rahmàn* : " And from the 'Ayn carry this passenger to Jidda, by the Wâdy Fâtima." — " I will carry him by Mecca, it is the nigher way." *Abd-er-Rahmàn, and Sleymàn* : " Nay, nay ! but by the Wâdy, — Abd-er-Rahmàn added ; This one goes not to Mecca," — words which he spoke with a fanatical strangeness, that betrayed my life ; and thereto Sleymàn rolled his head ! So that the dull cameleer began to imagine there must be somewhat amiss ! — he gaped on him who should be his charge, and wondered to see me so white a man ! I cut short the words of such tepid friends : I would ride from the 'Ayn in one course to Jidda, whereas the drudge asked many days. The camels of this country are feeble, and of not much greater stature than horses. Such camels move the Nejd men's derision : they say, the Mecca cameleers' march is *mîthil, en-nimml*, ' at the ants' pace.'

That jemmâl departed malcontent, and often regarding me, whom he saw to be unlike any of the kinds of pilgrims. [As he went he asked in our kâfily, what man I were ; and some answered him, of their natural malice and treachery, *A Nasrâny !* When he heard that, the fellow said ' *Wullah-Bullah*, he would not have conveyed me, — no, not for an hundred reals ' !] " Khalîl, there was a good occasion, but thou hast let it pass ! " quoth Abd-er-Rahmàn. — " And is it to such a pitiful fellow you would commend my life, one that could not shield me from an insult, — is this the man of your confidence ? one whom I find to be unknown to all here : I might as well ride alone to Jidda." *Sleymàn* : " Khalîl, wheresoever you ride in these parts, they will know by your saddle-frame that you are come from the east [Middle Nejd]." — And likewise the camel-furnitures of these lowland Mecca caravaners seemed to us to be of a strange ill fashion.

Whilst we were speaking Ibrahîm's servant shouted to remove ! The now half-naked and bare-headed caravaners loaded hastily : riders mounted ; and the Nejd kâfily set forward. — We were descending to Mecca ! and some of the rude drivers *yulubbûn* [the devout cry of the pilgrims at Arafát]; that is, looking to heaven they say aloud *Lubbeyk ! Lubbeyk !* ' to do Thy will, to do Thy will (O Lord) ! ' This was not a cheerful song in my ears : my life was also in doubt for those worse than unwary words of the son of Bessàm. Such tidings spread apace and kindle the cruel flame of fanaticism ; yet I hoped, as we had set out before them, that we should arrive at the 'Ayn ere that unlucky Mecca jemmâl. I asked our Annezy driver, why he craked so? And he — "Auh! how fares Khalîl? to-morrow we shall be in Mekky! and thus we cry, because our voyage is almost ended, — Lubbeyk-lubbeyk!"

The ihràm or pilgrims' loin-cloth remains doubtless from the antique religions of the Kaaba. I have found a tradition among Beduins, that a loin-cloth of stuff which they call *yémeny* was their ancient clothing. — Women entering the sacred borders are likewise to be girded with the ihràm; but in the religion of Islam they cover themselves with a sheet-like veil. Even the soldiery riding in the (Syrian or Egyptian) Haj caravans, and the officers and the Pasha himself take the ihràm: they enter the town like bathing men, — there is none excused. [The pilgrims must remain thus half-naked in Mecca certain days; and may not cover themselves by night! until their turning again from Arafát.] At Mecca there is, nearly all months, a tropical heat: and perhaps the pilgrims suffer less from chills, even when the pilgrimage is made in winter, than from the sun poring upon their weak pates, wont to be covered with heavy coifs and turbans. But if the health of anyone may not bear it, the Lord is pitiful, it is remitted to him; and let him sacrifice a sheep at Mecca.

I saw another in our kâfily who had not taken the ihràm, — a sickly young trader, lately returned from Bosra, to visit his Kasîm home; and now he went down, with a little merchandise, to Mecca. The young man had learned, in fifteen years' sojourning in the north, to despise Nejd, "Are they not (he laughed to me) a fanatic and foolish people? ha-ha! they wear no shoes, and are like the Beduins. I am a stranger, Khalîl, as thou art, and have not put on the ihràm, I might take cold; and it is but to kill a sheep at Mekky." I perceived in his illiberal nicety and lying, and his clay visage, that he was not of the ingenuous blood. He had brought down a strange piece of merchandise in our kâfily, a white ass of Mesopotamia; and looked to have a double price for her in Mecca, — where, as in other cities of the Arabic East, the ass is a riding-beast for grave and considerable persons. [*confer* Judg. v. 10.] I said to Abd-er-Rahmàn, who was weakly, "And why hast thou taken the ihràm?" He answered, 'that if he felt the worse by the way, he would put on his clothing again; and sacrifice a sheep in Mecca.' — These are not pilgrims who visit the sacred city: they perform only the ordinary devotion at the Kaaba ; and then they will clothe themselves, to go about their affairs.

From the Seyl we descend continually in a stony valley-bed betwixt black plutonic mountains, and half a mile wide : it is a vast seyl-bottom of grit and rolling stones, with a few acacia trees. This landscape brought the Scandinavian *fjelde*, earlier well-known to me, to my remembrance. The carcase of the planet is alike, everywhere : it is but the outward clothing that is diverse, — the gift of the sun and rain. They know none other name for this iron valley than *Wady es-Seyl*. In all yonder horrid mountains are *Aarab Haṭhèyl* [gentile pl. *el-Heṭheylân*], — an ancient name ; and it is said of them in the country, " they are a lineage by themselves, and not of kindred with the neighbour tribes." When Mecca and Tâyif cameleers meet with strangers coming down from Nejd, they will commonly warn them with such passing words, " *Ware the Haṭhèyl ! they are robbers.*" — The valley way was trodden down by camels' feet ! The Boreyda caravan had passed before us with two hundred camels, — but here I saw the footprints of a thousand ! I knew not that this is the Mecca highway to Tâyif, where there go-by many trains of camels daily. When the sun was setting we alighted — our last menzil — among the great stones of the torrent-valley. The height was now only 3700 feet.

—It had been provided by the good Bessàm, in case none other could be found at the station before Mecca, that his own man (who served his son Abd-er-Rahmàn by the way) should ride down with me to Jidda. Abd-er-Rahmàn now called this servant ; but the fellow, who had said " Ay-ay " daily in our long voyage, now answered with *lilla*, ' nay-nay — thus the Arabs do commonly fail you at the time ! — He would ride, quoth he, with the rest to Mecca.' Abd-er-Rahmàn was much displeased and troubled ; his man's answer confounded us. " Why then didst thou promise to ride with Khalîl ? go now, I entreat thee, said he ; and Khalîl's payment is ready : thou can'st not say nay." Likewise Ibrahîm the Emir persuaded the man ; — but he had no authority to compel him. The fellow answered shortly, " I am free, and I go not to Jidda ! " and so he left us. Then Ibrahîm sent for another in the kâfily, a poor man of good understanding : and when he came he bade him ride with Khalîl to Jidda ; but he beginning to excuse himself, they said, " Nothing hastens thee, for a day or two, to be at Mecca ; only set a price, — and no nay!" He asked five reals; and with this slender assurance they dismissed him: " Let me, I said, bind the man, by paying him earnest-money." Ibrahîm answered, " There is no need to-night; — in the morning!" I knew then in my heart that this was a brittle covenant; and had learned to put no trust in the evening promises of Arabs. — " Yâ Múthkir! let one of your Beduins ride with me to Jidda." — " Well, Khalîl, if that might help thee; but they know not the way." Ibrahîm, Abd-er-Rahmàn and the young companions were to mount presently, after supper, and ride to Mecca, — and then they would abandon me in this sinister passage. I understood later, that they had deferred riding till the morning light: — which came all too soon! And then we set forward.

It needed not that I should await that Promiser of over-night; who had no thoughts of fulfilling Ibrahîm and Abd-er-Rahmàn's words, — and they knew this. Though to-day was the seventeenth of our long marches from Aneyza; yet, in the sameness of the landscape, it seemed to me, until yesterday, when we passed es-Sh'aara, as if we had stood still. — The caravan would be at Mecca by midday: I must leave them now in an hour, and nothing was provided.

We passed by a few Beduins who were moving upward: light-bodied, black-skinned and hungry looking wretches: their poor stuff was loaded upon the little camels of this country. I saw the desolate valley-sides hoary with standing hay — these mountains lie under the autumn (monsoon) rains — and among the steep rocks were mountain sheep of the nomads; all white fleeces, and of other kind than the great sheep in Nejd. Now in the midst of the wady we passed through a grove of a treelike strange canker weed (*el-'esha*), full of green puff-leaves! the leafy bubbles, big as grape-shot, hang in noisome-looking clusters, and enclose a roll of seed. This herb is of no service, they say, to man or cattle; but the country people gather the sap, and sell it, for a medicine, to the Persian pilgrims; and the Beduins make charcoal of the light stems for their gunpowder. There met us a train of passengers, ascending to Tâyif, who had set out this night from Mecca. The hareem were seated in litters, like bedsteads with an awning, charged as a houdah upon camel-back: they seemed much better to ride-in than the side cradles of Syria.

I was now to pass a circuit in whose pretended divine law is no refuge for the alien ; whose people shut up the ways of the common earth ; and where any felon of theirs in comparison with a Nasrâny is one of the people of Ullah. I had looked to my pistol in the night ; and taken store of loose shot about me ; since I had no thought of assenting to a fond religion. If my hard adventure were to break through barbarous opposition, there lay thirty leagues before me, to pass upon this wooden thelûl, to the coast ; by unknown paths, in valleys inhabited by *ashràf* [sherîfs], the seed of Mohammed. — I would follow down the seyl-strands, which must needs lead out upon the seabord. But I had no food nor water ; and there was no strength left in me. — Ibrahîm who trotted by, gazed wistfully under my kerchief ; and wondered (like a heartless Arab) to see me ride with tranquillity. He enquired, " How I did ? and quoth he, seest thou yonder bent of the Wâdy ? when we arrive there, we shall be in sight of *'Ayn ez-Zeyma.*" — " And wilt thou then provide for me, as may befall ? " — " Ay, Khalîl ; " and he rode further : I saw not Abd-er-Rahmàn ! he was in the van with the companions.

The thelûl of one who was riding a little before me fell on a stone, and put a limb out of joint, — an accident which is without remedy ! Then the next riders made lots hastily for the meat ; and dismounting, they ran-in to cut the fallen beast's throat : and began with their knives to hack the not fully dead carcase. In this haste and straitness, they carved the flesh in the skin ; and every weary man hied with what gore-dropping gobbet his hand had gotten, to hang it at his saddle bow ; and that should be their supper-meat at Mecca ! they re-mounted immediately, and hastened forward. Between the fall of the thelûl, and an end of their butchery, the caravan camels had not marched above two hundred paces ! — Now I saw the clay banks of 'Ayn ez-Zeyma ! green with thúra ; — and where, I thought, in few minutes, my body might be likewise made a bloody spectacle. We rode over a banked channel in which a spring is led from one to the other valley-side. Besides the fields of corn, here are but few orchards ; and a dozen stems of sickly palms ; the rest were dead for fault of watering : the people of the hamlet are Hathèyl. I read the altitude, under my cloak, 2780 feet.

Here is not the Hejâz, but the Tehàma ; and, according to all Arabians, *Mecca is a city of the Tehàma*. Mecca is closed in by mountains, which pertain to this which we should call a middle region ; nevertheless the heads of those lowland jebâl (whose border may be seen from the sea) reach not to the brow of Nejd. [At el-Héjr, we found all that to be called Teháma which lies W. of the Aueyrid, although at first 3000 feet high, and encumbered with mountains : *v.* Vol. I. p. 463.]

In the (southern) valley-side stands a great clay kella, now ruinous ; which was a fort of the old Wahábies, to keep this gate of Nejd : and here I saw a first coffee-station *Kahwa* (vulg. *Gahwa*) of the Mecca country. This hospice is but a shelter of rude clay walling and posts, with a loose thatch of palm branches cast up. — Therein sat Ibrahîm and the thelûl riders of our kâfily ; when I arrived tardily, with the loaded camels. Sleymàn el-Kenneyny coming forth led up my riding-beast by the bridle to this open inn. The Kusmàn called *Khalîl !* and I alighted ; but Abd-er-Rahmàn met me with a careful face. — I heard a savage voice within say, "*He shall be a Moslem :*" and saw it was some man of the country, — who drew out his bright *khánjar !* " Nay ! answered the Kusmàn, nay ! not so." I went in, and sat down by Ibrahîm : and Abd-er-Rahmàn whispered to me, " It is a godsend, that we have found one here who is from our house at Jidda ! for this young man, *Abd-el-Azîz*, is a nephew of my father. He was going up, with a load of carpets, to et-Tâyif ; but I have engaged him to return with thee to Jidda : only give him a present, — three reals. Khalîl, it has been difficult ! — for some in the Kahwa would make trouble : they heard last night of the coming of a Nasrâny ; but by good adventure a principal slave of the Sherîf is here, who has made all well for you. Come with me and thank him : and we (of the kâfily) must depart immediately." — I found a venerable negro sitting on the ground : who rose to take me by the hand : his name was *Ma'abûb*. Ibrahîm, Sleymàn, and the rest of the Kusmàn now went out to mount their thelûls ; when I looked again they had ridden away. The son of Bessàm remained with me, who cried, " Mount ! and Abd-el-Azîz mount behind Khalîl ! " — " Let me first fill the girby." " There is water lower in the valley, only mount." " Mount, man ! " I said ; and as he was up I struck-on the thelûl : but there was no spirit in the jaded beast, when a short trot had saved me.

I heard a voice of ill augury behind us, " Dismount, dismount ! — Let me alone I say, and I will kill the kafir." I looked round, and saw him of the knife very nigh upon us ; who with the blade in his hand, now laid hold on the bridle. — " Ho ! Jew, come down ! ho ! Nasrâny (yells this fiend) ; I say down ! " I was for moving on ; and but my dromedary was weak I had then overthrown him, and outgone that danger. Other persons were coming, — " *Nôkh, nôkh !* cries Abd-er-Rahmàn, make her kneel and alight ! Khalîl." This I did without show of reluctance. He of the knife approached me, with teeth set fast, " to slay, he hissed, the Yahûdy-Nasrâny " ; but the servitor of the sherîf, who hastened to us, entreated him to hold his hand. — I whispered then to the son of Bessàm, " Go call back some of the kâfily with their guns ; and let see if the guest of Aneyza may not pass. Can these arrest me in a public way, without the *hadûd ?* " (borders of the sacred township). But he whispered, " Only say, Khalîl, thou art a Moslem, it is but a word, to appease them ; and to-morrow thou wilt be at Jidda : thou thyself seest — ! and wellah I am in dread that some of these will kill thee." — " If it please God I will pass, whether they will or no." " Eigh Khalîl ! said he in that demiss voice of the Arabs, when the tide is turning against them, what can I do ? I must ride after the kâfily ; look ! I am left behind." — He mounted without more ; and forsook his father's friend among murderers.

A throng of loitering Mecca cameleers, that (after their night march) were here resting-out the hot hours, had come from the Kahwa, with some idle persons of the hamlet, to see this novelty. They gathered in a row before me, about thirty together, clad in tunics of blue cotton. I saw the butcherly sword-knife, with metal scabbard, of the country, *jambîeh*, shining in all their greasy leathern girdles. Those Mecca faces were black as the hues of the damned, in the day of doom : the men stood silent, and holding their swarthy hands to their weapons.

The servitor of the Sherîf (who was infirm and old), went back out of the sun, to sit down. And after this short respite the mad wretch came with his knife again and his cry, ' that he would slay the Yahûdy-Nasrâny ' ; and I remained standing silently. The villain was a sherîf ; for thus I had heard Maabûb name him : these persons of the seed of Mohammed ' are not to be spoken against,' and have a privilege, in the public opinion, above the common lot of mankind. The Mecca cameleers seemed not to encourage him ; but much less were they on my part. [The sherîf was a nomad : his fellows in this violence were one or two thievish Hathéylies of the hamlet ; and a camel driver, his rafîk, who was a Beduwy. His purpose and theirs was, having murdered the kafir — a deed also of " religious " merit ! to possess the thelûl, and my things.]

When he came thus with his knife, and saw me stand still, with a hand in my bosom, he stayed with wonder and discouragement. Commonly among three Arabians is one mediator ; their spirits are soon spent, and indifferent bystanders incline to lenity and good counsel : I waited therefore that some would open his mouth on my behalf ! — but there was no man. I looked in the scelerat's eyes ; and totter-headed, as are so many poor nomads, he might not abide it ; but, heaving up his khánjar, he fetched a great breath (he was infirm, as are not few in that barren life, at the middle age) and made feints with the weapon at my chest ; so with a sigh he brought down his arm and drew it to him again. Then he lifted the knife and measured his stroke : he was an undergrown man ; and watching his eyes I hoped to parry the stab on my left arm, — though I stood but faintly on my feet, I might strike him away with the other hand ; and when wounded justly defend myself with my pistol, and break through them. Maabûb had risen, and came lamely again in haste ; and drew away the robber sherîf : and holding him by the hand, " What is this, he said, sherîf Sâlem ? you promised me to do nothing by violence ! Remember Jidda bombarded ! — and that was for the blood of some of this stranger's people ; take heed what thou doest. They are the Engleys, who for one that is slain of them send great battleships ; and beat down a city. And thinkest thou our lord the Sherîf would spare thee, a bringer of these troubles upon him ? — Do thou nothing against the life of this person, who is guilty of no crime, neither was he found within the precincts of Mecca. — No ! sherîf Sâlem, for *Hasseyn* (the Sherîf Emir of Mecca) our master's sake. Is the stranger a Nasrâny ? he never denied it : be there not Nasâra at Jidda ? "

Maabûb made him promise peace. Nevertheless the wolvish nomad sherîf was not so, with a word, to be disappointed of his prey : for when the old negro went back to his shelter, he approached anew with the knife ; and swore by Ullah that now would he murder the Nasrâny. Maabûb seeing that, cried to him, to remember his right mind ! and the bystanders made as though they would hinder him. Sâlem being no longer countenanced by them, and his spirits beginning to faint — so God gives to the shrewd cow a short horn — suffered himself to be persuaded. But leaping to the thelûl, which was all he levelled at, " At least, cries he, this is *náhab*, rapine ! " He flung down my coverlet from the saddle, and began to lift the great bags. Then one of his companions snatched my headband and kerchief; but others blamed him. A light-footed Hathèyly ran to his house with the coverlet; others (from the backward) plucked at my mantle: the Mecca cameleers stood still in this hurly-burly. I took all in patience; and having no more need, here under the tropic, I let go my cloak also. Maabûb came limping again towards us. He took my saddle-bags to himself; and dragging them apart, made me now sit by him. Sâlem repenting — when he saw the booty gone from him — that he had not killed the stranger, drew his knife anew; and made toward me, with hard-set (but halting) resolution appearing in his squalid visage, and crying out, that he would put to death the Yahûdy-Nasrâny: but now the bystanders withheld him. *Maabûb:* " I tell thee, Sherîf Sâlem, that if thou have any cause against this stranger, it must be laid before our lord the Sherîf; thou may'st do nothing violently." — " Oh! but this is one who would have stolen through our lord's country." — " Thou canst accuse him; he must in any wise go before our lord Hasseyn. I commit him to thee Sâlem, *teslîm*, in trust: bring him safely to Hasseyn, at et-Tâyif." The rest about us assenting to Maabûb's reasons, Sâlem yielded, — saying " I hope it may please the Sherîf to hang this Nasrâny, or cut off his head; and that he will bestow upon me the thelûl." — Notwithstanding the fatigue and danger of returning on my steps, it seemed to make some amends that I should visit et-Tâyif.

CHAPTER XVII

TÂYIF. THE SHERÎF, EMIR OF MECCA

Maabûb and Sâlem. The Nasrâny captive. Troubled day at the 'Ayn. Night journey with caravaners. Return to es-Seyl. The Seyl station. The Nasrâny assailed again. A Mecca pilgrimage. An unworthy Bessàm. A former acquaintance. 'Okatz. The path beyond to et-Tâyif. Night journey. Alight at a sherîf's cottage near Tâyif. Poor women of the blood of Mohammed. Aspect of et-Tâyif. The town. The Nasrâny is guest of a Turkish officer. Evening audience of the Sherîf. Sherîf Hasseyn, Emir of Mecca. The Sherîf's brother Abdillah. Turkish officers' coffee-club. A bethel stone. Zeyd, a Bîshy. Harb villages and kindreds. Sâlem brings again his booty. A Turkish dinner. " What meat is for the health." Three bethels. Mid-day shelter in an orchard.

THUS, Maabûb who had appeased the storm, committed me to the wolf! He made the thieves bring the things that they had snatched from me; but they were so nimble that all could not be recovered. The great bags were laid again upon the weary thelûl, which was led back with us; and the throng of camel-men dispersed to the Kahwa shadows and their old repose. — Maabûb left me with the mad sherîf! and I knew not whither he went.

Sâlem, rolling his wooden head with the soberness of a robber bound over to keep the peace, said now, 'It were best to lock up my bags.' He found a storehouse, at the Kahwa sheds; and laid them in there, and fastened the door, leaving me to sit on the threshold: the shadow of the lintel was as much as might cover my head from the noonday sun. — He eyed me wistfully. "Well, Sâlem (I said), how now? I hope we may yet be friends." "Wellah, quoth he — after a silence, I thought to have slain thee to-day!" — The ungracious nomad hated my life, because of the booty; for afterward he showed himself to be little curious of my religion! Sâlem called me now more friendly, " Khalîl, Khalîl ! " and not Nasrâny.

— He left me awhile; and there came young men of the place to gaze on the Nasrâny, as if it were some perilous beast that had been taken in the toils. "Akhs ! — look at him ! this is he, who had almost slipped through our hands. What think ye? — he will be hanged? or will they cut his throat? — Auh ! come and see ! here he sits, Ullah curse his father ! — Thou cursed one ! akhs ! was it thus thou wouldst steal through the béled of the Moslemîn?" Some asked me, "And if any of us came to the land of the Nasâra, would your people put us to death with torments?" — Such being their opinion of us, they in comparison showed me a forbearance and humanity! After them came one saying, he heard I was a hakîm; and could I cure his old wound? I bade him return at evening and I would dress it. "Thou wilt not be here then!" cries the savage wretch, — with what meaning I could not tell. Whatsoever I answered, they said it was not so; "for thou art a kafir, the son of a hound, and dost lie." It did their hearts good to gainsay the Nasrâny; and in so doing it seemed to them they confuted his pestilent religion.

 I was a passenger, I told them, with a general passport of the Sultan's government. One who came then from the Kahwa cried out, 'that he would know whether I were verily from the part of the Dowla, or a Muskôvy,' — the man was like one who had been a soldier: I let him have my papers; and he went away with them: but soon returning the fellow said, 'I lied like a false Nasrâny, the writings were not such as I affirmed.' Then the ruffian — for this was all his drift — demanded with flagrant eyes, 'Had I money?'—a perilous word! so many of them are made robbers by misery, the Mother of misdeed. — When Sâlem came again they questioned me continually of the thelûl; greedily desiring that this might become their booty. I answered shortly, 'It is the Bessàms'.' — 'He says *el-Bessàm!* are not the Bessàm great merchants? and wellah *melûk*, like the princes, at Jidda!'

 — Sâlem, who was returning from a visit to Mecca, had heard by adventure at the Kahwa station, of the coming down of a Nasrâny: at first I thought he had it from some in the Boreyda caravan. "It was not from them of Boreyda, he answered, — Ullah confound all the Kusmàn! that bring us kafirs: and billah last year we turned back the Boreyda kâfily from this place." — The Kasîm kâfilies sometimes, and commonly the caravans from Ibn Rashîd's country, pass down to Mecca by the Wady Laymûn. I supposed that Sâlem had some charge here; and he pretended, 'that the oversight of the station had been committed to him by the Sherîf.' — Sâlem was a nomad sherîf going home to his menzil: but he would not that I should call him Beduwy. I have since found the nomad sherîfs take it very hardly if any name them Beduw; and much less would the ashràf that are settled in villages be named *fellahîn*. Such plain speech is too blunt in their noble hearing : a nomad sherîf told me this friendly, — " It is not well, he said, for they are ashrâf."

Now Sâlem bade me rise, and led to an arbour of boughs, in whose shadow some of the camel-men were slumbering out the hot midday. Still was the air in this Tehâma valley, and I could not put off my cloak, which covered the pistol ; yet I felt no extreme heat. When Sâlem and the rest were sleeping, a poor old woman crept in ; who had somewhat to say to me, for she asked aloud, ' Could I speak Hindy ? ' Perhaps she was a bond-servant going up with a Mecca family to et-Tâyif, — the Harameyn are full of Moslems of the Hindostany speech : it might be she was of India. [In the Nejd quarter of Jidda is a spital of such poor Indian creatures.] Some negro bondsmen, that returned from their field labour, came about the door to look in upon me : I said to them, ' Who robbed you from your friends, and your own land ? — I am an Engleysy, and had we met with them that carried you over the sea, we had set you free, and given you palms in a béled of ours.' The poor black men answered in such Arabic as they could, ' They had heard tell of it ; ' and they began to chat between them in their African language. — One of the light sleepers startled ! and sat up ; and rolling his eyes he swore by Ullah, ' He had lost through the Engleys, that took and burned a ship of his partners.' I told them we had a treaty with the Sooltân to suppress slavery. ' I lied, responded more than one ferocious voice; when, Nasrâny, did the Sooltân forbid slavery ? ' ' Nay, he may speak the truth, said another ; for the Nasâra lie not.' — ' But he lies ! ' exclaimed he of the burned ship. — ' By this you may know if I lie ; — when I come to Jidda, bring a bondman to my Konsulato : and let thy bondservant say he would be free, and he shall be free indeed ! ' — ' Dog ! cries the fellow, thou liar ! — *are there not thousands of slaves at Jidda, that every day are bought and sold?* wherefore, thou dog ! be they not all made free ? if thou sayest sooth : ' and he ground the teeth, and shook his villain hands in my face.

Sâlem wakened late, when the most had departed : only a few simple persons loitered before our door ; and some were bold to enter. He rose up full of angry words against them. ' Away with you ! he cries, Ullah curse you all together ; Old woman, long is thy tongue — what ! should a concubine make talk : — and up, go forth, thou slave ! Ullah curse thy father ! shall a bondman come in hither ? ' — This holy seed of Mohammed had leave to curse the poor lay people. But he showed now a fair-weather countenance to me his prisoner : perhaps the sweet sleep had helped his madman's brains. Sâlem even sent for a little milk for me (which they will sell here, so nigh the city) : but he made me pay for it excessively ; besides a real for a bottle of hay, not worth sixpence, which they strewed down to my thelûl and their camels. Dry grass from the valley-sides above, twisted rope-wise (as we see in the Neapolitan country), is sold at this station to the cameleers.

It was now mid-afternoon : an ancient man entered ; and he spoke long and earnestly with Sâlem. He allowed it just to take a kafir's life, but perilous : ' the booty also was good he said, but to take it were perilous ; ay, all this, quoth the honest grey-beard, striking my camel-bags with his stick, is *tóm'a* (pelf). But thou Sâlem bring him before Hasseyn, and put not thyself in danger.' *Sâlem :* " Ay wellah, it is all tóm'a ; but what is the most tóm'a of all ? — is it not the Nasrâny's face ? look on him ! is not this tom'a ? " I rallied the old man (who was perhaps an Hathèyly of the hamlet, or a sherîf) for his opinion, ' that the Nasâra are God's adversaries.' His wits were not nimble ; and he listened a moment to my words, — then he answered soberly, " I can have no dealings with a kafir, except thou repent : " so he turned from me, and said to Sâlem, " Eigh ! how plausible be these Nasrânies ! but beware of them, Sâlem ! I will tell thee a thing, — it was in the Egyptian times. There came hither a hakîm with the soldiery : wellah Sâlem, I found him sitting in one of the orchards yonder ! — *Salaam aleyk !* quoth he, and I unwittingly answered, *Aleykom es-salaam !* — afterward I heard he was a Nasrâny ! akhs ! — but this is certain, that one Moslem may chase ten Nasâra, or a score of them ; which is oft times seen, and even an hundred together ; and Sâlem it is *íthin* (by the permission of) *Ullah !* " " Well, I hope Hasseyn will bestow on me the thelûl ! " was Sâlem's nomad-like answer.

— Seeing some loads of India rice, for Tâyif, that were set down before the Kahwa, I found an argument to the capacity of the rude camel-men ; and touching them with my stick enquired, " What sacks be these ? and the letters on them ? if any of you (ignorant persons) could read letters ? Shall I tell you ? — this is rice of the Engleys, in sacks of the Engleys ; and the marks are words of the Engleys. Ye go well clad ! — though only hareem wear this blue colour in the north !

but what tunics are these ? — I tell you, the cotton on your backs was spun and wove in mills of the Engleys. Ye have not considered that ye are fed in part and clothed by the Engleys!" Some contradicted: the most found that I said well. Such talk helped to drive the time, disarmed their insolence, and damped the murderous mind in Sâlem. But what that miscreant rolled in his lunatic spirit concerning me I could not tell: I had caught some suspicion that they would murder me in this place. If I asked of our going to Tâyif, his head might turn, and I should see his knife again; and I knew not what were become of Maabûb. — They count thirty hours from hence to et-Tâyif, for their ant-paced camel trains: it seemed unlikely that such a hyena could so long abstain from blood.

Late in the day he came to me with Maabûb and Abd-el-Azîz; who had rested in another part of the kahwa! — surely if there had been right worth in them (there was none in Abd-el-Azîz), they had not left me alone in this case. Maabûb told me, I should depart at evening with the caravan men; and so he left me again. Then Sâlem, with a mock zeal, would have an inventory taken of my goods — and see the spoil! he called some of the unlettered cameleers to be witnesses. I drew out all that was in my bags, and cast it before them: but "*El-f'lûs, el-f'lûs!* cries Sâlem with ferocious insistence, thy money! thy money! that there may be afterward no question, — show it all to me, Nasrâny!" — "Well, reach me that medicine box; and here, I said, are my few reals wrapped in a cloth!"

The camel-men gathered sticks; and made watch fires: they took flour and water, and kneaded dough, and baked '*abûd* under the ashes; for it was toward evening. At length I saw this daylight almost spent: then the men rose, and lifted the loads upon their beasts. These town caravaners' camels march in a train, all tied, as in Syria. — My bags also were laid upon the Bessàm's thelûl: and Sâlem made me mount with his companion, *Fheyd*, the Beduin, or half-Beduin master of these camels. — "Mount in the shidàd! Khalîl Nasrâny." [But thus the radîf might stab me from the backward, in the night!] I said, I would sit back-rider; and was too weary to maintain myself in the saddle. My words prevailed! for all Arabs tender the infirmity of human life, — even in their enemies. Yet Sâlem was a perilous coxcomb; for if any-one reviled the Nasrâny in his hearing, he made me cats' eyes and felt for his knife again.

In this wise we departed ; and the Nasrâny would be hanged, as they supposed, by just judgment of the Sherîf, at et-Tâyif : all night we should pace upward to the height of the Seyl. Fheyd was in the saddle ; and the villain, in his superstition, was adread of the *Nasrâny !* Though malignant, and yet more greedy, there remained a human kindness in him ; for understanding that I was thirsty he dismounted, and went to his camels to fetch me water. Though I heard he was of the Nomads, and his manners were such, yet he spoke nearly that bastard Arabic of the great government towns, Damascus, Bagdad, Mecca. But unreasonable was his impatience, because I a weary man could not strike forward the jaded thelûl to his liking, — he thought that the Nasrâny lingered to escape from them !

A little before us marched some Mecca passengers to et-Tâyif, with camel-litters. That convoy was a man's household : the goodman, swarthy as the people of India and under the middle age, was a wealthy merchant in Mecca. He went beside his hareem on foot, in his white tunic only and turban ; to stretch his tawny limbs — which were very well made — and breathe himself in the mountain air. [The heat in Mecca was such, that a young Turkish army surgeon, whom I saw at et-Tâyif, told me he had marked there, in these days, 46° C.] Our train of nine camels drew slowly by them : but when the smooth Mecca merchant heard that the stranger riding with the camel-men was a Nasrâny, he cried, " Akhs ! a Nasrâny in these parts ! " and with the horrid inurbanity of their (jealous) religion, he added, " Ullah curse his father ! " and stared on me with a face worthy of the koran !

The caravan men rode on their pack-beasts eating their poor suppers, of the bread they had made. Sâlem, who lay stretched nomad-wise on a camel, reached me a piece, as I went by him ; which beginning to eat I bade him remember, " that from henceforth there was bread and salt between us, — and see, I said, that thou art not false, Sâlem." — " Nay, wellah, I am not *khayin*, no Khalîl." The sickly wretch suffered old visceral pains, which may have been a cause of his splenetic humour. — He bye and bye blamed my nodding ; and bade me sit fast. " Awake, Khalîl ! and look up ! Close not thine eyes all this night ! — I tell thee thou mayest not slumber a moment ; these are perilous passages and full of thieves, — the Hathèyl ! that steal on sleepers : awake ! thou must not sleep." The camels now marched more slowly ; for the drivers lay slumbering upon their loads : thus we passed upward through the weary night. Fheyd left riding with me at midnight, when he went to stretch himself on the back of one of his train of nine camels ; and a driver lad succeeded him. Thus these unhappy men slumber two nights in three : and yawn out the daylight hours, — which are too hot for their loaded beasts — at the 'Ayn station or at the Seyl.

The camels march on of themselves, at the ants' pace. — " Khalîl ! quoth the driver lad, who now sat in my saddle, beware of thieves ! " Towards morning, we both nodded and slumbered, and the thelûl wandering from the path carried us under a thorny acacia : — happy I was, in these often adventures of night-travelling in Arabia, never to have hurt an eye ! My tunic was rent ! — I waked ; and looking round saw one on foot come nigh behind us. — " What is that ? " quoth the strange man, and leaping up he snatched at the worsted girdle which I wore in riding ! I shook my fellow-rider awake, and struck-on the thelûl ; and asked the raw lad, ' If that man were one of the cameleers ? ' — " Didst thou not see him among them ? but this is a thief and would have thy money." The jaded thelûl trotted a few paces and stayed. The man was presently nigh behind me again : his purpose might be to pull me down ; but were he an Hathèyly or what else, I could not tell. If I struck him, and the fellow was a cameleer, would they not say, ' that the Nasrâny had beaten a Moslem ? ' He would not go back ; and the lad in the saddle was heavy with sleep. I found no better rede than to show him my pistol — but I took this for an extreme ill fortune : so he went his way. — I heard we should rest at the rising of the morning star : the planet was an hour high, and the day dawning when we reached the Seyl ground ; where I alighted with Sâlem, under the spreading boughs of a great old acacia tree.

There are many such menzil trees and shadows of rocks, in that open station, where is no Kahwa : we lay down to slumber, and bye and bye the sun rose. The sun comes up with heat in this latitude ; and the sleeper must shift his place, as the shadows wear round. " Khalîl (quoth the tormentor) what is this much slumbering ? but the thing that thou hast at thy breast, what is it ? show it all to me." — " I have showed you all in my saddle-bags ; it is infamous to search a man's person." — " Aha ! said a hoarse voice behind me, he has a pistol ; and he would have shot at me last night." — It was a great mishap, that this wretch should be one of the cameleers ; and the persons about me were of such hardened malice in their wayworn lives, that I could not waken in them any honourable human sense. *Sâlem:* " Show me, without more, all that thou hast with thee there (in thy bosom) ! " — There came about us more than a dozen cameleers.

The mad sherîf had the knife again in his hand ! and his old gall rising, " Show me all that thou hast, cries he, and leave nothing ; or now will I kill thee." — Where was Maabûb ? whom I had not seen since yester-evening : in him was the faintness and ineptitude of Arab friends. — " Remember the bread and salt which we have eaten together, Sâlem ! " — " Show it all to me, or now by Ullah I will slay thee with this knife." More bystanders gathered from the shadowing places : some of them cried out, " Let us hack him in morsels, the cursed one ! what hinders ? — fellows, let us hack him in morsels ! " — " Have patience a moment, and send these away." Sâlem, lifting his knife, cried, " Except thou show me all at the instant I will slay thee ! " But rising and a little retiring from them I said, " let none think to take away my pistol ! " — which I drew from my bosom.

What should I do now ? the world was before me ; I thought, Shall I fire, if the miscreants come upon me ; and no shot amiss ? I might in the first horror reload, — my thelûl was at hand : and if I could break away from more than a score of persons, what then ? — repass the Rî'a, and seek Sh'aara again ! where 'Ateybân often come-in to water ; which failing I might ride at adventure ; and though I met with no man in the wilderness, in two or three days, it were easier to end thus than to be presently rent in pieces. I stood between my jaded thelûl, that could not have saved her rider, and the sordid crew of camel-men advancing, to close me in ; they had no fire-arms. — Fheyd approached, and I gave back pace for pace : he opened his arms to embrace me ! — there was but a moment, I must slay him, or render the weapon, my only defence ; and my life would be at the discretion of these wretches. — I bade him come forward boldly. There was not time to shake out the shot, the pistol was yet suspended from my neck, by a strong lace : I offered the butt to his hands. — Fheyd seized the weapon ! they were now in assurance of their lives and the booty : he snatched the cord and burst it. Then came his companion Sâlem ; and they spoiled me of all that I had ; and first my aneroid came into their brutish hands ; then my purse, that the black-hearted Siruân had long worn in his Turkish bosom at Kheybar. — Sâlem feeling no reals therein gave it over to his confederate Fheyd ; to whom fell also my pocket thermometer: which when they found to be but a toy of wood and glass, he restored it to me again, protesting with nefarious solemnity, that other than this he had nothing of mine! Then these robbers sat down to divide the prey in their hands. The lookers-on showed a cruel countenance still; and reviling and threatening me, seemed to await Sâlem's rising, to begin ' hewing in pieces the Nasrâny.'

Sâlem and his confederate Fheyd were the most dangerous Arabs that I have met with; for the natural humanity of the Arabians was corrupted in them, by the strong contagion of the government towns. — I saw how impudently the robber sherîf attributed all the best of the stealth to himself! Sâlem turned over the pistol-machine in his hand: such Turks' tools he had seen before at Mecca. But as he numbered the ends of the bullets in the chambers, the miscreant was dismayed; and thanked his God, which had delivered him from these six deaths! He considered the perilous instrument, and gazed on me; and seemed to balance in his heart, whether he should not prove its shooting against the Nasrâny. " Akhs — akhs! cried some hard hostile voices, look how he carried this pistol to kill the Moslemîn! Come now and we will hew him piecemeal: — how those accursed Nasrânies are full of wicked wiles! — O thou! how many Moslems hast thou killed with that pistol?" " My friends, I have not fired it in the land of the Arabs. — Sâlem, remember 'Ayn ez-Zeyma! thou camest with a knife to kill me, but did I turn it against thee? Render therefore thanks to Ullah! and remember the bread and the salt, Sâlem."

— He bade his drudge Fheyd, shoot off the pistol; and I dreaded he might make me his mark. Fheyd fired the first shots in the air: the chambers had been loaded nearly two years; but one after another they were shot off, — and that was with a wonderful resonance! in this silent place of rocks. Sâlem said, rising, " Leave one of them!" This last shot he reserved for me; and I felt it miserable to die here by their barbarous hands without defence. " Fheyd, he said again, is all sure? — and one remains?"

Sâlem glared upon me, and perhaps had indignation, that I did not say, *dakhîlak*: the tranquillity of the kafir troubled him. When he was weary, he went to sit down and called me, " Sit, quoth he, beside me." — " You hear the savage words of these persons; remember, Sâlem, you must answer for me to the Sherîf." — " The Sherîf will hang thee, Nasrâny! Ullah curse the Yahûd and Nasâra." Some of the camel-men said, " Thou wast safe in thine own country, thou mightest have continued there ; but since thou art come into the land of the Moslemîn, God has delivered thee into our hands to die : — so perish all the Nasâra ! and be burned in hell with your father, Sheytàn." " Look ! I said to them, good fellows — for the most fault is your ignorance, ye think I shall be hanged to-morrow : but what if the Sherîf esteem me more than you all, who revile me to-day ! if you deal cruelly with me, you will be called to an account. Believe my words ! Hasseyn will receive me as one of the ullema ; but with you men of the people, his subjects, he will deal without regard." " Thou shalt be hanged, they cried again, O thou cursed one ! " and after this they dispersed to their several halting places.

— Soon afterward there came over to us the Mecca burgess ; who now had alighted under some trees at little distance. From this smooth personage, a flower of merchants in the holy city — though I appealed to his better mind, that he should speak to Sâlem, I could not draw a human word ; and he abstained from evil. He gazed his fill ; and forsook me to go again to his hareem. I watched him depart, and the robber sherîf was upbraiding me, that I had " hidden " the things and my pistol ! — in this I received a shock ! and became numbed to the world : I sat in a swoon and felt that my body rocked and shivered ; and thought now, they had mortally wounded me with a knife, or shot ! for I could not hear, I saw light thick and confusedly. But coming slowly to myself, so soon as I might see ground I saw there no blood : I felt a numbness and deadness at the nape of the neck. Afterward I knew that Fheyd had inhumanly struck me there with his driving-stick, — and again, with all his force.

I looked up and found them sitting by me. I said faintly, " Why have you done this ? " *Fheyd :* " Because thou didst withhold the pistol." " Is the pistol mine or thine ? I might have shot thee dead ! but I remembered the mercy of Ullah." A caravaner sat by us eating, — one that ceased not to rail against me : he was the man who assailed me in the night, and had brought so much mischief upon me. I suddenly caught his hand with the bread ; and putting some in my mouth, I said to him, " Enough, man ! there is bread and salt between us." The wretch allowed it, and said not another word. I have never found any but Sâlem a truce-breaker of the bread and salt, — but he was of the spirituality.

— There came one riding to us on an ass! it was Abd-el-Azîz! He and Maabûb had heard the shots, as they sat resting at some distance yonder! For they, who were journeying together to et-Tâyif, had arrived here in the night-time; and I was not aware of it. Maabûb now sent this young man (unworthy of the name of Bessàm) to know what the shots meant, and what were become of the Nasrâny, — whether he yet lived? Abd-el-Azîz seeing the pistol in Sâlem's hands and his prisoner alive, asked, 'Wherefore had he taken away the man's pistol?' I said to him, "You see how these ignorant men threaten me: speak some word to them for thine uncle Abdullah's sake." But he, with sour fanatical looks; "Am I a Frenjy?"— and mounting again, he rode out of sight.

After these haps; Sâlem having now the spoil in his hands, and fearing to lose it again at et-Tâyif, had a mind to send me down to Jidda, on the Bessàm's thelûl. — "Ha! Khalîl, we are become brothers; Khalîl, are we not now good friends? there is nothing more betwixt us. What sayest thou? wilt thou then that we send thee to Jidda, and I myself ride with thee on the thelûl?" — But I answered, "I go to visit the Sherîf, at Tâyif; and you to accuse me there, and clear yourselves before him; at Jidda you would be put in prison." Some bystanders cried, "Let him go to et-Tâyif."

— A messenger returned from Maabûb, bidding Sâlem, Khalîl and Fheyd come to him. As we went I looked back, and saw Fheyd busy to rifle my camel-bags! — after that he followed us. The young Bessàm was sitting under the shadow of some rocks with Maabûb. — "Are you men? quoth Maabûb, are you men? who have so dealt with this stranger!" I told him how they robbed me, and what I had suffered at their hands: I was yet (and long afterward) stunned by the blows on the neck. *Maabûb:* "Sherîf Sâlem, thou art to bring this stranger to our lord Hasseyn at et-Tâyif, and do him no wrong by the way. How canst thou rob and wound one who is committed to thy trust, like the worst Beduin thieves? but I think verily that none of the Beduwy would do the like." *Sâlem:* "Is not this a Nasrâny? he might kill us all by the way; we did but take his pistol, because we were afraid." *Maabûb:* "Have you taken his silver from him and his other things, because ye were afraid? — I know thee, Sâlem! but thou wilt have to give account to our lord the Sherîf:" — so he dismissed us; and we returned to our place.

It came into my mind, bye and bye, to go again to Maabûb: the sand was as burning coals under my bare feet, so that after every few steps I must fall on my knees to taste a moment's relief. — Maabûb was Umbrella-bearer of the Sherîf; and an old faithful servitor of his brother, the late Sherîf. "Wherefore, I asked, had he so strangely forsaken me hitherto? Or how could he commit me to that murderous Sâlem! whom he himself called a *mad sherîf*; did he look to see me alive at Tâyif? — I am now without defence, at the next turn he may stab me; do thou therefore ride with me on the thelûl!" — "Khalîl, because of an infirmity [sarcocele] I cannot mount in a saddle." When I said, I would requite his pains, the worthy negro answered, "That be far from me! for it is my duty, which I owe to our lord, the Sherîf: but if thou have a remedy for my disease, I pray thee, remember me at et-Tâyif." — The young Bessàm had fever with a daily crisis. It came on him at noon; and then he who lately would not speak a word to shelter the Frenjy's life, with a puling voice (as they are craven and unmanly), besought me to succour him. I answered, 'At et-Tâyif!' Had he aided me at the first, for his good uncle's sake, I had not now been too faint to seek for remedies. I promised, if he would ride with me to-night, to give him a medicine to cut the fever, to-morrow: but Arabs put no trust in distant promises.

It drew to the mid-afternoon, when I heard we should remove; and then the foolish young Bessàm bade me rise and help to load the carpets on his camel. I did not deny him; but had not much strength; and Maabûb, blaming the rashness of the young man, would have me sit still in the shadow. — Maabûb rode seated on the load of carpets; and when the camel arose under him, the heavy old negro was nigh falling. Once more I asked him, not to forsake me; and to remember how many were the dark hours before us on the road.

I returned hastily to our menzil tree. The caravaners had departed; and the robber sherîf, who remained with the thelûl, was chafing at my delay: he mounted in the saddle, and I mounted again back-rider. — Sâlem had a new companion, who rode along with us, one Ibrahîm of Medina, lately landed at Jidda; and who would soon ride homeward in the 'little pilgrimage.' Ibrahîm hearing what countryman I was began to say, "That an Engleysy came in the vessel with him to Jidda; — who was wellah a good and perfect Moslem! yesterday he entered Mecca, and performed his devotion: — and this Engleysy that I tell you of, sherîf Sâlem, is now sojourning at Mecca, to visit the holy places." — Ibrahîm was one who lying under our awning tree, where he had arrived late, had many times disdained me, crying out despitefully, " Dog ! dog ! thou dog ! " But as we rode he began to smile upon the Nasrâny betwixt friendly and fiendly : at last quoth he, " Thou wast at Hâyil ; and dost thou not remember me ? — I have spoken with thee there ; and thou art Khalîl." — How strange are these meetings again in the immensity of empty Arabia ! but there is much resort to Hâyil : and I had passed a long month there. The light-bodied Arabian will journey upon his thelûl, at foot-pace, hundreds of leagues for no great purpose : and little more troubles him than the remembrance that he is absent from his household and children. " Thou hast known me then a long time in these countries ; now say on before these strangers, if thou canst allege aught against me." — " Well none, but thy misreligion."

Ibrahîm rode upon a dromedary ; his back-rider was an envenomed cameleer ; who at every pause of their words shook his stick at me : and when he walked he would sometimes leap two paces, as it were to run upon the kafir. There was a danger in Sâlem's seeing another do me wrong, — that in such he would not be out-done, and I might see his knife again : so I said to Ibrahîm (and stroked my beard), " By thy beard, man ! and for our old acquaintance at Hâyil ! — " Ibrahîm acknowledged the token ; and began to show the Nasrâny a more friendly countenance. " Ibrahîm, did you hear that the Engleys are a bad people ? " " Nay, *kullesh tâyib*, good every whit." — " Are they the Sultan's friends, or foes ? " — " His friends : the Engleys help him in the wars." *Sâlem :* " Well Khalîl, let this pass ; but tell me, what is the religion of the Nasâra ? I thought surely it was some horrible thing ! " — " Fear God and love thy neighbour, this is the Christian religion, — the way of Aysa bin-Miriam, from the Spirit of Ullah." — " Who is Aysa ? — hast thou heard this name, Ibrahîm ? " — " Ullah curse Aysa and the father of Aysa, cries Ibrahîm's radîf. Akhs ! what have we to do with thy religion, Nasrâny ? " Ibrahîm answered him very soberly, " But thou with this word makest thyself a kafir, blaspheming a prophet of the prophets of Ullah ! " The cameleer answered, half-aghast, " The Lord be my refuge ! — I knew not that Aysa was a prophet of the Lord ! " " What think'st thou, Sâlem ? " — " Wellah Khalîl, I cannot tell : but how sayest thou, *Spirit of Ullah !* — is this your kafir talk ? " — " You may read it in the koran, — say, Ibrahîm ? " — " Ay indeed, Khalîl."

There were many passengers in the way; some of whom bestowed on me an execration as we rode-by them, and Sâlem lent his doting ears to all their idle speech: his mind wavered at every new word. — "Do not listen to them, Sâlem, it is they who are the Nasâra!" He answered, like a Nomad, "Ay billah, they are Beduw and kafirs; — but such is their ignorance in these parts!" Ibrahîm's radîf could not wholly forget his malevolence; and Sâlem's brains were beginning again to unsettle: for when I said, "But of all this ye shall be better instructed to-morrow:" he cried out, "Thou liest like a false Nasrâny, the Sherîf will cut off thy head to-morrow, or hang thee: — and, Ibrahîm, I hope that our lord will recompense me with the thelûl."

We came to a seyl bed, of granite-grit, with some growth of pleasant herbs and peppermints; and where holes may be digged to the sweet water with the hands. Here the afternoon wayfarers to Tâyif alight, to drink and wash themselves to prayerward. [This site is said to be *Okâtz*, the yearly parliament and vaunting place of the tribes of Arabia before Islâm: the altitude is between 5000 and 6000 feet.] As we halted Abd-el-Azîz and Maabûb journeyed by us; and I went to ask the young Bessàm if he would ride with me to-night, — and I would reward him? He excused himself, because of the fever: but that did not hinder his riding upon an ass. — Sàlem was very busy-headed to know what I had spoken with them; and we remounted.

Now we ascended through strait places of rocks; and came upon a paved way, which lasts for some miles, with steps and passages opened by blasting! — this path had been lately made by Turkish engineers at the Government cost. After that we journeyed in a pleasant steppe which continues to et-Tâyif.

We had outmarched the slow caravan, and were now alone in the wilderness: Ibrahîm accompanied us, — I had a doubtful mind of him. They said they would ride forward: my wooden dromedary was cruelly beat and made to run; and that was to me an anguish. — Sâlem had responded to some who asked the cause of our haste, as we outwent them on the path, 'that he would be rid of the Nasrâny:' he murmured savage words; so that I began to doubt whether these who rode with me were not accorded to murder the Nasrâny, when beyond sight. The spoilers had not left me so much as a penknife: at the Seyl I had secretly bound a stone in my kerchief, for a weapon.

At length the sun set : it is presently twilight ; and Ibrahîm enquired of Sâlem, wherefore he rode thus, without ever slacking. *Sâlem :* " But let us outride them and sleep an hour at the mid-way, till the camels come by us. — Khalîl, awake thou and sleep not ! (for I nodded on his back ;) Auh ! hold thine eyes open ! this is a perilous way for thee : " but I slumbered on, and was often in danger of falling. Bye and bye looking up, I saw that he gazed back upon me ! So he said more softly, " Sleepest thou, Khalîl Nasrâny ? — what is this ! when I told thee *no* ; thou art not afraid ! " — " Is not Ullah in every place ? " — " Ay, wellah Khalîl." Such pious words are honeycombs to the Arabs, and their rude hearts are surprised with religion. — " Dreadest thou not to die ! " — " I have not so lived, Moslêm, that I must fear to die." The wretch regarded me ! and I beheld again his hardly human visage : the cheeks were scotched with three gashes upon a side ! It is a custom in these parts, as in negro Africa ; where by such marks men's tribes may be distinguished.

Pleasant is the summer evening air of this high wilderness. We passed by a watering-place amongst trees, and would have halted : but Ibrahîm answered not to our call ! — he had outridden us in the gloom. Sâlem, notwithstanding the fair words which lately passed between them, now named him " impudent fellow " and cursed him. " And who is the man, Sâlem? I thought surely he had been a friend of thine." — " What makes him my friend ? — Sheytàn ! I know of him only that he is from Medina." — Bye and bye we came up with him in the darkness ; and Ibrahîm said, ' They had but ridden forward to pray. And here, quoth he, is a good place ; let us alight and sup.' They had bread, and I had dates : we sat down to eat together. Only the radîf held aloof, fearing it might be unlawful to eat with a kafir : but when, at their bidding, he had partaken with us, even this man's malice abated. — I asked Ibrahîm, Did he know the Nejûmy family at Medina ? " Well, he said, I know them, — they are but smiths."

We mounted and rode forward, through the open plain ; and saw many glimpsing camp-fires of nomads. Sâlem was for turning aside to some of them ; where, said he, we might drink a little milk. It had been dangerous for the kafir, and I was glad when we passed them by ; although I desired to see the country Aarab. — We came at length to the manôkh or midway halting-place of passengers ; in the dim night I could see some high clay building, and a thicket of trees. Not far off are other outlying granges and hamlets of et-Tâyif. We heard asses braying, and hounds barking in nomad menzils about us. We alighted and lay down here on the sand in our mantles; and slumbered two hours: and then the trains of caravan camels, slowly marching in the path, which is beaten hollow, came by us again: the cameleers lay asleep upon their loads. We remounted, and passing before them in the darkness we soon after lost the road: Ibrahîm said now, they would ride on to et-Tâyif, without sleeping; and we saw him no more.

In the grey of the morning I could see that we were come to orchard walls; and in the growing light enclosures of vines, and fig trees; but only few and unthriving stems of palms [which will not prosper at Tâyif, where both the soil and the water are sweet]. And now we fell into a road — a road in Arabia! I had not seen a road and green hedges since Damascus. We passed by a house or two built by the way-side; and no more such as the clay beyts of Arabia, but painted and glazed houses of Turkey. We were nigh et-Tâyif; and went before the villa of the late Sherîf, where he had in his life-time a pleasure-ground, with flowers! [The Sherîfs are commonly Stambûl bred men.] — The garden was already gone to decay.

Sâlem turned the thelûl into a field, upon our right hand; and we alighted and sat down to await the day. He left me to go and look about us; and I heard a bugle-call, — Tâyif is a garrisoned place. When Sâlem returned he found me slumbering; and asked, if I were not afraid? We remounted and had ado to drive the domedary over a luke-warm brook, running strongly. So we came to a hamlet of ashràf, which stands a little before et-Tâyif; and drew bridle a moment ere the sunrising, at the beyt of a cousin of Sâlem.

He called to them within, by name! — none answered. The goodman was on a journey; and his wives could not come forth to us. But they, hearing Sâlem's voice, sent a boy, who bore in our things to the house; and we followed him. This poor home in the Mecca country was a small court of high clay walling; with a chamber or two, built under the walls. There we found two (sherîf) women; and they were workers of such worsted coverlets in yarns and colours as we have seen at Teyma. [Vol. I. p. 345.] — And it was a nomad household; for the hareem told me they lived in tents, some months of the year, and drank milk of the small cattle and camels. Nomad-like was also the bareness of the beyt, and their misery : for the goodman had left them naught save a little meal ; of which they presently baked a cake of hardly four ounces, for the guests' breakfast. Their voices sounded hollow with hunger, and were broken with sighing ; but the poor noble-women spoke to us with a constant womanly mildness : and I wondered at these courtly manners, which I had not seen hitherto in Arabia. They are the poor children of Mohammed. The Sultàn of Islam might reverently kiss the hand of the least sherîf ; as his wont is to kiss the hand of the elder of the family of the Sherîfs of Mecca (who are his pensioners — and in a manner his captives), at Stambûl.

It had been agreed between us, that no word should be said of my alien religion. Sâlem spoke of me as a stranger he had met with in the way. It was new to me, in these jealous countries, to be entertained by two lone hareem. This pair of pensive women (an elder and younger) were sister-wives of one, whom we should esteem an indigent person. There was no coffee in that poor place ; but at Sâlem's request they sent out to borrow of their neighbours : the boy returned with six or seven beans ; and of these they boiled for us, in an earthen vessel (as coffee is made here), a thin mixture, — which we could not drink ! When the sun was fairly risen, Sâlem said he would now go to the Sherîf's audience ; and he left me. — I asked the elder hostess of the Sherîf. She responded, " Hasseyn is a good man, who has lived at Stambûl from his youth ; and the best learned of all the learned men here : yet is he not fully such as Abdullah (his brother), our last Sherîf, who died this year, — the Lord have him in His mercy ! And he is not white as Abdullah ; for his mother was a (Galla) bond-woman." — It seemed that the colour displeased them, for they repeated, " His mother was a bond-woman ! — but Hasseyn is a good man and just ; he has a good heart."

Long hours passed in this company of sighing (hunger-stricken) women ; who having no household cares were busy, whilst I slumbered, with their worsted work. — It was toward high noon, when Sâlem entered. " Good tidings ! 'nuncle Khalîl, quoth he : our lord the Sherîf sends thee to lodge in the house of a Tourk. Up ! let us be going ; and we have little further to ride." He bore out the bags himself, and laid them on my fainting thelûl ; and we departed. From the next rising-ground I saw et-Tâyif ! the aspect is gloomy, for all their building is of slate-coloured stone. At the entering of the town stands the white palace of the Sherîf, of two stories ; and in face of it a new and loftier building with latticed balconies, and the roof full of chimneys, which is the palace of Abdillah Pasha, Hasseyn's brother. In the midst of the town appears a great and high building, like a prison ; that is the soldiers' quarters.

— The town now before my eyes ! after nigh two years' wandering in the deserts, was a wonderful vision. Beside our way I saw men blasting the (granite) rock for building-stone. — The site of Tâyif is in the border of the plutonic steppe, over which I had lately journeyed, an hundred leagues from el-Kasîm. I beheld also a black and cragged landscape, with low mountains, beyond the town. We fell again into the road from the Seyl, and passed that lukewarm brook ; which flows from yonder monsoon mountains, and is one of the abounding springs which water this ancient oasis. The water-bearers — that wonted sight of Eastern towns ! went up staggering from the stream, under their huge burdens of full goat-skins ; — there are some of their mighty shoulders that can wield a camel load ! Here a Turkish soldier met us, with rude smiles ; and said, he came to lead me to the house where I should lodge. The man, a Syrian from the (Turkish) country about Antioch, was the military servant of an officer of the Sherîf : that officer at the Sherîf's bidding would receive me into his house.

The gate, where we entered, is called *Bab es-Seyl* ; and within is the open place before the Sherîf's modest palace. The streets are rudely built, the better houses are daubed with plaster : and the aspect of the town, which is fully inhabited only in the summer months, is ruinous. The ways are unpaved : and we see here the street dogs of Turkish countries. A servant from the Sherîf waited for me in the street, and led forward to a wicket gate : he bade me dismount, — and here, heaven be praised ! he dismissed Sâlem. " I will bring thee presently, quoth the smiling servitor, a knife and a fork ; also the Sherîf bids me ask, wouldst thou drink a little tea and sugar ? " — these were gentle thoughts of the homely humanity of the Prince of Mecca !

Then the fainting thelûl, which had carried me more than four hundred and fifty miles without refreshment, was led away to the Sherîf's stables ; and my bags were borne up the house stairs. The host, *Colonel Mohammed*, awaited me on the landing ; and brought me into his chamber. The tunic was rent on my back, my mantle was old and torn ; the hair was grown down under my kerchief to the shoulders, and the beard fallen and unkempt ; I had bloodshot eyes, half blinded, and the scorched skin was cracked to the quick upon my face. A barber was sent for, and the bath made ready : and after a cup of tea, it cost the good colonel some pains to reduce me to the likeness of the civil multitude. Whilst the barber was doing, the stalwart Turkish official anointed my face with cooling ointments ; and his hands were gentle as a woman's, — but I saw no breakfast in that hospice ! After this he clad me, my weariness and faintness being such, like a block, in white cotton military attire ; and set on my head a fez cap.

This worthy officer, whose name and style was *Mohammed Kheiry, Effendy, yâwer* (aide de camp) *es-Sherîf*, told me the Sherîf's service is better (being duly paid) than to serve the Dowla : he was *Bîm-bashy*, or captain of a thousand, in the imperial army. Colonel Mohammed was of the *Wilayat Konia* in Anatoly. He detested the corrupt officiality of Stambûl, and called them traitors ; because in the late peace-making they had ceded provinces, which were the patrimony of Islam : the great embezzling Pashas, he exclaimed, betrayed the army. With stern military frankness he denounced their Byzantine vices, and the (alleged) drunkenness of the late Sultan ! — In Colonel Mohammed's mouth was doubtless the common talk of Turkish officers in Mecca and et-Tâyif. But he spoke, with an honest pride, of the provincial life in his native country ; where is maintained the homely simplicity of the old Turkish manners. He told me of his bringing up, and the charge of his good mother, " My son, speak nothing but the truth ! abhor all manner of vicious living." He remembered from his childhood, ' when some had (but) broken into an orchard by night and stolen apples, how much talk was made of it ' ! Such is said to be the primitive temper of those peoples ! — And have here a little talk, told me by a true man, — the thing happened amongst Turkoman and Turkish peasants in his own village, nigh Antioch. " An old husbandman found a purse in his field ; and it was heavy with silver. But he having no malice, hanged it on a pole, and went on crying down the village street, ' Did ye hear, my neighbours, who hast lost this purse here ? ' And when none answered, the poor old man delivered the strange purse to the Christian priest ; bidding him keep it well until the owner should call for it."

— Heavy footfalls sounded on the stair ; and there entered two Turkish officers. The first, a tall martial figure, the host's namesake and whom he called his brother, was the Sherîf's second aide de camp; and the friends had been brothers in arms these twenty years. With him came a cavalry aga; an Albanian of a bony and terrible visage, which he used to rule his barbarous soldiery; but the poor man was milder than he seemed, and of very good heart. He boasted himself to be of the stock of Great " Alexander of the horns twain "; but was come in friendly wise to visit me, a neighbour of Europa. He spoke his mind — five or six words coming confusedly to the birth together, in a valiant shout: and when I could not find the sense; for he babbled some few terms that were in his remembrance of Ionian Italian and of the border Hellenes, he framed sounds, and made gestures! and looking stoutly, was pleased to seem to discourse with a stranger in foreign languages. The Captain (who knew not letters) would have me write his name too, *Mahmûd Aga el-Arnaûty*, *Abu Sammachaery* (of) *Praevaesa*, *Jûz-bashy*. Seven years he had served in these parts; but he understood not the words of the inglorious Arabs, — he gloried to be of the military service of the Sûltàn! though he seldom-times received his salary. This worthy was years before (he told me) a *kawàs* of the French Consulate in Corfu; where he had seen the English red frieze coats. " Hî Angli — huh-huh! the English (be right strong) quoth he. But the Albanians, huh! — the Albanians have a great heart! — heart makes the man! — makes him good to fight! — Aha; they have it strong and steadfast here!" and he smote the right hand upon his magnanimous breast. The good fellow looked hollow, and was in affliction: Colonel Mohammed told me his wife died suddenly of late; and that he was left alone with their children. — The other, Mohammed Aga, was a man curious to observe and hard to please, of polite understanding more than my host: he spoke Arabic smoothly and well for a Turk. In the last months they had seen the Dowla almost destroyed in Europe: they told me, ' there was yet but a truce and no sure peace; that England was of their part, and had in these days sent an army by sea from India, — which passed by Jidda — an hundred thousand men!' Besides, the Nemsy (Austria) was for the Sûltàn; and they looked for new warfare.

Toward evening, after a Turkish meal with my host, there entered a kawàs of the Sherîf; who brought a change of clothing for me. — And when they had clad me as an Arab shekyh; Colonel Mohammed led me through the twilight street, to the Sherîf's audience : the ways were at this hour empty.

Some *Bîsha* guards stand on the palace stairs ; and they made the reverence as we passed to the Sherîf's officer : other men-at-arms stand at the stairs' head. There is a waiting chamber ; and my host left me, whilst he went forward to the Sherîf. But soon returning he brought me into the hall of audience ; where the Sherîf Emir of Mecca sits daily at certain hours — in the time of his summer residence at et-Tâyif — much like a great Arabian sheykh among the *musheyikh*. Here the elders, and chief citizens, and strangers, and his kinsmen, are daily assembled with the Sherîf : for this is the mejlis, and coffee-parliament of an Arabian Prince ; who is easy of access and of popular manners, as was Mohammed himself.

The great chamber was now void of guests : only the Sherîf sat there with his younger brother, Abdillah Pasha, a white man and strongly grown like a Turk, with the gentle Arabian manners. Hasseyn Pasha [the Sherîf bears this Ottoman title !] is a man of pleasant face, with a sober alacrity of the eyes and humane demeanour ; and he speaks with a mild and cheerful voice : his age might be forty-five years. He seemed, as he sat, a manly tall personage of a brown colour ; and large of breast and limb. The Sherîf was clad in the citizen-wise of the Ottoman towns, in a long blue *jubba* of pale woollen cloth. He sat upright on his diwan, like an European, with a comely sober countenance ; and smoked tobacco in a pipe like the " old Turks." The simple earthen bowl was set in a saucer before him : his white jasmine stem was almost a spear's length. — He looked up pleasantly, and received me with a gracious gravity. A chair was set for me in face of the Sherîf : then Col. Mohammed withdrew, and a servitor brought me a cup of coffee.

The Sherîf enquired with a quiet voice, " Did I drink coffee ? " I said, " We deem this which grows in Arabia to be the best of all ; and we believe that the coffee plant was brought into Arabia from beyond the (Red) Sea." — " Ay, I think that it was from Abyssinia : are they not very great coffee-drinkers where you have been, in Nejd ? " Then the Sherîf asked me of the aggression at 'Ayn ez-Zeyma ; and of the new aggression at the Seyl. " It were enough, he said, to make any man afraid. [Alas ! Hasseyn himself fell shortly, by the knife of an assassin,— it was the second year after, at Jidda : and with the same affectuous cheerfulness and equanimity with which he had lived, he breathed forth his innocent spirit ; in the arms of a countryman of ours, Dr. Gregory Wortabet, then resident Ottoman Officer of Health for the Red Sea.] — But now you have arrived, he added kindly ; and the jeopardy (of your long voyage) is past. Take your rest at Tâyif, and when you are refreshed I will send you down to the English Consul at Jidda." He asked, ' Had I never thought of visiting et-Tâyif ? — it had been better, he added, if I were come hither at first from the Seyl ; and he would have sent me to Jidda.' The good Sherîf said further, " Neither is this the only time that Europeans have been here ; for — I think it was last year — there came one with the consul of Hollanda, to visit an inscription near the Seyl ; — I will give charge that it may be shown to you, as you return." I answered, ' I knew of one (Burckhardt) who came hither in the time of the Egyptian warfare.' — The Sherîf looked upon me with a friendly astonishment ! [from whence, he wondered, had I this knowledge of their home affairs ?] — The then subtle Sherîf of Mecca, who was beguiled and dispatched by the old Albanian fox Mohammed Aly, might be grand uncle of this worthy Prince.

" And how, he asked, had I been able to live with the Beduw, and to tolerate their diet ? — And found you the Beduw to be such as is reported of them [in the town romances], or fall they short of the popular opinion [of their magnanimity] ? — Did you help at the watering ? and draw up the buckets hand over hand — thus ? " And with the Arabian hilarity the good Sherîf laid-by his demesurate pipe-stem ; and he made himself the gestures of the nomad waterers ! (which he had seen in an expedition). There is not I think a natural Arabian Prince — but it were some sour Waháby — who might not have done the like ; they are all pleasant men. — " I had not strength to lift with them." He responded, with a look of human kindness, " Ay, you have suffered much ! "

He enquired then of my journey ; and I answered of Medáin Sâlih, Teyma, Hâyil : he was much surprised to hear that I had passed a month — so long had been the tolerance of a tyrant ! — in Ibn Rashîd's town. He asked me of Mohammed ibn Rashîd, ' Did I take him for a good man ? ' — plainly the Sherîf, notwithstanding the yearly presents which he received from thence, thought not this of him : and when I answered a little beside his expectation, " He is a worthy man," Hasseyn was not satisfied. Then we spoke of Aneyza ; and the Sherîf enquired of Zâmil, " Is he a good man ? " Finally he asked, ' if the garments [his princely gift] in which I sat clad before him, pleased me ? ' and if my host showed me (which he seemed to distrust) a reasonable hospitality ? Above an hour had passed ; then Colonel Mohammed, who had been waiting without, came forward ; and I rose to take my leave. The Sherîf spoke to my host, for me ; and especially that I should walk freely in et-Tâyif, and without the walls ; and visit all that I would. — Colonel Mohammed kissed the venerable hand of the Sherîf, and we departed.

We returned through the streets to the market-place ; and went to sit on the benches before a coffee-house. This is the Turkish Officers' Club, where they come to drink coffee and the nargîly, and play at chess. We found a kaimakàm, a kâdy, a young army surgeon and other personages ; who were sitting on the benches to wear out their evening hours, and discoursing with the civil gravity of Orientals. The coffee taverner served us with a smiling alacrity ; and after salutations I became of those Ottoman benchers' acquaintance. The surgeon — a Stambûly — questioned me in the French language, which he spoke imperfectly. ' Were I a *medecin ?* ' and repeated to them with wonder, in Turkî, that I answered, *non !* for they heard-say I had professed the art, in my travels. But the kâdy responded, " Englishmen are thus by nature, they will not lie." The surgeon asked further, ' If I had any thought of visiting Mecca ? He had read in the French language of some European who lived several years in Medina and Mecca ! ' — Now Maabûb went by : and seeing me, he came to salute us. " This is that worthy man ! quoth Col. Mohammed, who saved your life at 'Ayn ez-Zeyma : — Maabûb, our lord the Sherîf is beholden to you for that good deed, and for the care you have spared us. Wellah if you had not been at the 'Ayn, Khalîl had been slain yesterday by that cursed Sâlem." *Maabûb*: " By good fortune I was at the 'Ayn, in time to save Khalîl from a sherîf mejnûn (madman) ; who would not let him pass by to Jidda."

— The young surgeon told me, ' He had seen that inscription of which the Sherîf made mention : the letters were all the same as in French ! and he could read them plainly — HIPPOCRATES ! ' And afterward another told me, he could read the inscription, — it was PHILIP OF MACEDON ! — These were spirits, only good to be set to divinity studies : they wear the livery, but are aliens from the mind of Europe ! A second military surgeon, who came in, said, ' et-Tâyif was too dry to be wholesome; and there was much fever here this year: a fetid marsh beyond the town, corrupted the night air.' They looked for the (tropical) rain to fall in the next moon; and this commonly lasts four, five or six weeks at et-Tâyif. — *Is not the border of the monsoon rain the just division between Arabia Felix and Arabia Deserta?* Notwithstanding the great altitude of the plain about Tâyif [nearly six thousand feet], snow is never seen here. The Turkish surgeons — of a somewhat light and disdainful humour — were contemned as "ignorants" by the military and townspeople! who with Oriental perversity are impatient of the slow and uncertain cures of medicine. — The Pasha, or military governor, of this province has his summer residence at et-Tâyif: his titular seat is Jidda.

We rose, and I went with the kâdy and my host, to visit a block lying before the man-of-law's house: they say it is an idol, *el-'Uzza*. I beheld by the light of their lanterns an untrimmed mass of scaly grey granite, without inscription (fig. p. 549), — one of the thousand crags of these mountains; and which haply lay here before the founding of et-Tâyif. — To rub and kiss the black stone built in the Kaaba wall, is even now Mohammedan religion: in like wise you may see poor devout men in the northern Arab countries throng to kiss the mahmal camel, returned from Mecca; and how they fervently rub their clothing on him. But the kâdy and Col. Mohammed told me, "There are some cursed ones in the town, who when they are sick will come hither by night to rub themselves secretly on this stone. The stones (they said further) were oracles, in the days of ignorance, and Sheytàn spake out of them." [We read that in the ancient Kaaba were diverse idols; and amongst them the images of Jesu and Miriam. Mohammed when he re-entered Mecca, more than a conqueror, gave the word to destroy them all; and they are accounted, by the (fabulous) Arabic schoolmen, three hundred and sixty! — or one for every day in the year, which we have seen to signify no more than '*a great many*': *v.* Vol. I. p. 61 and 83, and Vol. II. p. 179.]

On the morrow the Sherîf sent one of his Bîshy guards, to attend me;—a Beny Sâlem (Harby) villager, of negro blood, from *Jebel el-Figgera*, between Medina and Yanb'a: *Zeyd* was his name, a worthy young man, who had some knowledge of letters. The Bîshy (negro) guard are not drawn only from Wâdy Bîsha, neither are all the villagers of that valley of African blood; but the Bîshy soldiery are any likely fellows that come in and offer themselves to serve the Sherîf. Zeyd put off his jingling gunner's belt, and sword-knife; and lying down on the floor, Beduin-wise, he drew from his bosom a little book of devotion; and began to patter to himself, casting from time to time a pious eye upon me. And when I stayed to observe him; " Thou art good, quoth he, thou art not a kafir, and lackest but to learn the way unto Ullah." I asked him of his dîra and of his tribe. He said, " All the Harb country seyls to the Wady el-Humth." I asked, " And is the head of that great valley in the Wady Laymûn?" He answered, " It is likely." All the Harb may be divided, he told me, into Beny Sâlem and *Mosrûh*. I enquired of their settlements. *Zeyd*: " I will tell thee all that I know, — and thus the Sherîf bade me: the villages of Mosrûh are *Râbug, Klèys, el-Khereyby* (near Mecca), *es-Suergîeh*, and others, I have them not all in mind. But the Beny Sâlem villages, between el-Medina and Yanb'a, and in *Wâdy Ferr'a*, — a long valley, with Aarab Beny 'Amr and *el-'Ub-beda*, are these; — *el-Jedeyda, Umm-Theyàn, Kaif, el-Kissa, el-Âb, el-Hamra, el-Khorma, el-Wàsita, el-Hassanîeh, el-Faera, el-'Alîy, Jedîd, Beddur*, and (his own) *J. el-Figgera*; and in Wâdy Yanb'a are *Sweyga, Shâtha, en-Najjeyl, Medsûs*." Of the Lahabba (cutters of the pilgrim caravans), he said; " they are, Mosrûh, a fendy of 'Auf: the rest of 'Auf are not robbers. He is the most set-by among the Lahabba who is the best thief; and because they had it from their fathers, they would not leave their misdoing for a better trade of life. Their strength is six hundred guns" [two hundred perhaps or less]. I asked, " How durst they molest pilgrims? and you, the rest of Harb, why do ye not purge your dîra from those children of iniquity?" But Zeyd thought it could not well be, of a thing long time suffered! — The Arabs see not beyond their factions; and, having so little public spirit, there rise no leaders among them. Zeyd said further; ' The fendies of Harb, of Beny Sâlem kindred, are:

el-Hamda,	*el-Mo'ara,*
es-Sobh,	*Wélad Selîm,*
el-Motàl'ha,	*Beny Temîm* [not the Nejd nation],
Mohamîd,	*es-Sa'adîn,*
Rahala,	*el-Huâzim* and *el-Hejélla,*
Beny 'Amr,	*eth-Thoàhirra,*
el-Guâd,	*Mozayna,*
el-Wuffiàn,	*el-Henneytát,*
es-Serràha,	*el-Jemélla!*

and of Mosrûḥ kindred are,

- Sa'adî,
- Laḥabba (" all Haj-way robbers "),
- ez-Z'bèyd,
- Bíshr,
- el-Ḥumràn,
- Seḥely,
- Beny Ass'm,
- Beny 'Amr (of the Férr'a — not those of Beny Sâlem)
- el-Jeràjera,
- el-'Ubbeda,
- el-Juâberra,
- Beny 'Aly (sheykh el-Fúrn),
- el-Ferúdda,
- el-Jàhm,
- Ahl Ḥàjjur,
- Beny Ḥasseyn. (These last are all ashràf.) '

Col. Mohammed entered, — and then Sâlem : whom the Sherîf had commanded to restore all that he and his confederate robbed from me. The miserable thief brought the pistol (now broken !), the aneroid, and four reals, which he confessed to have stolen himself from my bags. He said now, " Forgive me, Khalîl ! and, ah! remember the *zád* (food) and the *melh* (salt) which is between us." " And why didst thou not remember them at the Seyl, when thou tookest the knife, a second time, to kill me ? " *Col. Mohammed*: " Khalîl says justly ; why then didst thou not remember the bread and salt ? " — " I am guilty, but I hope the Sherîf may overlook it ; and be not thou against me, Khalîl ! " I asked for the purse and the other small things. But Sâlem denying that they had anything more ! Col. Mohammed drove him out, and bade him fetch them instantly. — " The cursed one ! quoth my host, as he went forth : the Sherîf has determined after your departure to put him in irons, as well as the other man who struck you. He will punish them with severity, — but not now, because their kindred might molest you as you go down to Jidda. And the Sherîf has written an injunction, which will be sent round to all the tribes and villages within his dominion, ' *That in future, if there should arrive any stranger among them, they are to send him safely to the Sherîf* ' : for who knows if some European may not be found another time passing through the Sherîf's country ; and he might be mishandled by the ignorant people. Also the Sherîf would have no after-questions with their governments."

The good and wise Sherîf Hasseyn might have tolerated that a (Christian) European should visit Mecca (in which were nothing contrary to the primitive mind of Islam). — Word was now brought to him from the city of that British subject before mentioned ; whom some in Mecca would have violently arrested as a Nasrâny. Col. Mohammed told me, he was detained there at present ; and had called several persons to witness, that they had seen and known him in a former pilgrimage. — The Sherîf wrote again, 'that if the stranger were proved to be a Moslem he should be suffered to dwell in Mecca ; but if no, to send him with a sufficient guard to his consul at Jidda.' — I spoke earnestly in the matter so soon as I came thither a few days later, that the consular arm should be extended to shelter a countryman in danger. *Answer*: "If any Englishman be in Mecca, he went there without our knowledge : had he come to us, we would have dissuaded him ; and now if he be in trouble, that is his own folly, and let him look to it!"

I walked in the town with the Albanian ; but he with his (ferocious) kawàs's countenance repulsed the indiscreet thronging of the younger and idle sort ; and buffeting some of them with his hands, he cried terribly *es-súla! es-súla!* to the prayers with you! till, sorry that he so fondly beat the people, (since he seemed not to hear my words), I held his arm perforce ; — for would it not be said in the town, "We saw Moslems beaten to-day by occasion of the Nasrâny." So we came again to the coffee house in the market square ; which is encompassed by open shops and stalls, as it were a fair, and in the midst is a stand of lamps. Mahmûd showing me all this with his hand, asked with that disdainful distrust which the Orientals have of their own things, 'Had I ever seen so wretched a place?'

I returned to my host's ; and there came in Sâlem and Fheyd — very chopfallen, to restore the rest of the stolen trifles : the cameleer was detained at et-Tâyif for this cause : he could not look to his cattle and his carrier's trade ; moreover he dreaded some bodily chastisement. *Col. Mohammed*: "How big was the stick, wherewith this man beat you?" and he showed me those they held in their hands. When I responded, "Less than his club-stick, and bigger than this *bakhoora*," Sâlem exclaimed, "Ullah! how truly the Nasrâny speaks! he would not magnify it ;" and they thanked me. — "The villains! quoth my host, as they departed, — when you had entered the Sultan's borders and looked to be arrived among friends, that they should assail you!"

Before the sun set Col. Mohammed brought me into an inner chamber to dinner ; he called also the Bîshy soldier : and we sat down about a stool, with a tray upon it, in which were many little Turkish messes. But we guests, one from a Harb village and the other lately come from the desert life, were not very fain to eat of his delicates ; for which we should bye and bye feel the worse. — When they asked, ' How had I fared among the Beduw ? ' I praised the simple diet of Arabia. *Zeyd*: " And, have you heard the saying of the sheykh of Harb — when he supped with the Haj Pasha ? — ' I praise not, said the Beduwy, your town victual ! I had rather satisfy myself with rice and mutton, boiled ; which I hold to be best for the health : and I will show it you.' — Wellah the sheykh took some of the Beduin supper and put it in a pot ; he took likewise of the Pasha's mess and put it in a pot : and he buried them both together. On the morrow he took up the two pots, in the sight of the Pasha : and the Beduin's meat was not spoiled ! but the Pasha's pot had bred worms, — so that the Pasha loathed both the sight and the smell of it ! ' Now tell me, said the Beduwy, should we choose to fill our bellies with the more corruptible meat ? ' ' Wellah thou hast prevailed,' quoth the Pasha ! "

The Sherîf would — Col. Mohammed told me — that I should see and be informed of everything ; and my host encouraged me to make drawings of all that I should see at et-Tâyif. Zeyd and another Bîshy were appointed to accompany me. — On the morrow I went to visit the three idol-stones that are shown at Tâyif. El-'Uzza, which I had seen in the small (butchers') market place, is some twenty feet long : near the end upon the upper side is a hollowness which they call *makám er-ras*, the head place ; and this, say they, was the mouth of the oracle. Another and smaller stone, which lay upon a rising-ground, before the door of the chief gunner, they call *el-Hubbal* : this also is a wild granite block, five or six feet long and cleft in the midst " by a sword-stroke of our lord Aly." [So at Kheybar, *v*. p. 97.] A derwîsh who approached, to gaze on me, and uttered querulous cries, was immediately chased away by the Bîshies. There went by a venerable man of the middle sort of citizens ; who, when he saw me stand before the stone said, sighing,

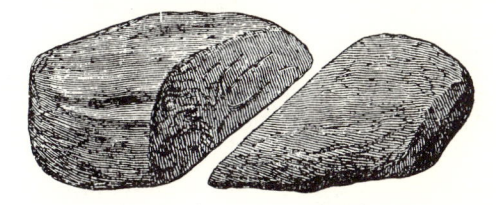

"Alas! there can be no place of the Moslemîn which is not entered by them; and now they come here!"

We passed out of the further town gate by the beautiful mesjid of Abdullah son of Mohammed's uncle Abbas. There is a gracious harmony in this ancient white building, which has two cupolas: some part of the walls were lately rebuilt. A little without the gate we came to the third reputed bethel-stone. This they name *el-Lâta* [which is Venus of the Arabs, says Herodotus] : it is an unshapely crag; in length nearly as the *'Uzza*, but less in height, and of the same grey granite. I saw the end of a miner's drill — and there a wound — in the stony flank! the deed, they told me, of some road-maker, two years before; the mechanical iconoclast would have ruined Sheytàn with a powder-blast: but there flew no more than a shiver of the tough crystalline mass — and it serves to manifest the nature of the mineral.

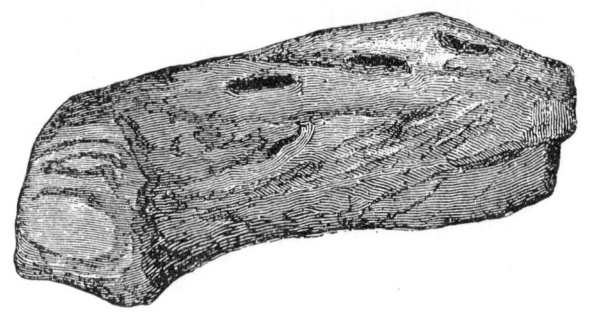

— Even the rocks in the infancy of human nature are oracles and saviours : and gods of the Arabian wilderness [till our VII. century] were such rude idol-stones ! reputed inns of their deities, — menâhil, rather than the gods themselves. [*Confer* Gen. xxviii. 17 : and even the Highest is called " a rock " in the Hebrew poets.] The bethels are untrimmed; though (we have seen) that Beduins might very well fashion a block to any rude similitude. There were some shallow pits or basins in the upper side of this Lâta stone, as the *makàm er-ras* in the 'Uzza; but they seem rather to be natural. Now these gods are no gods; for the generations that feared them — fear, that delightful passion and persuasion in religion ! — are dead : —vain is the religious wisdom which stands by deciduous arguments, to fall upon better knowledge ! and these " fears " of the Arabian fathers lie now in the dirt forsaken by human worshippers.

Zeyd brought me to an orchard ; where we might pass the midday heat under thick trees. — On this side of the town I saw not much greenness ; but a rough, blackish wilderness [as it might be of lavas]. The fruit of the market gardens of et-Tâyif is sent to Mecca and Jidda: beyond the brooks they are watered out of shallow pits, drawn by the small Arabian oxen. We entered the *bustàn* of a rich stranger, *el-Kâdy Músr*, one who commonly lives at et-Tâyif ; but he was absent in these days. The women of the garden rose as they saw us, and veiled their faces. — Then they spread a carpet under their great tree ; and brought leaning pillows ; and one gathered cactus fruit for the guests. Another sat down to make us coffee, which she boiled — as they use here — in a simple earthen cruse, of ancient form ; another prepared the nargîly : a maiden child served us with a gracious forwardness, and diligence. After coffee the hareem left us to slumber. Then Zeyd lying along and leaning on his elbow drew forth his book again ; and whilst he read his face was full of pensive religion ; but that was no occasion in him of a sour fanaticism, as in ill natures. — The young man had lately forsaken his Harb-village for fear of the sheykh. The sheykh of J. el-Figgera receives a Haj-road surra, paid partly in *ardubs* of grain ; which he distributes to the heads of households : but Zeyd's pretence, who being now of manly years required his part [not five reals' worth], was disallowed. The young man, in his anger, threatened death to the sheykh : and after that he thought he might no longer abide. He took his arms, and passed the mountains to Mecca ; where, being of good stature, he was admitted to be of the Emir's armed service.

CHAPTER XVIII

WADY FÂTIMA

Ghraneym. His unequal battle with the Kahtân. A second audience of the Sherîf. The tribes of ashràf. The dominion of the Sherîf. Gog and Magog. The *Rób'a el-Khâly*. Tâyif in fear of the Muscôv. The Koreysh. Set out to ride to Jidda. "The English are from the Tâyif dîra." A love-sick sherîf. A renowned effigy. The maiden's mountain. New dates. The Wady Fâtima. Tropical plants. The shovel-plough. Another Harra. Bee-hive-like cottages. The Tehâma heat. A rich man in both worlds. Mecca-country civil life and hospitality. A word of Saûd Ibn Saûd when he besieged Jidda. A thaif-Ullah. A poor negro's hospitality. End of the valley. The Mecca highway to Jidda. Sacred doves. Witness-stones. Apes of the Tehâma. A wayside Kahwa. — Jidda in sight! Melons grown in the sand without watering. Works and cisterns of Jidda water-merchants. Eve's grave. Enter the town. — A hospitable consulate.

THE Albanian meeting us as we re-entered the gate, led me on, by a street-like space betwixt the (ruinous) clay wall of Tâyif, and the town houses, to his barrack yard: where he showed me the cavalry horses, all Syrian hackneys; that stand always saddled. So he brought me homeward by the coffee club. I found there a certain Sheykh *Ghraneym*, of Aneyza; and with him sat a sheykh of el-Asîr. We drank round and discoursed together; and the Asîry sheykh, who seemed to be well studied in the Arabic tongue, entertained me gently, without any signs of fanatical misliking: — in the form of his speech I perceived nothing new. As for the patrician of Aneyza he received the Engleysy — thus honoured by the Sherîf — with a bowing-down complaisance. Ghraneym was a kinsman of Zâmil; and it seems had persuaded himself that he should have been emir before him: and for wanting of his will he had chosen to want his country; and live of a small pension at Mecca, which the Sherîf granted him. [Such is the bountiful custom of Arabian Emirs toward fugitive strangers.] It was told me here, 'Ghraneym would be in danger of his head if he returned home': when I said this afterwards to some of his townsmen, at Jidda, they laughed; and answered, 'that when he would, Ghraneym might return and live in Aneyza.'

Ghraneym told me, he was formerly chief of the English dromedary post for India! — the bag is now carried through the northern deserts from Damascus in eight days incessant riding to Bagdad! by Ageyl. [A tradesman of Aneyza in our kâfily told me, that upon a time he had ridden from el-Kasîm to et-Tâyif — almost 360 miles; and home again, in fifteen days! He used a diet of vetches to revive his jaded thelûl. Mehsan Allayda once mounted after the Friday midday prayer at el-Ally; and prayed next Friday in the great mesjid at Damascus — about 440 miles distant: but in such a course there is peril of the dromedary dying; the way being ten to twelve thelul journeys, at better leisure. The Haj-road post-rider stationed at M'aan can deliver a message at Damascus — about 220 miles distant — at the end of three days. El Héjr to Teyma — 75 miles, is one long thelûl journey; and from Kheybar to Medina — 72 miles, is counted a thelûl journey. A thelûl in good plight may be made to run 70 miles a day for short distances, and 60 to 65 miles daily for a week, and 50 miles daily for a fortnight. She has a shuffling gait, moving the legs of either side together, which is easy to the rider.] He questioned me further, 'Might there not be made a railroad through Arabia, passing by Aneyza and reaching to Mecca?' I said, that there wanted only an occasion for the enterprise. Since all northern Arabia (without the Hejâz and west of the Tueyk mountains) is a high plain country, it were but the cost of laying the rails for eight or nine hundred miles, from Syria to es-Sh'aara. From thence the broken country is but few miles to es-Seyl; and the rest an easy descent to 'Ayn ez-Zeyma.

— We chatted of the defeat of Kahtân. And Ghraneym said he was sorry he had not been at home: he would have lent me a mare, that I might have ridden out to see the Beduin manner of fighting. He was learning at Tâyif to ride with stirrups; and showed me his galled ankles. Ghraneym told us then of a marvellous adventure of his in the desert warfare: the man, who was a patrician, neither vaunted nor lied! and his tale was confirmed to me at Jidda, by some of Aneyza, not much his friends. *Ghraneym*: " I have once fought with the Kahtân! — it was near *es-Shibbebîeh*, in the Nefûd. — I was riding with a score of horsemen from Aneyza, when we lighted unawares [riders among the dunes may ofttimes not see a furlong about them] upon six hundred [a great number of] Kahtân riders. — I said then in my heart, Must I cast down arms and clothes, and forsake my mare; and go away naked [the desert robbers might suffer a man to pass thus, — if no blood be between them;] but I thought, that were an indignity. Then we settled ourselves on our mares, and rode to meet the Kahtân! who, seeing us galloping against them, were as men confused! for they supposed that some great ghrazzu of the town was at hand: — and wellah, they turned and fled!" Ghraneym and his men pursuing took three Kahtân mares, and returned to Aneyza. — There is so little concert among Beduins, that sometimes a multitude may be discomfited almost as one man! Ghraneym asked further, 'how Aneyza seemed to me?' He derided the fanaticism of the Waháby populace, and their expelling the Engleysy.

I was called the same evening to the Sherîf. There was now a full audience sitting round the bay of the hall, upon the diwan: in the midst of them, under a window, is the seat of the Emir Sherîf.

A chair was set for me again in face of the good Sherîf: who discoursed with the stranger so long that his great pipe was thrice burned out and replenished; and I thought continually, 'how excellent is his understanding!' At first the Sherîf enquired, what opinion I had of the air of et-Tâyif? I put him in mind of that mire beyond the town, and he answered, musing, "We had much wet last season: but this year, he added cheerfully, I will have it laid dry." He asked of the monuments [so much magnified among koran readers] at Medáin Sâlih. I responded frankly, 'that the houses of the citizens had been of clay; the chambers hewn in the rock were sepulchral; that in the floors of the chambers are hewn sepulchres.' The tolerant Sherîf acquiesced, soberly musing and smoking; and doubtless he mused (though my words sounded contrary to the letter of the koran), that a studied European were unlikely to be mistaken. *The Sherîf:* " Are there bones in the chambers?" — "The hewn sepulchres in the monument-chambers are full of human bones; I found also grave-clothes, and a resinous matter, wherewith doubtless the carcases were embalmed." — "Wonderful!" said the Sherîf: then turning himself to the audience, he spoke to them of the mummies of Eygpt. "How marvellous! quoth he, that the human flesh has been preserved these three thousand or four thousand, or more years, in which time even stones decay!" He enquired, 'If I were pleased with et-Tâyif? and what had I seen to-day?' I answered, We had visited the three crags, which were worshipped in the "Ignorance": — I felt the good Sherîf shrink at this word, and almost he changed countenance; for between them and us is brittle ground ; and I might provoke some fanatical words of the grave persons sitting about him. I hastened therefore to speak of the epitaphs at el-Héjr, — that they are Nabatean ; whereas the not far-off el-Ally inscriptions are Himyaric. The Sherîf wondered to hear me say, that *Himyâry* is to this day spoken in a district of el-Yémen ! — but that was immediately confirmed to him by a Yémeny sheykh sitting among his audience, who was from those parts. The Sherîf spoke again of the epigraph near es-Seyl ; and he requested me to send him a copy of my transcription, from Jidda. [I had found no inscriptions in Middle Nejd : but there is one, of five or six lines, in el-Wéshm — at the watering *Mâsul es-Sudda*, in a seyl bed under *Jebel Shotb*, of the Tueyk mountains — which is renowned among them ; for in the people's tradition it betokens a gold-mine !]

Among the company sate a big, black-bearded pilgrim-citizen of Câbul ; who spoke without fault in the Arabic tongue. — Now he called to me suddenly, " And wilt thou afterward visit Câbul ? " " Câbul, no Sir ; I should be in doubt of losing my head there ! " and then I said to the Sherîf, " They are jealous of the Engleys ; but as the Muscovite threatens from beyond, we may become better friends." The Sherîf mused and smiled ; and said to me in a peaceable voice, " Perhaps they are still somewhat barbarous in those parts ! — and what think you of India ? " — I answered quickly, " *Ummed-dinya !* Mother of the world." The Sherîf wondering and musing repeated my words to the company : — for they suppose that little England has grown to her greatness only of late, " of the immense tribute of India." Finally the good Sherîf said, ' I spoke well in Arabic : where had I learned ? ' [I pronounced, in the Nejd manner, the *nûn* in the end of nouns used indifferently, and sometimes the Beduin plurals ; which might be pleasant in a townsman's hearing.] — And then Hasseyn turning to the audience, began to speak with a liberal warmth, of the good instruction of late years, in all the field of Arabic letters, of so many young men in the Lebanon mountains, [Nasâra, issued from the American College at Beyrût. — The Sherîf visited Beyrût some years ago, when a private man, for the health of a tisical son ; who soon after deceased.] He spoke further of the many [European] books of necessary knowledge, which are every year translated and impressed in that Levantine town : he had been highly pleased with the Encyclopædia. " I have the first parts, quoth the Sherîf, and even now I take pleasure to read in them. You may find in those volumes a history of everything, — which is admirable ! Take for example, A chair (*kúrsy*) ! I find the word by the alphabet : and first there is the etymology, which is manifestly not Arabic ; and then a history of chairs from the beginning, in all nations."

When he understood that I had been in Andalûs, the Sherîf began to ask of all that I had seen there : he heard from me with pleasure of the " great river-valley " — yet named from the Arabic, Guádalquîver (Wád' el-Kebîr) ; that the market-streets in many towns stand over the Moorish sûks ; and that much remains in the country speech and customs of the old Móghrebies. — And whither, he asked kindly, would I go now ? I answered, ' To Aden, to repose awhile there ; and afterward to India.' [The gentle Sherîf made my host enquire further of me on the morrow, ' What means should I find to go forward, from Jidda ? ' — It is their settled opinion, that the Franks, notwithstanding their common faith, are at any such adventures sordid surmisers, unkind to each other and far from all hospitality. And I learned that this had been the Turkish officers' talk the other evening at the coffee-club.]

—Hasseyn is of the ashràf tribe *el-Abàdella*. The ashràf or prosperity of *Hásan* and *Hasseyn*, Mohammed's grandchildren, the sons of Fâtima, and Aly (afterward Calif), are grown in less than fifty generations to a multitude ; which may be, I suppose, fifteen thousand persons ! in the Mecca country and el-Yémen ; where they are divided in at least twenty tribes : some of them, as the *Thuy Hásan*, in el-Yémen, are said to be well-nigh as strong as the great Beduin nation of 'Ateyba ! — The nomad tribes of ashràf were thus named to me by a nomad tribesman of the Sherîf [sherîf Nâsir] who afterwards accompanied me to Jidda : — *El-Abàdella*, *es-Shenàberra*, *Thu Júdullah* (whereof was Sâlem, who would have stabbed me), *Thu Jazzàn* ; *el-Hurruth* ; *el-Men'ama* ; *Thu es-Surrùr* ; *Thu ez-Zeyd*, whereof *'Abd-er-Muttelib*, sometime Sherîf before the lately deceased Abdullah [he was deposed by the Sultan : but, Hasseyn murdered, 'Abd-er-Muttelib was sent again from Stambûl, and restored to his former dignity. He sat once more two years, — and was finally deprived by the Turk] ; *Thu Eḥamûd* ; *Thu Suâmly* ; *el-Faur* ; *Thu Hasseyn* ; *el-Barràcheda* ; *el-Aranta* ; *er-Ruâge* ; *Thuy 'Ammir* ; *el-Heyàderra* ; *Thuy Hásan* ; *Thuy Jessàs* ; *eth-Thâleba* : and besides these there is the great tribe *es-S'ada*, which although descended from Fâtima, are not named ashràf. — There are sherîfs and posterity of the blood of the Néby in all great towns of

Islam, and even in the desert tribes : such was my old Fejîry friend Zeyd es-Sbeykàn [Vol. I. p. 398]; whose was one of the best and least fanatical heads! The ashràf tribesmen give not their daughters in marriage to any not ashràf; but they take wives where they will, and concubines at their list; and all their seed are accounted ashràf.

When we were again at home, Còlonel Mohammed enquired, ' And how seemed to me the Sherîf?' I answered, " A perfect good man : " but my host preferred to speak of his deceased lord Abdullah. He said, ' Had I been at et-Tâyif a little earlier, I might have beheld a wonderful muster of the wild nomad people of the country, in their tribes and kindreds, to welcome-in the new Sherîf : three days, they ate and drank [compare 1 Chron. xii. 39], and made merry with shouting and firing their long guns. — The Sherîf's agent in Jidda had sent up on the Prince's account, to Tâyif, "fifty tons" [perhaps sacks] of rice, for their entertainment.' The Mohammedan succession is not, we have seen, from sire to son : a son of the late Sherîf, a goodly young man, was yet dwelling at et-Tâyif.

The Estates of the Sherîf Prince reach beyond Wâdy Bîsha. He is eldest son of the Néby's house, and Emir of Mecca; but the Sherîf has nevertheless some unruly subjects, who from time to time have refused to pay him tribute. — If he send forth an expedition to reduce the rebels, he will (like the Arabian Emirs) take the field himself, with his Bîshy guard (and some Ottoman soldiery). Three years ago, Col. Mohammed was in such an outriding toward Wâdy Runnya : and then he saw the Arabian khála, — " which, said he, is not so empty as one might think. For it was marvellous how many of those half-naked, sun-blackened wretches did start up every day before us, where we looked not for them ! But oh ! that wandering without way, the sun and the sand burning; and the thirst ! I can remember one day, when we found but a well of foul water, how glad we were to fill the girby and drink. I was, in that expedition, with two more officers of the Dowla; and we went clad in this sort — ! [in military or European wise]. The people came out from their villages, to gaze on us, as we sat in the tents; and they whispered together, ' *Look there ! these be three Nasrânies !* ' " But the three military Turks were little pleased to be noted thus; and the Sherîf vouchsafed, that in any future expedition, they should go clad as the rest.

— Col. Mohammed asked me, somewhat earnestly ! ' Whether I had a mind to visit Wâdy Bîsha, and the country toward Wâdy Dauâsir ? in which case the Sherîf would give me a letter of safe conduct ! ' — Perhaps Hasseyn would have favoured me as a friendly traveller ; and hope to save his government, for the time to come, from other Frenjies' adventuring themselves in the country. — Though I formerly desired to see those parts, I felt now that I must forsake it to go down without delay to the sea-coast.

They love not the (intruded) Turks. — Zeyd taught me thus (from his book), the divine partition of the inheritance of the world ; — " Two quarters divided God to the children of Adam, the third part He gave to *Ajûj* and *Majûj* (Gog and Magog), a manikin people parted from us by a wall ; which they shall overskip in the latter days : and then will they overrun the world. Of their kindred be the (gross) Turks and the (misbelieving) Persians : but you, the Engleys, are of the good kind with us. The fourth part of the world is called *Rob'a el-Khâly*, the empty quarter : " by this commonly they imagine the great middle-East of the Arabian Peninsula ; which they believe to be void of the breath of life ! — I never found any Arabian who had aught to tell, even by hearsay, of that dreadful country. Haply it is nefûd, with quicksands ; which might be entered into and even passed with milch dromedaries in the spring weeks. Now my health failed me ; and otherwise I had sought to unriddle that enigma.

Even here in the mountain of et-Tâyif, was the fear of the Muscôv. The soldier-servant of my host told me, that the retreat which I heard sounded (when I arrived), a little before sunrise, was of the last watch of the citizen volunteers ! " The first guard, he said, assemble at sunset, and patrol without the walls ; and so do the watches that succeed them, all night, — for dread of any surprise of the Nasâra ! " — there was not yet a telegraph wire to Mecca. This honest Syrian, a watch-mender by trade, looked forward to the term of his military service, when he would settle himself at Mecca ; where he hoped to earn, he said, " five reals every day," — which seems impossible.

A war contribution was collected in the Estates of the Sherîf, — the sum, Col. Mohammed said, was about five thousand pounds : and he himself had conveyed it to Stambûl. He found the capital changed ;

and he thought, for the worse ! — He passed the Suez canal and landed at Port Said : where he became the guest of the Russian consulate ! — for as yet the jehâd was not with Russia, but with the revolted provinces. The chests of silver money, gathered from the needy inhabitants of Arabia the Happy, were landed on the quay ; and he was in dread lest any of them should miscarry : but the consul, giving his kawàs charge of them all, bade him fear nothing ; and brought the Ottoman guest to his house and the Muscovite hospitality. — When he arrived at Stambûl, Col. Mohammed deposited the chests at the Porte : but he was left, day after day, without an answer. At length, to his relief, he was recalled to the Porte ; where a precious casket was delivered to him ; in which was a letter, of the Sultan's own hand, and a gift for the Sherîf.

— Besides fruits at Tâyif, they have plenty of all things necessary : the most flesh meat is 'Ateyba mutton ; white curd cheese is brought in by the Koreysh. The Koreysh (gentile pl. *el-Korásh*), Mohammed's tribesmen of the mother's side, are now a poor and despised kind of Beduw in the Mecca country ; and that is, said sherîf Nâsir, (see p. 556), " *because their fathers contemned the rasûl.*" Yet they are reputed to be of some great insight in the nomad landcraft ; and the people name them *Beny Fàhm,* ' children of understanding.' " There be, said Nâsir, of the Koreysh, who can declare by the footprints, if a man be wedded ; and whether a woman be maiden or wife. If a Koreyshy lost a strayed nâga, with calf ; and he find the footprint of her young one, even years afterward, he will know that it is his own."

— It was the fourth daylight of my reposing at et-Tâyif: and the Bessàm's weary and footsore thelûl being now somewhat refreshed, and judged able to bear me to Jidda (30 leagues distant), I should set out before evening. [There are two ways down to the Teháma and Jidda from et-Tâyif ; — a path which descends steeply from the *Kora* (or *Kurra*) mountains and leaves Mecca not far off upon the right hand ; and that of the Seyl and 'Ayn ez-Zeyma, through the Wady Fâtima. The good Sherîf — by the mouth of Col. Mohammed — desired me to choose between them : I left it to their good pleasure.] About midday I went with Col. Mohammed to take leave of the Sherîf ; but come to the palace stairs, we heard, ' that he had a little before re-entered to the hareem ' ; that is, his public business despatched, the worthy man was reposing — and perhaps reading the *Encyclopædia,* in the midst of his family. The noon heat is never heavy at et-Tâyif : I found at this hour 90° F. in the house ; and the nights were refreshing.

When it drew to evening, my bags were sent forward upon the thelûl to the place where I should mount with my company. Colonel Mohammed and the Albanian aga brought me forward on foot ; and Zeyd the Bîshy came along with us : he had asked, but could not obtain permission, to accompany me to Jidda. We went first to the palace of Abdillah Pasha, to take leave of him : but he was ridden forth with Hasseyn, and a sheykhly company, to breathe the air, under yonder black mountains (whose height may be nearly 8000 feet). Beyond the Seyl gate, we came to a tent in a stubble field — where I saw the straw stacked in European wise ! It was the lodging of some men that were over the Prince's camel herd. There my thelûl was couched ; and I saw two thelûls lying beside her, which were of the men appointed to ride with me to Jidda — by the Wady Fâtima : these were the nomad sherîf Nâsir, a gatherer of the Sherîf's tribute, and two (negroes) of the Bîshy guard. I found them smearing creosote in the thelûls' nostrils ! which, they told me, was good, to preserve them from ill airs in the tepid lower country. — So town Arabs cast creosote into wells of infected water.

After leave-taking I mounted, with my company and one of the overseers, Hásan, a merry fellow who would ride some leagues with us. When we had journeyed a mile and the sun was setting, they alighted by an orchard side, where was a well, to wash and pray. I found here less than five fathoms to the ground-water, which was light and sweet : the driver, who held up his ox-team, told me, it sinks a fathom when the rain fails. — We rode on by fruit grounds and tilled enclosures, for nearly three miles, — but they are not continuous : and beyond is the wilderness. This year the vines — which at (tropical) Tâyif bear only deformed clusters of (white) berries, had been partly devoured by locusts : the plants lie not loosely on the soil, as in Syria ; but are bound to stakes, set in good order. I saw many ethel trees — here called *el-aerîn* — grown in the orchards, for building timber. And the fig tree is called (as the wild fig beside certain desert waters — [v. Vol. I. p. 488] *hamâta*. Some olive trees which now grow in the mountains of et-Tâyif (at an height of 6000 feet at least) were brought from Syria. Those plants flourish under the tropic with green boughs, but will not bear fruit ; and are called here (by another name) *el-'etîm*. The living language of the Arabs dispersed through so vast regions is without end, and can never be all learned; the colocynth gourd *hámthal* of the western Arabians, *shérry* in middle Nejd, is here called *el-hádduj*.

— " Khalîl, quoth Hásan, thy people is of our country! for we have a book wherein it is written, that the Engleys went forth (in old time) from this dîra:" he told me, as we rode further, that it was since the héjra! There are others who fetch the Albanians out of this country! — of like stuff may be some ancient Semitic ethnologies. The twilight was past; and we were soon riding in the night. — " Eigh! Khalîl, said Hásan, sleepest thou? but tell me whether is better to journey on our camels or on your ship-boards? the Arabs are the shipmen of the khála and the Engleys are cameleers of the sea." We met some long trains of loaded camels marching upwards to et-Tâyif: and outwent other which descended before us to the Holy City. The most of these carried sacks — oh! blissful sweetness! in the pure night air, — of rose blossoms; whose precious odours are distilled by the Indian apothecaries in Mecca. This is the *'atr*, which is dispersed by the multitude of pilgrims through the Mohammedan world. The cameleers were lying along to slumber uneasily upon their pacing beasts: one of them who was awake murmured as we went by, "There is one with you who prays not!" Sherîf Nâsir, hearing the voice, cursed his father with the bitter impatience of the Arabs. — ' Intolerable! quoth he; that such a fellow should speak injuries of one riding in their company.' Our Bîshies lightened the loads of some of those sleepers, taking what they would of the few sticks which the camel-men carried for fuel, to make our coffee fire: and then they trotted forward to kindle it. After half an hour we found them in a torrent bed a little apart from the common road, seated by a fire, and the coffee-water ready. Here then we alighted on the sh'aeb to sup and pass the night: this desert stead was midway, they told me, between et-Tâyif and the Seyl.

The crackling and sweet-smelling watch-fire made a pleasant bower of light about us, seated on the pure sand and breathing the mountain air, among dim crags and desert acacias; the heaven was a blue deep, all glistering with stars,

> *that smiled to see*
> *the rich attendance on our poverty:*

we were guests of the Night, and of the vast Wilderness. We drew out our victual, dates and cheese and bread, and filled a bowl with clear water of et-Tâyif : only Nâsir could not eat. Alas! for the adventure of my coming to et-Tâyif ; and the Sherîf's commandment, that he should accompany me to Jidda, — it was this which should have been his bridal night ! The gentle nomad sherîf loved a maiden of 'Ateyba, a sheykh's daughter, with a melting heart. He was freshly combed and trimmed : and it was perchance her slender fingers that had tressed the long hair of his unmanly beauty in a hundred little lovelocks ; and shed them in the midst like a Christ ! The love-longing man, who might be nearly thirty-five years of age, sat silent and pensive ; and in his fantasy oft smiling closely to himself ; but the Bîshy companions made mirth of his languishing. I gave the sick man tea, with much sugar ; which though a Nomad he was used to taste in Mecca houses. — When we had supped, Hásan rode away upon his *Omanîeh*, to visit his family in some hamlet few miles beside the way : the 'Ateyba neighbours call their thelûls *hadùj*, a mocking word ; for it is as much as ' old toothless jade ; ' they say also *hurra*. — " All this path is full of thieves, beware Khalîl ! ' quoth the Bîshies, who now settled themselves to sleep about me ; and made their arms and bundles their pillows : " for these road thieves, quoth they, can rob a thing from under a sleeping man's head."

Ere dawn we remounted : and when the long summer day began to spring we saw a lean Beduwy on a thelûl, riding towards us. — It was Mûthkir ! who yesterday left the kâfily in the heat of Mecca ; and ascended to salute the new Sherîf : he hailed me, and stayed to speak with us. We fell again into that paved path with steps, and descended in strait passages. A nomad family met us (of Hathèyl or Koreysh) removing upward : they were slight bodies and blackish, a kind of tropical Arabs ; and in my unaccustomed seeing, Indian-looking : the housewife carried a babe riding astride upon her haunch bone ; and this is not seen in northern Arabia. Old stone-heaps here and there mark the way : some — as in all sands of the Arabs — are places of cursing and sites of mischance [*Confer* Josh. vii. 26 and viii. 29 ; 2 Sam. xviii. 17], where the idle passenger flings one stone more [— At the jin or ground-demon ?] : in other is some appearance of building.

When we were nigh the Seyl, they led me down, beside the way, in a short wild passage, the *Rî'a ez-Zelâla* ; where, as the Sherîf commanded, they would show me the famous inscription. They drew bridle in the midst before a grey crag ; on whose wall-like face I dimly descried a colossal human effigy — to the half length, and an epigraph. I dismounted, and went through the brambles (which grow in these tropical mountains) to the image, — which is but dashed with a stone on the hard granite ; and may be hardly better discerned at the first sight in the sunshine, than the man in the moon. The ancient, a great man before and behind, seems to sit and hold in his hand a (camel) staff ; and ranging therewith are two lines of Himyaric letters : the legend is

perpendicular. — We read, that in heathen times of Arabia men worshipped a rock in these parts. [*v. Die Alte Geogr. Arabiens*, § 355.] If the image be an idol, such was haply the *Abu Zeyd* of the Nejd Bishr ; [*v.* Vol. I. p. 349, and the fig. in *Doc. épigr.*] — certain it is that such images on the desert rocks are renowned among the Aarab.

My companions showed me four or five more inscriptions in this passage. They were Kufic : and I rode further, glad to be released of the pain of transcribing them, — for he is a weary man who may hardly sustain the weight of his clothing. I perceived then that Nâsir was unlettered, like the Beduins ! yet to save his estate of sherîf, he would not frankly acknowledge it. From thence we had hardly two miles to the Seyl : where we arrived early, and alighted to pass the hot hours.

This station is doubtless one of the most notable in the Peninsula ; a landing place of pilgrims from Nejd ; and of merchants, from the north parts, trading to Bocca or Mecca. — We hear traditions in Arabia of other pilgrimage-places of the ancient religions, as *Gârat Owsheyfîa* or *et-Teyry* (betwixt *Thermedda* and *Owsheyfy*, in el-Wéshm), where the Arabs think they see 'praying-places,' turned every way ; and Siddûs.

We slumbered out the meridian hours in the shadows of rocks : at the assr we set forward. — This third time I must remeasure the long valley to 'Ayn ez-Zeyma : to-day it seemed less direful, since I rode in the sun of the Prince's favour. Nâsir showed me, bye and bye, at our left hand *Thull'a el-Bint*, the maiden's mountain ; and the three companions lifting their right hands to a pinnacle which is seen like a column on the airy crest, shouted the legend, "Yonder pillar was a goat-herdess of the Aarab ; and she became a stone when Mohammed cursed the people of this valley, for not giving ear to his preaching. And the *bint* stands as she was spinning, when the judgment fell upon them : — ay, and were you there you might see the distaff in her hand, and the goats, some lying down beside her, and some as it were at pasture, and some reared on their hind legs that seem to crop of the wild boughs ! — Now they are black stones, wherein you may discern evidently all the form of a maid, and of her cattle — the horns and every part !" Nâsir told us 'he once climbed up thither, to see the wonder ; and that he had found all this, wellah.' — Here is a tale of the ignorant (so fain to mystify themselves and others) which they have matched to the stones ; and then they would take the stones for a testimony of their pretended miracle !

Lower in the valley Nâsir showed me much heaped gravel by the way side : the Sherîf had caused a well to be sunk there, — a sebîl for passengers : the pit, he said, was digged to great depth, yet they found no water ; but it springs of late. — In the twilight we came again to the 'Ayn ez-Zeyma ; and alighted among the stones in the midst of the wady. — Nâsir confirmed to me, 'that here is Teháma ; and Sh'aara, he said, is in Nejd : the country above the Seyl and the salt-coasts of the

Kisshub and the Harras seyl towards el-Medina,' — that is down to the Wady el-Humth. Since I recovered my aneroid from the violent hands of Sâlem and Fheyd, I had not much hope in it: nevertheless I now read the height which I had found here seven days before. For Tâyif I had a probable altitude of 6000 feet. The delicate little instrument is yet uninjured. — A man of the hamlet brought us of the first-ripe dates, *bellah róttub*, for our money: the day was about the ninth of August. There was a hum of gnats about us; and from the lower valley resounded a mighty jarring of frogs: I had not heard these watery voices since Kheybar, — *Urk-kiow-kúr-kúr-kúr-kreûrk!*

At the rising of the morning star *Zóhra* we remounted, to come to our noon shelter before the great (Teháma) heat. We held the Wâdy bottom; and after a half-hour rode by a place of orchards, *Sôla* — in the mouth of the nomads, *Sâla*. Here is a great spring and enclosures of lemons and mulberries, the patrimony of the Sherîf; the husbandmen are his bond-servants. Not three miles lower, I saw at our right hand, as the day was dawning, a valley mouth *el-Mothîch*; which is the outlet of Wady Laymûn, that descends from the Seyl into Wady Fâtima, the valley wherein we were now riding since 'Ayn ez-Zeyma. In Wady Laymûn are villages of the Hurrath, ashràf: the Sherîf Prince has possessions among them also; the Aarab in the mountains are Hathèyl. In that valley is the 'Ayn Laymûn: the wady above is desolate, toward the Seyl. Through the Mothîk lies the *derb es-sherky* or east Haj road from Medina, and the *derb-es-sultâny* from el-Kasîm and East Nejd. The stations from Mecca are *Barrûd*, where are shadows of fig-trees, and wells of cool water; then *el-Bértha*, *bîr Hathèyl*, a well in the midst of the Wady Laymûn; then *eth-Therrîby* [which is *That 'Irk*], where are ruins of a village; then *el-Birket fî Rúkkaba*, where are ruins; then *el-Muslah*, where is a cistern and some ruins; and left of the road is seen the village *el-Ferèya*: then *Hàtha*, where are corn fields and some ruins; afterward *el-'Ayn ibn Ghróbon* with palms at the water and some ruins; then *es-Sfeynah*, *Swergíeh*; — and so forth. I saw a village, *Jedîda*, in the valley mouth, with palms and corn fields, watered by springs and green with the tall flaggy millet; which is sown after the early (wheat and barley) harvest: and they reap this second grain, upon the same plots, in the autumn. — Nâsir told me that the corn grounds between et-Tâyif and el-Yémen (the altitude may be about 6000 feet) are watered only from heaven!

The Fâtima valley beyond is a wide torrent-strand without inhabitant ! We went by some high banks walled below with untrimmed (basalt) blocks,—in Europe we might call such ancient work Cyclopean : the nomad Nâsir answered, "It is of the Beny Helál." Those torrent banks are overgrown with a kind of wild trees, *thánthub*, all green stalks, having prickles for leaves, and bitter tasting ; Nâsir says it is a medicine for the teeth. Here, in the tropical Teháma, I saw the gum acacia thorns beset with a parasite plant (*el-gush'a*), hanging in faggot-like bunches of jointed stalks ; it is browsed only by goats.

A little lower we see where human industry has entered to guide and subdue this desert nature, — how by thwarts of bushes, when the waste valley seyls, the water is set over to the (right) side ; and led down upon a strand, which is cleared of stones for tillage. Lower in the wady that rain-water passes by a channel into a large field enclosed with high earthen banks ; and below it are other like field enclosures. When the valley seyls the enclosures are flooded with shallow water, which should stand seven or eight days. The gravel and grit soil is to be sown immediately after ; and the corn which springs will grow up (they say) till the harvest, without other watering. Simple and sufficient is every device of the Arabs ; and thus they eat bread of this forlorn stony wady. — Beyond I saw great banked works in making, after the manner in Egypt. They dig and carry soil by the ploughing of oxen, — at every turn of the plough-shovel there is transported a barrowful of earth ; and it is surprising to see how soon a rampart is heaped up : the name of the place is *ez-Zibbâra*. I saw here some signs of a better ancient tillage : for in riding, over higher ground, to cross a reach of the valley, we found old broken stone channels for the irrigation of gardens and orchards.

From thence appeared an huge blackness — a mountain platform before us, with a precipice of more than 1000 feet, bordering the valley side : plainly another Harra ! Nâsir answered me, "It is the *Harrat Ajeyfa*." — Yonder vulcanic flood lies brimming upon the crystalline mountains : a marvel — howbeit some other vulcanic fields come down in stages — to make the forehead sweat ! "The hilliân are high, and distant," said Nâsir : I saw none in this horizon. Harrat Ajeyfa, one of the great train of Harras, is said to be continent with the 'Ashîry [p. 508.] According to both Múthkir and Nâsir the Harras lie disposed like a band, betwixt the Harameyn [which we have seen to be the shape of the Kheybar and the Aueyrid Harras].

I questioned Nâsir of the Wadies south of Tâyif towards Wady Bîsha. — Two 'hours,' he said, from et-Tâyif, is *W. Wídj* ; — then two 'hours' to *W. en-N'khîb* ; then one day to *W. Líeh* ; then one day to *W. Bissel*. [These valleys have a length of nearly five journeys, and their courses are northward, till they are lost in the sands : in all of them are villages.] There are four days to *W. Turraba*, with Aarab B'goom and villages. This valley reaches to *el-'Erk* (not distant from Shukera in el-Wéshm) ; where after rains the seyl waters are gathered to a standing meer, and the Beduw come to encamp upon it : then three days to W. Sbey'a or Runnya ; which others say are two valleys, — the villages *Khorma* and *Konsolîeh* are in the former, and in the second, er-Runnya, a great palm village. There are villages in all the length of W. Bîsha, which are often at enmity one with another. *Beny Uklib* and *Sharân* are the Aarab of that country. The Wady head is in el-Asîr : the length of its course is many journeys ; and the seyl waters die away in the sand.

The Wady Fâtima is here most desolate : seldom any man passes. Nâsir had been in this part but once in his life, upon some business of the Sherîf. There grows nothing in the waste ground of grit and gravel, but hard bent plants, which exhale a moorish odour in the sun. Seeing that loose sand full of writhen prints, (mostly of the small grey lizard, here called *el-khossî*), the younger Bîshy cried out, "Wellah in this wady is nothing but serpents!" We passed the head of a spring, that is led underground by an old rude conduit (of stone) to the first oasis-village in W. Fâtima, *Imbârak*, — an hour lower.

When we rode by Imbârak I saw the date clusters hanging ruddy ripe in all the heads of the palm trees ; and on the clay banks, which overlie the valley gravel, much green growth of thúra. Also here first I saw the beehive-like cottages of straws and palm branches (made in Abyssinian wise), which are common in this country ; " They are, said Nâsir, for the servants of the ashrâf."— From henceforward all is loose gravel and sand-ground down to Jidda. The next palm village is three miles lower, *er-Rayyân*. These W. Fâtima oases are settlements about springs. The villagers are ashrâf, husbandmen, and nearly black-skinned ; their field labourers are both free men and bond. — I praised the nomad life : " Ay, said Nâsir, the nâga's milk is sovereign." And he told us, ' how upon a time as he rode with only few in company to the southward from et-Tâyif, for the Sherîf's business, they were waylaid by some Beduins of those parts ; and that he ran upon his feet beside the thelûls till the assr, running and firing ; and was yet fasting ! — Those Aarab (he answered me) would not have assailed him, if they had known him to be a sherîf ; — but how should they believe it, if he had told them ? '

We felt the heavy stagnant heat of the tropical lowland ; and my companions, when they had drunk all in the water-skin, were very impatient of the sun. Hàmed, the younger negro, was bye and bye weary of his life : he alighted, and wilfully forsaking his rafîk and us, went away on his feet ! — We approached Rayyân and saw that he held over to the palms, a mile distant. I asked, " What is amiss ! will he not return ? " His companion answered, " He may return, if he will, or go to Jehennem ; " and Nâsir cursed his father. But the raw fellow, who went but to appease his eager thirst, came-in to us, an hour later, at our noon resting place. [Perhaps this young negro had been chosen to accompany me, because he had conversed with the Franks : for Hàmed, to win a little silver to purchase arms and make himself gay, had served some months with the stokers on board a French steam-ship passing by the Red Sea.] Rayyân lies in the midst of the now large and open valley. We rode on the east part to a little bay ; and alighted, before a new stone cottage, of good building : we were now in a civil country, as Syria, — Meccan Arabia. Here dwelt a man who was rich in both worlds ! ministering of his wealth unto the poorer neighbours and to the public hospitality. — They think it unbecoming to ride up to a sherîf's house ! we dismounted therefore when half a furlong distant, and led forward our thelûls ; and halted nigh his door. A moment after, the host, who was sheykh of the place and swarthy as an Abyssinian, came forth to meet us ; and led us into his hall, which, built of stone, and open, with clean matted floor, resembled a chapel ; and a large Persian carpet was spread upon the north side, for the guests. — We had seen a new hamlet of flat-roofed stone cottages about his house, with a well, which were all of this good man's building ; and some straw cabins for his old servants : he stretches forth his hand likewise to the poor nomads, whose tents were pitched beside him. — There wanted two hours to midday, nor was the day very sultry : yet I found in the house 99° F.

So soon as it could be made ready, we were served to breakfast: yard-wide trays were borne-in full of hot girdle-bread and samn, with the best dates, and the bountiful man's bowls of léban. When we had eaten, and he heard of my adventure at 'Ayn ez-Zeyma, the good sheykh said, looking friendly upon me, ' And were I come to him at that time, he would have sent me forward to Jidda. — Yet why could I not become a Moslem, and dwell here alway in the sacred country, in the Sherîf's favour? he read it, in my eyes, that I was nigh of heart to the Moslemîn.' — A sheep had been slain for us; and it was served for our dinner at the half-afternoon. So civil a house and this hospitality I had not seen before in the Arabian country.

After leave-taking we led forth our thelûls about an hundred paces, as when we arrived, and remounted. And now leaving the Wady, which reaches far round to the Westward, we ascended over the desert coast; from whence I beheld again that lowering abrupt platform of the mighty Harra. — Some poor men went by us with asses, carrying firewood to market: Nâsir said, they were *Korásh*.— At sunset my company dismounted by a well, *Bîr el-Ghrannem*, to pray; and I saw now by their faces that Mecca lay a little south of eastward. Long lines of camels went up at our left hand, loaded with the new dates of W. Fâtima for Mecca. We passed forth, and at a seyl rode over the Syrian pilgrim road (*Derb el-Haj es-Shâmy*); from hence to Mecca might be twenty-two miles. The night fell dimly with warm and misty air; and we knew, by the barking of dogs, that the country was full of nomads. Three hours after the sun, we came again to the W. Fâtima; where alighting in a sandy place, we lay down to sleep.

Rising at day-break, the fourth of our journey, I saw before us an oasis village, *Abu She'ab*, and many nomad booths: the Aarab were *Laheyân*, of Hathèyl, said Nâsir. That village is mostwhat of the beehive-like dwellings — which are called *'usha* — made of sticks and straws; before every one was a little fenced court: some of their *'ushas* seemed to be leaning for age; and some were abandoned for rottenness, — it is said they will last good fifty years; and are fresh and wholesome to dwell in. Here is an high but rude-built fortress of stone, now ruinous, a work of the old Wahábies. Our path lay again in the Wady: we rode some miles; and passed over a brook, two yards wide, running strongly! — all this low Teháma is indeed full of water; yet none flows down to the sea. Here we met a family of *Aarab Daed*,

Hathèyl, removing : the women wore short kirtles to the knee, and slops under ! Their skins were black and shining ; and their looks (in this tropical Arabia) were not hollow, but round and teeming : a dog followed them. Besides Hethèylân and other Beduins, there are certain Heteym in this Teháma, both above and below Jidda. We often saw wretched booths of nomad folk of the country, which for dearth of worsted cloth were partly of palm matting. The most indigent will draw now to the oases, to hire themselves out in the date gathering ; — when godly owners are good to the weak and disherited tent-dwellers ; that nevertheless must eat the sweet of the settlements with hard words in their ears : and are rated as hounds for any small fault.

About nine o'clock we came to the oasis-village *ed-Dôeh* ; and alighted a little without the place, at a new 'usha ; which had been built by a rich man, for the entertainment of passengers. — The good Sherîf, careful for my health by the way, had charged Nâsir to bring me to the houses of worthy and substantial persons ; to journey always slowly, and if at any time they saw me fainting in the saddle, they were to alight there. The cabin was of studs and fascine-work a foot in thickness, firmly bound and compacted together ; and the walls, four-square below, were drawn together, in a lofty hollow overhead. My companions thought that our pleasant 'usha, which was a sure defence from the sun and not small, might have cost the owner a dozen crowns (less than £3). By the village is a spring, where the long-veiled women of the country, bearing pitchers of an antique form set sidewise on their heads, come to draw water.

The altitude was now only 1100 feet. We felt cool as we sat in our shirts in the doorless 'usha, with a breathing wind, yet I found 102° F. A field-servant of the household — a thick-set, great-bearded husbandman from Tâyif — who had brought us out the mat and cushions, wiping his forehead each moment exclaimed, " Oh ! this Teháma heat ! " The valley is here dammed by three basaltic bergs (*Mokesser, Th'af, Sídr*) from the north wind ; and quoth the host, who entered, " The heat is now such in W. Fâtima, that the people cannot eat : wellah there is no travelling, after the sun is up." I asked, What were the heat at Jidda? " *Ouf!* he answered, insufferable." *Nâsir :* " Khalîl, hast thou not heard what said Saûd ibn Saûd when — having occupied Mecca — he laid siege to Jidda [1803]; and could not take the place : ' I give it up then, I cannot fight against such a hot town : surely if this people be not fiends, they are nigh neighbours to the devil.' "

— A Beduin lad looked in at the casement ! Then all voices cried out roughly, " Away with thee ! " " *Ana min dîrat beyt Ullah,*" I am from the circuit of God's House ! answered the fellow vaingloriously : but for all that they would not let him enter. Our host, a young man, rated the weled fiercely ; " Get thee, he cried, to the next *'usha* — sit not here ! To the palms with thee ; *fî kheyr wâjid,* where thou shalt find to eat, and that enough : begone now ! " But the poor smell-feast removed not for all their stormy words : — there will none lay hand upon a *thaif-ullah* ! After we had been served (with mighty trays of victual) to breakfast, he with some other wretched persons were called in, to eat of that much which remained over of the rich man's hospitality. " But host ! will our bags be safe ? cries (the nomad) Nâsir, now that he (the Beduwy) lad has come in ? " — " Ay, since he has broken bread with you." That young tribesman, who then acknowledged himself an Hathèyly, rose from meat smiling malevolently ; and at the wash-pot rinsed his hands delicately : so turning without a word he went his way. — Afterwards as we were slumbering, there entered another Beduwy : " I thirst," quoth he : but hardly they suffered him to drink at the beak of the ewer, and then all their hard voices chided him forth again ! — We stayed over to dinner, which was ready for us wayfarers at the half-afternoon. The host had killed a fat sheep, that they served with rice in three vast chargers ; and thereby was set a great tray of the pleasant new dates : nor were our beasts forgotten.

We remounted and rode by wretched Beduin booths of *Aarab el-Meyatân* ; a tribe, said Nâsir, by themselves. I saw with wonder how all this low wilderness is full of nomads : their skin is of a coffee colour. — When the sun was about to set my companions alighted, and prayed north-eastward. Here in the desolate wâdy bottom, of sand and gravel, grows much of a great tropical humth which they call *humth el-aslah* ; of whose ashes the nomads make *shúb el-'bíl,* camel alum, a medicine for their great cattle. — Nâsir would have ridden all night, to arrive by the morrow early at Jidda : but the love-longing man was jaded ere we were at *Hádda*, the last village in Wady Fâtima. And coming in the dark to an inhabited place, "Well, let us sleep, quoth he ; here are the Sherîf's possessions, and all the people are his servants." We alighted at an 'usha, upon a little hill ; where dwelt a simple negro family. The poor soul, who was of the Bîshies' acquaintance, kindled a fire and prepared coffee for us ; and strawed down vetches [here called *bersîm*, as in Syria] for our thelûls. But this seemed to be no pleasant site, and we breathed a fenny air. Whilst I slumbered under the stars, the lovesick Nâsir levied a new hospitality, of that poor man, who was too humble to sit at coffee with us. Nâsir, a sherîf, and the Sherîf's officer, was wont to have it yielded to him in this world : he yielded also to himself, and was full of delicacy, unlike the honest austerity of the Beduw. — I was wakened at midnight to another large hospitality ! and to hear the excuses of the poor negro, for setting before us no more than his goat, and a vast mess of porridge.

We remounted at the rising of the dog-star ; and rode half an hour in a plain : and fell then into the *derb es-sultâny*, or highway betwixt Mecca and the port town of Jidda. — Long trains of camels went by us, faring slowly upward ; and on all their backs sat half-naked pilgrims, girded only in the *îhrâm*. They were poor hajjies of India and from el-Yémen, that had arrived yesterday at Jidda : and they went up thus early in the year to keep the fasting month, with good devotion, in the Holy City. — I saw, in the morning twilight, that the W. Fâtima mountains lay now behind us [they may be seen from Jidda], and before us an open waste country (*khobt*), of gravel and sand, — which lasts to the Red Sea. We had yet the seyl-bed from W. Fâtima, at our left hand ; and the roadway is cut by freshets which descend from the mountains — now northward. Two hours from Hádda we passed by some straw sheds, and a well ; the station of a troop of light horse, that with certain armed thelûl riders are guardians of the sacred highway. Not much beyond is a coffee-house : there is a Kahwa at every few miles' end, in this short pilgrim road.

Doves flitted and alighted in the path before us. The rafîks told me, ' It were unlawful to kill any of them, at least within the bounds ! for these are doves of the Háram ; which are daily fed in Mecca of an allowance (that is twenty *ardubs* monthly) of wheaten grain. When it is sprinkled to them, they flutter down in multitudes, though perhaps but few could be seen a moment before : they will suffer themselves to be taken up in the people's hands.' By this road-side, as in all highways of the border countries, lie many skeletons of camels; for the carcases of fallen beasts are abandoned unburied. [If any beast or hound die in the city, it is drawn forth without the gates.] We rode by a *wély*, the grave of a saint — commonly a praying place in the unreformed, or not-Waháby country — all behanged with (offered) shreds of pilgrims' garments.

Then I saw by the highway-side a great bank of stones; which now encroaches upon the road. "Every hajjy, said my companions, who casts a stone thereon has left a witness for himself [*confer* Josh. xxiv. 27]; for his stone shall testify in the resurrection, that he fulfilled the pilgrimage." — The wilderness beside the way is grown up with certain bushes, *reym*; and Nâsir said, 'The berries, with the beans of the sammar (acacia) are meat of the apes whose covert is the thicket of yonder mountain!' We saw a lizard [like that called *wurrùr*, a devourer of serpents, in Nejd], a yard in length, which carries his tail bent upward like the neck of a bird. The road now rises from the Wady ground: and we soon after descended to a Kahwa and dismounted; and leaving our thelûls knee-bound, we went-in to pass the hot hours under the public-roof. — Whilst the landlord, a pleasant man, was busy to serve us, I drew back my hot kerchief. But the good soul, seeing the side-shed hair of a Frenjy! caught his breath, supposing that I arrived thus foot-hot from Mecca. Then smiling, he said friendly, "Be no more afraid! for here all peril is past." — Near that station I found certain Aarab, *Âbida*, watering their (white-fleeced) flocks at a well digged in the seyl: when their camels were driven in, I hardly persuaded one of those nomads to draw me a little milk (for here is a road and much passage). On the brow above was a station of the dromedary police.

— When the sun was going down from the mid-afternoon height, we set forward: a merry townsman of Mecca, without any fanaticism, and his son, came riding along with us from the station. "Rejoice, Khalîl! quoth my rafîks, for from the next brow we will show thee Jidda." — I beheld then the white sea indeed gleaming far under the sun, and tall ships riding, and minarets of the town! My company looked that I should make jubilee. — In this plain I saw the last worsted booths of the Ishmaelites; they also are named *Bîshr*.

In the low sand-ground before the town are gardens of little pumpkins and melons which grow here — such is the tropical moisture — without irrigation ! My companions who now alighted beckoned to a negro gardener, and bade him bring some of his gourds, for our refreshment ; promising to give him money, to buy a little tobacco. — I commended the poor bondman when he denied us his master's goods ; but they cursed his father, and called him a niggard, a beast and a villain. As my companions delayed, I would have them hasten toward the town, because the sun was setting. But the negroes answered, " We cannot enter thus travel-stained ! we will first change our garments." — To this also they constrained me ; and decked me, " as an *emir el-Aarab*," with the garments which the good Sherîf had given me.

We remounted ; and they said to me, with the Arabian urbanity, " When we arrive, thus and thus shalt thou speak (like a Beduwy — with a deep-drawn voice out of the dry wind-pipe), *Gowak yâ el-Mohâfuth ! keyf 'endakom el-'bíl ? eth-thémn el-ghrannem eysh ; wa eysh ijîb es-samn ?* ' The Lord strengthen thee, O governor ! what be the camels worth here ? — the price of small cattle ? and how much is the samn ? ' Now I saw the seabord desert before us hollowed and balked ! — the labour doubtless of the shovel-plough — and drawn down into channels towards the city ; and each channel ending in a covered cistern. Rich water-merchants are the possessors of these *birkets* : all well-water at Jidda is brackish, and every soul must drink cistern-water for money. By our right hand is " the sepulchre of *Hawwa*," in the Abrahamic tradition the unhappy Mother of mankind : they have laid out " Eve's grave " — a yard wide — to the length of almost half a furlong [*v.* Vol. I. p. 434] : such is the vanity of their religion ! — which can only stand by the suspension of the human understanding. We passed the gates and rode through the street to " the Sherîf's palace " : but it is of a merchant (one called his agent), who has lately built this stately house, — the highest in Jidda.

On the morrow I was called to the open hospitality of the British Consulate.

THE END

APPENDIX TO VOLUME TWO

The Geology of the Peninsula of the Arabs *is truly of the Arabian simplicity : a stack of plutonic rock, whereupon lie sandstones, and upon the sand-rocks, limestones (diagram 1). There are besides great landbreadths (such as the Hauran in Syria) of lavas and spent volcanoes. The old igneous rocks are grey and red granites and traps and basalts ; I have found these lying through the midst of upland Arabia [from J. Shammar to Jidda, 500 miles]. The sand-rock is that wherein are hewn the monuments of Petra, and Medáin Sâlih ; and which I have followed from thence to the southward, nearly to Medina [500 miles]. To the same sand-beds pertain the vast sand deserts or* nefûds *of Arabia. The Haj-way from Damascus lies over a high steppe of limestones, [for more than 200 miles], through Ammon, Moab, and the mountains of Seir, to M'aan (in Edom). In Mount Seir is the same limestone with great flint veins which we see under Bethlehem, beyond the Dead Sea (diagram 2). I have found only a few cockle-shells in the limestone of M'aan, and in Arabia ; and some beautiful lobster-like print in the limestone (without flints) of the desert of Moab.*

In the wide-spread sand-rock of Arabia is often seen the appearance of strata and layers of quartz pebbles (v. fig.) ; but I have never found any forms of plants or animals. — And this view of plutonic, of sand, and of limestone rocks, and vulcanic countries or harras, *will be found, I am well persuaded, to hold for the breadth and length of the Peninsula. The region not unknown to me, between Damascus and Mecca, may be almost* 200,000 *square miles.*

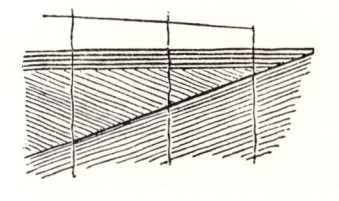

The harras, *in the western border of Northern Arabia, beginning at Tebûk, —* (diagram 3), *last nearly* 650 *miles to the Mecca country.* [*Other harras, not marked in the map, and only known to me by name, are the* Harrat el-Hamra — *near the* Wady Dauâsir, *and* Harrat es-Sauda — *in Jebel Tueyk.*]

(Diagrams 1, 2, 3, *see next page*)

DIAGRAM 1.

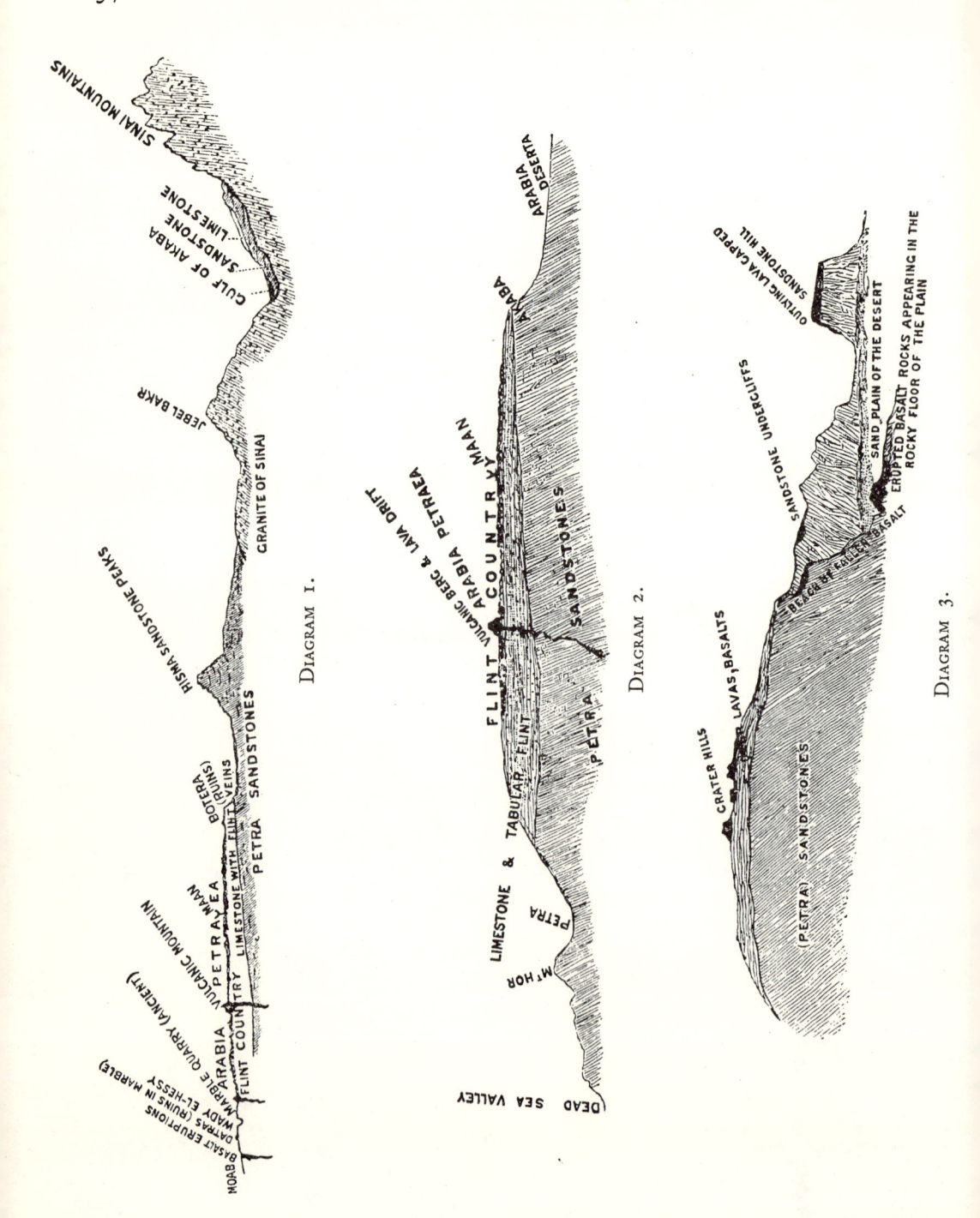

DIAGRAM 2.

DIAGRAM 3.

INDEX AND GLOSSARY
OF ARABIC WORDS

INDEX AND GLOSSARY OF ARABIC WORDS

ʿ*A* [and sometimes *aa* or *â*] is here put for ع: this Ar. letter is a sort of ventriloqual *a*, or ᵃₐ sounded with (as it were) an affected deepness and asperity in the larynx.

ʿ*Aad*, ancient tribe in S. Arabia, 61, 136.

Aʿaddi ʿaley-na (verb. عدي ; comp. *taad*, 287;) pass unto us, 606.

ʿ*Aarab*, the nomad Arabs; despised by townsfolk and oasis-dwellers as witless and idle robbers, 54, 132; dissolute, 143; in their mouths signifies *the people*, 265, 321.

ʿ*Aarab Zamil*, II. 445.

Aaron, *v.* Harûn.

el-*Âb*, Harb vill., II. 546.

Ab el-Ghrennem, patriarch of the Belka Arabs, 65.

Aba Rasheyd, Harrat, II. 204.

el-ʿ*Abàdella*, tribe of ashràf of which was the Sherîf Hasseyn, II. 556.

J. *Abàn, v. Abànàt*.

Abànàt, mountains, 668; II. 315, 335, 489, 490, 491.

ʿ*Abâra* (عِبَارً), manner, wise.

ʿ*Abbas*, uncle of Moh., II. 550.

Abbasîeh, a sandstone coast near the Misma, 621.

ʿ*Abd*, slave; in Arabia it signifies one of the black races of Africa, whether bond or libertine, 596.

ʿ*Abd-el-ʿAzîz, el-Bessàm*, II. 518, 526, 532, 535.

ʿ*Abd-el-ʿAzîz*, a former Emir of Boreyda, II. 347.

ʿ*Abd-el-ʿAzîz el-Metaab, Ibn Rashîd*, II. 40, 41, 273.

ʿ*Abd el-Azîz*, a servitor of Ibn Rashîd: he brings a gift-horse from his master to the Hâj Pasha at Medáin Sâlih, 238, 241, 242, 636, 637. When the Hâj arrived he went to lodge in the Pasha's tent, 636, 637.

ʿ*Abd-el-ʿAzîz, er-Romàn*, a Teyma sheykh, 377, 591, 609, 610, 613.

ʿ*Abd el-ʿAzîz*, Sultan, 98, 650; II. 400, 540.

ʿ*Abd-el-Hâdy*, a Kheybar villager, II. 94-101 [also called in derision *Abu Summakh*, 100].

ʿ*Abd-el-Kâder*, the Algerian Sherîf Prince and Imâm [since deceased], resident at Damascus, 40, 165, 207; II. 326.

ʿ*Abd-el-Kâder*, a young kellâ keeper, named after the Prince, 128, 130, 162.

ʿ*Abd-er-Rahmàn*, the great mosque of, at Cordoba, II. 426.

ʿ*Abd-er-Rahmàn*, son of ʿAbdullah el-Bessâm, II. 432, 482, 488, 503, 510-519.

ʿ*Abd-el-Wâhâb, v. ʿAbdullah*.

Abda, Shammar, II. 52, 56.

B. ʿ*Abdillah*, Harra, II. 378.

ʿ*Abdillah Pasha*, brother of Sherîf Hasseyn, II. 539, 542, 560.

ʿ*Abdullah ibn ʿAbbas* (uncle of Moh.); mosque of — at Tâyif, II. 550.

ʿ*Abdullah, ʿAbd-er-Rahmàn, el-Bessàm*, the elder, *v. sub* Bessàm.

ʿ*Abdullah Abu Néjm*, horse broker at ʿAneyza, II. 417, 418.

ʿ*Abdullah el-ʿAly*, Emir of Khúbra, II. 433, 441.

ʿ*Abdullah el-ʿAzîz, el-Mohammed*, late Emir of Boreyda, II. 459.

ʿ*Abdullah el-Bessàm*, the younger, II. 376-7, 383. His worthy and popular manners, 385-91, 397, 422.

ʿ*Abdullah*, a former Emir of Boreyda, II. 347.

ʿ*Abdullah*, a [Christian] stranger, who visited Hâyil in Telâl's time, 656.

ʿ*Abdullah*, a younger brother of Hamûd el-ʿAbeyd, II. 44, 45, 280, 282.

ʿ*Abdullah*, a slave of the Emir at Hâyil, II. 18.

ʿ*Abdullah el-Kennèyny, v. sub* Kennèyny.

ʿ*Abdullah weled Mahanna*, brother of Hásan, Emir of Boreyda, II. 341, 345, 346, 347, 350, 351, 353, 355, 356, 373, 408. His sister, 408.

ʿ*Abdullah el-Moslemanny*, a renegade Jew in Hâyil, 648, 653, 654; II. 59, 271.

ʿ*Abdullah ibn Rashîd*, 503; first Prince of J. Shammar, 639, 669; II. 19, 28, 31, 39, 41, 45, 65, 70.

INDEX AND GLOSSARY

'Abdullah ibn S'aûd, ii. 29, 50, 196, 368, 394, 424; driven from er-Riâth, 453, 454.

'Abdullah ibn Sellàm, a Jew of ancient Kheybar, who converted to Mohammed's religion and received the name, ii. 206.

'Abdullah, Sherîf of Mecca before his brother Hasseyn, ii. 190, 196, 537-40.

'Abdullah, es-Siruân (Abu 'Aly), ii. 98-109, 112-115, 120, 123, 135, 138-41, 145-55; 165, 174, 180-4; his letters to the Pasha of Medina, 146, 147, 183; embezzler of his soldiers' pay, 102, 147; 192-4, 197-8, 204, 207-8, 216-8, 221-3, 227-30, 232, 234-5, 241, 272, 299, 308; his Medina tales, 148-50, 151; his soldiering, 150; wived at Kheybar, 151; his account of his stewardship, 153; his shooting, 165; his violence, 181, 222; his assurances, 218; his dread of camphor, 229; he beats rebellious villagers, 234; he taxes the neighbour Heteym 241; 529.

'Abdullah, son of *Tollog,* a Mahûby, 513, 516, 532, 542, 543.

'Abdullah el-Yahŷa, son of the patriot and companion of Zâmil, at 'Aneyza, ii. 377, 410, 458, 459, 460.

'Abdullah ibn Yahŷa ibn Selèym, former Emir of 'Aneyza, ii. 459, 461, 462, 463.

'Abdullah, son of Zâmil Emir of 'Aneyza, ii. 365-6, 385, 431.

Aβηβζι, name in an inscription, 408.

Aβη<small>C</small>ακιων, name in an inscription, 408.

'Abeyd ibn Rashîd, brother of 'Abdullah, first Emir of Jebel Shammar, conductor of the military expeditions; a warlike man and poet, of the old Waháby straitness; father of Hamûd: he deceased two years after the death of Telâl, about the year 1870; 306, 502, 636, 642, 647, 650, 652, 654, 669, 670; his palms, 636, 660, 665, 670; his coffee-house, 646, 649, 656, 660, 665; ii. 17, 32, 41-44, 51, 69; kassâd, 42; warrior, 42; his old age 42; his family, 42-4; expelled the Ânnezy of el-Hâyat, 44; 301, 460, 462.

'Abeydillah, a Sehammy, 441-7, 449.

J. el-Abiath, or *el-Baitha,* in the Harrat Kheybar, district of *Theraieh el-Lahîb,* el-Heteymy. The nomads look upon this mountain as (part of) the water-shed between the great wadies el-Humth and er-Rummah, and in it they say are the highest seyl-strands or heads of the W. er-Rummah, ii. 90, 237.

'Abîda, a fendy of Kahtân, ii. 52, 56.

'Abida, Aarab near Jidda (perhaps the same as *el-'Ubbeda, Harb*), ii. 573.

Abishai, Joab's brother, his slaughter of the Edomites, 83.

Abraham defeats Chedorlaomer, 61; reported founder of the Ka'aba, 101; his city (Hebron), 493; 500; ii. 405.

Abu, abûy, father, 350, 361.

Abu 'Aly ('Abdullah es-Siruán), ii. 230, 234.

Abu Bâkkar (or *Búkkr*), a chief personage at Medina, ii. 225.

Abu Bátn (Selmàn ibn Shamàn), a Howeyty sheykh, 449-50.

Abu Daûd (Sleymàn), sheykh *'Ageyl es-Sham,* 49; ii. 61, 464.

Abu Fâris, a worthy Syrian vaccinator who wandered in Arabia, 295; was a year with the Beduins, visited the oases as far as Kasîm, and was esteemed by his nomad hosts, *ib.*; in Hâyil, 295-297, 342; ii. 310, 410.

"*Abu Fâris,*" a second, or *Sleymàn,* 295; he was less hardy, his humiliation before the Aarab when he received tidings of the massacre of Christians in Damascus, 296.

[*Abu Feyd,* a site not distant from Boreyda, where are springs.

Abu Khalîl, or *Ibrahîm er-Romàn, v. Ibrahîm.*

Abu Krûn [Kurûn], a Mahûby, 543.

Abu Middeyn, a Kheybar villager [*midd. i.e.* modius, a measure], ii. 220.

Abu Moghrair, v. Ybba M. (2).

Abu ['Bû] Ras, a Moorish negro trader, formerly of Kheybar, ii. 93.

Abu Rashîd, a Medân merchant, lodging at el-Ally, 196.

Abu Rashîd, a driver in the Hâj, 102.

Abu Robai, v. Gériat — .

Abu Sa'ad, an old Mu'atter at Damascus; tale of, 103.

Abu Sammakh, ii. 100.

Abu Shamah, 427, 502.

Abu Selim, a Moorish hakîm, rides down from Damascus with Mehsan Allayda; and they are robbed by a ghrazzu in the (Hâj) way, 481, 482; ii. 206.

Abu Sháhr, bunder on the Persian side of the Gulf, ii. 487.

Abu Shauk, the hedgehog, 371.

Abu She'ab, oasis vill. in W. Fâtima, ii. 567.

Abu Sinnán, a dog's name, 474.

Abu Sinûn (Mohammed), a Moor, formerly of a kellâ garrison, settled in his nomad wife's tribe (the Moahîb), a carrier of rice from

OF ARABIC WORDS   581

el-Wejh, 241, 283, 405, 430, 438, 441, 446, 447; his fortune, 447-9; 453, 454, 456, 458, 459, 462, 463, 475, 518, 519, 521, 540, 548, 552.
J. Abu Táḥa, 121.
Abu Tawfîsh (perhaps *tawfîz*, توفيز , haste), the cholera disease, 519.
Abu Thain, a pool in the 'Aueyrid, 470.
Abu Zeyd, a fabulous heroic personage, effigy of [*v. Doc. Épigr.* pl. XLVIII], 348, 349-50, 381, 479.
'*Abûd*, hasty-bread baked under the embers, 172, 568; II. 239.
Abyssinia, 203, 275, 289, 665; II. 154; beehive-like cabins in W. Fâtima, like those of —, 567.
Abyssinians: Further — or Gallas, *qd. v.* II. 102.
Acacia, *v. Tolh, Sammara, Sillima, Siála*. The possessed — at el-Héjr, 316, 324; gum arabic and pitch from, 411, 425, 426; camels browse the thorny boughs full of mimosa-like leaves, 425; and the small cattle browse them, *ib.*, 486; II. in the Kheybar Harra, 89, 90, 109; small herb springing under the north side of, 248; growth of —s a sign of ground-water, 493; sammar trees, 502, 506; — bushes trodden round by gazelles, 507; danger of the thorns in riding under an —, 528; — in the Mecca Teháma beset with a parasite plant, 566.
Acre ('*Akka*), 114.
'*Ad, v. 'Aed*.
Adam, 341, 434, 590; II. 102, 115, 191.
Beny Adam, the children of Adam, mankind:— compared with the jân, II. 212, 214, 215, 558.
Ádamy, pl. *ouádam* [a Persian Gulf word, in Nejd], one of the children of Adam, a man, II. 215, 426, 488.
'*Adan* (عَدَن), a sand dune of the Nefûd, II. 359.
'*Adanát*, pl. of '*Adan, qd. v.*, II. 339, 357.
Adders of the desert, 358, 373.
Aden ['*Aden*], II. 227, 449, 470, 556.
Ádilla, a dog's name, 474, 530.
W. *Adîra, v* W. *el-Hâsy*.
'*Adu*, enemy, II. 97, 443.
'*Adu ed-dîn*, II. 154.
Aduàn, a fendy of Ma'azy, 474.
Aduàn, a dog's name, 474.
W. *Adzîz*, II. 508.

'*Aed* [or '*Ad*, عد] — like *jau* — a watering place digged in low ground, II. 269.
Aelius Gallus, a Roman knight, general of Augustus' military expedition in Arabia, II. 196; his opinion of the Arabians and of their desert country, *ib.*
El-'Aerîn (العرين, the *ethla* tamarisk), II. 560.
Aerolith, 412, 478.
Afâra, a kinship of Kheybar villagers, II. 153.
Afarît, a fendy of Shammar, II. 56.
'*Afarît*, pl. of '*afrît*, 415.
Affârim! (Turk. آفریم) II. 397.
el-'*Affery* (class. اعفر, عفراء), the small never-drinking gazelle of the sand deserts, II. 164.
'*Affinîn* ['*Afinîn*], or '*Affûn*, pl. of '*affn*, corrupt persons, 355, 424.
'*Affn* ['*affn*], putrid, rotten.
'*Affûn* ['*afûn*], vulg. pl. of '*affn*, 367.
'*Afia* ['*aafia*], health! 532.
'*Afîf*, an ancient well in the desert between Kasîm and Mecca, II. 497-8, 499, 500, 502.
el-*Aflâj* [*v. W. Dauâsir*], II. 52, 425. According to Hámed en-Nefîs, these are names of vill. in el-Aflâj (the head is two thelûl journeys from er-Riâth);— *Siah, Leyla, Khúrfa, er-Rautha, el-Bidde'a, ib.*
Africa: Arabs have long ago wandered over the face of—, without leaving record, 198; antelopes of—, 372; II. 227, 406: gashed cheeks are tribes' marks, 536.
African blood, 603.
'*Afrît*, evil *genius loci*, 87, 213.
el-'Afu, id. *qd. v. 'Afuah*.
'*Afuah*, the same as '*afia*, thanks.
Afûn, corrupted, II. 378.
'*Âfy aleyk, el-'âfy*, 307.
Aga (*Âghra*), captain.
el-'*Agab*, the small swart-brown eagle of the desert, 374, 439; II. 240.
el-'*Agab*, pl. of '*akaba*, 341.
el-'*Agaba* (*Aarab*), 61.
'*Agâl, v. Meyshub, Maasub*, head cord of the Beduin kerchief, 189, 484.
el-'*Agàl Ullah* (العقل الله), 280.

Aged persons; many in 'Aneyza, II. 422.
el-*Âgel*, a desert station N.-W. of Teyma, 341.

el-Ágella [perhaps *Áḳilla*, which signifies 'where the ground-water is near,' but the wells here are 7 fath.], a hamlet of J. Shammar; II. 34, 266, 267, 290.

Ágerra, mare's name, II. 253.

'*Ageyl*, the dromedary riders of Nejd in the Ottoman Government service, 46, 49; called by the nomads *el-'Ageylát*. — camp at M'aan, 72, 91, 140, 198, 256, 257, 596, 625; II. at Kheybar, 97, 106, 109, 141-4, 150, 152, 190, 191; an 'Ageyly at Kheybar who had seen the Nasrâny at Damascus, 110; an 'Ageyly from Kasîm at Kheybar, 111; death of the sick Kasîm 'Ageyly, 208; 221, 222, 225, 227, 230, 232, 235, 248, 249, 261, 263, 268, 269, 272, 287, 292, 299, 308, 319, 415, 441, 482, 553.

'*Ageylát*, v. '*Ageyl*.

el-Ageylát, kindred of B. 'Atîeh, 95.

Aghrûty, II. 26, 27.

'*Agîd*, conductor of a foray, 234, 293, 364, 379, 480.

W. 'Agîg by Sh'aara, II. 508.

el-'Ágorra or *Shuk el-Ajûz*, *qd. v.*, 423, 483, 512, 535.

Ague-cake (*Táhal*, *qd. v.*); the throbbing enlarged spleen, left after fevers, especially the Hejâz and Kheybar fever, 597.

Ahab took an oath of his neighbours in the matter of Elijah, 310.

Ahl el-aard [*v. Ján*], 177; II. 16.

Ahl Aṭhab (*adab*), 657.

Ahl byût sha'ar, Booth-dwellers or Nomads, 317. [*v. Hâthir.*]

Ahl Gibly, southern Aarab, 270, 385, 393, 465.

Ahl Hàjjur, a fendy of Harb Mosrûh, II. 547.

Ahl hàwâ, II. 137.

Ahl kellimy, 508.

Ahl es-Shemâl, Aarab of the north, 465, 503.

Ahl Theyma, 328.

Ahl ṭîn, dwellers in clay houses, settled folk, 317.

el-Aḥmar, the south mountain of the Abànât, II. 491.

Ahmed, a prophet that was to come, *i.e.* Mohammed, feigned by the Moslem doctors to be foretold in the Evangelists (a barbarous blunder in the Korân), II. 24.

Ahmed (brother of M.) *en-Nejûmy*, II. 95, 101, 103, 134, 158; comes to Kheybar, *ib.*, and prospers, 159; 162; his children died in their tender years; coffee and tobacco tippler; sick in the pestilence, *ib.*; 178, 190, 194, 208, 217, 233.

Ahrâr, pl. of *Ḥarra* (أَحْرَارٍ *pl. of* حَرَّة), vulc. country, II. 204.

Aîda, a dog's name, 474.

Aïnàt, a kindred of the Fuḳara tribe, 270.

Air, the Arabs very imaginative of the quality of the air, 250, 485.

"Air-measure," II. 99.

Aisûn, butterfly, 496.

Aitha, camel's name, 321.

'*Ajâj*, v. '*Ajjâj*.

'*Ajamy*, Persian.

'*Ajeyfa Ḥarra*, II. 378, 566.

'*Ajilân*, nimble, a dog's name, 474.

J. *Ajja*, or *Âja*, [the course of, is N.-E. to S.-W. as delineated in the map], 464, 626, 628, 632, 635, 663, 667, 668, 669; II. 24; is greater than Selma, 24, 77, 267 [also pronounced Ejja], 269, 279, 286, 287, 490.

'*Ajjâj* (عَجَاج), the sand driving wind; '*ajâj*, عَجَاج, is the sandy dust : — of Sinai, 67, 96; II. 246, 267.

Âjjidát, (Ḳasim word, perhaps عقدات), town-wall, II. 340, 426.

Âjjilla, mtn. in the way betw. Ḳasim and Mecca, II. 500.

'*Ajjr* (عاقر), the word explained, 240; II. 33, 39.

Aj(k)eyl, a villager of Teyma, 575-7, 580-1.

Ajlâb, "fetched," said of drove-beasts (whether camels or horses), 633.

el-'Ajmàn, a great tribe of Southern Aarab, from Nejràn, and reputed to descend from a Persian legion. — in the N. are the same Aarab, and sometimes they return to el-Yémen. II. Great sheykh of — taken captive by the Turks; and wounded in the late jehâd by a ball in the arm, 275, 381, 453.

Ajûj (Yajûj) wa Majûj, Gog and Magog, II. 558.

[*el-Ak (Ach)*, a passage in the Tueyk mountains.

'*Aḳaba*, interpreted, 90.

'*Aḳaba Ayla* or '*A. el-Mísry*, 84; 474.

'*Aḳaba es-Shemîya*, 89, 90, 94, 96, 97, 120.

'*Akarît*, pl. of '*akarût*, a villanous Syrian and Egyptian word.

Akhbâra-'d-Dúal, a book, 642.

Akhdar [*Khûthr* of the Bed.]; *Wady el-*, 96; *Boghraz el-*, 116; *Kellat el-*, 116, 117; 119, 135, 219, 238, 241, 445, 448, 453, 464; ii. 197.

el-Akhma, undercliffs of the Harra upon the plain of Medáin S., 179, 525, 529, 555, 557, 563.

Akhu, brother: the Bed. — 406; ii. 255.

Akhu Noora, ii. 39.

Akhŷey (dim. of *akhûy*), my little brother, 379.

Akilla, desert site where the ground-water is near.

Akka (عُكَّة), a skin for samn, ii. 230.

'Akkâm (عُكَّم), the word interpreted, 41, 97, 102, 104; discourse of religion, 104; 111, 117, 121; A Christian — in the Haj, 124, 126.

Alarm in the way by night, 564; in the desert, 387, 567; ii. 494; in the caravan menzil, 508.

Albanians, 114 (*el-Arnaût*), ii. 97, 98, 110, 111, 144, 145, 191, 207; an — aga at Tâyif, 541, 548, 552, 560; " the — were from the Tâyif country," 561.

Ale, a kind of, in Galla-land, ii. 186.

el-'Alem, a considerable mountain in sight, to the southward, from Seleymy, ii. 306. [In a rude chart made for me by 'Abd. el-Bessàm, is written in this place, *Jebâl Rîk el-Ashmât el-'Alam*.]

'Alemny b'es-sahîh, ii. 100.

Aleppo [*Hâleb*]; felts of, 41; 42, 138, 580; ii. 64, 371; — boils, 511.

Alexander the Great [*Iskander Thu el-Kurneyn*]: his " tomb " at Rabbath Moab, 60; *Epoque grecque de*, 673; ii. 541.

Alexandria in Egypt, ii. 276, 387; Ômar burned the library at, 387.

'Aleyî, vill. in el-'Aruth, ii. 57.

'Aleyk 'àhad Ullah wa amàn Ullah, in mâ akhûnak, ii. 479.

Aleykom es-salaam, response to the greeting with peace, *Salaam 'aleyk*.

Aleynak sâdik (perhaps *'alemnak s*.), 492.

Alfred, king, his words of Ireland, 462.

Algeria [and, v. *'Abd-el-Kader*]: the Sáhara of, 129; 130, 132, 484, 629.

Algerian derwishes, 249.

'Alîa, wife of Abu Zeyd, effigy of, 348, 350.

'Alîy, vill. of B. Sâlem, Harb, ii. 546.

Allah, i.e. *el-ilâh*, the God; *vulg. Ullah*, 214.

Allàyda, the sheykhs' fendy of Wélad 'Aly, 271, 363, 370, 435, 437, 480; ii. 111, 206.

'Allowîn Beduins, a kindred of the Howeytát, 84.

Allowîy, reputed patriarch of el-Ally, 189.

el-Ally [*'Aly* or *'Ala* pron. *el-Êlly*, *el-'Ely*, so Wallin writes correctly from the sound *'Elah*. The litteral *el-'Ola* is never heard in the mouths of the villagers or Beduins, as neither el-Hîjr for they all say el-Héjr. I have but once heard a stranger — he was from *Feyd* in J. Shammar — pron. thus; and he said *el-'Ulla*]. It is said in that country, with much likelihood, " The 'Alowna are from the Jeheyna and from Egypt." El-Ally is about 8 m. below el-Héjr: these (Hejâz) villagers wear not the *haggu*. [Bar. alt., mean of 11 observ., 693-5 *mm*. Visited 27 Dec. 1876–6 Jan. 1877, and thrice revisited in the summer of 1877], 128; 134, 135, 178, 179; the first settlement of, 182; coffee at, 182; single marriage common in, 183; lemon groves, 185; people of a quiet behaviour, 184, 186; they are reputed " scholars " by the Nomads, 186; their speech, *ib*. and 242; their town often called the medina or city, *ib*., 524; here is the beginning of the Hejâz, *ib*.; was never subject, 186; their free-will tax to Medina, *ib*.; the old Waháby upon a time came against them, *ib*.; the oasis in W. Kôra, *ib*.; the village justice, *ib*.; inscriptions, 187; sûks or wards of the town, 187; kahwas, *ib*.; the townspeople go always armed, *ib*.; ancient names of the place, *ib*.; Beny Sókhr rights at, 189; rain, *ib*.; houses, *ib*.; African aspect, *ib*.; squalid looks of these villagers, *ib*.; the women, *ib*.; tolerant ignorance of the most, 191; a pasha banished to—, 193; the brook (2½ ft. deep), *ib*.; altitude of —, 193; well-pits, 194; humped kine, *ib*.; orchards, *ib*.; the townspeople sell their fruits, *ib*.; many of their young men go up with the yearly Hâj to Damascus, *ib*.; pumpkins, *ib*.; they will pay no " brotherhip " to the Beduw, *ib*.; the oasis land, *ib*.; the population, *ib*.; they sell dates and corn to the Beduw for silver, and exchange dates for the rice of Wejh carriers, 195; we see here the simplest kind of trading, *ib*.; el-Ally dates, *ib*.; the town site shut under the Harra, *ib*.; Medân tradesmen lodging at,

INDEX AND GLOSSARY

196; practice of medicine at, 197; fanaticism, *ib.*; and of the children, 198; robbers lurking about, 199; a son of a Christian at, 199; built of stones carried from el-Khreyby, 200; el-Mubbiát, 203; *Korh, ib.*; *J. Shakhúnab,* 205; 209; written *el-'Ola,* 229, 232, 234, 235, 236, 237, 242; 'Alowna come to the Hâj market, 239; 241, 247, 248, 315, 322, 326, 329; mosques at, 331; 338, 340; 355, 392, 396, 400, 403, 405, 413, 420, 455, 461, 463, 465, 485, 487, 488; the 'Alowna koran readers, 493; 502, 511; fever, 523; 525, 527, 528, 538, 540, 543, 553; iniquitous dealing in, 555; the beautiful sight of the oasis palms in the summer, *ib.* and 556; these villagers' gibing humour, 556; 557, 560, 563, 580, 592-3, 600, 610, 625; II. 85, 94, 96, 122, 132, 135, 195; their palm-stems are banked up, 416; water-snails in the brook, 451; [*v.* also *Búndur 'Alúshy* and *Baith Naam* ;] 555.

Alms, none asked an — at Teyma, 330.

'Alowna, sing. *'Alowwy,* the townspeople of el-Ally (*qd. v.*), 181, 185, 189, 194, 406.

'Alowwy v. 'Alowna.

Alpine rat, 371.

Alum [*v. Shúb*]; water tasting of —, II. 501.

'Aly, old blind father of Abdullah, Emir of Khubbera, II. 437-9, 442.

'Aly 'aḳlu, II. 33.

'Aly, second or executive Emir at 'Aneyza, II. 365-6, 371-2, 395, 431-3, 447, 467, 474, 476.

'Aly, a negro sergeant of the Emir at 'Aneyza, II. 363-6, 371-3, 405, 430-4.

'Aly, a poor kassâd of B. 'Atîeh, 544-5.

'Aly el-Aŷid, a neighbour at Hâyil, 664-5; II. 17, 272, 277.

el-'Aly, a fendy of Bishr, 376.

'Aly, a villager of Gussa, II. 266, 292, 293.

el-'Aly, Harb. *v.* B. 'Aly.

B. *'Aly,* a division of Harb Mosrûh in Nejd, II. 306, 318, 324, 327, 331; some of these tribesmen, though called kafirs, are very religious, 332; 334, 335, 547.

'Aly, a poor Harby of B. 'Aly, II. 312; 318; he accounts himself a homicide, *ib.*

Ibn *'Aly,* a principal family at Hâyil, II. 31.

'Aly houn-ak (علي هونك), 530.

'Aly, religious sheykh and villager at Kheybar, II. 154, 194.

'Aly laḥyaty, 309.

'Aly, a follower of Mâjid el-Hamûd, 666; II. 25, 72.

'Aly, son-in-law of Mohammed, 4th calif, 108, 657; II. 97; *Mesjid* — at Kheybar, 93, 97; 145; *'Ayn* —, [27° C.], 93; 258, 549, 556.

'Aly el-Rasheyd, of Bosra and 'Aneyza: he travelled with *Yûsef Khâlidy* through the chief countries of Europe, II. 448, 451, 470.

'Aly es-Sweysy, 328.

'Aly, a younger son of Zâmil and said to resemble him, II. 463.

Amalek, the ancient tribe of, II. 388.

Amân, a Galla freedman and 'Ageyly at Kheybar, comrade of the Nasrâny, II. 101, 124-7, 134-8, 143-5; his tale of a Christian who came to Medina, 176-7; 180; his tale of Galla-land, 185-191; he was stolen in his childhood, *ib.*; his life in the Hejâz, *ib.*; 192-4; 202, 207-8; tale of jins, 211; 228; his farewell, 235.

'Amân or *Omân,* the Arabian Gulf province of, II. 389, 460, 462, 489.

el-'Amâra, a corn settlement upon the river, above Bosra, II. 371, 449.

Amaziah, of the House of David, king of Judah; his cruelty to the Edomites, 83.

'Ambar ('Anbar), a Galla officer at Hâyil, II. 65, 271.

Amber beads, 336.

'Am'dàn, pl. of *'amûd,* pillar; stakes of the Bed. booth so-called, 262, 265, 266; — of locusts, 380.

Ameah Hakràn, or *el-Moy She'ab,* II. 505.

'Amed (اعمد), sally or go over to seek fellowship, 491.

America, called in Arabic *Dínya el-jedîda,* the New World, 647, 652; II. 28.

American seamen, 168; — missionary, 581, 631.

Amiable bloody ruffian, An, 130.

'Amiḳ, sometimes pron. *ghramiḳ,* II. 317.

'Amm, 360.

'Ammàn, v. Rabbath Ammon.

Ammar, *v.* Hallat Ammar.

Ammarát, a fendy of Bíshr, 376.

'Ammatak (thine uncle's wife), thy hostess, 257.

Ammera, a dog's name, 474.

Ammon, plains of, 56; children of, succeeded the Zamzummim, 61; land of, neighbour to the nomads, 82; to compare with an English county, 83; II. 575.

OF ARABIC WORDS 585

Amo (Span.), 361.
Amos, the herdsman prophet; words of, 412.
Beny 'Amr, a division of Harb Mosrûḥ, II. 155, 547.
Beny 'Amr, of Harb Beny Sâlem, II. 546.
'Amr Ullah, II. 279.
Amsterdam, a tome printed at, 654.
'Amûd, a pillar, v. 'am'dàn.
Amûd, a fendy of Shammar, II. 56.
W. Amudán, in the Teháma, 469.
Amulet, v. ḥijâb.
Ana abûk, 361.
Ana ajizt, 172, 539.
Ana akhtak, 361.
Ana akhu chokty, II. 39.
Ana bi wéjhak yâ sheykh, 311.

Ana efla yowwella (انا افلا ايوالله), 307.

Ana meyet, 91.
Ana min dîrat beyt Ullah, II. 571.

Ana nusîk (انا انسك), 311.

Ana sabáktahum, words of Moh. Ibn Rashîd, II. 31.

Ana ṣúrt nuzîlak (انا صرت نزيلك), 311.

Ana ummak, 361.
Ana ússhud! I bear witness, 307.
Ana weled abûy, II. 39.

Ana werrîk, II. 139. (انا اوريك); verb. ورّي for أري: they say commonly in Nejd werrîny, show me).
el-Anâbis, Ḥarrat, near Medina, II. 204.
['Anâg, young goat (Moahib).
Anatoly [Gr.-Turk.] the land of the sun-rising, the Levant; Ottoman Province of Asia Minor.
'Anâz, patriarch of the Ânnezy, 94, 270; his son Musslim, ancestor of the B. Wáhab, ib.
'Anâz [v. plate VI], great crater hill upon the Ḥarrat el-'Aueyriḍ, 449, 450, 451, 456, 465, 470.
Andalûs (Andalusîa), II. 182, 426, 556.
'Aneybar, a Galla officer of the Prince at Hâyil, 655; II. 65, 265, 271-9, 281-4, 299, 314, 342, 345.
'Aneyza [عنيزة Ibn 'Ayiṭh: v. Black Stone], "metropolis of Néjd," chief town of el-Ḳaṣîm; on the right border of the W. er-Rummah. Bar. height (mean of 9 observ.), 689 mm. The site of this town, which lies as the midway between Bosra and Mecca, is said by her citizens to be the centre of the Peninsula. [29 April—16 July, 1878.] 49, 212, 295, 527, 638, 658; II. 37, 42, 47, 55, 58, 60, 67, 311, 315, 317, 339, 346, 347, 349, 350, 352, 354, 355, 357-365; aspect of, 365; wards or parishes in, 367; half of the town are Wahábies, 368; house-building at, ib.; foreign merchants of, 367, 371, et passim; breakfast in, 371, 374; tradesmen to the Aarab robbed in the desert, 373; dinner in, 378; the sûks, 374, 380; aspect of the citizens, 375; franklins walk in the streets with long wands, 376; distribution of the day-time in, 379; tradesmen in, 380; the founding of, 381; Umm Nejd, ib.; a pleasant civil liberty at, 384; labourers and well-drivers at, 385; the miserable ask alms from door to door, ib.; coffee drinking at, 385, 396; the town of — is greatly increased of late years, 386; trading in 'Aneyza and Hâyil, 390; crimes at, 395; they take no booty from their enemies, 396; no breeding of horses at —, 417, 418-9; — is partly built upon a torrent bed, 422; ingenuous vocations are husbandry and camel and horse-dealing, 415, 416, 418, 428; — a good civil town more than other, 429; crafts, ib.; driven from —, 437; wars of —, 458-62; water at —, 464; dates of, 466; caravan from Bosra, 468, 470; the sámn caravan, 472, 481, 485, 488; great foray of the town with el-Meteyr against Kahtân, 473-81; 495-6; 543; 552.

Anezy, kellâ, 68.

Anfâd, pl. of nef'd (نفد), q. v.

Angel visions [v. Melûk and Ménhel], 496; in the books of Moses, 497; in the N.T., 498; II. v. also 81.

Anmâr, an Arabian patriarch, II. 393.

el-Ânnezy ('Anezy), the great Ishmaelitish nomad nation; their number, sub-tribes and dîras, 94, 171, 241; in W. Hanîfa, 270, 314, 360, 371, 376, 378; compared with B. Israel, ib.; their ancient dîra, ib.; 389, 430, 435, 444, 464, 474, 579, 597, 622, 630, 633; northern, 661; II. 27, 29; of el-Hâyat, 44; Abdullah ibn Rashîd deputed to govern, 45; 51, 64, 80; are landowners at Kheybar, 91, 92; ancient seats of the, 132; 134, 141, 156, 205; the Southern, 235; 240, 263, 285, 290, 298, 299, 308; booths of, 322, 342; the — lately of el-Kasîm now in Syria, 428; the founder of the Waháby reform reported to have been of —, 454; called the *Wáilyîn*, 476; 492, 508.

'*Antara* or '*Antar* [*ibn Shiddád, ibn 'Aad*; his mother's name was *Zbîby*, a slave woman], hero poet of the Arabian antiquity before Mohammed. He was a nomad of the desert country between el-Héjr and Medina. — is author of one of the Moallaka poems, 162, 204, 220, 362, 411, 669; II. 305.

el-'Antarîeh, a camping-ground, Fejîr dîra, 259.

Antelope, the Arabian, [*v. Wothŷhi*], 98, 325, 373.

Antilibanus mountains, II. 171.

Antimony used to paint the eyes, *v. Kaḥl*.

Antioch, II. 157, 539, 540.

"Antiquities," 328, 348, 428; II. 266, 272, 313.

Ants in the desert, 373; II. ant-hills sifted for bread, 418.

el-'Anûz, the Ânnezy Bed. nation, II. 80.

Anvil, 582.

A'orfy, a kind of pipe-heads wrought in stone by the Nomads, II. 200.

Apes of the Mecca Country, II. 573.

"The Apostle's Country," II. 91, 98.

Apothecaries, Indian, in Mecca, II. 561.

April heat in the desert, 387; II. 288; — showers at 'Aneyza, 434.

el-'Arab 'akl-hum nâḳiṣ, II. 422.

'*Araba, Wady, el-*, 75, 81, 84, *v. el-Ghrór*.

Arabia, *v. Beled el-'Arab*. Price of camels in, 275; invaded and carried by the world's changes, 289, 295, 298; the waste land of the Aarab, 316, 325; 396; hitherto nearly unknown to us, 469; II. the Turk would extend his dominion in, 48; Europeans have always a false opinion of, 196; desert —, *ib.*; ever full of alarms, 197, 222.

Arabia, ancient, 328, 434; II. 197.

Arabia the Happy [Εὐδαίμων or *Felix*], 135, 407; II. 196.

Arabia Petraea, 67.

Arabian race, feminine aspect of, 279; lastingness of the, with little change, notwithstanding their marvellous levity, 289; most miserable of mankind, 481; II. accounted Beduw by the dwellers in the Arabic settled countries, 47, 75; Arabians are never rightly merry, 103; it is well to be at peace with the Arabs, 254; slender Nejd Arabs, 279.

"Arabian tales;" in Damascus and other great border cities are found innumerable written romances in the people's hands treating (and chiefly magnifying the simple magnanimity) of the desert life, 306.

Arabian travel, the art of, 96; 113, 117, 121, 251; II. journey like a fever, 276.

Arabic authors, 196.

Arabic speech [*v. Loghra*], 168, 196; of the Bed., 307; of the Fukara and the Moahîb, 307; a multitude of book words are unknown to the Bed., 400; Koran — was perhaps never the tongue of the upland tribes, *ib.* and *v.* 228; II. Hejâz and Nejd —, 192; of the northern towns, 389; in el-Ḳaṣîm, 426; of the Meteyr, 475; — of el-'Asîr, 552.

L'Arabie avant Mahomet d'après les Inscr., 224.

The Arabs are wanderers (but not out of the way), II. 195; the nomads are barren minded in the desert, 302.

'*Araby*, the Arabic tongue.

Aradát, a fendy of Bíllî, 430.

'*Arafát*, II. 513-4.

Aramaic inscr. at Teyma, 581.

Araméenne l'écriture, 224.

el-Aránta, a tribe of ashrâf, II. 556.

el-'Arár (عرار), a tree, II. 24.

el 'Arbân, the tribes.

['*Arbân!* a multitude of kindreds and tribes, more than one can recount.

Arbiters in the Nomad tribes, a kind of justices after the tradition of the desert; they are other than the great sheykhs, 186, 551; II. in the oases, 153.

Archery, the ancient, 289, 613.

Architecture, sculptured, at Medáin S., 673-4; of the Arabs, II. 348.

Arcosolium (a form in architecture), 674.

Arctic dîra, tale of, and the wonder and mirth of the Aarab hearers, 321.

Arḍ ba'al (interpreted), 78.

Arḍ Jiddàr, 91, 92.

Arḍ el-Kelby, 73.

Arḍ (es) Ṣuwwán [*v. J. Sherra*], the Flint Land, is all the east part of the Mountain of Edom (which is covered with gravel, therewith being some vulcanic drift), from whence it reaches far eastward toward Jauf, 67, 68, 86, 217.

OF ARABIC WORDS

Ardub, a corn measure in the Turkish cities, II. 551, 572.
Areyj, a night station in the desert north of Teyma, 341.
Areymîsh, a camel's name, 321.
'*Aridàn*, mountain in the desert Kasim-Mecca, II. 501.
el-Arîsh, Nefûd of, II. 261.
Ark of B. Israel, 268.
Armenia, *Tiflis* in, II. 110.
Armies in Arabia [*v*. Ibrahîm Pasha, Aelius Gallus], II. 196.
Armour: many Beduin sheykhs possess old shirts of mail (*Daûdy* or Davidian *qd. v*.), and some have caps of steel; which they do on in the day of battle, when (being come in sight of their foemen) they light from the thelûls to mount upon their led mares, II. 36, 480.
Arnon, *v. Wady Mójeb*.
Aroa, a fendy of Jeheyna, 166.
Arrabûn, earnest-money, II. 299.
el-'Arrafej (عَرْفَج), a sweet-smelling Nejd pasture bush, 371.
Arrak'i, desert site between Hâyil and Kuweyt, II. 61.
Ἀρρη κώμη, 669.
Arrow heads of iron, found by hunters in the mountains of Arabia, 613.
Artesian well: Kenneyny's project of boring at 'Aneyza, II. 370, 379.
Artificers [*v. Sunná*]: — at Hâyil, II. 20; Semitic —, 348; — at 'Aneyza, 429.
Artillery of Ibn Rashîd, 636, 638, 658. [*v*. Cannon.]
el-'Aruth, 241, 264; II. 22, 47, 57, 377, 381, 424. ['*Erjah*, *Múnfuha*, *Hýer*, *Otherummah*, are villages and towns in this Province. — Hámed en-Nefîs.]
'*As*' (عَسِي) *Ullah sahîh*, II. 197.
'*As*' *Ullah, temmém*, II. 139.
Ashâb en-Néby, the companions of the Prophet, II. 93.
Asheyfát, an affinity of Kheybar villagers, II. 153.
Ashîrat, tribe, 270, 293.
'*Ashîry Harra*, II. 378, 508, 566.
el-'Ashrâf, pl. of sherîf, the "eminent" seed of Mohammed, II. 517; 'they are not to be spoken against,' 519; they are villagers and nomad tribes, but would not be named *Fellahîn* or *Beduw*, 523, 537-8. The fendy B. Hasseyn of Harb Mosrûh are all —, 547, 556; — give not their daughters to tribesmen without, but they take wives where they will, 557, 567. Ghrazzus would spare any —, 568. It is not becoming to ride up to a sherîf's house, 568.
Ashteroth Karnaim, 60.
Asia, first coffee-drinking in, 289.
Asiatic hearts full of corruption and iniquity, 376.
Asiatic religions; mystery of priests' cutting and wounding themselves, II. 137.
Asîly, of the root or lineage (*asl*), II. 146.
el-'Asîr, a province of el-Yémen, 464; II. 51, 362, 552, 567.
'*Askar*, soldier.
Askar, son of Misshel-el-Auájy, 379-80, 614, 621-30.
Asl (root), the spring of a kind or lineage.
el-Asmîeh, or *Jériat el-Fejîr*, II. 116, 118; those villagers are not Kheyâbara, *ib.*; rich and bountiful sheykh of, *ib.*; 153.
Asnâm (pl. of *sánam*), idols, II. 51.
Ass: the — will eat the colocynth gourd, 173; reckoned unclean, 298; hardly less than the camel a beast of the desert, 324, 475; the Solubby —, 324, 327; asses are easily lent to strangers in the oases without hire, 585; II. in the Nejd oases, 20, 24; names of —es, 253; an — gelding, 301; Mesopotamian white —, 469, 514; Solubby —, 497, 499; 502, 535, 537, 569.
B. *Assad*, tribe, anciently in J. Tŷ, II. 381.
Beny *Ass'm*, a fendy of Harb Mosrûh, II. 547.
el-Assr ['*asr*], the sun at half afternoon height, time of the third prayer, 178, 368, *et passim*.
Assyrian monuments, 229; — architecture, 227; II. — colonists in Syria, 285.
Asthma, II. 296.
Aswâk, pl. of *sûk*, II. 126.
'*Asyîn*, rebels to the Dowla, II. 182.
[*Ât*, unsalted (Western Arabia).
Âtàfa, *v. Âtéyfa*.
'*Ateja* (عَاتِكَة), Bed. fem. name, 514.
Atèwy, a sheykh at Kheybar, II. 152.
el-Ateyàt, fendy of 'Ateyba, II. 457.
'*Ateyba* [gentile pl. *el-'Ateybân*] a great tribe or Bed. nation; their dîra is all that high desert lying between et-Tâyif and el-Kasîm; they boast themselves friends of the Sherîf of

Mecca; they have been in every fortune the allies of 'Abdullah ibn S'aûd, 389; II. 38, 51, 52, 67, 168, 303, 304, 306, 307, 315, 320, 321; their dîrat in Nejd is bounded by the W. er-Rummah, *ib.*; 323, 336, 357, 365, 381, 384, 394, 445; — assailed by S'aûd ibn S'aûd, 453; 455, 456, 457, 492, 493, 494, 495, 502, 505, 506, 507, 509, 556, 559, 562.

Atèyfa, or *Âtafa* (from عطف), a damsel that mounted in a litter upon her camel is the living standard of her tribesmen in battle, 101; II. 329.

el-Ateyfát, a kindred of Kheybar villagers, II. 153.

el-'Athab (perhaps العذب), the cowpox vaccination, II. 403.

Athan 'lak 'oweyish, shall I prepare thee a little victual? 489.

Atheba, Bed. fem. name, 514.

el-'Atheyb, wells between Medáin Sâlih and el-Ally, 180, 557.

Athubba (اذنب!), wild bees of the desert, 426.

Beny 'Atîeh ['Atîyyah] or *el-Ma'azy*, 94, 97, 115, 219, 220, 234, 237, 270, 311, 380, 393, 435, 449, 453, 464, 513, 537, 544-5; II. 37, 38, 200. [Some kindreds of — are, *er-Robillát, el-'Ageylát, es-Sidenyîn, el-Kuthéra, es-Sbût.*]

Atonement; none between certain tribes, 449.

[*El-Atòylî*, watering of many wells in dîrat Wélad Sleymàn, of Nejd Bishr.

'*Atr, v. 'Attar.*

Atsha, camel's name, 321.

'*Attar*, ['*atr*], perfume, Attar of rose of Mecca, II. 484, 561.

el-Atthar, (Sbéya) vill. in Middle Nejd, II. 425.

Atûla, mountain between Kasîm and Mecca, II. 499.

Atullah, a rich Teyma villager, 583.

J. *Atwa*, beside Kheybar, II. 90, 109, 197.

'*Auâfy*, health! 446.

'*Auájy*, the sheykhs' fendy of Bishr in Nejd, 376, 567, 609, 611, 614, 618, 627, 628; II. 123, 140, 243, 245, 253, 272, 297, 300.

Auâzim (sing. *Azimy*), an old Heteym kindred, II. 194, 195.

'*Aud*, a spice, 137.

Auda, a dog's name, 474.

el-Auellîn, those of the former world, of old time, 328, 441; II. 239.

'*Aueynât Masállat el-Amân*, a phantom oasis (it may be mirage) seen near Teyma, 598.

'*Aueyrid Ḥarra* (and v. *Ḥarra*), 355, 431, 432, 441, 445, 451, 463; is three members, 463, 464; how formed, 464-6, 478, 485, 486, 502, 525, 529, 541; II. 506, 518, 567.

el-'Aueyrid in J. *Shammar*, 464, 669.

'*Auf* (a great clan of Harb), II. 174, 307; *warrahum ma fî shûf, ib.*; 546.

'*Aufy*, tribesman of 'Auf, II. 441.

August in the Mecca country, II. 565.

Augustus Caesar, sends an army to reave the riches of *Arabia Felix*, II. 196-7.

'*Auhellàn*, assembling place of the southern kafîlies near 'Aneyza; there are said to be "certain ancient caves hewn in the sand-rock and inscriptions," II. 488, 489.

'*Aul*, a camping ground in J. Shammar, II. 296, 299, 304.

'*Aunâk!* II. 26.

W. '*Aûrush*, in the Harra, 355, 463, 487, 488, 495, 524, 539.

[*Aûshez, 'Arab Shammar*, the people of Teyma.

Australian Continent, pouched rats of the, II. 261.

Austria, v. *el-Nemsa*; —n money current at Hâyil, II. 23.

'*Authèym*, a hamlet in Ibn Rashîd's country, II. 330.

Auwàd, a kâdy at Hayil, II. 57-8.

Auwàd, a village kâdy at Kheybar, II. 153, 222.

el-Auwâli Ḥarra, near Medina, II. 204.

Auweytha, fem. Bed. name, 514.

Avenger of the blood, II. 453.

'*Awaj*, awry, 307.

el-Ayathát, vill. in W. Dauâsir, II. 425.

'*Aŷb*, shame, 273, 630.

'*Aŷd*, a Mahûby, 459, 460.

'*Aŷd eth-thahîa*, 178; II. 109, 137.

'*Aŷd-ak mubârak*, 606.

Aydân, stems of palms, II. 134.

Ayeyna, in W. Hanîfa, II. 424.

'*Aŷid ibn Mertaad*, a hospitable sheykh, 619.

'*Ayîna*, springs and ruins; a summer station of the Aarab in *el-Ḥisma*, 93.

Ibn '*Ayiṭh*, a negro religious sheykh at 'Aneyza, II. 377, 383, 385, 425-6.

Ayla, village site at the head of the '*Akaba* Gulf, 84; view of —, 85.

el-Âyn, "the evil eye," 378.

OF ARABIC WORDS

el-'Ayn (ez-Zeyma, qd. v.), ii. 512.
'Ayn 'Aly, a spring at Kheybar [27° C.], ii. 97.
'Ayn ibn Ghróbon, station on the E. Hâj road, ii. 565.
'Ayn er-Reyih, a spring at Kheybar [29.5° C.], ii. 219.
'Ayn Selelîm, a spring near Kheybar [28° C.], ii. 206.
'Ayn es-Sweyna, vill. in W. es-Sirr, ii. 424.
'Ayn ez-Zeyma, station before Mecca in the way to et-Tâyif, ii. 488, 517, 553, 564, 565, 569.
'Aysa-bin-Miriam [v. Îsa, Messîh], 'Jesus son of Mary from the Spirit of Ullah,' 104, 493, 521, 560; the colour, lineaments and daily life of —, 642 ; ii. 396, 482, 534.
'Aysa, a Fejîry Beduin, 615.
'Aysh, a corn-food, 377.
'Aysht (a'asht) ! thanks, 565.
el-'Ayûn [Raud' el-'Ayûn, — Ibn Ayith], an oasis in el-Kasîm, her people are el-Missennid, of Shammar lineage ; 49; ii. 37, 336, 476.
'Ayûn bilâ sinûn, 546.
'Azab, said of camels pasturing apart from the menzils, 304, 507 ; ii. 81.
'Azîz, beloved.

Azzuâl (أزوال), pl. of zôl, qd. v.

Bab, gate.
Bab el-'Aarab, ii. 225.
Bab el-'Aly ('Aaly), the 'Porte,' ii. 174, 398, 559.
Bab Tooma (St. Thomas's gate) at Damascus, 104.
Babe : a nomad mother in the Mecca country carries her — riding astride upon her haunch bone, ii. 562.
Babel, the words of Isaiah concerning —, 212 ; tower of —, 434.
Bab es-Seyl, gate at et-Tayif, ii. 539.
Bâch(k)ir, to-morrow, 524.
el-Bâdia, the great waste wilderness, 265.
Baedi, a camping site in the H. Kheybar, ii. 253.
Bagdad, 42 ; caravan servant of —, 53, 108 ; — clothing, 338 ; — kerchiefs, 606 ; — wares, 630 ; — carpets, 638 ; tea from —, 641, 643 ; — mantles, 648 ; — Jew at Hâyil, 648, 653 ; 651, 653, a — caravan lost in the wilderness, 654,; 655 ; ii. 20, 28, 29, 34, 58, 65, 68, 69, 70, 145, 146, 275, 277, 282, 337, 338, 348, 352, 365, 380, 383, 385, 386, 389, 403, 469, 489, 527, 553.

Baggl and Bùggila (بكّال, بكّ), 305 ; dry milk shards, v. Mereesy, ii. 81.
Bàghrila, she mule, 586.
Bahâim, brute beasts, 355.
Bahhir! (بحِّر), Look ! behold ! 375.
Bahr eth-Thellam, 462.
Bairàm, festival after their month of fasting, 567; — at Teyma, 608, 610, 611.
Baith Naam, an ancient name of el-Ally, 189.
el-Baitha, a mountain in the Harrat Kheybar, ii. 237.
(2) el-Baitha, a mountain nigh Medina upon the north, ii. 237.
Baitha Nethîl, a great watering place of many (some say "eighty") wells, of Bîshr, in Nejd, 626, 633 ; ii. 81, 85, 253, 300.
Bak'a, between Hâyil and Kuweyt, ii. 61.
Bakhîl, niggard, 477.
Bakhorra (read Bakûra, باكورة) camel driving-stick, with a bent handle, 264, 349; ii. 548. [v. Mishaab, Mehján.]
el-Bakht, the hap.
Bakhûr, v. incense.
J. Bákr in W. Líthm, 84.
Bakr el-Wahashy, vulg. in Syria for the Wothýhi, qd. v.
Bakshîsh, 556.
Balloon, a Beduin sheykh asks of the —, 451.
Bâmiya, a pot-herb, 644.
Banks, street clay benches made by the house-doors in the oases, 526 ; ii. 127, 136, 155.
Banna (pron. Bunna), a Bed. woman's name, 514.
Barâd, temperate coolness of the air, 435.
W. Bárada, near Damascus [therein they show "the grave of Abel," and "the blood of Nimrod" (dark stains in the rock of the valley side)] : gentile superstitions in —, 497. [The sites are Umm es-Shekkakîf, and the rocky brow between the villages Bekkeya and Herreyry.] ii. 137.
Barâhimma (or Beny Ibrahîm, qd. v.), Jeheyna, settled at Yanb'a-the-Palms, ii. 202.
Bàrak, (bayrak), banner.
Barakát, a fendy of Billî, 469.

INDEX AND GLOSSARY

Barbary States, 129, 358, 415, 433, 503-4; — horses, 420; — coast, II. 178; 451; — sores, 511.
Barefoot, Southern Beduw are —, 265, 291.
BARI, a word used for Arabia in some Assyrian inscriptions — it may be from the Ar. *barîyeh*, desert-land (Sir Henry C. Rawlinson), 229.
Baris (Paris), 647; II. 448.
Barley: — bread, 253, 255; — grown in W. Thirba, 487; — harvest, 635; II. — eaten in the public hostel at Hâyil, 74.
el-Barràcheda, a tribe of ashràf, II. 522.
Barraga, 127.
Ibn Barrák, a division of Heteym, II. 253, 556.
Ibn Barrák, sheykh of the Ibn Barrák, great sheykh of the Beny Rashîd, Heteym, *v. Kâsim ibn Barrák*.
Barrows [*v. Namûs* and *Rijjûm*]: — of the H. 'Aueyrid, 428, 432, 441, 457, 478, 479, 494; II. — in the H. Kheybar, 120, 237, 239, 266.
Barrûd, a village in middle Nejd [*id. qd. Bessàm*], II. 377.
(2) *Barrûd*, station near Mecca, II. 565.
Barter, in Arabian traffic, 338.
Basalt, 423, 465, 478; columnar —, 442; Plutonic — in J. Ajja, 633; and II. 77, 78, 115, 254, 260, 266, 267, 321, 490, 493, 494, 497, 501, 566.
Bashan, plains of, 50.
Bashy Bazûk, II. 157-8, 168 — 170; the name interpreted, 170; their desperate manners, *ib.*; — expeditions, 196.
Bast: of some — the nomads make matches for their long guns; and of some they twist well-rope, II. 317, 452.
Batanea (*en-Niggera*), 314.
el-Bâtin, the bed of the W. er-Rummah N. of el-Kasîm thus called, II. 420.
Bâtin el-Ghrôl, 90.
el-Bat'neyn, a fendy of 'Ateyba; II. 457.
Battâl, bad, idle, II. 26.
Bawl Iblîs, the devil's water (tobacco), 289, 494.
Bayâdiyyeh, a sect of Mohammedans, to which pertain the people of Nejrân and of Mascat, II. 350.
Bayir, a site in the Syrian desert, 164.
B'dûr, a kind of Ânnezy, 377.
Beacons of heaped stones [*v. mantar*], 117, 428.
Beads in the Galla slave traffic, II. 186.
Bear, the constellation, 321.
Bear rock, in W. Sâny, 118.

Bear of the Lebanon mountains, II. 171.
Beard [*lahỳat, dûkn*]: — taken for a sign that an Arabian has not hungered, 240; — to signify *honour*, 292, 309, 311, 462; to swear by the —, 309; — dyed with saffron (the Persian manner), 98, 637, 648; II. 473; 'By thy —,' 534.
Beatrix, antelope; *v. Wothŷhi*.
Beatta (بياتة, *v. Bîat*), a sort of draughts played by the Arabs, 585 [*v. minkala*], II. — at Kheybar, 136.
Beautiful women, 362, 363, 511; Thahir's daughter, 546; 671.
Bébàn, pl. of *bab*, gate, door; it may signify a street-like row of doors, 143, 149, 150; they say bébàn el-Héjr, b. el-Wejh, b. el-Ally.
Béda, a ruined village in the Tehàma " 24 hours from el-Wéjh " [there are said to be " five monuments like those at el-Héjr "], 456, 463.
Bédan, pl. *bedûn*, the great wild goat [*v. W'aûl*], 173, 325, 372, 406, 477, 535, 612; — in captivity at Hâyil, 665; II. 24, 108, 116; a giant —, 164.
Bedaùwy, formal pl. of *Beduwy*; vulg. *Beduw*, 265.
Beddur, village of B. Sâlem, Harb, II. 546.
el-Bedîya, village in el-Yémen, II. 52.
Bedówna, a poor kindred of Heteym, 135.
Bedr Honeyn, a cave at — where the first Moham. "martyrs" lie buried, II. 180.
Bédr ibn Jôhr, prince of old Teyma, 331, 600.
Bédr el-Telâl, ibn Rashîd, murders his uncle Metaab with a shot, II. 28, 29; he is slain, 31, 32.
Beds, 526.
Beduins: their cheerfulness and hilarity, 258; — mildness and forbearance at home, 274, 307; abandoned to usage of coffee and tobacco, 288; — frenetic in the field; their ill humour, 308; their musing melancholy, devout in their natural religion, 283, 302, 398, 518; — fathers of hospitality, 269; the settled life to them, for a while, is refreshment, *keyif*, 240, 276, 355; — easily turn to husbandry, 276; their countenance grave with levity, 288; their listless drooping gravity, 303; their minds distempered by idleness and malice, 308, 469; their murderous wildness towards an adversary, 294, 315; "the Beduwy's mind is in his eyes," 299; the cheerful musing Bed. talk,

OF ARABIC WORDS 591

305 ; — very credulous of aught beyond their ken, 306 ; their fantasy is high and that is clothed in religion, 306 ; — are iniquitous lovers of their private advantage, 306 ; their civil understanding, 307 ; some turns of their discourse, 307 ; their eloquent utterance, *ib.* ; they are smiling speakers, *ib.* ; their mouths full of cursing and lies and prayers, 309 ; their deceitful hearts, *ib.* ; their maledictions, *ib.* ; they are melancholy despisers of their own things, 316, 518-9 ; "the — are all robbers," 319 ; their fanaticism, 343 ; in their tents is the peace and assurance of Ullah, 274, 308 ; they toil not, 285 ; they are constrained to be robbers, *ib.* ; *Mel'aun el-weyladeyn*, of cursed kind, *ib.* ; they lie down at midnight and rise with the day, *ib.* ; they are day sleepers, 291 ; their slumbering indolence, 299 ; which is austere, 305 ; they are full of great words, 294, 325, 355 ; in that extreme living men become wild men, 302 ; their barbarous meddling curiosity, mistrust and haggling and glosing and petulant spirit, 308 ; their hypocrisy and iniquity, 308 ; their leave-taking austere and ungracious, 312 ; destitute — in the oases, 330 ; their head-colds, 330 ; they ride fasting in the ráhlas, 346 ; the — are factious spirits and infirm heads, sudden to strive, 361 ; their disputes, *ib.* ; — peacemakers, *ib.* ; they compare themselves with game scattered in the wilderness, 370 ; of any gift of food they keep a kindly remembrance, 370; of no extraordinary vision, 375 ; suffer from eye-diseases, *ib.*; Arabians are very tender of other men's opinions, 377 ; herdsmen they are naturally of the contemplative life, 385 ; the Hâj road tribes, pensioners of the Dowla, are the least manly and welfaring —, 389-90 ; the Beduin tribes are commonwealths of brethren, if any lose cattle by a ghrazzu it will be made up by the general contribution, 85, 390 ; their good-humour, 399 ; their meditations always of treachery, 401, 413 ; 'all the — are Sheyatîn,' 404 ; Arabs of the settled countries have too ill an opinion of the faith of the Nomads, 405 ; their half-feminine raging of the tongue, 309 ; they clamour in their grief, 409 ; they have good heads to adventure at an height, 409 ; every one has two faces, 414 ; their patience of evil times and of fasting, 355, 394, 415 ; they are very short breathed in any enterprise, 420 ; their pleasant deceitful words, 422 ; — not hospitable in a journey, 423 ; and yet they will aid one another, and the stranger with humanity, 424, 446, 459 ; leprosy common among the misdieted —, 437 ; their hilarity and melancholy, 450 ; their life is a long holiday wedded to a divine simplicity, 490 ; their ignorance in religion, 492 ; — seldom homely thieves, 384, 510 ; — have no experience of public burdens, 500 ; their presumptuous opinion of themselves, distempered with melancholy, 514 ; the — are naturals in religion, 517 ; half imbecility very common among —, 518 ; very sensible of ferments and damps, 523 ; their homely malice, 539 ; — incline in natural things to incredulity, 545 ; stern delicacy of the desert life, 549 ; — worship the aphrodisia and the galliûn, 559 ; — timid and ill at ease in the towns, 250, 330, 529, 563-4 ; a Bíshr, 'Ageyly, 625 ; the desert tribes send no aid to the Sultan, 587 ; — excel the settled dwellers in patience of the long journey, but are not good to be day labourers, 594 ; — absent from home are very impatient to return to their households, 144, 608 ; in their greediness to spoil the stranger the Arabs are viler than any people, 621 ; the — are in suspense at a strange meeting in the wilderness, 624 ; after the greeting with peace, there is no more doubt of any evil turn, *ib.* ; — 'Ageyl, 625 ; — think it no day of their lives wherein they have not sipped coffee, 625 ; — given to tobacco smoking, *ib.*; II. — in battle, 36 ; — in the band at Hâyil, 49 ; — cursed by town-dwellers, 139 ; and compared to locusts, 142 ; — warfare, 142-3 ; — mild by nature to the guest, 232, 240 ; — are easily cast down by derision, 240 ; in all — is a spirit of barter, 314; — "are kafirs," 317 ; — though blackened in the sun, and with dirt and smoke, their skins are whitish, 327 ; — soon home-sick, 329, 333 ; in — is an easy wit in all that is not too far from their minds, 349 ; their feline and chameleon nature, 394 ; they clamour in their causes, 463 ; "the — are altogether deceitful," 474 ; there is ever a wrangling among them in the division of the booty, 481 ; the easy humour of all —, 495 ; Mecca country —, 516, 536 ; sometimes a multitude of — may be discomfited almost as one man, 554 ; — about

W. Fâtima, 569, 571, 573; of the Tehâma near Jidda, 573, 574.
Bedûn, pl. of bédan, the wild goat.
el-Beduw, vulg. pl. of Bedúwy, 265.
Beduwîa, fem. of Beduwy, 333.
Beduwiyát, pl., Bed. women, II. 39.
Bedúwy, inhabiter of the bâdia or great waste land.
Beer, a kind of — in Galla-land, II. 186.
Bees: — of the Christian Kerakers, 66; — of the desert (athubba), 426.
Beetles, 174; II. 328; burier — of 'Aneyza, 451.
[Begeya, hamlet of "forty houses" a few miles E. of Hâyil.
Beggar, a religious gentleman — of Medina, II. 274, 390.
Bejaida, v. Bejaija.
Bejaija, or Bejaida, a division of Bíshr; II. 80, 242, 245, 299, 300; — loghrat, 267, 300.
Bélah, the ripening date berries, 571.
Belais, a kindred of Ânnezy, 377.
Béled, country, the soil, 285, 303; II. — at Kheybar signif. a palm-yard, 119.
Béled el-Aarab, the Arabian Peninsula, 89.
Béled amân, II. 45.
Béled el-'Asîr, v. el-'Asîr.
Béled mât, a died-out place, 635.
Béled er-Rûm, Greek lands, II. 110.
Belka country, the name interpreted, 56; the land described, ib.; — limestone changed to marble by erupted rocks, 59; Patriarch of the — Arabs, 65; — wasted by the B. Helál, 433, 445; II. 38.
Belka, Kellât el- —, 52, 59.
Bell, a cattle — used by certain Beduw, 464.
Bellah, (Bélah, q. v.), the ripening dates: — rottub, moist dates, II. 565.
Bellezzîeh, a small corn settlement in Ibn Rashîd's country, II. 322.
el-Bellush, the morbus gallicus, 436.
Benâna, a watering-place in J. Shammar, II. 305, 321.
Benât, maidens, pl. of bint.
Benât et-Tî, or Tîh; the best Heteym thelûls so named, II. 261.
Beneyyi, a Mahûby, 459, 485.
Bengal rice, II. 188.
Benison, The, 437.
Bény el-Bint, the maiden's bower (ruins of a dam), near Kheybar, II. 201.
Berber, — race, 129.

Berdàn (بردان), a coarse kind of cool white (worsted) mantles, which are woven at el-Ally, 190.
Berger, M. Philippe —, Note par — sur Medáin Sâlih, 227-28.
Berkô'a, woman's face-cloth or veil, 619.
Bernéta [It. berretta], the Frankish hat; than which nothing, in the clothing of Franks, seems more contemptible (in the Mohammedan countries): they say in scorn, Ullah yelbisak bernéta, 'the Lord put on thy head a bonnet,' i.e. make thee one altogether like a swine-eating Nazarene, that cannot look up to heaven.
Bérni, a kind of date at el-Ally, 195.
el-Berrarîj, a fendy of 'Ateyba, II. 457.
Bersîm, vetches, II. 572.
el-Bertha bîr Hatheyl, station near Mecca, II. 565.
Besamna, name of an Arabian town in Pliny, II. 377.
Bess, it sufficeth! 296, 313, 418, 543.
Bessàm, vill. id. qd. el-Barrûd.
Bessàm, a wealthy family of many households at 'Aneyza, II. 376. [Middle Nejders are called — at Jidda, ib.] The most of them were Wahábies, and lenders of money in el-Kasîm, 377, 415; 436, 441, 442, 458, 482, 523.
el-Bessàm ('Abdullah 'Abd-er-Rahmàn), a Jidda merchant of 'Aneyza. A very good man and constant friend to the Nasrâny in 'Aneyza. He is of the above-named family, that came from Osheyjir [Usheykir] in el-Wéshm (others say from el-'Arûth) 60 years before; his kindred, II. 376; his worthy nature, 376-383; his hospitality, 387, 390, 402; his tolerance, ib.; his charity, ib.; his tale of Ômar, 387; his study of the Arabian antiquity, ib.; his middle fortune and integrity, 390; his comity, 391; his goodness to strangers, 397; 422; 425, 432, 446; 483; his patriotism, 398; 473; [v. 'Abd-er-Rahman el-B.], 482; 486, 488, 491, 499, 503, 512, 513, 515-8, 523, 532, 533, 559.
Bessàm, a travelled —, II. 402.
Bessàm, another — household, II. 404.
Beth Gamul, v. Umm Jemâl.
Bethel-stones at et-Tâyif, II. 545, 549, 550, 554.
Bethlelem, II. 56, 81, 575.
Bethra (بثر) et-tamr, II. 511.
B'ethrak (perhaps a childish turn for b'ithnak), 666.

el-Bettera (which sounds like an Ar. corruption of Pétra); ruins of a town in Mount Seir, 86.
Bewitched persons [*v. sub* Evil eye, Witchcraft, Fascinated, *Mishûr*], ii. 467.
Beylàn, Turkoman village in Upper Syria, ii. 157.
el-Beyrih, yesterday, or this forenoon, 526.
Beyrût, 481; a gardener of — living with the Aarab in Arabia, 559; a learned American missionary of —, 631; ii. 193, 370, 389, 447, 555.
Beyt, pl. *byût*, abode, booth, Semitic house, whether tent or stable dwelling.
Beyt Akhreymát, a beautiful monument at Medáin Sâlih, 156; with upper rank of pilasters, and loculi in the bay of the frontispice, which is nevertheless a little wanting in geometrical symmetry, *ib.*, 673-4.
Beyt el-mâl, treasure house (at Hâyil), 664; ii. 281.
Beyt (or *Kasr*) *es-Sâny*, a lofty monument at Medáin Sâlih, 151, 153, 238.
Beyt es-shaar, abode or booth of hair, the Nomad tent, which is made of worsted or hair-cloth, 147, 266, *et passim*.
Beyt es-Shereyfa, a Medina family descended from a jin woman, ii. 212.
Beyt es-Sheykh, a principal monument at Medáin Sâlih, 149; in the funeral chamber are 20 *loculi* and 3 deep recesses.
Bezîr, v. *Kasr es-Shebîb*.
B'goom Aarab, ii. 507, 567.
Bî wéjhy, ii. 29.
Bîa'a el-má, ii. 498.

Bîât (بيات), game at Kheybar, ii. 136.
[*v. Beatta.*]
Biddîa, a hamlet of J. Shammar, ii. 34, 77.
(2) *Biddîa*, village in el-Aflâj [*v. Bedîya*], ii. 425.
el-'bil [for *el-íbil*], the camels of a tribe, 357, 387.
B'il kheyer insh' Ullah, ii. 463.
Billah [*b'Illah*], *i.e.* by Ullah, the common Beduin oath.

Billî (بِلِّي), named *jíd* or patriarch of the Billî tribe, 430; his sons *M'khâlid* and *Kh'zâm*, *ib.*
Billî (sing. *Belûwy*), an ancient Tehâma tribe, 142, 164, of the Red Sea border. They pronounce *j* as the Egyptians (*g*); — carriers of Wejh rice to el-Ally, 195; 240, 267, 312, 360, 380, 382, 390, 422, 425, 426, 429, 430, 435, 436, 440, 444, 455, 460, 463, 464, 465, 469, 472, 511, 512, 537, 543, 610; ii. 38, 167, 322.
Billy, Bed., *v. Billî*.
Bîm-bashy, captain of a thousand, colonel.
Bint, daughter, girl; also young married woman until she have borne a child, 272, 420.

Bintu (بِنْتُو); word taken from the Frankish *venti*), the English sovereign, ii. 23.
Bîr, well.
Bîr el-Ghrannem (well of the flocks), in the Fukara dîra, but now of the Wélad 'Aly, a journey below Medáin Sâlih, 142, 179, 229, 271, 465.
(2) *Bîr el-Ghrannem*, by W. Fâtima, ii. 569.
[*Bîr el-jedîd*, a kellâ on the Hâj road, S. of el-Héjr.
Bîr en-Nâga, 133, 167.
Birds [*v.* Falcon, Waterfowl, Partridges, Gattà, Habâra]: crows, 174; swallows, 174, 495; blue-rock pigeons, 174; the eagle, *agab*, 374; the *rákham*, 374; the owl, 349; hawks, 349, 374; no chittering of — in the desert, 286; 367; but the sweet-voiced *swedyîa*, 452; small — of the khála fly in to water at Thirba, 495; cry of some fruit-eater — in the oasis, 555; fly-catcher, 559; migratory water — shot at Teyma, 583; a flight of some great white fowl seen flying from the sea, northward, in Sinai, 584; the Arabians have not learned to desire the captivity of any singing —, 582; ii. 56, 240; a night — which they called *sirrûk*, 287; a flight of cranes seen in Nejd, 288; little — chittering after rain in the khála, 330, 331; night —, 331; little — in el-Kasîm whose song ascends on the gamut, 445.
Birds : sculptured sepulchral — of the monuments at el-Héjr, 148, 153, 209; the soul-bird, *ib.*
Birket, cistern.
Birket el-Engleysy, a cistern without the northern gate of Medina, ii. 223.
Birket Mo'addam, v. *Mo'addam*.
el-Birket fî Rúkkaba, station on the E. Hâj road, ii. 565.
Birkets of water-merchants at Jidda, ii. 574.

J. (Thul'a or *Tor) Bîrrd [Bird],* a sandstone mountain that marks the border of the Fukara tribe toward Nejd, 271, 346, 395, 618.

Bîsàn, a Galla word for water, ii. 102.

Biscuit: caravan —, 42, 246, 252.

W. (el) Bîsha, or *Bîshy, qd. v.:* according to *Jeyber* this valley seyls into the W. Dauâsir. The negro villagers are fewer than the white people and Beduins. [Other hearsays: some villages are *er-Roshel, en-Nejîa, el-Jinneyny, el-Ageyly, el-Hîfa, el-Hàzzemy,* el-Báḳara, el-Jébel, Suhàn, Nimràn.] ii. 52, 191, 227, 350, 449, 453, 545, 557, 567.

Bishr, a great sub-tribe of Ânnezy in the W. Nejd, 166, 240, 271, 273, 306, 315, 343, 344, 347, 350, 354, 357, 363, 373, 376; a great ghrazzu of — takes a ghrazzu of W. Aly, 379, 380; 391, 413, 415, 457, 487, 537, 541, 550, 567, 595, 608, 609, 610, 613, 614; Nejd — resemble Bed. of the North, *ib.,* 614, 617, 618, 624, 631, 633; ii. 34, 35, 39, 87, 92, 108, 112, 122, 139, 141-4, 195, 216, 231, 234-5, 238, 242, 244, 263, 289, 292, 300, 320; good pasture but few waters in dîrat —, 322, 563.

Bishr, a fendy of Harb, Mosrûh, ii. 547.

Bishr Aarab near *Jidda,* probably of the above, ii. 573.

Bishrîa, woman of Bíshr, 365.

el-Bîshy, negro armed band serving the Sherîf Emir of Mecca; — a man serving in the 'Ageyl at Kheybar, ii. 191, 227, 300; 542, 545, 546, 548, 549, 557, 560-2, 567, 572.

Bismillah, in the name of Ullah, 446.

J. Biss, near Sh'aara, ii. 508.

W. Bissl, ii. 567.

Bîurúldi (Turk.), a circular passport, 207.

Bizr et-támr, ii. 511.

Black stone: the — of 'Aneyza, said to be in Bessàm's jeneyny, ii. 473. It is difficult to understand that which they relate of the —, as this (written down for me by a litterate): " The name of *'Aneyza* is from a berg upon which it is built; it is a black berg in a plain which is called *Falj* between Tharîyya and el-Boṣra!" And elsewhere he says, " The names of Boreyda and 'Aneyza are from two little bergs in them."

Black stone in the wall of the Ka'aba, ii. 545.

Blackness, said of death, calamity and evil, 143.

Blaspheme, the Semites cannot —, 308.

Blasphemy, a —, 578; ii. 263.

Blaṭ, Ḳellâ, 56.

Blind: — persons would have the hakîm restore their sight, 299.

Blood ransom [*v. Midda*], 499, 539.

Blood eaten in ignorance, 612.

Blood to be covered with dust, 540; slaughter — smelled to but refused by the nomad's hounds, 547.

Blood-guiltiness, 414, 491.

Blood-sprinkling: — upon breakland, 177, 499; — upon building and the like, 177, 499; — or smearing upon the booty of cattle, 499; and of a man's own cattle, 547; ii. — on building, 118; — upon the rock at Kheybar, where they laboured to open a spring, 219.

Bloody. Amiable — ruffian, 130.

Bludàn, a village in Antilibanus, ii. 172.

Blunderbuss, Haj Nejm's —, 129, 413, 418.

Boabat (بوابة) *Ullah,* the gate of the *Medân* quarter of Damascus, looking towards Medina and Mecca, 43, 120.

Bocca (an old pronunciation of Mecca), ii. 564.

Boghrâz (strait between cliffs), a Turkish word used on the Hâj road, 116, 127, 180.

Bokhâra, the city of —, ii. 274, 278. The erudite of — are said to speak the best (that is koran) Arabic.

Bokhŷta, Bed. fem. name, 514.

Bombay, 577; — *Gazette,* skein silk wrapped in shreds of the —, in the sûk at Hâyil ii. 20; — calico, 23; Arabian sale-horses in —, 59; merchant Jews in —, 146, 368, 376; Nejd colony in —, 389, 399; 417-9, 425, 466.

Bone-setter, *v. Jábbar.*

Bones: — of beasts unburied, never far to seek in the Arab countries, ii. 387; Ômar's tessera, *ib.;* camels where they find a white — will halt to champ it, 496; — of beasts by the highways, 573.

Book: a cabalistical —, 213; a Nejder's opinion of the Nasrâny's —s, 243; Nomads' opinion of the same, 315, 321, 327, 347, 631; a printed Hebrew — at Hâyil from the salvage of a lost Bagdad caravan, 654; ii. 99, 100, 102, 146; the Nasrâny's —s sent to the Pasha of Medina, 181; the same restored, 221, 227: but certain volumes were stolen (at Medina), *ib.;* some Heteymies wonder in seeing them, 242, 246; the Nasrâny buries his —s in a thob's hole at Âul, 303; an Arabic — lent by Sâlih, 472

Boots, Arabian Bed. not wearers of —, 291, 294.

Boreyda [بُرَيْدَة — Ibn 'Ayith], a great clay-built town in the Nefûd of el-Kasîm, on the left border of the W. er-Rummah, and distant 10 or 11 miles [1⅛ hrs. thelûl riding, 1¾ hrs. for a footman — between running and walking; 2 hrs. on horseback to go and come] from 'Aneyza. The thin clay wall of the town was rebuilt in 1873. Ibn 'Ayith says that ' the names of Boreyda and 'Aneyza are from bergs in them.' 49, 603, 658; II. 37, 40, 67, 112, 208, 274, 309, 315, 318, 321, 322, 336, 338, 339, 340; crumbling aspect of —, 340, 345; fanatical citizens of —, 345-6; the sûks, 348; 349, 353; palms and population of —, 355; 357, 358, 360, 361, 364, 365, 367, 373, 375, 377, 386, 388, 392, 394, 404, 408, 417, 418, 419, 436, 438, 441, 443, 447, 451, 455, 459, 460, 476, 479, 481, 485, 490, 498, 506, 508, 515, 523.

Borghrol, household wheaten diet of Syria, made of seethed grain, which is toasted in the sun. It is boiled to be eaten, 164; II. a kind of — in Nejd, 341, 380.

Borj [from Gk. πύργος], a tower of defence, 147; — at Medáin, 133; monuments in the — rock, 147, 174, 673; a cross mark under the — —, 176; the — rocks, 177, 235, 549, 554.

Borj Selmàn, a desert ground in the Fejîr dîra, 255, 257, 328.

Borma, or *Burma*, ruined town in Mount Seir, 68.

Borrûd, village W. of *Shúkra*, II. 424.

Borusia (Prussia), 168, 657; II. 398.

the Bosforus, II. 400.

Boṣra [Bos(t)ra Metropolis; in Syria called *Bosra éski Shem*] : ruins of — in the Hauran, 51.

Bosra in Edom, 70; tale of a sheykh from Hebron who came to —, 77; fruitful vineyards of —, 78.

Boṣra on the Tigris, 243; II. 336, 337, 368, 371, 377, 383, 389, 394, 398, 412, 420, 422, 448, 449, 468, 487, 514.

[*el-Bosŷta*, part of the Nefûd about Wady Sirhàn, so called.

Bothra, mountains [Heteymies say also *Búthra*; some Ânnezy men say *Búshra*], II. 85, 251, 255.

Bottîn (بطين), said of a blunt hilly height, 285, 471.

Bou, Moorish Arabic for *Abu*, II. 93.

Boughs: trail (*jurrat*) of lopped — seen in the desert, a sign of the Aarab menzils, II. 243.

Box : Bed. housewife's —, *v*. Coffer.

Boys ride out to the ghrazzus, 567; II. 480.

Bracelets of Teyma women, *v*. *Hadŷd*, 336.

Brain of slaughtered sheep or goat, eaten by (Bed.) women only, 547.

Braitshàn, a Shammar Bed. sheykh, II. 263, 264, 292, 294.

Bread baked under the embers [*v*. *'Abûd*], 172, 253, 302; II. — in diverse languages, 26; their girdle- — is sour and tough, 347.

the Bread and Salt, 269, 296, 319, 357, 446, 500, 551, 571, 620; II. 272, 284, 362, 527, 531, 547.

Breakfast, Bed. *fuk er-rîj* (فك الريق, loose the fasting spittle). The nomad —, 262, 265; 376; 489.

Bribes, not current in Hâyil, 659; but used by the Shammar princes in their dealing with the Dowla, *ib*. II. 35.

Bride : an Harb —, II. 308; another —, 319.

Bride-money, 281, 336, 363, 519, 539, 591.

'*Brik* [*Ibrîk*], metal ewer in Ar. chambers, 574.

Brîm (بريم), II. 375. [*v*. Haggu and *Hágub*.]

Broken : men already infirm and — at the middle age are common among the Arabs, II. 520.

Brook : the — at el-Ally, 193. There is another ancient conduit under the earth, higher in the valley towards el-Héjr; but it is choked with sand-drifts, and lying without their bounds, the 'Alowna have not opened it : this last may have brought water to el-Khreyby; —s of Kheybar, *v*. *sub* Kheybar; — of Tâyif, II. 537, 551; in W. Fâtima, 569.

Broom : bushes of — in the Arabian wilderness, 442, 448, 472; *et passim*; — is very seldom browsed by camels. [I have only seen camels browse it in the Nefûd of el-Arîsh.]

Broth, and camel milk, 551.

"Brothership," tax for brotherhood of the Beduins, *v*. *Khûa*.

Brown-haired Beduin women, 435, 511.

Brûssia, *v*. *Borusia*.

Buckets [v. *Dullu*]; Bed. — of leather, at the watering, 335, 395, 428, 506.
Buffalo, 320.
[" *W. el-Bûg*, in the E. part of the 'Aueyrid Harra, N. of W. Thirba: therein are springs and some ruins."
Buggân, a dog's name, 474.
Búggila (بكل), dry milk shards, v. *Baggl*, *Mereesy*.
Bugle-call at Tâyif, ii. 537.
Builders; Arab Moslems are mostly clay — 62, 185.
el-Bukkeríeh, palm village (Sbeya colony) in el-Kasîm, 49; ii. 320, 435, 437, 441, 442.
Bukkra (*búkra*), camel or thelûl cow with her first calf, 370.
Bulbul (Pers.), the nightingale.
Bull: a — sacrificed for the health of the sick, ii. 163; householders at el-Hâyat slay a — for their guests' supper, 232.
Bullah! ana khálaft 'aleyk! 542.
Bullets, a Nomad casting —, 538; lime-stone balls used for —, 548; ii. — on the Harra, 120.
el-Bûma, a mare's name, ii. 252.
Búnder el-Telâl ibn Rashîd, 656, 670; ii. murders his uncle Met'aab, 28; and is slain by his uncle Mohammed, 30, 31, 32, 40, 195.
Búnder's orphan child, ii. 40, 41.
Búndur, port of merchandise.
Búndur 'Aulánshy or *'Alúshy* or *'Alút*, ancient names of el-Ally, 189. [Sheykh Dâhir wrote —

بندر علوت بندر علاوشى.]

el-Bunn (البن), coffee powder, 286.
Burckhardt at Petra, 79; ii. — at Tâyif, 543.
Búrghrol, v. *Borghrol*.
Burial of the dead, 211, 498.
Burjésba, a desert site, 344.
Búrjess, a young Allaydy sheykh, and exile among the Fukara, 292.
Burnûs, white mantle of the Moors of Barbary, 129.
Burr [*barr*], land, high desert, 330.
Burr el-'*Ajam*, 94.
Burying ground [v. *Mákbara, Namûs, Rijjûm*, graves], 50, 349; — on the Harra, 441, 478.
Busatîn, pl. of *bustân*, qd. v.
Bussîyeh, fem. Bed. name, 514.

Bustân, pl. *busatîn* (a Pers. word used in Syria and in the Hejâz), an orchard ground, 526, 551.
Bustány, a printer of Beyrût [since deceased], ii. 370.
Butcher from el-Ally, 525; at Teyma, 573, 611; — market at Hâyil, 661; — trade illiberal, 662; ii. 65, 76; — at 'Aneyza, 363; — market, 365; — at Khubbera, 440, 449; *fatîrs* slaughtered in the great Nejd caravans, 505.
el-Búthenah, hamlet of Jeheyna, at Yanb'a-the-Palms, ii. 202.
J. Búthra, or *Búshra* [v. *Bothra*].
Bútm, a kind of oak, 497.
Butter [v. also *Samn*]: 111; — making, 262, 370, 429; ii. 83.
Butterfly [v. *Aisûn* and *Sherrára*]. I saw no — in Nejd, nor moths in Arabia, though they are common in Sinai; in W. Thirba, 496.
By-the-life-of-Ullah, a lawful oath, ii. 27.
By-thy-life, an oath of the Beduins, but blamed by the Wahábies, 647; ii. 27.
Byût, pl. of *beyt*, qd. v.
Buzzard, in the desert (v. Hawks), 349, 374, 409, 584.
Byzantine corruption, 659.

Cable, well —, of palm fibre, 593; ii. — of bast, 317, 452.
Câbul, the city of —, ii. 274, 555.
Cactus: a great round jointed — of the desert above Mecca, *el-ghrullathî* (qd. v.), ii. 507; " Indian fig " — fruit, 551.
Caddis-worms at Kheybar, ii. 219.
Caesarea Philippi, site of —, 486.
Cairns upon the crest of Sumrâ Hâyil, 668; ii. in the *Rí'a* above *es-Seyl*, 509. [v. *Mantar*.]
Cairo, 436.
Calf, camel-, meat, 499.
Calico of Manchester and Bombay, 168; ii. 23.
Calif [*Khâlîfa*], successor of the Apostle, title, at first of humility, assumed by Ômar; and since usurped by the Ottoman sultans, ii. 387.
Camel (Ar. *jemel*) v. *G'aud, Howwâra, Bukkra, Nâga, Fâtir, Líbney, Hej, Jítha, Thènny, Rôbba, Siddes, Shágg en-Naba, Wafîat, Muftir, Thelûl*, etc. The Arabian — has one hump; and it is incredible to Arabs that any

camel-kind should have two, or a double hump. The way measured by — marches, 53; — descends steep places uneasily, 90; skeletons of —s reported to be strewed by the Hâj way, 96 (but *cf.* II. 573); —s which faint and fall by the long way, 96; — riding painful at first, 96, 99; caravan —s march tied, 90, 96; Bed. —s go loose; Hâj —s and Bed. —s, 105; —-litter, 105; deceased pilgrim lady sewed in a — skin, 106; —-master, 114; Néby Sâlih's prodigious —; *v. Nâga*; —s frayed by wolves, 259; —s *jezzîn* in the spring season, 260, 284; they are then strong and lay up flesh, 260, 397; — calls, 261; the — made to kneel, 262; a — of the common charity, 263; *Aban*, the Nasrâny's —, 249, 321; — wounded, 321-2; the — a profitable possession, 275; price of —s in Arabia, 275; — brokers, 274-5; Fukara nâgas lie an hour before the milking, 302; a foster nâga for every mare, 304; a — to carry the mare's water, *ib.*; milking time, 304; no —s in the Nasâra countries, 317, 320; —s languish in the summer, 323; when they have little or no water the Nomads rinse their hands in — urine, 253; Nomad women wash their babes in the same, 279; men and women wash their long hair in it, 279, 385; Nejd could not be inhabited without the —, 336; new-born — calves are carried in the ráhla, 346; bearing —s, 346; seeking the strayed — of another, 347; —'s fired, 354; the horny sole under the —'s breast (*zôra*), 369; — -riding which breaks the back of the unwont, is easy to the inured, 346, 424; — paths in the desert, 348; — -dung (*jella*) for fuel, 348; the yeaning nâga, 369; the new-born calf, *ib.*; the bereaved — mother mourns and her eyes stand full of tears, 369; their —s' excrements are pure in the sight of the nomads, 253, 534; — milk, 257, 349, 370, 535; the *búkra* or cow-camel with her first calf, 370; price of well- —s at Teyma in corn and dates, 377; Fukara —s taken by a ghrazzu, 387 *et seq.*; value of the same, 389, 613; —s of the Fukara, 389, 390; the law, if cattle be lost, 390; —s strayed, 395; a new — bought, 401; —s named after their teeth, 401; —s could not lie at el-Ally above two days because of the flies, 405; —s vexed by flies in the Belka, 56; — -ticks, 408; —s browse the thorny acacia boughs, 425; —s in the Bed. kúfl, 426, 428; Harra-bred —s, 427; an enemy's life assessed at five —s, 449, 539; —s sick in a murrain, 475; — wool, 476; well —s, 375, 500; —s may die of suffocation in the hot winds, 536; — at Teyma, 593, 610; — in el-Kasîm, 593; —s coming home to the milking, 505; — at the watering, 505-7; the Bed. —s and thelûls may lie three days fasting at the market villages, 526; —'s kick is heavy, 565; well- — harness, 593; a phantom —, 472; roaring of —s grudging to be loaded, 618; a white —, 443; a — sold for a crown, in a year of dearth and murrain, 665; II. — stealing, 229; — -hump boiled down to lard, 231; the —'s lips are fenced with bristles, 239; ? whether — urine might be drunk in deadly thirst, 290; the common alighting place, where passengers make their —s kneel, and they themselves are received to the public hospitality [*v. Manôkh*]; the *zôra* or stay under the —'s chest, 290; the — seems beautiful in the wilderness, *ib.*; goats in an evening menzil skipping upon the couching —'s backs (as if they were rocks), 302; milk of —s which have fed in a pasture of wormwood is bitter, 305; —s of the Southern tribes are commonly blackish, 306; [Northern tribes prefer the dun colour in —s; for the black, they say, are of uncertain nature, headstrong and savage, and not so well shaped]; the males or bearing —s may be distinguished, by their leanness, at a distance, 321; — masters of Boreyda, 345; — flesh sold at 'Aneyza, 371; well —s at 'Aneyza, 382; —s increase in stature in the northern dîras, 428; —s will fall on their knees and wallow in sandy places, 496; they discern not their food by sight only, but in smelling, *ib.*; the unruly — yields being caught by the beard or by the nose, 501; little danger of his teeth, *ib.*; the grown camel lacks the upper front teeth, *ib.*; 'Ateyba —s seen near Sh'aara were mostly brown-haired, 507; the Mecca country —s are of little stature, 513, 516. [The — kicks backward, especially at dogs, and forward also, striking downward.]

Camp, *v. Menzil.*
Camphor, *v. Kafûr.*
[Cancer was not an uncommon disease at Hâyil, II. 19.]
Candles brought as an acceptable present to the Emir Ibn Rashîd, II. 276.
Canker. Mohammedan religion a —, II. 406.

Cannon in the Hâj, signal shot to march and to halt, 45, 57; — borne upon mules' backs, 49; 220, 239, 243, 254; Ibn Rashîd's —, 636, 638; II. old rude — shot lying in 'Aneyza, 460.
Canticles; the paramour excuses her swarthiness, 143.
Cap or bonnet of the ancient Arabians, 203, 613; II. 197.
Caravan [v. *Kâfila Kúfl*], distance that the Hâj caravan march in an hour, 54.
Caravan robbers, v. *'Aûf, Lahabba*.
Caravaners: —'s names of camping places and waymarks, 88, 118, 134 [v. *Shuk el-'Ajûz, Mufarish er-Ruz, Mûbrak en-Nâga, Medáin Sâlih, el-Howwâra*]: II. — of el-Kaṣîm [v. *Jemmâl*], 311, 335, 337; — expert in land-craft, 494; march of the —, 496; their impatience, *ib*.; 503; they taste flesh meat (by the way) every few days, 505; 507, 508; Mecca —, 513-521; 561, 572; — of Syria, 526.
Card-play in the Hejâz, 193; II. 193.
Carpets, 246, 257, 345, 414, 546, 574; II. 250, 257.
Carriage and demeanour [v. Gait] of the people of Nejd and Beduw, 242, 329, 526, 549; — of the 'Alowna, 527.
Castor-oil plant, 644; II. — grown to a tree at Kheybar, 165.
Cat: the — not commonly seen in Nejd villages, 338; II. — in Hâyil, 20; — at Kheybar, 208.
Cattle: skeletons of —, 96; the loss of — by tribesmen in the general adventure of the tribe is restored out of the common contribution, 390; if a tribe be bereaved of their —, their friendly neighbours will tax themselves to help them, 390; if a private man be bereaved of his —, without the general adventure, his friends will help him, 391; II. 262.
Cattle calls, for camels, v. *Wolloo-wolloo! Weeaho-weeaho! Wôh-ho? Hutch! Gluck!* [*Illuk-hèylo!* a cry to cheer the great cattle], 261, 477.
Cattle-pool in W. el-Ḥasy, 66-7.
Caucasus, war against the Russian invaders in the —, 130.
Cauterizing, 322, 540; II. 287.
Cedars, the grove of — of Lebanon, II. 414.
Ch: ك is commonly pron. — in vulgar Nejd Ar.
Chai, v. Tea.

Chair-sitters, 303.
Chalk, 471.
Change of garments, v. *sub* Garments.
Charcoal: — coffee-hearth, 332; — for smith's fire, 355; — for gunpowder, 410; ancient — found at Medáin Sâlih, 411; II. — for gunpowder, 165, 516; Mecca — burners, 509.
Charity is cold in the wilderness, 91.
Charms for love, 511.
Châsim, v. Kâsim.
Chaucer, II. 150.
J. *Chebàd (Kebàd)* in the Bíshr dîra, 348, 368.
(2) J. *Chebàd*, nigh Seyleymy, II. 306.
Cheeks gashed of some tribesmen near Mecca, II. 536.
Cheese: — -makers, nomad —, II. 230; — made by certain of Meteyr, 317.
Ch(k)ef Marhab, the 'rose of Jericho,' 347.
[el-*Cheffy* [*Keheyfy*, sometimes even pron. *Chuwa*], village of "a hundred" houses on the way from Boreyda to J. Shammar.
Beny *Chelb* or *Kelàb*, 328.
Ch[k]essab (كسب), booty, 234, 499.
Cheyf-ent, 480.
Cheyf Nasrâny? II. 69.
Child: a beautiful —, II. 428.
Children (nomad): female — anciently buried living, 281; — are ruled by entreaties, 282, 283; — playing at horses, 384; parents' love for their —, 397, 408; fanaticism of —, 479-480; —'s pastimes, 479; herding —, 479, 490, 519; hungry — climb date palms, 585; II. naked child in the winter of Nejd, 251; naked nomad — in the S., 507; — wearing a girdle of thongs, 509.
Children (oasis), fanaticism of, 198; 594; II. 273, 285; — taught letters in the Nejd towns, 472.
Chin: the younger Syrians shave the —, II. 46.
China Seas, wares from the —, 247; II. 23.
Chôl (steppes), 68; II. 279.
Cholera in Damascus 1875, 40; — in the Hâj, 120; a pilgrim who in appearance dead of the — was buried by the Hâj way; and he revived and returned to Damascus, 121; 246 [v. *Abu Tawfish*], 519, 629, 635, 670; II. 197.
Christen: some Mohammedan mothers in outlying Syria bring their sick and lunatic children to the (Greek) priest to be —ed; and they themselves will drink (they think it an help to fecundity) the dust of the church floor and be sprinkled with "holy water," 100.

OF ARABIC WORDS

Christian cruelties in the late war, II. 198.
a Christian and a Friar seen at Medina, II. 177.
Christian names (probable), in inscr., 408.
Christian religion, v. Religion.
Christian religion defended, 341-3; II. 98.
"Christian wife" of the Emir Ibn Rashîd, 642; II. 39.
Christians (Syrian): massacre of — at Damascus, 103; 341; 373; the old — hermits, 520-1.
Christians murdered: — at Medina and Mecca, 124; II. 68; a — in Medina, and his martyr's death, 176-8; a — of Tripoli —, 193.
Christians: Mohammedan fables of the —, 191, 341; II. 241.
False Christs in Syria, 214.
Chrysolite (vulcanic crystals of —) from the 'Aueyrid Harra, 451.
Circass women (that are sold), 655.
Circumcision, fables of the — in certain southern tribes, 170; — festival, v. Muzayyin, 385-6; 387; 437; — called "purification," ib.; 457; certain Turkomans not circumcised, II. 176; a "Frenjy" renegade who was circumcised in Mecca, 189.
Cisterns (birket) of the Hâj road, 44, 48, 97, 116; II. — of the water-merchants at Jidda, II. 579.
Citron: the —, 338, 644.
Clay: Mohammedans mostly — builders, 62, 185, 268; II. — under the lavas at Kheybar, 110, 129; — under the Nefûd in Ḳaṣîm (of the Rummah valley), 355, 422.
Clay-house, the stable dwelling (of clay) is called in Arabic ḳaṣr; —s of certain Beduins, Howeytát, Fejîr, W. 'Aly, 276, 671; II. 19, 141, 206.
Clothiers' street in 'Aneyza, II. 365.
Clothing of the Arabs [v. 'Agâl, Ma'aṣub, Mandîl, Thorrîb Thôb]: — often half nakedness, 67, 246, 614. Calico tunic (thôb), 189, 506; some women's tunics, 421; Arabians adventure abroad in their worst — for fear of forays, 172; II. 153; a home-spun mantle of tent cloth, 252; the woman's garment in Kasîm, 471.
Clothing: change of —, the princely custom of Ibn Rashîd, v. Garments.
Club-stick of the Beduins, v. Dubbûs.
Cockle-shells in the limestone of M'aan, 471; II. 575.
Cocoa-nut palm (in Bombay), II. 466.
Cod-liver oil, II. 411.

Coffee [v. Dellàl, Fatya, Gutîa, Bunn, Baḥar, Surbût]: — sellers by the Hâj way, 58, 246; — assemblies and hearth, 286-9, 292, 303, 321; — drinking, 67, 252, 263, 286-9, 393; — making, 259, 264, 284, 288, 332; — Sybarites in the desert, 288; Bed. abandoned to — and tobacco, 288, 289; — courtesy, 287; — customs the same in all N. Arabia, 289; rhythmical pounding of —, 286; — mortar, 286, 329; use of — in Arabia, 289; — first brought from Further Abyssinia, 289; great secular — trees in Galla-land, 289; — drinking there, ib.; smoke rising in the Bed. menzil is sign of a — fire, 292; "to —," 330; charcoal — hearth, 332; "where no — there no merry company is," 400; Nejd — hearth with many pots, 578, 638; Nejd —, 614; danger in the — of Princes, 656; II. — in Galla-land, 187; where — is there is the less hospitality, 265; — -drinking little used among Heteym, 303; the ringing — mortar, a sound of hospitality, 309; — lords, ib.; — tipplers, 328; — -drinking in el-Kasîm, 363, 376, 402; the Nejders are — tipplers, 411; — at Khubbera, 437; Arabian — tree from Abyssinia, 542; excessive — drinking in Nejd, ib.; — boiled at Tâyif in earthen vessels, 538, 551.
Coffee-bower in el-Kaṣîm [v. Maashush], II. 445.
Coffee-hall, the great — at Hâyil, 638, 663; II. 53, 59.
Coffee-host at el-Helàlîeh, II. 443.
Coffee-houses in the Mecca country, II. 542, 544, 548, 572.
Coffer: Bed. sheykhly housewives' —, 268.
Colic, a Bed. remedy [massage] for the —, II. 229.
Colocynth gourd: — deadly to man, is eaten by the goat, the ass, the porcupine [v. Hamthal, Shérry, Hádduj], 173, 510; II. 265, 561.
Colonel; vility of a Turkish —, II. 142; thieving of another —, 228, 245.
Comb found in the Nasrâny's bags, II. 99.
Comforter, the Paraclete of the Gospel of S. John, interpreted (a barbarous blunder) in the Korân, Aḥmed, II. 24.
Compass, II. 100.
Condiments, called by the Bed. dawwa, 297.
Conduits: old —, 487, 600; II. 566.
Constantine's vision, 50.
Constantinople [v. Stambûl], 98, 248, 289.
Consulate: — at Damascus, 39, 207, 251, 481; II. 182, 270, 278; hospitable — at Jidda, 574.

War Contribution from the estates of the Sherîf of Mecca, II. 558-9.
Cooking : — fires in the Hâj, 46, 126 ; — of simple messes, the Arab housewives' excellent —, II. 200 ; hunters' —, 260 ; cooks in the caravan fellowships, 490, 498.
Copt : a (Christian) — who came to show his grief to Ômar, the first Calif, at Medina, II. 387.
Cordoba, in Spain, II. 426 ; the great mosque of —, ib.
Corfu : the English garrison in —, II. 110, 541.
Corn : bruised —, 624 ; — market at Hâyil, 637 ; price there of — in a famine year, II. 21 ; — is always dear in Arabia, 382 ; the — trade, 390 ; camels treading out the —, 446 ; — they say comes up better in brackish ground, 464.
Cough, 597 ; II. 77.
Coverlets of worsted [v. Ekîm] made in Arabia, II. 537.
Cow : the wild —, v. 'Othŷahî and Wothŷhi.
Cow, v. kine ; II. — milk [v. Milk]; a — sequestered at Kheybar, 147.
Cow-pox, II. 403.
Crane : a — (sa'ady) shot at Teyma, 584 ; II. 288.
Creosote smeared in the nostrils of camels, and cast into wells, II. 560. [Bed. smear sick and mangy camels with —.]
Crickets : chirping of — in the wells of 'Aneyza, II. 451.
Crimea, the war in the —, 198, 318 ; II. 198.
Crimes : — revealed by enchantments, II. 209-210 ; — at 'Aneyza, 395 ; the punishment of —, ib.
Cristiani, compared with Moslemîn, II. 476.
Cross : a Greek — embroidered on a Hâj litter, 100 ; a — mark upon the Borj rock at el-Héjr, 176.
Croton oil remedy, 472, 510.
Crow : the — a bird of the desert, 173 ; II. 56, 240.
Crowbar, v. Tools.
Crystal : fragments of — in the soil shining as diamonds, 118 ; II. 120, 244.
Cucumbers, in Teyma, 582.
Cupping, blood-letting, 540.
Curses, v. Maledictions.

Dab, a snake, pl. *dîbàn* (or *deyban*).
Daed, Aarab of Hathèyl, II. 569.

ed-D'aika (الدعيكة), circuit of desert in the way from el-Kasîm to Mecca, II. 501.
Dafîna, water-pits in the khála betw. el-Kasîm and Mecca, II. 500.
el-Dâha, a desert station N. of Teyma, 341.
Dâhir, sheykh of el-Ally, 181-187 ; he is sheykh by inheritance, 181 ; his carefulness for the Nasrâny, 193 ; discourse of philosophy with —, 195-6 ; 199, 202-205.
[ed-Dâhy, the Bed. say *Thâhy*, wide waterless land, the Nefûd between Teyma, Jauf and Hâyil.
ed-Dajîn, a fendy of 'Ateyba, II. 457.
Dakhálakom or Dakhîlakom, O ye ! I am your dakhîl (*qd. v.*).
el-Dakhîl, ' one who enters to another,' *i.e.* in being come as it were under his roof he requires his protection, 380 ; II. 301.
Dakhîl, a valiant Kheybar villager, hunter, and post to Medina, II. 153, 176, 180, 181, 183, 216-18, 227, 232.
Dakhîlak, I become thy dakhîl, II. 297.
Dakhîlullah, a Kheybar villager, a *menhel*, II. 125-9, 138, 226.
Dalèyel, Bed. fem. name, 514.
Dalîl (a shewer of the way, lodesman): — el-Hâj, 96, 109 ; — in forays, 271.
el-Dâm, village in Wady Dauâsir, II. 425.
Dam ; an ancient — in J. Ajja, 632.
Damascene [v. Shwân]: — kellâ keepers, 165 ; sons of —s traders to Arabia, 196 ; a — saves Ibrahîm Pasha's Syrian troops by a distinction of speech, 197 ; 244, 247 ; the — Christians without courage, 295 ; sons of —s among the Fukara, 363 ; 485, 589 ; II. a — tradesman who came to Hâyil, 46, 66.
Damascus, Ar. *es-Sham* or *es-Shem* [*v.* also *Medân*], oasis-metropolis of *es-Sham* or Syria ; — in the days of the Hâj, 41 ; the street called Straight, 43 ; massacre of Christians at —, 103, 107, 110, 111, 113, 114, 119, 120, 125, 129, 132, 139, 144, 174 ; — Christians in daily fear of massacre, 178, 190, 191, 193, 196 ; the former massacre, 198 ; 204, 205-208, 214 ; *el-Moristàn, ib.*; 217, 236, 238, 240, 244, 246, 250, 251, 252, 253, 254, 270, 295, 296, 303, 314 ; — " the world's paradise," 316 ; 319, 338, 420, 435, 444, 469, 480, 481, 497, 510, 522, 553, 556, 581, 585, 607, 625 ; II. 48, 61, 65, 66 ; — ostrich feather merchant with the Hâj, 86 ; apricot orchards of —, 171-2 ; — of our fathers' days,

ib. [the Ottoman governor is said to have been slain who first imposed a tax in —, which was but of an halfpenny upon every household !]; aspect of the great Syrian city, *ib.*; 177, 181, 218, 264, 278, 312, 326, 337, 338, 349, 354, 363, 390, 416, 464, 465, 482, 527, 537, 553, 575.

Ibn Dammûk, an Heteymy sheykh, II. 304.

Ibn Dammûk (min el-Khluîeh), a fendy of Heteym, II. 253.

Damsels to wed, 589, 590.

the Dance, 70, 387, 438, 607, 608; II. 137.

Dandelion : the wild — in the desert mountains, 349.

Dánna, a camel name, 321.

Dàr, said at Teyma for house, 329, 332.

Dàr el-'Aarab, a camping ground worn in the desert soil, 428; II. 295.

Dàr el-Ḥamra, a well-built kellâ but now ruinous and without door, and seldom occupied, 48, 119, 120; cholera in the Hâj at —, 120; 121, 258, 271, 315, 347.

Dàr el-Múghr, a Hâj station, 115.

Daràwessha, a kindred of Howeytát, 68.

Dardanelles, the English fleet passed the —, II. 398.

Dareyem, a sheykh of Teyma, 596.

Darraga (دَرَقَة, target), the Hejâz buckler, 189.

Dartford, *v.* Gunpowder.

Darýesh, a Mahûby sheykh, 508, 515, 523, 532, 537, 548, 564, 565.

Dat Ras, palace-like ruins in the high plain of Kerak, 59.

Dates [*v. Ḥelw, Berni*]: — of Tebûk, 112; — of Teyma, 112, 338; — of Mogur, 629; — of Gofar, 634; Bed. provision of —, 268; — as food, 190; the new — berries (*belaḥ*), 319, 489, 555, 560, 566, 569, 571; 578; currency of — at Teyma, 377, 597, 603; — harvest at Teyma, 608-9; — good to be eaten with sour milk or mereesy, 338; Bed. pitched by an oasis pilfer no — from the villagers' trees, 585; — at Hâyil, the worst, 638; II. [*v. Shúḳra, Rótḥ.*] Sweyfly —, 21; Ibn Rashîd's question, 26; price of — in Hâyil and Gofar, 76; — of Kheybar, 94; — stones for camels are merchandise in the Hejâz, 199; — of J. Shammar, 292; — in 'Aneyza sold by weight, 375; — kinds there, 466; — of W. Fâtima, 565, 570, 571. Date-eaters, 190, 272, 605.

Dathyna, *v. Dafîna.*

Aarab Dauâsir, II. 453.

W. Dauâsir [called in that country *el-Wady*, *v. el-Aflâj*], 248; II. 52, [Names of villages in —, according to Hàmed en-Nefîs, —*el Ḥammam, es-Shotibba, es-Ṣoleyl, Tammerra, el-Dam* (three hamlets), *el-Loghrf, el-Ferr'a* (which is three or four villages), *es-Showŷg, el-Ayaṭhat*; others name *eth-Théllum*], 350, 365, 425, 453, 558, 575.

Daûd (David), 560, 658.

Daughters in an Arab household, 130, 281, 282, 366.

David, his cruelty to the Moabites, 62; his cruelty to the Edomites, 83; — a captain of the outlaws, 361; II. —'s daughter Tamar, 45; such as — are the Semites, 53, 407.

David shirts of mail, II. 36, 42, 480.

Dawwa, medicines (also condiments), 297.

Day, arctic —, 320.

Dead [*v.* Grave], a sacrifice for the —, 282; memory of the —, *ib.*; II. the slain in battle are left unburied by their victorious foemen, 480.

Dead Sea, 50; 75; 85; II. 575, 576.

Deaf: a — man at Khubbera, II. 439.

J. Debby, a mountain nigh Seleymy, II. 306.

Debîbat es-Shem, 91.

Dedan, 343.

Deformed persons: a cripple boy, 263, 357; none among the Moahîb, 519.

Deffafîat, a sounding sand-hill, 352.

Deghrèyma, Bed. fem. name, 514; II. an ass-mare name, 253.

Dehgreyrát, a fendy of Shammar, II. 56.

Deh ! Ar. imitative word; the sound of a gun-shot, 319, 393.

ed-Deheysa, an ass-mare name, II. 253.

ed-Dehússa, a fendy of '*Ateyba*, II. 457.

ed-Deir, a frontispice at Petra, 81.

"Delhi boil," II. 511.

Dellàl (دَلاَل), coffee-pots, 264.

Dellâl (دَلَّال), crier or running broker in the Arabic town sûks, 661; II. 63, 380.

[*ed-Dellam*, "four hundred" houses, between *el-Harik* and *el-Ḥauta.*

ed-Dellamîeh, a watering in Kasîm, II. 476.

Delta, the — in Egypt, 591.

Demons, *v.* Jân.

Deposit : the — is held sacred, 219; Nomads bury tents and stuff in sand hillocks, or lay up in certain their secret caves, 323; or in villages,

323 ; a mantle left hanging on a thorn in Sinai, 323 ; — in Sinai " Nasarene houses," 323 ; — in Hâj-road kellâs, 323 ; II. 263, 326.

Deraan, a kindred of Ânnezy, 377.

Derâhim [from the Greek δραχμή], money, II. 344.

Derb el-bukkra [*v.* Map]; a camel path between Tebûk and Dar el-Ḥamra, 481. [The Bed. say ' that a *bûkra* whose calf was left behind her about el-Héjr came limping again thither from Tebûk — her fore-limbs being tied — in four days.']

Derb el-Ḥâj [nearly the ancient Gold-and-Frankincense Road]: the Hâj way in the wilderness, 47, 51, 271 ; words of an ancient Arabic poet, *ib.*; held by landmarks, 96 ; reported strewed skeletons by the —, 96 ; — " passed by the Thorreyid," 485, 566 ; II. 37, 38, 155, 173, 204, 569.

Derb es-Sherky, or the East Hâj Road between the Harameyn, II. 393, 565.

Derb es-Sultâny, between Jidda and Mecca, II. 572.

Derb Zillâj, 620.

Derrûby (a Solubby kindred), 327.

Derwîsh, pl. *derawîsh* (a poor man, a *fakîr*): a Persian —, 43 ; a dying — in the Hâj, 91 ; an imperial charity for pilgrim derwishes, 92 ; a lost — arrives at Medáin Sâlih, 138 ; his death, 140 ; a — arrived at M'aan alone and on foot from Mecca, 139 ; a — in the returning Hâj, 251 ; — of the Medân, 252, 316 ; a — may savagely rebuke a Prince and go unpunished, 558 ; II. an Asiatic religious mystery of certain — wounding themselves without after hurt, 137.

Desert (Ar. *khála, qd. v.*): the Arabian — described, 95 ; silence of the —, 286, 322 ; eternal squalor of the —, 414 ; 477 ; II. dewless and silent —, 294.

Deserters from the Turkish army, 198 ; II. 309, 361, 362, 364, 390.

" Desolate Places," 135 ; 452.

Dewless Arabia, 468, 491 ; II. 451.

Deybàn, serpents [or perhaps ثُعْبَان which is sing.], 486.

[*Deyd* (better *deys*), teat of the nâga.

W. *Deydibbàn* (W. *el-Ḳora, qd. v.*), 187.

Ḍeyiḳ eṣ-ṣudr (ضِيق الصَّدْر), the straitness or anguish of the breast in affliction, constraint of heart ; heart-ache, home-sickness.

Diamonds : morsels of glassy quartz taken for diamonds, 118 ; II. 120, 244.

Diànat el-Mohammedía, II. 403.

Dîbàn, ruined village in Moab, 65.

Dibba (class. دُبَّاء), pumpkin, 194.

Dibon, *v. Dîbàn.*

ed-Dillum, a place in Middle Nejd, II. 425.

ed-Dîmn (الدِّمْن), II. 416.

Dimṣ (دِمْص), basaltic blocks (upon the 'Aueyrid), 427.

Dîn el-'Aarab, the nomad custom of life, 430. [Commonly *dîn* signif. religion, II. 403.]

Dîn néjis, II. 443.

Dinner : — of chief persons at Hâyil, 649 ; II. — at 'Aneyza, 378 ; Turkish —, 548-9.

Dînya el-jedîda, the New World, 647.

Dîra, circuit of the Nomads or oasis settlement, 55, 303 ; II. 266.

Dîrat er-Rasûl, the Medina country, II. 68, 114.

Diseases, *v.* Maladies.

Dissolution. An evil spirit sowed in man the seeds of —, 520.

Distances, account of —, 54, 322.

Distracted persons : a Christian Syrian cure for —, II. 412.

Divination, 205, 301, 347, 510.

el-Diwán (or *Lîwan*) at el-Héjr, 160 ; sculptured tablets in the — passage, 162, which an epigraph shows to have been idol-stones, *ib.*; conduit in the same, *ib.*, 228, 559 ; II. the clean sanded sitting-place on the ground in Kasîm orchards, 361.

Doàdamy, desert vill. S. of el-Wéshm, II. 492.

Doctor [*v. Ḥakîm*]; a military —, who came to cure, and the same day he perished of the cholera at Kheybar, II. 145.

Documents épigraphiques recueillis dans le nord de l'Arabie par M. Charles Doughty. Paris, Imp. nat. 1884 [64 pages de texte et 57 planches in-4°, avec une introduction et la traduction des inscriptions nabatiennes de Medain Saleh, par M. E. Renan.] — Vol. published by the Académie des Inscriptions et Belles Lettres, 224.

Doeg the Edomite, 83.

ed-Dôeh, oasis-vill. in W. Fâtima, II. 570.

Dog-star, 537; ii. 572.
Dogmàn, a kindred of Ânnezy, 377.
Dogmân, a dog's name, 474.
Dogs [v. Greyhound]:— in the Hâj, 109; town — must keep their quarters, 109; 338; the only life mishandled by the Aarab, 353, 382, 439; — eating locusts, 382; — wolf-eaters; — of the Fejîr; they resemble the street dogs of Syria, 382; Bíllî —, 382; — go not out with the flocks, 382; — receive little sustenance from man's hand, *ib.*; are spurned by the Aarab, *ib.*; half reasonable behaviour of —, *ib.*; — a sort of police of the Bed. menzils: they worry about the heels of strange comers, 383; they fall upon any baggage of strangers which is left abroad, *ib.*; men who are thieves of food called —, *ib.*; Bíllî —, 429, 473; 507; ii. — not seen by day in Nejd villages, 20; "betwixt the — and the wolf," 267; — of the Nomads, 295; distant barking of — a sign of the nomad menzils, 311, 329; a — which robs human food may be killed, 334.
Dogs' names: some — that are also names of nomad tribes or kindreds mentioned in this work. See the elench of names, 473, where Dogmàn (also a kindred of Ânnezy), *Ammera* (*cf.* Ammarát a fendy of Bishr), *Tôga* (*cf.* Shammar-Tôga), *Aduân, Simrân,* (*cf.* Ibn Sim'ry), *Shalân.*
Dokân, a shop: the Nasrâny's — at 'Aneyza, ii. 366, 371.
J. Dokhàn, 135.
W. Dokhàn(a), in the 'Aueyriḍ Harra, 463 [in the mouth are ruins of a place "wider than el-Ally, and of a great kellâ." — *Thàhir.*]
Dokhân (lit. smoke), the tobacco leaf (*qd. v.*).
Dókhany, a watering-place in el-Kasîm, ii. 476, 479, 480, 484, 492.
Dôm (دُوْم), or branched wild nut, palms, 134, 463, 468; ii. 117, 202, 466.
ed-Dôma, ass-mare name, ii. 253.
Dónnebil, camel's name, 321.
Doolàn, a Fehjy at Medáin Sâlih, his fable-talk of the ghrôl, 92, 173; and of the B. Kelb, and of Kheybar, 171; 173, 222, 233, 234, 237, 362, 409, 410, 411, 417-18, 565.
Doublûn, double gold piece (from the French or Spanish), ii. 23.
Doves [v. Pigeons]:— of el-Irâk, at Hâyil, 640; ii. — of Mecca, 572.

Dówla, the (Ottoman) Government, 48, 87 *et passim*; by nomad children regarded as a tribe, 271; 399, 417, 419, 458, 500, 657.
Dowlâny, one of the people of the settled countries under the Ottoman Government.
Dragon-flies in the grove of W. Thirba, 495; ii. — over the springs at Kheybar, 220.
Draughts: Ar. game of — (*beatta*), 560, 585. *v. Minḳala.*
Dreams: presages drawn from — at Kheybar, ii. 114.
Drift: block — in the high plain beyond Jordan, 43; vulcanic — near M'aan, 68; and in W. Sâny, 118; — before Dàr el-Hamra, 120; — in the plain of el-Héjr, 123; ii. — at *Mleylîeh,* 204.
Drinking, after meat, 551.
Dromedary [v. *Thelûl*], a light camel for riding. The difference between a — and an ordinary camel is like that between a riding and a draught-horse: dromedaries are bred from dromedaries: value of —, 413.
Dropsy (*istísḳa*): woman at Teyma sick of the —, 576; man with —, 596, 621; ii. 482.
Drought: a great — in Middle Nejd, ii. 428.
Drugs, simple medicines in the hands of the Nomad hareem [v. Spices, Perfumes, Witchcraft], 247, 297, 350, 540.
Druses: the — defeat the troops of Ibrahîm Pasha, 197; 341, 590, 653; ii. 64, 401.
Du'aa, the informal prayer of the spirit, 612; ii. 88.
ed-Dubb, rock in W. Sâny, 118.
Dubba (دَبِي s. دَبَا), the imperfect brood of latter locusts, 244, 351.
Dubbel, a station in the desert N.W. of Teyma, 341.
Dubbilân, a dog's name, 474.
Dubbûs (دَبُّوس), Arab mace, [v. *Ganna*]:— wasm or cattle-brand of the Heteym and Sherrarát, *v.* fig., 167, 425, 443, 583; ii. 144, 200, 261.
Dubbush (دَبِش), small cattle, the sheep and goats [v. *Ghrannem*], 59; — milked at sunset; and only in the best spring weeks or in good pasture again in the morning, 304, 355 *et passim*; Ibn Rashîd's —, 664.

604 INDEX AND GLOSSARY

ed-Duffîr [v. *eth-Thuffîr*], sheykh ibn Sweyd, once Aarab of the Héjr dîra, 167.

Dukṣa (دُقْسَة), a minute Nejd grain, 336.

Dulàb in the kellâ at Medáin Sâlih, the well machine, 167.

Dullû (دَلُو), bucket, 335. [v. *Suâny*.] a dumb man at Hâyil, II. 22-3, 63-4.

ed-Dumm thekîl, the burden of blood is very sore, 414.

Dungola, 604.

Durf ed-Drawish (ظَرْف الدراويش), a seyl in J. Sherra, 68.

Dustmen of the Háram at Medina : the Nejumies become —, II. 158.

Dutch, v. Flemish.

Dye : the nails and palms stained yellow with henna, at el-Ally [Hejâz ; — I have not seen this custom in Nejd], 184 ; grey beards dyed with saffron, 98, 637, 648 [I have seen old Bed. women in the Héjr country whose hair was stained thus] ; worsted —d by Arabian women, 190, 346 ; — fungus, 402 ; 523 ; II. — plant whose blossoms are used to stain the parting of the hair in Kasîm, 361.

Dzat (*That*, ذَات), Hâj, kellâ, 97.

Eagle, v. *Rákham*, *Ágab* ; the —'s life "a thousand years," 211 ; the greater — not seen in the Arabian deserts, 374.

Ears of fallen enemies cut off by the Turks, II. 144.

Earthenware vessels not used now in Arabia, 602 ; the potsherds in ruined sites are of the ancients (v. Potsherds).

Eat [v. Hospitality]: the brain of slaughtered beasts eaten by women only, in the desert, 547 ; II. women and children under age — not with the housefather and the guests, 161 ; the Arabs nimble —ers, 259 ; manner to — with the Arabs, 378 ; the Moham. Arabs will — and drink with any man, 396.

Ebbeden, never, 287 ; II. 57.

Eclipse of the moon : — at Teyma, 333 ; 558.

Edom [v. also Mount Seir]: vulcanic rocks in —, 59 ; the king of —, 62 ; uplands of —, 65, 67 ; usage of sitting house-wise in Howeytát tents in —, 75 ; the better parts of — are a land "flowing with milk," 75 ; and full of small cattle, 78 ; tillage in —, 78 ; Nomad peasants in —, ib.; wisdom ascribed (in the Bible) to the inhab. of —, 82 ; — neighbour land to the nomads, 82 ; tent-dwellers of —, 82 ; — the land of Uz, ib.; — and Israel rivals, 83 ; kingdom of — to compare with an English county, 83 ; David set garrisons in —, ib.; the voice of — detesting the iniquitous house of Jacob, 83 ; maledictions of the Hebrew prophets against her, ib.; the name, 86, 308, 462 ; II. 421, 575.

Effendy el-Fàiz, sheykh of B. Sókhr in Moab ; his dishonourable dealing with a guest and a stranger, 55.

Eflah! (افلا) 307 ; II. 225, 258.

'Εγρα (*Ptol.*), v. *el-Héjr*.

Egypt, 129, 196, 199 ; mummies of —, 229 ; 275, 322, 334, 373, 433, 503-4 ; speech of —, 522 ; 595, 658, 665 ; II. 39, 59, 103, 200; footprints seen in a monument opened in —, 239 ; 310, 314, 382, 387, 389, 402, 426, 454, 468 ; " Nile sores," 511.

Egyptian Hâj way in Arabia, 84 ; an — 'Ageyly at Kheybar, II. 97, 98 ; 174, 193, 197, 202, 208, 407, 414 ; — soldiery at the work of the Suez Canal, 450 ; — occupation of the Mecca country, 454, 525, 543 ; — mummies, 554 ; 566.

J. *Éhad* (thus pron. by Nejders, but written أَحَد), or J. *Hamzy*, near Medina, 187 ; II. 145.

Eherrij (هَرِّج)! speak, discourse, II. 179.

Eherris (أَحْرِز), I may have power over, 516.

Ejja, v. J. *Ajja*.

'*Ekîm* (عَكِيم), a kind of sleeping carpet made at Teyma, 345 [called sometimes *kotîfy*].

" EL brought Israel out of Egypt," 373.

Elbow. Summer passed on the —, 490.

Elephant [Ar. *el-Fîl*, qd. v.], 506 ; II. 116, 186.

Elijah, the prophet, 116, 118.

Elisha, his charge to the confederate kings of Israel and Judah against the king of Moab, 62 ; his derwishes, 173.

Eljy, village by Petra, 78, 80, 82, 218.

el-'Elk (علك), a kind of gum caout-chouc, juice of a Nefûd plant *el-móṭṭi* (أمطي), II. 200.

Ellathi thábah, II. 41.

Eloquence, 167, 168 ; — in the desert and in the oases, 306 ; the Arabs study to be eloquent, 307 ; II. 148-9, 162.

el-'Elûm, the liberal sciences, 643.

Elyâs, the patriarch, brother of *Keys*, II. 381.

Embroidering : women's industry of — at Hâyil, II. 20 ; — at 'Aneyza, 375.

Emesa, now *Ḥums* in N. Syria, 104, 140.

Emir, he in whom is the *amr* or word of command, 575.

Emir *el-Ḥâj* or *Sîr Amîn*, 43, 109, 129, 220 ; 248-9 ; II. 176.

Emir *el-kâfily*, v. *Ibrahîm*, II. 488, 491.

Ems, yesterday. In el-Ally this is said in the afternoon of the same day morning : thus they account the natural day from midday to midday, 526.

Enchanter, v. *Sáhar, Múndel, Móghreby*.

Enchantments as remedies (v. *Ḥijâb*), II. 150 ; — to reveal crimes, 209-10, 395 ; — to defeat the maleficence of demons, 211 ; — to discover treasures [v. *Treasure*].

Encyclopedia Bustâny, II. 370, 386, 555, 559.

el-Engéll, a water in the Nefûd of el-Wéshm, II. 452.

el-Engleys [*Inkalîz*], the English, 129, 334 ; words of the — learned by Bed., 365 ; their speech is rugged-like, 562 ; the Bed. question of —, 271 *et passim* ; — the Sultan's uncles, 318 ; II. — metals in the sûk at Hâyil, 23 ; — *jabâbara*, 104 ; — naval commanders of Turkish warships, 105 ; an — family at Tiflis, 111 ; Amm Mohammed would learn the — tongue, 178 ; — they suppose to be subject to the Sultan, 182 ; — in India, 226 ; — at Aden, 227, 397 ; — red coats, 541 ; — " not of Gog and Magog," 558.

el-Engleyssy, a kind of Bed. matchlocks, 504 ; a kind of pistols, 505.

English shippers on the Persian Gulf, 108 ; II. 504.

Enhaj ! (verb نهج = نهش comp. I. 621), II. 161.

Enjahsah, a ruined site in Moab, 61.

el-Enjîl (εὐαγγέλ-), the book of the Gospel of Jesus, 342, 521, 584 ; II. 24, 411.

Ensheyfa, a watering place in the Teháma, 445.

Enshèynish, a ruined site in Moab, 59.

Entha, female, said commonly of a woman of the poorer condition, 280 ; II. 292.

Ent kelb, " thou an hound ! " 586.

Envelope of a certain letter with a Syrian bishop's seal, seen at Hâyil, 643.

Enzân, a mountain coast in the Teháma, 463.

ἔπαρχος, governor of a province, a word found in the Aramaic inscriptions of Medáin Sâlih, 227.

Ephraim, Syrian father and commentator of the Gospels in that tongue, II. 414.

Epilepsy, II. 412, 414.

Epitaphs of Medáin Sâlih, v. *Inscriptions*.

Erb'a, a fendy of 'Ateyba, II. 457.

Érbah, village ruins and bergs near Teyma, 601, 617.

Erbeylát, a fendy of W. 'Aly, 271.

Eremite Fathers, 521 ; II. 150.

el-'Erk, in el-Wéshm, II, 567.

Erḳa (أرق), mount ! II. 94.

'Er'n (عرن), a kind of (scarlet) tan-root used by the nomad housewives, 268, 426.

el-'Erudda [perhaps Yakut's *'Orda*], a great watering place of the Fukara, 395, 396, 400, 404, 420, 421, 422, 438.

Esau : slaughter of the children of —, 83, 84.

el-'Esha (عشّة), a tree-like canker weed, II. 516.

Eskîny má, II. 296.

Èslam, a fendy of Shammar, II. 56.

Ésm'a (اسمع) ! listen, 562.

el-Ésmar, a mountain, v. *el-Éswad*.

el-'Esomma, a fendy of 'Ateyba, II. 457.

Estranghélo, l'ecriture, 224.

el-Éswad or *el-Ésmar*, the northern mountain of the *Abànát*, II. 491.

el-Éswad, a driver in the Hâj, 102-3 ; 105, 107, 108-9, 110, 117, 118 ; his tale of a cholera year, 120 ; 123, 126, 127.

Ethbah-hu ! II. 505, (comp. *thábah*, II. 41).

INDEX AND GLOSSARY

el-Éthelly, ruined site, probably of *Járada* or *Jarda*, the old metropolis of Ḳaṣîm, "in face of er-Russ over W. er-Rummah," II. 388, 479.

Éthla pl. *éthel*, (اَثْل), long tamarisk timber of Arabia, grown in the oases for building, 185, 638; II. — ware bowls, 20; 560.

J. *Éthlib*, in the Héjr plain, 123, 134, 136, 173, 176, 205, 233-5, 408, 409, 410, 411, 549.

J. *Ethmâd* (pl. of *Thámmad*), II. 255.
J. *Ethnân*, II. 89, 246, 247.
Ethn'asher kelb, II. 310.

el-'Etîm (عَلَم), the olive tree brought from Syria is thus called at et-Tâyif, II. 560.
Etna, II. 370.

Éṭrush (اطرش), drive forward! 458.

Etymologers, 327.
Euphrates valley, II. 70, 355.
Europe, 168, 169, 476, 503, 505, 506, 536, 580, 591, 602; II. 274, 275, 407, 448, 449, 471, 541.
Euting: Prof. Julius —, 581. [*Correction*: the here mentioned inscription is not that found by Euting and Huber who visited Teyma some years later. Prof. Euting found there another inscribed stone, not mentioned in this work, which the brother of *Seydàn* (581) showed them. The inscription of 24 lines which has been deciphered by Professors Euting and Nöldeke [*Sitzungsber. der k. Ak. der Wiss. zu Berlin* 1884 (No. xxxv.), p. 813-820] is of great antiquity and of the highest value. This inscription has been likewise translated by M. E. Renan: the stone is now in Paris.
"Eve's grave," 434; II. 574.
Evening: the long — in the tents, 302; — at el-Héjr, 405.
The Evil: a people that worship Sheytàn and —, 578.
Exiles in the nomad menzils, 271, 291, 292, 362, 363, 491, 549, 551.
Exodus: the pillar of cloud and fire in —, 380.
Exorcists, 301; II. 17-18.
Ey khábar? what tidings? II. 192.

Eyâd (اياد), an Arabian patriarch, II. 393.

Eyâd, a Bishry (of the Medina 'Ageyl service) at Kheybar; he conveys the Nasrâny to Ḥâyil, II. 123, 232, 234-299; his person, 261; he is out of taste of the Bed. life, 262.
Eyâda ibn Ajjuèyn, an Heteymy sheykh, II. 79, 82, 83, 84, 85, 249-251, 262.
el-Eyàlla, a fendy of 'Ateyba, II. 457.
'*Eyàr*, reputed founder of the '*Eyarîeh* and brother of *Owshâz*, II. 421.
el-'Eyarîeh or *Menzil 'Eyàr*, ruined site, "of the most ancient settlement" in the parts of el-Ḳaṣîm, upon the W. er-Rummah, near 'Aneyza; it was, they say, of B. Temîm, II. 417-422, 446, 451, 460.
Eye: the evil —, 378; eye-struck, 598.
Eye-salver: a Moghreby — in Arabia, 480; II. a Nejd —, 374.
Eye-washes, 382.
Eyes: diseases of the — among Arabs, *v.* Ophthalmia. Custom to paint the — with antimony [*v. Kâhl*], 279; spitting on —, 576; II. good eye-sight, 249, 256.
Eysh b'hu, what aileth him? 491.
'*Eyyâl 'amm*, 360.
'*Eyyâl es-sheukh*, 666.
Ezekiel: handstaves mentioned in the book of —, 189; hell in —, 212; 309, 475; 540; II. 59, 171.
Ezion Gaber, *v. Ayla.*
ez-Zerka, 51.

Fables of the East, 214, 433.
Hâj Fables, 77, 111, 127, 170.
Factions of the Arabs, — of kindreds, — in the oases: 50; — at M'aan, 73; — at Teyma before Ibn Rashîd's government, 329; II. — and usury are the undoing of the Arab countries, 415.
Faddaghra, fendy of Shammar, II. 56.
el-Faera, vill. of B. Sâlem, Harb, II. 546.
Fáhd (فَهْد), a wild cat, 373; a — bred up to hunting, *ib.*; II. 164.
Fáhd, a distracted elder son of 'Abeyd ibn Rashíd, 647; II. 23, 42-3, 72.
Fáhd, elder son of Motlog, great sheykh of W. 'Aly, a wooden-headed young man: his foolish questions, 271; 375, 379, 415.
Fáhd, a younger son of Rasheyd, foreign merchant of 'Aneyza, II. 449, 467, 468, 475.

Beny Fàhm (*v. Koreysh*), II. 559.
Fâiz, a Mahûby, 457, 610.
Fakir, an indigent man '*aly sebîl* (upon the way of faith in) *Ullah*', a derwish, *qd. v.*, 104.
Fâlaj, sing. of *Aflâj*, *qd. v.*, II. 52.
Falcon (*sokr*): the —, 349, 408-9, 563, 566, 583, 618. [Fukara friends counselled me to carry a — to Hâyil for a present to Ibn Rashîd; the Emir, they said, would take it well and receive me more favourably.]
Falconry, 408, 618.
Famine in the Kheybar dîra, II. 132.
Fanaticism [*v.* Zelotism]: — of the Bed., 343, 357, 423, 425, 435; — is of their barren minds and weak nature, 449; 551, 599; Turkish —, 419; II. 76, 154; — in Kasîm, 346, 352-4, 401, 403-5, 430-1, 482.
Far'aoun, Pharaoh: *Kasr* — at Petra, 79; *Khasna* —, 80, 81; *Wady* —, 79.
Fáras, mare.
Fardûs, a Fehjy, 219.
Farhàn, a villager of el-Ally, 525.
Fâsid, depraved, dissolute, corrupt, 143, 532.
el-Fasîha, Bed. fem. name, 514.
Fasting, II. of the Moslems [*v.* Ramathàn], 461. the Fat and the sweet comfort the health of the weak dieted, II. 108.
el-Fátha or the "opening" of the koran, III; II. 24.
Fatalism: the — of the Mohammedan religion explained, 197, 381; II. 378.
Fâtima, daughter of Mohammed, II. 97, 556.
W. Fâtima, near Mecca, 536; II. 204, 513, 559, 560, 565, 566; works for tillage in —, *ib.* 567, 569, 572.

Fâtir (فاتر), a decrepid camel, 497.

Fattish (فَتِّش) *b'il kitàb! fécher* (perhaps *fassir*, فَسِّر), 'Search and make divination by the book,' 511.

Fatya (probably فَتِيَّة), coffee-gear basket, 264.
el-Faur, a tribe of the ashràf, II. 556.
Feather: a — bound upon the foreheads of Bed. maidens for an ornament, 385; — merchant, *v.* Ostrich.
Fedd'an, a fendy of Bishr, 376.
el-Féha, Bed. fem. name, 514.

Fehját (sing. *Féhjy*), a poor and very small Heteym kindred, clients of the Fukara, and hereditary servants of the kellâ at Medáin Sâlih, 135, 138; they boast themselves to be the Children of 'Antara, 162, 411; 177, 218, 234, 235, 237, 315, 328; — eat the owl, 349, 656; 349, 362; their lineage, *ib.*; are they *Yahûd Kheybar?* *ib.*; 406, 411, 412, 417, 418, 426, 447, 554, 565; a — family dwelling as settlers at Teyma, 611; II. 84.
Féhjy, sing. of *Fehját*, *qd. v.*
el-Fejîr (for *Fakîr*, — *v.* the letter *J*), pl. [only] *el-Fúkara*, 261, 270; — name of the fendy or kindred of sheykhs in a sub-tribe [anciently called *el-Menâbaha*] of Ânnezy. This name of their sheykhly family is now extended to all the tribesmen, who are called *el-Fukára*. They are the Aarab of Medáin Sâlih and of the desert marches N. and W. from thence to Teyma and to the border of Nejd; a twin tribe of the *Wélad Aly*, and named together with them the *Beny Wáhab*: a tribesman of either will say of himself, *ana Wahâby*. — There is an old quarrel between these sister tribes for the ground-right of the kellâ at *el-Héjr*, and for possession of the Hâj surra thereof. *v. el-Fúkara*.
Fejjuân, a dog's name, 474.
Féjr, a Teyma villager, 584, 616; his wife, 591.
el-Féjr, the dawn, 399.
W. Fellah, v. W. el-Hâsy.
Felûs, money, 665.
Feminine humour, the Aarabs of —, "kind friends and implacable enemies," II. 254.

Fen el-ma'aziba (فين المَعْزِبَة؟) II. 257.

Fen Rubbuk? 518.
Fenced cities, 72.

Féndy (فِنْد), a kindred and natural division in a tribe.

Fenjèyl [(فنجيل)] *فنجال* for *fenjèyn*, 286.

Fenjèyn, the small coffee-cup of the Arabs, 286, 287.
Ferâ, v. Ferrâ.
[*el-Fer'a*, district between el-Kherj and el-Aflâj, with four towns and vill., *Hauta, Harik, Helwa, Náam*: — M. en-Nefîs.
[*el-Fer'a*, a village in el-Wéshm.

Ferâdessa, a kindred of Heteym, ii. 240, 253.

Feraij (فُرَيِّق), dim. of *ferîj*, *qd. v.*

Feràya, a Fejîry tribesman, 578.

[*el-Fèrdat* and *Merrâra*, mountains N. of *J. Mîsma.*

el-Feréya, Meteyr village on the *Derb es-Sherky*, ii. 393, 565.

Fergusson: Mr. James —, his opinion of the (nail) holes in certain frontispieces of the Medáin Sâlih monuments, 151.

Ferîj (فُرِيق), [dim. *feraij*, pl. *ferjàn* — where *j* is for *k*], lit. a partition, a nomad hamlet, ii. 250 *et passim.*

Ferjàn (فُرْقان), nomad hamlets or " divided " menzils of kindred, 263; ii. 250.

Ferjèyn, a peak in the desert S. of el-Kasîm, ii. 493.

Fernèyny, whirligig, 480. [Comp. *Amroulkeys, Mo'all.* 58.]

el-Ferra (or *Ferâ*), a valley bottom of the *W. Jizzl*, W. of the Harrat el-'Aueyrid, 217, 463.

el-Ferrâ, (فرع, Nasir es-Smîry), on the middle Hâj way, oasis village of Harb Beny 'Amr, *Mosrûh*, between the Harameyn, 463; ii. 103, 155, 163; — described, 194; 547.

Wady Ferr'a, with Aarab B. 'Amr, Harb B. Sâlem, and el-Ubbeda, ii. 546.

el-Ferr'a, village in el-Kasîm, ii. 452.

el-Ferr'a, great village in the South country, between er-Riâth and W. Bîsha [in Wady Dauâsir], ii. 52, 425.

Ferrah, a Shammar Beduwy, ii. 293.

Ferth, cud, ii. 260.

el-Ferúdda, fendy of Harb Mosrûh, ii. 547.

Ferujja, a kindred of Ânnezy, 377.

el-Fesas, station between Hâyil and el-Kuweyt, ii. 61.

Fever: el-Ally —, 405, 523; the Hejâz —, 523; — at Kheybar, ii. 112, 145, 150, 238; a remedy for —, 150.

Feyd, a village in the dominion of Ibn Rashîd, 335; ii. 34.

Feyd el-'Abeyd, Ibn Rashîd, ii. 44.

Feyd (فائد), booty, 499.

Fèysal, a child of Hamûd ibn Rashîd, ii. 18, 45, 69.

Fèysal ibn S'aûd, ii. 50, 453, 458, 459, 460.

Feytháh, village between W. es-Sirr and Shûkra, ii. 424.

Fez, one of the Barbary provinces, 129, 562; city of —, *ib.*

Fheyd, a Bed. or half-Bed. Mecca caravaner, companion of Sâlem, ii. 526, 527-32, 547-8, 565.

Fî ahl-ha, 302, 400.

Fî amân illah, ii. 379.

Fî kheyr wâjid, ii. 571.

Fî kull makân, ii. 63.

Fî tarîk, 642.

Fiction: an honest legal —, 539.

Fig trees in the waste [v. *el-Úthub, el-Hamâta*], 486, 488, 495, 568.

El-figgera (فُقْرَة), pl. *el-fúggar*: the brow of the Harra about Kheybar so called, ii. 92; ruins on —, *ib.*; depth of the lava at the Wady sides, 110, 112, 115, 118, 123, 138, 142, 163.

J. el-Figgera, vill. of B. Sâlem, Harb, ii. 545, 546, 551.

el-Fîl, the elephant, 506.

Filigrane or thread work: artificers in — of gold at 'Aneyza, ii. 429.

Fire: the cheerful or sweet smelling watch — of sticks and desert bushes, 118, 258, 294, 302, 303, 304, 580; — kindled of resinous bushes in the rain, 618; 619; ii. glimpsing camp —s of the Nomads appearing in the dark wilderness, 287, 311, 503, 536.

" Fire is half bread," 580.

Fire: ashes of an antique — appearing in the side of a loam pit, in Kasîm, ii. 422.

' Fire of hell ': the dread of — in Moslem hearts, ii. 409.

Firewood: — sold at Hâyil, 637; ii. — gatherers, 76.

Firing; remedy of —, *v.* Cauterize.

Firmàn: " a — of the Sultan must be obeyed," ii. 104, 105, 274, 277; the Sultan's — respected in Nejd, 388.

Fishes in the brooks of the Peraea, 66; at *el-Akhdar*, 117; ii. — [*hût*], in the brooks of Kheybar, 96.

J. Fittij, a mountain near Hâyil, 668.

Flamingies, Flemish seamen, 168.

Fleas in the Belka (and Hauràn], 56.

OF ARABIC WORDS   609

Flemish or Dutch seamen, 168.

Flesh: cured — (ḳourmah, Turc. قَاوُرْمَهْ)
of Damascus used in the Hâj caravan, 110;
stinking — meat eaten by Arabians, 612;
II. sun-dried — at 'Aneyza, 371; — scorched
in gobbets for their caravan journeys will last
good a month, 484.
Flies: — at Medáin Sâlih, 147, 558; — in the
Belka, 56; — at el-Ally, 189, 405, 529;
— in the wilderness, 452; — a sign of the
palm settlements nigh at hand, 627; II. — at
Hâyil, 26; — sign of an oasis nigh, 90;
— at desert waterings, 329, 498.
Flint instruments found in the gravel at M'aan
in J. Sherra, 68, 74-77.
"Flint land": the —, 86; v. Arḍ Ṣuwwán.
Flowers: the N. Arabians have not learned to
cherish —, 582.
Flowrets in the desert, 259, 620, 635; II. 500.
F'lûs (fish scales), silver or gold money, v. Fulûs.
Foal; a strange — adopted by a dry mare, II. 484.
Fódil, a Bíllî sheykh, 429, 641.
Footprints: among the Aarab of the N.W. parts
of Arabia is little skill to discern footprints.
Zeyd es-Sbeykàn knew only his wife's —.
II. — might remain till the next rain were
there no wind, 239; — of ostriches, 246;
pretended lore of the B. Faḥm, 559.
Forage; wild — for the Bed. horses, 302.
Forelock, braided —, v. "Horns."
el-Fosîha, Bed. fem. name, 514.
Fox [v. Ḥoṣenny]: the — in the khála, 96; it
is eaten by the Beduw, 372, 656; II. black
— of the Harra (Kheybar), 163.
France, v. Fransa.
Francesco Ferrari, II. 65-8.
Franciscan monks [v. Friar]: a convent of —
was suffered of old to dwell at Damascus,
II. 172. [In the massacre, many of those
friars were slain and their monastery was
sacked.]
Frank [v. Frenjy]: a — molested at Petra,
218; the —s uxorious, ib.; —ish button,
437; —ish medical missionaries in Syria,
481; II. 426.
Frankincense [v. Incense]: — road, 135; 407;
old — country in Arabia the Happy, II. 196.
Frankish words and letters learned by some
Nejd Arabians at the trade ports, II. 386, 388.

Frankistàn [word not heard in Arabia], land of
the Franks, Europe.
Fransa, France, 168, 245; II. 398.
"French beans," II. 107.
French: — conquest of Algeria, 130, 168;
657; II. an Italian hajjy seen passing by
Hâyil speaks in the — language, 65;
Algerians disarmed by the —, 174; letter
in — from Sábry Pasha of Medina to the
Nasrâny at Kheybar, 221; a Bîshy who
had served sometime on board a — ship, 568.
Frenchmen in the work of the Suez Canal, II. 450.
Frenjy (pl. el-Afrenj), a Frank, 218, 252, 456,
458; II. 110; a — or Frank-like stranger
who visited Mecca, 189; — or outlandish,
308; — word, 450.
Friar: convent of Franciscan —s at Damascus,
II. 172; a — in Medina, 178.
Friday: — accounted an unlucky day, 510;
II. rest-day and religious week-day of the
Mohammedan religion, 160; — in 'Aneyza,
376; — markets in Kasîm oases-towns,
423; 440, 459, 484.
Friendship, II. 233.
Fringes and tassels, v. tassels.
Frogs: small yellow — in the springs of
Kheybar, II. 219; — of the Mecca country,
451, 565.
Fruits freely bestowed upon strangers, 570;
II. 171.
Fuára, a watering of B. 'Aly, Harb, II. 326.
Fuddân, a hide of land, II. 136.
Fuggar, II. 120.
Fueyhy, a fendy of Bíllî, 430.
Fuèylik, a plain between Semîra and el-Kasîm,
II. 329.
el-Fúggera (Fuḳara), 550.

Fúk er-rîg (or rîj فَكّ الرِّيق), loose the
(morning or fasting) spittle, (489), and II. 362.
el-Fúḳara or el-Fejîr (qd. v.): Ânnezy Aarab
of el-Héjr [v. B. Wáhab], their wandering
ground is between Bîr el-Ghrannem, el-Héjr,
Birket Mo'atham, Teyma and J. Birrd;
59, 104, 117; their border N., 119, 128, 135,
164; they of old expelled B. Sókhr, 167;
234, 241, 253, 262-3; — are Ahl Gibly;
their fendies and ancient name and kindred
and lineage, 270; their dîra, 271; their
number ib.; — women open-faced, 272;

clay-houses of — sheykhs, at Kheybar, 276; 292, 293; the — sheykhs, *ib.*; 287-8; the — are of the fanatical tribes, 294; speech of —, 307, 311; a difficult year for — 314, 315; *El-Kleyb, Sheykh Fendy*, a kindred of — in the N., *ib.*; — horsemen, 318; 323, 332, 340; — fugitives, 344; 362, 363, 371, 376, 378, 380, 382, 388; their cattle and possessions, *ib.* 389, 391; 393, 394, 395, 396, 399, 404, 406, 420, 421, 422, 427, 429, 430, 435, 445, 447, 449, 470, 475, 483, 500-1, 537, 545, 547, 548, 549-50; — called despitefully *el-Fúggera, ib.*; and 596, 600, 607, 608, 614, 615, 617, 641; II. 34, 92, 118, 141, 142, 197, 200.

el-Fúlsifa, philosophy, 195.

Fulûs (or *flûs, qd. v.*), 218, II. 43, 366.

Fumm es-seyf, 505.

Funeral customs, of the Beduw, 498.

Fúrja, fem. Bed. name, 514.

Furkân (الْفُرْقَان); *el-Koran el-*, 584.

el-Fúrn, B. 'Aly, a kindred of Harb Mosrûh, II. 335, 547.

Furrk' (*Farkâ*, probably from فرقع) *'ayn abûy!* [a Beduin saying, in anger; that can only be proffered by one who has lost his father], 312.

yâ Furrka! 312, 618.

el-Fushîla, Bed. fem. name, 514.

Fustân, the Albanian man's kilt or petticoat, II. 110.

Futîs, the thing that is dead of itself, 324.

Futûr, or breakfast, 578.

Future life: Bed. with difficulty imagine any, 282.

Fuzzna (فَزَّنَا, verb فوز), the word explained, 235.

G: where — is written in this work in Arabic words, the hard sound is intended, namely of ق in the Nejd and Arabian speech. G (hard) for ج is heard but seldom in Nejd Arabia. For the soft sound of G, (ج) *J* is here used.

Gá', (*gá'a* قاع), *v. Khóbra*; clay bottom where winter rain is ponded, II. 260, 338, 424.

Gaaja, a kindred of Anneyzy, 377.

el-Gá (*Ḥá'a*), an open place in 'Aneyza, II. 363, 403, 430, 445.

el-Gabîd, a fendy of midland Heteym, II. 253.

Gabbily, mountain in the great desert S. of el-Kaṣîm, II. 493.

el-Gâbily, to-morrow, 456; II. 330.

Gadyta, i.e. *J. es-Sh'eyb, qu v.*

Gahwa, v. Kahwa.

el-Gaila (الْقَائِلَة, some Bed., as the Moahîb, say *el-jaila*), the sun rising towards noon, 399, 442.

W. Gaila, in the 'Aueyrid, 463.

Gait [*v.* Carriage]; half-feminine — of the Bed. sheykhs, 549; II. 309.

Galilee: lake of —, 486.

Galileo: his invention of the telescope in Europe, II. 165.

Galla-land 'is a high and admirable region (beyond Christian Abyssinia). The — families dwell dispersedly in beehive-like cottages, whereabout they till as much land as may suffice them: they are rich in great-horned kine. Horses (there of great stature) abound among them. The lion is not uncommon: the giraffe is found in that country, but not the elephant. There are many tribes, with such diversity of speech betwixt them, that the far removed may not easily understand each other. The Galla people are raw meat-eaters, and drink a sort of ale, besides milk; they of their abundance are good and hospitable to strangers. Wild coffee trees great as oaks are seen in —. There is plenty of grain-gold in their wadies. The climate is very temperate. The Gallas go clothed only with a loin-cloth. There is a smiths' caste amongst them, which marry not with the people of the land. Money they use not, and have no need of foreign wares, save salt, that is not found in their soil).' [*Amân.*] 289; II. 185-8.

Galla: the — slaves are commonly called *Habûsh* (Abyssinians) in Arabia; 106, 242, 289, 586, 597, 603, 640, 646, 655; II. 18, 65, 97, 102; their tongue, *ib.*; — bond-women, *ib.*; 98, 107, 127, 134, 137, 144, 149, 151, 152, 154; — slave traffic, 187-9; — women taken to wife by the Sherîfs of Mecca, 190; 191; beautiful — women, 225; 236, 271, 281, 282, 340, 349; — mother of the Sherîf, 538.

OF ARABIC WORDS

Galliûn (*ḳalyûn*], tobacco pipe, 167 ; the Bed. —, 277, 288-9, 290 ; II. *a'orfy*, 200, 240.
Gallus ; Aelius —, II. 196-7, 387.
Game : great — are white-haired on the sand-plains, 372, 441, 612 ; and swarthy upon the black Harra, 441.
Gámel, hard Egyptian pron. for *jémel* (camel).
Gamerèyn, 61.
Games [*v*. *Bîât*, *Minḳala*, Pastimes] ; children play at horses, 384.
Ganna (قَنّ), *v*. *Dubbûs*, club-stick of the Arabs, 443, 583.
Gâra (قَارَة), the oasis soil [said by the Bed. pitched at Teyma], 597.
Gârat el-Ḥajâj or *el-Ḥajîa*, between Termidda and Shuggera, II. 452.
Gârat Owsheyfîa or *et-Teyry*, II. 564.
Garden : en-Nejumy's herb and fruit — ground at Kheybar, II. 129 ; the only — in Desert Arabia, 190, 537.
W. *Gârib*, a valley of the 'Aueyrid, 465, 478, 483, 485.
Garlic, II. 229.
Garments : change of — ; the princely custom of Ibn Rashîd to give —, 394, 554 ; II. 35, 50, 59, 70, 276.
Garra (perhaps قَرّة), *v*. *Mergab*, the watch-tower of Kasîm villages, II. 337.
Garr'a, *v*. (*Gassa*).
Garrôra (قَارُورَة), a phial, glass bottle for medicine, 300.
Gassa, misprint for *Garr'a* [perhaps the same as *Gerr'at el-Musalîkh*], Kasîm village in the principality of Boreyda, II. 337, 339.
Gathowra, a fendy of Bishr, 376.
Gatta fowl (*ḳáta*), II. 88, 240.
G'atûny, pl. *gey'atîn*, qd. v.
G'aud (قَعُود), young camel, 401, 586.
el-Gâyth (القيظ), midsummer, 261.
Gaza (Ar. *Ghrazza*), 214 ; Beduins of —, 274 ; a corn staple, 275, 323.
Gazelle, Ar. *ghrazál* pl. *ghrazlán* [*v*. *Thobby*] : the —, 89, 325, 372 ; the roe of the Scriptures, *ib*. ; 372, 426 ; — in the vulcanic country colour of basalt, 441 ; — fawns brought up by the Nomads, 477 ; 507 ; — dams said to have suckled a new-born babe, exposed, 563 ; 642, 644 ; — in captivity at Hâyil, 604, 665 ; II. 116 ; the *affery* and *iddimy*, 164 ; a — fawn of three days can outstrip any man running, *ib*. ; 239, 304 ; — fawns taken by the nomad greyhound, 304 ; live — fawns sold at 'Aneyza, 371 ; great horns of —, 497 ; a — buck, 500 ; acacia bushes in the khála trodden round by —, 507.
Gazette : Arabic —, II. 398, 425, 472.
G'dah, a fendy of Jeheyna, 166.
Gelding, an ass —, II. 301.
Gell'a, *v*. *Kellâ*.
Gems, 360.
Genealogies, 270 ; II. Tree of —, 57.
Genna, a mountain, II. 305-7, 311, 320.
Gennaṣ (قَنّاص), hunter of great game, II. 116.
Geography, [*v*. Map, Topography], 469 ; book of —, 591, 631 ; 657 ; II. 57.
Geology, *v*. Basalt, Granite, Gravel, Harra, Lava, Loam, Sandstone, Trap ; view of the — of Arabia, II. 575, *et seq*.
St. George, 116, 522.
Gerabis, Heteym of the Red Sea bord, II. 86. [A Noâmsy ghrazzu foraying by the Jeheyna dîra drove off a camel-herd of the — and returned with them. The women of their menzil, when they came home, went forth to meet them with dancing and singing : but their old sheykh Ibn Nômus, as he sat in his tent, hearing that the booty had been taken from the —, said, ' he thought it wellah no time to be merry, seeing that these were cattle reaved from some of their own kins-folk ; ' and he afterward sent to restore them. — *Ghroceyb*.]
Gerasa, now *Jerash*, 49.
el-Gerèyeh, ruined village near Kheybar, II. 117.
Gèreyih, ruined site near Tebûk, 110, 545.
el-Géria (the village), a ruined site in W. Thirba, 433, 487 ; II. 337.
Gériat Abu Robai, village ruins at Kheybar, II. 117.
Gerîsh, a jau near Teyma, 340.
German matches, 630 ; old — cannon at Hâyil, 658 ; II. — pack of cards, at Kheybar (from Medina), 193 ; 429.

INDEX AND GLOSSARY

Gerŷa, hamlets of tents, of Beduin husbandmen in the Harra, 463.
el-Gerŷen, village in el-Wéshm, ii. 452.
[*Gesérrah*, an end of J. Tueyk.
Gestures, Semitic sacramental —, 181, 311; examples of —, *ib*.
Gey'aṭin (فياطين), pl. of *G'aṭûny*, indigent Bed. squatters at Kheybar, ii. 119, 123, 133, 143, 151, 205, 228, 263.
Ghosts in W. Thirba, 496, 530.
Gh-r (غ); as for this Arabic letter the ordinary transliteration *gh* is surely insufficient. The Ar. letter is pronounced like the guttural rolling *r* in France [*grasseyer les R*] and in some parts of Germany: there is no difference, save that the Arab utterance is somewhat more vehement than the European. When however غ is the last letter in an Arabic word, the *r* is hardly heard. In the transcription of Arabic words I have resolved this (in our sense) compound letter into its roman equivalent *gh-r*, wherein there seems to be nothing more *incompositum* than in our (χρ) *ch-r*.
Ghradîr eṭ-Ṭeyr, near Kheybar, ii. 202.
Ghradîr Umm Ayásh, Hâj camping ground in the desert, 88.
Ghradràn (pl. of *ghradîr*), certain tarns near Kheybar so called, ii. 204.
Ghraibat es-Shems, the going down of the sun, 400.
Ghrallàb, camel's name, 321.
Ghramîḳ (غميق), in dialect for *'amîk*, ii. 317.
Ghrânim, a smith at Hâyil, 652-3, 660; ii. 23.
Ghrannem (*v. Dubbush*], small cattle, 59, 262, 304; — milked at sunset, 368; and only in good spring pastures in the morning as well, 304; 385; 474-5; ii. — more profitable (for the butter) than great cattle, 314.
Ghranèym, an 'Aneyza sheykh at Tâyif, ii. 552; — his wonderful encounter with Kahtân, 553.
el-Ghrárb, or West Country, 417, 420.
Ghrarîb, stranger, 479.
Ghrashîm, rude, uncunning.
Ghrassanite rulers, 52.
Ghráṭṭa (*ghraṭṭha*)! cover it from sight, 489.
Ghraymàr, a watering of Harb in Nejd, ii. 329.

Ghrazzài (غازٍ pl. غزّي), a warfaring, on an expedition, ii. 265, 272.
Ghrazzu (غزو), a foray, rode (It. razzia), 135, 172, 218, 230, 234, 235, 238, 290, 293, 301, 309, 318, 363, 378; a — taken by a —, 379, 380; Fukara camels robbed by a —, 389 *et seq.*; tribesmen's losses by —s made up by a common contribution (85), 390; —s are the destruction of the Aarab, 391; salvage of robbed cattle, 396; 413, 415; a great — seen passing in the Héjr plain, 537; weariness and peril in the —, 553; a great — in the field a brave spectacle, 379, 567; ii. 90, 139, 265; Ibn Rashîd's —s, 323, 455, 494; murderous — of Kahtân against Meteyr, 393; — of 'Aneyza and Meteyr against Kahtân, 474-81; conscription for the same in 'Aneyza, 474; — in el-Yémen, 568. [Nomads asking Nomad friends of a — of theirs use to add, 'Please Ullah, there was none hurt?']
el-Ghrenèym, a mountain in sight from Teyma, 328, 569, 576, 601, 617.
el-Ghrerb, little West Oasis of Teyma, 581-2.
Ghrerra (غُرّة), ruddle, shepherds' red clay or chalk, 162, 176.
Ghreyth, a fendy of Shammar, ii. 56.
Ghrobny, a divorced wife of Zeyd es-Sbeykan, 278.
Ghroceyb, an Heteymy sheykh, rafîk of the Nasrâny, to Kheybar, ii. 85-95, 247, 249, 250, 251, 306.
Ghrôg (prob. روق), a horse; Kasîm word, seldom used, ii. 419.
Ghrôl (or *ghrûl*, غول), the —, 92, 93, 131, 173.
el-Ghrôl, a watering in the great desert S. of el-Kasîm, ii. 493, 499.
Ghrólfa, a desert ground so named, ii. 296.
Ghrôr [*v. W. el-'Arabia*], the —, 64, 70, 83; the same word in the mouth of the Bed. used for a waste upland, 395.
Ghrormûl el-Mosúbba (or *Umsubba*), a camping ground, 348, 566.
Ghróṣb, perforce, 667.

OF ARABIC WORDS

Ghróṭtha (غَضَا), a tamarisk kind which grows in sand country, and is excellent firewood, 93; II. 346, 434, 445.

[*Ghroweysh* (غَوَاش, *noise, tumult*), once heard in the sense of children, at Hâyil.

el-Ghrullathî (غَلْثِي), great round and ribbed jointed cactus of the S. 'Ateyba desert, II. 507.

el-Ghrúnemy, v. Solubba.

Ghrunèym, a smith at Hâyil, brother of Ghrânim, 652-3.

Ghrúta of Damascus, II. 416.

Ghrurrub, a desert site N. of Teyma, 164.

Giants, 434; the vulgar opinion of — in the land in former ages derided by young litterates of 'Aneyza, II. 422.

Gibello [from the Ar. *jebel*]; mount Etna is thus called by the Sicilians, II. 370.

Gift: the Arabs little grateful for —s, but it be of food, 313; Ibn Rashîd's princely — [*v.* Change of garments, Bribes], 238, 249, 659; II. 67, 225, 276.

Gilead, 50; — described, 55; II. poor village families dwelling in the summer under oaks in —, 421.

Ginger cakes: a sort of — prepared in el-Kasîm for the caravans, II. 484.

Ginniyát, English sovereigns, II. 23, 67.

Giraffe, II. 116, 186.

Girby, water-skin of goat (the best) or else sheep skin, without seam. The — is laid upon green sprays in the nomad tent, 268; II. the Meteyr housewives suspend the — in a trivet of canes, 475.

Girdle of leathern thongs, worn by children and women in the S., II. 509.

el-Gírmella, ass-mare's name, II. 253.

el-Girṭ (القَرْط), a sharp rush at Kheybar, II. 109.

Girtha, Bed. fem. name, 514.

el-Girthîeh, ass-mare's name, II. 253.

Gitthera, Bed. fem. name, 514.

Glass: broken — is commonly seen in ruined sites of Arabia, though not now used in the country, 203, 602; [and *v.* Potsherds]: no glazed windows seen in Nejd, 640, 647, 652.

Gledes, *v.* Hawks.

Globe of clay, figure of the earth, made by the Nasrâny at Kheybar, II. 146.

Gluck! a Bed. cluck signif. astonishment in the discovery of aught that seems to be to their detriment, 321; II. — camel call, 85.

Gnats at 'Aneyza, II. 451; at a desert well, 498; 565.

"Gnat houses" in Sinai, 431.

Gô (جَوّ), a seyl bed, 346.

Gô, Kasîm, vulg. for *ḳoom*, II. 426.

Goâra (*Kauâra*], hamlet of 30 houses (Shammar) on the way from Boreyda to Jebel Shammar.

Goat: the wild —, *v. Bédan* and *W'aûl*.

Goat [*v.* Sacrifice, Hospitality]: the — will eat the colocynth gourd, 173; — herds of the nomads, 474-6; lost —s have become wild in the khála, 477; price of —s at Hâyil, 662; II. blood of a — sprinkled upon new building, 118; —s not seen mingled with sheep flocks of some Harb and Shammar in Nejd, *v.* 256; —s skip upon the chines of couching camels, 302.

Goayîeh, desert village S. of el-Wéshm, II. 492.

Gôba, watering in the 'Ateyba desert, II. 500.

Gôfar, village: قفار; and the Bed. say *Jiffàr.* 631, 633-5, 655, 661, 663, 668, 669, 672; II. 17, 34, 36, 50, 65, 76, 77, 271, 283, 284, 287, 319.

Gog and Magog, II. 558.

Golbân, pl. of *j(ḳ)ellîb*, II. 317, 480, 493, 495.

Gold: — traffic of the Timbuctû caravans from Morocco, 562; II. sand shining like scaly —, 62; grain- — in further Abyssinia, 187; pits "where they have taken out —," 502.

Gold and Frankincense traffic: of this there is no tradition in the country; — road, 135, 407. *v.* Incense.

Goldsmiths of 'Aneyza, II. 429.

Gôm (قَوْم), pl. of *g(ḳ)omâny, qd. v.*

Gomâny (قوماني), an enemy, adversary, 133, 364, 396, 513, 567; II. 300.

Goom! ḥubb 'amm-ak, II. 428.

Goom, ṣully 'ala dînak yâ Musslim! 579.

Goom! úṭlub rubbuk, 599.

Goom yâ sûl! 558.

Wâdy el-Gôras, at Kheybar, II. 202.

Gorèytha Ḥarra, near Medina, II. 204.

INDEX AND GLOSSARY

Gorh, v. *Korh*.
Gorma, Bed. fem. name, 514.
Goṛṣ, girdle-bread, II. 108.
Gòrta (Turk. قورت for قورد. wolf, hyena), a kind of wild cat, II. 164.
Gòṭar (قَوْطَر), went, Bed., 196, 299.
Goṭṭha, a Mahûby lass, 548.
GOUKH, an Aramaic word found in the Héjr inscriptions, 674.
Gourds at Teyma, 593.
Gowwak (قَوَّك for قَوَّاكَ اللهُ), the Lord strengthen thee [the answer is *Ḥullah!* or *Ullah gowîk!*], 197, 376, 399, 567.
Gowak yâ Mohâfuth! etc., II. 574.
Gowwich, v. *Gowwak*.
Graaf, ruins of a town in Mount Seir, 82.
Grace, Arabian, 333.
Gránada, in Spain, II. 426.
Granite, *Ḥajr el-krà*, 451; Beduins work mill-stones of —, *ib.*; 462, 470, 626, 628, 629, 632, 635; II. 78; — mill-stones, made by Beduins, 200; 255, 266, 267, 287, 305, 313, 321, 490, 491, 493, 494, 495, 501, 508, 535, 545, 550, 563.
Grapes: sold at Kaṣîm, 338; white — at 'Aneyza, ripening in the end of June, II. 482.
Grashimîn, rude, ignorant, II. 207.
Grass [v. *Nuṣṣy*]; knot- —, forage for Hâj caravan camels, 135, 218; v. *Thurrm*; a wild barley —, II. 263.
Graûty, a fendy of Bíllî, 430.
Grave [v. Burial of the dead] : —s of pilgrims by the way side, 106, 117; religion of the Semitic —, 282, 496; —s of children in the khála, 349; —s in the Arabian wilderness, 434; — of the Auellîn, 441; 450; a lone Bed. —, 563; superstition of the — in Syria, 671; II. —s of those who perished in a plague at Kheybar, 117; a soldier's —, 144; Kheybar the — of the soldiery, 145; —s of the Auellîn, 239.
Grave-yard, v. *Máḵbara*.
Gravel, of Mount Seir, 67; — between Medowwara and *Thàt Hâj*, 97; beds of minute quartz grains, from the sandstone, 120, 121.
Graya, a fendy of Bíllî, 430.

Greece: custom of the elder generation of Greek women to cover the neck, 510; lang. of —, II. 57, 541.
(Greek) light-house people, v. 523; II. — workmen of the Suez Canal, 450.
Greenness of herbs in the desert, 97.
Greyhounds : Bed., 173, 371, 372; — take the fox, the gazelle fawn and the hare, 372, 382, 566; II. 304.
Greyth, a Teyma villager, 580.
Grûn, a fendy of Jeheyna, 166.
Guâd, an affinity of Kheybar villagers, II. 153.
(2) *el-Guâd*, a fendy of Ḥarb B. Sâlem, II. 546.
Guádalquiver (Rio), *i.e.* Ar. *Wâd' el-Kebîr*, II. 556.
Gubba, Nefûd village near Hâyil, II. 58.
Guest, v. sub Hospitality.
Guestship [v. Hospitality] : — in the desert, 269, 276, 552; — in Hâyil, 661; — in the border towns and oases, 269; Zeyd's tale of — in the towns, *ib.*; II. 112.
el-Gueyîn, a fendy of Bíllî, 430.
Gueyría, ruinous conduit and cistern by the old way between M'aan and Aḳaba Ayla, 85.
Gulf: v. Persian —.
Gum arabic distilled from the boughs of a kind of the desert acacia (*tolh qd. v.*), 411, 425.
Gum-mastica, a sort of — which flows from a wild tree (*el-'aràr* عَرْعَر), in J. Ajja, II. 24.
Gûm! hŷakom Ullah wa en Nêby, eflah! (قُمْ حَيَّاكُم اللّٰهُ والنبيّ افلا), II. 258.
W. *Gumm'ra*, II. 90.
Gunners' shroud : by a desert water, 544; — at Teyma, 583.
Gunpowder, v. Gunsalt : [Hall's Dartford — seen at Hâyil], II. 23; 35, 37, 165; the stems of *el-'esha* burned for —, 516.
Guns, v. Matchlocks.
"Gunsalt" (saltpetre) which is boiled out of saturated earth by the Arabs, 137, 160, 410; II. 492.
J. *Gurs*, II. 239.
el-Gúsh (القَشّ, القِشّ), the Bed. household gear and baggage, 267.
el-Gúsh (القَشّ), the wild bushes, 609.
el-Gush'a (قَشْعَة), a parasite plant in the Teháma of Mecca, II. 566.

el-Gussa, hamlet of J. Shammar, ii. 34, 265, 266, 292.

Gussha (القشّة), pasture bushes, 303.

Gutîa (probably قطعيّة), coffee-cup box, 286.

Guwah, a tower in the wilderness of Ammon, also called *Kaṣr es-Shebîb* or *Bezîr*, 51.
Guwiyîn, pl. of *ḳûwy*, strong.
Gypsum [*v. Jiṣṣ*], fretwork pargetting in el-Kaṣîm, ii. 346.

Ḥ is put for the Ar. letter ح, a sort of long-drawn *h* or $\overset{h}{h}$ (which we hear in sighing, and in the coughing of men and beasts).

Habalîs, pl. of *hablûs, qd. v.*

Ḥabâra (حُبَارَى), a bird, probably a kind of bustard, ii. 238.

e.-Ḥábash, Abyssinia [*v.* Galla-land], 289; ii. Galla fable of an Abyssinian empire, 185; 225.
Hábashy, a Galla bondsman.
Hábashy, Abyssinian language, 203.
Habîb, beloved.
Habîb Ullah, 88. *v.* Mohammed.
yâ Habîby, O my beloved one! 282.
Hablûs, pl. *habalîs* [a word heard only in the Teyma and Héjr country], rover on foot, landlober, a murderous thief in the desert [such I have heard called *henshûly*, in Middle Nejd], 179, 220, 322, 364, 393, 398, 399, 404 — Can this be a Beduin form of *Iblîs* or διάβολος?
Habûsh, pl. of *Hábashy*, Gallas.
Hâchim, v. ḥákim.
Hadâd, a mountain coast, said to be so named, in the Teháma, 463.

Ḥadâj (حِدْج, حِدَاجَة), camel pack saddle, 258.
el-Hadda, village in the south country, ii. 52.
Hadda, last village in W. Fâṭima, ii. 571.
el-Haddâj, the well-pit of Teyma: 329, 330; — described, 335; wherefore thus called, 336, 377; fall of the — steyning, and the Nasrâny accused thereof, 378; — rebuilt and falls again, 574-5; 577; 579; 582-3, 593-5; ancient stonework of —, 594; project to rebuild —, 595; 600, 602, 608.
el-Háddefa, Beduin fem. name, 514.
Jelîb ibn Haddîf, ii. 499.

el-Ḥadduj (الحَدَج), the colocynth gourd, ii. 561.
Haderûn, (we are) ready! 46.
el-Hadèyd, an affinity of Kheybar villagers, ii. 153.
Hadû, herding song, 306.
el-Hadûd, the bounds of Mecca, ii. 488, 519.

Hadùj (هدوج), dromedary, ii. 23, 562.

Hâdy, a *Tuàly* Beduin, 540.
Hâdy, a Kheybar villager, ii. 96.

Hadŷd (حديد), bracelet of the forearm, 336.

Ḥâf (حَافّ), said of food to be eaten unseasoned, *i.e.* without sámn), ii. 230, 263.
el-Hâfera, a dog's name, 474.
Hâfirat Zeylûl, a hamlet in J. Shammar, ii. 267.
el-Hafr, site in the W. er-Rummah, between Hâyil and Kuweyt, ii. 61.
Hág eth-thúbʿa, '(the stranger is) due to the hyena,' 518.
Hág Ullah! ii. 107.

Haggu (حَقّ), [*v. Hágub, Brîm*]; 384, 421; 561; — worn even by the Princes at Hâyil, 648. [It is not worn at el-Ally.] ii. — worn by women only in ʿAneyza, 375 (yet it is commonly worn in el-Kaṣîm); 509.

Hágub (حقاب), ii. 375. [*v.* Haggu.

el-Hahlih, ruined vill. site in Moab, 61.
Hail, strength.
Hair [*v.* "Horn"]: — which they let grow to the natural length; nomad men and women comb out their —, every few days, in camel urine, 279; Beduin maidens in the circumcision festivals have their — loosed, and combed down upon their shoulders, 385; 516.
Hâj: a magical appearance as of the —, ii. 209.
el-Hâj, a kellâ, 97, 98.

616 INDEX AND GLOSSARY

Ḥâj : Egyptian — way and caravan in Arabia, 84 ; II. 174, 197, 202, 514.
Ḥâj el-Kaṣîm, II. 383, 447, 449.
Ḥâj : the *Moghréby* — will pay no toll to the Beduw in Arabia, II. 173-5.
Ḥâj : Persian —, *v.* Persian pilgrimage.
Ḥâj (*es-Shem*), the great Syrian convoy of pilgrims to Mecca [*v. Takht er-Rûm, Emir el*- —, *Muḥâfiz el*- —, *Kasra el*- —, *Pasha el*- —, *Derb el*- —]. Their number (in 1876), 45 ; — camp fires, *ib.*; — camp at night, 46 ; night march lighted by links, 46 ; by paper lanterns, 112 ; the — treasurers at Damascus are Christians, 48 ; yearly cost of the —, *ib.*; the *surra, ib.*; the guard of soldiery, 49, 128 ; the caravan *hour* may be reckoned 2½ miles, 54 ; the — camp levied, 57 ; sellers of coffee, victual, and sweetmeats by the wayside, 58, 126 ; — attacked by Beduw, 94 ; — march by landmarks, 95 ; *dalîl el*- —, 96 ; reported skeletons of camels strewed by the roadside, 96 ; — the most considerable caravan of the East, 96 ; — camels faint by the way, *ib.*; day and night marches, 89, 96 ; signal rockets, 96 ; resting-whiles, *ib.*; women and children in the —, 99 ; they might as well ride in wagons, 100 ; *Mahmal* camel, 101 ; motley army of the —, 101 ; serving men in the —, 97 ; their salary, 101, 102 ; the — is now much diminished from its former glory, 97 ; diet of the Syrian drivers, 101 ; — camels, 105 ; sick Persians riding in the —, 106 ; Syrian proverb against the —, 107 ; old hajjies commonly less fanatic, 107 ; *Muḥâfiz el*- —, 109 ; *Kasra el*- —, *ib.*; dogs in the —, 109 ; a cock in the —, 110 ; supper fires, *ib.*; cured flesh and fresh mutton used in the —, 110 ; the *sûk*, 111 ; — biscuit, 111 ; villages which stood once by the — way, 112 ; — treasury, 113 ; a Nasrâny in the —, 123 ; tale of a Christian akkâm in the —, 124 ; miseries of the —, 138 ; fable of the Jews of Kheybar, cutters of the —, 170 ; return of the — to Medáin Sâlih, 246 ; departure from Medáin Sâlih, 249 ; the returning — much diminished, *ib.*; the — menzil, 251, 252 ; prices of victual in the — market, 252 ; B. Sókhr carriers in the —, 54, 253 ; 411, 418, 435 ; II. 65-8, 173, 183, 197, 201, 218, 224, 226, 495, 514.
Ḥajellán, sheykh of a small nomad tribe of *Shobek* in Edom, 66.
Ḥajellán palace at Boreyda, II. 346-7.

el-Hajîa or *Gârat el-Hajâj*, between Shuggera and Thermidda, II. 583.
Hajîn, dromedary, II. 23.
B. Hajir, a tribe of Southern Aarab, II. 381.
Ḥajjâj, pl. of Ḥâj.
Ḥájjar, district in East Arabia, II. 276.
Hajjilân, a dog's name, 474.
Ḥajjir, a considerable palm oasis of Meteyr, between el-Fer'a and Mecca, II. 393.
Ahl Ḥájjur, a fendy of Harb Mosrûḥ, II. 547.
el-Ḥajnowwy [perhaps Ḥaknowwy], outlying granges of er-Russ, II. 489.
Hajŷa, Aarab-el, 66.
Ḥâkim, one who executes justice, a Ruler, 596 ; II. 28, 495.
Ḥakîm, (a wise man), a professor of medicine, leech : 53, 118, 252, 299, 480 ; II. a Móghreby — at Hâyil, 16, 17, 18 ; the profession of healing procures favour and entrance among them, *ib.*; Persian — at Hâyil, 18, 33, 70 ; a leech at 'Aneyza, 402 [*v. Mudowwy, Ustâd, Vaccinnator.*]
el-Ḥakîm [hu] Ullah, 299.
J. Hakràn, between el-Kasîm and Mecca, II. 504, 505.

Hâ'l hazza (ها الْحَزَّة), II. 268.

[Hâ'l hôf (ها الْحَوْف), on this wise, common locution of the Moahîb children.
Ḥalâl, that which it is lawful to do, 269, 298 ; our lawful own (of cattle), 389, 392 ; II. 302.
Haleyfa, hamlet of J. Shammar, II. 34.
Haléyma, a Fejîr tribesman dwelling with the Moahîb, 537.
el-Hálhal, part of the bed of W. Jellâs near Kheybar, II. 161, 204-5, 216.
Ḥalîb, milk, 198, 261.
Halif yemîn, 309.
W. Halîfa, in dialect or mistake for W. Hanîfa.
Hall, Dartford, *v.* Gunpowder.
Halla [Bíshr *loghra, id. qd. Hilla*], a cinder-hill on the Harra, II. 247.

Hallat 'Ammár (حَلَّة عَمَار) : fable of —, 97.

Halleyfát, a fendy of 'Ateyba, II. 457.

Hállughra (read haluka, حَلْقَة), nose-rings of village women. [*v. Zmèyem.*]
Haltîta, gum asafœtida, 297.
Ḥam, son of Noah, 580 ; II. 191.

Ḥamâṭa (حَمَاطَة), pl. ḥamâṭ, a kind of wild fig tree, 488, 498; ii. — at et-Tâyif is said for the orchard fig tree, 560.
Ḥamd, praise.
el-Ḥamda, a tribe of Beny Sâlem, Harb, ii. 546.
Ḥamda, a woman's name (id. qd. Ḥamdy), ii. 242.
Ḥamdân, a Kheybar villager, ii. 199.
Ḥamdân, a kindred of the Fuḳara tribe, 270.
El-ḥamdu lillahî, Rub el-alamîn, 111.
Ḥamdy, wife of Abu Sinûn, 449, 470, 473, 475, 507, 513, 518, 519, 530-1, 534, 540, 542.
Ḥámed, (حمد). Note: this is the vulg. Nejd. pronunciation of the name Aḥmed; v. Vol. ii. 24.
Ḥámed [v. Aḥmed] a prophet that was to come, [i.e. Mohammed] feigned by the Moslem doctors to be foretold in the Evangelists, ii. 24.
Ḥámed, the thób so called, 371.
Ḥámed, a young Kheybar villager, ii. 236-42.
Ḥámed en-Nefîs, son of a late treasurer at er-Riâth, ii. 425.
Ḥámed, a negro Bîshy soldier, who had served sometime with the stokers on board a French steamship, ii. 549, 560, 568.
Ḥámed es-Sâfy, a foreign merchant of 'Aneyza, trading in Bagdad, ii. 383, 385-6, 397, 410, 412, 417, 422, 427, 446, 447, 486.
Ḥámed, a Shammary rafîk, dwelling with Harb, ii. 321-41.
Ḥámed, son of Tollog the Moahîb sheykh, 498, 513-16, 523, 532, 540, 544, 545, 548, 551, 554, 611.
Ḥámed el-Yahya es-Sâliḥ, a young patrician of 'Aneyza, ii. 410, 427, 484.
B. Ḥameydy, a Beduin tribe in Moab renowned for their good horses, 64-5; ii. 66.
Ḥameydy, father of Moṭlog sheykh el-Fejîr, 293.
el-Ḥameydy, a kind of tobacco, 394, 642; ii. 34, 282, 288, 297, 319.
Ḥamîn (حمين), hot season between March and April at Kheybar, ii. 128.
[el-Ḥammâda (الحمّادة), desert between el-Wéshm and the Tueyk mountains.
Ḥammâm, bath.
Ḥámmàm es-Shízm, a pool of Stygian water, 435.
Hamman (Syrian), the purse, 279.

el-Hammam, village in W. Dauâsir, ii. 425.
Hammam, ruins at M'aan, 71, 214.
Hammazàn, a fendy of Shammar, ii. 56.
Hammering of stones by the Bed. into pipe-heads and mill-stones, 238, 288, 451; for bullet-casting, 538; ii. 200.
Hámmr, village in the S. country, ii. 52.
Ḥamô! or better Ḥamû! is shouted for Hámed to a person afar off, ii. 237.
el-Ḥamra, Harb village, ii. 546.
el-Ḥamthal, or perhaps hanṭhal, الحنظل [v. Shérry, el-Ḥáduj], the colocynth gourd, qd. v.
Ḥamûd ibn Rashîd, cousin of the Prince: 642, 647-51, 652; his diet, ib., 649; his popular carriage, 651; 655, 656, 657; — a kaṣṣâd, 650, 657; 664, 665; ii. 17, 18; a wife of his, 18; 24-32, 36, 41-5, 51, 56, 58, 61-3, 68-75, 265, 276, 280, 377, 390; his brethren, 42-5; his daughter, 45.
Ḥamzy, uncle of Mohammed, ii. 145; Jebel H. [v. 'Ehad], ib.
Ḥánash (حنش), a snake, ii. 78.
Hand: the — given as a pledge of one's troth, 309; —s wiped after eating, in the desert, 551; ii. pain of cutting off the thief's —, 344, 395.
Hand-cart: a — at 'Aneyza, ii. 379.
Hand-clapping, 333, 387.
Handicraftsmen in 'Aneyza, ii. 429.
Hanging-stone: fable of the —, 493.
Hâni (هني), health! 446.
B. Hanîfa, from whom the family of Ibn S'aûd, 270.
W. Hanîfa, 245, 270, 434; ii. 424.
Hánnas ibn Nômus, sheykh of the Noâmsy, Heteym, 614, 618; ii. 80, 81.
el-Ḥáram, the forbidden (Temple qd. v.). There are three Hárams of the Catholic Mohammedans where entrance is forbidden unto unbelievers; these are the temples of Mecca, Medina, and Jerusalem. ii. — of Medina, 148, 180, 214.
el-Ḥarameyn, dual of háram above, 41, 43, 102, 124, et passim; ii. 32, 155, 173, 174, 307, 567.
Ḥarámy, pl. haramîyeh, law-breaker, thief: punishment of a caravan —, 52; 355; ii. 342.

618 INDEX AND GLOSSARY

Ḥarâr (حِرَار), a pl. of Ḥarra, vulcanic country, ii. 204.

Ḥârat, a town quarter or ward, 331.

el-Ḥarb [not *Beny Ḥarb*, which is an 'Annezyism], a great Beduin nation between the Harameyn and in Nejd: [Tusun Bey brother of] Ibrahim Pasha defeated by —, 49; 133; Saadîn, a fendy of —, 166; a fable of the —, 169-70; 182; their speech, 186; 276, 541, 543; a — woman caroling in the date harvest at Teyma, 608; 625; ii. 34, 35, 38, 80, 103; — speech of the Medina dîra, 107; 132, 155, 163, 169, 173, 174; — of the *Ferrâ*, 194; *Hâzim* a fendy of —, *ib.*; 202; — villagers of Yanb'a, *ib.*, 228; 257, 285; aspect of — tents, 295; 298, 299, 303, 306, 308, 309, 310; speech of the Medina —, 315; horsemen of —, *ib.*; 317, 319, 320-22; their dîrat in Nejd is bounded by the W. er-Rummah, 321; booths of —, 322; 324, 327-9, 332, 333, 357, 456, 491, 492, 510, 545; the divisions, fendies and villages of —, 546-7.

Harb el-awwel, at 'Aneyza, ii. 459.

Harb eth-thâny, at 'Aneyza, ii. 459.

Hare of the desert, 110; 349, 371; —s perish in a murrain, 476; —s taken by falconry, 618, 642; ii. 260, 500.

Ḥareem pl. *ḥorma*, a woman [*v.* Woman, Wife]: in the Haj, 121; their — are like flowers in our houses, that one day will be cast out: — in the ráhla, 258; little or no jealousy of their —, among Nomads, 272; the woman's lot, 277-9; — more than the men in number, 278; a strange custom of Arabic —, a help to fecundity, 279; they paint the eyes with antimony, *ib.*; — praying, 279, 558; *el-entha*, the female sex in the Semitic opinion, 279, 280; Nomad women have a liberty, 280, 281, 367; — child-bearing, 281, 467, 468; female births buried living, 281; female children unprofitable in the nomad household, 130, 281; their skill in simples, 297, 350, 485; witchcraft of the —, 350; clothing of Teyma —, 336-7; tobacco-sick —, 356; — infirmer in the sentiment of honour, 383; brown-haired —, 435; feminine talk, 456; Moahîb younger — cover the throat and lower jaw in presence of a stranger, 510; names of —, 514; Bed. — have not long hair, 516; "for the — anything is good enough," 583; religious — with child or nursing fast in Ramaṭhán, 586; the — sing not, 607; the Mohammedan Arabians are become as churls towards their —, 634; the woman's face is blotted out in Nejd, 619, 634; ii. wimpled —, 65; 302; — in 'Aneyza, 376, 471; maleficent drinks said to be given by the —, 412; — at et-Tâyif, 537-8, 551.

el-Hareỳry or Harrîry, the little Harra, below el-Ally, 134, 457, 463, 465, 468.

el-Hareỳry, a fendy of Bíllî, 430.

Ḥari(k)ch, in East Nejd, ii. 455.

[el-Harik, vill. of an "hundred and fifty" houses between ed-Dellam and el-Aflaj.

Ḥarr, hot, 338.

Ḥarrâm [*ḥarâm*], that which is not lawful to do (for them that fear God), 269, 298, 367; ii. 301, 302. *v.* Halàl.

Ḥarra(t) (حَرَّة), lava field, vulcanic country.

the Ḥarras [pl. Ḥarâr or Aḥrâr, (أَحْرَار)] of Arabia, 465, 668; ii. 85, 204; the Southern —, 378; they are disposed like a band, 566, 575.

Harrat 'Aashîry, ii. 378, 508, 566.

Harrat Aba Rasheyd, ii. 204.

Harrat B. Abdillah, ii. 204, 378.

Harrat el-Abiath, *v.* Harrat el-Abyaḍ.

Harrat el-Abyaḍ, ii. 90, 237 [*v. J. el-Abiâth.*]

Harrat 'Ajeyfa, ii. 378, 566.

Harrat Beny 'Ammr [*v.* Map].

Harrat el-Anábis, ii. 204.

Harrat el-'Aueyriḍ [and *v.* 'Aueyriḍ], between Tebûk and el-Ally: 115; 117, 118, 121, 123, 180, 199, 209, 213, 233, 238, 241; winter snow sometimes seen upon the —, 243; 323, 336, 372, 396, 402, 405, 420, 423, 425-30, 438, 440, 441, 443, 445, 448; aspect of the —, 115, 121, 180, 238, 402, 423, 440, 451-453, 459, 462-68, 471; Nomad menzils upon the —, 429, 431, 435, 440, 443, 450, 452, 455; waterings upon the —, 427, 453, 471, 479; difficult passage upon the —, 451, 455; 456, 457, 462-5, 468, 470, 472, 473, 476, 477, 478, 483, 486, 487, 488, 490, 495, 502, 509, 510, 515, 519, 523, 524, 525, 529, 536, 537, 541, 543, 547, 548, 557, 594, 610, 641; ii. 38, 70, 87, 120, 200.

Harrat el-Auwâli, ii. 204.

Harrat Batn el-Ghról, 90.

Harrat el-Ethnân, ii. 89. [Some waterings in the — are *Shújwa, Nebuàn, B'aija.*]

Ḥarrat el-Ḥamra, near the W. Dauâsir ("two thelûl journeys long"), ii. 575.
Ḥarrat Jehèyna, ii. 378.
Ḥarrat el-Kesshub [v. *Harrat el-Kisshub*], ii. 67, 204.
Ḥarrat Kheybar [I have heard this *Harra* called also *el-Ḥàzm*]: 243, 444, 457, 468, 618; ii. 42, 45, 70, 84, 85, 86, 87; the Arabs of the country have no tradition of burning mountains and flowing of lavas, 88; limits of the —, 89, 90, 92; 109, 110; stones of the —, 116; 119, 120, 138-44, 161, 164, 181, 192; the — toward Medina, 201, 205, 216, 217, 223, 229, 234, 237; depth of the lava border, 239, 301, 506; cattle paths in —, 238; wilderness of lavas and in part of lava stones, *ib.*; altitude, *ib.*, 239; border of the —, *ib.*, 245; appearance of steam seen in the —, 247; aspect of the —, *ib.*; crater-hills, *ib.*, 249; east border of —, 250, 254, 255; — 420. [The great vulcanic eruption which was seen from Medina A.D. 1256 is recorded in *Samhûdi's History of Medina*, p. 40 *sqq.* of the Arab. text.]
Ḥarrat el-Khúthery, 462, 464.
Ḥarrat el-Kisshub [Nâsir es-Smîry wrote كشب and pronounced *Kisshub*: others say *Kesshub*, *Kesshab*, or *Kusshub*], ii. 204, 378, 393, 456, 502, 506, 508, 565.
Ḥarrat el-Kusshub, v. *Ḥ. el-Kisshub*.
Ḥarrat el-Medina, ii. 204, 508.
Ḥarrat en-Nukheyl, south of Medina [v. Map] — N. es-Smîry.
Ḥarrat Rodwa, ii. 378.
[*Ḥarrat er-Rûka* : — is N.W. of J. Biss, says Nâsir es-Smîry.
Ḥarrat es-Sauda, in Jebel Tueyk, ("half a day long and wide"), ii. 575.
Ḥarrat es-Sŷdenyîn, 464.
Ḥarrat Terr'a, v. *Ḥ. Ṭurr'a*.
Ḥarrat Ṭurr'a, ii. 378, 502.
Harûn (Aaron): the name —, 73. *Jebel Saidna*, 75; —, v. Mount Hor, 80.
Harûn : 'Ayn —, 80.
Harvest: barley — was at el-Ally in the last week of March, and wheat — in the first week of April. The — is ready at Teyma early in April. At Kheybar (and Medina) the wheat — is reaped in the first week of April. The — in J. Shammar is about three weeks later. Barley — in el-Kasîm is at the end of April, and wheat is reaped a few days later. Millet (*thúra*) sown upon the same plots is reaped in the autumn.
el-Ḥáṣa, the stone (malady), 616.
el-Ḥása, a province of East Arabia, now under the Turks, 444; ii. 275; a stitcher of cotton quilts from — settled at Hâyil, 283; 367, 381, 454, 460.
Ḥásan, son of 'Aly and Fátima, grandson of Mohammed, ii. 556.
Ḥâj Ḥásan, garrison soldier at Medáin Sâlih, 128, 129, 168, 172, 178-9, 180, 184, 185, 206, 219, 220, 241, 403, 404, 409, 410, 414, 417, 418, *et seq.*, 485.
Hásan, a cameleer of 'Aneyza, ii. 434-7, 442-7.
Hásan, a cameleer of Boreyda, ii. 355, 357-9, 361.
Hásan wéled Maḥanna, Emir of Boreyda, ii. 37, 39, 339, 343, 345, 347, 348, 352, 353, 392, 438.
Hásan ibn Salâmy, a young Teyma sheykh, 573-575, 594.
Hásan, overseer of the Sherîf's cattle, ii. 560-2.
Haseyn, son of Amm Mohammed, ii. 136, 159-163, 205-7, 212, 229.
Hashîah (حشية), a skin of dates (Medina), ii. 132.
Hâshy (حاشية), a dromedary, ii. 23.
el-Ḥassanîeh, village of B. Sâlem, Harb, ii. 546.
Beny Ḥassèyn, a fendy of Harb Mosrûḥ, they are all Ashrâf, ii. 547.
Ḥasseyn (*Ḥasèyn*), son of 'Aly and Fátima, grandson of Moh. (and brother of Ḥásan), ii. 556.
Ḥasseyn, Pasha, Sherîf Emir of Mecca, ii. 520, 525, 531, 532, 538, 542-60.
el Ḥassîd, ruins of a dam in a Wady of that name near Kheybar, ii. 201.
Wady el-Ḥassîd near Kheybar, ii. 201.
el-Ḥâsy, Wady, 59, 65. Kellât —, 66.
Hât-hât-hât, ii. 151.
Hátab 'lil nár, 'Fuel for hell-fire,' 518.
Hàtha, station on the E. Hâj road, ii. 565.
Haṭhariyát, women of the settlements, ii. 39.
Haṭheyl (هذيل gentile pl. *Heṭheylàn*), an ancient tribe in the Mecca country, ii. 512, 515, 517, 519, 521; discourse of an old —y at the 'Aŷn, 525; 527, 528, 565, 569, 570.
Hâthi, Meteyr village on the Derb es-Sherky, ii. 393.

620 INDEX AND GLOSSARY

Ḥáthir (ḥáthr), settled folk (v. Ahl Ṭín), 317.

Ḥáthíra (حَظِيرَة), or haṭhàr; sheep-pen of lopped boughs, ii. 243.

J. Hatthon, N. of et-Ṭâyif, ii. 507.

Haurán, a vulcanic country in Syria beyond Jordan: *it is such as the Ḥarras of Arabia and may be reckoned unto them.* Ruins in the —, 44, 51; villagers of Ma'an remove to the —, 73; —, the land of bread to the Southern Beduins, 314, 319; 395, 643, 653, 674; ii. 64, 338, 575.

Ḥauṭa (حَوْطَة), an orchard ground (at Teyma), 581, 585, 602, 603, 608, 617.

Ḥauṭa, a considerable town of B. Temîm in middle Nejd, ii. 425.

[el-Ḥauṭa (Beny Temîm) town of "five hundred" houses, in the district el-Fer'a between el-'Arùth and el-Aflâj.

Ḥáwas, (probably حَوَاس senses), good natural wit, ii. 156.

Ḥawḍ, camel-trough of leather at the watering, 506.

Hawks, v. Falcon, 349, 374, 408, 656.

Ḥawwa (Mother Eve), 341; ii. her "grave" at Jidda, 574.

Ḥawwáma, (حَوَامَة), shawms made of a green grass stalk, and blown by Beduin herdsmen and children in the spring time, ii. 137.

Hay: wild —, bartered at el-Ally, 554; 626; sold in Hâyil, 637; ii. 21; — sold at 'Ayn ez-Zeyma, 525.

Hayapa, tribe of ancient Arabia so named in the Assyrian inscriptions, 229.

el-Ḥâyaṭ (الحَايَط) a negro village of Ibn Rashíd in the Harrat Kheybar nigh the heads of the W. er-Rummah: there is a strong welling but brackish spring, ii. 34, 42, 44, 70, 81, 89, 93, 118, 158, 166, 195, 205, 223, 229. The hospitable villagers and sheykh of —, 232; poor nomad women (Jeheyna and Heteym) married to negro villagers of —, *ib.*; 235, 237, 247, 251, 252, 301-2; Ánnezy Aarab formerly Beduin landlords at — and Howèyaṭ, *ib.*

Ḥayâtak, ii. 27.

Ḥayer, Sbeya village in el-'Arùth, ii. 381.

Hàyer, said to be an old name of Ḥáyil, 669.

Hayfa, name of a Bíllî woman.

Ḥáyil (حَائِل), village capital of Jebel Shammar and seat of Ibn Rashíd's government, in West Nejd. [Bar. alt., mean of 15 observ., 663 *mm*.] 22 Oct.–20 Nov., 1877; 1 and 2 April, 1878. 223, 241, 243, 249, 254, 271, 296, 312, 325, 327, 330, 333, 338, 340, 347, 372, 375, 385, 393, 394, 434, 464, 527, 541, 547, 554, 577, 580-1, 594, 595-6; exorcists at —, 598; 603, 606, 608, 611, 613, 618, 621, 625, 626, 627, 630, 631-7; — sûk, 636; Prince's quarters, 638; — town rather than oasis, 667; description of —, 667; foundation of —, 669; — was named Hàyer, *ib.*; — before Ibn Rashíd's rule, *ib.*; population, *ib.*; ii. town administration, 20; artificers at —, 20; women's industry at —, *ib.*; ancient —, *v. S'weyfly*; 15-48; 49-76; 83, 85, 93, 99, 105, 132, 183, 195, 222-4, 232, 235, 237, 243, 250-2, 258, 265, 267-83, 284; slender Shammar inhabitants of —, 285; 289, 293, 298, 299, 309, 310, 314, 320, 321, 334, 335, 342, 348, 352, 367, 375, 377, 378, 390, 393, 395, 438, 491, 495, 524, 543.

Ḥayzàn, an Auájy tribesman, 617-8, 621.

Ḥayzàn, a fendy of midland Heteym, *v.* Ḥeyzan.

Ḥayzàn, sheykh of the intruded Kahtan in el-Kasîm, ii. 51-5, 335, 393; his end, 479-80; his sister is slain and his brother, *ib.*

Ḥázam (حَزَام), gunner's belt, ii. 96, 245.

Hazardry unknown in the Waháby countries, ii. 429.

Hàzim, a fendy of Harb, but reviled as Solubba or Heteym, ii. 195, 319.

Hazkiyal, Ezekiel the prophet, ii. 59.

Ḥázm (حَزْم), a kind of monticule in the desert, the — "is black with some herbage," 668; ["—, says Ibn Ayith, is of rough soil whereon there are stones."]

el-Ḥázzam, part of the desert land so called between el-Kasîm and Mecca, ii. 500.

Ḥazzel, a watering place in the Ruwàlla dîra, ii. 269, 428.

Hazzeym es-Seyd, a grove of acacias with cattle pits between Kasîm and Mecca, ii. 504.

Headaches esteemed a sign of death, 318.

Head, Mr. Barclay: his note of the money of ancient Arabia, 229.

OF ARABIC WORDS 621

Heads of their slain enemies cut off by the Turks, II. 143.
Head-stalls of dromedaries made by the Beduin housewives, 518.
Heaps of stones, whether to mark a way, or graves, or places of cursing, 65, 121, 403, 478; "— in the furrows of the fields" in Moab, 62; — in Edom, 86; — which are beacons [v. Mantar], 117, 668; II. 509, 562; great bank of stones, which pilgrims have cast up by the Jidda-to-Mecca way side, 573.
Heat, v. Summer.
J. el-Hébeshy, a considerable basalt mountain near Semîra, II. 324, 327, 328.
Hebrân, a berg in the H. Kheybar, II. 231, 251, 253.
Hebrew law [v. Moses], 291; — letters, 653; — lineaments, 654; — names in inscriptions, 408.
Hebron, v. Khalîl.
Heddajor, a seyl-bed at Teyma, 340.
Hedgehog; the — in the desert, 371; 584. v. Kunfuth.
Hedîeh kellâ, one day from Kheybar; 127, 204; II. 202.

Héj (حِق), three-year-old camel, 401.

Hejâz, a part of Arabia lying betwixt Néjd or highland Arabia and the hot lowland border or Tehâma; it signifies border-land or hedge-land: therein is Medîna, 179; the great Wady of the —, 181; villagers in the — oases dwell in upper rooms, 181; sober — humour, 184; — Arabic, 186, 190; 272, 326, 330, 331, 396, 444, 462, 463, 482, 525, 526, 528, 584, 610; II. 32, 38, 74, 94, 98, 101, 103, 110, 135, 173, 176, 189, 190, 199, 202, 234, 237, 243, 246, 307, 326, 381, 388, 426, 449, 455, 456, 466, 517, 553.
el-Hejella, a fendy of Harb B. Sâlem, II. 546.
Jebâl Hejjûr, wild mountains lying between the Harrat Kheybar and the W. el-Humth, II. 90, 234, 239, 242.
el-Héjr [v. Medáin Sâlih], in the Koran el-Hijr (v. sub Ullah): Έγρα, Ptol. Hejra Plin. [4 Dec. 1876–13 Feb. 1877, and thrice revisited in the summer and autumn], 120, 123, 134, 135; — is all that country between Mûbrak en-Nâga and Bîr el-Ghrannem, 142; — the old caravan staple of these countries, has decayed almost without leaving record, 154; successions of tribes which have possessed —, 166; 172; catastrophe of —, 175; there was yet a small village in the tenth century, 177; 180, 183, 184, 195, 197; God's great curse over the villages of the plain of —, that they should never rise again, 200; 205, 209, 212, 222, 234, 238, 250, 260, 271, 288, 315, 322, 326, 355, 364, 378, 395, 399, 403, 406, 407, 410, 413, 421, 424, 427, 433, 454, 457, 461, 465, 469, 485, 486, 487, 496, 529, 537, 547, 550, 553, 554, 558, 564, 566, 567, 586, 602, 610, 620, 636, 641; II. 16, 19, 69, 148, 176, 518, 553, 555.
el-Héjr (port of Hejra emporium), on the Red Sea, [the site is not known], 154; II. 196.
Hejra (Plin.) v. el-Héjr, 135, 408.

Héjra (حِجْرَة), summer or "flitting" tent, 257, 266, 351, 471.

Hejûr, a kindred of the Fukara tribe, 270.
Helaima, a mountain near Teyma, 328.
B. Helál, ancient heroic Beduins of Nejd, 61, 62, 162, 166, 255, 260; Beduin rhapsodies of the —, 306, 434; tradition of the —, 432-4; 668; II. 204, 253, 355, 443, 509, 566.
el-Helalát, a pl. form, the B. Helál, 428.
el-Helàlîeh, a town (old colony of Sbeya) in el-Kasîm, II. 433, 435, 437, 442.
Helbon, village in Antilibanus, II. 171.
el-Hélissa, a fendy of 'Ateyba, II. 457.

Hellayey (حَلَيِّة), a lesser crater-hill, II. 247.

Hellowát (حَلَاوَات), crater-hills, II. 247.

Hellowîa (حَلْوِيَّة), the same as Helwîa, a milk bowl, 477.

Helly, pl. of hilla (حَلَّة sing. حَلَّة), qd. v. and v. Hilliân.
Helw, sweet, 562.
Helw, a kind of date at el-Ally.
[el-Helwa, village between the head of the Aflâj and W. Dauâsir.
Helwàn, mountain east of Teyma, 341, 351, 368, 618.
Thull'a Helwàn, north of Teyma, 340.

Helwîat en-Nâga (حَلْوِيَّة الذَاقَة), or H. en Néby, 180, 200.

Hemorrhoids: the disease of —, II. 405.

INDEX AND GLOSSARY

Henàba (هنابة), milk-bowl, 477.

Henakîeh, village, 187; II. 204; anciently of the Ruwàlla, 205.

Ḥenna (حنّا) is said by Beduins for *naḥn*.

Ḥenna el-úmera, 'we are the Emirs,' II. 367.
Ḥenna mâ na ṣadiḳîn billah, 343.
Ḥenna mamlukîn, we are thralls (of Ibn Rashîd), II. 46.
Ḥenna râḥil, 551.
el-Ḥennaba, ass-mare's name, II. 253.
Hennânia, a kinship of the Kheybar villagers, II. 153.
el-Ḥenneytát, a fendy of Harb B. Sâlem, II. 546.

Henshûly (هنشولة, desert thieves), II. 382.

'Herb stem': solemn oath upon the —, 309, 622.
Herbs and blossoms of the desert, 259; II. 500.
Herding maidens, 350, 367.
Herdsmen: — will milk for passengers, 256 [*v.* Hospitality]; — at the evening fire, 303; mirth and song of the Bed. —, 306, 308, 320, 395; II. wages of —, 264; —'s questions, 265, 294, 305; 474, 476.
Hermits: the old Christian —, 520-1; II. 412.
Hermon, Mount, 43; — called by the Arabian Beduins *Towîl éth-Thalj*, 45.
Herodotus, II. 149, 407, 550.
el-Herreyik, village in el-Wéshm, II. 452.
Hesban, *v.* Heshbon.
Heshbon; ruined site (*Hesban*) said to be of —, 57; fish-pools of —, *ib.*

Ḥess ez-zillamy (حسّ الزلمة), man's voice, 200; the human — in the dry desert is clear and well sounding, 307.
el-Ḥessánna, a fendy of 'Ateyba, II. 457.
el-Heteym, gentile pl. *el-Heteymàn* [*v. Sherarát, Fehját, Sweyfly, Bedowna, Noâmsa, Beny Rashîd, Gerabîs*; and *v.* Fendies of —, II. 253]: a great nomad nation and widely dispersed in N. Arabia. Their lineage is uncertain and perhaps alien; and therefore by the Arabians they are not accounted Beduw (326), 135; 166, 238, 311; — of fairer looks than the Beduw, 324; 326, 362, 474, 553, 603, 614; — of the Nefûd, 621; II. 34, 35, 38, 71, 73, 75, 77, 79, 80; the Beduw mingle not in wedlock with the —, *ib.*, and 81; 82, 84, 85; lineage of —, 86; — of less cheerful temper than the Beduw, *ib.*; Midland and Seabord —, *ib.*, 87, 89, 132, 147, 156; a hubt of — taken by a ghrazzu near Medina, 167; *Auâzim*, 194; certain — in the Teháma of Mecca, 195; — of the Kheybar dîra, 199, 217, 223; — cheese makers, 230, 231; certain poor women wedded (with black men) in the negro village of *el-Hâyat*, 232; 236, 237, 238; — not so civil minded as the Beduw, 240-1, 295-307; *Ferâdissa, Ibn Simry*, 240; — menzils, 241, 242, 243, 244; Southern — taxed by Ibn Rashîd and Medina, 241; they commonly pay a khûa to all the powerful about them, *ib.*; thus they are thriving more than the Bed., *ib.*; their thelûls are the best in the country, *ib.*, and 261; they are more robust than Beduw, 241, 261; and their hareem more beautiful, 241, 300; *Sueyder* —, 242; many poor Bed. households sojourn with Heteym, *ib.*; 243, 248, 249, 250, 251, 261; the — have few or no horses, 252, 269; — are more than the Beduw well nourished with milk and well armed, 269; 264, 272, 295, 296, 297, 298; — ill coloured, 300, 301; coffee-drinking hardly seen among —, 303; 305, 306, 310-1, 313; their name a reproach, 317; booths of —, 295, 332; 456, 492; — in the Teháma of Jidda, 570.

Heṭheylân, gentile pl. of *Haṭheyl*, II. 515.
Hetigy, village ruins in Edom, 75.
el-Heyàderra, tribe of Ashràf, II. 556.
Heyennîeh, a site in the Nefûd towards Jauf, II. 265.
Hèykal, temple, 601.
Ibn *Ḥeyzán*, an Heteymy sheykh, II. 242.
Ḥeyzán, a fendy of Midland Heteym, II. 253.
el-Hîara, a kinship of Kheybar villagers, II. 153.

Ḥijâbs (حجاب), or amulets, 197, 300, 301; in mediaeval Europe such were not seldom written by Jews, 301; they are yet found among Oriental Christians. The Arabs desire —, *ib.*, 510; II. 16, 28, 150; —, a veil, 400.
el-Ḥíjr, Koran spelling of *el-Héjr*, 134, 135; what is —, 229.
el-Hilâl, v. Moon.

OF ARABIC WORDS

Ḥilla or ḥilly (cf. Ḥilleya, Ḥalla, Ḥelleyey, Ḥillât], pl. ḥilliân, or ḥilly, or ḥellowât — class. حِلَّة pl. coll. حِلَاّ ; a hill (always black), cinder-hill or crater of extinct vulcanic eruption in the Harras, 448, 451, 465; II. 85, 90; — of the Medina Harra, 204, 247; — of the Harrat el-Kisshub, 502, 506; — of the Harrat Ajeyfa, 566.
Ḥilliân, v. Ḥilla.
Ḥimmarît (حميرية), small copper money found upon the plain within the cliffs of the monuments at el-Héjr, 153-4.
Himyaric letters (v. Inscriptions,] 158, 177, 184, 202, 260, 350, 408, 429, 525; II. 57, 563.
Ḥimyâry, old language of el-Yémen; and yet spoken corruptly in some districts, II. 555.
el-Hind, India.
Hindostani, vulgar speech of India, II. 274, 275, 402; a poor woman at ʻAyn ez-Zeyma speaks in —, 524.
Hindy, Indian; — sword, 265 [and v. Sword]; — art, i.e. arithmetic, 321, 568; II. an — apothecary, 166; — pilgrims, ib., 226.
Hinûd (pl.), people of India.
"Hippocrates;" a Turkish surgeon reads an Himyaric inscription —, II. 544.
Hirfa, wife of Zeyd es-Sbeykan, 257, 258, 259, 262, 263-4; — described, 271, 272; —'s flight, 273-4; — brought home, 273, 277; 294; — skilled in leech-craft, 297; 302, 329, 352, 364-5, 365, 376, 383, 399.
el-Ḥisma, or Ḥessma, an high and cragged plain country of sandstones, extending from above Petra to Tebûk in Arabia, 85; height of —, 85; 94, 96, 98, 112, 273, 474; II. — sandstone, 90.
History: in the oases of Nejd there are perhaps none other records of former times than their written contracts and songs, 591, 600.
Ḥʼmá (حمي), reserved circuits for common pasture about villages in the desert, II. 268, 310.
Hollanda [v. Flamingy], II. 543.
"Holy (City)," el-Ḳuds [v. Jerusalem], 493; II. 26, 56.
Holy Fair, 247.
Homan, v. Hammam.

Homicide, v. Murder, Midda.
Honey, 66, 319; wild — in the rocks about Kheybar, II. 108; — of J. Roḍwa, ib.
Honour and conscience, Semitic feeling of —, 382, 667.
Hoopoe: the — in the Nejd oases, II. 452.
Mount Hor (Jebel Saidna Harûn): a shrine of Aaron upon —, 73, 75, 80, 81.
Horèymla, a populous town in East Nejd, II. 424.
Ḥoreysh, a Mahûby, 524-6, 529-533, 534, 538, 542, 543, 546, 565, 623.
Ḥórma (she that is forbidden, to other than her spouse), woman, pl. ḥareem, 257, 280.
Horn-like braided forelock of some tribeswomen, 429, 464, 519; II. 243.
Horned heads: an ancient sculpture of —, 60.
"Horns," Joseph's, 373.
Horns of the great wild goat, 372; — of the Wʻothŷhi (antelope), 373; — of the (Bible) reem, ib.; — of the reindeer, 320.
"Horns," the braided side-locks of Beduins called —, 211, 279, 516, 543; II. 30, 262.
Horse-brokers: Nejd —, II. 417.
Horsemen: Beduin — in Moab, 54; in Mount Seir, 70; the Fuḳara esteemed a tribe of —, 317; — of the Southern Bed. do not exercise themselves upon their mares, 385; II. — of Harb, 315; — of Meteyr, 480; — of ʻAteyba, 507.
Horse-riding; feats of —: a (Christian) stranger who visited Hâyil and showed —, II. 39; — race in Bombay, 59-60; 417.
Horses: children play at —, 384.
Horses [v. Mare]: — in the Hâj, 58, 100, 106, 109; — of Europe to be esteemed pack- —, 317; — are they think of the Aarab, ib.; (the five strains of Arab —, ib.;) — of the Aarab and Nejd —, 70, 238, 249, 334, 351; — seldom impetuous, 353; common colour of —, ib.; firing —, 353; — in battle, 379; Barbary —, 420; Ibn Rashîd's sale- — for India, 657; his stud in Hâyil, 660; Nejd — undergrown, 661; 664; II. Ibn Rashîd's former yearly present of — to Ibn Saʻûd, 28, 35, 46; Ibn Rashîd's stud, 35; his sale- — shipped at Kuweyt, 61 note; a beautiful mare, 67; the Abyssinian —, 186; Nejd — and some of their names, 252-3; the Aarab make small account of stallions, 253; the Aarab have only entire —, 301; — sent from Kasîm to Bombay, 376; no breeding or sale of — in any Nejd town, 417; "ʻAneyza —," 418; the

INDEX AND GLOSSARY

Arabian — are hollow-necked, 419; they are good weight-carriers, *ib.*; the Waháby stud most treacherously taken by Kahtân, 454; Syrian cavalry — at Tâyif, 552.
Hosea, the prophet: words of —, 61.
el-Hosenîeh, a seyl-bed at Teyma, 340.
[*Hosennat*, the tuft of the tail of the jerbo'a.
el-Hósenny, a fendy of Ruwàlla, 376.
Hósn, Jeheyna hamlet of Yanb'a-the-Palms, II. 202.
Hospitality [*v.* Guest, Guestship]: — of the kellâ at Medáin Sâlih, 144, 164, 165; 181; the virtue of — an imitation of the heavenly Providence, 256, 269; 493; the nomads' — to the Nasrâny stranger, 357, 429, 446, 523, 546, 550, 619; decay of — reproved by a phantom camel, 472; 624, 625; public — at Gofar, 634; at Hâyil, 662-3; II. 64, 68, 82, 83, 85, 86, 95, 107, 109, 112; the Arabian —, 112, 118, 171; the host is the servant of his guests, *ib.*; 132, 195; — at el-Hâyat, 232; 233, 240, 242, 243, 244; — must not be stretched to ask a provision of water in the desert, *ib.*; 248, 250, 251, 252, 257-8; a town opinion of the Beduin —, 259; — is more scant in coffee-sheykhs' booths, 265; 266, 267, 285, 287, 290; the nomad guest enters the beyt of — with demure looks, 296; 302; regard of guests not to lay a burden on their hosts, 325; 334; herdsmen milk for passengers, 305, 306, 321, 335; an Harb woman upbraids the decay of —, 309; sorry —; 316, 334; — of el-Kasîm, 337, 438; — in the Mecca country, 568-72.

Hosseny (حُصَيْنِي, classical ابو الحصين), the fox, *qd. v.*, 372; taken by their greyhounds and eaten by the Fukara, *ib.*; II. 163.
el-Hóseny, [*v.* Hósenny] an Ânnezy sub-tribe now in the North near Aleppo; they are a sister tribe of the Fukara, and of them is said to be the family of Ibn Sa'ûd the Waháby, 270, 376.
Hostel: the public — at Boreyda [*munôkh es-sheukh*], II. 340-5; — at 'Aneyza [*menzil es-sheukh*], 390, 464.

[Hóth, حظ, luck (Bishr 'Ageylies).

Hound, *v.* Dog.
House: the Arabian —, 389.

House-building: — at el-Ally, 185; — at Teyma, 330; at Môgug, 629; — at Hâyil, 147, 669; II. 19; — at Boreyda, 340, 348; — at 'Aneyza, 368, 375; — at Khubbera, 440.
Household: mildness of the Arab —, 353.
House-rent at 'Aneyza, II. 368.
"Houses of hair:" the Beduin booths of worsted so called by them, namely *beyt esh'ar*. 'The conquerors of Islam shall be repulsed at the —,' 587.
Hòwama, a dog's name, 474.
el-Howayrîa, a sounding sand-hill, 352.
Howèyat (little *Hâyat*), a palm-hamlet of 40 houses in the border of the Kheybar Harra, II. 70, 301; Ânnezy Aarab were formerly landlords at —, *ib. v. Ibn Mujàllad.*
Howeych(k)im, a villager of el-Ally, 556-7, 563.
Howeytát (sing. *Howeyty*), a Beduin nation, 55; — *Ibn Jeysey*, of Petra, 68 and 175, 75; — land-tillers near Gâza, 84; speech of the —, 85; their bodily aspect, 85, 274-6; *Saidîn*, kindred of —, 86, 179; — robbers about el-Ally, 199-202; their footsteps known, 199, 274; *Terabîn* —, *ib.*, 274; their circle villages of tents and tillage near Gâza, *ib.*; the — country, *ib.*; *Tiáha* and *Seydeîn* — kindreds about Gâza, *ib.*; — husbandmen of palms in the Teháma, *ib.*; *Suáki* clan of —, *ib.*; — Syrians, *ib.*; their descent is obscure, 276; 387, 388, 436, 443, 449, 450, 464, 503, 529; II. 38, 348.
W. el-Howga, 164.
Howihih, a ruined site in Moab, 61.
Howsa, site in the desert, 164.
Howsha, Beduin fem. name, 514.
[*W. Howtha*, a valley in the W. flank of the 'Aueyrid Harra above W. Thirba.

Howwàr (حُوار), yearling camel calf, male, 401.
el-Howwâra (yearling camel calf, fem.), 499; a mountain platform crag in the plain of el-Héjr, an outlyer of the Harra; thus called in the Syrian caravans [but not known by this name to the Beduw]. The Syrians fable that — is the rock which opened her womb to receive the orphan foal of Néby Sâlih's prodigious camel, 137; fable of a vast treasure upon the height of —, 213; 529, 548.
el-H'roof, a kindred of Bíllî Bed., 429-30.
Hu *sâdik!* 642.

el-Huâzim, a fendy of Harb B. Sâlem, ii. 546.

Hub (حَبّ) *el-Frenjy*, the morbus gallicus, 437.

Húb et-támr, a disease of ulcers, (the " Aleppo boil ") chiefly on the shanks, ii. 511.

Húbbal (هُبَل), a bethel-stone (so-called) at et-Tâyif, ii. 549.

Hubbâra, ass-mare's name, ii. 253.

Huber, Charles — of Strassburg, 581; he travelled in Arabia in part of 1879 and part of 1880: he visited Jauf, Hâyil, Teyma, Medáin Sâlih, el-Ally, Kheybar, el-Kasîm. In 1884 Huber returned to Arabia with Prof. Julius Euting; and revisited Jauf, Hâyil, Teyma, Medáin Sâlih and el-Ally: where he separated from his companion, and journeyed towards Jidda. In re-ascending from Jidda Huber was shot by his (Harb) rafîks, near *Rabugh*.

Hubt, (هبط) a company of marketing nomads, ii. 76, 199.

Hud (هود), (a prophet in Arabia before Mohammed): a pretended grave of —, 49; ii. 51.

Huddebân, a dog's name, 474.

Hulk (حَلق), long neck of the camel, ii. 496.

yâ *Hullah!* or *Hullah!* well met! the hearty Bed. response [of Ânnezy in W. Nejd] to the greeting *gowwak*, the Lord strengthen thee.

Humanity of the Semitic salutations, 480, *et passim*.

el-Humeydát, sing. *Humída*, the villagers of Tebûk so called, 135.

el-Hummu (الحُمّ), a dry dead heat, 423, 462.

el-Humràn, a fendy of Harb Mosrûh, ii. 547.

Hums, v. Emesa.

Humṣîs (حَمصيص), sorrel, *qd. v.*

Humth, a bush in the Arabian desert which is good camel meat, 217; ii. — *el-aṣlah* (الاصلح?), ii. 571.

Wady *el-Humth* [الحَمض] named from the abounding of that plant in its bed. This great valley of the Hejâz, which is compared by the Arabians to the Wady er-Rummah, was unknown to European geographers until the winter of 1876, when Mr. Doughty traced it, from el-Héjr. 134, 181, 187, 204, 217, 457, 463, 465, 468, 469, 594; ii. 38, 87, 90, 132, 173, 201-4, 234, 237, 242, 510, 546, 565.

Hungary: Bed. matchlocks called *el-Májar*, 504.

Hunger: indigent life of — in the desert, 263, 284, 447, 488-90, 500, 505, 520, 526, 535, 602, 612.

Hunter: Solubby —s, 324-5, 612; Nomad —s of the *W'othŷhi*, 373; the Beduw are uncunning —s, 173-4; 406-7; Thahir, 535-6; ii. the Shammar princes —s of *bedûn* in J. Ajja, 24; an Heteymy —, 86; Solubby and Bed. —s, *ib.*; the Bed. unready —s, 238-40; Solubby —, 256; Solubby —s' fire by a well side in the khála, 497.

Hunters' roast, 371; ii. 55, 164, 260.

el-Húrda, an outlying corn land at Kheybar, ii. 91, 92, 134, 136, 206.

Hurr (حُرّ), a dromedary stallion, 280, 438; ii. 304.

Hurra, dromedary, ii. 23, 562.

Hurra (حُرَّة), a kind of basalt, 668.

el-Hurrath, a tribe of the Ashràf of the Mecca country, ii. 556, 565.

Hurrî (حُرّي), v. *Hurra*, a kind of basalt, 668.

Husbandry of Beduins [*v. sub* Howeytát, W. Thirba, W. 'Aurush.]

Husbandry [*v.* Palms, Irrigation]: oasis —, 177, 193, 337; poor livelihood of many owners of the soil, 570; — of a new well-ground at Teyma, 602; value and payment for oasis-ground at Teyma, *ib.*; ii. — at Kheybar, 115; 131, 135, 416; — at 'Aneyza, 464-5.

el-Husn, old acropolis at Kheybar, ii. 93, 104, 121-2, 141-3, 152, 165.

Hût (حُوت), fish, ii. 96.

Hút! (هَت), vulg. *hút*, a chiding call to camels, ii. 496.

Hutch! (perhaps for *hut-ak, hut-ik*), a camel call, 261.

INDEX AND GLOSSARY

Huṭhb (حَضْب), sing. *huṭhba*, hilly mountain coasts, 285.
el-Huṭheba, mountain near el-Ally, 180.
Hŷ! v. Hŷak!

Hŷak! (for حَيَّاكَ اللهُ), speed thee, II. 180.

Hyâtak, by thy life, 312.
Hyena, Ar. *ṭhùbbʻa*; the — follows the evil odour of the Hâj, 96; 141; 203; — eaten by certain Beduw, 372; 373, 498, 518, 656.
Hŷha, mare's name, II. 253.
Hypochrondria [*v.* Melancholy], II. 18, 412.
el-Hŷza, a well in the Nefûd, 351, 352, 392.

IBADID, a tribe of ancient Arabia mentioned in the Assyrian inscr., 229.
Iblis [διάβολος], the devil; — his "water" [tobacco], 289, 494; — an exclamation of impatience at Teyma, 592, 604; II. 442.
Ibn, son (of); in names beginning with — look for the second name.
Ibn akhy, 361.

Ibn juâd (ابن جواد), son of bounty, a worthy person, II. 361.
Ibn Nâhal (Khâlaf), a rich and sheykhly tribesman of Harb, II. 299-302, 305-11; a camel dealer, 310; 313-14; a merchant Beduwy, *ib.*; his wealth and ventures, 314-15; 318; 320; 327.
Ibn Rashîd, v. Rashîd.
Beny Ibrahîm, or *Barâhima*, a fendy of Jeheyna settled at Yanbʻa-the-Palms, 166; II. 202.
Ibrahîm, an Algerian man-at-arms at Hâyil, II. 36, 48.
Ibrahîm, a farmer at ʻAneyza, II. 361-2.
Ibrahîm of ʻAneyza, son-in-law of Rasheyd; he had laboured in the work of the Suez Canal, II. 449-51, 467-8.
Ibrahîm, a townsman of the armed band at Hâyil, II. 75, 271, 280-2.
Ibrahîm el-Kâdy, a Kheybar villager, II. 103, 114; his wives and children, 128, 140, 153, 236.
Ibrahîm of Medina, II. 533-7.
Ibrahîm Pasha: [his brother *Tusun Bey*] defeated by Harb, 49; — seizes Kerak, 62; troops of — closed in and massacred by the Druses, 197; II. 398, 414, 431, 454, 490.

Ibrahîm abu Khalîl er-Roman, 599; his report of many antique inscribed (tomb-)stones near Teyma, 601.
Ibrahîm es-Sâlih, of er-Russ, II. 453.
Ibrahîm es-Sennad, a W. ʻAly sheykh, 552.
Ibrahîm, a cameleer of Shuggera, II. 424-5.
Ibrahîm, an Egyptian at Teyma, 591; his fair daughter, *ib.*
Ibrahîm, a nephew of Zâmil, and emir of the great ʻAneyza caravans, II. 488, 491, 494-5, 503-5, 509, 512-18.
J. Ibrân, 626.

el-Iddimy (آدَم fem., أَدْماء) the greater (drinking) gazelle, II. 164.
Idolatry: the ancient — of Arabia, 289; II. "— of the Nasâra," 51, 396; idol-stones shown at et-Tâyif, 549; 563.
Idumea, *v.* Edom.
Iftaḥ ʻayûnak, 574.

Íghrtebig! (اغْتَبِق), II. 258; the Ignorance:
el-Jahalîat or time of the old heathen — in Arabia, 281; 342; 607; II. 452.
Ihrâm, the loin-cloth of pilgrims that enter Mecca, II. 511-14, 572.
Íjrî! II. 161.

Ikh-kh-kh! (اِخْ) guttural hissing to a camel, to kneel down, 262; II. 290.
Ikhtiyarîn, pl. of *ikhtiyàr(î)*, good, worthy, 470; 533.

[*Ílluk-ḥeylo!* (probably اعْلُقْ حَيَّ هَلا), a camel-call; to cheer the camels to pasture or water.
Images of animals scored upon the desert rocks, 175, 260, 479, 613.
Imâm: the —, ʻAneyza, II. 396.
Imbârak, captain of the band at Hâyil, 644; II. 47, 55, 62, 63, 70-5.
Imbârak, a village of *W. Fâṭima*, II. 567.
(2) *Imbârak*, Harb hamlet of Yanbʻa-the-Palms, II. 202.
Imbârak! imbârak! la tuktillu el-Moslemîn, II. 461.
Imbecility common among the Aarab [*v. Mejnûn*], 517, 546, 570; II. 312. Every third man in the desert life is broken-headed, 313, 323, 520.

Ímshy hâl-ak (أَمْشِي حَالك), II. 498.

Incense, *bakhûr* [*v.* Gold and Incense trade road], anciently the riches of Arabia Felix. The S. Arabian — trade to foreign nations is the oldest of which we have any record. The *regio thurifera* of Pliny, λιβανωτοφόρος χώρα of Ptol., is named HOLY LAND in a hieroglyphic inscription, of the 17th century B.C., which is a monument of an Egyptian expedition to S. Arabia; from whence they fetched frankincense, myrrh, and incense trees in pots. — and spice matter in the sandy floors of the tombs at el-Héjr, 137; — brought now from the Malay Islands to Mecca, and thence dispersed through Arabia, *ib.*; the Arabians use it as a perfume, *ib.*; *bakhûr* found at *el-Mubbiát*, 203; 212, 228; — used in sacrificing, 500; II. — burned about a victim, 163; — used to safeguard us from the influence of malign spirits, 211.

India (*el-Hind*), a land of the Moslemîn, 186; perfumes from —, 247; well-drawing in —, 336; — rice, 438, 469, 653, 657; II. 35, 69, 146; Indian pilgrimage, 166; 188, 210, 226, 274, 275, 277, 278, 348, 352, 378, 399, 402, 403, 411, 417, 419, 471, 495, 511, 524, 525, 541, 552, 555, 561, 562, 572.

art-Indian (arithmetic), 321, 568. [*v. Hindy.*]

Indigo, 336.

Indolent barren-mindedness of the Arabs, 299; 392; 474.

Infirmities, *v.* Maladies.

Inflammation : the Arabs forbid to use water in every kind of —, 597.

INɪ N..., word or name in an inscription, 408.

Ingenious ; the Arab nomads are surely the least — of all peoples, 358.

Inhaddem beytich (انهَدَم بيتك), 586.

Inny mâ adeshurak, I will not forsake thee, 310.

Inoculation [*v.* Vaccination, *el-'Athab*], 297; II. 375, 403.

Inscriptions : the earliest notice of the — at Medáin Sâlih was that left by Mr. Doughty in Vienna, in the hands of Prof. Hochstetter, president of the R. I. Austrian Geographical Society, by whom it was published (rendered into German) in the Society's *Mittheilungen*, 1876, p. 268-72, as follows :—

UEBER DIE BERÜHMTEN " TROGLODYTEN-
STADTE " IN ARABIEN.

Dieselben liegen zwischen Mâan in Idumäa und Medina, nahe der Pilgerstrasse. Ich zweifle nicht an der Existenz jener " Städte ;" ich hörte darüber von mehreren Leuten, welche alle in gleicher Weise, bis zum Pascha zu Damaskus, berichteten. Sie ähnlen Petra und sind derartig beschaffen, "als ob sie von denselben Maurermeistern aufgeführt worden wären." Über jeder Thüre befindet sich eine alte Inschrift mit der Gestalt eines Vogels, eines Falken oder Adlers mit ausgebreiteten Flügeln. Fünf dieser " Städte " [cliffs in which are the ranges of hewn monuments] sind in ebensoviele Berg eeingehauen und liegen nahe an einander; sie sind voll antiker Ziehbrunnen unten im Sande und in den darunter liegenden Felsen versunken. Die Araber nennen die Troglodytenstädte gemeiniglich *Hedger* (*Hidjr*) und die Pilger Medáin Sâlih. Der ausgezeichnete Reisende Burckhardt hörte von diesen Städten und wurde nur durch Krankheit verhindert, dieselben zu besuchen; er spricht davon im Anhange seines Tagebuches. Er glaubt, dass die Inschriften einer Art von architektonischen Schmuckes seien, welchen die unwissenden Araber missverstanden hätten; aber ich habe sichere Beweise dafür, das sie wirkliche Inschriften seien. — Ich vermuthe, dass sie 1 oder 2 sehr seltenen Idumäischen Inschriften ähnlich sein dürften, welche ich in Petra [*v.* p. 81] fand. (C. M. D.)

Some account of the — which Mr. D. saw at Medáin Sâlih (and in other parts of Arabia, mostly in the Héjr and Teyma country) was published soon after he returned from Arabia, in the *Proceedings of the R. A. S. Bombay*, and in Kiepert's *Globus*. Passing by Paris in May 1883, he showed many of them to M. Renan. After some further delay of sixteen months they were published in a (special) volume by the *Académie des Inscriptions et Belles Lettres*.

— at Petra, 79-81 ; 84 ; — near Medowwara, 97 ; — in Boghrâz el-Akhdar, 116 ; — in W. es-Sâny, 118 ; — of Khubbat et-Timathíl, 119 ;— over the kellâ door, Medáin Sâlih, 127 ; 176 ; at el-Ally, 184, 187, 461 ; — at el-Khreyby, 200, 202 ; the 'Alowna's opinion of —, 203 ; Kufic money, *ib.*; the Medáin Sâlih epitaphs impressed, 209, 466 the translations of these by M. Ernest Renan,

224-9; 230, 251; — in the Mézham, 250, 408; — at M'kuttaba, 260; — commonly found about watering and alighting places, and called *Timathîl el-Helalát*, 260; — at Teyma, 335; — at Ybba Moghrair, 349; a Nabatean — in the way between Teyma and el-Héjr, 402; — in Ethlib, 176, 410; — in the Teháma side of the Harra (not copied), 429; — in the Akhma, 525; — in Teyma, 580, 581, 583; — near Hâyil, ii. 57; Kufic — near Kheybar, 116; — of heathen Arabia, near Kheybar, *ib.*; — at *Mâsul es-Sudda* in el-Wéshm, 555; — in the *Ri'a ez-Zelâla*, 563.
Insha 'llah (or *Insh' Ullah*), if the Lord will.
Insh' Ullah ma teshûf es-shurr, 307.
Intermarriage: in the Arabian kindreds is a natural jealousy of their blood. The Heteym, Sherarát, Sunn'a, Solubba, the African *muwelladîn*, and all of whom it is said (ما لهم أصل) *mâ li-hum aṣl*, use to marry only within their own kin, 54, 326, 437.
Invention: the Arabs barren of all —, 329, 330, 334.
el-'Irâk, 330, 573, 614, 619, 631; ii. 56, 283, 333, 371, 375, 409, 480.
Iram (إِرِم), 93.
Ireland, King Alfred's words of —, 462.
Irkuḍ! ii. 161.
J. Irnàn, 341, 348, 367, 377, 619, 620.
Iron, 327; —stone, 328, 331, 582; — sold at Hâyil, ii. 23.
Irrigation: oasis — at el-Ally, 193; — at Teyma, 335, 337, 584, 593, 600; — at Hâyil, 636; 665; ii. — at Kheybar, 136, 206, 220; — at Gofar, 285; — at 'Aneyza, 382, 416, 464.
Irtugh(r) (imperat. from اِرْتَغِي), "he drank froth,"), 305.
Irzûm, a sounding sand-hill, 352.
Îsa, v. *'Aysa*.
Isaiah the prophet: he speaks of a Moabitish multitude, 61; words of —, 74, 78, 82, 211, 212, 343, 527.
Ishmael [v. *Ismayîn*] "father of the North Arabians:" the land of —, 95, 270, 326; ii. 45, 48, 51, 381, 477.
Iskander (Czar Alexander), ii. 398.
Iskander, v. Alexander.

Iskanderîa (Alexandria), ii. 387.
Islâm (they that do submit themselves unto the divine governance): decay of the militant —, 133; the nations of —, 142, 318, 342; the dire religion of —, 141, 198, 551; ii. Mohammed's religion makes numbness and deadness in some part of the understanding, 21; duty of a Moslem, 53; the institution of —, 405-6, 407. [*v.* Fatalism, *Mohammed*, *Moslem*, Zelotism, Circumcision, Fasting.]
el-Islâm kulluhu 'aŷb, ii. 226.
Islimt, I become a Moslem, ii. 179.
Ismaiel Pasha, the (former) ruler of Egypt, ii. 110.
Ismayîn, Arabic vulgar form of Ishmael, used by the Kahtân Beduins, ii. 51; the same is commonly heard amongst Moslems in Syria.
B. Israel [and *v. sub* Moses]: taking into account the Semitic vulgar wise in narration to multiply a true number by tens, the " 600,000 men " of — that ascended from Egypt might signify 60,000, or probably 6000 men; which were nearly the strength of all the tribes together of Ânnezy, that is now the greatest nomad people of Arabia and Syria. And we should the better understand the Mosaic record of their oppression in Egypt, their hard fighting with Amalek tribesmen, their journeys and passage of the strait Sinai valleys; and thereafter their long and not always victorious national strife with the dukes of petty states on both sides of Jordan. 75, 88, 100, 268, 308-9, 378, 381, 391, 497, 579; land of —, 642; ii. 56, 407.
J. 'Iss [*'Ayṣ*], below el-Ally, 134.
W. el-'Iss [*'Ayṣ*], below el-Ally, 134.
(2) *W. el-'Iss* [*'Ayṣ*], in the Jeheyna dîra, 134, 468, 470.
Issherub wa keyyif râsak, ' drink (tobacco) and solace thee,' 587.
Isshrub wa erwîk, drink and quench thy thirst, 444.
Iṣṭabal 'Antar, 204.
Istíska, the dropsy, *qd. v.*
Istughrfir Ullah, 551.
Italia, ii. 419.
Italian: — seamen, 168; — quarantine officers in the Levant, 454; ii. an — seen in the passing Persian Pilgrimage, at Hâyil, 65-8; ancient —s, Roman soldiers, in the Arabian expedition under Gallus, ii. 196; — workmen in the labour of the Suez Canal, 450.

OF ARABIC WORDS 629

Ithin Ullah (إِنْ الله), ii. 525.

J (ج): this letter is sounded in many words for *k* (ق) by Beduins and oasis-dwellers in Nejd; ex. *Fejîr*, for Fakîr, though the pl. be always *Fukara*; *'ajr* for *'aakr*; *hej*, three-year-old camel, for *hek*; *jedûm*, a hatchet, for *kedûm*; *jéria* (also *géria*), a village; *jaila* (also gaila), noonday; *'Ajeyl*, for 'Akeyl, a man's name; *ferîj* for *ferîk*; *jellîb*, a well, though the pl. be always *golbân*; *jett*, vetches, for *kett*; *jiddŷha*, milk-bowl, for *kudayha*; *jírby* (but more often gírby), a water-skin; *nejîm* for *nekîm*; *rîj* (also rîg), spittle. So in names of Nejd towns and sites: *Jiffâr* for Kâfar; *Khórj*, for Khark; *Usheyjir* for Usheykir; *Jîsan Mejelly* for Kîsan —. ج is seldom pronounced g in Nejd; ex. *Magid* (sometimes heard in Hâyil) for Majid.

Jaafar, a fendy of Shammar, ii. 52, 56.
Jâb-hum Ullah, ii. 477.
Jabâbara, pl. of *jabbâr*, ii. 284.
Jábbar [*jâbr*], 'bone setter' or military surgeon, 252.
Jabbâr, a high-handed, tyrannical person.
el-Jabbâr, a deceased sheykhly personage at Hâyil, ii. 31.
Jabbok, *v. ez-Zerka*.
Jackal: the — (a fruit eating animal) is not found in desolate Arabia, ii. 164.
Jacob, 526; ii. 407.
Jacob's bridge, 114.
Ibn *Jad*, an Howeytát sheykh nigh Ma'an, 85.
Jaddar (Bishr), cattle path in the Harra wilderness, *v. Jiddar*, ii. 238.
Jael broke the faith of the desert, 95.
Jáffila, Bed. fem. name, 514.
el-Jahalîat, the olden time of (heathen) ignorance, 281, 342, 607, *et passim*.
Jáhash, an ass.
Jàhil [*jâhl*], ignorant, 377.
el-Jàhm, fendy of Harb Mosrûh, ii. 547.
el-Jahrâ, near Kuweyt, ii. 61.
W. Jaida, valley in the Hareyny, 463, 543.
Jam(*n*)*bîeh* (جنبية), sword-knife of the Mecca lowland country, ii. 519.
James I.: tobacco brought to Stambûl in his days, 290.
ej-Jammera, an ass-mare name, ii. 253.

Jân, pl. of *jin*, demons; called also *ahl el-ard*, or "earth-folk," 177: they inhabit seven stages under the earth, 301; an half are Moslemîn and an half are kafirs, *ib.*; lunatic affections and diseases ascribed to their influence, 300, 301; exorcism is therefore the great skill in medicine, 598, 607; ii. the — described, 17; blood sprinkling to the —, 118, 219; 201; Amm Mohammed's Medina lore and tales of the *jin* world 209-15; an half part of all who bear the form of mankind are —, 211; many dogs and cats are —, *ib.*, 213; Amàn's tale of a well possessed by the — at Jidda, 211; a *jin* enters into a woman, 212; the — resemble mankind and are mortal, *ib.*; a citizen of Medina takes to wife a *jin* woman, 212-14; a *jin* city under the earth, 213; a just kâdy of the —, 214-5; a *jin* in the likeness of a serpent is slain, 215; wonderful building of wells *etc.* ascribed to the —, 246.

Janâbak, ii. 55.
Jannah, ruined site of an old settlement of B. Khâlid Aarab near the site of (the later founded) 'Aneyza, ii. 381; —, when founded, *ib.*; the people of —, overcome by those of 'Aneyza, forsook the place, *ib.*
Jar, Jeheyna hamlet of Yanb'a-the-Palms, ii. 202.
Jâr Ullah, a corn merchant at Hâyil, 654-5.
Jâra (جَارَة), Bed. housewife, 364, 371, 414, *et passim*.
Jarâd, locusts.
Jarada, (*Jâreda*, *Járida*, *Jar'da*), old ruined metropolis of el-Kasîm; (prob.) the site which is now named *el-Ethelly*. Ibn Ayith wrote for me, " الجريدة lies to the right of er-Russ and to the north about 3 ' hours.' " And again he wrote " at *el-Jarida* are vestiges of an old town by the side of Wady er-Rumma west of er-Russ and between them is the Wady. There are wells and granges of the people of er-Russ." The situations of these places on the map may perhaps be amended thus,—

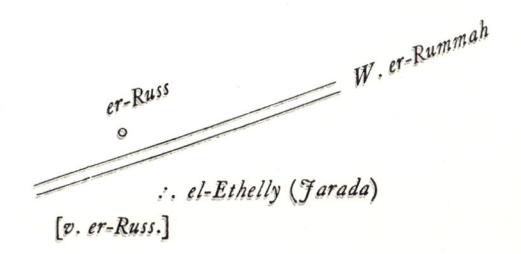

```
                              W. er-Rummah
  er-Russ
       o
              ∴ el-Ethelly (Jarada)
```
[*v. er-Russ.*]

INDEX AND GLOSSARY

Jarda, or *Jorda*, v. *Járada*.
Jardanîa, ruined town in J. Sherra, 68.
Jarfa, near Kerak, 61.
Jâsim, v. *Kâsim*.
Ibn *Jâsy*, v. *Jeysey*.
el-*Jau*, a valley-like passage between the Harras, above Medáin Sâlih, 167, 445, 451, 462, 464; — divides the *Ahl Gibly* and *Ahl es-Shemâl*, 464; 476; possessed trees in —, 496; 537.

Jau (جوّ), pl. *jiân*, watering place in low ground, 340, 464.

Jauf (el-Âmir), the ancient *Dûmat el-Jendel*, a great oasis and suburbs in the S. of the Syrian desert, and on the border of the Nefûd. [*Jauf* signifies a hollow or bottom ground.] The *Sunn'a* of — are greatly esteemed in all N.-W. Arabia and in the lands beyond Jordan, for their skill in metal and marble working (coffee mortars and pestles). There is a salt traffic from the neighbourhood of — to the Hauran, whither there come every year many poor Jaufies to labour for the Druses. 329, 340, 354, 376, 565, 587, 652, 664; II. 20, 33-5, 37, 44, 46, 47-9, 64, 200, 265, 460.

Javanese pilgrims to Mecca, II. 512.
Béled Jawwa (Java, the Malay Islands).
Jaysh, the Bed. and town sense of the word, 478.
Jâzy, a Fejîry, 553.
el-*Jebâl*, rugged mountains in the Nejd Bishr dîra, 348, 368.
Jebbâra, a fendy of Wélad 'Aly, 271.
Jebel, mountain.
EL-JEBEL, *i.e.* J. Shammar, the dîra of Ibn Rashîd, 502, 503, 554, 608, 627, 662, 669; II. 21, 292.
Jebel Tar [always so pronounced by the Morocco Moor Haj Néjm: he did not say *Jebel Tarik*], Gibraltar, 129.
Jebèyly, in W. *Hanîfa*, II. 424.
el-*Jedèyda*, Harb village, II. 546.
Jedîd, village of B. *Sâlem*, Harb, II. 546.
Jedîda, village at the mouth of W. *Laymûn*, II. 565.

Jedûm (قدوم), hatchet, 324.

Jefèyfa, village, 629; II. 34.
Jehâd [strife for the Religion], warfare, 130, 178, 198, 251, 317, 521; 'one Moslem prisoner exchanged for ten of the Nasâra,' 553; 587; II. the Russian and Turkish war, 65, 147, 198, 275, 278, 398, 472.

Jéhemma (جهمة), the dusk of the dawning light, "betwixt the dog and the wolf," II. 267.

Jehendem Pasha, a late governor of Mecca, II. 130.
Jehennem (Hebr.) hell, the place of the damned, 493.
Jeheyna, gentile pl. el-*Jehîn* [these sea-bord Aarab pronounce J hard as the Egyptians, and may probably name themselves *Geheyna*]: a considerable ancient Beduin tribe of nomads and settlers, that have remained, since the first Mohammedan ages, with their neighbours the Bíllî, in the Tehâma of the W. el-Humth. They are praised as "religious" tribesmen and observers of the old hospitality. In number they are as "twice the B. Wáhab," — that were 600 tents nearly. Some divisions and fendies of — are *el-Kleybát*, *Aroa*, *G'dah*, *Merowân*, *Zubbiân*, *Grûn*, *B. Ibrahîm*, *Sieyda*, *Seràsera*, *el-Thegîf*, *el-Hosseynát*. 92, 134, 182, 241, 380, 420, 436, 468, 470, 620, 626; II. 38, 111, 137, 149, 195; — of, the Rodwa, 202; — of Yanb'a, *ib.*, 228; poor — women wedded to negro villagers of el-Hâyat, 232; a foray of—, 241.

Jehèyna Harra, II. 378.
Jehoshaphat: monuments in the valley of — at Jerusalem, 80, 673.
Jehovah, 269, 312.
Jelàmy, the small brown lizard of the desert, 373.
Jeljul, ruined site in Moab, 61.

Jella (جلة), camel dung; — used for fuel, 348; 586, 607; II. a rahla of nomads traced by the —, 239, 246; 451.

Ibn *Jelladàn*, a fendy of midland Heteym, II. 253.
el-*Jellâs*, a great ancient kindred of Ânnezy, 271, 376.
Wady *Jellâs*, at Kheybar, 377; II. 92, 117, 134, 143, 204, 205.
J(k)ellîb, pl. *golbân*, a well; II. 317.
Jellowwy ibn S'aûd, sometime governor of 'Aneyza for the Waháby, II. 458, 459.

OF ARABIC WORDS 631

Jellowwy, a young Mahûby tribesman, living in exile with the Fukara, 578.
Jemân, a fendy of Bíllî, 430.
Jémel, a camel.
el-Jémélla, a fendy of Harb. B. Sâlem, II. 546.
Jemla, a hill near Medina, 327.
Jemmâl, camel master, II. 67, 311.
Jemmamîl, pl. of *jemmâl*, II. 311, 345.
Jenèynat el-Kâdy, upon the derb el-Hâj, 118.

Jenèyny (جُنَينة), pleasure ground; the palm orchards are so called at 'Aneyza, II. 379.
Jèrad and *jeràd*, plurals of *jurda* or *jorda*, dune in the Nefûd, II. 357.
Jeraida, a site in the Teyma desert, 164.
el-Jeràjera, fendy of Harb Mosrûh, II. 547.
Jerash, v. Gerasa.
Jerbo'a, the spring-rat of the desert, 371, 656; II. 261; the — (they say) ruminates, *ib*.
J. Jerbûa, 344.
Jeremiah the prophet: his words against Rabbath Ammon, 56.
Jerèyda (v. *Jeraida*), 164, 328, 348.
el-Jereyfa, village in el-Kasîm, II. 452.
Jèriat is said by the Ânnezy of Kheybar for *kèriat*.
Jèriat Bishr, the chief village of Kheybar, II. 91, 93, 118, 122, 153.
Jèriat el-Fejîr, or *el-Asmîeh*, the least of the three villages of Kheybar, II. 91, 116.
Jèriat W. Aly, or *Umm Kîda*, a village of Kheybar, II. 91, 95, 110, 111.
Jericho, II. 339.
Jerîd, javelin.

Jerm (جرم), pl. *jerûm*, goat-skins to hold butter; they must be well smeared within, with date syrup, II. 488.
el-Jerràr, an affinity of Kheybar villagers, II. 153.
Wady *Jerrîr*, the great affluent from the eastward of the W. er-Rummah, II. 500; words attributed to W. er-Rummah, *ib*., which Ibn Ayith wrote:

فانّه يرويني كلّ وادٍ يحسيني الّا الجرير

Jerrîsh, (حريش) *porridge*, 79.

Jèrula (غربل *to sift*; جرول stones, pebbles), II. 129.

Jerûm, pl. of *jerm*, *qd. v.*
Jerusalem [*el-Kuds*, THE HOLY], 57, 61, 80, 182, 280, 493, 498, 673, 674; II. 26, 178, 190, 339, 448.
Jeshurun, 'the darling,' that is Israel, 83.
Aarab *Jessàs*, 326.
Jesus C.: Inscription at Teyma of four or five centuries before —, 581; era of —, 673; II. a faithful disciple of —, 177-8; 396, 414; images of — and of Mary in the old Ka'aba, 545.

Jet (قتّ), a kind of vetch which is grown for the well-camels' provender in the oases of Kasîm, II. 361, 417, 465.
el-Jethémma, a fendy of 'Ateyba, II. 457.
Jethro, the Midianite, 130, 135, 367.
Jew (v. *Yahûd*): Teyma of the —s, 231; — musicants at Damascus, 607; II. "Jews'-houses," ruined stone buildings about Medina, 201.
Jewels [v. Bracelet, Nose-ring, Ornament]: women's — at el-Ally, 190, — among the Fukara, 268.
Jewish sculptures, 268; — visage, 292.
Jèyber, a Kahtâny, and man of trust of the Emir at Boreyda, II. 345, 346; his nature, 349-54; his wives, 351; 455.
el-Jèyn, a desert station north of Teyma, 341.
Ibn *Jèysey* (a Howeytát sheykh of the Petra dîra), and his Aarab, 68, 218, 388.
Jezîrat el-'Arab, the Arabian Peninsula, II. 182.
Jezzîn (pl. form; sing. جازي), [said of the great cattle in spring time when] abstaining from water, 260, 284; II. 248, 289.
Jiâfera, a kindred of Bishr, 376.
Jid, or patriarch (*qd. v.*) of a tribe or oasis: — of el-Ally, 189, 270, 527; II. 56, 286.

Jidda (جدّة), the Red Sea port of Mecca, 99, 208, 434, 462, 536; II. — bombarded, 104, 105, 144, 154, 177, 181, 186; — staple town of the African slavery, 187; 189; a well at — possessed by the jân, 211; 276, 314, 354, 364; slave market, 375; 376, 378, 397, 425, 432, 438, 442, 447, 457, 483, 486, 487, 488, 495, 499, 510, 512, 513, 515, 516, 518, 519, 520, 523; — slave traffic, 524; 532, 533, 541, 542, 543, 547, 548, 551, 552, 553, 555, 557, 559, 560, 562, 567, 569, 570, 571, 572; — besieged by Sa'ûd ibn Sa'ûd, 571; 574.

INDEX AND GLOSSARY

Jidda (perhaps *jidra*, قِدْرَة), Beduin caldron, 268.

Jiddàr, v. Ard Jiddàr.

Jiddàr, pl. *jiddrân* (جِدَارٍ pl. جُدْرَان), cattle paths in the Harra, II. 87, 90, 238.

Jiddŷha (قَدْيحَة), a milk basin, 477.

Jídery (small-pox, *qd. v.*), 297.

Jíffar (*Jífar*) Bed. pronc. of *Kàfar* (*qd. v.*) vulg. *Gófar,* great B. Temîm vill. near Hâyil, 634.

Jildîyyah, a mountain near Hâyil, 668.

el-Jimerîeh, mare's name, II. 253.

Jin [*jinn*], 92. v. pl. *Jân*.

Jindal, Aarab ibn — sheykh es-Suàlma, a kindred of Ânnezy, 377.

Jinnat ed-dinnea (Damascus), 316.

el-Jinny, 164.

Jips, read *jîbs* (جِبْس), gypsum, *v. jiss,* II. 20, 129.

Jîr-ak! (جَارَك) a Beduin formula as much as to say, "the affair is mine, trouble not my interest therein," 143.

Jîsan [*Kisan*] *Mejelly,* plain near Hâyil, 668.

Jiss (حِصّ), gypsum or pipe-clay, 578, 636, 638, 653; II. 20, 40, 129; — used as soap, *ib.*; pargetting with —, 346, 367, 373.

Jîth'a (جَذَع), four-year-old camel, 401.

Jízak Ulla kheyer, 307; II. 69.

Jizzat (جِيزَة for زِجَّة) *en-Nasâra* (341), 492.

W. *el-Jizzl,* 134, 181, 187, 217, 453, 463, 465, 468.

Joab, David's sister's son: his cruelty to the Edomites, 83.

Job, 321; the *reem* (رِئْم) or "unicorn" described in —, 373, 529, 558; II. 220, 345.

St. John, 213; II. 24.

St. John Baptist: "disciples of —," II. 231.

Jonas, sepulchre of —, 216.

Jonathan son of Saul, 310, 312.

Jorda, ancient metropolis of el-Kasîm, *v. Járada* and *el-Éthelly*.

Jorda, a Nefûd dune, *v. Jurda*.

Jordan River: lands beyond —, 40, 50, 66, 131, 308, 469, 486; II. 66, 264, 338, 339.

Joseph, the patriarch, 308, 312, 336, 373.

Josephus, 56.

Journey; the — in the Arabian desert like a fever, 484; II. 276; 507.

Jowla, mountain in the Teháma, 451, 462, 463.

Jowwár (class. جِوَار) pl. of *jára,* a wife, 258, 516.

Ju'a, hunger, 435.

el-Juâberra, fendy of Harb Mosrûh, II. 547.

Juba; II. 326.

Jubba (جُبَّة), long coat of stuff worn by substantial persons in the Turkish towns, II. 542.

Judah, 527.

Judgment, the day of —, 143, 493.

Juhâl, ignorants, pl. of *jâhil,* 355, 592.

July heat in el-Kasîm, II. 464.

Jumma'a (جَمَاعَة), the company and alliance of a man's kindred and partizans, 527.

Jummàr, a young village woman of the blacks at Kheybar, II. 191; 220.

Jummàr (جُمَّار), pithwood of the palm tree, II. 205 [the sweet wood next the pith, chopped small, is given, at Kheybar, to kine, to fatten them], 393.

June: spring and light summer showers commonly fall in Kasîm till —, II. 434, 482.

Jupiter's moons: the clear eyesight of Mohammed en-Nejûmy could even discern —, II. 165. [The like is reported by Wrangel of certain Samoyedes. Sabine's transl.]

Júrda (جُرْدَة), or *jorda,* pl. *jérad* and *jerád,* a dune in the Nefûd, 'with clay seams and plants growing upon it,' [but — is properly ground bare of herbage,] II. 357.

Jurdy (جُرْدَة), government relief expedition sent down to Arabia from Damascus, to meet the returning Hâj, at Medáin S.: the —, 40, 100, 128, 238-9, 243; — officers, 213, 244; 246, 248-9, 254, 294, 483; II. 197.

OF ARABIC WORDS 633

Jurn (جُرن), antique stone troughs so called at Medáin Sâlih, and el-Khreyby, 175, 180, 200.

Jurn (جُرن), clarified-butter skin, II. 230.

Jurraba (جُرباء), mangy thelûl, II. 342.

Justice [v. *Kady*, Arbiter] : a Christian has no hope in Moham. —, 215, not even amongst the Beduw, 396 ; — in the oases, 187 ; — in the desert administered by the sheykh and the council of the elders, 291 ; the desert — is upright, mild, expedite, and the sheykh's word is final, 291 ; there is no crime that may not be redeemed, 291 ; their law is not binding without the religion, 460.

K (ك): the people of Nejd in general pronounce this letter *ch*. [A like change is found in English, *ex*. spea*k*—spee*ch*, cool—*ch*ill.]

K (ق), a sort of guttural *k*, *g-k* nearly, pronounced deeply, with a strangling, in the throat. In the mouths of the people of Nejd this letter sounds commonly as *g hard* ; and is sometimes *g soft* or *j* [v. *J*].

el-Ká (*el-Ká'a* القَع), a Hâj menzil near Tebûk, 111.

el-Ka'aba, the *Beyt-Ullah* (Beth-el) or "God's house, built by Abraham;" the tower-like cell or chamber which stands in the midst of the court of the temple of Mecca. It is covered with a veil (*thôb*) ; and the "*black stone*" (which is of the kind of idol-stones of old heathen Arabia) is built into one of the walls. 101, 141, 578 ; II. 514, 515, 545.

Ka'abeny 'Arab, 112 (v. sub Tebûk), 578.

Ka'ak, biscuit cake of Damascus, 370, 633.

Kabâil, pl. of *kabîla*, qd. v.

Kabîla, a tribe, pl. *kabâil*.

Kábr ed-dunnia, II. 145.

Kábr es-Sâny, 668.

Kabshàn, basalt mountain and watering-place in the great desert S. of el-Kasîm, II. 493.

Kády (Nejd, *káthy*), a justice, 181 ; the village kâdies handle no bribes, nor pervert justice, 187 ; — at Hâyil, 659.

a *Kády* at Tâyif, II. 544, 545.

el-Kády Músr, a foreign dweller at et-Tâyif and possessor of an orchard there, II. 551.

Káfar, great B. Temîm vill. a few miles S. of Hâyil, vulg. *Gófar*, qd. v. and Bed. *Jífar*.

Káfer, a village near Boreyda, II. 339.

Káfila, a caravan [Bed. *kúfl*, qd. v.].

Kàfir, pl. *kuffâr* and *kafirûn* ; a reprobate, one not of the saving religion, one of the heathen, 71, 280, *et passim*.

Kafûr, camphor : II. their opinion of —, 229.

Káhatîn (قَحاطين), gentile pl. of *el-Kahtân*.

Kahl (better *kúhl*) or antimony used to paint the eyes ; they think it gives them beauty and preserves the sight : 279, 637, 647.

el-Kahtân [not *Beny* — which is *loghrat Ânnezy* ; gentile pl. *el-Kahatîn*] : a noble-blooded tribe of Southern Aarab, but reputed to exceed all other Aarab in fanatical wildness and cruel malice, 289 ; atrocious circumcision fabled to be used amongst them, 170 ; their stock, 270; 326, 389, 435, 464, 522, 661 ; II. 51-6 ; — not Beny —, 51 ; '*Abda Shammar* from a fendy of —, 52 ; noble ancestry of —, 53 ; — reputed to be *anthropophagi*, 55 ; it is reported that they drink human gore, and kill tobacco-drinkers, *ib*. ; the maws of fowls are their sepulchres, 56 ; 235, 342, 344, 345, 346, 350, 353, 354, 392-5 ; 436, 442 ; treachery in battle of —, 453, 454, 455 ; — a word of reproach, 467 ; 468, 472 ; expedition of Meteyr and 'Aneyza against —, 473-9 ; oath of the defeated sheykhs, that there should be no treachery, 479, 480, 481, 484, 489, 553-4.

Káhwa (vulg. *gáhwa*), coffee.

Káhwa (vulg. *gáhwa*), coffee house or coffee tent, 183 ; kahwas of the sheykhs at el-Ally, 184 ; II. the — or coffee tavern on the Mecca roads, 518, 573.

Káhwajy, coffee-server, 526 *et passim*.

Kahwat Abeyd, 646, 660.

Kaif, a B. Sâlem Harb village, II. 546.

Kaimakàm, at Maan, 115 ; II. at et-Tâyif, 544.

el-Kalandâry, 115.

el-Kàmîm, mountain in the desert between Kasîm and Mecca, II. 504.

el-Kamûs, or 'Ocean' Lexicon of the Arabic tongue, 457 ; II. 58.

Kanakîna, quinine, 641.

634

INDEX AND GLOSSARY

[*Ḳʻar* (قَعْر)], low bottom in the desert.

Ḳáramak Ullah, 663.
Karîm, bountiful, 477.
Karra, v. *Khára*.
Ḳaṣaṣîd, pl. of *Ḳaṣṣâd*, qd. v.
el-Ḳaṣîm, a province of Middle Nejd [whose lat., says Ibn Ayith, is 25°: the people of — are called *el-Ḳuṣmân*, qd. v.], 253, 295, 305, 330, 335, 338, 420, 444, 518, 522, 536, 547, 576, 638, 661, 665; ii. 18, 32, 37, 41, 42, 47, 51, 55, 60, 64, 71, 97, 111, 146, 240, 274, 297, 300, 308, 311, 312, 315, 317, 319, 320, 323, 327, 332, 335, 336, 337-42, 345, 346, 350, 355, 373, 393, 394, 419, 426, 428, 434; *Ḳusmàn* sojourning in the North, 439; 441; the currency of —, 447, 450, 456, 460, 465, 471, 490, 492, 493, 494, 498, 506, 514, 539, 553, 565.
Ḳâsim ibn Barák (or *Barrák*), great skeykh of the Midland Heteym, ii. 75, 78-82; his sister, 81; 296, 305, 306.
Ḳaṣr, pl. *ḳaṣûr*, signifies in desert Arabia a stable dwelling (which is in those countries of clay), and sometimes a cluster of houses enclosed by a wall: at Háyil and er-Riâth el-— signifies the princely residence or castle. 147, 570; 636; ii. 322, 325.
Ḳaṣr ʻAd ibn Shaddâd, ii. 52.
Ḳaṣr Arbŷiyyah, ruined suburb of Hâyil, 669.
el-Ḳaṣr [*Ḳaṣr el-Asheruwát*], village of J. Shammar (the wells are of 30, others say of 10, fathoms), ii. 34, 76, 267, 269.
Ḳaṣr Besîr, ancient tower in Moab, 51.
Ḳaṣr el-Bint, monument at Medáin S., 145, 146, 174; — *bebàn*, 149, 211, 673-4.
Ḳaṣr: the — or Prince's hostel at Boreyda, ii. 341.
Ḳaṣr Hajellân, at Boreyda, ii. 345, 347-54.
Ḳaṣr: the — or castle at Hâyil, 636, 637, 638, 645, 658, *et passim*; ii. — when founded, 19; 27, 28, 31, 39, 46, 272, 276, 280, 348, 455.
Ḳaṣr of an orchard in el-Ḳaṣîm, ii. 446.
Ḳaṣr en-Néby, an ancient cottage near Kheybar so called, ii. 116.
Ḳaṣr: the — or Princely residence at er-Riâth, ii. 455.
Ḳaṣr (or *Beyt*) *es-Ṣâny*, at Medáin S., 151, 153, 238.
Ḳaṣr es-Shebîb, v. *Shebîb*.
Ḳaṣr Zellûm, at Teyma, 339-40; inscription stone in —, 340; 601.

Kasra (كَسْرَي) *el-Ḥâj*, 109.
Ḳassab, village in el-Kasîm, ii. 452.
Ḳaṣṣâd [pl. *ḳaṣaṣîd* v. also *Shaʻer*, *Nâdem*], riming poet in the desert tribes, 306; their recitation, ib.; —s of Bishr were the best in the Teyma circuit; — of B. ʻAtîeh, 544.
Ḳaṣîda, song, qd. v.; —s of ʻAbeyd ibn Rashîd, 306; 513, 414.
Ḳaṣṣûr B'thèyny, the scuplured frontispices at el-Héjr [but in this work used to distinguish the western bébàn], 151, 213.
Ḳasyîn, pl., cruel, ii. 284.
Kaṭʻa 'l-ḳalb, heart cutting, 627.
Katálny et-taab (*tʻab*) *wa ej-jûʻa*, ii. 473.
Ḳathâfa, a woman's name, 179.
Káthir Ullah fóthilakom, the Lord multiply thy virtuous bounty, 446.
Káthir Ullah lebànakom, the Lord multiply thy food of milk, 447.
el-Kâthy, (Nejd pron. of *ḳâḍy*), a name, ii. 469.
Katràn kellâ, 58.
Ḳawàs, javelin-man (lit. archer): their kawasses precede great officers (and European consuls) in their formal passages abroad, ii. 106, 318, 541.
" Kedar. Black tents of," 266.
Kef (Bed. *Chef*), hand or palm, 347.

Keffy (كَفِّي), 313.

B. *Kelàb*, or *Chelb*, 328.
Kelàm Ullah, God's word, 342.
Beny Kelb, fable of the —, 171.

Kellâ (قَلْعَة), redout or stronghold, (147); which upon the Derb el-Ḥâj is a tower to defend a cistern of water, 47; Ḥâj-road —s surprised by the Beduw, 128; provision and cost of the —s, 164-5; 248.
el-Kellâ, a pinnacle near el-Ally, 180.
el-Kellâ, Medáin Sâliḥ; a building four-square, 60 feet upon a side and near 30 high. [v. M. Sâliḥ and the Fig. p. 416.]
Kellâjy, a kellâ-keeper upon the Ḥâj way, 125, 127, 235, 248.

el-Kennèyny, [read *el-Khennèyny*, الخنيني]: Abdullah el-, of ʻAneyza; a corn merchant at Bosra: he was a beneficent friend of the Nasrâny; ii. 367; his house, 368; his mother, 369; his books, 370; 376, 379,

OF ARABIC WORDS

397, 398, 411, 415, 417-22, 423, 426, 429, 431, 434, 437, 442, 446, 447, 472, 475; breakfast with —, 374; 379, 381; his palm-ground, 370, 382-3; his kindness to the European stranger, 386; 397, 468, 473, 483; his thoughts for his son, 388; his mind, *ib.*; his youth, his trading and good fortune, 389; his grain trade (at Bosra), *ib.*; 390, 410; his fatal malady, 411; 481, 483, 486, 487, 488, 503, 510; his farewell, 487; his end, *ib.*

Ker-ker-ker-ker, (imagined) sound of a meteor in the sky, 510.

Kerak, a town in Moab, and very strong site [Mr. D. sojourned in — a fortnight, in June 1875], 52, 57, 59, 60; — called el-Medina, 62; (perhaps Kir of Moab, 60;) husbandry at —, 61, 72; the people of —, 62; — taken by Ibrahîm Pasha, 62; — might be occupied without bloodshed, 63; Christians at —, *ib.*; 63, 65; Christian homicide at, 64; mere-stone of B. Hamèydy nigh —, 64; strife of the Kerakers with the B. Hamèydy, for the price of the "Moabite stone," 65; — wives of the next kellâ garrison; 66; — summer camps, 63, 74; (the kingdom of Moab to compare with an English county, 83); 450.

Jebel Kerak, 59, 70, 355.
Wady Kerak, 66.

Kerakô (Turk. قراول, vulg. قراقول, قراغول), sentinel, 46.

Kerdûs, the old name, some say, of *Siddûs*, II. 355.

Kériatèyn, a Syrian village, 579, 603, 619.
Kerrèya, *v.* sub *Kirreya*.
Kerwa, *v. Kirwa*.
Kesmih, vill. near Damascus, 43.
Ketèyby, cistern, 44.

Kethbàn (كثبان), pl. of *kethîb*, *qd. v.*

Kethîb (كثيب), pl. *kethbàn*, sand dunes (of the Nefûd), II. 339, 357.

Key: Bed. house-wife's —, 268; II. wooden gate- —, 352.
Keyf 'murak? how do thy affairs prosper? 197.
Keyf uṣbaḥt? 111.

Kèyif (كيف), pleasance, solace, 276, 587, 658; II. 466.

Keys, an Arabian patriarch, II. 381, 393, 394.
Keys, the tribe, II. 477.
Kezâz, a berg in el-Kasîm, II. 476, 492.
K'fa, a kindred of Solubba, 326.
el-Khábar? Weysh el-'ellûm? II. 305.

Khadŷjy (خديجة), Bed. fem. name, 514.

Wâdy Khâfutha, II. 90, 242.
J. Khâl, in the desert between el-Kasîm and Mecca, II. 501, 502.

el-Khála (الخلا), [*v.* Desert], the empty land, the waste desert, 177, 285, 305, 393; 404, 433; — a land under no rule, 319; 320; II. 62.

Khálaf el-'Ammr, sheykh of Teyma, 332, 575-9, 581, 591, 593-4, 596, 606.
Khálaf, an Allàydy sheykh living in exile with the Fukara, 265, 273, 296, 364, 390, 553.
Khálaf ibn Náhal, *v. Ibn Náhal*.

Khálaf Ullah 'aleyk yâ m'azzîb (معزب), the Lord requite thee, O host, 446.
Khàlas, an end! 296, 575, 671.
Khàlatak (read *khàltak*), II. 82.
B. Khâlid, a tribe whose name was the greatest in Nejd before the Waháby, II. 367, 378, 381.
Khâlid, a fendy of Wélad 'Aly, 271.
Khâlid bin Walîd, II. 421.
Khâlif(a), calif, vicar, II. 182.
Khalîl, a sheykh of Kerak.
el-Khalîl, (city of) the Friend (of God), *i.e.* Hebron, where Abraham dwelt, 72, 78, 493; Jebel —, the mountainous country about —, 64, 77, 82.
el-Khamâla, a kindred of the Fukara tribe, 270, 278, 422, 553, 560.
el-Khámr, the fermented (wine), 352.
Khân ez-Zebîb, site on the Hâj road in the desert of Edom, 89.
Khân ez-Zeyt, site on the Hâj road, in Moab, 57.
Khànjar, [*v.* also *Kiddamîyyah* and *Shibrîyyah*], the Bed. crooked girdle-knife, 505; II. 518.
Khanzir, swine.
Khanzîra, village under Kerak, 64.

Khàra (خرا), II. 32, 161.

Khark (vulg. *el-Khorj*), a town of Middle Nejd, II. 425.

el-Khárram, or *Khúrram*, 620-1, 626, 629, 630; II. 71, 87.
Kharûf, male lamb, 475.
el-Khâsira, a site in the desert nigh Hâyil on the N., II. 61.
Khathrâ, desert site between Ḥayil and Kuweyt, II. 61.
el-Khátm, the seal, *i.e.* the Koran scripture, 584.
Khawâja [*v. Mu'allem*], title of Jews and Christians in the civil (or border) Arabic countries, 551.
Khayin, treacherous, II. 527.
Khedéwy (خديو), title of the Pasha of Egypt, II. 110.
el-Kheréyby, Harb village near Mecca, II. 546.
el-Kheréysy, a part of the citizens of 'Aneyza so called, II. 411, 458-61.

[*Kheréyṭa* (خريطة), bag (Western Aarab).

[*el-Kherj*, district between el-'Aruth and the Aflâj, with seven villages: *ed-Díllum, el-Yemâma, N'ajàn, es-Sellumîeh, el-Aṭṭhar, es-Seyeh*. — M. en-Nefîs.
Kheyâbara, negro villagers of Kheybar: — despised by the strangers there, II. 104; they are dull peasants, 105; they speak Medina Arabic, 106, 112; — often comely, 94, 128, 137, 151; — are reputed niggards and inhospitable, 109, 131; but *v.* 131-2; their ancestry, 111-2, 114; these villagers commonly live with one wife, 112; their fear of the magical arts of the Nasrâny, 112, 115, 146, 160; their hope of his finding hid treasures, 121; their religion, 114, 116; they praise the dates of their valleys, 119; — poor and miserable in their abundant valleys, 131-2; they rest from labour at noon, 136; — 'a light and whimsical people', 137, 152; malice and fanaticism of the —, 154, 155, 156; — wives, charitable to strangers, 190; — fishing in the tarns, 204; — eat no poultry, nor leeks, 208, 221; Abu Middeyn, 220; 233, 238, 342.
el-Khéyba, an ass-mare's name, II. 253.
Kheybar [28 Nov. 1877—17 March, 1878], 119, 170, 171, 176, 192, 202, 204, 238, 254, 300, 312; — patrimony of Ânnezy, 314, 319; 323, 346, 377, 379, 381, 382, 389, 391, 413, 414, 435, 444, 458, 470, 474; *Abu Selîm* at —, 482; 485, 500-1, 524, 526, 528, 532, 538, 553, 557, 580, 595, 596, 597, 602, 608-9, 627; II. 21, 35, 37, 42, 45, 67, 69, 70, 71, 79, 80, 84, 86, 89, 90, 91; Medina government at —, 92; the — valleys, 110, and *v.* the map, 203; the old Mohammedan conquest of —, 93; — resembles an African village, 94; spring waters of —, 95, 96; 97; they are warm, sulphurous and not brackish, 110, 117; — grave-yard, 96; all horror at —, 97, 98, 102, 109, 192; Medina salesmen come to the autumn fair at —, 107; bride-money at —, *ib.*; marriage, *ib.* 128; lava of the Figgera seen to be about 50 feet thick at the valley sides, 110; underlying clays and sandstone, *ib.*; site and view of —, 112, 113; husbandmen's tools from the coast, 115; diviners come to raise the hid treasures of —, 121; witches of —, 124-6; 129; few young children seen at —, 128; — women, *ib.*; custom to labour for each other, 130, 206; clays underlie the lava valley sides, 110, 129; custom to break up the tough basalt rock by firing it, 130, 219; the abundance of their humble life at —, 108, 131; house-building at —, *ib.*; husbandry at —, *ib.*, 135; — dates, 94; date measures, 132; a wasteful young man of —, 131; the — valleys a proverb in the desert, 132; Mosaic —, *ib.*, 145; the Ânnezy conquest of —, 132; those ancient Aarab denied to the — villagers their daughters in marriage for ever, 133; the Beduin land-partnership, 133-4; former tyranny of the Beduw at —, 96, 135, 140, 151; a stranger may be a partner in their corn husbandry, 134; irrigation, 136; — villagers surprised by a passing ghrazzu, 138; Bed. warfare at —, 142-4; misery of the stranger's life at —, 110, 144; Ottoman soldiery at —, pilferers of the date fruit, 144; cholera and fever at —, 145, 150, 238; — the grave of the soldiery, 145; fabulous opinions of —, 146; captivity at —, 146, 218; Medina government of —, 147, 153; the village cleansed, 145; the housewives are compelled to sweep before their own doors, or be beaten, 145; contribution of firewood, 151-2; — is three sûks, 152; sedition, *ib.*; the number of inhabitants, 153; — palms, 118, 119, 198; autumn fair at —, 156, 158; Beduin warfare at —, 117, 123; the ancient inhabitants of the — valleys, 116; barrows on the lava-field about —, 120, 237; — fever, 120, 162; [In the summer

OF ARABIC WORDS 637

months of most heat the villagers sit in their ground chambers.] — to Medina is five marches, 201 ; topography, 201-4 ; — "cheese," 205 ; — kine, *ib.*; a Beduwy built for himself a clay summer house ; and, as he entered it, the lintel fell on his neck and slew him, 206 ; cottages at —, 207 ; chickens robbed, 208 ; — mountains, *ib.*; an 'Ageyly's grave said to have been violated, in the night-time, by the — witches, 208 ; 216-232 ; 233, 234, 237, 239, 241, 243, 249, 252, 261, 263, 268, 272, 273, 275, 279, 291, 293, 299, 308, 403, 412, 420, 435, 442, 451, 512, 529, 549, 553, 565, 566 ; the spring-time returns, 218 ; labour to enlarge a spring-head, *ib.*; springs are tepid at —, 219 ; irrigation rights, 220 ; waterer's dial, *ib.*; — an "island," 223 ; Ibn Rashîd desires to recover —, 225 ; famine at —, 232 ; altitude and air of —, 233-4 ; season to marry the palms, *ib.*; neither Hejâz nor Nejd, *ib.*; depart from —, 234-6 ; fenny ground, 237.

Kheyr, good : — *Ullah*, the Lord's bounty, common world's good as food, 256, 384, 627.

Kheyr-el-barr, the best of the land or the land's wealth, *v. sub Kheybar*, II. 132.

Kheyt-beyt, (حَيْت بَيْت), nothingness, 221.

el-Khiarát, a fendy of midland Heteym, II. 253.

Khíbel (خَبِل), lunatic, 647.

Khidâd, ruins of a village, 78.
el-Khithr, St. George or Elijah, 116.
el-Khlûa or *Kheluîy*, *v. Solubba*.
Kh'lûy (pl. *khlûa*), a lonely passenger in the *khála*, II. 257.

Khôaf (خَائِف, خَوَاف), a trembling coward, II. 102.

Khóbra (خَبْرَاءُ), [and *v. Gá*], loam-bottom where winter rain is ponded, II. 260, 338.

Khóbt, a flat country, II. 572.
[*Khorbêb'ha*, wady and géria in the Ḥarreyry below el-Ally.
el-Khorj (*Khark*), a town in Middle Nejd, II. 425.

Khórma, Sbeya village in W. es-Sbeya, II. 381, 567.
el-Khorma, village of B. Sâlem, Harb, II. 546.
Khormán (حِرْمان, deadly and hungered), 489.
el-Khosâba, ass-mare's name, II. 253.
Khôsh (خُوش), excellent, a Pers. Gulf word, II. 426.
Khossî, small grey lizard, II. 567.
Khóthra, a Bed. woman's name, 514.
Khótr (probably *ḳotr*, قُوطَر, *v. Gôṭar*), go down to, 523.
Khôweylid, a seyl-bed at Teyma, 340.
el-Khrèyby [dim. of *Khurbet*, ruin], site of Himyaric ruins near el-Ally. Mr. Doughty found there many (Himyaric) inscriptions : an underground aqueduct, which is seen above, may have led water to —, *v.* Brook ; [*el-Khreyby* is *Kériat Héjr*, 200 ;] 180, 184, 199 ; — described, 200 ; inscriptions at —, 200, 202 ; sepulchral cells hewn in the cliff, 202 ; image-tablets, *ib.*, human figure and sculptured head, 202-3-5 ; tablets with little basins, *ib.*, 203 ; is el-Khrèyby Thamudite Hejra ? 229 ; 529, 545, 556, 602.
el-Khrèymy, a palm planting of the Emir, near Hâyil, 668.
el-Kh'tâm, a mountain in the Harrat Kheybar, II. 240.

Khûa (خُوَّة ; *akhu*, brother), the tax paid by oasis-dwellers or by weaker nomad kindreds to Beduin tribes about them, to purchase (the security of) their *brotherhood*, 164 *et passim*.

Khûak (خُوك), thy companion, fellow, brother (in the way), II. 293.

Khubbat (perhaps قُبَّة) *et-Timathil*, a rock scored over with inscriptions, 119.
Khubbera [or *Khóbra*. Ibn 'Ayith wrote for me الخبرا], an oasis in el-Ḳasîm, 49 ; II. 37, 433-41 ; the town is silent, 440 ; population of —, 441 ; 447, 467, 487, 489, 490.

el-Khubbu b'il-Wady Mahàjja [haply the necropolis of ancient Teyma], 601.
Khubithîn, plur., malignants, II. 284.
el-Khuèyra (الخويّرة), 'a nâga that sweats much,' 513, 541-2, 621, 661 ; II. 286.
Khùiân, companions, like brothers, in the way, II. 293.
Khumsha, a fendy of Bishr, 376.
Khurbet, ruin [this word is often joined to the names of ruined places in the N.], 61.
Khurbet er-Rumm, 94.
Khurrfa, village in el-Aflâj, II. 425.
Khúrussy, a fendy of Shammar, II. 56.
Khûsa, a knife, 505.
Khussherkîsh, Fejîr camping ground, 259.
Khusshm, naze, snout of an animal, and (always in Arabia) said for the human nose, 285 ; II. 112.
Khusshm es-Sefsáfa, a headland rock at Kheybar, II. 109, 116.
el-Khúthar, site near Boreyda, II. 355.
el-Khuthéra (pronounced *kh'therra*), a nomad kindred of B. 'Atîeh, named of their shekyh's fendy *el-Khúthery*, 116 ; their country, *ib.*, 462, 464 ; their border southward, 119, 238.
Khúthera, II. 263.
Khutherân, a kindred at Kheybar, II. 153.
Khúthery, pl. *Khuthéra*, Bed. of W. el-Akhdar, 116, 119.
Khúthery Harra, 462, 464.
el-Khúthr, valley and kellâ, *v.* Akhdar.
Khuzèyn, a dog's name, 474.
Khuzna, treasure.
Kh'zâm, son of Bîllî, 430.
el-Kibd, the liver ; said by the Bed. of visceral diseases, 298.
Kiddamîyyah, prob. قدّاميّة, [also named *khánjar* and *shibrîyyah*], the Bed. crooked girdle-knife, 505 ; II. 54, 469.
Kids, 346, 368.
Kilâb, pl. of *kelb*, hounds, 355.
Kilâb el-khála, *v.* Solubba.
Kine : — of el-Ally, 194, 338 ; wild —, *v.* Bakr el-Wáhashy, II. 20 ; great-horned — of the Gallas, 186 ; — of Kheybar, 205 ; — of el-Yémen, *ib.*; — of el-Hâyat, *ib.*, 232 ; — of el-Kasîm, 336 ; — in 'Aneyza, 374 ; — to draw wells at et-Tâyif, 551, 560.
Kinîsy, synagogue, church.
el-Kîr [vulg. *Chîr*], a berg near Dókhany water, II. 492.

Kir of Moab, *v.* Kerak.
[*el-Kirr*, village of tents of Bed. husbandmen, one day S. of Béda, in the Teháma.
Kirra, *v.* kirwa.
el-Kirrân, an affinity of Kheybar villagers, II. 153.
el-Kirrèya (from أقر), a reading of words chosen out of the Koran ; which they think a remedy for poisonous bites of serpents and insects, and in exorcism, 358 ; II. 17.
Kirwa or *kerwa* or *kirra* (كروة and كرا), hire, 238.
Kiss : — a sacramental gesture, 311 ; the salutation with a —, 376, 414 ; II. to — the hand toward, in sign of devout acquiescence with thankfulness, 83, 199 ; the — of suppliants, 478. [I have seen a Bed. sheykh — *Ibrahîm es-Sennad*, an Allaydy of the Medina dîra — kiss the hem of the garment of the clerk of the Jurdy at Medáin Sâlih, entreating him in the matter of his surra, 428.]
el-Kissa, Harb village, II. 546.
Kisshub [diversely pronounced — *Kesshub*, *Kesshab*. Sheykh Nasîr es-Smîry wrote كشب, and he pronounced Kisshub.
Kitâb, book.
Kitchen of the public guest-house at Hâyil, II. 74.
el-Kleb, tribe *v.* Ibn et-Tubbai.
el-Kleyb 'Aarab, an ancient tribe, 326.
el-Kleybát, a fendy of Jehèyna, 166.
Kleyfát, a kindred of Ânnezy, 377.
Kleys, Harb village, II. 546.
el-Klîb, tribe *v.* Ibn et-Tubbai.
Knife, *v.* Khûsa, Rîsh : few of the Southern Aarab possess any —, 505 ; II. 260.
Koátcheba, a kindred of Ânnezy, 377 ; also a well in the Nefûd between Teyma and Hâyil, *v.* Map.
Koba, *v.* Gôba, II. 500.
Koleyb, name, II. 476.
Kôm, stock, II. 112.
Konsolîeh, village, II. 567.
Konsul (Consul), II. 105-6.
Konsulato, II. 106, 278.
W. *Koora*, *v.* W. Kora (3).
Koowy ! (كُوْع), lean easily on a cushion, II. 179.
Kòr ! (Turk. كور, fool), II. 161.

OF ARABIC WORDS

W. Kora (وادي القُرَي, v. W. el-Kurra), between el-Ally and el-Medina, 187, 193, 203.
(2) W. Kôra, in the Ḥareyry, 468.
(3) W. Kora, of the Ḥarrat Kheybar, 468; ii. 202.
J. Kora (vulg. Kurra), mountains near et-Tâyif, ii. 559.
el-Kôrân (ḳára, read), the Legend or (sacred) Reading (unto salvation), 134, 135, 136, 300, 331; — fables of Medáin Sâlih, 127, 135-6; — Arabic, 307; 342, 358, 400, 521, 584; 666; ii. 24; tongue of the —, 339, 426.
Ḳoreysh, gentile pl. Ḳorásh, the nomad kindred of Mohammed, now poor and despised tribesfolk, ii. 231, 381, 559; called Beny Fáhm, ib.; 562, 568.

Ḳorḥ (قُرْح); named, in the medieval Mohammedan authors, 'a busy trading town in the W. el-Kora above Medina:' the site is now not known, it might be Korḥ, 203-4.
[Koronát, the states of Europe; word used by the foreign merchants at 'Aneyza.
Koseyr, a Red Sea (African) port, ii. 110.
Kottîb, a scribe; or perhaps khotîb, 591.
Ḳouk, a Hebr. word compared with Goukh in the (Aramaic) monumental epitaph, of el-Héjr, 674.
el-Kowwâ, misprinted for es-Sowwa, ii. 253.
Kremer, Alfred von —, ii. 448.
Kreybîsh, a Mahûby lad, 542.
Krîm (Crimea), 318.
Ḳrûn, "horns," braided fore and side locks of the Arabians, qd. v.
K'seyberra, old ruined site near Yanb'a-the-Palms, ii. 202.
Kubbak, cast thee off, 223.
el-Kuds ("the Holy"), Jerusalem, 493.
Kudsh, pack-horses, 317.
Kûfa, ruins of —, 657.
el-Kuffâr, pl. of kàfir, heathen; commonly said of Jews and Christians, 137, 269, 324, 355.
Kufic (Kúfy):— writing, 203, 224; ii. — inscriptions, 116, 563.

Ḳúfi (قُفْل), Bed., convoy (townsfolk say ḳáfila), 420, 421-2; — march in the day's heat, 423.
Kul wàḥed 'aly dîn-hu, 191; ii. 103.

Kum(n)bâz, the man's gown of the civil border countries, 625, 644.
Kúmr, girdle, 620.
[Kúnfid, village near Béda in the Tehâma.
Ḳúnfuth (قُنْفُذ), the hedgehog, 371.
Ḳurbân [Hebr. and Ar. قُرْبان; a bringing near unto God], religious sacrifice.
Kurd, 114; Hâj kellâ garrisons were formerly of —s, 165; —y Aga at Ma'an, 214; ii. 97; Amm Mohammed's father, 157, 191.
ΚΥΡΙΑΚΟC, name or word in an inscription near Medáin S., 408.
Kurmel, Nabal's village, 78.

Kurn el-Menâzil (قرن المنازل), ancient name of a station at the height of Nejd, (now es-Seyl, qd. v.) whence those who arrive from Nejd go down in one or two marches to Mecca, ii. 427, 512.
W. el-Kurra, v. W. el-Kôra (وادي القُرَي, valley of the villages).
Kurra (or Kora) mountains near eṭ-Tâyif, ii. 559.
Kúrsy (chair), ii. 556.
Kurunîyah, villagers of Shammar kindred, in el-'Aruth, ii. 57.
el-Kurzân, a fendy of 'Ateyba, ii. 457.
Kuseyby, village of "two hundred" houses on the way from Boreyda to J. Shammar, ii. 339.
Kusmân, the people of el-Ḳasîm. The — followed faintly with the Waháby warfaring against 'Aneyza, ii. 430.
Kuss marrat-hu or ummhu, 312.
Kus umm-ha! ii. 268.

Kuṭ'aat ghránem (قِطْعَة غَنَم), a flock of sheep, 355.
Kuweyt, a free town on the Persian Gulf. ii. 35, 61, 305, 336, 337, 365, 366, 381, 394, 417, 449, 469, 483, 491.

La! 'ameymy, ii. 30.
La ilâh ill' Ullah, wa Mohammed rasûl Ullah (There is no God but the Lord our God, and M. is the Apostle of God); the Mohammedan confession of faith, 199, et passim.

La túnshud (لا تَنْشُد), 627.

INDEX AND GLOSSARY

La'ab (لَعَّاب ?), a playfellow.
Laanat Ullah aleyk, II. 161, 468.
Laban, the Syrian, 648.
Lâba(t), pl. *lûb* (لابَة pl. لُوب), lava, 468 ; II. 88, 237.
Lâbat el-Agûl, near Medina, II. 204.
Labbeyk (vulg. *lubbeyk*, *qd. v.*), II. 26.
Labourers: field — at 'Aneyza, II. 467-8 ; in W. Fâtima, 567, 570.
el-Lahá, ass-mare's name, II. 253.
Lahabba, a fendy of 'Aûf, Harb; they are robbers of the pilgrim caravans between the Harameyn, II. 174-6, 546, 547.
Laheyân Aarab, of Hatheyl, II. 569.
Lahyat-hu taîba, 311.
Lambs [*v. Kharûf, Tully, Rókhal*], 346, 368, 475.
Lance: the horseman's — (*shelfa* or *romhh*), 259, 332, 379.
Land: value of oasis — at Teyma, 602 ; II. at Kheybar, 117, 134, 158 ; — at 'Aneyza, 379.
Land-knowledge: the Beduins have little — beyond their own borders, 271, 349, 450, 469.
Landmarks of the Hâj march, 95, 96.
"Land of the Beduw, The," 255.
"Land which eateth up the inhabitants thereof," 477.
Language: the Beduin speech [*v*. Arabic and *Loghra*], 196, 238, 388, 624 ; II. 66.
Lantern, 46, 112.
Lapland nomads, 320.
Lark, of Syria, 86.
el-Lâta (اللات), a bethel-stone so named at Tâyif, II. 550.
Latákia, a seabord town in the N. of Syria, 214.
La tanshud, Ask not of it, 627.
Laudanum, II. 229.
Laughter a delight among the Aarab, 492, *et passim*.
Lava drift upon J. Sherra, 68 ; — by the Hâj way in W. Sâny, 118 ; — upon the plain of el-Héjr, 174, 423, 426, 429, 478 ; — in Arabic *lâba* (*qd. v.*) 468 [and *v. Harra*]; II. trachytic basalt near the Harrat Kheybar, 83 ; — of that Harra, 85, 87, 89, 90, 115-16 ; — millstones made by Beduins, 200 ; 227.
W. *Laymûn* (prob. contracted from W. *el-Aiman*, ' the right-hand valley ;' Prof. M. J. De Goeje.) in the Mecca country, II. 67, 488, 510, 523, 546, 565.

Lazzarino Cominazzi, old trade mark upon the best Bed. matchlocks, 504.
el-Lazzáry, that kind of Bed. matchlocks [*v*. Lazzarino, above], 504 ; II. 28.
Lead: hijabs written against —, 300 ; II. 28 ; pigs of — in Hâyil sûk, 23.
Learning in the oases of Arabia : — at el-Ally, 186, 492 ; — at Teyma, 591-2 ; — at Hâyil and in el-Kasîm, II. 56, 57 ; — at Kkeybar, 97, 99.
Lében, sour milk, commonly buttermilk, 81, *et passim*.
Lebanon mountains (*Jebel Libnàn*), II. 348, 370, 398 ; Maronite convents in —, 412, 555.
Lebeid, author of one of the Moallakát, II. 503.
Leechcraft of the hareem, 396.
Leeks: wild — in the desert, 255 ; II. the Kheyâbara eat no —, 208.
Léja, a lava field of the Hauran, 197.
el-Lejîma, Bed. fem. name, 514.
Lejûn (Legio), a ruined town in the Peraea, 58.
Lemons: sweet — at Tebûk, 112 ; — at el-Ally, 185, 194, 246 ; — at Teyma, 338, 582 ; — at Hâyil, 644 ; II. — of the Mecca country, 565.
Leopard [*v. Nímmr*], 373.
Leprosy, 436, 437, 655 ; II. 18.
Letters: the Arabians' opinion of the magical use of —, 511 ; II. 88, 112.
Leviticus: the locust might be eaten by the Hebrews, 381.
Ley tahowwam ? (لَيْ (لِأَيِّ) يُحَوِّمُ), 518.
Lêyla, village, II. 52.
Leyta, village in el-Aflâj, II. 425.
Libbun, ruined site near Kérak, 61.
Jebel Libnàn, the Lebanon range of mountains, II. 399.
Libney (لِبني), camel of the second year, 401.
Lichen; none in droughty Arabia, 442.
Lie: "the — is shameful," 283 ; — an easy defence and natural stratagem, *ib*.; — indulged by the Arabian religion, *ib*.; yet the Aarab say *el-kîthb mâ-hu zain* ; their common lying, 425 ; II. 95 ; " the — is better than the truth," 368.
W. *Lîeh*, near Tâyif, II. 567.
Lightning, 632 ; II. 81, 83, 290, 331.
Lilla, i.e. lâ-lâ, no-no, II. 515.

Limestone : — soil from Damascus to Ma'an, 55, 59, 70, 78, 79 ; in the Jehèyna dîra, 470 ; in the 'Aueyrid, 471 ; in the Harrat Kheybar, II. 90 ; in Moab, 575.
Lion, 506, 518 ; II. in Galla-land, 186 ; at Tâyif, 190.
Lira fransâwy, the French 20-franc piece, II. 23.
W. *Lithm*, between the Gulf of Akaba and Mount Seir, 84.
Litter : camel, mule and horse —s in the Hâj [v. *Takht er-Rum*], 45, 100, 101 ; the Pasha's —, 45, 101, 105 ; Beduin camel —s [v. *Múksir*], 484 ; II. 329 ; Mecca camel —s for hareem, 516.
Liveing, F.R.S., Prof. G. D.: note by — of the spice matter found in the tombs of Medáin Sâlih, 228-9.
el-Liwàn, at M. Sâlih, 160 ; the word explained, 207, 674.
Lizards in the desert, 349, 373, v. *Jelàmy* ; II. 567. [v. *Khossí*.]
Loam : ashes of an ancient hearth shown in the sides of a — pit, II. 421.
Lobster-like impressions in the limestone of Moab, II. 575.
Lock : the wooden — in Arabic countries, 158 ; 185 ; 577, II. 19.
Locusts [v. *Dubba*, *Jarâd*]: 209 ; — cured for food, 244 ; 255, 258, 351, 380-1, 412-13, 442, 472 ; murrain of —, 476, 500 ; diet of —, 520 ; 538, 546, 569 ; II. 91, 95, 119 ; Bed: compared to —, 142 ; — for food, 268 ; 292 ; parched — set to sale in Boreyda, 349 ; — hunters, 358 ; 466, 560.
Loghra(t) [v. *Rótn*], the manner of speaking proper to every tribe and dîra, 307-8, 388 ; II. 79.
Loghrat et-Teyr, a speech as the voices of birds, 562.
el-Loghrf, village in W. Dauâsir, II. 425.
Londra (London), II. 448.
Lost : Beduin boy — in a long ráhla, 347.
Lot : cities of — (*Medáin Lût*), 82, 136.
Love abides not in the desert, 278 ; mother's love, 398 .
Lubbeyk ! (or *labbeyk*, qd. v.) II. 26, 513.
St. Luke, 213.
Lullul-lullul-lullul-la, the *zullerghrît* (زلاغيط commonly زغاريت, Syrian word), or joyful cry of 'Arab women, 233, 392.
Lunatic, v. Imbecility, *Mejnûn*.

Mâ'aleyk ... The word understood is باس, *bâs*, evil ; " there shall no evil be upon thee, thou hast nothing to fear," II. 101.
Mâ b' ak kheyr, there is not any good in thee, II. 384.
Má el-'enab, 656.
Mâ fî árzal minhum, 564.
Mâ láhu kalb, he has no heart, 616.
Mâ lihu lahya, 311.
Mâ li-hum asl, 326.
Mâ ly ghreyr Ullah ! 299.
Mâ n' âsh (ما نَعَاش), we have nothing to eat, 565.
Mâ sâb-hu, it attained him not, 297.
Má es-Sáma (مَاء السَّمَاء), a sebîl of good water at Hâyil, 636, 638, 660 ; II. 65, 75.
Mâ yarúdd (ما يَرُدّ), II. 26.
Má yet'aabûn, they (the Beduw) toil not, 285.
Má yunf'a, II. 389.
Maa salâmy, the Arabic Semitic valediction, Go in Peace.
Maa samawwy ! (a childish mockery for *maa salâmy*), II. 442.
Ma'abûb, a negro, umbrella-bearer to the Sherîf Emîr of Mecca ; he saved the Nasrâny from the knife of a nomad sherîf, at '*Ayn ez-Zeyma*, II. 518-22 ; 526, 532-4, 544.
Ma'an (معان), Hâj station, the ninth from Muzeyrîb, a village in Edom : 43 ; camp established at —, 48, 58, 70 ; — a *merkez*, 71 ; public ware-room at —, 72 ; shops, *ib*.; factions, 73 ; villagers accounted to be of Jewish blood, 73 ; water-mine or well-gallery (made like an adit) (*serdâb*) and wells at —, 74 ; flint instruments, 74, 77 ; outlying corn plots, 74 ; a tale told at —, 77 ; 82, 86, 87, 88, 94, 95, 96, 115, 129, 130, 131, 139, 214, 218, 247, 341, 357, 388, 578, 613 ; II. 48, 64, 238, 289, 349, 553, 575.
Mâana lôn (prob. for ما معنا لُون), we have nothing left, 520.
Ma'araka (مَعْرَقَة), Bed. pad saddle [v. Saddle], II. 484.

642 INDEX AND GLOSSARY

Maʻasub (مَعْصُوب), head cord (which is commonly of twisted camel-wool) of the Bed. kerchief, 484.

Maatuk, an Heteymy sheykh, II. 296-312; his family, 298, 300.

Maʻaun (مَاعُون), clarified-butter skin, II. 230.

Maʻaz, patriarch of el-Maʻazy, 94, 270.

Mʻaazib مُعَزِّب host, II. 257, *et passim*; [the host and his family are called *maʻâzîb* [مَعَازِيب].

Maʻaziba (المَعْزَبَة), the place of entertainment, II. 257.

el-Maʻazy, commonly called *Beny ʻAtîeh*, *q.v.*: 94; their genealogy, 270; 464; 474; II. 286.

Macalister, F.R.S., Prof. A.: note by — of the sepulchral linen, leather and resinous matter found in the Nabatean tombs at el-Héjr, 229.

Máfrak, kellâ, 47.

Mágdala in Abyssinia, II. 185.

Mághrib (townsmen's word in the border lands, not used by Arabians), the sunsetting, 400.

Magical art [*v.* Letters, Divination, Hijâb, Sáhár, Treasure, Witchcraft], 213, 316; II. 108, 112, 120-1.

Magnanimity: the Arabian — serves the time and is not unto death, 310, 575.

Magnesia, called "English salt," 670; II. 27.

Magnify: large speaking of the Arabs, they are wont to —, 325, 469.

Magog and Gog, II. 558.

Máhal (مَحَل), an extreme barrenness of the desert soil; where no seasonable rain has fallen, 626, 635; II. 255, 266, 306.

Mahâl (مَحَال), Nomads' pulley-reels for drawing up water from deep wells, 324; II. 497.

Mahál el-Mejlis, a principal monument at Medáin Sâlih (so named by those of the kellâ): the epitaph, 156-7, 673-4.

Mahál el-Wái, old words written upon a rock at Kheybar, II. 205.

Máhallîb (pl. مَحَالِيب), milk bowls, 477.

Mahanna, usurping Emir of Boreyda, II. 338, 347, 358, 460.

Mahanna, sheykh of the Sehamma, Bíllî, 429-30, 438, 439, 440, 447, 455, 523-4, 547, 553, 557, 630, 641; his mother, 435; his son, 436; 441; II. 67.

Mahjil, Aarab ibn —, sheykh el-Esshàjir, a kindred of Ânnezy, 377.

Maḥʼleb nâkat neby Sâlih, the nâga's milking pail, at el-Khrèyby, 200.

Máhmal (مَحْمَل) camel in the Hâj, 101; II. 545.

Mahmûd, soldier-secretary of the Hâj station at Maʻan, 87, 108; II. 48-9, 348.

Mahmûd Ag(hr)a, el-Arnaûty, II. 541.

Mahmûd, a tradesman of Teyma, 339.

Mahûby, v. Moahîb.

Maibi, a reputed ancestor of the Solubba, 326.

Maidens, Bed. [*v.* Shepherd —, Marriage]: — in the circumcision festivals, 385.

Mail: shirts of — worn by Arabian sheykhs in the day of battle, II. 36, 480.

el-Májar, a kind of the Bed. matchlocks, 504.

Májid [which some few in Hâyil — but not the princely family — pronounce *Mâbid*], son of Hamûd ibn Rashîd, 649, 656; his tutor, 657; 664, 666-7; 671; II. 18, 22, 23, 24, 40, 41, 43; 57; —'s tutor, 58; 72.

Majûj, Magog, II. 558.

Makam, sacred place of sepulture, 51.

Makám er-râs, a hollow in a bethel-stone at et-Tâyif, II. 549, 550.

Mákbara [*v.* Namûs, Rijjûm], burying ground: — of the Fejîr, 395; ancient — upon the ʻAueyrid, 441, 495; — at Hâyil, 671; II. — at S'weyfly, 21; ancient — on the Harrat Kheybar, 239.

Makhʻaul, hamlet in the dominion of Ibn Rashîd, II. 34, 329.

Mákhzan el-Jindy, 563.

Mákhzans, the guest chambers at Hâyil, 638, 661; II. 16, 17, — described, 19, *et passim*.

Mákruha, thing unseemly, not convenient, II. 266.

Malachi: the prophecy of — against Edom, 83.

Maladies: the Arabs think themselves always ailing; their common diseases [*wajʻa*] are: el-kibd, visceral infirmities, 614; er-rihh, rheums, neuralgia; the old cough, 597; fevers (Oases and Hejâz —); ague cake (*tahal*), 597; the stone (*el-hasa*), 615; morbus gallicus; ophthalmia; ʻ fascination;' leprosy;

atrophy; the falling sickness; dropsy; 11. phthisis; cancer; sores; stranguria; tetter; senile itch; — at Hâyil, 18, 19; — at 'Aneyza, 366, 374; wen in the throat, 494.

el-Malakîeh, one of the four orthodox sects of Islam, 186.

Malay Islands; incense and spices from the —, 137, 246.

Maledictions: Bed. —, 309, 586, *et passim*.

[*'Beny Mâlik, dirat-hum bejîla* (حِيلَة), barr *el-Hejâz*: many villages.'

Mambûl, said in mockery for Stambûl, 207.

Manchester clothes the Aarab, in part, 168; 11. 23.

Mandîl, kerchief, 11. 262.

Manèm, a sleeping place (in a public kahwa), 11. 270.

Mangy camel cattle (*v. Jurruba*: Beduins daub their — camels with pitch]: 11. 184, 221, 295.

Mankind, in the opinion and estimation of the Ar., are but simple grains under the throne of God of the common seed of Adam, 313.

Man, the enigma, 520.

Manôkh, [*manûkh* or *manâkh*] place of kneeling down of camels; where passengers alight, and are received to the public hospitality, 11. 270, 536.

Mantar (مَنْظَر), cairns or beacons of stones by the Hâj-way side, way-marks, as at Ma'an and el-Akhdar, 117. [*v.* Cairns.]

Mantle: scarlet —, a common flattering gift of Ottoman governors to sheykhs of tribes and those free Oasis villages that acknowledge the supremacy of the Dowla, 85, 182, 219; 11. 335, 377.

Map of Arabia: a sufficient — may be made in the manner of Ptolemy by diligent cross-reckoning of camel marches, 53, 322; 11. 99. The Itinerarium, attached to these vols., was laid down (but without the aid of chartographers) by such reckonings from Ma'an, Medina, Hâyil, Jidda [whose situations I have accepted from *H. Kiepert's* excellent *Karte zu Ritter's Erdkunde*]. It is an art to question the Nomads and Oasis-dwellers, in topography; they are unwont (*v.* Vol. 11. p. 426) to such exercises of the mind, and of an easy conscience (*tibi assentari*); and that which may be gathered from the words of their best relaters, is ever mingled with doubt and contradictions. [*v.* 'Black Stone of 'Aneyza.']

We must compare together the relations of several persons (which is oftentimes difficult); and (saving their itineraries) I believe that a traveller can build-in little on such infirm ground, of parts which remain without his proper knowledge. In this kind I have adventured only in el-Wéshm; to include sites of interest to the rest of the work. An Orientalist at Damascus, Jidda, Bosra or Bagdad, might not only competently learn the Nejd speech; but — communing with the Nejders, that sojourn, or come in their traffic to those places — he could very well enquire out, if such were possible, the geography of Nejd. Hitherto Europeans dwelling in the Arabic cities have had nearly no conversation with the Arabs! It seems that even Arabists had no cognisance of the 'Ageyl! — Prof. Wetzstein, meeting, upon a time, with two or three Nejders in Damascus, enquired of them learnedly concerning their country, and has recorded their answers: but these have need of an Interpreter, being partly true and some part fable-talk (so that I was not able to make any use of them when advancing to the verity of things in Arabia), as that fetching up the Wady الرُمَّن ("*Rummen!*") from the Teháma of Wejh! and the 12½ hrs. [it is 2 hrs., — 11 miles nearly] thelûl-riding between Boreyda and 'Aneyza.

It would be unreasonable to look for the precision of navigators in a traveller's chart of a country, where one may hardly pass, in the midst of mortal dangers, and he should not be seen to carry instruments. Since the *Itinerarium* was published, first in Kiepert's *Globus*, and then by the R. Geogr. Society, every chartographer of those parts of Asia has founded upon my labours; which I trust to be such that no time shall overthrow them. The map is now coloured geologically; so that the nature also of the soil may be comprehended at a glance.

Marâkish, Morocco, 562.

Marbût el-hoṣàn, a rock in the plain of Medáin Sâlih, 411.

March: breathless heat in —, in the desert (1877), 322; 346; 11. — at Kheybar (1878), 233; — wind on the Harra, 238; 239, 246, 267.

Mare [*v.* Horse], the Arabian —. The desert horses are without gall towards mankind;

infants play about them, a child may lead them: they will enter their master's tent in the noonday heat, and stand sheltering amongst sleeping men. Ibn Rashîd's gift—, 238, 249; value of —s, *ib.*; 258, 292, 302, 304; to every nomad — a foster camel, *ib.*; the — is a chargeable possession, in the wilderness, *ib.*; their impatience of thirst, *ib.*; the Bed. master milks first for his —, *ib.*; milk a necessary diet of the desert —s, 304; the *rabèyby* stringed from the —'s tail, 306; the Fukara —s, 318; the nomads' knowledge of horses, 318; Zeyd's —, 350, 353; the — a sheykhly possession, *ib.*; a — lost by a ghrazzu, 388; Bed. — not branded, *ib.*; nomad — shod, 353, 422; Bed. sheykhs ride with a halter and often barebacked, 422; Mahanna's — perishes of thirst, 439; the desert — will drink more than the camel, 507; a — upon three legs, 583; —s ridden with the sharp Syrian bit may be reined-up suddenly in full career, 636; II. 262, 263; Ibn Rashîd's troops of —s and horses, 269; 'Ateyba —s, 457; —s mounted in the warfare of 'Aneyza and Meteyr against Kahtân, 475, 477; a present of two —s of their booty sent from the battle-field by el-Meteyr to Ibn Rashîd, 479; a dry — adopts a strange foal, 484.

Mâreb: dam-breach of —, 434; II. 51.
Márḥab, last sheykh of old Jewish Kheybar, 347, 362; II. 97, 112.
Márḥabà, welcome!
Maria Theresa dollars, II. 23.
Mârid (مارد), a tower in Jauf, II. 47.

Marra, woman, 273.
Marràn, a watering place, in the desert-way between el-Kasîm and Mecca, II. 506.
Marrat, village in el-Wéshm, II. 452.
Marriage: the Mohammedan —, 278; 342; — among the nomads, 363-7; — of cousins, 272, 519; — between the town and the desert, 290, 333, 525; — of nephew and aunt, 555; 589; II. 62; — is easy among them, 376.
Marsiman, a tribe of ancient Arabia named in the cuneiform inscriptions, 229.
Martyr: a Christian — at Medina, II. 176.
Martyrs (*shahûd* شهيد, pilgrims which die and are buried by the way side), 91, 117.
Mary, mother of Jesus [*v.* Miriam], 510, 522.

el-Màs, camel's name, 321.
Masc(k)at, a Gulf coast town in the province of 'Omân, II. 350.
Mashàrîf es-Shem, 89.
M'ashush (معشّش) [*v.* Mujúbbub], coffee-bower in Kasîm orchards, II. 445, 451, 452.
[Masîr (مَعْصِر, إِعْصَار pl. أَعَاصِير and معاصير)] an eddy of wind in the desert: Moahib.
Mask: sculptured — -like heads in the frontispices at Medáin Sâlih, 211.
Máskhara, a masking, 480.
Masons: Christian — sent to repair the kellâ at Medáin Sâlih, 41, 134, 198.
Másr, a site at Kheybar, II. 119.
Massage, remedy for the colic, II. 229.
Mâsul es-Sudda in el-Wéshm: a renowned inscription at —, II. 555.
Masully, praying-stead, 236, 496; II. 25, 160, 271.
Mátar, a Solubby at Teyma, 613; his words of the *w'othŷhi* and of the ancient archery, *ib.*
Matàra or *zemzemîyeh*, the leathern bucket-bottle of travellers; which is hung from the saddle, 41.
Matches (German) sold in Nejd towns, 630; II. 429.
Matchlocks: Beduins' opinion of their —, 241, 399; the kinds of —, 503-4; II. 256, 324.
Mâṭha tarîd, what wouldst thou? II. 57.
M'athûd (مِعْضَد, مِعْضَاد), Bed. bracelet of the arm, 506.
Matîn (مَتِين), sound and strong, 532.
Màṭîyah (مَطِيَّة), a dromedary, II. 23.

Matting: palm-plait — in the oases, II. 20.
Mâ úkdar, I am not able, II. 311.
Mauritius (the island of —): — sugar, II. 389.
Mausoleum: a — near Rabbath Ammon, 57.
Maweyrid (موارد), watering place [though in appearance a pl. form — seems to be used in the sing. by the Beduw], 505; II. 505.
May: the oasis-fever began at el-Ally in —, 405; II. the end of — (1878), 430.
Meal-times at 'Aneyza, II. 374.

Meat: Damascus preserved — in the Hâj (*kaurma*); II. — scorched in gobbets in el-Kasîm for the caravan journeys, that will last good a month, 484.

Mecca [read *Mekka*, vulg. *Mekky*: of old — was pron. *Bokka*, *qd. v.*]: 43, 58, 96, 98, 101, 106, 107, 109, 111, 120, 124, 127, 129, 137, 139; hospital for sick pilgrims in —, *ib.*; alms bestowed upon poor strangers in —, *ib.*; 141, 165, 171, 182; yearly popular riots in —, 189; 239, 246, 247, 248, 250, 271, 289, 305, 336, 434, 435, 455, 462, 465, 477, 496, 498, 510, 512, 519, 536, 547, 578, 650, 668; II. 29, 38, 62, 64, 65, 67, 68, 85; — vulg. *Mekky*, 103; 105, 111, 173, 174, 180, 187, 189, 195, 196, 197, 213, 228, 231, 243, 276, 288, 304, 314, 337, 345, 375, 376, 378, 381, 383, 393, 394, 406, 411, 427, 429, 438, 449, 456, 459, 462, 472, 480, 481, 482, 484, 487; price of sámn in —, *ib.*; 488, 490, 493, 494, 495, 496, 498, 506, 508, 509, 510, 511, 512, 513, 514, 515, 516; — a city of the Teháma, 517; 519, 520, 521, 527, 530; a wealthy burgess of —, 531; 533; summer heat in —, 527; 537, 539, 540, 542, 543, 544, 547, 548, 551, 552, 553; attar of rose distilled by Indian apothecaries in —, 511; 556, 557, 558, 559, 562, 564, 568, 569, 571, 572, 573, 575.

Mecca country, II. 204, 559, 568.

Medáin, ruins in Moab, 61.

Medáin Lût, 82, 136.

Medáin Sâlih (cities of Sâlih, the prophet; vulg. *Medáin*): the Syrian caravaners' name for the hewn monuments in the crags of el-Héjr (*v. sub* Inscriptions) on the Hâj road, six removes (or three thelûl journeys) N. of Medina. Mr. Doughty (the first European who visited el-Héjr) found the "Troglodyte cities" to be sandstone cliffs with the funeral monuments sculptured in them of an antique town, and like those which are seen in the "Valley of Moses" or Petra, 39, 40, 41, 42, 47, 55, 65, 80, 81, 82, 87, 92, 104, 117, 119, 121, 122, 123, 125; — a *merkez*, 71; the "Cities of Sâlih," 123, 125, 127, 135, 136; the Hâj camp at —, 125; the Jurdy camp at —, 238, 246; the kellâ, 125, 126; —, taken by Bed., 128; — described, 133; provision and cost of —, 164; the kellâ towers and garrisons, 165; artillery in the kellâ, 133; the garrison, 128; the subverted country, 133; the kellâ repaired by Christian masons, 134; the birket, 134; garden and palms, 134; the koran fable of el-Héjr, 135, 136; ancient wells, 144; the *Kasr el-Bint*, 145; the sandstone rock, 147; a first sculptured monument with an epigraph and bird, 148; hewn bays of the monuments which were sculptured from above downward, 147, 151; the aspect is Corinthian, with Asiatic pinnacles, the pilasters, *ib.*; the cell, 147; the sculptured birds, 148, 154; all the monuments are sepulchral, 149; mural *loculi*, *ib.*; grave-pits, grave-clothes, mummy odour, human bones, 149; *Beyt es-Sheykh*, *ib.*; old money found at —, 153-4; beds of potsherds and broken glass, 153; ornaments of the pediments, 156; craftsmasters of the sculptured monuments, 156; the titles of the monuments could not be read by the (Mecca) caravaners in Mohammed's time, 157; probably the monument chambers had been already violated, 158; it seems that not a marble plate has been used in their monuments, *ib.*; the *Diwán*, 160; the day in the kellâ, 164, 167; quarries in the plain, 171, 176; the town was clay-built, and of small houses, 176; husbandry in the plain, 177; 180, 192, 203, 204-208; burial of the dead in the monuments, they were shrouded in linen and leather and embalmed with spices, 212; 222, 229; the epitaphs deciphered by M. Renan, 224-7; note par M. Berger, 227-8; is — Nabatean Hejra? 229; 231, 238-9, 244; return of the Hâj, 246; prices in the Hâj market, 246; 248, 251, 254, 294, 323, 329, 346, 352, 358, 400, 402, 403; picture of the kellâ, 416; strife in the kellâ, 417-19; 425, 446, 466, 471, 485, 530, 558, 565, 566, 575, 580, 585, 603, 621, 641, 673-4; II. 92, 111, 135, 183, 218, 367, 543, 554, 575. [*v. el-Héjr*].

el-Medân, village quarter of Damascus, 41, 43, 103, 111, 196, 252, 270, 339; II. 290.

Meddián or *Middián*, a ruined village in the Teháma in the lat. of el-Héjr [there the Beduins say is 'a brook flowing to seaward'], 456.

Medega, a measure at Kheybar, II. 132.

Medeybîa, ruined town in Moab, 59.

Med'hunna, clarified-butter skin, II. 230.

Mediator: commonly among three Arabians is one —, II. 520.

Medicine [*v. Hakîm*]: practice of —, 197, 252, 294-7; they will give the praise to Ullah and not pay the hakîm, 299; 300; II. 111, 112, 128, 150, 192, 208, 225, 229, 230.

INDEX AND GLOSSARY

Medicine [*dáwa*] : an effervescing drink, 297 ; the Arabs use even unclean things for —, *ib.* ; 298-301 ; the tedious preparation of —s, 299 ; 596 ; Hamûd enquires of an enabling —, 647 ; II. Heteym women buy the Nasrâny's —, 85 ; the — -box opened at Kheybar, 99 ; — given to Muharram, 110 ; 150, 241-2 ; their religion permits them to seek —s, 404 ; 411, 428-9.

Medina (city, pl. *medáin* and vulg. *mudden* (مدن) : —*t en-Néby*, the Prophet's City [before Mohammed the town was called *Yáthrib*] ; also called *Medinat el-munûwra,* ' the illuminated or illustrious city' [the common sort of devout Moslems think they see in approaching her a luminous haze resting over Medina]. 43, 58, 108, 127, 130, 134, 139, 140, 162 ; el-Héjr to —, 169, 171, 177, 187 ; dissolute living at —, 193 ; 204, 217, 238, 240, 242, 247, 248, 250, 251, 254, 266, 294, 297, 299, 300, 312, 327, 350, 379, 396, 410, 482, 496, 500, 524, 538, 557, 558, 584, 596, 610, 620, 658, 662 ; II. 35, 37, 65, 75, 92 ; — government at Kheybar, 92, 95, 141 ; 97, 99, 103, 105 ; — Arabic, 106 ; — now a half-Indian city, 107 ; yet in part truly Arabian, *ib.* ; 109-11, 114, 115, 124, 129-32, 137, 139-41, 144-53, 155-63 ; wages of journeymen field labourers at —, 158 ; 165, 166 ; old Bashy Bazûk of —, 168-70 ; young ribalds of —, 172, 176-8, 181, 183, 184, 192-5 ; 197 ; citizens of — serving of their free will in the wars, 198 ; 199, 201-6, 209, 212, 214, 216-8, 220-8 ; *Birket el-Engleyssy,* 223 ; 232-4, 237, 241, 268 ; — *Mûbrak thelûl en-Néby, ib.* ; 269, 272-8, 284, 285, 301, 303, 306, 310, 314, 315-6, 318, 326-7, 332, 334, 337, 375, 387, 390, 406, 429, 481, 508, 512, 533, 536, 544-6, 553, 565, 575.

Medina, Pasha of [*v. Sábry*], II. 99, 102, 139, 140, 147, 149, 153 ; the — in council, 176 ; 180, 181 ; letter to the —, 188 ; 'Abdullah Siruân's new letter to the —, 183 ; 197, 218 ; letter in French from the — to the Nasrâny at Kheybar, 221 ; 222, (226), 227-8, 249, 270 ; his passport, *ib.,* 272, 276 ; 297, 299.

Meddowwara, *Kellâ,* 97, 131, 138.
Med'hunna, butter skin, II. 230.
Medsûs, village of B. Sâlem, Harb, II. 546.

Mehàditha, water in the way from Middle Nejd to Mecca, II. 507.
Mehai, a ruined town in Moab, 59.
Mehaineh, ruined site in J. Kerak, 61.

Mehján (مِحْجن), *v.* also *Mish'aab, Bakorra,* camel-driving stick with a (cut) double hook, 264.

[el-Mehmel, a great " valley " between el-Arùth and Wady Siddeyr : M. en-Nefîs. Towns and villages of — are *Thadich* (" two hundred " houses), *el-Bîr, es-Sforrát* (three villages), *el-'Alîa, el-Wasṭa, es-Siffilly, el-Burra, Otherumma* (metrop., " four hundred " houses), *Otheythia, Horeymla, Siddûs.*

Mehnûwara, ruined site in J. Kerak, 61.
Mehrûd, ruined site in J. Kerak, 61.
Meḥsan, the blind ; a bountiful Allayda sheykh, 240, 245, 480-2 ; II. 91, 553.

Meḥsan, a Fejîry sheykh whose wife was Zeyd's sister, 265, 400-1, 421, 550, 560, 562, 563, 564, 566-72, 574, 584 ; his fortune, 585 ; his impatience with his wife and children, 586, and benevolence with his friends, 587-9, 597, 601, 605, 612, 615-6 ; his wife, 572-3 ; 586.

Mejanîn, pl. of *mejnûn, qd. v.*
Mejarîd, an affinity of Kheybar villagers, II. 153.

Mejdûr (مجدور), one sick of the small-pox : hole dug in the desert for the cure of a —, II. 240.

Mejellád (مجلّد), a measure of dates at Kheybar, II. 132.

Mejîdy : Turkish silver dollar [3*s.* 8*d.* nearly] named after the Sultan *'Abd-el-Majîd.*

Mejlis, the sitting or assembly, the sheykhly council or congregation of elders, the daily parliament of sheykhs and men of age in a tribe (or town), 141, 290-1 ; evening —, 292 ; 294, 314, 398 ; Ibn Rashîd's — at Hâyil, 656 ; II. 19, 46, 73.

Mejlis : the open place or market-place in every oasis-town of Kasîm is called —, II. 340, 364 ; 365, 431, 433, 436, 440, 458, 463.

Mejmaá, a town in Middle Nejd, II. 338.
Mejnûn [from *jin*], one troubled in his mind, in possession of the *jân,* a foolish or distracted person, 296, 355, 642 ; II. 28.

OF ARABIC WORDS   647

Mekky, vulg. for *Mecca* (*Mekka*), II. 495.
Meláika (*v. Melûk*), the angels or fairy-like jinns, 497, 530.
Melancholy: musing — of the Aarab, 282, 305, 306, 316, 355, 385, 450, 514, 518, 521, 612.
Mel'aun el-weyladèyn, 286, 343.
Mel'aunát ej-jins, II. 160.
Mel'aunnîn, pl., accursed ones.
Melḥ, salt.
Melons, 176, 405, 487, 528, 555, 578, 593; II. 464; a kind of little — grown without irrigation nigh Jidda, 574.
Melûk [*v. Melaika* and *Ménhel*], the Power of the air, 497; II. 407.
Melûn Tâlibu, ruined hamlet near Môgog, 628.
Memlahát Teyma, 340.
Menâbaha, ancient name of the Fukara tribe, 270.
Menâhil, pl. *ménhel*, qd. v.
el-Menajîm, a fendy of 'Ateyba, II. 457.
el-Men'ama, a tribe of the Ashrâf, II. 556.
Menhél, pl. *menâhil* [*v. el-Melûk*], descending place of angels or fairy-like jinns: — in Thirba, 495, 496 [cf. Acts vii. 30, 35]. Sacrifice and slumber of the sick at the menhels, 497; — trees, 496; 538, 598; II. a manmenhel, 127; 231; 550.
Ménzil, alighting place, the camping ground of a caravan or of Nomads: ring- — of Bed. near Ma'an, 85; 252; the Fejîr pitch dispersedly and not in any formal order, 256, 263; pleasant to sojourn in the wandering village, 513; approach a nomad — by night, 622; II. ring- — of certain Harb, 334.
Menzil 'Eyár, II. 420.
Menzil el-Ḥâj (a camping place of the Hâj), 121, 252, 484.
Menzil el-Ḥâj, at Hâyil, (sketch, 667).
Menzil B. Helâl, site near Boreyda, II. 355.
Menzil es-sheukh, the public hostel at 'Aneyza, II. 390.
Mer'ai, a Fejîry herdsman.
Mêrbrak, village ruins in Edom, 81.
Merchant: —s to the Aarab in the Hâj, 111; Beduins playing the —, 195, 354; II. —s' principals in 'Aneyza and Hâyil, 390.

Merdàha (مِرْدَاهَة), a sling, 479.

Mérdumma, mountain between el-Kasîm and Mecca, II. 500.

Mereesy, or *Marîsa* (مَرِيسَة), *v. Thiràn*, *Buggila*, *Baggl*, *Muṭhîr*: dry milk, milk shards, 305; — good to take upon expeditions, *ib.*; dates may be eaten with —, 338; — a cooling drink, *ib.*; a kind of wormwood mingled with —, 425; diet of —, 520, 521, 535, 553; II. provision of — for the journey, 87; — making, 244, 316.
Mergab er-Ràfa, near 'Aneyza, II. 418.

Mergab (مَرْقَب) or *Garra*, *q. v.*, the watch-tower of el-Kasîm villages, II. 336; —, a watch-rock, 499.

Mérguba (مَرْقَبَة), the Bed. housewife's (pedlar's round in-folding) mirror, 268.
[*Merimsát*, a forsaken valley "with a spring and ruined village" nearly in face of the Khrèyby above el-Ally.
Merjàn of *Bejaida*, *Bíshr*, a young 'Ageyly at Kheybar, II. 123; he accompanied the Nasrâny to Hâyil, 235, 237-48; 249-73; 284-99.
Merkez, a centre: upon the Syrian Hâj way — signifies a principal rest-station of the pilgrimage; such are Ma'an and Medáin.
el-Meròwḥa, a fendy of 'Ateyba, II. 457.
Merowîn, a fendy of Jehèyna, 166.
[*Merrára*, mountain N. of J. Misma, *v. Fèrdat*.

Mèrshaḥa (مِرْشَحَة), pad-saddle. [*v.* Saddle.]

Ibn *Mertaad*, Aarab, 619.
J. *Merzûm*, 483.
Mes'âed, sheykh of the Beduins of el-Akhḍar, 116.
Mesakîn, pl. of *meskîn*.
Mesgeda, word deciphered in an (Aramaic) inscription at el-Héjr, 674; and this has become the Arabic word *mesjid* [which the Spanish corrupted to *mezquita*, whence the French and our word mosque], *ib.*
el-Méshab, open place before the castle at Hâyil, 637, 638, 640, 645, 650, 658-61, 662; II. 16, 17, 19, 28, 31, 53, *et passim*.
J. *Meshàf*, by the way between el-Kasîm and Mecca, II. 500.
el-Meshâhada [at Hâyil], citizens of Méshed 'Aly, 656-7; II. 284.
Méshed 'Àly, town at the ruins of *Kûfa*, 656, 658, 668; II. 29, 43, 64, 65, 67, 258-9, 277, 282.

Meshetta, ruins, 55.
Meshetta, a fendy of Wélad 'Aly [*v. Umshetta*], 55, 271.
Mesîhiyûn, pl. of *Mesîhy*, 642.
Mesîhy, Christian, 642.
Mesjid [*v. Mesgeda*]; place of kneeling down to worship [from this Arabic word we have received — through the Spanish — the French word mosque]; —s at el-Ally, 182, and Teyma, 331; — at Hâyil, 650, 658; strangers may repose in the —s, 331, and II. 404.
Meskîn, village near Damascus, 44.
Meskîn [Span. mezquino, French mesquin, It. mesquino], a pitiful person, 296, 355: a common word in the (Mohammedan) Arab's speech, when-as they would say *poor man!*
Mesopotamia ['land amidst the rivers']; 129, 139, 379, 389, 394, 455, 457, 518, 584, 641, 656; II. 29, 33, 44, 62, 64, 66, 67; the foreign colour of Nejd is —n, 338; 345, 349, 375, 426, 456, 469, 473, 514.
'Messenger of Ullah,' *v. Mohammed.*
Messîahi (Christian) religion [*v. Mesîhi*]: the —, 66, 177; II. 57, 406.
Messias: a false — in Syria, 214-15.
el-Messîh, the Messiah, 341, 342.
el-Mestewwy: Nefûd —, in el-Wéshm, II. 452.
Met'aab ibn Rashîd, who was prince after Telâl, 300, 655, 671; II. 28-31, 39-41, 46, 271, 273.
Metaad, a Mahûby, 499.
Metals: seeking for —s, 327; II. iron, lead, and tinning — in the sûk at Hâyil, 23; art to transmute —s, 166.
Meteor: a —, 253, 321; Beduin of the —, 273; 510, 520; II. 494.
Meteyr, vulg. *Umteyr* [*Muteyr*], a considerable Bed. tribe of the South, 576, 661; II. 31, 306, 317; "a Meteyry cannot keep himself from treachery," *ib.*; 357, 373, 381; foray of Kahtân against —, 393; 394, 445; — in battle with Kahtân and 'Ateyba, 453-4; 468, 470, 472, 473, 474; their speech and aspect, 475; great ghrazzu of — against Kahtân, 473-81; great sheykh of — sick of a dropsy, 482; 492; a — sheykh who slew Hayzàn and other Kahtân sheykhs in battle, 480.
Methàlitha, bergs by the desert way between Kasîm and Mecca, II. 500.

Metówali, Mohammedan schismatics, of the Persian faith, in Syria, II. 285.
el-Meyatân, *Aarab* in W. Fâtima, II. 571.
Meyhsub [if this word were rightly written down, it may be another pronc. of *ma'asub, qd. v.*], head-cord of the Nomads' kerchief, 484.
el-Mèzham, place of thronging, called by the Syrian caravaners *Mûbrak en-Nâga* (*qd. v.*), 123, 205, 229, 250, 352; fig. of —, 407 (and *v.* Index under *fig.* W. Thirba); 408, 486.
Mez'ûna (read *meṣuna* مَصُونَة), beautiful (woman), 365, 511; II. 329.
M'hai, site in the desert near Teyma, 328.
Miblis, a beautiful Mahûby woman, wife of Tollog, 498, 511-12.
Midd (modius), a corn measure, 444.
Midda (مُدَّة properly suspension of hostility; class. *dia*), ransom for blood, 449, 523-4, 539, 547; II. 153; valued in silver, 800 reals, 167; 236.
Middiân [*Midyan* مَدْيَن], a ruined village in the Tehàma, 456 [*v. Meddiàn.*]
Middle rocks: a name used in this work to distinguish the middle *bébàn* at el-Héjr, 151.
Midianite: —s, 135; — daughters of Jethro, 367; II. the tribe of *Midiàn*, 388.
Migrations of Nomad tribes, 94, 189, 314, 433; II. 428.
Mijwel, a young Fejîry sheykh, 265, 396.
Mîl (ميل), needle or pillar; the — at Siddûs, 246.
Mile-stones, 68.
Military service in free Arabian townships falls upon the substantial citizens, II. 474.
Milk [*v. Orghra, Roghrwa, Irtugh*]: — suffices for meat in the desert, 222; 368-71; nomad herdsmen milk their camels for passengers, 256-7, *et passim* [*v. sub* Hospitality]; camels —ed by men and lads only, 304; camel —, 256, 349, 369, 520; Bed. woman — the small cattle, 59, 261, 304, 368; the spring season of —, 304; — of the small cattle lasts through the few spring weeks only, 304, 366-70, 477, 479, 489; nâgas are in — eleven months, 304; — for the desert mares, 304-5; —ing of the Nomad's cattle, 305; — is food and health at a draught, *ib.*; the

pleasant — -bowl, 256, 477; the several kinds of —, 370; — of goats and nâgas savours of their pasture, 370; butter- — is *kheyr Ullah*, 477; Nomad hospitality of —, 641; II. — the best nourishment; boiled, 'it enters into the bones,' 83; cow- — accounted medicinal, 125; a saying of Moh., of spilt —, 258; the nâga of any good hump yields rich —, 286; virtue of camel- —, 290; — of camels and goats, which have fed upon wormwood is bitter, 305; "whole —," 306; poor 'Aneyza women will sell thee a little — if they have any, 429, 473; — sold at 'Ayn ez-Zeyma near Mecca, 525; — hardly given to passengers by Bed. of the Mecca road, 573.
Mill-stones: antique — at Medáin Sâlih and Petra, 175, 238; — made by Beduins, 323, 451; II. — made at Kheybar, 200; and by the Beduw of lava, granite or sand-stone, *ib.*; the noise of —, *ib.*
Millet, *v. Thùra.*
Mimosa bushes, 426.
Min, from.
Min? who?
Min 'ashîraty, 585.
Min ha'l shoṭṭût, II. 473.
Min hâtha? II. 505.
Min khulk Ullah, II. 407.
Min y'ámir-ly (من يعمر لي), 356.
Mine: a powder — fired at Boreyda, II. 347.
Minḳala (منقلة), vulg. *mùngola*, the board of an Arab game of draughts, 585. [*v. Bîát.*]
Minnîeh, mountains in the great desert S. of er-Russ, II. 493.
Minsilla, ass-mare name, II. 253.
Miracles of the East, 214-17; II. 413, 564.
Mirage, 74, 110, (598).
Miriam, mother of Jesus, 341; 560; II. 396; images of — and Jesus in the old Ka'aba, II. 545.
Miriam, a woman's name (commonly of slaves) in Arabia, 514.
'*Miriam*'s nails,' 470.
Mirror, *v. Merguba.*
Mîry, tribute, II. 33.
Mish'aab (مشعب), or *Mehján*, v. also *Bakorra*, camel-driving stick with a (cut) double-hook, 264.

Mishlah, a light mantle.
Mishmish, apricots of Damascus, II. 171.
Míshûr [*v. Sáhàr*] enchanted, II. 443.
Mishwat [perhaps *Musháwwat*, hard favoured], a Mahûby, 443, 444, 505, 513, 516, 519, 531, 532, 539, 542, 547, 548, 564.
Miskeh, a desert village near the borders of el-Kasîm, II. 323, 492.
J. *Misma*, 340, 395, 621, 622, 624, 626.
Misshel el-Auájy, 'Sheykh of the seven tribes,' 376, 609; — praised as a mighty spearsman, 610; 611, 614, 618, 619, 620; — the owner of more than two hundred camels, 620; 621; II. 71, 140-3, 253.
Missionary physicians in Beyrût, 481.
Míthil el-jerâd, 547.
Míthil el-mawt, 412.
Míthil en-nimml, II. 513.
Míthil es-seyd, 355.
Míthil ṭájir, II. 463.
el-*Míthnib* [المذنب — Ibn. 'Ayith] a town of es-Sedèyr, few hours W. of 'Aneyza, II. 385, 424.
Mizamîr, songs to the pipe [the Psalter], 658; II. 205.
Mizàn el-Ḥaḳ, a missionary book in Arabic thus called, II. 399.
Mizmàr (مزمار), pl. *mizamîr*, double reed pipe at Kheybar, II. 137; its shrilling sound [as it were of profane levity] offends the religious ears of good Moslems, *ib.*, 205.
M'khâlid, son of *Billî*, 430.
Mleylîeh, a site on the Hâj road above Medina, II. 204.
el-*M'nîf*, a part of J. Ajja, 667-8-9.
[*Wady Mnîkh el-Mishgár* or *el-Kelabby*, in the Tueyk mountains.
Moab, now (part of) *el-Belka*, *qd. v.*; plains of —, 56, 59, 62, 64, 65; fearful sacrifice of a king of —, 60; king of — a sheepmaster, 61; '— is God's washpot,' 62; — a neighbour land to the Nomads, 82; tent-dwellers of —, *ib.*; sculptured ornaments of, 88; 450; II. 66, 421, 575.
"Moabite stone," the —, 65.
Mo'addam (Bed. *Mo'aththan*), *kellâ* and *birket*, 119, 130, 259, 603.
Moahîb, Abu Shâmah [*Muwahîb*] sing. *Mahûby*: a fendy of *Sb'aa* (*qd. v.*), Ânnezy; their dîrat is the Harrat el-'Aueyrid, with the

plain borders upon both sides. The Sb'aa, they say, came from the Nejd province el-Ḥasa, where some of their kindred yet remain and are settlers. The Sb'aa are now Aarab of the *Shimbel* near *es-Sófa*, in the Syrian desert N.-E. of Damascus, 117. They expelled B. Sókhr from the *Jau*, 167, 445; their generations are thirteen in that Harra country, 167, 445; 241, 276; their speech, 307; 311, 312; their secret deposit-cave, 323; — husbandmen, 355; 360, 380, 390, 396, 405, 420, 427, 430, 436, 441, 443, 444, 445, 447-50, 453, 461, 464, 472, 476, 479; the *ráhla* of —, 483; 487, 496, 498, 500, 501, 502, 503, 505, 506, 511; a brother of the sheykh shot himself, 516; 519, 523, 524, 537, 543, 544, 548, 549, 550, 551, 552, 554, 564, 565; all their great cattle reaved at once by a ghrazzu, 567-8; 609, 610, 641.

Mo'allaḳ el-Hamèydy, part of the Harra near el-Ally, 180.

Moallakát, the —, v. *Muallakát*.

el-Moâra, fendy of Harb B. Sâlem, ii. 546.

Moâtidal mountains near el-Ally, 180.

Mogeyra : wells below el-Héjr in the W. 'Aly dîra, 378, 602.

Moghrair, is perhaps cave, 350.

Moghrâreba, pl. of *Móghreby*, qd. v.

el-Moghrássîb : a kindred of the Fukara tribe, 270.

Móghreby, a man of the *Móghrib* or land of the sunsetting, an Occidental, a Moor: their valour, 131, 132; a — diviner comes to el-Héjr, 213; — eyesalver, v. *Abu Selím*; ii. Moors in Hâyil, 18, 47, 48, 93; a — diviner who made enchantments at Kheybar, 121; — pilgrims, 172-4; the old Moors of Spain, 182; — enchanter at Jidda, 211; 282, 303; a young — pilgrim, sometime captive among Kahtân, delivered by the ghrazzu of 'Aneyza, 480.

Mógug, village in J. Shammar, 629, 630, 631, 635, 665, 670; ii. 19, 34, 77, 269.

Mogŷil (or *mogèyil* or *mogèyl* مَقِيل), the noon resting of passengers in a march, ii. 491, *et passim*.

Mohâfuz, guardian. [*v. Muhâfiz* and *Muhafûth*.]

Mohamîd, a fendy of Harb. B. Sâlem, ii. 546.

Mohammed (he was citizen of Mecca of a sheykhly family), preacher and founder of the religion of Islâm. [He is called *Habîb Ullah*, 88; *en-Néby, ib.*; *er-Rasûl*, 112, 342; the First before every creature, 522; and Seal of the Prophets of Ullah, 342.] His infirm law of marriage, 63; 88, 104, 108, 112; Persian schismatics in the Hâj burned at Medina, for defiling —'s tomb, 108; his preaching of fables, which persuaded the fantastic superstitious fears of the people, 127; el-Héjr a fable in —'s time, 135; his religion grew as an Arabian faction, 141, 289; it is become the faith of a tenth part of mankind, 141; — mild and politic, 186; 270, 281, 326, 342; — bade spare the Christian hermits, 521; growth of —'s faction, 527; 562, 579, 605, 653; ii. 24 [*v. Hámed*]; " —'s cottage " at Kheybar, 116; 166, 174; 178, 179; his sepulchre at Medina, 178, 197; danger of blaspheming that name, 193; 201, 207, 231, 274, 362; his sweet-blooded religion, 376; 387, 391, 396; his religious language, 399; 400; the personage and doctrine of —, 405, 406-7; 467, 482, 517, 542, 545, 550, 556, 557, 564.

Mohammed ibn 'Abd-el-Wâhâb, founder of the Waháby reformation, ii. 454.

Moḥammed Ag(hr)a, second Turkish aide-de-camp of the Sherîf, ii. 541.

Moḥammed Aghra, el-'Ajamy, Persian mukowwem in the Syrian Hâj caravan, 43, 44, 99, 100, 125, 126, 247.

Moḥammed 'Aly, an Albanian, ruler of Egypt (in the time of Napoleon), ii. 454, 543.

Moḥammed 'Aly, el-Mahjûb, kellâjy : 127, 128; his mingled nature, 130-3; his tales, 130-1 : — resists the Hâj Pasha, 132; 133, 137; — receives a lost derwîsh, 138; his Turkish promises, 142; comedy of M. 'Aly and Zeyd, 142; 144, 149; his words of the Beduw, 164; his tales, 167, 169; his saw of ' the three kinds of Arabic speech,' 168; his soldiering life, 169; 181, 204-8, 214, 217; his tale of a Frenjy at Petra, 218; 219, 220, 230, 232, 237, 239, 242, 244, 245, 248, 250, 397, 418; ii. 48, 49, 367.

The '*Sheykh Mohammed*,' a citizen of 'Aneyza, ii. 407-8.

Mohammed, a clothier at 'Aneyza, ii. 408.

Moḥammed ed-Deybis, a Fejîry, 230, 235, 405, 406, 408, 553.

Moḥammed ed-Dûgy, 55.

Moḥammed Kheiry, effendy, *yâwer es-Sherîf* (the Sherîf's aide-de-camp at et-Tâyif),

OF ARABIC WORDS 651

11. 539-42, 544-9, 557-60; carries the war-contribution of the Sherîf's subjects to Stambûl, 558-9.
Mohammed, the young son of 'Abdullah el-Khenneyny, 11. 389, 487.
Mohammed el-Kurdy, a police-soldier at Kheybar, 11. 110, 193, 208.
Mohammed, half-Beduin soldier lad at Medáin S., 128, 130, 178-9, 181, 220, 222, 358, 403, 404, 417 et seq., 550, 563.
Mohammed Mejelly, sheykh of Kerak, 64, 65.
Mohammed en-Nefîs, son of a late treasurer at er-Riâth.
Mohammed en-Nejûmy, a Kurdy on his father's side; his mother was of Harb: magnanimous friend of the Nasrâny stranger at Kheybar, 557; 11. 101, 102; his mother's Harb village, 103; 106, 159; — speaks Medina (or Harb) Arabic, 107; his cottage, 108, 109; 115, 116; his traffic, ib.; his hunting, ib.; 153, 217; his corn and palm grounds 117, 118; his wife, 119, 127, 160, 212, 229; his little daughter, 128, 225; his mare, 129, 180, 236; his nature, 129-30, 154; 131-2, 134-5-6-7-8-9, 144-5-6, 150-4-5, 197; 224; his younger brother was slain by a ghrazzu in the way to Kheybar, 137, 166-7; that brother had been initiated in a religious mystery, 137; — captain of the Kheybar villagers in the Bed. warfare, 142-3; his son Hasseyn, 136, 159-63, 205-7, 212; his wife's brother, 143, 216; his camel stealing, 228-9; 232; — was, since the Medina occupation, established at Kheybar, 144, 158; his disdain of those black villagers and of 'Abdullah and 'Aly, 154, 160; his fable of the ostrich and the camel, 155; his valiant defence of the Nasrâny, ib.; his family, ib., 157, 159, 225; his magnanimous goodness to all men, 155-6; his easy natural religion, 130, 159-60, 162; — a gunsmith, 156, 166; his father, 157; his riotous youth at Medina, 158, 162, 172, 226; he became a dustman of the temple, 158; — becomes a salesman at Medina, ib.; — bankrupt, goes to Kheybar and prospers, ib.; and becomes an autumn salesman there, ib.; his projects, 159; his mirth and cheerfulness, 159-62, 178, 191; a strong chider in his household, 160-1; his good shooting, 164-5, 238; — makes gunpowder, 165; his uncommon eyesight, 165; his grudges of conscience, 168; — wounded, 169; he saves a Moorish hâjjy from his robber fellows, 173-4; his tale of a Christian who came (by adventure) to Medina and suffered there a martyr's death, 176-8; he had seen another Christian, and a 'friar,' at Medina, 178; he would have redeemed his Nasrâny guest, with his mare, from the Siruân, 180; his tales of the Ferrà, 194; — visits Hâyil, 195; — in his youth would have gone, a warfaring for the faith, to the Crimea, 196; 198; his mother, 199; an old project in company with another strong man to lead a colony from Medina, to occupy some good waste soil nigh Kheybar, 201-2; his map of Kheybar and the Medina Harras, 202-4; — finds a skeleton twenty paces of length, laid bare in the bank of a seyl, 204; — goes for palm-sets to the Hálhal, ib., 205, 218-236; 308; his discourse of the jân, 209-215; his defence of the Nasrâny, 207, 216, 218; — a just salesman for his clients, 217; his tale of a young Medina tradesman among the Shîas (at el-Meshed), 224; the Nejûmy family, 225; his worthiness, 226; seditious words of his generous impatience, 230; 234; his tale of the virtue of wedduk, 231; a saying of —, 233; his farewell, 236; his opinion of the blood eaten in flesh meat 260; 403, 512.
Mohammed ibn Rashîd, v. Ibn Rashîd.
Mohammed Sa'îd, Pasha: a Kurdy, Pasha of the Hâj, 40; 87; — governor of the Peraea, 65, 89; 90; his history, 113-5, 131, 132, 140, 214, 220, 230, 248-9; 254, 459; 11. 48; — speaks an honourable word for the Nasrâny, 218.
Mohammed ibn Sa'ûd, a muttowwa, brother of Fèysal, 11. 460.
Mohammed es-Sherâry, Hâj post, 162, 217, 553.
Mohammed abu Sinûn, v. Abu Sinûn.
Mohammed Tâhir, effendy, clerk of the Jurdy, 239, 251, 254.
Mohammedans (in the Arab countries) are commonly clay builders, 62.
W. Mójeb, the brook Arnon, 58, 66.
Mokesser, a basalt berg in W. Fâtima, 11. 570.
Mokha coffee, 11. 334.
Môna [v. Mûna], place of pilgrimage near Mecca, 101; 11. 68.
el-Monasîr, a fendy of 'Ateyba, 11. 457.
Monastery: a Maronite — in Lebanon, 11. 412.

Money: — of ancient Arabia, 153-4; *note* by Mr. Barclay V. Head, 229; 338, 410; some Aarab can hardly count —, 430 [and this is reported by Syrian traders to the Ruwàlla]; II. — stolen at Hâyil, 63; the Nasrâny's — robbed by the Turkish lieutenant at Kheybar, 101; the rate of usury in el-Kasîm, 368-9.

Móngora, a fendy of Bíllî Aarab, II. 167.

Mons regalis, *v. Shobek.*

Monsoon (Ar. *mowsim* موسم, season of the year): the —, II. 417, 493, 516, 539; is not the — the just division between A. Felix and A. Deserta? 545.

Monte Nuovo, a crater-hill at Puteoli, nigh Naples, that was cast up in one eruption, 466.

Montenegro, 522.

Monuments de Medáin Sâlih, 673-4.

Moon: eclipse of the —, 333; the new — (*hilâl*), 412; which is welcomed-in by the nomads, *ib.*; the Jews blow rams' horns in the new —, 412; 'to look on the — at the full is not wholesome,' 491; sleeping in the moonlight blackens the face, 491; the — of Ramathan, 558; II. " Do the Nasâra see the — ?" 58; greeting the new —, 247, 331.

Moors [*v. Móghreby*]: the Arabic-speaking people of Barbary. Garrisons of — in the Hâj-road towers; at el-Akhḍar, 117; at Medáin, 126, 128, 167; reputed men of violence, 127, 373; pride of —, 131-2; — in Damascus, 165; — are well accepted by the Arabians, 166; el-Ally founded by —, 182; 204, 280, 412, 414, 415, 419; the — are of sterner metal than the Arabians, 420.

Morbus Gallicus [among tribes trading to the coast towns, as the Bíllî, or to Medina as the Heteym; it is common at Hâyil], 436; II. 18, 241.

Moríah, mount —, 493.

el-Moristàn (المارستان), a sort of hospital for distracted persons at Damascus, 215.

Morning star, II. 528.

Morocco [*v. Marâkish*], 128, 453, 497, 562; II. 153.

Morphia, a medicine, 299.

Beny Morr, *v. Murra.*

Morra: Aarab —, *v. Murra.*

Mortar, to pound in: ancient — in some ruins nigh Kheybar. Coffee —, *v. sub* Coffee. II. 117; coffee — at 'Aneyza, 385; rhythmical smiting of the —, *ib.*

Mortrâb, ruined village, 74.

Moseilima, "the false Prophet," 246.

Moses [*Mûsa, qd. v.*]: by — is here intended the Pentateuch (whether written by — or not; like as we say HOMER of the Iliad, whether that be all Homer's work or not): camping-grounds of Israel in the desert, 88; the caravan of B. Israel, 100; 130, 268; — or law of Israel, 280, 282, 291, 308, 342; a sublime word in —, 361; 372, 391, 397, 412, 497, 623; II. 149, 362; tribes of the times of —, 338; 407. [*v.* also Exodus, Leviticus.]

Moslem (vulg. *Musslem, Misslim*), pl. *Moslemîn* [from *sellm*, submit], the people submitted unto the divine providence, 282: " None are less Moslems than the Moslemîn," 342, 457; duty of a —, 387; it is perilous to trust a second time to their tolerance, 404, 549.

Moslemanny, a convert to the religion of Islam, a neophyte Moslem, 199, 653.

el-Moslemîn, pl. of *Moslem*, used in Nejd for " those of our part, or townsmen," II. 476.

Mosque, *v. Mesjid.*

Mosrûh, a great division of Harb, II. 546-7.

el-Motàl'ha, a fendy of Harb B. Sâlem, II. 546.

Mothâbara, a fendy of Midland Heteym, II. 253.

a Mother's love, 278, 280, 398.

Motheyîf (مُضَيِّف), id. qd. *Mothîf, qd. v.*

el-Mothîch (prob. المَضيق), mouth of Wady Laymûn, II. 565.

Mothîf (مَضيف), guest-house at Hâyil, 636, 638, 646, 658, 662, 663; yearly cost of the —, 663; II. 29; provision for the way given to visiting strangers from the —, 284; 348.

Mothîf at 'Aneyza, II. 464.

Motlog Allayda, sheykh of the Wélad Aly, 219, 271, 272, 363, 414, 532; II. 91, 141, 207.

Motlog el-Hamèydy, sheykh of the Fejîr or Fukara, 128, 133, 259, 290; his nature, 292-3; 294, 311, 322, 357, 375, 376, 388, 389, 391, 393, 394, 396, 397, 398-9, 421, 422, 429, 438, 470, 537, 548, 549-60, 564, 609, 641; II. 33.

Motlog, a Harb Beduin, II. 312-20.

OF ARABIC WORDS

Mottehma, village ruins in Mount Seir, 75.

el-Mótti (امطي), a shrub of the Nefûd, from which there flows a sort of gum caoutchouc, II. 200. [*v.* '*Elk.*]

Motullij, a Solubba kindred, 327.

Mount of Olives, II. 339.

Moveables : few — in Arab houses, 334, 603, 646.

el-Mowla, the Lord God, II. 100.

el-Moy, or *el-Moy She'ab* or *Ameah Hakràn*, on the way between Kasîm and Mecca, II. 505.

Mozàyna, a fendy of Harb. B Sâlem, II. 381, 546.

'*Mraikhàn*, a fendy of W. 'Aly, 271.

Mu'afin (مَعَافِين pl. of معفون), musty, 514.

Mu'allakát, the few elect poems which have been preserved of pre-Islamite Arabia : they are of the age before Moh., 328 ; II. 50, 58, 503.

Mu'allem, master in a handicraft, school-teacher : in the mouths of Moslems — is an honourable title of Jews and Christians, who are 'the people of the Scriptures,' 343 ; II. 348.

Muâmir, deceased brother of Tollog sheykh of the Moahîb, Abu Shamah, 519.

Muâra, basket of palm mat at Kheybar, II. 129.

Mu'atterîn pl. of مَعَتِّر (in Damascus), loose-living persons, 102 ; II. 170-1.

Mubârak (مبارك), a spice, 137.

el-Mubârak (disease), 437.

el-Mubbiát [Kady Mûsa wrote ال مابيات; *Wahîby* is another name for the place]: site of ruined villages, about five miles below el-Ally, 203, 602.

Mûbrak en-Nâga (مَبْرَك الناقةِ), 123 ; (Bed. *el-Mézham*, qd. v.), 136, 142, 177, 250, 405, 407-8.

Múbty, too tardy, 526.

Mudd yédak! 649.

Mudérris, a studied man, II. 214.

Mudîr el-Màl at Ma'an, 72.

Mudowwy (مدوي مداوي), apothecary, man of medicine [*v. Hakîm*]; 298 *et passim.*

Muéthin, v. *Muetthin.*

Muetthin, he who utters the formal cry (*el-íthin*) to the canonical prayers ; whether from a mosque or in the field, 107 ; 562 ; II. 332.

Mueylih, 464.

Mufârish er-Rúz, Syrian caravaners' name of a camping site near el-Héjr, 121.

el-Mufarrij (or *Mufúrrij*) of 'Aneyza, steward of the Prince's hall at Hâyil, 638, 640, 646, 662; II. 64, 74, 272, 377 ; his sister is put to death for child murder at 'Aneyza, 395.

el· Mufeyrij, a fendy of 'Ateyba, II. 457.

Mùfter (مفطر), eight-year-old camel, 401.

Mughraz, tower in the desert of Moab, 52.

el-Mugótta, a fendy of 'Ateyba, II. 457.

Muhâfiz, guardian of the pilgrimage, 109.

Muhafûth (مَحْفُوظ), title of Ibn Rashîd, 669 ; II. 27, 45.

Muhâkimîn, II. 444.

Muhállif, a kindred of Kheybar villagers, II. 153.

Muharram, an Albanian 'Ageyly at Kheybar, II. 98, 109, 110-11 ; death of —, 192-4 ; sale of his goods, 193 ; 208.

Muházimîn (محزوم), they who go girded with the gunner's belt, II. 96.

Ibn Mujállad, a sub-tribe of Ânnezy formerly of el-Kasîm, II. 42 ; their sheykh desperately defies 'Abeyd ibn Rashîd, *ib.*; 51.

Mujeddir, vaccinator, 296.

Mujellad (مجلَّد), a skin of dates at el-Ally, *v. Shenna*, 195 ; II. 132.

el-Mujjir (مَجِّر = مَجَرَّة), the milky way, 321.

Mujúbbub [*v. M'ashush*], coffee bower in 'Aneyza orchards, II. 451.

Múk'aad, sitting place (of the men) in an Arab house or booth, 267 ; — in the oasis (or clay) house, 332.

Mukâry, (*kíra*, hire) a carrier upon pack beasts, 124.

Wady Mukhèyat, II. 247.

el-Mukhtelif, II. 77.

Mukkarîn, (sing. ماكر or مكّار), deceitful persons, 219, 264.

B. *Muklib*, v. *Sherarát.*

Mukowwems (مقوّم), camel-masters in the Hâj, 41, 42, 44.

Muḵṣir (مقصّر, in Burckhardt), Bed. camel saddle crates or litters, in which are carried the sheykhly housewives, 483; II. 329.

Mulberries, of the Mecca country, II. 565.

Mules in the Hâj, 100; kellâ —, to drive the well-machine, 47, 165.

Muleteer in Edom, 78.

Mumbir (*munbir*) *er-Rasûl*, a mountain [*v. Sherarat*].

Mummies of Egypt, II. 554.

Mûna [*v. Mona*] near Mecca, II. 453.

Munâkh (vulg. *munô'kh qd. v.*), a 'couching place' of camels, 634; II. 340.

Munbir, pulpit.

Mundel (منذل), a revealer of secret things by enchantments, II. 209-10.

Múngola, the field in the game of *beatta*, a kind of out-door draughts, 585.

Munôkh, [*v. Munâkh*] *es-Sheukh*, at Boreyda, II. 340.

Muntar B. 'Atîeh, 328.

Múntefik, *Thuèyny el-*, II. 381.

Murabb'a (مربّع), made fat of the rabîa or spring pasture, 404.

Murâd, who succeeded Sultan 'Abd-el-'Azîz; he was shortly afterward deposed, 587.

Murder [*v.* Homicide, Crimes]: — of an old wiver at Kheybar, II. 236; — of a little maiden at 'Aneyza, 393; — of Suez Canal labourers, 450.

Murra or *Morra*, a tribe of Beduins in the South: a tribesman of —, 248; II. 381, 453, 455.

B. *Murra* or *Morr*, a Solubby kindred, 326; 327.

Murrains, 391, 472, 475; II. 263, 428.

el-Murràshedda, a fendy of 'Ateyba, II. 457.

Mûsa, Moses, 104, 130, 560; II. 26, 578.

'*Ayn Mûsa*, 80.

Mûsa the *ḵâdy*, at el-Ally, 187; — of B. Sôkhr lineage, 190; 526, 528, 557, 563.

Wady Mûsa, Moses' valley, or Petra, 78, 79, 127, 218.

Musâfir, a wayfaring man, 569, 575.

el-Musellîkh, a fendy of Ruwàlla, 376.

Musherif, high overlooking ground, 471.

Musheyikh, II. 418, 542.

Mushîr, field marshal, II. 104.

Mushowwam (مشوّم?) a camel-broker in the B. 'Aly, Harb, speech, II. 331.

Múshrak, II. 125.

Mushrakîn (pl. of *mushrak*), idolaters, 503.

Mushy, a dog's name, 474.

Musicants of Damascus, 607.

el-Muskôv, the Russian people, 98, 130, 250, 521; II. 57; the Nasrâny at Kheybar mistaken for a spy of the —, 99; 275, 278, 523; fear of the — at Tâyif, 558.

Musky, poisoned in his drink, II. 28.

el-Muṣlah, station on the E. Hâj road above Mecca, II. 565.

Musslim, son of '*Anâz*, jid or patriarch of the Ânnezy, 270.

el-Mustajidda, village of J. Shammar: — is "less than Teyma," II. 34, 67, 322, 326.

Musubba or *Umsubba*, 348, 568.

Muṣullies, v. Maṣully.

Mutasállim, commissary (for the Prince Ibn Rashîd), 595; II. 35.

Múthir, a poor Bishry at Kheybar, II. 263.

Múthir, or better *muthîr* (مضير), name for milk shards or mereesy in the Mecca country, 305.

Múṭhkir, an 'Ateyba sheykh, who rode rafîk in the 'Aneyza sámn kâfily, II. 492-516; 562, 566.

Múthur (مضر), an Arabian patriarch, II., 381, 393, 492.

Mutton; a sharp-set man had eaten a —, 520; price of — at Hâyil, 662; II. — at 'Aneyza, 371.

Muṭṭowwʻa (مطوّع), religious elder (*Kaṣîm*), II. 396, 423, 433, 440.

Muwalladîn, home-born persons of strange blood, 603.

Muzayyin (مزيّن), circumcision festival, 385; the chorus of maidens, *ib.*; the guest-supper, 387; the guests, *ib.*; dancing men, *ib.*; hand-clapping, *ib.*; 437-8; II. 280.

Muzeyrîb, assembling place of the Syrian Hâj Caravan nigh forty miles S. of Damascus, 42, 43, 44, 45, 47, 50, 65, 87, 92, 96, 106.

el-Muzzeh'ma, a fendy of 'Ateyba, II. 457.

Ibn *Múzzeyed*, *Aarab* —, a kindred of Ruwàlla, 376.

Myrtle: a shrub like the —, 541.

OF ARABIC WORDS

Nabal, 78.
Nabatean: the — people, 68, 276; — inscriptions, v. sub Inscriptions and Medáin Sâlih, 218, Appendix, p. 224-9; — sculptured architecture, 673; — royaume, 674 [About the time of Jesus C. the — kingdom extended from Bost(t)ra to el-Héjr in Arabia.]
Nablus, 70.
Nabût (نَبُوت or نَابُوت v. Shûn), quarter-staff of the Hejâz Arabians, 189.
Nâdem, a poet, 306.
Nâga, Beduin for Naḳa, a cow-camel: Néby Sâlih's —, 123; — and calf, 136.
"the Nâga's milking-pail," 180, 200.
Nagûs, a tomb, 432; — perhaps from νέκυς [corr.; this conjecture is erroneous], 457. The Syrian Bustâny says in his Lexicon, that Nâmûs is used in Syria for ناووس tomb: since the ق is hardly sounded by Syrians, ناووس stands here for [ناقوس].
J. Nagûs, a sounding sand-drift in Sinai, 352.
Nâgûs (ناقوس), the sounding board in the belfry of the Greek Monasteries, 352; a bell, 457.
Naha, Beduin fem. name, 514.
Náhab (náhb), rapine, ii. 520.
Nails, iron — among European wares sold in Nejd, ii. 429.
Najàn, a village in Middle Nejd, ii. 425.
en-Najjeyl, village of B. Sâlem, Harb, ii. 546.
Naked Beduin children (and that even by night and in cold weather), 346, 519; ii. 251.
Náḳsh, scored inscription, 601.
Nâmûs (ناموس), pl. nawamis, v. Nagûs: in old Arabic — is a lair, especially a hunter's lair, 457; certain cells of dry stone building in Sinai called —, 431, 457; opinion of Sir Henry C. Rawlinson, ib.; ii. 120.
Ibn Nâmus [v. Nômus], sheykh of the Noàmsy, Heteym, ii. 263.
Namûs (ناموس), ardour and incitation of the spirits (pd. Gallis verve, elan), the sting of anger, 207; ii. 228.
Naós, perhaps corrupted to Pers, navús, 457.
Nargîly (for narjîly; called also shîsha), the water-pipe, 58, 106, 109, 113.
Nàsar, a poor man of Ḥums in the pilgrimage, left sick at Medáin Sâlih, 140.

el-Naṣâra (sing. Naṣrâny), the Christian people or nations: the — esteemed by Mohammedans of better faith than themselves, 219, 257; — of better blood and human nature, 318, 590; — of better religion than the wild Bed., 221, 440, 492; "One Moslem may chase an hundred —," 318; "One Moslem prisoner exchanged for ten —," 553; "Do meteors fall upon the heads of the — ?" 321; the pre-Islamic inhabitants of Arabia called —, 276, 326, 432, 442, 487, 595; all arts derived to them from the —, 330; 451, 503, 580, 630, 649, 665; the Arabian (perchance Montanist) tradition of the wedlock of the —, 341, 492; the — "falsifiers of the former Scriptures," 342, 658; — "People of the Scriptures," 342; and therefore "teachers," 343; — "are idolaters, they make unto God partners," 343; — are, they think, one kindred, 432; land of the —, 434; — a people of their word, 508, 582; Yahûd and — 'cannot utter the Lord's name,' 518; '— cannot look up to heaven,' 522; is smoke-drinking blamed amongst the — ? 528; — encourage the Moslems to pray in their religion, 579; "Sleep in the house of the —," 579; — 'uncles' sons of the Yâhûd,' 580; war of the — and Islam, 587; fasting of the —, 588; 'no kind of wedlock observed among the —,' 341; 492, 590, 656; 'Are the — polite nations?' 656; ii. — cannot look up to heaven, 63, 244; the — may everywhere pass freely save to the Harameyn, 103, 105; riches of the —, 106, 163; — said to be born out of the sea, 191; — reputed great strikers, 198; — "inhabit a city walled with iron, in the sea," 241; 'the — sicken not as other men,' 281; war with the —, v. Jehâd; behind how many floods dwell the — ? 303; some strangers, passengers in Nejd, reputed —, 302; their probity, 310; — will fall down into hell fire, 328; they are children of the Evil One, 368; "the — be not followers aright of the doctrine of Jesus," 396; 397-402; 412; lands and cities of the —, 448; opinion of the — at 'Aneyza, 411, 467.
Nasarene, Christian.
the Nasarene country (which in Syria we hear named el-Belâd, and more seldom Frankistán; and among the foreign merchants in el-Kasîm, el-Koronát), a land without camels, 317; without palms, 318, 319; peaceable, 320; without Beduins, ib.; — very populous, 318, 321.

[*Nasera* Beduins, near Ḥodèyda.
Sherîf Nâṣir, a tribute gatherer of the Sherîf Emir of Mecca, II. 457, 560-74.
Sheykh *Nâṣir es-Smîry*, a Khâlidy [corr. a Sbeyay] of 'Aneyza, II. 376; and one of the Jidda merchants, 378-81, 397, 415, 418, 419, 431.
Naṣr, victory, II. 69.
Nàṣr, an Auájy tribesman, 623, 627-30; 634-7.
Naṣr, a Harby at Hâyil, 655.
Naṣr, Ibn Rashîd's secretary, 640, 642, 643, 659; II. 61, 74.
Naṣr, a Shammary of el-'Irâk, 631-3.
Naṣrâny: "it is lawful to kill a —," 237, 308, 316; the Nomads' jealousy of the — among them, 294; the — an enigma to them, 315; the name — was a reproach and execration, 317; 459; 479; 'a — three spears' length of stature,' 491; 'a — may not wed ere he shall have slain a Moslem,' 590; "With a — who need keep any law?" II. 254, 288, 297.
Naṣrâwy, the same as *Naṣrâny* (I have heard also in Arabia the fem. *Nasrawîa*), II. 75, 78.
Nature: 520; the Temple of —, II. 138.
Navûs (Pers.), a cemetery, 457.
Nazareth, 198; II. 415.
Neapolitan seamen: dark-coloured — mistaken for slaves, 168; II. 178.

Nebb'a (نَبْع), a gnarled mountain bush, II. 509.

Nebhanîeh, village in el-Kasîm, II. 315.
Néby, prophet: *en-* —, the Prophet, *i.e.* Mohammed, *qd. v.*
Nedowwer el-ḥâky wa el-ḳáhwa, II. 115.
Needles and thread, for gifts in the khála, 619.

Nef'd, pl. *anfâd* (انْفَاد, نَفْد), dunes of the Nefûd so called, II. 339.
Néfer, a common soldier of the Hâj-road kellâs, 165, *et passim*.

Neffera (نَافِرَة, shy), II. 238.

Nefs, spirit, wind, II. 412.

Nefûd (Bessàm wrote نَفُود: *v. Néfd*] deep sand desert. In the map I have accounted the —s with the Petra sandstones; and believe them to be such as our "greensands." There are tongues of Nefûd in all the vastity of the Arabian peninsula: in el-Wéshm they say, "The Nefûd reaches in the north to Jauf el-'Amir, and southward to Sunn'a [Sán'a]." This is like their saying of the southern Harras, "they stretch between Mecca and Kheybar"; but we have seen that they are not continuous, 95; — between Gâza and Egypt, 274; — between Teyma and Jauf, 340, 347, 351, 354, 367, 376, 392, 617, 626, 668; II. 46, 64, 87, 164, 287, 456; — *el-Arîsh*, 261; — el-Kasîm, 37; 49, 55, 260, 315, 329, 336-9, 347-8, 352, 335, 357-60, 365, 367, 373, 375, 382, 388, 392-4; the cottage floors in 'Aneyza are of deep-strewn — sand, 404; 408, 417, 418, 420, 427, 428, 434-5-6, 440-2-5-6, 451, 460-4-7-8, 481, 487-8-9; border of the — southward, 490, 553; — of el-Wéshm, 452, 467-8; the —s of Arabia, 575.
Néfur et-Ṭarik, mountain in the way to Mecca from Middle Nejd, II. 507.
Negâba, said to be the name of a mountain coast in the Teháma, 463.
Negaes, ruined site in J. Kerak, 61.
Negro: there are a multitude of —es in Arabia; they are bond-servants in oases and nomad tribes, and freed men; and the posterity of such. There are some whole villages of — blood in Arabia, as Kheybar and el-Hâyat. Sometimes a poor white village or nomad woman (of Heteym, of Jeheyna) will wed with a welfaring — villager! and I have known an Heteymy wedded with a black woman of el-Hâyat. [The children of an Heteymîa wedded with a negro of the kellâ at el-Héja were black-skinned, but they had the fine lineaments of Arabs, 603.] — woman in the Hâj, 99; a young — at Teyma, 339; — Beduin woman, 421; —es joy to be well adorned, 600; II. —es in Arabia, 97, 191, 363; a young — pargetter at 'Aneyza, 373; 446, 486; — women in 'Aneyza, 471; — bondsmen at 'Ayn ez-Zeyma, 524; a — host in W. Fâtima, 572; a — gardener, 574. [*v.* Slaves.]
Nejd, the inner highland of north Arabia, 177; humour of —ers, 181, 183, 186; — manners, 242; Waháby —, 270, 272, 289; people of —, 328-9, 331, 343; — could not be inhabited without the camel, 336; 338; 371, 376, 473, 527, 542, 566, 578, 585, 596; devout —, 599; 605, 609, 611, 632, 635, 656, 658, 662; West —, 305, 328, 330, 669; population of nomad —, 318; — Arabians are called Beduw in the border lands, 589; — tribes, 663; II. East —, 18, 28, 47, 53, 222, 260; Middle —, 196; — manners, 27; — a plain, 329; — urbanity, 39; 52; — wilder-

ness, 60; — Arabians, 64, 111; — Arabia, 192, 199, 234; nomad women veiled, 243; — tribes are commonly dispersed in *fcrjàn*, 250, 257; 308; murrain in —, 263, 288; the trade of — east of Teyma pertains to the Persian Gulf, 337; the vulgar Arabic speech of —, 426.

W. *Nejid* (two Wadies thus named, which descend to opposite parts from one mountain of that name) in the Teháma-Shéfa, 463.

Néjis, foul, impious, 543, 613, 657.

Néjis ed-dínya, II. 447.

Nejjàb, postman, 47, 162, 208, 217; II. 208.

Néjjar (read *nejr* نَجْر), antique stone troughs so called at Medáin Sâlih, 175; 180.

Nejjel, village ruins in Mount Seir, 75.

en-Nejjilla, ass-mare's name, II. 253.

Wady Néjl, in the Teháma-Shéfa, 463.

Nejm, a star, an aerolith, 412, 478; II. 157.

Nejm : Hâj —, warden of the kellâ at Medáin Sâlih, 128, 129, 134, 137, 153, 168, 179, 181, 204, 206, 207, 208, 209, 213, 220, 233, 234, 235, 236, 242, 323, 327, 358, 403, 405, 409, 410, 412 *et seq.*, 415, 417 *et seq.*, 420, 485, 550, 560, 562-3, 585, 603; II. 135.

Nejowwazak (جَوّز for زَوّج) *bint*, 366.

Nejràn, a city in el-Yémen, 522; II. 196; "the inhabitants are in religion *Bayâdiyyeh*, like the people of Maskat" (Sleymàn Abu Daûd. Sheykh el-'Ageyl at Damascus), 350.

Nejûmy [Ar. for the Kurdish *Yelduzely*], family name of Amm Mohammed, II. 157; the elder —, *ib*.; 169, 209; 315, 536.

Nelnokh, village ruins in Moab, 61.

el-Némsa, Austrian Empire and Germany, 657, II. 541.

Nenhash, (perhaps for *nahájj*, نهش=نهج), 621.

Neskhi, l'ecriture —, 224.

Nesma (نَسْمَة), II. 115.

Nessellem 'aleyk (Bed. valediction), 313; II. 297.

Nettle : — at Kheybar, II. 138, 163, 253.

N. Testament, 480, 498; II. 24.

Níbs (*níbz*), said in jesting wise, 514.

Niggera, the — (Batanea), 314.

Niggera (نَقَرَ), sunken bays in the Harra lavas so called, II. 253, 254.

Night : — in the wilderness of Arabia, 302, 330, 384, 421, 424, 453; arctic —, 320; the cheerful summer — in the khála, 321, 384; coolness of the summer —, 520, 531.

Nightshade weed, 350.

Nikkel, a ruined site in Moab, 59.

Nile : the —, 129, 604; II. a — village, 110, 187; Nile sores, II. 511.

Nimmr [*nímr*], the Arabian leopard, 373, 428; II. 164.

Nimrân, a dog's name, 474.

Nimrod [of whom the Moslems say, "He slew his father and took his own mother to wife"], II. 32.

Thulla'an en-Nír, between el-Kasîm and Mecca, II. 495.

Nîş (نِيص), the porcupine, 173.

Nitre, prepared by the Bed., 410.

W. *en-N'kîb*, near Tâyif, II. 567.

en-N'kussha, a fendy of 'Ateyba, II. 457.

Noâba, an affinity of Kheybar villagers, II. 153.

Noah : "tomb" of — at Kerak, 63; II. 191, 414.

Nôakh! [*nûwwkh*,] make (the camel) kneel, 444.

Noâmsy, a kindred of Heteym, clients of the Auájy, Bíshr, 614.

Noàsera, a kindred of Ânnezy, 377.

Nôkh (read *nûwwkh*, نوخ)! make the camel kneel, II. 78, 519.

Ibn *Nômus* [*Nômas*], family name of the sheykhs of the Noâmsy, II. 80, 86; their dîra, 89, 253, 263.

Noora, a woman's name, II. 39.

Nose-medicines, 485.

Nose-ring : the woman's —, at el-Ally, 190; — among the Bed., 268, 385; II. 243, 321.

November : cold — nights in J. Shammar, II. 76.

Noweyr, wife of *Maatuk*, an Heteymîa, II. 298, 302, 304.

Nuhéj نُهَيج (from هيج), we will flit, 537.

Numbers : the fabulous enumeration of Hebrews and Arabs, 61, 83, 100, 171; Zeyd counts by tens, 387; II. 545.

Numedal, a valley in Norway, 476.

Nûn, the Arabic letter *n*, sounded in the ending of nouns pronounced indefinitely, in Nejd, 632.

en-Nuṣeyrîeh (النَّصِيرِيَّة), an idolatrous Mohammedan sect in Northern Syria, II. 401.

Nûshud el-Jemâl (ناشد الجمل), father of the patriarch *Wâil*, 270.
el-Nussîr, a kindred of Ânnezy, 377.
Nuṣṣy (نصي), a kind of barley grass, in the desert, 135 ; ii. 363, 493 ; valley sides in the Mecca country hoary with —, 516.
Nuzzân, a dog's name, 474.

Oaks : evergreen — in the mountains of Edom, 78 ; — in the Harra, 425.
Oasis [perhaps the Ar. *Wady*]: all the Arabian —es were colonies of Bed., 276 ; — -dwellers are of more sound understanding than the Nomads, 322, 361 ; — life bare of superfluous cares, 582 ; ii. 6 ; — Arabs are full of petulant humour, 408.
Oath : (as all Arabs) the Bed. incessantly take God's name in vain, crying out, *Ullah! Wellah! Billah!* 309 ; Bed. —s, 309-12 ; to swear by the religion, 309 ; *hâlif yemîn (wa hyat hâtha el-'aûd, wa Rubb el-mabûd inny mâ adeshurak)*, 310; words to clear oneself of another's suspicion, *ib.*; certain forms of oaths which are received among them as binding, *ib.*; — of denial, *ib.*; to swear upon the sword, *ib.*; —s that are binding between enemies, 310 ; ii. 82, 292.
Occidental : the — nations, 420 . [*v.* Franks, *Frenjy.*]
Ochre : chamber walls in Hâyil painted with —, 638, 646, 651, 653.
Odours : Arabs very imaginative of all —, 250, 440, 485.
Oedipus : a Beduin —, 237.
Officer : an Ottoman — who disputed with Zeyd, ' Whether nigher unto God were the life of townsfolk or of the Nomads,' 269.
Og : the great " bed " of —, 57.
Ogre [*v. Ghrôl*]: the —, 90.
Oil for the lamps of the temples of Medina and Mecca carried in the Hâj, 72 ; of a tree which is better than samn, 319 ; — of the rock, 647, 651.
'Okâtz [pronc. by Nejders '*Okâth* عكاظ], probable site of —, ii. 535.
O*killa* named ' the slave of Márhab, last sheykh of Mosaic Kheybar ; after the (Mohammedan) conquest of the place he gathered the dispersed villagers and became their head,' ii. 132 ; he was slain by the Beduw, *ib.*
Oleander, *v.* Rose-laurel, 486.

'Omân, commonly pronounced in Nejd '*Amân* : the Arabian Gulf Province of —, ii. 389, 462, 489.
'Omanîa, thelûl of '*Oman*, ii. 489, 562.
'Omar [*pronc.* in Nejd '*Amar*], first calif : mosque of —, 493 ; ii. justice and simplicity of —, 387, 421.
Ophthalmia : (the eyeballs of the weak-dieted Arabs, baked all day in the sunny drought, are very subject to night chills), 81, 299, 364; 375, 436, 576; rheumatic —, 597, 598, 601 ; ii. 129, 289, 334, 385.
Orange : the — is not planted in the Arabian oases, 194.
Orchard at eṭ-Ṭâyif, ii. 551. [*v. Jenèyny, Hauta, Béled.*]
Oreymát, a kindred of Harb in Nejd, which have no great cattle, ii. 333.
Orghra or *roghrwa* (رغوة), the sweet froth of new drawn milk, 305.
Orientalism : that fantastic — which is as it were the odour of a lady's casket, is not Arabian but foreign, 96, 131, 631 ; — of the great border cities, 301-6 ; — of the Nomads, 306 ; [*v. Kaṣṣâd.*] They are credulous of aught beyond their ken, 306 ; they tell of bygone adventures in the desert, *ib.* ; ii. — of the Arabs, 120.
Orion, 321.
Ornaments [*v.* Bracelet, Nose-ring, Jewel] of the women of el-Ally, 190 ; — of the Beduin maidens and women, 268, 385 ; — sold at Hâyil, 637.
Oshèyjir [*Ushèykir*], oassi in el-Wéshm (" three hundred " houses): from hence came the Bessàm family, about the year 1818, to 'Aneyza, ii. 452.
Osmully, Syrian vulg. for *Osmanli*, Ottoman, a Turk.
Ostrich in Arabia, 126, 173 ; —es perish in a murrain, 476; ii. 86; value of — skins, *ib.*; 246.
'Otheym, hamlet of five houses, in the dominion of Ibn Rashîd, ii. 34.
Otheythia, oasis in el-Wéshm, ii. 452.
'Othŷ'hi, v. W'othŷhi.
Ottoman : — Empire [*v. Dowla*]: all now ruinous in the — countries, 43 ; — criminal government, 113, 115, 132 ; pious foundation of some — Sultans, 92 [*v. Selîm,* '*Abd-el-'Azîz*]; — rule in Syria, 113 ; Bed. opinion of the — government, 132, 143, 270, 271 ; ii. — corruption and misrule deplored by the Arabians, 397 ; 401, 455.

OF ARABIC WORDS

Ouadam, pl. of *Adamy* (*qd. v.*) a man.
Oweyish, a dog's name, 474.
Owèynat el-Béden, site near Medina, 127.
Owl; the — in the desert, 349; it is eaten by Fehjies, *ib.*, 656.
Owlàd el-wáṭan, children of the soil, 197.
Owshâz, "founder of *el-Owshazîeh* and brother of 'Eyàr," II. 421.
el-Owshazîeh, an ancient town site near 'Aneyza, II. 418.
Owsheyfy [*v. Gârat Owsheyfîa*], a place in el-Wéshm, II. 564.
Ozmáṭ (بقسماط, بشماط), caravan biscuit, 164, 252.

P: this letter is wanting in Arabic. [*v.* II. 22.]
Palestine, a bare limestone country of little natural beauty, 130, 216; graves of patriarchs in —, 434; — renferme peu de monuments antérieurs à l'époque grecque, 673-4; II. 401.
Palm bast, for well-ropes, II. 452.
Palm-leaf plait (for mats) at el-Ally, 190; at Kheybar, II. 198.
Palmistry, 301, 492, 533, 598.
Palms: [There are no wild — in the Arabian desert soil, saving few seedlings by watering places, 395; there grow half-wild — in some sites of spring waters as in J. Ajja and by the lower valley ground of Kheybar.] Male and female —, 134; no — in the land of the Nasâra, 318; husbandry of — at el-Ally, 194; at Teyma, 328, 330, 337, 608; in Hâyil, 665; II. half wild — in Ajja, 24; — of Kheybar, where they are innumerable, 119, 198; — off-sets, 204; season to marry the —, 232, 236; male —, *ib.*; no — at Semîra, 325; — of Gassa, 337; — of Boreyda, 355; — of 'Aneyza, 358, 382.
Palmyra, [*v. Todmor*] sulphurous stream of —, 193; the ancient city, 211; L'ecriture de —, 224; 579, 603, 619; II. 219, 428.
Papers: the Kheyâbara suspicious of the Nasrâny's buried —, II. 112, 114.
Paradise: the Moslem —, 132; II. 159.
Παράκλητος [*v. Aḥmed*], II. 24.
Pargeters: — at Hâyil, II. 20; — in el-Kasîm, 346, 367. [*v. Jiss.*]
Parliament of the tribe, *v. Mejlis*.
Partridge: the rock —, 367, 440, 480, 496; II. 77, 205, 238.

Pasha (Ar. *basha*) of the Hâj (*v. Mohammed Sa'id*), 40, 48, 49, 54, 65, 87, 89, 94, 106; — guardian and paymaster, 109, 113, 132; his provision, 110, 113; his life, 113-15; he is his own camel-master, in the Hâj, his Kurdish avarice, his daughter, his brother, his palace at Damascus, 114; his great pavilion, 117; 127, 140, 206, 246, 254.
Passport: circular — [*Bîurúldi*], II. 100; 183; — of Ibn Rashîd, 74, 99, 146, 181, 232, 282; British —, 181, 183.
Pastimes [*v.* Game, *Biât, Minḳala*]: no manly — among the Bed., 385; children's —, *ib.*, 479-480.
Pasture-bushes [*v. Gussha*], 303, 322.
Path; beaten — in the khála, near oases upon common ways, 629, 635.
Patriarch [*v. Jid*], the Semitic —s, 270, 282; — of el-Ally, 189.
Patriotism and religion, 599.
St. Paul, II. 373.
Peacemaker, 362, 417.
Peleg, II. 52.
Peninsula (of Arabia), *v.* Arabia, 289, 295, 311, 325, 378, 420, 469, 657; II. 182.
Pensioners of Ibn Rashîd, 663, 671.
Peppermint in the dry seyls in the steppe of eṭ-Ṭâyif, II. 427, 510, 535.
Perfumes [*v.* Incense, *Áttar*], 247, 297, 485, 498.
Περίκλυτός [*v. Aḥmed*], II. 24.
Persia, 71, 98-9.
Persian: —s in the Syrian Hâj, 42, 43; singing, 43; 44, 46; 87; their apparel, 98; — woman and dames, 99; 110, 111, 125; 250; — aga, *v. Mohammed Aghra*, 99; — lordlings, 100; — standard, 71; — consulate, 104; pilgrimage of a — lady deceased, 106; — cock on pilgrimage, 110; 352; II. — small money in the bazaar of Hâyil, 23; — calligraphy in Arabic documents, 100; "— cartridges," 144; — camel-bags, 228; — language, 388; — manner of drinking tea, 397; the —s are of Gog and Magog, 558.
Persian Gulf, 108, 338, 601; — words, 654; 664; II. 23, 231, 337, 375, 411, 419, 487, 494, 504, 511.
Persian hakîm, *v. Ḥakîm*.
Persian pilgrimage caravan through Ibn Rashîd's country, 641, 651; II. 63-4-5-6, 302, 320.
Persian (schismatic) religion, 108, 214, 522; —s in the Hâj burned in the fury of their (Sunnî) fellow pilgrims at Medina for despite done to

660 INDEX AND GLOSSARY

the tomb of Moh., 108; II. their malignant curiosity in not eating with other men, 224; —s in Syria, 285; 401; — pilgrims, 516.
Pest, pestilence [*v el-Wába*, Cholera, Fever], 432; II. 21, 403.
Pestle: coffee —, called *surbût* (*qd. v.*) by the Aarab of the Western dîras, 288; — of limestone, 329; II. — of stone, wrought by Bed., 200.
Petra, *Wady Mûsa*, 78-83, 85; hewn monuments (mostly sepulchral) at — and Medáin Sâlih compared, 82; 147; — sandstone rock (79) compared with that of el-Héjr, 147; the *Sîk* compared with the Diwán passage at Medáin Sâlih, 160; the *Khazna Far'aôun* compared with the Diwán, *ib.*; 211; Moh. 'Aly's tale of a Frank and his wife at —, 218; 486; 673, 674; II. 19; the ancient —, 196; 575.
Phantom camel, 472; — oasis, 598.
Pharaoh, 79, 160, 312.
Philadelphia, *v.* Rabbath Ammon.
Philemon, the Comic Poet, who died laughing [he was 274 B.C.], 92.
"Philip of Macedon': a Turkish army surgeon at Tâyif affirms that he can read an Himyaric inscr. — ! II. 544.
Philosophy (*v. el-Fúlsifa*): the Platonic —, 195-196.
Phlebotomists; Bed. —, 540.
Phoenician coast, 560; II. 284, 401.
Phthisis, II. 411.
Physician [*v. Mudowwy, Ḥakîm*]: what must be the Arabian —, 298-301.
Piastre, a Frankish (Ital.), word, used by Franks in the East; it is half a groat at Damascus.
Pictures: book of —, 382, 415.
Piedmontese Hâjjy, at Hâyil, II. 65-6-8.
Pigeons, blue rock-, which haunt about water holes in the desert [*Lubeid* 69]: — at Medáin Sâlih, 174, 495; II. 91, 253, 505.
Pilaw, a Turkish mess of boiled rice and mutton, 650.
Pilgrimage of the Religion, 41. [*v. Ḥâj.*]
Pilgrimage caravans of el-Kasîm, *v. Ḥâj el-Kasîm*.
Pilgrimage; 'the little —' to Medina, II. 512.
Pilgrimage: places of ancient — in Arabia, II. 512, 564.
Pillar of cloud and fire spoken of in Exodus, 380; —s of locusts, *ib.*
Pillars: — at Ma'an, 71; ancient — at *Khurbet er-Rum*, 94; — at el-Ayîna, 93; — at Teyma, 331, 581.

Pimpernel: wild — springing in the desert after showers, 259.
Pincers worn by the Bed. housewives, to pluck thorns out of the soles of the bare feet, 268.
Pison: "the river —," II. 191 [W. Bîsha].
Pistol-case found in the Nasrâny's bags, II. 100.
Pistols: 219; few — in the hands of the Southern Bed., 379; 388, 397, 413, 414, 504; II. 469.
Pitchers of antique form borne upon their heads by women going to draw water in W. Fâṭima, II. 570.
Pithwood of date palm, *v. Jummàr.*
Plagues; bred in the Mecca pilgrimage, 141, [*v. Wába.*]; 477, 629, 635, 670.
Plain *el-Fuèylik*, II. 329.
Plato, 196, 522.
Play: children —ing at horses, 384, 480, 623.
Pleiades, 321.
Pliny, 135; II. 197, 377.
Plough, a stake shod with iron, 84.
Plum tree: the — at el-Ally, 194; — blossoms in March at Teyma, 329.
gentile Plural forms of some Arabian tribes and kindreds (such are not seldom of the family name of the Sheykh): ['*Arbân*, many peoples and names]; *es-Sokhûr* (of Beny Sókhr); *Anûz* (of Ânnezy); *Jehîn* (of Jehèyna); *Fuḳara* (of el-Fejîr); *Noâmsy* (of Ibn Nomas); *Heteymân* (of Hetèym); *Noàsera* (of Nussîr); *Barâhimma* (of Beny Ibrahîm); *Shubâramy* (of Shubramy); *'Ateybân* (of 'Ateyba); *Ḳahatîn* (of Ḳahtân); *Korásh* (of Ḳorèysh); *Heṭheylân* (of Haṭhèyl); so *Zuàmil* (of Zâmil); *Waylyîn* (the children of Wayil, the Ânnezy); *el-Wahûb* (of Beny Wáhab).
Plutonic country [*v.* Granite, Basalt, Trap], 451; II. — of Jebel Shammar, 239, 244, 246, 256; — from a little S. of er-Russ to Mecca, 490.
Pockets: none are made in Bed. clothing, 268.
Poets: unlettered desert —, 306.
Poison, 297, 460, 642, 662; II. 27.
Pomegranate: —s sold to the Haj at Tebûk, 112; 570 *et passim*; — a bitter-sweet, and such should be a worthy man in the opinion of the Arabs, 615.
Pool: well and irrigation — at 'Aneyza, II. 464-5.
Porcupine, 173, 371, 656.
Porch of audience at 'Aneyza, II. 463.

OF ARABIC WORDS

Porridge [v. Borghrol] : — (jerrîsh) the diet of the Peraean Beduins and villagers, 60, 79 ; — of samh, 357 ; — the evening meal at Teyma, 605.
Port Sa'id, ii. 559.
" Porte : " the — (Bab el-'Aly), 251 ; ii. 174, 398, 559.
Posture of the Beduw reposing upon the soil, 303.
Potsherds : ancient — and broken glass in the site of Medáin Sâlih, 153, 410 ; — in the site called el-Mubbiát, 203 ; ii. 422.
Poultry bred in Nejd villages, 338 ; ii. 20, 207.
Poverty in the oases not base, 582.
Power of the Air, 496, 498. [v. Menhel el-melûk.]
Ppahppah ! voice of a dumb Arabian, ii. 22.
Praevaesa, town in Albania, ii. 541.
Pray [v. Du'a] : their formal —ers, 236 ; women —ing, 279, 558 ; hardly an half of the men in the Nejd tribes have learned to —, 279, 286, 292 ; they wash with sand, ib. ; 292, 456 ; the Lord's prayer, ib. ; —ers in the Arctic dîra ; —ing-places in the desert, 236, 496 [v. Masully] ; ii. —er-banks at Hâyil, 25 ; —ing-places in the desert, 271 ; ' A young man should begin to — when he is married,' 162 ; —ing-places of old heathen Arabia said to be seen in certain bergs in Nejd, 564.
Prisoners in war, v. Jehâd.
Pro Deo et Patria (for God and the Fatherland), motto read on a Beduin's cutlass, 505.
Promises : ' — of overnight,' a Bed. proverb, 425 ; their — to a kafir are not binding, 310 ; ii. 82 ; Nomad lying —, 91.
Prophets : the Hebrew —, ii. 407.
Provender gathered by Bed. visiting Hâyil for their dromedaries, which must lie there two or three days, 626.
Proverbs [riming — of the tribes, v. 592] : ' God increased 'Annezy, but has put divisions among them,' 378 ; ' Promises made in the night-time be not binding by day-light,' 425 ; ' There be none less Moslems than the Moslemîn,' 457 ; ' The stranger for the wolf,' 518 [ii. 301] ; ' Sup with the Jew, but sleep in the house of the Nasrâny,' 579 ; ii. ' Kheybar the grave of the soldiery,' 145 ; ' The Dowla a stone whereupon if any one fall . . .,' 151 ; ' The Dowla hath a long arm,' 235 ; ' All is not Khúthera and Tunis,' 262 ; ' Betwixt the dog and the wolf,' 267 ; ' The Lord may work much mercy before the morning,' 278 ; ' We have a religion and they have a religion,' 302 et passim ; ' Every man is justified in his own faith,' ib., et passim ; ' Nothing is seen beyond 'Auf,' 307 ; ' A prudent man will not reveal his name in strange company,' 451.
Provinces : the notion of — may be somewhat foreign to the understanding of Nejd Arabians ; they speak of Ibn Rashîd's dîra as Jebel Shammar ; but el-Kaṣîm, el-Wéshm etc. are in their minds as wadies. An erudite Nejder, 'Abd-el-'Azîz of Herrmah in Siddîr, whom I found living at Bombay, in describing these countries, wrote for me Wady el-Kaṣîm, Wady Sidîr, Wady el-Wéshm, Wady el-Kharj. And Ḥàmed en-Nefîs spoke of Wady el-Mehmel and Wady el-Arûth.
Provision for the way given out to passengers from the public kitchen at Hâyil, ii. 284.
Psalms : the locust named in the —, 381.
the Psalter in Arabic, 658.
Ptolemy, the geographer, 134, 135, 669.
Pulse : they think an hakîm should know all a sick man's state in only handling his —, 298 ; ii. 70, 383.
Pumice, 174, 423, 451, 479.
Pumpkins (dibba), 178, 194, 487, 555, 593, 605, 637.
" Purged like Tollog," 472.
Purification (circumcision), 387, 437-8.
Pyrrhic dancing, 70.
Pythagoreans, ii. 348.

Queen : the — of England, 186, 492 ; ii. 282.
Quern-stones, v. Mill-stones.
Quilts : a stitcher of cotton — in Hâyil, ii. 283.
Quinine : 299, 563 ; — used effectually in a plague, 670 ; ii. 73, 84, 338.

Rabba, v. Rabbath Moab.
Rabbath Ammon, 56 ; words of Jeremiah against —, 57 ; the Christians of Kerak would have occupied —, 63.
Rabbath Moab (Rabba), 59, 60.
Rabèyby (رَبَابَة) : one-stringed viol of the Arabians ; the —, 81, 138, 306 ; — forbidden at Teyma, 332 [yet I have heard it played upon at Môgug] ; 384, 412, 587.

Rabî'a, the tender spring of herbs in the waste, after the autumn or winter showers, 244; it is the life of the Nomads' cattle, 259, 260, *et passim*; II. 259.

Sheykh Rabî'a, II. 477.

Rabugh, Harb village near the Red Sea above Jidda, II. 546.

Rachel, *v. Rókhal*.

Radîf (pl. *ráduffa* رُدَفاء or رُدَافي), dromedary back-rider, 379.

Ráduffa (*v. radîf*), II. 90.

Rafîk [pl. *rufaká*], a way-fellow, 142, 276, 320; faith of the —, 405, 425, 430; II. duty of the younger — to serve in his company, 245; 255; he who abandons his — is despised, and no honest person should thereafter receive him, 288.

Râfuthy, a heretic, II. 361.

Rafýa, an oasis of er-Russ, II. 490.

Rágel, Egyptian for *rájil*, a man.

er-*Ràha*, district of the Harra, 117.

Ráhab (friar): a — in Medina, II. 178; Mohammed's precept concerning —s, *ib.*

er-*Rahabba*, an open place in the Bíshr village of Kheybar, II. 136, 156.

Rahala, a fendy of Harb B. Sâlem, II. 546.

Rahamna wa rahamkom Ullah, es-sulât 'aly el-jennèyzat el-hâthera, II. 214.

er-*Raheydân*, mare's name, II. 252.

er-*Rahîfa*, camel's name, 321.

Rahîl (رَحِيل), about to remove (as the Nomads).

Ráhla (رَحْلَة): the removing and journeying of the Nomads, 257; a — described, 261; 345-7; a summer —, 483; II. 329.

Rahma(t), mercy (*rahm*, the womb), the movement of the bowels and instinction to lovingkindness: — *Ullah!* 307.

Rahn, a pledge.

Rahôl (رَحُول) a dromedary, II. 23; 335.

Rahýel el-Hameydy, brother of Motlog, 265, 332, 352, 353, 354, 357, 388, 389, 392, 393, 421, 554, 557; II. 141.

Railroad: " might a — be laid through Nejd to Mecca ? " II. 553.

Rain in Arabia: the —s in Northern Arabia and W. Nejd are very partial. In 1876, rain to wet the ground had not fallen for three years at el-Héjr. Showers fell all day there, with chill damp air and dark gusty skies, on 29 Dec. at el-Ally. On the 10 Jan. 1877 we heard thunder in the afternoon, and the Harra was veiled with bluish mist; rain fell for some hours and the wilderness was full of plashes: which were mostly sunk up again on the morrow. The next day was rainy. Showers fell again on the morning of the 30th. In the last days of March, 1877 (the time of barley harvest at el-Ally) we had clouds and some showers by night in the Teyma wilderness. After very hot summer months the bright weather changed in the Teyma country to clouded skies and gusts of wind on 2nd Oct.; rain fell tempestuously the same evening; and we had showery days and rainy nights until the 14th. In the country between Hâyil and Kheybar it rained one or two nights in the last week of November. The autumn rain fell that year abundantly in the Nefûd toward Jauf and in the northern wilderness toward Sûk es-Sheukh: but very little had fallen in the basin of W. el-Humth. In 1878 I saw showers in the evening of the 4th April, and a tempest of rain and lightning in the afternoon of 19th April, near Semîra; and some light and almost daily showers in May, at 'Aneyza (where early summer showers fall yearly at that time). The deserts between el-Kasîm and Mecca are watered yearly by seasonable rains, which at Tâyif fall commonly for 4, 5, or 6 weeks, from the end of August. 189, 209, 351, 353, 608, 612, 613, 616, 618, 619, 620; depth of the —, 626; " What of the — ? " 627; 632; II. — near el-Hâyat, 81, 83, 85; ponded — on the Harra, 87, 90; 116; — -pools in the Harra, 239; tropical — at Mecca, 197; 265, 290, 329-31.

Rainbow: triple —, II. 330; *v.* note by Prof. P. G. Tait, 356.

Rain-pools, 628.

Râ'iyat, (راعِيَة, intensive from *râ'y* راعي a pastor); which word the Bed. seem to use in the sense of lord or ruler, 427; they say of one so long a guest that he is an ally of the household, — or *askar el-beyt*; and so — *el-Haddaj* is said at Teyma for one of the owners of the Teyma well.

Rajajîl (رَجَاجِيل) *es-shéukh*, the Prince's armed band at Hâyil, 655, 659-62; II. 22, 35, 36, 37, 47, 49, 63, 67, 265, 272.
Rájjàl, a manly man [Dowlâny Ar. heard at el-Ally].
Rájil, a man.
Rájul ṣadûḳ, 641.
Rákham, small white carrion eagle; the —s hover over the nomad menzils in the desert, and are migratory birds, 298, 374, 439, 583, 584, 656; II. 240, 512.
Rakhŷeh, *v.* Rakŷyeh.
Rakŷyeh, Meḥsan's daughter, 365, 514.
Ramaṭhân (vulg. *Ramaḍán*, Turk. *Ramazán*), the Mohammedan month of fasting, 48, 102, 186, 279; zelotism in —, 557, 558; 569, 598; watching for the new moon of —, 578; —, a month of weariness and of evil deed, 570; 574; the Nasrâny eats without regard of —, 575, 584; — breakfast at sun-set, 577; — supper after midnight, 578; 580; religious women, even being with child or nursing, fast in —, 586; passengers fast not in —, 594; 596, 597; — ended, 605; 606, 607, 608, 611; II. duty of Moslems to fast in —, 53; 276, 400.
Ramta, a camping place, 46.
Rape: wild — kind, springs with the new herb in the desert, 259.
Râs, the head.
Râs el-'Aŷn, fountain head, at el-Ally, 200.
Rashèyd, a foreign merchant of 'Aneyza: his outlying palms, II. 377, 445, 446-7-8-9; 465-7-8-9-70, 475-6, 481-2; his family story, 449, 469-70-1.
Rashèyd, an officer of Zamil's, II. 404, 431-2-3.
Rashîd, a lettered Beduwy of Ânnezy, II. 56, 57.
Rashîd, ancestor of the Hetèym, II. 86.
Beny Rashîd, the midland Hetèym, II. 79, 86, 195, 305.
Ibn Rashîd: princely family of —, *v.* 'Abdullah, 'Abeyd, Telâl, Met'aab, Bunder, Bédr, Mohammed, Ḥamud, Mâjid, 'Abd-el-'Azîz, Fáhd, Feyd, Sleymàn, 'Abdullah, Feysal, 'Aneybar, 'Ambar; their wasm, 166; II. the princely family, 39 *et seq.*; the sheykhly children, 45.
Ibn Rashîd: Mohammed —, Prince of West Nejd. His country, 59, 88, 119, 223, 235; — came to the Emir's dignity by bloodshed, and that was of his kindred, 236; 238, 240, 241, 242, 249, 279, 290, 314, 315, 329, 330, 332, 333, 334, 335, 338, 344, 377, 378; his tax, 394; 413, 414, 436, 470, 496, 500, 502, 503, 516, 527, 546, 550, 554; government of —, 587, 595, 596, 606, 609, 610; — accepts three thelûls of the Moahîb booty, 610; — accounted *néjis* by many pious persons, 613; 631, 633, 636, 670; his ancestry, 640; an audience of —, 640-5; erudite in their letters and a kaṣṣâd, 643; the Hâyil Princes are clad like the Nomads, 648; his daily mejlis, 658-61; his manner of government, 595-6, 622, 651, 660, 670; another audience, 651; his popular carriage, 651; he was formerly conductor of the 'Persian Hâj,' *ib.*; his wealth in cattle &c., 664; riches, 664; his soldiery, 664; II. Arabian Princes take no thought for public remedies, 21; — allied with his cousin Ḥamûd el-'Abeyd, 29-30, 32; a new audience, 25-8; he could speak Persian, 26-7; his popular manners, 33; 38, 45-6-7, 52, 56; his government, 33, 47; — pitiless in battle, 36; — of great understanding, 27, 33, 46; his oath, 39; tragedies in the princely family, he slays Bunder el-Telâl and becomes Prince, 28-32, 40, 41; his revenue and private wealth, 34; his treasury, 48; his severity, 32, 47; he is '*ajr*, 33, 39, 40; his wives, and one of them is reported to be a *Nasrawîa!* 39; — formerly conductor of the Persian Hâj, 27, 65; dominion of —, [*v. J. Shammar*], 34, 35, 37; his is to-day the greatest name in Nejd, 45, 46, 51; — called an oppressor even in Hâyil, 46, 72; — reoccupies Jauf, 47; — receives Abdullah ibn Sa'ud, 50; a passport of —, 74, 99, 146, 181, 183; 61, 73, 89, 100, 195, 222, 223, 225, 232, 240, 248; 266; his former taxing Kheybar, 140, and oppressive rule there, 156, 230; his loss of Kheybar, 140; 144, 148; — "weakens the tribes," 241; his armed service, 245; the men of his armed band are mounted on Sherary thelûls, 261, 262; 264, 265, 266, 269, 270-2-3-6, 280-2-3-4-5; his spring forays, 269; custom of military service at Hâyil, 272; his alliance with Boreyda, 274; 285, 296-9, 302-3-6; 314; his Hâj caravan, 320; his tax-gathering in the desert, 321, 326; his strong name a shelter, 322, 323; 334, 342, 357-8, 364, 367, 377, 394; the power of —, 406; 453, 455, 456, 459, 462, 477, 479, 491, 493, 494, 543.

INDEX AND GLOSSARY

Rashîd es-Shûbramy, Sheykh of Semîra, II. 325.
Rashîdy, one of the house of Ibn Rashîd, II. 30.
Rasûl, messenger, apostle [*v. Mohammed*].
dîrat er-Rasûl, II. 91, 98.
Rat: the desert spring —, 349, *v. Jerbo'a*; the Alpine —, 371; the common — eaten in certain Hejâz villages, as Kheybar, 584; herb eating — at Kheybar, II. 138.
er-Rauth, a village of *el-Kasîm*. II. 336, 339, 340.
Rautha, pl. riâth, (روضة (رياض)), a green site of bushes where winter rain is ponded in the desert, II. 260.
er-Rautha, village in el-Aflâj, II. 425.
(2) *er-Rautha*, a village in J. Shammar, II. 34, 322; fever at —, *ib.*
Rawlinson: Sir Henry C. —, 229; his opinion of the word *namûs*, 457.
Rayis, foreman.
Rayyàn, oasis village in W. Fâtima, II. 567-8.
Rayyàn, a Noâmsy Heteymy, 618.
'Reading' over the sick, 358, 373; [*v. Kirreya*] — to the Bed., 400.
Real (from the Spanish) a crown, a dollar. In the dominion of Ibn Rashîd the common — is the *Mejidy* (the source of it is the Ottoman surra, paid to the Beduins of the Syrian Hâj road). In the Mecca trade the Maria Theresa thaler is the common currency. The — in el-Kasîm is mostly the Spanish, which comes to them in the Gulf Traffic.
Reals; a Kahtân wife that saved her husband's —, II. 476.
Rebibel, an old English word [Arabic *rabèyby*], 306.
Beny Rechab, II. 146.
Red lead, specific, 437; II. 162.
Red Sea, 85, 94, 217, 275, 276, 323, 400, 462, 465, 619; II. 234, 288, 572.
Reem (رٍم) [*v.* "Unicorn"], 373.
Religion: — of the Beduins, 58; discourse of —, religious saws fall to the humour of the Arabs, 236; Semitic — the growth of the soil in their souls, 308; — the principal business and pastime of their lives, and without which a man should have no estimation amongst them, 308; Christian and Moham. —, 341-3, 406, 492; devilish iniquity of —, 424, 551; natural — in hospitality, 447; — and patriotism, 599; II. 21, 24, 159-60;

the Arabs credulous in —, 59; — a chimera of self-love, malice and fear, 350; — a blood passion in the people of Moses and Mohammed, 362; the Mohammedan —, 370-3; the — of Islam is conformable to human nature, 399-400, 405-7.
Remedies [*v.* Medicines]: — for fever, II. 150, 184; — for colic, 229.
Renan, M. Ernest; his translation of the Aramaic monumental inscriptions of el-Héjr, 224-7; his opinion of the bethels of the Liwàn Passage, there, 228.
a Renegade lands at Jidda and visits Mecca and Medina, II. 189; another — in Mecca, 533, 547-8.
the Resurrection, 493; II. 573.
to Return upon the Moslemîn puts their tolerance to a dangerous proof, 404, 549.
Revel, old English word, the Span. rabel, Ar. *rabèyby*, 306.
Reym (رَيم), bushes in the Tehàma of Jidda, II. 573.
Rhapsodies of the Beduins, 306. [*v. B. Helál.*]
Rheums of the Beduins, 484.
Rhubarb, "an horrible medicine," II. 208; "a good medicine indeed," 241.
Rhythmical: labour of the Arabs —, 286, 506; — knocking, 404.
Rî'a (رِيعَة), a passage in a cleft or gap of the mountains.
er-Rî'a, above *Kurn el-menâzil*, II. 509, 529.
Rî'a Agda, near Hâyil, 669.
Rî'a es-Self, 632-3.
Rî'a ez-Zelâla (wherein is the Himyaric effigy and inscription), near *es-Seyl*, II. 562.
er-Riâth ('the gardens, or green places, in the desert'), the Wahâby metropolis in East Nejd: 434; II. 28, 45, 50, 51, 52, 56, 71, 196; signification of the name, 260; 350, 424, 425, 453, 454, 455, 459, 462, 476. [The Derb el-Hâj from el-Riâth passes by *es-Sòkhn*, vill., *er-Ruèytha*, vill., *el-Greyîeh*, desert vill., *J. Merdumma* or *Mutherumma* [*v. Rautha.*]
Ribaldry of the Bed., 308; the herdsmen's grossness is in the Semitic nature, 308; — in Israel, *ib.*; Palestine and the lands beyond Jordan defiled by the ancient dwellers in them, 308; the offence of lying with cattle, 308.

OF ARABIC WORDS

Ribshàn, a fendy of Jellàs, 377.
Rice : India — from el-Wejh is the diet of North-Western Arabia as far inland as the Fukara, 195, 420, 438, 448 [v. Temmn.] II. Bengal —, 188 ; a fermented drink made from —, 189 ; Arabian — shippers in Bombay, 389 ; — from Jidda for Mecca and Tâyif, 525.
Riddles at the Arabian coffee-hearth, 237.
Rifle, European, seen in Hâyil, 653 ; II. — used by the Emir, 36.
er-Rîhh (اريح), said by the Bed. for all kinds of rheums, 298.
Rîj for rîẓ, II. 362.
Rijjûm [rijûm] ; (vaulted) stone heaps, 431 ; [called 'Nasarene houses,' v. Namûs], 457, 487, 492 ; — described, 494, 542 ; II. 120, 313, 509.
Rikàb (ركاب), dromedary, 393 ; II. 23.
Rikb el-Héjr, 172, 412, 490.
er-Rimth (الرمث), a saline bush of the deserts ; the old dry sticks are used by the Nomads for fire-wood ; — is browsed by camels, and is to them, say the Nomads, ' as flesh-meat unto man ; ' but — eaten alone will give colic, 250, 279 ; II. used (dried and beaten) instead of soap, 129.
Rîsh (ريش), a pen-knife, 505.
[W. Rissha, in which lies the Hâj road from Shuggera ; begins some say near Sh'aara.
Risshàn, an ancient tower in the desert of Moab, 52.
the River country [v. Mesopotamia], II. 381.
Rîzelleyn, dual, a pair of vile fellows.
J. Roaf, in the Nejd Bíshr dîra, " great as J. Birrd," 395.
Ròbb'a el-Khâly (ربع الخالي), the great unknown sandy desert of South-East Arabia, II. 558.
er-Robba, a small village in Middle Nejd, II. 424.
Ròbb'a (Roba'a رباع), six-year-old camel, 401.
Robillát, a kindred of B. 'Atîeh, 97.
Rock, strange forms of sandstone —s in the Fukara dîra, 285.

Rocket : signal —s in the Hâj, 120 et passim.
J. Roḍwa, between Yanb'a and Medina : II. " wild men " in —, 108, 149, 202.
Roḍwa Harra, II. 378.
the Roes of the Scriptures, v. Gazelle.
Roghrwa (رغوة) or orghra (qd. v.), the sweet froth of milk from the udder, 305.
Rohòl, a dromedary, v. Rahôl.
Ròkhal, pl. rokhâl (رخل pl. رخال), young female, especially of sheep, but also of goats and camels, 475 ; II. 293.
Roman : — ruins in the Land beyond Jordan, v. Gerasa, Ammân, Bost(t)ra, Umm Jemâl, Umm Rosàs, Lejûn, Rabba, Dat Ras, Jardanîeh, Bozra, 'Uthera, Graaf, &c.; — ensign board, 116 ; II. — military expedition in Arabia, 196-7, 387 ; piece of — money found at Hâyil, 273 ; rottenness of the — power in the age of Mohammed, 387.
er-Romàn : name of a sheykhly family at Teyma, 339 ; 'Abd-el-'Azîz —, 377.
Romhh (or shelfa), horseman's lance, 262, 332, 379.
er-Romla, Beduin feminine name, 514.
" Rose of Jericho : " plants of the — in the desert, 347.
Rose-laurel, 486.
Roses of et-Tâyif, II. 510 ; from them is distilled attar of roses in Mecca, 561.
Ròtb, moist, good, II. 466.
Rotl, 114.
Ròthm (رضم), basaltic blocks upon the 'Aueyriḍ Harra, 427.
er-Rotham, a seyl-bed at Teyma, 340.
Ròtn (not pure Arabic ; and seldom heard in the mouths of Bed., other than those dwelling near Medina) رطن [properly the speech of a foreigner], II. 258, 426.
Rowsa, a sounding sand-hill in the Nefûd, 352.
er-Ruâge, a tribe of Ashràf, II. 556.
Rúb'a (Ròb'a) ed-dínga, 669.
Rubb, Lord.
Rubba, a Mahûby herdsman, 470, 475, 485, 499.
Rubbâ (ربّ), fellowship, 206, 296, 661 ; II. 19.

Yâ Rubby! Ah (my) Lord (God)! [Hebr. Rabbi], 307, 471.

Rubî'a (رَبِيعَة), an Arabian patriarch, II. 393.

Ruèyht (ruèyt), hast slaked thy thirst? II. 296.

Rueytha, one of the oases of er-Russ, II. 490.

Rúfaka, pl. of *rafîk.*

Ruffian, An amiable bloody —, 130.

Rûh-hu, commonly a desert man will not name —, his own soul (himself), to a stranger, II. 453.

Ruhh! begone, 380; II. 167.

Ruins and inscriptions in Arabia are attributed to the Yahûd or Nasâra.

Ruins, stupendous Roman, 49.

er-*Rúkhsa,* ass-mare's name, II. 253.

er-*Rukka,* water-pits in the desert, south of er-Russ, II. 492.

er-*Rukkaba,* a part of the high desert between el-Kasîm and Mecca, II. 506-7.

Rûm (Romans, *i.e.* Byzantines), the Greeks, 440; II. 450.

J. Rumm, mountains near el-Ally, 180.

W. er-Rummah الرُّمَّة, [*v. el-Bâtin*], and called in the country *el-Wady* [*qd. v.*], a great dry valley and seyl-bed of Northern Arabia, "whereunto flow seventy considerable wadies:" *Bessàm.* Its winding course from the heads in the Harrat Kheybar to the outgoing at Zbeyer near Bosra is "forty camel marches"; — compared with the W. el-Humth, 217; head and outgoing of the —, 243, 444, 668; II. 39, 61, 70, 81, 87, 132, 238, 260, 305, 306, 321, 322, 326, 335, 338, 339, 346; — an ancient affluent of Euphrates, 355; come to the —, 358; 375, 377, 388, 392, 393, 417, 419; — near 'Aneyza, 420; the course of — hardly to be discerned in el-Kasîm, *ib.*; the length of —, *ib.*; the seyling of —, *ib.*; 434, 436, 445, 459, 460, 461, 476, 477, 481, 489, 491, 495, 500 [*v. W. Jerrîr*]. Rummah is interpreted old fretted rope, *ib.*

Rúmmaky (رُمَّكَة), a mare, II. 419.

W. Rumútha, 464.

Runnya, v. *Rúnya.*

Wady Runnya, II. 449, 557, 567.

Rúnya, or *Runnia,* Sbeya village in Wady es-Sbeya, II. 381.

Rupî, the rupee, money of India, II. 166.

Rushdân, a dog's name, 474, 530, 542.

Russ (رَسّ), is said in the signification of watering the land out of (shallow) pits, II. 465.

er-*Russ* (place of pits for watering), an oasis town in el-Kasîm. The site of er-Russ is according to Ibn Ayîth north of the W. er-Rummah, and el-Éthelly is beyond the Wady to the north-west, [*v. sub Járada*]. 49; II. 37, 55, 388, 433, 438, 439, 453, 476, 484, 489; — is three oases [*er-Ruèytha, er-Rafya* and *Shinâny*], 490; 498, 500.

Russia [*v. Muskov*], II. 275, 398; —n consulate at Port Sa'id, 559.

er-*Ruthán,* a fendy of 'Ateyba, II. 457.

Ruwàlla, a great sub-tribe of Ânnezy in the north, 234, 271, 358, 376, 388, 565; II. 37, 92, 134, 205, 269; the — were aforetime at Semîra, 326.

S. There are two letters in the Arabic alphabet for which we must write *s,* namely سِ, which sounds as simple *s,* and صِ, which is pronounced nearly as *ç* in French; and here written *ṣ.*

Sa'adi, a fendy of Mosruh, Harb, II. 547.

Saadîn, a fendy of Harb above Medina, 166, 543; II. 546.

Sa'ady (prob. سَعْدِي), a long-legged migratory water-fowl, like a crane, seen at Teyma in September, 584.

Saafa, mare's name, II. 253.

Sa'at, an hour.

Sabeans on the Persian Gulf, II. 231.

Sâbera, Bed. fem. name, 514.

Sabigát, mare's name, II. 253.

Sabra, a site at Petra, 81.

Sábry Pasha, Governor of Medina; his letter in French to the Nasrâny at Kheybar, II. 221-2. [*v. Medina.*]

Sàbt, the sabbath, 192.

Sabûny, soap, II. 100.

Sacrifice (*thubîha*): — for the dead, 282, 337, 400, 490, 499, 500; — of hospitality [*v.* Hospitality]; — for the life and health of man, 490, 499; — for the health and safety of cattle, 490, 499, 547; — to the *jân*, 177, 499; — for the birth of a son, 490, 499; at the "purification," 437; — to *melaika* or angels, 497; — to consecrate their booty of cattle taken in an expedition, 499; *kurbân*, 500; — with the burning of incense, 500; the communion with God in man's —, 500; the victim's head to be turned toward Mecca, 547; II. — for the health, 163; — with incense, *ib.*; the victim's head is toward Mecca, *ib.*; the year's mind slain, 275. [*v.* Blood-sprinkling.]

es-S'ada, a tribe of Ashrâf, II. 556.

Sádaka, that which one giveth of his own, in the faith of God, to the relief of another, 493; II. 302.

Saddle: Beduin sheykhs of the Syrian borders ride with the wooden medieval — and stirrups of Damascus; but the Arabian Beduins, beginning with those in the Syrian desert, ride upon a pad *ma'araka* (مِعْرَقٌ, *qd. v.*)

(Dowlâny Ar. *mèrshaha* مِرْشَحَة), with a slender girth, without stirrups, and guide their mares with a halter only, II. 417.

Saddle-bags: Camel —, 99; 397; — made by the Bed. hareem, 518.

Sadûk; *rájul* —, 641; II. Aarab —, 393.

Saera, mare's name, II. 252.

Saffron [*v.* Dye]: 637; an infusion of — will, it is said, stay all haemorrhages, II. 156.

Sáfr, a month, II. 234.

Es-Sâfy, Hàmed [*Beyt es-Sâfy, Hârat es-Seffafîr*, Bagdad]: a young 'Aneyza citizen trading at Bagdad, II. 383.

Sàg, v. Sâk, II. 442.

Sah [read *sa'a*, صاع], measure of capacity: it is at Medina and Kheybar nearly 5 pints, at el-Ally 3, at Hâyil 2½, at Teyma 2. 338; II. 132.

Sahah (صَحَاح)! health, 446.

Sáhar, a magician.

Sáhara of Algeria, 484, 629.

es-Saheyn (الصُّحَين), an open place in the Kheybar village, II. 99, 137, 239.

Sahîby, my friend, 513.

Sâhilat el-Khamasshîeh, a plain by Hâyil, 668-9.

Sa'îd, a negro resident for Ibn Rashîd at Teyma, 333-5, 595.

Beny Sa'îd, once Aarab of the Héjr dîra, 167.

Sâiehh, [*v. Sûwahh*], a world's wanderer, 315.

Saiyeh, a fendy of Shammar, II. 56.

Sajjèydy, a kneeling carpet, 650.

Sâk, or *Sàg*, a solitary mountain in the plain of el-Kasîm, II. 335, 476.

es-Sakhf, a water station of Shammar Aarab, II. 266.

Sâla or *Sôla*, *qd. v.*

Salaam [*salâm*], peace: — *'aleyk*, Peace be with thee, the greeting of the Moslemîn: the Nasrâny is blamed for using it, 551; II. 26, 397.

Salâmîn, village, 44.

Salâmy, a Mahûby, 541, 543.

Salâmy, a Teyma sheykh, 594.

es-Salat wa es-salaâm 'aleyk, yâ auwel khulk Illah wa khâtimat rusul Illah, II. 332.

Beny Sâlem, a division of Harb, II. 257, 259, 308, 321, 324, 326, 329, 334, 545; — a great division of Harb, 546.

Sâlem, a Beduin 'Ageyly at Kheybar, II. 98, 109, 122, 123.

Sâlem, an Harby sheykh of Aarab Oreymât in Nejd, II. 334.

Sâlem, a nomad Sherîf of the tribe *Thu Jûdullah*, who would have slain the Nasrâny at *'Ayn ez-Zeyma*, II. 518-39, 544, 547, 548.

Sâlema, a Mahûby woman, 471, 514, 531, 538.

Salesman: a certain fanatical — of 'Aneyza, II. 425.

Salewwa (سَلِعْوَة), a jin, ogre, 93.

Saleyta (prob. سليطة), a light and cheap calico stuff, of the Persian Gulf trade, 338.

Salîb, the cross of Christians, 198.

Sâlih, a fabulous prophet of Arabia before Mohammed: he was a prince of the Thamudites, 123, 136, 180.

Sâlih, or *el-Fejîr*, the sheykhs' kindred of the Fukara, 270.

Sâlih, a caravaner of 'Aneyza, II. 494.

Sâlih, a younger son of Motlog sheykh el-Fejîr, 559.

Sâlih, a personage at Hâyil, 651.

Sâlih, an Heteymy rafîk, II. 75-82, 251-2, 255.

Sâlih el-Khenneyny, II. 368.

Sâlih, sheykh of Kheybar, II. 99-101, 125, 135, 136, 139, 140, 146-7, 148, 150, 153-4, 183-4, 222, 236.

668　INDEX AND GLOSSARY

Ṣâliḥ el-Moslemány, the son of a Christian foreigner that became a Moslem, el-Ally, 199, 203, 205, 555.

Ṣâliḥ el-Rashèyd, of 'Aneyza, II. 448-9, 468, 472-5.

Ṣâliḥ, Zeyd es-Sbeykàn's old hind, 274, 572, 584, 585, 615.

Sâlim Ibn ez-Zîr, 326.

s-Sàlmî, watering of many wells in dîrat Wélad Sleymàn, of Nejd Bíshr.

Salt : rock — for the nomad pot, 267 ; — from Teyma, 340 ; — crust in the desert, 340 ; — on wounds, 359 ; II. — crust in the Kheybar Harra, 88, 109 ; *súb'kha* at Kheybar, 92 ; Suakim — carried in the Galla-land slave traffic, 186 ; — used to sprinkle corn land, 464 ; — -plains under the Harrat Kisshub, 502-3-5-6.

es-Salt, village in the Peraea, 57.

Salutations [*v. Salâm, Gowwak, Marhába*] : grace and humanity of the Semitic —, 333, 480. [The salutation of Beduin friends in West Nejd meeting again after an absence is commonly in suchwise ; *Cheyf ent*, how dost thou ? *Answer* : *Cheyf ent ?* — *L'alak* (لَعَلَّكْ) *tâyib*, perhaps thou art well ? — *'Asâk* (عساك) *tâyib*, and please God thou art well ? — *Ṭâyib yâ Ṭâyib*, well, ay, thou good man ! — *El-ḥamd lillah*, the Lord be praised therefore ! — *Ullah yirḍâ* (يرضي) *'aleyk*, and the Lord be well pleased with thee.]

Samaritan Syria, II. 284.

Sammara (sam'ra سَمْرَة), a kind of acacia tree, II. 109 ; which is very good fuel, *ib.*, 139, 205, 435 ; the pleasant beans of the — are meat for the apes of the Teháma of Jidda, 573.

[*Sammaṭ* or *summaṭ* (سماط), unsalted, *v. Ât.*

Sammḥ (سَمْح), plant, 357, 603.

Sámn, clarified butter [*v. Butter*], 74, 111 ; price of —, 209 ; — is the poor Nomad's market ware, 305 ; — brought to sell by Nomads, from Jauf, 354 ; worth of —, 391 ; price paid for — for the Mothîf at Hâyil, 663 ; II. making —, 83, 251, 319 ; the sweet lees of —, 84 ; Nomad housewives' gift of — to a stranger guest, 84 ; it is — which makes the oasis diet wholesome, 230 ; names of — skins, *ib.* ; they must be inwardly well-daubed with date syrup. The best — has the odour of wine, 230 ; — the health of man in the khála, they think that — gives them force, *ib.* ; Ibn Nahal's merchandise of —, 314 ; — as much in Arabia as a man's money, 459.

Sámn caravan of 'Aneyza to Mecca (yearly between mid-summer and autumn), II. 481 ; 487-518 ; the day's march, the noon station and evening menzil, 488-90.

Samra [*v. Sumra*], II. 21.

Samuel, hand-staves mentioned in the book of —, 189.

yâ Sámy (يا سَمِّي) ! O my namesake, II. 91.

Sand : —s of Arabia [*n. Nefûd*], 91, 95 ; the Nomads wash with — to prayer-ward, 292 ; the — surface is cool soon after sun-set but remains long warm at little depth, 302 ; — -drift hummocks about desert bushes, 250, 322 ; — soil is not seen rippled in inner Arabia, 323 [yet it may be strongly rippled on the Red Sea-bord, as in Sinai : the — also of the inland Nefûds is driven up in waves]. The — at the head of the *Mézhan* shows perfectly the fosse-form of driven snow on the weather side of rock, bush or stone ; where is an eddy, and that which was borne forth in the wind is cast back and falls down a little short of the obstacle (*v. Fig.*).

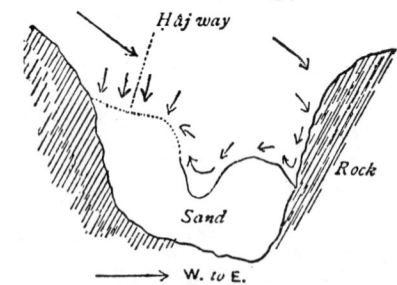

" Sand grouse," *v. Gatta.*

Sandals (Ar. *na'l*), 265 ; in the desert life the best are cut from the saturated camel-leather of old date sacks, 268 ; but the best of all are made from the thick hide of the w'othyḥi bull, 613 ; 644, 645 ; II. 26, 68 ; 116.

OF ARABIC WORDS

Sandstone [v. sub Petra and Medáin Sâlih], 96, 121; 424; — of the 'Aueyrid, 441; II. of the Harrat Kheybar, 84, 88, 89; — of the Kheybar valleys, 110, 116, 246, 336; — of el-Kasîm, 355.

Ṣâny (صانع), pl. ṣunnʿa, a smith. The ṣunnʿa or smiths' caste in Arabia are not accounted of ingenuous blood. They may marry with Heteym, but not with Beduins; who in their anger revile them as 'Solubba'! They are braziers, tinners, blacksmiths, farriers, and workers in wood and stone in the tribes and oases: thus they are villagers and nomads. The ṣunnʿa may commonly be distinguished by their lineaments from the ingenuous Arabians. Artificers, they are men of understanding more than their ingenuous neighbours. Yet such is sometimes the rudeness of Arabian smiths' work, that it seems to have been wrought in the dark, 178, 258; farriers, 322, 353; some settled and some nomads, 327, 328; in a Nasrâny they look for artifice, 580; II. — in Hâyil, 20 [in that town I have heard Ustâd said in this sense]; —ies snibbed as Solubba, 319; artificers in Hâyil, 429.

Waḍy es-Ṣâny, 118.

Sâra, a low sandstone coast, II. 335-6.

Sarâbta, a fendy of Bíllî, 430.

Sarah, a woman's name, 514.

SARGON, king of Assyria: an expedition of — in Arabia, 229.

Ṣárhah سَرْحَة (a bush): a menhel —, 497.

Ṣarṣar (صرصر), a destroying wind which fell upon the Thamudites, 136.

Sarûk, a common thief, II. 334.

Satan [v. Sheytân], 130.

Saʿud ibn ʿAbd-el-ʿAzîz, Emir of eth-Therʿeyyeh, who with Moh. ʿAbd-el-Wâhâb founded the Waháby reformation, II. 454.

Saʿud ibn Saʿud (the elder), II. 571.

Saʿud ibn Saʿud, II. 50, 315, 368; — assails the ʿAteyba and is miserably defeated, 453-5; his decease, 455, 474.

Ibn Saʿud, el-Waháby (qd. v.): this sheykhly house is said by the Fukara to be of (their sister tribesfolk) el-Hosseny qd. v.; but in Nejd they are said to be of Beny Hanîfa, ancient Ânnezy Aarab in the wady of that name since the days of Mohammed, 186, 270, 649, 652; II. 196, 307, 321, 338, 377, 392, 414, 424 [v. ʿAbdullah —], 443, 456-7-8-9, 460-2, 479.

Saul, 312, 361, 506.

Sausages: great (mutton) —, sold in the sûk of Boreyda, II. 349.

Sawra (Sowra, Sôra, Stôra, Stoora), Hâj road kellâ, four days above Medîna, two days from Kheybar; there is a clay house and four Arab servitors (probably Bedowna), 119, 127, 135, 140, 166, 414.

Sayàl, a kind of police troopers with the Hâj, 49.

Sayer (ساير), sally, 294.

Sbá, a fendy of Bishr, 376.

es-Sbʿaa [v. el-Moahîb]: a considerable subtribe of Ânnezy: some say they are from the province of el-Hása in East Nejd: their seats were afterward upon the W. er-Rummah between Kheybar and el-Kasîm. Now they are Aarab of the Shimbel dîra in the wilderness of Syria, 444, 451, 579; II. 56, 64, 134, 253.

Sbeya, an Aarab tribe of Nejd (Keysites), founders of many oases in el-Kasîm, as ʿAneyza, Búkerîeh, el-Helàlîeh, II. 367; — in el-ʿArûth, 381; — in W. es-Sbeya, ib. 442.

W. es-Sbeya, in the borders of Nejd and the Hejâz, II. 381, 567.

Derb Wâdy Sbeya, between el-Kasîm and Mecca II. 499.

Sbeydy (زبادي), a small wild tuber plant in the desert, 255.

Sbeyîeh, a village in el-Kasîm, II. 315.

Sbût, a fendy of B. ʿAtîeh, 464.

a Scandinavian valley, 'murrain of hares in,' 476; — salutation [Tak for sidst], II. 251.

Schoolmaster: — at Mogug, 631; II. — at Hâyil, 58, 271, 277.

Schools in the Arabian oases: — are held in the mosques at el-Ally in Ramaṭhàn, 186. There are no — in Teyma; II. — in Hâyil, 58-9; — at Kheybar, 97.

Scorpions in the desert, 373; the sting is not dangerous, ib., 485.

the Sea, is they know not what, II. 191.

the 'Seal,' i.e. the koran, 584; '— of the Prophets,' i.e. Mohammed, 342.

Seamen : Nasâra, — ii. 188.
Searing irons, 322.
Sebbâ, Bed. fem. name, 514.
[*Sebba'an*, small vill. of 50 houses, in J. Shammar on the way to el-Kasîm, *v.* Map.
es-Sebbàha, fendy of 'Ateyba, ii. 457.
Sebîl, the way ; commonly said of fountains by the way side, made for the relief of passengers. 'I am upon the — *Ullah*' is often the pious response of a poor person, if one ask him of his living ; the tobacco pipe called — is an earthenware tube, 288 ; 356.
Secretary : Ibn Rashîd's —, *v. Násr.*
Sects of *el-Islam*, *v.* Sunni and *Shî'a, Malakîeh, Râfuthy.*
Sedeyr, a province of E. Nejd, *v. Siddîr.*
[*Seffer* (سَفَر, the rising of the sun), light :

used in el-Kasîm.
Seffua, mountain in the desert between Kasîm and Mecca, ii. 501.
Séfn, shipping, ii. 303.
el-Sefsáfa [over the source 29° C., in the basin 28° C.], spring at Kheybar from which the villagers draw water (which smacks of sulphur), ii. 96, 109, 112, 116, 138, 141, 142, 160, 165, 218.
Sehamma, a fendy of Billî, 267, 429, 430, 431, 435, 437, 445, 455, 460, 511, 523, 641.
Sehely, a fendy of Harb Mosrûh, ii. 547.
Seherân, a dog's name, 474.
Seir, Mount [*v. J. Sherra* and Edom], 67, 70, 81 ; ii. 348, 575.
Seleyma [or *Soleyma*], a desert village of Shammar in Ibn Rashîd's country, ii. 302, 306, 310, 316, 320.
Beny *Seléyta* (or *Seyléyta*), nomad clients of the B. Sókhr, 54 ; the sheykh's hospitality, *ib.*
Selim, an 'Alowwy exile at Teyma, 580.
Selim, a Mahûby, son of Thâhir, 539-40.
Selim, son of Zeyd es-Sbeykán, 142, 258, 278, 371, 399, 400.
Selim, Sultàn : — a benefactor and builder on the Hâj way of the kellâts of Ma'an, Birket Mo'addam and Medáin, 71, 119.
Sélla, village in the south country, ii. 52.
Ibn *Sellem*, an ancient villager of Mosaic Kheybar, ii. 206.
Sellímt (سَلِّمْتُ) ! I grant it you, 307.

es-Sellummîeh, in Middle Nejd, ii. 425.
Sellût, an affinity of Kheybar villagers, ii. 153.

Selma, a woman's name, 514.
J. *Selma*, 635 ; — is less than J. Ajja, ii. 24, 322.
Sem, 'son of Noah,' 580 ; ii. 191.
Sema, heaven, 522.
Semîly or *Semîla* (سميلة for تميلة), milk-bag

or skin (commonly of sheep's leather) made like a girby, for milk. The semíla, being sour, sours fresh milk which is poured into it. Nomad housewives rock the — upon their knees till the butter come : and that may be found bye and bye in a lump at the skin's mouth. 262, 305, 324, 370, 429 ; ii. 330.
Semîra, a desert village in the dominion of I. Rashîd, 147 ; ii. 34, 67, 302, 321, 324-5 ; villagers of, *ib.*, 456.
Semitic nature, 95, 101 ; their fox-like subtlety without invention, 329 ; ii. they can be banded only by the passion of religion and their greediness of the spoil, 387, 401 ; — arts, 426.

Senna (سَنَا) plant, 483, 510, 635.

Sentinel : a sepoy —, ii. 278. [*v. Kerakô.*]
Septuagint : "Unicorn" in the — translation, 373, and *v.* Reem.
Sepulchre [*v. Medáin Sâlih, el-Ally, el-Khrèyby*]; the Semitic East a land of —s, 211 ; " — of Jonas," 216 ; les innombrables tombeaux, taillés dans le roc ... de ces régions, sont postérieurs à Alexandre, 673.
Serahîn, a fendy of the Moahîb, 445, 479, 502, 505, 525-6, 529, 531, 543, 544, 547, 550, 565.
Serai, a palace.
Seràserra, fendy of Jehèyna, 166.
St. Sergius, 522.
Serifat (زَرِيبَة), ii. 243 ; a pen of boughs for

small cattle.
Serpents, 55 ; the Nomads' dread of, 294, 357 [*v. Umm-jenèyb*]; remedy of 'reading' over serpent bites ; remedy of searing the wounded flesh, 358 ; the ligature, 359 ; friendly magnanimity to suck the envenomed wound, *ib.*; certain stones, as onyxes, accounted good to be laid to the bites of —, 359-60 ; many snakes and adders in the desert, 373, 495 ; ii. 324.
es-Serràha, fendy of Harb B. Sâlem. ii. 546.
Servia, 522.

OF ARABIC WORDS

Settàm, a young Fejîry, a ward of Zeyd, 263. [Guardians among Beduins are said to oftentimes "devour" their wards' inheritance. "A guardian will deliver his own to the ward (not at any set time, but) so soon as the young man be grown sufficient to the charge": Zeyd es-Sbeykàn.]
Settatásher kelb, II. 310.
Sevilla (in Spain), II. 426.
Sewing and embroidering: women's industry of — at Hâyil, II. 20; — at 'Aneyza, 429.
Ṣeyàd, light hunter with hawk and hound, II. 116.
Ṣeyadîn (صَيَادِين), Beduin petty tradesmen [from the old صَيْدَلانِي or صَيْدَنانِي pl. صَيَادِنَة], II. 76, 319.
es-Ṣeyd, beasts of the chase, 355.
Seyd, a Tehàma mountain, 464.
Seydàn, a Mahûby sheykh, 524, 531-2, 542-3, 564.
Seydàn, a young sâny at Teyma, 580-2, 590.
Seydeîn, a clan of Howeytát near Gâza, 275.
es-Seyeḥ, vill. in Middle Nejd, II. 425 [perhaps the same as *Siaḥ, qd. v.*].
Seyf, sword.
Seyfîeh, a seyl-bed at Teyma, 340.
Sèyid, v. *Séyyid*.
Seyl, pl. *seúl*, torrent; used also commonly [as we say torrent] of the dry bed, 68; — strands are called *sh'aeb* (شعب) *qd. v.*; —s below Ma'an, 88; none seen in vast desert land-breadths, 120, 260; II. sometimes, being suddenly flushed by rain in their upper strands, a head of water flows down with dangerous fulness and force; and men and cattle overtaken are in danger to perish therein, 251.
es-Seyl, the ancient *Kurn el-Menâzil*, a journey N. of Mecca, II. 427, 488, 510, 515, 527-8, 535, 539, 542-3, 553-5-9, 561-2-3-4-5; — a notable station, 563-4.
Bab es-Seyl, a gate of Tâyif, II. 539, 560.
Seyl el-Arem: fable of the —, 434.
Seyl, of Hâyil, II. 21.
Wady es-Seyl, the valley descending from *es-Seyl* to 'Ayn ez-Zeyma, II. 515.
Seyyid, religious nobleman of the blood of Moh., 207; II. 283.

Seyyid Maḥmûd, a chief Meshedy trader at Hâyil, 656, 658.
Sfá, a mountain, II. 296, 299, 302.
'Sfàn, a desert station N. of Teyma, 341.
es-Sferry (السَّفَرِي), fall of the year, 261, 488.
Sfeynah, Meteyr vill. on the Derb es-Sherḳy, II. 393, 565.
S'goor, a fendy of Bishr, 376.
'Sgoora, a kindred of the Fukara tribe, 270.
Shaab en-Naam, an ancient name of el-Ally, 189.
Shaaba, desert district, in J. Shammar, II. 260.
Sha'abân, a month, 540.
Sh'aara [in Nejd], a watering place of many wells in the desert, few m. N. of *Ḳurn el-Menâzil*, II. 507-8, 516, 529, 553, 564.
Shaara, desert vill. S. of el-Wéshm, II. 492.
Sh'aara, ass-mare's name, II. 253.
Shâba, mountain near the vill. Therrîeh in the desert S. of el-Kasîm, II. 492.
Shadows, blissful — of the Harra, 423.
Sh'aeb (شعب), pl. *sháebân*, seyl strand, II. 237.
Shaeḥ (شيح), a kind of southernwood, 425, 472.
Shâer (*shâ'ir*), a poet, 306.
Shâfy, a villager of Teyma, 582, 602.
J. Shâfy, 85.
Shàgg en-nâba (شاق الناب), eight-year-old camel, 401.
Shahûd, martyrs, *qd. v.*
Shájr, tree.
Ibn Shalân, great sheykh of the Ruwàlla, II. 29.
Shalân, a fendy of Jellás, Ânnezy Aarab, 377.
Shalân, a dog's name, 474.
es-Sham, the Land-of-the-left-hand, the northwest country, or Syria: (the wilderness of) — is 'a land of milk' say the Beduw in Arabia. 56, 314, 657 *et passim*.
es-Sham, metropolis of *es-Sham* or Syria, Damascus, *qd. v.*
Shamir, a tribe of southern Aarab, II. 381.
Shammah, v. *Shemmîa*.
Shammar [vulg. *Shummar*, v. the rime, 592], a great (mingled) Beduin tribe: a part of them are in the N. [el-'Irâk] and part in West Nejd, where their oases are Hâyil, Teyma, etc., 236; speech of —, 329; 389, 390, 406, 421, 573, 578; *es*- — *'ayûnuhum ḥumr*, 592; hospitality

of —, 592; 622, 625, 627; no natural amity betwixt Ânnezy and —, 622; 631-4; northern —, 633, 661; certain half-resident poor — tribesmen at Hâyil, 671; II. 34-5-7; a kindred of — in el-'Arùth, 57; 77; — flocks, *ib.*; 144, 262-3; their tents are lofty, *ib.*; 264-5-6-9, 285, 292, 299, 310, 315, 320; booths of —, 322; the — dîra praised for its many waters, *ib.*; 333, 426, 491.

Jebel Shammar, or *Dîrat ibn Rashîd*, in which are the Ajja and Selma low mountain ranges, 253, 329, 335, 338, 464, 594, 609, 633, 635, 652, 669; villages in — made desolate by the plague, 635; II. Nomad spirited people of —, 21; state of —, 28; revenues, population, military power, 34-7; 41-5, 52, 56, 195, 223, 326, 336-7, 459, 476, 490, 575.

Shammar Prince [*v. Ibn Rashîd*], 119, 236, 333, 487, 596.

Shammar-Toga, a fendy of Shammar, in el-'Irâk, II. 56.

Shâmy, pl. *Shwâm*, citizen of es-Sham, a Damascene, II. 307.

Sharân, Aarab of the W. Bîsha country, II. 567.

Shaṭâra, a mastery, 573.

Shâtha, B. Sâlem, Harb. vill., II. 546.

esh-*Shazlîeh* (الشاذلية), a heterodox sect of el-Islâm [in Damascus], II. 400.

Sh'brâmy, cattle-pits in the desert betw. Kasîm and Mecca, II. 500.

es-*She'ab*, a site in the great desert S. of el-Kasîm, II. 493.

J. She'aba, in the great desert S. of el-Kasîm, II. 495.

es-*She'abîn*, a fendy of 'Ateyba, II, 457.

es-*She'adda*, a fendy of 'Ateyba, II. 457.

J. She'ar, between Kasîm and Mecca, II. 495.

Shebbaan, II. 93.

Shebîb ibn Tubbai [*v. Ibn et-Tubbai*], 'an ancient ruler of the lands beyond Jordan,' 51, 52, 61; *Kasr es-* —, 51, 52.

Shebrûm, desert site near the head of Wady Jerrîr, II. 500.

Sheep of the Arabian wilderness [*v. Kharûf, Tully, Rókhal*], 78, 391, 473-6; 'sand-struck' —, 476; Arabian —'s wool, 476; — -shearing, *ib.*; — many slaughtered for supper by a ghrazzu, 537; the —'s great lap-tail, 550; price of — at Hâyir, 662; II. — -pen made of lopped boughs, used by the Aarab, 243 : — flocks not mixed with goats, 256; — of Europe and of the Arabic East compared, 275; the — of Harb in Nejd are mostly black fleeces; — flocks of the *Oreymât*, 333; pilgrims who have not taken the *ihrâm* are to sacrifice a — in Mecca, 514; small mountain — of the Mecca country, 516.

Shéfa, the lower mountainous land seaward under the Harrat el-'Aueyriḍ, 451, 462, 463, 465.

Shehîeh, hamlet in el-Kasîm, II. 443.

[*Shelásh*, son of *Foḍil* sheykh of the Seḥamma, Bíllî.

Shelfa (شَلْفَة), or *romḥ*, horseman's lance, 262, 379, 504.

W. *Shellâl*, in the 'Aueyrid, 495, 534, 537, 540-1, 543, 547, 554.

Shellalî, a kindship of Kheybar villagers, II. 153.

es-*Shem*, v. es-*Sham*.

[*Shemân*, instantly, word heard among the nomads of the Belka and the Medina dîra; from the Turk. شمن .

Shemlán, a fendy of Bishr, 376.

[esh-*Shemmâsiyya* : village a few miles E. from Boreyda; — Ibn 'Ayith.

Shemmîa : vill. by Ma'an, 71, 72, 73, 74, 90; (Shammah, 71 ;) wells at —, 72.

es-*Shenàberra*, a tribe of Ashrâf, II. 556.

Shenna (شَنَّة), a skin of dates at el-Ally, 195 ; v. *Mujellad*.

Shepherd [*v. Ass*]: Zeyd's —, 293 ; —s lop down acacia boughs for their stock, 426 ; Mahûby —s, 473-5.

Shepherd lasses in the desert, 350, 367.

Sher'aan, a mountain in the midst of the Fejîr dîra, 490.

es-*Sherâfa*, an outlying palm-ground near Hâyil, II. 271.

Sherarát, a nomad tribe between Ma'an and Jauf; their dîra comes down nearly to Tebûk ; they are of Heteym kindred (326), and by the Arabians are not accounted Beduw; theirs are the best thelûls of Arabia, 93 ; 97-9 ; the — are the B. *Múklib*, 98 ; the *Sweyfly* a kindred of —, 117 ; 166 ; — reckoned to the B. Helál, *ib.*; 326, 328, 340, 388, 392, 396, 475, 480, 553, 603, 611, 612 ; II. 35-7, 46-8, 86 ; thelûls of the —, 241 and 261 ; 289, 290, 319.

es-*Sherg*, East oasis, at Teyma, 582.

OF ARABIC WORDS

Sherîf, religious nobleman of the blood of Mohammed, 238. [*v. Ashràf.*]

the *Sherîf Emir* of *Mecca* : his style is, His Excellency ... Pasha, the Sherîf, Governor of the glorious Mekka : ii. 190, 196, 394, 459, 512 ; '*Abdullah*, the former —, *v. sub* '*Abdullah*. Ḥaseyn [the Sherîf Ḥaseyn was stabbed in the bowels at half-past six o'clock in the morning of the 14th March, 1880, as he entered Jidda, by one disguised as a Persian derwish. The wounded Prince was borne into his Agent's house ; and in the next hours, feeling himself little the worse, he made light of the hurt ; and sent comfortable tidings of his state to the great ones and to his kindred in Stambûl. But an intestinal hemorrhage clotted in the bowel ; and Ḥaseyn, who lived through that night, was dying toward morning ; and he deceased quietly, at ten o'clock, in the arms of his physician. — The assassin, who had been snatched by the police-soldiery from the fury of the people, was cast into prison : but nothing is known of his examination. — Yet it was whispered, among the Ottoman officers, That the Sherîf had been murdered *because he favoured the Engleys !*], 510, 518-9-20-1-3-7, 530-1-2-5-7-8-9 ; audience of the —, 542-4 ; 545-6-7 ; an injunction of the —, *ib*.; 552 ; second audience of the —, 554-6 ; 557 ; the estates of the —, *ib*.; the people of the country come to es-Tâyif to welcome-in the new —, *ib*.; expedition of the late — against certain his unruly subjects, *ib*.; the — would have given a safe-conduct to the Nasrâny, to travel further in his estates, 558-559-60-2-4 ; his possessions in the Mecca country, 565 ; 567-8 ; 570, 572-4.

a *Sherîf*, gentleman-beggar of Medina, ii. 274-275-6-7-9, 352.

the *Sherîf* of *Suâka*, ii. 202.

es-Sherḳiyîn, Orientals ; the people of Middle Nejd are so called at Mecca and Jidda, ii. 377.

Sherm, a bay, in Sinai, 90.

Sherôra [*Sharûrâ* in *Yakut*], high landmark mountain near Tebûk : the akkams call it *Mumbir er-Rasûl*, 112.

J. *Sherra* (الشَّرَا), Mount Seir, or the mountain of Edom [comp. Sp. Sierra, and It. Serra, a precipice of the Val del Bove, Etna], 67 ; limestone of —, *ib*.; height oft —, 67 ; flint instruments from —, 68, 76, 77 ; 82, 276 ; ii. 37. [*v. Ard Sawwán.*]

Sherrâbs, (tobacco) bibbers, 528.

Sherrân, an affinity of Kheybar villagers, ii. 153.

Sherrâra شَرَارَة (spark), a butterfly, 496.

Shérry (شَرِي), colocynth gourd [*v. Ḥámṭhal, Hádduj*], ii. 561.

Sheukh, pl. of *sheykh*, qd. v. They are nobles of the blood of the *Jid* or patriarch, 293 ; they govern with a homely moderation, 361 ; 376, 445.

Sheyabîn Aarab, of 'Ateyba, ii. 507.

J. *es-Sh'eyb* [This, Bessam says, is *Gadyta* of the old itineraries], in the desert way between Kasîm and Mecca, ii. 500.

Sheybàn, a mountain, 117, 464.

Sheykh, pl. *sheukh*, an elder [the dignity of a — in free Arabia is commonly more than his authority]: a great — should bear himself as a nobleman, 258, 287 ; and with mild impartiality, 293, 302 ; the dignity is theirs by inheritance, 293 ; he is *agîd* ; his share in the booty, 293.

Sheykh el-Áueyrid, 449.

Sheykh el-musheyik, sheykh of the sheykhly council or mejlis, chief of the sheykhs. With these words Amm Mohammed, in his laughing humour, commonly saluted any lad that met with us in the way (at Kheybar).

Sheykha, fem. of *sheykh*, said among Bed. of a sheykhly woman, 272, 365, 492, 518.

Sheyṭàn, Satan : — an exclamation in crosses and evil hap, and used to check the perversity of froward persons, 78, 258 ; 377, 404, 494 ; a people that worship —, 578.

es-Sh'hebba, a fendy of 'Ateyba, ii. 457.

Shî'as (شِيعَة): Persian (schismatic) Mohammedans, 108 ; ii. tale of a young Medina tradesman among the Meshed —, 224.

es-Shibbebîeh, granges in the Nefûd, a few hours S. of 'Aneyza, ii. 489, 553.

es-Shibberîeh, water pits in the Nejd Harb dîra, ii. 322.

Shibrîyyah شِبْرِيَّة [also *Khánjar* and *Kiddamîyyah*], Bed. crooked girdle-knife, 505.

INDEX AND GLOSSARY

Shidád (شداد), camel riding saddle, 334, 377; II. 20, 513.
es-Shiffa, a part of the desert land so called, between Kasîm and Mecca, II. 500.
es-Shî-îl (*shîl*, *qd. v.*) II. 489.

Shîl! (شيل) lift the loads, load, carry.

Shimbel (شُنْبِل) a corn measure), name of an Ánnezy dîra in Syria, 444, 619.
Shimmer, patriarch of the Shammar, II. 56.
Shinány, one of the oases of er-Russ, II. 490.
Ship : a — made to sail under water, 451 ; II. ' what is a — ? ' (told to the black villagers of Kheybar), 105 ; loss of a Turkish war- —, which was commanded by an Englishman, *ib.*
Shirt : Beduin —, *v.* Tunic, *Thôb*.
Shirt-cloth, brought by Medân, Gâza, Teyma, J. Shammar and Kasîm tradesmen upon camels to the nomad menzils in the wilderness, 111, 196, 238, 246, 247, 275.
es-Shitá (Bed. *es-Shtá*), winter time, 261.

Shittr (شَنْتَر), a Persian word, for dromedary, which is often heard at Hâyil, II. 23.
Sh'káky, a town in the Syrian desert near Jauf, II. 34, 37, 269.
Shôbek, (Mons Regalis, of the Crusaders, 75), village of Mount Seir, 51, 70; corn very cheap at —, 72, 75 ; camp of Shobekers, 75 ; the sheykh, *ib.* ; 75, 355.
Shooting at a mark : *Májid* —, II. 23.
Shops in Hâyil, 637, 661 ; II. — in 'Aneyza shut in the absence of a great foray of the townsmen, 474.

es-Shór (الشُّوري), the counsels (of the Nomads), 290.
Shòrafat en-Nejid, a mountain in the Teháma, 463.
es-Shotb, II. 89.
J. Shotb, in el-Wéshm, II. 551.
es-Shotibba, village in W. Dauâsir, II. 425.
Shottifa, mare's name, II. 253.
Shovel-plough, to remove and heap up earth, II. 566, 574.
Shower : a — caused the defeat of a sortie of the besieged 'Aneyza citizens, II. 461.
es-Showŷg, vill. in W. Dauâsir, II. 425.

'Shu bitekûn ent ? (اي شَيْءٌ هُوَ) بتكون انت, II. 224.

Shubàramy, the people of Semîra, so named after their sheykh *Rashîd es-Shûberamy*, II. 325.
Shubb ej-jemâl (شَبّ الجِمَال), a kind of rock-alum used as a camel medicine, 340.
Shubb el 'bîl, like the above, II. 571.
es-Shûberamy, family name of the sheykh of Semîra, II. 325.
Shubúb, young men.
es-Shûel, mare's name, II. 253.
Shûf! behold !

Shûf f'il ghraib (شوف في الغَيْب), 388.

Shuggéra [*Shukkra*], chief town of *el-Wéshm*, the townsfolk are *Beny Zeyd* and *es-Suedda*, descended, they say, from Kahtân, II. 374, 377, 419, 424, 452, 492.
es-Shuggera, mare's name, II. 253.
Shuggery : a certain — field labourer in Rasheyd's orchard, a good teller of tales, II. 452-3-5, 465-6, 471, 479.
Shujjer [perhaps *Shúkir*], ancient village in el-Wéshm, II. 452.
Shuk el-'Ajûz, a desert site on the Hâj road, above Medáin S., so named by the Syrian caravaners (*el-Agorra* of the Beduw), 121, 254, 423.
Shukkûk, village near Boreyda, II. 339.
Shúkkra, chief town in el-Wéshm, *v. Shuggera* and *Shukera*, II. 567.

es-Shukkra (الشُّقْرَاء), a date kind, II. 466.

Shûn (perhaps the same as شُوم), quarter-staff, 189. *v. Nabût*.

Shurma (شُرَماء), cleft-lips, II. 260.

Shurrma, a watering by the desert way between Kasîm and Mecca, II. 502-5.
Shwâm, pl. of *Shâmy*, Syrians or Damascenes.
Shwóysh, a Mahûby, 450, 499, 511, 523, 564, 610.
Sîah, village in el-Aflâj, perhaps the same as *Seyeh* and *Sihh*, *qd. v.*, II. 425.
Siah, dans le Haouran, 674.

Siála (سَيَالة), a kind of acacia trees, II. 109.

OF ARABIC WORDS

Sicily : lavas of —, 468 ; seamen of —, 168 ; II. the Arabs in —, 370.

the Sick [v. Malady]. The — in the Hâj, 105-6; — at Teyma, 575 ; II. — of the Persian Hâj left at Hâyil, 70.

es-Sídd, a dam in *Wady Líthm*, 84.

Siddes (سديس), seven-year old camel, 401.

Siddîr [*Sidîr* or *Sedeyr* or *Sudeyr*], Province or Wady in E. Nejd. In Wady Siddîr [named of the *sidr* tree] which has a northerly course and ends at *Asheyrah* are these towns and villages : *Zilfy, el-Aggál, eth-Themèyil, el-Ghrât, el-Khîs, er-Ruèytha, el-Mejm'aa* (metrop., " three hundred " houses), *Herrmah,* " two hundred " houses (Ânnezy), *el-Júwy, Jelâjil,* " an hundred and fifty " houses, *el-Dakhella,* " sixty " houses, *et-Tuèym,* " forty " houses (deep wells and antique fortress), *el-'Aud* (hamlet), *er-Rautha es-Sedeyr* (" two to three hundred " houses and formerly metrop.), *el-Attar,* " an hundred " houses (Sbey'a), *el-Auwdy* (considerable ancient village), *Ash'aera,* " an hundred " houses, *Temeyr, el-Hauta es-Sedeyr.*

Siddûs, 245 ; II. 346, 355 [v. *Kerdûs*], 424, 564.

Sidényîn, a kindred of B. Atîeh, 115.

Sídr (سدر), an apple-thorn tree, in some deserts it grows even to great timber [as in Sinai], II. 164, 202, 238.

Sídr, a basalt berg in W. Fâṭima, II. 570.

Siena in Italy : adit-like well-galleries at —, 74 [such in Syria are called *serdab,* — Pers. *sard*, cold, and *âb*, water].

Sieyda, a fendy of Jehèyna, 166.

Sihh (*Sîh*), village in the south country, v. *Siah* and *Sèyeh*, II. 52.

The *Sîk* (سيق), a strait passage betwixt *Eljy* and *Wady Mûsa*, 80, 81 ; pavement and tablets in —, 80 ; — compared with the Diwàn passage at el-Héjr, 160, 162.

Silk : skein — from India, seen at Hâyil, II. 20.

W. es-Síllima, a valley of the Kheybar wadiân, II. 109, 117.

Sillima (سَلَمَة pl. سَلَم), pl. *slîm*, a kind of acacia trees, II. 109.

Sìllimát, a fendy of Bíshr, 376.

Silver : a — bullet, 300 ; as money, 338, 602.

Silvestre de Sacy : mémorie de —, 224.

Simm, poison.

Simples, v. Medicines : skill of the hareem in —, 297, 350.

Simrân, a dog's name, 474.

Ibn Sim'ry or *eth-Thiàbba*, a fendy of Heteym, 474 ; II. 240, 242, 248, 253.

Simûm (سَمُوم): the — wind, 141, 403, 430, 536 ; II. 506, 511.

Sinai : '*ajâj* in —, 67 ; travels in —, 69 ; vulcanic dykes in —, 84 ; 90, 94 ; — very barren, 109, 203 ; — Beduw, 250, 275 ; " Written valley " in —, 260, 323 ; J. *Nagûs*, 352 ; the sounding-board (*nagûs*) in the monastery, 352, 374 ; leopard traps in —, 428 ; 431-2 ; the monastery, 432 ; *namus* in —, 432, 457 ; 469, 584 ; II. Beduins of —, 200 ; Beduin summer houses in —, 207 ; 287 ; the extreme barren desert soil of —, 305 ; 414, 450, 451, 501.

Sinaïtique, l'écriture, 224.

Sing [v. Song]: the Arabian —ing, 81, 138 ; Solubby —ing, 607 ; women — not, 607 ; —ing women of the Time of Ignorance, 607.

Sinjâra, a fendy of Shammar, II. 56.

Sîr Amîn, v. *Emir el-Hâj*.

W. *Sirhân*, in the Sherarát dîra, II. 37, 46.

Wady es-Sirr (in el-Wéshm): hamlets in — are *el-Feytha, er-Rîshîy, et-Torrofíy, 'Ayn es-Sweyna*. In — are *el-Owsheyeyn* two *gârats* " with vestiges of the B. Helál," II. 452.

Sirrûk (سَرُّوق), a thievish night-bird so called, II. 288.

Sîrûr, a Galla 'Ageyly at Kheybar, II. 98-102, 109, 112, 134-5, 152-4, 193, 230.

Skeirát, a ruined village site, in W. Sodr (near el-Ally), 326.

Skull : a — found, without the field of (the Beduins') battle, at Kheybar, II. 117.

Slaves and Slavery : African — brought up every year in the Hâj, 250 ; 334 ; Galla —, 289, 603 ; Timbuctû — traffic, 562 ; Heteymy woman wedded with a negro —, 603 ; value of negro —, 604 ; the most — are from the Upper Nile countries, 604 ; a poor — woman that had been robbed from Dongola, 604 ; tolerable condition of — in Arabia, 604-5 ; they receive their freedom early, and some substance, from good house-fathers, 605 ;

11. the head of the Mohammedan — trade is Mecca-Jidda, 68 ; — in Hâyil, 71 ; a householder may wound his bond-servant, 149 ; — of the same household are accounted brethren, 190 ; — in Jidda, 375 ; Zanzibar — traffic, 389 ; Jidda and Mecca — traffic, 524.

Sleep : to slumber sitting in a company about the hearth is unbecoming, 291 ; the Beduins are day- —ers, *ib.*; they reverence the —er, 292 ; they — not after vespers, 290, 491 ; nomads — upon their breasts, 303 ; ' — in the house of the Nasrâny,' 579 ; 11. a common —ing place for strangers at 'Aneyza is the deep-sanded roof of a mesjid, 404.

J. Sleih, under the 'Aueyrid H., 431.

es-S'lèyb, v. *es-Solubba*.

Sleymàn, Solomon, qd. v.

Sleymàn, of el-'Ally, a tobacco seller among the Fukara, 355, 356.

Sleymàn Abu Daûd, sheykh of the 'Ageyl in Syria, v. *Abu Daûd*.

Sleymàn (Solomon), a Syrian vaccinator called Abu Fâris, 295-7.

Sleymàn, a worthy younger son of Bessàm, 11. 487.

Sleymàn, brother of Ḥamûd el-'Abeyd, 11. 44.

Sleymàn, a personage in Hâyil [Ḥamûd's uncle of the mother's side], 648, 656 ; 11. 25-7, 43, 265.

Sleymàn el-Khenneyny, a *jemmâl*, 11. 381, 483-518 ; his drivers, 487-513 ; his company in the *sámn kâfily* to Mecca, 489-90.

Sleymàn, a young villager of Teyma, 329, 336, 343.

W. Sleymàn, a sub-tribe of Bishr in Nejd, 376 ; 624 ; 11. 195.

Slîm, pl. of *Sillima*, a kind of acacia, 11. 109.

Sling (*merdàha* مِرْدَاهَة), 480 ; 11. — a weapon of the ancient Arabians, 196.

Small-pox (*jídery*): — in the Hâj, 243, 246 ; — and cholera the destruction of Nomad Arabia, *ib.*, 628 ; 11. a Beduin cure of sweating, 240 ; calamity of a great sheykh of Aarab who was forsaken by all men, *ib.*; — in 'Aneyza, 374 ; — treatment there, *ib.*, 403, 410, 472 ; the Beduin treatment is such in the western dîras according to *Mohammed ed-Deybis* : ' If a tribesman be found to have the jídery the rest will make haste to remove from him : and his household, having made a bower with bushes, for their sick (it is commonly under the lee of a mountain), they will leave with him such things as they can provide (it may be two milch goats and dates and corn) for his sustenance : moreover they procure someone to watch him and help him, — that is always a person who has had the malady, or has been inoculated ; and who if the sick (*mejdûr* مَجْدُور) die may bury him. In their opinion, the disease comes to them from Mecca (*i.e.* in the Hâj). About half of the *mejdûrs* die. If the sick recover, he and his companion, when forty days are out, will wash their flesh and their clothing, and the goats and the stuff that was with them, and shave their heads ; and they may now return to the Aarab. According to others the clothes of the small-pox-man are buried ; and any infected tent: after a year it may be taken up. The Liwàn at el-Héjr is ofttimes a shelter for *mejdûrs*.

Smell : the Beduins very imaginative of all odours, 250, 485.

Smile. Men yield half their soul with the —, 492.

es-Smîry : sheykh Nâsir —, v. *Nâsir*.

Smith, Arabian (*v. Ṣâny*): nomad —, 322, 324 ; —s farriers, *ib.*, 353 ; 11. —s' caste in Abyssinia, 187 ; Solubby farriers, 301, 315 ; 'Aneyza —s, 429.

Smoke rising in a menzil the sign of a coffee fire, 292.

Smyrna, 454.

Snails : land- — not seen in Nejd ; — in Barbary, 11. 451 ; water- — in Arabian brooks, *ib.*

Snakes, v. Serpents.

Snake-stones, or certain stones, as onyxes, good to cure the bites of serpents, 360.

Snow in Arabia, 45, 243, 341 ; 11. 60.

Soap (*ṣabún*): it is Syrian —, 189 ; made of the oil olive, which may be found in Arabia ; 11. 429.

Sobh, a tribe of B. Sâlem, Harb, 11. 546.

W. Sódr, a valley of W. el-Humth below el-Ally, 326, 465.

Beny Sókhr, Beduin pl. *es-Sokhûr* : a considerable tribe of Beduins in Moab and Ammon, 51 ; they had many horses, 54 ; — routed by a military expedition, *ib.*; Hâj carriers, *ib.*, 253 ; — accounted treacherous, 54 ; their sheykh, *ib.*; they were of old Southern Aarab, of the dîrat el-Héjr, 166 ; — fabled to be sprung of the rock (*sókhr*); — driven from the Héjr dîra

OF ARABIC WORDS

by the Moahîb and Fejîr, 167, 445; 182, 189, 253; — once masters of el-Ally, 189; — of Teyma, 331; a ghrazzu of — robs many camels of the Fukara, 388; response of their elders to the messenger bearing the complaint of the Fukara, 396; Tebûk of old subject to —, 578; II. 38, 66; 264; " — are of B. Temîm," 382.

Ṣokr (صقر, the Latin *sacer*), falcon.

Sôla, or Sàla: orchards of the Sherîf at —, near 'Ayn ez-Zeyma, II. 565.
Solder, 327.
Soldiers of the Sultan [*v. 'Askar*, Deserter], 412.
es-Soleyil, *v. Suleyl*, town in W. Dauâsir, II. 425.
"Solomon father of David," 196, 280, 533, 658; II. 58, 414, 452.
Solubba, *sing. Solubby* (in Syria they are called *es-Slèyb*): beauty of their children, 324; their hunting and gipsy labour, 324-7; cattle surgeons, 324; *the precept of their patriarch*, 324; they have no milch cattle, 324; they are despised by the Bed., *ib.*; they only of all men are free of the Arabian deserts, *ib.*; they have no citizenship, *ib.*; they ride and remove on ass-back, *ib.*; their asses, *ib.*; 325, 327; in landcraft they outgo the Bed., 325; their inherited landlore, 325; they wander from Syria to South Arabia, 325; — called *el-Khlûa* and *Kilâb el-khála*, *ib.*; *el-Ghrúnemy*, *ib.*; their lineage unknown, 326-7; *Maibî*, 326; *Aarab Jessàs*, *ib.*, and *Klèyb*, *ib.*; *Aarab K'fâ*, *ib.*; *Beny Murra*, fellowship of *Sàlim ibn ez-Zôr* from the hill *Jemla, Motullij, Derrûby*; are the Solubba a remnant of some ancient Aarab? *ib.*; *Ṣulb el-Aarab*, *ib.*; the — are ' rich,' 327; they bury their money, *ib.*; certain — are said to be cattle-masters in Mesopotamia, 327; a — at Hâyil, *ib.*; the — hold to circuits, *ib.*; their abject looks, *ib.*; their women go a-begging in the Aarab menzils, *ib.*; Syrian *Slèybies* clad in gazelle skins, 328; the — booth, *ib.*; 354; 359; 396; — hunters, 407; 549; a — singing, 607; II. Nomads not Beduins reviled as —, 195; — come tinkering to Kheybar, 199; tale of a — who slays his faithless jâra, 231-2; — household, with the Heteym near Kheybar, from *Wady Suffera*, 243; a kindred of Heteym snibbed as —, 253; 256; — come tinkering to an Heteym menzil, 301;

— gelding an ass, *ib.*; — eat carrion, *ib.*; 315; the name of — a reproach, 319; — riding on their asses in the desert, 324; 327; — said to be founders of the villages *es-Shaara, Doàdamy* and *Goayîeh*, 492; — hunters' fire by a well in the khála, 497; — hunters' custom to drink before dawn, *ib.*; 499. [A weakly Beduin child is sometimes named *Solubby* — as we have seen such called by the names of wild beasts — " that if it pleased Ullah he might not die ": I have known an Heteymy sheykh, *Ibn Khlûy*, whose father was thus named.]
Solubbîa, Solubby woman, 552, 587.
Solubby, one of the nomad kindred of hunters and tinkers, *es-Slèyb* or *Solubba*.
" Son of the way," *Ibn es-sefr*, 117.
Songs of the Aarab [*v. Kaṣṣîda*] to the one-stringed viol, 81, 138; 306; strangers may hardly understand them, 169; the *hadû* or herding-song, 306; — of the Bed. at labour, 395, 506; — of the wilderness, 513, 514; — of war, 567; II. 256; braying-wise of —, likened by the ancient poet 'Antar to the hum of flies, 305; saddle —, *ib.*, and 331.
Sons are beloved in the Arabian household, 258, 281, 282, 283, 590.
Sooltan, *v. Sultân*.
Sorbonne, conférence faite à la —, par M. Ph. Berger, 227.
Sordidatus (said of one who is miserably clothed, to move pity in the spirits of any that have power over him).
Sores: — springing of themselves and such probably as the " Aleppo boil," II. 511.
Sorrel: wild — of the desert (*humsîs*), 222, 255, 259.
Soṭwḥ (a sword-wound in the hip; probably سطوح), 475.

Soul, The, 521.
Southernwood [*v. Shaeh*], 88; II. 77.
Sowra, ass-mare's name, II. 253.
es-Sowwa [misprinted *el-Kowwâ*], ass-mare's name, II. 253.
Sowwân, a dog's name, 474.
Spade, *v.* Tools.
Spain, 503; reals of —, II. 23, 447.
Sparrows, 584; II. 17.
Spears, *v. Romḥ, Shelfa*.
Spenser: the divine Poet Edmund — 31; some words of — (' for short time — *etc.*'), 50.
Sphinx: enigma of —, 237.

678 INDEX AND GLOSSARY

Spices [v. Perfumes, 'Aud Bakhûr, Mubârak : Bahàr بهار], 247, 286, 297.

Spiders in the grove of W. Thirba, 495.
Spinning: women —, 262, 476, 490.
Spitting to heal the sick, 576; — upon a lock, 577; II. — upon water for a remedy, 184.
Sprenger: Prof. Aloys —, 93, 403, 669; II. 191, 303, 500, 563.
Spring season of the new herbage and of milk in the wilderness, v. Rabî'a.
Springs of water at el-Ally, 193; — in J. Ajja, 632; — at Fuâra, II. 326; — near 'Aneyza, 358; — in the Wady es-Sirr, 452.
Spy (jassûs), 316-7; the treacherous enemy [and though he were a guest, he may be put to death], 317, 320.
Stables: Arab — in Bombay, II. 418; 466.
Stambûl, 109, 129, 183, 193, 207, 220, 249, 461-2, 587, 652; II. 105, 147, 177; 181, 183, 274, 398, 448, 472, 537, 538, 540, 556, 558.
Standard of the Hâj [v. Mahmal], 101.
Stars: Bed. knowledge of the — by their names, 321; aeroliths, 412; in August, at el-Héjr, the lesser — were commonly dimmed in the first night hours; Moh. Nejûmy could see the — at noonday, II. 165.
Stealing of food not very shameful amongst the Bed., 384.
Steel, for striking fire with the flint, 324, 580.
Stick: camel — [v. Bakorra, Mish'aab مشعب, Mehjàn], 349, 398.
Stirrups, Arabians ride without —, 69; II. 417.
Stone (the disease), 616.
Stone-buck, v. Bédan.
Stone-casting: none better to cast stones than the Arabs, II. 260, 430.
Stone-hewing at 'Aneyza, II. 382, 414, 429.
Stoora, a station on the Hâj road, four marches above Medina [v. Sawra], below el-Héjr, II. 201.
Storks (or cranes), 584; II. 288.
Strabo, II. 197.
Stranger: —s (exiles) in the nomad menzils, 263; they prefer the opinion of a —, 518; 'the — to the wolf,' 319, 518; II. a Christian — who came to Hâyil and showed feats of horse-riding: he became a Mosleman, and Ibn Rashîd, they say, took his sister to wife,

39; a certain one-eyed — at Hâyil, 275-6-7; some —s passengers in Nejd, who were reputed 'Nasâra,' 302; a mechanical — brought down by 'Aly el-Rasheyd to 'Aneyza, to set up pumping gear, 449.
ΣΤΡΑΤΗΓΌΣ (military leader), a word found in the epitaphs at Medáin Sâlih, 227.
Stygian water: pool of —, 435.
es-Suâda, ass-mare's name, II. 253.

Ṣûah, pl. of ṣah (read ṣu'a pl. of ṣa'a, صاع pl. صوع), a standard measure.

Suâka, hamlet of Harb, Yanb'a-the-Palms, II. 202; Sherîf of —, ib.
Suâki, a kindred of Howeytát dwelling in the Nefûd of el-Arîsh, 275.
Suâkim, head of the Galla-land slave traffic and salt staple, II. 186.

Suâlif سوالف, tales (properly of the past), 492.

Suàlma, a fendy of Jellàs, 377.

Suâny, sing. sâniyeh (سانية pl. سواني): draw-wheel frames of the wells of irrigation in Nejd oases, 335, 644; II. 21.

Subbâk (سبعك الله)! — answer yussbâk ent (يسبعك انت), 302, 586; II. 319.

Súbbakha (سبخة), salt crust upon the soil, (Kheybar vulg. summakha), II. 92, 109, 117, 131, 145, 419, 502, 503, 505, 506.
Subbîa, a sounding sand-hill, 352.

Subîa (سبية), a fermented drink, made from rice, II. 189.

Sudàn, black men, 480, 562.
es-Suedda (of Kahtân): the people of Shuggera are partly —, II. 452.
es-Suergîeh, Harb village, II. 546.
Sueygy [v. Suaka], Harb hamlet at Yanb'a-the-Palms.
Suez, 432, 438; II. — Canal, 397, 450-1, 468, 559.
Ṣuffa (ṣáfa), the ground rock, 284.

Ṣuffa (صُفَّة), an upper house-chamber at Kheybar, II. 94. [In the summer months of most heat the villagers use to sit in their lower chamber or ground-floor.]
W. es-Suffera, II. 243.
es-Suffuk, desert site near Kheybar, II. 141.
Sufra, the leathern tray or mat which the Arabs set under their dish of victual, 190.
Sugar: the sweet [dates, honey, sugar] is much accounted-of by the Arabians (living in hunger and nakedness) as very good for the health; Arab — traders to the Mauritius, II. 389.
Sújwa or *Shújwa*, a kellâ below el-Héjr, 127, 128, 166, 204, 469; II. 202.

Sûk (سوق)! drive on! drive up cattle, whence to pay, 363.
Sûk, street or bazaar (lit. drift-way).
Sûk er-Ruwàlla, a site near Kheybar, II. 205.
Sûk es-Sheukh, II. 456.
es-Ṣulât, the Prayer, II. 129; — *el-akhîr*, 380.
el-Suléyl, v. *es-Soleyil*, village, II. 52.
Ṣull yâ, ta'all ṣull! II. 332.

Ṣully 'alâ hâ 'l ghrádâ صَلّ عليَ ها الغادَة (this tender girl!) II. 410.
Ṣully 'aly en-Neby, give glory to the Prophet, II. 53.
Ṣully Ullah 'aley-hu, 341.
Sulphur, for gunpowder, purchased from Medina, 410; II. demons cannot abide the smell of —, 212; cattle pits tasting of —, 506. [The thermal springs of (Palmyra,) el-Ally, Thirba and Kheybar taste of —.]
Wady es-Sulsilla, the lower main valley at Kheybar, II. 202.
Súltàn: the Ottoman Sultan called *Sûltàn el-Islâm*, 595; his authority as Calif — howbeit conquered by the sword — is acknowledged by all orthodox Moslems, II. 388; 538; rescript of thanks from the — to the Sherîf, 559.
Derb es-Sultány, between el-Kasîm and Mecca, II. 499, 500-2, 565.
Sum! v. *Summ*.
Summ: the word explained, 662; II. 269, 273.

[Correction to p. 662, (سَمّ قْلّ بسم الله) say *bismillah!*]
Súmmakha (salt-crust), v. *Súbbakha*.

[*Summat* (سامط), unsalted (Western Arabia).
v. *Ât*.
Summer not yet ended in Arabia, on the 24th Nov. 1876, 90
the Summer: — day in the khála, 367; withering drought in April (harvest month in the oases), 387; 400, 423; — upon the 'Aueyrid, 453; — at Wejh, 522; — at el-Ally, 526, 555; — in Thirba, 490, 537; — in the Héjr plain, 550, 554, 558, 560, 563, 566-7; last — heat at Teyma, 585, 587; II. — heat at Kheybar, 145; — in el-Kasîm, 339.
Summer-famine, 520.
Samrâ, dual form of Samrâ, qd. v.; — Hâyil, 633, 667, 668; II. 15, 76, 270.

Súmṭ (سمط), stony places in the (Nejd Harb) desert, II. 322.
Sun: Arabians impatient of the burning — -light, 354, 394; midday — nearly vertical in May, 405; summer heat, 367, 400, 423, 453, 484, 489-90. Arctic summer — at midnight, 320.
Sun-rising in Arabia, 112, 367; II. 294, 331.
Sun-setting in Arabia, 111, 346; coming-home of the cattle and herdsmen at —, 59; the nomads return to their households to sup at the —, 293, 415; after — the inflamed air and sand are quickly cool, 302, 490.
Sunday esteemed an unlucky day in which to begin any work (at Kheybar), II. 218.
Sunna, the Mohammedan Talmud, 99.
Ṣúnn'aa, pl. of *Ṣâny*, a smith, qd. v., 324; they are aliens in Arabia, 326, 603.
Sunnî, an observer of the *Sunna* or Catholic traditions of Mohammed, 108; II. 224.
Supper: the — hour of the Nomads, 302; 'Sup with the Jew' (prov.), 579; II. — the chief meal in Arabia, 435; an Harb sheykh disputes with a pasha, 'Whether the town food or the simple diet of the Aarab be better for the health?' 548.
Sûr: the — of Mosaic Teyma, 331, 601, 602.
Surbût (probably from the Syrian *sharbît* שְׁרָבִיט, سَربوط), Bed. coffee pestle, 288.
Surgery [v. Firing, Cupping], 485.
Ṣurra(t), 'bundles of money,' paid to the Beduins [v. *Hâj*], 48; — *el-Bint*, 94; 112, 128, 239; the Fejîr —, 389; 408, 436.

INDEX AND GLOSSARY

Suryân (سُرْيَان, pron. *Sírian*), running channels of the oasis irrigation, Teyma, 593, 607.

Sûs, in Morocco, II. 153.

Suspicion: the Arabs (naturally of bad faith) are full of —, 132.

es-Sûta, a fendy of 'Ateyba, II. 457.

Sûwahh سُوَاح (v. *Sâiehh*), world's wanderer, 315, 316, 435, 461; II. 59, 121.

Swallows in the desert [near the Red Sea bord]: black and grey —, 177; dun —, 495.

The sweet and the fat comfort the health of the weak dieted, 319; II. 108.

Swergîeh, a Meteyr village by the E. Hâj way, between the Harameyn; but the villagers are mostly Ashrâf descended from Hasèyn, II. 393, 565.

W. *Swergîeh*, II. 393.

Sweydîa سَوَادِيَة, (in other parts called *Umm Sâlema*, qd. v.), a bird haunting among rocks of the Arabian wilderness, 452.

S'weyfly, a suburb of Hâyil, destroyed by the plague, 669; II. 19, 21, 22; — was ancient Hâyil, 21.

es-Sweyfly a kindred of the Sherarát, 117, 135.

Sweyga, Beny Sâlem Harb vill., II. 546.

Sweylmát, a fendy of Bishr, 376.

Sweymly, a fendy of Billî, 430.

Swimming: Bed. —, 594.

Swine, 506, 584, 642, 656.

Sword (Ar. *seyf*): the best Bed. —s, 265; 273, 503-5; Oriental —s, 505; 'the mouth of the —,' *ib.*; Hamûd's —, 649; the — is valued by the Arabians as a sure weapon, *ib.*; 653; II. only Bed. strangers and persons who have served the Dowla may carry the — in Medina, 155; the son of the Emir's house and officers of the Emir carry the — in 'Aneyza, 404; 463; — the key of Mohammed's paradise, 406; 444.

Swordsman: a certain — at Hâyil, II. 282.

Swoysh, v. Shwoysh.

Sybarites of the desert life, 286; II. 238.

Synagogue: fable of a buried — at Kheybar, 482; II. 206.

Syria [v. *es-Sham*], 74, 78, 89, 114, 129; troops of —, 130; 134, 137, 162, 165, 169, 171, 196, 208; — a land of sepulchres, 211, 213; 244, 275, 294, 314, 315; —n wilderness, 328; 332, 338, 341, 353, 355, 373, 389; 395, 403, 412, 428, 433, 445, 451, 455, 469, 475, 476, 481, 486, 497, 501, 522, 579, 603, 607, 633, 641, 654, 658, 665, 673, 674; II. 37, 38, 46, 47-8, 50-1-9, 64-8, 104; speech of —, 106, 144; 157; hackneys of —, *ib.*; hospitality in —, 171; 174, 183, 190, 193, 264, 284, 289, 304, 328, 337-8, 348, 370, 382, 398-9, 400-1; superstitious —n Christianity, *ib.*; —ns sterile in invention, *ib.*; 415; — eaten up by usurers, 416; 426-8; 429, 440, 509, 516; —n soldier at Tâyif, 539, 558; —n hackneys of the Turkish soldiery at Tâyif, 552; 553; vines and olives of —, 560; 568, 572, 575.

Syrian *kellâ* keepers, 165, 170.

Syrie Centrale, par M. le Marquis de Vogüé, 673.

T: there are two *T*-like letters in the Arabic alphabet, namely ت which sounds like our *t*, and ط which sounds nearly as the Irish pronounce *t*, with a little thickness and explosion of the breath. I could not ofttimes discern these differences in the common speech: when (as in names) the *t* is certainly ط I have distinguished that letter by writing under it a dot (*ṭ*).

Ta'ad hennéyi (تَعَدّ هَنَا), 287.

Ta'al ḥubbiny (تَعَال حِبِّني), II. 63.

Ta'al yâ mel'aun, II. 176.

Ta'am طعم (*ej-jídery*), vaccination lymph, 297.

Beny *Taâmir*, an ancient Nejd tribe, formerly in the dîra which is now of the Nejd Shammar and Meteyr in the N., II. 286, 304, 420.

Tabernacle of Israel, 269.

Ṭâga (طَاقَة), casement, II. 94.

Ṭáhal (طُحَل) (ague-cake, qd. v.), after the Hejâz or oasis fever, 597, II. 238, 374.

et-Ṭâif (v. *Ṭâyif*).

Taifát, fendy of Wélad Aly, 271.

OF ARABIC WORDS

Tájir, tradesman, II. 314.

Takht er-Rûm (تَخْت الروم), camel litter, of great personages in the Hâj, 105-6, 109, 127, 246.

Tales: Oriental —, 168-71; II. 150.

Taliâny, Italian, *qd. v.*

Talisman, *v. Hijâb.*

Talk: Firelight evening —, 492, *et passim*; II. 150, 174, *et passim.*

J. *Tâly*, 629.

Tamar, David's daughter, 336; II. 45.

Tamarisk [*v. Ethla, Turfah, Ghróttha*], 185, 425; II. — in el-Kasîm, 339; Arabia might become a — wood, 356; 419, 445.

Tam(n)bûr, 70, 181; II. 136-7, 142.

Tamerlane, 650.

Tammerra, village in W. Dauâsir, II. 425.

Támr, dates; — *el-Hind* (read *támr Hindy*, tamarind), II. 385.

Tamyîz (تَمْيِيز), divination, 205.

Tannûr, girdle-pans of iron plate, 246, 645.

Tape-measure found in the Nasrâny's bags, II. 100.

Tarbûsh, the féz or red cap of the Ottoman countries, 556, 624; II. 338.

Târiba, a sheykh and arbiter of the Wélad Aly, 551.

Tarkîy, pl. *terâgy* (طراقي) طرقيّة, *v. Turkiêh*, a small company of passengers, II. 266.

Tassels and fringes are to the Semitic humour, 268, 385, 476.

T'âus (prob. دعص), dunes of the Nefûd so called, II. 339. The sing. is *T'îs*.

Tax [*v. Zíka, Míry*]: Ibn Rashîd's — in the settlements, 338; — upon the nomad stock, 394, 502; — of the Dowla upon the nomad cattle, 500; II. 34; Ibn Rashid's — formerly at Kheybar, 140, 241; 147, 273, 285, 321, 326; the old Wáhaby exactions at 'Aneyza, 458.

Táyib, good, well.

et-Tâyif, an ancient town in the highland above Mecca enclosed by ruinous clay walls; summer residence of the Sherîf, Emir of Mecca, and villegiatura of Mecca citizens: 325; II. 190, 231, 492-3, 506-10-1-2-5,

516-8, 521-4-5-6-7, 532-3-5-7; enter —, 538; the town, 539-60; orchards of —, 537, 551, 560, 565, 566; plenty of all things at —, 559; vines of —, 560; roses of — for distilling attar, 561; 564, 567-8, 570.

Tchôl (Steppes of) *Bagdad* [*v. Chôl*], 68.

Tea: the Persian — -drinking in the Hâj, 58; — -making, 352, 401, 418; — is cordial in great fatigue and languishing, 460, 489; 641; II. 228, 397.

Tebûk oasis, 94, 95, 112, 113; '*Arab el-Kaabeny*, 112; '*Ayn* —, 113; *Yarmûk, ib.*; 115, 118, 130, 135, 238, 346, 447, 448, 453, 454, 464, 470, 480, 481, 540, 545, 546; — of old subject to B. Sókhr, 578; II. 85, 510, 575.

Teeth of the Beduins, 546; battle of the — at Arabian dinner, II. 378.

Teghrurriz el-ghrannem (تَغرز الغَنَم), 489.

Tegúf [thou stand still, Medina vulgar; class. تَقِف], II. 195.

Teháma (تهامة), hot low-land, commonly said of the sea-bordering country as far down as Mecca (and beyond), 164, 217, 267, 275, 276, 326, 382, 426, 429, 430, 431, 434, 436, 449, 450, 451, 453, 455, 462-4, 469, 471, 502, 521, 536, 537, 550; II. 466.

Teháma of the Wady el-Húmth below Kheybar, II. 234.

Teháma of Mecca, II. 195, 451, 496, 506, 517, 524, 559, 564, 565, 569.

Tekhálliny aném fî hothnak, II. 324.

Telâl ibn Rashîd, the second Prince of J. Shammar, 300, 517, 633, 636, 642, 656, 671; II. 19, 28-44, 271, 460.

The Telegraph, a matter of wonder to the Arabs, 647, 651; II. 370; none yet to Mecca, 558.

TEMA, Teyma in the Bible, 343, 600.

Temathîl el-Helalát, imagery of the B. Helál, *v.* p. 260.

Temîm, patriarch of the B. Temîm, II. 286.

Beny Temîm: — of Gofar, 634, 669; II. of el-Kasr, 269; — of Gofar, 285, 325, 337; — of el-Kasîm, 349, 355, 367, 378, 382; — of Zanzibar, 389; 405; — of *el-'Eyarieh*, 421; — of el-Hauta, 425; — of 'Aneyza, 429; in them is the spirit of industry, and a good plain understanding,

682 INDEX AND GLOSSARY

ib.; the founder of the Waháby reformation was of —, 454; battle of — with the *Tubb'a el-Yémen*, 477; 487.
(2) B. Temím, Harb, a fendy of B. Sâlem, II. 546.
a *Beny Temîmy* "learned" personage at 'Aneyza, II. 405.
Temmn [better *témn* تمن], river rice from Mesopotamia, 195, 619, *et passim*; II. 320.
Tempests in Arabia, II. 81, 330-1. *v.* Rain.
Temple of Ullah: the *Beyt Ullah* at Mecca [*v. Háram, Ka'aba*], 247; the Háram of Medina, II. 158.
Temût, thou wilt die, 459.
Tent [*v. Beyt es-sh'ar, Héjra*]: 82; every Beduin — is sanctuary, 95, 268, 274; the Beduin booth described, 257; is set up by the women, 258, 262; 263, 265, 448; — divided into the open men's and the women's or householding apartment, 267-9; coffee assemblies, 286 (*v.* Coffee); the inner place about the hearth is the higher seat, 287; the Beduin booth is four-square only (though there be some mention in the ancient poems of round tents), 328; II. — building wise of Ânnezy and Shammar, 263; —s of Harb and Heteym, 295; the men's "sitting place" and the apartment of the hareem not always on the same sides of the nomad —, *ib.*; a long and lofty triple tent (Harb), 310; canvas —s of 'Aneyza citizens, 382.
Terabîn, a clan of Howeytát Bed. in the Nefûd of *el-Arîsh*, 274-5.
Terâgy, pl. of *tarkîy, qd. v.*, small wayfaring companies in the desert, II. 266.
Terâny billah, yâ sheykh; wa bak ana dakhîlak, 311.
Terky, a Harby tribesman dwelling at Medina, II. 327-8-9-30, 335.
Terky, a Kahtân sheykh, brother of Hayzàn; they were slain, both of them and their sister, in one day, II. 480.
Térrai, a seyl-bed, 351.
Tèrras (Turk. ترس), II. 161.
Teslîm, the entrusting to the keeping of another, 422, 447; II. 521.
Tessera: Ômar's —, II. 387.
Teyâmena, the people of Teyma, 242, *et passim*.
Teyma oasis تيماء [27 Feb.–1 March, 1877; and 2 Sept.–10 Oct. in the same year];

anciently called (they say) *Tôma*: the Bib. Tema. The villagers of — are '*Aarab Aushez*, of *Shammar*. Dates of —, 112; colonists from — at el-Héjr, 177; 178, 192; "miracles of Khalîl" at —, 217, 223, 238, 241, 242, 254, 261, 275, 288, 295, 315, 327; the sterile ground, which lies about — 328, 569; 329; the situation and aspect, the turrets, plum (or almond) trees in blossom, altitude, 329; *Sleymàn* of —, *ib.*; — a Nejd colony of Shammar, 329; the well-pit Haddàj, their palms, their speech, clothing, spacious houses, *ib.*; — was never wasted by plagues, the town always thriving, *ib.*; their antique wells, *ib.*; — surrendered to 'Abeyd ibn Rashîd, *ib.*, 340; they sink no wells for themselves, 330; few destitute persons, 330; Old — of the Jews, 331; the *Sûr, Bedr ibn Jòher, ib.*; New —, B. Sókhr, *ib.*; fever unknown: unwholesome water, 331; — men and women, *ib.*; 331; no aged persons seen, 331; women not veiled, *ib.*; number of houses and quarters and mesjids; the great mosque (may probably stand) upon the site of an ancient temple, 331, 581-2; coffee-halls; the charcoal coffee hearth, 332; *dâr*, said for house; very small coffee; their well-built spacious houses, *ib.*; the Resident for Ibn Rashîd, 333; a building of old —, 335; an inscription, *ib.*; — women, *ib.*, 336; husbandry, 337; corn harvest in April, 337; fruit trees, *ib.*; Teyma is not Nejd, 338; dates of —, cattle and poultry, *ib.*; little silver; date currency, *ib.*; the government tax, 338; tradesmen strangers from Hâyil, and Damascenes in —, 338; town walls of old —, 339, 569; the oasis a loam bottom in the high desert, the salines, 340; way to Jauf, 340; — mentioned in the Towrat, 343; old Teyma, 344; *ekîm* carpets made at —, 345; 346, 353, 355, 359, 375, 376, 377, 378, 392, 401, 403, 406, 413, 426, 436, 455, 503, 523, 546, 551, 560, 566, 567, 569, 570, 571, 578, 580, 581; — is three oases, 582; 583, 585, 587, 589, 590, 591; the Teyâmena are *juhâl*, 592; 593; well-camels hired by the month for an hundred measures of dates, 593; Jewish —, 594, 600; 596-7, 598; the old town wall, 600; *Bédr ibn Jôher*, 600; Emir Samuel, *ib.*, 600; are there hidden springs at —, 600; site of old —,

OF ARABIC WORDS

600; shivers of silex in —, *ib.*, 601; reported necropolis of ancient Teyma, 601; the ancient oasis of —, 601-2; the oasis is not walled by a sûr, 603; paths in the oasis, 603; 605, 607, 608, 610, 612, 613, 615; departure from —, 617, 618; 619, 620, 625, 629, 641, 654; II. 21, 34, 35, 85, 132, 135, 195, 260, 289, 322, 336-7, 464, 537, 543, 553.

Teymâny, a man of Teyma.
et-Teyry or Gârat Owsheyfîa, II. 564.

T-h: there are three (or four, if we reckon ظ) th-like letters in Nejd Arabic [Th was signified in the old English by a proper letter, and indeed by two; —þ, to express the sharp t sound of th in *thing*, and ð to express the dull d sound of th in *seethe* — soð] : — ث or þ nearly, ذ or ð nearly, and ض or þ-ð nearly. This last, somewhat sharper in sound and *crassior* than ð, is a propriety and grace of the Nejd speech. When we pronounce ض as the people of Nejd, the tip of the tongue is not put to the edge of the upper front teeth as when we pronounce simple ð, but behind the teeth and pressed to the teeth more than when we pronounce simple þ; the sound is nevertheless nearer to ð. This Nejd ص we might compare also with the (South) Spanish lisping z for example in *plaza* (pronc. *plàtha*). For ث I have used Th, i.e. þ; and for ذ and ض (not seldom also for ظ), since I might not always distinguish them, Ṭh, i.e. ð and þ-ð.

W. Thá, a valley of the 'Aueyrid, 463.

Thá el-melûk (داء الملوك), the morbus gallicus, 437.

Thâbit, a fendy of Shammar, II. 56.
Th'af, basalt berg in W. Fâṭima, II. 570.
Thafja, a mountain between Teyma and Tebûk, 341.
Tháhab el-asfr, gold, 385; — el-abiath, silver, 392.
Ṭhâhir, a villager of Teyma, 576.
Ṭhâhir, a Mahûby, 519, 534-40.

Ṭhâhir's daughter, 546.
'ayd eth-Ṭhahîa: a Mohammedan festival, 178.
eth-Ṭhâhy, the waterless Nefûd land between Teyma, Jauf, and Hâyil.
Thaif, a guest, pl. *theûf*, 269.
Thaif-Ullah, a guest whom God sendeth: every stranger is a —; and, for the reverence of Ullah, there should none do him wrong or molest him.
Thaifullah, Wélad 'Aly lad, 435.
Thaifullah, a Heteymy, II. 83-4.
Ṭhail, horse tail, sheep's tail, 550; II. (podex), 55.

Thakîf (ثقيف), tribe, II. 381.

eth-Th'al, mountain by the way between Kasîm and Mecca, II. 500.
eth-Thâleba, a tribe of Ashrâf, II. 556.

Thalûk, perhaps ذلوق, a pleasant-tasting wild bush in the desert which is often chewed by the Nomads, 255.
Ṭhâmin, one of whom is taken surety for another, 574.
Thámmad, mountains, v. *Ethmâd*.
Wady Thammud, near Kheybar, II. 201.

Thamûd (ثمود), ancient tribe of South Arabia, where, defeated by 'Aad, says the koran tradition, they wandered northward, and settled in the plain of el-Héjr, under mount Ethlib: 61; destruction of —, 135, 136, 151, 229; Thamudite plain of el-Héjr, 246.

Than-ak, perhaps الدانك for ولدانك, thy progeny (heard at Hâyil).

Thanthub (تنضب, tanthub), a kind of wild trees in the Teháma of Mecca, II. 566.
Thanwa, a Mahûby woman, 548.

Thàr (ثار) el-Emîr, 660.

Thàt el-Hâj, Ḳellâ, 97.
Thàt 'Irk, i.e. eth-Therrîby, qd. v.
el-Thegîf, a kindred of Jeheyna, II. 195.
Thelûl, the dromedary or riding camel [as a riding horse to a draught horse, such is the thelûl to the common or draught camel,

jémel, ba'yer] : 51 ; ghrazzu of — riders, 379 ; the — in battle, *ib.* ; the Bed. housewife receives as he alights, and she discharges her husband's —, 392 ; —s sold for two or three reals in a year of murrain, 665 ; II. gait of — -calf, 85 ; — not sure-footed in miry ground, 237 ; —s of the Heteymàn, 241, 261 [*v. et-Tîh*] ; —s of the Sherarát, *ib.*, ; 'Ageyl —s, 221, 245 ; Howeytát —s, 261 ; the — in warfare, 323 ; in a murrain —s could be purchased for two reals, 428 ; a braying — might be muzzled with the halter, 436 ; —s of private persons always standing in the house-yards at 'Aneyza, 459 ; centaur-like aspect of the — -rider regarded from the backward, 501 ; if a — put a limb out of joint the accident is without remedy, 517.

Thelûl-riding, 623 ; II. examples of —, 553.

Themîla (ثَمِيلَة), pl. *themèyil*, shallow water-holes of the Beduw, digged with their hands, 501, 622 ; II. the digging of a —, 322.

Thènny (ثَنِي), five-year-old camel, 401.

Thennŷib, mountain in the desert between Kasîm and Mecca, II. 501.

eth-Ther'eyyeh in W. Hanîfa ; the old Waháby metropolis, II. 424 ; — was destroyed by Ibrahîm Pasha, 454.

Thérmidda, a populous town in el-Wéshm, II. 424, 452, 564.

Therrai, a lake plash near J. Bírrd, 395.

eth-Therríby (ضَرِيبَة) which, says Bessàm, is THAT 'IRK), station on the E. Hâj road near Mecca, II. 565.

Therrîeh, desert village near the borders of el-Kasîm, II. 323, 492.

Wady Therry in the Tehàma, 469.

Therrya, fem. Bed. name, 514.

eth-Therrŷeh, elder son of Motlog, sheykh el-Fejîr, 222, 265, 391, 555, 559 ; — 'sheykh of sheykhs,' 559 ; 567, 576.

Theûf, pl. of *thaif*.

Theûf Ullah, guests of Ullah ; all strangers are accounted such, 269.

Theydi(k)ch, a place in Middle Nejd, II. 424.

Theyma : *ahl* —, 328.

eth-Thíabba or *Ibn Simra*, a fendy of Midland Heteym, II. 253.

eth-Thib, the wolf.

Thief in the Hâj : punishment of a —, 52, 108 ; II. thieving in 'Aneyza, 396, 428.

Thimble : Bed. housewife's —, 268.

Thiràn (probably from classical أَثَر), 305 ; dry milk shards, *v. Mereesy*.

W. Thirba : bees in —, 426 ; 429, 454, 457, 463, 466 ; — described, 486, 488 ; husbandry in —, 487, 495 ; 490 ; wells in —, 487-8, 495 ; the grove of wild fig trees in —, 488, 495 ; the great thorn, 495 ; 501, 502, 530, 534, 537, 542, 565, 567, 610, 611 ; II. 451, 483. [See Fig.]

Thirru (ضِرو a single one is ضِرْوَة), a tree with leaves like the mountain ash [the same as *thirwa, qd. v.*], II. 89.

Thirst : the Arabians impatient of —, 525 ; II. — in the 'Aneyza sámn caravan, 503.

Thirwa, a kind of evergreen oak, *v. Thirru*, above, 497.

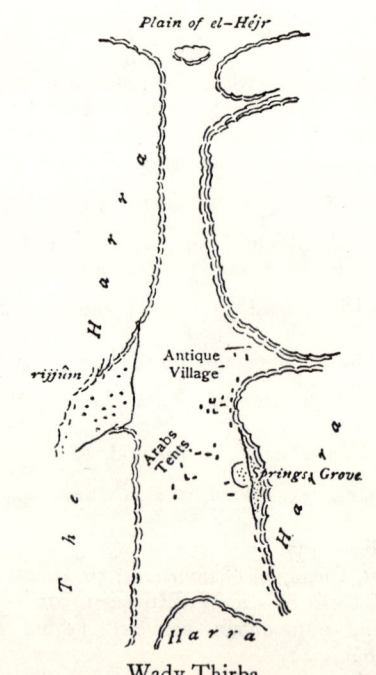

Wady Thirba.

eth-Thoàhirra, a fendy of Harb B. Sâlem, II. 546.

OF ARABIC WORDS 685

[*Thôb* ثَوْب, the Arabian tunic of calico, which is called *ḳamîṣ* in Syria.

eth-Thôb (الثَوْب), tapet-covering of the Ka'aba at Mecca, 101.

Thôb (ضَبّ), a saurian in the desert, 110, 371; called *Sheykh Ḥamed*, *ib.*; 656; II. 220, 303, 304.

Thobby (ظَبْي), the gazelle (N. T. Tabitha), v. Gazelle.

Thofîra (ضُفَيْرَة), II. 129.

eth-Thóhr, the sun at midday height, 399.
Tholfa, village in el-Kasîm, II. 443.
Thór (steer), Aaron's calf, 191.
Thorèyih, a hamlet in the great desert, S. of el-Kasîm, II. 492.
eth-Thorrèyid or *Sorrèyid*, a strait in the under-cliffs of the 'Aueyrid, 465, 485, 501.

Thorrîb (probably ضَرِيب), Nomad kerchief, 484.

eth-Thów, the light, II. 108.
Thread; every — or cord of the Arabs is a twine of two strands, 593; II. 452.
"Three hundred" signifies very many, 60, 83; II. 134. [They say likewise, 'In el-Hása are 300 springs.'] — prophets, 179; — images in the Ka'aba, 545.
Threshing-floors in Kasîm are plots of the common ground, II. 446.
Thûy 'Ammîr, a tribe of the Ashrâf, II. 556.
Thû Ehamûd, a tribe of the Ashrâf, II. 556.
Thûy Hásan, a great tribe of the Ashrâf, II. 556.
Thû Hasseyn, a tribe of the Ashrâf, II. 556.
Thû Ithbeyt, a fendy of 'Ateyba, II. 457.
Thû Izzyàd, a fendy of 'Ateyba, II. 457.
Thû Jazzàn, a tribe of the Ashrâf, II. 556.
Thûy Jessàs, a tribe of the Ashrâf, II. 556.
Thû Júdullah, a tribe of the Ashrâf, II. 556.
Thû Suâmly, a tribe of the Ashrâf, II. 556.
Thû es-Surrur, a tribe of the Ashrâf, II. 556.
Thû ez-Zeyd, a tribe of the Ashrâf (whereof 'Abd el-Muttelib), II. 556.
Thúbb'a, the hyena, *qd. v.*
Thubîḥa, beast for slaughter, 128.

Thuèyba, a fendy of W. 'Aly, 271.
Thuèyny el-Múntefik, II. 381.
Thuèyny er-Romàn, a Teyma sheykh, 604, 609, 614.
eth-Thueyrát, desert site, a thelûl journey from 'Aneyza, where the W. er-Rummah is barred by sand-banks, II. 420.
eth-Thuffîr [and v. *Ḍuffîr*] tribe now about Sûk es-Sheukh and Zbeyer, 661; II. 29, 30, 37.
Thúkr, virile, II. 398.
Thullâ [*Thul'aa*] lit. rib, and dim. *Thulley'a*, used commonly by the Beduw for mountain, 285, *et passim*.
Thull'a el Bint, near es-Seyl, II. 564.
Thúlm, mountain in the desert between Kasîm and Mecca, II. 501.
Thûm, garlic, II. 229.

Thumma (ظَمْء), thirst, 435.

eth-Thumràn, ass-mare's name, II. 253.
Thunder, II. 290, 331.
Thunma, a small wild plant with tubers, in the desert, 255.
Thùra, a kind of millet, 337; II. 95, 116, 119, 190, 517, 565, 567.

Thurbàn (ظَرِبَان (ضَرِبَان)), an animal, perhaps fabulous, 371.

Thurghrud, hamlet in the Harrat Kheybar, II. 34, 247, 254, 297, 298.
Thurrambàn, a beast [perhaps the same as *Thurbàn* above, *qd. v.*], II. 164.

Thurrm (probably ثَرم), knot-grass, forage for the great Hâj camels, and even for the soldiers' hackneys, 105, 117, 135; II. 499.
eth-Thuy Bàt, a fendy of 'Ateyba, II. 457.
Thyme, 644.
et-Tî, v. *Tîh*.
Tiáha, a kindred of Howeytát, dwelling about Gâza, 275.
Tiberias (town by the lake of —), 114.
Tiberius, 131.
Ticks, camel —, 408.
Tidings are not often carried certainly or speedily in Arabia, II. 315.
Tiflis, in Russian Armenia, II. 110, 111.
et-Tîh or *Tî*, phantom thelûl male, II. 261.
Timathîl, pl. of *timthàl*, images: the Himyaric scored inscriptions in the desert, thus called

by the Bed., 119, 260, 350, 479; 561; images of men upon the rock holding bows in their hands, and on their heads is portrayed a long cap, 613; II. 510.

Timbuctû, 562.

Tiryâk, II. 27.

Tittun (Turk. تُوتُون), tobacco, 355, et passim.

Toadstools : certain — used for dye by Nomad women, 402.

et Toâla, a fendy of W. 'Aly, 271.

Tobacco pipe [v. Galliûn, Sebîl, A'orfy], 288; — wrought in stone by the Bed., 288.

Tobacco [v. Tittun, Dokhân, Hameydy]: Persian —, 43; Bed. women 'smoke-drinkers,' 277; the use of — in Arabia, 288, 289; — first brought by English shippers to Constantinople, ib.; Bed. abandoned to coffee and —, ib., 289, 290; yet some have it in aversion, ib.; — is bawl Iblis, ib., 494; — tolerated in Nejd, 289; — bibbers in the oases, ib.; some who wean themselves from it, ib.; — and coffee distemper their weak bodies, ib.; — grown at Teyma, 337; — in Wady Thirba, 487; the Nomads dote upon —, 355, 356; a — seller in the tribe, 355; verses of a Bed. maker, 356; 525, 568, 630, 642; II. green — of Kheybar, 104; their — fields to be taxed, 151; — tipplers, 266, 271, 299; — tolerated within doors in Kasîm, 366, 411.

J. Tobey(k)ch, a considerable mountain [which is, according to the saying of Moh. ed-Dèybis. of red sandstone] between Tebûk and Ma'an, 341.

Tòdmor [Bib. Tadmor], Palmyra, qd. v.

et-Toèym, hamlet in el-Wéshm, II. 452.

Tôga, a dog's name, 474.

Tokhfa, mountain in the great desert S. of el-Kasîm, II. 493.

Ṭólâ (tol'a, طَلْع), the shooting fruit-stalks of the palm, when spring begins, II. 234, 236, 268.

Tolerance of the Beduw and oasis-dwellers, 295, 404, 445.

et-Toleyhát, a seyl bed at Teyma, 340.

Ṭolh, the gum acacia : the — timber, which is heavy, is used for ship-building on the Arabian Red Sea coast as at el-Wejh, and by sanies in the nomad country for their wood-work. The other kinds of acacia are reckoned too brittle to serve them. 316, 371, 411, 426, 436, 568; II. 109; tale of a possessed —, 231; 243.

Ṭóllog, a Harb Beduin, brother of Motlog, II. 312, 315, 316, 318, 319, 320-1.

Ṭóllog Abu Shâmah, sheykh of the Moahîb Abu Shamah, 427, 447, 449, 450, 455, 456, 458, 459, 460, 461, 471, 472, 483, 498, 499, 501, 502, 503, 506; his family, 508, 511-6, 519, 523-4, 528, 532, 534, 535, 537, 543, 544, 546, 548, 549, 550, 552, 554, 564, 610, 641.

Ṭóm'a ed-dinya, II. 409.

Ṭóm'a (طَمَع), cupidity, gain, 540, 576; II. 168, 525.

Tôma, said to be an ancient Arabian name for Teyma, 343.

Tomatoes, sold to the Hâj at Tebûk, 112.

Tómbac, a Persian tobacco-like drug leaf, for the nargily, or water-pipe, 100.

Tombeaux en Palestine, 673.

J. Tommîeh, in W. er-Rummah [Bessam says "it is a square-cut mountain, which may be seen from far off"], 668.

Tools : husbandmen's — at Hâyil, II. 23 ; — at Kheybar, 114.

Topography, 311, 316. [v. Map, Distances.] Art to examine the Arabs, 469.

et-Ṭôr, mountain in Beled Asîr, II. 51.

J. Ṭôr, the mountainous peninsula of Sinai, II. 26.

Ṭôr, sea village in Sinai, and port of the monastery, 352, 584.

Torrent bed, limestone tubers in a —, 71, 73.

Tourk, Turk, II. 137.

Tow (تَوْ, properly just now, but little time ago), too early.

Tówara, Beduin tribe of Sinai, 431 ; II. 200.

Tower : — in the desert, 52 ; watch — in the Gospel parable, 329; private —s of the oases, ib.; II. watch- —s at Kheybar, 92 ; sepulchral —, 116; public — of the Kasîm oases [v. Mergâb, Garra], 336, 436, 440.

Tower-mark on a rifle [English] in Hâyil, 653.

Ṭowîl (طَوِيل), any tall peak or berg serving for a landmark, thus called by the Bed., 285.

Towîl, a desert station N. of Teyma, 341.
Towîl éth-Thálj (Mount Hermon), 45.
Towîl el-'Ummr, ii. 26.
et-Towîlán, a singular natural landmark, 347-8.
Towrát, the volume of Moses' books, the Pentateuch, 191, 342, 343; ii. 24.
Towwâla, sing. Tuâly, a fendy of W. 'Aly, 488.

Towwy (طَوَي), building up, 593.

Tradesmen: — in Hâyil, their trading principals, 658; ii. — from el-Kasîm, 64; Mesopotamian —man at Hâyil, 70.
land-Traffic, in Arabia 355.
Trang! sound of a pistol-shot, ii. 169.
Trap rock, ii. 240, 242, 260, 266, 267, 287.
Travel: art of — in Arabia, 95; — may be comprehended in one word *humanitas*, 305; 576, 632; the first movement of the mind in Arabs is the best, ii. 79; 235, 288.
Treasure: a — fabled to lie upon the Howwâra, 213; a — raised at Ma'an, 214; the fable of Geryeh, 545; the fable of a — in a mountain, 545; seekers of —, 213, 316; hidden —, 158, 335; the Semitic nomads dream all their lives of hid —s, 306, 316; 433, 547; ii. 121, 421.
Treasury at Hâyil, 338, *v.* Beyt el-mâl.
Tree-worship, *v.* Menhel-trees.
Trefoil [*v.* Jét], for the well-camels' provender in el-Kasîm, ii. 465.
Tribes: the greatest Arabian — are not a multitude, 171.
Tribute [*v.* Tax, Mîry, Zika]: the Sultan receives a — from Boreyda, ii. 388.
Tripes: Zeyd's half a cart-load of —, ii. 279.
Tripoli in Syria, ii. 193.
Trivet stones remaining in the desert, 348.
Trove-money, 602.

Tùahí! (from وَعَي), ii. 89.

et-Tuâl 'Aly, a mountain near Hâyil, 668.
Tuâly, tribesman of the Towwâla, a fendy of Wélad 'Aly, 496, 540.
Ibn et-Tubbai, a tribe; they are also called el-Klîb or Kleb, 52.
Tubb'a: battle of the — el-Yémen against the Wâilyîn (before the Héjra), ii. 476.
et-Tûbj, a strait valley descending from Kheybar to Wady el-Humth, 595; ii. 202, 236.

J. Tuèyk, mountains lying N. and S. in the midst of Nejd, ii. 51, 52, 70, 385, 553, 555, 575.
Tuèym, a kinship of Kheybar villagers, ii. 153.
Tufa: vulcanic —, 427; ii. 87.
Tûlahu thelàthy armâh, ii. 491.

Tully (طلي), pl. *tulliân*, male lamb, 475; ii. 293.
Tumân, a fendy of Shammar, ii. 56.

Tunb (طنب) el-beyt, tent-cords, 266.

Tunic (*thôb*), the (calico) shirt of men and women, which is made in Arabia with long sleeves to the feet, 189, 336, *et passim*.
Tûnis, 129, 433; ii. 263.

Tûrfah (طرفاء), a kind of tamarisk which is good firewood, 453.
Turin, ii. 66.
Turk [*v.* Dówla]: —ish juggling, 113; corrupted Stambûly —s, 129, 130, 143; —ish bribes, 142; worthy —s, 239; —s are chair-sitters, 303; —ish soldiery, 300, 504; —s love silver and to be well mounted, 596; —ish military violence, 604; ii. —ish soldiery, 48, 92, 110, 147, 557; 97; —ish courtesy, 103; —ish speech, 130, 151; 388; —ish governors, 137, 141, 151; all offices venal, 144; 191; —ish military expedition in Arabia, 196; 243, 270; —s in el-Hása, 275; 308, 397, 442, 454; the —s in el-'Asîr, 362; 388, 541; —ish shippers, 504; —ish army surgeons at Tâyif, 527, 544, 545; —ish soldier there, 538; 558; street dogs of —ish places, 539; homely simplicity of the old —ish manners, 540; —ish officers, *ib.*; —ish dinner, 541, 549; —ish officers' coffee club, 544, 552, 556; —ish officers, in an Arabian expedition from Tâyif, mistaken by that country people for Nasâra, 557; " the —s are of Gog and Magog," 558.
Turkey, 510, 657 [*v.* Dówla]; ii. 537.
Turkî, the Turkish language.

Turkîeh (طرقية), a wayfaring company, 523.

Turkoman: certain —s not circumcised, ii. 176; 319.

INDEX AND GLOSSARY

[*Turmus*, a circuit of the open desert, so named, E. of J. Selma, on the way from el-Kasîm to Hâyil, *v.* Map.
Turquoise, their opinion of the virtue of this stone, ii. 211.
Turrʻa, Ḥarra, ii. 378.
Turraba, oasis N. of Tâyif, ii. 507, 567.
Turrʼfa, a dog's name, 474.

et-Ṭursh (طُرْش), the driven flocks and great cattle of the Nomads, 346, 476.
Ṭwoyel Saʻîda, a mountain, 328.

Jebel Ṭŷ (جبل طيّء), *i.e. J. Ajja* and *Selma.*
Tyrant, *v. Jabbâr*: the Bed. great sheykh should be no —, 293.

el-ʻUbbeda, Harb Mosrûḥ, ii. 547.
Ubbeyt, a great watering near Teyma, 340.
Ûdkhul hareemakom (v. Dakhîl), 296.
Ûdkhul ʻalʼ Ullah, 307.

Ugglot! (اَقْلَطْ), approach, come in, the response from within when one knocks, at ʻAneyza, ii. 404.
ΥΙΟΥ ΒΕΝΙΑΜΗΝ, name in an inscription, 408.
Ûkhruju fî kulli el-âlam, 643.
Beny Ûklib, Aarab of the W. Bîsha country, ii. 567.
Ûktub-ha! 644.
Ulcers, horrible open, 437.
Ullah: the formal writing of this word الله
(*el-îlah,* the god) in Roman letters is *Allah*; but no Arab could well understand a Frank who pronounced God's name thus; we must say *Ôllah* nearly or *Ullah.* We have here to do with the vulgar and not with book Arabic [which may be sometimes even erratic, as the name written *el-Héjr* in the koran; whose pronunciation *Héjr* we have conserved in Ptolemy and Pliny and in the speech of the Nomads].
Ullah! exclamation of surprise and invocation.
Ullah: the peace and assurance of —, 269, 274, 307; the koran —, 353.

"*Ullah,*" in old Arabic scored inscriptions, at Kheybar, ii. 116.
Ullah akhbar, God Almighty! 139, 518; this invocation is the cry of the Mohammedans entering into battle, ii. 143.
Ullah âlem, 657.
Ullah gowwîk, 376.
Ullah hadîk, 307.

Ullah ḥy-îk! (الله حيَّاكَ) ii. 258.

Ullah karîm, 612.
Ullah er-Rahmân er-Rahîm, 518.
Ullah yáfukkʼny minch, the Lord loose me from thee, 586.

Ullah yʻaŷna-kom (الله يعينكم), ii. 324.

Ullah yerham weyladeyk, yuhâdy weyladeyk ilʼ ej-jínna, 307.
Ullah yesellîmk, 307.
Ullah yethkirak bʼil kheyer, 307.
Ullah ia yubârak fîk, la yujibʼ lak el-kheyr, 496.
Ullah yubèyith wejh-ak, ii. 103.
Ullah yulʻaan abu haʼ ʼl hubûb, ii. 246.
Ullah yulʻaan Thegîf, ḳuddam tegûf, ii. 195.
Ullah yúnṣur es-Sooltân, 317.

Ullah yusullaṭ (يسلَّط), *ʻaleyhim,* ii. 54.

Ullah yuṭowil ʻumr hâʼl weled! ii. 248.
Ullah yuwaṣṣelak bʼil-kheyer, 307.
ʻ*Ullema* (pl. of ʻ*além,* a learned man), the doctors, 133, 270.
Umgassur, an ancient oasis-town in N.-Western Arabia, 602.

Umjemmîn (مقيمين), *el-Aarab — el-yóm,* the people will abide in standing booths (sojourn in this menzil to-day, without removing), 261.
Umjeyd: Aarab Ibn—sheykh ʻAbdillah, a kindred of Ânnezy, 377.
Umm Arkab, a berg at Hâyil, 668.
Umm Arthama, desert site between J. Shammar and Kuweyt, ii. 61.
Umm Jemâl, a ruined city, of basalt building, in the Hauran, 50; inscription upon a church lintel, 50; the manner there of building, *ib.*

Umm-jenèyb (أمّ جنيب), an adder, 358.

Umm Kîda, or *Jèriat W. 'Aly, qd. v.*, a village of Kheybar, II. 110-3; speech of —, 112; 117, 121, 140, 153, 234.
Umm Meshe'aib, a site in the great desert south of el-Kasîm, II. 494.
Umm Nejd (i.e. *'Aneyza*), II. 381.
Umm Rosàs, a ruined city in the Peraea, 57.
Umm Rúkaba, red trachyte bergs at Kheybar, II. 206.
Umm Sâlema, a little sweet-voiced solitary bird of the desert rocks: called in other parts *Sweydîa, qd. v.*, II. 255.
Umm es-Sghrar, mare's name, II. 253.
Umm es-Sûf, mother of wool, 514.
Umm Theyân, Harb village, II. 546.
Umm Tŷeh, granges of er-Russ, II. 491.
J. Ummry, in the desert south of er-Russ, II. 492.
Ummshásh, a watering-place in the Teháma, 431, 445.
Ummthail, a dog's name, 474.
Umseylmy, i.e. *Moseilima*, 246.
Umsheyrifa, a desert ground, 328.
Umshetta, a fendy of Wélad 'Aly, 55, 271.
Umsubba or *Mosubba*, 348, 568.
Umteyra, a woman's name, 514.
Un'aam Ullah 'aleyk', II. 259.
Uncleanness: ceremonial —, 623.
Unicorn [*v. Reem*], 373.
Unseir, a kindred of Ânnezy, 377.
Úrhum yâ Rubb! khálkat, elati ent khalakta: úrhum el-mesakîn, wa el-ju'aanîn, wa el-'aryanîn! úrham yâ 'llah, — yâ 'llah! 612.
Urine. Rock oil said in Hâyil to be made from human —, 647.
Urraie! (from راي, with following يا), II. 69.
el-'Urruk, wages paid for *the sweat* of the labourer, II. 338.
'Usha (عشّ), bee-hive Abyssinian-like cabins in W. Fâtima thus called, II. 567, 569.
[*Ustâd* (اُستاذ Pers.), artificer, said by Mâjid at Hâyil to the Nasrâny hakîm.
Ustibbah (اصطبح), II. 259.
el-'Usshb (العشب), the sappy spring herb, 260.

J. Usshúb, a great crater hill in the 'Aueyrid Harra, 449.
Usshud! II. 177.
Usury: the Beduins count no — in their dealings among themselves, 362; II. — in el-Kasîm, 382, 415, 441.
'Utherah, ruined town in Mount Seir, 74, 82; II. 348.
el-Úthub (اُثب), a barren wild fig-tree, 486.
"*el-'Uzza*" (العُزّي), idol-stone at et-Tâyif, II. 545-9-50.
Uzziah king of Judah built towers in the wilderness, 52.

Vaccination [*v*. Inoculation, *el-'Athab*, Smallpox], 149, 197, 244, 254, 294-5, 297, 321; II. 428.
Vaccinator, at Damascus, 294; — in Arabia, *v. Abu Fâris.* [*v. Jídery, Mujedder, Mejdûr, Ta'am.*] II. a Christian — (impostor) who feigned to vaccinate at Hâyil, and was afterward met-with, they say, and slain by Bed. in the desert, 18; 403 [*v. el-'Athab*], 410.
'Valley-of-Saints,' II. 412-4.
Valleys: — of the Peraea how formed, 66.
Veil: Howeytát women in the mountain of Edom not —ed, 75; the woman's —, 280; Zeyd's opinion of —, 280; II. — of Heteym hareem, 81, 86; 243; — in the Nejd oases, 404.
Venus of the Arabs (*el Lâta* اللات), II. 550.
Vesical diseases in Arabia, 576; II. a — which is common in Africa, II. 190.
mount Vesuvius: — in eruption, 441; 452, 466, 471.
Vibrating water stream; river-valley-terraces formed by — (pointed out by the Author, in a treatise of the Jöstedal Norw. glaciers, in 1866), 486.
Vienna; Zündhölzer, 630; II. 448.
Vines at el-Ally, 194; — at Teyma, 338, 574; at Hâyil, 656; II. no — (saying one at Umm Kîda) at Kheybar, 129; — at Teyma and 'Aneyza, 464, 482; — at Tâyif, 560.
Viol of the desert, *v. Rabèyby*, 81, 306.

Vipers of the desert, 357-60.
Vision; no extraordinary — of the Beduw, 375.
Vocabulary: an Arabic — read to the Nomads, 400.
Vogüé, Marquis de —; note par le —, 673-4.
Voice: sweet cadence of a woman's —, 536.
Volcanoes [v. Harra, Hilliân]: vulcanic bergs in J. Sherra, 68; — in the 'Aueyrid, 427, 431, 441, 449, 451, 452-3, 468, 471.
Volunteer defenders of eṭ-Ṭâyif, ii. 558.
Vultures not seen in the Arabian deserts, 374.

Waar, rugged-like, 562.
Wa ent sélim, ii. 295.
[Wa éntom ... common form of the (Western) nomads in enumerating tribes and kindreds, ex. ' And you the Wélad 'Aly, and you the Moahîb, and you the Sehamma —.'
Wa fúkkny rubby, ii. 150.
Wa hu fî baṭn-ak, ii. 30.
Wa hyât, by the life of, 309, 312.
Wa hyât dúḵny, 309.
Wa hyât ibny, 312.
Wa hyât el-messîeh hâṭha (وحـيـاة المسّي هذا), 312.
Wa hyat ruḵbátak, ii. 292.
Wa hyât ruḵbaty, 312.
Wa hyât Ullah, 309.
Wa hyat weyladich, 312.
Wa low (وَلَوْ), and it were so? ii. 313.
Wa shûghrol-hum bez en náhab, ii. 140.
Wâba, the plague, 629, 635, 670; ii. 21, 197, 201.
Wábar (وبر), a rodent animal in the desert mountains, 371, 656; ii. the — is said by hunters to ruminate, 261.
Wabbar, v. Wábar.
Wâbissa, a fendy of Bíllî, 430.
Wâd' el-Kebîr, the Guádalquíver, ii. 556.
Wadda, a dog's name, 474.
Wadiàn, pl. of wâdy.
Wâdy, pl. wadiàn, low valley ground. In names beginning Wady el- look under the second name.
Wâdy, a Fejîr Beduwy, 138, 172, 173, 234, 235, 237, 409, 414.

Wâdy Mûsa, v. Petra.
el-Wâdy [v. W. er-Rummah], ii. 408, 419, 439, 445-6, et passim.
Wâdy es-Sírr, in el-Wéshm, ii. 424.
Wafîyat (وفِيّ), eight-year-old camel, 401.
Wâga, a dog's name, 474.
el-Wàgilla, ass-mare's name, ii. 253.
Wagons might be used for carriage in the Hâj, 100.
Beny Wáhab [vulg. gentile pl. el-Wahûb], — the Menâbaha, Hosseny, Fejîr and Wélad 'Aly. Their jid or patriarch is Musslim, a son of the Ânnezy ancestor 'Anâz. The Bíshr, Jellàs, and Ruwàlla (all Ânnezy), are sometimes accounted also to the B. Wáhab. A tribesman of the Fukara or Wélad 'Aly will say of himself ana Wahâby. 204, 270-1, 331, 344, 368, 392; ii. 35, 86.
Wahabite tribes, 55.
el-Wahâby (الوَهّابي): Prince 'Abdullah ibn Sa'ud —, 55, 332; ii. 27, 45; — driven from his government by his young brother Sa'ud, becomes a fugitive in W. Nejd, 50; marries a sister of Ibn Rashîd, ib.; and after her death a sister of Ḥamûd, 51; v. Abdullah ibn Sa'ud.
Wahâby zeal, fanatical humour and doctrine, 95, 242, 245, 289; ii. 56, 222, 362, 366, 368, 390, 397, 423, 429, 447, 470, 484, 491, 503, 554, 573; — reformation, i. 585, 598, 599; ii. 25, 27; the founding of the reformation, ii. 454; — Nejd, i. 272, 279, 312, 527, 619, 669; ii. 332; state, government and power, i. 527; ii. 37, 39, 45, 50, 276, 337, 367, 381, 394, 406, 414, 443, 569; ruin of the —, 453-4-5; second warfare with Âneyza, 459-61; metropolis, [v. er-Riâth], 196, 260, 459; — was a reproachful word in Âneyza, 455; — expedition in 'Omân, 462.
Wàhamy (وَهْمِي), ii. 137.
Wahîby, another name of el-Mubbiát, qd. v.
Wàil, v. Wayil.
Wâilyîn, sons of Wayil or the Ânnezy, ii. 476.
Wâjed, 313.
Wajjâ (wáj'a), a pain or disease, 298, 337.
Wajjàj, a buried well-pit at Teyma, 600.
Wajjid, fem. Bed. name, 514.

Wajjidàn, a fendy of 'Ateyba, II. 457.
el-*Waḵbâ*, station in the khála between J. Shammar and Kuweyt, II. 61.

Wákh'm (وخم), filth, foul air, 185.

Wakîd (وكيد), it is well ascertained, 587.

Wallin (Georg), a learned young Swedish Arabist; who in 1845 — travelling as a Mohammedan doctor of the law — passed the northern Nefûd from Jauf to Hâyil, and visited Medina. In 1848 he journeyed anew in Arabia : setting out then from Mueylih (on the Red Sea coast) he passed over part of the 'Aueyrid Ḥarra, near Tebûk, and went to Teyma and Ḥâyil. Wallin died not long after he had returned to Europe. A usage among certain B. Atîeh, to ring a cattle-bell, mentioned by —, 464.

Wàly : the — governor of the *Weliát* or Province of Syria, 39, 207 ; II. 100, 183.

War [v. *Jehâd*, *Ghrazzu*]: — of the Bed. is not to the extinguishing of tribes, 380 ; II. — in Kasîm, 392-3 ; 'Aneyza citizens take no booty in —, 396 ; 'Aneyza —s, 456-62 ; —ing together of Arabians like a —fare of Gipsies, 460.

Warak (وراءك *back!*), a word in the mouths of 'Aneyza children, II. 384.

Wardship, v. sub. *Settàm*.

Wareysîeh, a landmark berg in the desert between Kasîm and Mecca, II. 495.

Washing : — before prayers with sand, 292 ; — with water, 453, 585 ; — after the conjunction of wedded folk, 623 ; Arabs love to wash themselves, 632.

Wâsiṭ, a suburb of Hâyil, now in ruins, 669-70 ; II. 21.

el-*Wàsita*, Beny Sâlem, Harb, vill., II. 546.

Wásm, pl. *wasûm* : the token or cattle-brand of every family, kindred or tribe is called — ; the Arabian *wasûm* oft-times resemble the Himyaric letters (*v. p.* 166), 94, 158, 167; they are found battered upon the rocks, in every nomad dîra : and those marks are the only certain records of the former occupation of tribes, 166, 167, 185 ; 396 ; II. 67.

Wasps of mankind, 449.

Watch : account of distances kept by the —, 322 ; Gulf —es, 664 ; Syrian soldier at Tâyif a — -mender, II. 558.

Water : — scant by the Hâj way, 47, 48, 66, 101, 119, 120, 247 ; penury of — in the khála, 253, 259, 284-5, 298, 551 ; all Arabian ground- — is lukewarm, 554, 629 ; — cooled in the girbies, 554 ; Arabs forbid to use — in any inflammation, 597 ; one of the most wasting excesses of the body, to drink — to bedward, 598 ; brackish — an occasion of fever, 636 ; II. 21 ; — at Kheybar, 95, 205 ; — in the desert full of vermin, 239 ; seeking — by the way, 247, 255, 266, 295 ; caravaners are niggards of — in the journey, 496-498, 503 ; channels, cisterns and — -merchants at Jidda, 574 ; — at el-Ḳaṣr, 269.

Water, temperature of springs and wells : the well at Medáin 66° F.; the brook at el-Ally 92° F.; spring in W. Thirba 83° F.; — at Kheybar 81°-84° F.

Water-bearers, at eṭ-Ṭâyif, II. 539.

Water-fowl in passage at Teyma (in September), 584 ; II. at Kheybar, 205.

Water-pit, opening a — at Kheybar, II. 115, 117, 129, 130. [*v. Themîla.*]

Watershed : — of the soil near Ma'an, 68 ; — between the Dead and Red Seas, 85 ; II. — in the Harrat Kheybar between W. el-Ḥumṭh and W. er-Rummah, 87.

Water-skins, *v. Girby.*

Water snails : small turreted — in the lukewarm brooks of el-Ally and Kheybar, 193 ; II. 219.

Waterers' labour in the desert, 506-7, 524 ; II. 329 ; Hostile Waháby — before 'Aneyza, 460 ; caravan —, 496-7, 506.

Waters : Bed. — in the khála, *muèyrid* [*v. el-Hŷza, el-'Erudda, Baiṭha Nethîl, Ummshásh,* etc.], 290 ; Zeyd finds a water, 350 ; 368, 421, 428, 540 ; 544 ; II. 329.

Wa'ul (sing. وعْل): the great wild goat is thus named in Syria and by Ḳaḥtân in Arabia. [*v. Bédan.*], 372.

Wâyil, father of the Ma'azy and Ânnezy tribes, 270 ; II. 286, 393, 476.

Wâyil, a Mahûby sheykh, 531-2, 548, 550, 554, 611.

Weapons : the older are the more esteemed, 504; II. — of the ancient Arabians, 196.

Wedding : a — at Teyma, 333.

Wedduk (وَدَك), lard of the camel's hump : II. a tale of —, 231.

Weeaho! (وَرْه ?) a call to camels, 428.

Weed: few — -kinds in the Arabian oases, II. 451.

el-Wéjh (vulg. *el-Wésh*), a Red Sea village port nearly opposite to Medáin Sâlih: rice from —, 195; 217, 241, 275, 322, 326; sea salt from —, 340; 396, 401, 405, 411, 420, 425, 429-30, 435, 437, 438, 448, 453, 454, 455-6, 459, 462, 463, 464, 521, 540, 550, 557, 578; II. 110.

Wélad 'Aly (a fem. pl., signifying tribeswomen of the —, is *Wélad 'Aliât*), a great sub-tribe of Ânnezy: they are two half tribes, whose fendies are named at p. 271. The *dîrat* of those in the N. (where they have sojourned, it is said, about 40 years, and are rich in great cattle) is nigh upon the Hauran in Syria. The southern half-tribe — sister tribe of the Fukara — are treacherous and fanatical Aarab. They remain in their ancient wandering ground; which is reckoned from Stôra, four days above Medina, unto two days N. of el-Héjr. 55, 119, 128, 153, 162, 217, 219, 221, 233; 235, 238, 239, 240; — landlords at el-Héjr, 241, 242, 250, 270, 271; clay houses of certain — sheykhs at Kheybar, 276; 292, 314, 344, 363, 378; a ghrazzu of — taken by a ghrazzu of Bishr, 379, 380; 390, 391, 402; two — sheykhs slain by Hâj Néjm, 153; 410, 413, 414, 420, 435, 479, 480, 488, 532, 551-3, 563, 609; II. 16, 34, 91, 111, 132, 141, 206, 242.

Wélad Selîm, a fendy of Harb B. Sâlem, II. 546.

Wéled, young man.

Wéled 'ammy, 360.

Wéled Mahanna (*Hásan*), Emir of Boreyda, II. 37, 365.

Well [Ar. *Bîr*]: kellâ —s, 47; 136; 179; ancient —s at Teyma, 330, 583; child let down into a —, 554; —s in the desert, 568; 600; ancient — at Teyma opened, 602; — at Hâyil, 644, 665; II. -making in el-Kasîm, 355; Khenneyny's project of boring Artesian —, 370, 379; —-labour at 'Aneyza, *ib.*, 382, 451, 465-6; cost of — at 'Aneyza, *ib.*; —s at Khubbera, 445; —s in Rasheyd's palm ground, 447, 465; labouring lads bathing in the orchard —, *ib.*; a caravaner of 'Aneyza fell down into the deep 'Afîf —, 497; —s at et-Tâyif, 551, 560.

Well-camels, *v.* Camel.

Well-drivers, 593-4; II. 451.

Well-rope, 593; nomad — sometimes made of twisted bast, II. 317, 452.

Well-sinkers, 330; II. 421, 429.

Wellah, lit. By God, but it is come to signify verily, indeed; the Beduins say commonly *billah* (*qd. v.*); they say also *wellah-billah* and *wullah-bullah*, 309; *wellâhi, wellâhi-billâhi*, 309.

Wellah Fulàn! II. 295.

(Welsh mutton): small Mecca country sheep compared with —, 473.

Wély, grave of a saint, II. 573.

Wen in the throat, seldom seen in Nejd Arabia, II. 494.

Wennys (وَنيِس for أَنيِس), a word said by Mishwat, a Mahûby: the sense may be unseen powers, 509.

el-Wéshm, a province of middle Nejd, II. 338, 419, 424, 444, 452, 455, 466; inscription in —, 555; 564, 567.

the West Country (States of Barbary): 417, 420, 562; II. 'From that quarter of the world shall come the great danger upon el-Islam,' 303.

Weyley! (وَيْلي) woe is me, 437; II. 478.

Wèyrid, a Fejîry, 578.

Wèyrid (وَرْد) [the provision of water fetched from a watering], the watering, 506, 544, 547.

Weysh 'aad (وَيْش عاد), II. 74.

Weysh 'aleyk, II. 292.

Weysh yúnsurhu? II. 69.

Wheat: small grained — in the Arabian oases; price of — at Teyma, 338; II. — at 'Aneyza, 382.

Wheel: hand-cart on —s seen at 'Aneyza, II. 379; —-wrights: *suâny* —s in the oases, 379; 429.

Whistling: a Beduwy —, 607.

White, the hue of cheerfulness, 143; II. 373.

Widd el-ghrarîb ahlhu a'an el-ájnaby, II. 298, 302, 333.

W. Widj, near Tâyif, II. 567.

Widow: a Syrian — weeping by her husband's grave, 282; II. a bountiful negro — at Kheybar, 107; a beneficent — woman at et-Tâyif, 190.

OF ARABIC WORDS   693

Wife [*v. Hareem*, Woman]: the Bed. —'s remedy in an unhappy marriage, 273 ; 342 ; 363 ; ii. "A — should be come of good kin, and be liberal," 160.
Wilàyat Konia, ii. 540.
Wild cow : the —, *v. Wothŷhi*.
Wild goat, *v.* Goat.
Wild ox, *v. Wothŷhi*, 372 ; ii. 116.
Winchester rifle, ii. 364.
Wind in Arabia [*v. sub. 'Ajjâj, Fejîr, Medáin Sâlih, Moahîb*, March, Sand], ii. 238.
Windows in Arabia are casements to the air, 330, 640 ; ii. 369. [*v. Tâga*.]
Wine : not remembered by Beduins, 289 ; a kind of — made at Hâyil, 656 ; ii. "Was there — in the world before Jesus Christ ? " 414.
Wings : images of angels and gods vainly made with —, 373.
Winter : cold — nights at Medáin, 243 ; on the Harra, 453.
'Witchcraft of the hareem,' 297 ; ii. witches of Kheybar, 124-6, 208-9.
el-*Withanîn*, a fendy of 'Ateyba, ii. 457.
Witr, a mountain, 117, 464.

Wittr or *withr* (وِثْر), pad set under the camel pack-saddle frame, 258.
Wòh-ho ! a call to camels, 261, 428.
Wolf in the desert, 96, 372, 452 ; — eaten by the Bed. who account the flesh medicinal, 372 ; [the — was eaten in medieval Europe ! *ib.*] ; Zeyd's saying, *ib.*; name of — is often given to sickly (Moslem and Christian male and female) children, in Syria, 374 ; 'The stranger to the —,' 319 ; 473-4, 477, 518, 656 ; ii. sleight of the — in hunting, 163-4 ; "Betwixt the dog and the —," 267 ; 334.
Wolverine, *v. Fáhd*.
Wolloo-wolloo-woolloo ! a camel call, 261.
Woman [*v. Hareem*, Wife] : 277-8 ; "the best —," ii. 150 ; a — must be kept in subjection, 160 ; beautiful Heteym —en, 242, 300 ; a certain Harbîa chideress, 309 ; —en shopkeepers at Boreyda, 349 ; —en are jealously veiled in Nejd, 404 ; —en of 'Aneyza come forth to the battle, 460 ; townswomen taught to read in Nejd, 472 ; a — messenger in battle, 478 ; —en wailing for the dead in battle, 481 ; Beduin —en in W. Fâtima, 570 ; oasis — there, *ib.*
Woodgatherers [*v.* Firewood], ii. 21, 76, 139.

Woodgrouse, note of the —, 536.
Wool : Bed. housewives' —, 268, 356, 476, *et passim*.
World : "the — fadeth away," 104.

Worma (ورماء), Bed. fem. jesting name, 514.

Wortabet : Dr. Gregory —, ii. 543.

Wothŷhi (وَضِيَحة) [vulg. pronunciation nearly *Oth-thŷ'hî*, *v. Bakr el-Wáhashy*], the wild ox, probably the *Reem* or Unicorn of Scripture : It is an antelope (*Beatrix*). 98, 325, 372, 373 ; hunting the —, 373 ; the — described, 561 ; 613 ; is fleetest of all game, *ib.*; the meat esteemed above other venison, *ib.*; the bull's hide, for sandals, brought to Ma'an, *ib.*; the horns, which are common at Teyma, are used there for tent-pegs, *ib.*; 642 ; a pair of live —ies in the Prince's garden at Hâyil, 644 ; ii. — of the Kahtân dìra in el-Yémen, 52 ; scored images of —ies on the rocks, at Kheybar, 116, 455.
Wotton, Sir Henry — : a merry saying of his, 40.
el-*Wuffiàn*, a fendy of Harb B. Sâlem, ii. 546.

Wurrùr (or *warrer*, وَرَر for class. وَرَل or وَرَن), a great lizard, ii. 573.
Wúttid, a mountain in the Teháma, 451, 462, 463.

Yâ ahl el-karîm, ii. 385.
Yâ ent râkabin, 514.
Yâ fárkah ! 618.
Yâ hulla, 614.
Yâ latîf ! 263.
Yâ mâl ej-ju'a, ii. 496.
Yâ mâl et-teyr, ii. 496.
Yâ mâl eth-thubbah (or perhaps الضبعة), ii. 496.
Yâ Rasûl Ullah ! ii. 114.
Yâ Rubby ! ana 'ajist min hâl-y, wa ent tekúbbny, 'O Lord, I am weary of my being ...,' 471.
Yâ Tawîl el-'Ummr ! ii. 70.

Yaarud 'aley (يَعْرِض عَلَيّ), ii. 74.

Yâfet (Japheth) son of Noah, 580 ; ii. 191.
[*Yagût*, I knew two persons thus named at Hâyil ; one of them was a son of the renegade Jew.

694   INDEX AND GLOSSARY

Yahûd (sing. *Yahûdy*) Juda or the Jews: Damascus —, their part in the massacre of the Christians, 104; Mohammedan fable of the —, 191; pre-Islamic Arabians called —, 326; 328, 442; — "falsifiers of the Scripture," 342; the Arabians do not well distinguish between — and Nasâra, 343, 377, 487, 579-80; both words are used among them as injuries, 251, 417, 595, 615; — and Nasâra 'cannot utter the Lord's name,' 518; — "Sup with the —," 579; a renegade Jew at Hâyil, *v. 'Abdullah el-Moslemanny*; II. — in el-Yemén, 54, 163, 178, 402.

Yahûd Kheybar: the fabulous "Jews of Kheybar"; the Fehját (Heteym) pretend that they come of the old Jewish people of Kheybar, and that they are the —; in the talk of the neighbour Bed., the Wélad 'Aly and Fukara (who have land rights there) are snibbed as —. 170, 362, 435, 550; 600; 641; II. 92, 98, 146, 174.

Yahûdy: a certain — who visited el-Ally, Teyma and Kheybar, and perished at Kheybar, 192-3; 328, 330; II. 121; words of a certain — of el-'Irâk, 409.

Yahŷa eṣ-Ṣâliḥ, patriot, sheykh of a great ward of 'Aneyza, II. 373, 410-11, 427, 458-9; a song made of —, 461; his wife, 411; 473; 484.

Yahŷa, son of the Emir 'Aly of 'Aneyza, II. 394.

Yajiddûn (يَجَدُّون) *en-núkhl*, 608.

Yaḳṭ'a 'umrak, 519.
Yakubb-hu, 592.
el-Yâm, an Arabian lineage, II. 381.
Yanb'a el-Baḥr, Yanb'a-at-the-Sea; the port of *Y. en-Núkhl*, one journey distant, 134, 217; II. 108, 122, 157, 177, 196, 202.
Yanb'a en-Núkhl, Yanb'a-at-the-Palms, an oasis in the Tehâma, 166, 599, II. 202, 545, 546.
Wady Yanb'a, II. 546.
Yáthrib, old name of Medina, 43.
Ybba said for *Abu*, 350.
Ybba Moghrair, a cragged sandstone mountain, with a pool, in the dîrat Bíshr, 348, 368, 619.
(2) *Ybba Moghrair*, a watering-place "greater than Baitha Nethîl" between the dîras of Harb and 'Ateyby, four days E. of Medina, in the way to el-Kasîm. [*v*. Map.]

Year: the Mohammedan — is of 354 days; the (lunar) months are alternately of 30 and 29 days.

Yegôtarun, v. Gôtar.
Yéhia, name, *v. Yahŷa*, II. 426.
Yel'aan Ullah abu hâ l ras, II. 496.
Yelduz, Kurdish name of the family Nejûmy, II. 157.

[*Yellah yâ sitterak!* (يا الله يا سِتْرك) Lord, thy protection!) Men say this in el-Kasîm, in indolently rising.

el-Yemâma, town of E. Nejd: "two hundred" houses, II. 425.
el-Yemâna, misprint for *el-Yemâma*, qd. *v*.
el-Yémén (Lane-of-the-right-hand), Arabia Felix, 61, 136, 169; Ottoman troops in —, 198; 246, 276, 289; II. 51, 54, 55, 57, 142, 205, 276, 309, 361, 375, 418, 424, 453-4-5, 476, 482, 555-6, 565, 572.
Yémeny, a man of el-Yémen.
Yémeny (stuff), II. 514.
Yemmen, wells of the Auájy, II. 245.
Yerḥamak Ullah, II. 379.
Yeterôha, a district of the *Hejjûr* mountains, II. 242.
Yeteyr, "it will rise and fly away," 381.
Ymgebâs, perhaps *Umm Jebas*, the desert owl, 349.
Yoktân, 270.

el-Yôm nejîm (نَقِيم) cf. *Umjemmin*), II. 498.

Yugaialûn (يقَيِلون) [*v. Gaila*] they take rest at noon, 485, 594.

Yuḥáshimûn (يَحْشُمون), they respect), 595.

Yuhowwishûn (يهوّشون), they chide together, 502.

Yujassas, spying out, II. 247.
Yuḳdur Ullah! 307.
Yulubbûn: II. 513.
Yun'aam Ullah 'aleyk, II. 379.
Yunâny, language of Javan (Ionian, or Greek), II. 57.

[*Yúnṭun* يَنْطُن from نَطَ, they weave (Moahîb).

Yurussun (from رَسّ) *el-má*, II. 465.

Yûsef Khâlidy, II. 448.

Yusbʿak ent! (يَسْبَعَكَ انتَ), 312.

Yuṣuddirûn (يصدّرون), they (the camels) breast upward, 507, 540, 548.

Zaʿal, displeasure, II. 309.

Zabṭîyah (ضَبْطِيَّة), police soldiery in Syria, II. 48, 97.

Zâd (زاد), food, II. 547.

Zahlán read *Zaʿalán*, sorrowful, 273.

Zâmil, Emir of ʿAneyza, II. 357, 362, 363, 364, 365; his mild and prudent nature, 384, 404, 408, 424, 442, 443; 366-7, 370-1-2-3, 376-377, 385, 393-4-5-6; his proclamation to the Kahtân, 395; Friday lecture in —'s coffee-hall, 396; 423, 430-1-2-3; 445-6-7; 460; his words to stay the slaughter, 461; his family, 462; son of a former Emir, 463; his prudence and philosophy, *ib.*; his daily life, *ib.*; his dues, *ib.*; 464; 467-8, 472-3; he rides with the town against the Kahtân, 474-475; 476-7-8-9, 480-1-2; 488, 491, 544, 552.

Zanzibar slave traffic, II. 389.

Zared: the brook —, 66.

ez-Zbèyd, a fendy of Ḥarb Mosruḥ, II. 547.

Zbeyer near Bosra; there is the outgoing of the great W. er-Rummah, 243; II. 70, 449.

ZHƟOC, word or name in an inscr., 408.

Zehme, Albrecht: his work *Arabien und die Araber seit hundert Jahren*, II. 303.

ez-Zelakát (الزلاقات), 121.

Zélamat (زَلَمَة), pl. *zílm*, an upland word in Syria and Western Arabia; a carl, a fellow, a man of the people. 92, 202, 335, 363, 371.

Zellûm, a seyl-bed, Teyma, 340.

Zelotism [*v.* Fanaticism], springs in envious depraved natures, 599; II. 352, 372, 384, 423.

Zemmel (زِمِل), carriage camels.

Zemzemîeh (زَمْزَمِيَّة) (or *Matàra*), pilgrims' saddle bottle — for Zemzem water (*cf.* Jordan-bottle, or Jordan, of medieval English pilgrims to Palestine), 41. [Zemzem is the springing well in the court of the Kaʿaba.]

Zenaiba, name of a rising ground in the H. ʿAueyrid, 440.

Zerka, *Wady* and *Kellâ*, 51, 66, 108, 120, 165.

Zêy êl-fîl, like unto the elephant, 506.

Beny Zeyd, the people of Shuggera in el-Weshm, II. 452; — of *Shaara*, *Doàdamy* and *Goeyîeh*, 492.

Zeyd, a *Ḥarby* of *J. el-Figgera*, one of the Bîshy soldiery at Tâyif, II. 545-6-9, 558, 560.

Zeyd, porter of the Castle at Hâyil, a Moghreby, II. 47, 71, 279, 280-1.

Zeyd es-Sbeych(k)an, 270; a principal sheykh of the *Fúḳara Aarab*: he had married six wives, 137; comes to the kellâ at Medáin Sâlih, 142-144; a philosopher, 143; 148-9; his grandsire, who was great-sheykh of the tribe, brought husbandmen of Teyma to till the good soil at Medáin, 177; 222, 230, 249, 252, 254, 256, 257; a lordling, 258; 259; Zeyd's menzil, 260, 262; his family, *ib.*, 263; 270; Zeyd sparing of coffee, 259, 263, 264; his illiberality, 376, 616; disputes with an officer of the Hâj, whether nigher unto God were the life of townsfolk or of the Beduw, 269; his relation of the genealogies of the Fúḳara and kindred tribes, 270; his wives, 271-4; 277, 278; his opinion of the wife's veil, 280; knows all the rocks in his tribe's dîra, 285; his courtesy, 287; 293, 302, 303, 304, 306, 316, 317, 319, 321, 322, 323, 328, 329, 332, 335, 339, 343, 344, 348, 349, 350, 352, 354, 355, 357, 362, 364, 365, 368, 372, 375, 376, 378, 388, 389, 390, 391, 393, 395, 396, 397, 398, 399, 400, 401, 402, 404, 421, 427, 438, 447, 462, 549, 550, 552, 553, 557, 560, 567, 571, 572, 573, 576, 584, 586, 607, 608, 614, 615, 616, 617; II. 118, 141, 557.

W. *Zeydîeh*, a Kheybar valley, II. 109, 116, 117, 122, 143.

ʿAŷn ez-Zeyma, (hamlet of Haṭheyl, station between Ḳurn el-Menâzil and Mecca, II. 512-513-7-526, 528, 530, 542-4, 553-9, 564, 565, 569.

Zîarra, a kinship of Kheybar villagers, II. 153.

ez-Zibbâra, a site in W. Fátima, II. 566.

Zibdâny, a village in Antilibanus, 497 [the grove of the broken crocks, called *Umm es-Shukkakîf*, is upon a rocky hill near *Bludân*; the cave of the pots is on a high ground near *Bekkayeh* in the way to the Moslem village

696 INDEX AND GLOSSARY

Herrèyry. At Zibdâny is *Makàm Néby Abdàn* whereunto the village people make yearly a religious festival procession.

Zighreybîeh, a rautha near 'Aneyza, II. 420.

Zíka, tribute, 344; II. duty to pay —, 53, 285.

Zíkma, cold in the head, 330.

W. *Zilèyly*, in Sinai, 432.

Zílfa (زِلْفَة), a milk bowl, 477.

ez-*Zílfy*, a town in (W.) Sedeyr, II. 432, 468.

Derb *Zillâj*, 620.

Zillamy, v. *Zélamat*.

Zion; "the Controversy of —," 83.

Zmèyem (زمَيْم), 385, the nose-rings (mostly of gold) worn by Beduin women in their feasts; village women have them commonly of silver and name them *hálluka*, qd. v.

Zmurrûd, Kellâ, 127, 204.

Zófr Miriam umm Sinnakît, certain petrified shells so named, 470.

Zóhra (زُهْرَة), the morning star, II. 565.

Zôl pl. *azzuâl* (زُول ,ازوال) the uncertain looming of aught in distant sight, II. 256, 499.

Zôra (زُورَة), the pillar-like stay under the chest of the camel, which (when the great beast is couched) bears-up the weight of his long neck; it is soled with horny skin, 369; II. 290.

Zuâmil, the men of Zâmil; the people of 'Aneyza so called by Beduins in their manner to name a tribe after the sheykh. [*cf. el-Fejîr.* — The like was an old usage in some European languages: we often read it in Froissart.] II. 477.

Zuâra, a kindred of the Fukara tribe, 270.

Zûba, a fendy of Shammar, II. 56.

Zubbàla, a fendy of Bíllî, 430.

Zubbiàn, a fendy of Jehèyna, 166.

Zuggimân, a dog's name, 474.

ez-*Zumèyl*, a fendy of Shammar, II. 56.

Zündholzer (Vienna —): from the sûk of Hâyil, 630; II. — sold in 'Aneyza, 429.

ez-*Zurán*, a fendy of 'Ateyba, II. 457.

Zymát, an uncertain word written down from the mouths of the (Heteym) speakers, II. 303.

NOTE TO THE 1921 EDITION

[I desire here to record my grateful remembrance of the kindly aid which I received from the eminent Scholars (the late) Prof. M. J. De Goeje and Prof. Edward C. Sachau, whilst this Index was passing through the Press; in giving me the formal equivalents in Arabic letters, of not a few words which I wrote down in Arabia, as I heard them; and those chiefly from the lips of the Nomads. — C.M.D.]

NOTE TO THE 1936 EDITION

The proofs of this edition have been read by Mr. A. C. Fifield, who read the 1921 edition under the author's supervision; and the necessary alterations to the headlines and Index pagination have been made by the same hand.

**A CATALOGUE OF SELECTED DOVER BOOKS
IN ALL FIELDS OF INTEREST**

A CATALOGUE OF SELECTED DOVER BOOKS IN ALL FIELDS OF INTEREST

CONDITIONED REFLEXES, Ivan P. Pavlov. Full translation of most complete statement of Pavlov's work; cerebral damage, conditioned reflex, experiments with dogs, sleep, similar topics of great importance. 430pp. 5⅜ x 8½. 60614-7 Pa. $4.50

NOTES ON NURSING: WHAT IT IS, AND WHAT IT IS NOT, Florence Nightingale. Outspoken writings by founder of modern nursing. When first published (1860) it played an important role in much needed revolution in nursing. Still stimulating. 140pp. 5⅜ x 8½. 22340-X Pa. $3.00

HARTER'S PICTURE ARCHIVE FOR COLLAGE AND ILLUSTRATION, Jim Harter. Over 300 authentic, rare 19th-century engravings selected by noted collagist for artists, designers, decoupeurs, etc. Machines, people, animals, etc., printed one side of page. 25 scene plates for backgrounds. 6 collages by Harter, Satty, Singer, Evans. Introduction. 192pp. 8⅞ x 11¾. 23659-5 Pa. $5.00

MANUAL OF TRADITIONAL WOOD CARVING, edited by Paul N. Hasluck. Possibly the best book in English on the craft of wood carving. Practical instructions, along with 1,146 working drawings and photographic illustrations. Formerly titled *Cassell's Wood Carving.* 576pp. 6½ x 9¼. 23489-4 Pa. $7.95

THE PRINCIPLES AND PRACTICE OF HAND OR SIMPLE TURNING, John Jacob Holtzapffel. Full coverage of basic lathe techniques—history and development, special apparatus, softwood turning, hardwood turning, metal turning. Many projects—billiard ball, works formed within a sphere, egg cups, ash trays, vases, jardiniers, others—included. 1881 edition. 800 illustrations. 592pp. 6⅛ x 9¼. 23365-0 Clothbd. $15.00

THE JOY OF HANDWEAVING, Osma Tod. Only book you need for hand weaving. Fundamentals, threads, weaves, plus numerous projects for small board-loom, two-harness, tapestry, laid-in, four-harness weaving and more. Over 160 illustrations. 2nd revised edition. 352pp. 6½ x 9¼. 23458-4 Pa. $6.00

THE BOOK OF WOOD CARVING, Charles Marshall Sayers. Still finest book for beginning student in wood sculpture. Noted teacher, craftsman discusses fundamentals, technique; gives 34 designs, over 34 projects for panels, bookends, mirrors, etc. "Absolutely first-rate"—E. J. Tangerman. 33 photos. 118pp. 7¾ x 10⅝. 23654-4 Pa. $3.50

CATALOGUE OF DOVER BOOKS

THE DEPRESSION YEARS AS PHOTOGRAPHED BY ARTHUR ROTHSTEIN, Arthur Rothstein. First collection devoted entirely to the work of outstanding 1930s photographer: famous dust storm photo, ragged children, unemployed, etc. 120 photographs. Captions. 119pp. 9¼ x 10¾.
23590-4 Pa. $5.00

CAMERA WORK: A PICTORIAL GUIDE, Alfred Stieglitz. All 559 illustrations and plates from the most important periodical in the history of art photography, *Camera Work* (1903-17). Presented four to a page, reduced in size but still clear, in strict chronological order, with complete captions. Three indexes. Glossary. Bibliography. 176pp. 8⅜ x 11¼.
23591-2 Pa. $6.95

ALVIN LANGDON COBURN, PHOTOGRAPHER, Alvin L. Coburn. Revealing autobiography by one of greatest photographers of 20th century gives insider's version of Photo-Secession, plus comments on his own work. 77 photographs by Coburn. Edited by Helmut and Alison Gernsheim. 160pp. 8⅛ x 11.
23685-4 Pa. $6.00

NEW YORK IN THE FORTIES, Andreas Feininger. 162 brilliant photographs by the well-known photographer, formerly with *Life* magazine, show commuters, shoppers, Times Square at night, Harlem nightclub, Lower East Side, etc. Introduction and full captions by John von Hartz. 181pp. 9¼ x 10¾.
23585-8 Pa. $6.95

GREAT NEWS PHOTOS AND THE STORIES BEHIND THEM, John Faber. Dramatic volume of 140 great news photos, 1855 through 1976, and revealing stories behind them, with both historical and technical information. Hindenburg disaster, shooting of Oswald, nomination of Jimmy Carter, etc. 160pp. 8¼ x 11.
23667-6 Pa. $5.00

THE ART OF THE CINEMATOGRAPHER, Leonard Maltin. Survey of American cinematography history and anecdotal interviews with 5 masters—Arthur Miller, Hal Mohr, Hal Rosson, Lucien Ballard, and Conrad Hall. Very large selection of behind-the-scenes production photos. 105 photographs. Filmographies. Index. Originally *Behind the Camera.* 144pp. 8¼ x 11.
23686-2 Pa. $5.00

DESIGNS FOR THE THREE-CORNERED HAT (LE TRICORNE), Pablo Picasso. 32 fabulously rare drawings—including 31 color illustrations of costumes and accessories—for 1919 production of famous ballet. Edited by Parmenia Migel, who has written new introduction. 48pp. 9⅜ x 12¼. (Available in U.S. only)
23709-5 Pa. $5.00

NOTES OF A FILM DIRECTOR, Sergei Eisenstein. Greatest Russian filmmaker explains montage, making of *Alexander Nevsky,* aesthetics; comments on self, associates, great rivals (Chaplin), similar material. 78 illustrations. 240pp. 5⅜ x 8½.
22392-2 Pa. $4.50

CATALOGUE OF DOVER BOOKS

A MAYA GRAMMAR, Alfred M. Tozzer. Practical, useful English-language grammar by the Harvard anthropologist who was one of the three greatest American scholars in the area of Maya culture. Phonetics, grammatical processes, syntax, more. 301pp. 5⅜ x 8½. 23465-7 Pa. $4.00

THE JOURNAL OF HENRY D. THOREAU, edited by Bradford Torrey, F. H. Allen. Complete reprinting of 14 volumes, 1837-61, over two million words; the sourcebooks for *Walden,* etc. Definitive. All original sketches, plus 75 photographs. Introduction by Walter Harding. Total of 1804pp. 8½ x 12¼. 20312-3, 20313-1 Clothbd., Two-vol. set $70.00

CLASSIC GHOST STORIES, Charles Dickens and others. 18 wonderful stories you've wanted to reread: "The Monkey's Paw," "The House and the Brain," "The Upper Berth," "The Signalman," "Dracula's Guest," "The Tapestried Chamber," etc. Dickens, Scott, Mary Shelley, Stoker, etc. 330pp. 5⅜ x 8½. 20735-8 Pa. $4.50

SEVEN SCIENCE FICTION NOVELS, H. G. Wells. Full novels. *First Men in the Moon, Island of Dr. Moreau, War of the Worlds, Food of the Gods, Invisible Man, Time Machine, In the Days of the Comet.* A basic science-fiction library. 1015pp. 5⅜ x 8½. (Available in U.S. only) 20264-X Clothbd. $8.95

ARMADALE, Wilkie Collins. Third great mystery novel by the author of *The Woman in White* and *The Moonstone.* Ingeniously plotted narrative shows an exceptional command of character, incident and mood. Original magazine version with 40 illustrations. 597pp. 5⅜ x 8½. 23429-0 Pa. $6.00

MASTERS OF MYSTERY, H. Douglas Thomson. The first book in English (1931) devoted to history and aesthetics of detective story. Poe, Doyle, LeFanu, Dickens, many others, up to 1930. New introduction and notes by E. F. Bleiler. 288pp. 5⅜ x 8½. (Available in U.S. only) 23606-4 Pa. $4.00

FLATLAND, E. A. Abbott. Science-fiction classic explores life of 2-D being in 3-D world. Read also as introduction to thought about hyperspace. Introduction by Banesh Hoffmann. 16 illustrations. 103pp. 5⅜ x 8½. 20001-9 Pa. $2.00

THREE SUPERNATURAL NOVELS OF THE VICTORIAN PERIOD, edited, with an introduction, by E. F. Bleiler. Reprinted complete and unabridged, three great classics of the supernatural: *The Haunted Hotel* by Wilkie Collins, *The Haunted House at Latchford* by Mrs. J. H. Riddell, and *The Lost Stradivarious* by J. Meade Falkner. 325pp. 5⅜ x 8½. 22571-2 Pa. $4.00

AYESHA: THE RETURN OF "SHE," H. Rider Haggard. Virtuoso sequel featuring the great mythic creation, Ayesha, in an adventure that is fully as good as the first book, *She.* Original magazine version, with 47 original illustrations by Maurice Greiffenhagen. 189pp. 6½ x 9¼. 23649-8 Pa. $3.50

CATALOGUE OF DOVER BOOKS

AMERICAN ANTIQUE FURNITURE, Edgar G. Miller, Jr. The basic coverage of all American furniture before 1840: chapters per item chronologically cover all types of furniture, with more than 2100 photos. Total of 1106pp. 7⅞ x 10¾. 21599-7, 21600-4 Pa., Two-vol. set $17.90

ILLUSTRATED GUIDE TO SHAKER FURNITURE, Robert Meader. Director, Shaker Museum, Old Chatham, presents up-to-date coverage of all furniture and appurtenances, with much on local styles not available elsewhere. 235 photos. 146pp. 9 x 12. 22819-3 Pa. $6.00

ORIENTAL RUGS, ANTIQUE AND MODERN, Walter A. Hawley. Persia, Turkey, Caucasus, Central Asia, China, other traditions. Best general survey of all aspects: styles and periods, manufacture, uses, symbols and their interpretation, and identification. 96 illustrations, 11 in color. 320pp. 6⅛ x 9¼. 22366-3 Pa. $6.95

CHINESE POTTERY AND PORCELAIN, R. L. Hobson. Detailed descriptions and analyses by former Keeper of the Department of Oriental Antiquities and Ethnography at the British Museum. Covers hundreds of pieces from primitive times to 1915. Still the standard text for most periods. 136 plates, 40 in full color. Total of 750pp. 5⅜ x 8½.
23253-0 Pa. $10.00

THE WARES OF THE MING DYNASTY, R. L. Hobson. Foremost scholar examines and illustrates many varieties of Ming (1368-1644). Famous blue and white, polychrome, lesser-known styles and shapes. 117 illustrations, 9 full color, of outstanding pieces. Total of 263pp. 6⅛ x 9¼. (Available in U.S. only) 23652-8 Pa. $6.00

Prices subject to change without notice.

Available at your book dealer or write for free catalogue to Dept. GI, Dover Publications, Inc., 180 Varick St., N.Y., N.Y. 10014. Dover publishes more than 175 books each year on science, elementary and advanced mathematics, biology, music, art, literary history, social sciences and other areas.